EQUITY AND THE LAW OF TRUSTS

EQUITY AND THE LAW OF TRUSTS

Eleventh Edition

PHILIP H PETTIT MA

of the Middle Temple, Barrister
Emeritus Professor of Equity, Universities of Bristol and Buckingham

OXFORD
UNIVERSITY PRESS

OXFORD
UNIVERSITY PRESS

Great Clarendon Street, Oxford OX2 6DP

Oxford University Press is a department of the University of Oxford.
It furthers the University's objective of excellence in research, scholarship,
and education by publishing worldwide in

Oxford New York

Auckland Cape Town Dar es Salaam Hong Kong Karachi
Kuala Lumpur Madrid Melbourne Mexico City Nairobi
New Delhi Shanghai Taipei Toronto

With offices in

Argentina Austria Brazil Chile Czech Republic France Greece
Guatemala Hungary Italy Japan Poland Portugal Singapore
South Korea Switzerland Thailand Turkey Ukraine Vietnam

Oxford is a registered trade mark of Oxford University Press
in the UK and in certain other countries

Published in the United States
by Oxford University Press Inc., New York

British Library Cataloguing in Publication Data

Data available

Library of Congress Cataloging in Publication Data

Data available

Typeset by Newgen Imaging Systems (P) Ltd., Chennai, India
Printed in Great Britain
on acid-free paper by
Ashford Colour Press Ltd, Gosport, Hampshire

ISBN 978-0-19-956102-5

5 7 9 10 8 6 4

PREFACE

The single major task in preparing this new edition has been to make the considerable revisions necessary as a consequence of the provisions of the Charities Act 2006, the text of which runs to 182 pages, nearly twice that of the Charities Act 1993. One difficulty has been that not all the provisions of the Act have been brought into force at the time of writing. Much of the Act is already in force, and most of the remainder will either come into force on 1 April 2009, or is expected to be brought into force on 1 October 2009. The text has been written on the assumption that this expectation will be fulfilled. The same course has been taken with regard to the Supreme Court Act 1981 which it is envisaged will be renamed as the Senior Courts Act 1981 on 1 October 2009 under the provisions of the Constitutional Reform Act 2005. The relevant sections of the Civil Partnership Act 2004 and the Mental Capacity Act 2005 that were referred to in the previous edition have now been brought into force. Thus, inter alia, the enduring power of attorney has been replaced (with savings) by a lasting power of attorney.

In response to comments that I have received I have somewhat expanded the introductory chapter and set out the most familiar maxims of equity. Further I have, of course, attempted to take full account of the decisions of the courts since the last edition. Perhaps the most revolutionary was the House of Lords decision in *Stack* v *Dowden* where the majority of their Lordships abandoned the resulting trust in the context of the family home in favour of the common intention constructive trust. Only Lord Neuberger adopted the traditional resulting trust approach. Another House of Lords decision is *Barlow Clowes International Ltd (in liq)* v *Eurotrust International Ltd* where their Lordships considered their earlier decision in *Twinsectra Ltd* v *Yardley* on the meaning of dishonesty in the context of a claim for knowing assistance. They admitted that there was 'an element of ambiguity' in the earlier decision, which they sought to clarify. Commentators, however, have not been persuaded that it is simply a case of clarification, and views have been expressed that their Lordships have delivered a volte face, and that the decision in *Barlow Clowes* is radically different from that in *Twinsectra*.

Other interesting cases include *Hanchett-Stamford* v *A-G* on the situation where a non-charitable unincorporated association is reduced to one member; *Nelson* v *Greening & Sykes (Builders) Ltd* which decides that where an equitable owner declares a bare trust of his interest he does not 'disappear from the picture'; *Cooper* v *PRG Powerhouse Ltd* on the *Quistclose* trust; *Yeoman's Row Management Ltd* v *Cobbe* on proprietary estoppel; and *Sieff* v *Fox* on the rule in *Re Hastings-Bass*. There are, as usual, numerous injunctions cases, particularly in breach of confidence and invasion of privacy cases, and on freezing injunctions.

One change that has been made in the content of this work is the omission of the equitable doctrines of conversion and reconversion; satisfaction, ademption and performance; and election. These no longer play a part in undergraduate courses, which are now commonly trusts courses rather than equity courses. The updated material is however available in the Online Resources Centre.

All the staff of my publishers with whom I have had dealings have been very helpful and efficient and I wish to record my thanks to them. I would also like to express my gratitude to the OUP for taking responsibility for the tables and the index.

I have endeavoured to state the law as at the end of October 2008, with one or two additions being possible at the proof stage.

Philip H Pettit
January 2009

ADDENDUM

It is understood that the introduction in the Lords of a Perpetuities Bill to implement the proposals made by the Law Commission in 1998, referred to at p 222, infra, is imminent. Such a Bill is unlikely to prove controversial.

The Law Commission in Consultation Paper 154 (1999), referred to at p 232, infra, made certain proposals relating to Illegality and Trusts. In a second Consultation Paper, No 189 (2009), it makes revised proposals. It hopes to publish a final report in Autumn 2009.

March 2009

CONTENTS

TABLE OF CASES

TABLE OF LEGISLATION

UK Secondary legislation

ABBREVIATIONS

The following abbreviations have been used in relation to legal periodicals

AALR	Anglo American Law Review
Adel LR	Adelaide Law Review
Alberta LR	Alberta Law Review
ALJ	Australian Law Journal
All ER Rev	All England Law Reports Annual Review
Am JLH	American Journal of Legal History
ASCL	Annual Survey of Commonwealth Law
Auck ULR	Auckland University Law Review
Bond LR	Bond Law Review
BTR	British Tax Review
CBR	Canadian Bar Review
CC	Charity Commission
CCL	Charity Commission leaflet
CJQ	Civil Justice Quarterly
CLJ	Cambridge Law Journal
CLP	Current Legal Problems
CLPR	Charity Law and Practice Review
CLY	Current Law Yearbook
Calif LR	California Law Review
Cambrian LR	Cambrian Law Review
Cant LR	Canterbury Law Review
CLWR	Common Law World Review
Co Law	Company Lawyer
Col LR	Columbia Law Review
Conv	Conveyancer and Property Lawyer (New Series)
Crim LR	Criminal Law Review
Dal LJ	Dalhousie Law Journal
Deak LR	Deakin Law Review
Dec Ch Com	Decisions of the Charity Commissioners
Denning LJ	Denning Law Journal
E & L	Education & the Law
EG	Estates Gazette
EHR	English Historical Review
ELJ	Education Law Journal
ET & PJ	Estates Trusts & Pensions Journal
Fam Law	Family Law
GLR	Griffiths Law Review
HLR	Harvard Law Review
ICLQ	International and Comparative Law Quarterly
Ind LJ	Industrial Law Journal
Ir Jur NS	Irish Jurist (New Series)

JBL	Journal of Business Law
JLH	Journal of Legal History
JMCL	Journal of Malaysian and Comparative Law
JPEL	Journal of Planning and Environmental Law
JSW & FL	Journal of Social Welfare and Family Law
Jur R	Juridical Review
KCLJ	Kings College Law Journal
Law Com CP	Law Commission Consultation Paper
Law Com No	Law Commission Report Number
LJ	Law and Justice
LMCLQ	Lloyd's Maritime and Commercial Law Quarterly
Lpool LR	Liverpool Law Review
LQR	Law Quarterly Review
LS	Legal Studies
LSG	Law Society's Gazette
L Teach	Law Teacher
McGill LJ	McGill Law Journal
Mal LR	Malaya Law Review
Man LJ	Manitoba Law Journal
Mich LR	Michigan Law Review
MLJ	Malaya Law Journal
MLR	Modern Law Review
Mon LR	Monash University Law Review
MULR	Melbourne University Law Review
New LR	Newcastle Law Review
NILQ	Northern Ireland Law Quarterly
Nott LJ	Nottingham Law Journal
NLJ	New Law Journal
NYULR	New York University Law Review
NZLJ	New Zealand Law Journal
NZULR	New Zealand Universities Law Review
OLR	Ottawa Law Review
Osg Hall LJ	Osgoode Hall Law Journal
Otago LR	Otago Law Review
Ox JLS	Oxford Journal of Legal Studies
PCB	Private Client Business
PLJ	Property Law Journal
Pub L	Public Law
QITLJ	Queensland Institute of Technology Law Journal
QLJ	Queen's Law Journal
QLSJ	Queensland Law Society Journal
RLR	Restitution Law Review
RR	Review of the Register leaflet issued by the Charity Commission
S Ac LJ	Singapore Academy of Law Journal
SCLR	Supreme Court Law Review (Canada)
SJLS	Singapore Journal of Legal Studies

Sol Jo	Solicitor's Journal
Stat LR	Statute Law Review
Sydney LR	Sydney Law Review
T & E	Trusts and Estates
T & ELJ	Trusts & Estates Law Journal
T & ELTJ	Trusts & Estates Law & Tax Journal
TL & P	Trust Law and Practice
Tru LI	Trust Law International
Tulane LR	Tulane Law Review
UBCLR	University of British Columbia Law Review
UNSWLJ	University of New South Wales Law Journal
U Penn LR	University of Pennsylvania Law Review
UQLJ	University of Queensland Law Journal
UT Fac L Rev	University of Toronto Faculty Law Review
U Tas LR	University of Tasmania Law Review
UTLJ	University of Toronto Law Journal
UWALR	University of Western Australia Law Review
VUWLR	Victoria University of Wellington Law Review
WILJ	West Indies Law Journal
Yale LJ	Yale Law Journal

Case references   Where footnote references to English cases decided since the Judicature Acts are not followed by an indication of the court in which they were decided, it can be assumed that the decision was at first instance in the High Court.

Reports   In Chapters 13 and 14, the 'Reports' referred to are the annual reports of the Charity Commission for England and Wales (previously Charity Commissioners for England and Wales), published in pursuance of para 11 of Sch 1A to the Charities Act 1993 inserted by the Charities Act 2006, s 6(2) and Sch 1. This paragraph replaces similar provisions previously contained in the Charities Act 1993 and the Charities Act 1960.

1

HISTORY OF THE
COURT OF CHANCERY
AND INTRODUCTION
TO EQUITY

The words 'equity' and 'trust' are part of everyday language and, like many words, have more than one meaning. Which is the appropriate meaning depends on the context, and both have special meanings as part of the language of the law.

In a non-technical sense, the primary dictionary meaning of 'equity' is fairness, and lawyers sometimes use it in this sense. This concept indeed, as we shall see, lies behind its legal meaning. In the world of finance, 'equity' is the word used to describe a company's ordinary share capital and an investment in 'equities' means an investment in the shares of a company; as will be explained, 'equities' in the law of trusts has a different meaning, except when used in connection with trustees' power of investment.

The legal meaning of 'equity' has been moulded by history. In the early years after the Norman Conquest, justice continued to be dispensed by local courts on the basis of local custom. Later, particularly under Henry II in the twelfth century, royal justice developed bringing into being a 'common law', which applied throughout the kingdom. The subsequence emergence of 'equity', and its relationship to the common law, are explained in the first three sections of this chapter.

The word 'trust' primarily carries with it the concept of confidence in the integrity and competence of a person or institution. The trust, as a legal institution, regulates the way in which a person or body holds property not for his own benefit, but for the benefit of others. Most of this book is concerned with the 'trust' in this sense. What is known in the USA as 'antitrust legislation' has nothing to do with the trust in this sense: it is concerned with arrangements between commercial organizations to defeat competition and keep up prices—that is, what we think of as competition law. The history of the trust, and the meaning of equitable interests and equities, are considered in sections 4 and 5. The chapter concludes with short sections on trusts and taxation, and trusts and conflict of laws.

1 HISTORY OF THE COURT OF CHANCERY[1]

If law be regarded in general terms as the rules enforced in the courts for the promotion of justice,[2] equity may be described as that part of the law which, immediately[3] prior to the coming into force of the Supreme Court of Judicature Acts 1873 and 1875[4] on 1 November 1875, was enforced exclusively in the Court of Chancery and not at all in the courts of common law—Common Pleas, Exchequer, and King's Bench. Although, in origin, the jurisdiction of the Court of Chancery was undoubtedly based on moral principles designed to remove injustices incapable of being dealt with in the common law courts, equity was always, at least until the Judicature Acts, essentially a supplementary jurisdiction, an appendix or gloss on the common law.[5] In some sense, this remains the case, although developments in equitable doctrine since that date have been said to render the description of equity as an appendix to the common law 'an utterly misleading statement of equity's place in the scheme of things today'.[6] It is accordingly not really possible to define it successfully; it can only be described by giving an inventory of its contents or in the historical terms set out above.

The position at the end of the thirteenth century, even after the last of the three common law courts to evolve out of the Curia Regis had become separate, was that a residuum of justice was still thought to reside in the King. If, therefore, the common law courts for any reason failed to do justice, an aggrieved person might petition the King or the King's Council. The Lord Chancellor, in addition to being the Keeper of the Great Seal and the head of the Chancery, which by this time had become an important department of state, was the head of the King's Council and, from early times, petitions seeking the King's 'extraordinary justice' were referred to him. As early as the reign of Edward I, petitions are to be found addressed to the 'Chancellor and the Council'. This procedure steadily became more frequent and, by the end of the fourteenth century, petitions began to be addressed to the Chancellor alone. The petition would pray that the person we now call the 'defendant' should be brought before the Chancery to be examined and dealt with appropriately, and his presence was enforced by a writ of subpoena—that is, an order that he should appear before the Chancery on pain of forfeiting a sum of money. There, he would be examined on oath, and questions of both law and fact would be determined. However they were addressed, the petitions were, in fact, dealt with by the Chancellor, although at first purely

---

[1] For a fuller account, see Holdsworth, *History of English Law*, vol I, p 395 *et seq*; *Potter's Historical Introduction to English Law*, 4th edn, p 152 *et seq*; Kerly, *History of Equity*; and also Milson, *Historical Foundations of the Common Law*, 2nd edn, p 82 *et seq*.

[2] This begs the real question, 'what is justice?', which is, however, outside the scope of this book, being a question for jurisprudence and philosophy. Of course, in practice, many matters that justice would demand are not enforced in the courts for various reasons, many being unsuitable for judicial enforcement, and some of the rules enforced fail to achieve justice either generally or in a particular case.

[3] Before 1842, the Court of Exchequer had an equity jurisdiction. The statement following in the text relates to the central courts and disregards the Palatine Courts (abolished by the Courts Act 1971) and the county courts.

[4] Now replaced by the Supreme Court Act 1981, renamed as the Senior Courts Act 1981 by the Constitutional Reform Act 2005, as from 1 October 2009.

[5] Maitland, *Equity*, 2nd (Brunyate) edn, p 18. See also (1997) 113 LQR 601 (A J Duggan).

[6] See (1994) 110 LQR 238 (A Mason).

as a delegate of the Council. As the practice became habitual and references frequent, the Chancellor and his office the Chancery acquired the characteristics of a court, although so far as is known it was not until 1474 that the Chancellor made a decree upon his own authority.[7]

The cases referred to the Chancellor and the Chancery fall into two main groups: firstly, cases in which the law was defective; and secondly, those in which there was theoretically a remedy at common law, but the petitioner was unable to obtain it because of the disturbed state of the country, or the power and wealth of the other party, who might be able to put improper pressure on the jury or even the court. For a long time,[8] the latter was the most important and frequent type of case to be dealt with. In exercising jurisdiction in cases of this kind, it is unlikely that the Chancellor regarded himself as administering a separate system of law—indeed, he was not. It was a jurisdiction that was a cause of considerable complaint and it may well be that the Chancellor's powers would have disappeared at about the end of the fourteenth century if it had not been for the other head of jurisdiction, which must now be considered.

During the early period of growth of the common law, there was rapid development as the Chancery created new writs to meet new cases. Moreover, the common law judges had a wide discretion to do justice, particularly in the informal procedure by plaint or bill (as opposed to actions begun by writ), and in proceedings in the General Eyre. At first, therefore, there was little scope for a jurisdiction to remedy the defects of the common law. However, this early rapid development ceased with the Provisions of Oxford in 1258, and only proceeded slowly after the controversial[9] *in consimili casu* clause of the Statute of Westminster the Second in 1285, so that it is fair to say that, by the end of the thirteenth century, the common law formed a rigid system that was unadaptable, or at least could only be slowly adapted, to meet new types of case. Moreover, plaints without writ, for reasons that are not fully explained, apparently ceased to be available in the fourteenth century and, at about the same time, General Eyres virtually ceased to be held. Consequently, hardship increasingly often arose because of defects in the law and petitions began to be brought on this ground. In giving relief in these cases, new law was being created and it was this new law that became known as 'equity', in contrast to the 'common law' dispensed in the common law courts.[10]

For a long time, there was close consultation between the Chancellor and the common law judges as to the types of case in which relief should be granted. Moreover, the

---

[7] Although he seems to have dismissed a petition without consulting the Council nearly a century before. For a discussion of an early Tudor debate on the relation between law and equity, see (1998) 19 JLH 143 (G Behrens).

[8] The change seems to have taken place during the reign of Henry VI. The business of the Court of Chancery multiplied three times between 1420 and 1450, by which time nine-tenths of its work was concerned with uses: see (1970) 86 LQR 84 (Margaret E Avery).

[9] See (1931) 31 Col LR 778 (T F T Plucknett); (1931) 47 LQR 334 (W S Holdsworth); (1936) 52 LQR 68 (P A Landon); (1936) 52 LQR 220 (T F T Plucknett); (1937) 46 Yale LJ 1142 (Elizabeth Dix); Fifoot, *History and Sources of the Common Law*, p 66 et seq; Kiralfy, *The Action on the Case*, p 19 et seq; J H Baker, *An Introduction to English Legal History*, 4th edn, p 61 et seq.

[10] In addition to the equitable jurisdiction known as the 'English side' simply because the pleadings were in the native language, there was the relatively unimportant and largely separate 'Latin side' of the jurisdiction, so called because the records were kept in Latin. This comprised certain specialized matters such as questions relating to royal grants and inquisitions relating to the Crown's property rights, and the ordinary common law jurisdiction in personal actions brought by or against officers of the court.

Chancellor sometimes sat in the common law courts and common law judges might be asked to sit in Chancery. This reduced the risk of conflict from the point of view of person-alities; from the point of view of principle, conflict between the jurisdictions was reduced by the fact that it was a cardinal rule of the Court of Chancery that equity acts *in per-sonam*. Thus, in the central institution of equity jurisdiction, the trust, the Chancellor never denied that the trustee was the legal owner of the trust property, but merely insisted that the trustee should deal with it in accordance with the trust for the benefit of the ben-eficiaries. This remains the law today. Thus, as Scott J has observed:[11] 'The jurisdiction of the court to administer trusts...is an in personam jurisdiction.' Failure to comply with the Chancellor's order would be a contempt of court, which was punishable by imprisonment until the trustee was prepared to comply with the order. Originally, this procedure *in per-sonam*, against the person of the defendant, was the only process of the Court of Chancery for enforcing its decrees.[12]

Nonetheless, conflict did arise in the sixteenth century as the Chancellor extended and consolidated his jurisdiction, and the dispute centred on what became known as 'common injunctions' issued by the Chancellor, who contended that, even though a judgment was technically good, he was entitled to set it aside where it had been obtained by 'oppres-sion, wrong and a bad conscience'. By a 'common injunction', he would restrain parties to an action at common law either from proceeding with their action at law, or, having obtained judgment, from enforcing it. The dispute finally came to a head under James I, when Coke was Chief Justice and Ellesmere Lord Chancellor. The validity or invalidity of these injunctions would, it was recognized, determine the question whether legal suprem-acy was vested in the common law courts or the Chancery. The matter was referred by the King to Bacon, the Attorney-General, and other counsel, and in due course he accepted their advice that the injunctions were valid and, in 1616, accordingly issued an order in favour of the Chancery. This proved to be a final settlement of the dispute, although it was not fully accepted by the common lawyers until the end of the century.

From a broad point of view, the settlement did not prove altogether satisfactory by rea-son of the defects that grew up in the Court of Chancery during the latter part of the seventeenth and the eighteenth centuries. There was corruption and abuse of the process of the court,[13] an inadequate number of judicial staff, too many and incompetent officials, an over-elaborate system of rehearing and appeals, and a generally unsatisfactory organ-ization, which led to such expense, delays, and injustice that the business of the court declined. After piecemeal reforms beginning with the appointment of a Vice-Chancellor in 1813 and becoming much more numerous after the Whig victory in 1830, the Court of Chancery finally ceased to exist as a separate court as a result of the major reorganization of the whole judicial system by the Judicature Acts 1873 and 1875. Its jurisdiction was transferred to the Supreme Court of Judicature, most of the jurisdiction at first instance being assigned to the Chancery Division of the High Court.

---

[11] *Chellaram v Chellaram* [1985] Ch 409, 428, [1985] 1 All ER 1043, 1053.

[12] Sequestration was introduced towards the end of the sixteenth century and now there are various pow-ers for the court to make vesting orders, etc. See, eg, Trustee Act 1925, ss 44 *et seq*; Supreme Court Act 1981, now renamed as the Senior Courts Act 1981, s 39.

[13] The Chancery became very ready to issue injunctions by reason of the profits that thereby accrued and litigants were able to use them purely as delaying tactics. See (1988) 11 UNSWLJ 11 (C J Rossiter and Margaret Stone).

It should be added, in conclusion, that limited jurisdiction in equity matters is given to the county courts, the relevant statute now being the County Courts Act 1984.[14]

2 JURISDICTION OF THE COURT OF CHANCERY

Originally, as we have seen, the Chancellor did not have any clearly defined jurisdiction, but dispensed an extraordinary justice remedying the defects of the common law on grounds of conscience[15] and natural justice, a function for which he was well qualified, as he was commonly an ecclesiastic, well versed in both the civil and canon law. He was, indeed, sometimes called the 'Keeper of the King's Conscience'. In the absence of fixed principles, the decision at first depended to a large degree upon the Chancellor's personal ideas of right and wrong; thus Selden,[16] in the mid-seventeenth century, observed that equity varied according to the conscience of the individual Chancellor, in the same way as if the standard measure were a Chancellor's foot. This state of affairs began to be less true in the later seventeenth century, as the principles of equity began to become more fixed. Cases in the Chancery began to be reported around the middle of the century and were increasingly cited, relied on, and followed in subsequent cases. The Chancellors began to say that although they had a discretion, it should be exercised not according to conscience, but in accordance with precedent.[17] Lawyers rather than ecclesiastics became appointed Chancellors, the last of the non-legal Chancellors being Lord Shaftesbury, who held office during 1672–73. With his successor, Lord Nottingham (1673–82), often called the 'father of modern equity', the development of a settled system of equity really began, to be continued under succeeding Chancellors—notably, Lord Hardwicke (1736–56)—and completed in the early nineteenth century by Lord Eldon (1801–06 and 1807–27). The result of their work was to transform equity into a system of law almost as fixed and rigid as the rules of the common law. Accordingly, Lord Eldon could observe[18] 'Nothing would inflict on me greater pain, in quitting this place,[19] than the recollection that I had done anything to justify the reproach that the equity of this court varies like the Chancellor's foot', and it has since been bluntly stated[20] that 'This Court is not a Court of conscience'. By the early nineteenth century, equity had become simply that part of the law enforced in the Court of Chancery.

---

[14] Section 23 and SI 1981/1123. So far as the estates of deceased persons and trusts are concerned, there is jurisdiction where the estate or fund subject to the trust does not exceed in amount or value the sum of £30,000. There is unlimited jurisdiction in certain equity proceedings (but excluding proceedings under the Variation of Trusts Act 1958) by written consent of the parties under s 24, as amended.

[15] See (2001) 46 McGill LJ 573 (D R Klinck) for an interesting account of the meaning of conscience in early equity, its development from the fifteenth to the nineteenth centuries, and its position in current Canadian equity. Klinck further considers the meaning of 'conscience' in (2005) 31 QLJ 207. See also (2007) 27 Ox JLS 659 (M Macnair).   [16] *Table Talk of John Selden* (ed Pollock, 1927), p 43.

[17] See an article entitled 'Precedent in equity' in (1941) 57 LQR 245 (W H D Winder).

[18] *Gee v Pritchard* (1818) 2 Swans 402, 414.   [19] That is, the Court of Chancery.

[20] *Per* Buckley J in *Re Telescriptor Syndicate Ltd* [1903] 2 Ch 174, 195, 196.

A related matter is whether it is any longer open to equity to invent new equitable interests. Although there is no fiction in equity as there has been said to be at common law that the rules have existed from time immemorial,[21] and although 'it is perfectly well known that they have been established from time to time—altered, improved and refined from time to time. In many cases we know the names of the Chancellors who invented them',[22] yet it is in principle doubtful whether a new right can now be created. Extrajudicially Lord Evershed observed[23] that s 25(11)[24] of the Judicature Act 1873 put a stop to, or at least a very severe limitation on, the inventive faculties of future Chancery judges, and Lord Denning said, again extrajudicially,[25] that 'the Courts of Chancery are no longer courts of equity.... They are as fixed and immutable as the courts of law ever were'. The Court of Appeal, moreover, has observed[26] that if a 'claim in equity exists, it must be shown to have an ancestry founded in history and in the practice and precedents of the courts administering equity jurisdiction. It is not sufficient that because we may think that the "justice" of the present case requires it, we should invent such a jurisdiction for the first time', and again, more recently, that *the creation of new rights and remedies is a matter for Parliament, not the judges*'.[27] Further, so far as an equitable interest in land is concerned, s 4(1) of the Law of Property Act 1925 provides that, after 1925, such an interest is only capable of being validly created in any case in which an equivalent equitable interest in property real or personal could have been created before 1926.[28] In principle, it is very doubtful, therefore, whether new equitable interests can any longer be created, except through the extension and development of existing equitable interests by exactly the same process as extension and development may take place at law. As to that process, an Australian judge has observed:[29]

> It is inevitable that judge made law will alter to meet the changing conditions of society. That is the way it has always evolved. But it is essential that new rules should be related to fundamental doctrine. If the foundations of accepted doctrine be submerged under new principles, without regard to the interaction between the two, there will be high uncertainty as to the state of the law, both old and new.

---

[21] This has been said to be a fairy tale in which no one any longer believes. In truth, judges make and change the law. The whole of the common law is judge-made and only by judicial change in the law is the common law kept relevant in a changing world. See *Kleinwort Benson Ltd v Lincoln City Council* [1999] 2 AC 349, [1998] 4 All ER 513, HL, esp *per* Lord Browne-Wilkinson at 358, 518, and Lord Goff at 371, 378, 534, 535.

[22] *Per* Jessel MR in *Re Hallett's Estate* (1880) 13 Ch D 696, 710, CA—said, however, to be 'rather an overstatement' by Lord Evershed in the 1954 Lionel Cohen Lectures entitled 'Aspects of English equity', p 13.

[23] (1953) 6 CLP 11, 12.

[24] This subsection is discussed at p 8 *et seq, infra*. Lord Evershed's point is that the subsection necessarily proceeded upon the view that the rules of equity were then a known body of established doctrine.

[25] (1952) 5 CLP 8.

[26] *Re Diplock* [1948] Ch 465, 481, 482, [1948] 2 All ER 318, 326. CA; affd sub nom *Ministry of Health v Simpson* [1951] AC 251, [1950] 2 All ER 1137, HL; *Thompson v Earthy* [1951] 2 KB 596, [1951] 2 All ER 235.

[27] *Per* Megaw LJ giving the judgment of the court in *Western Fish Products Ltd v Penwith District Council* [1981] 2 All ER 204, 218, CA.

[28] See (1952) 16 Conv 323 (F R Crane). Cf *Hanchett-Stamford v A-G* [2008] EWHC 330 (Ch), [2008] 4 All ER 323, *per* Lewison J at [31].

[29] *Allen v Snyder* [1977] 2 NSWLR 685, 689, *per* Glass J A. See also *Lonrho plc v Fayed (No 2)* [1991] 4 All ER 961, [1992] 1 WLR 1 at 969, 9, per Millett J; *Kleinwort Benson Ltd v Lincoln City Council, supra*, HL.

The proper approach is, it is submitted, that stated by Bagnall J in *Cowcher v Cowcher*,[30] who said:

> I am convinced that in determining rights, particularly property rights, the only justice that can be attained by mortals, who are fallible and are not omniscient, is justice according to law; the justice which flows from the application of sure and settled principles to proved or admitted facts. So in the field of equity the length of the Chancellor's foot has been measured or is capable of measurement. This does not mean that equity is past child-bearing;[31] simply that its progeny must be legitimate—by precedent out of principle. It is well that this should be so; otherwise no lawyer could safely advise on his client's title and every quarrel would lead to a law suit.

Of recent years, some common law lawyers have sought to give equity a much wider and less precise jurisdiction. Such a development is, it is submitted, not only contrary to precedent and the historical development of equity, but is undesirable for the reasons given by Bagnall J and unnecessary by reason of the improvements in the machinery for law reform,[32] which enable defects in the law to be corrected by legislation more rapidly than in the past.

It is convenient to mention briefly at this point that one distinction between the common law and equity lay in the remedies available. In general, the only remedy available at common law, apart from a real action for the specific recovery of certain interests in land,[33] was damages, and a plaintiff who established his right and the breach of it by the defendant was entitled to this remedy as a matter of right, no matter how little merit there might seem to be in his claim. Equity, on the other hand, had no power,[34] until statute intervened,[35] to award damages at all, although in some circumstances it might award monetary compensation for breach of trust or the infraction of a fiduciary duty.[36] However, it invented a variety of remedies, the grant of which is always in the discretion of the court; the most important are specific performance and injunction. As we shall see, these are orders *in*

---

[30] [1972] 1 All ER 943, 948, [1972] 1 WLR 425, 430; *Harris v Digital Pulse Property Ltd* (2003) 197 ALR 626.

[31] But in [1982] Cambrian LR 24, Goulding J said extrajudicially that whether or not equity is past childbearing, she ought to be.

[32] In particular, the establishment of the Law Commission.

[33] See Cheshire and Burn, *Modern Law of Real Property*, 17th edn, p 28; Holdsworth, *History of English Law*, vol III, p 3 *et seq*.

[34] Or, if it had, which is, perhaps, the better view, from a very early time considered it to be ordinarily undesirable to exercise it. See (1992) 109 LQR 652 (P M McDermott), a revised version of which appears in his book *Equitable Damages*, ch 1, and p 514 *infra*. Extrajudicially, Lord Millett has said that 'damages for breach of trust' (or fiduciary duty) is a misleading expression, the use of which should be stamped out: (1998) 114 LQR 214. See also (1999) 37 Alberta LR 95 (J Berryman); (1999) 37 Alberta LR 114 (P M Perell).

[35] Lord Cairns' Act (Chancery Amendment Act 1858). Note that the remedy of damages is available in cases of breach of confidence, '*despite the equitable nature of the wrong, through a beneficent interpretation of Lord Cairns' Act*' (as to which, see p 567 et seq, *infra*): *A-G v Guardian Newspapers Ltd (No 2)* [1990] 1 AC 109, 286, [1988] 3 All ER 545, 662, *per* Lord Goff, HL. See *Seager v Copydex Ltd* [1967] 2 All ER 415, [1967] 1 WLR 923, CA.

[36] In Australia, it has been said to be '*an equitable monetary remedy which is available when the equitable remedies of restitution and account are not appropriate*': *O'Halloran v R T Thomas and Family Property Ltd* (1998) 45 NSWLR 262; and see *Duke Group Ltd (in liq) v Pilmer* (1999) 153 Fed LR 1 at p 165 *et seq* and on appeal sub nom *Pilmer v Duke Group (in liq)* (2001) 180 ALR 249: See (1982) 13 MULR 349 (I E Davidson); *Day v Mead* [1987] 2 NZLR 443, noted (1989) 105 LQR 32 (M Vennell); (1993) 67 ALJ 596 (L Aitken); (1994) 24 VUWLR 19 (C Rickett and T Gardner). See also (2006) 73 T & ELTJ 7 (R Dew) and p 514, *infra*.

personam directing a person to do or not to do some specified thing, and disobedience of such an order is a contempt of court. An equitable remedy may be awarded both to enforce a right recognized only in equity and also to enforce a legal right, although this will only be done where the common law remedy of damages is regarded as inadequate.

3 FUSION OF THE ADMINISTRATION OF LAW AND EQUITY

The reorganization of the courts carried out by the Judicature Acts 1873 and 1875 produced one Supreme Court administering both law and equity. Although for the sake of convenience the High Court, dealing with cases at first instance, was divided into divisions,[37] every judge of each division was, by s 24[38] of the 1873 Act, given the power and duty to recognize and give effect to both legal and equitable rights, claims, defences, and remedies. Further, by s 25, provision was made for situations in which the rules of law and equity were in conflict. After dealing specifically with a number of particular cases, it was provided[39] in general terms that in all other cases in which there was a conflict or variance between the rules of equity and the rules of common law with reference to the same matter, the rules of equity should prevail.

(A) THE EFFECT OF SS 24 AND 25[40]

Before the Judicature Acts, there were cases in which common law and equity had different rules that might give rise to inconsistent remedies. In such cases, the equitable rule would ultimately prevail by means of the grant of a common injunction.[41] Section 24(5) abolished the common injunction, but even without this, the result in any particular case would have been the same as before the Act in litigation in the High Court, because, as we have seen, every judge was bound to have regard to all equitable rights, claims, defences, and remedies.

Curious as it was that, prior to the Acts, there should have been different rules relating to the same subject matter in different courts, it would have been even more strange if these conflicting rules had continued to exist when both were being administered in the same court, notwithstanding provisions as to which rule should prevail. What s 25(11) does, after dealing with particular cases, is to provide that in all courts, where there are conflicting rules, in the sense referred to above, the legal rule is abolished and the equitable rule

---

[37] Originally five, now three—namely, Chancery, Queen's Bench, and Family Divisions.

[38] Now replaced by s 49 of the Supreme Court Act 1981, now renamed as the Senior Courts Act 1981.

[39] Judicature Act 1873, s 25(11), now replaced by s 49 of the Supreme Court Act 1981, now renamed as the Senior Courts Act 1981.

[40] See, generally, Maitland, *Equity*, 2nd (Brunyate) edn, pp 16–20, 149–159; Meagher, Gummow, and Lehane, *Equity: Doctrines and Remedies*, 3rd edn, p 36 *et seq*; (1975) 39 Conv 1 & 236 (J T Farrand and P Jackson); (1982) 26 Am JLH 227 (D O'Keefe).

[41] See p 4, *supra*, and p 610, *infra*.

is to replace it for all purposes. The court in such cases has henceforward only one rule to enforce.

It should be stressed that, in many cases, there were differences between the rules of common law and equity that did not result in conflict, and to which ss 24 and 25 had no application. Thus, for example:

(i)   the common law would award damages for breach of a voluntary contract made by deed, or for breach of a contract of personal service,[42] but in neither case was a remedy available in equity. Equity would not however restrain a plaintiff from obtaining his common law remedy;

(ii) in some cases, common law and equity might give different, but compatible, remedies. For instance, in a case of nuisance common law would give damages for the injury suffered by the plaintiff, while equity would grant an injunction restraining further commission of the tort;

(iii) in relation to the tort of conversion, this was a common law cause of action and the common law did not recognize the equitable title of the beneficiary under a trust. It recognized only the title of the trustee, as the person normally entitled to immediate possession of the trust property. An equitable owner had no title at common law to sue in conversion, unless he could also show that he had actual possession or an immediate right to possession of the goods claimed.[43] Again, the House of Lords has rejected as insupportable the proposition that 'a person who has the equitable ownership of goods is entitled to sue in tort for negligence anyone who for want of care causes them to be lost or damaged without joining the legal owner as a party to the action'.[44]

Such cases remain unaffected by the Judicature Acts.

Reverting to s 25(11), this provision was applied in *Berry v Berry*[45] to prevent a wife succeeding in an action on a separation deed. The deed had been varied by a simple contract, which was no defence to an action at law, but the equitable rule was that such a variation is effective and that rule prevailed. Again, in *Walsh v Lonsdale*,[46] there was an agreement for a lease of a mill for seven years at a rent payable quarterly in arrears, with a provision entitling the landlord to demand a year's rent in advance. No formal lease was ever executed and the lease, as such, was accordingly void at law.[47] The tenant entered into possession and paid rent quarterly in arrears for some eighteen months, at which time a year's rent was demanded in advance. On failure to pay, the landlord distrained and the action

---

[42] See Chapter 28, section 2(D), *infra*.

[43] *MCC Proceeds Inc v Lehman Bros International (Europe)* [1998] 4 All ER 675, CA.

[44] *Leigh and Sillivan Ltd v Aliakmon Shipping Co Ltd* [1986] 1 AC 1, 14.

[45] [1929] 2 KB 316, DC. For other examples, see *Job v Job* (1877) 6 Ch D 562; *Lowe v Dixon* (1885) 16 QBD 455. See also *Raineri v Miles* [1981] AC 1050 [1980] 2 All ER 145, HL.

[46] (1882) 21 Ch D 9, CA. Dicta of Jessel MR in this case, which appear to suggest that the distinction between legal and equitable interests has been abolished, are misleading. See Megarry and Wade, *Law of Real Property*, 7th edn, [17.046], stressing that the doctrine of *Walsh v Lonsdale* depends upon the availability of specific performance, and cf the same judge's orthodox statement of the position in *Salt v Cooper* (1880) 16 Ch D 544 at 549, CA. His decision was affirmed on appeal without comment on his remarks on this point. See also (1987) 7 Ox JLS 60 (S Gardner); *Chan v Cresdon Pty Ltd* (1989) 168 CLR 242, 89 ALR 522.

[47] Section 3 of the Real Property Act 1845, now replaced by s 52(1) of the Law of Property Act 1925.

was for damages for illegal distress. The tenant contended that, having gone into possession and paid by reference to a year, he was a yearly tenant upon such of the terms of the
agreement as were not inconsistent with the yearly tenancy, that the provision for payment
of a year's rent was inconsistent, that the landlord accordingly was not entitled to make the
demand, and that the distress was unlawful. This argument represented the common law
view before 1875. The court, however, held that the equitable view must prevail—namely,
that this being an agreement of which specific performance would be granted, the rights
and liabilities of the parties must be ascertained as if the lease had actually been executed
containing all of the agreed terms.[48]

(B) FUSION OF LAW AND EQUITY, OR MERELY FUSION OF THEIR ADMINISTRATION

The orthodox view is that there has merely been a fusion of administration, 'the two streams
of jurisdiction, though they run in the same channel, run side by side and do not mingle
their waters'.[49] More recently, the view has been expressed that law and equity themselves
are fused.[50] This view has been put most clearly and most authoritatively by Lord Diplock
in *United Scientific Holdings Ltd v Burnley Borough Council*:[51]

> My Lords, if by 'rules of equity' is meant that body of substantive and adjectival law, that
> prior to 1875, was administered by the Court of Chancery but not by courts of common
> law, to speak of the rules of equity as being part of the law of England in 1977 is about as
> meaningful as to speak similarly of the statutes of Uses or of Quia Emptores. Historically
> all three have in their time played an important part in the development of the corpus
> juris into what it is today; but to perpetuate a dichotomy between rules of equity and rules
> of common law which it was a major purpose of the Supreme Court of Judicature Act
> 1873 to do away with, is, in my view, conducive to erroneous conclusions as to the ways in
> which the law of England has developed in the last 100 years.

It is respectfully submitted that these propositions cannot be accepted. Baker has pointed
out[52] that no one thinks that the rules of equity have remained unchanged since 1875—
they have developed in the same way as rules of common law. As to the comparison with
Quia Emptores, Baker observes that this is still in force today and is said to be 'one of the
pillars of the law of real property'.[53] Most importantly, it is a complete misapprehension to

---

[48] The principle of *Walsh v Lonsdale*, *supra*, has been held to be applicable twice, eg where V agrees
to sell the fee simple to P, who agrees to grant a lease thereof to T: *Industrial Properties (Barton Hill) Ltd
v Associated Electrical Industries Ltd* [1977] QB 580, [1977] 2 All ER 293, CA. See Maitland, *Equity*, 2nd
(Brunyate) edn, pp 16–18, and cf Hohfeld, *Fundamental Legal Conceptions*, p 121 *et seq*.

[49] *Ashburner's Principles of Equity*, 2nd edn, p 18; (1954) 70 LQR 326 (Lord Evershed); (1961) 24 MLR 116
(V T H Delaney); Megarry and Wade, *Law of Real Property*, 7th edn, [5.019]; (1977) 93 LQR 529 (P V Baker);
(1977) 6 AALR 119 (T G Watkin). See (1993) 5 Cant LR 299 (J Maxton); (2003) 26 UNSWLJ 357 (M Tilbury);
(2006) 29 UNSWLJ 38 (D A Hughes).

[50] *Per* Lord Denning in *Errington v Errington* [1952] 1 KB 290, 298, [1952] 1 All ER 149, 155, CA. A case
for integration is made in [2002] CLP 223 (Sarah Worthington).

[51] [1978] AC 904, [1977] 2 All ER 62, 68, HL. These views were adopted by Peter Smith J in *WWF—World
Wide Fund for Nature v World Wrestling Federation Entertainment Inc* [2005] EWCH 184 (Ch), [2006] FSR
663, revsd [2007] EWCA Civ 286, [2008] 1 All ER 74, without comment on this point. See also Lord Simon at
83, 84, and *Canson Enterprises Ltd v Boughton & Co* (1991) 85 DLR (4th) 129.

[52] (1977) 93 LQR 529.   [53] Megarry and Wade, *Law of Real Property*, 7th edn, [2.018].

think that it was a purpose of the Judicature Acts to do away with the dichotomy between rules of equity and rules of common law. Introducing the second reading, the Attorney-General said[54] in terms that 'The Bill was not one for the fusion of law and equity' and he went on to explain what the purpose of the Bill was:

> The defect of our legal system was, not that Law and Equity existed, but that if a man went for relief to a Court of Law, and an equitable claim or an equitable defence arose, he must go to some other Court and begin afresh. Law and Equity therefore, would remain if the Bill passed, but they would be administered concurrently, and no one would be sent to get in one Court the relief which another Court had refused to give.... Great authorities had no doubt declared that law and Equity might be fused by enactment; but in his opinion, to do so would be to decline to grapple with the real difficulty of the case. If an Act were passed doing no more than fuse law and Equity, it would take 20 years of decisions and hecatombs of suitors to make out what Parliament meant and had not taken the trouble to define. It was more philosophical to admit the innate distinction between Law and Equity, which you could not get rid of by Act of Parliament, and to say not that the distinction should not exist, but that the Courts should administer relief according to legal principles when these applied, or else according to equitable principles. That was what the Bill proposed, with the addition that, whenever the principles of Law and Equity conflicted, equitable principles should prevail.

The orthodox view was recently reasserted by Mummery LJ,[55] who observed that the Judicature Acts:

> were intended to achieve procedural improvements in the administration of law and equity in all courts, not to transform equitable interests into legal titles or to sweep away altogether the rules of the common law, such as the rule that a plaintiff in an action for conversion must have possession or a right to immediate possession of the goods.

Although it is clear that the decision in a case may well depend upon an amalgam of rules from both common law and equity, as in *Walsh v Lonsdale*,[56] and although on a broader canvas one may regard the law of real property, for instance, as an amalgam of statute, common law, and equity, it is accordingly submitted that to talk of the fusion of law and equity is misleading. The facts, inter alia, that the trust has been unaffected, and there is still duality of legal and equitable ownership,[57] that in the law of property legal rights and equitable rights, even though for some purposes equivalent as in *Walsh v Lonsdale*, may have different effects, for instance, as regards third parties, that purely equitable rights can still only be enforced by equitable remedies,[58] and that the writ *ne exeat regno* is only available in relation to an equitable debt,[59] are inconsistent with the idea conveyed by the phrase 'fusion of law and equity'. Also, the language of s 49 of the Supreme Court Act 1981, now renamed as the Senior Courts Act 1981, which replaces s 25(11) of the Judicature Act

---

[54] Hansard 3rd Series vol 216, 644, 645. See, to the same effect, *Salt v Cooper* (1880) 16 Ch D 544, 549, *per* Jessel MR; (1995) 9 Tru LI 35, 37 (Lord Millett).

[55] *MCC Proceeds Inc v Lehman Bros International (Europe)* [1998] 4 All ER 675, 691, CA.

[56] (1882) 21 Ch D 9, CA.

[57] See *Joseph v Lyons* (1884) 15 QBD 280, 287, *per* Lindley LJ, cited by Mummery LJ in *MCC Proceeds Inc v Lehman Bros International (Europe), supra*, CA, at 691.

[58] Thus an equitable owner cannot purely as such sue in conversion: *MCC Proceeds Inc v Lehman Bros International (Europe)*, CA, *supra*. Now, however, there is statutory power for the court to award damages in lieu of or in addition to an injunction or specific performance: Supreme Court Act 1981, now renamed as the Senior Courts Act 1981, s 50. See [1996] CLJ 36 (A Tettenborn).   [59] See p 710, *infra*.

1873, appears to assume the continued separate existence of rules of equity and rules of the common law.

Those who refer to the fusion of law and equity commonly make little effort to explain precisely what they mean by the phrase, nor do they deal with the arguments set out above. Recently, moreover, Lord Browne-Wilkinson was careful to refer to the fusion of the administration of law and equity,[60] and Lord Millett, writing extrajudicially,[61] has observed that the opinion that the Judicature Acts had the effect of fusing law and equity to the extent that they have become a single body of law rather than two separate systems of law administered together is now widely discredited. He referred with approval to the view of a New Zealand judge[62] that: 'Neither law nor equity is now stifled by its origin and the fact that both are administered by one court has inevitably meant that each has borrowed from the other in furthering the harmonious development of the law as a whole.'

4 USES AND TRUSTS

(A) HISTORY OF THE TRUST

Maitland called[63] the trust 'the greatest and most distinctive achievement performed by Englishmen in the field of jurisprudence'. It is the outstanding creation of equity. Under a trust, in the most general terms, trustees, who are not permitted to profit from their trust,[64] are required to hold property of which they are the legal owners for the benefit of other persons, the cestuis que trust or beneficiaries.

Even before the Conquest, cases have been found of land being conveyed to one man to be held by him on behalf of or 'to the use of'[65] another, but for a considerable time this only seems to have been done for a limited time and a limited purpose, such as for the grantor's family while he went on a crusade. From the early thirteenth century, the practice grew up of conveying land in a general way for more permanent purposes. For various reasons, a landowner might convey land by an ordinary common law conveyance to persons called 'feoffees[66] to uses' directing them to hold the land for the benefit of other persons, the cestuis que use, who might indeed be or include the feoffor himself. After early doubts, the common law refused to take any account of the uses—that is, the directions given to

---

[60] In *Tinsley v Milligan* [1994] 1 AC 340, [1993] 3 All ER 65, 86, 90, HL: his reference to 'the fusion of law and equity' in *Lord Napier and Ettrick v Hunter* [1993] AC 713, [1993] 1 All ER 385, 406, 408, [1993] 2 WLR 42, 65, 66, HL, can, perhaps, be regarded as a loose shorthand. See, generally, (1993) 5 Bond LR 152 (Fiona Burns); (1994) 110 LQR 260 (A Mason); [1994] Conv 13 (Jill Martin); (2002) 22 Ox JLS 1 (A Burrows).

[61] (1995–96) 6 KCLJ 1, reprinted (1995) 9 Tru LI 35. Hayton & Marshall, *Law of Trusts and Equitable Remedies*, 12th edn, [1.33], say that it is a fallacy to assume that law and equity have been fused into a new body of principles.

[62] Somers J in *Elders Pastoral Ltd v Bank of New Zealand* [1989] 2 NZLR 180, 193.

[63] *Selected Historical Essays* 129 (1936). There is no institution quite like the trust in civil law systems based on Roman law: see (1974) 48 Tulane LR 917 (J H Merryman). See also (1980) 25 McGill LJ 42 (Yves Caron) on the trust in Quebec, and W A Wilson (ed), *Trusts and Trust-like Devices*; [1997] CLJ 175 (N G Jones).

[64] Unless authorized by the trust instrument, statute, or the court—see Chapter 19, p 441 *et seq, infra*.

[65] From the Latin *ad opus*—Pollock and Maitland, *History of English Law*, 2nd edn, vol II, p 228.

[66] The mode of conveyance was normally feoffment with livery of seisin, and the person conveying the land was accordingly the 'feoffor'; the person receiving it, the 'feoffee'.

the feoffees to uses, who, although they were bound in honour, could not be sued either by the feoffor or the cestuis que use. The common law in fact treated the feoffees to uses as the unfettered owners of the property and completely disregarded the claims of the cestuis que use.

It was clearly highly unsatisfactory that feoffees to uses should be able to disregard the dictates of good faith, honour, and justice with impunity,[67] and, from the end of the fourteenth or the early fifteenth centuries,[68] the Chancellor began to intervene and compel the feoffees to uses to carry out the directions given to them as to how they should deal with the land. The Chancellor never, however, denied that the feoffees to uses were the legal owners of the land; he merely ordered the feoffees to uses to carry out the directions given to them and failure to carry out the order would be a contempt of court, which would render the feoffees liable to imprisonment until they were prepared to comply.

The device of the use was adopted for various purposes. It enabled a landowner, for example, to evade some of the feudal dues that fell on the person seised of land, to dispose of his land by his will, to evade mortmain statutes, and more effectively to settle his land. The use developed considerably during the fifteenth and early sixteenth centuries, so much so that it was said, in 1500, that the greater part of the land in England was held in use[69] and the rights of the cestui que use were so extensive that it became recognized that there was duality of ownership. One person, the feoffee to uses, was the legal owner according to the common law—a title not disputed by the Chancellor. But the feoffee to uses had only the bare legal title; beneficial ownership was in the equitable owner, the cestui que use. A stop was put to the development of the use in 1535, however, when, largely because the King was losing so many feudal dues by the device of the use, the Statute of Uses[70] was passed to put an end to uses, or at least severely to limit them. In cases in which the Act applied, the use was 'executed'—that is, on the one hand, the feoffees to uses were deprived of their seisin of the land (indeed, they commonly dropped out of the picture altogether) and, on the other hand, the equitable estates of the cestuis que use were turned into equivalent legal estates carrying seisin. Although the Act executed the vast majority of uses, there were cases to which it did not apply—those in which, for instance, the feoffees to uses had active duties to perform—and thus the use never became completely obsolete.

One special case that should be mentioned was the use upon a use, as where land is limited to A and his heirs to the use of B and his heirs to the use of C and his heirs. It was decided before 1535 that C took nothing in such a case: A had the legal fee simple, B the equitable fee simple, but the limitation to C was repugnant to B's interest and accordingly void. After the Statute of Uses, the second use was still held to be void,[71] although the first use was executed so as to give B the legal fee simple and leave A, like C, with nothing at all. Eventually, however, by steps that are not very clear,[72] the Chancellor, at about the

---

[67] There may have been a remedy in the ecclesiastical courts, at least after the death of the feoffor: see (1979) 70 Col LR 1503 (R H Helmholz).

[68] See J H Baker, *An Introduction to Legal History*, 4th edn, p 251, n 12, and (1982) 98 LQR 26 (J Barton).

[69] Y B Mich 15 Hen VII 13 pl 1, *per* Frowike C J.

[70] For background, see (1967) 82 EHR 676 (E W Ives).

[71] *Tyrrel's Case* (1557) 2 Dyer 155a. But see (1966) 82 LQR 215 (J L Barton); (1993) 14 JLH 75 (I N G Jones).

[72] The political background was that, after the abolition of military tenure in 1660, the King ceased to have any substantial interest in the maintenance of feudal dues.

middle of the seventeenth century[73] or perhaps earlier,[74] began to enforce this second use and it had become a well-established practice by the end of the century. As a matter of terminology, the second use thus enforced became called a 'trust', and, as a matter of drafting, the basic formula was '*unto and to the use of B and his heirs in trust for C and his heirs*'. B took the legal fee simple at common law, but the use in his favour prevented the second use being executed by the Statute of Uses, leaving it to be enforced in equity as a trust. The result was to restore duality of ownership, B being the legal and C the equitable owner. The use was, in effect, resuscitated under the name of 'trust'.

In the opinion of Lord Browne-Wilkinson,[75] it remains a fundamental principle that equity operates on the conscience of the owner of the legal interest. So, in the case of a trust, the conscience of the legal owner requires him to carry out the purposes for which the property was vested in him ('express' or 'implied' trust) or which the law imposes on him by reason of his unconscionable conduct ('constructive' trust). Accordingly, he cannot be a trustee if and so long as he is ignorant of the facts alleged to affect his conscience—that is, until he is aware that he is intended to hold the property for the benefit of others in the case of an express or implied trust, or, in the case of a constructive trust, of the factors that are alleged to affect his conscience. Extrajudicially, Lord Millett has expressed a different view,[76] observing that a resulting trust can arise even if the recipient is unaware of the transfer or of the circumstances in which it was made, and he is unpersuaded by the explanation given by Lord Browne-Wilkinson of the cases[77] in which this has occurred. Lord Browne-Wilkinson, it has been contended, exaggerates the role that conscience plays in the law of property.[78] Maybe the better view is that a resulting trust arises as soon as the property is transferred, but the transferee does not become subject to a fiduciary duty, or liable for breach of trust, until he is aware of his position.[79]

Once a trust is established, as from the date of its establishment, the beneficiary has, in equity, a proprietary interest in the trust property,[80] which proprietary interest will be enforceable in equity against any subsequent holder of the property (whether the original property or substituted property into which it can be traced) other than a purchaser for value of the legal interest without notice. Moreover, if the trustee becomes bankrupt, the trust property is not available to the trustee's creditors, but remains subject to the trust and unaffected by the bankruptcy.

The trust has become a much more highly developed institution than the use had ever been and has since been, and now is used for a wide variety of purposes. In developing the trust, equity in general followed the law and permitted equitable estates to be created

---

[73] But later than *Sambach v Dalston (or Daston)* (1635) Toth 188, sub nom *Morris v Darston* Nels 30, according to the orthodox view. See (1958) 74 LQR 550 (J E Strathdene); (1957) 15 CLJ 72 (D E C Yale); A W B Simpson, *A History of the Land Law*, 2nd edn, p 201 *et seq.*

[74] At least ten years before *Sambach v Dalston, supra*, and perhaps as early as 1560, if not before: see (1977) 93 LQR 33 (J H Baker); [2002] Cambrian LR 67 (N G Jones).

[75] See *Westdeutsche Landesbank Girozentrale v Islington London Borough Council* [1996] AC 669, 705, [1996] 2 All ER 961, 988, HL.

[76] In Cornish et al (eds) *Restitution: Past, Present and Future*, p 201.

[77] Including *Re Vinogradoff* [1935] WN 68, discussed *infra*, p 178.

[78] (1988) 12 Tru LI 226 (W Swadling).

[79] See (1998) 114 LQR 399 (Millett LJ); Hanbury and Martin *Modern Equity*, 17th edn, [10.002]; *Port of Brisbane Corporation v ANZ Securities Ltd (No 2)* [2002] QCA 158, [2003] 2 Qd R 661.

[80] See (2004) 120 LQR 108 (R C Nolan).

corresponding to the legal estates recognized in the common law courts, and these equitable estates were commonly made subject to incidents and rules corresponding to those applying to the equivalent legal estates. Exceptionally, however, the Chancellor regarded himself as entitled to depart from the legal rule where he considered it to be unduly technical or inequitable.

(B) PURPOSE FOR WHICH A TRUST IS SET UP

(i) Introduction

Although cases do arise where the whole legal estate is vested in a trustee and the whole equitable interest in a sole beneficiary, it is seldom that such a simple trust is deliberately created. Much more common is some species of settlement constituted by a will, or *inter vivos* upon marriage or on some other occasion, whereby provision is made for a family. The avoidance of taxes may well dictate the form that a family settlement shall take and, indeed, may be a primary reason why any settlement is made, just as landowners took advantage of the use before 1535 in order to evade the payment of feudal dues. In addition to, or as part of, tax saving, the objects of a family settlement may include the more equal distribution of funds among the members of the family, the passing of wealth to future generations, born or unborn, and making provision for minors, spendthrifts, or those members of the family who, by reason of mental or physical disability, are unable to provide for themselves. And the 'family' provided for may be a mistress and illegitimate children.

(ii) Forms of family trust

The forms of trust that may be used include the following.

(a) *The life interest trust*   In its classic form, this entitled the life tenant to the income and use of the trust assets, but he had no recourse to capital, which had to be retained for the beneficiaries in remainder. The modern life interest trust is a flexible instrument under which wide powers are usually given to the trustees that enable them, in effect, to vary the beneficial interests. In outline, a typical modern life interest trust made by a parent-settlor might provide for the beneficial interests along the following lines.

(1) Direct the trustees of the trust fund:
   (i)   to pay the income to son George for life;
   (ii)   subject to (i), to pay the income to George's widow for life;
   (iii) subject to (i) and (ii), to pay or apply the income until a specified date within the perpetuity period to George's issue (whether present or future) and their wives/husbands/widows/widowers in such shares as they shall, in their absolute discretion, think fit;
   (iv)   from the specified date, hold both capital and income of the trust fund for George's surviving children, and, if more than one, in equal shares absolutely (the issue of any deceased child to take its parent's share by substitution);
   (v)   on failure of (i)–(iv), to hold both capital and income of the trust fund upon trust for Charity X.

(2) Notwithstanding the provisions in clause (1), confer on the trustees power to apply all or part of the capital of the trust fund for any purpose they consider to be for the benefit of any of the persons in (i)–(iii) for the time being in existence, or transfer or pay all or part of such capital to any one or more of such persons being of full age.

(3) Confer on the trustees power to add individuals to or exclude individuals from the persons specified in (iii), either permanently or for a specified period.

Many, perhaps most, family trusts arise under wills. Commonly, after disposing of his personal chattels, and making pecuniary and specific legacies, a testator will give the residue of his estate to trustees on trust for his wife for life, with remainder to his children on reaching the age of eighteen in equal shares (the issue of any deceased child to take his or her share by substitution). The will may confer on the wife a right to call for all, or part, of the capital to be paid to her. A testator who makes a will along these lines probably expects that his widow will be sufficiently provided for by her life interest, but sets up a safety net that will operate if, for instance, she incurs long-term nursing home fees for which the life interest is inadequate.

(b) *Discretionary trusts*[81]   These may be useful to enable trustees to take account, inter alia, of the changing circumstances and needs of the beneficiaries, who may not even be in existence when the trust was created. Thus, for example, a wealthy settlor might, in order to avoid or reduce liability to income tax, capital gains tax, and inheritance tax, transfer funds to trustees and direct them to hold both income and capital on trust during the perpetuity period for the 'discretionary beneficiaries'. These might be defined as:

(1) (i)   the settlor's widow;
   (ii)   the issue (whether present or future) of the settlor's paternal grandfather (excluding the settlor);
   (iii)   the spouse for the time being and any widow or widower of the individuals referred to in clause (1)(ii) (excluding any spouse of the settlor);
   (iv)   power may be given to the trustees to add individuals (other than the settlor or his wife) to, or remove individuals from, the class in 1(ii) above.

(2) The trustees may be given power in their absolute discretion to pay, or apply for their benefit, income or capital of the trust fund to such of the discretionary beneficiaries as they think fit. It is important that the trustees should be given, by the settlor, a letter explaining his non-binding wishes as to how they should exercise their discretionary powers. In order to obtain the maximum tax benefits, the settlor and his wife must be excluded from actual and potential benefit.

(3) There will be an ultimate trust at the end of the perpetuity period for, say, the issue of the settlor then living, although the trust funds would be expected to have been fully distributed long before that date.

(c) *Protective trusts*[82]   These may be used to protect assets against both spendthrift beneficiaries and outside claimants.

---

[81] See p 77 *et seq, infra*.   [82] See p 81 *et seq, infra*.

(d) *Specialized trusts to take advantage of tax reliefs* These include trusts for disabled persons, which may attract relief from income tax, inheritance tax, and capital gains tax,[83] and, in relation to inheritance tax, trusts for the young children of a deceased testator, known as 'bereaved minor trusts'[84] and 'age 18–25 trusts'.[85]

(iii) Use of tax havens

Lord Walker recently observed[86] that it:

> has become common for wealthy individuals in many parts of the world (including countries which have no indigenous law of trusts) to place funds at their disposition into trusts (often with a network of underlying companies) regulated by the law of, and managed by trustees resident in, territories with which the settlor (who may be also a beneficiary) has no substantial connection. These territories (sometimes called tax havens) are chosen not for their geographical convenience ... but because they are supposed to offer special advantages in terms of confidentiality and protection from fiscal demands (and, sometimes, from problems under the insolvency laws, or laws restricting freedom of testamentary disposition, in the country of the settlor's domicil). The trusts and powers contained in a settlement established in such circumstances may give no reliable indication of who will in the event benefit from the settlement. Typically it will contain very wide discretions exercisable by the trustees ... in favour of a widely-defined class of beneficiaries. The exercise of those discretions may depend on the settlor's wishes as confidentially imparted to the trustees ... As a further cloak against transparency, the identity of the true settlor may be concealed behind some corporate figurehead.

(iv) Blind trusts

A blind trust arises where the settlor transfers property to a trustee, commonly on a resulting trust for himself, giving the trustee full power to deal with the trust property without reference to him, and restricting the right of the settlor to information about the trust property and the dealings of the trustee with it. A blind trust may be set up, for example, by a politician, to make it impossible for him to be attacked on the ground of conflict of interest.[87]

(v) Unit trusts[88]

These provide a simple way for an investor to have a varied portfolio, thereby spreading his risk. A unit trust is set up under a trust deed made between parties known as the 'trustee' and the 'manager'. It is, in essence, the same institution as a particular kind of deed of settlement company known as a 'management trust', which became familiar in about the middle of the nineteenth century. Following the Companies Act 1862, the management trust was held

---

[83] See the Inheritance Tax Act 1984, s 89; the Taxation of Chargeable Gains Act 1992, s 3, Sch 1, para 1, as amended; the Finance Act 2005, ss 23–45, Sch 1.

[84] Inheritance Tax Act 1984, ss 71A–71C, 71H, inserted by the Finance Act 2006, s 156, Sch 20, para 1(1).

[85] Inheritance Tax Act 1984, ss 71D–71H, likewise inserted. It has not been possible, since 22 March 2006, to set up an accumulation and maintenance trust: s 71(1A), likewise inserted by para 2(1), (3).

[86] In *Schmidt v Rosewood Trust Ltd* [2003] UKPC 26, [2003] 2 AC 709, [2003] 3 All ER 76, at [1].

[87] See [1999] PCB 29 (Judith Morris); [1999] PCB 292 (D Hochberg and W Norris).

[88] See (2002) 36 T & ELJ 13 (E Nugee) and *CPT Custodian Property Ltd v Commissioner of State Revenue* [2005] HCA 53, [2006] WTLR 447. Note that the so-called 'investment trust' is not a trust at all, but a company formed to acquire and hold property by way of investment. In accordance with the principles of company law, the shareholders have no direct beneficial interest in the property so acquired.

to be illegal in *Sykes v Beadon*[89] and all but one were wound up or registered as companies under the Companies Act. That one, however—the Submarine Cables' Trust—continued in existence and successfully contended[90] before the Court of Appeal in the following year that *Sykes v Beadon*[91] had been wrongly decided. Nevertheless, no more management trusts appear to have been created until the early 1930s, when the institution was reintroduced and became known as the 'unit trust'.[92] Unit trust deeds vary widely in their terms, but the general principle is that securities are vested in the trustee under the trust deed, initially on trust for the manager. The beneficial interest thus held by the manager is divided up into a large number of units, subunits, or shares, which are offered to the public at a price based on the market value of the securities plus an initial service charge. The investor who purchases units accordingly becomes the beneficial owner of an undivided share of the securities in proportion to the number of units he holds.[93] Many matters are dealt with in the trust deed: provision is made, inter alia, for the remuneration of the trustee and the manager out of income, for the manager to repurchase shares from unitholders who wish to dispose of their investment, and for resale by the manager to new investors, although units may be dealt with on the market in the usual way, and for the duration of the trust, which has usually been fixed, with perhaps unnecessary caution,[94] at less than twenty-one years to avoid the possible infringement of the rule against perpetuities. Even so, however, the trust deed commonly provides for an extension of the trust if the unitholders so desire. Unit trusts may be either fixed or flexible. The fixed trust under which the portfolio of investments is normally bound to remain unaltered has become unpopular,[95] and the flexible trust, which gives the manager power to switch securities, is much more common. It gives the unitholder the benefit of the manager's financial skill and acumen, but correspondingly makes him dependent upon the manager's ability, or lack of it, and integrity.[96] The trustee has considerable control over the manager by reason of the fact that the trust deed must provide for requiring the manager to retire from the trust if the trustee certifies that it is in the interest of the beneficiaries under the trust that he should do so. Further, an investigating authority may appoint inspectors to investigate and report on the administration of any authorized unit trust scheme, if it appears that it is in the interests of unitholders to do so or the matter is one of public concern.[97] No inspector has yet been appointed under this provision.

(vi) Pension scheme trusts[98]

These are of great importance, but they are of quite a different nature from traditional trusts. The traditional trust is one under which the settlor, by way of bounty, transfers property to

---

[89] (1879) 11 Ch D 170.   [90] In *Smith v Anderson* (1880) 15 Ch D 247, CA.   [91] *Supra*.

[92] The longest surviving unit trust is thought to be the M & G General Trust, launched as the First British Fixed Trust on 22 April 1931.   [93] See *Costa & Duppe Properties Pty Ltd v Duppe* [1986] VR 90.

[94] Cf *Re AEG Unit Trust (Managers) Ltd's Deed* [1957] Ch 415, [1957] 2 All ER 506.

[95] The court had to consider a fixed unit trust in *Re Municipal and General Securities Co Ltd's Trust, Municipal and General Securities Co Ltd v Lloyds Bank Ltd* [1950] Ch 212, [1949] 2 All ER 937.

[96] It is understood that there has been no case involving an authorized unit trust in which investors have suffered a loss through dishonesty of the managers of the trust. Statutory protection is given to the investor by the Financial Services Act 1986.

[97] Financial Services and Markets Act 2000, s 284, which, in subs (11), defines 'investigating authority' as the Financial Services Authority or the Secretary of State.

[98] See Nobles, *Pensions Employment and the Law*; (1992) 6 Tru LI 119 (Lord Browne-Wilkinson); (1996) 75 CBR 221 (Eileen Gillese); [1997] Conv 89 (Marina Milner), arguing that a new form of trust is evolving;

trustees to be administered for the beneficiaries as objects of his bounty. Normally, there is no legal relationship between the parties apart from the trust. The beneficiaries have given no consideration for what they receive. The settlor, as donor, can impose such limits on his bounty as he chooses. In a pension scheme, by contrast, the benefits are part of the consideration that an employee receives in return for the rendering of his services. In many cases, membership of the pension scheme is a requirement of employment. Beneficiaries of the scheme, the members, far from being volunteers have given valuable consideration. The company employer is not conferring a bounty.[99]

Although, on the one hand, it is clear that, in general, the principles applicable to private trusts as a matter of trust law apply equally to pension schemes,[100] on the other hand, in view of the differences referred to, it is dangerous to apply uncritically in the field of pension funds concepts that have been developed in the field of private trusts. Thus, while in a private trust it is axiomatic that a trustee should not be asked to exercise a discretion as to the application of a fund amongst a class of which he is a member, if, under a pension scheme, an employer has a power of amendment in relation to a pension fund that has not been wound up, he is entitled to exercise it in any way that will further the purposes of the scheme, and his exercise of the power will not necessarily be invalid because the employer may benefit directly or indirectly.[101] The Goode Committee report[102] concluded that criticism of trust law as the basis for pension schemes following the Maxwell affair was largely misplaced. It endorsed the view that had been expressed in the great weight of evidence submitted to the Committee that trust law, in itself, is broadly satisfactory and should continue to provide the foundation for interests, rights, and duties arising in relation to pension schemes, although some of its principles required modifications in their application to pensions.

[2005] Conv 229 (D Hayton). See also (2000) 14 Tru LI 130 (S E K Hulme); (2002) 16 Tru LI 74 (D Pollard); (2002) 16 Tru LI 214 (Lord Scott).

[99] *Mettoy Pension Trustees Ltd v Evans* [1991] 2 All ER 513, 537, 549, [1990] 1 WLR 1587, 1610, 1618, *per* Warner J; *Stannard v Fisons Pension Trust Ltd* [1992] IRLR 27, CA; *Air Jamaica Ltd v Joy Charlton* [1999] 1 WLR 1399, PC, noted [2000] Conv 170 (C Harpum); (2000) 116 LQR 15 (C E F Rickett and R Grantham) *Re UEB Industries Ltd Pension Plan* [1992] 1 NZLR 294. See (1990) 4 TL&P 94 (D Higgins); (1990) 4 TL&P 156 (I Pittaway); (1990) 53 MLR 377 (R Nobles); (1991) 5 TL&P 56 (P Docking); [1992] 1 GLR 210 (S Travers); (1993) 56 MLR 471 (G Moffat); [1993] Conv 283 (D Hayton); (1994) 14 LS 345 (R Nobles).

[100] *Cowan v Scargill* [1985] Ch 270, 292, [1984] 2 All ER 750, 764, *per* Megarry V-C; *Wilson v Law Debenture Trust Corpn plc* [1995] 2 All ER 337, 347, *per* Rattee J. Although there are no special rules of construction applicable to pension schemes, the courts' approach to the construction of the relevant documents should be practical and purposive, rather than detached and literal, so as to give reasonable and practical effect to the scheme: see *National Grid Co plc v Mayes* [2000] ICR 174, CA, revsd [2001] UKHL 20, [2001] 2 All ER 417, HL, without comment on this point. In Canada, a pension trust has been said to be a classic trust: *Schmidt v Air Products of Canada Ltd* [1994] 2 SCR 611; *Bathgate v National Hockey League Pension Society* (1994) 16 OR (3d) 761, 776. Similarly in New Zealand: *Stuart v Armourguard Security Ltd* [1996] 1 NZLR 484. See (2003) 17 Tru LI 129 (K Rowley).

[101] *British Coal Corpn v British Coal Staff Superannuation Scheme Trustees Ltd* [1995] 1 All ER 912, said to have been wrongly decided on another point by Lord Hoffman and Lord Scott in *National Grid Co plc v Mayes, supra*, HL. See also *Jefferies v Mayes* (1997) Times, 30 June.

[102] Report of the Pension Law Review Committee, 1993, Cm 2342, [4.1.12] and [4.1.14]. The Report includes an extensive (although not exhaustive) bibliography. See (1993) 7 Tru LI 191 (D A Chatterton); (1994) 8 Tru LI 35 (Vinelott J).

(vii) Employee trusts

An employee trust is a specialized form of discretionary trust, usually set up by a corporate employer, although it can be set up by an individual employer, in which the actual and potential beneficiaries are defined by reference to their employment by a specified employer or a particular group of companies. These trusts are set up with the intention of encouraging loyalty and commitment from the employees, and are commonly drafted in a form that carries considerable tax advantages.

(viii) Other trust situations

Under the 1925 property legislation, a trust arises in all cases of beneficial co-ownership of land.[103] One result of this is that where the family home is owned, whether by a married couple or an unmarried couple, it is usually subject to a trust. Again under the 1925 legislation, a trust arises when a person dies intestate[104] and in relation to the proceeds of a sale where a mortgagee has exercised his power of sale over the mortgaged property.[105] Clubs and societies, unincorporated bodies of all kinds, and most charities commonly have their funds and property vested in trustees, and under time-sharing schemes the villas or apartments to be time-shared are usually vested in a trustee.[106]

A trust may also come into being as part of commercial arrangements. An example of this is *Barclays Bank Ltd v Quistclose Investments Ltd*.[107]

(C) CONCLUSION

One might sum up the present position by saying that, in the complexity of modern society, there are few aspects of human activity that do not run more smoothly through the assistance of the trust concept.[108] However, after observing that the trust has become a valuable device in commercial and financial dealings in the modern world, Lord Browne-Wilkinson issued a valuable warning.[109] The fundamental principles of equity, he said, apply as much to such trusts as they do to the traditional trusts in relation to which those principles were originally formulated. But if the trust is not to be rendered commercially useless, it is important to distinguish between the basic principles of trust law and those specialist rules developed in relation to traditional trusts, which are applicable only to such trusts and the rationale of which has no application to trusts of quite a different kind.

---

[103] The amendments to the law made by the Trusts of Land and Appointment of Trustees Act 1996 do not affect the validity of this proposition.

[104] Administration of Estates Act 1925, s 33.   [105] Law of Property Act 1925, s 105.

[106] See (1987) 84 LSG 19 (J Edmonds). The rules of the European Holiday Timeshare Association are partly based on the Public Trustee Rules 1911 (as amended).

[107] [1970] AC 567. [1968] 3 All ER 651, HL, and see p 174, *infra*. As to trusts in business and commerce, see Underhill and Hayton, *Law of Trusts and Trustees*, 17th edn, [1.97]–[1.138]. See also (1981) 13 MULR 1 (H A J Ford); (1983) 21 Alberta LR 395 (D W M Waters); [1987] JMCL 1 (D W M Waters); (1987) 3 QITLJ 17 (D G Gardiner); [1993] JBL 24 (G M D Bean); (1992) 15 UNSWLJ 256 (Sarah Worthington); (1997) 107 Yale LJ 105 (J H Langbein)

[108] See *per* Roxburgh J in *Re a Solicitor* [1952] Ch 328, 332, [1952] 1 All ER 133, 136. See also (1986) 36 UTLJ 186 (A I Ogus). For speculation as to the future, see [2000] PCB 94, 163, 244 (D Hayton).

[109] In *Target Holdings Ltd v Redferns (a firm)* [1996] AC 421, 435, [1995] 3 All ER 785, HL . See pp 514 and 515, *infra*.

5 EQUITABLE INTERESTS AND EQUITIES

(A) DEFINITION AND DISTINCTION

It would no doubt be as satisfying to the reader as to the author to have clear definitions of these terms and certainty as to what rights come within each category, and the consequences that thereby attach to them. This, however, is by no means the position, nor, perhaps, is it surprising since equity has grown by filling in gaps in the common law and is still in the process of development. Before discussing the matter, something should be said about the distinction between property rights and personal rights. Lord Wilberforce[110] has stated that before an interest can be admitted into the category of property, 'it must be definable, identifiable by third parties, capable in its nature of assumption by third parties, and have some degree of permanence and stability'. All of the Law Lords in that case agreed that the right in question—that of a deserted wife to remain in the former matrimonial home—was a personal and not a property right. The owner of a property right can normally: (i) in case of dispute, recover the property itself as opposed to merely recovering damages payable out of no specific fund; (ii) transfer his right to another; and (iii) enforce his right against at least some third parties. But a property right can exist without all of these elements being present.[111]

With this in mind, let us first turn to consider equitable interests, of which the interest of a beneficiary under a trust is the earliest and prime example. This is a proprietary interest that can be assigned *inter vivos* or disposed of by will, and is normally binding on third parties—unless a third party can establish that he is a bona fide purchaser for value of a legal estate, without notice, actual or constructive, of the equitable interest. In course of time, the Court of Chancery came to protect other rights unrecognized by the common law and, in 1965,[112] Lord Upjohn regarded the list set out by Professor Crane[113] as being complete. It comprised, in addition to beneficial interests under trusts, equitable mortgages, vendor's liens, restrictive covenants, and estate contracts.

In other cases in which equity intervened to protect a plaintiff, the effect was not to confer on him an equitable interest and he would be said to have an equity or a mere equity. Unfortunately, the picture is far from clear. In the widest sense, an equity includes the right of the plaintiff in every case in which he can call upon equity to mitigate the rigours of the common law. However, when used in contradistinction to an equitable interest as denoting a right that, in some circumstances, may bind successors, it was said by Lord

---

[110] *National Provincial Bank Ltd v Ainsworth* [1965] AC 1175, 1248, [1965] 2 All ER 472, 494, HL. See, generally, Meagher, Gummow, and Lehane, *Equity: Doctrine and Remedies*, 3rd edn, p 103 *et seq*; (1996) 16 LS 200 (J Hill). See also [2002] CLJ 423 (Christine Davis).

[111] For a careful analysis of a beneficiary's proprietary right, see (2006) 122 LQR 232 (R C Nolan), who says that a beneficiary's proprietary rights under a trust consist principally in the beneficiary's primary, negative, right to exclude non-beneficiaries from the enjoyment of trust assets. Infringement of this primary right will generate secondary rights by which a beneficiary may also prevent access to assets by non-beneficiaries, including the right to claim misapplied assets or other assets representing them.

[112] In *National Provincial Bank Ltd v Ainsworth* [1965] HL, *supra*, at 1238, 488.

[113] (1955) 19 Conv 343. It is submitted that at least equitable easements and profits should be added to the list. Note that an equitable charge, unlike an equitable mortgage, does not give the chargee an equitable interest in the land: *Bland v Ingram's Estates Ltd* [2001] Ch 767, [2002] 1 All ER 221, CA.

Upjohn[114] to be a word of limited application: the term includes the right of a grantor to have a conveyance that he has made set aside on the ground of the grantee's fraud or undue influence,[115] the right to rectification of a document that incorrectly embodies the agreement between the parties,[116] and the right of consolidation of mortgages. Lord Upjohn went on to say that it was not possible for a mere equity to bind a purchaser unless such an equity is ancillary to, or dependent upon, an equitable estate or interest in land, and summed up the position thus: 'A mere "equity" naked and alone is, in my opinion, incapable of binding successors in title even with notice; it is personal to the parties.' The deserted wife in the case before him had only a personal equity, which did not bind the purchasers. But if a tenant has a lease that does not accurately set out the agreed terms of the tenancy and a right to have the lease rectified, a purchaser of the reversion with notice will be bound by the equity that is ancillary to the tenant's property interest.

According to Neave and Weinberg,[117] 'the expression "an equity" has come to be used in the sense of a proprietary interest ranking at the bottom of a hierarchy of proprietary interests consisting of legal interests, equitable interests and equities'. Neave and Weinberg argue that equities fall into two groups, which they call 'defined equities' and 'undefined equities'. By 'defined equities', they mean those in relation to which there is no doubt about the plaintiff's entitlement to a remedy against the other party to the transaction, such as the right to have a conveyance set aside for fraud or a contract rectified where it does not represent the true agreement of the parties. In these cases, the enforcement of the plaintiff's right is no more discretionary than where he seeks to assert an estate contract against the vendor. A defined equity is a proprietary interest. 'Undefined equities' are at a different stage of development. Where the facts do not fall into any established category, the court has first to be persuaded to give a remedy against the other party to the transaction. The court has a wide discretion whether to accept that there is a personal equity. If it does, the next question is whether it is enforceable against third parties so as to become an equity in the proprietary sense. If the court provides the remedy sufficiently often, the equity may be converted into a defined equity, and, ultimately, both defined and undefined equities may become equitable interests. Neave and Weinberg's view stresses flexibility: they consider that the use of the equity device enables the court to modify the rigid structure of legal and equitable interests.

It is indeed difficult to find two writers who share the same view. Wade[118] suggested that the dividing line between equitable interests and mere equities is the discretionary character of the latter, but nevertheless admitted that this puts the right of a purchaser under an estate contract in the wrong category, since he relies on the discretionary remedy of specific performance. Maudsley[119] submitted the test should be whether the 'interest' is

[114] [1965] AC 1175, [1965] 2 All ER 472, HL.

[115] Contrast *Gross v Lewis Hillman Ltd* [1970] Ch 445, [1969] 3 All ER 1476, CA (right of purchaser to rescind a purchase of land for misrepresentation).

[116] See *Blacklocks v J B Developments (Godalming) Ltd* [1982] Ch 183, [1981] 3 All ER 392; *Boots the Chemist Ltd v Street* (1983) 268 EG 817; *Nurdin & Peacock plc v D B Ramsden & Co Ltd* [1999] 1 EGLR 119. See also *Itco Properties Ltd v Mohawk Oil Co* (1988) 62 Alta LR (2d) 42, 91 AR 76, in which a right to rectification was held to be assignable.   [117] (1978–80) 6 U Tas LR 24, 115.

[118] [1955] CLJ 160–161. See also (1955) 71 LQR 482 (R E Megarry).

[119] *Hanbury & Maudsley's Modern Equity*, 13th edn, p 873.

capable of being bought and sold in the marketplace, but accepted that this test would put at least restrictive covenants in the wrong group.

Although the distinction is far from clear, it may yet be of importance where a question arises as to the priority of competing interests. Moreover, in relation to registered land, the Land Registration Act 2002[120] now provides that both an equity by estoppel[121] and a mere equity have effect from the time at which the equity arises as an interest capable of binding successors in title.

(B) EQUITABLE RULES AS TO PRIORITIES

The rules relating to priorities are complex: they depend, in the first instance, on the kind of property that is being dealt with, and have, since 1925, been much affected by statutory provisions as to registration and in relation to overreaching. For present purposes, it will suffice to mention the bare essentials of the basic equitable rules.[122]

(i)   *Estates and interests rank in order of their creation*   This is the primary rule because it is always applied in the absence of special circumstances and it establishes the burden of proof.[123]

(ii) *The superiority of the legal estate*   Someone with a legal estate or interest may gain priority over an earlier equitable interest. In order to do this, he must establish that he is a bona fide purchaser for value[124] of a legal estate without notice, actual or constructive, of the prior equitable interest.[125]

(iii) *The rule giving priority to the owner of a legal interest only applies where, as it is said, the equities are equal*   'Equity' is here used in yet another sense: what is meant is that the owner of a legal interest may be postponed if there is fraud, misrepresentation, or gross negligence on his part.

(iv) *Where there are two competing equitable interests, the primary rule again applies that they rank in order of their creation, again subject to the proviso that the equities are equal.*[126]   Thus the primary rule applied to the equitable interests in *Cave v*

---

[120] Section 116.   [121] See p 203 *et seq, infra.*

[122] These rules were not relevant in *Bristol and West Building Society v Henning* [1985] 2 All ER 606, [1985] 1 WLR 778, CA, or in *Equity and Law Home Loans Ltd v Prestidge* [1992] 1 All ER 909, [1992] 1 WLR 137, CA, in which the owner of the equitable interest had consented, or was deemed to have consented, to the creation of the mortgage, which accordingly had priority. See (1996) 3 Deak LR 147 (H Long); [2006] Conv 509 (P Omar).

[123] *A-G v Biphosphated Guano Co* (1879) 11 Ch D 327, CA.

[124] Note that the common law rule that the court does not inquire into the adequacy of consideration is not relevant here. The concept of 'purchaser for value' is based on equity, which looks at the substance not the form. Thus, on the assignment of a lease, the liability of the assignee for rent, the tenant's obligations, and the indemnity to the assignor suffices to render him a purchaser for value: *Nurdin & Peacock plc v D B Ramsden & Co Ltd* [1999] 1 EGLR 119.

[125] See *Macmillan Inc v Bishopsgate Investment Trust plc (No 3)* [1995] 3 All ER 747, [1995] 1 WLR 978, noted (1996) 10 Tru LI 20 (G Virgo); *MCC Proceeds Inc v Lehman Bros International (Europe)* [1998] 4 All ER 675, CA; *State Bank of India v Sood* [1997] Ch 276, [1997] 1 All ER 169, CA. See also [1997] Conv 431 (J Howell).

[126] See *Snell's Principles of Equity*, 31st edn, [4.03]; *Lloyds Bank v Bullock* [1896] 2 Ch 192; *Capell v Winter* [1907] 2 Ch 376, 382; *Jacobs v Platt Nominees Pty Ltd* [1990] VR 146; *Secureland Mortgage Investments Nominees Ltd v Harmore & Co Solicitor Nominee Co Ltd* [1991] 2 NZLR 399.

Cave,[127] in which a sole trustee purchased land out of trust moneys in breach of trust, the conveyance being taken in the name of his brother. The brother created first a legal mortgage and then an equitable mortgage. It was held that the legal mortgagee had priority by virtue of his legal estate, but that, the equities being equal, the primary rule applied to give the beneficiaries under the trust priority to the equitable mortgagee. The equities were not, however, equal in *Rice v Rice*,[128] in which a vendor indorsed a receipt on, and handed the title deeds over to, a purchaser without having received the purchase money. Although the vendor still retained an equitable interest, his vendor's lien for the purchase price, it was held that a subsequent equitable mortgagee of the property without notice of the lien had priority although later in point of time, because the vendor's conduct had led him to assume that there was no competing equitable interest.

(v)   *Where, however, the competition is between an equitable interest and a mere equity, the position is analogous to that between a legal estate and an equitable interest, ie the bona fide purchaser of an equitable interest takes free from a prior equity of which he has no notice.*[129]   The fullest judicial discussion of the matter is in the Australian case of *Latec Investments Ltd v Hotel Terrigal Pty Ltd*.[130] In that case, a mortgagee purported to exercise its power of sale in favour of a wholly owned subsidiary. The circumstances were such that the exercise of the power of sale was fraudulent. The purchaser created an equitable charge on the land in favour of a third party who had no notice of the circumstances of the sale. Five years later, the mortgagor sought to have the sale set aside, and he succeeded against the mortgagee and the purchaser. It was unanimously held, however, that he was bound by the equitable charge of the third party, by the majority on the ground that the mortgagor's right to have the sale set aside was a mere equity,[131] and against that the plea of the bona fide purchaser for value without notice, even of an equitable interest, could successfully be put forward. Accordingly, as against the third party, the mortgagor could not establish his equity of redemption and there was therefore no prior equitable interest to which his conveyance could be held subject.

It is submitted that the courts retain considerable flexibility because of the proviso that the rules only apply '*where the equities are equal*'. Even the purchaser of a legal estate will be bound if he takes with notice of a prior equitable interest, and the existence of the proviso

---

[127] (1880) 15 Ch D 639; *Wu v Glaros* (1991) 55 SASR 408.

[128] (1854) 2 Drew 73; *Re King's Settlement* [1931] 2 Ch 294; *Abigail v Lapin* [1934] AC 491, PC; *Heid v Reliance Finance Corpn Pty Ltd* (1984) 154 CLR 326. Contrast *Capell v Winter* [1907] 2 Ch 376.

[129] *Cave v Cave, supra*; *Westminster Bank Ltd v Lee* [1956] Ch 7, [1955] 2 All ER 833; *National Provincial Bank Ltd v Ainsworth* [1965] AC 1175, [1965] 2 All ER 472, HL; *Taylor Barnard Ltd v Tozer* [1984] 1 EGLR 21; *Mid-Glamorgan County Council v Ogwr Borough Council* (1993) 68 P & CR 1, CA. But see (2002) 118 LQR 296 (D O'Sullivan).

[130] (1965) 113 CLR 265, [1966] ALR 775. Taylor J, although he agreed with Kitto and Menzies JJ in the result, considered that the plaintiff had an equitable interest but there was an impediment to his title that a court of equity would not remove. See also *Blacklocks v J B Developments (Godalming) Ltd* [1982] Ch 183, [1981] 3 All ER 392; [1995] Denning LJ 153 (J Reeder and G Kinley).

[131] It makes no difference that, where the question is whether the plaintiff can assign it in his lifetime or leave it by his will, the right to have a conveyance set aside for fraud may be regarded as an equitable interest: *Stump v Gaby* (1852) 2 De GM & G 623; *Gresley v Mousley* (1859) 4 De G & J 78; *Dickinson v Burrell* (1866) LR 1 Eq 337.

may enable the courts to avoid grappling with the difficulties raised by the uncertainties as to the distinction between equitable interests and mere equities.

6 THE MAXIMS OF EQUITY

At one time, the maxims of equity were regarded as the fundamental principles of equity on which the whole of the equitable jurisdiction was based. This view has long since been abandoned and they are best regarded not as rules to be literally applied, but as indicators of the approach that equity takes to particular problems. Of the large number of alleged maxims of equity, twelve are now commonly referred to, and these will now be considered.

(A) 'EQUITY WILL NOT SUFFER A WRONG TO BE WITHOUT A REMEDY'

Reliance cannot be placed on this comprehensive maxim in modern law, but, historically, it lies behind the Chancellor's intervention on the grounds of conscience and natural justice. It can be regarded as justifying the grant of an injunction to restrain a tort where the common law would only award damages or, indeed, in the case of a *quia timet* injunction, give no remedy at all. Another example is the appointment of a receiver by way of equitable execution, which enabled a creditor who was unable to enforce his judgment by a common law writ to obtain satisfaction out of certain assets of the debtor.[132] The pre-eminent example is the protection given to the beneficiary under a trust.

(B) 'EQUITY FOLLOWS THE LAW'

As we have seen,[133] in enforcing a trust, the Chancellor never denied the title of the legal owner, but insisted that he hold it for the beneficiaries. He fully recognized the various legal estates and interests, and followed the law by developing corresponding interests in the equitable estate. As we shall see,[134] in the case of an executed trust, equity followed the law and gave a strict construction to technical words, but it did not follow the law blindly and would depart from the legal rule if it considered that the circumstances merited it: thus, in the case of an executory trust, it did not feel bound to construe technical words in a technical way.

(C) 'WHERE THE EQUITIES ARE EQUAL, THE FIRST IN TIME PREVAILS'

This maxim is sometimes quoted in its Latin form, *Qui prior est tempore, potior est jure.* It, and the following maxim, both deal with the priority of competing interests, and both were considered in the preceding section.

---

[132] See p 684, *infra*.   [133] See p 4, *supra*.   [134] See p 73, *infra*.

(D) 'WHERE THE EQUITIES ARE EQUAL, THE LAW PREVAILS'

(E) 'HE WHO COMES INTO EQUITY MUST COME WITH CLEAN HANDS'

A claimant will not obtain relief in equity where his conduct has been improper in rela-tion to the transaction that he seeks to enforce. In *Overton v Banister*,[135] an infant, by fraudulently misrepresenting his age, induced his trustees to pay him money. He was not permitted to claim the usual protection of infancy when suing for the money again on reaching his majority, arguing that the previous payment was in breach of trust. Again, a tenant under an agreement for a lease, who is in breach of his obligations thereunder, can-not compel a lease to be granted.[136] That the improper conduct must be related to the claim is demonstrated by *Duchess of Argyll v Duke of Argyll*,[137] in which the claimant was not disentitled to an injunction to restrain the defendant from publishing confidential matter by reason of the fact that it was her adultery that led to a divorce.

(F) 'HE WHO SEEKS EQUITY MUST DO EQUITY'

This is closely relater to the previous maxim, but looks to the future, rather than the past. A claimant will not be granted an equitable remedy unless he is prepared to fulfil his legal and equitable obligations relating to the matter in dispute, and to act fairly towards the defendant. The discretionary nature of equitable remedies is to be contrasted with the common law position where, if a party has made out his case, the court is bound to give him a remedy no matter how unworthy his claim might be. There are many examples of the application of this maxim: thus unfairness or hardship on the defendant or oppression or sharp practice on the part of the claimant may be a ground for refusing to grant a decree of specific performance,[138] and rescission will not be granted unless *restitutio in integrum* is possible.[139] An injunction will not be granted unless the claimant is both able and will-ing to carry out any obligations he has undertaken towards the defendant.[140] The maxim lies at the basis of the equitable doctrine of election.[141]

(G) 'DELAY DEFEATS EQUITIES'

This maxim is sometimes stated in the form 'equity assists the diligent not the tardy', or, in Latin, *Vigilantibus non dormientibus aequitas subvenit*. It lies at the basis of the concepts of laches and acquiescence, considered later.[142]

(H) 'EQUALITY IS EQUITY'

This is sometimes stated in the form 'equity is equality', but the meaning is the same which-ever way it is put. Where two or more persons are concurrently entitled to an interest in

---

[135] (1844) 3 Hare 503.   [136] *Coatsworth v Johnson* (1885) 55 LJQB 220, CA.
[137] [1967] Ch 302, [1965] 1 All ER 611. See also *Tinsley v Milligan* [1994] 1 AC 340, [1993] 3 All ER 65, HL, and *Tribe v Tribe* [1996] Ch 107, [1995] 4 All ER 236, CA, both discussed p 225, *infra*.
[138] See p 667, *infra*.   [139] See p 696, *infra*.   [140] See p 599, *infra*.
[141] See the Online Resource Centre.   [142] See pp 534, 597, and 672, *infra*.

property, then, in the absence of any provision or agreement applying to the situation, equity treats them as equally entitled. This is at the basis for equity's preference for a tenancy in common over a joint tenancy: in a joint tenancy, the rule of survivorship operates arbitrarily in favour of longevity. The maxim is also applied to an implied trust in default of appointment.[143]

(I) 'EQUITY LOOKS TO THE INTENT RATHER THAN THE FORM'

Equity concentrates on the substance of a transaction, rather than its form. Thus, it may hold that a trust has been created even though the word 'trust' has not been used,[144] that a covenant, although positive in wording, is in substance negative and enforceable as a restrictive covenant,[145] and it will refuse to grant an injunction that would, in substance, amount to a decree of specific performance where such an order would not be granted directly.[146] It will not grant specific performance of a voluntary contract even though contained in a deed.[147]

(J) 'EQUITY LOOKS ON THAT AS DONE WHICH OUGHT TO BE DONE'

Equity commonly treats a contract to do a thing as if that thing were already done. A well-known example is the doctrine of *Walsh v Lonsdale*,[148] under which a person who, for valuable consideration, has entered into an agreement for a lease is treated as if he were an actual lessee, and a vendor under a contract for the sale of land is treated as a constructive trustee for the purchaser, although in a modified sense.[149] It is the basis of the equitable doctrine of conversion,[150] and the rule in *Howe v Earl Dartmouth*.[151]

(K) 'EQUITY IMPUTES AN INTENTION TO FULFIL AN OBLIGATION'

This is usually listed as one of equity's maxims, although it is of limited application. It puts a favourable construction on what a person has done, and is one of the bases of the equitable doctrines of satisfaction, ademption, and performance.[152]

(L) 'EQUITY ACTS *IN PERSONAM*'

As we have seen,[153] equity enforced its decrees by a personal order against the defendant: breach of the order would be a contempt of court, for which he was liable to imprisonment. Provided that the defendant is within the jurisdiction of the court, it does not

---

[143] See p 37, *infra*.   [144] See the discussion of precatory trusts, p 47 *et seq*, *infra*.
[145] *Tulk v Moxhay* (1848) 2 Ph 774.
[146] See, eg, *Page One Records Ltd v Britton* [1967] 3 All ER 822.   [147] See p 653, *infra*.
[148] (1882) 21 Ch D 9, CA.   [149] See p 164, *infra*.   [150] See the Online Resource Centre.
[151] (1802) 7 Ves 137 and p 429 *et seq*, *infra*.   [152] See the Online Resource Centre.
[153] See p 4, *supra*.

matter that the subject of the dispute is outside it.[154] It does not necessarily follow that the interests of the beneficiary under a trust are purely personal. This difficult matter is discussed later.[155]

7 TRUSTS AND TAXATION

As we have noted, in many cases, the stimulus to create a settlement may not be so much a wish to provide for the family as a desire to reduce the incidence of taxation. It is clear, however, that there are very real limits as to what can be done. Basically, a settlor cannot both have his cake and eat it, and if he wishes to reduce the incidence of tax, it can only be by, in effect, giving his property to other persons, although the gift may be by way of trust or settlement under which the interests of individual beneficiaries are restricted. Tax considerations may not only be the reason why a trust or settlement is made or why it is made in a particular way, but may also be the reason why the provisions of a trust may be sought to be varied, perhaps with the assistance of the court under the Variation of Trusts Act 1958.

It will be realized that the various taxes have their own textbooks, and there are also specialized books dealing with the taxation of trusts and settlements, and even with what is called 'tax planning'. A vital distinction exists between 'tax evasion'—that is, non-payment of taxes that one is under a legal duty to pay—which is clearly illegal and may result in criminal proceedings, and 'tax avoidance'—that is, the arrangement of one's financial affairs so that no liability or a reduced liability to tax accrues—which is perfectly legal. Although there are judicial dicta that disapprove of schemes that have been entered into to avoid tax, there are many more judgments recognizing the right of individuals to dispose of their capital and income so as to attract the least amount of tax.[156]

The courts themselves have, indeed, been prepared to give their assistance in the creation of tax avoidance schemes, in particular under the Variation of Trusts Act 1958, although Lord Denning MR has observed:[157] 'The avoidance of tax may be lawful, but it is not yet a virtue.' More recent cases, however, indicate an increasingly critical approach by the courts to the manipulation of financial transactions to the advantage of the taxpayer.[158]

It is not proposed to attempt to deal with any of the above-mentioned taxes even in outline, but it seems desirable, at this early stage, to stress the practical importance of tax considerations. Fortunately, however, an understanding of equity and trusts does not demand a knowledge of tax law, although it will be found that numerous points of trust law have been decided in litigation with the Inland Revenue (now HM Revenue and Customs). It should be noted, however, that, in a tax statute, a word may have a different meaning from the one that it has in ordinary trust law.[159]

---

[154] *Penn v Lord Baltimore* (1750) 1 Ves Sen 444.   [155] See p 83 *et seq, infra*.

[156] See *per* Viscount Sumner in *Levene v IRC* [1928] AC 217, 227.

[157] *Re Weston's Settlements* [1969] 1 Ch 223, 245, [1968] 3 All ER 338, 342.

[158] *W T Ramsay Ltd v IRC* [1982] AC 300, [1981] 1 All ER 865, HL; *Furniss v Dawson* [1984] AC 474, [1984] 1 All ER 530, HL; *Craven v White* [1989] AC 398, [1988] 3 All ER 495, HL; *Fitzwilliam v IRC* [1993] 3 All ER 184, [1993] 1 WLR 1189, HL; and see (1984) 43 CLJ 259 (D Hayton).

[159] See *J Sainsbury plc v O'Connor* [1991] 1 WLR 963, CA.

8 TRUSTS AND THE CONFLICT OF LAWS

The Recognition of Trusts Act 1987 brings into force for the United Kingdom the main provisions of the Hague Convention on the Law Applicable to Trusts and on their Recognition,[160] the purpose of which is to establish common principles between states on the law of trusts and to deal with the most important issues concerning their recognition. It is intended, in particular, to assist civil law countries, which are not generally familiar with the trust concept, to deal fairly, expeditiously, and effectively with trust issues arising within their jurisdiction. It does not make much change of substance to the existing law in the United Kingdom, although some points are clarified. The Convention applies only to trusts created voluntarily and evidenced in writing, but so far as the United Kingdom is concerned, it is extended by s 1(2) to any other trusts of property arising under the law of any part of the United Kingdom or by virtue of a judicial decision, whether in the United Kingdom or elsewhere.

Article 6 provides that a trust shall be governed by the law chosen by the settlor. The choice must be express or be implied in the terms of the instrument creating or the writing evidencing the trust, interpreted, if necessary, in the light of the circumstances of the case. Where no applicable law has been chosen, Art 7 provides that a trust shall be governed by the law with which it is most closely connected.

In ascertaining the law with which a trust is most closely connected, reference shall be made in particular to:

(i)   the place of administration of the trust designated by the settlor;

(ii)   the situs of the assets of the trust;

(iii)   the place of residence or business of the trustee;

(iv)   the objects of the trust and the places where they are to be fulfilled.

The law specified by Arts 6 or 7 governs the validity of the trust, its construction, its effects, and the administration of the trust.

---

[160] Cmnd 9494. See (1987) 131 Sol Jo 827 (T Prime); (1987) 36 ICLQ 260 (D J Hayton); (1987) 36 ICLQ 454 (Ann Wallace). See also Dicey, Morris, and Collins, *Conflict of Laws*, 14th edn, ch 29.

2

THE TRUST CONCEPT

It is commonly observed that no one has succeeded in producing a wholly satisfactory definition of a trust, although the general idea is not difficult to grasp. The general idea is expressed by saying that the trustee is the nominal owner of the trust property, but that the real or beneficial owner is the cestui que trust, or, alternatively, that the trustee is the legal owner, the cestui que trust the equitable owner. Although adequate to give the general idea, neither statement is altogether satisfactory as a definition, because neither covers, for instance, cases in which a sub-trust has been created, such as where trustees hold a fund on trust for X and Y in equal shares, and X and Y both declare themselves trustees of their respective shares for their children. In such a case, under the head trust, the trustees are nominal owners, but X and Y can hardly be regarded as the real or beneficial owners; under the sub-trust, it is clear that X and Y are not the legal owners at all, but are trustees of the respective equitable half-shares.

Having regard to the above considerations, a trust can be said to exist whenever equity imposes on a person (the trustee) an obligation to deal with property[1] of which he is the owner,[2] either for the benefit of other persons[3] (the beneficiaries or cestuis que trust),[4] any one of whom may enforce the obligation, or for a charitable purpose, which may be enforced at the instance of the Attorney-General, or for some other purpose permitted by law, although unenforceable.[5]

According to Lord Browne-Wilkinson,[6] it would be wrong to say that if the legal title is in A, but the equitable interest in B, A necessarily holds as trustee for B; there are many cases in which B enjoys rights that, in equity, are enforceable against the legal owner, A, without A being a trustee, for example, an equitable right to redeem a mortgage, equitable

---

[1] This may comprise any proprietary interest that a person can, at law or in equity, transfer or assign. See p 50, *infra*.

[2] He may be either the legal owner or the equitable owner. For example, A may be a trustee (under the head trust) holding the legal title to Blackacre on trust for B and C in equal shares, and B (under a sub-trust) may be a trustee holding his equitable half-share on trust for D, E, and F in equal shares.

[3] A trustee (except, it seems, a trustee under a half-secret trust—see p 133, *infra*) can himself be a beneficiary, but a sole trustee cannot be the sole beneficiary: *Re Cook* [1948] Ch 212, [1948] 1 All ER 231.

[4] This seems to be the correct plural of cestui que trust, not 'cestui que trusts' or 'cestuis que trustent': (1910) 26 LQR 196 (C Sweet).

[5] See, generally, (1899) 15 LQR 294 (W G Hart); [2002] 61 CLJ 657 (P Parkinson). As to unenforceable trusts, see p 59 *et seq*, *infra*.

[6] In *Westdeutsche Landesbank Girozentrale v Islington London Borough Council* [1996] AC 669, 707, [1996] 2 All ER 961, 989, HL, in which 'mortgagor' is misprinted as 'mortgagee' in both reports. *Don King Productions Inc v Warren*, per Lightman J at first instance [1998] 2 All ER 608, 630; affd [2000] Ch 291, [1999] 2 All ER 218, CA. See also *R v Chester and North Wales Legal Aid Area Office (No 12), ex p Floods of Queensferry Ltd* [1998] 1 WLR 1496, CA.

easements, restrictive covenants, and the right to rectification. Even in cases in which the whole beneficial interest is vested in B and the bare legal interest is in A, A is not necessarily a trustee, for example, where title to land is acquired by estoppel as against the legal owner; a mortgagor who has fully discharged his indebtedness enforces his right to recover the mortgaged property in a redemption action, not an action for breach of trust. Lord Millett, writing extrajudicially,[7] is not, however, convinced, and considers that a trust exists whenever the legal title is in one party and the equitable title in another.

A fuller understanding of the trust can be obtained by comparing it with other legal concepts. These comparisons will be made in the following sections of this chapter.

1 TRUST AND BAILMENT

Blackstone[8] has caused some confusion by defining bailment as 'a delivery of goods in trust, upon a contract expressed or implied, that the trust shall be faithfully executed on the part of the bailee'. It may well be that the bailee is, in a popular sense, entrusted with the goods lent, hired out, deposited for safe custody, or whatever it may be; there is, however, no trust in the technical sense and the concepts are distinct. It is indeed better to define 'bailment' as a delivery of personal chattels upon a condition, express or implied, that they shall be redelivered to the bailor, or according to his directions, when the purpose of the bailment has been carried out. Bailment was a recognized common law institution, while trusts, of course, were only recognized by courts of equity. Apart from historical and procedural differences, bailment applies only to personal property, while the trust concept applies to all kinds of property. The essential difference is, perhaps, that the bailee has, as it is said, only a special property in or special ownership of the goods bailed, the general property or general ownership remaining in the bailor, while the trustee is the full owner. Consequently, the bailee cannot, as a rule,[9] pass a title to the goods that will be valid as against the bailor, but a trustee can pass a good title to someone who acquires legal ownership bona fide for value without notice of the trust.

2 TRUST AND CONTRACT

Again, there is the historical distinction that contract was developed by the common law courts, while the trust was a creature of equity. In general, the purposes are different: a contract usually represents a bargain between the contracting parties giving each some advantage, while the beneficiary under a trust is commonly a volunteer, and the trustee himself usually obtains no benefit from the trust at all.[10] It is of the essence of a contract that the agreement is supported by consideration, but, in the case of a trust,[11] there is no need for

---

[7] In Cornish et al (eds) *Restitution: Past, Present and Future*, p 204.

[8] *Commentaries*, Book II, p 451; see Maitland's *Equity*, 2nd (Brunyate) edn, Lecture IV.

[9] There are important exceptions, eg under the Factors Act 1889; estoppel.

[10] See Chapter 19, *infra*.

[11] Provided that it is completely constituted: see Chapter 6, p 100 *et seq*, *infra*.

consideration to have been given in order for it to be enforceable. This distinction is blurred by the fact that a contract by deed is enforceable at law without value having been given.

3 TRUST AND AGENCY

It is sometimes said that an agent is a trustee for his principal of property belonging to the principal committed to his charge, either generally,[12] or, according to Keeton and Sheridan,[13] only where there is some special, confidential relationship. There is no doubt that a principal can commonly exercise the same remedies against his agent as a cestui que trust can against his trustee, but Professor Powell has pointed out[14] that this 'does not necessarily mean that an agent is a trustee or that a trustee is an agent. It means simply that agents and trustees have something in common—and that "something in common" is that they both hold a fiduciary position which imposes on them certain obligations'. Thus both agents and trustees are under a duty not to let their interests conflict with their duties, not to make any unauthorized profits, and to keep proper accounts.

There are, however, considerable differences. Thus the relationship of principal and agent is created by their agreement, but this is not so in the case of trustee and beneficiary. The trustee does not represent the beneficiaries, although he performs his duties for their benefit, as the agent represents his principal. Further, the trustee does not bring his beneficiaries into any contractual relationship with third parties, while it is the normal function of an agent to do so. Again, the concept of a trust necessarily involves the concept of trust property over which the trustee has at least nominal control, but an agent need never have any control over any property belonging to his principal. An agent is subject to the control of his principal, but a trustee is not subject to control by the beneficiaries except in the sense that the beneficiaries can take steps to compel him to carry out the terms of the trust. Further, it may be observed that the statutory provisions relating to trustees do not, in general, apply to agents. It may, however, be a matter of some difficulty to decide on the facts whether a particular transaction sets up a trust or agency, nor are the institutions mutually exclusive.[15]

An agent may become a constructive trustee. If, for instance, his principal directs him to buy Blackacre and he purports to buy it for himself, he will be held to be a constructive trustee of it for his principal;[16] likewise, if his principal transfers property to him for sale, investment, or safe custody;[17] also, where he receives property on behalf of his principal, provided that he is under a duty to keep it separate from his own property.[18]

---

[12] See (1898) 14 LQR 272 (S Brodhurst); (1933) 49 LQR 578 (W S Holdsworth); (1954) 17 MLR 24 (F E Dowrick); [1975] CLP 39 (J D Stephens); *Neste Oy u Lloyds Bank plc* [1983] 2 Lloyd's Rep 658.

[13] *Law of Trusts*, 12th edn, p 246.

[14] *Law of Agency*, 2nd edn, p 25; F E Dowrick, op cit; *Ian Scott & Co v Medical Installations Co Ltd* (1981) 258 EG 556 illustrates the fiduciary nature of an agent's position. See also *Brandeis (Brokers) Ltd v Black* [2001] 2 All ER (Comm) 980; [2007] 92 T & ELTJ 26 (G Rosenberg).

[15] See (1892) 8 LQR 220 (C Sweet); Scott, *Law of Trusts*, 4th edn, vol I, p 95.

[16] *Longfield Parish Council v Robson* (1913) 29 TLR 357.

[17] See *Re Hallett's Estate* (1880) 13 Ch D 696; *Burdick v Garrick* (1870) 5 Ch App 233.

[18] *Lyell v Kennedy* (1889) 14 App Cas 437; *Foley v Hill* (1848) 2 HL Cas 28; *Aluminium Industrie Vaassen BV v Romalpa Aluminium Ltd* [1976] 2 All ER 552, [1976] 1 WLR 676; *Clough Mill Ltd v Martin* [1984] 3 All

4 TRUSTS AND POWERS[19]

(A) BASIC DISTINCTION

A power can be sufficiently defined for present purposes as an authority vested in a person to deal with or dispose of property not his own.[20] It can be distinguished from a trust succinctly: a trust is imperative; a power, discretionary. One type of power in particular that is liable to be confused with a trust is a special[21] power of appointment. This is a power given to someone (called the 'donee' of the power) under a trust or settlement authorizing him to appoint some, or all, of the trust property among a limited class of persons (called the 'objects' of the power). The donee of the power can choose whether to make an appointment or not, and if, by the end of the period during which the power can be exercised, he has failed to make a valid appointment, whether intentionally or unintentionally, the objects of the power can do nothing about it and the court has no jurisdiction to intervene.[22] If there is a gift over in default of appointment, it will take effect; if not, there will be a resulting trust for the testator's[23] estate. Suppose, however, that instead of a person being given a mere power of appointment, a fund is given to trustees on trust to divide it among an ascertainable class of persons: in such case, even though the trustees have been directed to divide it in such shares as they in their absolute discretion should think fit,[24] they would be under a duty to make the division and, in case of a failure to distribute, any potential beneficiary could apply to the court, which would see to it that the division took place.

It will have been observed that, in the illustration of a power just given, reference was made to a power of appointment arising under a trust. Since 1925, most powers, including

---

ER 982, [1985] 1 WLR 111, CA. As to bribes received by an agent, see *A-G of Hong Kong v Reid* [1994] 1 AC 324, [1994] 1 All ER 1, PC.

[19] See, generally, [1970] ASCL 187 (J D Davies); (1971) 29 CLJ 68 (J Hopkins); (1971) 87 LQR 31 (J W Harris); (1974) 37 MLR 643 (Y Grbich); (1976) 54 CBR 229 (M C Cullity); (1977) 3 Mon LR 210 (Y Grbich); (1992) 5 Cant LR 67 (N P Gravells).

[20] *Freme v Clement* (1881) 18 Ch D 499; *Re Armstrong* (1866) 17 QBD 521.

[21] Contrast a general power of appointment, under which the person to whom it is given may appoint to himself and make himself owner. In addition to general and special powers, there are powers in a hybrid category. See (1949) 13 Conv 20 (J G Fleming); (1954) 18 Conv 565 (F R Crane). These 'hybrid' or 'intermediate powers'—ie powers exercisable in favour of anyone, with certain exceptions—may be validly conferred upon trustees. They enable trustees to deal with virtually all eventualities and, at the same time, make the maximum tax savings. See *Re Manisty's Settlement, Manisty v Manisty* [1974] Ch 17, [1973] 2 All ER 1203; *Re Hay's Settlement Trusts* [1981] 3 All ER 786, [1982] 1 WLR 202; (1974) 33 CLJ 66 (J Hopkins). In the following discussion, 'power' means a special or intermediate power of appointment. There is no rule of law against testamentary delegation that prevents the use of wide powers of appointment in wills: *Re Beatty's Will Trusts* [1990] 3 All ER 844, [1990] 1 WLR 1503; noted (1991) 107 LQR 211 (J D Davies); *Gregory v Hudson* (1998) 45 NSWLR 301.

[22] The court does, of course, have jurisdiction to see that a person does not exceed the power given to him. Thus an appointment that goes beyond the limits set to the power by the terms of the power itself or by law is known as an 'excessive execution' of the power and is void, eg appointment to grandchildren under a power to appoint to children. Again, an appointment is void if it is a 'fraud on the power', or, in more modern parlance, an improper use of the power for a collateral purpose. See [2007] PCB 131, 191 (P Matthews); (2007) 22 UNZLR 496 (P Devonshire).

[23] Or for the settlor (or his estate) if the trust is created *inter vivos*.

[24] That is, a discretionary trust: see p 77, *infra*.

all powers of appointment, are equitable only and can therefore only subsist behind a trust or settlement. Accordingly, the real question is whether a particular provision in a trust instrument confers a power or imposes a trust. The fact that the provision is contained in a trust instrument does not mean, on the one hand, that an individual who, under a trust, is given a power of appointment is thereby necessarily constituted a trustee; nor, on the other hand, does it prevent a trustee being given a mere power of appointment, although where a power is given to a trustee *ex officio* he is not in the same position as an individual.

At one extreme, if a mere power is given to an individual, he is under no duty to exercise it or even to consider whether he should exercise it. He owes no duty at all to the objects of the power. He is free to release the power even if he does so because, as a consequence, he will receive some benefit from one or other of the persons who take in default of appointment.[25] The objects can only complain if there is an excessive execution of the power, or if the appointment made constitutes a fraud on the power. At the other extreme, if property is given to trustees on discretionary trusts, the court will see to it that the trust is carried out.

In between these two extremes is the case in which a power is given to a trustee *ex officio*.[26] In this case, by reason of his fiduciary position, the trustee, unlike an individual, is under a duty to consider[27] whether and in what way he should exercise the power, and cannot refuse to consider whether it ought to be exercised. As explained by Megarry VC in *Re Hay's Settlement Trusts*:[28]

> Normally the trustee is not bound to exercise [a mere power], and the court will not compel him to do so. That, however, does not mean that he can simply fold his hands and ignore it, for normally he must from time to time consider whether or not to exercise the power, and the court may direct him to do this.

The decision of the trustees in the exercise of their discretion will not normally be interfered with by the court. If, for some reason, the trustees cannot exercise the power, the remedies available in discretionary trusts[29] have been held to be equally available.[30]

It is not always easy in practice to decide whether, on its true construction, a particular provision constitutes a power or a trust, as appears from a series of cases culminating in *McPhail v Doulton*.[31] In that case, the judge at first instance and a majority in the

---

[25] *Re Greaves' Will Trusts* [1954] Ch 434, [1954] 1 All ER 771, CA; *Re Gulbenkian's Settlement Trusts* [1970] AC 508, 518, [1968] 3 All ER 785, 787, HL, *per* Lord Reid.

[26] A power given to trustees *ex officio* is not capable of being released: *Re Wills's Trust Deeds* [1964] Ch 219, [1963] 1 All ER 390; *Re Manisty's Settlement* [1974] Ch 17, [1973] 2 All ER 1203, in the absence of words in the trust deed authorizing them to do so; *Muir v IRC* [1966] 3 All ER 38, [1996] 1 WLR 1269, CA. Note that although an employer is not to be treated as a fiduciary when he exercises powers vested in him under a pension scheme, he owes an implied obligation of good faith to his employees: *National Grid Co plc v Mayes* [2001] UKHL 20, [2001] 2 All ER 417, HL.

[27] The duty of the trustees is to give properly informed consideration to the exercise of their powers: see *Stannard v Fisons Pension Trust Ltd* [1992] IRLR 27, CA. See (2008) 22 TruLI 81 (D Hayton).

[28] [1981] 3 All ER 786, 792, [1982] 1 WLR 202, 209. No hint is given to the significance of the word 'normally' on either occasion when it is used: *Re Gulbenkian's Settlement Trusts, supra*, HL at 518, 787, *per* Lord Reid; *McPhail v Doulton* [1971] AC 424, 449, [1970] 2 All ER 228, 240, *per* Lord Wilberforce. See *Vestey v IRC (No 2)* [1979] 2 All ER 225, esp at 235; affd [1980] AC 1148, [1979] 3 All ER 976, HL.

[29] See *McPhail v Doulton, supra*, HL at 457, 247, *per* Lord Wilberforce, and p 80, *infra*.

[30] *Mettoy Pension Trustees Ltd v Evans, supra* (pension fund surplus: trustee, the company, in liquidation), noted (1991) 107 LQR 214 (S Gardner); [1991] Conv 364 (Jill Martin). See also [1992] JBL 261 (R Nobles).

[31] *Supra*, HL. See *Pearson v IRC* [1981] AC 753, [1980] 2 All ER 479, HL.

Court of Appeal held that the trustees had a mere power, while the House of Lords unanimously agreed that the relevant provision constituted a trust. In the House of Lords, Lord Wilberforce observed[32] how narrow and artificial the distinction could be:

> what to one mind may appear as a power of distribution coupled with a trust to dispose of the undistributed surplus, by accumulation or otherwise, may to another appear as a trust for distribution coupled with a power to withhold a portion and accumulate or otherwise dispose of it.

(B) SPECIAL POWER OF APPOINTMENT—MERE POWER OR TRUST POWER

The inherent difficulty in understanding the relationship between trust and power is not helped by the terminology used. In this context, a power is commonly referred to as a 'mere power', 'bare power', or 'power collateral'—these terms appear to be synonymous—in order to distinguish it from what is variously called a 'trust power', a 'power in the nature of a trust', or a 'power coupled with a duty'. A power will be a trust power where, although at first sight it may appear to be a mere power, it is held that, on the true construction of the instrument, there is an element of trust. It will later be submitted that the term 'trust power' is used in two quite different senses.

The question whether a power is a mere power or a trust power has often arisen in family trusts where the person to whom a power of appointment has been given has died without exercising it and where there is no gift over in default of appointment. In such a case, if the court holds that the power is a mere power, then, as we have seen, the objects have no claim and there will be a resulting trust; if, however, the court holds that the power is a trust power, in default of appointment, there will be held to be a trust in favour of the objects of the power. A leading case is *Burrough v Philcox*,[33] in which a testator gave his surviving child, in the events that happened, power 'to dispose of all my real and personal estates amongst my nephews and nieces or their children, either all to one of them, or to as many of them as my surviving child shall think proper'. No appointment was made and the court held that the effect of this provision was to create a trust in favour of the nephews and nieces, and their children, subject to a power of selection in the surviving child, and that since the power had not been exercised, the nephews and nieces and their children took equally. As Lord Cottenham explained:[34]

> when there appears a general intention in favour of a class, and a particular intention in favour of individuals of a class to be selected by another person, and the particular intention fails, from that selection not being made, the court will carry into effect the general intention in favour of the class.

In such a case, it is the duty of the donee of the power to execute it and 'the court will not permit the objects of the power to suffer by the negligence or conduct of the donee, but fastens upon the property a trust for their benefit'.

---

[32] *Supra*, at 448, 240, HL.
[33] (1840) 5 My & Cr 72; *Brown v Higgs* (1803) 8 Ves 561 (affd (1813) 18 Ves 192, HL).
[34] *Burrough v Philcox* (1840) 5 My & Cr 72 at 92.

Whether a power is a mere power or a trust power is a question of 'intention or presumed intention to be derived from the language of the instrument'.[35] It is clear, however, that a gift over in default of appointment, although not upon some other event,[36] is conclusive against the power being a trust power, because it is inconsistent with an intention to benefit the objects of the power if the donee fails to exercise it.[37] This is so even though the gift over is itself void for some reason.[38] An ordinary residuary gift is not, however, a gift over for this purpose.[39]

Where there is no gift over, there is no 'inflexible and artificial rule of construction'[40] to the effect that a trust must be implied.

Although Evershed MR thought it 'clear that, where there is a power to appoint among a class, there will prima facie be implied a gift over in default of appointment to all the members of the class in equal shares',[41] it is submitted that the better view is that the court will be unwilling to infer a trust from a power in the absence of some other indication of an intention to benefit the class. Thus it was held that there was a mere power and no trust: in *Re Weekes' Settlement*,[42] in which a testatrix, having given her husband a life interest in certain property, gave him 'power to dispose of all such property by will amongst our children'; in *Re Combe*,[43] in which, following life interests to his wife and son, a testator directed his trustees to hold the property 'in trust for such person or persons as my said son ... shall by will appoint, but I direct that such appointment must be confined to any relation or relations of mine of the whole blood'; and in *Re Perowne*,[44] in which a testatrix gave her husband a life interest in her estate and continued, 'knowing that he will make arrangements for the disposal of my estate, according to my wishes, for the benefit of my family'.

In most of the family trust cases in which the court has decided that the power is a trust power, the court has held that the power remains a power, but, finding an intention on the part of the testator to benefit the objects of the power in any event, has implied a trust in their favour in default of appointment. Thus, in *Re Wills' Trust Deeds*,[45] Buckley J said that it really turns on:

> the question whether on the particular facts of each case it was proper to infer a trust in default of appointment for the objects of the power. The court did not, and, I think, could not compel the donee personally to exercise the power but carried what it conceived to be the settlor's intention into effect by executing an implied trust in default of appointment.

Where the court holds that a trust is to be implied in default of appointment, it determines logically whom the beneficiaries under the trust should be. A typical case is *Walsh v Wallinger*,[46] in which a husband left property to his wife 'trusting that she will, at her decease, give and bequeath the same to our children in such a manner as she shall appoint'. Since the wife's power of appointment could only be exercised by will, an appointment

---

[35] *Per* Evershed MR in *Re Scarisbrick's Will Trusts* [1951] Ch 622, 635, [1951] 1 All ER 822, 828, CA.
[36] *Re Llewellyn's Settlement* [1921] 2 Ch 281.   [37] *Re Mills* [1930] 1 Ch 654, CA.
[38] *Re Sprague* (1880) 43 LT 236.   [39] *Re Brierley* (1894) 43 WR 36, CA.
[40] *Per* Tomlin J in *Re Combe* [1925] Ch 210, 216.
[41] *Re Scarisbrick's Will Trusts* [1951] Ch 622, 635, CA.   [42] [1897] 1 Ch 289.
[43] [1925] Ch 210, [1925] All ER Rep 159.   [44] [1951] Ch 785, [1951] 2 All ER 201.
[45] [1964] Ch 219, [1963] 1 All ER 390.
[46] (1830) 2 Russ & M 78; *Re Arnold's Trusts* [1947] Ch 131, [1946] 2 All ER 579. For the special position in which there is a trust power in favour of relations or members of the donee's family, see *IRC v Broadway Cottages Trust* [1955] Ch 20, [1954] 3 All ER 120, CA, and cases there cited; *Re Poulton's Will Trusts* [1987] 1 All ER 1068, [1987] 1 WLR 795.

by the wife could only be made to children living at her death. No appointment having been made, the court held that there was an implied trust in default of appointment for those children only who survived the wife,[47] as being those whom the testator presumably intended to benefit. It is always a question of the construction of the particular instrument and some cases cited in this context do not really involve an implied trust at all. An example is *Lambert v Thwaites*,[48] in which the trust was, in effect, to sell real estate and divide the proceeds 'amongst all and every the children [of RW] in such shares and proportions, manner and form' as RW should, by will, appoint. It was held that, on its true construction, this was a trust for all of the children of RW, subject, however, to the power of appointment. The children accordingly obtained vested interests liable to be divested if the power of appointment was exercised. RW having died without exercising the power, all of his children, including the estate of his deceased son Alfred, took equal shares.

It may be added that where the court holds that there is an implied trust in default of appointment, it applies the maxim 'equality is equity' and divides the property among the beneficiaries equally.[49]

(C) TRUST IN DEFAULT OF APPOINTMENT OR DISCRETIONARY TRUST

As has just been seen, in most of the family trust cases in which a power has been held to be a trust power, the court has implied a trust in default of appointment. In other cases,[50] however, it has also been called a trust power where the court has held that the power was of a fiduciary character that the donee of the power was under a duty to exercise, and that if he should fail to exercise the power, the court would in some way see to it that the duty was carried out. As Lord Eldon said in *Brown v Higgs*,[51] 'the court adopts the principle as to trusts and will not permit his [ie the donee of the power] negligence, accident or other circumstances to disappoint the interests of those for whose benefit he is called upon to execute it' but will 'discharge the duty in his room and place'.

This second construction has been adopted in a number of cases concerning large benevolent funds, such as *McPhail v Doulton*,[52] in which the trustees were directed to make grants out of income 'at their absolute discretion ... to ... any of the officers and employees or ex-officers or ex-employees of the Company or to any relatives or dependants of any such persons'. As already mentioned, in that case, all of the Law Lords agreed that it was a case of a trust, not a mere power. Although they differed on other points going to the very validity of the trust, they also agreed that, if the trust were valid, the trustees would be under a fiduciary duty to exercise the power, and that if the trustees were to fail to exercise it, then the court would do so.[53]

---

[47] That is, the estates of children who had predeceased their mother got nothing.

[48] (1866) LR 2 Eq 151, Kindersley VC observed, at 157: 'In the case now before the Court there is in express terms a direct gift to the children.'

[49] *Wilson v Duguid* (1883) 24 Ch D 244; *Re Llewellyn's Settlement* [1921] 2 Ch 281; *Re Arnold's Trusts, supra*.

[50] For example, *Brown v Higgs* (1803) 8 Ves 561; affd (1813) 18 Ves 192, HL, although it has not by any means always been so regarded, and was one of the few cases cited in *Re Wills' Trust Deeds, supra*; *Burrough v Philcox* (1840) 5 My & Cr 72, in which dicta can be found to support both views; *Re Leek* [1967] Ch 1061, [1967] 2 All ER 1160; (affd [1969] 1 Ch 563, [1968] 1 All ER 793, CA). See (1971) 29 CLJ 68 (J Hopkins).

[51] *Supra.*   [52] [1971] AC 424, [1970] 2 All ER 228, HL.

[53] As to how the court would exercise the power, see p 80, *infra*.

It is unfortunate that the term 'trust power' has been used in these two different senses: viz (i) where the court implies a trust in default of appointment; and (ii) where it holds the power to be of a fiduciary nature, which it will itself exercise if necessary. It is, indeed, somewhat curious, as well as unfortunate, because a trust power in the second sense is indistinguishable from what is usually referred to as a 'discretionary trust'—that is, a trust under which the trustees are given a discretionary and fiduciary power to decide which of the class of potential beneficiaries shall take.[54] Indeed, in further proceedings in *McPhail v Doulton*,[55] the term used is 'discretionary trust' and not 'trust power'. It is to be hoped that this will become the accepted terminology and that the term 'trust power' will be restricted to the case in which a trust is implied in default of appointment.

A trust power in the sense of a discretionary trust has been described as intermediate between trusts and powers: it is, it is submitted, essentially a trust and is in most respects treated as such, but in one important respect, as will be seen shortly, it has been virtually assimilated to a mere power.

It should be added that the courts have, in fact, seldom discussed,[56] and often do not seem to have recognized the existence of, the two different senses in which the term 'trust power' is used. What has usually happened in practice is that the court has, in substance, discussed either the question 'is it a mere power or is there an implied trust in default of appointment?' or, alternatively, the question 'is it a mere power or a discretionary trust?'. Assuming that the courts in future distinguish between the two senses of trust power, it seems a clear inference from *McPhail v Doulton*[57] that, in the case of a 'trust power' for a large class or classes of beneficiaries, the second sense—that of discretionary trust—is likely to be thought more appropriate, although it may well be that where the trust power is in favour of a small defined class of persons, the court will prefer to imply a trust in default of appointment.

(D) MERE POWERS AND DISCRETIONARY TRUSTS

As we shall see,[58] the assimilation of the rules as to certainty for powers and discretionary trusts has removed the main practical reason for having to distinguish between them. Certain differences remain, however, and in appropriate circumstances may be of considerable importance. There is still a vital distinction where the power or trust is not exercised. In the case of a mere power, the property goes to the persons entitled in default of appointment, either by express or implied gift over, or by way of resulting trust, while in the case of a discretionary trust, the beneficiaries will not be allowed to suffer by reason of the default of the trustees and the court will in some way ensure that the trust is executed.

Another distinction was suggested by Lord Wilberforce in *McPhail v Doulton*:[59]

As to the trustees' duty of enquiry or ascertainment, in each case the trustees ought to make such a survey of the range of objects or possible beneficiaries as will enable them to carry out

---

54 See p 77, *infra*. See also [1984] Conv 227 (R Bartlett and C Stebbings).
55 *Re Baden's Deed Trusts (No 2)* [1972] Ch 607, [1971] 3 All ER 985; affd [1973] Ch 9, [1972] 2 All ER 1304, CA.
56 Chitty J noted the distinction in *Wilson v Duguid* (1883) 24 Ch D 244, 249, but said that, in that case, there was a plain implication of a trust in default of appointment and no need to refer to the concept of a duty to be exercised by the trustees. See (1962) 26 Conv 92 (M G Unwin); (1967) 31 Conv 364 (F R Crane).
57 *Supra*, HL.   58 See p 53 *et seq*, *infra*.
59 [1971] AC 424, 457, [1970] 2 All ER 228, 247, HL. See, generally, (1990) 4 TL & P 117 (Fiona Spearing).

their fiduciary duty. A wider and more comprehensive range of enquiry is called for in the case of [discretionary trusts][60] than in the case of powers.

In so far as it relates to powers, this rather vague dictum is dealing with, and is restricted to, powers given to trustees. An individual to whom a mere power is given is normally under no fiduciary duty to survey the range of objects at all. Where trustees have a power that they have decided to exercise, it has been cogently argued[61] that the distinction drawn by Lord Wilberforce is invalid and that the duty of the enquiry should be the same as in a discretionary trust. The fiduciary obligation at this stage should be the same. There is no justification for allowing one fiduciary to discharge his duty by a lower, or higher, standard than another. The difference appears at the earlier stage previously discussed.[62]

In *Re Hay's Settlement Trusts*,[63] Megarry VC considered how, in the case of a power given to trustees, the duty of making a responsible survey and selection should be carried out in the absence of any complete list of objects. The trustee, he said:

> must not simply proceed to exercise the power in favour of such of the objects as happen to be at hand or claim his attention. He must first consider what persons or class of persons are objects of the power.... In doing this, there is no need to compile a complete list of the objects, or even to make an accurate assessment of the number of them: what is needed is an appreciation of the width of the field.

Having applied his mind to the 'size of the problem', he can then consider in individual cases whether, in relation to other possible claimants, a particular grant is appropriate, although he is not required to make an exact calculation whether, as between deserving claimants, A is more deserving than B.

(E) UNENFORCEABLE TRUSTS OR TRUSTS OF IMPERFECT OBLIGATION

These trusts, as the alternative names imply, constitute an exception to the principle that trusts are imperative; powers, discretionary. In these trusts, the trustees cannot be compelled to carry out their duties; they are, in substance, powers rather than trusts, and are admittedly anomalous and exceptional. They are discussed later.[64]

5 TRUSTS AND THE ADMINISTRATION OF ESTATES OF DECEASED PERSONS

Although different in origin, trusts having been developed by the Lord Chancellor and the jurisdiction over personal representatives having been at first exercised only in the ecclesiastical courts, it is not now possible to draw a clear line between trustees and personal representatives. In fact, a person may well be at the same time both trustee and personal representative in relation to the same estate, although not in relation to the same item

---

[60] Lord Wilberforce actually used the term 'trust powers'.   [61] (1974) 38 Conv 269 (L McKay).
[62] See p 34, *supra*.   [63] [1981] 3 All ER 786, [1982] 1 WLR 202. See [1982] Conv 432 (A Grubb).
[64] See p 59 *et seq, infra*.

of property.[65] The main principles that produce this somewhat confusing situation are as follows.

(i)   Until the coming into force of s 50 of the Administration of Justice Act 1985, the rule was that a personal representative retained his office for the whole of his life,[66] unless that grant was originally of a limited duration, or was subsequently revoked by the court. An example of a limited grant is where a minor is appointed sole executor. In this case, a grant of administration is made to his parents or guardians for his use and benefit until he attains the age of eighteen years. Such a grant automatically deter-mines on his attaining that age or earlier death. As to revocation, this may occur for various reasons: for example, if it appears that the presumed deceased is still alive. The 1985 Act now empowers the court to appoint a substituted personal representative in place of the existing personal representative or representatives or any of them, or to remove one or more, but not all, of the existing personal representatives.

(ii) In a number of cases, of which *Re Ponder*[67] is perhaps the best known, it has been held that a personal representative who has paid all expenses and debts, cleared the estate, and completed his duties in a proper way, becomes *functus officio*[68] as such, and holds the residue not as a personal representative, but as a trustee, and can accordingly exercise the statutory power to appoint new trustees. Some doubt was cast upon this view by a reserved judgment of a strong Court of Appeal in *Harvell v Foster*,[69] in which an administrator was held liable as such[70] when all of the duties of his office had been performed save the distribution of the net residue, which was impossible by reason of the minority of the residuary legatee. Danckwerts J criticized dicta in this case in *Re Cockburn*[71] and had no doubt that a personal representative who has completed his duties in a proper way can appoint new trustees. There seems, in fact, to be no necessary conflict between *Re Cockburn* and *Re Ponder*, on the one hand, and *Harvell v Foster*, on the other, if it is accepted, as it was by the Court of Appeal in the last-men-tioned case, disapproving on this point Sargant J's view in *Re Ponder*, that the offices of personal representative and trustee are not mutually exclusive. On this basis, he can, *qua* trustee, exercise the statutory power to appoint new trustees,[72] while, *qua* personal representative, he remains liable for any failure to carry out his duties as such.

     It should be observed that until the estate, whether of a testator[73] or an intestate,[74] is fully administered, the residuary legatees, or the next of kin of an intestate, are

---

[65] See [2006] Conv 245 (T Prime).

[66] *Re Timmis* [1902] 1 Ch 176, 183, *per* Kekewich J; *George Attenborough & Son v Solomon* [1913] AC 76, 83, HL, *per* Haldane LC; *Harvell v Foster* [1954] 2 QB 367, [1954] 2 All ER 736, CA, *per* Evershed MR; *Re Aldhous* [1955] 2 All ER 80, [1955] 1 WLR 459.

[67] [1921] 2 Ch 59; *Re Yerburgh* [1928] WN 208; *Re Cockburn's Will Trusts* [1957] Ch 438, [1957] 2 All ER 522. See (1991) 11 Ox JLS 609 (Chantal Stebbings).

[68] As to this term, see [1990] Conv 427 (Chantal Stebbings).

[69] *Supra*. See (1955) 19 Conv 199 (B S Ker).

[70] The action was actually against the sureties in the administration bond. As to sureties, see now the Supreme Court Act 1981, now renamed the Senior Courts Act 1981, s 120.   [71] *Supra*.

[72] But where land is concerned, see *Re King's Will Trusts* [1964] Ch 542, [1964] 1 All ER 833; [1976] CLP 60 (E C Ryder) and p 42 fn 82, *infra*.

[73] *Stamp Duties Comr (Queensland) v Livingston* [1965] AC 694, [1964] 3 All ER 692, PC. See [1992] Conv 92 (Julie Maxton).

[74] *Eastbourne Mutual Building Society v Hastings Corpn* [1965] 1 All ER 779, [1965] 1 WLR 861.

not to be regarded as the beneficial owners of the unadministered assets. The personal representatives hold the assets in full ownership without distinction between legal and equitable interests. It is also true, however, that they hold them for the purpose of carrying out the functions and duties of administration, not for their own benefit, and that these functions and duties may be enforced by creditors and beneficiaries. The result therefore is that a personal representative is in a fiduciary position with regard to the assets that come to him in the right of his office and for certain purposes, and in some aspects he is treated by the court as a trustee. But equity has never recognized or created for residuary legatees, or the next of kin of an intestate, a beneficial interest in the assets in the hands of the personal representatives during the course of administration.[75] One consequence of this is that personal representatives are not under the same duty as trustees to hold the balance evenly between the beneficiaries.[76] And the memoranda in *Crowden v Aldridge*[77] could not operate as assignments because, when they were signed, none of the residuary legatees had any beneficial interest in the estate. They constituted a direction to the executors varying their obligations in the administration and distribution of the estate.

(iii) The same persons are commonly appointed as executors and trustees by a testator. In the absence of an express assent, an implied assent to themselves as trustees will readily be inferred from their conduct where executors have completed their duties as such. This was of vital importance in *Attenborough v Solomon*[78] by reason of an important difference between the power of one of two or more trustees, and that of one of two or more personal representatives. Trustees can only act unanimously[79] and, accordingly, one of two or more trustees has no power to deal with or dispose of the trust property. By contrast, one of two or more personal representatives has full power to deal with or dispose of pure personalty, and it seems to make no difference whether he is an executor or an administrator. So far as land is concerned, whether freehold or leasehold, where there are two or more personal representatives, they must all concur in any contract or conveyance in respect thereof.[80]

In *Attenborough & Son v Solomon*,[81] the property involved was pure personalty, and what had happened was that, long after the debts and pecuniary legacies had been paid and the residuary account' passed, one of two persons appointed as executors and trustees pledged certain plate forming part of the residuary estate

---

[75] *Stamp Duties Comr (Queensland) v Livingston, supra; Re Leigh's Will Trusts* [1970] Ch 277, [1969] 3 All ER 432; *Marshall v Kerr* [1995] 1 AC 148, [1994] 3 All ER 106, HL. But note that, subject to the right of the personal representatives to resort to it for the purposes of administration, a specific bequest or devise belongs to the legatee or devisee as soon as the testator dies: *Re K* [1986] Ch 180, [1985] 2 All ER 833, CA. See (1965) 23 CLJ 44 (S J Bailey); Meagher, Gummow, and Lehane, *Equity: Doctrine and Remedies*, 3rd edn, p 96 *et seq*.

[76] *Re Hayes's Will Trusts* [1971] 2 All ER 341, [1971] 1 WLR 758 (power to sell to a beneficiary at estate duty valuation. Executors bound to consider interest of estate as a whole, but under no duty to consider effect between trust beneficiaries). See p 428 *et seq, infra*, as to duty of trustees.

[77] [1993] 3 All ER 603, [1993] 1 WLR 433, criticized [1994] Conv 446 (J G Ross and Martyn).

[78] [1913] AC 76, HL; *Phillipo v Munnings* (1837) 2 My & Cr 309; *Re Claremont* [1923] 2 KB 718.

[79] For discussion of this rule, see Chapter 16, section 3, p 400 *et seq, infra*.

[80] Administration of Estates Act 1925, ss 2(2), as amended by the Law of Property (Miscellaneous Provisions) Act 1994, s 16.   [81] *Supra*, HL. See [1984] Conv 423 (Chantal Stebbings).

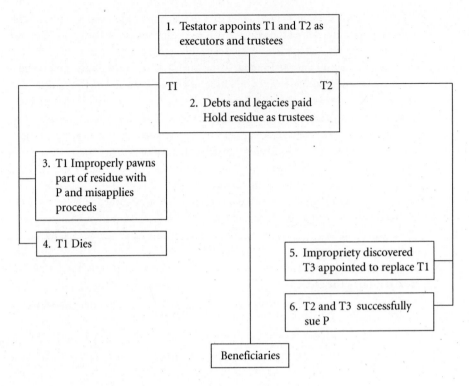

Figure 2.1 *Attenborough & Son v Solomon* [1913] AC 76, HL

with pawnbrokers and misapplied the money so raised. After the death of the pledgor, the transaction was discovered, and an action was brought by the surviving coexecutor and a new trustee against the pawnbroker to recover the plate. They were held entitled to succeed on the ground that the proper inference to be drawn was that, before the date of the pledge, the executors had assented to the trust disposition taking effect and held the plate not as executors, but as trustees. Since 1925, it should be noted that an assent to a legal estate in or over land must be in writing, even in the case of a personal representative assenting to himself as a trustee.[82]

---

[82] Administration of Estates Act 1925, ss 36(4) and 55(1)(vi)(vii); *Re King's Will Trusts* [1964] Ch 542, [1964] 1 All ER 833, criticized in (1964) 28 Conv 298 (J F Garner), and not followed in Ireland: *Mohan v Roche* [1991] 1 IR 560, noted [1992] Conv 383 (J A Dowling). According to this not-altogether-convincing decision, without a written assent, a personal representative who has become a trustee cannot, as regards land, take advantage of s 40 of the Trustee Act 1925 (discussed in Chapter 15, section 2) on the appointment of new trustees. Cf *Re Cockburn's Will Trusts* [1957] Ch 438, [1957] 2 All ER 522, apparently not cited in *Re King's Will Trusts, supra.* The most valuable discussion is in [1976] CLP 60 (E C Ryder). The Court of Appeal proceeded on the basis that *Re King's Will Trusts* was correctly decided in *Re Edward's Will Trusts* [1982] Ch 30, [1981] 2 All ER 941, CA, discussed [1981] Conv 450 (G Shindler) and [1982] Conv 4 (P W Smith). It seems that the rule is now so well understood and established in practice that its advantages in certainty outweigh the occasional practice difficulties, and Law Com No 184 accordingly does not recommend a change in the law. As to assents over personal property, see [1990] Conv 257 (Chantal Stebbings).

(iv) The amount of overlapping has been increased by the definition in the Trustee Act 1925[83] of a trustee as including a personal representative, where the context admits, and by the provisions of the Administration of Estates Act 1925,[84] which constitute an administrator an express trustee both on a total and partial[85] intestacy. Further, ss 1–9, 12, 13, and 15–18 of the Trusts of Land and Appointment of Trustees Act 1996[86] apply to personal representatives, but with appropriate modifications and without prejudice to the functions of personal representatives for the purposes of administration,[87] and the Trustee Act 2000 likewise applies to personal representatives with appropriate modifications.[88]

(v) The distinction between personal representative and trustee may also be relevant with regard to the Statutes of Limitation,[89] and by reason of the rule that a sole personal representative, whether or not a trust corporation, can give a valid receipt for capital money arising on a sale of the deceased's land, while there must be at least two trustees of a trust of land for this purpose, unless the sole trustee happens to be a trust corporation.[90] For most purposes, however, Jessel MR correctly summarized the position when he observed in Re Speight:[91] 'In modern times the Courts have not distinguished between...executors and trustees but they have put them all together and considered that they are all liable under the same principles.'

6 TRUST AND RESTITUTION

Restitution, which may be described as 'the law concerned with reversing a defendant's unjust enrichment at the claimant's expense',[92] has now been recognized by the House of Lords as a part of English law.[93] Burrows[94] states that it 'is most akin to, and belongs aside, contract and tort', but there is an overlap with the law of trusts. Thus both of the works cited include sections dealing with restitution in respect of benefits acquired in breach of fiduciary relationships, such as profits made by a trustee out of his trust.

In *Westdeutsche Landesbank Girozentale v Islington London Borough Council,*[95] Lord Goff observed that, in recent years, restitution lawyers, since certain equitable

---

[83] Section 68(1), (17).

[84] Section 33, as amended by the Trusts of Land and Appointment of Trustees Act 1996 and the Trustee Act 2000. Cf Land Transfer Act 1897, s 2, and *Toates v Toates* [1926] 2 KB 30, DC.

[85] Administration of Estates Act 1925, s 49, as amended.   [86] As amended.

[87] Trusts of Land and Appointment of Trustees Act 1996, s 18.   [88] Trustee Act 2000, s 35.

[89] See Chapter 23, section 3(D), p 529, *infra*.

[90] Law of Property Act 1925, s 27(2), as substituted by the Law of Property (Amendment) Act 1926, s 7, and Schedule, and amended by the Trusts of Land and Appointment of Trustees Act 1996.

[91] (1883) 22 Ch D 727, 742, CA; affd sub nom *Speight v Gaunt* (1883) 9 App Cas 1, HL.

[92] Burrows, *The Law of Restitution*, 2nd edn, p 1. See also Goff and Jones, *The Law of Restitution*, 7th edn, ch 1. S Headley [1995] CLJ 578 argues that emphasis on the theory of unjust enrichment has gone much too far.

[93] *Lipkin Gorman (a firm) v Karpnale Ltd* [1991] 2 AC 548, [1992] 4 All ER 512, HL; *Woolwich Equitable Building Society v IRC* [1993] AC 70, sub nom *Woolwich Building Society v IRC (No 2)* [1992] 3 All ER 727, HL.

[94] Op cit.   [95] [1996] AC 669, [1996] 2 All ER 961, HL, noted [1997] Conv 1 (AJ Oakley).

institutions—notably the constructive trust and the resulting trust—have been perceived
to have the function of reversing unjust enrichment, had sought to embrace those institutions within the law of restitution, if necessary moulding them to make them fit for
that purpose. Equity lawyers, on the other hand, were concerned that the trust concept
should not be distorted and also that the practical consequences of the imposition of a
trust should be fully appreciated. In the same case, Lord Browne-Wilkinson said that the
resulting trust is an unsuitable basis for developing proprietary restitutionary remedies.
However, he added, the remedial constructive trust, if introduced into English law, might
provide a more satisfactory road forward.[96]

[96] At 999. But see *Re Polly Peck International plc (in administration) (No 2)* [1998] 3 All ER 812, CA,
p 68 *et seq, infra.*

3

THE ESSENTIALS
OF A TRUST

Clearly, a valid trust cannot be created unless the purported creator of the trust has the power to create it and the purported beneficiaries have the ability to accept the equitable interests purported to be conferred on them. The capacity of a person to be a settlor or a beneficiary is dealt with in section 1 of this chapter. Section 2 considers what are known as 'the three certainties'; if any of these are absent, the purported trust will fail. The first, certainty of words, requires that it shall be clear that a legally binding obligation is imposed on the alleged trustee or trustees; the second, certainty of subject, that there shall be no ambiguity about either the property subject to the trust or the exact interests to be taken by the beneficiaries; and the third, certainty of objects requires that the beneficiaries shall be ascertainable. This leads on to section 3, which involves a consideration of the 'beneficiary principle', which requires that—with certain exceptions, of which the most important is the charitable trust—a trust, in order to be valid, must be for the benefit of individuals. One particular difficulty, considered in section 4, arises in connection with trusts for unincorporated associations by reason of the fact that such bodies do not have legal personality.

1 CAPACITY OF SETTLOR AND BENEFICIARIES

(A) CAPACITY OF SETTLOR

Capacity to create a trust is, in general, the same as capacity to hold and dispose of any legal or equitable estate or interest in property.

There are some special cases.

(i) Minors

A minor cannot, since 1925, hold a legal estate in land[1] and, accordingly, cannot settle it.[2] As regards other property, the position is similar to the rule in relation to contracts involving the acquisition of an interest in property of a permanent nature;[3] accordingly, an *inter vivos* settlement by a minor is voidable, in the sense that it will be binding upon the minor

---

[1] Law of Property Act 1925, s 1(6).   [2] He can, however, have an equitable interest.
[3] See Cheshire, Fifoot, and Furmston, *Law of Contract*, 15th edn, p 548 *et seq.*

after he comes of age unless he repudiates it on, or shortly after, attaining his majority.[4] So far as a settlement by will is concerned, a minor cannot make a valid will,[5] unless he is a soldier[6] being in actual military service, or a mariner or seaman being at sea.[7]

(ii) Persons lacking mental capacity

The Mental Capacity Act 2005[8] contains new provisions in relation to persons who lack capacity within the meaning of the Act. For the purposes of the Act, a person lacks capacity if he is unable to make a decision[9] for himself in relation to a matter because of an impairment, or a disturbance in the functioning, of his mind or brain, whether permanent or temporary.[10] A person is assumed to have capacity unless it is established that he lacks capacity, a question that has to be decided on a balance of probabilities after all practicable steps to help him to make a decision have been taken without success.[11] He is not to be treated as unable to make a decision merely because he makes an unwise decision,[12] nor can a lack of capacity be established merely by reference to a person's age or appearance, or a condition of his, or an aspect of his behaviour, which might lead others to make unjustified assumptions about his capacity.[13]

If a person lacks capacity in relation to a matter concerning his property and affairs, expressly including capacity to create a settlement of any of his property, whether for his own benefit or for the benefit of others, or to execute a will, the court may make appropriate orders on his behalf.[14] The court must exercise its powers in the best interests of the person who lacks capacity.[15]

Where the Act does not apply, the question is whether the person concerned is capable of understanding what he does by executing the deed in question when its general purport has been fully explained to him. For the making of a valid will, a high degree of understanding is required, including an understanding of the claims of all potential beneficiaries and the extent of the property to be disposed of. The same degree of understanding may be required in the case of an *inter vivos* gift or settlement, although here it varies with the circumstances of the transaction, and a much lower degree of understanding would suffice if the subject matter and value of a gift were trivial in relation to the donor's other assets.[16]

---

[4] *Edwards v Carter* [1893] AC 360, HL. The position is unaffected by the Minors' Contracts Act 1987.

[5] Wills Act 1837, s 7, as amended by Family Law Reform Act 1969, s 3.

[6] Including a member of the Royal Air Force: Wills (Soldiers and Sailors) Act 1918, s 5(2).

[7] Wills Act 1837, s 11, as amended by the Wills (Soldiers and Sailors) Act 1918. The privilege also extends to a member of the Royal Naval and Marine Forces when so circumstanced that, if he were a soldier, he would be in actual military service.

[8] The relevant provisions of the Act came into force on 1 October 2007, replacing provisions contained in the Mental Health Act 1983.

[9] What is meant by 'inability to make decisions' is defined ibid, s 3.

[10] Mental Capacity Act 2005, s 2(1), (2).   [11] Ibid, ss 1(2), (3), and 2(4).   [12] Ibid, s 1(4).

[13] Ibid, s 2(3).   [14] Ibid, ss 16(1), (2), (5), and 18(1)(h), (i).

[15] As to 'best interests', see ibid, s 4, which sets out the steps to be taken. Under previous legislation, it was said that the court should be guided by what it thought likely the person on whose behalf it was acting would himself do if he had capacity, but on the assumption that his circumstances in other respects were what they were in fact: see the Court of Protection decisions in *Re TB* [1967] Ch 247, [1968] 3 All ER 509; *Re C* [1991] 3 All ER 866; *Re S* [1997] 1 FLR 96.

[16] *Re Beaney* [1978] 2 All ER 595, [1978] 1 WLR 770. See [1984] Conv 32 and [1986] Conv 78 (A H Hudson). As to the burden of proof, see *Williams v Williams* [2003] EWHC 742 (Ch), [2003] All ER(D) 403 (Feb).

(B) CAPACITY OF BENEFICIARY

In general, anyone who can hold an interest in property can be a beneficiary under a trust. A minor can have an equitable interest in land, although he cannot hold a legal estate.[17] It should be added that a beneficiary may be a trustee, even a sole trustee, although a sole trustee cannot hold on trust for himself as sole beneficiary. No trust can exist where the entire estate, both legal and equitable, is vested in one person.[18] The legal title carries with it all rights. Accordingly, where the absolute owner at law and in equity pays money or transfers property to another under what turns out to be a void contract, it cannot successfully be contended that the transferor retains the equitable interest in the money or property transferred. The only question could be whether the circumstances were such as to impose a trust on the transferee.[19]

2 THE THREE CERTAINTIES

Lord Langdale's judgment in *Knight v Knight*[20] is frequently referred to as setting out the proposition that, in order for a trust to be valid, the 'three certainties' must be present: certainty of words, certainty of subject, and certainty of object. There was, however, nothing novel in this statement. Lord Eldon, for instance,[21] said that, in order for a trust to be valid, 'first, that the words must be imperative...; secondly, that the subject must be certain...; and thirdly, that the object must be as certain as the subject'. Each of these three certainties will now be considered in turn.

(A) CERTAINTY OF WORDS

Since 'equity looks to the intent rather than the form', there is no need for any technical expression to be used in order to constitute a trust.[22] It is a question in every case of construction of the words used to ascertain whether they (together with any admissible

---

[17] Law of Property Act 1925, s 1(6).   [18] *Re Cook* [1948] Ch 212, [1948] 1 All ER 231.

[19] *Westdeutsche Landesbank Girozentrale v Islington London Borough Council* [1996] AC 669, 706, 708, 709, [1996] 2 All ER 961, 989, 991, 992, HL, *per* Lord Browne-Wilkinson.

[20] (1840) 3 Beav 148; *Gibbons v St John's (City)* (2005) 746 APR 4. For a case in which the question of uncertainty arose in an unusual form, see *Muir v IRC* [1966] 3 All ER 38, [1966] 1 WLR 1269, CA. See (1979) 8 AALR 123 (T G Watkin); (1986) 8 U Tas LR 209 (J D Davies). Text above cited *Creaglean v Hazen* (1999) 551 APR 240.

[21] In *Wright v Aykyns* (1823) Turn & R 143, 157.

[22] Conversely, it has been held in New Zealand that the use of the word 'trust' in a statute does not necessarily give rise to a trust in the equity sense, and it is thought that the same would be true in England: *Wellington Harness Racing Club v Hutt City Council* [2004] 1 NZLR 82. In relation to a will, Hart J said, in *Re Harrison (decd)* [2005] EWHC 2957 (Ch), [2006] 1 All ER 858, [2006] 1 WLR 1212, at [13], that the mere fact that the words 'in trust' had been used was not, in itself, inconsistent with an intention that the testator's wife should be the absolute beneficial owner. Although doubtless true, a strong context is required to deny the prima facie construction of the word 'trust'. See the observations of Lewison J on the above dictum in *Re Harding (decd)* [2007] EWHC 3 (Ch), [2007] 1 All ER 747, at [9], [10], noting that Hart J decided that the words 'in trust' in the will that he was considering were incompatible with an absolute gift.

extrinsic evidence)[23] establish an intention to set up a trust. Thus, in *Re Kayford Ltd*,[24] members of the public paid money to the company for the future supply of goods. The company, having doubts as to its ability to deliver the goods, paid the money into a separate account on trust for the customers pending delivery. A trust was established. In contrast, in *Re B (Child: Property Transfer)*,[25] it was held that an order under the Guardianship of Minors Act 1971 transferring property from the father to the mother '*for the benefit of the child*' did not create a trust in favour of the child.

The question has often arisen under wills whether a trust is created where the testator has in terms expressed his confidence, wish, belief, desire, hope, or recommendation that the legatee or devisee will use the gift in a certain way, or whether, in such a case, the legatee or devisee takes beneficially with at most a moral obligation to use the gift in the way indicated. In the earlier cases,[26] the courts were very ready to hold that such precatory words set up what is commonly called a 'precatory trust'. Rigby LJ[27] has however, castigated this phrase as 'a misleading nickname', pointing out that if, as a matter of construction, precatory words are held to set up a trust, the trust so constituted is a perfectly ordinary trust with no special or unusual characteristics.

It is generally agreed that there was a change of approach by the courts during the nineteenth century. *Lambe v Eames*,[28] in 1871, is sometimes said to be the turning point,[29] but Lord St Leonards had pointed out the change of attitude more than twenty years before.[30] There is, in fact, no clear dividing line and even after *Lambe v Eames*[31] there are cases[32] in which the older approach is still adopted.

The proper attitude to precatory words is stated in the judgment of Cotton LJ in *Re Adams and the Kensington Vestry*,[33] in which it was held that there was no trust created by a testator who gave all of his property to his wife 'in full confidence that she will do what

---

[23] The Administration of Justice Act 1982, s 21, provides that extrinsic evidence, including evidence of the testator's intention, may be admitted to assist in the interpretation of a will in so far as any part is meaningless or ambiguous on its face or in the light of surrounding circumstances.

[24] [1975] 1 All ER 604, [1975] 1 WLR 279, criticized (1983) 21 Alberta LR 295 (D W M Waters) and discussed [1985] JBL 456 (P Richardson); (1006) 81 T & ELTJ 26 (S Kempster). Likewise, in *Re Chelsea Cloisters Ltd* (1980) 41 P&CR 98, CA (tenants' deposits—landlord company in liquidation); *Re Eastern Capital Futures Ltd* [1989] BCLC 371; *Re Lewis's of Leicester Ltd* [1995] 1 BCLC 428; *Re Branston & Gothard Ltd* [1999] BPIR 466; *Re Japan Leasing (Europe) plc* [2000] 2 WTLR 301; *OT Computers Ltd (in administration) v First National Tricity Finance Ltd* [2003] EWHC 1010 (Ch), [2007] WTLR 165. See the discussion in (1980) 43 MLR 489 (W Goodhart and G Jones); [1994] Denning LJ 93 (G McCormack).

[25] [1999] 2 FLR 418, CA, noted (1999) 11 T & ELJ 10 (S Webster). See also *Re H B Haina & Associates Inc* (1978) 86 DLR (3d) 262 (advance payments received by travel agent and deposited in so-called 'trust account': trust not established); *Re Multi Guarantee Co Ltd* [1987] BCLC 257, CA, discussed (1988) 85 LSG 36/14 (I M Hardcastle); *Customs and Excise Commissioners v Richmond Theatre Management Ltd* [1995] STC 257; *Re Holiday Promotions (Europe) Ltd* [1996] 2 BCLC 618. For a novel approach, see (1983) 33 UTLJ 381 (M Pickard).

[26] For example, *Palmer v Simmonds* (1854) 2 Drew 221; *Gully v Cregoe* (1857) 24 Beav 185.

[27] In *Re Williams* [1897] 2 Ch 12, 27, CA.   [28] (1871) 6 Ch App 597.

[29] For example, Cozens-Hardy MR in *Re Atkinson* (1911) 103 LT 860, 862, CA.

[30] *A Treatise of the Law of Property*, p 375 *et seq*, published in 1849. See also the argument of Mr Richards in *Knight v Knight* (1840) 3 Beav 148, 165 *et seq*.

[31] (1871) 6 Ch App 597.

[32] For example, *Curnick v Tucker* (1874) LR 17 Eq 320; *Le Marchant v Le Marchant* (1874) LR 18 Eq 414.

[33] (1884) 27 Ch D 394 at 410, CA. A similar case is *Re Hutchinson and Tenant* (1878) 8 Ch D 540. See, now the Administration of Justice Act 1982, s 22, which provides that, except where a contrary intention is shown, it is to be presumed that if a testator leaves property to his spouse in terms that in themselves would

is right as to the disposal thereof between my children, either in her lifetime, or by will after her decease'. He said:

> ...some of the older authorities went a great deal too far in holding that some particular words appearing in a will were sufficient to create a trust. Undoubtedly confidence, if the rest of the context shows that a trust is intended, may make a trust,[34] but what we have to look at is the whole of the will which we have to construe, and if the confidence is that she will do what is right as regards the disposal of property, I cannot say that that is, on the true construction of the will, a trust imposed upon her. Having regard to the later decisions, we must not extend the old cases in any way, or rely upon the mere use of any particular words, but, considering all the words which are used, we have to see what is their true effect, and what was the intention of the testator as expressed in his will.

Again, there was held to be no trust created in *Re Hamilton*,[35] and the legatees took beneficially where, after giving legacies to two nieces, a testator continued 'I wish them to bequeath them equally between the families of [O] *and* [P] in such mode as they shall consider right'.

Other cases illustrating the modern approach, and in which it was held that no trust was constituted, include *Mussoorie Bank Ltd v Raynor*,[36] in which a testator gave all of his estate to his wife 'feeling confident that she will act justly to our children in dividing the same when no longer required by her', *Re Diggles*,[37] in which the relevant words were 'it is my desire that she allows X an annuity of £25', and *Re Johnson*,[38] in which, after leaving half of his estate to his mother, the testator provided: 'I request that my mother will on her death leave the property or what remains of it...to my four sisters.'

The modern attitude does not, of course, prevent the court from holding that a trust is created by precatory words where, as a matter of construction, this appears to be the intention of the testator;[39] at any rate, according to Wynn-Parry J in *Re Steele's Will Trusts*,[40] if a testator uses language that is the same, *mutatis mutandis*, as that used in an earlier case in which it was held that a trust was constituted, he thereby shows an intention in like manner to set up a trust. If rightly decided, it is submitted that the principle of *Re Steele's Will Trusts*[41] should be restricted to cases in which the older authority comprises a more or less complex limitation that might reasonably be regarded as having been used as a precedent for the later will.

It may be added that the normal rules of construction apply to trust documents. However, a benignant construction may be given so as to save a gift for charity[42] and, in non-charity cases, a purposive construction may be given where appropriate. In two related unreported cases,[43] there was a discretionary trust for the settlor's children and remoter issue *born* 'during the Trust Period', which was defined as eighty years commencing at the date of the settlement. For many years, the trust was administered on the assumption that the

give an absolute interest to the spouse, but by the same instrument purports to give his issue an interest in the same property, the gift to the spouse is nevertheless absolute.

[34] Compare *Comiskey v Bowring-Hanbury* [1905] AC 84, HL.
[35] [1895] 2 Ch 370, CA. See esp *per* Lopes LJ at 374.   [36] (1882) 7 App Cas 321, PC.
[37] (1888) 39 Ch D 253, CA. Cf *Re Oldfield* [1904] 1 Ch 549, CA, in which, at first instance, Kekewich J said, 'a desire carries no obligation except a moral one'.
[38] [1939] 2 All ER 458, applied *Re the Will of Logan* [1993] 1 Qd R 395; *Re Atkinson* (1911) 103 LT 860, CA.
[39] *Comiskey v Bowring-Hanbury* [1905] AC 84, HL: *Re Burley* [1910] 1 Ch 215.
[40] [1948] Ch 603, [1948] 2 All ER 193. The earlier case here was *Shelley v Shelley* (1868) LR 6 Eq 540.
[41] *Supra.*   [42] See p 255, *infra.*
[43] I *Johnson v Rhodes* (1994) and E *Johnson v Rhodes* (1995), discussed by J Child in [2000] PCB 230.

settlor's children in being at the date of the settlement were included as potential beneficiaries. When this was challenged, it was held that 'born' should be construed as more or less
equivalent to 'living', and accordingly the trust had been correctly administered.

(B) CERTAINTY OF SUBJECT

The scope of trusts recognized in equity is virtually unlimited. There can be a trust of a
chattel or of a chose in action, or of a right or obligation under an ordinary legal contract,
just as much as a trust of land or money.[44] It even seems that there is no objection to a
party to a contract involving skill and confidence or containing non-assignment provisions becoming trustee of the benefit of being the contracting party as well as of the benefit
of the rights conferred.[45] In *Abrahams v Trustee in Bankruptcy of Abrahams*,[46] it was held
that where a person paid money to a lottery syndicate, she gained the right to have any
winnings received duly administered in accordance with whatever rules of the syndicate
then applied. That right was property that was capable of being held on a resulting trust.
And in *Swift v Dairywise Farms Ltd*,[47] it was held that a milk quota, which must be attached
to a holding of appropriate land, known as a 'euroholding', could be the subject of a trust.
If T held a quota on trust for B, then where B had no euroholding he could not, therefore,
require T to transfer the quota to him. He could, however, require T to realize the quota
and transfer the proceeds to him.

This requirement of certainty of subject is somewhat ambiguous,[48] because the phrase
may mean that the property subject to the trust must be certain, or that the beneficial
interests of the cestuis que trust must be certain.

(i) Certainty of subject matter[49]

It is abundantly clear that, in order to establish a trust, the trust property must be identifiable.[50] Where it cannot be clearly identified, the purported trust is altogether void as, for
instance, in *Palmer v Simmonds*,[51] in which the subject of the alleged trust was 'the bulk
of my said residuary estate'; nor was a trust established in *Re London Wine Co (Shippers)
Ltd*,[52] in which a company had stocks of wine in various warehouses, which it sold to

---

[44] See *Lord Strathcona Steamship Co Ltd v Dominion Coal Co Ltd* [1926] AC 108, 124, *per* Lord Shaw,
cited by Lightman J in *Don King Productions Inc v Warren* [1998] 2 All ER 608; affd [2000] Ch 291, [1999] 2
All ER 218, CA.

[45] *Don King Productions Inc v Warren* [1998] 2 All ER 608, 634, *per* Lightman J; affd [2000] Ch 291, [1999]
2 All ER 218, CA. But a provision in the contract prohibiting a party from declaring himself a trustee would
be effective. See also *Barbados Trust Co v Bank of Zambia* [2007] EWCA Civ 148, [2007] 2 All ER (Comm)
445, discussed (2007) 70 MLR 848 (A Trukhtanov); (2008) 124 LQR 517 (M Smith).

[46] [1999] BPIR 637, noted (2000) 18 T & ELJ 21 (D Unwin).

[47] [2000] 1 All ER 320, noted [2000] All ER Rev 247 (P J Clark), affd [2001] BCLC 672, CA, on different
grounds.   [48] See (1940) 4 MLR 20 (G Williams).

[49] See (1986) 61 Tulane LR 45 (Jane Baron), [2002] 61 CLJ 657 (P Parkinson).

[50] See *Westdeutsche Landesbank Girozentrale v Islington London Borough Council* [1996] AC 669, [1996]
2 All ER 961, HL, *per* Lord Browne-Wilkinson, at 988.

[51] (1854) 2 Drew 221; cf *Bromley v Tryon* [1952] AC 265, [1951] 2 All ER 1058, HL, and on another point,
Richardson v Watson (1833) 4 B & Ad 787.

[52] (1975) 126 NLJ 977. See *Re Goldcorp Exchange Ltd (in receivership)* [1995] 1 AC 74, [1994] 2 All ER 806,
PC, discussed [1995] RLR 83 (P Birks); *Re Stapylton Fletcher Ltd* [1995] 1 All ER 192, [1994] 1 WLR 1181,
noted (1995) 16 Co Law 111 (J Breslin); [1995] 48(1) CLP 113 (Alison Clarke).

various customers, the intention being that the wine purchased should become the property of the customers, but stored by the company at the customers' expense. It was argued that if the legal title had not passed to the customers, there was a trust in their favour. The court seems to have accepted that there was an intention to create a trust, but held that it nevertheless failed on the ground of uncertainty of subject matter, because there was never any segregation or appropriation of the wine within the warehouse until actual delivery of the wine to a purchaser. This last decision seems right in principle, but the subsequent Court of Appeal decision in *Hunter v Moss*[53] causes difficulties. In that case, it was held at first instance that the requirement of certainty does not apply in the same way to trusts of intangible assets such as, in the case before the court, fifty out of 950 indistinguishable shares. In such cases, it was held, the question of certainty depends not on the application of any immutable principle based on the requirements of a need for segregation or appropriation, but rather on whether, immediately after the purported declaration of trust, the court could, if asked, make an order for the execution of the purported trust. On this basis, the trust was upheld. The Court of Appeal expressly agreed with the conclusion of the judge below on the uncertainty point and should, perhaps, be treated as accepting his reasoning, although it has been much criticized, it is thought rightly, by most of the commentators,[54] arguing that intangible assets are not in a different position from tangible. Nor is the analogy drawn by the court with a demonstrative legacy of shares valid, because a trust of such shares will become completely constituted only when the particular shares have been vested in the trustee. The Australian courts have, after careful consideration, declined to follow *Hunter v Moss*.[55]

It may be added, as to the segregation of funds, that Watkins LJ, giving the judgment of the court, said in *R v Clowes (No 2)*[56] that the effect of the authorities seemed to be:

> that a requirement to keep moneys separate is normally an indicator that they are impressed with a trust, and that the absence of such a requirement, *if there are no other indicators of a trust*, normally negatives it. The fact that a transaction contemplates the mingling of funds is, therefore, not necessarily fatal to a trust.

Further the courts are slow to introduce trusts into everyday commercial transactions.[57]

Sprange v Barnard[58] illustrates the way in which the question has arisen in a number of cases. In that case, a testatrix gave property to her husband 'for his sole use' and continued 'at his death, the remaining part of what is left, that he does not want for his own wants and

---

[53] [1994] 3 All ER 215, [1994] 1 WLR 452, CA. The decision was followed by Neuberger J in *Re Harvard Securities Ltd* [1997] 2 BCLC 369, noted (1998–99) 9 KCLJ 112 (Theresa Villiers). Cf *Re CA Pacific Finance Ltd (in liq)* [2000] 1 BCLC 494 (Hong Kong CFI).

[54] See [1993] Conv 466 (Alison Jones); (1994) 28 L Teach 312 (P Luxton); [1994] CLJ 448 (M Ockleton); All ER Rev 1994 250 (P J Clarke); (1995) 110 LQR 335 (D Hayton). Contra J Martin in [1996] Conv 223. See also [1999] JBL 1 (Sarah Worthington).

[55] *White v Shortall* [2006] NSWSC 1379, (2006–07) 206 Fed LR 254.

[56] [1994] 2 All ER 316, 325, CA; *Bank of Montreal v British Columbia (Milk Marketing Board)* (1994) 94 BCLR (2d) 281; *Air Canada v M & L Travel Ltd* (1994) 108 DLR (4th) 592.

[57] See *Neste Oy v Lloyds Bank plc* [1983] 2 Lloyd's Rep 658, 665, *per* Bingham J, cited with approval in *R v Clowes (No 2)*, *supra*, CA. See also *Re ILG Travel Ltd* [1995] 2 BCLC 128, in which the agreement was held to take effect as an equitable charge.

[58] (1789) 2 Bro CC 585 (principle of case valid although decision perhaps doubtful); cf *Re Last* [1958] P 137, [1958] 1 All ER 316. Cf *Re Jones* [1898] 1 Ch 438 (absolute gift—gift over of what remains void for repugnancy).

use, to be divided between' a brother and sisters. It was held that there was no trust, since it was uncertain what would be left at the death of the husband. The husband accordingly took absolutely. In practice, the question of certainty of subject is often associated with that of certainty of words. In giving the advice of the Privy Council in *Mussoorie Bank Ltd v Raynor*,[59] Sir Arthur Hobhouse observed:

> uncertainty in the subject of the gift has a reflex action upon the previous words, and throws doubt upon the intention of the testator, and seems to shew that he could not possibly have intended his words of confidence, hope, or whatever they may be—his appeal to the conscience of the first taker—to be imperative words.

(ii) Certainty of beneficial interests

If there is certainty of words and the property subject to the trust is clearly identified, the trust will be valid. If, however, the beneficial interests to be taken are not certain, those interests will fail for uncertainty and the trustees will hold on a resulting trust for the settlor, as in *Boyce v Boyce*,[60] in which a testator devised two houses to trustees on trust to convey one to Maria 'whichever she may think proper to choose or select' and the other to Charlotte. Maria predeceased the testator and it was accordingly held that Charlotte had no claim. There is no uncertainty, however, where there is a discretion given to the trustees to determine the exact quantum of the beneficial interests, or where the words used by the testator are a sufficient indication of his intention to provide an effective determinant of what he intends. Thus, in *Re Golay*,[61] the testator directed his executors to let T 'enjoy one of my flats during her lifetime and to receive a reasonable income from my other properties'. It was held, a little surprisingly, perhaps, that the words 'reasonable income' directed an objective determinant of amount that the court could, if necessary, apply and, accordingly, the gift did not fail for uncertainty. Again, in other circumstances, the court may cure an apparent uncertainty by applying the maxim that 'equality is equity'. Further, if there is an absolute gift in the first instance, and trusts are engrafted or imposed on that absolute interest that fail for uncertainty, or indeed any other reason, then the absolute gift takes effect so far as the trusts have failed.[62]

(C) CERTAINTY OF OBJECTS[63]

(i) Need for ascertainable beneficiaries

For reasons that will appear, in considering what test for certainty of objects has to be applied in order that a disposition shall be valid, it is sensible to consider not only the rules that apply to trusts, but also those that apply to powers. Moreover, it will be convenient to discuss, first, a mere power, then, a fixed trust—that is, where the interest of the beneficiaries is determined by the settlor and is not dependent upon the discretion of the

---

[59] (1882) 7 App Cas 321, 331, PC.

[60] (1849) 16 Sim 476; *Re Double Happiness Trust* [2003] WTLR 367 (Jersey Royal Court). Cf *Guild v Mallory* (1983) 41 OR (2d) 21.

[61] [1965] 2 All ER 660, [1995] 1 WLR 969. See (1965) 81 LQR 481 (R E Megarry).

[62] *Lassence v Tierney* (1849) 1 Mac & G 551; *Hancock v Watson* [1902] AC 14, HL.

[63] See, generally, 1971 CLP 133 (Harvey Cohen); (1971) 87 LQR 31 (J W Harris); (1971) 29 CLJ 68 (J Hopkins); (1973) 5 NZULR 348 (Y F R Grbich); (1980) 9 Sydney LR 58 (R P Austin); (1988) 20 OLR 377 (D R Klinck).

trustees—and finally a discretionary trust. There is no need to consider separately a trust power in the first sense[64]—that is, where the court implies a trust in default of appointment—because this simply comprises a mere power followed by a fixed trust, to each of which the appropriate test must be applied separately. In this last case, it could happen that the power would be valid, but the trust in default void for uncertainty.[65] It should be noted that we are not here concerned with cases in which there is a condition or description attached to one or more individual gifts; in such cases, uncertainty as to some other persons who may have been intended to take does not in any way affect the quantum of the gift to persons who undoubtedly possess the qualification.[66]

(ii) Test for a mere power

So far as a mere power is concerned, the law is 'that the power is valid if it can be said with certainty whether any given individual is or is not a member of the class and does not fail simply because it is impossible to ascertain every member of the class'.[67] Thus, in *Re Coates*,[68] it was held that the following provisions in a will conferred a valid power on the wife:

> if my wife feels that I have forgotten any friend I direct my executors to pay to such friend or friends as are nominated by my wife a sum not exceeding £25 per friend with a maximum aggregate payment of £250 so that such friends may buy a small memento of our friendship.

In this case, Roxburgh J applied the dictum of Lord Tomlin in *Re Ogden*:[69] 'The question is one of degree in each case, whether having regard to the language of the will, and the circumstances of the case, there is such uncertainty as to justify the court in coming to the conclusion that the gift is bad.' In this sort of case, as Harman J said in *Re Gestetner Settlement*,[70] 'there is no duty to distribute, but only a duty to consider', and it is not necessary that all of the possible members of the class should be considered, provided that it can be ascertained whether any given postulant is a member of the class or not.

Shortly before the House of Lords decision in *Re Gulbenkian's Settlement Trusts*,[71] there had been cases[72] proposing a less stringent test—namely, that if you could find a person clearly within the description of the class intended to be benefited, the power would be good, even though you might be able to envisage cases in which it would be difficult or impossible to say whether a person was within the description or not. This test was decisively rejected in *Re Gulbenkian's Settlement Trusts*,[73] which was followed in *McPhail v Doulton*,[74] but the judgments in the subsequent proceedings in the latter case, reported as *Re Baden's Deed Trusts (No 2)*,[75] have somewhat confused the position. The test laid down in the two House of Lords decisions was, it will be recalled, whether 'it can be said with certainty that any given individual is or is not a member of that class'.[76]

---

[64] See p 37, *supra*.   [65] Compare *Re Sayer* [1957] Ch 423, [1956] 3 All ER 600.
[66] *Re Barlow's Will Trusts* [1979] 1 All ER 296, [1979] 1 WLR 278, discussed [1980] Conv 263 (Lindsay McKay); (1979) 30 NILQ 24 (R Burgess); (1983) 98 LQR 551 (C T Emery).
[67] *Per* Lord Wilberforce in *McPhail v Doulton* [1971] AC 424, [1970] 2 All ER 228, HL.
[68] [1955] Ch 495, [1955] 1 All ER 26; *Re Sayer Trust, supra.*
[69] [1933] Ch 678, 682, [1933] All ER Rep 720, 722.   [70] [1953] Ch 672, 688.
[71] [1970] AC 508, [1968] 3 All ER 785, HL.
[72] *Re Gibbard* [1966] 1 All ER 273, [1967] 1 WLR 42; *Re Leek*, at first instance [1967] Ch 1061, [1967] 2 All ER 1160; *Re Gulbenkian's Settlement Trusts*, in the Court of Appeal [1968] Ch 126, [1967] 3 All ER 15.
[73] *Supra*, HL.   [74] *Supra*, HL.   [75] [1973] Ch 9, [1972] 2 All ER 1304, CA.
[76] Emphasis added.

The majority of the Court of Appeal in *Re Baden's Deed Trusts (No 2)*[77] held, in effect, that a power[78] may be valid even though there may be a substantial number of persons of whom it is impossible to say whether they are within the class or not, provided, according to Megaw LJ, that, as regards at least a substantial number of objects, it can be said with certainty that they fall within it. Sachs LJ said that so long as the class of persons to be benefited is conceptually certain,[79] evidential uncertainty as to whether or not a given individual is within the class does not matter. The power can only be exercised in favour of persons who are proved to be within it. 'Conceptual certainty' refers to the precision of language used by the settlor to define the class of person whom he intends to benefit; 'evidential certainty' refers to the extent to which the evidence in a particular case enables specific persons to be identified as members of those classes. The latter is sometimes confused with 'ascertainability', which refers to the extent to which the whereabouts or continued existence of persons identified as beneficiaries or potential beneficiaries can be ascertained.[80] Stamp LJ, however, gave a forceful dissenting opinion, arguing in substance that this would be to bring in by the back door the test decisively rejected by the House of Lords in *Re Gulbenkian's Settlement Trusts*[81]—namely, that the trust is good if there are individuals, or even one, of whom you can say with certainty that he is a member of the class, notwithstanding that there may be others whose status is uncertain. The House of Lords test, in his view, requires it to be possible to say positively of any individual that he either is, or alternatively is not, within the class.

Lastly, reference should be made to a point made by Templeman J in *Re Manisty's Settlement*.[82] After holding that a power cannot be uncertain merely because it is wide in ambit, and that it does not matter that the power does not attempt to classify the beneficiaries, but only to specify or classify excepted persons, he went on to say that, in his view, a capricious power could not be validly created:

> A power to benefit "residents of Greater London" is capricious because the terms of the power negative any sensible intention on the part of the settlor. If the settlor intended and expected the trustees would have regard to persons with some claim on his bounty or some interest in an institution favoured by the settlor, or if the settlor had any other sensible intention or expectation, he would not have required the trustees to consider only an accidental conglomeration of persons who have no discernible link with the settlor or with any institution. A capricious power negatives a sensible consideration by the trustees of the exercise of the power.

Megarry VC in *Re Hay's Settlement Trusts*[83] sounded somewhat unenthusiastic about these dicta, observing that he did not think that Templeman J had in mind a case in which the settlor was, for instance, a former chairman of the Greater London Council. In any case, he said, an intermediate power cannot be void on this ground.

---

[77] *Supra.*

[78] Technically, the case concerned a discretionary trust to which, as we shall see, the same principles now apply.

[79] For example, 'first cousins' as contrasted with 'someone under a moral obligation'.

[80] This last point is made by C T Emery (1982) 98 LQR 551, to whom the author is indebted for the above definitions. See *McCracken v A-G for Victoria* [1995] 1 VR 67, in which the judge thought it not always easy to discern the boundary between the two kinds of uncertainty.   [81] *Supra*, HL.

[82] [1974] Ch 17, 27, [1973] 2 All ER 1203 , 1211; criticized (1974) 38 Conv 269 (L McKay).

[83] [1981] 3 All ER 786, [1982] 1 WLR 202.

(iii) Test for a fixed trust

As regards fixed trusts, Lord Evershed MR observed, in *Re Endacott*,[84] that: 'No principle perhaps has greater sanction or authority behind it than the general proposition that a trust by English law, not being a charitable trust, in order to be effective, must have ascertained or ascertainable beneficiaries.' In the present context, there is some danger of confusion by reason of the fact that the most elaborate consideration of what is meant by 'certainty of beneficiaries' has been in relation to discretionary trusts at a time when it was thought that they were to be treated for this purpose in the same way as fixed trusts. Until the House of Lords decision in *McPhail v Doulton*,[85] the law in relation to discretionary trusts was that, where there was a trust for such of a given class of objects as the trustees should select, it was essential that the trustees should know, or be able to ascertain, all of the objects from which they were enjoined to select by the terms of the trust. The duty of selection being a fiduciary one, it was considered that trustees could not properly exercise their discretion unless and until they knew of what persons exactly the class consisted among whom they were called on to make their selection. Likewise, if the trustees failed to act and the court was called upon to do so, it was thought, prior to *McPhail v Doulton*,[86] that the court could only act by way of equal division, which would be impossible unless there was a complete list of potential beneficiaries.[87]

The relevant date for deciding whether the membership of the class was ascertainable or not was the date on which the trust came into existence.[88] The fact that it might be difficult or expensive to ascertain the membership of the class did not matter. Thus, in *Re Eden*,[89] Wynn-Parry J stated 'it may well be that a large part, even the whole of the funds available, would be consumed in the inquiry. To say the least of it, that would be very unfortunate, but that cannot of itself constitute any reason why such an inquiry, whether by the trustees or by the court, should not be undertaken'. In order to hold the trust valid, the court had to be satisfied affirmatively that there was at least a probability of the objects being completely ascertained.[90]

So far as concerns the ascertainment of the objects of a fixed trust, the above propositions still seem to represent the law.[91] Suppose, for instance, that a whimsical testator were

---

[84] [1960] Ch 232, 246, [1959] 3 All ER 562, 568, CA.   [85] [1971] AC 424, [1970] 2 All ER 228, HL.

[86] *Supra*, HL. For the present position, see p 80, *infra*.

[87] See *IRC v Broadway Cottages Trust* [1955] Ch 20, [1954] 3 All ER 120, CA, *per* Jenkins LJ; *Re Gulbenkian's Settlement Trusts* [1970] AC 508, [1968] 3 All ER 785, HL. See also *Re Ogden* [1933] Ch 678, [1933] All ER Rep 720, in which a gift of residue, to be distributed among such political bodies having as their object the promotion of Liberal principles as the residuary legatee should select, was held to be a valid trust on evidence that the class benefited was capable of ascertainment.

[88] *Re Hain's Settlement* [1961] 1 All ER 848, [1961] 1 WLR 440, CA; *Re Culbenkian's Settlement Trusts, supra*, HL.

[89] [1957] 2 All ER 430, 435, [1957] 1 WLR 788, 795.

[90] *Re Saxone Shoe Co Ltd's Trust Deed* [1962] 2 All ER 904, [1962] 1 WLR 943, *per* Cross J, who also referred to a qualification applying to discretionary trusts that cannot apply to fixed trusts—namely, that there is no need to trace persons in whose favour the trustees can say in advance that they will not exercise their discretion. In a fixed trust *ex hypothesi* all the members of the class must take.

[91] See *OT Computers Ltd (in admnistration) v First National Tricity Finance Ltd* [2003] EWHC 1010 (Ch), [2007] WTLR 35. See also [1984] Conv 22 (P Matthews), whose views are, it is submitted, effectively refuted by Jill Martin [1984] Conv 304 and D J Hayton [1984] Conv 307. In Australia, in *West v Weston* (1997–98) 44 NSWLR 657, the rule was modified in a case in which there was a gift to the issue of the testator's four grandparents equally per capita. Some three years after the testator's death in 1975, issue had been ascertained and

to direct trustees to divide a fund equally between a class of persons, such as the objects of the trust in *McPhail v Doulton*.[92] In such a case, the trust would seem to be void for uncertainty unless the test of certainty set out above could be satisfied.

(iv) Test for a discretionary trust

Turning to discretionary trusts, as already mentioned, prior to the House of Lords decision in *McPhail v Doulton*,[93] a discretionary trust was treated in the same way as a fixed trust and the consequence was that the validity of a disposition might have depended upon the technical question of whether it fell on one side or other of the narrow dividing line between 'trust' and 'power'. The result met with judicial criticism. For instance, Harman LJ, referring to what he called this 'most unfortunate doctrine', said[94] 'it ought to make no difference to the validity of the provisions of the deed whether, on a minute analysis of the language used in this clause, it should be construed as creating a trust or a power...the fact that it does is an absurd and embarrassing result'. The House of Lords has now decided, by a bare majority, that 'the test for the validity of [a discretionary trust][95] ought to be similar to that accepted by this House in *Re Gulbenkian's Settlement*[96] for powers, namely that the trust is valid if it can be said with certainty that any given individual is or is not a member of the class'.[97] The doubts as to whether the word 'similar' meant resemblance rather than identity have been silenced by *Re Baden's Deed Trusts (No 2)*,[98] which makes it clear that the test to be applied to mere powers and discretionary trusts is precisely the same.

In relation to trusts, Lord Wilberforce in *McPhail v Doulton*[99] further observed that, even where the meaning of the words used is clear, the definition of beneficiaries may be so hopelessly wide as not to form *'anything like a class'*, so that the trust is administratively unworkable. This proposition does not apply to powers. The courts have a much more limited function[100] in respect of powers and cannot be called upon to administer them.[101] It should be added that it has been strongly contended[102] that the proposition rests upon no satisfactory basis and should be discarded. The possible bases examined and rejected were the need for common attributes among the beneficiaries, mere size, inability of the

---

it was possible that more might come to light. The rule, it was held, will be satisfied if, within a reasonable time after the gift comes into effect, the court can be satisfied on the balance of probabilities that the substantial majority of the beneficiaries have been ascertained that that no reasonable inquiries could be made that would improve the situation.

[92] [1971] AC 424, [1970] 2 All ER 228, HL. The objects are set out at p 37, *supra*.   [93] Ibid.

[94] *Re Baden's Deed Trusts* [1969] 2 Ch 388, 397, [1969], 1 All ER 1016, 1019, CA; revsd sub nom *McPhail v Doulton*, HL, *supra*.

[95] Lord Wilberforce actually used the phrase 'trust powers'.

[96] *Supra*, HL. See also *Re Beckbessinger* [1993] 2 NZLR 362.

[97] Per Lord Wilberforce in *McPhail v Doulton* [1971] AC 424, [1970] 2 All ER 228, HL. Hopkins in (1971) 29 CLJ, at 101, raises the question as to the application of the new rule to discretionary trusts of capital as opposed to income. It is submitted that it should apply equally to both.

[98] *Supra*, CA, and *per* Brightman J at first instance, [1972] Ch 607, [1971] 3 All ER 985.

[99] [1971] AC 424, 457, [1970] 2 All ER 288, 247, HL discussed in *Re Manisty's Settlement* [1974] Ch 17, [1973] 2 All ER 1203; *Re Hay's Settlement Trusts* [1981] 3 All ER 786, [1982] 1 WLR 202.

[100] Primarily to determine whether a power is valid and, if so, whether a particular exercise of the power is within its scope.

[101] *Re Hay's Settlement Trusts, supra*. But see (1991) 107 LQR 214 (S Gardner) suggesting that the question may need to be reconsidered in the light of *Mettoy Pension Trustees Ltd v Evans* [1991] 2 All ER 513, [1990] 1 WLR 1587; see p 34, *supra*.   [102] (1974) 38 Conv 269 (L McKay).

trustees to perform the administrative duties, and inability of the court to execute the trust. However, Megarry VC in *Re Hay's Settlement Trusts*[103] indicated that, had he not already held the discretionary trust void on other grounds, he would have held it void as being administratively unworkable. Further, Lord Wilberforce's dictum was applied and the trust held void in *R v District Auditor, ex p West Yorkshire Metropolitan County Council*,[104] in which Lloyd LJ said that there was a fundamental difficulty in that a trust with as many as two-and-a-half million potential beneficiaries would be quite simply unworkable: the class was far too large.

(v) Trusts for purposes

The fundamental rule that the object of a trust must be certain applies equally to trusts for purposes. Thus trusts for philanthropic,[105] or patriotic,[106] or public,[107] or benevolent[108] purposes are all void, because these words have no technical legal meaning and the court would accordingly be unable to determine whether the trustees had or had not carried out their trust by applying the trust funds in any particular way. Similarly, trusts for 'the formation of an informed international public opinion' and 'the promotion of greater co-operation in Europe and the West in general' are void as being too vague and uncertain,[109] and a trust to apply the subject matter for such purposes as the donee may think fit is also void for uncertainty.[110] Again, in *Re Challoner Club Ltd (in liq)*,[111] in which the officers of a club deposited donations received from members as a rescue fund in a separate bank account not to be used until the future of the club was known, no trust was created, since the terms of the intended trust were not certain. The money in the account was therefore part of the club assets for the purposes of the liquidation, despite the assurances to the contrary that the officers had given to the members. Charity, however, is a term of art and, even though there may be uncertainty in the sense that no particular charitable purpose is specified, or only referred to in vague terms, this does not matter, provided that the gift is exclusively for charitable purposes. In another sense, charity is one and indivisible, and, if necessary, a scheme will be made to specify the particular charity that is to benefit.[112]

(vi) Consequences of failure of trust for uncertainty

In any case in which there is uncertainty of objects, assuming that the other two certainties are present, the trustee cannot take beneficially, but will hold the trust property on a resulting trust for the settlor, or, where the trust arises under a will, for the persons entitled to the residue, or on intestacy, as the case may be.

---

[103] *Supra.* See [1982] Conv 432 (A Grubb); (1986) 8 U Tas LR 209 (J D Davies); [1990] Conv 24 (I Hardcastle).

[104] [1986] RVR 24, DC, noted (1986) 45 CLJ 391 (C Harpum).

[105] *Re Macduff* [1896] 2 Ch 451, CA.

[106] *A-G v National Provincial and Union Bank of England* [1924] AC 262, HL.

[107] *Houston v Burns* [1918] AC 337, HL.

[108] *Chichester Diocesan Fund v Simpson* [1944] AC 341, HL.

[109] *Re Koeppler's Will Trusts* [1984] Ch 243, [1984] 2 All ER 111; revsd [1986] Ch 423, [1985] 2 All ER 869, CA, but approved on this point.

[110] *Re Pugh's Will Trusts* [1967] 3 All ER 337, [1967] 1 WLR 1262.

[111] (1997) Times, 4 November.   [112] See Chapter 14, section 7, p 328 *et seq, infra.*

3 THE BENEFICIARY PRINCIPLE

Even where the purpose of a trust is clearly defined so that the trust cannot be said to be void for uncertainty, further difficult problems may arise where the object of a trust is a non-human beneficiary, such as a dog, an unincorporated association, or a non-charitable purpose.[113] The basic principle, subject perhaps to the possibility of review of the decisions by the House of Lords and with the exception of charitable trusts, is that 'a trust to be valid must be for the benefit of individuals'.[114] This is the principle stated by Grant MR in *Morice v Bishop of Durham*,[115] that 'there must be somebody in whose favour the court can decree performance', restated by Harman J in *Re Wood*,[116] who observed 'that a gift on trust must have a cestui que trust', and since affirmed by Roxburgh J in *Re Astor's Settlement Trusts*,[117] and the Court of Appeal in *Re Endacott*.[118] Accordingly, it has been said:[119] 'A gift can be made to persons (including a corporation) but it cannot be made to a purpose or to an object; so, also, a trust may be created for the benefit of persons as cestuis que trust, but not for a purpose or object unless the purpose or object be charitable.' The idea behind this seems to be that, otherwise, the validity of the trust would depend upon the whim of the trustee and 'a court of equity does not recognize as valid a trust which it cannot both enforce and control'.[120] This 'beneficiary principle', which operates to invalidate non-charitable purpose trusts, may, however, be held to be inapplicable in certain situations and is also subject to exceptions.

Before considering the situations in which the beneficiary principle does not operate, one should note that it has recently been argued that the principle is unduly restrictive and that a settlor should be able to confer enforcement rights on persons other than the beneficiaries (including himself), so that non-charitable purpose trusts would be valid, so long as they are administratively workable and are limited to a valid perpetuity period.[121]

---

[113] For a full and penetrating discussion, see Morris and Leach, *The Rule Against Perpetuities*, 2nd edn, p 307 *et seq*. See also (1977) 40 MLR 397 (N P Grave*lls)*, where the case for the validation of public purpose trusts is argued; Equity and Contemporary Legal Developments (ed S Goldstein), p 302 (R B M Cotterrell). Cf *R v District Auditor, ex p West Yorkshire Metropolitan County Council* [1986] RVR 24, DC; *Rowland v Vancouver College Ltd* (2001) 205 DLR (4th) 193.

[114] *Per* Lord Parker, in *Bowman v Secular Society Ltd* [1917] AC 406, 441, HL.

[115] (1805) 10 Ves 522; affg (1804) 9 Ves 399 at 405.

[116] [1949] Ch 498, 501, [1949] 1 All ER 1100, 1101.

[117] [1952] Ch 534, [1952] 1 All ER 1067; *Re Shaw* [1957] 1 All ER 745, [1957] 1 WLR 729; compromised, [1958] 1 All ER 245n, CA.

[118] [1960] Ch 232, [1959] 3 All ER 562, CA. Yet two years later, in *Re Harpur's Will Trusts* [1962] Ch 78, [1961] 3 All ER 588, CA, Evershed MR, who was a member of the court in *Re Endacott*, observed, at 91, 592, that a trust to apply income, restricted to the perpetuity period, 'for certain named purposes such as the trustees think fit, some of the purposes being charitable and some not charitable' would be valid.

[119] *Leahy v A-G of New South Wales* [1959] AC 457, 478, [1959] 2 All ER 300, 307, PC, *per* Viscount Simonds; *Re Recher's Will Trusts* [1972] Ch 526, [1971] 3 All ER 401.

[120] *Per* Roxburgh J in *Re Astor's Settlement Trusts, supra,* at 549, 1075.

[121] (2001) 117 LQR 96 (D Hayton), (2003) 17 Tru LI 144 (J Hilliard); [2007] Conv 440 (M Pawlowski and Jo Summers).

(A) SITUATIONS OUTSIDE THE SCOPE OF THE BENEFICIARY PRINCIPLE

(i) Re Denley's Trust Deed[122]

It was held in this case that a distinction must be drawn between 'purpose or object trusts which are abstract or impersonal' and which are void on the principle set out above, and a trust that 'though expressed as a purpose, is directly or indirectly for the benefit of an individual or individuals'. Such a trust, Goff J said, is in general outside the mischief of the principle that every trust must have a certain cestui que trust. He accordingly held valid a trust for the provision of a recreation or sports ground, during a period limited within the perpetuity period, for the benefit of what he held to be an ascertainable class. One interpretation of this decision is that, in this sort of case, the need for enforceability is met by the existence of *factual* beneficiaries—that is, persons who, although not actually cestuis que trust, are interested in the disposal of the property.[123] Vinelott J, in *Re Grant's Will Trust*,[124] however, considered that *Re Denley's Trust Deed*[125] fell altogether outside of the categories of gifts to unincorporated associations and purpose trusts. He could:

> see no distinction in principle between a trust to permit a class defined by reference to employment to use and enjoy land in accordance with rules to be made at the discretion of trustees on the one hand, and, on the other hand, a trust to distribute income at the discretion of trustees amongst a class, defined by reference to, for example, relationship to the settlor. In both cases the benefit to be taken by any member of the class is at the discretion of the trustees, but any member of the class can apply to the court to compel the trustees to administer the trust in accordance with its terms.

(ii) Contractual situations

In some circumstances, it may be held that, on a true analysis of the facts, there is no trust and the matter is one of contract. Thus it was held in *Conservative and Unionist Central Office v Burrell*,[126] in which funds were contributed to a treasurer of the party, that he held them subject to a mandate to use them in a particular way. No trust arose, except the fiduciary relationship inherent in the relationship of principal and agent.[127]

(B) EXCEPTIONS TO THE BENEFICIARY PRINCIPLE

There are admitted exceptions to the beneficiary principle. These have been said 'properly [to] be regarded as anomalous and exceptional',[128] perhaps 'concessions to human weakness

---

[122] [1969] 1 Ch 373, [1968] 3 All ER 65, applied in *Re Lipinski's Will Trusts* [1976] Ch 235, [1977] 1 All ER 33. There are difficulties in reconciling this decision with dicta in *Leahy v A-G of New South Wales, supra*. See [1968] ASCL 437 *et seq* (J D Davies); (1969) 32 MLR 96 (J M Evans); (1970) 34 Conv 77 (P A Lovell); (1973) 37 Conv 420 (L McKay). See also *Strathalbyn Show Jumping Club Inc v Mayes* (2001) 79 SASR 54.

[123] See (1980) 39 CLJ 88 (C E F Rickett); [1982] Conv 118, 177 (A R Everton).

[124] [1979] 3 All ER 359, [1980] 1 WLR 360. See (1980) 43 MLR 459 (B Green). Cf *Re Bowes* [1896] 1 Ch 507 (trust to lay out £5000 on planting trees on settled estates; held persons entitled to estate entitled to have the money whether actually so laid out or not).

[125] *Supra.*   [126] [1982] 2 All ER 1, [1982] 1 WLR 522, CA.

[127] See [1982] NZLJ 335 (C E F Rickett); [1983] Conv 150 (P Creighton); [1983] 133 NLJ 87 (C T Emery).

[128] *Per* Roxburgh J in *Re Astor's Settlement Trusts, supra*, at 1074, 547, and *per* Evershed MR in *Re Endacott, supra*, CA.

or sentiment',[129] or 'merely occasions when Homer has nodded'.[130] They are known as 'unenforceable trusts' or 'trusts of imperfect obligation', and seem to be restricted to trusts arising under wills in which the legacy will fall into a residuary gift if the unenforceable trust is not carried out.[131] The court can indirectly enforce the trust in such a case by obtaining an undertaking from the trustee to apply the legacy towards the unenforceable purpose and giving the residuary legatees liberty to apply if the undertaking is not carried out. Evershed MR in *Re Endacott*[132] referred with apparent approval to the classification of these exceptions put forward by Morris and Leach[133] into five groups, as follows.

(i) *Trusts for the erection or maintenance of monuments or graves*   If the tomb can be regarded as part of the fabric of a church,[134] or the trust is for the maintenance of a churchyard in general,[135] the trust is charitable and clearly valid. Equally clearly, a trust for the maintenance of a tomb or a monument not in a church for ever or for an indefinite period is void as offending against the rule against perpetual trusts.[136] A trust for the erection of a monument to the testator or some member of his family, or for the maintenance of a tomb has, however, been held valid, where it would not continue beyond the perpetuity period.[137] Although valid, such a trust is unenforceable, in that no one can compel the trustee to carry it out; if he wishes to perform it, however, no one can prevent him from doing so, and only if and in so far as he chooses not to do so will there be a resulting trust for the residuary legatees. The rule that the trust must not continue beyond the perpetuity period,[138] sometimes called the 'rule against perpetual trusts', is generally thought to have been entirely unaffected by the Perpetuities and Accumulations Act 1964.[139]

(ii) *Trusts for the saying of masses, if these are not charitable*   Trusts for the saying of masses in public have been held to be charitable.[140] Where masses are to be said privately, such trusts are not charitable. They might, perhaps, be valid unenforceable

---

[129] Ibid.   [130] *Per* Harman LJ in *Re Endacott, supra*, at 250, 571, CA.

[131] *Re Astor's Settlement Trusts, supra. Sed quaere*—there will always be someone entitled to the fund if the unenforceable trust is not carried out, either under the intestacy rules, or by way of resulting trust or otherwise, who could be given liberty to apply.

[132] *Supra.*

[133] Morris and Leach, *The Rule Against Perpetuities*, 2nd edn, p 301, and see [2007] Conv 148 (J Brown). For an Australian view, see (1987) 14 UQLJ 175 (P Jamieson).

[134] *Hoare v Osborne* (1866) LR 1 Eq 585; *Re King* [1923] 1 Ch 243.

[135] *Re Vaughan* (1886) 33 Ch D 187, *per* North J, at 192: 'I do not see any difference between a gift to keep in repair what is called "God's House" and a gift to keep in repair the churchyard round it which is often called "God's Acre"'; *Re Manser* [1905] 1 Ch 68; *Re Eighmie* [1935] Ch 524.

[136] *Hoare v Osborne, supra; Re Vaughan, supra; Re Elliot* [1952] Ch 217, [1952] 1 All ER 145; *Pedulla v Nasti* (1990) 20 NSWLR 720 (trust for the 'erection and maintenance of a vault or chapel in which to house my ashes' held void for perpetuity). See Chapter 11, section 2, p 222, *infra*.

[137] *Trimmer v Danby* (1856) 25 LJ Ch 424 (legacy to his executors in the will of the artist J M W Turner 'to erect a monument to my memory in St Paul's Cathedral, among those of my brothers in art' held valid but unenforceable. The executors chose to carry it out); *Pirbright v Salwey* [1896] WN 86; *Re Hooper* [1932] 1 Ch 38. In *Mussett v Bingle* [1876] WN 170, it was either assumed the monument must be erected within twenty-one years or the point was not taken, although the trust for the maintenance of the monument was held void for perpetuity.

[138] As to what is meant by the perpetuity period, see p 222, *infra*.

[139] The relevant section is s 15(4).

[140] *Re Hetherington* [1990] Ch 1, [1989] 2 All ER 129. See pp 264 and 280, *infra*. The law in Australia is similar: *Crowther v Brophy* [1992] 2 VR 97.

trusts,[141] provided that they are restricted to the perpetuity period, with like effects to those referred to under (i) above.

(iii) *Trusts for the maintenance or benefit of animals in general, or of a class of animals are charitable*[142]   A trust for the benefit of specific animals is, however, not charitable, but, in several cases,[143] such a trust has been held to be a valid unenforceable trust, if restricted to the perpetuity period, again with like effects to those referred to under (i) above. It may be observed that in the only case in which this point was discussed,[144] the judge, North J, did not treat animal cases as exceptions to a rule, but dissented from the view that the court will not recognize a trust unless it is capable of being enforced by someone.

(iv) *Trusts for the benefit of unincorporated associations*   There is no difficulty where the purposes of the association are charitable: the trust will not then be void either for uncertainty, perpetuity, or unenforceability. Cases of non-charitable associations were said to form a more doubtful group by Morris and Leach,[145] and recent decisions indicate that this group should be deleted as an exception. Other difficulties in connection with unincorporated associations are discussed below.

(v) *Miscellaneous cases*   The most commonly cited case is *Re Thompson*,[146] in which a testator gave a legacy of £1,000 to his friend G W L, to be applied to him, in such manner as in his discretion he might think fit, towards the promotion and furtherance of fox hunting. Clauson J refused to accept the argument based on *Morice v Bishop of Durham*[147] that the trust was invalid and indirectly enforced the trust in the usual way by requiring an undertaking from the trustee to apply the legacy towards the object expressed in the will, and giving the residuary legatees liberty to apply to the court in case the trustee failed to carry out his undertaking. Such a trust would now seem to be illegal and void as a consequence of the Hunting Act 2004.

Finally, it should be mentioned that, in the present state of the authorities, it seems impossible to accept the attractive proposition that an unenforceable trust should be allowed to take effect as a power.[148] In two cases,[149] the Court of Appeal has made clear statements to the contrary, observing, for instance, in *IRC v Broadway Cottages Trust*:[150] 'We do not think a valid power is to be spelt out of an invalid trust.' If, however, a provision is drafted as a mere power to appoint for a specific non-charitable purpose limited in its exercise to the perpetuity period, it seems it may well be valid.[151] The donee of the power may exercise

---

[141] *Bourne v Keane* [1919] AC 815, HL.   [142] See Chapter 13, section 3(K), p 271, *infra*.

[143] *Pettingall v Pettingall* (1842) 11 LJ Ch 176; *Mitford v Reynolds* (1848) 16 Sim 105; *Re Dean* (1889) 41 Ch D 552; *Re Haines* (1952) Times, 7 November. See (1983) 80 LSG 2451 (P Matthews).

[144] *Re Dean, supra*.   [145] Op cit, p 310.   [146] [1934] Ch 342.   [147] *Supra*.

[148] Morris and Leach, *The Rule Against Perpetuities*, 2nd edn, p 391 *et seq*. See the American Law Institute's Restatement of Trusts, 2d (1959), para 124.

[149] *IRC v Broadway Cottages Trust* [1955] Ch 20, [1954] 3 All ER 120, CA; *Re Endacott* [1960] Ch 232, [1959] 3 All ER 562, CA.

[150] [1955] Ch 20, 36, [1954] 3 All ER 120, 128, CA. See *Daniels v Daniels' Estate* [1992] 2 WWR 697, in which a gift of residue to his executors 'to distribute as they see fit' failed for uncertainty of object, reversing the decision at first instance that the clause conferred a valid general power of appointment.

[151] *Re Douglas* (1887) 35 Ch D 472, CA.

it if he wishes to do so, and, if he does not, the property will pass to the persons entitled in default of appointment, or be held on a resulting trust for the settlor or his estate.

4 TRUSTS FOR THE BENEFIT OF UNINCORPORATED ASSOCIATIONS

Viscount Simonds has referred to the difficulties arising out of 'the artificial and anomalous conception of an unincorporated society which, though it is not a separate entity in law, is yet for many purposes regarded as a continuing entity and, however inaccurately, as something other than an aggregate of its members'.[152] It is now clear that, in the case of a gift to an unincorporated non-charitable association, one must first construe the gift and then decide what results flow from that construction. It appears from *Re Recher's Will Trusts*[153] that there are four possible interpretations of such a gift.

(i) *As a gift to the individual members of the association at the date of the gift for their own benefit as joint tenants or tenants in common, so that they could at once, if they pleased, agree to divide it amongst themselves, each putting his share into his own pocket* The association on this construction is used in effect as a convenient label or definition of the class that is intended to take. On the basis that the gift is to the individual members, it follows that any member, after severance if he took as a joint tenant, can claim an *aliquot* share whether or not he continues to be a member of the association and irrespective of the wishes of the other members. In *Leahy v A-G of New South Wales*,[154] it was observed that it is by reason of this construction:

> that the prudent conveyancer provides that a receipt by the treasurer or other proper officer of the recipient society for a legacy to the society shall be a sufficient discharge to executors.[155] If it were not so, the executors could only get a valid discharge by obtaining a receipt from every member. This must be qualified by saying that, by their rules, the members might have authorized one of themselves to receive a gift on behalf of them all.

This first construction may even be given to a gift for the general purposes of the association,[156] although it may clearly not be contemplated that the individual members shall divide it amongst themselves, provided that there is nothing in the

---

[152] *Leahy v A-G of New South Wales* [1959] AC 457, 477, [1959] 2 All ER 300, 306, PC. There are three essential characteristics of an unincorporated association—namely: (i) there must be members of the association; (ii) there must be a contract binding the members *inter se*; (iii) there must by a matter of history have been a moment in time when a number of persons combined or banded together to form the association.

[153] [1972] Ch 526, [1971] 3 All ER 401, following *Leahy v A-G of New South Wales, supra*, PC and *Neville Estates Ltd v Madden* [1962] Ch 832, [1961] 3 All ER 769. See (1965) 29 Conv 165 (J A Andrews); (1971) 8 MULR 1 (P W Hogg); (1973) 47 ALJ 305 (R Baxt); [1985] Conv 318 (Jean Warburton). Cf *Artistic Upholstery Ltd v Art Firma (Furniture) Ltd* [1999] 4 All ER 277, [2000] FSR 311.

[154] [1959] AC 457, 477, [1959] 2 All ER 300, 306, PC.

[155] But even this will not save the gift where there is, in fact, no association. Thus the gift to the Oxford Group failed in *Re Thackrah* [1939] 2 All ER 4. See E O Walford, op cit.

[156] *Bowman v Secular Society Ltd* [1917] AC 406, HL: *Re Ogden* [1933] Ch 678.

THE ESSENTIALS OF A TRUST

constitution of the society to prohibit it.[157] It would, however, be very difficult to give this construction to a gift by name to a society engaged in philanthropic work.[158]

(ii) *As a gift not only to present members, but also to future members for ever or for an indefinite period* On this construction, unless the duration were limited to the perpetuity period, it would, prior to the Perpetuities and Accumulations Act 1964, have failed for perpetuity. Since that Act, it is submitted that it will not fail for perpetuity, but will operate in favour of those members ascertained within the perpetuity period.[159]

(iii) *As a gift to the trustees or other proper officers of the association on trust to carry into effect the purposes of the association* On this construction, the rule in *Morice v Bishop of Durham*[160] applies and the gift will fail for the want of a beneficiary. It is only if, on this construction, the gift were to be held valid—which, it is submitted, is not the case—that unincorporated associations would constitute an exception to the beneficiary principle, because each other construction is based on a gift to individuals.

(iv) *As a gift to the existing members of the association beneficially, but on the basis that the subject matter of the gift is given as an accretion to the funds of the association and falls to be dealt with in accordance with the rules of the association by which the members are contractually bound* inter se[161] On this construction, the gift will be valid. Although beneficially entitled, an individual member cannot claim to be paid out his share. His share will accrue to the other members on his death or resignation, even though such members include persons who become members after the gift took effect.[162] This fourth construction was held to be the proper way in which to construe the gift to the Anti-Vivisection Society in *Re Recher's Will Trusts*[163] itself. The gift would accordingly have been held good had the society still

---

[157] *Re Clarke* [1901] 2 Ch 110. Cf *Re Drummond* [1914] 2 Ch 90; disapproved *Leahy v A-G of New South Wales, supra.*

[158] *Re Haks* [1972] Qd R 59.

[159] Perpetuities and Accumulation Act 1964, ss 4(4) and 3(1) and (4), and see [1976] ASCL 421 (J Hackney). The effect of the Act is not considered by Vinelott J in *Re Grant's Will Trusts* [1979] 3 All ER 359, [1980] 1 WLR 360, nor by Brightman J in *Re Recher's Will Trusts* [1972] Ch 526, [1971] 3 All ER 401, who restated the old rule that, if construed as a gift to all members, present and future, beneficially, it would be void for perpetuity.

[160] (1805) 10 Ves 522; affg (1804) 9 Ves 399; *Re Grant's Will Trusts, supra.*

[161] In [1995] Conv 302 (P Matthews), it is argued that whether a gift falls within (i) or (iv) is 'a matter of construction *of the rules themselves* and has nothing to do with the donor's intentions'. Simon Gardner, however, in [1998] Conv 8, persuasively contends that the donor's intention is significant in determining whether the gift is to the members 'on account of the club', or in their personal capacity.

[162] This is not easily reconciled with the Law of Property Act 1925, s 53(1)(c), which requires the disposition of an equitable interest to be in writing, and there are also difficulties in regard to infant members. See [1971] ASCL 379 (J Hackney).

[163] [1972] Ch 526, [1971] 3 All ER 401. See *Universe Tankships Inc of Monrovia v International Transport Workers' Federation* [1983] 1 AC 366, [1982] 2 All ER 67, HL, discussed (1983) 133 NLJ 515 (J McMullen and A Grubb); (1982) 45 MLR 561, (1983) 46 MLR 361 (B Green). The same construction was applied to the local branch of a trade union in *News Group Newspapers Ltd v SOGAT 1982* [1986] ICR 716, CA. (The funds of the local branch, an unincorporated association, were accordingly not subject to the writ of sequestration of the

been in existence, but, on the facts, it was held to fail because the Society had been dissolved before the testatrix died.

In *Re Lipinski's Will Trusts*,[164] the matter was more complicated in that there was a gift by will to an association 'to be used solely in the work of constructing the new buildings for the association and /or improvements to the said buildings'. This purpose was within the powers of the association and was one of which the members were beneficiaries. Oliver J held that the gift was valid:

> Where the donee association is itself the beneficiary of the prescribed purpose,...the gift should be construed as an absolute one [on the fourth construction] the more so where, if the purpose is carried out, the members can by appropriate action vest the resulting property in themselves, for here the trustees and the beneficiaries are the same persons.

Alternatively, he continued, the same result is reached by applying the principle of *Re Denley's Trust Deed*[165] and treating the gift as one of the specification of a particular purpose for the benefit of ascertained beneficiaries, the members of the association for the time being. It was, he thought, significant that the members could, by an appropriate majority, alter their constitution so as to divide the association's assets among themselves. This last point was stressed by Vinelott J in *Re Grant's Will Trusts*,[166] who accepted that the expectation of the donor or testator that the association would employ the gift in the furtherance of the expressed purpose may not be fulfilled. Although neither of the last two cases cited was referred to by Lewison J in *Hanchett-Stamford v A-G*,[167] he adopted a similar approach. The thread, he said, running through the cases is:

> that the property of an unincorporated association is the property of the members, but that they are contractually precluded from severing their share except in accordance with the rules of the association, and that, on its dissolution, those who are members at the time are entitled to the assets free from any such contractual restrictions. It is true that this is not a joint tenancy according to the classical model, but since any collective ownership of property must be a species of joint tenancy or tenancy in common this kind of collective ownership must, in my opinion, be a sub-species of joint tenancy, albeit taking effect subject to any contractual restrictions applicable as between members.

On a dissolution, the then members of the dissolved association have beneficial interests in its assets. If an association reaches the point at which there is only one member remaining, as happened in the *Hanchett-Stamford* case, then it must cease to exist; one cannot associate with oneself, and since the members' rights are based on contract, a contract must cease to bind once there is no other party who can enforce it. The same legal principle

funds of SOGAT 1982.) See also *Re Horley Town Football Club* [2006] EWHC 2386, [2006] WTLR 1817, noted [2007] Conv 274 (P Luxton); [(2007) 85 T & ELTJ 4 (M O'Sullivan).

[164] [1976] Ch 235, [1977] 1 All ER 33. See [1976] ASCL 419 (J Hackney); (1977) 40 MLR 231 (N P Gravells); (1977) 41 Conv 179 (K Widdows); (1980) 39 CLJ 88 (C E F Rickett); (1977) 9 VUWLR 1 (I McKay).

[165] [1969] 1 Ch 373, [1968] 3 All ER 65, discussed p 59, *supra*.

[166] [1979] 3 All ER 359, [1980] 1 WLR 360, in which the members did not fully control the funds and the gift failed. See (1980) 130 NLJ 532 (A M Tettenborn).

[167] [2008] EWHC 330 (Ch), [2008] 2 P & CR 102.

applies as in the case in which, at the time of dissolution, there is more than one member. The sole surviving member is accordingly entitled to the assets beneficially.[168]

Exceptionally, as in *Cunnack v Edwards*,[169] the combined effect of the rules of the association and statute may make a claim by the members impossible. In this case, the Crown will take the assets as *bona vacantia*.

---

[168] On this point declining to follow the *obiter dictum* of Walton J in *Re Bucks Constabulary Widows' and Orphans' Fund Friendly Society (No 2)* [1979] 1 All ER 623.

[169] [1896] 2 Ch 679, CA.

4

CLASSIFICATION AND
JURISTIC NATURE
OF TRUSTS

Trusts may be classified in several different ways. This is not merely an academic exercise: the category into which a trust falls may have important practical consequences. Thus, for example, as we shall see, the requirements of writing that apply to express trusts of land do not apply to resulting, implied, or constructive trusts, and charitable trusts have considerable advantages in relation to taxation when compared with private trusts.

Section 1 of this chapter considers numerous classifications, the first being that into express, implied, resulting, and constructive trusts. A clear case of an express trust would arise where a settlor conveyed property to trustees and directed them to hold the property on trust for specified persons, and this would equally be so if, without signing any document, he declared unequivocally that henceforth he would hold his shares in XYZ plc on trust for a named child. Where there is no unequivocal declaration of trust in so many words, the court may nevertheless be prepared to infer a trust from a person's words and actions. In some circumstances, the court presumes that there is a trust: if, for instance, a settlor were to set up a trust that directed the trustees to hold the trust property on trust for X and Y in equal shares but, unknown to him, X and Y had died in a car crash on the previous day, and the trust therefore failed, the trustees could not, of course, keep the trust property for themselves, but they would hold it on what is known as a 'resulting trust' for the settlor.

In other circumstances, the court may impose what is called a 'constructive trust'. Suppose a trustee, quite improperly, gives an item of the trust property to his girlfriend as a birthday present. The girlfriend, although knowing nothing of the trust and innocently assuming that the item had been purchased by the trustee out of his own money in the normal way, will hold it as a constructive trustee for the beneficiaries under the trust.

Section 2 explains what is meant by a 'discretionary trust', under which the beneficiaries do not have fixed interests in the trust property, but have interests dependent on the exercise by the trustees of a discretionary power given to them by the trust instrument. It will also consider a 'protective trust', designed for the protection of a spendthrift.

Section 3 discusses the nature of a trust.

1 CLASSIFICATION

(A) EXPRESS, RESULTING, IMPLIED, AND CONSTRUCTIVE TRUSTS

There is no generally agreed classification and it has even been judicially suggested[1] that the boundaries of constructive trust may have been left deliberately vague, so as not to restrict the court by technicalities in deciding what the justice of a particular case may demand. Nevertheless, it may be important in particular contexts to be able to put a trust in one category or another. Thus, as a general rule, a declaration of trust of land must be evidenced by writing, but this rule does not apply to resulting, implied, and constructive trusts;[2] and although the appointment of a minor as an express trustee is void,[3] he can hold property as a trustee upon a resulting trust.[4]

(i) Express trust

'An express trust is one which is deliberately established and which the trustee deliberately accepts.'[5]

(ii) Implied trust

The term 'implied trust' is used in more than one sense, although it is doubtful whether it is really a distinct category.[6] In one sense, an implied trust may be said to arise where the intention of the settlor to set up a trust is inferred from his words or actions: for example, precatory trusts.[7] Implied trusts in this sense are probably best regarded as express trusts, in that the trust is expressed, albeit in ambiguous and uncertain language. Again, as mentioned below, many, perhaps all, resulting trusts depend upon the implied intention of the grantor. Some accordingly treat resulting and implied trusts as synonymous, although others consider implied trust as synonymous with constructive trust.

(iii) Resulting trust

The term 'resulting trust' seems to be limited to three[8] fairly well-defined categories: firstly, where a man purchases property and has it conveyed or transferred into the name of another or the joint names of himself and another when the beneficial interest will normally, as it is said, result to the man who put up the purchase money; secondly, where there is a voluntary conveyance or transfer into the name of another or into the joint names of the grantor and another where likewise there is prima facie a resulting trust for the grantor; and thirdly, where there is a transfer of property to another on trusts that

---

[1] *Per* Edmund Davies LJ in *Carl-Zeiss-Stiftung v Herbert Smith & Co (No 2)* [1969] 2 Ch 276, 300, [1969] 2 All ER 367, 381, CA. See, generally, (1998) 114 LQR 399 (P J Millett); (1999) 18 NZULR 305 (C E F Rickett).

[2] Law of Property Act 1925, s 53(2).   [3] Law of Property Act 1925, s 20.

[4] *Re Vinogradoff* [1935] WN 68.

[5] *Per* Tipping J in *Fortex Group Ltd v MacIntosh* [1998] 3 NZLR 171.

[6] See [2002] NZLJ 176 (Nicky Richardson).   [7] See pp 48, 49, *supra*.

[8] The first two categories were treated as one by Lord Browne-Wilkinson in *Westdeutsche Landesbank Girozentrale v Islington London Borough Council* [1996] AC 669, [1996] 2 All ER 961, HL.

leave some or all of the equitable interest undisposed of. Again, there is a resulting trust, whether the reason is that there is no attempt to dispose of part of the equitable interest, as where property is given to trustees on trust for X for life, and nothing is said as to what is to happen after X's death, or that a purported disposition fails, as where a declared trust is void for uncertainty.

In *Re Vandervell's Trusts (No 2)*,[9] Megarry J classified the first two categories as 'presumed resulting trusts', because they depend upon the presumed intention of the grantor, while the third category he called an 'automatic resulting trust', because it does not depend on any intentions or presumptions, but is the automatic consequence of the transferor's failure to dispose of what is vested in him. In *Westdeutsche Landesbank Girozentrale v Islington London Borough Council*,[10] Lord Browne-Wilkinson doubted Megarry J's analysis of the third category, stating that, in his view, if the settlor has expressly, or by necessary implication, abandoned any beneficial interest in the trust property, there would be no resulting trust but the undisposed-of equitable interest would vest in the Crown as *bona vacantia*.

Chambers[11] has suggested that all cases of resulting trust arise by operation of law when property has been transferred to another and the provider of that property did not intend to benefit the recipient: it depends on lack of an intention to benefit the recipient. The resulting trust, he contends, is an equitable response to this lack of intention and actively reverses unjust enrichment. Although this view has powerful extrajudicial support,[12] it has also met with severe criticism.[13] In *Carlton v Goodman*,[14] the alternative theories were considered, but since, on the facts, they both led to the same result, it was not necessary to decide between them.

Most recently, Swadling[15] has argued that the explanation of the 'presumed' resulting trust is the same today as it was in the seventeenth century—namely, that the primary fact of the voluntary transfer or purchase in the name of another gives rise to a presumption of the secondary fact that the transferor declared a trust in his own favour. The 'automatic' resulting trust, however, in his view, 'still defies legal analysis'.

(iv) Constructive trust[16]

There are two distinct types of constructive trust: namely, (a) the institutional constructive trust; and, (b) the remedial constructive trust. Only the first of these is presently recognized as valid in English law.[17]

---

9 [1974] Ch 269, [1974] 1 All ER 47; revsd [1974] Ch 269, [1974] 3 All ER 205, CA, without discussing this classification. See *Allen v Rochdale Borough Council* [2000] Ch 221, [1999] 3 All ER 443, CA.

10 *Supra*, HL, at 708, 991.

11 *Resulting Trusts*. See also *Equity and Contemporary Legal Developments* (ed S Goldstein), p 335 (P Birks), and [2002] 16 Tru LI 104, 138 (R Chambers) on resulting trusts in Canada.

12 See Lord Millett in (1998) 114 LQR 399.   13 (1996) 16 LS 110 (W Swadling).

14 [2002] EWCA Civ 545, [2002] 2 FLR 259.   15 (2008) 124 LQR 72.

16 See [1999] CLJ 294 (L Smith); (1999) 37 Alberta LR 133 (L I Rotman). Ormiston JA recently observed, 'The subject of constructive trusts has over the years become contentious and differences in analysis have tended to confuse rather than inform': *Nolan v Nolan* [2004] VSCA 109, [2004] WTLR 1261 (Australia).

17 See *Re Sharpe (a bankrupt)* [1980] 1 All ER 198, 203, [1980] 1 WLR 219, 225, *per* Browne-Wilkinson J; *Halifax Building Society v Thomas* [1996] Ch 217, 229 [1995] 4 All ER 673, 682, CA, *per* Peter Gibson LJ; *Westdeutsche Landesbank Girozentrale v Islington London Borough Council* [1996] AC 669, 714–715, [1996] 2 All ER 961, 997, HL, *per* Lord Browne-Wilkinson; *Re Polly Peck International plc (in administration) (No 2)*

(a) *The institutional constructive trust*   Under such a trust:

> the trust arises by operation of law as from the date of the circumstances which give rise to it: the function of the court is merely to declare that such a trust has arisen in the past. The consequences that flow from such a trust having arisen (including the possibly unfair consequences to third parties who in the interim have received the trust property) are also determined by rules of law, not under a discretion.[18]

In English law, the constructive trust is a substantive institution, in principle like any other trust. Express trusts and constructive trusts are two species of the same genus.

Common situations in which a constructive trust will be imposed are:

(i)   where a stranger to the trust, not being a bona fide purchaser for value without notice, is found in possession of trust property—he will be compelled to hold it on trust for the beneficiaries as a constructive trustee;

(ii)   where a trustee makes some profit out of his trust—he will be compelled to hold it as a part of the trust property;

(iii)   under a contract for the sale of land when the vendor is a constructive trustee for the purchaser until completion.

It should be remembered, however, that 'where there is an express declaration of trust, the doctrine of constructive trusts cannot be used so as to contradict the expressly declared trust. The doctrine of constructive trusts is one which applies in circumstances in which there is no declared trust'.[19]

In *Paragon Finance plc v D B Thakerar & Co (a firm)*,[20] Millett LJ explained that the term 'constructive trust' is used to describe two entirely different situations. Firstly, it covers cases:

> where the defendant though not expressly appointed as trustee, has assumed the duties of a trustee by a lawful transaction which was independent of and preceded the breach of trust and is not impeached by the plaintiff. The second covers those cases where the trust obligation arises as a direct consequence of the unlawful transaction which is impeached by the plaintiff.
>
> A constructive trust arises by operation of law whenever the circumstances are such that it would be unconscionable for the owner of property...to assert his own

---

[1998] 3 All ER 812, CA; [1980] Conv 207 (J Martin); (1998) 114 LQR 399 (P J Millett). Note, however, *Ocular Sciences Ltd v Aspect Vision Care Ltd* [1997] RPC 289, in which Daddie J, at 411–416, appears to regard constructive trust as a remedy, although, on the facts, no trust was imposed. He said, at 416, 'the imposition of a constructive trust is part of the equitable armoury of the court'.

[18] *Westdeutsche Landesbank Girozentrale v Islington London Borough Council, supra*, HL, per Lord Browne-Wilkinson. But in the Australian case of *Muschinski v Dodds* (1985) 160 CLR 583, a constructive trust was expressly imposed only from the date of publication of reasons for the judgment so as to safeguard the legitimate interests of third parties. This would seem to be appropriate only in the case of a remedial constructive trust and it is to be noted that, in *Muschinski v Dodds*, Deane J saw the constructive trust both as 'remedy' and 'institution', but having a predominantly remedial character. See also *Parsons v McBain* (2001) 109 FCR (Aust) 120.

[19] *Pink v Lawrence* (1977) 36 P & CR 98 at 101, CA, per Buckley LJ; *Goodman v Gallant*, [1986] Fam 106, [1986] 1 All ER 311, CA. See also *Pettitt v Pettitt* [1970] AC 777, [1969] 2 All ER 385, HL, esp per Lord Upjohn at 813, 405.

[20] [1999] 1 All ER 400, CA, at 408–409, and per Lord Millett in *Dubai Aluminium Co Ltd v Salaam* [2002] UKHL 48, [2003] 2 AC 366, [2003] 1 All ER 97, at 130–131, and extrajudicially in (1998) 114 LQR 399.

beneficial interest in the property and deny the beneficial interest of another. In the first class of case...the constructive trustee really is a trustee. He does not receive the trust property in his own right but by a transaction by which both parties intend to create a trust from the outset and which is not impugned by the plaintiff. His possession of the property is coloured from the first by the trust and confidence by means of which he obtained it, and his subsequent appropriation of the property to his own use is a breach of that trust...In these cases the plaintiff does not impugn the transaction by which the defendant obtained control of the property. He alleges that the circumstances in which the defendant obtained control make it unconscionable for him thereafter to assert a beneficial interest in the property.

The second class of case...arises when the defendant is implicated in a fraud. Equity has always given relief against fraud by making any person sufficiently implicated in the fraud accountable in equity. In such a case he is traditionally though I think unfortunately described as a constructive trustee and said to be 'liable to account as constructive trustee'. Such a person is not in fact a trustee at all, even though he may be liable to account as if he were. He never assumes the position of a trustee, and if he receives the trust property at all it is adversely to the plaintiff by an unlawful transaction which is impugned by the plaintiff. In such a case the expressions 'constructive trust' and 'constructive trustee' are misleading, for there is no trust and usually no possibility of a proprietary remedy; they are 'nothing more than a formula for equitable relief'.[21]

(b) *The remedial constructive trust* In some other jurisdictions, the view is taken that express and constructive trusts are distinct concepts and not two species of a single genus.[22] Canada has been a pioneering jurisdiction in this respect and has developed the remedial constructive trust as a remedy for unjust enrichment.[23] A Canadian judge has explained the distinction thus:[24]

In a substantive constructive trust, the acts of the parties in relation to some property are such that those acts are later declared by a court to have given rise to a substantive constructive trust and to have done so at the time when the acts of the parties brought the trust into being...In a remedial constructive trust...the acts of the parties are such that a wrong is done by one of them to another so that, while no substantive trust relationship is then and there brought into being by those acts, none the less a remedy is required in relation to property and the court

---

[21] *Per* Ungoed-Thomas J in *Selangor United Rubber Estates Ltd v Cradock (No 3)* [1968] 2 All ER 1073, 1097, [1968] 1 WLR 1555, 1582; see *Governor and Company of the Bank of Scotland v A Ltd* [2001] 3 All ER 58, CA. But see (2004) 67 MLR 16 (S B Elliott and C Mitchell).

[22] See *Scott on Trusts*, 4th edn, vol V, sections 461, 462; American Restatement of the Law of Restitution, § 160.

[23] As to Australia, see *Baumgartner v Baumgartner* (1988) 62 ALJR 29; *Bryson v Bryant* (1992) 29 NSWLR 188, noted (1994) 16 Sydney LR 412 (Joellen Riley); (1997) 113 LQR 227 (Rebecca Bailey-Harris); *Parij v Parij* (1998) 72 SASR 153; *Lloyd v Tedesco* [2002] 25 WAR 360, noted (2002) 16 Tru LI 182 (J Edelman). In Australia and New Zealand, the preferred basis seems to be unconscionability: (1994) 8 Tru LI 74 (M Bryan). As to New Zealand, see *Gillies v Keogh* [1989] 2 NZLR 327, in which Cooke P said, at 331, that 'reasonable expectations in the light of the conduct of the parties are at the root of the matter'; *Phillips v Phillips* [1993] 3 NZLR 159 (referring to 'the reasonable expectation test'); *Commonwealth Reserve I v Chodar* [2001] 2 NZLR 374, (1996) 6 Cant LR 369 (Nicky Richardson); [1999] NZLJ 175 (S Trew). The extensive recent literature includes: (1991) 14 NZULR 375 (I S R Scott); [1991] Conv 125 (C Rickett); (1993) 43 UTLJ 217 (P Parkinson); [1991] NZLJ 90 (R Fardell and K Fulton); (1992) 7 Auck ULR 147 (J Dixon); (1993) 109 LQR 263 (S Gardner); *The Frontiers of Liability* (ed P Birks) vol II, p 165 (D W M Waters), p 186 (S Gardner), p 204 (J Eekelaar), p 214 (P Birks), p 224 (J D Davies); (2000) Deak LR 31 (S Evans).

[24] Lambert JA in *Atlas Cabinets and Furniture Ltd v National Trust Co Ltd* (1990) 68 DLR (4th) 161.

grants that remedy in the form of declaration which when the order is made creates a constructive trust by one of the parties in favour of another party.

Lord Browne-Wilkinson has described a remedial constructive trust succinctly[25] as a 'judicial remedy giving rise to an enforceable obligation: the extent to which it operates retrospectively to the prejudice of third parties lies in the discretion of the court'. It 'depends for its very existence on an Order of the Court; such Order being creative rather than simply confirmatory'.[26]

The Canadian development, which originated as a remedy in property disputes between married and unmarried couples,[27] has been extended beyond family property cases.[28] It has been said[29] not to expunge the constructive trust in situations in which English courts of equity traditionally find a constructive trust, but it is applied in circumstances in which the familiar principles of English law would lead to the same result.[30]

Lord Denning sought to introduce a similar approach in several cases in the 1970s. Thus, in *Hussey v Palmer*,[31] he defined a constructive trust as 'a trust imposed by law whenever justice and good conscience require it ... It is an equitable remedy by which the court can enable an aggrieved party to obtain restitution'. Lord Denning's view may well have influenced the Canadian development, but it has not prevailed in English law.[32] However, in *Re Polly Peck International plc (in administration) (No 2)*,[33] Nourse LJ referred to several cases[34] in which judges have accepted the possibility that the remedial constructive trust may become part of English law. But, he pointed out, the judicial observations in those cases were both obiter and tentative. A remedial constructive trust, he continued, gives the court a discretion to vary proprietary rights, which is something that no court has power to do without the authority of Parliament. Statutory authority, such as the Variation of Trusts Act 1958 and the Matrimonial Causes Act 1973, is required to give the court

---

[25] In *Westdeutsche Landesbank Girozentrale v Islington London Borough Council* [1996] AC 669, 714, 715, [1996] 2 All ER 961, 997, HL.

[26] Per Tipping J in *Fortex Group Ltd v MacIntosh* [1998] 3 NZLR 171; *Commonwealth Reserve I v Chodar* [2001] NZLR 374. See [1999] LMCLQ 111 (C Rickett and R Grantham); [2001] 5 Deak LR 31 (S Evans).

[27] See *Pettkus v Becker* (1980) 117 DLR (3d) 257; *Sorochan v Sorochan* (1986) 29 DLR (4th) 213; *Rawluk v Rawluk* (1990) 65 DLR (4th) 161; *Peter v Beblow* (1993) 101 DLR (4th) 621; *LeClair v LeClair Estate* [1998] 9 WWR 182. See also (1999) 37 Alberta LR 1 (M McInnes); (1999) 37 Alberta LR 173 (R Chambers).

[28] See *LAC Minerals Ltd v International Corona Resources Ltd* (1989) 61 DLR (4th) 14; *Soulos v Korkontzilas* (1997) 146 DLR (4th) 214, noted (1997) 31 UBCLR 341 (K B Farquhar); (1997) 76 CBR 539 (L D Smith); (1998) 114 LQR 14 (L Smith); (1999) 10 SCLR 461 (L I Rotman).

[29] In *Soulos v Korkontzilas, supra*, at 222, 223. See (1997) 42 McGill LJ 437 (S Hoegner); (1998) 25 Man LJ 513 (M McInnes).

[30] See *Re Polly Peck International plc (in administration) (No 2)* [1998] 3 All ER 812, 831, CA, per Nourse LJ.

[31] [1972] 3 All ER 744, [1972] 1 WLR 1286, CA. See also *Cooke v Head* [1972] 2 All ER 38, [1972] 1 WLR 518, CA; *Eves v Eves* [1975] 3 All ER 768, [1975] 1 WLR 1388, CA.

[32] See *Burns v Burns* [1984] Ch 317, [1984] 1 All ER 244, CA; *Grant v Edwards* [1986] Ch 638, [1986] 2 All ER 426, CA.

[33] *Supra*, CA.

[34] *Metall und Rohstoff AG v Donaldson Lufkin & Jenrette Inc* [1990] 1 QB 391, [1989] 3 All ER 14, CA; *Re Goldcorp Exchange Ltd (in receivership)* [1995] 1 AC 74, [1994] 2 All ER 806, PC; *Westdeutsche Landesbank Girozentrale v Islington London Borough Council, supra*, HL. See the valuable article by Birks in (1998) 12 Tru LI 202. See also *Re Esteem Settlement* [2003] JLR 188 (Jersey Royal Court), noted PCB 153 (Zillah Howard).

jurisdiction to vary proprietary rights. Extrajudicially, Lord Millett has said that the remedial constructive trust is unlikely to take root in England.[35]

(B) TRUSTS OF LAND

Prior to 1997, when land was settled on trust, in nearly every case the land would be either settled land under the Settled Land Act 1925, or held upon trust for sale under the Law of Property Act 1925.[36]

If the land was settled land, as defined in the Settled Land Act 1925,[37] the beneficiaries were treated as having equitable interests in the land, even if the land was in fact sold and was represented by capital money in the hands of the trustees of the settlement.[38] The powers of management were normally vested in the tenant for life.[39] Social changes, the effects of taxation, and the complexity of the provisions of the Settled Land Act 1925 had the result that few new settlements were being created. Provisions in the Trusts of Land and Appointment of Trustees Act 1996[40] have taken account of this and made it impossible to create a new settlement under the 1925 Act, although existing settlements continue so long as there is relevant property subject to the settlement.[41] Land vested in trustees on charitable, ecclesiastical, or public trusts was before 1997 deemed to be settled land,[42] but since 1996, no land held on such trusts is, or is deemed to be, settled land even if it was, or was deemed to be, settled land before 1997.[43]

Where, before 1997, land was conveyed to trustees in fee simple upon trust to sell it and to hold the proceeds of sale on trust for X for life with remainder to Y absolutely, a trust for sale governed by the Law of Property Act 1925 would have been created. The trustees would have been under a duty to sell the land[44] and the powers of management were vested in them.[45] Moreover, under the doctrine of conversion, the beneficiaries were treated as having interests in personalty, not in the land, even while the land remained unsold. Trusts for sale were also created by statute, as noted below.

Very considerable changes were made by the Trusts of Land and Appointment of Trustees Act 1996. The trust for sale is now subsumed within the definition of a 'trust of land' in the 1996 Act, as meaning any trust of property that consists of or includes land. It includes any description of trust (whether express, implied, resulting, or constructive), including a trust for sale and a bare trust.[46] Although it is still possible to create a trust for

---

[35] Cornish et al (eds) *Restitution: Past, Present and Future*, p 199.

[36] An exceptional case was that in which a trustee held land on a bare trust for a beneficiary absolutely entitled. Note, however, *Wilson v Wilson* [1969] 3 All ER 945, [1969] 1 WLR 1470, in which Buckley J held that the trustees in that case held on a statutory trust for sale for one of them alone. Harpum, in [1990] CLJ 277, says that it is quite impossible to find a trust for sale in such circumstances.

[37] Section 1, as amended. The primary case is where land is limited in trust for any persons by way of succession. By s 1(7), it cannot be settled land if it is held on trust for sale.

[38] Ibid, s 75(5).　　　　[39] Ibid, Pt II, as amended.

[40] Section 2(1), slightly qualified by subss (2), (3). The Act came into force on 1 January 1997.

[41] Ibid, s 2(4).　　　　[42] Settled Land Act 1925, s 29 (repealed with savings).

[43] Trusts of Land and Appointment of Trustees Act 1996, s 1(5).

[44] But with power to postpone the sale indefinitely: Law of Property Act 1925, s 25 (repealed).

[45] Although these could often be delegated under s 29 of the Law of Property Act 1925 (repealed).

[46] Trusts of Land and Appointment of Trustees Act 1996, s 1(1), (2). The definition includes a trust created, or arising, before 1997. It does not include settled land or land to which the Universities and College Estates Act 1925 applies: s 1(3).

sale, the doctrine of conversion no longer applies, whenever the trust came into being.[47] Beneficiaries under a trust of land have equitable interests in the land itself. Moreover, in the case of every trust for sale of land created by a disposition, there is to be implied, despite any provision to the contrary made by the disposition, a power for the trustees to postpone sale of the land and the trustees are not liable in any way for postponing sale of the land, in the exercise of their discretion, for an indefinite period.[48] The practical consequence would seem to be that the land will be retained unless the trustees agree to sell it.

It may be added that, for the purpose of exercising their functions as trustees, the trustees of land have in relation to the land subject to the trust all of the powers of an absolute owner.[49]

(C) STATUTORY TRUSTS

In contrast to the trusts considered above, which were either set up by act of parties or imposed by a court of equity, a trust may be created by statute in specified circumstances. Among the most important are the trust arising on intestacy under s 33 of the Administration of Estates Act 1925, as amended by the Trusts of Land and Appointment of Trustees Act 1996 and the Trustee Act 2000, and the trust imposed by ss 34 and 36 of the Law of Property Act 1925, as likewise amended, in cases of undivided shares and joint tenancy of land. Prior to the 1996 Act, these provisions imposed a trust for sale, but since that Act, they impose a trust without a duty to sell.[50]

A limited special case is a trust of service charge money set up under s 42 of the Landlord and Tenant Act 1987.[51]

(D) EXECUTORY AND EXECUTED TRUSTS

This is a division of express trusts. Although, as Lord St Leonards pointed out in *Egerton v Earl Brownlow,*[52] in one sense, all trusts are executory in that there is always something to be done, the terms 'executory' and 'executed' are used, he continued, with a technical meaning.

An executed trust arises when the settlor has been his own conveyancer—that is, where he has defined exactly the interests to be taken by the beneficiaries or, in other words, has set out the limitations of the equitable interests in complete and final form.

An executory trust arises when he has merely expressed his general intention as to the way in which the property shall go, the limitations really only being intended as instructions as to the mode in which a formal settlement should ultimately be made.[53] The doctrine of executory trusts, however, has its limits. Before it can be applied, it must be possible to ascertain from the language of the document directing the setting up of the trust, at least

---

[47] Ibid, s 3(1), (3). There is an exception in relation to wills of testators who have died before 1997: ibid, s 3(2).

[48] Ibid, s 4.   [49] Ibid, s 6(1). See p 462, *infra.*

[50] Trusts of Land and Appointment of Trustees Act 1996, s 5, Sch 2, paras 3–5, Sch 4.

[51] Discussed (1990) 140 NLJ 785 (R Dickson).   [52] (1853) 4 HL Cas 1, 210.

[53] See *Stanley v Lennard* (1758) 1 Eden 87; *Jervoise v Duke of Northumberland* (1820) 1 Jac & W 559; *Davis v Richards and Wallington Industries Ltd* [1991] 2 All ER 563, [1990] 1 WLR 1511. See also *per* Lord Colonsay in *Sackville-West v Viscount Holmesdale* (1870) LR 4 HL 543, 570.

in general terms, the trusts that one is to impose on the property to be settled. It was held that this could not be done, and the trust accordingly failed, in *Re Flavel's Will Trusts*,[54] in which a testator left a share of residue to trustees 'for formation of a superannuation bonus fund for the employees' of a named company.

The importance of the distinction between 'executory' and 'executed' trusts lies in their construction. In the case of an executed trust, equity will follow the law and give a strict construction to technical words: if strict conveyancing language with a definite legal meaning is used in the creation of a trust of an equitable estate, it is not competent to a court to disregard that legal meaning even though a contrary intention may appear from the rest of the deed.[55] However, even in an executed trus,t the use of untechnical expressions may enable the court to give effect to the settlor's intentions.[56] By contrast, in the case of an executory trust, the court is not bound to construe technical expressions in a technical way, but can look at the whole instrument in order to discover what is the real intention of the settlor, or testator, and order the formal settlement to be drafted so as to fulfil, so far as possible, these real intentions.[57]

Most cases on executory trusts have been cases on marriage articles, where the articles direct a more formal conveyance to be made and themselves express the limitations in an informal manner, but executory trusts may arise under wills,[58] or indeed under *inter vivos* dispositions other than marriage articles.[59] It may be added that the practical importance of the distinction between executed and executory trusts has been considerably reduced as a result of the abolition[60] of the rule in *Shelley's Case*,[61] and the provisions of ss 60 and 130 of the Law of Property Act 1925, as amended.

(E) PRIVATE AND CHARITABLE TRUSTS

A private trust is for the benefit of an individual, or a number or class of specified persons, all of whom must be definitely ascertained within the perpetuity period; a public or charitable trust has as its object charity in a technical sense and usually requires an element of public benefit. The definition of 'charity', and the advantages and disadvantages of charitable trusts, are discussed in Chapter 13.

(F) COMPLETELY AND INCOMPLETELY CONSTITUTED TRUSTS

This distinction is discussed in Chapter 6.

(G) SIMPLE AND SPECIAL TRUSTS

The distinction has not been fully worked out by the courts. The term 'bare trust', which seems to be synonymous with 'simple trust' or 'naked trust', has been the subject of

---

[54] [1969] 2 All ER 232, [1969] 1 WLR 444; *Pengelly v Pengelly* [2007] WTLR 1619.

[55] *Re Bostock's Settlement* [1921] 2 Ch 469, CA.   [56] *Re Arden* [1935] Ch 326.

[57] See *per* Lord Westbury in *Sackville-West v Viscount Holmesdale* (1870) LR 4 HL 543, 565; *Re Bostock's Settlement* [1921] 2 Ch 469, CA.

[58] *Re Spicer* (1901) 84 LT 195.   [59] *Mayn v Mayn* (1867) LR 5 Eq 150.

[60] By the Law of Property Act 1925, s 131, as amended by the Trusts of Land and Appointment of Trustees Act 1996.   [61] (1581) 1 Co Rep 93b.

conflicting views in several cases in which the point has arisen on the construction of that term in a statute. Hall VC, in *Christie v Ovington*,[62] took the view, in connection with s 5 of the Vendor and Purchaser Act 1874, that a bare trustee was 'a trustee to whose office no duties were originally attached, or who, although such duties were originally attached to his office, would, on the requisition of his cestuis que trust, be compellable in equity to convey the estate to them, or by their direction'. Jessel MR, in *Morgan v Swansea Urban Sanitary Authority*,[63] criticized this definition on two grounds: firstly, he said, the concept of a trustee necessarily connotes duties, and the definition would be meaningless unless 'duties' means active duties in the sense of trusts to sell or lease or something of that sort; secondly, he said that, as it stands, the second part of the definition is totally unhelpful, since in any trust all the cestuis que trust, if *sui juris*, can together compel the trustees to convey the estate. It would, he said, have a meaning, if it continued 'and has been requested by them so to convey it', because, after such request, it would be wrong of the trustee to continue to hold the estate. However, Jessel MR's own view was that a bare trustee meant a trustee without any beneficial interest.

Jessel MR's view is supported by *Re Blandy Jenkins' Estate*,[64] in which the point arose under the Fines and Recoveries Act 1833,[65] and by the opinion of Kenyon CJ in the older case of *Roe d Reade v Reade*.[66] On the other side, the view that the test is whether the trustee has active duties to perform was applied in *Re Docwra*,[67] *Re Cunningham and Frayling*,[68] and *Schalit v Joseph Nadler Ltd*,[69] although in the last case the earlier cases were not referred to. This view, or a variant of it, also seems to be the one preferred by textbook writers.[70] The matter was discussed by Gummow J in the Australian case of *Herdegen v Federal Comr of Taxation*,[71] who pointed out that the meaning may vary from statute to statute. In construing the statute before him, he combined the two views referred to above and said that 'bare trustees' meant:

> those trustees who have no interest in the trust assets other than that existing by reason of the office and the legal title as trustee and who never have had active duties to perform or who have ceased to have those duties, such that in either case the property awaits transfer to the beneficiaries or at their direction.

A bare trust of land is a 'trust of land' within the Trusts of Land and Appointment of Trustees Act 1996[72] and the trustees of such a trust accordingly have, in relation to the land subject to the trust, all of the powers of an absolute owner.[73]

If a trust is not a simple one, it is a special one. On the basis that, under a special trust, the trustee has active duties to perform, a further subdivision can be made into 'ministerial' and 'discretionary', according to the degree of judgment and discretion that the trustee is required to exercise.

---

[62] (1875) 1 Ch D 279. See, generally, [2005] PCB 266 (P Matthews).

[63] (1878) 9 Ch D 582. The view of Jessel MR was preferred by Mason P in *Chief Comr of Stamp Duties v ISPT Pty Ltd* (1997) 45 NSWLR 639.

[64] [1917] 1 Ch 46.   [65] Sections 27 and 22.   [66] (1799) 8 Term Rep 118.

[67] (1885) 29 Ch D 693.   [68] [1891] 2 Ch 567.   [69] [1933] 2 KB 79, [1933] All ER Rep 708, DC.

[70] Underhill and Hayton, *Law of Trusts and Trustees*, 17th edn, [4.1]–[4.4]; *Lewin on Trusts*, 17th edn, p 13. Cf *Worthing Rugby Football Club Trustees v IRC* [1985] 1 WLR 409.

[71] (1988) 84 ALR 271; *Burns v Steel* [2006] 1 NZLR 559.   [72] Section 1(1), (2a).

[73] Ibid, s 6. See Chapter 21, section 9, *infra*.

(H) FIXED AND DISCRETIONARY TRUSTS

In a fixed trust, the trust instrument sets out the share or interest that each beneficiary is to take and, accordingly, each beneficiary is the owner of the specified interest that he has been given.

Trustees are often given discretions of varying kinds—for example, as to how the trust funds should be invested—but the phrase 'discretionary trust' means a trust under which the trustees are given a discretion to pay or apply income or capital, or both, to or for the benefit of all, or any one or more exclusively of the others, of a specified class or group of persons, no beneficiary being able to claim as of right that all or any part of the income or capital is to be paid to him or applied for his benefit. They may even be given power to include or exclude any person (or charity) from the class of potential beneficiaries,[74] either permanently or for a specified period.

The trustees may thus have power to decide both who shall benefit and what the benefits shall be. A potential beneficiary cannot be said to be the owner of an equitable interest unless and until the trustees exercise their discretion in his favour. Discretionary trusts are further discussed below.[75]

(I) TRUSTS IN THE HIGHER SENSE AND TRUSTS IN THE LOWER SENSE

Where it is alleged that the Crown is a trustee, the real position may be that there is a governmental obligation or 'trust in the higher sense'. Although this is no mere moral obligation, it is not enforceable in the courts and is outside the scope of this book. A 'trust in the lower sense' or 'true trust' is an equitable obligation originally created by the Court of Chancery and fully enforceable in the courts.[76] Whether an instrument has created a true trust or a trust in the higher sense is a matter of construction, looking at the whole of the instrument in question, its nature and effect, and its context.

2 DISCRETIONARY AND PROTECTIVE TRUSTS

(A) LIMITATIONS UPON CONDITION AND DETERMINABLE INTERESTS

One might think that a gift to X for life or until he becomes bankrupt would have the same effect as a gift to X for life on condition that, if he becomes bankrupt, his interest shall

---

[74] Re Manisty's Settlement [1974] Ch 17, [1973] 2 All ER 1203.   [75] Infra, p 77.

[76] Tito v Waddell (No 2) [1977] Ch 106, [1977] 3 All ER 129. See also Guerin v R (1984) 13 DLR (4th) 321, discussed (1985) 30 McGill LJ 559 (J Hurley), (1986) 18 OLR 307 (Darlene M Johnston); Aboriginal Development Commission v Treka Aboriginal Arts and Crafts Ltd [1984] 3 NSWLR 502; Principal Savings & Trust Co v British Columbia (1994) 20 Alta LR (3d) 388. Note Philipp Bros v Republic of Sierra Leone [1995] 1 Lloyd's Rep 289, CA, in which it was held that the payment of aid by the European Commission to the Republic of Sierra Leone did not give rise to a claim that the money was held on trust. Nor is cash belonging to a prisoner paid into an account under the control of the governor held by him as a trustee: Duggan v Governor of Full Sutton Prison [2004] EWCA Civ 78, [2004] 2 All ER 966.

determine. In law, however, a distinction must be drawn between a 'determinable interest', where the determining event is incorporated in the limitation so that the interest automatically, and naturally determines if and when the event happens, and a 'grant upon a condition subsequent', where an interest is granted subject to an independent proviso that the interest may be brought to a premature end if the condition is fulfilled.[77] In the latter case, if for any reason the condition is void, the grant becomes absolute and the interest will not be liable to premature determination.[78] These principles apply in general to all estates and interests in property, but, for present purposes, we are concerned with their effect upon life interests.

Conditions that have been held void include conditions intended to secure the premature determination of the interest granted on alienation[79] or bankruptcy.[80] There is no doubt, however, that the corresponding determinable limitation—that is, a grant of a life interest to X until he attempts to alienate the same or becomes bankrupt—is perfectly valid,[81] and in dealing with life interests the courts, it seems, will not be astute to construe a provision as a condition if it can be constructed as a determinable limitation.

An important restriction on the validity of such a determinable limitation is that a man cannot settle his own property on himself until his bankruptcy, so as to defeat the claim of his trustee in bankruptcy,[82] although there is no objection to a limitation that takes effect so as to defeat a particular alienee.[83] Where a man does settle property on himself, and, as is usually the case, the life interest is determinable not only on bankruptcy, but also upon other events such as an attempted alienation or charge, then, on the one hand, if bankruptcy is the first determining event to happen, the life interest will vest indefeasibly in the trustee in bankruptcy and will no longer be capable of being determined by the happening of any subsequent specified determining event;[84] on the other hand, if one of the other determining events is the first to happen, the life interest will automatically come to an end and, if the life tenant subsequently becomes bankrupt, the bankrupt will have no interest in the property to pass to his trustee in bankruptcy.[85]

(B) DISCRETIONARY TRUSTS[86]

A discretionary trust may be exhaustive—that is, where the trustees are bound to distribute the whole income, but have a discretion as to how the distribution is to be made

---

[77] For a discussion of the distinction, see Megarry and Wade, *The Law of Real Property*, 7th edn, [9.093]–[9.096].   [78] *Sifton v Sifton* [1938] AC 656, 677, PC.

[79] *Brandon v Robinson* (1811) 18 Ves 429; *Rochford v Hackman* (1852) 9 Hare 475; *Re Trusts of the Scientific Investment Pension Plan* [1999] Ch 53, [1998] 3 All ER 154, i`n which the distinction was said to be '*not a particularly attractive one, being based on form rather than substance*'. See, generally, *Re Brown* [1954] Ch 39, [1953] 2 All ER 1342; (1943) 59 LQR 343 (G Williams). As to bankrupts and their rights under an annuity contract or pensions scheme containing a restriction against alienation, see *Krasner v Dennison* [2001] Ch 76, [2000] 3 All ER 234, CA; *Rowe v Sanders* [2002] 2 All ER 800, CA.

[80] *Re Dugdale* (1888) 38 Ch D 176. See *Money Markets International Stockbrokers Ltd (in liq) v London Stock Exchange Ltd* [2001] 4 All ER 223.   [81] See, eg, *Brandon v Robinson* (1811) 18 Ves 429.

[82] *Wilson v Greenwood* (1818) 1 Swan 471, 481, fn; *Mackintosh v Pogose* [1895] 1 Ch 505; *Re Wombwell* (1921) 125 LT 437.

[83] *Re Johnson, ex p Matthews* [1904] 1 KB 134, DC.   [84] *Re Burroughs-Fowler* [1916] 2 Ch 251.

[85] *Re Richardson's Will Trusts* [1958] Ch 504, [1958] 1 All ER 538; *Re Detmold* (1889) 40 Ch D 585; *Re Brewer's Settlement* [1896] 2 Ch 503.

[86] See (1957) 21 Conv 55 (L A Sheridan); (1967) 31 Conv 117 and [1968] BTR 351 (A J Hawkins); [1977] Mon LR 210 (Y Grbich); [1982] Conv 118, 177 (Ann R Everton).

between the objects; alternatively, according to the cases cited below, a discretionary trust may be non-exhaustive, in which case the trustees have a discretion not only as to how the distribution is to be made, but also as to whether and to what extent it is to be made at all. It is submitted that the term 'non-exhaustive discretionary trust' in fact conceals the two alternatives referred to by Lord Wilberforce in *McPhail v Doulton*[87] viz a power of distribution coupled with a trust to dispose of the undistributed surplus, by accumulation or otherwise, and a trust for distribution coupled with a power to withhold a portion and accumulate or otherwise dispose of it. The distinction between these alternatives does not appear to have been raised in *Gartside v IRC*[88] and it is submitted that it is only if the provision there in question was construed in the latter sense that it should properly have been called a 'discretionary trust'. It was, in fact, consistently so called by their Lordships, although the language of the will is similar to that given as a typical example of a mere power by Russell LJ in *Re Baden's Deed Trusts*.[89]

The nature of the interest of a discretionary beneficiary has been discussed in relation to statutory provisions relating to estate duty, a tax that has now been abolished. In *Gartside v IRC*,[90] which involved a non-exhaustive trust, Lord Reid made it clear that the objects of a discretionary trust do not have concurrent interests in the income, nor do they have a group interest. They all have individual rights: they are in competition with each other and what the trustees give to one is his alone. The reference to a class or group of objects under a discretionary trust is merely a convenient form of reference to indicate individuals who satisfy requirements to qualify as objects who may separately receive benefits under the exercise of the discretion. Subsequently, Cross J, in *Re Weir's Settlement*,[91] and Ungoed-Thomas J, in *Sainsbury v IRC*,[92] have taken the same view in the case of an exhaustive trust. The cases cited also lay down that the separate 'interest' of each separate object is unquantifiable and of a limited kind. What he has is a right to be considered as a potential beneficiary, a right to have his interest protected by a court of equity, and a right to take and enjoy whatever part of the income the trustees choose to give him. He could accordingly go to the court if the trustees were to refuse to exercise their discretion at all, or exercise it improperly.[93]

---

87 [1971] AC 424, 448, [1970] 2 All ER 228, 240, HL.

88 [1968] AC 553, [1968] 1 All ER 121, HL. Cf *Pearson v IRC* [1981] AC 753, [1980] 2 All ER 479, HL (decided by a bare majority in the House of Lords, which disagreed with all the judges below). There seems much to be said for the dissenting speech of Lord Russell of Killowen. The analysis of trust law by Fox J at first instance in [1980] Ch 1, 14–15, [1979] 1 All ER 273, 281–282, repays study. As pointed out by Vinelott J in *IRC v Berrill* [1982] 1 All ER 867, [1981] 1 WLR 1449, there is nothing in the speeches in the House of Lords casting any doubt on its accuracy or completeness.

89 [1969] 2 Ch 388, 400, [1969] 1 All ER 1016, 1022, CA; revd sub nom *McPhail v Doulton* [1971] AC 424, [1970] 2 All ER 228, HL. In *Re Weir's Settlement* [1971] Ch 145, 164, [1970] 1 All ER 297, 300, CA, Russell LJ referred to *Gartside v IRC*, supra, HL as 'a case of a non-exhaustive discretionary power or trust'.

90 [1968] AC 553, [1968] 1 All ER 121, HL.

91 [1969] 1 Ch 657, [1968] 2 All ER 1241; revsd [1971] Ch 145, [1970] 1 All ER 297, CA, without casting doubt on relevant dicta in court below.

92 [1970] Ch 712, [1969] 3 All ER 919.

93 *Tempest v Lord Camoys* (1882) 21 Ch D 571, CA; *Martin v Martin* [1919] P 283, CA; *Gartside v IRC*, supra, HL. See p 489 et seq, infra. The preceding six lines of the text were quoted with implicit approval in *Quinn v Executive Director and Director (Westman Region) of Social Services* [1981] 5 WWR 565.

He has also, it has been said,[94] a right to have the trust property properly managed and to have the trustee account for his management. It follows from what has been said that it is very difficult to explain where the equitable interest lies in the case of discretionary trusts. Perhaps the true view is that the beneficial interest is in suspense until the trustees exercise their discretion.[95]

The rights of a potential beneficiary under a discretionary trust are, in fact, similar to those of the object of a mere power given to trustees in their fiduciary capacity.[96] He has merely a hope, not an entitlement, that it will be exercised in his favour.[97] The main difference lies in the fact that the object of a mere power has no ground of complaint if, after due consideration, the trustees decide not to exercise the power at all. Further, although 'the discretion of the trustees ought to be exercised promptly in every case where its exercise is obligatory',[98] with such necessary limitations on absolute obligations as the necessities of the case demand,[99] the consequences of non-exercise are quite different in the two situations. If the trustees do not exercise a merely permissive power within a reasonable time, it ceases to be exercisable and the trusts in default operate. But in the case of a trust, where the trustees are under a duty to distribute, but neglect to do so within a reasonable time, the court has allowed trustees, willing and competent to do so, to repair their own inaction.[100] It should be added that an object of a discretionary trust may renounce his right to be considered as a potential beneficiary and, at any rate, if he does so for valuable consideration, he thereupon ceases to be an object of the trust.[101]

If an object of a discretionary trust assigns his interest or becomes bankrupt, it is clear that the assignee or trustee in bankruptcy cannot, any more than the discretionary beneficiary could have done, demand payment of any part of the fund.[102] If the trustees exercise their discretion in favour of a discretionary beneficiary by paying or delivering money or goods to him, or even, it seems, by appropriating money or goods to be paid or delivered to him, the title to the money or goods passes to the assignee or trustee in

---

[94] *Per* Powell J in *Spellson v George* (1987) 11 NSWLR 300, 316, cited with approval in *Schmidt v Rosewood Trust Ltd* [2003] UKPC 26, [2003] 2 AC 709, [2003] 3 All ER 76. See p 402, *infra*.

[95] See *Barclays Bank Ltd v Quistclose Investments Ltd* [1970] AC 567, [1968] 3 All ER 651, HL; *Re Northern Developments (Holdings) Ltd* (6 October 1978, unreported) but discussed in *Carreras Rothmans Ltd v Freeman Mathews Treasure Ltd* [1985] Ch 207, [1985] 1 All ER 155, esp *per* Peter Gibson J at 222, 166. But see *Twinsectra Ltd v Yardley* [2002] UKHL 12, [2002] 2 AC 164, [2002] 2 All ER 377 *per* Lord Millett at [90]–[92]. Note, however, that Lord Millett did not refer to the discretionary trust.

[96] See *Vestey v IRC (No 2)* [1979] Ch 198, [1979] 2 All ER 225; affd [1980] AC 1148, [1979] 3 All ER 976, HL.

[97] *Re Smith* [1928] Ch 915.

[98] *Re Locker's Settlement Trusts* [1978] 1 All ER 216, 219, [1977] 1 WLR 1323, 1326, *per* Goulding J.

[99] *Re Gourju's Will Trusts* [1943] Ch 24, 34, *per* Simmonds J. But they cannot validly exercise their discretion in advance: *Re Vestey's Settlement* [1950] 2 All ER 891, 895, CA, *per* Evershed MR (not reported on this point in [1951] Ch 209). See also *Re Allen-Meyrick's Will Trusts* [1966] 1 All ER 740, [1966] 1 WLR 499; *Re Gulbenkian's Settlement Trusts (No 2)* [1970] Ch 408, [1969] 2 All ER 1173.

[100] *Re Locker's Settlement Trusts, supra*; *Breadner v Granville-Grossman* [2001] Ch 523, [2000] 4 All ER 205. As to the position if they are not willing, see p 80, *infra*.

[101] *Re Gulbenkian's Settlement Trusts (No 2)* [1970] Ch 408, [1969] 2 All ER 1173.

[102] *Re Smith* [1928] Ch 915; *R v Barnet Magistrates' Court, ex p Cantor* [1998] 2 All ER 333, [1999] 1 WLR 335, QBD.

bankruptcy.[103] And, where the trustees have actually paid the discretionary beneficiary after notice of an assignment or bankruptcy, they have been held liable to the assignee or trustee in bankruptcy for all the money paid.[104] It seems, however, that the trustees can validly expend the whole or any part of the fund for his maintenance, for instance, in paying a hotel keeper to give him a dinner, or in paying the rent of the house in which he is living,[105] and in respect of any such payment an assignee or trustee in bankruptcy will have no claim.[106]

The position is quite different where the trustees are bound to apply the whole fund for the benefit of a particular person, even though they may be given a discretion as to the method in which the fund is to be applied for his benefit. In this case, the beneficiary, if *sui juris*, is entitled to demand payment of the whole fund, which will pass to an assignee or trustee in bankruptcy.[107] Similarly, where two or more persons together (constituting a closed class) are the sole objects of an exhaustive discretionary trust and between them entitled to have the whole fund applied to them or for their benefit, although no one by himself may be able to demand any payment, they can, if *sui juris*, all join together and require the trustees to pay over the fund to them.[108] Similarly, they may agree and assign to a third party all of the capital or income as the case may be of the trust fund, when the trustees will become obliged to pay it to the third party.[109] But where the class is not a closed class, even a sole member of the class for the time being cannot claim an immediate entitlement to the income so long as there exists a possibility that another member of the class could come into existence before a reasonable time for the distribution of the accrued income has elapsed.[110]

A quite separate problem is what should happen if trustees fail to execute a discretionary trust. Being a trust, the court will see to it that it does not fail and, before *McPhail v Doulton*,[111] it was thought that all that the court could do was to order equal division. This, it will be recalled, is the reason why, before that decision, it was thought that a discretionary trust would only be valid if you could get a complete list of potential beneficiaries. In that case, however, it was held that the court was not so restricted, but may execute a trust power by appointing new trustees, or by authorizing or directing representative persons of the classes of beneficiaries to prepare a scheme of distribution, or even, should the proper basis for distribution appear, by itself directing the trustees so to distribute.[112]

---

[103] *Re Coleman* (1888) 39 Ch D 443, CA.

[104] *Re Neil* (1890) 62 LT 649; *Re Bullock* (1891) 60 LJ Ch 341. According to *Re Ashby* [1892] 1 QB 872, however, the trustee in bankruptcy or assignee can only claim to the extent to which sums are paid in excess of the amount necessary for the mere support of the object of the trust.

[105] *Re Allen-Meyrick's Will Trusts* [1966] 1 All ER 740, [1966] 1 WLR 499.

[106] *Re Coleman, supra; Re Bullock, supra.*

[107] *Green v Spicer* (1830) 1 Russ & M 395; *Younghusband v Gisborne* (1844) 1 Coll 400; *Re Smith* [1928] Ch 915. See Chapter 16, section 6, p 409, *infra.*

[108] *Re Smith, supra; Re Nelson* [1928] Ch 920n, CA; *Sir Moses Montefiore Jewish Home v Howell & Co (No 7) Pty Ltd* [1984] 2 NSWLR 406.

[109] See *Re Weir's Settlement* [1969] 1 Ch 657, 683, [1968] 2 All ER 1241, 1248, at first instance; *Sainsbury v IRC, supra,* at 725, 927; *Thorn v IRC* [1976] 2 All ER 622, [1976] 1 WLR 915.

[110] *Re Trafford's Settlement* [1985] Ch 32, [1984] 1 All ER 1108.

[111] [1971] AC 424, [1970] 2 All ER 228, HL.

[112] See *per* Lord Wilberforce in *McPhail v Doulton, supra,* at 457, 247; applied *Mettoy Pension Trustees Ltd v Evans* [1991] 2 All ER 513, [1990] 1 WLR 1587. See (1967) 31 Conv 117 (A J Hawkins); (1971) 29 CLJ 68 (J Hopkins).

(C) PROTECTIVE TRUSTS[113]

Protective trusts may be set out expressly,[114] or the instrument may incorporate the statutory provisions in s 33 of the Trustee Act 1925,[115] which take effect subject to any modifications contained in the instrument creating the trust. Section 33(1) provides as follows:

> Where any income, including an annuity or other periodical income payment, is directed to be held on protective trusts for the benefit of any person (in this section called 'the principal beneficiary') for the period of his life or for any less period, then, during that period (in this section called 'the trust period'), the said income shall, without prejudice to any prior interest, be held on the following trusts, namely:
>
> (i) Upon trust for the principal beneficiary during the trust period or until he, whether before or after the termination of any prior interest, does or attempts to do or suffers any act or thing, or until any event happens, other than an advance under any statutory or express power,[116] whereby if the said income were payable during the trust period to the principal beneficiary absolutely during that period, he would be deprived of the right to receive the same or any part thereof... [and thereafter] ...
>
> (ii) ...upon trust for the application thereof for the maintenance or support,[117] or otherwise for the benefit, of all or any one or more exclusively of the other or others of the following persons (that is to say)—
>
>   (a) the principal beneficiary and his or her spouse or civil partner, if any, and his or her children or more remote issue,[118] if any; or
>
>   (b) if there is no spouse or civil partner or issue of the principal beneficiary in existence, the principal beneficiary and the person who would, if he were actually dead, be entitled to the trust property or the income thereof or to the annuity fund, if any, or arrears of the annuity, as the case may be:
>
>   as the trustees in their absolute discretion, without being liable to account for the exercise of such discretion, think fit.

Subsection (3) specifically provides that nothing in the section shall validate any trust that would otherwise be invalid,[119] such as a settlement by a man of his own property on himself until bankruptcy.[120]

It is not necessary in order to invoke the section to use the actual words mentioned therein, provided that the reference is sufficiently clear. In *Re Platt*,[121] a gift to be held 'for a protective life interest' was held to be effective, and in *Re Wittke*,[122] a gift of income 'upon protective trusts for the benefit of my sister' was also held to be adequate, consequent

---

[113] Sometimes called 'spendthrift trusts'. See (1957) 21 Conv 110 (L A Sheridan).

[114] See, eg, *Re Munro's Settlement Trusts* [1963] 1 All ER 209, [1963] 1 WLR 145, in which it is pointed out that a beneficiary under a discretionary trust is in a somewhat different, and perhaps stronger, position than a mere expectant heir.

[115] As amended by the Family Law Reform Act 1987, s 33(1), Sch 2, para 2, and Sch 3, para 1, and the Civil Partnership Act 2004, s 261(1) and Sch 27, para 6.

[116] Even if this clause is omitted in an express protective trust, a consent to an advancement will not normally cause forfeiture of the determinable life interest: *Re Rees' Will Trusts* [1954] Ch 202, [1954] 1 All ER 7.

[117] The trustees may apply the income to the maintenance and support of the principal beneficiary without regard to any debt he may owe to the trust estate: *Re Eiser's Will Trusts* [1937] 1 All ER 244.

[118] Including illegitimate children or issue: s 33(4), inserted by the Family Law Reform Act 1987.

[119] Trustee Act 1925, s 33(3).   [120] See p 77, *supra*.

[121] [1950] CLY 4386. Cf *Re Trafford's Settlement* [1985] Ch 32, [1984] 1 All ER 1108.

[122] [1944] Ch 166, [1944] 1 All ER 383.

upon the decision as a question of construction that the sister was intended to take a life interest.

It is, of course, a question of construction of the particular terms of the relevant clause in s 33 or the express limitation, as the case may be, whether a particular event determines the interest of the principal beneficiary. Where the protective trusts under s 33 have applied, events that have been held to have this effect have included the Trading with the Enemy Act 1939 and Orders[123] made thereunder, whereby money payable to a person resident in enemy territory was directed to be paid to the Custodian of Enemy Property,[124] and an order made in the Probate Divorce and Admiralty Division of the High Court that the principal beneficiary should charge his interest with the payment of £50 per annum,[125] but not an order diverting a part of the income from a husband to a wife in priority to the protective trust.[126] Decisions on express provisions, differing to a greater or lesser extent from the provisions of s 33, suggest that the interest of the principal beneficiary under s 33 would be determined, inter alia, by the trustee impounding part of the income of the principal beneficiary in order to repair a breach of trust by the trustee in paying part of the trust fund to the principal beneficiary at his own instigation,[127] or an order of sequestration of the income,[128] but not by an order of the court under s 57 of the Trustee Act 1925 varying the effect of the trusts,[129] nor by a garnishee order,[130] nor by an authority to the trustees to pay dividends from trust shares to creditors, if no dividend is in fact declared.[131]

There is no reason why there should not be a series of two or more protective trusts in favour of the same beneficiary: for example, the first trust until he attains the age of 30, the second for the remainder of his life thereafter. This would give the principal beneficiary a second chance to enjoy the income as of right, and thus prevent a youthful indiscretion from making him dependent on the discretion of the trustees for the rest of his life.[132]

---

[123] Trading with the Enemy (Custodian) Order 1939 (SR&O 1939/1198). Later orders of this kind contained a proviso that vesting in the Custodian of Enemy Property should not take place if it would cause a forfeiture, eg The Trading with the Enemy (Custodian) (No 2) Order 1946 (SR&O 1946/2141).

[124] Re Gourju's Will Trusts [1943] Ch 24, [1942] 2 All ER 605; Re Wittke [1944] Ch 166, [1944] 1 All ER 383; cf Re Harris [1945] Ch 316, [1945] 1 All ER 702; Re Pozot's Settlement Trusts [1952] Ch 427, [1952] 1 All ER 1107, CA, in which the protective trusts were not in the statutory form.

[125] Re Richardson's Will Trusts [1958] Ch 504, [1958] 1 All ER 538; Edmonds v Edmonds [1965] 1 All ER 379n, [1965] 1 WLR 58.

[126] General Accident Fire and Life Assurance Corpn Ltd v IRC [1963] 3 All ER 259, [1963] 1 WLR 1207, CA.

[127] Re Balfour's Settlement [1938] Ch 928, [1938] 3 All ER 259; cf Re Brewer's Settlement [1896] 2 Ch 503. As to impounding a beneficiary's income, see Chapter 23, section 3(C), p 528, infra.

[128] Re Baring's Settlement Trusts [1940] Ch 737, [1940] 3 All ER 20.

[129] Re Mair [1935] Ch 562. Cf Re Salting [1932] 2 Ch 57. As to the effect of s 57 of the Trustees Act 1925, see Chapter 22, section 2(B), infra.

[130] Re Greenwood [1901] 1 Ch 887; Permanent Trustee Co Ltd v University of Sydney [1983] 1 NSWLR 578.

[131] Re Longman [1955] 1 All ER 455, [1955] 1 WLR 197.

[132] See (1958) 74 LQR 182 (R E Megarry), and Re Richardson's Will Trusts [1958] Ch 504, [1958] 1 All ER 538.

3 NATURE OF A TRUST[133]

It may seem strange, although it is perhaps not untypical of English law, that although the trust is so highly developed an institution, it is impossible to say with assurance what is the juristic nature of the interest of a cestui que trust.[134] If one considers the traditional classification of rights into rights *in rem*, which are good against persons generally, and rights *in personam*, which are rights against a specified person or persons, the right of a cestui que trust seems to be rather less than one and rather more than the other. The traditional view that was insisted upon by Maitland[135] is that the interest of the cestui que trust is necessarily a right *in personam*. The main reason why Maitland thought that the contrary view untenable was the undoubted rule[136] that an equitable interest will not avail against a subsequent bona fide purchaser for value of a legal estate without notice of the trust—'such a purchaser's plea of a purchase for valuable consideration without notice is an absolute, unqualified, unanswerable defence, and an unanswerable plea to the jurisdiction of this court'.[137] This view is also consistent with the historical development of the trust under which the beneficiary could originally only sue the original feoffee to uses, then a rapidly increasing number of classes of persons, until ultimately it became convenient and possible, instead of listing the persons against whom the right could be enforced, to say that it was enforceable against everyone except the bona fide purchaser for value of a legal estate without notice.

This traditional view has met with some criticism. Scott[138] has argued that the right of the cestui que trust is a right *in rem* because it is available against persons generally, although there are some exceptions, in the same way as the owner of a cheque is regarded as having a right *in rem* to it, although he may be defeated by a holder in due course. Further, it has been suggested that the traditional view is not adequate to explain the rules as to following the trust property.[139] In so far as a cestui que trust can do this he is, it is said, exercising a right *in rem*, a proprietary right that is clearly greater than a right *in personam*. Moreover, the House of Lords, in *Baker v Archer-Shee*,[140] which depended upon the nature of a life interest in a settled fund, seems to have committed English law[141] to what is sometimes called the 'realist' view, which can hardly be reconciled with traditional theory. The majority of their Lordships[142] took the view that a beneficiary 'was sole beneficial owner of the interest and dividends of all the securities, stocks and shares forming part of the trust

---

[133] See (1967) 45 CBR 219 (D W M Waters); *Burns Philp Trustee Co Ltd v Viney* [1981] 2 NSWLR 216; *Connel v Bond Corpn Pty* (1992) 8 WAR 352.

[134] As to the interest of persons entitled to the estate of a deceased person, see p 40, *supra*.

[135] *Equity*, 2nd (Brunyate) edn p 106 *et seq*; (1917) 17 Col LR 467 (H F Stone). See, generally, Winfield, *Province of the Law of Tort*, p 108 *et seq*; (1954) 32 CBR 520 (V Latham).

[136] Now considerably affected by the provisions as to registration under the Land Charges Act 1972, which do not, however, apply to the ordinary trust interest.

[137] *Pilcher v Rawlins* (1872) 7 Ch App 259, 268, 269, *per* James LJ.   [138] (1917) 17 Col LR 269.

[139] See Chapter 24, section 2, *infra*.   [140] [1927] AC 844, HL; (1928) 44 LQR 468 (H G Hanbury).

[141] Contrast the law of New York: *Archer Shee v Garland* [1931] AC 212, HL.

[142] Lords Atkinson, Carson, and Wrenbury.

fund',[143] and, in a subsequent case,[144] the House unanimously agreed that this constituted the binding *ratio decidendi* of the former case. Thus Viscount Dunedin observed[145] that Viscount Sumner's opinion had been 'rejected by the majority on the view that there was in the beneficiary a specific equitable interest in each and every one of the stocks, shares, etc, which formed the trust fund', and Lord Tomlin said:[146]

> I do not think that it can be doubted that the majority of your Lordships' House in the former case founded themselves upon the view that according to English law...[the beneficiary] had a property interest in the income arising from the securities, stocks and shares constituting the American trust, and that but for the existence of that supposed property interest the decision would have been different.

Most recently, Lord Browne-Wilkinson has said[147] in terms that the owner of an equitable estate has a right *in rem* not merely a right *in personam*. It may be added that the traditional view was repeated by the Divisional Court in *Schalit v Joseph Nadler Ltd*,[148] but it can carry little weight, because *Baker v Archer-Shee*[149] does not even appear to have been cited.[150]

In the light of the considerations discussed, some modern writers have attempted to find a compromise solution. Thus Hanbury[151] regarded equitable interests as hybrids, not quite rights *in rem*, because of the doctrine of the bona fide purchaser, and not quite rights *in personam*, because of the doctrine of following trust funds, while Marshall[152] said that a cestui que trust always has a personal right and, in some cases, he has a real right also. There seems much to be said for treating the interest of a cestui que trust as *sui generis*, instead of trying to force it into a classification that is really inadequate. It may be added that the position is further complicated by the possibility of the registration of certain equitable interests under the Land Charges Act 1972. Whatever the nature of an equitable interest may be before registration, it would seem to become a right *in rem* by virtue thereof, since registration is deemed to constitute actual notice to all persons and for all purposes connected with the land affected.[153] An equitable interest under a trust, however, is not in general capable of registration, but one exception is under a contract for the sale of land where, on the one hand, the vendor is regarded as a constructive trustee for the purchaser,[154] and, on the other hand, the equitable interest of the purchaser is registrable as a land charge class C(iv) under s 2(4)(iv) of the Land Charges Act 1972. In such case, after registration, the purchaser would clearly seem to be properly referred to as the equitable owner of the subject matter of the contract.

---

[143] *Supra*, at 870, *per* Lord Carson. Cf *O'Rourke v Darbishire* [1920] AC 581, HL.

[144] *Archer-Shee v Garland* [1931] AC 212, HL; *IRC v Berrill* [1982] 1 All ER 867, [1981] 1 WLR 1449, and see *Pritchard v M H Builders (Wilmslow) Ltd* [1969] 2 All ER 670, [1969] 1 WLR 409; *Re Cuff Knox* [1963] IR 263; *Costa & Duppe Properties Ltd v Duppe* [1986] VR 90.

[145] *Archer-Shee v Garland, supra*, at 221.   [146] Ibid, at 222.

[147] In *Tinsley v Milligan* [1994] 1 AC 340, 371, [1993] 3 All ER 65, 86, HL.

[148] [1933] 2 KB 79, [1933] All ER Rep 708, DC.   [149] *Supra*.

[150] But see (1954) 32 CBR 520 at 537 (V Latham) for a contrary view.

[151] *Modern Equity*, 8th edn, p 446. See also Holdsworth, *History of English Law*, vol IV, p 432 *et seq* and, in relation to constructive trusts, (1985) 17 OLR 72 (Debra Rankin).

[152] Nathan & Marshall, *A Casebook on Trusts*, 5th edn, p 9, and see 12th edn by D Hayton and C Mitchell at [1.54] *et seq*.

[153] Law of Property Act 1925, s 198, as amended by the Local Land Charges Act 1975, s 17(2) and Sch 1. See also the Land Registration Act 2002, s 116.   [154] See p 163, *infra*.

None of the above cases was referred to in *Webb v Webb*,[155] in which the question was one of the construction of Art 16(1) of the Brussels Convention,[156] which provides that the courts of the contracting state in which the property is situated have exclusive jurisdiction, regardless of domicile, in proceedings that have as their object rights *in rem* in immovable property. On a reference from the Court of Appeal, the Court of Justice of the European Communities held that an action for a declaration that a person holds immovable property as trustee and for an order requiring that person to execute such documents as should be required to vest the legal ownership in the plaintiff does not constitute an action *in rem* for the purpose of Art 16(1) of the Convention, but an action *in personam*. The plaintiff is not claiming that he already enjoys rights directly relating to the property that are enforceable against the whole world, but is seeking only to assert rights against the alleged trustee. In the opinion of the Advocate-General, the dividing line lies between actions the principal subject matter of which is a dispute over ownership between persons who do not claim *inter se* any fiduciary relationship and actions concerning a breach of fiduciary duty that, if found to have been committed, will have effects *in rem*. In the latter case, the personal nature of the relations is the overriding factor.

---

[155] [1994] QB 696, [1994] 3 All ER 911, ECJ, noted (1994) 110 LQR 526 (A Briggs); (1994) 8 Tru LI 99. (P Birks); [1996] Conv 125 (Catherine MacMillian); *Ashurst v Pollard* [2001] Ch 595, [2001] 2 All ER 75, CA. Cf *Re Hayward (decd)* [1997] Ch 45, [1997] 1 All ER 32.

[156] The Convention on Jurisdiction and the Enforcement of Judgments in Civil and Commercial Matters 1968, set out in Sch 1 to the Civil Jurisdiction and Judgments Act 1982.

5

FORMAL REQUIREMENTS
OF EXPRESS TRUSTS

Apart from statute, there are no requirements as to writing or other formalities in connection with the creation of trusts or dealings with equitable interests, whether *inter vivos* or testamentary, and whether relating to real or personal property. The statutory provisions, however, are of wide ambit and must now be considered. Resulting, implied, and constructive trusts are not within the scope of this chapter, but, for the avoidance of doubt, it may be mentioned that the Law of Property Act 1925, s 53(2), expressly provides that s 53 does not affect the creation or operation of resulting, implied, or constructive trusts, and the Law of Property (Miscellaneous Provisions) Act 1989, s 2(5) provides likewise in relation to s 2 of that Act.

Most of this chapter is concerned with statutory provisions relating to *inter vivos* transactions. It concludes with a short section dealing with testamentary provisions.

1 *INTER VIVOS* TRANSACTIONS

(A) CONTRACTS TO CREATE A TRUST OR TO DISPOSE OF A SUBSISTING EQUITABLE INTEREST

(i) Land

Such contracts, if relating to land or any interest therein, come within the scope of s 2 of the Law of Property (Miscellaneous Provisions) Act 1989.[1] It provides as follows:

(1) A contract for the sale or other disposition[2] of an interest in land[3] can only be made in writing and only by incorporating all the terms which the parties have expressly agreed in one document or, where contracts are exchanged, in each.

(2) The terms may be incorporated in a document either by being set out in it or by reference to some other document.

---

[1] Replacing the Law of Property Act 1925, s 40(1). See [1989] Conv 431 (P H Pettit); [1989] LSG 86/39/15 (P Kenny and Ann Kenny); (1990) 106 LQR 396 (G Hill); (1990) 140 NLJ 105 (C J Davis, N P Gravells, and A M Pritchard); [1990] Conv 441 (Jean Howell); [1990] LS 325 (L Bently and P Coughlan); (1993) 22 AALR 499 (M Haley).

[2] 'Disposition' has the same meaning as in the Law of Property Act 1925–see p 91 *et seq, infra*.

[3] By s 2(6), as amended by the Trusts of Land and Appointment of Trustees Act 1996, 'interest in land' is defined as meaning any estate, interest, or charge in or over land.

(3) The document incorporating the terms or, where contracts are exchanged, one of the documents incorporating them (but not necessarily the same one) must be signed by or on behalf of each party to the contract.[4]

Signature is required by both parties and the effect of non-compliance is to make the contract a complete nullity.[5]

(ii) Pure personalty

There are no requirements of writing in connection with contracts to create a trust or to dispose of equitable interests in pure personalty.

(iii) Equitable interests in pure personalty and, semble, land

By way of qualification to what has been said in (i) and (ii) above, it should be said that a contract to assign an equitable interest may come within the scope of s 53(1)(c) of the Law of Property Act 1925 as being a 'disposition' of a subsisting equitable interest. This is discussed later.[6]

(B) DECLARATIONS OF TRUST *INTER VIVOS*

The more obvious use of the phrase 'declaration of trust' is to describe the case in which the settlor (S) expressly or by implication declares that henceforth he will hold specified property on certain trusts. Where S is the owner of the property both at law and in equity, the effect is that he remains the legal owner, but the equitable interest becomes vested in the beneficiaries under the newly created trust.

Where S is himself only the owner of an equitable interest under a trust, the effect is to create a sub-trust under which S remains the owner of the equitable interest, which he now holds on trust for the beneficiaries under the sub-trust. This was always the case where S had active duties to perform, but, until the recent decision in *Nelson v Greening & Sykes (Builders) Ltd*,[7] it was commonly thought that, if the trust declared by S, the owner of an equitable interest, was a bare or simple trust, he would 'disappear[s] from the picture',[8] the legal owner under the head trust becoming a trustee directly for the beneficiaries under the

---

[4] For the effect of a court order for rectification of one or more of the relevant documents, see s 2(4). Where one document incorporates another document, it is the first document that must be signed; it is no signature within the Act where the party whose signature is said to appear on a contract is only named as the addressee of a letter prepared by him: *Firstpost Homes Ltd v Johnson* [1995] 4 all ER 355, [1995] 1 WLR 1567, CA, noted [1996] CLJ 192 (A J Oakley). The Act applies equally to the variation of a contract within the Act: *McCausland v Duncan Lawrie Ltd* [1996] 4 All ER 995, [1997] 1 WLR 38, CA.

[5] See *J Pereira Fernandes SA v Mehta* [2006] EWHC 813 (Ch), [2006] 1 WLR 1543, [2006] 2 All ER 891 (email address not a sufficient signature for the purpose of s 4 of the Statute of Frauds 1677).

[6] *Infra*, p 91 *et seq.*

[7] [2007] EWCA Civ 1358, [2007] All ER (D) 270 (Dec), [2008] Times 22 January.

[8] *Per* Upjohn J in Grey v IRC [1958] Ch 375, 382, [1958] 1 All ER 246, 251; revsd on appeal [1958] Ch 690, [1958] 2 All ER 428. The CA decision was affirmed by HL on different grounds [1960] AC 1, [1959] 3 All ER 603. See *Grainge v Wilberforce* (1889) 5 TLR 436; *Corin v Patton* (1990) 92 ALR 1. In *Re Lashmar* [1891] 1 Ch 258, CA, in which it was held that the trustee disappeared from the picture, Lindley LJ expressly pointed out that *Onslow v Wallis* (1849) 1 Mac & G 506 was to be distinguished on the ground that there the trustee had duties to perform, and said that had there been any duties to perform in the case before them, the decision of the court would have been the other way. But see (1984) 47 MLR 385 (B Green).

sub-trust. In *Nelson's* case, the Court of Appeal held that the authorities did not bind the Court to hold that, in such circumstances, an intermediate trustee ceases to be a trustee. Lawrence Collins LJ, who gave the leading judgment, said that, when Lord Evershed in *Grey v IRC*[9] said that the practical effect would amount to the 'getting rid' of the trust of the equitable interest, it was not the same as saying that, as a matter of law, it does get rid of the intermediate trust. What he was saying was that, in the case of a trust and sub-trust of personal property, the trustees may decide that, as a matter of practicality, it is more convenient to deal directly with the beneficiary of the sub-trust.

In any event, Lawrence Collins LJ went on to say, the authorities had no application to a case, such as that before the Court, in which the trust property is the purchaser's interest in land created by the existence of an executory contract for sale and purchase. It thus remains faintly arguable that the old rule still applies in the case of a bare or simple intermediate trust of personal property.

The perhaps less obvious use of the phrase 'declaration of trust' is to describe an alternative mode in which a trust may be created—namely, by a transfer of the property to trustees and a direction to the trustees to hold the property on specified trusts, the direction to the trustees by the equitable owner really constituting the declaration of trust.[10]

(i) Land

As regards land or any interest therein,[11] s 53(1)(b)[12] of the Law of Property Act 1925 provides:

> A declaration of trust respecting any land or any interest therein must be manifested and proved by some writing signed by some person who is able to declare such trust or by his will.

Although the wording is somewhat different, the requirement of writing in s 53(1)(b) is generally thought to be the same as was required under s 40(1), now repealed, and reliance can accordingly be placed on decisions on the latter section. Thus the writing is only required as evidence of the declaration of trust,[13] and need not therefore be contemporaneous with it.[14] The writing need not be in any particular form,[15] but must contain all of the material terms of the trust,[16] and joinder of documents is permitted.[17] Under s 53(1) (b),

---

[9] *Supra*, CA, at 715.   [10] But see (1975) 7 OLR 483 (G Battersby).

[11] 'Land' is widely defined in the Law of Property Act 1925, s 205(1)(ix), as amended by the Trusts of Land and Appointment of Trustees Act 1996, as including, inter alia, land of any tenure (this includes leaseholds: *Re Brooker* [1926] WN 93; *Re Berton* [1939] Ch 200, [1938] 4 All ER 285), mines and minerals, buildings or parts of buildings, and other corporeal hereditaments, and also incorporeal hereditaments.

[12] Replacing s 7 of the Statute of Frauds 1677. Care must be taken in applying decisions on the old Act where there have been changes in the wording: see *Grey v IRC* [1960] AC 1, [1959] 3 All ER 603, HL.

[13] *Forster v Hale* (1798) 3 Ves 696; affd (1800) 5 Ves 308; *Re Holland* [1902] 2 Ch 360, CA. If it has been destroyed, secondary evidence may be admissible: *Barber v Rowe* [1948] 2 All ER 1050, CA.

[14] *Rochefoucauld v Boustead* [1897] 1 Ch 196, CA.

[15] See, eg, *Deg v Deg* (1727) 2 P Wms 412 (recital in deed); *Forster v Hale* (1798) 3 Ves 696; affd (1800) 5 Ves 308 (correspondence); *Cohen v Roche* [1927] 1 KB 169; *Hill v Hill* [1947] Ch 231, [1947] 1 All ER 54, CA.

[16] *Hawkins v Price* [1947] Ch 645, [1947] 1 All ER 689; *Tweddell v Henderson* [1975] 2 All ER 1096, [1975] 1 WLR 1496; *Ram Narayan v Rishad Hussain Shah* [1979] 1 WLR 1349, PC (writing insufficient where it omitted reference to chattels included in one indivisible contract for land and chattels), discussed [1980] Conv 92.

[17] *Timmins v Moreland Street Property Co Ltd* [1958] Ch 110, [1957] 3 All ER 265, CA; *Elias v George Sahely & Co (Barbados) Ltd* [1983] 1 AC 646, [1982] 3 All ER 801, PC, discussed (1983) 133 NLJ 841 (H W Wilkinson), and see (1958) 22 Conv 275 (G H L Fridman).

signature by an agent is not permitted; the signature must be by 'some person who is able to declare such trust'.[18] In the first type of declaration of trust, in which the owner of property declares himself to be a trustee thereof, he is clearly the person who must sign the writing. In the second type of declaration of trust, in which there is separation of the legal and equitable interests and the declaration of trust takes the form of a direction to the trustees by the equitable owner, it has been settled that it is the equitable owner who must sign the writing if it is to be effective.[19]

Section 53(1)(b) does not contain any express sanction for failure to comply with its provisions. The assumption of most textbook writers[20] is probably right: that since s 53(1)(b) merely requires writing as evidence, absence of writing does not make the declaration of trust void,[21] but merely unenforceable, as was previously the case under s 40(1).[22]

(ii) Pure personalty

There is no requirement of writing and a trust may accordingly be declared by unsigned writing, by word of mouth, and even by conduct.[23]

(iii) Equitable interests in real or personal property

By way of qualification to what has been said above, writing may be required in some cases under s 53(1)(c)[24] as a declaration of trust may also be a disposition within that section. It is thought[25] that this can only arise where the declaration of trust consists of a direction to the trustees by the equitable owner. It is now settled beyond dispute that, at any rate, where an equitable interest in pure personalty is concerned, such a declaration is a disposition within s 53(1)(c), although it does not, of course, fall within s 53(1)(b). The point arose in *Grey v IRC*,[26] in which, on 1 February 1955, a settlor transferred 18,000 shares to trustees to be held by them as nominees for himself. On 18 February 1955, he orally directed the trustees to hold the shares on specified trusts, and, on 25 March 1955, the trustees executed a deed of declaration of trust reciting the directions given to them on 18 February and declaring that they had been holding the shares on the specified trusts since that date. This deed was also executed by the settlor to testify the giving of the directions and their

---

[18] See (1984) 54 CLJ 306 (T G Youdan). Cf s 53(1)(c) discussed p 91 *et seq, infra*, and s 2 of the Law of Property (Miscellaneous Provisions) Act 1989, discussed p 85, *supra*.

[19] *Tierney v Wood* (1854) 19 Beav 330; *Kronheim v Johnson* (1877) 7 Ch D 60; *Grey v IRC* [1958] Ch 690 at 709, [1958] 2 All ER 428 at 433, CA; affd [1960] AC 1, [1959] 3 All ER 603, HL.

[20] See, eg, Underhill and Hayton, *Law of Trusts and Trustees*, 17th edn, [12.9]; (1984) 43 CLJ 306 (T G Youdan).

[21] Contrast the effect of s 53(1)(c) replacing s 9 of the Statute of Frauds, p 89, *infra*.

[22] *Leroux v Brown* (1852) 12 CB 801; *Britain v Rossiter* (1879) 11 QBD 123, CA; *Maddison v Alderson* (1883) 8 App Cas 467, HL; *Rochefoucauld v Boustead* [1897] 1 Ch 196, CA.

[23] *Kilpin v Kilpin* (1834) 1 My & K 520; *M'Fadden v Jenkyns* (1842) 1 Ph 153; *Jones v Lock* (1865) 1 Ch App 25; *Grey v IRC, supra*, CA, *per* Evershed MR at 708, 432, *per* Morris LJ at 719, 440. Both judges refer to 'personal property', but it is thought that they cannot have meant to include leaseholds.

[24] The nature of the requirement of writing under s 53(1)(c) and the effect of failure to observe it are dealt with at p 91 *et seq, infra*.

[25] If, which now seems very unlikely, the owner of an equitable interest in personal property 'disappears from the picture', were he to declare himself a bare trustee of that interest, the declaration would amount to a disposition within s 53(1)(c). See p 87, *supra*.

[26] [1960] AC 1, [1959] 3 All ER 603, HL. Cf *Parker v Parker and Ledsham* [1988] WAR 32.

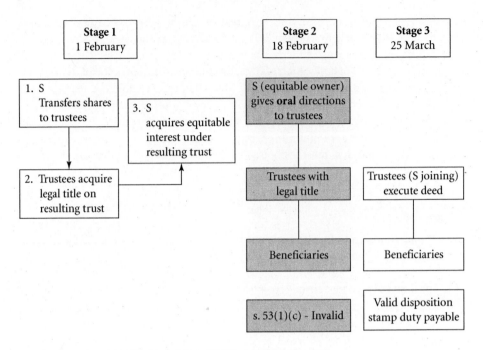

Figure 5.1 *Grey v IRC* [1960] AC 1, [1959] 3 All ER 603, HL

nature.[27] The object of dealing with the matter in this way was to avoid liability to stamp duty.[28] If the directions of 18 February were valid, they would, being oral, attract no duty themselves and the deed of 25 March would likewise attract no duty, because it would not be a 'disposition'. The House of Lords, however, held that the oral direction given by the settlor on 18 February was a purported disposition of an equitable interest within s 53(1)(c) and was thereby rendered invalid, because it was not in writing. Therefore, the deed of 25 March was an effective disposition attracting *ad valorem* stamp duty.

Where the declaration of trust is in respect of an equitable interest in land, writing is already required by s 53(1)(b).[29] It may, however, be important to know whether s 53(1)(c) also applies, as the requirement of writing, and probably the effects of absence of writing, differ[30] under the two provisions. Although the point is not referred to, the reasoning in *Grey v IRC*[31] would seem to apply equally to interests in land and interests in pure personalty.

---

[27] See *Grey v IRC per* Evershed MR in CA [1958] 2 All ER 428, 432.

[28] In (1984) 47 MLR 385 (B Green), it is pointed out that an effective scheme might have been for: (i) the settlor to declare himself a trustee on the specified trusts; (ii) the settlor to appoint the trustees as new trustee in his place, and to transfer the shares to them; and (iii) for the trustee to execute a deed of declaration of trust.

[29] *Tierney v Wood* (1854) 19 Beav 330.

[30] For the requirements and effect of s 53(1)(c), see below.

[31] *Supra.*

(C) DISPOSITIONS OF EQUITABLE INTERESTS *INTER VIVOS*

Section 53(1)(c) of the Law of Property Act 1925 provides:

> A disposition of an equitable interest or trust subsisting[32] at the time of the disposition, must be in writing signed by the person disposing of the same, or by his agent thereunto lawfully authorised in writing or by will.

Unlike s 53(1)(b), but like s 2 of the Law of Property (Miscellaneous Provisions) Act 1989, s 53(1)(c) requires that the disposition shall actually be in writing, and not merely evidenced in writing; signature must be by the person making the disposition, or, like s 2, but unlike s 53(1)(b), by his duly authorized agent. The requirement that the disposition must actually be in writing, if not complied with at the time, clearly cannot be rectified subsequently,[33] and accordingly it always seems to have been assumed that absence of writing makes the purported disposition void. This view seems to be implicit in two important decisions of the House of Lords: *Grey v IRC*[34] and *Oughtred v IRC*.[35] The disposition may be contained in more than one document, provided that there is sufficient reference in the signed document to the other or others.[36]

The meaning of the phrase 'disposition of an equitable interest or trust' has given rise to difficulties. Some points have been clarified by the courts, while others remain more or less uncertain.

(i) Direct assignment

The phrase clearly includes a direct assignment or transfer by a beneficiary of his equitable interest to another. It will accordingly be void if not in writing.

(ii) Direction to trustee

As was explained in the previous subsection, *Grey v IRC*[37] establishes that the term 'disposition' includes the case in which the equitable owner directs the trustee to hold the property in trust for a third party.[38]

(iii) Disposition to fiduciary

It was held in *Re Tyler's Fund Trusts*[39] that there is no need, where the assignee is to take in a fiduciary capacity, for the writing to contain particulars of the trust. In that case, a written direction by the equitable owner to the trustee telling him to hold the trust property on trusts previously communicated orally was held to be valid, the judge treating the equitable owner as having assigned his equitable interest to the trustee as a fiduciary. There is no necessary conflict between this decision and *Grey v IRC*,[40] but it is unfortunate that the earlier decision was not referred to.

---

[32] See *Kinane v Mackie-Conteh* [2005] EWCA Civ 45, [2005] WTLR 345 at [17].
[33] Except, of course, by a fresh independent disposition in writing.
[34] [1960] AC 1, [1959] 3 All ER 603. Cf (1959) 17 CLJ 99 (J C Hall).
[35] [1960] AC 206, [1959] 3 All ER 623, HL.
[36] *Re Danish Bacon Co Ltd Staff Pension Fund* [1971] 1 All ER 486, [1971] 1 WLR 248.
[37] *Supra*, HL.   [38] See pp 89–90, *supra*.   [39] [1967] 3 All ER 389, [1967] 1 WLR 1269.
[40] *Supra*, HL.

Figure 5.2 *Oughtred v IRC* [1960] AC 206, [1959] 3 All ER 623, HL

(iv) Contract to assign an equitable interest

In *Oughtred v IRC*,[41] there was a settlement under which shares were limited to O for life with remainder to her son P absolutely. By an oral agreement on 18 June 1956, made between O and P, it was agreed that, on 26 June 1956, they would effect an exchange: P would make over to his mother his reversionary interest in the settled shares and she, in exchange, would make over to him absolutely a separate block of shares in the same company, which were her absolute property. In an attempt to save liability to stamp duty, the agreement was carried into effect on 26 June by the execution of three documents: (i) a transfer of her own shares by O to P; (ii) a deed of release whereby O and P gave a release to the trustees in respect of anything done by the trustees in the execution of the trusts of the settlement; and (iii) a transfer (referred to as 'the disputed transfer') of the previously settled shares by the trustees to O. Stamp duty was claimed on the disputed transfer.

One contention by the Inland Revenue was that the oral agreement of 18 June could not, because of s 53(1)(c), effect a disposition of P's reversionary interest, which remained vested in him until the execution of the disputed transfer. The contrary argument was that the effect of the oral contract was to make P a constructive trustee of the reversionary interest in favour of O, under a well-settled principle discussed later,[42] so that the entire beneficial interest had already passed to her before the disputed transfer was executed and, as we have seen, a constructive trust is exempted from the requirement of writing by s 53(2). The transfer on this basis, it was said, would only operate on the bare legal estate and would not attract stamp duty.

The basis of the decision adopted by the majority was that, even if the oral agreement was effective to pass the equitable interest in the settled shares to the mother, the transfer,

---

[41] *Supra; Bishop Square Ltd v IRC* (1997) 78 P & CR 169, CA. See (1984) 47 MLR 385 (B Green). See also [2006] Conv 390 (P G Turner), discussing the Australian case of *Halloran v Minister Administering National Park and Wildlife Act 1974* [2006] HCA 3, (2006) 80 AJLR 519.

[42] See p 164, *infra*.

as the instrument by which the transaction was completed, was nonetheless a conveyance on sale within s 54 of the Stamp Act 1891, but different views were expressed as to whether s 53(2) applied. In *Neville v Wilson*,[43] the Court of Appeal applied what they described as the 'unquestionably correct' view of Lord Radcliffe that a specifically enforceable agreement to assign an interest in property creates an equitable interest in the assignee under a constructive trust, and that s 53(2) operates to exclude the requirement of writing under s 53(1)(c) in such a case.

(v) Disclaimer

This arose in *Re Paradise Motor Co Ltd*,[44] in which 350 shares had been transferred into the name of J by way of gift. By the time of the action, 300 shares had been re-transferred into the name of the donor, W, and the remaining shares were still in the name of J. The evidence established an attempted disclaimer by J of the gift, and it was held that this was effective, although merely oral, notwithstanding s 53(1)(c). The short answer, it was said, '*is that a disclaimer operates by way of avoidance and not by way of disposition*'. It is unfortunate that this was not further explained, particularly since, in s 205(1)(ii), 'disposition' is defined as including a conveyance, which is in turn defined as including a disclaimer. This definition, of course, applies only where the context does not otherwise require, which does not seem to be the case here.

(vi) Transfer by bare trustee of the legal estate

Vandervell v IRC[45] established that s 53(1)(c) does not apply to the case in which the equitable owner directs the trustee to transfer the legal estate to a third party and the transfer duly takes place. In that case, Mr Vandervell transferred money and shares in Vandervell Products Ltd ('the company') to a trustee company that he set up, called Vandervell Trustees Ltd, to be held on trust for his children. Later, he wished to found a chair of pharmacology at the Royal College for Surgeons and the plan was to arrange for the transfer of a block of shares in the company, held by a bank as his nominee, to the College and for dividends to be paid on the shares sufficient to found the chair. As part of the plan, the College agreed to give the trustee company an option to purchase the shares for £5,000. The trust on which the trustee company was to hold the option was not defined and it was decided that it was held on a resulting trust for Mr Vandervell, with unfortunate tax consequences for him. In pursuance of the plan, the bank, as legal owner of the shares, but holding them as a bare trustee, transferred them, as directed by Mr Vandervell, to the College.

In dismissing the argument that no beneficial interest passed to the College in the absence of a writing signed by the equitable owner, Lord Upjohn pointed out[46] that the

---

[43] [1997] Ch 144, [1996] 3 All ER 171, CA, noted [1996] Conv 368 (M P Thompson); [1996] CLJ 436 (R Nolan); (1997) 113 LQR 213 (P Milne); (1997) 6 Nott LJ 86 (G Watt).

[44] [1968] 2 All ER 625, [1968] 1 WLR 1125, CA; *Sembaliuk v Sembaliuk* (1985) 15 DLR (4th) 303; *Re Smith (decd)* [2001] 3 All ER 552. See Meagher, Gummow and Lehane, *Equity: Doctrine and Remedies*, 3rd edn, p 223; [1979] Conv 17 (G Battersby).

[45] [1967] 2 AC 291, [1967] 1 All ER 1, HL; (1966) 24 CLJ 19 (G Jones); (1967) 31 Conv 175 (S M Spencer); (1967) 30 MLR 461 (N Strauss); [1979] Conv 17 (G Battersby); (1984) 47 MLR 385 (B Green); [2002] 61 CLJ 169 (R C Nolan).

[46] At 311. There seems to be much to be said for Harman LJ's succinct statement in CA that '*s 53(1)(c) in dealing with dispositions of an equitable interest, only applies where the disponer is not also the controller of the legal interest*': [1965] 2 All ER 37, 49.

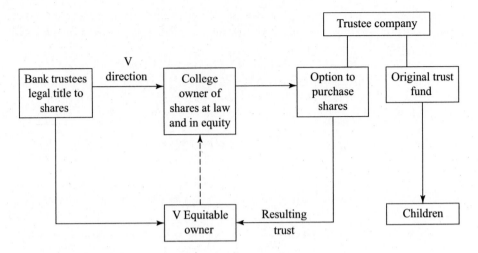

Figure 5.3 *Vandervell v IRC* [1967] 2 AC 291, [1967] 1 All ER 1, HL

object of the section is 'to prevent hidden oral transactions in equitable interests in fraud of those truly entitled, and making it difficult, if not impossible, for the trustees to ascertain who are in truth his [sic] beneficiaries'. However, he continued, when the beneficial owner 'owns the whole beneficial estate and is in a position to give directions to his bare trustee with regard to the legal as well as the equitable estate there can be no possible ground for invoking the section where the beneficial owner wants to deal with the legal estate as well as the equitable estate'. Accordingly, if the bare trustee, on the directions of the beneficial owner who intends the beneficial interest to pass, transfers the legal estate to a third party, that third party will also acquire the beneficial interest without any need for any further document. Although a convenient decision, its reasoning is not altogether convincing.

(vii) Declaration of new trusts by trustee with assent of beneficiary

In *Re Vandervell's Trusts (No 2)*,[47] the trustee company held an option to purchase shares in the company on such trusts as might be declared by the trustee company or Mr Vandervell and, as was seen above, pending such declaration of trust on a resulting trust for Mr Vandervell. It exercised the option by using moneys held on trust for Mr Vandervell's children, and informed the Revenue authorities that the shares would henceforth be held by it on the trusts of the children's settlement. Dividends on the shares received by the trustee company were paid to the children's settlement.

At first instance, Megarry J had held that there was nothing to negative the resulting trust for Mr Vanderwell, which applied to the shares themselves when the option had been exer-cised, and there seems much to be said for his view. The Court of Appeal, however, reversed his decision, though the *ratio decidendi* is not altogether clear. It is, perhaps, that the acts of

---

[47] [1974] Ch 269, [1974] 1 All ER 47; revsd [1974] Ch 308, [1974] 3 All ER 205, CA. This difficult decision is discussed in (1974) 38 Conv 405 (P J Clarke); [1974] ASCL 528 (J Hackney); (1985) 38 MLR 557 (J W Harris); (1975) 7 OLR 483; [1979] Conv 17 (G Battersby); (1984) 47 MLR 385 (B Green). For an interesting comparison of the judgment of Megarry J at first instance and Denning MR in the Court of Appeal, see (1987) 37 UTLJ 358 (D R Klinck).

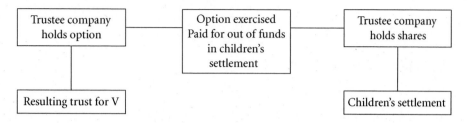

Figure 5.4 *Vandervell's Trusts (No 2)* [1974] Ch 269, [1974] 1 All ER 47; revsd [1974] Ch 308, [1974] 3 All ER 205, CA

the trustee company were sufficient evidence of a declaration of trust, which, made with Mr Vandervell's consent, without any need for writing, operated to create new equitable interests in the children, which automatically put an end to his equitable interest, and not by way of disposition of his equitable interest. It would presumably have been different if Mr Vandervell had declared the new trusts. It seems to have been regarded as significant that the trust for Mr Vandervell was a resulting trust. The comment has been made[48] that 'a "hard-case" may have been avoided; but as to what law the decision may have had, only clarification in future decisions will reveal'.

(viii) Surrender up of equitable interest

There seems little doubt but that a surrender is a disposition,[49] although it has been diffidently suggested that it may not be because it involves the extinguishment of a subsisting equitable interest, and extinction is not disposition.[50]

(ix) Nominations under staff pension fund

Megarry J thought[51] it very doubtful whether the section would apply to a nomination made under a staff pension fund, where a member had power to appoint a nominee to receive the moneys otherwise due to his personal representatives in the event of his death, and this view was accepted by counsel for the defendant in *Gold v Hill*.[52]

(x) Declaration of trust by equitable owner

As was explained above, this would seem to constitute a disposition if it were a case in which the equitable owner 'disappears from the picture'.[53] However, since the decision in

[48] J W Harris, op cit.

[49] See *per* Lord Hoffman in *Newlon Housing Trust v Alsulaimen* [1999] 1 AC 313, [1998] 4 All ER 1, HL (actual decision on meaning of 'disposition' in s 37(2) of the Matrimonial Causes Act 1973).

[50] (1960) BTR 20 (J G Monroe). The suggestion is not accepted by Meagher, Gummow, and Lehane, op cit, p 214.

[51] In *Re Danish Bacon Co Ltd Staff Pension Fund Trusts* [1971] 1 All ER 486, [1971] 1 WLR 248. The decision in that case that it was not a testamentary paper within the Wills Act 1837 was applied by the Privy Council in *Baird v Baird* [1990] 2 AC 548, [1990] 2 All ER 300, PC, noted [1990] Conv 458 (G Kodilinye); (1990) 4 TL & P 103 (Meryl Thomas).

[52] [1999] 1 FLR 54 (no difference where nomination expressed in the form of a trust).

[53] See p 87, *supra*.

Nelson v Greening & Sykes (Builders) Ltd,[54] it seems very unlikely that such a declaration will be held to constitute a disposition within s 53(1)(c).

(xi) Variation of Trusts Act 1958

The relationship between this Act and s 53(1)(c) is dealt with in Chapter 22, section 3.

(xii) Statutory definition of 'disposition' and 'equitable interest'

The House of Lords, in *Rye v Rye*,[55] held that 'conveyance' in s 205(1)(ii) of the Law of Property Act 1925, the definition section, applies only to an instrument in writing as distinct from an oral disposition. In the same subsection, 'disposition' is defined as including 'a conveyance and also a devise, bequest or an appointment of property contained in a will'. On the basis of the decision in *Rye v Rye*,[56] 'disposition' would likewise appear to be restricted to an instrument in writing. If this were to be so, an oral disposition would not be a 'disposition' within the meaning of the Act and would not be caught by s 53(1)(c). This would be a strange result. The point has not yet come before the courts, which might get over the difficulty by making use of the phrase *'unless the context otherwise requires'*, which governs all of the definitions in s 205.

Further, the definition of 'equitable interest' in s 205(1)(x)[57] is in terms of interests in or over land. It always seems to have been assumed, however, although the point has not been taken in the cases, that s 53(1)(c) applies equally to equitable interests in personalty, and it is now probably too late to argue to the contrary.[58]

(D) 'EQUITY WILL NOT PERMIT A STATUTE TO BE USED AS AN INSTRUMENT OF FRAUD'

All of the statutory provisions that have been discussed have their origin in the Statute of Frauds 1677, the purpose of which appears from its title—namely, to prevent the injustice that was thought likely to occur from perjury or fraud when oral evidence was admitted.[59] Although the Court of Chancery was bound by statute, it nevertheless regarded itself as having power to intervene where the strict application of the statute would actually promote the fraud that it was intended to prevent. Until the Law of Property (Miscellaneous Provisions) Act 1989, the leading example of the maxim heading this section was the equitable doctrine of part performance.[60] Since that Act, however, this doctrine has had no part to play in contracts concerning land.

In the leading case of *Rochefoucauld v Boustead*,[61] it was said:

> It is further established...that the Statute of Frauds does not prevent the proof of a fraud; and that it is fraud on the part of a person to whom land is conveyed as a trustee, and who knows it was so conveyed, to deny the trust and claim the land himself. Consequently, notwithstanding the statute, it is competent for a person claiming land conveyed to another to

---

[54] [2007] EWCA Civ 1358, [2007] All ER (D) 270 (Dec), [2008] Times, 22 January.

[55] [1962] AC 496, [1962] 1 All ER 146, HL.   [56] *Supra*, HL.

[57] As amended by the Trusts of Land and Appointment of Trustees Act 1996.

[58] See (1984) 47 MLR 385 (B Green).

[59] See (1947) 63 LQR (E Robel); [1983] Am JLH 354 (P Hamburger); (1984) 43 CLJ 306 (T G Youdan).

[60] See *Steadman v Steadman* [1976] AC 536, [1974] 2 All ER 977, HL.

[61] [1897] 1 Ch 196, 206, CA. Cf *Wratten v Hunter* [1978] 2 NSWLR 367.

prove by parol evidence that it was so conveyed upon trust for the claimant, and that the grantee, knowing the facts, is denying the trust and relying upon the form of conveyance and the statute, in order to keep the land himself.

It is not necessary that the actual conveyance shall have been fraudulently obtained, nor is there any need for the conveyance to include any express stipulation that the grantee is in so many words to hold as trustee: 'The fraud which brings the principle into play arises as soon as the absolute character of the conveyance is set up for the purpose of defeating the beneficial interest.'[62]

It is clear that the Court of Appeal in *Rochefoucauld v Boustead*[63] were actually enforcing the express trust, notwithstanding the absence of writing and the provisions of the statute. Lindley LJ, giving the judgment of the court, said in terms:

> The trust which the plaintiff has established is clearly an express trust... which both plaintiff and defendant intended to create. This case is not one in which an equitable obligation arises although there may have been no intention to create a trust. The intention to create a trust existed from the first.

This is how the decision was understood and applied by Ungoed-Thomas J at first instance in *Hodgson v Marks*,[64] in which the plaintiff had transferred a house to one Evans, it being orally agreed between her and Evans that the house was to remain hers although held in Evans' name. At first instance, no attempt was made to rely on s 53(2), which excludes from the operation of s 53(1) resulting, implied, and constructive trusts. In the Court of Appeal,[65] the actual decision was on the basis of s 53(2), but the Court seems to have taken the same view as Ungoed-Thomas J on the point being discussed, because it was observed: 'Quite plainly Mr Evans could not have placed any reliance on s 53, for that would have been to use the section as an instrument of fraud.'[66]

Unfortunately, the Court of Appeal in *Bannister v Bannister*,[67] although apparently intending to apply *Rochefoucauld v Boustead*,[68] treated it as a case of constructive trust and, for this reason, excluded from s 53(1); this view has been followed without discussion

---

[62] *Bannister v Bannister* [1948] 2 All ER 133, 136, CA; followed in *Staden v Jones* [2008] EWCA Civ 936, [2008] 2 FLR 1931.

[63] *Supra*, CA. See also *Davies v Otty (No 2)* (1865) 35 Beav 208, in which Romilly MR said: 'I am of opinion that it is not honest to keep the land. If so, this is a case in which, in my opinion, the Statute of Frauds does not apply.' However, he then went on to say that the plaintiff must succeed on the basis of resulting trust. The two grounds are inconsistent alternatives.

[64] [1971] Ch 892, [1970] 3 All ER 513.

[65] [1971] Ch 892, [1971] 2 All ER 684. The main point of the decision was whether the plaintiff had an overriding interest under s 70(1)(g) of the Land Registration Act 1925 (repealed). See (1971) 35 Conv 255 (I Leeming); (1973) 36 MLR 25 (R H Maudsley). See the much-criticized decision in *Peffer v Rigg* [1978] 3 All ER 745, [1977] 1 WLR 285, and comment in (1977) 93 LQR 341 (R J Smith); (1977) 36 CLJ 227 (D Hayton); (1977) 41 Conv 207 (F R Crane); [1985] CLJ 280 (M P Thompson). In Law Com No 254, para 3.44, it is said that it is generally assumed that the reasoning in that case cannot be supported.

[66] Ungoed-Thomas J thought that the defendant, a purchaser for value without notice from Evans, would likewise be unable to rely on s 53(1), but this point was left open in the Court of Appeal.

[67] [1948] 2 All ER 133, CA. On the plaintiff's oral undertaking that the defendant would be allowed to live in a cottage rent-free for as long as she desired, the defendant agreed to sell to him, at a price well below the contemporary value of the two cottages, that and an adjacent cottage. The conveyance executed in due course contained no reference to the plaintiff's undertaking. Subsequently, the plaintiff claimed possession of the premises occupied by the defendant and claimed that the alleged trust contained in the oral understanding was defeated by the absence of writing.

[68] *Supra*, CA.

in subsequent decisions. For example, in *Re Densham*,[69] Goff J said:

> To hold such an agreement unenforceable unless in writing…is in my opinion contrary to equitable principles, because once the agreement is formed it would be unconscionable for a party to set up the statute and repudiate the agreement. Accordingly, in my judgment he or she becomes a constructive trustee of the property so far as necessary to give effect to the agreement. That, in my judgment, was established long ago in *Rochefoucauld v Boustead*[70]…

As previously indicated, the court in *Rochefoucauld v Boustead* did not impose a constructive trust, and it is respectfully suggested that it is at least a little curious to say, in effect, that the express trust being unenforceable because it is not in writing, the court will impose a constructive trust to carry out the terms of the express trust. It is submitted that it would be much better in these cases to reach the same result by a straightforward application of the principle in fact laid down in *Rochefoucauld v Boustead*—namely, that, in a case of fraud, equity will allow an express trust to be established by parol evidence notwithstanding the statute. But it would be wrong to deny that the trend in recent cases[71] is in favour of constructive trust.

It has been pointed out that both *Rouchefoucauld v Boustead*[72] and *Bannister v Bannister*[73] were cases in which A had, in effect, transferred land to B, subject to an oral arrangement under which B was to hold it for the benefit of A. Different views have been put forward as to whether the principle of these cases would apply where B had agreed to hold for a third party, C.[74] It was held in *Staden v Jones*[75] that it would. In that case, following divorce, W transferred her half share in the family home to H, with a right to occupy it, on his written undertaking that her half share (or the proceeds of sale) would ultimately (no particular time specified) go to their daughter, D. H subsequently transferred both his own half share and W's half share into the joint names of himself and his second wife. D successfully established a constructive trust in her favour in proceedings against the second wife after the death of H.

Finally it should be observed that it is doubtful whether the maxim would be applied to a modern statute: 'It is no "fraud" to rely on legal rights conferred by Act of Parliament.'[76]

2 THE CREATION OF TRUSTS AND THE DISPOSITION OF EQUITABLE INTERESTS BY WILL

The provisions of the Law of Property Act 1925 do not affect wills,[77] but the requirements of the Wills Act 1837, which apply to both legal estates and equitable interests in all forms of property, both land and pure personalty, are even more stringent. Section 9 of the Act,

---

[69] [1975] 3 All ER 726, 732, [1975] 1 WLR 1519, 1525. See also *Neale v Willis* (1968) 19 P & CR 836; *Binions v Evans* [1972] Ch 359, [1972] 2 All ER 70, CA; *Allen v Snyder* [1977] 2 NSWLR 685.

[70] *Supra*, CA. See Hayton and Marshall, *Cases and Commentary on the Law of Trusts*, 12th edn, [2.19]–[2.29].

[71] Most recently, *Ashburn Anstalt v Arnold* [1989] Ch 1, [1988] 2 All ER 147, CA; *Staden v Jones, supra*, CA.

[72] *Supra*, CA.   [73] *Supra*, CA.

[74] See the contrasting views of Feltham in [1987] Conv 246, and Youdan in [1984] CLJ 306 and [1988] Conv 267.   [75] Supra, CA.

[76] *Midland Bank Trust Co Ltd v Green* [1981] AC 513, 530, [1981] 1 All ER 153, HL, *per* Lord Wilberforce.

[77] Law of Property Act 1925, s 55(a).

as substituted by s 17 of the Administration of Justice Act 1982, provides as follows:

No will shall be valid unless—

(a) it is in writing, and signed by the testator, or by some other person in his presence and by his direction; and

(b) it appears that the testator intended by his signature to give effect to the will; and

(c) the signature is made or acknowledged by the testator in the presence of two or more witnesses present at the same time; and

(d) each witness either—
  (i) attests and signs the will; or
  (ii) acknowledges his signature,
  in the presence of the testator (but not necessarily in the presence of any other witness),

but no form of attestation shall be necessary.

Failure to comply with the statutory requirements makes the purported will absolutely void.

It was at one time thought that the cases on fully secret and half-secret trusts[78] represented an exception to the operation of s 9, being a further application of the maxim that 'equity will not permit a statute to be used as an instrument of fraud'.[79] As will be explained later,[80] it can now be regarded as settled that there is no conflict between the rules relating to fully secret and half-secret trusts, and the provisions of the Wills Act 1837, and, accordingly, it would be inappropriate and indeed misleading to discuss the former in this section.

[78] Discussed in Chapter 7, p 127, *infra*.
[79] This was undoubtedly the principle upon which the doctrine of secret trusts was originally based, but in course of time the basis of the doctrine has changed.
[80] See p 128, *infra*.

6

COMPLETELY AND INCOMPLETELY CONSTITUTED TRUSTS

Beneficiaries under a trust may be 'volunteers'—that is, pure recipients of bounty, for example, where a person sets up a trust for family members—or they may have given consideration—for example, employees under a pension scheme trust—or be treated in equity as having given consideration as being within the marriage consideration. Section 1 of this chapter considers how a trust should be constituted—that is, set up.

Where everything necessary has been done and the trust has, as it is said, been completely constituted, it can be enforced equally by a person who has given consideration and by a volunteer. However, where the trust property is not vested in the trustee—that is, where there is merely an undertaking or covenant to create a trust—although it may be enforced by a beneficiary who has given consideration, it cannot be enforced by a volunteer. The maxim that 'equity will not assist a volunteer' applies. The position of a volunteer is discussed in section 2. Further considerations apply in the case of a trust of a chose in action: these are discussed in section 3, and this leads on to the difficulties surrounding the trust of the benefit of a contract for a volunteer.

Section 5 looks at trusts of future property, and the final section considers the exceptions to the maxim that 'equity will not assist a volunteer'.

1 THE PERFECT CREATION OF A TRUST

The classic statement of the law as to what is meant by the perfect creation, or complete constitution, of an *inter vivos* trust is to be found in the judgment of Turner LJ in the leading case of *Milroy v Lord*:[1]

> ...in order to render a voluntary settlement valid and effectual, the settlor must have done everything which, according to the nature of the property comprised in the settlement, was necessary to be done in order to transfer the property and render the settlement binding

---

[1] (1862) 4 De GF & J 264, at 274–275. Hayton and Marshall, *Cases and Commentary on the Law of Trusts*, 12th edn, [4.02, n 8], point out that, although treated as a voluntary settlement, the deed was, in fact, expressed to be made in consideration of one dollar. In *Mountford v Scott* [1975] Ch 258, [1975] 1 All ER 198, CA, payment of £1 was treated as valuable consideration enabling a decree of specific performance to be granted. See [1982] Conv 352 (S Smith); *Dean and Westham Holdings Pty Ltd v Lloyd* [1990] 3 WAR 235.

upon him. He may, of course, do this by actually transferring the property to the persons for whom he intends to provide, and the provision will then be effectual, and it will be equally effectual if he transfers the property to a trustee for the purposes of the settlement, or declares that he himself holds in trust for those purposes;...but, in order to render the settlement binding, one or other of these modes must...be resorted to, for there is no equity in this court to perfect an imperfect gift. The cases I think go further to this extent, that if the settlement is intended to be effectuated by one of the modes to which I have referred, the court will not give effect to it by applying another of those modes. If it is intended to take effect by transfer; the court will not hold the intended transfer to operate as a declaration of trust, for then every imperfect instrument would be made effectual by being converted into a perfect trust.

Each of the two alternative modes of constituting an *inter vivos* trust—the effective transfer of the trust property to trustees, or the declaration by the settlor that he is a trustee thereof—requires further consideration.[2]

It should be observed that a trust created by will cannot fail on the ground that it is incompletely constituted. On the death of the testator, the trust property will vest in his personal representatives, who[3] will be under a duty to vest it in the trustees appointed by the testator. As we shall see,[4] the trust will be enforceable even if, for example, all of the trustees appointed predecease the testator, or all disclaim the trust. The personal representatives in whom the trust property must, in every case, vest initially would, in such circumstances, themselves hold as trustees until other trustees were appointed.

(A) THE EFFECTIVE TRANSFER OF THE TRUST PROPERTY TO TRUSTEES

(i) Settlor the owner of the property both at law and in equity

Here, he must normally, if he intends to constitute the trust by transfer, vest the legal interest in the property in the trustee: exceptionally, if he cannot do this, the trust may nevertheless be effective if it can be established that the settlor has done everything in his power, according to the nature of the property given, to give the trustee a complete legal title. What is necessary to pass the legal title depends on the nature of the property: thus (a) in the case of land, whether freehold or leasehold, there must be a deed;[5] (b) in the case of personal chattels capable of passing by delivery, there must be either delivery or a deed of gift;[6] and (c) in the case of registered shares, there must be an appropriate entry in the company's register made in pursuance of a proper instrument of transfer.[7]

---

[2] See *Caroyo Property Ltd v Total Australia Ltd* [1987] 2 Qd R 11, in which Connolly J cited the text above.

[3] Subject to their rights and duties for the purposes of administration of the estate, eg to pay the deceased's debts.   [4] See p 357, *infra*.

[5] Law of Property Act 1925, s 52(1). When electronic conveyancing is introduced an appropriate document in electronic form will be regarded as a deed: Land Registration Act 2002, s 91(5).

[6] *Cochrane v Moore* (1890) 25 QBD 57, CA; *Re Cole* [1964] Ch 175, [1963] 3 All ER 433, CA; *Thomas v Times Book Co Ltd* [1966] 2 All ER 241, [1966] 1 WLR 911 (this concerned the original manuscript of *Under Milk Wood*); *Balding v Ashley* (1991) unreported, CA (registration of car in name of alleged donee ineffective, but handing over keys could constitute constructive delivery); and see [1953] CLJ 355 (J W A Thornely); (1964) 27 MLR 357 (A L Diamond). See *Richert v Stewards' Charitable Foundation* [2005] BCSC 211, [2005] WTLR 371.

[7] Including the statutory stock transfer form under the Stock Transfer Act 1963, as amended by the Stock Exchange (Completion of Bargains) Act 1976. Note, however, that neglect of inessential matters on a transfer

In *Milroy v Lord*,[8] the attempt to create a trust failed, the legal title not having been vested in the trustee due to the fact that the wrong form of transfer was used for the purpose of transferring the bank shares that were intended to constitute the trust property. This was distinguished in *Jaffa v Taylor Gallery Ltd*,[9] in which a physical transfer of the trust property to the trustees was held not to be required. The trust property, a painting, was in the hands of a third party as agent of the settlor. By a document, the settlor purported to give the painting to his three children. As two of the children were minors, the settlor 'placed their interests in the hands of trustees'. This last statement was not further explained, nor was it stated whether or not the document was under seal, which, as the law then stood, was needed for a valid deed. Each trustee agreed to act and was given a copy of the document. It was held that the declaration of trust constituted a transfer of property in the painting to the trustees, the judge observing that he 'could not conceive that a physical transfer had to take place and indeed it would be absurd so to find when one trustee was in Northern Ireland, another in England and when the third owner was the adult third plaintiff'.

Milroy v Lord[10] is also a leading authority for the rule that if a prospective settlor attempts to set up a trust by transferring property to a trustee and the attempted transfer is for any reason ineffective, it is impossible to construe it as a declaration of trust. Exactly the same principle applies where a prospective donor attempts to transfer property to a person beneficially and the transfer is ineffective. In neither case is there an equity to complete the imperfect gift by construing it as a declaration of trust, whether the imperfect gift was direct or through the intervention of trustees. There is a vital distinction between an intention to transfer property and an intention to retain it, albeit in an altered capacity as trustee. An intention to do the former, even though the execution is ineffective, cannot be construed as the latter, quite different, intention.[11] An illustration is to be found in *Richards v Delbridge*,[12] in which JD, who was possessed of certain leasehold business premises, indorsed and signed on the lease a memorandum in these terms: 'This deed and all thereto belonging I give to EBR from this time forth, with all the stock-in-trade', EBR being JD's infant grandson. JD shortly afterwards delivered the lease to EBR's mother on his behalf. Subsequently, after JD's death, it was claimed that there was a trust in favour of EBR. It was held, however, that there was no effective transfer of the lease[13] and, further, that the ineffective attempt to transfer could not be construed as a declaration of trust.

More recent cases have modified the strictness of the rule. Thus, although the legal title may remain vested in the settlor, an attempted transfer by him to a trustee may nevertheless be effective in equity and may enable an enforceable trust to be established

---

is not necessarily fatal to a transfer's validity, but may be treated as a mere irregularity and disregarded: *Re Paradise Motor Co Ltd* [1968] 2 All ER 625, [1968] 1 WLR 1125, CA. As to electronic transfer under the CREST system, see (1996) 146 NLJ 964 (R Pinner).

8 (1862) 4 De GF & J 264, See also *Re Wale* [1956] 3 All ER 280, [1956] 1 WLR 1346; *Spellman v Spellman* [1961] 2 All ER 498, [1961] 1 WLR 921, CA; (1992) 13 QL 86 (Suzanne Rigney).

9 (1990) Times, 21 March.   10 *Supra.*   11 See Maitland, *Equity*, 2nd (Brunyate) edn, p 72.

12 (1874) LR 18 Eq 11. See also the cases cited in fn 8, *supra.*

13 This would have required an assignment under seal: Real Property Act 1845, s 3, now replaced by Law of Property Act 1925, s 52(1).

where the settlor has done everything in his power to divest himself of the property in favour of the trustee.[14] Where this is the position, the property is regarded as effectively transferred in equity, the settlor retaining the bare legal title on trust for the transferee.[15] Thus, in *Re Rose*,[16] the deceased executed two transfers in proper form dated March 1943, each in respect of 10,000 shares in an unlimited company, one transfer being in favour of his wife beneficially, and the other in favour of his wife and X as trustees. At the date of their execution, the transfers and the related share certificates were handed to the transferees. The legal title to the shares could, of course, only pass by an appropriate entry in the register of the company, the articles of association of which authorized the directors to refuse to register any transfer. The transfers were, in fact, registered on 30 June 1943. The deceased died on 16 February 1947, and whether or not estate duty was payable on the shares transferred by the two transfers of 30 March 1943 depended upon whether the transfers were effective before 10 April 1943. Although the legal title clearly did not vest in the respective transferees until 30 June 1943, the principle set out above was laid down. It was accordingly held that, the deceased having 'done all in his power to divest himself of and to transfer to the transferees the whole of the right, title and interest, legal and equitable, in the shares in question',[17] the gift of the beneficial interest in the shares had been made and completed on 30 March 1943. Between that date and 30 June 1943, the deceased was a trustee of the bare legal title for the transferees.[18] Most recently, in *Pennington v Waine*,[19] it was held that the delivery of the share transfers required in *Re Rose*[20] may be dispensed with in circumstances in which it would be unconscionable to recall the gift. This further modification of the principle established by *Re Rose* arguably goes too far.[21] And it has been suggested that the satisfactory outcome of the case could have been reached by a different route.[22]

---

[14] The same principle applies to the case of a gift to a donee beneficially.

[15] The transferee may himself be a trustee, or may take beneficially.

[16] [1952] Ch 499, [1951] 1 All ER 1217, CA. It is submitted that this decision is unlikely to be upset, notwithstanding the criticisms in (1976) 40 Conv 139 (L McKay). See also [1998] CLJ (Sarah Lawrie and P Todd). It was applied in *Mascall v Mascall* (1984) 50 P & CR 119, CA (gift of land complete when father handed over transfer and land certificate to son, who was left to have transfer stamped and title in land register altered), discussed (1985) 82 LSG 1629 (H W Wilkinson), and see (1999) 50 NILQ 90 (A Dowling). See also *Re Fry* [1946] Ch 312, [1946] 2 All ER 106; *Re Rose* [1949] Ch 78, [1948] 2 All ER 971; *Vandervell v IRC* [1967] 1 AC 291, 330, [1967] 1 All ER 1, 18, HL, *per* Lord Wilberforce; *Corin v Patton* (1990) 92 ALR 1.

[17] *Re Rose* [1952] Ch 499, 515, [1952] 1 All ER 1217, 1225, *per* Jenkins LJ.

[18] The Court of Appeal actually considered the case of the transfer to the wife beneficially, saying that the same principle would apply in the case of the transfer to trustees, in which there would be a sub-trust in favour of the ultimate beneficiaries. See *Macmillan Inc v Bishopsgate Investment Trust plc (No 3)* [1995] 3 All ER 747, [1995] 1 WLR 978, noted [1995] LMCLQ 308 (Joanna Bird).

[19] [2002] EWCA Civ 227, [2002] 4 All ER 215, noted [2002] LMCLQ 296 (H Tjio and T M Yeo); (2003) 17 Tru LI 35 (D Ladds); [2003] PCB 393 (Judith Morris); [2003] CLJ 263 (Abigail Doggett); [2003] Conv 364 (J Garton). The statement in the text represents the opinion of Arden and Schiemann LJJ. Clarke LJ went even further. His view was that signing a share transfer form without delivery would constitute a valid equitable assignment where there was no intention of revoking it.

[20] *Supra*, CA.   [21] See (2002) 38 T & ELJ 4 (J N McGhee); [2003] Conv 192 (Margaret Halliwell).

[22] See [2006] Conv 411 (Chee Ho Than), arguing as one possibility that the case might have been decided on a contractual basis—namely, that the donor's agent communicated an offer to complete the transfer of shares in consideration of the donee completing Form 288A, which he did.

(ii) Settlor possessing merely an equitable interest in the property

Here, a trust[23] of that equitable interest can be completely constituted by an assignment[24] of that interest to trustees: there is no need for him to compel a transfer of the legal title, even if he can do so. As we have already seen, a disposition of an equitable interest must be in writing.[25] Thus, in *Kekewich v Manning*,[26] trustees held certain shares on trust for A for life with remainder to B absolutely. B, in effect, executed a voluntary assignment of his equitable revisionary interest to C upon trust for D. It was held, even on the assumption that the assignment was purely voluntary, that a valid trust was effectively created of the equitable interest, although the legal title, of course, remained vested in the original trustees.

(B) A DECLARATION OF TRUST

Whether the settlor has a legal or merely an equitable interest in property, he can completely constitute a trust by declaring[27] that he holds it on trust for the intended beneficiary. 'Where a declaration of trust is relied on the Court,' it has been said,[28] 'must be satisfied that a present irrevocable declaration of trust has been made.' A settlor, however, 'need not use the words, "I declare myself a trustee", but he must do something which is equivalent to it and use expressions which have that meaning'.[29] It is even possible for a declaration of trust to be implied from conduct.[30]

It may be added that although 'equity will not assist a volunteer' and thus will not perfect an imperfect gift or an incompletely constituted trust, it will not strive officiously to defeat a gift. Accordingly, the principle that, where a gift is incompletely constituted, the court will not hold it to operate as a declaration of trust does not prevent the court from construing it to be a trust if that interpretation is permissible as a matter of construction, which may be a benevolent construction.[31]

The evidence was held to establish a trust in *Paul v Constance*,[32] in which C, separated from his wife, the defendant, began living with the plaintiff as man and wife in 1967. C received £950 as damages for personal injuries in 1973, and he and the plaintiff decided to use it to open a deposit account, which, because they were not married, was put in the name of C alone. On many occasions, both before and after the deposit, C told the plaintiff that the money was as much hers as his. After C's death, it was held that, in the context of

---

[23] Strictly a sub-trust.

[24] In *Re McArdle* [1951] Ch 669, [1951] 1 All ER 905, CA. Jenkins LJ observed that: 'A voluntary equitable assignment, to be valid, must be in all respects complete and perfect so that the assignee is entitled to demand payment from the trustee or holder of the fund, and that the trustee is bound to make payment to the assignee, with no further act on the part of the assignor remaining to be done to perfect the assignee's title.' Cf *Re Wale* [1956] 3 All ER 280, [1956] 1 WLR 1346; *Letts v IRC* [1956] 3 All ER 588, [1957] 1 WLR 201.

[25] Law of Property Act 1925, s 53(1)(c).

[26] (1851) 1 De GM & G 176, and see *Gilbert v Overton* (1864) 2 Hem & M 110; *Ellison v Ellison* (1802) 6 Ves 656; *Chief Comr of Stamp Duties v ISPT Pty Ltd* (1997) 45 NSWLR 639.

[27] The formal requirements were discussed in Chapter 5.

[28] *Re Cozens* [1913] 2 Ch 478, 486, *per* Neville J.

[29] *Richards v Delbridge* (1874) LR 18 Eq 11, 14, *per* Jessel MR.

[30] See, eg, *Gray v Gray* (1852) 2 Sim NS 273; *Gee v Liddell* (1866) 35 Beav 621; and cf *Re Cozens* [1913] 2 Ch 478. See also *Secretary, Department of Social Security v James* (1990) 95 ALR 615.

[31] *Pennington v Waine* [2002] EWCA Civ 227, [2002] 4 All ER 215, *per* Arden LJ at [61].

[32] [1977] 1 All ER 195, [1977] 1 WLR 527, CA, applied *Rowe v Prance* [1999] 2 FLR 787, noted [1999] Fam Law 721 (M Pawlowski and K Everett); (1999) 10 T & ELJ (R Leonard); [2000] Conv 58 (S Baughan). Cf *Arthur v Public Trustee* (1988) 90 FedLR 203 (Aust).

their relationship, these words could properly be construed as equivalent to a declaration of trust by C of the moneys in the account for C and the plaintiff in equal shares. There was, however, held to be no declaration of trust in *Jones v Lock*,[33] in which a father died shortly after putting a cheque for £900 (received by the father in payment of a mortgage) into the hand of his nine-month-old baby saying 'I give this to baby; it is for himself', and then taking back the cheque and putting it away. And it seems that payments added to a cheque or credit card voucher in settlement of a restaurant bill by way of a tip are not held by the restaurateur on trust.[34] It should, however, be added that there is no need for the declaration of trust to be communicated to the cestui que trust.[35]

(C) THE INTERMEDIATE CASE

Until very recently, it had been thought that *Milroy v Lord*[36] laid down the methods discussed above as two discrete alternative ways of creating a trust. In the novel case of *T Choithram International SA v Pagarani*,[37] the facts did not fall squarely within either of the two methods. The facts, slightly simplified, were that the settlor (now deceased) executed a trust deed, of which he was one of the trustees, establishing a charitable foundation, and immediately afterwards orally purported to give all of his wealth to the foundation. His family had already been provided for. No transfers of his assets took place in his lifetime, although they were registered in the names of the surviving trustees of the foundation after his death. The Privy Council held that the gift 'to the foundation' could only mean 'I give to the trustees of the foundation trust deed to be held by them on the trusts of the foundation trust deed'. Although his words were apparently words of outright gift, they were essentially words of gift on trust. In one composite transaction on the same day, the settlor had declared that he was giving property to a trust that he himself had established and of which he had appointed himself one of the trustees. His conscience was affected, and it would be unconscionable and contrary to the principles of equity to allow him to resile from his gift. In the absence of special factors, where one of a larger body of trustees has the trust property vested in him, he is bound by the trust and must give effect to it by transferring the trust property into the names of all of the trustees. The trustees of the foundation accordingly held the assets on the trusts of the foundation trust deed.

2 THE POSITION OF A VOLUNTEER

(A) MEANING OF THE TERM 'VOLUNTEER'

A beneficiary under a trust is a volunteer unless either he has provided valuable consideration in a common law sense, or he is, as it is said, within the scope of the marriage

---

[33] (1865) 1 Ch App 25. Nor could it have been a gift, as the title to the non-bearer cheque could only have passed by endorsement.

[34] *Nerva v R L & G Ltd* [1995] IRLR 200. Cf *Shabinsky v Horwitz* (1973) 32 DLR (3d) 318.

[35] *Tate v Leithead* (1854) Kay 658; *Middleton v Pollock* (1876) 2 Ch D 104; *Standing v Bowring* (1885) 31 Ch D 282, CA. [36] (1862) 4 De G F & J 264.

[37] [2001] 2 All ER 492, [2001] 1 WLR 1, PC, noted [2001] CLJ 483 (J Hopkins); [2001] Conv 515 (C Rickett).

consideration. So far as value in the common law sense is concerned, reference may be made to the discussion of consideration in works on the law of contract,[38] but some explanation must be given of what is meant by 'marriage consideration'.

Marriage has been said to be 'the most valuable consideration imaginable'[39] and a settlement or trust made or agreed to be made before[40] and in consideration of marriage is accordingly regarded as made for value. The question is who can take advantage of this, or, in other words, who is within the scope of the marriage consideration.[41] It is now clear that only the husband, wife, and issue[42] of the marriage are within the scope of the marriage consideration.[43] Some other cases,[44] which held, or suggested, that other persons such as illegitimate children or children by a former or possible second marriage were within the marriage consideration, can now, it seems only be supported on the ground that the interest of such persons, on the special facts of the cases, were so intermingled with the interests of issue of the marriage that they could not be separated and the latter could only be enforced if the former were also admitted.

(B) THE POSITION BEFORE THE CONTRACTS (RIGHTS OF THIRD PARTIES) ACT 1999

The main importance of knowing whether or not a trust had been completely constituted arose in connection with the enforcement of the trust by a beneficiary thereunder who was a volunteer. If a beneficiary had provided valuable consideration, then he could have the trust enforced even though it had not been completely constituted—that is, he could enforce a contract or covenant to create a trust; but if he was a volunteer, even though he might be specially an object of the intended trust,[45] he would only succeed if the trust had been completely constituted.[46]

---

[38] See, eg, Cheshire, Fifoot, and Furmston, *The Law of Contract*, 15th edn, p 93 *et seq*. Note that a beneficiary under a pension scheme is not a volunteer—see p 18, *supra*.

[39] *A-G v Jacobs-Smith* [1895] 2 QB 341, 354, CA, *per* Kay LJ. Note, however the provisions of s 4(6) of the Land Charges Act 1972, as amended, which put a purchaser for money or money's worth in a better position than one who can only rely on the consideration of marriage. See also *A-G for Ontario v Perry* [1934] AC 477, PC.

[40] A post-nuptial settlement executed in pursuance of an ante-nuptial agreement would be regarded as made for value (*Re Holland* [1902] 2 Ch 360, CA); but neither a post-nuptial settlement made otherwise than in pursuance of an ante-nuptial agreement, nor a mere post-nuptial agreement.

[41] It is not entirely clear whether the formation of a civil partnership is to be treated as equivalent to marriage in this context under the Civil Partnership Act 2004. It is thought not. The Law of Property Act 1925, s 205(1)(xxi), provides that '"valuable consideration" includes marriage' and the 2004 Act, s 261(1), Sch 27, para 7, adds the words 'and formation of a civil partnership', but this definition is only for the purposes of the Act.

[42] Whether children or more remote issue: *Macdonald v Scott* [1893] AC 642, 650, HL, *per* Lord Herschell.

[43] *De Mestre v West* [1891] AC 264, PC; *A-G v Jacobs-Smith* [1895] 2 QB 341, CA; *Re Cook's Settlement's Trusts* [1965] Ch 902, [1964] 3 All ER 898. It is submitted that the position is unaffected by the Family Law Reform Act 1969.

[44] *Newstead v Searles* (1737) 1 Atk 264; *Clarke v Wright* (1861) 6 H & N 849, Ex Ch.

[45] *Re Cook's Settlement Trusts* [1965] Ch 902, [1964] 3 All ER 898.

[46] Note also that if an incompletely constituted trust is enforced by a beneficiary who has given valuable consideration, it enures for the benefit of a volunteer: *Davenport v Bishopp* (1843) 2 Y & C Ch Cas 451; affd (1846) 1 Ph 698.

(i) Beneficiary not a volunteer

Here, the law is unaffected by the 1999 Act. The beneficiary can enforce not only a completely, but also an incompletely, constituted trust. He can, if need be, compel his trustee to bring an action at law for damages for breach of the contract or covenant to create a trust; to such an action, the settlor, in appropriate circumstances, might plead the Limitation Act 1980. In most cases, however, the beneficiary would choose to assert his equitable rights based on the availability of the equitable remedy of specific performance, as a result of which the property contracted or covenanted to be settled would be regarded as subject to a trust. Thus, in *Pullan v Koe*,[47] there was a marriage settlement in 1859 that contained a covenant by the husband and wife with the trustees to settle the wife's after-acquired property of the value of £100 or upwards. In 1879, the wife had received £285, which she had paid into her husband's banking account, on which she had power to draw. Shortly afterwards, part of this sum was invested in two bearer bonds, which remained at the bank until the death of the husband in 1909 and, at the time of the action, were in the possession of the executors. The trustees of the marriage settlement, with the object of benefiting the widow and nine surviving children of the marriage, brought an action against the husband's executors. Any claim by the trustees at law for damages for breach of the covenant would long since have been barred by the Statute of Limitation, since the cause of action had arisen when the covenant was broken in 1879; the court, however, held that the moment at which the wife received the £285, it was specifically bound by the covenant and was consequently subject to a trust enforceable[48] in favour of the wife and children, being persons within the marriage consideration. It seems clear that the beneficiaries, not being volunteers, would have had their interests equally protected, even if the trustees had been unwilling to bring proceedings to enforce the covenant.

It should be noted, however, that even a beneficiary who has provided consideration will be unable to do more than compel his trustee to exercise his remedy at law, where the contract or covenant is one to which the remedy of specific performance is not appropriate so that there is never any property subject to a trust. This is commonly the position where there is a covenant merely to pay money, as in *Stone v Stone*,[49] in which case it was held that an action at law on the covenant to settle £1,000 being barred by the Statute of Limitation, the beneficiaries, although purchasers, were without remedy.

(ii) Beneficiary a volunteer: the equitable rules

If the trust is completely constituted, the fact that a beneficiary is a volunteer is irrelevant: he is just as much entitled to enforce the trust as a cestui que trust who has provided consideration. If, however, the trust is not completely constituted, a volunteer beneficiary will gain no assistance from a court of equity. This can be illustrated by *Re Plumptre's Marriage Settlement*.[50] In that case, under a marriage settlement made in 1878, certain funds coming from the wife's father were settled upon the usual trusts of a wife's fund,

---

[47] [1913] 1 Ch 9; *Sonenco (No 77) Pty Ltd v Silvia* (1989) 89 ALR 437.

[48] The claim could, of course, have been defeated by a bona fide purchaser for value without notice who acquired the legal title, but neither the husband, nor his executors claiming through him, were in this position.

[49] (1869) 5 Ch App 74. In *Pullan v Koe, supra*, a specific fund of money was impressed with a trust. Cf *Beswick v Beswick* [1968] AC 58, [1967] 2 All ER 1197, HL, discussed p 112, *infra*.

[50] [1910] 1 Ch 609; *Jefferys v Jefferys* (1841) Cr & Ph 138; *Re D'Angibau* (1879) 15 Ch D 228, CA.

with an ultimate remainder, in the events that happened, for the wife's statutory next of kin. The settlement contained an after-acquired property clause, which was held to cover a sum of stock given by the husband to the wife, which she subsequently sold and reinvested and which remained registered in her name on her death in 1909. The facts of this case, it will have been observed, are very similar to those in *Pullan v Koe*,[51] and it was likewise held that any action at law would be barred by the Statute of Limitation. By contrast with *Pullan v Koe*, however, the beneficiaries under the settlement who were seeking to enforce the covenant—that is, the next of kin—were not within the marriage consideration, but were mere volunteers. It was accordingly held that they could not enforce the covenant against the husband, as administrator of his wife's estate.

As appears from the above cases, the fact that the obligation is contained in a deed makes no difference in equity, which has no special regard to form.[52] It may well be asked, however, whether the trustees with whom the covenant is made can, or should, bring an action at law for damages, since the common law regards consideration and the formality of a deed as alternative requirements. On this question, it has been held that volunteers cannot compel trustees to take proceedings for damages and, further, that if the trustees ask the court for directions as to what they should do, they will be directed not to take any steps either to compel performance of the covenant or to recover damages through the failure to implement it. Thus, in the leading case of *Re Pryce*,[53] there was a marriage settlement under which the wife covenanted to settle after-acquired property. The beneficial limitations of funds brought into the settlement by the wife (including any after-acquired property) were successive life interests to the wife and the husband, remainder to the children of the marriage (of whom there were never, in fact, any), and an ultimate remainder to the wife's next of kin, who were, of course, volunteers. The husband was dead and the wife did not wish the covenant to be enforced. The court held that the trustees *ought* not to take any steps to compel the transfer or payment to them of the after-acquired property. Notwithstanding powerful academic criticism,[54] *Re Pryce*[55] and *Re Kay's Settlement*[56] were followed in *Re Cook's Settlement Trusts*.[57]

(iii) Beneficiary a covenantee

Even where the cestui que trust is a volunteer, there is a clear decision at first instance[58] that if the covenant is made with him, there is no answer to an action by him at common law on the covenant and substantial damages for breach thereof will be awarded. But, as a volunteer, he will not be able to obtain the equitable remedy of specific performance.

(iv) Performance of unenforceable covenant

It is clear that if the settlor has, in fact, transferred property to trustees in compliance with an unenforceable covenant to settle the same in favour of volunteers, he thereby completely

---

[51] [1913] 1 Ch 9, discussed *supra*, p 107.

[52] See, eg, *Jefferys v Jefferys, supra; Kekewich v Manning* (1851) 1 De GM & G 176.

[53] [1917] 1 Ch 234; *Re Kay's Settlement* [1939] Ch 329, [1939] 1 All ER 245. See 'Incompletely constituted trusts' by R H Maudsley in *Perspectives of Law* (ed R Pound), p 240.

[54] (1960) 76 LQR 100 (D W Elliott); (1962) 76 LQR 228 (J A Hornby). As to the position if trustees do not ask the court for directions, but choose to bring an action, see D W Elliott, op cit; [1988] Conv 19 (D Goddard); R H Maudsley, op cit, p 244; [1967] ASCL 392 (J D Davies).

[55] *Supra.*   [56] *Supra.*   [57] [1965] Ch 902, [1964] 3 All ER 898. See p 117, *infra.*

[58] *Cannon v Hartley* [1949] Ch 213, [1949] 1 All ER 50.

constitutes the trust and cannot thereafter claim to recover the property, which must be held by the trustees on the declared trusts.[59]

(v) Re Ralli's Will Trusts[60]

In this case, the testator, who died in 1899, left a half-share of his residue to his widow for life with remainder to his daughter, Helen, absolutely. By her marriage settlement in 1924, Helen covenanted to assign her revisionary interest in the testator's estate to the trustees on trust after her death, in the events that happened, for persons who were mere volunteers. The widow died in 1961, Helen having predeceased her without having executed an assignment of revisionary interest to the trustees. The plaintiff became the sole surviving trustee of both the will of the testator and Helen's marriage settlement. Helen's personal representatives claimed that her share of residue should be paid over to them, and that they would not then be compelled to pay it over to the plaintiff as trustee of the marriage settlement, as equity would not assist the beneficiaries thereunder being mere volunteers. The court held for the plaintiff on two grounds. The first ground was that, on the true construction of the settlement, Helen had effectively declared herself a trustee of her equitable reversionary interest. Secondly, Buckley J held that it was irrelevant that the plaintiff, the settlement trustee, had acquired the legal title as trustee of the will. The question was: who was entitled in equity? Helen, having covenanted to assign her share to the plaintiff would not be allowed to assert a claim in equity against him, and her personal representatives could be in no better position. The inability of the volunteers under the settlement to enforce their rights against Helen was irrelevant: it was sufficient for them to rely on their claim against the plaintiff as settlement trustee. The trust became completely constituted by the chance acquisition by the sole surviving trustee of the legal estate in a different capacity. If, as might easily have happened, the will trustee and the settlement trustee had been different persons, the result, disregarding the first ground, would have been quite different. Helen's personal representatives would then have been able to claim her share from the will trustee and the volunteers under the marriage settlement would have been unable to compel the enforcement of the covenant. Buckley J's reasoning is not entirely convincing and it is difficult to distinguish *Re Brooks' Settlement Trusts*,[61] which, if it had been cited to the judge, might well have persuaded him to a different conclusion, in favour of the argument put forward by Helen's personal representatives.

(C) CONTRACTS (RIGHTS OF THIRD PARTIES) ACT 1999

The law as stated above has been considerably modified by the Contracts (Rights of Third Parties) Act 1999, although never to the disadvantage of beneficiaries. The Act, which does not apply to contracts entered into before 11 May 2000,[62] provides that a person who is

---

[59] *Paul v Paul* (1882) 20 Ch D 742, CA; *Re Adlard* [1954] Ch 29, [1953] 2 All ER 1437; *Re Ralli's Will Trusts* [1964] Ch 288, [1963] 3 All ER 940.

[60] *Supra*. An analogy may be drawn with the rule in *Strong v Bird* (1874) LR 18 Eq 315, discussed *infra*, p 119 *et seq*.

[61] [1939] Ch 993, [1939] 3 All ER 920.

[62] Contracts (Rights of Third Parties) Act 1999, s 10(2). By s 10(3), a contract made on or after 11 November 1999 may expressly provide that the Act is to apply.

Figure 6.1 *Re Ralli's Will Trusts* [1964] Ch 288, [1963] 3 All ER 940

not a party to a contract[63] may, in his own right, enforce a term of the contract where the term purports to confer a benefit on him.[64] This includes a beneficiary under a contract or covenant[65] to create a trust. The third party must be expressly identified in the contract by name, as a member of a class or as answering a particular description, but need not be in existence when the contract is entered into.[66] It is provided, however, that these provisions do not apply if, on a proper construction of the contract, it appears that the parties did not intend the term to be enforceable by the third party.[67] There is available to the third party any remedy that would have been available to him in an action for breach of contract if he had been a party to the contract: this enables him to sue for damages and obtain substantial damages, but it is thought that a third-party volunteer will still be unable to obtain specific performance, because the Act does not appear to affect the rule that 'equity will not assist a volunteer'.[68]

The Act would not appear to affect the result in cases such as *Re Plumptre's Marriage Settlement*,[69] because the Limitation Act would defeat the claim at law as much at the

---

[63] As to the rights of a beneficiary who is a party to the deed, see *Cannon v Hartley* [1949] Ch 213, [1949] 1 All ER 50, and p 108, *supra*.

[64] Contracts (Rights of Third Parties) Act 1999, s 1(1)(b). On the Act generally, see (2001) 60 CLJ 353 (N Andrews); (2004) 120 LQR 292 (R Stevens). See also *Prudential Assurance Co Ltd v Ayres* [2007] EWHC 775 (Ch), [2007] 3 All ER 946, in which, however, on appeal [2008] EWCA Civ 52, [2008] 1 All ER 1266n, it was held that no question arose on the 1999 Act.

[65] It is clear from the Contracts (Rights of Third Parties) Act 1999, s 7(3) that s 1 of that Act applies both to a simple contract and a specialty.

[66] Ibid, s 1(3).

[67] Ibid, s 1(2). This would seem to leave scope for the same arguments as those considered *infra*, pp 115–117, as to whether there was a trust of the benefit of the covenant.

[68] See *Cannon v Hartley* [1949] Ch 213, [1949] 1 All ER 50. Of course, a mere promise without consideration and not by deed remains unenforceable.

[69] *Supra*.

instance of the next of kin as of the trustee.[70] Further, as noted above, the position in equity is unchanged by the Act. However, in a case such as *Re Pryce*,[71] in which there is no case for the application of the Limitation Act, the next of kin should be able to sue for damages unless the defendant could establish that the parties did not intend the term to be enforceable by a third party, although as volunteers they would still be unable to claim specific performance.[72]

Any right or remedy of the third party that exists or is available apart from the Act is unaffected by it,[73] and the right, if any, of the trustees to sue the settlor is likewise unaffected.[74] We will, therefore, go on to consider how equity sometimes enabled the volunteer to protect his interest, although the volunteer beneficiary is likely to prefer to proceed under the Act.

3 TRUSTS OF A CHOSE IN ACTION

(A) THIRD-PARTY CONTRACT—ACTION FOR DAMAGES BY CONTRACTING PARTY

There is no difficulty over the concept of a chose in action constituting the trust property: to give a simple illustration, if A owes B £250, B may assign the debt to trustees on trust for X and Y equally so as to create an effective trust. Suppose, however, A enters into a contract with B under which A is to confer some benefit upon C. At common law, the rule was that only a person who is a party to a contract can sue on it:[75] this meant that C would be unable to sue either directly or indirectly for the benefit that A had agreed with B to give him. As we have just seen, this rule has been reversed by the Contracts (Rights of Third Parties) Act 1999. This does not affect the rule that if A fails to confer the benefit on C, B, the promisee, can sue A, the promisor, although the nature of the remedy that the court will grant will depend on the circumstances of each case.[76] It is expressly provided that the 1999 Act does not affect any right of the promisee to enforce any term of the contract.[77]

B has always been able to bring an action for damages for breach of contract. The general principle is that a claimant may only recover damages for a loss that he has himself suffered.[78] One exception, as we shall see,[79] is where he entered into the contract as trustee for C, when he can obtain substantial damages measured by the loss to C, but which he

---

[70] Ibid, s 3(2)(b).

[71] *Supra*. If the trustees were asked to sue by the beneficiaries, it is thought that they would be wise to seek the directions of the court rather than rely on *Re Pryce*.

[72] Lewin, *The Law of Trusts*, 18th edn, p 351, suggests that, in the case of a marriage contract, beneficiaries outside the marriage consideration could obtain specific performance.

[73] Ibid, s 7(1).   [74] [1939] Ch 993, [1939] 3 All ER 920.

[75] *Tweddle v Atkinson* (1861) 1 B & S 393. See *Darlington Borough Council v Wiltshier Northern Ltd* [1995] 3 All ER 895, CA and authorities therein cited.

[76] *Snelling v John G Snelling Ltd* [1973] QB 87, [1972] 1 All ER 79.   [77] Section 4.

[78] See, eg, *Alfred McAlpine Construction Ltd v Panatown Ltd* [2001] 1 AC 518, 522, sub nom *Panatown Ltd v Alfred McAlpine Construction Ltd* [2000] 4 All ER 97, 100, HL, *per* Lord Clyde, but see also *per* Lord Goff at 538, 120.

[79] See p 114, *infra*.

must hold for C's benefit. The 1999 Act[80] provides that where B has recovered in respect of C's loss, in any proceedings brought by the third party under the Act, the court must reduce any award to him to the extent appropriate to take into account of the sum recovered by B.

(B) EQUITABLE REMEDIES FOR CONTRACTING PARTY

As an alternative to damages, according to the circumstances, some equitable remedy may be available. Thus, all of the Law Lords agreed in *Beswick v Beswick*,[81] as indeed had the judges in the Court of Appeal, that, in an appropriate case, B could obtain a decree of specific performance against A, compelling him to confer the agreed benefit on C, even though the obligation of A may merely be to make a money payment. If damages would be nominal, this has been said to be an argument in favour of, rather than against, the availability of specific performance.[82] In other circumstances some other remedy, such as an injunction, may be appropriate.[83]

It will be useful to consider the application of these principles to the facts of *Beswick v Beswick*.[84] In this case, one Peter Beswick agreed with his nephew, the defendant, to assign to him the goodwill and assets of the business of a coal merchant carried on by him in consideration of the defendant employing him as consultant to the business for the remainder of his life at a weekly rate of £6 10s 0d; and for the like consideration, the defendant agreed to pay, after Peter Beswick's death, an annuity of £5 per week to his widow. Peter Beswick died intestate, having been duly paid £6 10s 0d per week during his lifetime. Having made one payment of £5 to his widow, the defendant repudiated his liability. The widow took out letters of administration to Peter Beswick's estate, and brought an action suing both personally and as administratrix. The claim in the personal capacity failed, but as administratrix, it was held that, the legal remedy of damages being inadequate, she was entitled to a decree of specific performance.[85] Under the Contracts (Rights of Third Parties) Act 1999, she would, on similar facts, now be able to bring an action in her personal capacity for damages, but still not, it is thought, for specific performance.

It should be added that Lord Denning MR appears to have taken the view that in the sort of third-party contract under discussion, if the contracting party B can obtain specific performance, the same remedy is directly available to the third party, C. In *Neale v Willis*,[86] a husband borrowed £50 from his mother-in-law to assist in buying a house, on the express undertaking that the house would be in the joint names of his wife and himself. He broke the undertaking and had the house conveyed into his name alone. Lord Denning observed correctly that, following *Beswick v Beswick*,[87] the mother-in-law could have obtained specific performance. Counsel had, however, pointed out that this was an action by the wife—the third party—and that the mother-in-law was not even a party to the action. Lord Denning expressed himself unimpressed by this distinction and was

---

[80] In s 5.

[81] [1968] AC 58, [1967] 2 All ER 1197, HL. See also *Gurtner v Circuit* [1968] 2 QB 587, [1968] 1 All ER 328, CA.   [82] But see p 649, *infra*.

[83] See *Snelling v John G Snelling Ltd, supra,* and (1973) 36 MLR 214 (A Wilkie).   [84] *Supra*, HL.

[85] Note that, as administratrix, the widow stood in the shoes of Peter Beswick and was not a volunteer; nor was she a trustee.

[86] (1968) 19 P & CR 836, CA.   [87] *Supra*, HL.

prepared to enforce the agreement at the instance of the wife. It is respectfully submitted that *Beswick v Beswick*[88] cannot be called in aid in this way to support an action by a third party. Their Lordships in that case, as we have seen, drew a clear distinction between the widow *qua* third party suing personally and the widow *qua* administratrix suing in her representative capacity. It was only in the latter capacity that her claim succeeded. Lord Hodson[89] made explicit what is implicit in the speeches of the other Law Lords when he said: 'although the widow cannot claim specific performance in her personal capacity...' It is accordingly respectfully submitted that the opinion of Lord Denning in *Neale v Willis*[90] is wrong on this point, although it may well be that the case itself is rightly decided on the other ground[91] supported by the other members of the court.

(C) OTHER RELEVANT COMMON LAW PRINCIPLES

A further rule at common law is that B cannot require A to confer the benefit on him instead of C: A is fully entitled to insist on carrying out the contract according to its terms by conferring the benefit on C.[92] If he does so, B cannot sue C at common law in an action for money had and received.[93] It may be, however, that prima facie C could be called on to account to B in equity, on the basis that he holds on a resulting trust for B who has furnished the consideration.[94] The presumption of a resulting trust, if it exists, will often, in practice, be rebutted by the presumption of advancement,[95] or proof of an intent that C should take the property for his own use and benefit. Apart from presumptions, whether the parties intended C to be a mere nominee, or to take for his own use and benefit, is a question of construction of the agreement read in the light of all of the circumstances that were known to the parties.[96]

Previously, A and B could freely come to a fresh agreement, releasing the old one, or varying it as they wished,[97] or B could simply release A from his obligation. The Contracts (Rights of Third Parties) Act 1999, however, now limits their powers where a third party has a right under the Act to enforce a term of the contract.[98] Section 2(1) provides[99] that, in such a case, A and B cannot, by agreement, rescind the contract, or vary it in such a way as to extinguish or alter C's entitlement under that right without his consent.[100] The section applies if either:

(i) C has communicated his assent[101] to the term to A;

(ii) A is aware that C has relied on the term; or

---

[88] *Supra*, HL.

[89] *Supra*, at 81, 1207. The distinction is also clearly drawn by Ormrod J in *Snelling v John G Snelling Ltd* [1973] QB 87, [1972] 1 All ER 79.   [90] *Supra*.

[91] The principle applied in *Bannister v Bannister* [1948] 2 All ER 133, CA, discussed *supra*, p 97.

[92] *Re Stapleton-Bretherton* [1941] Ch 482, [1941] 3 All ER 5; *Re Schebsman* [1944] Ch 83, [1943] 2 All ER 768, CA; *Re Miller's Agreement* [1947] Ch 615, [1947] 2 All ER 78.   [93] *Re Schebsman, supra*.

[94] *Re Policy No 6402 of the Scottish Equitable Life Assurance Society* [1902] 1 Ch 282; and see the cases cited in fn 11, *supra*. See also (1944) 7 MLR 123 (G Williams).

[95] See Chapter 9, section 2(D), p 181, *infra*.

[96] *Beswick v Beswick* [1968] AC 58, [1967] 2 All ER 1197, HL.

[97] *Re Schebsman, supra*, CA; *Green v Russell* [1959] 2 QB 226, [1959] 2 All ER 525, CA.

[98] That is, under s 1.   [99] Subject to any express term of the contract: ibid, s 2(3).

[100] As to the power of the court to dispense with consent, see ibid, s 2(4)–(6).

[101] The assent may be by words or conduct, but must have been received by A: ibid, s 2(2).

(iii) A can reasonably be expected to have foreseen that the third party would rely on the term and C has, in fact, relied on it.

(D) INTERVENTION BY EQUITY

In some circumstances, the above rules may be qualified by the intervention of equity:[102] this will be so if it can be established that B has constituted himself a trustee for C of the benefit of the contract. If this can be shown, B, as trustee for C, can sue A and recover substantial damages, the measure of damages being the loss suffered by C.[103] If B refuses to sue, C, the beneficiary, can himself bring proceedings, but he must join B in the action as co-plaintiff, if he consents, or as defendant, if he refuses.[104] It is important to observe that if a trust is established, it is not open to A and B to release A from his obligation to benefit C or in any way to vary it.[105] It may also be noted that it is not essential for C to be ascertained at the date of the contract.[106]

The problem is to know in what circumstances B will be regarded as a trustee: no satisfactory test can be suggested, and it has been said that 'the way in which the court will decide a novel case is almost completely unpredictable'.[107] What can be said with a fair degree of confidence is that the onus of establishing a trust is a heavy one–: 'the intention to constitute the trust must be affirmatively proved',[108] or, as was said in another case,[109] 'It is not legitimate to import into the contract the idea of a trust when the parties have given no indication that such was their intention'. Although this seems to represent the present state of the law in England, one sympathizes with the difficulty felt by Fullager J in *Wilson v*

---

[102] In other cases by the intervention of the legislature, eg Road Traffic Act 1988, s 148(7). There are also some exceptions at common law: see *Alfred McAlpine Construction Ltd v Panatown Ltd* [2001] 1 AC 518; sub nom *Panatown Ltd v Alfred McAlpine Construction Ltd* [2000] 4 All ER 97, HL.

[103] *Lamb v Vice* (1840) 6 M & W 467; *Robertson v Wait* (1853) 8 Exch 299; *Lloyds v Harper* (1880) 16 Ch D 290, CA.

[104] *Gandy v Gandy* (1885) 30 Ch D 57, CA; *Vandepitte v Preferred Accident Insurance Corpn of New York* [1933] AC 70, PC; *Harmer v Armstrong* [1934] Ch 65, CA. But the courts will be astute to disallow use of this 'procedural shortcut' in a commercial context where it has no proper place: see *per* Lightman J in *Don King Productions Inc v Warren* [1998] 2 All ER 608, 634; affd [2000] Ch 291, [1999] 2 All ER 218, CA. Cf *Bradstock Trustee Services Ltd v Nabarro Nathanson (a firm)* [1995] 4 All ER 888, [1995] 1 WLR 1405; *Baxter International Inc v Nederlands Produktielaboratorium voor Blaedtrans-fiesapparatour BV* [1998] RPC 250.

[105] *Re Schebsman* [1944] Ch 83, [1943] 2 All ER 768, CA; but see *Hill v Gomme* (1839) 5 My & Cr 250, in which the contrary is suggested; *Re Empress Engineering Co* (1880) 16 Ch D 125, 129, CA; *Re Flavell* (1883) 25 Ch D 89, 102, CA.

[106] *Swain v Law Society* [1980] 3 All ER 615, 624, [1980] 1 WLR 1335, 1344, *per* Slade J. The decision was reversed [1981] 3 All ER 797, [1981] 1 WLR 17, CA, without casting any doubt on this dictum, and eventually restored by the House of Lords on different grounds [1983] 1 AC 598, [1982] 2 All ER 827.

[107] (1944) 7 MLR 123 (G L Williams), and see (1948) 21 ALJ 455 and 22 ALJ 67 (J G Starke). Barrington J said, in the Irish case *Cadbury Ireland Ltd v Kerry Co-operative Creamery Ltd* [1982] ILRM 77, that the courts were more ready to infer that the promisee in a contract is a trustee for the third party where the promisee has some contractual or fiduciary duty to the third party. The Australian courts have recently shown a greater willingness to infer a trust: see (1995) 14 U Tas LR 143 (D M Dwyer).

[108] *Vandepitte v Preferred Accident Insurance Corpn of New York* [1933] AC 70, 79–80, PC; *Burton v FX Music Ltd* [1999] EMLR 826.

[109] *Re Schebsman, supra,* CA, *per* Lord Greene, MR, at 89. Moreover, it has been said that 'the concept of constructive trusteeship of promises which confer a benefit on a cestui que trust is not capable in private law of extension to promises which impose a burden on a cestui que trust': *Swain v Law Society, supra,* HL, at 612, 833, *per* Lord Diplock.

Darling Island Stevedoring and Lighterage Co Ltd[110] in understanding the reluctance of the courts to infer a trust in some of the cases, particularly perhaps in the insurance cases.

Fletcher v Fletcher[111] is an interesting and important case. Here, the settlor, by a voluntary deed, covenanted with trustees that if A and B (his natural sons, at that time infants) or either of them should survive him and attain full age, his personal representatives should, within twelve months of his death, pay £60,000 to the trustees on trust for A and B or such one of them as should attain the age of twenty-one. A and B both survived the settlor, but B died without attaining full age. The trustees refused to sue, but the court held that this fact did not prejudice the right of A to recover payment of the debt out of the assets of the convenantor. In the course of the judgment, Wigram VC said:[112] 'One question made in argument has been, whether there can be a trust of a covenant the benefit of which shall belong to a third party; but I cannot think there is any difficulty in that ...' There was held to be a completely constituted trust of the chose in action, the benefit of the covenant, which the beneficiary could enforce if the trustee failed or refused to act. In the light of the attitude shown by the courts in subsequent cases, it has been doubted whether, on similar facts, a court today would find an intention to create a trust.[113]

Numerous cases have arisen in connection with policies of insurance. Two points emerge from the cases:[114] (i) the mere fact that A takes out a policy that is expressed to be for the benefit of B or on behalf of B does not constitute a trust for B; and (ii) the mere fact that the policy provides that the policy moneys are to be payable to B does not create a trust in favour of B. The more recent decisions in the higher courts suggest that the burden of establishing a trust is not easy to discharge.[115] In particular, it has recently been said that trusts should not lightly be implied in commercial affairs.[116] However, if the policy moneys are actually paid over to the third party, the third party will, even in the absence of a trust, be entitled to retain them as against the assured's estate, provided that, under the contract, the policy moneys were to be paid out for his own use and benefit.[117]

The same problem has arisen in cases in which a partnership deed, or a deed of dissolution of partnership, contains a covenant by the surviving partner. Again, the latest

---

[110] (1956) 95 CLR 43, and see the valuable judgments in *Trident General Insurance Co Ltd v McNiece Bros Pty Ltd* (1988) 80 ALR 574.

[111] (1844) 4 Hare 67. *Re Cavendish Browne's Settlement Trusts* [1916] WN 341 may also be explained on the same basis. Cf *Colyear v Lady Mulgrave* (1836) 2 Keen 81, in which the covenantee was not intended to be a trustee. For a full discussion of the cases up to 1930, see (1930) 46 LQR 12 (Corbin).

[112] (1844) 4 Hare 67, 74.

[113] [1979] CLP 1 (C E F Rickett); Hanbury and Martin, *Modern Equity*, 17th edn, at [4.020], point out two difficulties of this decision: firstly, that positive evidence of the intention to create a trust of the benefit of the covenant is lacking; secondly, that a trust of such a chose in action should be created by the covenantee and not the covenantor, and, on the facts, the covenantee did not originally know of the arrangement, and as soon as he did, wished to decline the trust. J D Feltham, however, in (1982) 98 LQR 17, thinks that, in the case of a voluntary covenant, one should look to the intention of the settlor who, in the absence of evidence to the contrary, should be presumed to intend a trust for the volunteer beneficiary.

[114] *Re Webb* [1941] Ch 225, [1941] 1 All ER 321, in which the earlier cases are reviewed; *Re Foster's Policy* [1966] 1 All ER 432, [1966] 1 WLR 222; *Swain v Law Society, supra*, HL. Cf (1993) 22 AALR 221 (W Anderson).

[115] *Vandepitte v Preferred Accident Insurance Corpn of New York* [1933] AC 70, PC; *Re Schebsman* [1944] Ch 83, [1943] 2 All ER 768, CA; *Green v Russell* [1959] 2 QB 226, [1959] 2 All ER 525, CA. A trust was established in *Royal Exchange Assurance v Hope* [1928] Ch 179, CA: *Re Gordon* [1940] Ch 851; *Re Foster's Policy, supra*.

[116] See *E D & F Man (Sugar) Ltd v Evalend Shipping Co SA* [1989] 2 Lloyd's Rep 192, 202.

[117] *Beswick v Beswick* [1968] AC 58, [1967] 2 All ER 1197, HL.

cases suggest that it is far from easy to establish a trust,[118] although in an earlier case[119] a covenant in a partnership deed was held, in the events that happened, to constitute the personal representative of the deceased partner a trustee, notwithstanding the fact that the existence of the trust would have disabled the partners from cancelling or varying the partnership deed in so far as doing so might affect the trust.

The above rules are unaffected by the Contracts (Rights of Third Parties) Act 1999,[120] but may well cease to be called on in practice in view of the direct rights given to third parties by s 1.[121]

4 TRUSTS OF THE BENEFIT OF A CONTRACT AND VOLUNTEERS

Some of the cases just considered seem to offend against the maxim previously discussed[122] that 'equity will not assist a volunteer'. Assuming that the intention to create a trust has been established, the difficulty is to establish that the trust has been completely constituted by the vesting of the trust property in the trustee and, indeed, of what the trust property consists.

One answer to the difficulty is said to be that the maxim does not apply to a completely constituted trust and that, in such cases, the trust property—that is, a chose in action, the benefit of the contract—is fully vested in the trustee. This view explains cases such as *Fletcher v Fletcher*,[123] but should, it seems, have produced a different result in *Re Pryce*[124] and *Re Kay's Settlement*,[125] and, at first sight, seems inconsistent with the principle frequently laid down by Lord Eldon, which has been repeated in and formed the basis of subsequent decisions, that there is a vital distinction between the case in which the trust has been completely constituted by the transfer of the property, and the case in which the matter 'rests in covenant, and is purely voluntary',[126] when equity will refuse to give any assistance towards the constitution of the trust. As to *Re Pryce*[127] and *Re Kay's Settlement*,[128] the answer, it has been contended,[129] is that these cases were wrongly decided, while as to Lord Eldon's rule, the point is said to be that the trust of the benefit of the contract or covenant is completely constituted. Lord Eldon's rule prevents the volunteer from claiming specific performance of a covenant to settle specific property, and disables him from claiming

---

[118] *Re Miller's Agreement* [1947] Ch 615, [1947] 2 All ER 78.

[119] *Re Flavell* (1883) 25 Ch D 89, CA not cited in either of the cases in the two previous notes.

[120] Section 7(1).   [121] See p 109, *supra*.   [122] See p 105 *et seq*, *supra*.

[123] (1844) 4 Hare 67, discussed at p 115, *supra*; *Williamson v Codrington* (1750) 1 Ves Sen 511; *Cox v Barnard* (1850) 8 Hare 310; *Gandy v Gandy* (1885) 30 Ch D 57, CA.

[124] [1917] 1 Ch 234, and see p 108, *supra*.

[125] [1939] Ch 329, [1939] 1 All ER 245, and see p 108, *supra*.

[126] *Ellison v Ellison* (1802) 6 Ves 656, 662, *per* Lord Eldon. See also *Re D'Angibau* (1879) 15 Ch D 228, CA; *Re Plumptre's Marriage Settlement* [1910] 1 Ch 609; *Re Kay's Settlement*, *supra*. See (1988) 8 LS 172 (M R T MacNair).

[127] [1917] 1 Ch 234.   [128] [1939] Ch 329, [1939] 1 All ER 245.

[129] See (1960) 76 LQR 100 (D W Elliott); (1961) 78 LQR 228 (J A Hornby); (1965) 23 CLJ 46 (G Jones); (1966) 29 MLR 397 (D Matheson); (1996) 70 ALJ 911 (D Wright).

that such specified property is subject to the trusts of the settlement unless and until it is conveyed to the trustees, but, according to this argument, even a volunteer should be able to compel the trustees to sue for damages for breach of the covenant, because the right to sue—that is, the benefit of the contract—is held by the trustee on a completely constituted trust.

These arguments were not accepted by Buckley J in *Re Cook's Settlement Trusts*,[130] who followed *Re Pryce* and *Re Kay's Settlement* without disapproval. The judge said that a covenant to settle future property was not a property right and, accordingly, was not capable of being made the subject of an immediate trust. The covenant before him was, he said, 'an executory contract to settle a particular fund or particular funds of money which at the date of the covenant did not exist and might never come into existence...The case...involves the law of contract, not the law of trusts'. It is not clear why the benefit of the covenant did not constitute a property right, although the actual decision may be right on the ground that there was no intention to create a trust of the promise. The benefit of a contract is equally a chose in action whether it relates to present or future property.

Although there has been some academic support[131] for *Re Pryce* and the cases that follow it, there has been further forceful criticism.[132] It is suggested, notwithstanding the closely reasoned and persuasive arguments of the critics, that *Re Pryce, Re Kay's Settlement*, and *Re Cook's Settlement Trust* are not likely to be overruled. There is, after all, something of a paradox in the proposition that a contract to create a trust that equity would not permit trustees to enforce in the Court of Chancery should give rise to a remedy at common law. Even on the basis that there is a trust of the benefit of the contract or covenant, an argument could be put forward not only to deprive the volunteers of any right to compel the trustees to sue, but also to deprive the trustees of power to choose whether to sue or not—namely, that the trusts attaching to the benefit of the contract or covenant are not necessarily the same as those that will attach to any property actually transferred thereunder. The reluctance of equity to assist volunteers might lead the court to hold that the volunteer has no equitable interest in the benefit of the contract, and, on this basis, if all of the beneficiaries under the settlement are volunteers, the whole equitable interest in the benefit of the contract would result to the settlor, on which basis the court would surely, and rightly, direct the trustees not to sue, even if an application of the *Saunders v Vautier*[133] principle does not enable the settlor himself to do so. But if, as in *Davenport v Bishopp*,[134] someone who has or is deemed to have furnished consideration enforces the covenant as he may, the trusts of the settlement, including the interests of volunteers, will naturally attach to the property that actually comes into the hands of the trustees.

On this last view, the main difficulty is to discover the intention of the settlor. If, as in *Fletcher v Fletcher*,[135] the intention is to create an immediate trust of the benefit of the covenant at law in favour of volunteers, the trust is completely constituted as from the moment at which the covenant is executed and the volunteer beneficiaries have

---

[130] [1965] Ch 902, [1964] 3 All ER 898; [1966] 30 Conv 286 (M C Cullity and H A J Ford); [1982] Conv 280 (M W Friend); (1986) 60 ALJ 387 (S Lindsay and P Ziegler).

[131] [1967] ASCL 387 *et seq* (J D Davies); (1969) 85 LQR 213 (W A Lee).

[132] (1975) 91 LQR 236 (J L Barton); (1976) 92 LQR 427 (R P Meagher and J R F Lehane); [1988] Conv 19 (D Goddard).

[133] See Chapter 16, section 6, p 409, *infra*.   [134] (1843) 2 Y & C Ch Cas 451.

[135] (1844) 4 Hare 67.

immediate equitable rights that they can enforce by compelling the trustees to sue on the covenant. If, however, the intention is not to give volunteers any equitable rights in the benefit of the covenant, they have no rights that they can enforce either directly or indirectly, unless and until property is actually transferred to the trustees under the covenant. And in construing the settlement, to ascertain the intention, one would have to bear in mind that, as we have seen,[136] the intention to create a trust must be affirmatively proved.

The difficulties discussed above are now increasingly unlikely to arise because, as we have seen,[137] the Contracts (Rights of Third Parties) Act 1999 enables a third party to sue directly in relation to contracts entered into after 10 May 2000.[138]

5   TRUSTS OF FUTURE PROPERTY

Future property—for example, the hope a person may have that he will take under the will or on the intestacy of a living person,[139] or under the exercise of a special power of appointment,[140] future royalties,[141] and the proceeds of any future sale of specific property[142]—cannot be owned for the simple reason that they do not exist and, for the same reason, cannot be assigned either at law, or in equity,[143] or held on trust. So far as trust is concerned, it makes no difference whether the alleged settlor has (a) purported to make a voluntary assignment to trustees on declared trusts, or (b) declared himself a trustee of the future property for specified beneficiaries.

Suppose, however, that the future property materializes: for example, the hope of the settlor that he will receive a legacy is fulfilled on the death of the testator. In principle, in neither situation will the beneficiaries have an enforceable claim, because 'equity will not assist a volunteer'. An illustration of situation (a) is *Re Ellenborough*,[144] in which, by a voluntary settlement, X purported to assign to trustees property to which she might become entitled under her brother's will. On the death of her brother, she received property under his will, but was unwilling to transfer it to the trustees. It was held that she was entitled to refuse to do so. If, however, the second ground of the decision in *Re Ralli's Will Trusts*[145] is valid, it would seem that if the brother's executors had happened to be the same persons as

---

[136] See p 114, *supra*.   [137] See p 109, *supra*.

[138] See the Contracts (Rights of Third Parties) Act 1999, s 10(2), and note the qualified extension in s 10(3).

[139] *Re Lind* [1915] 2 Ch 345, CA; *Wu Koon Tai v Wu Yau Loi* [1997] AC 179, PC.

[140] *Re Brooks' Settlement Trusts* [1939] Ch 993, [1939] 3 All ER 920. Note that, in this case, he had a mere expectancy: if, however, a person is entitled to property in default of appointment, he has a vested interest liable to be divested by the exercise of the power of appointment, and this interest can be owned, assigned and held on trust.

[141] *Re Trytel* [1952] 2 TLR 32. See *Performing Right Society Ltd v Rowland* [1997] 3 All ER 336.

[142] *Re Cook's Settlement Trusts* [1965] Ch 902, [1964] 3 All ER 898.

[143] *Meek v Kettlewell* (1842) 1 Hare 464; affd (1843) 1 Ph 342; *Re Ellenborough* [1903] 1 Ch 697.

[144] *Supra*. X had, by the settlement, likewise covenanted to assign property to which she might become entitled under her sister's will. This property had been transferred to the trustees and it was not suggested that it was not held by them on the trusts of the voluntary settlement. The transfer can be regarded as a confirmation of the declaration of trust: *Re Bowden* [1936] Ch 71; *Re Adlard* [1954] Ch 29, [1953] 2 All ER 1437. See *Re Plumptre's Marriage Settlement* [1910] 1 Ch 609 and p 106, *supra*.

[145] [1964] Ch 288, [1963] 3 All ER 940. See p 109, *supra*.

the trustees of the voluntary settlement, X would not have been able to call for the transfer of the property, but it would have been held upon the trusts of the settlement. In situation (b), the trust will be enforceable if the declaration is confirmed after the property has been received by the settlor.[146]

The position is quite different if the settlor has received valuable consideration for creating the trust. Just as an assignment of future property for valuable consideration is effective in equity, which construes the assignment as a contract binding the conscience of the assignor and binding the subject matter of the contract when it comes into existence,[147] so in the case of a trust of future property created for valuable consideration, once it materializes into existing property, it is treated in equity as being held on trust for the beneficiaries.[148] The settlor's conscience is bound so that he cannot keep it for himself.[149]

6 EXCEPTIONS TO THE MAXIM THAT 'EQUITY WILL NOT ASSIST A VOLUNTEER'

(A) THE RULE IN *STRONG V BIRD*[150]

Where a donor has attempted to make an immediate gift *inter vivos* of either real[151] or personal[152] property to a donee, which gift has failed by reason of the fact that the legal formalities necessary for the proper transfer of title to the particular property in question have not been complied with, then if the donee has subsequently become the executor or administrator[153] of the donor, the gift is considered to have been perfected by the vesting of the legal title in the donee. For the rule to apply, it is necessary to show that the testator had, up to the moment of his death, a continuing intention that the gift should have been given at the time when it was given[154] and, where the donor has appointed the donee his executor, that the testator had not any intention inconsistent with an intention to bring

---

[146] *Re Northcliffe* [1925] Ch 651.

[147] *Tailby v Official Receiver* (1888) 13 App Cas 523, HL; *Re Ellenborough, supra*. A devisee of land comprised in an unadministered estate can enter into a binding contract to sell it in the same way as he can contract to assign a future chose in action: *Wu Koon Tai v Wu Yau Loi* [1997] AC 179, PC.

[148] *Holroyd v Marshall* (1862) 10 HL Cas 191; *Tailby v Official Receiver, supra*, HL; *Re Lind* [1915] 2 Ch 345, CA. See *Pullan v Koe* [1913] 1 Ch 9, and p 107, *supra*.   [149] *Re Ellenborough, supra*.

[150] (1874) LR 18 Eq 315. Meagher, Gummow, and Lehane, *Equity: Doctrine and Remedies*, 3rd edn, pp 735 *et seq*, point out that *Strong v Bird* did not, in fact, lay down the rule attributed to it and that the rule is based on a misconstruction of the decision. See [1982] Conv 14 (G Kodilinye); [2006] Conv 432 (J Jaconelli).

[151] *Re James* [1935] Ch 449.

[152] The rule applies to the release of a debt, as in *Strong v Bird, supra*, itself.

[153] *Re James, supra*, followed in *Re Gonin* [1979] Ch 16, [1977] 2 All ER 720, in which, however, Walton J expressed doubt as to whether it was right in principle. It seemed wrong to him that it should depend on the chance of who should manage to obtain a grant of letters of administration. The editorial note to this case in (1977) 93 LQR 485 is to the effect that these doubts are unjustifiable in the light of the reasons given in *Re Stewart* [1908] 2 Ch 251, which are set out below, but Ford and Lee, *Principles of the Law of Trusts*, 3rd edn, [3340] regard it as a 'questionable extension'. It makes no difference that the donee is merely one of several executors or administrators, because, in the eye of the law, the whole of the property vests in each personal representative: *Re Stewart* [1908] 2 Ch 251; *Re James* [1935] Ch 449.

[154] *Re Pink* [1912] 2 Ch 528, CA; *Re Freeland* [1952] Ch 110, sub nom *Jackson v Rodger* [1952] 1 All ER 16, CA; *Re Gonin, supra*; *Benjamin v Leicher* (1998) 45 NSWLR 389.

about the result flowing from the appointment.[155] The rule does not apply where there is a mere promise to make a gift in the future,[156] or where there is an intention to give, and the gift is not completed because the intending donor desires first to apply the subject matter of the contemplated gift to some other purpose.[157] The rule in *Strong v Bird* has been said[158] to rest on two grounds: firstly, that the vesting of the property in the personal representative at the donor's death completes the imperfect gift made in the lifetime; and, secondly, that the intention of the donor to give the benefit to the donee is sufficient to countervail the equity of the beneficiaries under the will. An Australian judge has said[159] that the rule should not, in the twenty-first century, be extended at all.

(B) *DONATIO MORTIS CAUSA*[160]

'The principle of not assisting a volunteer to prefect an incomplete gift does not apply to a donatio mortis causa',[161] although it is not in every case that the assistance of equity is required. A *donatio mortis causa* has been described as:

> a singular form of gift. It may be said to be of an amphibious nature, being a gift which is neither entirely inter vivos nor testamentary. It is an act inter vivos by which the donee is to have the absolute title to the subject of the gift not at once but if the donor dies. If the donor dies the title becomes absolute not under but as against his executor. In order to make the gift valid it must be made so as to take complete effect on the donor's death.[162]

The title of the donee can never be complete until the donor is dead[163] and, accordingly, the *donatio* will fail if the donee predeceases the donor.[164]

If there has been a delivery of the subject matter of the *donatio* such as would suffice to constitute an effective *inter vivos* gift, death makes the conditional gift unconditional and the *donatio* becomes effective and complete without any further act being necessary. Where, however, delivery would be ineffective to transfer the title in the case of an *inter vivos* gift, as in the case of land or many choses in action, it may nevertheless suffice to constitute a valid *donatio mortis causa*.[165]

In such case, the legal title will be held by the personal representatives on trust for the donee, and the donee will, if need be, be able to compel the personal representatives to lend

---

[155] *Re Pink, supra.*

[156] *Re Innes* [1910] 1 Ch 188, although it was held to apply in *Re Goff* (1914) 111 LT 34, in which there was an intention to give only if the donor predeceased the donee. See Waters, *The Law of Trusts in Canada*, 2nd edn, pp 168, 169; [1982] Conv 14 (G Kodilinye).

[157] *Re Freeland, supra,* CA.   [158] See, eg, *Re Stewart* [1908] 2 Ch 251, 254–255, *per* Neville J.

[159] *Blackett v Darcy* [2005] NSWSC 65, [2006] WTLR 581, *per* Young CJ.

[160] See, generally, Borkowski, *Deathbed Gifts.* The pages in a previous edition corresponding to pp 119 and 120 were cited by Glennie J in *Armstrong v Hachen Estate* (2000) 598 APR 110, 151–154.

[161] *Per* Lindley LJ in *Re Dillon* (1890) 44 Ch D 76, 83, CA, citing *Duffield v Elwes* (1827) 1 Bli NS 497.

[162] *Re Beaumont* [1902] 1 Ch 889, 892, *per* Buckley J. A *donatio*, like a testamentary gift, is liable to inheritance tax. As to whether the subject matter of a valid *donatio* is liable for the deceased's debts, see [1978] Conv 130 (Shan Warnock-Smith). As to the degree of mental competence required, see *Re Beaney* [1978] 2 All ER 595, [1978] 1 WLR 770, and p 46, *supra.*

[163] *Duffield v Elwes, supra; Delgoffe v Fader* [1939] Ch 922, [1939] 3 All ER 682.

[164] *Tate v Hilbert* (1793) 2 Ves 111, 120; *Walter v Hodge* (1818) 2 Swan 92, 99.

[165] *Ward v Turner* (1752) 2 Ves Sen 431; *Re Wasserberg* [1915] 1 Ch 195.

their names to any necessary action, on receiving an appropriate indemnity.[166] It is where the transfer has been inchoate or incomplete that equity allows an exception to the rule that it will not complete an imperfect gift.

In order for a *donatio mortis causa* to be effective, there are three conditions that must be complied with, as follows.[167]

(i) The gift must be made in contemplation, although not necessarily in expectation, of impending death.[168] This requirement will readily be treated as satisfied where it was made during the donor's last illness, but it is not necessary that the donor should be *in extremis* when the gift is made.[169] The reported cases all contemplate death through illness, but, on principle, there seems no reason why the contemplation of death from some other source should not be equally effective.[170] But, of course, a merely general contemplation of death, on the ground that everyone must die at some time or other, is inadequate. Prior to the Suicide Act 1961, which provided that suicide should no longer be a crime, it had been held[171] that a purported *donatio mortis causa* in contemplation of suicide was not valid, as it would otherwise allow the donor to give effect to his gift by means of committing a crime. By virtue of the Act, this reason is no longer applicable, although it is arguable that such a *donatio mortis causa* should not be recognized on grounds of public policy. It does not matter that death actually occurs from a disease[172] other than that contemplated.[173]

(ii) The gift must be made on the condition that it is to be absolute and perfected only on the donor's death, being revocable until that event occurs. It must be distinguished, on the one hand, from an intention to make an immediate or irrevocable gift[174] and, on the other hand, from an attempted nuncupative will.[175] It may be revoked by the donor in his lifetime and will automatically be revoked by his recovery from a possibly terminal illness.[176] If it is revoked, the donee will thereafter hold any property that has been transferred as trustee for the donor.[177] The condition need not be express and will readily be implied where the gift is made in expectation of death.[178] Probably, somewhat illogically, the better view

[166] *Duffield and Elwes, supra; Delgoffe v Fader, supra; Re Lillingston* [1952] 2 All ER 184.

[167] *Sen v Headley* [1991] Ch 425, 431, [1991] 2 All ER 636, 639, CA, *per* Nourse LJ.

[168] It is thought that the test is subjective. Some support for this view can, perhaps, be drawn from *Re Miller* (1961) 105 Sol Jo 207, although the point was not taken and the *donatio* failed on other grounds. But see the Canadian case of *Thompson v Mechan* [1958] OR 357, in which the alleged *donatio* failed because, inter alia, the donor could not properly be said to have contemplated dying from 'a cause that exists only in his fancy or imagination'—that is, air travel.

[169] *Walter v Hodge* (1818) 2 Swans 92, 100, *per* Plumer MR; *Saulnier v Anderson* (1987) 43 DLR (4th) 19.

[170] See the discussion in *Agnew v Belfast Banking Co* [1896] 2 IR 204.

[171] *Re Dudman* [1925] Ch 553.

[172] Or, probably, from any other source, including suicide not contemplated at the date of the gift: *Mills v Shields* [1948] IR 367.

[173] *Wilkes v Allington* [1931] 2 Ch 104.

[174] If the intention is to make an *inter vivos* gift, which is incomplete and accordingly fails, it cannot be treated as a *donatio mortis causa* even though this might validate it: *Edwards v Jones* (1836) 1 My & Cr 226.

[175] *Solicitor to the Treasury v Lewis* [1900] 2 Ch 812.

[176] Or the cessation of the possibility of death from the other contemplated source, as the case may be.

[177] *Staniland v Willott* (1852) 3 Mac & G 664; *Re Wasserberg* [1915] 1 Ch 195.

[178] *Gardner v Parker* (1818) 3 Madd 184; *Re Lillingston* [1952] 2 All ER 184.

is that the necessary condition may be implied notwithstanding the fact that the donor knows that there cannot be any recovery.[179] In his lifetime, the *donatio* will be revoked by the donor recovering dominion over the subject matter of the gift,[180] but not by the mere fact of the donor taking the property back for safe custody.[181] It is said to be impossible, however, to revoke a *donatio mortis causa* by will, because death makes the gift complete,[182] although a *donatio* may be satisfied by a legacy contained in a subsequent testamentary instrument.[183]

(iii) There must be a delivery of the subject matter of the gift, or the essential indicia of title thereto, which amounts to a parting with dominion. This means, primarily, physical delivery of the subject matter of the *donatio* with intent to part with the dominion and not merely, for instance, with intent to ensure its safe custody.[184] Failure to part with the dominion inevitably means failure of the *donatio mortis causa*, as, for instance, in *Bunn v Markham*,[185] in which the property was, by the deceased's directions, sealed in three parcels and the names of the intended donees written thereon. The deceased declared that they were intended for the named donees and directed that they should be given to them after his death. The parcels were then replaced in the chest to which the deceased retained the key, and it was held that there was no sufficient delivery and accordingly no effective *donatio mortis causa*. Again, there is no delivery if the donee refuses to accept it.[186]

Delivery, however, need not be by the donor personally into the hands of the donee. It may be made by a duly authorized agent of the donor,[187] although it must, of course, be made before the donor dies;[188] or likewise to an agent for the donee,[189] but mere delivery to an agent of the donor is ineffective,[190] unless he can be regarded as a fiduciary agent holding on trust for the donee.[191] Again, an antecedent delivery of the chattel—that is, anterior to the date of the actual gift—is adequate, even though made *alio intuitu*,[192] for example, for safe custody only, and it seems that words of gift subsequently followed by delivery may suffice.[193] Further, a *donatio mortis causa* is not invalidated by the fact that it is expressed to be subject to an express charge or trust, even to an indefinite extent, for example, to pay funeral expenses.[194]

[179] *Wilkes v Allington* [1931] 2 Ch 104, 111, *per* Lord Tomlin; *Re Lillingston, supra*; *Re Mustapha* (1891) 8 TLR 160.

[180] *Bunn v Markham* (1816) 7 Taunt 224.   [181] *Re Hawkins* [1924] 2 Ch 47.

[182] See, eg, White and Tudor's *Leading Cases in Equity*, 9th edn, vol I, p 355.

[183] *Jones v Selby* (1710) Prec Ch 300, in which satisfaction was said to be equivalent to a revocation: *Hudson v Spencer* [1910] 2 Ch 285.

[184] *Hawkins v Blewitt* (1798) 2 Esp 663.   [185] (1816) 7 Taunt 224.

[186] *Cant v Gregory* (1894) 10 TLR 584, CA.   [187] *Re Craven's Estate* [1937] Ch 423, [1937] 3 All ER 33.

[188] *Hardy v Baker* (1738) West temp Hard 519; *Re Miller* (1961) 105 Sol Jo 207. Mellows, *The Law of Succession*, 5th edn, p 526, suggests that the Post Office could be treated as a fiduciary agent with a duty to deliver the insurance policy to the addressee, so that there was sufficient delivery. See also Borkowski, *Deathbed Gifts*, p 66.

[189] *Moore v Darton* (1851) 4 De G & Sm 517 (perhaps a doubtful decision on the facts).

[190] *Powell v Hellicar* (1858) 26 Beav 261; *Farquharson v Cave* (1846) 2 Coll 356.

[191] *Mills v Shields* [1948] IR 367. There seems to be no English authority to support this qualification, but see fn 185, *supra*.

[192] *Cain v Moon* [1896] 2 QB 283, DC; *Birch v Treasury Solicitor* [1951] Ch 298, [1950] 2 All ER 1198, CA.

[193] *Re Weston* [1902] 1 Ch 680.

[194] *Hills v Hills* (1841) 8 M & W 401; *Re Ward* [1946] 2 All ER 206; *Birch v Treasury Solicitor, supra*.

It is settled, however, that delivery of the key to the box or other receptacle or place in which the subject matter of the alleged *donatio* is contained may be a sufficient delivery of such subject matter if the requisite intent appears.[195] The better view, it is submitted, is that this is not to be regarded as a symbolic delivery, but as giving to the donee the means of getting at the subject matter, and correspondingly depriving the donor of his power of dealing with it,[196] and, further, that it applies not only to bulky articles, but also to things that are incapable of actual manual delivery.[197] Even where delivery of the key only transfers a partial dominion over the subject of the donation, as where the key to a safe deposit at Harrods Ltd, was handed over, but under the terms of the contract of deposit, the contents would only be handed over to anyone other than the actual depositor on production, in addition to the key, of a signed authority and the giving of a password, this may be sufficient delivery and equity will complete the imperfect gift.[198] Delivery of a key will be equally effective if it merely gives the donee the means of getting at another key that, in turn, gives access to the place in which the subject matter of the *donatio* is contained.[199] But if the donor retains a duplicate key, it seems there is no effective delivery, for the donor is still able to deal with the subject matter and cannot be said to have parted with dominion.[200] For the same reason, there can be no *donatio mortis causa* if the alleged donor parts with possession of a locked box or other receptacle, but retains possession of the key.[201]

There may be more difficulty where the subject matter of the alleged *donatio mortis causa* is not a chattel capable of actual delivery as explained in the preceding paragraphs, but is a chose in action. There will be no problem where there has been such delivery of a banknote,[202] or a negotiable instrument, other than one drawn by the donor,[203] in such a condition that mere delivery of the document will effect a transfer of the chose in action that it represents; nor in any other case in which the formalities of transfer have been carried out so as to pass the legal title.[204] Where, however, the title to the chose in action does not pass by mere delivery of

[195] *Jones v Selby* (1710) Prec Ch 300; *Re Mustapha* (1891) 8 TLR 160. In *Trimmer v Danby* (1856) 25 LJ Ch 424, the artist J M W Turner had delivered the key to a box containing certain bonds to his housekeeper of some forty years. Despite evidence of an intention of gift, the alleged *donatio* failed on the ground that the delivery of the key was in her capacity as a housekeeper for the purpose of safekeeping. Cf (1956) 19 MLR 394 (A C H Barlow).

[196] *Birch v Treasury Solicitor, supra*; contra, *Jarman on Wills*, 8th edn, vol 1, p 47.

[197] It is submitted that decisions such as *Jones v Selby, supra*, and *Re Mustapha, supra*, are to be preferred on this point to dicta in other cases, eg *Re Wasserberg* [1915] 1 Ch 195.

[198] *Re Lillingston* [1952] 2 All ER 184; *Re Wasserberg, supra*.

[199] *Re Lillingston, supra*, 'it does not matter in how many boxes the subject of a gift may be contained or that each, except the last, contains a key which opens the next, so long as the scope of the gift is made clear', *per* Wynn-Parry LJ [1952] 2 All ER 184, 191.

[200] *Re Craven's Estate* [1937] Ch 423, 428, [1937] 3 All ER 33, 38, *per* Farwell J. This was distinguished in relation to an alleged *donatio mortis causa* of a car in *Woodard v Woodard* [1995] 3 All ER 980, CA, noted (1991) 5 Tru LI 124 (Debra Jill Morris); [1992] Conv 53 (Jill Martin); [1994] 144 NLJ 48 (M Pawlowski). Here, the donee already had possession of the car and one set of keys, but the vehicle registration document and a second set of keys (the existence of which was doubtful) were not handed over. Note that the question was said not to be so much one of dominion as one of intention.

[201] *Re Johnson* (1905) 92 LT 357; *Reddel v Dobree* (1839) 10 Sim 244.

[202] *Miller v Miller* (1735) 3 P Wms 356; *Re Hawkins* [1924] 2 Ch 47.

[203] See p 126, *infra*.   [204] *Staniland v Willott* (1852) 3 Mac & G 664.

any document, and where there has been no formal transfer of the legal title, it is the law that for the purposes of a *donatio mortis causa* delivery of the appropriate document may be regarded as equivalent to a transfer and equity will complete the imperfect gift. The question of what are the appropriate documents that must be delivered is to be answered by applying the test propounded by the Court of Appeal in *Birch v Treasury Solicitor*[205]—namely, 'that the real test is whether the instrument "amounts to a transfer"[206] as being the essential indicia or evidence of title, possession or production of which entitles the possessor to the money or property purported to be given'.[207] In that case, it was held that the choses in action respectively represented by a Post Office Savings bank book, a London Trustee Savings bank book, a Barclays Bank deposit book, and a Westminster Bank deposit account book were each the subject of a valid *donatio mortis causa* by delivery of the appropriate book. Other cases have held valid the *donatio mortis causa* of a bond,[208] bills of exchange, cheques, and promissory notes payable to the donor, even though unendorsed and therefore not transferable by delivery,[209] a banker's deposit note,[210] national savings certificates,[211] an insurance policy,[212] guaranteed investment certificates,[213] and even a mortgage.[214] In the case of an intangible thing such as a chose in action, parting with dominion over the essential indicia of title will usually suffice for the parting with dominion over the subject matter of the gift.[215] The unfortunate plaintiff failed, however, in the New Zealand case of *Wilson v Paniani*,[216] in which there was no doubt but that the deceased donor intended to make a gift of the sum represented by the cheque that she had received from her pension fund and handed over to the plaintiff. The plaintiff paid the cheque into her bank account, but the pension fund, which had discovered that it was only about half the sum to which the donor was entitled, stopped it prior to issuing a new cheque for the larger sum. The donor, on being informed of this, reaffirmed her intention that the plaintiff should have the sum represented by the original cheque, and indicated that the balance should go to children and grandchildren. The donor died shortly afterwards, and, two days later, a cheque for the increased amount was paid into her estate account. The plaintiff failed because all that she had been given was the right to recover such funds as the cheque given to her would produce, which was nil, and there was no dealing with the second cheque or its proceeds to give rise to a *donatio mortis causa* in respect of it or any part of it.

[205] [1951] Ch 298, 311, [1950] 2 All ER 1198, 1207, CA.

[206] Adopting the phrase uttered by Lord Hardwicke LC in *Ward v Turner* (1752) 2 Ves Sen 431, 444.

[207] It is no longer regarded as necessary that the document handed over contain a record of all of the essential terms of the contract. Cf *Re Weston* [1902] 1 Ch 680; *Delgoffe v Fader* [1939] Ch 922, [1939] 3 All ER 682.

[208] *Gardner v Parker, supra*; *Re Wasserberg* [1915] 1 Ch 195.

[209] *Re Mead* (1880) 15 Ch D 651; *Clement v Cheesman* (1884) 27 Ch D 631.

[210] *Re Dillon* (1890) 44 Ch D 76, CA.   [211] *Darlow v Sparks* [1938] 2 All ER 235.

[212] *Witt v Amis* (1861) 1 B & S 109; *Amis v Witt* (1863) 33 Beav 619.

[213] *Saulnier v Anderson* (1987) 43 DLR (4th) 19.

[214] *Duffield v Elwes* (1827) 1 Bli NS 497, followed without comment in *Wilkes v Allington* [1931] 2 Ch 104.

[215] *Sen v Headley* [1991] Ch 425, 436, [1991] 2 All ER 636, 645, CA, *per* Nourse LJ, giving the judgment of the court.

[216] [1996] 3 NZLR 378.

Dicta of Lord Eldon in *Duffield v Elwes*[217] led to the common assumption that these cannot be a *donatio mortis causa* of land. In *Sen v Headley*,[218] it was held that, admitting the doctrine of *donatio mortis causa* to be anomalous, there was no justification for an anomalous exception. A *donatio mortis causa* of land is neither more nor less anomalous than any other and is capable of being made provided, of course, that the general requirements for such a gift are satisfied. The facts of that case were that the deceased had uttered words of gift, without reservation, when in hospital, knowing he did not have long to live and when there could have been no practical possibility of his ever returning home. He had parted with dominion over the title deeds by delivering to the plaintiff the only key to the steel box in which they were kept. The plaintiff had her own set of keys to the house and was in effective control of it. This was held to constitute parting with dominion over the house.

(iv) It is commonly stated that some things cannot form the subject matter of a *donatio mortis causa*. These seem to fall into two categories.

(a) Firstly,[219] it was stated in *Moore v Moore*[220] that railway stock, and in *Re Weston*[221] that building society shares are not a proper subject of a *donatio mortis causa*. In *Re Weston*, the court held that the building society shares were not distinguishable from the railway stock in *Moore v Moore*,[222] which, in its turn, merely followed *Ward v Turner*,[223] which was treated as deciding that the South Seas annuities, the subject of the case, could not be the subject of a *donatio mortis causa*. It is submitted that *Ward v Turner* should be regarded as deciding not that South Sea annuities could never be the subject of a *donatio mortis causa*, but that the delivery of the receipts in that case did not 'amount to a transfer'. It is noteworthy that Lord Hardwicke in his judgment said that, after acceptance of the stock, the receipts 'are nothing but waste paper, and are seldom taken care of afterwards'. If *Ward v Turner*[224] is properly to be explained on this ground, it would undermine the authority of *Moore v Moore*[225] and *Re Weston*[226] on this point. These latter cases, moreover, are not easy to reconcile with *Staniland v Willott*,[227] in which it was held that a valid *donatio mortis causa* was constituted by a complete transfer of shares in a public company. On the view now being suggested, this second category altogether disappears. Support for this view from a different angle may be found in the unwillingness of the court in *Sen v Headley*[228] to accept anomalous exceptions to the rule, as already noted in connection with a *donatio mortis causa* of land.

---

[217] *Supra.*

[218] *Supra*, CA, noted [1991] Conv 307 (M Halliwell); [1991] CLJ 404 (J W A Thornely); (1993) 109 LQR 19 (P V Baker).

[219] See, generally, (1966) 30 Conv 189 (A Samuels). In Australia, it has been held, in *Public Trustee v Bussell* (1993) 30 NSWLR 111, that a delivery of share certificates can be a valid *donatio mortis causa*: they constitute indicia of title and handing them over is a delivery of part of the means of getting at the property.

[220] (1874) LR 18 Eq 474. [221] [1902] 1 Ch 680, but see (1947) 204 LTJo 142.

[222] (1874) LR 18 Eq 474. [223] (1752) 2 Ves Sen 431.

[224] *Supra*. See *per* Lord Harwicke LC at 444. [225] *Supra*. [226] *Supra*.

[227] (1852) 3 Mac & G 664. See also *Re Craven's Estate* [1937] Ch 423, [1937] 3 All ER 33.

[228] [1991] Ch 425, [1991] 2 All ER 636, CA.

(b) Secondly, it is clear that there cannot be a valid *donatio mortis causa* of the donor's own cheque or promissory note.[229] The point here is that a man's own cheque or promissory note is not property when given by the donor to the donee; a cheque is merely a revocable order to the banker to make the payment to the person in whose favour the cheque is drawn and the gift of a promissory note is merely a gratuitous promise. It may be otherwise if a cheque has actually been paid during the donor's lifetime,[230] or immediately after the death before the banker has been apprised of it,[231] or negotiated for value.[232]

(v) The onus is on the donee to prove the alleged *donatio mortis causa* and where a claimant's case depends entirely on his own evidence, the court must scrutinize it very carefully. However, the uncorroborated evidence of the claimant may suffice if the court is satisfied as to its truthfulness.[233]

(C) STATUTORY PROVISIONS

Occasionally, statute will complete an imperfect gift. A legal estate in land is not capable of being held by a minor.[234] A purported conveyance of a legal estate in land to a minor or minors is accordingly not effective to pass the legal estate. However, the Trusts of Land and Appointment of Trustees Act 1996 provides[235] that it is to operate as a declaration that the land is held in trust for the minor or minors.

(D) PROPRIETARY ESTOPPEL

The effect of this principle,[236] which is discussed later, may sometimes be to complete an imperfect gift.

---

[229] *Re Beaumont* [1902] 1 Ch 889; *Re Leaper* [1916] 1 Ch 579; *Re Swinburne* [1926] Ch 38, [1925] All ER Rep 313, CA (actually a decision on an *inter vivos* gift); *Curnock v CIR* [2003] WTLR 955. See [2005] 67 T & ELTJ 4 (Catherine Finely).

[230] *Bouts v Ellis* (1853) 17 Beav 121; affd (1853) 4 De G M & G 249. It is enough if it has been accepted by the banker during the donor's lifetime; *Re While* [1928] WN 182; *Re Beaumont* [1902] 1 Ch 889.

[231] *Tate v Hilbert* (1793) 2 Ves 111; *Lumsden v Miller* (1980) 110 DLR (3d) 226.

[232] *Tate v Hilbert, supra*; *Rolls v Pearce* (1877) 5 Ch D 730.

[233] *Re Dillon* (1890) 44 Ch D 76, CA; *Birch v Treasury Solicitor* [1951] Ch 298, [1950] 2 All ER 1198, CA.

[234] Law of Property Act 1925, s 1(6).

[235] Section 2, Sch 1, para 1. This paragraph also deals with a conveyance to a minor and a person of full age, and cases previously coming within s 27 of the Settled Land Act 1925 (repealed by the 1996 Act).

[236] *Infra*, p 203 *et seq*.

7

SECRET TRUSTS AND MUTUAL WILLS

The first section of this chapter considers two cases: firstly, that in which a will apparently gives property to a legatee or devisee beneficially, but in which that person has agreed with the testator that he will hold it as a trustee for others; and secondly, that in which the will gives it to him expressly as a trustee, but does not state what those trusts are, although they had, in fact, been communicated to him by the testator in his lifetime and accepted by him.

The second section deals with the situation in which two persons, in pursuance of an agreement to that effect, make wills containing, *mutatis mutandis*, similar provisions, including a term not to revoke the will. Questions may arise as to the position if the survivor nevertheless purports to revoke his will and makes a new one, containing different provisions.

1 FULLY SECRET AND HALF-SECRET TRUSTS[1]

(A) THE PRINCIPLE UPON WHICH SECRET TRUSTS ARE ENFORCED

A typical case of a fully secret trust would be that in which a testator had left property by his will to X absolutely, on the face of the will for his own benefit, but where, in fact, during his lifetime, the testator had informed X that the property left to him by will was not for his own benefit, but for certain persons or charitable purposes, and where X had promised to carry the testator's intention into effect. From early times, the Court of Chancery would, in such cases, compel X to carry out the trusts, although difficulty was felt in reconciling the result with the provisions of s 9 of the Wills Act 1837,[2] which requires a testamentary disposition to be made in a specified form. At first, the accepted explanation was that this was an application of the maxim that we have already met, that 'equity will not permit a statute

---

[1] See, generally, (1947) 12 Conv 28 (J G Fleming); (1963) 27 Conv 92 (J A Andrews); [2000] Conv 40 (Diana Kincaid). A survey of the use of secret trusts in reported in [2003] Conv 203 (Rowena Meager). For the position in New Zealand, see (1995) 6 Cant LR 108 (Nicky Richardson); *Brown v Pourau* [1995] 1 NZLR 352, noted [1996] Conv 302 (C E F Rickett).

[2] Prior to this Act, the Statute of Frauds 1677, and see p 98, *supra*.

to be used as an instrument of fraud';[3] it would be fraud on the part of the secret trustee to rely on the absence of the statutory formalities in order to deny the trust and keep for himself property that he well knew the testator did not intend him to enjoy beneficially. While the fraud theory can explain why the secret trustee cannot keep the property for himself, it does not adequately explain why it enforces the secret trust in favour of the secret beneficiary, rather than merely requiring the secret trustee to hold the property on a resulting trust for the testator's estate.

More recent cases, however, appear to establish that there is no conflict with the Wills Act 1837, since the trust operates outside or, as it is said, dehors the will. Where the will is executed in proper form, X will be able to establish his legal title to the property; if the intention of the testator had been communicated to X by the testator in his lifetime, and X has acquiesced, his conscience will be bound in equity and he will be compelled to hold the property on trust for the persons or purposes indicated by the testator.[4] This trust is not regarded as a testamentary disposition coming within the Wills Act, but as a trust within the ordinary equity jurisdiction. There will, of course, be no secret trust if the evidence shows that the testator intended to impose not a binding obligation, but a mere moral obligation, on the alleged secret trustee.[5]

A half-secret trust differs from a fully secret trust in that the will declares that the property is given to X on trust, although the trusts are not expressed in the will, but have likewise been communicated to X by the testator during his lifetime.[6] Although there are authorities going back as far as the seventeenth century, there was greater difficulty in establishing their validity. So long as the basis was thought to be fraud, the difficulty was that even if the intended beneficiaries did not take, it was clear that the secret trustee could not keep the property for himself, as he was expressed to be a mere trustee in the will. If the Wills Act were to apply to invalidate the secret trust, there would be a resulting trust to the estate. In *Blackwell v Blackwell*,[7] however, it was finally established that half-secret and fully secret trusts are enforced on the same principles.

The modern view was well expressed by Megarry VC in *Re Snowden (decd)*,[8] who said 'the whole basis of secret trusts... is that they operate outside the will, changing nothing that is written in it, and allowing it to operate according to its tenor, but then fastening a trust on to the property in the hands of the recipient'. Two cases may be mentioned as illustrations.

---

[3] See, eg, *Jones v Badley* (1868) 3 Ch App 362, *per* Lord Cairns; *McCormick v Grogan* (1869) LR 4 HL 82, *per* Lord Hatherley. D R Hodge in [1980] Conv 34 argues in favour of this maxim as the basis of secret trusts, and does not think it inconsistent with the secret trust being outside the will.

[4] See, eg, *Cullen v A-G for Ireland* (1866) LR 1 HL 190, *per* Lord Westbury; *Re Blackwell, Blackwell v Blackwell* [1929] AC 318, HL. Patricia Critchley, however, in (1999) 115 LQR 631, rejects the 'dehors the will' doctrine and, with qualifications, accepts the fraud theory. Emma Challinor contends, in [2005] Conv 492, that secret trusts are a covert device by which the courts avoid the statutory formalities of the Wills Act 1837, and proposes their abolition (or at least fundamental revision).

[5] *Kasperbauer v Griffith* [2000] 2 WTLR 333, CA, noted [1998] 1 T & ELJ 20 (E Hailstone), in which it was doubted whether a secret trust could be created over the death benefit in a pension scheme, which the testator did not own or control and which he could never bring into his own ownership or dispose of as he willed.

[6] See p 133, *infra*, for the position as to the time of communication in the case of half-secret trust. In *Jankowski v Pelek Estate* [1996] 2 WWR 457, the court was divided as to whether the trust was fully secret or half-secret.

[7] *Supra*, approving *Re Fleetwood* (1880) 15 Ch D 594; *Re Huxtable* [1902] 2 Ch 793, CA.

[8] [1979] Ch 528, 535, [1979] 2 All ER 172, 177. But see (1999) 115 LQR 631 (Patricia Critchley).

In *Re Gardner*,[9] there was a secret trust and one of the beneficiaries thereunder had prede-ceased the testatrix. Although a gift by will lapses if the beneficiary predeceases the testator, it was held that the share of the deceased beneficiary did not lapse, but passed to her per-sonal representative, since her title arose not under the will, but by the trust created[10] during her lifetime by communication and acceptance thereof by the secret trustee. In *Re Young*,[11] the problem arose in an acute form. Section 15 of the Wills Act 1837[12] provides that a legacy to an attesting witness is ineffective; the facts were that one of the attesting witnesses was a beneficiary under a secret trust. It was held that he did not take under the will and that he was therefore unaffected by the statutory provisions. 'The whole theory,' it was said,[13] 'of the formation of a secret trust is that the Wills Act 1837 has nothing to do with the matter.' It may be added that where it is the secret trustee, and not the beneficiary thereunder, who predeceases the testator, or where the secret trustee disclaims the devise or legacy, the better view is, perhaps, that the secret trust fails in the case of a fully secret trust, on the ground that it only affects the property by reason of the personal obligation binding the individual devisee or legatee.[14] In the case of a half-secret trust, however, the trust may well be good, on the principle that equity will not allow a trust to fail for want of a trustee.[15]

There is no general agreement as to whether secret trusts are express or constructive. Snell,[16] for example, deals with secret trusts under the head of express trusts, but adds that they are 'better classified as constructive'. Underhill and Hayton[17] treat secret trusts within the division dealing with express trusts 'because of their affinity with express trusts', but nevertheless say that they should be categorized as constructive trusts. Thomas and Hudson[18] come down in favour of the constructive trust. Hanbury[19] adopts a split view—that half-secret trusts are express, but that fully secret trusts 'can be enforced under either head'—while Sheridan[20] considered that although half-secret trusts are express, fully secret trusts are constructive. But, it may be asked, as the trust operates outside the will, why should the fact that the existence of the trust is disclosed in the will alter the character of the trust? It is submitted that secret trusts are express trusts, being based on the expressed intention of the testator communicated to and acquiesced in by the secret trustee.[21] On this basis, one runs into the difficulty that s 53(1)(b) of the Law of Property

---

[9] [1923] 2 Ch 230. See [2004] Conv 388 (M Pawlowski and J Brown).

[10] Although it illustrates the present point well, it is difficult to see how the beneficiary could have obtained a transmissible interest before the trust was completely constituted by the trust property vesting in the secret trustee on the death of the testatrix. [11] [1951] Ch 344, [1950] 2 All ER 1245.

[12] Now modified by the Wills Act 1968, which allows the attesting witness-legatee to take if the will is duly executed without his attestation. Section 15 invalidates only beneficial gifts. Accordingly, attestation by the trustee under a half-secret trust would not affect the validity of the half-secret trust, and this may well also be the position in the case of a fully secret trust.

[13] *Per* Danckwerts J at 350, 1250.

[14] *Re Maddock* [1902] 2 Ch 220, 231, CA, *per* Cozens Hardy LJ; contra *Re Blackwell, Blackwell v Blackwell* [1929] AC 318, 328, HL, *per* Lord Buckmaster.

[15] See p 357, *infra*. [16] *Principles of Equity*, 31st edn, [22.29] *et seq*.

[17] *Law of Trusts and Trustees*, 17th edn, [12.79] *et seq*. Hayton and Marshall, *Cases and Commentary on the Law of Trusts*, 12th edn, pp 120, 121, not surprisingly, take a similar view. See also (1972) 23 NILQ 263 (R Burgess).

[18] *Law of Trusts*, [28.49] *et seq*. [19] *Modern Equity*, 17th edn, [5.015].

[20] (1951) 67 LQR 314 (L A Sheridan).

[21] See (1991) 5 Tru LI 69 (P Coughlon) citing the Irish case of *Re Prendiville* (5 December 1990, unre-ported), a half-secret trust case.

Act 1925[22] would seem to require writing where the subject of the secret trust is land. This was, in fact, held to be the case in *Re Baillie*,[23] which concerned a half-secret trust, but more recently, in *Ottaway v Norman*,[24] a fully secret trust of land was held valid on parol evidence. In this case, the trust seems to have been treated as constructive rather than express, but there was no discussion of this point and no reference was made to any possible requirement of writing. However, even if a secret trust is express, it is arguable that it should be enforced notwithstanding the absence of writing by an application of the maxim that 'equity will not permit a statute to be used as an instrument of fraud'.[25]

It should be added that, in *Nichols v IRC*,[26] it was conceded by counsel that the doctrine of secret trusts applies to *inter vivos* gifts, and reference was made to *Bannister v Bannister*;[27] which has already been discussed. It is suggested, however, that the better view is that of Pennycuick J who observed, in *Re Tyler's Fund Trusts*,[28] 'It is probably true to say that the particular principles of law applicable to secret trusts are really concerned only with trusts created by will'.

(B) EVIDENCE

The alleged secret trust must, of course, be established by evidence. It was not established in *Re Snowden*,[29] in which it appeared that the testatrix had simply left the residue to her brother,[30] as a matter of family confidence and probity, to do what he thought she would have done if she had ever finally made up her mind. There was no real evidence that she intended the sanction to be the authority of a court of justice and not merely the conscience of her brother.

As to the standard of proof, there are no special rules as to the evidence required to establish a secret trust. Where no question of fraud arises, the standard of proof is the ordinary civil standard of proof that is required to establish an ordinary trust. According to Megarry VC, if a secret trust can be held to exist in a particular case only by holding the legatee guilty of fraud, then no secret trust should be found unless the standard of proof suffices for fraud.[31] It is, however, submitted that the principles on which secret trusts are enforced today never make it necessary to establish fraud on the part of the legatee and that, accordingly, the ordinary civil standard of proof is always appropriate.[32]

---

[22] See p 88, *supra*.

[23] (1886) 2 TLR 660. In *Re Young* [1951] Ch 344, [1950] 2 All ER 1245 (trust held to have been validly established by parol evidence; no point was taken on s 53(1)(b)).

[24] [1972] Ch 698, [1971] 3 All ER 1325, but the evidence did not establish a secret trust in the residuary estate.   [25] See *Rochefoucauld v Boustead* [1897] 1 Ch 196, CA, and p 96, *supra*.

[26] [1973] 3 All ER 632; affd on different grounds [1975] 2 All ER 120, [1975] 1 WLR 534, CA.

[27] [1948] 2 All ER 133, CA, discussed *supra*, p 97.

[28] [1967] 3 All ER 389, 392, [1967] 1 WLR 1269, 1275. The dictum of Pennycuick J requires slight modification to cover the analogous cases referred to in the next following paragraph, *infra*. The phrase 'created by will' is not a very happy one, but the meaning seems clear.

[29] [1979] Ch 528, [1979] 2 All ER 172. There seems much to be said for the suggestion that the evidence pointed to a secret trust in favour of the testatrix's relatives, subject to a power of selection in her brother: see [1980] Conv 341 (D R Hodge).   [30] Who died six days after the testatrix.

[31] *Re Snowden* [1979] Ch 528, [1979] 2 All ER 271; *Re Riffel Estate* (1988) 64 Sask R 190; *Glasspool v Glasspool* (1999) 53 BCLR (3d) 371. Contra *Ottaway v Norman* [1972] Ch 698, 712, [1971] 3 All ER 1325, 1333, *per* Brightman J.

[32] As argued by C E F Rickett in (1979) 38 CLJ 260; (1979) 43 Conv 448 (F R Crane).

(C) FULLY SECRET TRUSTS

As already indicated, the essential factors that must be present in order to raise a trust are the communication of the intention of the testator to the secret trustee and his express or tacit[33] promise to carry out the testator's intention, on the faith of which the testator either makes a disposition in favour of the secret trustee,[34] or leaves an existing disposition unrevoked.[35] A trust is raised in exactly the same way if, on the strength of such a promise by an intestate successor, a man fails to make a will,[36] or if he destroys a codicil so as to revive the effect of prior testamentary provisions in favour of the secret trustee.[37] In most of the cases, the obligation imposed on the secret trustee is to make some form of *inter vivos* transfer, but in *Ottaway v Norman*,[38] the doctrine was held to apply equally where the obligation was to make a will in favour of the beneficiary under the secret trust.

The communication to the secret trustee, which may be through an authorized agent,[39] must take place during the testator's lifetime, although it does not matters whether it is before or after the date of the will. If, however, the alleged secret trustee only learns of the alleged trust after the death of the testator, the trust will be ineffective. On the death, the property passes under the will to a beneficiary whose conscience is perfectly clear and his absolute title will not be affected by anything he may subsequently learn about the testator's intentions, which have not been expressed in compliance with the Wills Act 1837. Thus, in *Wallgrave v Tebbs*,[40] the testator bequeathed £12,000 and devised certain lands to T and M as joint tenants. Neither T nor M had ever had any communication with the testator about his will, or about any of his intentions or wishes with respect to the disposition of his property. The evidence showed that the testator wished certain charitable purposes to be carried out, and felt confident that T and M would carry them out. T and M claimed to take the property absolutely free from the trust, although they admitted that they would, if they succeeded, apply the property substantially as the testator wished. It was held that, in the absence of any communication in the testator's lifetime, T and M took absolutely.

It is not sufficient to communicate merely the fact of the trust to the secret trustee: the details of the trust must also be communicated to and accepted by him. If there is merely communication and acceptance of the fact of the trust, the secret trustee will hold on trust for the residuary devisees or legatees, or the persons entitled on intestacy if there is no residuary gift, or if residue is given on a secret trust.[41] He cannot take beneficially, as he

---

[33] If the intention is communicated to the secret trustee, it seems that silence on his part will normally be treated as consent to act: *Moss v Cooper* (1861) 1 John & H 352. But mere knowledge of the testator's intention has been held, in Singapore, not to suffice: *Kamla Lal Hiranand v Harilela Padma Hari* [2000] 3 SLR 696, citing text above (in earlier edn).

[34] *Drakeford v Wilks* (1747) 3 Atk 539.   [35] *Moss v Cooper* (1861) 1 John & H 352.

[36] *Stickland v Aldridge* (1804) 9 Ves 516; *Re Gardner* [1920] 2 Ch 523, CA.

[37] *Tharp v Tharp* [1916] 1 Ch 142; compromised on appeal [1916] 2 Ch 205, CA.

[38] [1972] Ch 698, [1971] 3 All ER 1325—the secret trustee was beneficially entitled for life. It was observed in this case that, if a will contains a gift that is in terms absolute, clear evidence is needed before the court will assume that the testator did not mean what he said. The decision is not without its difficulties: see (1973) 36 MLR 210 (S M Bandali); [1971] ASCL 382 (J Hackney).

[39] *Moss v Cooper, supra*, in which the question of communication through an unauthorized agent was raised, but not answered.

[40] (1855) 2 K & J 313. See *Jones v Badley* (1868) 3 Ch App 362. See also (1997) 18 JLH 1 (Chantal Stebbings).

[41] The same result would follow if the trusts were communicated, but were void for uncertainty, illegality, or other cause.

Figure 7.1 Illustrates significance of communication date of the trust

has accepted the position of trustee, but communication of the particular trusts after the death by an unattested paper is not permitted, as this would be a means by which a testator could evade the provisions of the Wills Act 1837.[42] It would, however, probably be a sufficient communication if the details of the trust were handed over to the secret trustee by the testator during his lifetime in a sealed envelope, even though this was marked 'Not to be opened until after my death'.[43]

Difficulties have arisen where there has been communication to one, or some only, of two or more secret trustees.[44] If the gift in the will is to two or more persons as tenants in common, then only the person, or persons, to whom the secret trust was communicated in the testator's lifetime are bound by it; the other person or persons take their respective shares beneficially.[45] Where the gift is to persons as joint tenants, a curious distinction is drawn between the cases in which one, or more, of the secret trustees have accepted the trust prior to the execution of the will, and the case in which the acceptance was subsequent to the will (although, of course, during the testator's lifetime). In the first case, all of the joint tenants are bound by the trust,[46] on the ground that no one can take a benefit that has been procured by fraud. For no satisfactory reason, this principle does not apparently apply in the latter case, in which only the person or persons who have accepted the trust are bound by it.[47]

---

[42] *Re Boyes* (1884) 26 Ch D 531.

[43] *Re Boyes, supra; Re Keen* [1937] Ch 236, [1937] 1 All ER 452, CA, in which, arguing by analogy, Lord Wright MR said '*a ship which sails under sealed orders is sailing under orders though the exact terms are not ascertained by the captain till later*'.

[44] The propositions below are disputed in (1972) 88 LQR 225 (B Perrins), in which it is argued that in every case in which there has been a communication to X (one of two secret trustees X and Y) only, yet it is alleged that X and Y are both bound by the secret trust, the question is whether the gift to Y in the will was induced by the promise made by X to the testator.

[45] *Tee v Ferris* (1856) 2 K & J 357; *Re Stead* [1900] 1 Ch 237.

[46] *Russell v Jackson* (1852) 10 Hare 204; *Re Stead, supra.*

[47] *Moss v Cooper* (1861) 1 John & H 352; *Re Stead, supra.*

(D) HALF-SECRET TRUSTS

Here, as we have seen, the will expressly states that the gift is on trust, so there is no possibility of the secret trustee claiming beneficially. The problem, accordingly, is whether he holds on trust for the residuary devisees or legatees, or the persons entitled on intestacy, if there is no residuary gift or if residue is given, or whether the secret trusts communicated to and accepted by him can be enforced. There are, however, rather more difficulties and uncertainties in the relevant law than in the case of fully secret trusts.

What may, perhaps, be called the 'primary' rule is the rule that evidence as to the alleged half-secret trust is inadmissible if it contradicts the terms of the will. Thus, in *Re Keen*,[48] the testator bequeathed £10,000 to X and Y 'to be held upon trust and disposed of by them among such person, persons or charities as may be notified by me to them or either of them during my lifetime'. As a matter of construction, it was held that the will referred to a future notification and the court held that evidence of a prior notification was inadmissible, as it would be inconsistent with the express terms of the will. Another aspect of this rule is that a person named as trustee in the will is not permitted to set up any beneficial interest in himself,[49] although it is a different matter if, on its true construction, the will gives property to a person conditionally on his discharging the testator's wishes communicated to him.[50]

A further problem arises in connection with this rule where the will gives property to persons in some such terms as in *Re Spencer's Will*[51] 'relying, but not by way of trust, upon their applying the sum in or towards the object privately communicated to them' by the testator. In that case, the Court of Appeal held that evidence would be admissible to show that the legatees had, in fact, accepted a secret trust,[52] although it is not made clear how this is to be reconciled with the rule, as such evidence would contradict the terms of the will. Indeed, it seems doubtful whether the point was argued. This decision was distinguished in *Re Falkiner*,[53] in which it was held that the true inference was that the alleged secret trustee, knowing the contents of the will, had agreed to give effect to the testatrix's wishes in accordance with the scheme of the will, which included a provision that there should be no trust or legal obligation.

Turning to another matter, the most important distinction between fully secret and half-secret trusts is that, in the latter case, the communication to and acceptance of the trusts will not merely be ineffective if it takes place after the testator's death, but even if it takes place during his lifetime but after the execution of his will. It has been said that:[54]

> A testator cannot reserve to himself a power of making future unwitnessed dispositions by merely naming a trustee and leaving the purposes of the trust to be supplied afterwards nor can a legatee give testamentary validity to an unexecuted codicil by accepting an indefinite trust, never communicated to him in the testator's lifetime.

---

[48] [1937] Ch 236, [1937] 1 All ER 452, CA. See also *Re Spence* [1949] WN 237.

[49] *Re Rees' Will Trusts* [1950] Ch 204, [1949] 2 All ER 1003, CA; *Re Huxtable, supra*; *Re Pugh's Will Trusts* [1967] 3 All ER 337. Cf *Re Tyler's Fund Trusts* [1967] 3 All ER 389, [1967] 1 WLR 1269.

[50] See, eg, *Irvine v Sullivan* (1869) LR 8 Eq 673.   [51] (1887) 3 TLR 822, CA.

[52] This, of course, would be a fully secret trust, not a half-secret trust.

[53] [1924] 1 Ch 88, applied in *Re Stirling* [1954] 2 All ER 113, [1954] 1 WLR 265. The distinction lacks plausibility, according to Waters, *The Law of Trusts in Canada*, 2nd edn, p 230.

[54] *Per* Viscount Sumner in *Re Blackwell, Blackwell v Blackwell* [1929] AC 318, 339, HL.

On this basis, it has been stated that, in the case of a half-secret trust, communication cannot be effective if made after the date of the will. This argument, which, if valid, would apply equally to fully secret trusts, is, it is submitted, invalid as it fails to take into account the basis of the secret trusts—that is, that they operate entirely outside the will. The secret trustee, whether it is a fully secret or half-secret trust, should, on principle, take the property bound by an equitable obligation if he has accepted the trust at any time during the testator's lifetime, whether before or after the date of the will being irrelevant. However, although not finally settled, the weight of dicta favours the view that, in the case of half-secret trusts, the communication and acceptance of the trust must be prior to, or contemporaneous with, the execution of the will,[55] and the contrary view seems to have been considered unarguable in *Re Bateman's Will Trusts*,[56] the most recent case. In Australia, however, the courts have refused to apply the English rule and have held that a half-secret trust can be communicated at any time before the testator's death, as in the case of a fully secret trust.[57]

Where a testator makes a gift to two or more persons who, on the face of the will, are trustees, who always hold as joint tenants, it is clear, assuming that the law as stated in the preceding paragraph is correct, that if there had been no communication of the trusts by the time that the will was executed, the trustees would hold the property on trust for the residuary devisees or residuary legatees, or the persons entitled on intestacy if there is no residuary gift or if it is a gift of residue.[58] Where the trust has been communicated to and accepted before the date of the will by one, or some only, of the trustees, the position seems to be the same as in fully secret trusts—that is, the gift being to them as joint tenants, acceptance by one binds all.[59] What has been said is subject to the qualification that, as we have already seen, if the evidence as to communication contradicts the terms of the will, it is inadmissible; so, if the will states that the trusts have been communicated to all of the trustees, evidence of communication to one only would seem to be inadmissible.[60]

---

[55] *Johnson v Ball* (1851) 5 De G & Sm 85; *Blackwell v Blackwell, supra*; *Re Keen* [1937] Ch 236, [1937] 1 All ER 452, CA. The apparent rule is criticized by Holdsworth (1937) 63 LQR 501 and by Parker and Mellows, *The Modern Law of Trusts*, 8th edn, p 127, but approved (1972) 23 NILQ 263 (R Burgess) and [1981] Conv 335 (T G Watkin), who would like to see the rule extended by statute to fully secret trusts. See also [1992] Conv 202 (J Mee) discussing the different rule in Irish law. The unsatisfactory position is, perhaps, due to confusion with the probate doctrine of incorporation by reference, under which a document not properly executed in accordance with the provisions of the Wills Act 1837 may be incorporated in the will and granted probate. In order for this to happen, the document sought to be incorporated must already be in existence when the will is executed and referred to therein as an existing document in terms enabling it to be clearly identified. See *Re Schintz's Will Trusts* [1951] Ch 870, [1951] 1 All ER 1095. It has recently been argued, contrary to what is said above, that the incorporation doctrine is the basis of the half-secret trust: [1979] Conv 360 (P Matthews). Counterarguments are put in [1980] Conv 341 (D R Hodge). An alternative view accepts the distinction between fully secret and half-secret trusts, and explains it in terms of the extrinsic evidence rule: [1985] Conv 248 (B Perrins); D Wilde seeks to justify it, in [1995] Conv 366, on the ground that a fully secret trust is commonly set up without legal advice, while a half-secret trust almost always involves a solicitor.

[56] [1970] 3 All ER 817, [1970] 1 WLR 1463.

[57] *Legerwood v Perpetual Trustee Co Ltd* (1997) 41 NSWLR 532. Moreover, the English courts have refused to apply the rule to the analogous case of nomination under a life insurance policy: *Gold v Hill* [1999] 1 FLR 54.

[58] The same result would follow if the trusts were duly communicated in time, but were void for uncertainty, illegality, or other cause. See, eg, *Re Hawksley's Settlement* [1934] Ch 384.

[59] *Re Young* [1951] Ch 344, [1950] 2 All ER 1245.

[60] *Re Spence* [1949] WN 237. Cf *Re Keen* [1937] Ch 236, [1937] 1 All ER 452, CA, in which the will referred to communication to the trustees 'or one of them'.

The last point to be mentioned was decided in *Re Cooper*.[61] In that case, the testator bequeathed £5,000 to two persons as trustees on the face of the will, and the trusts were duly communicated to them by the testator and accepted prior to the execution of the will. Subsequently, the testator executed a codicil, whereby he in effect increased the legacy to £10,000, the trustees *'knowing my wishes regarding the sum'*. The increase of the legacy was never communicated to the trustees by the testator. It was held that the secret trusts were effective as to the first £5,000, but failed as to the additional £5,000 given by the codicil.

2 MUTUAL WILLS[62]

Mutual wills are generally regarded as a case of constructive trust.[63] They arise where two persons, usually, but not essentially,[64] husband and wife, have made an agreement as to the disposal of their property, and each has, in accordance with the agreement, executed a will, the two wills containing, *mutatis mutandis*, similar provisions. The mutual wills may give the survivor only a life interest,[65] or, it seems, after some hesitation, an absolute interest.[66] In either case, it may well be a term of the agreement that the wills shall not be revoked,[67] and if one or the other nevertheless purports to revoke his mutual will, various problems may arise.

In the first place, it is quite clear that a will cannot be made irrevocable.[68] In *Re Hey's Estate*,[69] a husband and wife made mutual wills in 1907. The husband died in 1911 and his will was duly proved, under which the wife took certain benefits. Subsequently, the wife executed a codicil in 1912 and a fresh will in 1913. These later instruments were made in breach of a definite agreement between the husband and wife in 1907, when the mutual wills were executed, that they should be irrevocable. It was held that the will of 1907 was nonetheless revocable, because our testamentary law regards revocability as an essential characteristic of a will and probate was accordingly ordered of the will of 1913.

It by no means follows, however, that an agreement such as that entered into by the husband and wife above in 1907 is worthless. At law, an action for damages will lie for breach of a covenant or contract not to revoke a will (otherwise than a revocation by a subsequent marriage) at the suit of the other party,[70] and it is arguable that an intended beneficiary under the mutual will may now sue directly under the Contracts (Rights of Third Parties) Act 1999.[71] Further, in equity, a mutual will of which probate will not be granted may be enforced under a trust. Equity takes the view, where two persons have agreed to make and have in fact executed mutual wills, and where it was a term of the agreement that such

---

[61] [1939] Ch 811, [1939] 3 All ER 586, CA.

[62] See, generally, (1951) 15 Conv 28 (G Boughen Graham); (1970) 34 Conv 230 (R Burgess); [1982] Conv 228 (K Hodkinson); (1982) 79 LSG 1305 (T Prime); (1988) 138 NLJ 351 (F H G Sunnocks); [1997] Conv 182 (A Harper); [2005] 29 MULR 390 (Rosalind Croucher). See also (1989) 105 LQR 534 (C E F Rickett).

[63] See *Re Cleaver* [1981] 2 All ER 1018, [1981] 1 WLR 939; C E F Rickett in (1982) 8 Adel LR 178.

[64] *Lord Walpole v Lord Orford* (1797) 3 Ves 402.

[65] For example, *Dufour v Pereira* (1769) 1 Dick 419—the earliest and leading case on mutual wills.

[66] *Re Green* [1951] Ch 148, [1950] 2 All ER 913; disregarding doubts suggested by *Re Oldham* [1925] Ch 75.

[67] Except, of course, as a result of a subsequent agreement.   [68] *Vynior's Case* (1609) 8 Co Rep 81b.

[69] [1914] P 192.   [70] *Robinson v Ommanney* (1883) 23 Ch D 285.   [71] See p 109 *et seq, supra*.

wills should not be revoked, that the first of them to die does so with the implied promise of the survivor that the agreement shall hold good. Accordingly, if the survivor revokes[72] or alters his will, as we have seen he can, his personal representatives will take his property upon trust to perform the agreement, because the will of the one who has died first has, by his death, become irrevocable.[73] The principle has been held to apply equally whether or not the survivor takes any benefit under the will of the first to die.[74]

Similar principles[75] apply in the case of a joint will, as is illustrated by *Re Hagger*.[76] In that case, under the joint will, the survivor was to have a life interest in certain joint property with remainders over. The husband and wife agreed not to revoke the joint will. The wife was the first to die and, subsequently, but before the death of the husband, one of the remaindermen died. The husband subsequently made a fresh will inconsistent with the joint will. It was held that, from the death of the wife, the husband held the property upon the trusts of the joint will and, accordingly, there was no lapse of the share of the beneficiary who survived the wife, but predeceased the husband, and his share was payable to his personal representatives as part of his estate.

In order to establish the trust, it is not sufficient to establish an agreement to make mutual wills followed by their due execution: it is essential that an agreement not to revoke them be proved. This agreement, although it does not restrain the legal right to revoke, is the foundation of the right in equity.[77] Such an agreement will not be implied from the mere making of mutual wills. In *Re Oldham*,[78] it was pointed out that 'the fact that those two wills were made in identical terms connotes no more than an agreement of so making them'; other evidence, which may consist of recitals in the mutual wills,[79] or of evidence outside them[80] must be brought to establish the agreement not to revoke them. The agreement, if it relates to land, is deprived of any legal effect as a contract by s 2(1) of the Law of Property (Miscellaneous Provisions) Act 1989. However, it was held in *Healey v Brown*,[81] in the absence of writing, that there was a constructive trust of the share in what had been the matrimonial home of the first to die, but a dictum of Morritt LJ in *Re Goodchild (decd)*[82] was held to inhibit a constructive trust of the survivor's share.

Even assuming that an agreement not to revoke the mutual wills is established, a trust is not created at once, and, indeed, may never arise at all. Clearly, the parties may release each other from their bargain by mutual agreement and it seems that, during their joint

---

[72] This includes revocation by a subsequent marriage: *Re Goodchild (decd)* [1997] 3 All ER 63, [1997] 1 WLR 1216, CA.

[73] *Dufour v Pereira* (1769) 1 Dick 419; *Stone v Hoskins* [1905] P 194; *Thomas and Agnes Carvel Foundation v Carvel* [2007] EWHC 1314 (Ch), [2007] 4 All ER 81, [2008] 2 WLR 1234. Cf *Staib v Powell* [1979] Qd R 151.

[74] *Re Dale* [1994] Ch 31, [1993] 4 All ER 129, discussed [1994] NLJ Charities Supp 34 (D Brown); (1994) 144 NLJ 1272 (P O'Hagan); (1995) 58 MLR 95 (A H R Brierly).

[75] The Canadian courts have held that it is easier to infer an intention not to revoke from the terms of the will alone in the case of a joint will as opposed to mutual wills: *Re Grisor* (1980) 101 DLR (3d) 728.

[76] [1930] 2 Ch 190.

[77] *Gray v Perpetual Trustee Co Ltd* [1928] AC 391, PC; *Re Cleaver* [1981] 2 All ER 1018, [1981] 1 WLR 939; *Re Goodchild (decd), supra*, CA; *Lewis v Cotton* [2001] 2 NZLR 21, noted [2002] 36 T & ELJ centre pages (Zandra Houston); *Osborne v Estate of Osborne* [2001] VSCA 228, [2002] ITELR 804; *Birch v Curtis* [2002] EWHC 1158 (Ch), [2002] 2 FLR 847, noted (2002) 43 T & ELJ 14 (D Rowell). But see (2003) 27 MULR 217 (Julie Cassidy).

[78] [1925] Ch 75.   [79] *Re Green* [1951] Ch 148, [1950] 2 All ER 913.

[80] *Re Heys' Estate* [1914] P 192.

[81] [2002] WTLR 849, noted (2002) 41 T & ELJ 7 (D Jackson); [2003] Conv 239 (Christine Davis).

[82] *Supra*, CA, at 76, 1230. See also *Humphreys v Green* (1882) 10 QBD 148, CA.

lifetimes, either may revoke his will separately, provided that he gives notice of the revocation to the other party.[83] Such other party thereby acquires an opportunity to alter his own
will and the ground upon which a trust is raised ceases to exist. Further, even though no
notice be given during their joint lives, where the one who dies first has departed from the
bargain by executing a fresh will revoking the former one, the survivor, who has, on the
death of the other party to the agreement, notice of the alteration cannot, on the one hand,
claim to have the later will of the deceased set aside or modified, or indirectly enforced by
way of declaration of trust or otherwise.[84] On the other hand, the survivor will no longer
be bound by the agreement and can leave his entire estate uninhibited by the terms of the
mutual will, and this is so even where the will of the first to die has not been revoked, but
merely varied by a codicil, at least where the alteration is 'not insignificant'.[85] In such cases,
therefore, no trust will ever come into being. The principles giving rise to a trust have,
however, been held to be applicable in a case in which a party, not being the first to die,
has, by reason of senile dementia, lost the capacity to revoke his will and make a new will.
The wife was in this position in *Low v Perpetual Trustees WA Ltd*,[86] and the personal representatives of the husband, who was the first to die and who had made a fresh will, were
held to hold his estate upon trust to perform the terms of the mutual wills.

In practice, the most difficult problem may well be to ascertain exactly what property is
subject to the trusts. It was said, in *Re Hobley (decd)*,[87] that the legal principles that apply to
mutual (or joint) wills, if not revoked, oblige the survivor to leave not only any estate inher-
ited from the first to die, but also the whole of his or her own estate, whenever acquired, on
the agreed terms. This is, of course, subject to the terms of the mutual (or joint) wills. Thus,
in *Re Hagger*,[88] the facts of which have already been mentioned, it was held that the joint
will effected a severance of the joint interest of the husband and wife, and the trust operated
as from the wife's death, not only on her interest in the property, but also on the interest of
the surviving husband. Contrast *Re Green*,[89] where the mutual wills of husband and wife
were in identical form, *mutatis mutandis*. Apart from certain specific real property, the
husband divided his residue into two equal shares: one moiety being considered as his own
personal estate and the other moiety as the equivalent to any benefit that he had received
from his wife by reason of her predeceasing him, as in fact happened. The husband subsequently revoked his first, mutual, will and, after the husband's death, the court held that

---

[83] *Dufour v Pereira, supra.*

[84] *Stone v Hoskins* [1905] P 194. But there may be a claim for damages where there has been unilateral
revocation in breach of contract. The decision in *Stone v Hoskins* was doubted in the Australian case of *Bigg
v Queensland Trustees Ltd* [1990] 2 Qd R 11, in which the plaintiff and the deceased (his wife) had executed
mutual wills leaving their property to each other and, on the death of the survivor, to their respective children by previous marriages. By later wills, the deceased revoked her mutual will, appointed the defendant as
executor and altered the disposition of her property. The plaintiff made and continued to make investments
in the deceased's name in the belief that the mutual will still stood. It was held that the defendant held all of
the deceased's estate on trust for the plaintiff. However, in (1991) 54 MLR 581, C E F Rickett points out that
this was not an action against a survivor and, in his opinion, was not a mutual wills case at all. In his view,
the primary remedy was in contract, with the possibility of claims in restitution or reliance on promissory
estoppel. See (1991) 21 QLSJ 121 (M Weir).

[85] *Re Hobley (decd)* [2006] WTLR 467. See [1998] PCB 332 (A Norris and H Legge).

[86] (1995) 14 WAR 35. An Australian case, but it is thought the English courts would come to the same
conclusion.

[87] *Supra*. See the discussion in (1951) 14 MLR 136 (J D B Mitchell).   [88] *Supra.*

[89] [1951] Ch 148, [1950] 2 All ER 913.

the trust operated only on one half of the husband's residuary estate—that is, the moiety that he had notionally received from his wife. The other moiety passed under his fresh will.On a slightly different point, it was said in *Re Hobley (decd)*[90] that the survivor is not prevented from using the available assets in his lifetime, or even disposing of them by gift, unless expressly prohibited by the agreement.

As has been mentioned in connection with *Re Hagger*,[91] the same principles apply where two persons have executed a joint will.[92] In such cases, on the death of one of the joint testators, probate will be granted of so much of the joint will as becomes operative on his death.[93] The survivor of joint testators will be bound by a trust in the same way and to the same extent as if they had executed mutual wills.

It is thought that similar principles would be applied in analogous situations. There do not seem to be any English cases, but in Canada, they have been applied where the agreement is subsequent to the making of the wills, and where the agreement is that, if one party makes a change in a particular part of his will (having a right under the agreement to do so), the other party will make a corresponding change. In this last case, if the survivor does not make the change, equity will treat the case as if he had done so and compel the personal representatives to distribute the estate on that basis.[94]

[90] *Supra.*   [91] *Supra.*

[92] It was at one time thought that a joint will was impossible, but there is now no doubt that it can be valid: see, eg, *Re Duddell* [1932] 1 Ch 585, [1932] All ER Rep 714. Joint wills are rare in practice, and Underhill and Hayton, *Law of Trusts and Trustees*, 17th edn, [35.54], n 2, states that they are to be deprecated and that practitioners should do their utmost to ensure that separate wills are drafted. See (1996) 139 Sol Jo (R Shah). See also *Re Ohorodynk* (1979) 97 DLR (3d) 502, appeal dismissed (1980) 102 DLR (3d) 576; criticized (1979) 29 UTLJ 390 (T G Youdan).

[93] *Re Piazzi-Smyth's Goods* [1898] P 7.

[94] *Re Fox* [1951] OR 378. See (1979) 29 UTLJ 390 (T G Youdan).

8

CONSTRUCTIVE TRUSTS

As will be realized, it is impossible to make an exhaustive list of constructive trust situations, but a discussion of some of the more common and important circumstances that have been held to give rise to a constructive trust follows. As a general principle, it may be said that property subject to a constructive trust must have come into the hands of the alleged trustee as a result of unconscionable dealing or in breach of a fiduciary obligation.[1] In addition, as we have seen, some take the view that secret trusts and mutual wills are enforced on the basis of constructive trust, and also cases such as *Rochefoucauld v Boustead*[2] and *Bannister v Bannister*.[3]

The first two sections in this chapter deal with aspects of the principle that a trustee is not permitted to make a profit out of his trust: any such profit will be held by him as a constructive trustee for the beneficiaries under his trust. The next section examines the circumstances in which a person who is not an appointed trustee will nevertheless be held liable as a constructive trustee of trust property that comes into his hands. The final sections consider three particular limited situations. One important example of the constructive trust—the common intention constructive trust—is considered in a subsequent chapter.

1 THE RULE IN *KEECH V SANDFORD*[4]

Where a trustee who held a lease for the benefit of a cestui que trust has made use of the influence that his situation has enabled him to exercise to obtain a new lease, he will be compelled in equity to hold the new lease thus acquired as a constructive trustee for the benefit of the cestui que trust. The length to which the doctrine has been carried is exemplified by *Keech v Sandford*[5] itself. In that case, the rule was still adhered to despite express proof of the lessor's refusal to renew the lease for the benefit of the cestui que trust, the court apparently taking the view that to relax the rule would give the trustees too great an opportunity to defraud the beneficiaries. The renewed lease is regarded in equity as an accretion to, or graft upon, the original term and subject accordingly to the same trusts.

---

[1] *French v Mason* (1998) Times, 13 November.   [2] [1897] 1 Ch 196, CA. See p 96 *et seq, supra*.

[3] [1948] 2 All ER 133, CA; followed in *Staden v Jones* [2008] EWCA Civ 936, [2008] 2 FLR 1931.

[4] (1726) Sel Cas Ch 61. See (1972) 36 Conv 159 (D R Paling), in which the pleadings are transcribed. Many of the relevant cases are reviewed in *Re Biss* [1903] 2 Ch 40, CA. See also (1969) 33 Conv 161 (S Cretney); (1974) 38 Conv 330 (D Paling); (1987) 1 TL & P 171 (Fiona Spearing).

[5] *Supra*, applied *Warman International Ltd v Dwyer* (1995) 128 ALR 201, noted [1995] LMCLQ 462 (P Jaffey). See *A-G for Hong Kong v Reid* [1994] 1 AC 324, [1994] 1 All ER 1, PC.

The doctrine is not restricted to cases in which the old lease was renewable by custom or agreement: it applies also where there is no obligation to grant a new lease, and notwithstanding the fact that the old lease has expired.[6]

The principle that a trustee who renews a lease will be treated as a constructive trustee of the renewed lease or, to put it another way, the presumption of personal incapacity to retain the benefit, has been extended to other cases in which there is a fiduciary relationship. Apart from the case of the trustee, there are other persons in connection with whom the presumption cannot be rebutted[7]—namely, personal representatives,[8] agents, tenants for life,[9] and presumably, in most cases, as a result of the Law of Property Act 1925,[10] joint tenants and tenants in common. In some other cases—namely, mortgagors,[11] mortgagees,[12] and partners[13]—the presumption of personal incapacity has been said to be 'at most a rebuttable presumption of fact'.[14] These seem to be the only cases in which any such presumption arises, and the Court of Appeal in *Re Biss*[15] expressly disapproved of dicta[16] suggesting that if any person, only partly interested in an old lease, obtained from the lessor a renewal, he must be held a constructive trustee of the new lease, whatever might be the nature of his interest or the circumstances under which he obtained the new lease.

In *Re Biss*[17] itself, it was held that the principle in *Keech v Sandford*[18] did not apply. In that case, a lessor granted a lease for seven years of a house in which the lessee carried on a profitable business. On the expiration of the term, the lessor refused to renew, but allowed the lessee to remain as tenant from year to year at an increased rent. During that tenancy, the lessee died intestate, leaving a widow and three children, one being an infant. The widow alone took out administration to her husband's estate, and she and the two adult children, one of whom was a son, continued to carry on the business under the existing yearly tenancy. The widow and son each applied to the lessor for a new lease for the benefit of the estate, which he refused to grant but, having determined the yearly tenancy by notice, he granted to the son, who had never become an administrator of his father's estate, 'personally' a new lease for three years at a still further increased rent. The widow, as sole

---

6 *Pickering v Vowles* (1783) 1 Bro CC 197.

7 *Re Biss* [1903] 2 Ch 40, CA; *Re Knowles' Will Trusts* [1948] 1 All ER 866, CA.

8 Including an executor *de son tort: Mulvany v Dillon* (1810) 1 Ball & B 409.

9 *James v Dean* (1808) 15 Ves 236; *Lloyd-Jones v Clark-Lloyd* [1919] 1 Ch 424, CA and now see ss 16(1) and 107 of the Settled Land Act 1925, as amended by the Trustee Act 2000.

10 Sections 34 and 36, as amended by the Trusts of Land and Appointment of Trustees Act 1996. But not if the legal estate is vested in outside trustees. In such case, there is no fiduciary relationship, either in the case of tenants in common—*Kennedy v de Trafford* [1897] AC 180, HL—or of joint tenants—*Re Biss, supra.*

11 *Leigh v Burnett* (1885) 29 Ch D 231.

12 *Nelson v Hannam and Smith* [1943] Ch 59, [1942] 2 All ER 680, CA.

13 *Clegg v Edmondson* (1857) 8 De GM & G 787; *Chan v Zacharia* (1983) 53 ALR 417. But see *Thompson's Trustee v Heaton* [1974] 1 All ER 1239, [1974] 1 WLR 605, the note in (1975) 38 MLR 226 (P Jackson) and Oakley, *Constructive Trusts*, 3rd edn, p 159, suggesting that the presumption should be irrebuttable in the case of partners. The duty of good faith continues to subsist until the partnership affairs have been finally wound up and settled, and the assets of the partnership have been distributed: *John Taylors (a firm) v Masons (a firm)* [2001] EWCA Civ 2106, [2005] WTLR 1519, in which Arden LJ said it may be that the rule, in its application to partnerships, is too harsh in modern circumstances.

14 *Re Biss, supra*, at 56, *per* Collins MR; *Harris v Black* (1983) 46 P & CR 366, CA (not applied where two trustees were joint beneficiaries and one of them did not wish to apply for a new tenancy under the Landlord and Tenant Act 1954, Pt II). Cf *Glennon v Taxation Comr of Commonwealth of Australia* (1972) 127 CLR 503.

15 *Supra.*   16 *Per* Lord Bathurst LC in *Rowe v Chichester* (1773) Amb 715.   17 *Supra.*

18 *Supra.*

administratrix, applied to have the new lease treated as taken by the son for the benefit of the estate. The court, however, in the absence of a fiduciary relationship, held the son entitled to keep the lease for his own benefit.

Another way in which the rule in *Keech v Sandford*[19] has been extended is by its application to the acquisition by a trustee of the reversion expectant on a lease. The earlier cases, however, laid down a distinction for which no really satisfactory justification can be put forward.[20] This was that the rule applied to the purchase of reversions on leases when the leases were renewable by custom or agreement,[21] on the ground that it deprived the beneficiaries of the chance of renewal for their benefit, but not where there was no right or custom of renewal.[22] This distinction does not appear to have been mentioned to the Court of Appeal in *Protheroe v Protheroe*,[23] in which it was held that the purchased reversion was held on trust although there was presumably no right or custom of renewal. It was a case in which the husband held the lease of what had been the matrimonial home as trustee for himself and his wife in equal shares, and after the parties had separated and the wife had filed a petition for divorce, he purchased the freehold reversion. It was held that the freehold reversion must be regarded in equity as acquired on the same trusts as the lease.

It should be observed that where a man is held to be a constructive trustee under the rule in *Keech v Sandford*,[24] he is entitled to a lien on the property for the expenses of renewal,[25] and the costs of permanent improvements,[26] and he is entitled to be indemnified against the covenants in the new lease.[27] If the lease comprises business premises upon which the trustee carries on a business, he will be accountable for the whole of the profits, although allowances may be made for his time, energy, and skill.[28]

2 OBLIGATION TO ACCOUNT AS A CONSTRUCTIVE TRUSTEE FOR PROFITS RECEIVED BY VIRTUE OF HIS POSITION AS TRUSTEE

Various cases may be mentioned to illustrate the wide principle, continually restated, that 'whenever a trustee, being the ostensible owner of property, acquires any benefit as the owner of that property, that benefit cannot be retained by himself, but must be surrendered for the

---

[19] *Supra.* See *Owen v Williams* (1773) Amb 734; *Giddings v Giddings* (1827) 3 Russ 241.

[20] See (1969) 33 Conv 161 (S Cretney) for a historical explanation, coupled with the opinion that the distinction is now irrelevant.

[21] *Re Lord Ranelagh's Will* (1884) 26 Ch D 590; *Phillips v Phillips* (1885) 29 Ch D 673, CA. Cf *Griffith v Owen* [1907] 1 Ch 195.

[22] *Longton v Wilsby* (1897) 76 LT 770; *Bevan v Webb* [1905] 1 Ch 620. And see *per* Wilberforce J at first instance in *Phipps v Boardman* [1964] 2 All ER 187, 202.

[23] [1968] 1 All ER 1111, [1968] 1 WLR 519, CA. See (1968) 32 Conv 220 (F R Crane) and (1968) 31 MLR 707 (P Jackson). See also *Thompson's Trustee v Heaton* [1974] 1 All ER 1239, [1974] 1 WLR 605; *Metlej v Kavanagh* [1981] 2 NSWLR 339 and note in (1975) 38 MLR 226 (P Jackson).

[24] *Supra.*   [25] *Isaac v Wall* (1877) 6 Ch D 706; *Re Lord Ranelagh's Will* (1884) 26 Ch D 590.

[26] *Mill v Hill* (1852) 3 HL Cas 828; *Rowley v Ginnever* [1897] 2 Ch 503.

[27] *Mill v Hill* (1852) 3 HL Cas 828.   [28] *Re Jarvis* [1958] 2 All ER 336, [1958] 1 WLR 815.

advantage of those who are beneficially interested'.[29] The object of the equitable remedies of account or the imposition of a constructive trust is to ensure that the defaulting fiduciary does not retain the profit; it is not to compensate the beneficiary for any loss. It does not depend on whether the beneficiaries actually suffered any loss. The strict rule requires a trustee or fiduciary to disgorge all of the profits that he has made from the transaction that has involved the breach of duty.[30] However, it has recently been said[31] that:

> ...it may be appropriate for a higher court one day to revisit the rule on secret profits and to make it less inflexible in appropriate cases, where the unqualified operation of the rule operates particularly harshly and where the result is not compatible with the desire of modern courts to ensure that remedies are proportionate to the justice of the case, where this does not conflict with some other overriding policy objective of the rule in question.

Such a possible development is opposed by Conaglen[32] in favour of the long-standing orthodoxy, rejecting the argument of Longbein[33] that fiduciary doctrine's strict prohibition of conflicts between duty and interest should be relaxed where the fiduciary has acted in the best interests of the beneficiaries.

The principle applies equally to a custodian trustee,[34] and to other persons in a fiduciary position,[35] including agents,[36] solicitors,[37] company directors,[38] company promoters,[39] and partners,[40] although its application and precise scope must be moulded according

---

[29] Per Lord Cairns LC in *Aberdeen Town Council v Aberdeen University* (1877) 2 App Cas 544, 549, HL; *A-G for Hong Kong v Reid* [1994] 1 AC 324, [1994] 1 All ER 1, PC. See *Re Edwards' Will Trusts* [1982] Ch 30, [1981] 2 All ER 941, CA (access strip conveyed to trustee in consequence of his occupation of property as trustee). See also (1989) 48 CLJ 302 (I M Jackman).

[30] *United Pan-Europe Communications NV v Deutsche Bank AG* [2002] 2 BCLC 461, 484, CA, *per* Morritt LJ; *Murad v Al-Saraj* [2005] EWCA Civ 959, [2005] WTLR 1573, noted (2006) 76 T & ELTJ 22 (R Ticehurst), in which all three members of the court considered *Warman International Ltd v Dwyer* (1995) 128 ALR 201. Clarke LJ interpreted that case as deciding that the court had a discretion to order disgorgement of only a proportionate share of the profits, but Arden and Jonathan Parker LJJ disagreed, and held that the restriction of the relief granted was limited solely by causation.

[31] *Murad v Al-Saraj, supra*, CA, *per* Arden LJ, at [83], and see (2006) 122 LQR 11 (M McInnes).

[32] [2006] CLJ 278.   [33] (2005) 114 Yale LJ 929.

[34] *Re Brooke Bond & Co Ltd's Trust Deed* [1963] Ch 357, [1963] 1 All ER 454, in which, however, the court authorized the custodian trustee to retain the profits.

[35] As to what is meant by a 'fiduciary' obligation or relationship, see Finn, *Fiduciary Obligations*; (1989) 68 CBR 1 (J R M Gautreau); (1989) 9 Ox JLS 285 (R Flannigan); *Hospital Products Ltd v United States Surgical Corpn* (1984) 55 ALR 417, discussed (1986) 6 Ox JLS 444 (R P Austin); (1986) 8 U Tas LR 311 (D S K Ong); *News Ltd v Australian Rugby Football League Ltd* (1996) 139 ALR 193, 310–314; *LAC Minerals Ltd v International Corona Resources Ltd* (1989) 61 DLR (4th) 14; *Estate Realties Ltd v Wignall* [1991] 3 NZLR 482; *Hodgkinson v Simms* (1994) 117 DLR (4th) 151; *Pilmer v Duke Group Ltd (in liq)* (2001) 180 ALR 249 (held there was no fiduciary duty), noted [2001] CLJ 480 (M D J Conaglen); (1990) 69 CBR 455 (D W M Waters); [1990] LMCLQ 4 (J D Davies); [1990] LMCLQ 460 (P Birks); (1991) 108/109 LJ 4 (G Jones).

[36] See, eg, *Parker v McKenna* (1874) 10 Ch App 96, 118, *per* Lord Cairns.

[37] *Brown v IRC* [1965] AC 244, [1964] 3 All ER 119, HL. See also *Alimand Computer Systems v Radcliffes & Co* (1991) Times, 6 November (solicitors trustees of funds paid to them by clients as stakeholders).

[38] *Regal (Hastings) Ltd v Gulliver* (1942)[1967] 2 AC 134n, [1942] 1 All ER 378, HL; *Selangor United Rubber Estates Ltd v Craddock (No 3)* [1968] 2 All ER 1073, [1969] 1 WLR 1773; *Guinness plc v Saunders* [1990] 2 AC 663, [1990] 1 All ER 652, HL. See [1986] JBL 23 (D W Fox); (1985) 23 Osg Hall LJ 203 (Lord Wedderburn); (1994) 45 NILQ 1 (J P Lowry) (arguing for greater flexibility in the application of the principle to company directors). See (2006) 122 LQR 449 (R Flannigan).

[39] *Jubilee Cotton Mills Ltd v Lewis* [1924] AC 958, HL.

[40] *Aas v Benham* [1891] 2 Ch 244, CA; *Thompson's Trustee v Heaton* [1974] 1 All ER 1239, [1974] 1 WLR 603. In *Fraser Edmiston Pty Ltd v AGT (Qld) Pty Ltd* [1988] 2 Qd R 1, it was held that a fiduciary

to the nature of the relationship.[41] In *Reading v A-G*,[42] there was held to be a fiduciary relationship between the Crown and an army sergeant stationed in Cairo who, on several occasions, while in uniform, boarded a private lorry and escorted it through Cairo, thus enabling it to pass the civilian police without being inspected. The Crown was held to be entitled to the money that he received for the misuse of his uniform and position. In the Court of Appeal in that case, it was said[43] that, in this context:

> a fiduciary relation exists (a) whenever the plaintiff entrusts to the defendant property tangible or intangible (as, for instance, confidential information) and relies on the defendant to deal with such property for the benefit of the plaintiff or for purposes authorized by him and not otherwise; and (b) whenever the plaintiff entrusts to the defendant a job to be performed, for instance, the negotiation of a contract on his behalf or for his benefit, and relies on the defendant to procure for the plaintiff the best terms available.

A claimant may have alternative remedies. In *Tang Man Sit (personal representative) v Capacious Investments Ltd*,[44] the classic example was said to be (1) an account of the profits made by a defendant in breach of his fiduciary obligations, and (2) compensation for the loss suffered by the claimant by reason of the same breach. The former is measured by the wrongdoer's gain, the latter by the injured party's loss. The claimant must choose between them when, but not before, judgment is given in his favour and the judge is asked to make orders against the defendant.

The cases can be loosely grouped as follows.

(A) FEES PAID TO TRUSTEE DIRECTORS

On one side of the line are *Re Francis*,[45] in which trustees were required to account for remuneration that they voted to themselves as directors by virtue of their holding of the trust shares, and *Re Macadam*,[46] in which trustees had power as such and, by virtue of the articles of the company, to appoint two directors of it. By the exercise of this power, they appointed themselves and were held liable to account for the remuneration they received for their services as directors,[47] because they had acquired it by the direct use of their trust powers. Cohen J observed:[48] '...the root of the matter...is: Did the trustee acquire the position in respect of which he drew the remuneration by virtue of his position as trustee?'

---

relationship existed although the partnership negotiations never matured into an agreement. See p 140, fn 13, *supra*.

[41] *New Zealand Netherlands Society Oranje Inc v Kuys* [1973] 2 All ER 1222, PC (officer of an unincorporated non-profit making society). See (1975) UTLJ 1 (E J Weinrib).

[42] [1951] AC 507, [1951] 1 All ER 617, HL. See (1968) 84 LQR 472 (G Jones).

[43] [1949] 2 KB 232, 236, [1949] 2 All ER 68, 70, CA.

[44] [1996] AC 514, [1996] 1 All ER 193, PC. Lord Nicholls, delivering the judgment of the Board, said that it was more accurate to refer to compensation rather than damages. In the case before them, nothing turned on the historic distinction between damages, awarded by common law courts, and compensation, a monetary remedy awarded by the Court of Chancery for breach of equitable obligation. He found it convenient therefore to use the nomenclature of damages, which had been adopted throughout the case.

[45] (1905) 92 LT 77.   [46] [1946] Ch 73, [1945] 2 All ER 664.

[47] The court, however, allowed remuneration under the inherent jurisdiction: see *Re Masters* [1953] 1 All ER 19, [1953] 1 WLR 81; *Re Keeler's Settlement Trusts* [1981] Ch 156, [1981] 1 All ER 888.

[48] [1946] Ch 82, [1945] 2 All ER 672.

On the other side of the line is *Re Dover Coalfield Extension Ltd*,[49] in which it was held that the directors were not liable to account for their remuneration. They had become directors before they held any trust shares, and although the trust shares were subsequently registered in their names in order to qualify them to continue as directors, it was not by virtue of the use of those shares that they either became entitled or continued to earn their fees. And from *Re Gee*,[50] in which the earlier cases were reviewed, it appears that if the use of, or failure to use, the trust votes could not prevent the appointment of the trustee to a remunerative position in the company, he will not be called upon to account; further, there is no reason why a trustee should not use the votes attached to his own shares, as opposed to those attached to the trust shares, in favour of his own appointment.[51] It may be added that there is, of course, no reason why, as in *Re Llewellin's Will Trusts*,[52] a testator holding a majority of shares should not effectively empower his trustees to appoint themselves as directors and arrange for their remuneration without being liable to account therefor.

(B) OTHER CASES IN WHICH TRUSTEES ACCOUNTABLE FOR PAYMENTS RECEIVED

In *Williams v Barton*,[53] the defendant, one of two trustees of a will, was clerk to stockbrokers on the terms that he should get a half-commission on business introduced by him. He persuaded his co-trustee to employ his firm, and was held accountable as a constructive trustee for the half-commission received by him. On principle, any payment made to a trustee to induce him to act in any particular way in connection with the trust business must be held by him as a part of the trust funds. Thus, in *Sugden v Crossland*,[54] a payment of £75 made to a trustee in consideration of his retiring from the trust and appointing the person making the payment as a new trustee was directed to be held as a part of the trust funds. A very curious case was *Re Payne's Settlement*,[55] in which an eccentric mortgagor devised the equity of redemption to the mortgagee, with whom he had no other relationship. The mortgagee happened to be a trustee, and it was held that he took the equity of redemption as a part of the trust estate.

(C) COURT ACTING TO PREVENT TRUSTEE PROFITING

The same fundamental principle may call for somewhat different action in different circumstances. Thus, in *Wright v Morgan*,[56] it was held that an option to purchase trust

---

49 [1908] 1 Ch 65, CA. Also *Re Lewis* (1910) 103 LT 495.

50 [1948] Ch 284, [1948] 1 All ER 498; *Re Northcote's Will Trust*, [1949] 1 All ER 442. *Re Gee* was distinguished in *Re Orwell's Will Trusts* [1982] 3 All ER 177, [1982] 1 WLR 1337.

51 It is not possible to split one's vote on a show of hands. A trustee shareholder, even though he had a larger personal shareholding, was accordingly held to be in breach of trust in voting for a resolution detrimental to the interests of his beneficiary: *McGratton v McGratton* [1985] NI 18, CA.

52 [1949] Ch 225, [1949] 1 All ER 487. Similarly, in *Re Sykes* [1909] 2 Ch 241, CA, a trustee was held entitled to retain profits made in supplying goods to the estate in connection with a business by virtue of a clause in the will. And see *Re Waterman's Will Trusts* [1952] 2 All ER 1054.

53 [1927] 2 Ch 9.   54 (1856) 3 Sm & G 192.   55 (1886) 54 LT 840.

56 [1926] AC 788, PC. Cf *Patel v Patel* [1982] 1 All ER 68, [1981] 1 WLR 1342, CA, a Rent Act case, in which it was held that trustees were not acting in breach of trust in seeking to live in a house subject to the trust

property could not be validly assigned to a trustee, as it would involve him in a conflict of duty and interest,[57] and, for the same reason, the court granted an injunction in *Re Thompson*[58] to restrain an executor carrying on the testator's business as yacht agent from setting up in competition.

An Australian case that it is difficult to categorize is *Malsbury v Malsbury*,[59] in which the court, relying on the *Keech v Sandford*[60] principle, held that there was a constructive trust. The property was held by the defendants, the plaintiff's son and daughter-in-law, under an express trust to allow him to live there for life as part of a family unit in which his son would be an integral part and in which he would be cared for as a member of the family. The son having divorced and left the property, the express trust was impossible of performance. It was held that the defendants could not withdraw from the plaintiff the essential rights reserved for him and yet require him to accept as fulfilment of the terms of the trust an arid right of residence. The defendants were constructive trustees of the property for themselves and the plaintiff in shares proportionate to their respective contributions towards its purchase.

(D) CASES INVOLVING OTHER FIDUCIARY RELATIONSHIPS

In *Regal (Hastings) Ltd v Gulliver*,[61] the essence of the matter, simplifying the facts slightly, was that the appellant company (Regal) formed a subsidiary company, A Ltd, which had an authorized share capital of £5,000, to acquire the leases of two cinemas. The prospective landlord required a guarantee of the rent by the directors unless the paid-up capital of A Ltd was fully subscribed. The directors were unwilling to give the guarantees and Regal could only put £2,000 into A Ltd. The directors, acting honestly and in the best interests of Regal, provided the remaining £3,000. In the events that happened, a purchaser bought the shares both in Regal and in A Ltd, paying for the latter the price of £3 16s 1d per share: the directors had subscribed for these shares at the price of £1 per share. The action was brought by Regal, now under the control of the purchaser, against the now ex-directors to recover the profits that they had made. The directors were held to be in a fiduciary relationship to the appellants, and liable to account.[62] The strict principle to be applied was thus

---

of which the beneficial owners were young children whom the trustees had adopted on the death of their parents.

[57] Even though the price was to be fixed by valuation, there would be a conflict in relation to the time of sale; the trustee, *qua* trustee, would want to sell when prices were high, but *qua* individual, would want the sale to take place when they were low.

[58] [1930] 1 Ch 203. Whether or not an injunction is granted may depend on the nature of the business. Cf *Moore v M'Glynn* [1894] 1 IR 74.

[59] [1982] 1 NSWLR 226.   [60] (1726) Sel Cas Ch 61.

[61] [1942] 1 All ER 378, subsequently reported in [1967] 2 AC 134n. The effect of the decision was a windfall for the purchaser, who, in substance, recouped much of the price that he had paid for A Ltd. The principle was extended in *CMS Dolphin Ltd v Simonet* [2001] 2 BCLC 704, noted (2002) 37 T & ELJ 9 (G Bennett), to a director who resigned to take advantage of a business opportunity of which he had knowledge as a result of his having been a director. The extent of the fiduciary obligation of an ex-director is considered by Perlie Koh in [2003] CLJ 403. See also (2003) 66 MLR 852 (S Scott); [2005] 71 T & ELTJ 16 (G Harbottle).

[62] The case was pleaded as a personal claim to account. Since the directors had the means to meet any judgment, it was not necessary to decide whether they were constructive trustees of the profits received: in principle, it is submitted that they were.

stated by Lord Russell of Killowen:[63]

> The rule of equity which insists on those, who by use of a fiduciary position make a profit, being liable to account for that profit, in no way depends on fraud, or absence of bona fides, or upon such questions or considerations as whether the profit would or should otherwise have gone to the plaintiff, or whether the profiteer was under a duty to obtain the source of the profit for the plaintiff, or whether he took a risk or acted as he did for the benefit of the plaintiff, or whether the plaintiff has in fact been damaged or benefited by his action. The liability arises from the mere fact of a profit having, in the stated circumstances, been made. The profiteer, however honest and well-intentioned, cannot escape the risk of being called upon to account.

The same principles were applied in the leading case of *Boardman v Phipps*,[64] in which the facts, somewhat simplified, were that B, at all material times, acted as solicitor to the trustees and for the co-appellant P, one of the beneficiaries. The trust property included shares in a private company. In 1956, B and F, the active trustee, a chartered accountant, considered that the position of the company was unsatisfactory and that something must be done to improve it. Following the 1956 annual general meeting of the company, B and P decided, with the knowledge of two of the three trustees, including F, that they should try to obtain control of the company by purchasing shares. The trustees had no power to invest trust moneys in shares of the company. B, purporting to act on behalf of the trustees as shareholders, obtained much information from the company, and in July 1959, after long and difficult negotiations, B and P purchased more than two-thirds of the shares, virtually all of the remainder being still held by the trustees. A considerable profit subsequently arose from capital distribution on the shares. It was accepted that B had acted with complete honesty throughout.[65] At the time of the purchase of the shares, the beneficiaries were absolutely entitled in possession to their respective shares (following the death of an annuitant in November 1958), which were in fact distributed in 1960. The action was brought by one of the beneficiaries, having an interest in five-eighteenths of the trust fund, claiming that B and P were constructive trustees of a corresponding five-eighteenths of the shares purchased, and were liable to account to him for the profit thereon. The claim succeeded, and was affirmed by the Court of Appeal and ultimately by the House of Lords (although here only by a bare majority), on the ground that both the information that satisfied B and P that the purchase of the shares would be a good investment and the opportunity to bid for them came to them as a result of B's acting, or purporting to act, on behalf of the trustees for

---

63 At 386, 144–145, applied *Patel v London Borough of Brent* [2003] EWHC 3081 (Ch), [2004] WTLR 577, discussed (2004) 60 T & ELJ 4 (J Small and D Radley-Gardner); *Murad v Al-Saraj* [2005] EWCA Civ 959, [2005] WTLR 1573; *Ultraframe (UK) Ltd v Fielding* [2005] EWHC 1658 (Ch), [2006] WTLR 835, noted (2008) 94 T & ELTJ 4 (Katherine Pawson).

64 [1967] 2 AC 46, [1966] 3 All ER 271, HL; *Swain v Law Society* [1981] 3 All ER 797, CA; reversed on different grounds [1983] 1 AC 598, [1982] 2 All ER 827, HL. See (1968), 84 LQR 472 (G Jones); [1978] Conv 114 (B A K Rider); (1979) 95 LQR 68 (A M Tettenborn); (1984) 134 NLJ 891 (E L Sagar). See also *Hanson v Lorenz and Jones* [1986] NLJ Rep 1088, CA, in which it was held that a solicitor is under no duty to account to his client for profit made from a joint venture in circumstances under which the client understood the terms and effect of the agreement, and those terms were fair; *Strother v 3464920 Canada Inc* [2007] SCC 24, [2007] 2 SCR 177, noted (2008) 124 LQR 21 (J Edelman).

65 Note *Badfinger Music v Evans* [2001] WTLR 1, in which it was held that although honesty is an important factor, it is not necessarily determinative. Remuneration was awarded to a party whose conduct was open to serious criticism, although the allegation of outright dishonesty was rejected.

certain purposes.[66] In so holding, the majority took the view that the claimant beneficiary was 'a fortunate man in that the rigour of equity enabled him to participate in the profits' and directed that payment should be allowed on the liberal scale to B and P, in respect of their work and skill in obtaining the shares and the profits in respect thereof.[67] However, as Lord Goff pointed out in *Guinness plc v Saunders*,[68] strictly speaking, any payment is irreconcilable with the fundamental principle that a trustee is not entitled to remuneration for services rendered by him to the trust.[69] It can, he said, only be reconciled with it to the extent that any such payment does not conflict with the policy underlying the rule. In his view, adopted in *Quarter Masters UK Ltd (in liq) v Pyke*,[70] such a conflict will only be avoided if the exercise of the jurisdiction is restricted to those cases in which it cannot have the effect of encouraging trustees in any way to put themselves in a position in which their interest conflicts with their duties as trustees. Lord Upjohn, dissenting, in the House of Lords, fully accepted 'the fundamental rule of equity that a person in a fiduciary capacity must not make a profit out of his trust, which is part of the wider rule that a trustee must not place himself in a position where his duty and his interest may conflict'. There seems, however, something to be said for his opinion that it was an over-rigid application of the rule to apply it to the facts of *Boardman v Phipps*,[71] and that the dictum of Lord Selborne LJ in *Barnes v Addy*[72] should have been applied: 'It is equally important to maintain the doctrine of trusts which is established in this court, and not to strain it by unreasonable construction beyond its due and proper limits.' If a defendant has breached his fiduciary duty of loyalty, he is liable in respect of any profits he has received: there is no requirement that the profit was obtained 'by virtue of his position'. The purpose of imposing a proprietary remedy is not to compensate the beneficiary, but to ensure that the fiduciary does not profit from his breach of duty.[73]

Another case is *Industrial Development Consultants Ltd v Cooley*,[74] in which the defendant was managing director of the plaintiff company. The defendant was privately offered

---

[66] It is not entirely clear whether the House of Lords held that B and P were constructive trustees, or merely personally liable: see [1994] RLR 56 (D Crilley).

[67] Account would, of course, also be taken of their expenditure. See also *O'Sullivan v Management Agency and Music Ltd* [1985] QB 428, [1985] 3 All ER 351, CA, noted (1986) 49 MLR 118 (W Bishop and D D Prentice), in which an appropriate allowance was made even though there was moral blameworthiness on the part of the fiduciary; *Estate Realties Ltd v Wignall* [1992] 2 NZLR 615 (likewise moral blameworthiness); *Re Berkeley Applegate (Investment Consultants) Ltd* [1989] Ch 32, [1988] 3 All ER 71; *John v James* [1991] FSR 397, 434. It has been suggested that it is unlikely that such an allowance will ever be granted again and that *Boardman* must be considered a mere aberration: [1995] Newc LR Vol 1 No 1 p 73 (D Cowan, L Griggs, and J Lawry). See also (2004) 21 NZULR 146 (J Palmer).

[68] [1990] 2 AC 663, [1990] 1 All ER 652, HL.

[69] For the principle and the qualifications to it, see p 442 *et seq, infra.*

[70] [2004] EWHC 1815 (Ch), [2005] 1 BCLC 245.   [71] *Supra.*

[72] (1874) 9 Ch App 244 at 251, CA.

[73] *United Pan-European Communications NV v Deutsche Bank AG* [2000] 2 BCLC 461, CA.

[74] [1972] 2 All ER 162, [1972] 1 WLR 443, doubted by J D Davies in [1998] SJLS 1, in a useful article on fiduciary liability. Cf *Plus Group Ltd v Pyke* [2002] EWCA Civ 370, noted [2003] CLJ 42 (P Koh); *Warman International Ltd v Dwyer* (1995) 128 ALR 201, in which the High Court of Australia held that the liability of a fiduciary to account does not depend upon detriment to the plaintiff or the dishonesty and lack of bona fides of the fiduciary; *Nottingham University v Fishel* [2000] IRLR 471 (mere fact person is an employee does not mean he owes fiduciary duties), noted (2001) 30 Ind LJ 100 (V Sims); *Bhullar v Bhullar* [2003] EWCA Civ 424, [2003] 2 BCLC 241, noted (2004) 120 LQR 198 (D D Prentice and J Payne). See also *Item Software (UK) Ltd v Fassihi* [2004] EWCA 1244, [2004] IRLR 928, noted (2005) 121 LQR 213 (A Berg); *Shepherds Investments Ltd v Walters* [2006] EWHC 836 (Ch), [2007] 2 BCLC 202; *Foster Bryant Surveying Ltd v Bryant*

a contract by a third party, who made it clear that he was not willing to contract with the plaintiffs. The defendant concealed the offer from the plaintiffs and obtained his release from his employment with them. About a week later, he entered into a contract with the third party. He was held liable to account to the plaintiffs for all of the benefit that he had received, or would receive, under the contract with the third party. He had been in a fiduciary relationship with the plaintiffs and, in breach of his fiduciary duty, had failed to disclose information of concern to the plaintiffs, and had indeed embarked on a deliberate course of conduct that had put his personal interest as a potential contracting party in direct conflict with his fiduciary duty as managing director of the plaintiffs. Whether the benefit of the contract would have been obtained for the plaintiffs but for the defendant's breach of fiduciary duty was held to be irrelevant.

The Privy Council took a much less strict view in *Queensland Mines Ltd v Hudson*.[75] Hudson was the managing director of Queensland, which was interested in obtaining mining exploration licences. At a late stage, Queensland ran into financial difficulties and could not proceed. Hudson resigned as managing director (although he remained on the board for ten years) and took the licences in his own name, although initially for and on behalf of Queensland. At a board meeting in 1962, Hudson gave his assessment of the likely risks and benefits of exploiting the licences, whereupon the board resolved not to pursue the matter further. Hudson went ahead on his own and, from 1966 onwards, received substantial royalties. The Privy Council held that Hudson was not accountable for the profit on two grounds. Firstly, the rejection of the opportunity to exploit the licences took the project outside the scope of Hudson's fiduciary duties to the company—which is difficult to reconcile with *Regal (Hastings) Ltd v Gulliver*.[76] It is, however, difficult to deny a conflict of interest where directors acquire for themselves an opportunity that they have rejected on behalf of the company. Secondly, that, at the 1962 board meeting, the board had given its fully informed consent to Hudson exploiting the licences in his own name, for his own gain, and at his own risk and expense. In order to be effective, however, consent should be given not by the board, but also by the shareholders in general meeting.[77]

The last case to mention is *Guinness plc v Saunders*,[78] in which it was held that money paid to W, a director of Guinness, by that company under a void contract was received by him as a constructive trustee, notwithstanding that, for the purposes of the action, it was assumed that he acted in good faith, believing that his services were rendered under a contract binding on the company.

Where property is acquired, in breach of fiduciary duty, with mixed trust money and personal money, it may be appropriate to restrict the profit or gain to be accounted for to a proportionate part of the total profit or gain. Relevant circumstances include the source from which and the time at which the personal contribution is made, and the nature of the profit gained by the acquisition. It has been held in Australia[79] that a fiduciary is liable for

[2007] EWCA Civ 200, [2007] 2 BCLC 239; *Ultraframe (UK) Ltd v Fielding* [2005 EWHC 1638 (Ch), [2006] WTLR 835; (2007) 91 T & ELTJ 8 (Jennifer Haywood).

  75 [1978] 18 ALR 1, PC; *Island Export Finance Ltd v Umunna* [1986] BCLC 460.

  76 [1942] 1 All ER 378, subsequently reported in [1967] 2 AC 134n.

  77 See (1979) 42 MLR 711 (G R Sullivan); [1980] Conv 200 (W J Braithwaite).

  78 [1990] 2 AC 663, [1990] 1 All ER 652, HL, noted [1990] Conv 296 (S Goulding); [1990] CLJ 220 (J Hopkins); (1990) 106 LQR 365 (J Beatson and D D Prentice).

  79 *Paul A Davies (Australia) Pty Ltd v Davies* [1983] 1 NSWLR 440; *Australian Postal Corpn v Lutak* (1991) 21 NSWLR 584. See (1993) 13 LS 271 (L Aitken).

the whole, and not merely a proportion, of the profit where trust moneys contributed to the purchase price, but the 'personal money' allegedly contributed by the fiduciary comprised only his personal liability on a mortgage on the security of the property acquired.

It seems that where a third party, having received confidential information, with knowledge or notice that the information has been imparted in breach of fiduciary duty, uses that information to acquire property, he will not be liable unless it would be unconscionable for him to retain the benefit thus obtained.[80]

(E) BRIBES

The general principle of the cases discussed above is that the fiduciary is not merely personally liable to account, as is clearly the case, but is also a constructive trustee of profits that he receives by virtue of his position. An Australian judge, Deane J, explained the position as follows:[81]

> Stated comprehensively in terms of the liability to account, the principle of equity is that a person who is under a fiduciary obligation must account to the person to whom the obligation is owed for any benefit or gain (i) which has been obtained or received in circumstances where a conflict or a significant possibility of conflict existed between his fiduciary duty and his personal interest in the pursuit or possible receipt of such a benefit or gain or (ii) which was obtained or received by use or by reason of his fiduciary position or of opportunity or knowledge resulting from it. Any such benefit or gain is held by the fiduciary as a constructive trustee.

Thus it was held in terms in *Guinness plc v Saunders*,[82] referred to above, that the director was, and always had been, a constructive trustee for Guinness of the £5.2m received by him in breach of his fiduciary duty.

In relation to bribes, Lord Templeman said, in *A-G for Hong Kong v Reid*,[83] that it had always been assumed that the law had been definitively settled by the Court of Appeal decision in *Lister & Co v Stubbs*,[84] in which it was held that, if a fiduciary accepts a bribe, his only obligation is to account for the sum he receives and he is not regarded as a constructive trustee of it. In *A-G for Hong Kong v Reid*,[85] the Privy Council refused to apply *Lister & Co v Stubbs*,[86] saying that it was not consistent with the principles that a fiduciary must not be allowed to benefit from his own breach of duty, that the fiduciary should account for the bribe as soon as he receives it, and that 'equity regards as done that which ought to be done'. From these principles, it follows that the bribe and the property from time to

---

[80] *Satnam Investments Ltd v Dunlop Heywood & Co Ltd* [1999] 3 All ER 652, CA, noted (1999) 143 Sol Jo 984 (M Draper), applied *Crown Dilmun plc v Sutton* [2004] EWHC 52 (Ch), [2004] WTLR 497, noted (2004) 61 TELTJ 16 (Rachel Nelson), in which Peter Smith J agreed with the criticism of the rule in Goff and Jones, *Law of Restitution*, 6th edn, [33.019]–[33.020].

[81] In *Chan v Zacharia* (1984) 53 ALR 417, 433, cited with evident approval by Walters J in *Jurley v BGH Nominees Pty Ltd (No 2)* (1984) 37 SASR 499, and by Morritt LJ in *Don King Productions Inc v Warren* [2000] Ch 291, [1999] 2 All ER 218, CA.

[82] *Supra.*

[83] [1994] 1 AC 324, [1994] 1 All ER 1, PC, noted [1994] CLJ 31 (A J Oakley); [1994] Conv 156 (Alison Jones); [1994] LMCLQ 189 (R A Pearce); [1994] Co Law 3 (R C Nolan); (1994) 5 Cant LR 374 (P Devonshire); (1995) 58 MLR 87 (T Allen); [1996] JBL 22 (D Cowan, R Edmunds, and J Lowry); [1996] 19 UNSWLJ 378 (C Rotherman); [1995] CLJ 60 (S Gardner). See also [1993] RLR 7 (Sir Peter Millett).

[84] (1890) 45 Ch D 1, CA, a much-criticized decision.

[85] *Supra*, PC. See *Secretary for Justice v Hon Kam Wing* [2003] 1 HK LRD 524.   [86] *Supra*, CA.

time representing it are held on a constructive trust for the person injured. A fiduciary, of course, remains personally liable for the amount of the bribe if, in the event, the value of the property then recovered by the injured person proves to be less than that amount. The advice of the Privy Council is, of course, technically not binding on the English courts. It does not seem unreasonable to assume, however, that if the point were to come to the House of Lords, their Lordships would take the same view as the Privy Council and would overrule *Lister & Co v Stubbs*.[87] In *Daraydan Holdings Ltd v Solland International Ltd*,[88] Lawrence Collins J said that, if he had not been able to distinguish *Lister & Co v Stubbs*, it would have been proper for him to apply the view of the Privy Council.

It may be added that not only is the bribed fiduciary liable, but an account of profits is available against the briber.[89]

3   STRANGERS TO THE TRUST

(A)   INTRODUCTION

Where trustees improperly allow trust property to come into the hands of strangers to the trust, the trustees will, of course, be personally liable for breach of trust. This, however, will not be an adequate remedy for the beneficiaries if the trustees do not have the means to repair the breach of trust, and the beneficiaries in that case will want to know whether, and to what extent, a stranger to the trust may be liable. There are three situations. Firstly, the stranger may be under no liability at all. On general principles, this will be the case if he can establish that he is a bona fide purchaser for value of a legal estate without notice.[90]

Secondly, as we shall see,[91] a beneficiary may have a proprietary remedy where he is able to trace the trust property into the hands of a third party who is what is known as an 'innocent volunteer'—that is, one who has acquired the trust property bona fide without notice of the breach of trust, but who has not given value. Where tracing is possible, the third party will be required to restore an unmixed fund to the trust (whether or not it retains its original form), or, where it has been mixed with property belonging to the innocent volunteer, there will be a declaration of charge. The innocent volunteer will not, however, be liable as a constructive trustee so as to be personally accountable if he has parted with the trust property without having previously acquired some knowledge of the existence of the trust.[92] Such accountability may arise if he loses his innocence and becomes liable in the third situation about to be considered.

---

[87] *Supra*, CA. See *Worcester Works Finance Ltd v Cooden Engineering Ltd* [1972] 1 QB 210, 217, [1971] 3 All ER 708, 711, CA, *per* Denning MR. For a contrary view, see [1994] RLR 57 (D Crilley); All ER Rev 1994, 366 (W J Swadling). Note, moreover, *A-G's Reference (No 1 of 1985)* [1986] QB 491, [1986] 2 All ER 219, CA, discussed p 538, *infra*, but not referred to in *A-G for Hong Kong v Reid*, PC, *supra*, and see (1994) 110 LQR 180 (J C Smith) on the possible effect of this last decision on the criminal law.

[88] [2004] EWHC 622 (Ch), [2005] 4 All ER 73, noted [2005] Conv 88 (Margaret Halliwell). See (2005) 121 LQR 23 (H N Bennett).   [89] *Fyffes Group Ltd v Templeman* [2000] 2 Lloyd's Rep 643.

[90] *Pilcher v Rawlins* (1872) 7 Ch App 259.

[91] See Chapter 24, pp 539, *infra*. See also (1986) 13 Co Law 44 (B Strong) (1987) 46 CLJ (D J Hayton).

[92] *Re Diplock* [1948] 2 All ER 318, 324, 325, 347, CA; affd sub nom *Ministry of Health v Simpson* [1951] AC 251, [1959] 2 All ER 1137, HL; *Re Montagu's Settlement Trusts* (1985) [1987] Ch 264, [1992] 4 All ER 308;

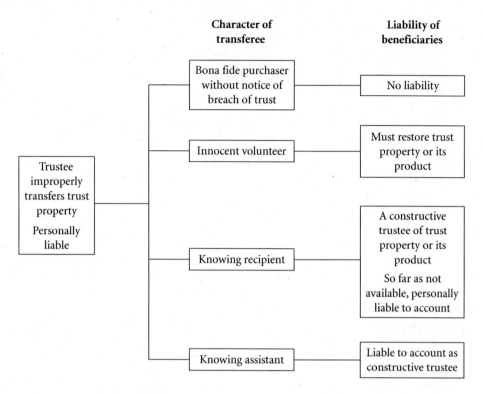

Figure 8.1 Strangers to the trust

Thirdly, as will now be discussed, the stranger may be liable as a constructive trustee—that is, he will not only hold any trust property in his hands as a trustee, but will also be personally accountable for any loss to the trust estate even though he may no longer have any of the trust funds in his possession or under his control.

The cases can be put under three heads:

(i)   trustee *de son tort,*

(ii)   recipient liability, or knowing receipt or dealing,[93]

(iii)   accessory liability,[94] or knowing assistance.

Agip (Africa) Ltd v Jackson [1992] 4 All ER 385, 403; affd [1991] Ch 547, [1992] 4 All ER 451, CA; *Westdeutsche Landesbank Girozentrale v Islington London Borough Council* [1996] AC 669, 705–706, [1996] 2 All ER 961, 988, HL, *per* Lord Browne-Wilkinson; *Bristol and West Building Society v Mothew (t/a Stapley & Co)* [1998] Ch 1, 22, 23, [1996] 4 All ER 698, 716–717, CA, *per* Millett LJ.

[93] In relation to the classification into heads (ii) and (iii), reference is often made to the dictum of Lord Selborne in *Barnes v Addy* (1874) 9 Ch App 244, at 251–252: '...*strangers are not to be made constructive trustees*...[unless they] *receive and become chargeable with some part of the trust property, or unless they assist with knowledge in a dishonest and fraudulent design on the part of the trustees.*'

[94] The preferred phase in *Royal Brunei Airlines Sdn Bhd v Tan* [1995] 2 AC 378, [1995] 3 All ER 97, PC. See, generally, (1987) 61 ALJ 281 (M J Bridle and J A Hooley); (1991) 135 Sol Jo 502 (Margaret Halliwell); *Equity and Contemporary Legal Developments* (ed S Goldstein), p 374 (G H Jones); (1991) 5 SJLS 26 (T Hans).

(B) TRUSTEE *DE SON TORT*

The phrase 'trustee *de son tort*' describes a person who, not being a trustee and not having authority from a trustee, takes upon himself to intermeddle with trust matters or to do acts characteristic of the office of trustee.[95] The expression seems to have been adopted by analogy with the expression 'executor *de son tort*' in the law relating to the administration of assets to cover the situation in which a stranger has positively assumed to act as trustee. This is consistent with the opinion of Ungoed-Thomas J in *Selangor United Rubber Estates v Cradock (No 3)*,[96] in which he distinguished between what he called:

two very different kinds of so-called constructive trustees.

(i) Those who, though not appointed trustees, take on themselves to act as such and to possess and administer trust property for the beneficiaries, such as trustees de son tort. Distinguishing features [include] (a) they do not claim to act in their own right but for the beneficiaries, and (b) their assumption to act is not of itself a ground of liability (save in the sense of course of liability to account and for any failure in the duty so assumed), and so their status as trustees precedes the occurrence which may be the subject of claim against them.

(ii) Those whom a court of equity will treat as trustees by reason of their action, of which complaint is made. Distinguishing features are (a) that such trustees claim to act in their own right and not for beneficiaries, and (b) no trusteeship arises before, but only by reason of, the action complained of.

Trustees *de son tort* are perhaps better described as 'de facto trustees'. In their relation with the beneficiaries, they are treated in every respect as if they had been duly appointed. They are true trustees and are fully subject to fiduciary obligations. Their liability is strict; it does not depend on dishonesty. Like express trustees, they cannot plead the Limitation Acts as a defence to a claim for breach of trust.[97] However, as Mann J explained in *Jasmine Trustees Ltd v Wells & Hind (a firm)*,[98] although they may have the same liability to the beneficiaries as validly appointed trustees, they do not have the same powers, for example, to appoint new trustees, as those given, whether by the trust instrument or by statute, to validly appointed trustees. Nor, it was held, are they 'trustees of the settlement' within the meaning of s 69 of the Taxation of Chargeable Gains Act 1992.

As to the second class of so-called constructive trustee, it has been said[99] that this type of constructive trust 'is merely the creation by the court by way of a suitable remedy to meet the wrongdoing alleged: there is no real trust and usually no chance of a proprietary remedy'.

---

[95] See *Mara v Browne* [1896] 1 Ch 199, CA; *Taylor v Davies* [1920] AC 636, 651, PC, *per* Viscount Cave; *Dubai Aluminium Co Ltd v Salaam* [2002] UKHL 48, [2003] 2 AC 366, [2003] 1 All ER 97 *per* Lord Millett, at [136]–[138]. There is a useful discussion in *Nolan v Nolan* [2004] VSCA 109, [2004] WTLR 1261 (Australia), noted (2004) 62 TELTJ 18. Note *Re Barney* [1892] 2 Ch 265, in which Kekewich J said that, in order to be a trustee *de son tort*, a person must have the trust property vested in him or at least have the right to call for a transfer.

[96] [1968] 2 All ER 1073, 1095, [1968] 1 WLR 1555, 1579, as was noted at p 69, *supra*. Millet LJ, as he then was, drew the same distinction in *Paragon Finance plc v Thakerar & Co (a firm)* [1999] 1 All ER 400, CA, applied in *Jasmine Trustees Ltd v Wells & Hind (a firm)* [2007] EWHC 38 (Ch), [2007] 1 All ER 1142, [2007] 3 WLR 810.

[97] See *Dubai Aluminium Co Ltd v Salaam, supra*, HL, *per* Lord Millett at [138].

[98] [2007] EWHC 38 (Ch), [2007] 1 All ER 1142.

[99] *Per* Jules Sher QC, sitting as deputy judge of the Chancery Division in *Coulthard v Disco Mix Club Ltd* [1999] 2 All ER 457, 479, [2000] 1 WLR 707, 731.

However, he is traditionally said to be 'accountable as a constructive trustee', a phrase that Lord Millet would like to discard, substituting the words 'accountable in equity'.[100]

(C) KNOWING RECEIPT OR DEALING—RECIPIENT LIABILITY

In this context, the word 'receipt' refers to the receipt by one person from another person of assets. Where a person enters into a binding contract, he doubtless acquires contractual rights, but it does not constitute a 'receipt' of assets; this may occur when the contract is completed.[101]

This head comprises situations in which a person:

(i)   knowingly receives trust property in breach of trust ('receipt of property constructive trust');[102] or

(ii) receives trust property without notice of the trust and subsequently deals with it in a manner inconsistent with the trusts of which he has become cognisant ('wrongful dealing constructive trust'); or

(iii) receives trust property knowing it to be such, but without breach of trust, and subsequently deals with it in a manner inconsistent with the trusts.[103]

In *Agip (Africa) Ltd v Jackson*,[104] these three cases were put into two separate categories, in each of which it is immaterial whether the breach of trust was fraudulent or not.

Head (iii) is that of a person, usually an agent of the trustees, who receives the trust property lawfully and not for his own benefit, but who then either misappropriates it or otherwise deals with it in a manner that is inconsistent with the trust. He is liable to account as a constructive trustee if he received the trust property knowing it to be such, although he will not necessarily be required in all circumstances to have known the exact terms of the trust.

Heads (i) and (ii) above relate to a person who receives for his own benefit trust property transferred to him in breach of trust. The claimant in these situations must show: firstly, a disposal of his assets in breach of fiduciary duty; secondly, the beneficial receipt by the

---

[100] *Dubai Aluminium Co Ltd v Salaam, supra*, HL, at [142].

[101] *Criterion Properties plc v Stratford UK Properties LLC* [2004] UKHL 28, [2004] 1 WLR 1846.

[102] The directors of a limited company are treated as if they were trustees of those funds of the company that are in their hands or under their control, and if they misapply them, they commit a breach of trust: *Belmont Finance Corpn v Williams Furniture Ltd (No 2)* [1980] 1 All ER 393, CA; *J J Harrison (Properties) Ltd v Harrison* [2001] EWCA Civ 1467, [2002] 1 BCLC 162, noted [2002] 152 NLJ 304 (S Bhandari). A claim in 'knowing receipt' has been held to fall within the Civil Liability (Contribution) Act 1975: *City Index Ltd v Gawler* [2007] EWCA Civ 1382, [2008] 2 WLR 950.

[103] *Re Montagu's Settlement Trusts* [1987] Ch 264, [1992] 4 All ER 308, *Lipkin Gorman v Karpnale Ltd* [1987] 1 WLR 987; affd in part, reversed in part [1989] 1 WLR 1340, CA; revsd in part [1991] 2 AC 548, [1992] 4 All ER 572, HL, relying on the law of restitution; *Baden v Société Générale pour Favoriser le Développement de Commerce et de l'Industrie en France SA* [1983] BCLC 325 (appeal dismissed [1985] BCLC, 258n, CA). As to the position in Canada, see *Banton v CIBC Trust Corporation* (2001) 197 DLR 212 and (2002) 81 CBR 171 (M McInnes). See [1996] JBL 165 (M Bryan).

[104] [1990] Ch 265, [1992] 4 All ER 385; affd [1991] Ch 547, [1992] 4 All ER 451, CA, *per* Millett J at first instance at 403, 404. For the judge's extrajudicial views, see *Equity and Contemporary Legal Developments* (ed S Goldstein), p 407 and (1991) 107 LQR 71. See also [1991] LMCLQ 378 (E McKendrick); (1994) 57 MLR 38 (S Fennell); (1995) 16 Co Law 35 (C E F Rickett); [1999] NZLJ 40 (C E F Rickett); [2005] 71 T & ELTJ 4 (A Learmouth).

defendant of assets that are traceable as representing the assets of the claimant; and, thirdly, knowledge on the part of the defendant that the assets he received are traceable to a breach of trust or fiduciary duty.[105] The receipt must be the direct consequence of the alleged breach of trust or fiduciary duty of which the recipient is said to have knowledge.[106]

Where there is a company intermediary, the court is entitled to pierce the corporate veil and recognize the receipt of a company as that of the individual in control of it if the company had been used as a device or facade to conceal the true facts, thereby avoiding or concealing any liability of that individual. It is, however, insufficient that the company had been involved in some impropriety not linked to the use of the corporate structure to avoid or conceal that liability. Nor can the court pierce the corporate veil merely on the grounds that it was necessary to do so in the interests of justice and no unconnected third party was involved.[107]

The Court of Appeal reaffirmed, in *Bank of Credit and Commerce International (Overseas) Ltd (in liq) v Akindele*,[108] the 'clear authority' of *Belmont Finance Corpn v Williams Furniture Ltd (No 2)*[109] that, although a knowing recipient will often be found to have acted dishonestly, it has never been a prerequisite of liability that he should. As Vinelott J stated, in *Eagle Trust plc v SBC Securities Ltd*:[110]

> ...in a 'knowing receipt' case it is only necessary to show that the defendant knew that the moneys paid to him were trust moneys and of circumstances which made the payment a misapplication of them. Unlike a 'knowing assistance' case it is not necessary, and never has been necessary, to show that the defendant was in any sense a participator in a fraud.

Citing this dictum with approval, Nourse LJ in *Akindele*[111] went on to say that, while in theory it is possible for a misapplication not to be fraudulent and the recipient to be dishonest, in practice such a combination must be rare.

Turning to the question of knowledge, Nourse LJ said that with the proliferation in the last twenty years or so of cases in which the misapplied assets of companies had come into the hands of third parties, there had been a sustained judicial and extrajudicial debate as to the knowledge on the part of the recipient that is required in order to found liability in knowing receipt. Expressed in the simplest terms, he continued, the question is whether the recipient must have actual knowledge (or the equivalent) that the assets received are traceable to a breach of trust or whether constructive knowledge is enough. He referred to

---

[105] *El Ajou v Dollar Holdings plc* [1994] 2 All ER 685, 700, CA, *per* Hoffman LJ; *Bank of Credit and Commerce International (Overseas) Ltd (in liq) v Akindele* [2001] Ch 437, [2000] 4 All ER 221, CA, noted (2000) 59 CLJ 447 (R Nolan); (2000) 14 Tru LI 224 (J E Penner); (2001) 15 Tru LI 151 (P Jaffrey); (2001) 21 Ox JLS 239 (Susan Thomas); [2001] RLR 99 (J Stevens). As to attribution of knowledge to a company, see *El Ajou v Dollar Holdings plc*, *supra*, CA; *K & S Corporation Ltd v Sportingbet Australia* (2003) 86 SASR 312 (first four categories of knowledge sufficient: on facts, no need to decide on fifth).

[106] See *Brown v Bennett* [1999] 1 BCLC 649, 655, CA, *per* Morritt LJ.

[107] *Trustor AB v Smallbone (No 2)* [2001] 3 All ER 987, [2001] 1 WLR 1177, noted (2003) 119 LQR 13 (Susan Watson).

[108] *Supra*, CA. Also in *Houghton v Fayers* [2001] 1 BCLC 511, CA.

[109] [1980] 1 All ER 393, CA (a decision said sometimes to have been overlooked in this context).

[110] [1992] 4 All ER 488, 501, [1993] 1 WLR 484, 497. See also *Polly Peck International plc v Nadir (No 2)* [1992] 4 All ER 769, 777, CA, *per* Scott LJ; *Agip (Africa) Ltd v Jackson*, [1990] Ch 265, 292, [1992] 4 All ER 385, 404, *per* Millet J, affd [1991] Ch 547, [1992] 4 All ER 451, CA.

[111] *Supra*, CA. Also in *Houghton v Fayers*, *supra*, CA.

dicta in a series of cases[112] that might be thought to provide strong support for the view that constructive knowledge is enough. However, as he went on to point out, in each of the Court of Appeal cases referred to, actual knowledge was found and, moreover, the decisions in the *Karak* case and the *Agip* case were based on knowing assistance, not knowing receipt. The seminal judgment, he said, was that of Megarry V-C in *Re Montagu's Settlement Trusts*.[113] The facts of that case were that, by a family resettlement in 1923, the future tenth Duke of Manchester assigned certain chattels to which he was entitled in remainder on the death of the ninth Duke to trustees upon trust, on the death of the ninth Duke, to select such chattels as they thought fit for inclusion in the settlement and to hold the remainder (if any) in trust for the tenth Duke absolutely. The ninth Duke died in 1947. No selection was ever made, and the chattels were released to the tenth Duke in 1948 and 1949. This was a breach of trust, because he was only entitled to receive what was left of the settled chattels after the selection had been made. The Duke's solicitor, who knew of the settlement and, at an earlier stage, had known of the effect of the clause relating to the chattels, informed the Duke in writing in 1948 that he was free to sell the chattels released. The tenth Duke died in 1977, having sold some of the chattels in his lifetime. One of the claims made in an action by the eleventh Duke was that the tenth Duke had become a constructive trustee of the chattels.

Megarry V-C drew a distinction between the equitable doctrine of tracing and the imposition of a constructive trust by reason of the knowing receipt of trust property. Tracing, he said, is primarily a means of determining rights of property, in relation to which the doctrine of the purchaser without notice is appropriate. Where chattels are traced into the hands of a volunteer, he may be liable to yield up any chattels that remain, or the traceable proceeds of any that have gone, but unless he is a constructive trustee, he will not be liable if the chattels have gone and there are no traceable proceeds. The imposition of a constructive trust, however, creates personal obligations that go beyond mere property rights. In considering whether a constructive trust has arisen in a case of knowing receipt of trust property, the basic question is whether the conscience of the recipient is sufficiently affected to justify the imposition of such a trust. This primarily depends on the knowledge of the recipient, and not on notice to him: 'The cold calculus of constructive and imputed notice does not seem to me to be an appropriate instrument for deciding whether a [person's] conscience is sufficiently affected for it to be right to bind him by the obligations of a constructive trustee.'[114] It must be admitted that judges and academics have not always been careful to maintain the distinction in their use of the words 'knowledge' and 'notice'.

The effect of Megarry V-C's decision, according to Nourse LJ in *Akindele*,[115] is that, in order to establish liability in knowing receipt, the recipient must have actual knowledge

---

[112] Including *Karak Rubber Co Ltd v Burden (No 2)* [1972] 1 All ER 1210, 1234, [1972] 1 WLR 602, 632, *per* Brightman J ; *Agip (Africa) Ltd v Jackson, supra*, at first instance *per* Millet J at 291, 403; *Houghton v Fayers, supra, per* Nourse LJ himself at 516.

[113] [1987] Ch 264, [1992] 4 All ER 308, adopted by Steyn J in *Barclays Bank plc v Quincecare Ltd* [1992] 4 All ER 363 and by Alliott J at first instance in *Lipkin Gorman (a firm) v Karpnale Ltd* [1992] 4 All ER 331, [1987] 1 WLR 987; revsd in part [1992] 4 All ER 409, [1989] 1 WLR 1340, CA; in turn revsd in part [1991] 2 AC 548, [1992] 4 All ER 512, HL. See (1992) 12 LS 332 (Helen Norman); *Equity and Contemporary Legal Developments* (ed S Goldstein), p 46 (J D Davies).

[114] *Per* Megarry VC in *Re Montagu's Settlement Trusts, supra*, at 273, 320. But see (1987) 50 MLR 217 (C Harpum).

[115] *Bank of Credit and Commerce International (Overseas) Ltd (in liq) v Akindele* [2001] Ch 437, 453, [2000] 4 All ER 221, 234, CA. There was already a line of cases holding that, in commercial cases, constructive

(or its equivalent) that the assets received are traceable to a breach of trust and that constructive knowledge is not enough. Hitherto, reference has often been made to *Baden v Société Générale pour Favouriser le Développement de Commerce et de l'Industrie en France SA*,[116] in which Peter Gibson J said that there were five categories of knowledge—namely:

(i) actual knowledge;

(ii) wilfully shutting one's eyes to the obvious—'Nelsonian knowledge';[117]

(iii) wilfully and recklessly failing to make such inquiries as an honest and reasonable man would make;

(iv) knowledge of circumstances that would indicate the facts to an honest and reasonable man;

(v) knowledge of circumstances that would put an honest and reasonable man on inquiry.

The essential difference between (ii) and (iii), on the one hand, and (iv) and (v), on the other hand, is that the former are governed by the words 'wilfully' or 'wilfully and recklessly'; (ii) and (iii) seem to be equivalent to actual notice; (iv) and (v), however, have no such adverbs and seem to be cases of constructive notice. They are cases of carelessness or negligence being tested by what an honest and reasonable man would have realized, or would have inquired about, even if the person concerned was, for instance, not at all reasonable. Megarry V-C, in *Re Montagu's Settlement Trusts*,[118] accepted the five categories of knowledge set out in the *Baden* case[119] as useful guides, but thought that the modern tendency in equity was to put less emphasis on the detailed rules that have emerged from the cases, and to give more weight to the underlying principles that engendered them. Nourse LJ in *Akindele*,[120] however, had grave doubts about its utility in cases of knowing receipt. He observed that the fivefold categorization had been put to the judge on an agreed basis, and that both counsel accepted that all five categories of knowledge were relevant, and neither sought to submit that there was any distinction for that purpose between knowing receipt and knowing assistance: the claim in constructive trust was based squarely on knowing assistance and not on knowing receipt. The purpose, he said, to be served by a categorization of knowledge could only be to enable the court to determine whether, in the words of Buckley LJ in *Belmont (No 2)*,[121] the recipient can 'conscientiously retain [the] funds against the company' or, in the words of Megarry V-C in *Re Montagu's Settlement Trusts*,[122] '[the recipient's] conscience is sufficiently affected for it to be right to bind him by the obligations

---

notice was not enough: *Eagle Trust plc v SBC Securities Ltd, supra; Cowan de Groot Properties Ltd v Eagle Trust plc* [1992] 4 All ER 700; *Eagle Trust plc v SBC Securities (No 2)* [1996] 1 BCLC 121. In other jurisdictions, constructive notice has been held sufficient even in the case of commercial transactions: *Equiticorp Industries Group Ltd v Hawkins* [1991] 3 NZLR 700; *Citadel General Assurance Co v Lloyds Bank Canada* (1997) 152 DLR (4th) 411, noted (1998) 114 LQR 394 (L Smith); (1999) 10 SCLR 461 (L I Rotman).

[116] [1983] BCLC 325 (appeal dismissed [1985] BCLC 258n, CA).

[117] As to blind-eye knowledge, see *Bank of Credit & Commerce International SA (in liq) (No 15)* [2004] EWHC 528 (Ch), [2004] 2 BCLC 279.

[118] *Supra.*   [119] *Supra.*

[120] *Bank of Credit and Commerce International (Overseas) Ltd (in liq) v Akindele* [2001] Ch 437, [2000] 4 All ER 221, CA.

[121] *Belmont Finance Corpn v Williams Furniture Ltd (No 2)* [1980] 1 All ER 393, 405, CA.

[122] *Supra.*

of a constructive trustee'. But if that is the purpose, Nourse LJ continued, there is no need for categorization. All that is necessary is that the recipient's state of knowledge should be such as to make it unconscionable for him to retain the benefit of the receipt. This he propounded as a single test of knowledge for knowing receipt. He accepted that difficulties of application could not be avoided, but it would enable the courts to give common-sense decisions in the commercial context in which claims in knowing receipt are frequently made. One of the difficulties will be to draw the line between dishonesty, which is not required for liability, and unconscionability, which is.

In *Re Montague's Settlement Trusts*,[123] Megarry V-C further agreed with the observation of Peter Gibson J in the *Baden* case[124] that 'the court should not be astute to impute knowledge where no actual knowledge exists'. And in *Re Clasper Group Services Ltd*,[125] Warner J said that 'in considering whether a particular person may be treated as having had knowledge of any of those kinds, the court must have regard to what Lawson J in *International Sales and Agencies Ltd v Marcus*[126] called the "attributes" of that person'. Thus in the *Clasper Group* case,[127] on the facts, the person in question was young, inexperienced, and in a lowly position, and because of this, his conscience was not affected in such a way as to constitute him a constructive trustee.

Megarry V-C further observed that a person is not to be taken to have knowledge of a fact that he once knew, but has genuinely forgotten: the test is whether the knowledge continues to operate on that person's mind at the time in question. Finally, Megarry V-C thought it at least doubtful whether there is a general doctrine of 'imputed knowledge' corresponding to 'imputed notice'.

In the light of his views as to the law, Megarry V-C held, on the facts, that the tenth Duke did not have any knowledge at any material time that the chattels that he was receiving or dealing with were chattels that were still subject to any trust. There was no reason why the solicitor's knowledge of the settlement at some earlier time should be imputed to the Duke so as to affect his conscience. Nor did his failure to inquire impose a constructive trust. Even if he had once known the relevant terms of the settlement, there was nothing to suggest that he remembered them when he received the trust property. Although the assignment of the chattels to him was a breach of trust, he did not become a constructive trustee of them.

Extrajudicially,[128] Lord Nicholls has suggested that it would be better if cases of misapplied property gave rise to restitutionary liability regardless of fault, but subject to a defence of change of position.[129] This is clearly not the law as it stands and, in *Akindele*,[130] Nourse LJ doubted whether it would, in fact, be preferable to fault-based liability in many commercial transactions. He did not think that, simply on proof of an internal misapplication of a company's funds, the burden should shift to the recipient to defend the receipt

---

[123] *Supra.*   [124] *Supra.*   [125] [1989] BCLC 143.   [126] [1982] 3 All ER 551, 558.

[127] *Supra.*

[128] Cornish, Nolan, O'Sullivan, and Virgo (eds) *Restitution Past, Present and Future: Essays in Honour of Gareth Jones*, pp 238–239. See the valuable article by J Dietrich and Pauline Ridge in (2007) 31 MULR 47.

[129] In Australia, unjust enrichment as the basis of recipient liability has been decisively rejected: *Farah Construction Pty Ltd v Say-Dee Pty Ltd* [2007] HCA 22, (2007) 235 ALR 209, noted (2007) 29 Syd LR 713 (H Atkin); (2008) 124 LQR 26 (Pauline Ridge and J Dietrich); [2007] CLJ 515 (M Conaglen and R Nolan); (2007) 21 TruLI 55 (D Hayton).

[130] *Supra*, CA.

either by a change of position or perhaps in some other way. Moreover, he said, if the circumstances of the receipt were such as to make it unconscionable for the recipient to retain the benefit of it, there would be an obvious difficulty in saying that it is equitable for a change of position to afford him a defence.

Finally, it may be noted that a claim in knowing receipt is one to recover compensation within s 6 of the Civil Liability (Contribution) Act 1978, and, accordingly, a defendant to such a claim may recover contribution from the defaulting trustee or any other person liable in respect of the loss to the trust estate.[131]

(D) THE ACCESSORY LIABILITY PRINCIPLE—KNOWING ASSISTANCE

In a much-quoted dictum in *Barnes v Addy*,[132] Lord Selborne said that a person would be liable as a constructive trustee if he had knowingly assisted in a dishonest and fraudulent design on the part of the trustees, even though no part of the trust property may ever come into his hands. In *Royal Brunei Airlines Sdn Bhd v Tan*,[133] the Privy Council said that something had gone wrong in the subsequent cases because of a tendency to cite, interpret, and apply Lord Selborne's dictum as if it were a statute, as a result of which the courts found themselves wrestling with the interpretation of the individual ingredients, especially 'knowingly', but also 'dishonest and fraudulent design on the part of the trustees', without examining the underlying reason why a third party who has received no trust property is being made liable at all. Moreover, the approach exemplified by *Belmont Finance Corpn Ltd v Williams Furniture Ltd*[134] leads to the conclusion that a third party who dishonestly procures or assists in a breach of trust, the trustee himself being perfectly innocent,[135] is not liable under the accessory liability principle—a conclusion that the Privy Council considered could not be right. What matters is the state of mind of the third party sought to be made liable, not the state of mind of the trustee. And, of course, as Treacy J observed,[136] 'a fiduciary or trust relationship and a breach of trust is a prerequisite to a claim against a stranger for knowing assistance'.

In *Royal Brunei Airlines Sdn Bhd v Tan*,[137] the Privy Council took the opportunity to review the law on what it preferred to call the 'accessory liability principle', and the

---

[131] *Charter plc v City Index Ltd (Gawler & Ors, Pt 20 defendants)* [2006] EWHC 2508 (Ch), [2007] 1 All ER 1049.

[132] (1874) 9 Ch App 244, CA.

[133] [1995] 2 AC 378, [1995] 3 All ER 97, PC (in which the relevant New Zealand cases are referred to); *Balfron Trustees Ltd v Peterson* [2002] Lloyd's PN 1. See also *Barlow Clowes International Ltd v Eurotrust International Ltd* [2004] WTLR 1365 (Isle of Man HC). For the Canadian approach, see *Air Canada v M & L Travel Ltd* (1994) 108 DLR (4th) 592; *3464920 Canada Inc v Strothen* (2005) 256 DLR 319 and (1995) 74 CBR 29 (T Allen). For the Australian approach, see *Farah Construction Pty Ltd v Say-Dee Pty Ltd* [2007] HCA 22.

[134] [1979] Ch 250, [1979] 1 All ER 118, CA.

[135] The trustee himself is, of course, liable for a breach of trust, even though innocent: see Chapter 23, section 1(a), p 512, *infra*.

[136] In *Abou-Rahmah v Abacha* [2005] EWHC 2662 (QB), [2006] 1 All ER (Comm) 247, affd [2006] EWCA Civ 1492, [2007] 1 All ER (Comm) 827, noted [2007] CLJ 22 (G Virgo).

[137] *Supra*, PC, noted [1995] CLJ 305 (R Nolan); (1995) 111 LQR 545 (C Harpum); (1995) 92/28 LSG 20 (J Snape and G Watt); (1995) 9 Tru LI 102 (G McCormack); 1996 LMCLQ 1 (P Birks); (1996) 112 LQR 56 (S Gardner); (1996) 140 Sol Jo 156 (Jill Martin); All ER Rev 1995, 323 (P J Clarke); (1996) 30 L Teach 111 (G Ferris); (1996) 59 MLR 443 (A Berg); 1995 RLR 105 (J Stevens). See, generally, (2004) 67 MLR 16 (S B Elliott

judgment of the Board delivered by Lord Nicholls was treated by the House of Lords in *Twinsectra Ltd v Yardley*[138] as correctly stating the law, although, as we shall see, there were, in that case, significant differences of interpretation. It may be noted that, in so far as a stranger who does not receive the trust property is made liable as a constructive trustee, there is an anomaly, because, on general principles, in order for a person to be a trustee, there must be trust property vested in him.[139] As previously explained,[140] although traditionally referred to as 'constructive trust', it is not really a case of trust at all, but one of personal accountability.

Lord Nicholls said that different considerations apply to cases of knowing receipt and accessory liability: the former is restitution-based, while the latter is not. In relation to accessory liability, with which alone the case was concerned, he dismissed out of hand, on the one hand, the possibility that a third party who does not receive trust property ought never to be liable directly to the beneficiaries merely because he assisted the trustee to commit a breach of trust or procured him to do so, and, on the other hand, that there is liability where a third party deals with a trustee without knowing, or having any reason to suspect, that he is a trustee, or, being aware that he is a trustee, has no reason to know or suspect that the transaction in question is inconsistent with the terms of the trust. Accepting, therefore, that, in some circumstances, a third party may be liable directly to a beneficiary, Lord Nicholls went on to identify the touchstone of liability, which, he said, was dishonesty or lack of probity, which is synonymous. The term 'unconscionable' is, he added, better avoided in this context. 'Dishonesty' means simply not acting as an honest person would in the circumstances, which is an objective standard, even though there is a subjective element in that conduct is assessed in the light of what a person actually knew at the time, as distinct from what a reasonable person would have known or appreciated. For the most part, it is to be equated with 'conscious impropriety'.[141] 'Nelsonian blindness' to the facts can also found liability, because honest people do not close their minds to obvious indications of improper conduct that come to their attention. Nor do they refrain from asking pertinent questions for fear of gaining actual knowledge of the suspected unpalatable truth. When called upon to decide whether a person was acting honestly, a court will look at all of the circumstances known to the third party at the time. The court will also have regard to personal attributes of the third party, such as his experience and intelligence, and the reason why he acted as he did. The third party's state of mind is to be judged by an objective standard in the light of his subjective knowledge.

Lord Nicholls summarized the overall conclusion of the Board as follows:

> ...dishonesty is a necessary ingredient of accessory liability. It is also a sufficient ingredient. A liability in equity to make good resulting loss attaches to a person who dishonestly

---

and C Mitchell), who argue that dishonest assistance yields a duplicative secondary liability comparable to secondary criminal liability. See also (2008) 124 LQR 445 (Pauline Ridge) discussing the remedies available.

[138] [2002] UKHL 12, [2002] 2 AC 164, [2002] 2 All ER 377 (although Lord Millett differed from the majority as to its interpretation), noted (2002) 118 LQR 502 (T M Yeo and H Tjio). See (2003) 44 T & ELJ 3 (J McDonnell).

[139] This was said by Lord Browne-Wilkinson in *Westdeutsche Landesbank Girozentrale v Islington London Borough Council* [1996] AC 669, 705, 706, [1996] 2 All ER 961, 988, HL, to be the only apparent exception to the general principle. See (1977) 28 NILQ 123 (R H Maudsley).

[140] See p 69, *supra*.

[141] See *Cowan de Groot Properties Ltd v Eagle Trust plc* [1992] 4 All ER 700, 761.

procures or assists in a breach of trust or fiduciary obligation.[142] It is not necessary that, in addition, the trustee or fiduciary was acting dishonestly, although this will usually be so where the third party who is assisting him is acting dishonestly. 'Knowingly' is better avoided as a defining ingredient of the principle, and in the context of this principle the *Baden*[143] scale of knowledge is best forgotten.[144]

It is not necessary, however, to show a precise causal link between the assistance and the loss.[145]

In *Twinsectra Ltd v Yardley*,[146] the House of Lords had to examine the meaning of the term 'dishonesty'. The majority view was most fully explained by Lord Hutton, who observed that the courts often draw a distinction between 'subjective dishonesty' and 'objective dishonesty'. There are, he said, three possible standards that can be applied. There is the purely subjective standard, whereby a person is only regarded as dishonest if he transgresses his own standard of honesty, even if that standard is contrary to that of reasonable and honest people. This standard has been rejected by the courts. Secondly, there is a purely objective standard whereby a person acts dishonestly if his conduct is dishonest by the ordinary standards of reasonable and honest people, even if he does not realize this. Thirdly, there is a standard that combines an objective and a subjective test, and which requires that, before there can be a finding of dishonesty, it must be established that the defendant's conduct was dishonest by the ordinary standards of reasonable and honest people, and that he himself realized that, by those standards, his conduct was dishonest. This 'combined test' was held to be the correct one. It was thought to be less than just for the law to permit a finding that a defendant had been 'dishonest' in assisting in a breach of trust where he knew of the facts that created the trust and its breach, but had not been aware that what he was doing would be regarded by honest men as being dishonest.

In a powerful speech dissenting on this issue, Lord Millett said that the question was not whether Lord Nicholls had used the word 'dishonesty' in a subjective or objective sense in the *Royal Brunei* case, but whether a plaintiff should be required to establish that

---

[142] Note, however, that in *Brown v Bennett* [1998] 2 BCLC 97, noted (1998) 114 LQR 357 (R B Grantham and C E F Rickett), Rattee J seemed to think that this head of liability was restricted to a breach of trust in relation to property, a breach of duty in relation to management not being sufficient. On appeal, [1999] 1 BCLC 649, CA, it was not necessary to decide the matter, which was said to be an arguable point. The Court of Appeal left it open in *Goose v Wilson Sandford & Co (a firm)* [2001] Lloyd's Rep PN 189, CA, cited in *Gencor ACP Ltd v Dalby* [2000] 2 BCLC 734. See also (2001) 117 LQR (C Mitchell).

[143] *Baden v Société Générale pour Favouriser le Développement de Commerce et de l'Industrie en France SA* [1992] 4 All ER 161: see p 156, *supra*.

[144] But this, S Gardner says, (1996) 112 LQR 56, cannot be right. An assessment of whether a certain action is dishonest requires reference to what the defendant knew as he performed it. And in *Bank of Credit and Commerce International (Overseas) Ltd (in liq) v Akindele* [2001] Ch 437, [2000] 4 All ER 221, 235, CA, Nourse LJ expressed the view that the categorization in *Baden* is often helpful in identifying different states of knowledge, which may or may not result in a finding of dishonesty for the purposes of knowing assistance.

[145] *Casio Computer Ltd v Sayo* [2001] EWCA Civ 661, at [15]; (2004) 67 MLR 16 (S B Elliott and C Mitchell).

[146] [2002] UKHL 12, [2002] 2 AC 164, [2002] 2 All ER 377, noted [2002] Conv 387 (M P Thompson); (2002) 146 Sol Jo 472 (M Pooles and S Charlwood); [2002] CLJ 524 (Rosy Thornton); (2002) 36 T & ELJ 4 (J R Martyn); (2002) 16 Tru LI 223 (J Glister); [2002] RLR 112 (C Rickett); [2003] Conv 398 (Georgina Andrews); [2006] NILQ 494 (A Woodcock). See also *Bank of Scotland v A Ltd* [2001] EWCA Civ 52, [2001] 3 All ER 58; US *International Marketing Ltd v National Bank of New Zealand* (28 October 2003, unreported), discussed (2004) 120 LQR 208 (T M Yeo). In New Zealand, opposing views have been expressed as to bringing back a subjective knowledge requirement: see [2004] NZLJ 454 (J V Ormsby, W Williams, et al) and 456 (C Cato); [2006] NILQ 494 (A Woodcock).

an accessory to a breach of trust had a dishonest state of mind,[147] or whether it should be sufficient to establish that he acted with the requisite knowledge (so that his conduct was objectively dishonest). Lord Millett preferred the objective approach, which, he said, accords with traditional doctrine. Consciousness of wrongdoing is an aspect of *mens rea* and an appropriate condition of criminal liability, but not of civil liability. For the purpose of civil liability, it should not be necessary that the defendant realized that his conduct was dishonest; it should be sufficient that it constituted intentional wrongdoing. As to the knowledge required, in his opinion, knowledge of the arrangements that constitute the trust is sufficient; it is not necessary that the defendant should appreciate that they do. The gravamen of the charge against the accessory is that he is assisting a person who has been entrusted with the control of a fund to dispose of the fund in an unauthorized manner. He should be liable if he knows of the arrangements by which that person obtained control of the money and that his authority to deal with the money was limited, and participates in a dealing with the money in a manner that he knows to be unauthorized. 'Knowing assistance', as he would prefer to call it, is the equitable counterpoint of the tort of wrongful interference with the performance of a contract, in which liability depends on knowledge and dishonesty is not required.

The speeches of the majority in *Twinsectra*—in particular, those of Lord Hutton and Lord Hoffman—appeared to many to give a defendant the possibility of a successful defence on the ground that he did not realize that honest men would regard his conduct as dishonest. In *Barlow Clowes International Ltd (in liq) v Eurotrust International Ltd*,[148] Lord Hoffman, delivering the advice of the Privy Council, said that there was an 'element of ambiguity' in some of the remarks in the speeches of Lord Hutton and himself. He explained these remarks as meaning that, in considering whether a defendant's state of mind is dishonest, an inquiry into the defendant's view about standards of honesty is not required. His knowledge of a transaction must be such as to render his participation contrary to normally acceptable standards of honest conduct; there is no requirement that he should have had reflections about what those normally acceptable standards are. Consciousness that one is transgressing ordinary standards of honest behaviour requires consciousness of those elements of the transaction that make participation transgress ordinary standards of honest behaviour. It does not require that one should have thought about what those standards are.

Barlow Clowes would at least appear to go some way to restoring the law to what it was generally thought to be before *Twinsectra*. Referring to the first instance judge as correctly stating the law, the Privy Council said:[149]

> In summary, she said that liability for dishonest assistance requires a dishonest state of mind on the part of the person who assists in a breach of trust. Such a state of mind may consist in knowledge that the transaction is one to which he cannot honestly participate (for example, a misappropriation of other people's money), or it may consist in suspicion combined with a conscious decision not to make inquiries which might result in knowledge...Although a dishonest state of mind is a subjective mental state, the standard by

---

[147] That is, so that he was subjectively dishonest in the sense used in *R v Ghosh* [1982] QB 1053, [1982] 2 All ER 689, CA. Note that, in the *Royal Brunei* case, *supra*, PC, Lord Nicholls said, at 389, 106: '*If a person knowingly appropriates another's property, he will not escape a finding of dishonesty simply because he sees nothing wrong in such behaviour.*'

[148] [2005] UKPC 37; [2006] 1 All ER 333, [2006] 1 WLR 1476.   [149] *Supra*, at [10].

which the law determines whether it is dishonest is objective. If by ordinary standards a defendant's mental state would be characterised as dishonest, it is irrelevant that the defendant judges by different standards.

Commentators[150] have not been persuaded that, as stated by the Privy Council, *Barlow Clowes* merely clarifies the decision in *Twinsectra*. Thus Ryan says:[151] '...the Privy Council has delivered something of a volte face via a judgment that disavows the existence of any divergence between its earlier advice in *Royal Brunei* and the later approach of the House of Lords in *Twinsectra*.' The most forthright comment is, perhaps, that of Akkouh, who observes:[152] '...it seems that the Privy Council were somewhat brazen to insist that their decision in [*Barlow Clowes*] merely clarifies an element of ambiguity present in reasoning of the majority of the House of Lords in *Twinsectra*. It is submitted that it radically alters the *Twinsectra* doctrine.' It is surprising that the Privy Council made no reference to the dissenting opinion of Lord Millett in *Twinsectra*, noted above.

In the most recent case, *Abou-Rahmah v Abacha*,[153] the Court of Appeal recognized the existence of the controversy, but found it unnecessary to enter into it for the purposes of the appeal, in which the defendants were unrepresented. They accepted that the law, as laid down in the *Twinsectra* case, as interpreted in the *Barlow Clowes* case, represented the law of England and Wales, but what that interpretation is is not entirely clear. Hopefully, it is a move towards the acceptance of the view of Lord Millett in *Twinsectra*.

There is a possible technical difficulty in relation to the doctrine of precedent, since *Twinsectra* is a House of Lords decision, while *Barlow Clowes* sets out the advice of the Privy Council, which traditionally is merely persuasive. Recent cases suggest a relaxation of the strict rules. Thus, in *Daraydan Holdings Ltd v Solland International Ltd*,[154] Lawrence Collins J indicated that, had it been necessary, he would have preferred the Privy Council case of *A-G for Hong Kong v Reid*[155] to that of *Lister & Co v Stubbs*.[156] Such a preference would, in his opinion, be appropriate particularly 'where the decision of the Privy Council is recent, where it was a decision on the English common law, where the Board consisted mainly of serving Law Lords, and where the decision had been made after full argument on the correctness of the earlier decision'. Again, in *R v James*,[157] it was accepted that, in some circumstances, a court may prefer a decision of the Privy Council to a prior decision of the House of Lords. There, the relevant cases were *A-G for Jersey v Holley*[158] and *R v Smith (Morgan)*.[159] The exceptional circumstances were: (i) that all nine of the Lords of Appeal in Ordinary sitting in *Holley* agreed that the result reached by the majority clarified definitively English law on the issue in question; (ii) that the majority in *Holley* constituted half

---

[150] Including [2006] Conv 188 (E D Ryan); [2005] Sol Jo 1475 (T Akkouh); [2006] 122 LQR 171 (T M Yeo); [2006] CLJ 18 (M Conaglen and Amy Goymour); (2006) 74 T & ELTJ 4 (R Wilson); (2006) 20 TruLI 122 (J E Penner); (2007) 83 T & ELTJ 20 (M Pawlowski); (2006) 17 KCLJ 103 (M Bryan); [2005] NZLJ 410 (Jessica Palmer); [2007] CLJ 22 (G Virgo). But see *AJIT Weekly Trade Mark* [2006] RPC 633 (the Appointed Person under the Trade Marks Act 1994).

[151] Op cit.   [152] Op cit.

[153] [2006] EWCA Civ 1492, [2007] 1 All ER (Comm) 827, discussed (2007) 83 T & ELTJ 20 (M Pawlowski); (2007) 89 T & ELTJ 4 (Margaret Halliwell).

[154] [2004] EWHC 622 (Ch), [2005] 4 All ER 73. See (2006) 122 LQR 349 (M Conaglen and R C Nolan).

[155] [1994] 1 AC 324, [1994] 1 All ER 1, PC.   [156] (1890) 45 Ch D 1, CA.

[157] [2006] EWCA Crim 14, [2006] 1 All ER 759.

[158] [2005] UKPC 23, [2005] 2 AC 580, [2005] 3 All ER 371.

[159] [2001] 1 AC 146, [2000] 4 All ER 289, HL.

of the Appellate Committee of the House of Lords; and (iii) that, in the circumstances, an appeal to the House of Lords on the issue would be a foregone conclusion. Arden LJ in *Abou-Rahman v Abacha* regarded the circumstances of that case as exceptional, but said that *Barlow Clowes* did not, in fact, involve a departure from or refusal to follow the *Twinsectra* case; rather it gave guidance as to the proper interpretation to be placed on it as a matter of English law.

It may be added that it may not be a prerequisite of liability for 'knowing assistance' that any property should have been received or handled by the defendant. Without deciding, the Court of Appeal referred to the issue whether the dishonest breach of trust in which the defendant assisted must have involved the misapplication of trust property or its proceeds of sale, and did not rule out the possibility of a claim in its absence.[160]

(E) POSSESSION BY AN AGENT OF TRUSTEES

The question has often arisen as to whether an agent of trustees, such as a solicitor, banker, or broker, has himself become a constructive trustee of trust property that has come into his hands. It is clear that, in this context, such an agent is a stranger to the trust, and the principles applicable to cases of knowing receipt and dealing[161] have been formulated in terms to cover the special case. In *Lee v Sankey*,[162] Bacon VC said:

> It is well established by many decisions, that a mere agent of trustees is answerable only to his principal and not to cestuis que trust in respect of trust moneys coming to his hands merely in his character of agent, But it is also not less clearly established that a person who received into his hands trust moneys, and who deals with them in a manner inconsistent with the performance of trusts of which he is cognisant, is personally liable for the consequences which may ensue upon his so dealing.

In other words,[163] 'an agent in possession of money which he knows to be trust money, so long as he acts honestly, is not accountable to the beneficiaries interested in the trust money unless he intermeddles in the trust by doing acts characteristic of a trustee and outside the duties of an agent'. On the one hand, in *Mara v Browne*,[164] trustees employed a solicitor who advised improper investments, which were actually carried through by him on being paid trust moneys for the purpose. It was held that the solicitor had acted only in his character of solicitor to the trustees and that, consequently, he was not liable as a constructive trustee in the sense of a trustee *de son tort*.[165] Of course, if he had acted dis-

---

[160] *Goose v Wilson Sandford & Co* [2001] Lloyd's Rep PN 189, CA.

[161] See [1991] LMCLQ 356 (Y C Tan). It is perhaps arguable that an agent in some respects may be in a different position from other strangers: *Carl Zeiss-Stiftung v Herbert Smith & Co (No 2)* [1969] 2 Ch 276, 299, [1969] 2 All ER 367, 380, CA, *per* Sachs LJ.

[162] (1872) LR 15 Eq 204; *Lord Napier and Ettrick v R F Kershaw Ltd* [1993] 1 Lloyd's Rep 10, CA, noted [1993] Conv 391 (Alison Jones); [1993] 143 NLJ 1061 (Jill Martin). This point was not discussed on appeal: [1993] AC 713, [1993] 1 All ER 385, HL.

[163] In *Williams-Ashman v Price* [1942] Ch 219, 228, [1942] 1 All ER 310, 313, *per* Bennett J, citing *Mara v Browne* [1896] 1 Ch 199, CA.

[164] *Supra.* See also *Barnes v Addy* (1874) 9 Ch App 244; *Re Blundell* (1888) 40 Ch D 370; *Goddard v DFC New Zealand Ltd* [1991] 3 NZLR 580. Also contrast *Bridgman v Gill* (1857) 24 Beav 302, with *Thomson v Clydesdale Bank Ltd* [1893] AC 282, HL, and *Coleman v Bucks and Oxon Union Bank* [1897] 2 Ch 243, a rather surprising decision on the facts.

[165] See p 152, *supra.*

honestly, he would have become accountable as a constructive trustee, or, in Lord Millett's preferred phrase,[166] 'accountable in equity', and his firm would have been vicariously liable. And even in the absence of dishonesty, a claim brought in due time against the solicitor for negligence in advising an improper investment would probably have succeeded, but at the time of the action, such a claim, unlike a claim for breach of trust, would have been statute-barred.

On the other hand, in *Lee v Sankey*,[167] trustees of a will employed solicitors to receive the proceeds of the sale of their testator's real estate. The solicitors improperly paid over the proceeds of sale to only one of the trustees, who subsequently became bankrupt, without the receipt or authority of the other. It was held that the solicitors were liable to make good the loss to the trust estate that accrued.

The law is reluctant to make a mere agent a constructive trustee. There must be a want of probity. As Sachs LJ said in *Carl-Zeiss-Stiftung v Herbert Smith (No 2)*,[168] 'professional men and agents who have received moneys as such and have acted bona fide are accountable only to their principals unless dishonesty as well as cognisance of trusts is established against them'. Accordingly, mere notice of a claim asserted by a third party is insufficient to render the agent guilty of a wrongful act in dealing with property derived from his principal in accordance with the latter's instructions, unless the agent knows that the third party's claim is well founded and that the principal accordingly had no authority to give such instructions.[169] And it has been held that banks do not become constructive trustees merely because they entertain suspicions as to the provenance of money deposited with them.[170]

4 THE VENDOR UNDER A CONTRACT
FOR THE SALE OF LAND

Numerous cases[171] from the middle of the seventeenth century onwards establish[172] the general proposition that, where there is a contract for the sale of land,[173] the purchaser becomes the owner in equity of the land or, as Lord Hardwicke put it,[174] the rule is 'that

---

[166] *Dubai Aluminium Co Ltd v Salaam* [2002] UKHL 48, [2003] 2 AC 366, [2003] 1 All ER 97, 131, in which he also said that *Re Bell's Indenture* [1980] 3 All ER 425, [1980] 1 WLR 1217, should be overruled. See (2002) 153 NLJ 405 (J Mitchell).

[167] (1873) LR 15 Eq 204.

[168] *Supra*, CA, at 380. See also *Eagle Trust plc v SBC Securities Ltd* [1992] 4 All ER 488, [1993] 1 WLR 484 (the order was set aside in the Court of Appeal and the plaintiff was given liberty to amend the writ and statement of claim—[1993] 1 WLR 508); *Winslow v Richter* (1989) 61 DLR (4th) 549.

[169] *Carl-Zeiss-Stiftung v Herbert Smith (No 2)*, *supra*, CA.

[170] *A Bank v A Ltd* (2000) Times, 18 July.

[171] See (1960) 24 Conv 47 (P H Pettit); [1984] Conv 43 (M P Thompson); [1987] Ox JLS 60 (S Gardner).

[172] The only dissenting voice seems to be that of Brett LJ in *Rayner v Preston* (1881) 18 Ch D 1, CA.

[173] Or other property where the contract is specifically enforceable: see *Neville v Wilson* [1997] Ch 144, [1996] 3 All ER 171, CA; *Michaels v Harley House (Marylebone) Ltd* [2000] Ch 404, [1999] 1 All ER 356, CA.

[174] *Green v Smith* (1738) 1 Atk 572 at 573. The purchaser's equitable interest is not destroyed if the vendor is a company that is placed in receivership by a debenture holder: *Freevale Ltd v Metrostore (Holdings) Ltd* [1984] Ch 199, [1984] 1 All ER 495, discussed [1984] Conv 446 (D Milman and S Coneys). See *Property*

the vendor of the estate is from the time of his contract, considered as a trustee for the purchasers'.[175] There are, however, difficulties, some of which are due to the fact that the nature of the trust and the duties of the vendor as trustee may undergo important changes. When the purchaser has paid the purchase price in full and has no other obligation to perform under the contract, the vendor is a trustee without qualification, a naked, bare, or mere trustee,[176] but until that state has been reached, he 'is only a trustee in a modified sense',[177] a 'quasi-trustee',[178] or as Jessel MR put it:[179] 'He is certainly a trustee for the purchaser, a trustee, no doubt, with peculiar duties and liabilities, for it is a fallacy to suppose that every trustee has the same duties and liabilities; but he is a trustee.'

The reason for the special position of the vendor-trustee is given by Lord Cairns in *Shaw v Foster*.[180] The vendor-trustee, he explained:

> was not a mere dormant trustee, he was a trustee having a personal and substantial interest in the property, a right to protect that interest, and an active right to assert that interest if anything should be done in derogation of it. The relation, therefore, of trustee and cestui que trust subsisted, but subsisted subject to the paramount right of the vendor and trustee to protect his own interest as vendor of the property.

For a full discussion of the special position of a vendor-trustee, reference should be made to works on vendor and purchaser;[181] for present purposes, it is sufficient to observe by way of illustration that, on the one hand, like any other trustee, he is under a duty to use reasonable care to maintain the property in a reasonable state of preservation,[182] although, by way of qualification, he will be under no liability to the purchaser for neglect or even misfeasance if the contract ultimately goes off.[183] Further, a vendor who, after entering into a contract for the sale of property, sold that property to another person for valuable consideration has been held accountable as a trustee to the original purchaser for the proceeds of sale.[184] And if the vendor has made a planning application, he may be under an obligation

---

Discount Corpn Ltd v Lyon Group Ltd [1980] 1 All ER 334, 330, *per* Goulding J; affd [1981] 1 All ER 379, [1981] 1 WLR 300, CA.

[175] See Chapter 30, section 2(b), available on the Online Resource Centre. The proposition seems not to apply to the grantor of an option: see (1984) 43 CLJ 55 (S Tromans).

[176] Such a trust has no existence except as the equitable consequence of the contract, with potentially fatal results if the contract was registrable under s 4(6) of the Land Charges Act 1972, as amended: *Lloyds Bank plc v Carrick* [1996] 4 All ER 630, CA, noted [1996–97] KCLJ 117 (Theresa Villiers); [1997] CLJ 32 (Nika Oldham); (1998) 61 MLR 486 (N Hopkins).

[177] *Royal Bristol Permanent Building Society v Bomash* (1887) 35 Ch D 390, 397, *per* Kekewich J.

[178] *Cumberland Consolidated Holdings Ltd v Ireland* [1946] KB 264, 269, [1946] 1 All ER 284, 286, *per* Lord Greene MR giving the judgment of the Court of Appeal.

[179] In *Earl of Egmont v Smith* (1877) 6 Ch D 469, 475; *Berkley v Poulett* [1977] 1 EGLR 86, 93, CA, *per* Stamp LJ.

[180] (1872) LR 5 HL 321, 339. See also *Bunny Industries Ltd v FSW Enterprises Pty Ltd* [1982] Qd R 712, in which this discussion is referred to; *Jerome v Kelly* [2004] UK HL 25, [2004] 2 All ER 935, *per* Lord Walker, at [30]–[32].

[181] For example, *Emmet on Title*, 19th edn, ch 6; (1959) 23 Conv 173 (V G Wellings). See also Law Com No 191, which recommends that this trust should remain unaltered; *Englewood Properties Ltd v Patel* [2005] EWHC 188 (Ch), [2005] 3 All ER 307; *Bevin v Smith* [1994] 3 NZLR 648.

[182] See, eg, *Cumberland Consolidation Holdings Ltd v Ireland, supra,* CA; *Phillips v Lamdin* [1949] 2 KB 33, [1949] 1 All ER 770. See also [1995] Cambrian LR 33 (A Dowling).

[183] *Plews v Samuel* [1904] 1 Ch 464.

[184] *Lake v Bayliss* [1974] 2 All ER 1114, [1974] 1 WLR 1073, noted (1974) 38 Conv 357 (F R Crane).

not to withdraw it without the consent of the purchaser.[185] On the other hand, by way of contrast with an ordinary trustee, the vendor-trustee is entitled to retain for his own benefit the rents and profits until the date fixed for completion, and is entitled to retain possession of the property until the contract is completed by payment of the purchase price.

It may be added that a property adjustment order in ancillary proceedings pursuant to the Matrimonial Causes Act 1973, s 24(1)(a), ordering a husband to transfer his interest in the matrimonial home to his wife likewise confers an equitable interest in the property on her, conditional only upon the making of the decree absolute.[186]

5 UNDERTAKING BY PURCHASER

In *Binions v Evans*,[187] the Tredegar Estate entered into an agreement with the defendant, the widow of a former employee, that she should be permitted to reside in a specified cottage rent-free for the remainder of her life or until she determined the arrangement by four weeks' notice. The Estate subsequently sold the cottage to the plaintiffs expressly subject to the agreement and, because of that provision, at a reduced price. Some months later, the plaintiffs brought proceedings for possession against the defendant. The majority of the Court of Appeal held that the effect of the agreement was to make the defendant a tenant for life under the Settled Land Act and the plaintiff accordingly bound by her interest. Lord Denning MR did not agree. He thought—wrongly, as it has now been held[188]—that she had from the outset a licence conferring an equitable interest in the land, but, on the hypothesis that this was not so, said that, on the sale at a reduced price 'subject to' the defendant's rights, the court would 'impose on the purchaser a constructive trust for her benefit, for the simple reason that it would be utterly inequitable for the purchaser to turn the widow out contrary to the stipulation subject to which he took the premises'.

It is now clear that Lord Denning went too far when he said that a constructive trust would be imposed whenever the owner of land sells it to a purchaser and, at the same time, stipulates that he shall take it 'subject to' a contractual licence. While taking this view in *Ashburn Anstalt v Arnold*,[189] the Court of Appeal was equally clear that the facts of *Binions v Evans*[190] did give rise to a constructive trust. In the circumstances, it was a proper inference that, on the sale to the plaintiffs, the intention of the Estate and the plaintiffs was that the plaintiffs should give effect to the tenancy agreement. If they had failed to do so, the Estate would have been liable to damages to the defendant.

---

[185] *Sinclair-Hill v Sothcott* (1973) 26 P & CR 490, doubted *Englewood Properties Ltd v Patel, supra.*

[186] *Mountney v Treharne* [2002] EWCA Civ 1174, [2002] 3 WLR 1760.

[187] [1972] Ch 359, [1972] 2 All ER 70, CA, applied *DHN Food Distributors Ltd v London Borough of Tower Hamlets* [1976] 3 All ER 462, [1976] 1 WLR 852, CA; *Lyus v Prowsa Developments Ltd* [1982] 2 All ER 953, [1982] 1 WLR 1044; [1983] 46 MLR 96 (P H Kenny); [1983] Conv 64 (P Jackson); (1984) 47 MLR 476 (P Bennett); *Ungurian v Lesnoff* [1990] Ch 206, [1989] 3 WLR 840, discussed [1990] Conv 223 (P Sparkes), (1991) 107 LQR 596 (J Hill), (1991) 5 Tru LI 12 (Bernadette Griffin); *Dent v Dent* [1996] 1 All ER 659, [1996] 1 WLR 683. *Binions v Evans* is discussed in (1972) 88 LQR 336 (P V Baker); (1973) 117 Sol Jo 23 (B W Harvey); (1972) 36 Conv 266 (Jill Martin); (1972) 36 Conv 277 (D J Hayton); (1975) 35 MLR 551 (A J Oakley); (1973) 32 CLJ 123 (R J Smith); (1977) 93 LQR 561 (J A Hornby). See also [1978] Conv 250; (2004) 120 LQR 667 (B McFarlane).

[188] See *Ashburn Anstalt v Arnold* [1989] Ch 1, [1988] 2 All ER 147, CA.

[189] [1989] Ch 1, [1988] 2 All ER 147, CA.   [190] [1972] Ch 359, [1972] 2 All ER 70, CA.

In *Lyus v Prowsa Developments Ltd*,[191] the plaintiff contracted with developers to buy a plot with a house to be built according to agreed specifications. Before the house was built or the contract completed, the developers went into liquidation and the bank mortgagees, who were not bound by the plaintiff's contract and were accordingly in a position to sell free from it, sold to the first defendants. It was, however, a term of the contract that the property was sold subject to, but with the benefit of, the plaintiff's agreement. The first defendants resold to the second defendants, subject to the plaintiff's contract so far, if at all, as it may have been enforceable against the first defendants. The plaintiff successfully contended that the 'subject to' clause imposed a constructive trust on the first defendants and it was admitted that, if this was so, the second defendants were similarly bound.[192] In approving this decision in *Ashburn Anstalt v Arnold*,[193] the Court of Appeal observed that there was no point in making the conveyance subject to the contract unless the parties intended the purchaser to give effect to it. Further, on the sale by the bank, a letter had been written to the bank's agents by the first defendant's solicitors, giving an assurance that their client would take reasonable steps to make sure that the interests of contractual purchasers were dealt with quickly and to their satisfaction. But there is no rule that the sale of land 'subject to' a contractual licence automatically gives rise to a constructive trust; rather the reverse is true. To establish a constructive trust, very special circumstances must be proved, showing that the transferee of the property undertook a new liability to give effect to provisions for the benefit of third parties. It is the conscience of the transferee that has to be affected and it has to be affected in a way that gives rise to an obligation to meet the legitimate expectations of the third party.[194] It has been suggested[195] that, if a 'subject to' clause does create a trust, the true analysis is that it arises because that is what the parties intended. It is therefore not a constructive trust at all, but rather an express trust.

6 EXECUTOR *DE SON TORT*

An executor *de son tort* is one who, without due authority, takes possession of, or intermeddles with, the property of a deceased person. Such a person may be, but is not necessarily, a constructive trustee.[196] There would appear to be no justification for imposing a constructive trust where the executor *de son tort* is a complete stranger, save in the most exceptional

---

[191] *Supra.* See [1985] CLJ 280 (M P Thompson); (1983) 80 LSG (Constance Whippman); [2000] Conv 398 (Susan Bright); *Bahr v Nicolay (No 2)* (1988) 62 ALJR 268. The position may be affected by the Contracts (Rights of Third Parties) Act 1999.

[192] *Quaere* whether this admission was rightly made. The way in which Dillon J distinguished *Miles v Bull (No 2)* [1969] 3 All ER 1585 is unconvincing vis-à-vis the second defendant. See (1983) 80 LSG 1783 (Constance Whippman) asking what was the fraud or unconscionable conduct on the part of the second defendant, and drawing attention to the failure to refer to the Land Registration Act 1925, ss 59(6) and 74 (both now repealed). The apparent force of s 74 is reduced by the decision in *Williams & Glyn's Bank Ltd v Boland* [1981] AC 487, [1980] 2 All ER 408, HL.

[193] [1989] Ch 1, [1988] 2 All ER 147, CA. See (1990) 20 VUWLR 23 (B Davies).

[194] *IDC Group Ltd v Clark* [1992] 1 EGLR 187; *Lloyd v Dugdale* [2001] EWCA Civ 1754, [2002] WTLR 863 noted [2002] Conv 584 (M Dixon).

[195] (1983) 133 NLJ 798 (C T Emery and B Smythe).

[196] See the full discussion in [1974] Conv 176 (F Hinks).

circumstances. But where, for instance, a widow enters into possession as executrix *de son tort* and seeks to establish title by adverse possession against her adult children, it would be quite a different matter. In *James v Williams*,[197] in which it has been pointed out[198] that the contrary Court of Appeal decision in *Pollard v Jackson*[199] was not cited, the intestate died leaving three adult children. No letters of administration were taken out, but William, one of the children, took it upon himself to take possession of the property as if he owned it. Nearly twenty-four years after the intestate's death, William himself was dead and the defendant claimed title to the property through him. One of the other children commenced proceedings against the defendant, contending that she was entitled to a one-third share in the property. The defence was based on the Limitation Act 1980, which provides for a twelve-year limitation period in an action to recover any land. The defence failed on the ground that, on the facts, William had been a constructive trustee of the property, and the plaintiff's claim was accordingly not barred by the Act.[200]

[197] [2000] Ch 1, [1999] 3 All ER 309, CA.

[198] By N Asprey in (2000) 20 T & ELJ 19; (2000) 150 NLJ 942 (G Miller).

[199] (1993) 67 P & CR 327, CA.

[200] By s 21(1) of the 1980 Act, no limitation period applies to an action by a beneficiary under a trust to recover trust property in possession of the trustee or previously received by the trustee and converted to his use. See p 529 *et seq, infra*.

9

RESULTING TRUSTS

As we have seen,[1] there are limited situations that give rise to a resulting trust. In the first section of this chapter, we shall consider cases in which the settlor has failed in whole, or in part, to declare comprehensive trusts of the property transferred to trustees, or in which those trusts fail in whole or in part. The position in which declared trusts fail because they are unlawful or illegal is considered in a later chapter.

The second section considers cases in which, absent a declaration of trust, property is transferred for no consideration by X to Y, or in which X buys property that is put into the name of Y. The last two situations are governed by similar principles and are therefore considered together. It is important to note that some of the cases cited in this section involve the family home to which, as explained in the following chapter, it has recently been held that the law of resulting trusts does not apply. However the principles laid down in these cases remain valid in other situations.

1 FAILURE TO DISPOSE OF THE EQUITABLE INTEREST

(A) THE PRINCIPLE INVOLVED

'*Equity,*' it has been said,[2] '*abhors a beneficial vacuum.*' Accordingly, where a settlor conveys or transfers property to trustees, but fails to declare the trusts upon which it is to be held, or where the expressed trusts fail altogether on the ground,[3] for instance, of uncertainty, or non-compliance with statutory requirements as to writing,[4] or where they fail partially on similar grounds, or because the trusts expressed only dispose of a part of the equitable interest, the entire equitable interest, or such part thereof as has not been effectively disposed of, remains vested in the settlor or, in technical language, is said to result to him, and the property is accordingly said to be held by the trustees upon a resulting trust for him.[5] *Ex hypothesi*, in these cases, the transfer is on trust and, accordingly, the resulting

---

[1] See p 67, *supra*.

[2] *Vandervell v IRC* [1966] Ch 261, 291, [1965] 2 All ER 37, 46, CA, *per* Diplock LJ. Cf dicta in *Wood Preservation Ltd v Prior* [1969] 1 All ER 364, CA, esp *per* Lord Donovan, at 367, and in *Conservative and Unionist Central Office v Burrell* [1980] 3 All ER 42, 61 *et seq*, *per* Vinelott J; affd [1982] 2 All ER 1, [1982] 1 WLR 522, CA. See, generally, (1999) 25 Mon LR 110 (J Glover); (2008) 124 LQR 72 (W Swadling).

[3] The special considerations that apply where the trusts fail on the ground of illegality, or because they offend against public policy, are discussed in Chapter 11, p 221, *infra*.

[4] *Hodgson v Marks* [1971] Ch 892, [1971] 2 All ER 684, CA. [5] Or, if he is dead, for his estate.

trust does not establish the trust, but merely carries back to the transferor the beneficial interest that has not been disposed of. The same principle applies to a devise or bequest by a testator to trustees upon trusts that fail similarly either altogether or in part, when the trustees will hold on a resulting trust, wholly or pro tanto, for the persons entitled to residue, or, if the gift that fails is a gift of residue, or if there is no residuary gift, then for the persons entitled on intestacy.[6] We have, indeed, already come across an application of the principle in connection with alleged half-secret trusts that have not been established.[7] Another illustration is where there has been a marriage settlement in contemplation of a particular marriage and the contract to marry has been '*definitely and absolutely put an end to*';[8] the trustees of the settlement will, in such a case, hold the property on a resulting trust for the person who put the property into the settlement. And the same result has been reached where a decree of nullity has been pronounced.[9]

Where the expressed trusts are in part valid, but do not exhaust the beneficial interest, there will be a resulting trust whether the expressed trusts are of a non-charitable or a charitable nature, unless the terms of the trust expressly or by implication exclude a resulting trust,[10] or, in the case of a charitable trust, the cy-près doctrine applies. A case involving a non-charitable trust was *Re the Trusts of the Abbott Fund*,[11] in which a fund had been raised by subscription for the maintenance and support of two distressed ladies. On the death of the survivor, a portion of the fund remained unapplied in the hands of the trustees. It was held that there was a resulting trust of the balance of the fund for the subscribers thereto. Again, in *Re Gillingham Bus Disaster Fund*,[12] following an accident in which a number of cadets were killed and injured, a fund was raised by subscription for the benefit of the victims and then to other worthy causes in memory of the boys who were killed. The trust for worthy causes was void for uncertainty. Consequently, it was held that the balance of the fund not applied for the benefit of the victims was held on a resulting trust for the subscribers. It was further held in that case that the position was unaffected by the fact that a large number of the subscribers, such as contributors to street collections, were, as it was assumed, unascertainable, but the better view seems to be that where money

<hr>

[6] See, eg, *Morice v Bishop of Durham* (1805) 10 Ves 522; *Chichester Diocesan Fund v Simpson* [1944] AC 341, [1944] 2 All ER 60, HL.

[7] See, eg, *Johnson v Ball* (1851) 5 De G & Sm 85; *Re Keen* [1937] Ch 236, [1937] 1 All ER 452, CA. The result is the same in a fully secret trust if the apparent beneficiary admits that he is or is proved to be a mere trustee: *Re Boyes* (1884) 26 Ch D 531.

[8] Per Pearson J in *Essery v Cowlard* (1884) 26 Ch D 191, 193. In this case, the parties had, in fact, lived together without marriage and had had three children; *Bond v Walford* (1886) 32 Ch D 238. For a case in which no trusts were sufficiently declared, see *Re Wilcock* (1890) 62 LT 317. Cf *Burgess v Rawnsley* [1975] Ch 429, [1975] 3 All ER 142, CA.

[9] *Re Ames' Settlement* [1946] Ch 217, [1946] 1 All ER 689, considered by Lord Browne-Wilkinson in *Westdeutsche Landesbank Girozentrale v Islington London Borough Council* [1996] AC 669, [1996] 2 All ER 961, 997–998, HL. See also *Re d'Altroy's Will Trusts* [1968] 1 All ER 181, discussed in (1969) 32 MLR 210 (J Tiley); *Re Rodwell* [1970] Ch 726, [1969] 3 All ER 1363. But note the power of the Divorce Court under the Matrimonial Causes Act 1973, s 24. Section 16 of the Act now provides that a decree of nullity in respect of a voidable marriage shall end the marriage from the date of the decree absolute and not retrospectively.

[10] *Davis v Richards and Wallington Industries Ltd* [1991] 2 All ER 563, [1990] 1 WLR 1511.

[11] [1900] 2 Ch 326.

[12] [1958] Ch 300, [1958] 1 All ER 37; affd [1959] Ch 62, [1958] 2 All ER 749, CA, although the present point did not arise on appeal.

is raised by means of entertainments, raffles, and sweepstakes, or street collections, the donor parts with his money out and out, and there is no resulting trust.[13]

Another type of case in which there may be a resulting trust is that in which the provisions of a settlement fail to cover the events that in fact happen. In *Re Cochrane's Settlement Trusts*,[14] there was a post-nuptial settlement in an unusual form. Husband and wife each brought property into the settlement, the beneficial limitations of which were that income was payable to the wife for life 'so long as she shall continue to reside with the husband' and after her death 'or the prior determination of the trust in her favour' to the husband for life with a gift over of capital, 'from and after the decease of the survivor of them'. The wife ceased to reside with the husband, who later died, leaving the wife surviving him. It was held that, during the remainder of the life of the wife, there were resulting trusts in favour of the estate of the husband and in favour of the wife of the income of their respective parts of the trust fund.

Where charitable trusts are declared that fail in whole or in part, there may likewise be a resulting trust, although here, as already mentioned, it will often be ousted by the cy-près doctrine, which will be discussed later in connection with charitable trusts. In the absence of the requirements for the application of the cy-près doctrine, there has been held to be a resulting trust both in cases in which the trust has failed altogether, and in cases in which the court has had to deal with a surplus after the particular charitable purpose has come to an end. In *Re Ulverston and District New Hospital Building Trusts*,[15] a fund was opened for the building of a new hospital, but the scheme became impracticable so that there was a total failure *ab initio* of the purpose of the fund. It was held that so far as money had been received from identifiable[16] sources, there was a resulting trust for the subscribers. There will likewise be a resulting trust for the subscribers where there is a surplus after the particular charitable trust has been fulfilled,[17] and for the settlor or his representatives where a charitable trust for a limited period or a limited purpose has come to an end.[18]

(B) THE PRELIMINARY QUESTION OF CONSTRUCTION

In various circumstances in which, at first sight, one might think that there was a resulting trust, it has been held that, on the true construction of the relevant documents, a resulting trust does not arise.

---

[13] *Re West Sussex Constabulary's Widows, Children and Benevolent (1930) Fund Trusts* [1971] Ch 1, [1970] 1 All ER 544, criticized on another ground (1971) 87 LQR 466 (M Albery); and see (1958) 74 LQR 190, 489 (P S Atiyah); (1973) 37 Conv 126 (Penelope Pearce and A Samuels).

[14] [1955] Ch 309, [1955] 1 All ER 222. The resulting trust may, however be ousted by the doctrine of acceleration—*Re Flower's Settlement Trusts*, [1957] 1 All ER 462, [1957] 1 WLR 401, CA; *Re Dawson's Settlement* [1966] 3 All ER 68—or the court may even, in a clear case, supply words to fill in a gap in the limitations, with the result that there will be no place for a resulting trust: *Re Akeroyd's Settlement* [1893] 3 Ch 363, CA; *Re Cory* [1955] 2 All ER 630, [1955] 1 WLR 725.

[15] [1956] Ch 622, [1956] 3 All ER 164, CA. See also *Re University of London Medical Sciences Institute Fund* [1909] 2 Ch 1, CA.

[16] As to anonymous subscribers, see the Charities Act 1993, s 14, as amended, and p 338, *infra*.

[17] *Re British Red Cross Balkan Fund* [1914] 2 Ch 419: the subscribers are entitled to the surplus rateably in proportion to their subscriptions. The actual decision is suspect, as the objects would seem to have been charitable, in which case the surplus should have been applied cy-près to some other charitable purpose: *Barlow Clowes International Ltd (in liq) v Vaughan* [1992] 4 All ER 22, CA. As to the cy-près doctrine, see p 332 *et seq*, *infra*.

[18] *Gibson v South American Stores (Gath & Chaves) Ltd* [1950] Ch 177, [1949] 2 All ER 985, CA; *Re Cooper's Conveyance Trusts* [1956] 3 All ER 28, [1956] 1 WLR 1096; *Bankes v Salisbury Diocesan Council* [1960] Ch 631, [1960] 2 All ER 372. See (1957) 21 Conv 213; note the effect of the Perpetuities and Accumulations Act 1964, s 12.

(i) Donor/settlor parts with his money out and out, without any intention of retaining any interest therein

If the settlor or donor has expressly, or by necessary implication, abandoned any beneficial interest in the property, there is no resulting trust and the undisposed-of equitable interest[19] necessarily falls to the Crown as *bona vacantia*. This, according to the better view,[20] is the position in relation to money raised by means of street collections. The result is even clearer in the case of money raised by means of entertainments, raffles, and sweepstakes. Here, as Goff J pointed out in *Re West Sussex Constabulary's Fund Trusts*,[21] it is quite impossible to apply the doctrine of resulting trusts for two reasons. Firstly, the relationship is one of contract and not of trust: the purchaser pays his money as the price of what is offered and what he receives; his motive need not be to aid the cause at all. Secondly, there is, in such cases, no direct contribution to the fund at all. It is only the profit, if any, which is ultimately received, and there may even be none.

(ii) Defunct voluntary associations

This situation was considered in a previous chapter.[22] It does not give rise to a resulting trust.

(iii) Gift subject to carrying out a particular trust

In some cases, the court has to decide whether, on the true construction of a will,[23] there is a gift to a donee on trust, when any property not required to carry out the expressed trust will be held on a resulting trust for the testator's estate,[24] or whether there is a beneficial gift to a donee subject to carrying out some specified trust or obligation, in which case, the donee will take beneficially any surplus remaining after the trust or obligation has been carried out.[25] Extrinsic evidence will not be admitted to show that someone who, on the construction of the will, is a mere trustee was intended by the testator to take beneficially.[26]

(iv) Trust for assistance of certain persons by stated means

In *Re Andrew's Trust*,[27] a fund was subscribed for the education of the children of a deceased clergyman. When the children were all of age and their education had been completed, there remained a surplus. It was held that it should be divided equally among the children and not on a resulting trust for the subscribers. It is interesting to compare this case with

---

[19] *Westdeutsche Landesbank Girozentrale v Islington London Borough Council* [1996] AC 669, [1996] 2 All ER 961, 991, HL, *per* Lord Browne-Wilkinson.

[20] *Re West Sussex Constabulary's Widows, Children and Benevolent (1930) Fund Trusts* [1971] Ch 1, [1970] 1 All ER 544. See also, in a very different context, *Universe Tankships Inc of Monrovia v International Transport Workers' Federation* [1981] ICR 129, CA; revsd [1983] 1 AC 366, [1982] 2 All ER 67, HL.

[21] *Supra.*   [22] See p 64, *supra.*

[23] The cases all seem to have arisen on wills, but there seems no reason why the same problem should not arise on an *inter vivos* disposition.

[24] This was the decision in *Re West* [1900] 1 Ch 84 and *Re Rees' Will Trusts* [1950] Ch 204, [1949] 2 All ER 1003, CA.

[25] This was the decision in *King v Denison* (1813) 1 Ves & B 260 and *Croome v Croome* (1888) 59 LT 582, CAS, affd (1889) 61 LT 814, HL.

[26] *Re Rees' Will Trusts, supra*, CA. Cf *Re Tyler's Fund Trusts* [1967] 3 All ER 389, [1967] 1 WLR 1262.

[27] [1905] 2 Ch 48; *Re Osoba* [1978] 2 All ER 1099; varied [1979] 2 All ER 393, [1979] 1 WLR 247, CA. See [1978] 37 CLJ 219 (C E F Rickett).

the somewhat similar facts of *Re the Trusts of the Abbott Fund*,[28] in which it will be recalled it was held that there was a resulting trust for the subscribers. If a trust is constituted for the assistance of certain persons by certain stated means, there is a sharp distinction between cases in which the beneficiaries have died and cases in which they are still living. If they are dead, as in *Re the Trusts of the Abbot Fund*, the court is ready to hold that there is a resulting trust, because the major purpose of the trust can no longer in any sense be carried out. But if the beneficiaries are still living, the major purpose of providing help and benefit for the beneficiaries can still be carried out even after the stated means have all been accomplished, and so the court will be ready to treat the stated means as being merely indicative and not restrictive. Accordingly, in *Re Andrew's Trust*,[29] the fund was treated as having been subscribed for the benefit of the children generally, with particular reference to their education. Accordingly, there was nothing to form the subject matter of a resulting trust.

(v) The rule in *Lassence v Tierney*[30]

Finally, mention should be made of the rule:

> that if you find an absolute gift to a legatee in the first instance, and trusts are engrafted or imposed on that absolute interest which fail, either from lapse or invalidity or any other reason then the absolute gift takes effect so far as the trusts have failed to the exclusion of the residuary legatee or next of kin[31] as the case may be.[32]

(C) THE *QUISTCLOSE TRUST*

This is a prime example of the use of equity in commercial transactions. In *Barclays Bank Ltd v Quistclose Investments Ltd*,[33] Rolls Razor Ltd had not got the funds to pay the dividend that it had declared. Quistclose agreed to lend the necessary money, nearly £210,000, on condition 'that it is used to pay the forthcoming dividend due on July 24 next'. A cheque for the exact amount was handed over and paid into a separate account at Barclays Bank, with which it was agreed the account would only be used to meet the dividend due on 24 July. Before that date, Rolls Razor went into liquidation and the dividend could no longer lawfully be paid. Barclays sought to set the sum in the separate account against Rolls Razor's

---

[28] [1900] 2 Ch 326. See p 171, *supra*.   [29] *Supra*.

[30] (1849) 1 Mac & G 551, also known as the rule in *Hancock v Watson* [1902] AC 14, HL; *Watson v Holland* [1985] 1 All ER 290. See (2006) 73 T & ELTJ 17 (Jo Summers and Helen Wholley).

[31] Who could, of course, only claim on a resulting trust.

[32] *Per* Lord Davey in *Hancock v Watson* [1902] AC 14, 22, HL.

[33] From *Barclays Bank Ltd v Quistclose Investments Ltd* [1970] AC 567, [1968], 3 All ER 651, HL, which was applied in *Re EVTR Ltd* [1987] BCLC 646, CA, discussed (1987) 131 Sol Jo 1439 (D W Fox); (1988) 85 LSG 36/14 (I M Hardcastle); *Lord v Australian Elizabethan Theatre Trust* (1991) 102 ALR 681, discussed (1992) 18 Mon LR 147 (Fiona Burns); *R v Common Professional Examination Board, ex p Mealing-McCleod* (2000) Times, 2 May, CA. But no trust in *Daly v Sydney Stock Exchange Ltd* (1986) 65 ALR 193, discussed (1987) 61 ALJ 241 (J G Starke), in which no condition was imposed on the loan. Nor in *Re Miles* (1988) 85 ALR 216, in which the *Quistclose* principle was said to be limited to cases involving the actual payment of money by the party claiming to be the beneficiary of a resulting trust, for the purpose of discharge of debts by the payee, that purpose having failed. Also distinguished in *Peter Cox Investment Pty Ltd (in liq) v International Air Transport Association* (1999) 161 ALR 105. See also (1993) 23 QLSJ 145 (Tina Cockburn); [1992] Ox JLS 333 (M Bridge); [1994] Denning LJ 93 (G McCormack); (2006) 80 T & ELTJ 21 (S Kempster); *The Quistclose Trust: Critical Essays*, ed W Swadling.

overdraft. It was decided that that money was held on trust for Quistclose. The fact that the contract between Quistclose and Rolls Razor was one of loan did not prevent a trust from arising.[34] Moreover, Barclays had notice that the money was trust money and not part of the assets of Rolls Razor, and was accordingly bound by the trust.

There has been much debate as to the correct analysis of the *Quistclose* trust. Dicta of Lord Wilberforce in that case[35] suggested that there were two successive trusts: a primary trust for payment to identifiable beneficiaries, such as creditors or shareholders; and a secondary trust in favour of the lender arising on the failure of the primary trust. The matter was considered in some detail by Lord Millett in *Twinsectra v Yardley*,[36] who pointed out several objections to this approach—in particular, that it could not apply to a trust for an abstract purpose. There was, he said, no reason to make an arbitrary distinction between money paid for an abstract purpose and money paid for a purpose that could be said to benefit an ascertained class of beneficiaries. Another theory is that there is a primary purpose trust under which the loan can only be used for a specified purpose. The beneficial interest is left in suspense until the stated purpose is carried out or fails. The difficulty with this, Lord Millett said, '(apart from its unorthodoxy)[37] is that it fails to have regard to the role which the resulting trust plays in equity's scheme of things, or to explain why the money is not simply held on a resulting trust for the lender'. Chambers'[38] view is that no trust is created at all. The borrower receives the entire beneficial ownership in the money, subject only to a contractual right in the lender to prevent the money being used otherwise than for the specified purpose. It is only if the purpose fails that a resulting trust for the lender comes into being. Lord Millett rejected this view[39] on the grounds, inter alia, that it provided no solution to cases of non-contractual payment and was inconsistent with Lord Wilberforce's description of the borrower's obligation as fiduciary.

The conclusion reached by Lord Millett, it is submitted rightly, is that, in cases such as these, the beneficial interest remains throughout in the lender subject only to the borrower's power or duty to apply the money in accordance with the lender's instructions. If the purpose fails, the money is returnable to the lender, not under some new trust in his favour that only comes into being on the failure of the purpose, but because the resulting trust in his favour is no longer subject to any power on the part of the borrower to make use of the money. In the latter case, money was loaned to a firm of solicitors on an undertaking that the money would be retained by them until such time as it was applied in the acquisition of property on behalf of Y and that it would be utilized solely for that purpose. Money in a client account is held on trust, and the only question is as to the terms of the trust.

[34] *Neste Oy v Lloyds Bank plc* [1983] 2 Lloyd's Rep 658; *Re E Dibbens & Sons Ltd (in liq)* [1990] BCLC 577. Normally, payment by way of loan is inconsistent with the creation of a resulting trust. In *Hussey v Palmer* [1972] 3 All ER 744, [1972] 1 WLR 1286, CA, it is submitted that the view of Cairns LJ, at 749, on this point is to be preferred to that of Phillimore LJ, at 748. See (1973) 37 Conv 65 (D J Hayton).

[35] *Supra*, HL, at 580, 654–6, applied in *Re Northern Developments (Holdings) Ltd* (1978, unreported), referred to in *Twinsectra v Yardley* [2002] UKHL 12, [2002 2 AC 164, [2002] 2 All ER 377, at [86].

[36] [2002 UKHL 12, [2002] 2 AC 164, [2002] 2 All ER 377, HL, noted (2003) 119 LQR 8 (T M Yeo and H Tjio); (2002) 16 Tru LI 165 (N Richardson); (2002) 16 Tru LI 223 (J Glister), and referred to as an 'authoritative analysis' in *Re Margaretta (in liq)* [2005] EWHC 582 (Ch), [2006] WTLR 1271. Alhough Lord Millett delivered a dissenting speech, there does not seem to have been any disagreement on this point. His observations on *Quistclose* were, however, obiter.

[37] This presumably refers to its conflict with the beneficiary principle.

[38] *Resulting Trusts.*

[39] Which could not, he thought, survive the criticisms of Lusina Ho and P St J Smart in (2001) 21 OJLS 267.

Here, the solicitors held the money on a resulting trust for the lender, but subject to a power to apply it towards the acquisition of property by Y in accordance with the undertaking.

Quistclose and *Twinsectra* were both cited in *Cooper v PRG Powerhouse Ltd.*[40] In this case, Mr Cooper, the claimant, resigned from PRG and, as a part of the resignation arrangements, he was to keep the Mercedes car purchased by him on credit on which PRG had been paying the instalments of the purchase price. He was, however, to pay £34,239 to PRG towards the balance of the purchase price, which PRG would pay to the supplier, together with its contribution of £3,000. The claimant paid the money to PRG, which did not pay it into a separate account. It sent a cheque for the combined sum to the supplier, but, unfortunately, went into administration before the cheque had been cleared and it was therefore dishonoured. On the facts, it was held that the payment to the company was for the specific purpose of settling the account with the supplier of the car. It was further held that the fact that the money was not paid into a separate account was not so critical as to prevent a purpose trust [sic] from arising. This is difficult to reconcile with Lord Millett's statement that the borrower must keep the money separate. It was further held that equitable principles of tracing applied (the account was, at all material times, in credit for a sum exceeding £34,239) and the claim should therefore succeed. Subject to the separation point, it was an appropriate case in which to apply the *Quistclose* principle. However, to say, as Evans-Lombe J did, that a purpose trust had been established is inconsistent with Lord Millett's conclusion: 'But the only trust is the resulting trust for the lender. The borrower is authorised or directed to apply the money for a stated purpose, but this is a mere power and does not constitute a purpose trust.'

(D) PENSION FUND SURPLUSES

Pension fund schemes vary widely and the position with regard to any surplus depends on the terms of the scheme. In the most usual type of scheme, the employee contributes a specified proportion of his salary and the employer's contribution is on a 'balance of cost' basis—that is, he has to contribute the sum required to bring the total contribution up to what is necessary to meet the funding level. In such a scheme, if, on dissolution, there is a surplus, it is not clear who is entitled to it. In *Re Courage Group's Pension Schemes*,[41] Millett J was of the opinion that any surplus arises from past overfunding not by the employer and employees pro rata to their respective contributions, but by their employer alone to the full extent of its past contributions and only subject thereto by the employees. Writing extrajudicially,[42] Vinelott J said that Millett J in that case gave '*compelling reasons for the conclusion that in the case of a balance of cost scheme the surplus belongs to the employer*'.[43]

In *Davis v Richards and Wallington Industries Ltd*,[44] Scott J distinguished between the proportion of the fund derived from employees' contributions and the proportion

---

[40] [2008] EWHC 498 (Ch), [2008] BPIR 492.

[41] [1987] 1 All ER 528, [1987] 1 WLR 495; *Wrightson Ltd v Fletcher Challenge Nominees Ltd* [2002] 2 NZLR 1, PC. See (2001) Tru LI 130 (N Davis).   [42] (1994) 8 Tru LI 35.

[43] But see s 37 of the Pensions Act 1995 providing safeguards to scheme members in relation to the payment of a surplus to the employer. See also *National Grid Co plc v Mayes* [2001] ICR 544, HL, noted [2001] 30 Ind LJ 318 (R Nobles).

[44] [1991] 2 All ER 563, [1990] 1 WLR 1511, noted [1990] Ind LJ 204 (R Nobles); [1991] Conv 366 (Jill Martin); [1992] Conv 41 (S Gardner); *Re UEB Industries Ltd Pension Plan* [1992] 1 NZLR 294; (1990) 4 TL & P 163

attributable to the employer's contributions. It was held that, in so far as the surplus was derived from the employer's overpayments, there was a resulting trust for it. However, a resulting trust was excluded in relation to the employees' contributions, because it would lead to an unworkable result and it would conflict with the statutory provisions giving tax advantages to an approved scheme: in so far as the surplus was so derived, it devolved in the Crown as *bona vacantia*.[45]

2 TRANSFER INTO AND PURCHASE IN THE NAME OF ANOTHER, AND RELATED CASES

(A) PURCHASE IN THE NAME OF ANOTHER, OR IN THE JOINT NAMES OF THE PURCHASER AND ANOTHER

Whenever someone buys either real or personal property and has it conveyed or registered or otherwise put into the name of another, or of himself and another jointly, it is presumed that the other holds the property on trust for the person who has paid the purchase money. The classic statement of the law is to be found in the judgment of Eyre CB in *Dyer v Dyer*:[46]

> The clear result of all the cases, without a single exception, is that the trust of a legal estate, whether freehold, copyhold, or leasehold; whether taken in the names of the purchasers and others jointly, or in the names of others without that of the purchaser; whether in one name or several; whether jointly or successive—results to the man who advances the purchase-money.[47]

Although *Dyer v Dyer*[48] refers only to interests in land, the principle has always been treated as equally applicable to pure personalty.[49] The same principle governs analogous

---

(Meryl Thomas); (1991) 5 TL & P 60 (R Ellison). See also *Re William Makin & Son Ltd* [1993] BCC 453, discussed (1996) 10 Tru LI 15 (Marina Milner); (2000) 14 Tru LI 66 (Lord Millett).

[45] A proportion of the fund derived from transfers from other schemes: this also devolved as *bona vacantia*.

[46] (1788) 2 Cox Eq Cas 92 at 93: cited with approval by Lord Upjohn in *Pettitt v Pettitt* [1970] AC 777, [1969] 2 All ER 385, HL. See *Carlton v Goodman* [2002] EWCA Civ 545, [2002] 2 FLR 259. In that case, although the woman had had a relationship with the man (now deceased), they had never lived together. The deceased had provided the deposit and discharged all of the payments on the property bought in their joint names. The woman's involvement in the purchase was limited to joining in the mortgage, as the deceased did not have sufficient income to finance a mortgage by himself: the involvement was so circumscribed and temporary that it could not fairly be described as a contribution to the purchase price. She therefore held the legal estate on a resulting trust for the deceased's estate. See also (2008) 124 LQR 72 (W Swadling) and p 68, *supra*.

[47] It has been held in Australia—*Little v Little* (1988) 15 NSWLR 43—that regard is to be had to contributions to the purchase money only, and not to incidental costs, fees, disbursements, or the aggregate costs of the acquisition.   [48] *Supra*.

[49] *The Venture* [1908] P 218, CA; *Re Policy No 6402 of the Scottish Equitable Life Assurance Society* [1902] 1 Ch 282; *Shephard v Cartwright* [1955] AC 431, [1954] 3 All ER 649, HL; *Bateman Television Ltd v Bateman and Thomas* [1971] NZLR 453, CA.

cases, as in *Re Howes*,[50] in which a testatrix put £500 on deposit at a bank in the name of her niece.[51] She never informed the niece of what she had done, retained the deposit note, and purported to dispose of the money by a codicil to her will. It was held that even though this was not strictly a purchase, the equitable principle gave rise to a resulting trust to the testatrix. It also applies in a similar way where there is a joint advance by two or more persons, but the conveyance or transfer is taken in the name of one only. For instance, if X advances £60,000 and Y advances £30,000 towards the purchase of property that is conveyed into the name of X alone, X will hold the property as to one third on a resulting trust for Y.[52] If the transfer had been to X and Y as legal co-owners, they would similarly hold the legal title on a resulting trust for themselves in the proportion of two to one.

There is no need for the conveyance or other instrument of transfer to contain any reference to the fact that the purchase price has been paid by someone other than the transferee. Parol evidence is always admissible to establish who in fact advanced the money,[53] and this is so even though the consideration is expressed to be paid by the nominal purchaser. The fact of the advance must, of course, be satisfactorily proved by evidence, which may, however, be circumstantial evidence, such as that the nominal purchaser had not the means to provide the purchase money.[54] Evidence must also show that the money was intended to be advanced by the person alleging the resulting trust in the character of purchaser: if the evidence merely established a loan of some or all the money used for the purchase, there would be no resulting trust and the person lending the money would be a mere creditor.[55] If the fact of the advance is established, absence of writing is immaterial, even in the case of land, since the statutory provisions as to writing expressly exclude the creation and operation of resulting, implied, and constructive trusts.[56]

The resulting trust of a property purchased in the name of another, in the absence of contrary intention, arises once and for all at the date on which the property is acquired. Because of the liability assumed by the mortgagor in a case in which moneys are borrowed by the mortgagor to be used in the purchase, the mortgagor is treated as having provided the proportion of the purchase price attributable to the moneys so borrowed. Subsequent payments of the mortgage instalments are not part of the purchase price already paid to the vendor, but are sums paid for discharging the mortgagor's obligations under the mortgage.[57] Payment for subsequent improvements to the property will not increase the

[50] (1905) 21 TLR 501; *Abrahams v Trustee of the Property of Abrahams* [1999] BPIR 637 (wife paid husband's share of informal lottery syndicate: presumption of resulting trust in respect of husband's share of winnings).

[51] She was not *in loco parentis* to the niece, so the presumption of advancement did not apply: see p 181 *et seq, infra.*

[52] *Diwell v Farnes* [1959] 2 All ER 379, [1959] 1 WLR 624, CA; *Bull v Bull* [1955] 1 QB 234, [1955] 1 All ER 253, CA. The presumption is that if the contributions are equal, they take jointly, but if their contributions are unequal, they take as tenants in common in shares proportionate to their contributions.

[53] *Heard v Pilley* (1869) 4 Ch App 548.

[54] *Willis v Willis* (1740) 2 Atk 71; *Groves v Groves* (1829) 3 Y & J 163.

[55] *Aveling v Knipe* (1815) 19 Ves 441; *Carlton v Goodman* [2002] EWCA Civ 545, [2002] 2 FLR 259.

[56] Law of Property Act 1925, s 53(2) replacing the Statute of Frauds (1677), s 8.

[57] *Curley v Parkes* [2004] EWCA Civ 1515, noted [2005] Conv 79 (M J Dixon) expressing surprise that no claim was made on the basis of constructive trust.

payer's interest under a resulting trust.[58] In *Laskar v Laskar*,[59] the mother having exercised her right to buy under the Housing Act 1985, the property was transferred into the joint names of the mother and her daughter, whose financial assistance had been needed to enable the purchase to proceed. The purchase having been made primarily as an investment, not as a home, mother and daughter held the legal title on a resulting trust for themselves in proportion to their contributions. It was held that the discount to which the mother was entitled by reason of her long tenancy should be treated as, in effect, a part of her contribution.

An attempt was made in *Savage v Dunningham*[60] to extend the principle of *Dyer v Dyer*[61] to an informal flat-sharing arrangement under which the tenancy agreement was in the name of the defendant, but the rent and other expenses were shared equally between the plaintiffs and the defendant. It was held that 'purchase money' does not include rent and, accordingly, the sharing of the rent[62] did not establish a resulting trust in favour of the plaintiffs. Rent, unlike purchase money, is not paid for the acquisition of a capital asset, but for the use of property during the term.

The presumption of a resulting trust may also apply where the parties were, at the relevant time, husband and wife. Further discussion of this aspect of resulting trusts will be found later in this chapter.[63]

As to a claim that there is a resulting trust, which involves setting up a transaction that is fraudulent, illegal, or contrary to public policy, see Chapter 11.[64]

It must be remembered that if there is a specific declaration in the conveyance as to the parties' interests, this will prevail. Thus if a transfer of property to X and Y were to contain an express declaration that the property is to be held by them as joint tenants, the fact that X may have paid all of the mortgage instalments in respect of the property would not be relevant in determining how the property was held.[65] The current form of transfer of registered land contains a box for the insertion of a declaration of trust specifying the beneficial interests.

(B) VOLUNTARY CONVEYANCE OR TRANSFER INTO THE NAME OF ANOTHER, OR INTO THE JOINT NAMES OF THE GRANTOR AND ANOTHER

It is necessary to draw a distinction between land and pure personalty.

   (i) As to land, the position is still curiously unsettled, not withstanding s 60(3) of the Law of Property Act 1925, which provides:

> In a voluntary conveyance a resulting trust for the grantor shall not be implied merely by reason that the property is not expressed to be conveyed for the use or benefit of the grantee.

---

[58] *Clarke v Harlowe* [2005] EWHC 3062 (Ch), [2005] WTLR 1475, noted (2005) 149 Sol Jo 1198 (M Pawlowski); (2006) 81 T & ELTJ 9 (Deborah Clark). Unless there is a specific agreement to the contrary or, exceptionally, such an agreement can be inferred: see *Harwood v Harwood* [1991] 2 FLR 274, CA. As to improvements to matrimonial property, see p 200, *infra*. See (1994) 8 Tru LI 43 (P Matthews) arguing that all subsequent payments and contributions are irrelevant in considering the initial share in the property under a resulting trust.

[59] [2008] EWCA Civ 347, [2008] 1 WLR 2695, noted [2008] 38 Fam Law 654 (M Pawlowski).

[60] [1974] Ch 181, [1973] 3 All ER 429.   [61] *Supra*.

[62] *A fortiori* the sharing of the other expenses.   [63] See p 183 *et seq*.

[64] Sections 3 and 7, *infra*.   [65] *Grindal v Hooper* (1999) 144 Sol Jo LB 33.

At first instance in *Lohia v Lohia*,[66] it was held that the effect of that section is that a voluntary conveyance does not give rise to a presumption of a resulting trust. On appeal, however, it was held to be unnecessary to decide the matter and the members of the court preferred not to express a concluded view, so the 'knotty question' remains unresolved.

(ii) As to pure personalty, it seems to be settled that, on a transfer into the joint names of the transferor and another, there is a presumption of a resulting trust for the transferor. A clear example is *Re Vinogradoff*,[67] in which a testatrix, during her lifetime, had transferred an £800 War Loan into the joint names of herself and her infant granddaughter who was aged four years. After the death of the testatrix, it was held that her granddaughter held the War Loan on a resulting trust for the testatrix's estate. According to Lord Browne-Wilkinson,[68] the resulting trust only comes into effect when the transferee becomes aware of the circumstances giving rise to it, but a different view has been expressed, extrajudicially, by Lord Millett.[69]

It also seems that there is a presumption of a resulting trust where there is a transfer into the name of another alone.[70]

(C) REBUTTING THE PRESUMPTION OF A RESULTING TRUST

It has been said that:[71]

Trusts are neither created nor implied by law to defeat the intentions of donors or settlors; they are created or implied or are held to result in favour of donors or settlors in order to carry out and give effect to their true intentions, expressed or implied...

Accordingly, the presumed intention of a person who purchases property in the name of another, whether alone or jointly, that that other shall be a bare trustee for him, will not prevail if evidence establishes that the true intention is otherwise. The same is true where there is a voluntary conveyance or transfer that gives rise to a presumption of a resulting trust. Even parol evidence[72] may suffice to establish that, at the relevant time, the true intention of the person who provided the purchase money or transferred the property was

---

[66] [2001] WTLR 101 on appeal (2002) 16 Tru LI 231.

[67] [1935] WN 68. See also *Batstone v Salter* (1875) 10 Ch App 431; *Standing v Bowring* (1885) 31 Ch D 282, CA; *Young v Sealey* [1949] Ch 278, [1949] 1 All ER 92.

[68] *Westdeutsche Landesbank Girozentrale v Islington London Borough Council* [1996] AC 669, [1996] 2 All ER 961, HL.

[69] In Cornish et al (eds) *Restitution: Past, Present and Future*, p 201. Also by W Swadling in (1998) 12 Tru LI 228.

[70] *Crane v Davis* (1981) Times, 13 May; *Fowkes v Pascoe* (1875) 10 Ch App 343 at 348; *Vandervell v IRC* [1967] 2 AC 291, [1967] 1 All ER 1, HL. See also *Seldon v Davidson* [1968] 2 All ER 755, [1968] 1 WLR 1083, CA, (not followed in Australia: *Joaquin v Hall* [1976] VR 788), in which it was held that a payment of money was prima facie a loan, not a gift, in the absence of circumstances raising the presumption of advancement—as to which see *infra*, p 181 *et seq*.

[71] *Per* Lindley LJ in *Standing v Bowring* (1885) 31 Ch D 282, 289, CA, and see, generally, *Vandervell v IRC*, *supra*, HL. The presumption was rebutted in *Aroso v Coutts & Co* [2002] 1 All ER(Comm) 241, noted (2001) 31 T & ELJ 9 (R Walford), and in *Vajpeyi v Yusaf* [2003] EWHC (Ch) [2004] WTLR 989, noted (2003) 147 Sol Jo 1301 (M Pawlowski).

[72] *Fowkes v Pascoe* (1875) 10 Ch App 343.

that the person into whose name the property was conveyed or transferred solely or jointly with his own should take some beneficial interest. The relevant time is, of course, the date of the purchase or transfer and, if the evidence establishes an intention at that time to make an absolute gift, the donor cannot subsequently change his mind and recall the property that he has had put in the then-intended donee's name.[73] The orthodox view is that the acts or declarations of a party are admissible both for and against the presumption if they take place before or substantially contemporaneously with the transaction, but, if they take place subsequently, only against the party who made them.[74] The rigid application of this view, which applies equally to the presumption of advancement discussed below, has been challenged by Fung[75] as being formulated on the basis of old authorities and the law of evidence at the time, and as failing to take account of changes in the rules relating to the admissibility of evidence.

It has been suggested[76] that, in the absence of any presumption of advancement, where a transfer or payment is made by mistake, or where there is a failure of consideration, the transferee holds the property on a resulting trust for the transferor, there being no positive evidence of donative intent. The better view,[77] however, seems to be that evidence of the mistake or failure of consideration is inconsistent with a presumed intention that the transferee is to be a trustee for the transferor and, accordingly, no resulting trust arises. There may, of course, be a personal restitutionary claim at common law.

Evidence to rebut a resulting trust may establish that there is no resulting trust at all, and that the person in whose name the property is purchased was intended to take absolutely and beneficially,[78] but it may merely rebut the presumption of a resulting trust in part, leaving it to prevail as to the remainder.[79] In particular, the courts, it seems, will be very ready to accept evidence, where there has been a purchase in or transfer into the joint names of the person providing the purchase money or transferring the property and another, that the intention was that the former should receive the income during his life—that is, to this extent, the resulting trust prevails—but that the property should belong to the other after his death—that is, the resulting trust is rebutted as to the remainder.[80] Indeed, in cases in which stock has been transferred or money paid into a bank account in joint names, the person providing the stock or money has been held entitled on the evidence not only to the income during his life, but also to sell and transfer the stock or withdraw the money. Nevertheless, on that person's death, an intention that the other should take beneficially what is left in the joint names had been established and held to be valid.[81]

---

[73] *Re Gooch* (1890) 62 LT 384; *Shephard v Cartwright, supra,* HL.

[74] *Shephard v Cartwright* [1955] AC 431, [1954] 3 All ER 649, HL.   [75] [2006] 122 LQR 651.

[76] *Equity and Contemporary Legal Developments* (ed Goldstein), p 335 (P Birks); Chambers, *Resulting Trusts.*

[77] (1996) 16 LS 110 (W Swadling); *Westdeutsche Landesbank Girozentrale v Islington London Borough Council* [1996] AC 669, [1996] 2 All ER 961, 985, 986, HL, per Lord Browne-Wilkinson. See [1997] JBL 48 (G McCormack); [1997] 10 Tru LI 84 (C Mitchell); (1977–78) 8 KCLJ 147 (P Oliver).

[78] *Currant v Jago* (1844) 1 Coll 261.

[79] *Napier v Public Trustee (Western Australia)* (1980) 32 ALR 153.

[80] *Fowkes v Pascoe* (1875) 10 Ch App 343, CA; *Batstone v Salter* (1875) 10 Ch App 431; *Standing v Bowring* (1885) 31 Ch D 282, CA; *Young v Sealey* [1949] Ch 278, [1949] 1 All ER 92. It is submitted that there is no difference in principle between realty and personalty: see (1966) 30 Conv 223 (E L G Tyler). See also (1992) 6 Tru LI 57 (J G Miller).

[81] *Beecher v Major* (1865) 2 Drew & Sm 431; *Young v Sealey, supra.* (Gift not defeated by the Wills Act 1837, although it appeared in fact to be testamentary in nature. The earlier decisions on similar facts were followed

It may be added that the presumption of a resulting trust naturally weakens with the passage of time, at any rate, if there has been acquiescence as where the person in whose name the property has been purchased is allowed to remain in possession.[82]

(D) THE PRESUMPTION OF ADVANCEMENT[83]

In addition to rebutting the presumption of a resulting trust by evidence as to the true intention, the existence of certain special relationships between the person who provides the purchase money or who transfers the property and the person into whose name the property is conveyed or transferred, either alone or jointly, gives rise to a presumption of advancement, which displaces the presumption of a resulting test.[84] Although the law is commonly expressed in such a way, it is perhaps more accurate to say that the special relationship will be treated as prima facie evidence that the person who paid the purchase money or transferred the property intended to make a gift to the person into whose name the property was conveyed or transferred.[85] In any case, evidence is admissible to rebut the presumption of advancement in whole or in part, and to reinstate wholly or partially the presumption of a resulting trust, by showing that the intention of the person who paid the purchase money or transferred the property was that he should retain the whole or some part of the equitable interest.

(i) Father and child

Perhaps the primary relationship that has consistently been held to give rise to a presumption of advancement is that of father and child. There have been many cases in which, on the purchase or transfer of property by a father into the name of his child,[86] the question has been whether the evidence was sufficient to rebut the presumption of advancement arising by virtue of the relationship. Thus, in the Canadian decision *B v B*,[87] a father bought an Irish Hospitals Sweepstake in the name of his twelve-year old daughter. It proved to be the winning ticket and won £50,000. It was held that the father had failed to discharge the onus upon him to rebut the presumption of advancement. The winnings accordingly belonged to the daughter. The fact that property is conveyed or transferred into the joint names of a child and a stranger does not prevent the presumption of advancement from applying.[88]

notwithstanding that the point on the Wills Act had apparently not been raised.) See also *Re Figgis* [1969] 1 Ch 123, [1968] 1 All ER 999; *Aroso v Coutts & Co* [2002] 1 All ER (Comm) 241; *Griffiths v Floyd* [2004] WTLR 667 (Isle of Man HC), and see (2004) 62 T & ELTJ 9 (S Phelps and Tamara Glassman).

[82] *Groves v Groves* (1829) 3 Y & J 163; *Clegg v Edmondson* (1857) 8 De GM & G 787.

[83] See [2007] Conv 340 (Georgina Andrews), in which it is contended that the presumption conflicts with the Human Rights Act 1998 and should be abolished, or at least equalized.

[84] See (2001) 26 T & ELJ 16 (H Landau).

[85] The corresponding sentence in the fourth edition applied in *Re Dagle* (1990) 70 DLR (4th) 201.

[86] There is no presumption of advancement on a purchase or transfer of property by a child into the name of its father.

[87] (1976) 65 DLR (3d) 460; *Casimir v Alexander* [2001] WTLR 939. It has been held in Canada that the presumption ceases to apply once the child reaches adulthood: see (2007) 123 LQR 529 (M McInnes); [2007] Conv 370 (J Glister), discussing *Pecore v Pecore* [2007] SCC 17, [2007] 1 SCR 795, and *Madsen Estate v Saylor* [2007] SCC 18, [2007] 1 SCR 838. In *Laskar v Laskar* [2008] EWCA Civ 347, [2008] All ER(D) 104 (Feb), Lord Neuberger, after noting that it is a relatively weak presumption, said that it is even weaker when the child is aged over eighteen and managing her own affairs.

[88] *Crabb v Crabb* (1834) 1 My & K 511.

The Privy Council, in *Comr of Stamp Duties v Byrnes*,[89] said that the fact that a son permits his father to receive the profits during his lifetime is not evidence that rebuts the presumption, as it is merely an act of reverence and good manners, but a later case shows that the retention of the title deeds to the property by the father may have a different result.[90] The presumption of advancement was rebutted in *Re Gooch*,[91] in which a father bought shares in a company in the name of his son in order to qualify the son to be a director. The son always handed the dividends received on the shares to his father and, later, handed over the actual share certificates. And it seems that the fact that the son is his father's solicitor is, by itself, a fact that will rebut the presumption.[92] Most recently, the view that has been applied in husband-and-wife cases,[93] that the presumption of advancement is a judicial instrument of last resort, has been held equally applicable in father-and-child cases. Evidence that a house had been put in the son's name to enable a mortgage to be obtained, and the existence of proposals that the beneficial interest should be shared, was held sufficient to rebut the presumption.[94]

The presumption of advancement also arises where a man is *in loco parentis*[95] to the person into whose name the property is conveyed or transferred—that is, where he has taken upon himself what is regarded in equity as the father's natural office and duty of making provision for the child.[96]

The mere relationship of mother[97] and child has been held not to give rise to any presumption of advancement,[98] the reason given being that equity does not recognize any obligation on the part of the mother to provide for her child. In practice, however, as Jessel MR observed,[99] 'in the case of a mother...it is easier to prove a gift than in the case of a stranger: in the case of a mother very little evidence beyond the relationship is wanted, there being very little additional motive required to induce a mother to make a gift to her child'. Moreover, it has recently been held,[100] so far as concerns the rule against double

---

[89] [1911] AC 386, PC.   [90] *Warren v Gurney* [1944] 2 All ER 472, CA.

[91] (1890) 62 LT 384. Also, in *Low Gim Siah v Low Geoh Khin* [2007] 1 SLR 795 (Singapore CA), but see (2008) 124 LQR 369 (K F K Low), citing *Lau Siew Kim v Terence Yeo Guan Chye* [2007] SGCA 54.

[92] *Garrett v Wilkinson* (1848) 2 De G & Sm 244.   [93] See p 183, *infra*.

[94] *McGrath v Walls* [1995] 2 FLR 114. See (1995) 139 Sol Jo 826 (A Kenny); *Lavelle v Lavelle* [2004] EWCA Civ 223, [2004] 2 FCR 418; *Kyriakides v Pippas* [2004] EWHC 646, [2004] 2 FCR 434.

[95] The meaning of the term *in loco parentis* seems to be the same here as in connection with satisfaction, discussed fully in Chapter 31, section 3(c), available on the Online Resource Centre.

[96] *Currant v Jago* (1844) 1 Coll 261; *Soar v Foster* (1858) 4 K & J 152; *Shephard v Cartwright* [1955] AC 431, [1954] 3 All ER 649, HL; *Re Paradise Motor Co Ltd* [1968] 2 All ER 625, [1968] 1 WLR 1125, CA. But see *Tucker v Burrow* (1865) 2 Hem & M 515, 526, 527.

[97] *A fortiori*, stepmother and stepchild: *Todd v Moorhouse* (1874) LR 19 Eq 69, 71.

[98] *Bennet v Bennet* (1879) 10 Ch D 474; *Gross v French* (1974) 232 Estates Gazette 1319; affd (1975) 238 Estates Gazette 39, CA; *Sekhon v Alissa* [1989] 2 FLR 94, noted [1990] Conv 213 (G Kodilinye); *Lattimer v Lattimer* (1978) 82 DLR (3d) 587. Contra, particularly in the case of a widowed mother, *Sayre v Hughes* (1868) LR 5 Eq 376; *Garrett v Wilkinson* (1848) 2 De G & Sm 244. In Australia, the presumption has been held to apply equally to a gift by a mother to a child: *Brown v Brown* (1993) 31 NSWLR 582; *Nelson v Nelson* (1995) 184 CLR 538. The corresponding paragraph in the fourth edition was cited in the Canadian case of *Cohen v Cohen* (1985) 60 Alberta Rep 234, in which Montgomery J said that whatever the law may have been in the past, today, there should be a presumption of gift when a mother transfers property to her child. The same view was taken in *Dreger v Dreger* [1994] 10 WWR 293 and *Nelson v Little Estate* (2004) 250 Sask R 237, although, in all of these cases, the presumption was rebutted by the evidence.

[99] In *Bennet v Bennet, supra*, at 479–480.

[100] *Re Cameron (decd)* [1999] Ch 386, [1999] 2 All ER 924.

portions,[101] that both parents should nowadays be taken to be *in loco parentis* unless the contrary is proved, and the law was stated in these terms in *Antoni v Antoni* in relation to the presumption of advancement generally.[102]

(ii) Husband and wife

(a) *Circumstances in which a dispute may arise*[103] Questions as to the beneficial ownership of property where the legal title is held by the husband, or by the wife, or by them jointly, may arise in at least three situations: (i) on the breakdown of a marriage; (ii) on the death of one or other of them, when there may be a dispute between the survivor and beneficiaries claiming under the deceased's will or the law of intestacy; (iii) where a third party has a claim against property that he alleges to be property of the husband or the wife, but in which the wife or husband, as the case may be, asserts a beneficial interest. The answer to these questions will sometimes, although for the reasons explained below, now rarely, depend on an application of the presumption of resulting trust and the presumption of advancement.

The first reason is that the court may have statutory power to settle the dispute without needing to determine the exact property rights of the parties. In matrimonial proceedings for divorce, nullity, and judicial separation, the courts have wide powers under the Matrimonial Causes Act 1973[104] to rearrange beneficial interests and thus to do what is just in all of the circumstances; under the Inheritance (Family Provision) Act 1975, where the will of the deceased or the law relating to intestacy, or a combination of the will and that law, does not make reasonable financial provision for the surviving spouse, the court may make orders to achieve such a result, including orders for the transfer of property comprised in the deceased's estate.

The second reason relates to the subject matter of the dispute. In most marriages, the major asset—often the only substantial one—is the family home, and this is the item most likely to be the subject of dispute. The House of Lords has recently held, in *Stack v Dowden*,[105] altering what had previously been thought to be the law, that the family home is governed by the rules relating to constructive trusts, and that the presumptions of resulting trust and advancement are not relevant.

Although it cannot be stated with absolute certainty, it is thought that the decision in *Stack v Dowden* does not apply to personal property or to real property other than the family home.[106] To these forms of property, the presumptions of resulting trust

---

[101] See Online Resource Centre.

[102] [2007] UKPC 10, [2007] AC 432, [2007] WTLR 1335. Although not applicable on the facts, it was assumed in *Laskar v Laskar* [2008] EWCA Civ 347, [2008] All ER (D) 194 (Feb), that it would otherwise apply in a mother–daughter relationship.

[103] Considered in a little more detail in connection with the family home in Chapter 10.

[104] Section 24, as amended. This section does not apply to formerly engaged couples, notwithstanding s 2 of the Law Reform (Miscellaneous Provisions) Act 1970, which provides that the rules applied to determine property disputes between husband and wife apply also to property disputes between formerly engaged couples: *Mossop v Mossop* [1988] Fam 77, [1988] 2 All ER 202, CA, noted [1988] Conv 284 (J E M). See *R v Harrow London Borough Council, ex p Coker* (1989) Times, 14 March, CA, an unusual case in which a third party sought, unsuccessfully, to rely on the presumption.

[105] [2007] UKHL 17, [2007] 2 All ER 929, discussed p 190 *et seq, infra*.

[106] This seems to be the view of the Law Commission: Law Com No 307, para A.25; also of Lord Neuberger, with whose judgment the other members of the court agreed, in *Laskar v Laskar* [2008] EWCA Civ 347, [2008] All ER(D) 104 (Feb), at [16], [17].

and advancement still appear to apply, although, curiously, the relevant authorities include family home cases to which they no longer apply—a point that must always be borne in mind.

(b) *General principles*   Firstly, property rights have to be ascertained as at the time of purchase or transfer, and the rights so ascertained cannot be altered by subsequent events unless there has been an agreement to vary them. In particular, as Lord Morris said in *Pettitt v Pettitt*,[107] the fact of a breakdown of the marriage is irrelevant in the determination of a question of where ownership lay before the breakdown: the breakdown will then merely have caused the need for a decision, but will not, of itself, have altered whatever was the pre-existing position as to ownership.

Secondly, as Lord Upjohn explained in the same case,[108] 'the beneficial ownership of the property in question must depend on the agreement of the parties determined at the time of its acquisition'.[109] If the agreement contains an express declaration of trust that comprehensively declares the beneficial interests in the property, there is no room for the application of the doctrines of resulting, implied, or constructive trusts unless and until the agreement is set aside or varied. It is only where there is no available evidence as to the beneficial interests that the doctrines of resulting trust and advancement come into play.[110] As to the latter, it can be taken as settled, in the light of clear statements by three of the Law Lords in *Pettitt v Pettitt*,[111] that the strength of the presumption is much diminished with changing conditions of society.

(c) *Purchase or transfer by a husband into the name of his wife, or into the joint names of his wife and himself*   The classic statement of the presumption of advancement

---

[107] [1970] AC 777, 803, [1969] 2 All ER 385, 397, HL. He added that it might be relevant on application under s 17 of the Married Women's Property Act 1882—see p 201, *infra*.

[108] *Pettitt v Pettitt, supra*, at 813, 405; *Pink v Lawrence* (1977) 36 P & CR 98, CA; *Brykiert v Jones* (1981) 2 FLR 373, CA (conveyance to husband or wife in 1948 contained express declaration of trust in favour of purchasers as joint tenants; marriage came to grief and wife left matrimonial home in 1951; wife entitled to assert her claim to a half-share on sale in 1981); *Bernard v Josephs* [1982] Ch 391, [1982] 3 All ER 162, CA; *Re Gorman (a bankrupt)* [1990] 1 All ER 717, [1990] 1 WLR 616, Ch D.

[109] The agreement may be in writing or oral: *Lloyds Bank plc v Rosset* [1991] 1 AC 107, 132, HL, [1990] 1 All ER 1111, 1118, HL; *Mortgage Corpn v Shaire* [2001] 4 All ER 364, [2001] 3 WLR 639.

[110] See *per* Slade LJ in *Goodman v Gallant* [1986] Fam 106, [1986] 1 All ER 311, CA, noted (1986) 45 CLJ 205 (S Juss); *Painter v Hutchinson* [2007] EWHC 758 (Ch), [2008] BPIR 170. This principle was applied in *Turton v Turton* [1988] Ch 542, [1987] 2 All ER 641, to the erstwhile home of an unmarried couple many years after they had parted. The woman was held to be entitled to her half-share under the trust although she had made no contribution directly or indirectly to the purchase price and had only lived with the man for about five years. See also *Wright v Johnson* [2001] EWCA Civ 1667, [2002] P & CR 210. But in *City of London Building Society v Flegg* [1988] AC 54, [1987] 3 All ER 435, HL, notwithstanding express trusts for named beneficiaries, the property was deemed to be held on resulting trusts for the named beneficiaries and the respondents (who had provided over half of the purchase price, but were not parties to the declaration of trust) as tenants in common.

[111] [1970] AC 777 [1969] 2 All ER 385, HL, *per* Lord Reid, at 793, 389, Lord Hodson, at 811, 404, and Lord Diplock, at 824, 414. Lord Upjohn, however, thought the presumptions as useful as ever, although he said that they only come into play in the absence of evidence. It was said that it '*must be applied with caution in modern social conditions*' in *Harwood and Harwood* [1991] 2 FLR 274, CA, although, on the facts of that case, there was nothing to displace it. It was held still to exist in Canada, and applied, in *Mehta Estate v Mehta Estate* (1993) 104 DLR (4th) 24 (happily married couple killed together in air crash), noted (1993) 22 Man LJ 185 (C H C Edwards).

in this situation is that of Malins VC in *Re Eykyn's Trusts*,[112] cited with approval by Lord Upjohn in *Pettitt v Pettitt*:[113]

> The law of the court is perfectly settled that when a husband transfers money or other property into the name of his wife only, then the presumption is, that it is intended as a gift or advancement to the wife absolutely at once ... And if a husband invests money, stock or otherwise, in the names of himself and his wife, then also it is an advancement for the benefit of the wife absolutely if she survives her husband, but if he survives her, then it reverts to him as joint tenant with his wife.

Although, as mentioned above, the House of Lords has stated that the strength of presumption is now greatly diminished, the Court of Appeal relied on it in *Tinker v Tinker*.[114] The Court did not attempt to explain why it applied the presumption without hesitation in this case, which contrasts with all of the other husband-and-wife cases since *Pettitt v Pettitt*,[115] in which the presumption has been treated as of little or no importance. All of the other relevant cases have, in fact, involved contributions to the purchase by both husband and wife—a situation that is discussed in (d) below—and *Tinker v Tinker*[116] may be distinguished on that ground, because, in that case, the husband had provided the whole of the purchase price of the house, which he had put into his wife's name. It may be that the strength of the presumption of advancement is less impaired in the situation under consideration—that is, where there has been a purchase or transfer by a husband into the name of his wife, and no contribution is made by the wife.

It has always, of course, been possible to rebut the presumption by evidence that no gift was intended. The older cases, particularly those in which the presumption of advancement was upheld, must, however, be read with care in the light of the change in the weight to be attached to the presumption. The presumption of advancement was rebutted in *Re Salisbury-Jones*,[117] in which the wife entered into a mortgage of her property under which the husband was a surety. When the husband was called upon to pay the money due under the mortgage, it was held that, in so doing, he was discharging a legal obligation and there was no question of his making a gift to his wife. He was therefore entitled as against her to all of the remedies of a surety.

The presumption has been applied not only to a once-and-for-all purchase or transfer, but also to analogous transactions, such as a purchase of land with the aid of an instalment mortgage that is paid off by the husband over a period of years, when the payment of each instalment is, as it were, a supplementary gift.[118] It may be noted that, by the Married Women's Property Act 1964, money derived from any allowance made by a husband for the expenses of the matrimonial home or for similar purposes,[119] or any property acquired out of that money, is to be treated as

---

[112] (1877) 6 Ch D 115, 118, in which it was held that the presumption of advancement was unaffected by the fact that the property was placed in the name also of another person. It makes no difference whether one is dealing with realty or personalty: see (1966) 30 Conv 223 (E C G Tyler).   [113] *Supra.*

[114] [1970] P 136, [1970] 1 All ER 540, CA, in which the evidence in fact supported the presumption.

[115] *Supra.*   [116] *Supra.*

[117] [1938] 3 All ER 459, applied to a guarantee of an overdraft; *Anson v Anson* [1953] 1 QB 636, [1953] 1 All ER 867.

[118] *Moate v Moate* [1948] 2 All ER 486; *Silver v Silver* [1958] 1 All ER 523, [1958] 1 WLR 259, CA.

[119] This phrase was held not to include mortgage repayments towards the purchase of the matrimonial home in *Tymoszczuk v Tymoszczuk* (1964) 108 Sol Jo 676, in which it was held that the Act was retrospective.

belonging to the husband and wife in equal shares, in the absence of any agreement between them to the contrary.

Special mention should be made of joint bank accounts[120] between husband and wife, in which both parties have power to draw cheques on the account. Prima facie in such a case, during their joint lives, each spouse has power to draw cheques not only for the joint benefit of both, but also for his or her own separate benefit, and, accordingly, if either spouse draws on the account to purchase a chattel or an investment in his or her name alone, that spouse will be the sole owner of the chattel or investment both at law and in equity. If the purchase were in joint names,[121] they would prima facie be joint tenants. And on the death of one spouse, the survivor will be entitled to the balance of the account.[122] These prima facie rules may be displaced by the evidence. On the one hand, this may rebut the presumption of advancement and show that a banking account placed in joint names is to be held beneficially for the husband[123] alone. Thus, in *Marshall v Crutwell*,[124] a husband in failing health transferred his banking account from his own name into the names of himself and his wife, and directed his bankers to honour cheques drawn either by himself or his wife. He afterwards paid considerable sums into the account. All cheques were thereafter drawn by the wife at the direction of her husband, and proceeds were applied in payment of household and other expenses. After his death, the wife claimed to be entitled to the balance, but it was held that the transfer of the account was not intended to be a provision for the plaintiff, but merely a mode of conveniently managing her husband's affairs. It has recently been observed,[125] however, that it is likely that, today, a court would take a different view of the facts.

The presumption was not rebutted in *Re Figgis*,[126] in which the joint account had been in existence for nearly fifty years, but had only been operated by the wife during the First World War, and, without the husband's knowledge, during his last illness. This case involved both a current and a deposit account, and, as to the latter, the judge observed that, in the nature of things, it was far less appropriate than a current account as a provision made for convenience. He added that even if the

---

This decision was doubted on both points by Goff J in *Re John's Assignment Trusts* [1970] 2 All ER 210n, [1970] 1 WLR 955. See Law Com No 175; (1985) 135 NLJ 797 (S P de Cruz).

[120] See (1969) 85 LQR 530 (M C Cullity).

[121] Vaisey J's dictum in *Jones v Maynard* [1951] Ch 572, 575, [1951] 1 All ER 802, 804, to the effect (*semble*) that if the husband draws on the account to purchase investments in his wife's name, the presumption of advancement will apply and the wife will be entitled, seems to be right on principle. It is less certain whether the general rule of a resulting trust for the wife (see p 187, *infra*) would apply to a similar purchase by the wife in the husband's name.

[122] The authorities for the above propositions are *Re Young* (1885) 28 Ch D 705; *Re Bishop* [1965] Ch 450, [1965] 1 All ER 249. The same principle was applied where a father transferred funds into a joint account with one of his children: *MacInnis Estates v MacDonald* (1995) 394 APR 321. See Law Com No 175. Cf *Public Trustee v Gray-Masters* [1977] VR 154, in which the parties were unmarried and it was held that the presumption of resulting trust was rebutted.

[123] *Hoddinott v Hoddinott* [1949] 2 KB 406, CA.

[124] (1875) LR 20 Eq 328; *Simpson v Simpson* [1992] 1 FLR 601. *A fortiori* where the account is fed by the wife alone, she alone is beneficially entitled: *Heseltine v Heseltine* [1971] 1 All ER 952, [1971] 1 WLR 342, CA.

[125] *Aroso v Coutts & Co* [2002] 1 All ER (Comm) 241, 249, *per* Lawrence Collins J.

[126] [1969] 1 Ch 123, [1968] 1 All ER 999.

current account had been opened merely for convenience, in his view, this could change and later become an advancement for the wife. On the other hand, where one spouse has drawn on the account to purchase an investment in his or her name alone, the evidence may show, as in *Jones v Maynard*,[127] that the parties intended '*a common purse and a pool of their resources*'.[128] In that case, the investment purchased out of the joint[129] account by the husband in his sole name was accordingly directed to be held by him as to one half on trust for his wife.

If, at the relevant time—that is, the time of the purchase or transfer—the relationship of husband and wife was in existence, the presumption of advancement will be applied notwithstanding that the parties were subsequently divorced,[130] or, in the case of a voidable marriage, that a decree of nullity has been pronounced.[131] The presumption may be even stronger where the parties were engaged to be married, provided that the marriage was subsequently duly solemnized.[132] There is, however, no presumption of advancement if the purported marriage is void.[133] Nor has the presumption ever been applied where a man and woman are living together without having gone through any ceremony of marriage at all.[134]

(d) *Purchase or transfer by a wife into the name of her husband, or into the joint names of her husband and herself*   Here, there is no presumption of advancement and, accordingly, the husband will hold on a resulting trust for the wife.[135] Thus, in *Mercier v Mercier*,[136] husband and wife had a joint banking account almost entirely composed of the wife's income. Land was purchased and paid for out of the joint account, but conveyed into the name of the husband alone. In holding that the husband held the property on a resulting trust for his wife, it was pointed out that there was no distinction in principle between payment out of capital or income. And in *Pearson v Pearson*,[137] in which the matrimonial home was conveyed into joint names, but the wife not only provided the initial payment, but also paid all of the mortgage instalments, it was held that the wife alone was entitled. In *Pettitt v*

---

[127] *Supra.*   [128] *Jones v Maynard, supra,* at 803.

[129] Technically, it seems, it was not a joint account, as it remained in the name of the husband alone, but it was said to be a joint account 'to all intents and purposes', because both spouses had power to draw on it.

[130] *Thornley v Thornley* [1893] 2 Ch 229.   [131] *Dunbar v Dunbar* [1909] 2 Ch 639.

[132] *Moate v Moate* [1948] 2 All ER 486. Cf *Zamet v Hyman* [1961] 3 All ER 933, [1961] 1 WLR 1442, CA, and see (1975) 119 Sol Jo 108 (E Ellis); (1976) 120 Sol Jo 141 (N V Lowe); *Cavalier v Cavalier* (1971) 19 FLR 199. There is a statutory presumption of gift in relation to an engagement ring, even though the marriage does not take place—Law Reform (Miscellaneous Provisions) Act 1970, s 3(2)—although the gift may be expressly made on the condition that it is to be returned if the agreement is terminated: ibid, s 3(1), and see *Shaw v Fitzgerald* [1992] 1 FLR 357.

[133] *Soar v Foster* (1858) 4 K & J 152: 'marriage' with deceased wife's sister, at that time illegal. So held, notwithstanding the judicial observation that '*any moralist would say that a man was bound to make provision for the woman with whom he had so cohabitated*'. Whether or not a decree of nullity has been pronounced would seem to be irrelevant.

[134] *Crisp v Mullings* (1974) 233 Estates Gazette 511, reversed without discussing this point (1975) 239 Estates Gazette 119, CA; *Napier v Public Trustee (Western Australia)* (1980) 32 ALR 153; *Calverley v Green* (1984) 59 ALJR 111, and see (1986) ALJ 31 (F Bates), (1985) 8 UNSWLJ 1 (Rebecca Bailey-Harris); (1986) 12 NZULR 79 (Julie K Maxton).

[135] *Re Curtis* (1885) 52 LT 244; *Rich v Cockell* (1804) 9 Ves 369. Law Com No 175 (1988) proposed that the presumption of advancement should apply equally to both spouses.

[136] [1903] 2 Ch 98, CA.   [137] (1965) Times, 30 November.

Pettitt,[138] however, Lord Upjohn observed:

> If a wife puts property into her husband's name it may be that in the absence of
> all other evidence he is a trustee for her, but in practice there will in almost every
> case be some explanation (however slight) of this (today) rather unusual course. If
> a wife puts property into their joint names I would myself think that a joint benefi-
> cial tenancy was intended, for I can see no other reason for it.

In *Heseltine v Heseltine*,[139] a wealthy wife transferred two sums of £20,000 to her
relatively poor husband for the purpose of equalizing their property for estate duty
purposes, and a further sum of £20,000 to enable the husband, as a candidate for
membership of Lloyd's, to sign a certificate that he was worth £90,000. One might
expect the court to have held that there was a presumption of a resulting trust,
rebutted by the evidence. In fact, after the break-up of the marriage, it was held that
all of these sums were held by the husband on trust for the wife. Lord Denning MR
called it '*a resulting trust which resulted from all the circumstances of the case*', but,
in fact, the court seems to have imposed a constructive trust, although it is doubtful
whether it was justified in doing so on the facts.

An established, although limited, exception to the presumption of a resulting
trust arises where a husband and wife are living together, and the wife consents to or
acquiesces in the husband receiving income from her property, when to that extent
only there will be a presumption of gift.[140] But if, without the wife's knowledge,
the husband were to sell the property and misappropriate the proceeds of sale, he
would not only be liable to replace the capital, but also to account for the income
that would have been produced after the date of the sale, because whatever the
position may have been as to income arising before that date, the wife, not having
known of the sale, could not have assented or acquiesced thereafter.[141] The same
principles underlie what is known as the 'equity of exoneration',[142] which has been
said not to have '*any less part to play now than it had in the days when the equitable
doctrine was being formulated*'.[143] This applies where a married woman charges her
property with money for the purpose of paying her husband's debts and the money
raised by her is so applied. In such case, she is prima facie regarded in equity and,
as between herself and him, as lending him and not giving him the money raised
on her property, and as entitled to have the property exonerated by him from the
charge that she has created. The presumption of the equity of exoneration, however,
may be rebutted by evidence showing that the proper inference is that the money
was intended to be given, not merely lent, as might be the case, for instance, where
the debts have been incurred with the assent of the wife in order to maintain the
husband and wife in a standard of living above their income.[144]

---

[138] *Supra*, at 815, 407; *Knightly v Knightly* (1981, unreported), noted 131 NLJ 479, CA.

[139] [1971] 1 All ER 952, [1971] 1 WLR 342, CA. Possibly, the wife could have had the transfers set aside on
the grounds of undue influence. This case also raises difficulties as to what has been called the 'floating trust'
concept, and the idea of a 'trust for the family': see (1971) 115 Sol Jo 614 (S Cretney).

[140] *Caton v Rideout* (1849) 1 Mac & G 599; *Edward v Cheyne (No 2)* (1888) 13 App Cas 385, HL. The presumption is, of course, rebuttable: *Re Young* (1913) 29 TLR 391.

[141] *Dixon v Dixon* (1878) 9 Ch D 587.

[142] *Clinton v Hooper* (1791) I Ves 173; *Hudson v Carmichael* (1854) Kay 613.

[143] *Re Pittortou* [1985] 1 All ER 285, 289, [1985] 1 WLR 58, 62, *per* Scott J.

[144] *Paget v Paget* [1898] 1 Ch 470, CA, explained in *Hall v Hall* [1911] 1 Ch 487; *Re Berry (a bankrupt)*
[1978] 2 NZLR 373.

It has recently been pointed out[145] that, in view of completely changed social conditions, the guide that the older cases can provide is often not very valuable. In considering how the equity of exoneration should work as between a husband and a wife, the courts should take into account the relationship that husbands and wives bear, or ought to bear, to one another in their family affairs in current times. On the facts in *Re Pittortou*,[146] in which the husband and wife were each beneficially entitled to a half-share subject to the building society mortgage, the wife was prima facie entitled, by the equity of exoneration, to require the second charge to secure the husband's debts to be met primarily out of the husband's share in the net proceeds of sale. But to the extent that the husband's indebtedness represented payments made for the benefit of the household, it should be discharged out of the proceeds of sale before division.

(e) *Contributions by both parties to purchase price of property*   Even before *Stack v Dowden*,[147] the role of the presumption of advancement had become negligible in relation to the family home, and it is doubtful whether it now carries any weight in relation to other forms of property.

(iii) The presumption of advancement and human rights

There is wide agreement that the presumption, which came into being in very different social conditions from those that pertain today, is outdated. Moreover, it has been persuasively argued[148] that the discriminatory nature of the presumption is in conflict with human rights legislation, and it has been contended accordingly that the presumption should be abolished or, at the very least, its application equalized.

---

[145] *Re Pittortou, supra,* citing the unreported decision of Walton J in *Re Woodstock (a bankrupt)* (19 November 1979).

[146] *Supra.* See *Official Trustee in Bankruptcy v Citibank Savings Ltd* (1995) 38 NSWLR 116.

[147] [2007] UKHL 17, [2007] AC 432 [2007] 2 All ER 929. See p 190 *et seq, infra.*

[148] [2007] Conv 340 (Georgina Andrews).

10

COMMON INTENTION CONSTRUCTIVE TRUSTS; PROPRIETARY ESTOPPEL; LICENCES

It might well be asked why three apparently disparate subjects should be included in the same chapter. The justification is that, in recent years, in a number of cases, mainly arising out of informal arrangements in a family setting, the court has taken the view that justice demanded that the claimant should have a remedy in circumstances in which it was at least doubtful whether he was entitled to one under existing rules as previously understood. The matters to be discussed concern the ways in which the courts have sought to achieve what they considered to be a just result. The different ways overlap and interact.

1 COMMON INTENTION CONSTRUCTIVE TRUST

(A) SHARED HOMES

(i) Background

The common intention constructive trust has been developed mainly in connection with disputes relating to claims to beneficial interests in the home shared by a cohabiting couple, who may be married or unmarried. It has long been settled that, in determining their property rights, the same principles apply between married and unmarried couples, although cohabitation in marriage or civil partnership, in contrast to a less permanently intended relationship, may have a bearing on the ascertainment of their common intention and on the determination of an appropriate apportionment of their rights to the property in which they live.[1] The leading case is the recent House of Lords decision in *Stack v Dowden*,[2]

---

[1] *Bernard v Josephs* [1982] Ch 391, [1982] 3 All ER 162, CA, noted [1982] Conv 444 (Jean Warburton); (1983) CLJ 30 (K Gray). See (1980) 96 LQR 248 (A A S Zuckerman); (1980) WILJ 3 (A J Bland).
[2] [2007] UKHL 17, [2007] AC 432, [2007] 2 All ER 929, noted [2007] 123 LQR 511 (W Swadling); [2007] Conv 352 (M Dixon); [2007] Conv 354 and (2007) 37 Fam Law 606 (M Pawlowski); [2007] CLJ 517

which has profoundly affected the law as previously understood and which appears to put shared home cases in a separate category.

Lord Neuberger, in *Laskar v Laskar*,[3] was of opinion that Baroness Hale, who gave the leading speech in *Stack v Dowden*, intended her reasoning to apply not only to cohabiting couples, but also to other personal relationships, at least where the property is purchased as a home for two (or indeed more than two) people who are the legal owners, citing her reference to 'the domestic consumer context'. Accordingly, he thought that HHJ Behrens had been right to conclude in *Adekunle v Ritchie*,[4] in the Leeds county court, that it applied to a case in which a house was purchased by a mother and a son in joint names as a home for them both.

Questions as to the beneficial ownership of the shared home, the legal title to which may be held in the name of one of them alone, or in both of them as joint tenants, may arise in one of three situations.

(a) *On the breakdown of the relationship*   Where, in the case of married couples, there are matrimonial proceedings, there will be no need to determine the parties' exact property rights, because the matter can, and should, be dealt with under the provisions of Pt 2 of the Matrimonial Causes Act 1973, as amended, which enable the court to do what is just in all of the circumstances. Questions of ownership yield to the higher demands of relating the means of each to the needs of each, the primary consideration being the welfare of children. There are corresponding provisions in relation to civil partners in the Civil Partnership Act 2004.[5] There are no statutory provisions relating to other cohabitants, who can only claim, if at all, under the law of trusts.[6]

(b) *On the death of one party*   Following the death of one party, there may be a dispute between the survivor and beneficiaries under the will, or intestacy of the deceased in relation to a claim by the survivor to a beneficial interest in an asset held by the deceased in his name at his death.[7] The question of who owns what remains important. In some cases, however, the problem may be solved by means of an application under the Inheritance (Provision for Family and Dependants) Act 1975, which created a scheme enabling specified persons for whom reasonable financial provision had not been made by the will, or the law relating to intestacy, or a combination of

---

(A J Cloherty and D M Fox); [2007] Conv 456 (M Dixon); (2008) 71 MLR 120 (N Piska); [2007] PCB 366 (Deborah Sevitt and J Freeman); (2007) L Teach 350 (R Lister); (2007) 37 Fam Law 533 (A Chandler); (2007) 37 Fam Law 712 (A Ralton); (2007) 37 Fam Law 924 (Rebecca Probert), applied *Murphy v Gooch* [2007] EWCA Civ 603, [2007] 3 FCR 96; *Fowler v Barron* [2008] EWCA Civ 377, [2008] 2 FCR 1; *Holman v Howes* [2007] EWCA Civ 877, [2008] 1 FLR 1217. See also *Abbott v Abbott* [2007] UKPC 55, [2008] 1 FLR 1451, noted (2008) 124 LQR 209 (Rebecca Lee). The most significant earlier House of Lords decisions are *Pettitt v Pettitt* [1970] AC 777; [1969] 2 All ER 385; *Gissing v Gissing* [1971] AC 886, [1970] 2 All ER 780; and *Lloyds Bank plc v Rosset* [1991] 1 AC 107, [1990] 1 All ER 1111.

[3] [2008] EWCA Civ 347, [2008] 1 WLR 2695, noted [2008] 38 Fam Law 654 (M Pawlowski).

[4] (2007, unreported). Cf *Laskar v Laskar* itself, in which mother and daughter bought the house primarily as an investment, not a home.

[5] Section 72 and Sch 5.

[6] The Law Commission has recommended legislation to deal with the situation: Law Com No 307, *Cohabitation: The Financial Consequences of Relationship Breakdown*.

[7] See *Re Cummins* [1972] Ch 62, [1971] 3 All ER 782, CA.

the two, to make a claim against the deceased's estate. The scheme was extended to cohabitants by the Law Reform (Succession) Act 1995 and to civil partners by the Civil Partnership Act 2004.

(c) *There may be a claim by a third party*   The most common situation in which this arises is a case such as that of *Lloyds Bank plc v Rosset*,[8] in which the wife contended that she had a beneficial interest in the house held in her husband's name that should not be subject to the claims of the bank with which her husband had an overdraft secured by a legal charge over the property. Another common case is that in which the party in whom the legal title is vested has become bankrupt and the other party seeks to resist a claim against the property made by the trustee in bankruptcy. In these sorts of case, it is vital to know whether a claim to a beneficial interest can be established.

(ii) Preliminary points

In *Stack v Dowden*,[9] the majority of the Law Lords agreed with the speech of Baroness Hale. Lord Neuberger agreed with the result, but reached it by means of the traditional resulting trust approach, which, as a consequence of the majority decision, no longer represents the law. The issue in the case was as to the effect of a conveyance into the joint names of an unmarried cohabiting couple of a dwelling house, which was to become their home, but without an explicit declaration of their respective beneficial interests. Early in her speech, Baroness Hale referred to two uncontroversial propositions: firstly, that an express declaration of trust is conclusive as to the beneficial interests of those who are party to the transaction, unless and until set aside on the grounds of fraud, mistake, duress, or undue influence, rectified, varied by a subsequent agreement, or affected by proprietary estoppel.[10] However, she continued, it been rightly decided[11] that a declaration in a Land Registry transfer that the survivor of the transferees (inevitably joint tenants at law) could give a valid receipt for capital money arising on a disposition of the land did not, in itself, amount to an express declaration of a beneficial joint tenancy. The amended form of transfer introduced in 1998 has a box for the insertion of a declaration of trust specifying the beneficial interests in the property. This will reduce the number of disputes, but not eliminate them, as completion of the box is not mandatory.[12] Secondly, she referred to the proposition that the severance of a beneficial joint tenancy results in a beneficial tenancy in common.

(iii) Establishing a common intention constructive trust

In the absence of an express declaration of trust, a party who claims a beneficial interest in the shared home of his or her partner where the legal title is held by the partner alone, or a larger interest than that of a joint tenant where the legal title is in joint names, will, applying the decision in *Stack v Dowden*, base his or her claim on a common intention constructive trust.

The starting point, it was said, where there is sole legal ownership, is sole beneficial ownership: the onus is on any non-owner to show that he has any interest at all. Likewise, the starting point where there is joint legal ownership is, at least in the domestic context, joint beneficial ownership: here, the onus is on a joint owner who claims to have other

---

   [8] *Supra*, HL.   [9] *Supra*, HL.   [10] See section (ii), p 183, and p 184, fn 110, *supra*.
   [11] In *Harwood v Harwood* [1992] 1 FCR 1; *Huntingdon v Hobbs* [1993] 1 FCR 45.
   [12] J Glister [2007] Conv 364 agrees that completion of the box is not mandatory, but not for the reason given by Baroness Hale in *Stack v Dowden*, *supra*, HL, at [52].

than a joint beneficial interest to establish it.[13] At one time, the question as to how the onus could be discharged would have been answered by the presumptions of resulting trust and advancement. But, Baroness Hale said:[14]

> The law has indeed moved on in response to changing social and economic conditions. The search is to ascertain the parties' shared intentions, actual, inferred or imputed, with respect to the property in the light of their whole course of conduct in relation to it.

As Lord Bridge famously explained in *Lloyds Bank plc v Rosset*,[15] there are two categories of case. In the first category are express common intention cases, in which, at some time prior to acquisition or exceptionally at a later date, there has been an express, although informal, agreement, arrangement, or understanding reached between them that, notwithstanding that the legal title is in one only, the property is to be shared beneficially between them, or, where they own the legal title jointly, that one of them is to have a larger interest than the other.

Cases in which the legal title was in one only of the parties include *Eves v Eves*,[16] in which the parties had lived together, intending to marry when they were free to do so, and had two children. A house was purchased in the man's name. He told the woman that it was to be their house, but that it would have to be in his name alone as she was under the age of twenty-one. This was simply an excuse to avoid a conveyance into joint names. She made no financial contribution, but did a great deal of work in the house and garden, 'much more than many wives would do'. After they had parted, she successfully claimed a share of the beneficial interest. Likewise, in *Grant v Edwards*,[17] in which the defendant told the plaintiff with whom he was cohabiting that her name was not to go on to the title because, if the property were acquired jointly, it would operate to her prejudice in the matrimonial proceedings between her and her husband. This showed that she was intended to have a beneficial interest: otherwise, no such excuse would have been needed. However, in a case such as *Stack v Dowden*, it was common ground that a conveyance into joint names would be sufficient, at least in the vast majority of cases, to surmount that hurdle.

In cases in the second category, there is no evidence to support a finding of an agreement or arrangement to share the beneficial interest (or for one party to have a larger interest than the other), however reasonable it might have been for the parties to have made such an agreement if they had applied their minds to the question. Here, the court, relying entirely on the conduct of the parties referable to the acquisition of a beneficial interest (or larger beneficial interest, where the legal title is held jointly) may infer from it a common intention to that effect. If, and in so far as, actual intention need not exist, it may be more accurate to say 'imputed' rather than 'inferred'. But it does seem necessary at least that the other party was aware of the conduct from which the common intention arises.[18] The court must not, however, impose its own view of what is fair upon the situation.

---

[13] Note *Gibson v Revenue and Customs Prosecution Office* [2008] EWCA Civ 645, [2008] 2 FLR 1622 (presumption of joint beneficial ownership unaffected by wife's guilty knowledge of tained source of husband's wealth).

[14] At [60]. See also *per* Lord Neuberger at [126], [127].   [15] *Supra*, HL, at 132, 133, 1118, 1119.

[16] [1975] 3 All ER 768, [1975] 1 WLR 1338, CA. There was insufficient evidence of an agreement or understanding in *Negus v Bahouse* [2007] EWHC 2628 (Ch), [2008] WTLR 97.

[17] [1986] Ch 638, [1986] 2 All ER 426, CA. In *Van Laethem v Brooker* [2005] EWHC 1478 (Ch), [2006] 2 FLR 495, at [67], Lawrence Collins J said that if the matter were free from authority, he would prefer a proprietary estoppel approach in 'excuse' cases.

[18] *Lightfoot v Lightfoot-Brown* [2005] EWCA Civ 201, [2005] 2 P & CR 377.

Lord Bridge[19] said that while direct contributions to the purchase price by a party who is not the legal owner, whether initially or by payment of mortgage instalments, would readily justify the court in drawing an inference of a common intention, it was 'at least extremely doubtful whether anything less will do'. Baroness Hale, in *Stack v Dowden*,[20] thought that Lord Bridge 'may have set the hurdle too high in certain respects', and in the same case, Lord Walker[21] said that the court should take a wide view of what is capable of counting as a contribution towards the acquisition of a residence. But these observations were strictly obiter, because there was no dispute in *Stack v Dowden* that each party had an interest: the dispute was as to the size of the respective shares.

It is nevertheless surprising that none of the opinions in *Stack v Dowden* refer to *Burns v Burns*.[22] In that case, which involved an unmarried couple, a house had been purchased and conveyed into the name of the man alone in 1963. There was no express trust, and no express agreement to create an interest for the benefit of the woman plaintiff, who had made no real or substantial contribution towards the purchase price either directly or indirectly. The court declined to infer a common intention that she was to have a beneficial interest merely from the facts that she had lived with the defendant, by whom she had two children, for nineteen years, had looked after the family's well-being by performing the domestic duties of the household, and had brought up their children, or from the fact that she had bought chattels for the household out of her earnings and had redecorated the house. She was not, May LJ said:

> entitled to any share in the beneficial interest in [the family] home even though over a very substantial number of years she may have worked just as hard as the man in maintaining the family, in the sense of keeping house, giving birth to and looking after and helping to bring up the children of the union.

In *Le Foe v Le Foe*,[23] however, the judge held, after citing *Burns v Burns*,[24] that, by virtue of the wife's indirect contributions to the mortgage, he was entitled to infer that the parties commonly intended that the wife should have a beneficial interest in the former matrimonial home. It remains at least doubtful whether a common intention can be inferred from domestic contributions alone.[25]

In the unusual case of *Re Share (Lorraine)*,[26] in which the property was in the sole name of the wife, it was her trustee in bankruptcy who sought to claim that she had a beneficial interest. It was held, however, that the husband was the sole beneficial owner. He had paid the deposit, all of the mortgage instalments and the insurance payments, and the evidence was that, at the time of the purchase (when the husband was married to a different woman), it was agreed that the property should belong to the husband alone.

---

[19] In *Lloyds Bank plc v Rosset* [1991] 1 AC 107, 132, 133, [1990] 1 All ER 1111, 1118, 1119, HL.

[20] *Supra*, HL, at [63].   [21] At [34].

[22] [1984] Ch 317, [1984] 1 All ER 244, CA, noted (1984) 43 CLJ 227 (R Ingleby); [1984] Conv 381 (S Coneys); *Thomas v Fuller-Brown* [1988] 1 FLR 237, CA; *Howard v Jones* [1989] Fam Law 231, CA (claim also failed in last two cases on ground of no common intention). See also *Winkworth v Edward Baron Development Co Ltd* [1987] 1 All ER 114, [1986] 1 WLR 1512, HL, noted [1987] Conv 217 (Jean Warburton), in which the wife was held to have no equitable interest, there being no connection between her contribution and the acquisition of the matrimonial home; [2003] Fam Law 834 (D Burles).

[23] [2001] 2 FLR 970, noted [2002] Conv 273 (M P Thompson).   [24] *Supra*, CA.

[25] *James v Thomas* [2007] EWCA Civ 1212, [2007] All ER (D) 373 (Nov0; [2008] Fam Law 424 (A Ralton).

[26] [2002] 2 FLR 88.

(iv) Detrimental reliance

The Law Commission,[27] in setting out the current law, has stated that it is the applicant's detrimental reliance on the common intention that makes it unconscionable for the legal owner to deny the applicant's beneficial interest. In cases of express common intention, the range of conduct and contributions that will count as reliance is wider than that which will give rise to an inferred common intention. In case of inferred common intention, the conduct from which the common intention is inferred will also constitute detrimental reliance. Thus, in *Midland Bank Ltd v Dobson*,[28] it had been the common intention of husband and wife when the family home had been purchased thirty years earlier that they should share the beneficial interest. However, the wife's claim failed: on the ground of resulting trust, because she had made no contribution directly or indirectly to the purchase price; and on the ground of constructive trust, because she had not demonstrated that she was induced to act to her detriment on the basis of a common intention of ownership of the house, or that there was otherwise any nexus between the acquisition of the property and something provided or foregone by her. There is little authority on what is necessary for a claimant to prove that she so acted, but there must be some link between the common intention and the acts relied on as a detriment. In *Grant v Edwards*,[29] Nourse LJ said that, in his view, the conduct required 'must be conduct on which the woman could not reasonably have been expected to embark unless she was to have an interest in the home'. In the same case, Browne-Wilkinson VC said:[30]

> Setting up house together, having a baby and making payments to general housekeeping expenses (not strictly necessary to enable the mortgage to be paid) may all be referable to the mutual love and affection of the parties and not specifically referable to the claimant's belief that she has an interest in the house.

However, he went on:

> once it has been shown that there was a common intention that the claimant should have an interest in the house, any act done by her to her detriment relating to the joint lives of the parties is... sufficient detriment to qualify. The acts do not have to be inherently referable to the house.

In *Churchill v Roach*,[31] all of the acts relied upon as constituting detriment occurred before the alleged common intention arose and could not therefore constitute the detrimental reliance required to establish a constructive trust.

It has been pointed out[32] that there is no reference in *Stack v Dowden* to detrimental reliance on any agreement, arrangement, or understanding, but it is not entirely clear what significance is to be attached to this omission. It will be remembered that there was no dispute in *Stack v Dowden*, but that each party had a share: the dispute was as to the size of the

[27] In Law Com 307, para A.36.

[28] [1986] 1 FLR 171, CA. See (1996) 16 LS 218 (Anna Lawson).

[29] [1986] Ch 638, 657, [1986] 2 All ER 426, 433, CA. See also *Ungarian v Lesnoff* [1990] Ch 206, [1989] 3 WLR 840, noted [1990] CLJ 25 (M Oldham); *Cooke v Cooke* [1987] VR 625.

[30] *Supra*, CA, at 439, applied *Lloyds Bank plc v Rosset* [1989] Ch 350, [1988] 3 All ER 915, CA. See (1991) 54 MLR 126 (S Gardner).

[31] [2004] 2 FLR 989.

[32] [2008] CLJ 265, in which Sir Terence Etherton makes the novel argument that the trust in *Stack v Dowden* is not an institutional trust, but a discretionary remedial trust for unjust enrichment.

respective shares. One view, however, is that the courts will, once a common intention has been established, no longer require the claimant to establish detrimental reliance. Thus Simon Gardner,[33] referring to the requirement, says 'its demise is understandable; if the common intention can be imputed—i.e. need not actually exist—it would be incoherent to expect [the claimant] to rely on it'.

(v) Quantification of the beneficial interest in the shared home

Baroness Hale in *Stack v Dowden*[34] referred to *Oxley v Hiscock*,[35] a conveyance into the sole name of one of the cohabitants, in which, on the first question—whether the other party had any beneficial interest—it was clearly to be inferred from the other's contribution towards the purchase price that she had. As to the second question—namely, the extent of that interest—Chadwick LJ said that the answer was that 'each is entitled to that share which the court considers fair having regard to the whole course of dealing between them in relation to the property'. Baroness Hale, however, preferred the way that essentially the same thought had been expressed by the Law Commission:[36]

> If the question really is one of the parties' "common intention", we believe that there is much to be said for adopting what has been called a "holistic approach" to quantification, undertaking a survey of the whole course of dealing between the parties and taking account of all conduct which throws light on the question what shares were intended.

This statement was preferred because it emphasized that the search was still for the result which reflects what the parties must, in the light of their conduct, be taken to have intended, yet did not enable the court to abandon that search in favour of the result that the court itself considers fair. It is not for the court to impose its own view of what is just upon the situation in which the parties find themselves.

The approach to quantification in joint names cases, Baroness Hale continued, should certainly be no stricter than the approach in cases in which the home has been conveyed into the name of one only. There are, however, differences between sole and joint names cases when trying to divine the common intentions or understanding between the parties. There seems to be no case in which a sole legal owner, absent a declaration of trust, has been held to hold the property on a beneficial joint tenancy. But this may well be the result where there are joint legal owners. The onus in a joint owner case will be on the party seeking to show that the parties did intend their beneficial interests to be different from their legal ones, and in what way.

The domestic context, Baroness Hale said, is very different from the commercial one, and each case will depend on its own facts. But many more factors than financial contributions may be relevant to divining the parties' true intentions. These include, inter alia, advice or discussions at the time of the transfer, the reasons why the transfer was into joint names, the reason why (if it be the case) the survivor was authorized to give a receipt for the capital money, the purpose for which the home was acquired, the nature of the parties' relationship, whether they had children for whom they both had responsibility to provide a home, how the purchase was financed both initially and subsequently,[37] and how they

---

33 In [2008] 124 LQR 422.   34 [2007] UKHL 17, [2007] AC 432, [2007] 2 All ER 929.

35 [2004] EWCA Civ 546, [2005] Fam 211, [2004] 3 All ER 703.   36 In Law Com No 278.

37 Where a parent contributes to a the purchase price of the family home (or a deposit on it) as a wedding present, this will normally be treated as a present to them both: *McHardy & Sons (a firm) v Warren* [1994] 2

discharged the outgoings on the property and other household expenses. When a couple are joint owners of the home and jointly liable for the mortgage, the inferences to be drawn from who pays for what may be very different from the inferences to be drawn when only one is owner of the home. The arithmetical calculation of how much was paid by each is also likely to be less important. It will be easier to draw the inference that they intended that each should contribute as much to the household as they reasonably could and that they would share the eventual benefit or burden equally. The parties' individual characters and personalities may also be a factor in deciding where their true intentions lay. In the cohabitation context, mercenary considerations may be more to the fore than they would be in marriage, but it should not be assumed that they always take pride of place over natural love and affection. There may also be reason to conclude that whatever the parties' intentions at the outset, they may have changed—for instance, if one party has alone been responsible for substantial improvements.

At the end of the day, Baroness Hale said, having taken everything into account, cases in which the joint legal owners are to be taken to have intended that their beneficial interests should be different from their legal interests will be very unusual. However, the facts of the case before the House were, in her opinion, exceptional and entitled the respondent to a 65 per cent share. Lord Walker thought[38] that the new approach pointed the way to making the outcome of the type of case before the court more predictable, so that parties can be advised with more confidence as to appropriate terms of settlement. Some commentators are less optimistic. One commentator[39] suggests that the decision is 'all things to all claimants' and speculates as to how much litigation there will be as parties attempt to prove that their case is also exceptional, and elsewhere[40] that the listed factors 'will lead to endemic uncertainty'. It remains to be seen whether the fears behind these comments will prove to be justified.

Lord Neuberger was unhappy with the different approach laid down by the majority to the ownership of the beneficial interest in a domestic context from that prevailing in a commercial context. In his opinion, the same principles should apply to assess the apportionment of the beneficial interest as between legal owners, whether in a sexual, platonic, familial, or commercial relationship. It is not entirely clear whether the new approach is applicable in a domestic context in relation to property other than the family home. It is thought probably not.[41]

(vi) Date of valuation of shares

Prima facie, if persons are entitled to property in aliquot shares as tenants in common under a trust, the value of their respective shares must be determined at the date when the property is sold, but that may have to give way to circumstances. For example, one of the

---

FLR 338, CA; *Midland Bank plc v Cooke* [1995] 4 All ER 562, CA; and see *Halifax Building Society v Brown* [1996] 1 FLR 103, CA (loan to finance deposit). It seems that post-acquisition factors are only to be taken into account in so far as they are indicative of the parties' common intention, which it is the duty of the court to identify: *Holman v Howes* [2007] EWCA Civ 877, [2007] 37 Fam Law 987.

[38] In *Stack v Dowden, supra*, HL, at [27].

[39] [2007] Conv 456 (M J Dixon), discussing *Abbott v Abbott* [2007] UKPC 53, [2007] All ER (D) 432 (Jul) and *Ritchie v Ritchie* (17 August 2007, unreported), Leeds county court.

[40] [2007] Conv 352 (M J Dixon).   [41] See p 183, *supra*.

parties may buy out the other, in which case the value of that party's share may have to be determined at a different date.[42]

Valuation is not to be made as at the date of separation, save in the unlikely circumstance that it was agreed that the parties' respective beneficial shares should be valued at that point of time if and when it should occur. The parties' separation will doubtless indicate that the purpose of the trust has failed and the effect may well be to trigger off a demand for a sale. But it does not give rise to any discretion in the court to impose on the parties a valuation of their interests at a date that is earlier than the date of the realization.

(vii) Improvements

So far as improvements to matrimonial property are concerned, s 37 of the Matrimonial Proceedings and Property Act 1970 provides[43] that where a husband or a wife makes a substantial[44] contribution to the improvement of real or personal property in which either or both of them has or have a beneficial interest, the party so contributing shall, unless otherwise agreed, be treated as having acquired by virtue of his or her contribution a share or an enlarged share, as the case may be, in that beneficial interest of such an extent as may have been then agreed or, in default of such agreement, as the court may, in all of the circumstances, consider just.

The Civil Partnership Act 2004[45] contains similar provisions in relation to civil partners.

(viii) Rights of occupation[46]

In many shared home cases, the relationship has broken down and one of the parties has left the property while the other continues in occupation. Some adjustment is called for. In such circumstances, the matter is governed by the Trusts of Land and Appointment of Trustees Act 1996, which applies generally and is not restricted to shared home cases, although this is probably its most common application. Section 12(1) gives a right of occupation to a beneficiary who is beneficially entitled to an interest in possession to land,[47] where the purposes of the trust include making the land available for his occupation, or the land is held by the trustees so as to be so available.[48] Both parties will therefore have a right of occupation. Section 13(1) gives the trustees power to exclude or restrict this right[49] and, under s 13(3), to impose reasonable conditions on any beneficiary in relation to his

---

[42] *Gordon v Douce* [1983] 2 All ER 228, 230, CA *per* Fox LJ. *Bernard v Josephs, supra,* CA; *Turton v Turton, supra,* CA. See [1987] Conv 378 (J Warburton); [1988] Fam Law 72 (J Montgomery); (1989) 86 LSG 31/31 (I M Hardcastle).

[43] The section was said by Lord Denning MR in *Davis v Vale* [1971] 2 All ER 1021, 1025, CA, to be declaratory of the pre-existing law. It is made applicable to engaged couples by the Law Reform (Miscellaneous Provisions) Act 1970, s 2. See (1970) 120 NLJ 1008 (R T Oerton) and the correspondence at 1082.

[44] As to what is meant by 'substantial', see *Samuels (WA)'s Trustee v Samuels* (1973) 233 Estates Gazette 149.

[45] Section 65.   [46] See, generally, [1998] CLJ 123 (D G Barnsley); [2006] Conv 54 (S Pascoe).

[47] As to the construction of this phrase, see Whitehouse and Hassall, *Trusts of Land, Trustee Delegation and the Trustee Act 2000,* 2nd edn, para 2.21, favouring what is thought to be the better view that a beneficiary under a trust for sale of land is included. Contra, the annotation to s 12 in Current Law Statutes 1996 (P Kenny).

[48] The right is excluded if the land is either unavailable or unsuitable for occupation by him: ibid s 12(2).

[49] The trustees must act reasonably: ibid, s 13(2).

occupation of land. Thus, in *Rodway v Landy*,[50] trustees were held entitled, in relation to a single building that lent itself to physical partition, to exclude or restrict one beneficiary's entitlement to occupy one part and, at the same time, exclude or restrict the other beneficiary's entitlement to occupy the other part. It was further held that a condition requiring a beneficiary to contribute to the cost of adapting the property to make it suitable for his occupation was a condition within s 13(3). The conditions that may be imposed include, under s 13(5), paying any outgoings or expenses in respect of the land, and, under s 13(6), paying compensation to a person whose right to occupy has been excluded or restricted.

In exercising their powers, the trustees of land must have regard to:

(a) the intentions of the creator(s) of the trust;

(b) the purposes for which the land is held; and

(c) the circumstances and wishes of each of the beneficiaries entitled to occupy the land.[51]

Moreover, they must not exercise these powers so as to prevent any person who is in occupation of land from continuing in occupation, or in a manner likely to result in any such person ceasing to occupy the land, unless he consents or the court has given approval.[52]

The 1996 Act provides that any person who is a trustee of land or has an interest in property subject to a trust of land may apply to the court for an order under that section.[53] On the application, the court may make any such order relating to the exercise by the trustees of any of their functions,[54] or declaring the nature or extent of a person's interest in property subject to the trust, as the court thinks fit.[55] In determining an application, s 15(1) provides that the matters to which the court must have regard include:

(a) the intentions of the person or persons (if any) who created the trust;

(b) the purposes for which the property subject to the trust is held;

(c) the welfare of any minor who occupies or might reasonably be expected to occupy any land subject to the trust as his home; and

(d) the interests of any secured creditor of any beneficiary.[56]

In addition, in an application relating to s 13, s 15(2) provides that the court must also have regard to the circumstances and wishes of each of the beneficiaries entitled to occupy the land.[57]

---

[50] [2001] 2 WLR 1775, CA, noted (2001) 30 T & ELJ 5 (R Pearce).   [51] Ibid, s 13(4).

[52] Ibid, s 13(7). In determining whether to give approval, the court must have regard to the matters set out in s 13(4): s 13(8).

[53] Section 14(1). In *Oke v Rideout* [1998] CLY 4876, discussed (1999) 4 T & ELJ 18 (M Warner), it was held that a trustee with no beneficial interest was entitled to apply despite a conflict of interest, but on the facts and applying the criteria in s 15, the application was refused.

[54] Including an order relieving them of any obligation to obtain the consent of, or to consult, any person in connection with the exercise of any of their functions.

[55] Ibid, s 14(2). See *Turner v Avis* [2007] EWCA Civ 748, [2007] 4 All ER 1103. The court may not, however, make an order under this section as to the appointment or removal of trustees: s 14(3). Following *Smith v Smith* (1975) 120 Sol Jo 100 on the corresponding provision of the Law of Property Act 1925, the discretion of the court would not be limited in any way by s 11 (consultation with beneficiaries).

[56] Discussed p 200, *infra*.

[57] As to an application other than one made under s 13 or one made under s 6(2), see s 15(3).

The above statutory provisions were held in *Stack v Dowden* to have replaced the doctrine of equitable accounting, and to give increased flexibility to the court to the benefit of families and to the detriment of banks and other chargees.[58] Old authorities should not be overthrown, but should be regarded with caution and, in many cases, are unlikely to be of great, let alone decisive, assistance.[59]

The above provisions in the 1996 Act only apply, however, where the beneficiary claiming compensation is entitled to occupy the land under s 12. Thus, where one of two sharing owners becomes bankrupt, his trustee in bankruptcy, although entitled for the benefit of the creditors to an interest in possession in the property subject to a shared home trust, has no right of occupation. In such a case, there is no scope for the operation of s 13. The old law applies under which the party remaining in possession will be debited with an occupation rent, but credited with half of any payments made in respect of mortgage instalments and other outgoings, the court having no discretion in the matter.[60]

There are special provisions on an application for the sale of land by a trustee of a bankrupt's estate. On such an application, the court must make such order as it thinks just and reasonable having regard to:

(a) the interests of the bankrupt's creditors;

(b) where the application is made in respect of land that includes a dwelling house that is, or has been, the home of the bankrupt or the bankrupt's spouse or civil partner, or former spouse or former civil partner—

   (i)   the conduct of the spouse or civil partner, or former spouse or former civil partner, so far as contributing to the bankruptcy,

   (ii) the needs and financial resources of the spouse or civil partner, or former spouse or former civil partner, and

   (iii) the needs of any children; and

(c) all of the circumstances of the case other than the needs of the bankrupt.[61]

Moreover, where an application is made after the end of the period of one year beginning with the first vesting of the bankrupt's estate in a trustee, the court must assume, unless

---

[58] *Stack v Dowden* [2007] UKHL 17, [2007] AC 432, [2007] 2 All ER 929. But in (2008) 22 TLI 11, Sir Gavin Lightman has made a powerful argument to the effect that the 1996 Act does not apply to past events, only to the present and future.

[59] *Mortage Corpn v Shaire* [2001] 4 All ER 364, discussed [2000] Conv 315 (S Pascoe); [2000] Conv 329 (M P Thompson); [2001] CLJ 44 (M Oldham); [2001] Fam Law 275 (M Pawlowski and S Greer). It remains a powerful consideration whether the creditor is receiving proper recompense for being kept out of his money: *Bank of Ireland Home Mortgages Ltd v Bell* [2001] 2 All ER Comm 920, CA, noted [2002] Conv 61 (R Probert); *Re MCA* [2002] EWHC 611 (Admin/Fam), [2002] 2 FLR 274. Note that, if the court refuses to order a sale, a mortagee can sue on the personal covenant, which will almost certainly force the mortgagor into bankruptcy: *Alliance and Leicester plc v Slayford* [2001] 1 All ER (Comm) 1, CA, noted [2002] Conv 53 (M P Thompson). See also (2005) 25 LS 201 (L Fox).

[60] *Re Barcham* [2008] EWHC 1505h, [2008] 2 FCR 643; *Dennis v McDonald* [1982] Fam 63,]1982] 1 All ER 590, CA; *Re Gorman (a bankrupt)* [1990] 1 All ER 717, [1990] 1 WLR 616; *Re Pavlou (a bankrupt)* [1993] 3 All ER 955, [1995] 1 WLR 1046; *Byford v Butler* [2003] EWHC 1267 (Ch), [2004] 2 FCR 454.

[61] Insolvency Act 1986, s 335A(1), (2) inserted by the Trusts of Land and Appointment of Trustees Act 1996 and amended by the Civil Partnership Act 2004. Where s 335A applies, s 15 of the 1996 Act is excluded: s 15(4). See *Judd v Brown* (1999) 79 P & CR 491, CA. In relation to the Human Rights Act 1998, see *Nicholls v Lan* [2006] EWHC 1255 (Ch), [2006] BPIR 1243, noted [2007] Conv 78 (M Pawlowski).

the circumstances of the case are exceptional, that the interests of the bankrupt's creditors outweigh all other considerations.[62]

It will be convenient to conclude this section by noting two points relating to a right of occupation, although they are not relevant in shared homes cases. Firstly, the right to occupy trust land does not extend to a beneficiary under a discretionary trust, but there is no reason why the trust instrument should not provide that the trustees may permit a discretionary beneficiary to occupy the trust land upon such terms and conditions as they think fit.

Secondly, if a settlor does not wish any beneficiary to enjoy a right of occupation, it is important that it should be clearly indicated in the trust instrument. The Act does not appear to contemplate the exclusion of s 12, but a statement of the intention of the settlor in the trust instrument is likely to be effective in practice.[63]

(ix) Section 17 of the Married Women's Property Act 1882[64]

This section provides as follows:

> In any question between husband and wife[65] as to the title or to possession of property, either party...may apply [to a court which] may make such order with respect to the property in dispute...as it thinks fit.

So far as title to property is concerned, it was finally settled by the House of Lords in *Pettitt v Pettitt*,[66] after a long series of cases demonstrating acute differences of opinion in the Court of Appeal, that s 17 is a purely procedural section that confers no jurisdiction to transfer any proprietary interest from one spouse to the other or to create new proprietary rights in either spouse.[67] By an extension contained in s 39 of the Matrimonial Proceedings and Property Act 1970, an application may be made for three years after the marriage has been dissolved or annulled. Usually, however, there is no point in going on with an application under s 17 once there has been a divorce. The proper course is to take out proceedings under the Matrimonial Causes Act 1973, which gives wide powers to the court to do what is just having regard to all of the circumstances.[68]

---

[62] Insolvency Act 1986, s 335A(3). See *Barca v Mears* [2004] EWHC 2170 (Ch), [2005] 2 FLR 1; *Dean v Stout (The trustee in bankruptcy of Dean)* [2005] EWHC 3315 (Ch), [2006] 1 FLR 725, in which Lawrence Collins J summarized the applicable principles; *Donohoe v Ingram (trustee in bankruptcy of Kirkup)* [2006] BPIR 417; *Nicholls v Lan*, supra. As to the effect of the Hunan Rights Act 1988, see *Foyle v Turner* [2007] EWCA Civ 748, [2007] BPIR 663. See also Insolvency Act 1986, s 337, and *Martin-Sklan vWhite* [2006] EWHC 3313 (Ch), [2007] BPIR 76.

[63] This may be backed up by a provision restricting the investment powers of trustees under s 6(1), (3), as amended by the Trustee Act 2000, Sch 2, para 45, so as to exclude buying land for beneficial occupation: see s 8(1). See also Trustee Act 2000, ss 8, 9(b).

[64] As amended. It applies also to previously engaged couples: Law Reform (Miscellaneous Provisions) Act 1970, s 2(2), and see *Shaw v Fitzgerald* [1992] 1 FLR 357.

[65] Including the parties to a polygamous or potentially polygamous union married according to the law of their domicile: *Chaudhry v Chaudhry* [1975] 3 All ER 687, point not decided on appeal [1976] Fam 148, [1976] 1 All ER 805n, CA.

[66] [1970] AC 777, [1969] 2 All ER 385, HL.

[67] The court has power to order a sale of the property. Having declared the respective shares of husband and wife in the property, it may order the sale by one party to the other of his or her share at the price defined by the declared value of the vendor's interest, and, in an appropriate case, may order payment of the sum so assessed: *Bothe v Amos* [1976] Fam 46, [1975] 2 All ER 321, CA.

[68] See *Fielding v Fielding* [1978] 1 All ER 267, CA.

It should be added that it is equally clear from *Pettitt v Pettitt*[69] that, where the question is not one of title to property, but whether an established property right can be enforced, it is agreed that the court has a discretion to restrain or postpone the enforcement of a spouse's legal rights, in relation, for instance, to sale of the property or to possession, having regard to the mutual matrimonial duties of the spouses.

The Civil Partnership Act 2004[70] contains similar provisions in relation to civil partners.

(x) Law Commission recommendations[71]

The Law Commission has recommended that legislation should create a scheme of general application under which couples satisfying statutory eligibility criteria would be entitled to apply for financial relief on separation, provided that they had not entered into an agreement disapplying the statutory scheme. It proposes that persons should be eligible to apply if either (a) they have lived together as a couple (not being married to each other or civil partners) in a joint household for a minimum period (a range of two or five years is suggested), or (b) they are cohabitants who have a child together.

It is recommended that the court should be given discretionary power to grant financial relief in accordance with a statutory scheme, based upon the economic impact of cohabitation. The party applying for relief must prove that the other party has a retained benefit, or that the applicant has an economic disadvantage, as a result of qualifying contributions that the applicant has made. Contributions are not limited to financial contributions and include future contributions, in particular to the care of the parties' children following separation. The discretionary factors to be taken into account by the court are set out. The first consideration is the welfare of any minor child of both parties. Other considerations are the financial needs and resources of each party, the welfare of any children living with either party, and the conduct of each party.

For the avoidance of doubt, the legislation should make it clear that a cohabitation contract governing the financial arrangements of a cohabiting couple is not contrary to public policy, and that opt-out agreements are to be taken to have been made for valuable consideration.

It is also recommended that appropriate amendments should be made to the Inheritance (Provision for Family and Dependants) Act 1975. The Report does not contain a draft Bill.

The government announced, in March 2008, that it would wait to see the result of legal changes in Scotland and, for the time being, would take no further action.[72]

(B) CASES OTHER THAN COHABITANT'S SHARED HOME

In principle, the common intention constructive trust is not restricted to cohabitants' shared homes, but there are few other reported cases in which such a claim has been made

---

[69] *Supra*. Note that the Family Law Act 1996, ss 30 *et seq*, as amended, confers rights of occupation on a spouse or civil partner in relation to a dwelling house that has been a home so long as the marriage or civil partnership subsists. See also Insolvency Act 1986, ss 335A and 336, as amended.   [70] Sections 66–68.

[71] Law Com No 307, *Cohabitation: The Financial Consequences of Relationship Breakdown*. See (2007) Fam Law 911, 998, 1076 (S Bridge); (2007) 37 Fam Law 407 (C Barton); [2008] Conv 197 (D Hughes, M Davis, and Louise Jacklin); [2008] Fam Law 351 (G Douglas, J Pearce, and H Woodward).

[72] See (2008) Times, 7 March.

successfully. One such case is *Re West Norwood Cemetery*,[73] in which P was the registered owner of exclusive rights of burial in Plot 177. According to the report, after the burial of his mother's remains in the Plot, P, one of seven children, made it clear to his siblings that he did not want the remains of his father (D) to be buried there. Nevertheless, five of P's siblings arranged for D's ashes to be buried in the plot, in all likelihood by forging P's signature on the burial form. When the burial authority discovered the facts, it petitioned the Consistory Court for a faculty for the exhumation of D's ashes. The court held that the grant to P of exclusive rights of burial was not definitive of those rights. About a quarter of the cemetery bill had been paid by other members of the family, including D, who had acted to his detriment by contributing without insisting that his name appear on the grant. The judge said that 'since there was a common intention among family members that D should have a right of interment in plot 177, a constructive trust was established and P had no right to refuse his consent to D's interment thereby defeating the common purpose of the trust'. The report fails to show what evidence there was that P, who had the legal title, shared this 'common intention', which was vital to the result. The judge continued by holding that the same result was achieved by the law of proprietary estoppel: by contributing to the project D and P's siblings had acted to their detriment in reliance on the belief that D would have a right to be buried there. The report does not show what evidence there was that P encouraged, or even acquiesced, in that belief. The necessary evidence to establish a constructive trust and/or proprietary estoppel may well have been before the court, but it does not appear in the brief report.

Another case is *Mollo v Mollo*,[74] in which a divorced couple bought a house in the woman's name, principally to serve as a home for their adult sons. It was decided that she held it for herself and her ex-husband in proportion to their contributions on the basis of constructive trust or proprietary estoppel. There are also several cases[75] in which such a claim has been assumed to be made on a valid basis, but has failed on the facts.

2   PROPRIETARY ESTOPPEL

(A)   THE PRINCIPLES INVOLVED

In *Dillwyn v Llewellyn*,[76] a father placed one of his sons in possession of land belonging to the father, and at the same time signed a memorandum that he had presented the land to the son for the purpose of furnishing him with a dwelling house, but no formal conveyance was ever executed. The son, with the assent and approbation of the father, built,

---

[73] (2005) Times, 20 April (Consistory Court).

[74] [2000] WTLR 227, discussed (2000) 17 T & ELTJ 7 (M Cohn and M Watson).

[75] For example, *Pratt v Medwin* [2003] EWCA Civ 906, [2003] 2 P & CR D 63; *Lalani v Crump Holdings Ltd* [2007] All ER (D) 127 (Jan); *James v Thomas* [2007] EWCA Civ 1212, [2007] All ER (D) 373 (Nov).

[76] (1862) 4 De G F & J 517. Cf *Ramsden v Dyson* (1866) LR 1 HL 129; *Plimmer v Wellington Corpn* (1884) 9 App Cas 699, PC; *Chalmers v Pardoe* [1963] 3 All ER 552, [1963] 1 WLR 677, PC. See, generally, (1983) 42 CLJ 257 (M P Thompson); (1984) 13 AALR 45 (E K Teh); [1988] Conv 346 (P T Evans); (1988) 23 Ir Jur NS 38 (L Bentley and P Coughlan); (1989) 12 Sydney LR 17 (S Stoljar); (1990) 10 Ox JLS 42 (M Garner); (1991) 13 Adel LR 225 (L Kirk); (1994) 14 LS 151 (Margaret Halliwell); [1996] Conv 193 (C Davis). See also (1993) 13 Ox JLS 99 (Christine Davis); (1996) 20 MULR 805; (1997) 19 Syd LR 32 (A Robertson); (2002) 146 Sol Jo (M Pawlowski).

at his own expense, a house upon the land and resided there. After the father's death, the question arose what estate, if any, the son had in the land. The judgment of Lord Westbury LC does not makes it clear whether he considered the case to be one of gift or of contract, but he did say, after repeating the rule that 'equity will not complete an imperfect gift', that the subsequent acts of the donor might give the donee a right or ground of claim that he did not have under the original gift. The ratio of his actual decision in this case seems to be that putting the son into possession and the subsequent expenditure incurred with the approbation of the father were grounds for equity intervening to complete the imperfect gift by compelling a conveyance of the fee simple to the son,[77] although it has been thought that the case is to be explained on a contractual basis.[78]

Scarman LJ, in *Crabb v Arun District Council*,[79] adopted a passage from the judgment of Fry J in *Willmott v Barber*,[80] in which he had, in effect, said that, in order for P (who may in fact be either plaintiff or defendant) to succeed in a plea of proprietary estoppel, he must establish five points—namely:

(i)   P must have made a mistake as to his legal rights.

(ii) P must have expended some money or must have done some act (not necessarily upon D's land) on the faith of his mistaken belief.

(iii) D, the possessor of the legal right which P claims it would be inequitable for D to enforce, must have known of the existence of his own right which is inconsistent with the right claimed by P.

(iv) D must have known of P's mistaken belief of his, P's, right.

(v)   D must have encouraged P in his expenditure of money or in the other acts which he has done, either directly or by abstaining from asserting his legal right.

However, it has now been said to be clear that it is not essential to establish the five 'probanda', as they are called,[81] although they continue to be referred to from time to time:[82] 'They are relevant only to cases of unilateral mistake, where the Defendant's only encouragement to the Claimant has been passive non-intervention.'[83] Accordingly, in *Taylor Fashions Ltd v*

---

[77] See (1963) 79 LQR 238 (D E Allan).

[78] For example, Wynn-Parry J at first instance in *Re Diplock* [1947] Ch 716, 781–784, [1947] 1 All ER 522, 549. See *J T Developments Ltd v Quinn* (1990) 62 P & CR 33, CA, in which, to found an estoppel, it had to be shown that the plaintiffs had created or encouraged an expectation that the defendants would have a new lease, and that the defendants had expended money on the property in reliance on the expectation and with the knowledge of the plaintiffs.

[79] [1976] Ch 179, [1975] 3 All ER 865, CA, noted (1976) 40 Conv 156 (F R Crane), and applied *Griffiths v Williams* [1977] LS Gaz R 1130, CA. See also *Western Fish Products Ltd v Penwith District Council* [1981] 2 All ER 204, CA; *Waltons Stores (Interstate) Ltd v Maher* (1988) 76 ALR 513; (1979) 8 Sydney LR 578 (J D Davies); [2001] 22 Adel LR 157.   [80] (1880) 15 Ch D 96.

[81] *Lloyds Bank plc v Carrick* [1996] 4 All ER 630, CA, *per* Morritt LJ, noted (1996) 112 LQR 549 (P Ferguson); [1996] Conv 295 (M P Thompson).

[82] See *Coombes v Smith* [1986] 1 WLR 808, in which the judge went through Fry LJ's five points and held that the plaintiff failed to establish any of them; *Matharu v Matharu* [1994] 2 FLR 597, CA, noted [1994] Fam Law 624 (J Dewar); (1995) 58 MLR 413 (P Milne); [1995] Conv 61 (Mary Welstead), in which the majority of the court held that the five points were established and the defendant was accordingly entitled to a remedy. The estoppel claim failed in *A-G of Hong Kong v Humphreys Estate (Queen's Gardens) Ltd* [1987] AC 114, [1987] 2 All ER 387, PC, which shows that, where there is an agreement subject to contract, it is very difficult to establish an estoppel preventing a party from withdrawing.

[83] *Yeoman's Row Management Ltd v Cobbe* [2008] UKHL 55, [2008] 4 All ER 713, *per* Lord Walker, at [58].

Liverpool Victoria Trustees Co Ltd,[84] Oliver J said that what is required is:

> a very much broader approach which is directed to ascertaining whether, in particular individual circumstances, it would be unconscionable for a party to be permitted to deny that which, knowingly or unknowingly, he has allowed or encouraged another to assume to his detriment rather than to inquiring whether the circumstances can be fitted within the confines of some preconceived formula serving as a universal yardstick for every form of unconscionable behaviour.

It has also been said that: 'The fundamental principle that equity is concerned to prevent unconscionable conduct permeates all the elements of the doctrine.'[85] The principle, in its broadest form, is that where one person (A) has acted to his detriment on the faith of a belief that was known to, and encouraged[86] by, another person (B) that he either has or is going to be given a right in or over B's property, B cannot insist on his legal rights if to do so would be inconsistent with A's belief.[87] There must be a sufficient link between the promises relied upon and the conduct that constitutes the detriment,[88] but the promises relied on do not have to be the sole inducement for the conduct: it is sufficient that they are *an* inducement.[89] Once it has been established that promises were made, and that there has been conduct by the complainant of such a nature that inducement may be inferred, then the burden of proof shifts to the defendant to establish that he did not rely on the promises.[90] The effect is that promises unsupported by consideration, which are initially revocable, may become binding and irrevocable as a consequence of the promisee's detrimental reliance. Thus, for example, if B gives repeated assurances to A that he will leave certain property to A by his will, and A acts to his detriment on the faith of those assurances, A may have a remedy in equity against B if B subsequently changes his mind.[91]

---

[84] [1982] QB 133n, [1981] 1 All ER 897, 915, 916, CA. Oliver LJ cited this after his elevation to the Court of Appeal in *Habib Bank Ltd v Habib Bank AG Zurich* [1981] 2 All ER 650, [1981] 1 WLR 1265, CA, and it received the approbation of the other members of the court. See also *Hammersmith and Fulham London Borough Council v Top Shop Centres Ltd* [1990] Ch 237, [1989] 2 All ER 655; *Lim Teng Huan v Ang Swee Chuan* [1992] 1 WLR 113, PC, noted [1992] Conv 173 (Say Hak Goo); *Austotel Pty Ltd v Franklin's Selfservice Pty Ltd* (1989) 16 NSWLR 582, (NSWCA); *Pridean Ltd v Forest Taverns Ltd* (1998) 75 P & CR 447, CA; *Jones v Stones* [1999] 1 WLR 1739, CA.

[85] *Gillett v Holt* [2000] 2 All ER 289, 301, CA, *per* Robert Walker LJ, noted (2000) 59 CLJ 453 (M Dixon), (2000) 15 T & ELJ 6 (J McDonnell); [2001] Conv 78 (M P Thompson). Where the pleadings fail to make the allegations normally necessary to support a claim on the basis of proprietary estoppel, the court may nevertheless grant relief on that basis if the evidence relied on would have supported such a plea: *Strover v Strover* [2005] EWHC 860 (Ch), [2005] WTLR 1245, noted (2006) 73 T & ELTJ 26 (Charlotte Simm).

[86] Or, it seems, merely allowed: *Inwards v Baker* [1965] 2 QB 29, 37, [1965] 1 All ER 446, 448, CA ; *Ward v Kirkland* [1967] Ch 194, [1966] 1 All ER 609.

[87] See *Re Basham (decd)* [1987] 1 All ER 405, 410, [1986] 1 WLR 1498, 1503, *per* Mr Nugee QC, cited by Balcombe LJ in *Wayling v Jones* (1993) 69 P & CR 170, 172, CA, and by Robert Walker LJ in *Gillett v Holt, supra*, CA, at 302, and noted [1987] Conv 211 (Jill Martin); (1988) 46 CLJ 216 (D J Hayton).

[88] See *Wayling v Jones, supra*, CA, at 173, cited *Gillett v Holt, supra*, CA; *Keelwalk Properties Ltd v Walker* [2002] EWCA Civ 1076, [2002] 3 EGLR 79.

[89] See *Wayling v Jones, supra*, CA, at 173, cited *Gillett v Holt, supra*, CA; *Amalgamated Investment and Property Co Ltd (in liq) v Texas Commerce International Bank Ltd* [1982] QB 84, [1981] 1 All ER 923, affd on other grounds [1982] QB 84, [1981] 3 All ER 577, CA; *Evans v HSBC Trust Co (UK) Ltd* [2005] WTLR 1289, noted (2006) 76 T & ELTJ 17 (Amanda Nelson).

[90] See *Wayling v Jones, supra*, CA, at 173, cited *Gillett v Holt, supra*, CA; *Greasley v Cooke* [1980] 3 All ER 710, [1980] 1 WLR 1306, CA; *Grant v Edwards* [1986] Ch 638, [1986] 2 All ER 426, CA.

[91] *Gillett v Holt supra*, CA. Generally, of course, a will may be revoked and a representation by a living person as to his testamentary intentions is not binding. It is the detrimental reliance that may prevent that

However, if there is a relevant unforeseen change of circumstances, the probable reaction of the just bystander (and it has been said that it is by reference to his conscience that these matters should be judged) might be that the assurance given could be rescinded by B and replaced by a different arrangement, and this would be the proper conclusion as long as it satisfied the equity that arose before the change of circumstances.[92]

The fundamental principle referred to in the previous paragraph does not, however, mean that a finding of unconscionable behaviour is sufficient to justify the creation of a 'proprietary estoppel equity'. The House of Lords recently gave careful consideration to the issue in *Yeoman's Row Management Ltd v Cobbe*.[93] The essential facts, slightly simplified, were that A, the owner of land with development potential, entered into an oral 'agreement in principle' with B (although some terms remained to be agreed) that B would, at his own expense, seek planning permission and, if this were obtained, A would sell the land to B who would carry out the development and sell off the residential units. B would make an up-front payment of £X to A and, when the units were sold, any profits over £2X would be equally divided between A and B. B obtained planning permission, but A sought to renegotiate the agreement, seeking a substantial increase in the sum representing £X. B would not agree with this and A would not proceed on the original terms. B brought legal proceedings against A and, at first instance and in the Court of Appeal, it was held that a case of proprietary estoppel was made out, and that B was entitled to compensation calculated by reference to the value of his expectations under the unenforceable and incomplete agreement. The proprietary estoppel conclusion was held to be justified by the unconscionability of A's conduct.

The House of Lords profoundly disagreed. Lord Scott stated the position clearly and succinctly thus:[94] 'Proprietary estoppel requires...clarity as to what it is that the object of the estoppel is to be estopped from denying or asserting, and clarity as to the interest in the property in question that that denial, or assertion, would otherwise defeat.' On the facts, there was clarity in neither respect. To treat a 'proprietary estoppel equity' as requiring neither a proprietary claim by the claimant nor an estoppel against the defendant, but simply as unconscionable behaviour is, he said, a recipe for confusion. The claim on the basis of proprietary estoppel was accordingly reversed.[95] Lord Scott added, obiter, that even if there had been a complete agreement, if it was void under s 2 of Law of Property (Miscellaneous Provisions) Act 1989, it would not become enforceable via the route of proprietary estoppel.

In reaching the same conclusion, Lord Walker said that the case failed on the fundamental point that, as persons experienced in the property world, both parties knew that there was no legally binding contract and that they could withdraw from negotiations without legal liability. Conscious reliance on honour, he said, will not give rise to an estoppel. He

---

person from changing his mind. See *Taylor v Dickens* [1998] 3 FCR 455 and the criticism of that decision in *Gillet v Holt, supra*, CA.

[92] *Uglow v Uglow* [2004] EWCA Civ 987, [2004] WTLR 1183.

[93] [2008] UKHL 55, [2008] 4 All ER 713.

[94] At [28]. He had noted at [18] that Oliver J in *Taylor's Fashions Ltd v Liverpool Victoria Trustees Co Ltd, supra*, at 144, referred to the expectation of 'a certain interest in land', as had Lord Kingsdown in *Ramsden v Dyson* (1866) LR 1 HL 129, 170.

[95] The claimant was, however, held to be entitled to a *quantum meruit* payment for his services, including outgoings, in obtaining the planning permission.

further said that the court should be very slow to introduce uncertainty into commercial transactions by over-ready use of equitable concepts such as equitable estoppel.

It was said in *Jennings v Rice*[96] that the expectation need not be focused on any specific property, but in a recent case, *Lissimore v Downing*,[97] it was said that that dictum must be read in context. In the opinion of the judge, the basic rule is that the representation made or assurance provided or expectation raised must relate to some specific property (which may include the whole of the B's property or his residuary estate), or be expressed in terms that enable an objective assessment to be made of what is being promised.

Somewhat surprisingly, under the doctrine of proprietary estoppel, a promise to confer an interest in property that is so equivocal in its terms that it would be incapable of giving rise to a binding contract may be capable of conferring on the promisee a right in equity to a transfer of the whole property. This is said to be an instance of equity supplementing the law.[98]

Finally it may be added, on general principles, that when a person seeks the aid of the court to override someone's strict legal rights on equitable grounds, aid will not be given to one who has violated the principle of equity that 'he who comes to equity must come with clean hands'.[99]

(B) DETRIMENTAL RELIANCE

It is settled law that detriment is required, but, in this context, 'detriment' is not a narrow or technical concept. The detriment need not consist of the expenditure of money or other quantifiable financial detriment, so long as it is something substantial. The requirement must be approached as part of a broad inquiry as to whether repudiation of an assurance is or is not unconscionable in all of the circumstances.[100] The issue of detriment must be judged at the moment when the person who has given the assurance seeks to go back on it. Whether the detriment is sufficiently substantial is to be tested by whether it would be unjust or inequitable to allow the assurance to be disregarded—that is, again, the essential

---

[96] [2002] EWCA Civ 159, [2003] 1 P & CR 100, citing *Re Basham* [1987] 1 All ER 405, [1986] 1 WLR 1498, and see *per* Robert Walker LJ in *Gillett v Holt, supra*, CA, at 302.

[97] [2003] 2 FLR 308.

[98] *Jones v Watkins* [1987] CA Transcript 1200, *per* Slade LJ, cited by Robert Walker LJ in *Gillett v Holt, supra*, CA.

[99] *J Willis & Son v Willis* [1986] 1 EGLR 62, CA (aid refused to one who had put forward a wholly fraudulent document. It seems to be a case of proprietary estoppel, although referred to as 'promissory estoppel', 'equitable estoppel' or 'quasi estoppel').

[100] *Gillett v Holt* [2000] 2 All ER 289, CA, discussed [2001] Conv 13 (R Wells), who argues that the decision does not make it easy to ascertain to what extent the court can take into account matters of a personal nature as opposed to matters that have a financial or property element. In *Greasley v Cooke* [1980] 3 All ER 710—see [1981] Conv 154 (Ruth Annand)—the plaintiffs had given assurances to the defendant that she could remain in the house that had been her home for many years for as long as she wished, and it was held that it was to be presumed that the defendant had acted on the faith of those assurances. The burden of proof was on the plaintiffs to rebut this presumption and, since they had failed to do so, an equity was raised in favour of the defendant, which should be satisfied by allowing her to stay on in the house for as long as she wished. In (1981) 125 Sol Jo 539, M P Thompson observed that the facts are difficult to distinguish from those in *Maddison v Alderson* (1983) 8 App Cas 467, not cited in *Greasley v Cooke*, in which the contrary conclusion was reached. A passage of the judgment of Lord Denning MR in *Greasley v Cooke*, at 713, which suggests that any action in reliance on an assurance is sufficient, whether or not the action is detrimental, has been explained by Dunn LJ in *Watts v Storey* (1983) 134 NLJ 631, CA.

test of unconscionability. The detriment, it has been said,[101] 'must truly hurt'. The detriment alleged must, of course, be pleaded and proved.[102] Further, it must be a personal detriment. Accordingly, in *Lloyd v Dugdale*,[103] the majority shareholder in a company was not permitted to rely on a form of derivative estoppel, derived from the company.

In order to show that the person to whom the assurance was made was induced to act to his detriment, it is not necessary to show that he would have left the maker of the assurance if the promise had not been made, but only that he would have left him if the promise had been withdrawn. Once the claimant shows that the promise was made, and that his conduct was such that inducement could be inferred, the burden of proof shifts to the maker of the promise to show that the claimant did not, on fact, rely on the promise.[104]

In *Gillett v Holt*,[105] at the defendant's suggestion, the claimant left school at the age of fifteen, against his headmaster's advice and despite his parents' misgivings, to work on the defendant's farm, which he continued to do for nearly forty years. With his wife and children, the claimant provided the defendant, a bachelor, with a surrogate family, and he was given repeated assurances that he would inherit the farm business. However, in 1995, he was summarily dismissed, and the last of a series of wills left him nothing; an earlier will had left everything to him. The Court of Appeal, reversing the judge below, had no hesitation in finding the necessary detriment: 'Mr Gillett and his wife devoted the best years of their lives to working for Mr Holt and his company, showing loyalty and devotion to his business interests, his social life and his personal wishes, on the strength of clear and repeated assurances of testamentary benefit.'[106]

(C) HOW THE EQUITY MAY BE SATISFIED[107]

If the equity is established, it is then for the court to say, in the light of the circumstances at the date of the hearing, taking into account the conduct of the parties up to that date, what is the appropriate way in which it can be satisfied.[108] However, the court approaches its task in a cautious way, in order to achieve 'the minimum equity to do justice to the plaintiff'.[109]

---

[101] Per Baron J in *G v G (Matrimonial Property: Rights of Extended Family)* [2005] EWHC 1560 (Admin), [2005] 1 FLR 62.

[102] *Gillett v Holt, supra,* CA; *Jiggins v Brisley* [2003] EWHC 841 (Ch), [2003] WTLR 1141. Cf *Christian v Christian* (1981) 131 NLJ 43, CA, in which the claim failed because the plaintiff had not shown a detriment; *Bostock v Bryant* (1990) 61 P & CR 23, CA, in which there was no detriment sufficient to make it unconscionable for the licence to be determined. See (1981) 44 MLR 461 (G Woodman); [1982] CLJ 290 (Susan J Burridge). The detriment was insufficient to establish a claim in *Churchill v Roach* [2004] 2 FLR 989, but a claim under the Inheritance (Provision for Family and Dependants) Act 1975 was established.

[103] [2001] EWCA Civ 1754, [2002] WTLR 863, noted [2002] Conv 584 (M Dixon).

[104] *Wayling v Jones* (1995) 69 P & CR 170, CA, noted (1995) 111 LQR 389 (Elizabeth Cooke); *Grundy v Ottey* [2003] EWCA Civ 1176, [2003] WTLR 1253, noted [2004] Conv 137 (M P Thompson).

[105] *Supra,* CA. See (2004) 130 PLJ 22 (Barbara Rich).

[106] Ibid, *per* Robert Walker LJ, at 310. Further examples are to be found in the cases referred to in the following section.

[107] Useful articles include (1997) 17 LS 258 (Elizabeth Cooke); (1998) 18 LS 360 (A Robertson); (1999) 115 LQR 438 and (2006) 122 LQR 492 (S Gardner); [2003] Conv 225 (M P Thompson).

[108] *Burrows and Burrows v Sharpe* [1991] Fam Law 67, CA, discussed (1992) 142 NLJ 320 (S Jones); [1992] Conv 54 (J Martin). See *Roebuck v Mungovin* [1994] 2 AC 224, in which Lord Browne-Wilkinson observed that the effect of an estoppel is to give the court the power to do what is equitable in all of the circumstances.

[109] The phrase used by Scarman LJ in *Crabb v Arun District Council* [1976] Ch 179, 198, [1975] 3 All ER 865, 880, CA, and cited by Robert Walker LJ in *Gillett v Holt* [2000] 2 All ER 289, 311, CA. See also *Grundy*

Thus, in *Dillwyn v Llewelyn*,[110] *Pascoe v Turner*,[111] and *Voyce v Voyce*,[112] there was an order for the conveyance of the fee simple estate; in *Taylor Fashions Ltd v Liverpool Victoria Trustees Co Ltd*,[113] there was a decree of specific performance of the renewal option in the lease; in *Unity Joint Stock Mutual Banking Association v King*,[114] a lien was imposed for the amount expended where a father had allowed his sons to occupy and expend money on his land. In other cases, such as *Campbell v Griffin*[115] and *Jennings v Rice*,[116] the claimant has been awarded a sum of money. As the cases cited demonstrate, in some instances, the estoppel claimant is acknowledged to have a property right; in others, a personal right only. It has been argued[117] that proprietary estoppel should give rise to a property right only if that is necessary to protect the claimant's reasonable reliance.

The law was reviewed by the Court of Appeal in *Jennings v Rice*,[118] in which a widow died at the age of ninety-three without children and wholly intestate, leaving an estate of £1.285m, including a house and furniture valued at £435,000. The claimant (the appellant in the Court of Appeal) was a self-employed bricklayer who started to work for the deceased as a part-time gardener in 1970 at the rate of 30p per hour. As time went on, his job was extended to running errands, taking the deceased shopping, and doing minor maintenance work in the house. In the late 1980s, she stopped paying him, but did give him £2,000 towards the purchase of his home. As the deceased became more physically incapacitated, the claimant came to perform other services, including personal services, for her and, after she suffered a burglary, the claimant began to stay overnight to provide security. On several occasions, the deceased led the claimant to believe that he would receive all or part of her property on her death. The claimant had clearly acted to his detriment in giving up spare time in the evenings and at weekends to look after the deceased, and eventually staying overnight, all unpaid. The judge at first instance, taking account of what the cost of full-time nursing care would have been, awarded the claimant £200,000. The respondent accepted the decision, but, in the appeal, the claimant asserted that he was entitled to the whole estate, or at least the house and furniture. In dismissing the appeal and affirming the judge's decision, Aldous LJ said:

> ...once the elements of proprietary estoppel are established an equity arises. The value of that equity will depend upon all the circumstances including the expectation and the detriment. The task of the court is to do justice. The most essential requirement is that there must be proportionality between the expectation and the detriment.

---

v Ottey [2002] EWCA Civ 1176, [2003] WTLR 1253; *Wormall v Wormall* (2004) Times, 1 December, CA (declaration satisfied minimum equity); (2004) 54 T & ELJ 8 (Barbara Rich).

[110] (1862) 4 De G F & J 517. See also *Jackson v Crosby (No 2)* (1979) 21 SASR 280.

[111] [1979] 2 All ER 945, CA. See p 210, fn 121, *infra*.

[112] (1991) 62 P & CR 290, CA, noted [1992] Conv 54 (Jill Martin).   [113] *Supra*.

[114] (1858) 25 Beav 72. See *Savva v Costa* (1981) 131 NLJ 1114, CA. In *Giumelli v Giumelli* [1999] ALJR 547, noted [1999] CLJ 476 (D Wright), the order was for the payment of a sum of money. See also (2001) 22 Adel LR 123 (Fiona Bruce).

[115] [2001] EWCA Civ 990, [2001] WTLR 981.   [116] [2002] EWCA Civ 159, [2003] 1 P & CR 100.

[117] By Sarah Bright and B McFarlane in [2005] CLJ 449.

[118] [2002] EWCA Civ 159, [2003] 1 P & CR 100, noted (2002) 118 LQR 519 (M Pawlowski); [2003] Conv 225 (M P Thompson); *Grundy v Ottey* [2003] EWCA Civ 1176, [2003] WTLR 1253; *Uglow v Uglow* [2004] EWCA Civ 987; [2004] WTLR 1183; *Thorner v Curtis* [2007] EWHC 2422 (Ch), [2008] WTLR 155, noted [2007] 10 T&E 4; (2008) 93 T & ELTJ 4 (M Pawlowski); *Hopper v Hopper* [2008] EWHC 228 (Ch), [2008] 1 FCR 587.

Robert Walker LJ agreed with Aldous LJ's decision, observing that the court must take a principled approach and cannot exercise a completely unfettered discretion according to the individual judge's notion of what is fair in any particular case. The equity arises not from the claimant's expectation alone, although this may be the starting point: it is the combination of this with detrimental reliance and the unconscionability of allowing the benefactor (or his estate) to go back on his assurances. Factors that may be taken into account include misconduct on the part of the claimant,[119] particularly oppressive conduct on the part of the defendant,[120] the need for a clean break,[121] a change in the amount of the benefactor's assets and his circumstances, the effects and potential effects of taxation,[122] and other claims that there may be on the benefactor's bounty. On the facts of the instant case, it would have been disproportionate to award the claimant the whole estate, or even the house and furniture valued at £435,000.[123]

Illustrative cases include *Inwards v Baker*,[124] in which the defendant was, in 1931, considering building a bungalow on land that he would have to purchase. His father, who owned some land, suggested that the defendant should build the bungalow on his land and make it a little bigger. The defendant accepted that suggestion and built the bungalow himself, with some financial assistance from his father, part of which he repaid. He had lived in the bungalow ever since. In 1951, the father died and, in 1963, the trustees of his will claimed possession from the defendant. The court held that the defendant was entitled to remain in possession of the bungalow as a licensee so long as he desired to use it as his home. In *E R Ives Investments Ltd v High*,[125] the facts were very different and the

---

119 See *J Willis & Son v Willis* [1986] 1 EGLR 62, CA, referred to in p 207, fn 99, *supra*.

120 *Crabb v Arun DC* [1976] Ch 179, [1975] 3 All ER 865, CA (defendants estopped from denying that the claimant had a right of way over their land. On the faith of their words and conduct, the claimant had sold off a portion of his land, leaving him, if the defendants had been allowed to succeed, with a useless piece of land to which there was no access). M P Thompson, op cit, has pointed out that there was some misunderstanding of this decision in *Jennings v Rice*, *supra*, CA. It was applied to an unusual set of facts in *Salvation Army Trustee Co Ltd v West Yorkshire Metropolitan CC* (1980) 41 P & CR 179.

121 *Pascoe v Turner* [1979] 2 All ER 945, [1979] 1 WLR 431, CA, noted [1979] MLR 574 (B Sufrin); (1979) 129 NLJ 1193 (R D Oughten), in which the deserted mistress was perhaps lucky, having spent only about £250 on repairs and improvements, for the court to order conveyance of the fee simple to her. The court took the view that the equity could, in all of the circumstances, only be satisfied by compelling the defendant to give effect to his promise and her expectations. Cf *Sledmore v Dalby* (1996) 72 P & CR 196, CA, noted (1997) 113 LQR 232 (M Pawlowski); [1997] CLJ 34 (P Milne); [1997] Conv 458 (J R Adams), in which the claimant had to be content with something less than his expectation, the need for proportionality being at the heart of the judgment.

122 *Gillett v Holt*, *supra*, CA (for facts, see p 208, *supra*).

123 Similarly, in *Campbell v Griffin* [2001] EWCA Civ 990, [2001] WTLR 981, noted (2001) 31 T & ELJ 17 (T Sisley); [2003] Conv 157 (M P Thompson), it would have been disproportionate to award the claimant a life interest in the whole property: he was entitled to the sum of £35,000 charged on the property worth £160,000; *Evans v HSBC Trust Co (UK) Ltd* [2005] WTLR 1289.

124 *Supra*, CA. See also *Jones (A E) v (F W) Jones* [1977] 2 All ER 231, [1977] 1 WLR 438, CA (a tenant in common entitled to one quarter of proceeds of sale of a house held on trust for sale held entitled to stay in possession of the house for the rest of his life without paying any rent to his stepmother, his deceased father's administratrix, who was entitled to the other three-quarters. He had given up work elsewhere and moved into the house, and also paid money, in the reasonable expectation, induced by his father, that it would be his home for the rest of his life); *Re Sharpe* [1980] 1 All ER 198, [1980] 1 WLR 219; *Matharu v Matharu* [1994] 2 FLR 597, CA; *Clark v Clark* [2006] EWHC 275 (Ch), [2006] WTLR 823.

125 [1967] 2 QB 379, [1967] 1 All ER 504, CA, followed in *Thatcher v Douglas* [1996] NLJR 282, CA. See (1967) 31 Conv 332 (F R Crane); (1967) 30 MLR 580 (H W Wilkinson); (1968) 32 Conv 96 (R E Poole); (1995) 59 MLR 637 (G Battersby).

application of the principle was varied accordingly. The defendant and the predecessors in title of the plaintiff had, in 1949, entered into an agreement whereby the defendant agreed that the foundations of the plaintiff's building should remain on the defendant's land, and it was further agreed that the defendant should have a right of access across the plaintiff's land. The agreement was never put into a formal document. Subsequently, the defendant, with the encouragement of the plaintiff's predecessors in title, built a garage, the only access to which was across the plaintiff's land. The plaintiff, who took with full knowledge of the facts, nevertheless brought an action for damages for trespass and an injunction to restrain the defendant from further trespass. On the basis of the above principle, the Court of Appeal affirmed the dismissal of the action by the county court judge.[126]

In *Baker v Baker*,[127] a father gave up his secure tenancy, and moved in with his son and daughter-in-law to a property partially bought with his money on the basis that he would live there rent-free for the rest of his life. The father left following a family dispute and it was held that what he was entitled to was compensation for the loss of rent-free accommodation for the rest of his life.

In relation to unregistered land, it seems to be accepted that a right arising from proprietary estoppel is capable of binding third parties. It is not registrable as a land charge and will not bind a purchaser for value without notice.[128] In relation to registered land, the Land Registration Act 2002[129] provides, for the avoidance of doubt, that an equity by estoppel has effect from the time at which the equity arises as an interest capable of binding successors in title, and, where the claimant is in actual occupation, it may constitute an overriding interest both in respect of first registration *and in* respect of registered dispositions.[130] It has been strongly argued[131] that the person whose conduct gives rise to a proprietary estoppel claim is personally liable to the claimant and may remain so even after the transfer of the relevant property to a third party. The authors of this view accept, however, that there is no authority that unequivocally supports it.

(D) FLEXIBILITY

The flexibility of equity is shown not only in the range of orders that have been made, tailored to the circumstances of the case, but also in the way in which it may be varied

---

[126] The court also relied on the principle of *Halsall v Brizell* [1957] Ch 169, [1957] 1 All ER 371, viz that he who takes the benefit (on the facts here, of keeping his foundations in the defendant's land) must accept the burden (of allowing the defendant the agreed access). It is probably necessary that the benefit and burden both arise under the same deed: *IDC Group Ltd v Clark* [1992] 1 EGLR 187. See *Tito v Waddell (No 2)* [1977] Ch 106, 289 *et seq*, [1977] 3 All ER 129 *et seq*; *Rhone v Stephens* [1994] 2 AC 310, HL: *Thamesmead Town Ltd v Allotey* (1998) 30 HLR 1052, CA; [1998] CLJ 522 (Christine Davis).

[127] (1993) 25 HLR 408, CA; *Cheese v Thomas* [1994] 1 All ER 35, [1994] 1 WLR 129, CA—both cases discussed (1994) NLJ 264 (Jill Martin); [1994] CLJ 232 (M Dixon). See also *Dodsworth v Dodsworth* (1973) 228 EG 1115, CA; *Griffiths v Williams* [1977] LS Gaz R 1130, CA.

[128] *Inwards v Baker* [1965] 2 QB 29, [1965] 1 All ER 446, CA; *E R Ives Instruments Ltd v High* [1967] 2 QB 379, [1967] 1 All ER 504, CA; *Williams v Staite* [1979] Ch 291, [1978] 2 All ER 928, CA; *Lloyds Bank plc v Carrick* [1996] 4 All ER 630, CA. But see *Ashburn Anstalt v Arnold, supra,* CA, and *United Bank of Kuwait plc v Sahib* [1997] Ch 107, [1996] 3 All ER 215, CA; (1984) 100 LQR 376 (S Moriarty); [1991] Conv 36 (G Battersby); (1994) 14 LS 147 (S Baughen).

[129] Section 116. See [2003] CLJ 661 (B McFarlane).   [130] Schedule 1, para 2; Sch 3, para 2.

[131] [2005] Conv 14 (Susan Bright and B McFarlane).

according to changing circumstances. Thus, in *Williams v Staite*,[132] Goff LJ said, 'In the normal type of case...whether there is an equity and its extent will depend...simply on the initial conduct said to give rise to the equity, although the court may have to decide how, having regard to supervening circumstances, the equity can best be satisfied', or, as Cumming-Bruce LJ put it in the same case, 'the rights in equity [do not] necessarily crystallize forever at the time when the equitable rights come into existence'. Thus, in *Crabb v Arun District Council*,[133] in which the court directed that the person setting up the equity should have an easement, the court felt that, had the matter been dealt with earlier, it would have ordered the party setting up the equity to make compensation; in *Dodsworth v Dodsworth*,[134] the court took into account the fact that the lady who had offered to share her house had died.

(E) RELATIONSHIP WITH CONSTRUCTIVE TRUST

According to Chadwick LJ in *Oxley v Hiscock*,[135] it is now accepted that, in cases concerning the property interests of unmarried couples in the quasi-matrimonial home, there is no difference in outcome whether the true analysis lies in constructive trust or proprietary estoppel,[136] and in *Yaxley v Gotts*,[137] all of the members of the court agreed that although there are large areas where the two concepts do not overlap, in the area of a joint enterprise for the acquisition of land (which may be, but is not necessarily, the family home) the two concepts coincide. In *Hyett v Stanley*,[138] again in a judgment agreed by all of the members of the court, it was said in terms that the two doctrines have not been assimilated. It has been contended[139] that there are fundamental distinctions between the two doctrines. In both cases, the claimant must show that he has acted to his detriment; however, in the case of constructive trust, a common intention must be established, while in proprietary estoppel, the unilateral act of the defendant must raise an expectation in the claimant that it would be unconscionable for the defendant to deny. Further, the evidentiary requirements for a constructive trust are more stringent than those for proprietary estoppel.

It should be noted that proprietary estoppel may enable a claimant to enforce an oral contract for the grant of an interest in land, notwithstanding s 2 of the Law of Property (Miscellaneous Provisions) Act 1989, provided that this does not run contrary to the public policy underlying the Act.[140]

---

[132] [1979] Ch 291, [1978] 2 All ER 928, CA.   [133] *Supra.*   [134] (1973) 228 EG 1115, CA.

[135] [2005] Fam 211, [2004] EWCA Civ 546, [2004] 3 All ER 703. See also *Van Laethem v Brooker* [2005] EWHC 1478 (Ch), [2006] 2 FLR 495.

[136] *Oxley v Hislock, supra,* CA, at 738.

[137] [2000] Ch 162, [2000] 1 All ER 711, CA, discussed (1999) 11 T & ELJ 4 (A Allston); [2000] NLJ Easter Supp 21 (P Milne); (2000) 59 CLJ 23 (L Tee); [2000] Conv 245 (M P Thompson); (2000) 116 LQR 11 (R J Smith); (2000) 63 MLR 912 (I Moore); [2000] All ER Rev 244–245 (P J Clarke); *Birmingham Midshires Mortgage Services Ltd v Sabberwal* (1999) 80 P & CR 256, 263, *per* Robert Walker LJ, noted (2000) 116 LQR 341 (C Harpum); (2000) 22 T&ELJ 16 (N Jones and P J Kirby). See also *S v S and M* [2000] EWHC 2892 (Fam), [2007] 1 FLR 1123.

[138] [2003] EWCA Civ 942, [2003] 3 FCR 253, not cited in *Oxley v Hiscock, supra,* CA.

[139] By P Ferguson in (1993) 109 LQR 114, but see (1993) 109 LQR 485 (D Hayton).

[140] *Yaxley v Gotts, supra,* CA; *James v Evans* [2000] 3 EGLR 1, CA; *Kinane v Mackie-Conteh* [2005] EWCA Civ 45, [2005] WTLR 345. See (2001) 30 Tru LI 21 (R Stone).

Lord Walker, who was one of the members of the court in *Yaxley v Gotts*,[141] said, in *Stack v Dowden*,[142] that he had become less enthusiastic about the notion that proprietary estoppel and common intention constructive trusts can or should be completely assimilated. He observed that the claim in proprietary estoppel was no more than a 'mere equity', which may do no more than lead to a monetary award, while a common intention constructive trust identified the true beneficial owner and the size of his beneficial interest.

(F) RELATIONSHIP WITH S 2 OF THE LAW OF PROPERTY (MISCELLANEOUS PROVISIONS) ACT 1989

As we have seen,[143] s 2(1) of the 1989 Act provides that a contract for the sale or other disposition of an interest in land is void if its provisions are not complied with. Problems may arise where there is, on the one hand, such a contract that fails to comply with the statutory requirements, and, on the other hand, facts that would prima facie establish a claim on the basis of proprietary estoppel.

The Court of Appeal had to consider the matter in *Yaxley v Gotts*.[144] The facts of that case were that the second defendant orally offered to give the plaintiff, a builder, the ground floor of a house that he was proposing to purchase, in return for which the plaintiff would convert the house and manage the property on behalf of the second defendant. In the event, it was the second defendant's son, the first defendant, who actually purchased the house. The plaintiff, believing the second defendant to be the owner, performed his side of the bargain, supplying labour, materials, and management services. The plaintiff and the defendants subsequently fell out, and the first defendant refused to grant the plaintiff an interest in the property. There were doubts in the Court of Appeal as to whether the first instance judge had found that there was an agreement between the plaintiff and the first defendant for the transfer or creation of an interest in the property. If there was not, s 2 would, of course, not be relevant.

If there was an agreement within s 2, the court was faced with what Robert Walker LJ[145] called 'the public policy principle'—namely, that the court will not grant a remedy that amounts to the direct or indirect enforcement of a contract that the law requires to be treated as ineffective. However, as Robert Walker LJ went on to explain,[146] this was not a problem in the case before him, because the facts gave rise to a common intention constructive trust, as established by Lord Bridge in *Lloyds Bank plc v Rosset*.[147] This brought into play s 2(5), which provides that nothing in the section affects the operation of resulting, implied, or constructive trusts. The other members of the court agreed with this analysis. Robert Walker LJ observed that a common intention constructive trust was 'closely akin to, if not indistinguishable from, proprietary estoppel', but his decision nevertheless seems to be dependent on an overlap between constructive trust and proprietary estoppel, and the existence of a constructive trust that engages s 2(5).

---

[141] *Supra*, CA.   [142] [2007] UKHL 17, [2007] 2 All ER 929.   [143] At pp 86, 87, *supra*.

[144] [2000] Ch 162, [2000] 1 All ER 711, CA; *Yeoman's Row Management Ltd v Cobbe* [2008] UKHL 55, [2008] 4 All ER 713.

[145] In *Yaxley v Gotts, supra*, CA, at 172, 718.

[146] At 177, 724, citing *Westdeutsche Landesbank Girozentrale v Islington BC, Kleinwort Benson Ltd v Sandwell BC* [1994] 4 All ER 890, 929, *per* Hobhouse J.

[147] [1991] 1 AC 107, 132, [1990] 1 All ER 1111, 1118. See p 194, *supra*.

Beldam and Clarke LJJ, however, seem to have been prepared to go further. They thought it permissible to take account of the policy behind the Law Commission proposals on which the 1989 Act was based, which showed an intention that the proposals should not affect the power of the court to give effect in equity to the principles of both proprietary estoppel and constructive trust. The general principle, Beldam LJ said,[148] that 'a party cannot rely on an estoppel in the face of a statute depends upon the nature of the enactment, the purpose of the provision and the social policy behind it'. Nor did he think it 'inherent in a social policy of simplifying conveyancing by requiring the certainty of a written document that unconscionable conduct or equitable fraud should be allowed to prevail'. As interpreted by Wright J in *James v Evans*,[149] in a judgment with which the other members of the court agreed, both Beldam and Clarke LJJ:

> indicated that in their views circumstances giving rise to a proprietary estoppel which might not at the same time bring about the creation of a constructive trust could be sufficient to have [the effect of displacing s 2(1)], provided that they did not run contrary to the public policy underlying the Act.

More recently, in *Kinane v Mackie-Conteh*,[150] the issue was said to be whether the circumstances justified a finding of proprietary estoppel overlapping with constructive trust and Neuberger LJ doubted whether s 2(5) would assist if there was 'merely a proprietary estoppel'.[151] The essential difference, he said:

> between a proprietary estoppel which does not give rise to a constructive trust, and one that does, is the element of agreement, or at least expression of common understanding, exchanged between the parties, as to the existence, or intended existence, of a proprietary interest, in the latter type of case.

On the facts, the requirement was satisfied and s 2(5) accordingly applied.

In her judgment, Arden LJ observed that a party seeking to rely on proprietary estoppel as a basis for disapplying s 2(1) is not prevented from relying in support of his case on the agreement that s 2(1) would otherwise render invalid. However, reliance on the unenforceable agreement only takes the claimant part of the way: he must still prove all of the other components of proprietary estoppel. In particular, he must show that the defendant encouraged or permitted the claimant in his erroneous belief: this is not satisfied simply by the admission of the invalid agreement in evidence. The cause of action, Arden LJ continued, is not founded on the unenforceable agreement, but on the defendant's conduct, which, when viewed in all relevant respects, is unconscionable. The court does not enforce the agreement made void by s 2(1), but provides a remedy for the unconscionability. The question did not arise for decision in *Yeoman's Row Management Ltd v Cobbe*,[152] but Lord Scott expressed the clear view that 'proprietary estoppel cannot be prayed in aid in order to render enforceable an agreement that statute has declared to be void'.

---

[148] This statement was unanimously approved in *Shah v Shah* [2002] EWCA Civ 527, [2001] 4 All ER 138.

[149] [2000] 3 EGLR 1, CA.   [150] [2005] EWCA Civ 45, [2005] WTLR 345.

[151] It has been submitted that a remedy should be not be restricted to the case in which proprietary estoppel overlaps with constructive trust: there should be no need to rely on s 2(5). Since no attempt is being made to enforce the void contract, s 2(1) would not be engaged. See [2005] Conv 247 (M D); [2005] KCLJ 174 (B McFarlane); (2005) 146 PLJ 11 (Laura McDonald); [2005] Conv 501 (B McFarlane).

[152] [2008] UKHL 55, (2008) Times, 6 September, at [29], in which *Kinane v Mackie-Conteh*, *supra*, was not referred to.

3 THE *PALLANT V MORGAN* EQUITY

The *Pallant v Morgan*[153] equity, as it has been called,[154] is closely related to proprietary estoppel and constructive trust. In that case, there was an agreement between the claimant's and the defendant's respective agents that they would not compete against each other for Lot 16 at auction, but that the defendant's agent alone should bid. The proper inference from the facts was that the defendant's agent, when he bid for Lot 16, was bidding at auction for both parties on an agreement that there should be an arrangement between the parties on the division of the lot if he were successful, as he was. There was too much uncertainty as to the terms of the arrangement for a decree of specific performance to be ordered, but the claimant was nonetheless entitled to a remedy. If the parties could not agree on a division, the property would have to be resold and the proceeds divided equally between them. Unlike proprietary estoppel, the claimant had not suffered any detriment as a consequence of his agent's agreement not to bid, because he would have been outbid by the defendant's agent. However, the defendant had obtained an advantage by keeping the claimant out of the bidding, as he obtained Lot 16 for less than he would have had to pay if the claimant had been bidding against him.

In *Banner Homes Group plc v Luff Developments Ltd*,[155] Chadwick LJ, observing that this was the first case in which the *Pallant v Morgan* equity had been before the Court of Appeal, laid down a series of relevant propositions, as follows.

(i)   A *Pallant v Morgan* equity may arise where the arrangement or understanding on which it is based precedes the acquisition of the relevant property by one of the parties to the arrangement. It is the pre-acquisition arrangement that colours the subsequent acquisition by the defendant and leads to his being treated as a trustee if he seeks to act inconsistently with it.

(ii) It is unnecessary that the arrangement or understanding should be contractually enforceable. Indeed, if it is, there is unlikely to be any need to invoke the *Pallant v Morgan* equity; equity can act through the remedy of specific performance and will recognize the existence of a corresponding trust.

(iii) It is necessary that the pre-acquisition arrangement or understanding should contemplate that one party (the acquiring party) will take steps to acquire the relevant property, and that, if he does so, the other party (the non-acquiring party) will obtain some interest in that property. Further, it is necessary that (whatever private reservations the acquiring party may have) he has not informed the non-acquiring party before the acquisition (or, more accurately, before it is too late for the parties to be restored to a position of no advantage/no detriment) that he no longer intends to honour the arrangement or understanding.

---

[153] [1953] Ch 43, [1952] 2 All ER 951. See [2001] Conv 35 (N Hopkins); (2003) 23 LS 311 (Sarah Nield).

[154] *Banner Homes Group plc v Luff Developments Ltd* [2000] Ch 372, [2000] 2 All ER 117, 137, CA, *per* Chadwick LJ, noted [2001] Conv 265 (M P Thompson).

[155] *Supra*, CA. See *Hooper v Gorvin* [2001] WTLR 575, criticized [2001] Conv 293 (P Kenny); *Cox v Jones* [2004] EWHC 1486 (Ch), [2004] 2 FLR 1010, noted [2004] Fam Law 7 (R Bailey-Harris); [2005] Conv 168 (R Probert); [2000] All ER Rev 244 (P J Clarke); *Yeoman's Row Management Ltd v Cobbe* [2008] UKHL 55, [2008] 4 All ER 713.

(iv) It is necessary that, in reliance on the arrangement or understanding, the non-acquiring party should do (or omit to do) something that confers an advantage on the acquiring party in relation to the acquisition of the property, or is detrimental to the ability of the non-acquiring party to acquire the property on equal terms. It is the existence of the advantage to the one, or detriment to the other, gained or suffered as a consequence of the arrangement or understanding that leads to the conclusion that it would be inequitable or unconscionable to allow the acquiring party to retain the property for himself, in a manner inconsistent with the arrangement or understanding that enabled him to acquire it.

(v) Although, in many cases, the advantage/disadvantage will be found in the agreement of the non-acquiring party to keep out of the market, that is not a necessary feature. Further, although there will usually be advantage to the one and co-relative disadvantage to the other, the existence of both advantage and detriment is not essential—either will do. What is essential is that the circumstances make it inequitable for the acquiring party to retain the property for himself in a manner inconsistent with the arrangement or understanding on which the non-acquiring party has acted.

4 LICENCES

(A) AT COMMON LAW

In the context of property law, a 'licence' is a purely personal permission that allows the licensee to do some act that would otherwise be a trespass and the traditional common law view is that it is not a proprietary interest.[156] The basic distinction at common law was between a bare licence, for example, permission to the child next door to enter to recover his ball, and a licence coupled with a proprietary interest in land or chattels, for example, a licence to the purchaser of felled timber on the vendor's land to enter the vendor's land to carry it away. The former was revocable at any time on reasonable notice,[157] even if under seal or made for valuable consideration; the latter was irrevocable until the purpose for which the licence was given had been fulfilled.

The common law approach is illustrated by *Wood v Leadbitter*,[158] in which the plaintiff bought a ticket for admission to the grandstand at Doncaster races. Having been forcibly removed after refusing to depart peacefully, he sued for assault. The defence was that, as his licence had been revoked, he was a trespasser and the defendant was entitled to remove

---

[156] As to what is meant by this phrase in this context, see *Hounslow London Borough Council v Twickenham Garden Developments Ltd* [1971] Ch 233, [1970] 3 All ER 326.

[157] *Ministry of Health v Bellotti* [1944] KB 298, [1944] 1 All ER 238, CA; *Greater London Council v Jenkins* [1975] 1 All ER 354, [1975] 1 WLR 155, CA. See [1996] CLJ 229 (Tamara Kerbel); [2001] CLJ 89(J Hill).

[158] (1845) 13 M & W 838. The decision turned very much on the pleadings. The only issue to be decided was whether the plaintiff continued to have the leave and licence of the defendant when he was removed. It was held that he had not, because it had been withdrawn. On the pleadings, the question did not arise whether or not the effect of the contract was to prevent the plaintiff from being treated as a trespasser until the races were over.

him using no more force than was reasonably necessary. The defence succeeded. It made no difference that he had given a valuable consideration for the privilege of going onto the stand.

(B) EQUITABLE INTERVENTION

(i) *Hurst v Picture Theatres Ltd*[159]

In this case, X, having bought a 6d tally, surrendered it to an usherette at a Kensington cinema and was shown to an unreserved seat. Under the mistaken belief that he had not paid, he was asked to see the manager and, on his refusal, was eventually removed by the porter under protest, offering no resistance. In an action for assault and false imprisonment, there was pleaded a right to revoke the licence and thereafter eject X as a trespasser. The ratio least stressed[160] by the court was that there was a contract by implication not to revoke the licence before its purpose had been fulfilled and that, because an injunction would lie to restrain the breach of such a contract, there was no justification for treating X as a trespasser. This ground was approved by both the Court of Appeal and the House of Lords in *Wintergarden Theatre (London) Ltd v Millennium Productions Ltd*,[161] and adopted by Megarry J in *Hounslow London Borough Council v Twickenham Garden Developments*.[162] These cases assume the possibility of an irrevocable licence entirely divorced from the grant of any interest of a proprietary nature.[163] As Megarry J explained in the last case mentioned, a licence is a contractual licence if it is conferred by a contract; it is immaterial whether the right to enter the land is the primary purpose of the contract or is merely secondary. It is not an entity distinct from the contract that brings it into being, but merely one of the provisions of that contract. A contractual licensee cannot be treated as a trespasser so long as his contract entitles him to be on the land, whether or not his contract was specifically enforceable. Not only may an injunction be granted to restrain a breach, but also, in an appropriate case, a decree of specific performance may be granted.[164] And in *Tanner v Tanner*,[165] in which it was held on appeal, reversing the judge below, that the defendant had a contractual licence to occupy the house so long as the children were of school age and the accommodation was reasonably required by the defendant, damages were awarded to compensate the plaintiff for having been wrongly turned out following the judgment at first instance.

It may be added that nowadays, particularly where informal family-type arrangements are involved, the courts may find a contractual licence on very slight evidence.[166]

---

[159] [1915] 1 KB 1, CA.

[160] The other ratios are untenable: that X had an 'interest' in seeing the picture, and that the absence of a deed of grant would be relieved in equity since the Judicature Acts.

[161] [1948] AC 173, [1947] 2 All ER 331.   [162] [1971] Ch 233, [1970] 3 All ER 326.

[163] Of course, the licence may be revocable according to its terms: *Abbeyfield (Harpenden) Society Ltd v Woods* [1968] 1 All ER 352n, [1968] 1 WLR 374.

[164] *Verrall v Great Yarmouth Borough Council* [1981] QB 202, [1980] 1 All ER 837, CA. See [2006] Conv 197 (A Dowling) discussing the Australian case of *South Dowling Property Ltd v Cody Outdoor Advertising Property Ltd* [2005] NSWCA 407.

[165] [1975] 3 All ER 776, [1975] 1 WLR 1346, CA. Lord Denning MR was prepared, if need be, to impose the equivalent of a contract on the defendant. See [1976] 92 LQR 168 (J L Boston). *Tanner v Tanner* was distinguished on the facts in *Coombes v Smith* [1986] 1 WLR 808.

[166] See, eg, *Horrocks v Forray* [1976] 1 All ER 737, [1976] 1 WLR 230, CA; *Hardwick v Johnson* [1978] 2 All ER 935, [1978] 1 WLR 683, CA; *Chandler v Kerley* [1978] 2 All ER 942, [1978] 1 WLR 693, CA.

(ii) Proprietary estoppel

If an equity is made out, in appropriate circumstances, it may be satisfied by conferring a licence. This, as we have seen,[167] was the decision of the court in *Inwards v Baker*,[168] *Re Sharpe*,[169] and *Greasley v Cooke*.[170] The terms of the licence vary according to the circumstances: in the first and last of these cases. as long as the plaintiff wished; in *Re Sharpe*,[171] until the loan was repaid.

(iii) Constructive trust

In *Re Sharpe*,[172] Browne-Wilkinson J felt bound by the authority of *Binions v Evans*[173] and *DHN Food Distributions Ltd v London Borough of Tower Hamlets*[174] to hold that, without more, an irrevocable licence to occupy gave rise to a property interest. The Court of Appeal has now held, in *Ashburn Anstalt v Arnold*,[175] that a contractual licence does not create a property interest, although the facts of a particular case may give rise to a constructive trust.

(iv) Reason and justice

In *Hardwick v Johnson*,[176] the majority of the court based their decision on contractual licence. Lord Denning MR, however, said the court would look at all of the circumstances and spell out the most fitting relationship, and would find the terms of that relationship according to what reason and justice require. He cited in support Lord Diplock's speech in *Pettitt v Pettitt*,[177] in which he said that the court imputes to the parties a common intention that they never in fact had by forming its own opinion as to what intention reasonable men would have formed in those circumstances. Yet, in *Gissing v Gissing*,[178] Lord Diplock himself recognized that the majority of their Lordships had rejected his view, and his speech in the latter case was in different terms. Lord Denning referred to constructive trust and personal licence as alternative relationships, and held that this was a personal, not a contractual, licence—that is, '*an equitable licence of which the court has to spell out the terms*'. With respect, the introduction of yet another category of licence—the equitable licence imputed in equity—simply adds more confusion to an already confused area. The approach of the majority is to be preferred, although it is arguable that a more natural inference from the evidence was that the contractual licence was conditional on the continuance of the marriage.[179]

(C) THE LICENSEE'S RIGHTS AGAINST THIRD PARTIES

(i) Contractual licences

The traditional view is that a licence is a purely personal transaction, creating no property rights, and does not affect a subsequent purchaser, even though he takes with

---

[167] See p 210, *supra*.   [168] [1965] 2 QB 29, [1965] 1 All ER 446, CA.
[169] [1980] 1 All ER 198, [1980] 1 WLR 219.   [170] [1980] 3 All ER 710, [1980] 1 WLR 1306, CA.
[171] *Supra*.   [172] *Supra*.   [173] *Supra*.   [174] *Supra*.
[175] [1989] Ch 1, [1988] 2 All ER 147, CA, and see [1980] Conv 207 (J Martin).
[176] [1978] 2 All ER 935, [1978] 1 WLR 683, CA.   [177] [1970] AC 777, [1969] 2 All ER 385, HL.
[178] [1971] AC 886, [1970] 2 All ER 780, HL.
[179] See (1980) 12 MULR 356 (I J Hardingham); *Chandler v Kerley* [1978] 2 All ER 942, 945, *per* Lord Scarman.

notice.[180] The only exception is a licence coupled with an interest in land where the proprietary interest is binding on the third party and probably similarly with an interest in chattels.

As we have seen, it is now clear that a contractual licence can be specifically enforced and its breach prevented by injunction. But as Lord Wilberforce pointed out in *National Provincial Bank Ltd v Ainsworth*,[181] *'this does not mean that the right is any less of a personal character or that a purchaser with notice is bound by it; what is relevant is the nature of the right, not the remedy which exists for its enforcement'*.

Lord Denning, however, took a different view in *Errington v Errington and Woods*,[182] maintaining that *'this infusion of equity means that contractual licences now have a force and validity of their own and cannot be revoked in breach of the contract. Neither the licensor nor anyone who claims through him can disregard the contract except a purchaser for value without notice'*. After a long period of uncertainty, the Court of Appeal positively affirmed the traditional view in *Ashburn Anstalt v Arnold*[183] and it seems the law can now be regarded as settled.

(ii) Estoppel licences

The position is considered in relation to proprietary estoppel at p 211, *supra*.

(iii) Contractual licence giving rise to constructive trust

If a contractual licence gives rise to a constructive trust, then it logically follows that a third party may be bound on ordinary trust principles. Lord Denning's view[184] that a constructive trust will be imposed whenever a purchaser takes property subject to a contractual licence can no longer be supported. The Court of Appeal, in *Ashburn Anstalt v Arnold*,[185] accepted, however, that, on the facts, a case involving a contractual licence could give rise to a constructive trust. Thus, as we have seen, it was said to have been right for a constructive trust to have been imposed in *Binions v Evans*[186] and *Lyus v Prowsa Developments Ltd*.[187] But the court will not impose a constructive trust unless it is satisfied that the conscience of the estate owner is affected. The mere fact that land is expressed to be conveyed 'subject to' a contractual licence gives notice to the purchaser, but does not necessarily imply that he is to be under an obligation, not otherwise existing, to give effect

---

[180] *King v David Allen & Sons, Billposting Ltd* [1916] 2 AC 54, HL; *Clore v Theatrical Properties Ltd* [1936] 3 All ER 483, CA. Cf *Pennine Raceway Ltd v Kirklees Metropolitan Council* [1983] QB 382, [1982] 3 All ER 628, CA (licensee 'interested in the land' for the purposes of the Town and Country Planning Act 1971, s 164, now repealed and replaced by the Town and Country Planning Act 1990, s 107).

[181] [1965] AC 1175, [1965] 2 All ER 472, HL. See (1972) 36 Conv 266 (Jill Martin); [1982] Conv 118, 177 (A Everton), who suggests the category of quasi-proprietary right for a licence.

[182] [1952] 1 KB 290, 299, [1952] 1 All ER 149, 155: as pointed out in *Ashburn Anstalt v Arnold* [1989] Ch 1, [1988] 2 All ER 147, CA, the actual decision can be supported on other grounds; *Binions v Evans* [1972] Ch 359, [1972] 2 All ER 70, CA; *DHN Food Distributors Ltd v London Borough of Tower Hamlets* [1976] 3 All ER 462, [1976] 1 WLR 852, CA.

[183] [1989] Ch 1, [1988] 2 All ER 147, CA, noted [1988] Conv 201 (M P Thompson); (1988) 51 MLR 226 (J Hill).

[184] See *Binions v Evans* [1972] Ch 359, [1972] 2 All ER 70, CA; *DHN Food Distributors Ltd v London Borough of Tower Hamlets, supra*, CA.

[185] [1989] Ch 1, [1988] 2 All ER 147, CA.

[186] [1972] Ch 359, [1972] 2 All ER 70, CA, discussed p 166, *supra*.

[187] [1982] 2 All ER 953, [1982] 1 WLR 1044.

to the licence. Moreover, a constructive trust of land should not be imposed in reliance on inferences from slender materials, and the case was not made out in *Ashburn Anstalt v Arnold*[188] itself.

(iv) Rights of licensees against a trespasser

Where the defendant is not claiming through the licensor, but is a mere trespasser, a licensee, whether or not he is in actual occupation, can obtain an order for possession, if that is a necessary remedy to vindicate and give effect to such rights of occupation as, by contract with his licensor, he enjoys. The remedy is not limited to a party with title to or an estate in the land, and is available to a licensee even though he has no right to exclude the licensor himself.[189]

---

[188] *Supra*, CA; *Canadian Imperial Bank of Commerce v Bello* (1991) 64 P & CR 48, CA.

[189] *Manchester Airport plc v Dutton* [2000] 1 QB 133, sub nom *Dutton v Manchester Airport plc* [1999] 2 All ER 675, CA, noted [1999] Conv 535 (E Paton and Gwen Seabourne). It is cogently argued that this case is wrongly decided (2000) 116 LQR 354 (W Swadling). A contractual licensee in possession has contractual rights against the licensor, but it is only the fact of possession that enables him to bring conversion or trespass against a third party who interferes with his possession. Cf *Hunter v Canary Wharf Ltd* [1997] AC 655, [1997] 2 All ER 426, HL, not cited in *Dutton*, in which it was held that only someone with a right to the land, such as a freeholder, a tenant in possession, or a licensee with exclusive possession, can sue in nuisance, and see *Countryside Residential (North Thames) Ltd v (1) a Child; (2) persons unknown* (2001) 81 P & CR 10, CA.

11

UNLAWFUL TRUSTS

It is against the policy of the law to enforce certain trusts, and the following are the more important categories of trust that are liable to be declared void. No attempt is made here to give an exhaustive list, and, in any case, there is no reason why a novel kind of trust should not be declared void on the ground of public policy. As Danckwerts LJ said in *Nagle v Feilden:*[1] 'The law relating to public policy cannot remain immutable. It must change with the passage of time. The wind of change blows on it.' Some cases are really isolated instances, such as *Brown v Burdett*.[2]

One instance of change relates to trusts for illegitimate children. The fact that a person is illegitimate has never prevented him from being a beneficiary under a trust, but in dispositions made before 1 January 1970, an illegitimate child might face two difficulties. Firstly, if he claimed under a gift to a class of children, he would have had to displace the presumption that 'children' means 'legitimate children'. Secondly, he would have had to establish that, on the facts, the rule that a disposition in favour of illegitimate children not in being when the disposition takes effect is void as being contrary to public policy did not apply. These difficulties do not arise in respect of a disposition made after 31 December 1969. By s 15(1) of the Family Law Reform Act 1969, now repealed and replaced by the Family Law Reform Act 1987, the presumption referred to was reversed, and by s 15(7), the public policy rule was abolished.

1 TRUSTS THAT OFFEND AGAINST THE RULE AGAINST PERPETUITIES

Since the Perpetuities and Accumulations Act 1964, it will only be rarely that the rule against perpetuities will make void a limitation contained in an instrument taking effect after the commencement of the Act.[3] Until amended by the Act, however, the rule was one of the commonest causes of the failure of a trust. In its unamended form, it laid down that a

---

[1] [1966] 2 QB 633, [1966] 1 All ER 689, CA, admittedly in a different context. In *Re Canada Trust Co and Ontario Human Rights Commission* (1990) 69 DLR (4th) 321, it was held that a trust premised on notions of racism and religious superiority was against public policy. However, a valid charitable trust when founded in 1923 and saved by the cy-près doctrine: see p 332 *et seq, infra*.

[2] (1882) 21 Ch D 667 (trust to block up a house for twenty years), applied *Re Boning* [1997] 2 Qd R 12. As to the validity of a testamentary direction for the destruction of a pet, see (1987) 9 U Tas LR 51 (P Jamieson).

[3] 16 July 1964. With one limited exception (in s 8(2)), the Act has no retrospective effect: s 15(5).

future interest[4] in any kind of property, real or personal, would be void *ab initio* if it might possibly vest outside the perpetuity period—namely, the compass of a life or any number of lives in being[5] at the time when the instrument creating it came into effect, and twenty-one years thereafter, with the possible addition of the period of gestation in the case of some person entitled being *en ventre sa mère* at the end of the period. The main alteration made by the 1964 Act was to change the rule from one concerned with possibilities to one concerned with actual events—the 'wait and see' principle. The Act[6] also enables the trust instrument to specify a perpetuity period of a fixed number of years not exceeding eighty. The rule is discussed at length in books on the law of real property.[7]

The government accepted Law Commission proposals[8] for reform in 2001, and it is understood that the introduction of a Bill to implement the proposals is imminent.

2   TRUSTS THAT OFFEND AGAINST THE RULE AGAINST PERPETUAL TRUSTS

Closely related to, and sometimes confused with, the rule against perpetuities is the rule that a gift that requires capital to be retained beyond the perpetuity period is void. This rule is sometimes known as the 'rule against inalienability', and it should perhaps be made clear that it cannot be evaded merely by giving a power to change investments sufficiently wide to enable the property given to be disposed of, if the proceeds of sale are required to be reinvested and the capital fund has to be retained in perpetuity. This rule, which does not apply to charities, is, like the rule against perpetuities, discussed in books on the law of real property.[9]

3   THE EFFECT OF DECLARING A TRUST VOID AS OFFENDING AGAINST THE POLICY OF THE LAW

In the types of case discussed in the two preceding sections, the usual result of an expressed trust being declared void will be that the property must be held on a resulting trust for the settlor, or, where the trust arises under a will, the property will fall into the residuary

---

[4] Since 1925 a future interest, other than a revisionary lease, must be an equitable interest under a trust. For a possible qualification, see (1908) 24 LQR 431 (D T Oliver).

[5] Including the life of a person *en ventre sa mère* at the relevant time. 'Lives' means 'human lives'. In so far as *Re Dean* (1889) 41 Ch D 552 suggests the contrary, it is generally thought to be wrong: see Morris and Leach, *The Rule against Perpetuities*, 2nd edn, p 63, and *Re Kelly* [1932] IR 250.   [6] In s 1.

[7] See, eg, Cheshire and Burn, *Modern Real Property*, 17th edn, p 517 *et seq*; Megarry and Wade, *The Law of Real Property*, 7th edn, [9.012] *et seq*; Morris and Leach, *The Rule against Perpetuities*, 2nd edn, and Supp.

[8] Law Com No 251 (1998).

[9] See, eg, Megarry and Wade, op cit, [9.137] *et seq*; Morris and Leach, op cit, p 321 *et seq*. See also [2006] LS 414 (I Dawson).

estate[10] of the testator. The particular provisions of the instrument creating the trust must, however, be taken into account. Suppose, for instance, the limitations under a trust were to X for life, with remainder for life to X's first son to become a barrister, remainder in fee simple to Y. Suppose further that, when the limitation came into effect, X had no children, although he subsequently had sons who survived him by more than twenty-one years. Before the Perpetuities and Accumulations Act 1964, the second limitation would have been void *ab initio* as infringing the rule against perpetuities, and even now will become void for the same reason if no son has become a barrister within twenty-one years of the death of X. Neither before nor after the Act, however, would there have been a resulting trust, but the vested remainder of Y would have been or would be accelerated.[11]

In the types of case discussed in the following three sections, the question is not strictly one as to the validity of the trust itself, but rather as to the validity of a condition to which the trust is made subject. It is a question of construction whether a condition is a condition precedent—that is, where the gift is not intended to take effect unless and until the condition is fulfilled—or a condition subsequent—that is, where the gift vests immediately, but is liable to be divested if and when the condition is fulfilled; the court in general, it seems, prefers the latter construction where the intention is not made clear.[12] If a condition subsequent is void,[13] the gift, whether of realty or personalty, remains good and is not liable to be determined by breach of the condition, the presence of a gift over being irrelevant. In the case of conditions precedent, it seems that a distinction has to be drawn between gifts of realty and gifts of personalty. If a gift of real property is made dependent upon a condition precedent that is void, the gift fails. In the case of a gift of personal property, where a condition precedent is illegal and void, a further distinction is drawn according to whether the illegality involves *malum in se*, or *malum prohibitum*. In the former case, the gift fails, as in the case of real property, but in the latter case the gift is good, and will pass to the donee unfettered by the condition. Unfortunately, 'the *difference between* malum prohibitum *and* malum in se *has never been very precisely defined or considered*'.[14] *Malum in se* seems to mean some act that is intrinsically and morally wrong, such as murder; *malum prohibitum* some act that offends against a rule of law but is not wrong in itself, such as smuggling. It has been held in Canada that a condition precedent in a will intended to promote the divorce of the testator's son from his wife is *malum prohibitum*.[15]

Finally, it was held, in *Re Hepplewhite's Will Trusts*,[16] that where a testator leaves a gift of personalty subject to several conditions precedent, some of which are valid and some of

---

[10] If the subject of the gift is residue, or if there is no residuary gift, it will become property undisposed of by will and devolve accordingly.

[11] Compare *Re Flower's Settlement Trusts* [1957] 1 All ER 462, [1957] 1 WLR 401, CA; *Re Allan's Will Trusts* [1958] 1 All ER 401, [1958] 1 WLR 220; *Re Boning* [1997] 2 Qd R 12, and see Perpetuities and Accumulations Act 1964, s 6; (1973) 32 CLJ 246 (A M Pritchard).

[12] See, eg, *Re Johnston* [1980] NI 229.

[13] The requirement of certainty is stricter for a condition subsequent than a condition precedent: *Blathwayt v Baron Cawley* [1976] AC 397, [1975] 3 All ER 625, HL; *Re Barlow's Will Trusts* [1979] 1 All ER 296, [1979] 1 WLR 278; *Re Waring's Will Trusts* [1985] NI 105. See (1977) 8 Sydney LR 400 (P Butt); [1980] Conv 263 (Lindsay McKay); (1982) 126 Sol Jo 518 (N D M Parry). On testamentary conditions generally, see (1998) 20 UQLJ 38 (K Mackie).

[14] *Per* Romer J in *Re Piper* [1946] 2 All ER 503, 505. See *Sheppard's Touchstone*, p 132; *Re Moore* (1888) 39 Ch D 116, CA; *Re Elliott* [1952] Ch 217, [1952] 1 All ER 145; (1955) 19 Conv 176 (V T H Delaney).

[15] *Re McBride* (1980) 107 DLR (3d) 233.　　[16] (1977) Times, 21 January.

which are invalid as contrary to public policy, the valid conditions are separable from the others and the gift is good subject thereto, but disregarding the invalid conditions.[17]

4   TRUSTS TENDING TO PREVENT THE CARRYING OUT OF PARENTAL DUTIES

The cases have usually arisen on the validity of a condition subsequent and, in deciding the matter, the courts have referred to the principle set out in *Sheppard's Touchstone*,[18] that 'if the matter of the condition tend to provoke or further the doing of some unlawful act, or to restrain or forbid a man the doing of his duty; the condition for the most part is void'. Thus, in *Re Sandbrook*,[19] a testatrix, having given the bulk of her residuary estate to trustees on trust for two grandchildren, declared that if one or both of them should 'live with or be or continue under the custody, guardianship or control of their father,... or be in any way directly under his control', they should forfeit their interest. It was held that the case fell directly within the principle laid down in *Sheppard's Touchstone*. The condition, Parker J said:[20]

> is inserted in the will with the direct object of deterring the father of these two children from performing his parental duties with regard to them, because it makes their worldly welfare dependent on his abstaining from doing what it is certainly his duty to do, namely, to bring his influence to bear and not give up his right to the custody, the control and education of his children.

It was accordingly declared to be void, with the result that the gift remained valid and not liable to be determined by breach of the condition. Similarly, in *Re Piper*,[21] in which a condition precedent in a will against residence with the father was held void as being calculated to bring about the separation of parent and child, the fact that the father had been divorced before the date of the will was held not to affect the matter. The condition was further held to be *malum prohibitum* and, accordingly, the gift to the children, being a gift of personalty, took effect free from it.

Dicta in *Blathwayt v Lord Cawley*[22] have, however, cast doubt on whether the principle was correctly applied in *Re Borwick*.[23] In that case, a condition subsequent under which children becoming Roman Catholics would forfeit their interests was held void on the ground that it operated to restrain or hamper their parents from doing their parental duty in regard to the religious instruction of their children. Their Lordships have now made it reasonably clear that not every condition that might affect or influence the way in which a child is brought up, or in which parental duties are exercised, is void on the principle set out above. In particular, a condition as to religious upbringing is not necessarily void

---

[17] Presumably only where it involves *malum prohibitum*.   [18] At p 132.

[19] [1912] 2 Ch 471. See also *Re Morgan* (1910) 26 TLR 398 (bequest to grandchildren on condition of living with mother if she and father live separately); *Re Boulter* [1922] 1 Ch 75 (condition against children residing abroad); *Re Johnston* [1980] NI 229.

[20] *Re Sandbrook* [1912] 2 Ch 471, 476.

[21] [1946] 2 All ER 503. See (1947) 11 Conv 218 (J H C Morris).   [22] *Supra*, HL.

[23] [1933] Ch 657.

because it may compel parents to make a choice between material prosperity and spiritual welfare for their children. A condition such as that, in *Re Sandbrook*,[24] with the direct object of deterring a father from performing his parental duty and from exercising any control at all over his children, is quite different from one tending to influence him to exercise his authority in a particular way. The mere fact that the existence of a condition may affect a parent's action does not necessarily mean that it is void as offending against public policy.

5 TRUSTS DESIGNED OR TENDING TO INDUCE A FUTURE SEPARATION OF HUSBAND AND WIFE, OR TO ENCOURAGE AN INVASION OF THE SANCTITY OF THE MARRIAGE BOND

Where a husband and wife have decided upon an immediate separation, trusts contained in a deed of separation entered into at that time are valid and will be enforced;[25] the point is that the separation in such case is not in any way induced by the trusts contained in the deed. By contrast, trusts that are made in contemplation of the future separation of a husband and wife then living together are void, because their existence might tend to bring about a separation that would not otherwise take place.[26]

A condition contained in a bequest to a married woman that she should live apart from her husband has been held[27] *contra bonos mores* and void on this ground. Again, in the case of the will of a testatrix giving her residue to her son absolutely with a proviso modifying the gift so long as the son's wife should be alive and married to him, but declaring that the absolute gift should take effect if the wife should die or the marriage be otherwise terminated, it was held that the provision was designed, or tended, to encourage an invasion of the sanctity of the marriage bond, and was, therefore, void as being against public policy.[28] The facts were somewhat similar and the decision the same in *Re Johnson's Will Trusts*,[29] in which a testator gave his residue of over £11,000 on protective trusts for his daughter for life, with a proviso cutting down her interest to £50 pa so long as she was married and living with her husband, but giving her the whole income in the event of her husband's death, or her divorce or separation from him. The result will be the same where the provision in question operates indirectly.[30]

The effect of each particular provision has to be carefully considered in every case. Thus, in *Re Lovell*,[31] a man, by his will, gave an annuity to his mistress, a married woman living

---

[24] [1912] 2 Ch 471.

[25] *Wilson v Wilson* (1848) 1 HL Cas 538; *Vansittart v Vansittart* (1858) 2 De G & J 249.

[26] *Westmeath v Westmeath* (1831) 1 Dow & Cl 519; *Re Moore* (1888) 39 Ch D 116, CA.

[27] *Wren v Bradley* (1848) 2 De G & Sm 49; *Re Freedman* (21 December 1942, unreported) referred to in *Re Caborne* [1943] Ch 224, [1943] 2 All ER 7.

[28] *Re Caborne* [1943] Ch 224, [1943] 2 All ER 7; *Re Hope Johnstone* [1904] 1 Ch 470.

[29] [1967] Ch 387, [1967] 1 All ER 553.

[30] See *Wilkinson v Wilkinson* (1871) LR 12 Eq 604 (condition against residence by wife in place where her husband lived and had his business).   [31] [1920] 1 Ch 122.

apart from her husband *'provided and so long as she shall not return to live with her present husband... or remarry'*. It was held that the provision was valid, as its object was not to induce her to continue to live apart from her husband and not to remarry, but to make provision for her until she returned to her husband or remarried. A similar decision was reached in *Re Thompson*,[32] in which a testator gave his daughter an annuity of £300, if still married to her present husband, but the income of the whole estate if she should become a widow, or remarried to another person, or divorced and not remarried to her present husband. It was held that the provision was not contrary to public policy, as the purpose was not to induce a divorce, but to prevent the income coming into the hands of the husband, regarded by the testator as a spendthrift. It has been suggested,[33] however, that this decision disregards the rule that the law looks to the general tendency of the disposition, and not to the possibility of public mischief occurring in the particular instance.

It may be added that it has recently been said[34] that there is nothing contrary to public policy in a cohabitation agreement governing the property relationship between adults who intend to cohabit, or who are cohabiting, for the purpose of enjoying a sexual relationship. The Law Commission[35] has said that it would expect this dictum to be followed, although it cannot be conclusively said that it represents the current state of English law.

6   TRUSTS IN RESTRAINT OF MARRIAGE

The law is difficult,[36] being complicated both by the differences in the rules relating to general and partial restraints, and also by the distinctions that have to be drawn between dispositions of realty, where the rules are based on the common law, and dispositions of personalty, where the rules adopted by the Court of Chancery came to it, with considerable modifications, from Roman Law by way of the ecclesiastical courts.[37]

So far as realty is concerned, there is no clear decision, but the weight of opinion is in favour of the view that a general restraint is prima facie void.[38] It seems, however, that whatever the form of the disposition, it will readily be treated as a limitation until marriage, which is valid, if the intention appears to be not to promote celibacy, but to make provision until marriage takes place.[39]

As far as personalty[40] is concerned, it is settled that a general restraint is prima facie void,[41] whether the restraint is general in so many words, or whether, although in terms

---

[32] [1939] 1 All ER 681.

[33] By Simonds J in *Re Caborne, supra*. Cf *Re Fentem* [1950] 2 All ER 1073; *Re Johnson's Will Trusts, supra*.

[34] *Per* Hart J in *Sutton v Michcon de Reya and Gawor & Co* [2003] EWHC 3166 (Ch), [2004] 1 FCR 837, at [22].   [35] Law Com No 307, Appendix A.21.

[36] 'Proverbially difficult', at least as to personalty, *per* Younger J in *Re Hewett* [1918] 1 Ch 458, 463.

[37] See *Re Whiting's Settlement* [1905] 1 Ch 96, 115–116, CA, *per* Vaughan Williams LJ; *Bellairs v Bellairs* (1874) LR 18 Eq 510, 513, *per* Jessel MR.

[38] White and Tudor, *Leading Cases in Equity*, 9th edn, vol I, p 487; *Jarman on Wills*, 8th edn, vol II, p 1528; (1896) 12 LQR 36 (C Williams). Contra *Theobald on Wills*, 16th edn, p 665.

[39] *Jones v Jones* (1876) 1 QBD 279, DC.

[40] Or a mixed fund representing the proceeds of sale of real estate and personalty: *Bellairs v Bellairs, supra*.

[41] *Bellairs v Bellairs, supra*; *Re Bellamy* (1883) 48 LT 212; *Re Hewett* [1918] 1 Ch 458.

partial, it is from its nature probable that in practice it would amount to a prohibition of marriage.[42] However, where the intention was not to promote celibacy, but, for instance, to make provision for the child of the person restrained,[43] or to ensure that, after the death of the person restrained, the property given would be dealt with in a particular manner,[44] the restraint has been held good. On principle, one might have thought that the court would not be entitled to look behind the general tendency of the provision, and examine its motive and intention in the light of the particular circumstances, and the ground of the public policy involved. However, in the cases above referred to, the court has regarded itself as entitled to make the necessary inquiry.[45] It is clear, however, that a gift until marriage is perfectly good,[46] the intention in such a case being assumed to be to provide for the beneficiary while unmarried, and not to prevent a marriage from taking place.

Partial restraints, whether with regard to realty or to personalty, are prima facie valid,[47] and accordingly the following conditions have been held good: against marriage with any person born in Scotland or of Scottish parents;[48] against marriage with a person who did not profess the Jewish religion and was not born a Jew;[49] against marriage with a domestic servant, or a person who had been a domestic servant;[50] against marriage with either of two named persons;[51] or against marriage without the consent of named persons.[52] For this purpose, a condition in restraint of a second or subsequent marriage, whether of a man or a woman, and whether the gift was by one spouse to the survivor, or by a stranger, is regarded as a partial restraint, and it is accordingly prima facie valid.[53]

There is, however, an important difference in the effect of a partial restraint imposed on realty and personalty, respectively. Lord Radcliffe[54] has stated the position in these words:

> For, whereas a condition subsequent in partial restraint of marriage was effective to determine the estate in the case of a devise of realty even without any new limitation to take effect on the forfeiture, so that a residuary devisee or heir came in of his own right,[55] it was early determined and consistently maintained that a condition subsequent in partial restraint of marriage, when annexed to a bequest of personalty,[56] was ineffective to destroy the gift

---

[42] *Re Lanyon* [1927] 2 Ch 264: marriage with a blood relation, however remote.

[43] *Re Hewett, supra*, in which the woman restrained was the testator's mistress and the child the fruit of their irregular union. See *Williams on Wills*, 8th edn, vol I, [35.2].

[44] *Re Fentem* [1950] 2 All ER 1073: a gift by a testatrix to her brother for life, with remainder to his personal representatives. The condition was attached only to the gift over after the brother's death.

[45] See also *Jones v Jones, supra*. Cf *Re Caborne* [1943] Ch 224, [1943] 2 All ER 7.

[46] *Morley v Rennoldson* (1843) 2 Hare 570; *Webb v Grace* (1848) 2 Ph 701.

[47] Unless void on some other ground, such as uncertainty. See, eg, *Clayton v Ramsden* [1943] AC 320, [1943] 1 All ER 16, HL; *Re Moss's Trusts* [1945] 1 All ER 207; *Blathwayt v Baron Cawley* [1976] AC 397, [1975] 3 All ER 625, HL; *Re Tepper's Will Trusts* [1987] Ch 358, [1987] 1 All ER 970.

[48] *Perrin v Lyon* (1807) 9 East 170.

[49] *Hodgson v Halford* (1879) 11 Ch D 959. Cf *Re Selby's Will Trusts* [1965] 3 All ER 386, [1966] 1 WLR 43 (condition precedent). See (1999) 19 LS 339 (D Cooper and D Herman).

[50] *Jenner v Turner* (1880) 16 ChD 188.

[51] *Re Bathe* [1925] Ch 377; *Re Hanlon* [1933] Ch 254.

[52] *Dashwood v Lord of Bulkeley* (1804) 10 Ves 230; *Lloyd v Branton* (1817) 3 Mer 108.

[53] *Leong v Lim Beng Chye* [1955] AC 648, [1955] 2 All ER 903, PC; *Allen v Jackson* (1875) 1 Ch D 399, CA.

[54] Giving the judgment of the Judicial Committee of the Privy Council in *Leong v Chye, supra*, at 660, 906.

[55] *Haughton v Haughton* (1824) 1 Mol 611; *Jenner v Turner, supra*.

[56] And possibly, where realty and personalty are given together: *Duddy v Gresham* (1878) 2 LR Ir 442.

unless the will in question contained an explicit gift over of the legacy to another legatee. And for this purpose a mere residuary bequest was not treated as a gift over.

In the latter case, where there is no gift over, the condition is said to be merely *in terrorem*— that is, intended merely in a monitory sense. Lord Radcliffe,[57] after emphasizing that it is impossible to give an account of the origin of the rule that is wholly logical, suggested that rather than base the rule on an artificial presumed intention, it is better to say simply that it is the presence in the will of the express gift over that determines the matter in favour of forfeiture.

7 TRUSTS THAT ARE NOT MERELY UNLAWFUL, BUT ALSO FRAUDULENT

As we have seen,[58] where the object of a trust is unlawful, in general, there will be a resulting trust for the settlor, or where the trust is declared by will, the property given will fall into the residuary estate of the testator. This is so not only when the trust offends against a technical rule such as the rule against perpetuities, but also where the trust is calculated to encourage an offence prohibited by statute.[59] Where, however, the object is not merely against the policy of the law, but is also fraudulent, further considerations have to be taken into account.

If the matter is still in the stage of contract or covenant, the fraud or illegality will, of course, make it unenforceable. This is not a matter of trust, but a matter of contract. As Lord Jauncey put it in *Tinsley v Milligan*:[60]

> it is trite law that the court will not give its assistance to the enforcement of executory provisions of an unlawful contract whether the illegality is apparent ex facie the document or whether the illegality of purpose of what would otherwise be a lawful contract emerges during the course of the trial.

We are concerned, however, to consider, at this point, cases in which a man, having conveyed or transferred property to another for some fraudulent and illegal purpose, subsequently claims that that other holds the property upon a resulting trust for him. The law on this matter was reviewed by the House of Lords in *Tinsley v Milligan*.[61] The facts

---

[57] *Leong v Lim Beng Chye* [1955] AC 648, 662, [1955] 2 All ER 903, 908, PC.

[58] See p 218, *supra*.   [59] *Thrupp v Collett* (1858) 26 Beav 125.

[60] [1994] 1 AC 340, [1993] 3 All ER 65, HL, discussed [1993] JBL 513 (A G J Berg); (1993) 143 NLJ 1577 (B Council); [1994] LMCLQ 163 (N Cohen); (1994) 57 MLR 441 (H Stowe); (1994) 45 NILQ 378 (S H Goo); (1994) 110 LQR 3 (R A Buckley); (1994) 14 Ox JLS 295 and (1995) 111 LQR 135 (N Enonchong); *Birkett v Acorn Business Machines Ltd* [1999] 2 All ER (Comm) 429, CA; *Barrett v Barrett* [2008] EWHC 1061 (Ch), [2008] BPIR 817. See also *Nelson v Nelson* (1995) 132 ALR 133, and for a comparative study with French law (1995) 44 AALR 196 (M Enonchong).

[61] [1994] 1 AC 340, [1993] 3 All ER 65, HL, applied *Lowson v Coombes* [1999] Ch 373, CA, noted (1999) 8 T & ELJ 3 (D Reade); [1999] Conv 242 (M P Thompson), in which a married man bought a house jointly with his mistress, but it was conveyed into her sole name with the illegal purpose of frustrating any potential claim by his wife under s 37(2)(b) of the Matrimonial Causes Act 1973; *Webb v Chief Constable of Merseyside Police* [2000] 1 All ER 209, CA; *Mortgage Express v Robson* [2001] EWCA Civ 887, [2001] 2 All ER (Comm) 881. See [2004] Conv 439 (Margaret Halliwell).

were that a house, to the purchase of which the parties contributed equally, was conveyed into the sole name of the appellant to enable the respondent to make false claims to the Department of Social Security (DSS) for benefits. The appellant claimed possession, and relied on the 'clean hands' doctrine to prevent the respondent from asserting a trust. The planned illegality of defrauding the DSS was, in fact, carried out, but without needing to make use of the conveyance, and the respondent, as it was said, 'made her peace with the DSS' soon after the action began, so there was no continuing illegality.

More recently, in *Tribe v Tribe*,[62] the plaintiff had transferred his shareholding in his family company to his son for a pretended consideration, which was not paid and was not intended to be paid. The transaction was carried out for the illegal purpose of deceiving his creditors by creating the appearance that he no longer owned any shares in the company. The illegal purpose, however, was never carried into effect: negotiations with the creditors were brought to a satisfactory conclusion without resorting to deception. When the plaintiff sought a retransfer of the shares, the son unsuccessfully contended that evidence of the illegal purpose could not be admitted in order to rebut the presumption of advancement in his favour.

In both of these last two cases, property had been put into the name of X with the mutual intention of concealing Y's interest in the property for a fraudulent or illegal purpose. Before *Tinsley v Milligan*,[63] the general rule was that, in such a case, Y could not recover the property irrespective of whether the presumption of advancement arose between the parties or not, but it now appears that a distinction must be made.[64] In any case, however, as Millet LJ has observed,[65] Y's action will fail if it would be illegal for him to retain any interest in the property. Thus, the claims rightly failed in *Curtis v Perry*,[66] in which a ship was registered in the name of one partner only to enable profits to be made by government contracts into which the other partner, who alleged a trust, could not enter, being a member of Parliament, and in *Ex Yallop*,[67] in which to admit the alleged resulting trust would have defeated the purpose of the statute requiring registration.

(A) WHERE THERE IS NO PRESUMPTION OF ADVANCEMENT

In *Tinsley v Milligan*,[68] all of the Law Lords agreed that, at law, property in chattels and land can pass under a contract that is illegal, and the transferee can enforce property rights so acquired provided that he does not need to rely on the illegal contract for any purpose other than providing the basis of his claim to a property right. It is irrelevant that the illegality of the underlying agreement was either pleaded or emerged in evidence: if the transferee has acquired legal title under the illegal contract, that is enough. Moreover, the same principles apply at law and in equity. Neither at law nor in equity may a party rely on his own fraud or illegality in order to found a claim or rebut a presumption, but the common law and equity alike will assist him to protect and enforce his property rights if he can do so without relying on the fraud or illegality.

---

[62] [1996] Ch 107, [1995] 4 All ER 236, CA noted [1996] CLJ 23 (G Virgo), applied *Painter v Hutchison* [2007] EWHC 758 (Ch), [2008] BPIR 170. See also (1996) 112 LQR 545 (F D Rose).

[63] [1994] 1 AC 340, [1993] 3 All ER 65, HL.

[64] In Australia, the distinction was rejected by all of the members of the court in *Nelson v Nelson, supra*.

[65] In *Tribe v Tribe, supra*, CA, at 252, 259.　　[66] (1802) 6 Ves 739.　　[67] (1808) 15 Ves 60.

[68] *Supra*, HL. See [1999] LMCLQ 465 (Imogen Cotterill).

This was the situation in *Tinsley v Milligan*,[69] in which it was not disputed that, apart from the question of illegality, the respondent would have been entitled in equity to a half-share in the property. In principle, this should be simply on the basis of a resulting trust by reason of her equal contribution to the purchase price, but Lord Browne-Wilkinson said that she had established a resulting trust by showing that she had contributed to the purchase price, and that there was a common understanding between her and the appellant that they should own the house equally. The clear theoretical distinction between a resulting and a constructive trust is again being blurred.

Whatever the basis of the equitable interest, there was no need for the respondent to allege or prove why she had allowed the house to be conveyed into the sole name of the appellant: 'The test is whether of necessity reliance is placed by the claimant on the illegality in proving his claim.'[70] Both Nourse and Millett LJJ in *Tribe v Tribe*[71] agreed that, where he can rely on a resulting trust, the transferor will normally be able to recover his property if the illegal purpose has not been carried out. However, where the illegal purpose has been carried out, Nourse and Millett LJJ expressed different views. Nourse LJ said that it was inherent in the decision in *Tinsley v Milligan*[72] that it makes no difference whether or not the illegal purpose has been carried into effect, as it clearly had been in that case. Millett LJ said that there is no invariable rule: a claim may fail where the illegal purpose has been carried out and the transferee can rely on the transferor's conduct as inconsistent with his retention of a beneficial interest.[73] It is not clear, however, what is the essential difference between the facts of *Tinsley v Milligan*[74] and the case put by Millett LJ—namely, that a transferor would not, in his view, be able to recover property transferred to a nephew in order to conceal it from creditors with whom he had subsequently settled on the footing that he had no interest in the property transferred.

In the most recent case, *Collier v Collier*,[75] although the dispute was between father and daughter, the case turned on whether the father could rely on an express agreement that his daughter would hold the leases that he had granted to her on trust for him, when the admittedly effective grants were intended to further an illegal purpose. It was held that he could not, unless he could resort to the doctrine of *locus poenitentiae*, which was not available on the facts. Mance LJ observed that if the presumption of advancement were to be applicable, the father would likewise fail, as he could only rebut it by disclosing his illegal purpose.

(B) WHERE THERE IS A PRESUMPTION OF ADVANCEMENT

In cases in which the presumption of advancement applies, such as *Tribe v Tribe*,[76] the plaintiff can only recover if he brings evidence that rebuts the presumption and shows that no gift was intended. It was held in that case that he can do this by leading evidence of an

---

[69] *Supra*, HL.

[70] *Per* Peter Gibson LJ in *Silverwood v Silverwood* (1997) 74 P & CR 453, 457, CA, in which *Tinsley v Milligan, supra*, HL, was applied.

[71] *Supra*, CA.   [72] *Supra*, HL.

[73] Millett LJ did not think that cases such as *Re Great Berlin Steamboat Co* (1884) 26 Ch D 616, CA (money placed to credit of a company to enable it to have a fictitious credit in case of inquiries at their bankers), had been impliedly overruled in *Tinsley v Milligan, supra*, HL.

[74] *Supra*, HL.   [75] [2002] EWCA Civ 1095, [2002] BPIR 1057.   [76] *Supra*, CA.

illegal purpose behind the transfer, provided that he has withdrawn from the transaction before the illegal purpose has been wholly or partly carried into effect. In the opinion of Millett LJ, voluntary withdrawal from an illegal transaction when it has ceased to be needed is sufficient. Unless and until the illegal purpose begins to be carried into effect, it is often said that he has a *locus poenitentiae*, but Nourse LJ said that this was a name that tended to mislead. Both Nourse and Millett LJJ refused to become embroiled in the application of that doctrine to executory contracts.

In *Tribe v Tribe* itself, the illegal purpose was not carried out, as we have seen, and the plaintiff was able to rebut the presumption of advancement. In *Gascoigne v Gascoigne*,[77] however, in which the husband intended to defeat his creditors by putting property in his wife's name while retaining the beneficial interest and had acted upon that dishonest intention, it was held that the wife was entitled to retain the property conveyed to her for her own use, notwithstanding that she was a party to the fraud; in *Tinker v Tinker*,[78] the husband, on the purchase of the matrimonial home, had it conveyed into his wife's name, to avoid its being taken by his creditors in case his business failed. It was found as a fact that he had acted honestly, not fraudulently. This evidence of his intention was held to strengthen the presumption of advancement and, accordingly, the husband had no claim to the house when the marriage broke up, although the wife had made no contribution to its purchase.[79]

(C) REIMBURSEMENT OF BENEFITS

In the Australian case of *Nelson v Nelson*,[80] Mrs Nelson had purchased property in the name of her children to enable her to obtain a subsidized loan from the Commonwealth by making a declaration that she did not own or have a financial interest in a house other than the one for which a subsidy was sought. The loan was obtained, but all of the members of the court were prepared to admit evidence to rebut the presumption of advancement,[81] tainted though it was by illegality and notwithstanding that the illegal purpose had been carried out. They held that there was a resulting trust in favour of Mrs Nelson. The majority, applying the maxim that 'he who seeks equity must do equity', went on to hold that Mrs Nelson must do equity by reimbursing the Commonwealth to the extent of the benefit that she had received. The minority allowed the appeal unconditionally, saying, however, that the Commonwealth should be informed and would presumably require repayment. The majority view has its attractions, but if a plaintiff, notwithstanding the illegality, is held to have an equitable property interest under a resulting trust, the English courts might well prefer the minority view. The maxim has normally been applied in relation to dealings between the parties, for example, where a person seeks to enforce a claim to an

---

[77] [1918] 1 KB 223, DC; *Re Emery's Investments' Trusts* [1959] Ch 410, [1959] 1 All ER 577.

[78] [1970] P 136, [1970] 1 All ER 540, CA, somewhat unconvincingly distinguished in *Heseltine v Heseltine* [1971] 1 All ER 952, [1971] 1 WLR 342, CA. See (1971) 115 Sol Jo 614 (S Cretney); (1980) 9 AALR 28 (G Kodilinye).

[79] Note, however, that such a conveyance into the wife's name may constitute a postnuptial settlement that the court has jurisdiction to vary under s 24(1)(c) of the Matrimonial Causes Act 1973.

[80] (1995) 132 ALR 133. See (1996) 10 Tru LI 51 (P H Pettit); (1996) 19 UQLJ 150 (P Butler); (1997) 60 MLR 102 (P Creighton); [1997] ALJ 195 (D Maclean); (1997) 19 Sydney LR 240.

[81] As to that presumption, see p 181, *supra*.

equitable interest in property, the court has required as a condition of giving effect to that equitable interest that an allowance be made for costs incurred, and for skill and labour expended in connection with the administration of the property.[82] In England, by reason of the decision in *Tribe v Tribe*,[83] the problem could only arise where there is no presumption of advancement.

8 LAW COMMISSION CONSULTATION PAPER 154[84]

The Law Commission considers that the law relating to the effect of illegality on trusts is in need of reform, by reason of the complexity and uncertainty of the law, and its potential to give rise to unjust decisions. While accepting the need to retain an illegality doctrine, it proposes the abandonment of the reliance principle laid down in *Tinsley v Milligan*[85] and *Tribe v Tribe*,[86] and the giving of a statutory discretion to the courts to declare an illegal trust to be invalid or valid. The court would be required to take into account:

(i)   the seriousness of the illegality;

(ii) the knowledge and intention of the illegal trust beneficiary;

(iii) whether invalidity would tend to deter the illegality;

(iv) whether invalidity would further the purpose of the rule that renders the trust 'illegal';

(v)   whether invalidity would be a proportionate response to the claimant's participation in the illegality.

The Commission further proposes that there should be no role for the 'clean hands' doctrine.

---

[82] *Re Berkeley Applegate (Investment Consultants) Ltd* [1989] Ch 32; [1988] 3 All ER 71.
[83] *Supra*, CA.   [84] The Law Commission intends to publish a report in Spring 2009.
[85] *Supra*, HL.   [86] *Supra*, CA.

12

VOIDABLE TRUSTS

In various circumstances in which it would be unfair to someone prejudiced thereby for an otherwise valid transaction to be allowed to stand, it may be set aside by the court, usually by virtue of statutory provisions. The first two sections of this chapter explain the relevant provisions of the Insolvency Act 1986, which enable certain transactions to be set aside for the benefit of a bankrupt's creditors, the powers being enlarged when the transaction was entered into with a positive intent to defraud creditors.

Section 173 of the Law of Property Act 1925 is noted briefly, but this is now of little practical importance. Much more important are the provisions contained in the Matrimonial Causes Act 1973 for the protection of a spouse or civil partner and the family, and those contained in the Inheritance (Provision for Family and Dependants) Act 1975. These are discussed in the fourth section of this chapter.

Apart from statute, sham trusts and what are known as 'illusory trusts', considered in the final two sections of this chapter, can also be set aside by the court.

1 TRANSACTIONS AT AN UNDERVALUE

(A) GENERAL

Where a settlor has become bankrupt, the relevant provisions of the Insolvency Act 1986 are designed to enable the trustee of the bankrupt's estate to recover the trust property for the benefit of the creditors. Section 339(1) provides that the trustee of the bankrupt's estate may apply to the court for an order under that section where an individual has been adjudged bankrupt and has, at a relevant time, entered into a transaction[1] with any person[2] at an undervalue. On such an application, the court may make such order as it thinks fit for restoring the position to what it would have been if that individual had not entered into that transaction.[3]

---

[1] See p 236, fn 16, for a case on the same words in s 423.

[2] The expression 'any person' in the corresponding provision dealing with companies (s 238) has been held to have its literal meaning, unrestricted as to persons or territory. The safeguards are that the court's power to make an order is discretionary and, in the case of persons who are abroad, the leave of the court must be obtained for service abroad: *Re Paramount Airways Ltd* [1993] Ch 223, [1992] 3 All ER 1, CA.

[3] Section 339(2). The value is to be assessed as at the date of the transaction: *Re Thoars (decd)* [2002] EWHC 2416 (Ch), [2003] BPIR 489. Cf s 423(2) discussed p 236, *infra*. See, generally, (1987) 17 Fam Law 316 (N Furey); [2001] CWLR 206 (A Keay).

(B) MEANING OF 'UNDERVALUE'

An individual enters into a transaction at an undervalue if:

  (a) he makes a gift to that person or he otherwise enters into a transaction with that person on terms that provide for him to receive no consideration,

  (b) he enters into a transaction with that person in consideration of marriage or the formation of a civil partnership, or

  (c) he enters into a transaction with that person for a consideration the value of which, in money or money's worth, is significantly less than the value, in money or money's worth, of the consideration provided by the individual.[4]

(C) THE RELEVANT TIME

A transaction at an undervalue can only be upset by the court if it was entered into at a relevant time. This is defined in s 341(1) as a time in the period of five years ending with the day of the presentation of the bankruptcy petition on which the individual is adjudged bankrupt.

Within the five-year period, a distinction is drawn between a time that is less than two years, and one that is two years or more, before the end of the five-year period. There are no qualifications if the transaction was entered into within two years of the bankruptcy, but within the period of two to five years before the bankruptcy, a time is not a relevant time unless the individual was insolvent at that time, or becomes insolvent in consequence of the transaction. However, this qualification is presumed to be satisfied, unless the contrary is shown, in relation to any transaction at an undervalue that is entered into by an individual with a person who is an associate of his.[5] For the purposes of these provisions, a person is insolvent if he is unable to pay his debts as they fall due, or the value of his assets is less than the amount of his liabilities, taking into account his contingent and prospective liabilities.[6]

---

  [4] Section 339(3), as amended by the Civil Partnership Act 2004, s 261(1), Sch 27, para 119. In the ordinary case, a transferee under a transfer made pursuant to a property transfer order under the Matrimonial Causes Act 1973 is regarded as having given consideration within s 339 that is equivalent to the value of the property being transferred, unless the case was an exceptional one in which it could be demonstrated that the property transfer order had been obtained by fraud or some broadly similar exceptional circumstance: *Hill v Haines* [2007] EWCA Civ 1284, [2008] 2 All ER 901, noted (2008) 38 Fam Law 123 (Margaret Hatwood and Sandra Bayne); (2008) 93 T & ELTJ 15 (Georgina Vallance-Webb); [2008] PCB 227 (G Miller); (2008) 38 Fam Law 418 (A Start and W Edwards); (2008) 124 LQR 361 (D Capper). Although not essential, it is preferable for the court to arrive at precise figures for the incoming and outgoing values where it is possible to do so: *Ramlort Ltd v Reid* [2004] EWCA Civ 800, [2004] BPIR 985.

  [5] Section 341(2). 'Associate' is defined in s 435. A person is an associate (i) of an individual if that person is the individual's husband or wife or civil partner, or is a relative, or the husband or wife or civil partner of a relative, of the individual or of the individual's husband or wife or civil partner, (ii) of any person with whom he is in partnership and the husband or wife or civil partner or a relative of any individual with whom he is in partnership, and (iii) of any person by whom he is employed. Further, a person in his capacity of trustee of a trust is, with certain exceptions, an associate of another person if the beneficiaries of the trust include, or the terms of the trust confer a power that may be exercised for the benefit of, that other person or an associate of that other person. 'Relative' is defined in s 435(8) as amended by the Civil Partnership Act 2004, s 261(1), Sch 27, para 122.

  [6] Section 341(3).

Special provisions are made in the case of criminal bankruptcy.[7] In this case, a transaction is treated as having been entered into at a relevant time if it was entered into at any time on or after the date specified in the criminal bankruptcy order on which the petition was based.[8]

(D) THE ORDER OF THE COURT

Without prejudice to the generality of the power of the court to make such order as it thinks fit,[9] s 342 spells out particular orders that the court may make. Under sub-s 1(a) and (b), these clearly include orders to direct trustees to vest appropriate property, whether in its original form or in any form that represents it, in the trustee of the bankrupt's estate. Further, the overall discretion of the court is wide enough to enable it to make no order where, exceptionally, justice so requires.[10]

The power of the court to make an order is not limited to the person with whom the bankrupt entered into the transaction, but a third party will be protected in his interest if he can show that he acquired it in good faith and for value.[11] However, it is presumed that the interest was acquired otherwise than in good faith if, at the time of its acquisition, the third party had notice of the relevant surrounding circumstances[12] and of the relevant proceedings,[13] or was in some way connected with either party to the original transaction.[14]

It may be added that the fact that a settlement or transfer of property had to be made in order to comply with a property adjustment order under the Matrimonial Causes Act 1973 does not prevent it being a transaction in respect of which an order may be made under s 339.[15]

---

[7] Under s 264(1)(d), repealed from a date to be appointed: Criminal Justice Act 1988, s 170, Sch 16. Note the power of the court to make confiscation orders under ibid, ss 71 *et seq*, as amended.

[8] Section 341(4). By subs (5), no order is to be made under s 339 where an appeal is pending. Both of these subsections are repealed from a date to be appointed by the Criminal Justice Act 1988, s 170, Sch 16.

[9] The court does not start with a presumption in favour of monetary compensation as opposed to setting aside the transaction: *Ramlort Ltd v Reid* [2004] EWCA Civ 800, [2004] BPIR 985. There are special provisions in relation to excessive pension contributions in ss 342A–342F, as inserted, or substituted for sections previously inserted, by the Welfare Reform and Pensions Act 1999.

[10] As was the case in *Singla v Brown* [2007] EWHC 405 (Ch), [2007] BPIR 424, [2008] 2 WLR 283.

[11] Section 342(2), as amended by the Insolvency (No 2) Act 1994, s 2(1).

[12] That is, the fact that the individual in question entered into the transaction at an undervalue: Insolvency Act 1986, s 342(4), as substituted by the Insolvency (No 2) Act 1994, s 2(3).

[13] A person has notice of the relevant proceedings if he has notice (a) of the fact that the petition on which the individual in question is adjudged bankrupt has been presented, or (b) of the fact that the individual in question has been adjudged bankrupt: Insolvency Act 1986, s 342(5), added by the Insolvency (No 2) Act 1994, s 2(3).

[14] Insolvency Act 1986, s 342(2A), added by the Insolvency (No 2) Act 1994, s 2(2). See (1994) 138 Sol Jo 710 (R Potterton and S Cullen).

[15] See s 39 of the Matrimonial Causes Act 1973, as amended by s 235(1) and Sch 8, para 23, of the Insolvency Act 1985, and s 439(2) and Sch 14 to the Insolvency Act 1986.

2 TRANSACTIONS DEFRAUDING CREDITORS

(A) GENERAL

The substance of ss 423–425 of the Insolvency Act 1986 is to empower the court to make an appropriate order to protect the interests of persons who are the victims of certain specific transactions. Section 423, like s 339, relates to transactions entered into[16] at an undervalue,[17] but, unlike s 339, is not restricted to transactions taking place within a certain period. It applies whether or not the transferor was about to engage in a risky or hazardous business when he entered into the transaction.[18] Again, s 423 applies whether or not insolvency proceedings have been taken while, as we have seen, s 339 only applies where an individual has been adjudged bankrupt. In these respects, s 423 is wider than s 339. In one respect, however, it is narrower: s 339 does not call f or any intent on the part of the bankrupt; all that has to be established is the transaction at an undervalue at a relevant time. Under s 423, the court only has jurisdiction if it is satisfied that the transaction was entered into for the purpose:[19]

(a) of putting assets beyond the reach of a person[20] who is making, or may at some time make, a claim against him, or

(b) of otherwise prejudicing the interests of such a person in relation to the claim which he is making or may make.[21]

The power of the court under s 423 is somewhat wider than under s 339. There is the same power in s 423(2) for the court to make such order as it thinks fit for '(a) restoring the position to what it would have been if the transaction had not been entered into', but while s 339(2) stops at that point, s 423(2) continues 'and (b) protecting the interests of persons who are victims of the transaction'. The word 'and' between (a) and (b) is to be read conjunctively.[22] A victim of a transaction is a person who is, or is capable of being, prejudiced by it.[23] It is not restricted to only those of the debtor's creditors that he had in contemplation when he

---

[16] *Department for Environment, Food and Rural Affairs v Feakins* (2004) Times, 20 December (a person can enter into a transaction at an undervalue by simply participating in an arrangement that resulted in the undervalued transaction); *Beckenham MC Ltd v Centralex Ltd* [2004] EWHC 1287 (Ch), [2004] BPIR 1112 (s 423 prima facie applies to a transfer by a trustee, but transaction will normally, but not always, be protected by s 423(2)).

[17] Defined in s 423(1) in similar terms to s 339(3), as amended, set out p 231, *supra*. Section 423 is concerned with actual value, not book value: *Pena v Coyne* [2004] EWHC 2684 (Ch), [2004] 2 BCLC 703. See *Agricultural Mortgage Corpn Ltd v Woodward* [1995] 1 BCLC 1; *Barclays Bank plc v Bean* [2004] 3 EGLR 71, and, generally, [1998] Conv 362 (G Miller).

[18] *Sands v Clitheroe* [2006] BPIR 1000.

[19] Note that the wording of s 423 is subjective: *Pagemanor Ltd v Ryan* [2002] BPIR 593. What must be shown is that the bankrupt was substantially motivated by one or other of the aims set out in s 423(3)(a) and (b) in entering into the transaction in question: *IRC v Hashim* [2002] EWCA 981, [2002] 2 BCLC 489, applied *Kubiangha v Ekpenyong* [2002] EWHC 1567 (Ch), [2003] BPIR 623. See (2002) 36 T & ELJ 21 (Suzanne Popovic-Monyag), discussing *Stone v Stone* (2001) 55 OR(3d) 491; [2003] Conv 272 (A Keay).

[20] The section does not require the applicant to establish that the purpose of the transaction was to put assets beyond the applicant's reach: *Jyske Bank (Gibraltar) Ltd v Spjeldnaes* [1999] 2 BCLC 101.

[21] Section 423(3). See *Midland Bank plc v Wyatt* [1997] 1 BCLC 242.

[22] *Chohan v Sagger* [1994] 1 BCLC 706, and see *Ram v Ram* [2004] EWCA Civ 1452, [2005] 2 FLR 63.

[23] Section 423(5). See *Chohan v Saggar* [1994] 1 BCLC 706, CA.

entered into the transaction under attack. Anyone who, in fact, proves to be prejudiced by the transaction may claim to be a victim.[24]

A claim under s 423 is a 'breach of duty' within s 32(2) of the Limitation Act 1980.[25]

(B) WHO MAY APPLY FOR AN ORDER

An application for an order under s 423 cannot be made except:

(a) in a case where the debtor has been adjudged bankrupt,...by the official receiver, by the trustee of the bankrupt's estate...or, (with the leave of the court), by a victim of the transaction;

(b) in a case where a victim of the transaction is bound by a voluntary arrangement approved under...Part VIII of the Act,[26] the supervisor of the voluntary arrangement or any person who (whether or not so bound) is such a victim, or;

(c) in any other case, a victim of the transaction.[27]

It is expressly provided[28] that whoever makes the application, it is to be treated as made on behalf of every victim of the transaction.

(C) THE ORDER OF THE COURT

Section 425 contains provisions corresponding to those in s 342,[29] modified only to allow for the fact that s 423, unlike s 339, is not restricted to cases in which the individual who entered into the transaction at an undervalue has been adjudged bankrupt.

(D) ASSET PROTECTION TRUSTS

The so-called 'asset protection trust'—the term is imprecise—has primarily been developed in the USA, and is designed to hold assets beyond the reach of creditors, including the revenue authorities. It has made little headway in England, partly, no doubt, because of the above provisions. Further, s 357 provides for criminal penalties, and a professional adviser involved in arranging such a trust to defraud creditors could become liable in a criminal conspiracy or in aiding and abetting a s 357 crime.[30] A trust, however, may be, and commonly is, drafted quite properly with the purpose and effect of avoiding tax, and the protective trust, as we have seen,[31] may operate to defeat the claims of the creditors of a spendthrift life tenant.

---

[24] *Sands v Clitheroe, supra; Giles v Rhind* [2008] EWCA Civ 118, [2008] 3 All ER 697.

[25] *Giles v Rhind, supra*, CA.

[26] That is, a proposal made by the debtor to his creditors for a composition in satisfaction of his debts or a scheme of arrangement of his affairs. The procedure under Pt VIII is additional to the provisions in the Deeds of Arrangement Act 1914.

[27] Section 424, as amended.   [28] Section 424(2).

[29] Discussed p 235, *supra*. In unusual circumstances, monetary compensation was ordered in place of setting aside the transaction in *Pena v Coyne (No 2)* [2004] EWHC 2685 (Ch), [2004] 2 BCLC 730. See *Moon v Franklin* [1996] BPIR 196.

[30] *Midland Bank plc v Wyatt* [1997] 1 BCLC 242, and see [1994] PCB 96 (R Citron and M Steiner); 239 (J McLeuchlan and M Steiner); [1997] PCB 77 (P Willoughby).

[31] See p 81 *et seq, supra*.

3 VOLUNTARY SETTLEMENT OF LAND FOLLOWED BY CONVEYANCE FOR VALUABLE CONSIDERATION

Under s 173 of the Law of Property Act 1925, a voluntary settlement of land made with intent to defraud a subsequent purchaser is voidable at the instance of such a purchaser being a bona fide purchaser for value. The onus of establishing an actual intent to defraud rests on the party alleging it.[32] This provision does not affect a bona fide purchaser for value who purchased the interest of a beneficiary under the settlement prior to the disposition for value.[33]

4 PROVISIONS FOR PROTECTION OF SPOUSE OR CIVIL PARTNER AND FAMILY

(A) SECTION 37 OF THE MATRIMONIAL CAUSES ACT 1973

By virtue of this section, a spouse or former spouse, or civil partner or former civil partner, who has brought proceedings for financial relief[34] against the other party may apply to the court for an order setting aside any 'reviewable' disposition[35] that the court is satisfied[36] was made with the intention—that is, the other party's subjective intention (which need not be the sole or even the dominant intention)—of defeating the claim for financial relief. It is open to the court to conclude that, in making the disposition, the other party knew and intended the inevitable result of his action.[37] If the application is made before financial relief has been granted, the claimant must show that if the disposition were set aside, the court would grant financial relief or different financial relief. A disposition is a 'reviewable disposition' unless it was 'made for valuable consideration (other than marriage) to a person who, at the time of the disposition, acted in relation to it in good faith and without notice of any intention on the part of the other party to defeat the applicant's claim for financial

---

[32] *Moore v Kelly* [1918] 1 IR 169.   [33] *Prodger v Langham* (1663) 1 Keb 486.

[34] Defined in s 37(1) by reference to specified provisions of the Act.

[35] 'Disposition' is defined by s 37(6) in terms wide enough to include a trust. The court may also restrain a threatened disposition of property, even though it be land situated abroad: *Hamlin v Hamlin* [1986] Fam 11, [1985] 2 All ER 1037, CA. See also *Shipman v Shipman* [1991] 1 FLR 250. The section only applies to transactions effected by the other party, and does not apply to transactions effected by a third party for the benefit of that other party: *McGladdery v McGladdery* [2000] 1 FCR 315, CA.

[36] As to the standard of proof, see *K v K* (1982) Times, 16 February, CA; *Kemmis v Kemmis* [1988] 1 WLR 1307, CA, noted [1989] Conv 204 (Jane Fortin); *Trowbridge v Trowbridge* [2002] EWHC 3114 (Ch), [2004] 2 FCR 79.

[37] *Kemmis v Kemmis, supra*, CA.

relief'.[38] 'Notice' includes constructive, as well as actual, notice.[39] This provision operates to protect intermediate bona fide dealing for value between the date of the disposition and the date of its being set aside.

Where the disposition was made three years or more before the application, the claimant must prove affirmatively the other party's intention to defeat the claim. Where, however, the disposition was made less than three years before the application, this intention is presumed, if the effect of the disposition would be to defeat the claim, or, where an order for relief is already in force, if it has had this effect: the presumption can be rebutted by evidence to the contrary, but the onus of proof in this case rests on the other party.[40]

(B) INHERITANCE (PROVISION FOR FAMILY AND DEPENDANTS) ACT 1975

This Act[41] enables the court to review dispositions (including dispositions by way of trust) effected by the deceased otherwise than for full valuable consideration and made with the intention,[42] although not necessarily the sole, or even the dominant, intention,[43] of defeating applications for financial provision in whole or in part. The Act applies to dispositions made less than six years before the date of the death of the deceased.

5 SHAM TRUSTS

What appears on the face of it to be a trust may be set aside as a sham if the truth of the matter is that the settlor retains full beneficial entitlement and there is no intention that the apparent beneficiaries shall obtain any benefit. The definition in *Snook v London and West Riding Investments Ltd*[44] is constantly cited—namely, that:

> if it has any meaning in law, [sham] means acts done or documents executed by the parties to the "sham" which are intended by them to give to third parties or to the court the appearance of creating between the parties legal rights and obligations different from the actual rights and obligations (if any) which the parties intend to create.

---

[38] Section 37(4). See *Whittingham v Whittingham* [1979] Fam 9, [1978] 3 All ER 805, *per* Balcombe J, affd CA on other grounds, at 813; *Green v Green* [1981] 1 All ER 97.

[39] *Kemmis v Kemmis, supra,* CA; *Sherry v Sherry* [1991] 1 FLR 307, CA, noted [1991] Conv 370 (Jane Fortin).

[40] Section 37(5). The onus was discharged in *Shipman v Shipman* [1991] 1 FLR 250.

[41] Sections 10–14. Under the Civil Partnership Act 2004, the 1975 Act applies in relation to a civil partnership as it applies to marriage: s 71, Sch 4, para 2.

[42] On a balance of probabilities.

[43] *Re Dawkins, Dawkins v Judd* [1986] 2 FLR 360; *Kemmis v Kemmis, supra,* CA.

[44] [1967] 2 QB 786, 802, [1967] 1 All ER 518, 528, CA ; *Raftland Pty Ltd v Federal Commissioners of Taxation* [2006] WTLR 657 (Aust); *Kensington International Ltd v Republic of the Congo* [2005] EWHC 2684 (Comm), [2006] 2 BCLC 296. Cf *Bhopal & Kaur v Wilia* (1999) 32 HLR 302, CA (oral agreement for a tenancy at a rent of £300 per month. Written agreement for tenancy at £450 per month to mislead vendor's bank held to be a sham giving rise to no legal rights or obligations). See [2008] CLJ 176 (M Conaglen); see also [2004] PCB 95 (D Harris); [1999] NZLJ 462 (R Holmes).

Arden LJ, in *Hitch v Stone*,[45] said that the authorities established the following points:

(i)   the court, in addition to examining the document itself, may examine external evidence;

(ii)   the test of intention is subjective—the parties must have intended to create rights and obligations other than those appearing on the face of document, and, further, must have intended to give third parties a false impression of what the rights and obligations created were;

(iii) the mere fact that the act or document is uncommercial, or artificial, does not mean that it is a sham—for it to be a sham, the parties must have intended to be bound by some other arrangement;

(iv)   the fact that parties subsequently depart from the terms set out in an agreement does not necessarily mean that they never intended that it should be effective and binding;

(v)   a trust deed is not a sham unless both the settlor and the trustee intended that the true arrangement should be different from that appearing in the trust deed.

It seems, however, that a sham transaction will remain a sham transaction even if one of the parties to it merely went along with the shamming, neither knowing nor caring what he or she was signing.[46]

Another apparent trust that may, perhaps, be set aside as a sham is what is sometimes referred to as a 'Red Cross trust'. This is a trust in a wide discretionary form set up with a single named beneficiary, such as 'the Red Cross', but with the trustees having wide powers to add the settlor and his family, and where there is evidence that the Red Cross is not intended to benefit.[47]

The nature of a trust is determined when it is created. A trust that is not initially a sham cannot subsequently become one, unless all of the beneficiaries, with the requisite intention, join together for that purpose with the trustees.[48] However, a trust that is initially a sham can subsequently lose that character. If a new trustee is appointed, he cannot become an unknowing party to an earlier sham. Once a new trustee becomes the legal owner of the trust property, provided that he exercises his powers and fulfils his duties in accordance

---

[45] [2001] EWCA Civ 63, [2001] STC 214, applied *Re Esteem Settlement* [2003] JLR 188 (Jersey Royal Court), discussed (2003) 52 T & ELJ 14 (K Lawrence and V Connolly). See *Midland Bank plc v Wyatt* [1995] 3 FCR 11; *Abdel Rahman v Chase Bank (CI) Trust Co Ltd* [1991] JLR 105 (Jersey Royal Court), noted [1993] PCB 94 (R C Lawrence III); *Re Nurkowski (a bankrupt), Hill v Spread Trustee Co Ltd* [2005] BPIR 842, appeal dismissed [2006] EWCA Civ 542, [2007] 1 All ER 1106, [2007] 1 WLR 2409 (no appeal on sham point); *Mackinnon v The Regent Trust Co Ltd* [2005] JCA 066, [2005] WTLR 1376. See also [1996] PCB 228 (P Willoughby); (1999) 6 T & ELJ 11 (C Syed); [1999] NZLJ 462 (R Holmes); [2000] PCB 28, 105 (J Mowbray); [2005] PCB 69 (D Hochberg); (2006) 74 T & ELTJ 24 (C Gothard and Henrietta Sargant); (2007) 21 TruLI 191 (P Matthews).

[46] *Midland Bank plc v Wyatt, supra*; *Minwalla v Minwalla* [2004] 2823 (Fam), [2005] 1 FLR 771, noted (2005) 70 T & ELTJ 18 (R Ticehurst). In further proceedings in *C I Law Trustees v Minwalla* [2005] JRC 099, [2006] WTLR 807, the Jersey Royal Court was prepared, in '*the unusual and particular circumstances*' of the case, to recognize and enforce the judgment of the English court, at least in part.

[47] This is sometimes called a 'black hole' trust. See [2002] PCB 42, 110 (P Matthews). See also *TR Technology Investment Trusts plc* [1988] BCLC 256, and the Isle of Man litigation in *Steele v Paz Ltd (in liq)* (10 October 1995, unreported), extracts from which appear in Butterworths' *Offshore Cases and Materials*, 1996, vol I, p 338.

[48] *A v A* [2007] EWHC 99 (Fam), [2007] 2 FLR 407.

with the terms of the trust instrument, the trust cannot be regarded as a sham, no matter what might have passed before.[49]

Although not a sham, it is convenient to note here that there is an irreducible core of obligations owed by the trustees to the beneficiaries and enforceable by them that is fundamental to the concept of a trust. If the beneficiaries have no trusts enforceable against the trustees, there are no trusts and an apparent trust document will have no effect as such. In so holding in *Armitage v Nurse*,[50] Millett LJ refused to accept that these core obligations included the duties of skill and care, prudence, and diligence. The duty of the trustees to perform the trusts honestly and in good faith for the benefit of the beneficiaries was, he said, the minimum necessary to give substance to the trusts, and, in his opinion, was sufficient.

However, it seems that commercial arrangements in the context of a specialized business environment will be upheld, even though their enforcement reduces the obligations of the trustee below the 'irreducible core'.[51]

6 ILLUSORY TRUSTS

Illusory trusts are really examples of sham trusts, but merit separate treatment, as they are subject to a long line of authority.

(A) TRUSTS FOR THE BENEFIT OF CREDITORS[52]

If a valid trust is created, it cannot be revoked, unless the settlement itself contains a power of revocation. There appears to be an exception to this rule where a debtor conveys or transfers property to trustees for the benefit of his creditors. Such a disposition is prima facie revocable by the debtor, but the true view in such a case is that the apparent beneficiaries have never acquired any equitable interest in the property at all. The trustees, in the eye of equity, hold the property conveyed or transferred to them on trust for the debtor himself absolutely. The debtor 'proposes only a benefit to himself by the payment of his debts—his object is not to benefit his creditors'.[53] The trustees are, in effect, mere mandatories or agents[54] of the debtor, who, it has been said:[55]

is merely directing the mode in which his own property shall be applied for his own benefit, and...the general creditors, or the creditors named on the schedule, are merely persons named there for the purpose of showing how the trust property under the voluntary deed shall be applied for the benefit of the volunteers.

---

[49] *A v A, supra.*   [50] [1998] Ch 241, [1997] 2 All ER 705, CA.
[51] See *Citibank NA v MBIA Assurance SA* [2007] EWCA Civ 11, [2007] 1 All ER (Comm) 475, noted (2007) 123 LQR 342 (S Trukhtanov). See also *Australian Securities and Investments Commission v Citigroup Global Markets Australia Pty Ltd* [2007] FCA 963, noted (2008) 124 LQR 15 (J Getzler).
[52] See, generally, (1957) 21 Conv 280 (L A Sheridan).
[53] *Bill v Cureton, supra*, at 511, *per* Pepys MR.
[54] See *Acton v Woodgate* (1833) 2 My & K 492, *per* Leach MR.
[55] *Garrard v Lord Lauderdale* (1830) 3 Sim 1, 12, *per* Shadwell VC; affd (1931) 2 Russ & My 451.

The deed, in substance, operates merely as a power to the trustees that is revocable by the debtor.

(B) WHERE THE TRUST BECOMES IRREVOCABLE

In various circumstances, the court will draw the inference that the prima facie rule does not represent the intention of the debtor, and that the deed accordingly creates a true trust for the benefit of the creditors, or, at any rate, some of them. This will clearly be the case as regards those creditors who have executed the deed,[56] or who have acted on the deed, for instance by forbearing to sue,[57] or have expressly assented, not necessarily formally, to the trust,[58] or where they have been expressly or impliedly told by the debtor that they may look to the trust property for the payment of their debts.[59] Mere communication of the trust to a creditor that is not dissented from by him may well be sufficient by itself to make the trust irrevocable, but the law on this point is confused.[60]

A deed has been held to be irrevocable where the obvious intention of the transaction would be frustrated if the debtor were to retain a power of revocation. Thus, in *New, Prance and Garrard's Trustee v Hunting*,[61] the debtor conveyed the property to trustees on trust to raise £4,200 to make good breaches of trust committed by the debtor. The obvious purpose, it was said, was thereby to mitigate the penal consequences of the breaches of trust, which purpose required the creation of an irrevocable binding trust.

The effect of the death of the debtor is not clear. If the trust is to commence only after the debtor is dead, it seems that it makes it irrevocable.[62] Where the trust is to pay either during the debtor's lifetime or after his death, the authorities are contradictory as to whether the death of the debtor makes the trust irrevocable.[63]

Lastly, it has been held that the mandatory theory does not apply to an assignment made to a creditor as trustee for himself and other creditors; the debtor cannot revoke such a deed after it has been communicated to the assignee.[64]

(C) DEEDS OF ARRANGEMENT ACT 1914

This Act considerably reduces the practical importance of the law as stated above. It provides that a deed of arrangement[65] made by a debtor for the benefit of his creditors generally, or, if he was insolvent at the date of the execution thereof, for the benefit of any three or more of them, shall be void if not registered with the registrar appointed by the Board of

---

[56] *Montefiore v Browne* (1858) 7 HL Cas 241; *Mackinnon v Stewart* (1850) 1 Sim NS 76; *Johns v James* (1878) 8 Ch D 744, CA.

[57] *Nicholson v Tutin* (1855) 2 K & J 18; *Re Baber's Trusts* (1870) LR 10 Eq 554.

[58] *Harland v Binks* (1850) 15 QB 713.   [59] *Synnot v Simpson* (1854) 5 HL Cas 121.

[60] In favour of a trust, *Adnitt v Hands* (1887) 57 LT 370, DC; *Re Sanders' Trusts* (1878) 47 LJ Ch 667; contra, *Cornthwaite v Frith* (1851) 4 De G & Sm 552; *Re Michael* (1891) 8 Morr 305, DC. See also *Mackinnon v Stewart, supra; Montefiore v Browne, supra.*

[61] [1897] 2 QB 19, CA; affd on another ground [1899] AC 419, HL. See also *Radcliffe v Abbey Road & St John's Wood Permanent Building Society* (1918) 87 LJ Ch 557.

[62] *Re Fitzgerald's Settlement* (1887) 37 Ch D 18, CA; *Priestley v Ellis* [1897] 1 Ch 489.

[63] In favour of a continued power of revocation: *Garrard v Lord Lauderdale, supra* (assumed without discussion); *Re Sanders' Trusts* (1878) 47 LJ Ch 667; contra, *Montefiore v Browne, supra; Priestley v Ellis, supra.*

[64] *Siggers v Evans* (1855) 5 E & B 367.   [65] Defined in s 1.

Trade within seven days of its execution.[66] Further, if a deed of arrangement is expressed to be, or is in fact, for the benefit of a debtor's creditors generally, it will be void unless it has received the written assent of a majority in number and value of the creditors within twenty-one days after registration.[67]

It should also be noted that a deed of arrangement affecting unregistered land may be registered under the Land Charges Act 1972,[68] and if not so registered, will be void as against a purchaser for valuable consideration.[69] In the case of registered land, the procedure to protect the priority of a deed of arrangement is to enter a notice in the register.[70]

---

[66] Section 2, subject to the Administration of Estates Act 1925, s 22(1).

[67] Deeds of Arrangement Act 1914, s 3, as amended by the Insolvency Act 1985, s 235 and Sch 8, para 22, and the Insolvency Act 1986, s 439(2) and Sch 14.

[68] Land Charges Act 1972, s 7(1).   [69] Ibid, s 7(2).

[70] Land Registration Act 2002, ss 32 and 87(1)(d).

13

CHARITABLE TRUSTS

The very fact that there are two chapters devoted to charitable trusts indicates that there are differences between them and non-charitable, or private, trusts. The differences must not be exaggerated: in most cases, the rules relating to charitable and non-charitable trusts are the same. However, there are some very important differences, which may go to the very validity of the trust—for instance, in relation to certainty, or perpetuity—or which may have important economic consequences—for instance, in relation to tax. The effect of these differences is the reason why it may be necessary to contend that a trust is, or is not, charitable.

Before entering into a legal analysis, it may be helpful to refer to the way in which the Charity Commission has summarized the essential characteristics of a charity. It has done so in the following terms:[1]

A charity:
- (a) has aims all of which are, and continue to be, recognized by law as exclusively charitable ie that are:
  - (i) directed to the provision of something of clear benefit to others in society;
  - (ii) not concerned with benefiting individuals in a way which outweighs any benefit to the public;
  - (iii) directed to things that overall are not harmful to humankind;
  - (iv) certain and lawful;
  - (v) not for the pursuit of party or other political aims;
- (b) is independent;
- (c) is able to show that any personal, professional or commercial advantage, is or will continue to be incidental to carrying out its charitable aims;
- (d) does not impose conditions on access or membership that in practice restricts the availability of facilities in a way that results in the organization as a whole not benefiting the public.

In the first section of this chapter, the most important of the differences between charitable and non-charitable trusts are considered; the second section establishes the legal meaning of 'charity' and 'charitable purposes', as laid down by statute. The third and fourth sections look in some detail at the different heads of charity, and the fifth section notes some purposes which have been held not to be charitable. The last two sections consider the overriding requirement of public benefit, which has acquired greater importance as a consequence of the Charities Act 2006, and the exceptional cases to which the requirement does not apply.

---

[1] See RR1—the first of a series of publications relating to the review of the register.

1 DIFFERENCE BETWEEN CHARITABLE AND NON-CHARITABLE TRUSTS

(A) CERTAINTY

(i) Basic position

The ordinary rule, as we have seen,[2] is that a private trust will fail if there is no certainty of objects, and thus, for instance, gifts for public or for benevolent purposes, or for worthy causes,[3] are void for uncertainty since the words used have no technical legal meaning. Where, however, there is a clear intention to give property for charitable purposes, the gift will not fail on that ground. 'Charity' and 'charitable' are words with a technical legal meaning, and, accordingly, if trustees are given discretion to distribute property amongst charitable objects, the court can determine whether any object chosen is charitable or not, and, as we shall see,[4] a procedure is available for selecting the objects of a gift to charity where the settlor or testator either makes no provisions for the purpose or the provisions are for any reason ineffective. The certainty required is certainty of intention to devote the property exclusively to charitable purposes. Thus a gift 'for the relief and benefit of the deserving poor and needy in the district in which I farmed' was held to be a valid charitable gift by a Canadian court in *Re Daley's Estate*.[5] The purposes being exclusively charitable, the vagueness of the emphasized phrase did not matter. But if an organization with several clearly charitable purposes has, in addition, one non-charitable purpose, it cannot be a charity.

Although a gift for charity may be good notwithstanding that the particular objects are left undefined by the trust instrument, the gift will nonetheless fail if the trust is drafted in such a way that it is possible, without a breach of trust, for the whole of the gift to be devoted to non-charitable purposes. It was for this reason that gifts have wholly failed in numerous cases, such as *Blair v Duncan*,[6] in which there was a bequest 'for such charitable or public purposes, as my trustee thinks proper', *Houston v Burns*,[7] in which residue was given 'for such public, benevolent or charitable purposes . . . as [my trustees] in their discretion shall think proper', and *A-G of the Bahamas v Royal Trust Co*,[8] in which residue was given 'for any purposes for and/or connected with the education and welfare of Bahamian children and young people'. In each of these cases, the words were construed disjunctively, so that the trustees, according to the terms of the trust, could quite properly have applied the whole fund for, in the first case, public, in the second case, public or benevolent, and in

---

[2] See Chapter 3, section 2(c), p 52, *supra*.

[3] *Re Gillingham Bus Disaster Fund* [1958] Ch 300, [1958] 1 All ER 37; affd [1959] Ch 62, [1958] 2 All ER 749, CA; *Re Atkinson's Will Trusts* [1978] 1 All ER 1275, [1978] 1 WLR 586; *A-G of the Cayman Islands v Wahr-Hansen* [2001] WTLR 345, PC.

[4] Chapter 14, section 7, p 328 *et seq, infra*.   [5] (1988) 64 Sask LR 175 (emphasis added).

[6] [1902] AC 37, HL.

[7] [1918] AC 337, [1918–19] All ER Rep 817, HL; *Chichester Diocesan Fund and Board of Finance Inc v Simpson* [1944] AC 341, [1944] 2 All ER 60, HL.

[8] [1986] 3 All ER 423, PC, discussed [1987] NLJ Annual Charities Review 20 (S P de Cruz); (1987) 131 Sol Jo 1537 (N D M Parry).

the third case, welfare purposes, none of which is exclusively charitable. A trust is charit-able only in so far as the trust funds are exclusively devoted to charitable purposes.[9] But it is not necessarily fatal that it is impossible for a benefit to be withdrawn after a beneficiary ceases to qualify.[10]

However, as Lord Millett has pointed out,[11] a charitable trust is not precluded from coexisting with a private trust either (so to speak) vertically or horizontally. Thus a testator may validly leave his estate to be held (by the same trustees) as to part on charitable trusts and as to part on private trusts.[12] Alternatively, a trust instrument may provide for trustees to pay or apply income for charitable purposes for twenty-one years and then to hold it on non-charitable trusts for individual beneficiaries.[13]

(ii) Charitable Trusts (Validation) Act 1954

The principle that, to be charitable, trust funds must be exclusively devoted to charitable purposes still remains in full force in respect of trust instruments coming into operation on or after 16 December 1952,[14] but is qualified by the above Act in respect of what the Act calls 'imperfect trust provisions' contained in instruments coming into operation before that date.

An 'imperfect trust provision' is defined[15] as one declaring the objects for which prop-erty is to be held or applied, and so describing those objects that, consistently with the terms of the provision, the property can be used exclusively for charitable purposes, but can nevertheless be used for purposes that are not charitable. Where the Act applies, an imperfect trust provision has effect as respects the period before commencement of the Act,[16] as if the whole of the declared objects were charitable, and as respects the period after the commencement, as if the provision required the property to be held or applied for the declared objects in so far only as it authorized use for charitable purposes.

The Act may apply not only to a gift that is expressed to be for charitable purposes as well as for other non-charitable purposes, but also to a gift such as, for example, a gift for worthy causes, in which charity is not expressly mentioned, but in which the terms of the gift in fact include both charitable and non-charitable purposes, and the gift can accord-ingly, in fact, be used exclusively for charitable purposes. One test might be to ask whether anyone, such as the founder or a person interested in a non-charitable application, would have a legitimate complaint if the whole were applied to charity.[17] It did not apply to a trust for institutions as opposed to one for objects or purposes.[18]

---

[9] The existence of a power to revoke existing charitable trusts and declare new non-charitable trusts does not affect the charitable nature of the original trusts unless and until they are revoked: *Gibson v South American Stores (Gath and Chaves) Ltd* [1950] Ch 177, [1949] 2 All ER 985, CA.

[10] *Joseph Rowntree Memorial Trust Housing Association Ltd v A-G* [1983] 1 All ER 288.

[11] In *Latimer v Commissioners of Inland Revenue* [2004] UKPC 13, [2004] 1 WLR 1466, sub nom *Re Crown Forestry Rental Trust* [2004] 4 All ER 558, at [31], noted (2004) 18 Tru LI 155 (D Morris).

[12] *Public Trustee v Commissioners of Inland Revenue* [1971] NZLR 77.

[13] *Re Sir Robert Peel's School at Tamworth, ex p the Charity Commissioners* (1868) LR 3 Ch App 543.

[14] The Act is more fully discussed in the 3rd edn, p 158 *et seq*. A strong argument for a new Act to similar effect to apply to future such dispositions is put by Sheridan in (1993–94) 2 CLPR 1. See the Report for 1977, paras 71–80.

[15] By s 1(1).   [16] 30 July 1954.

[17] *Ulrich v Treasury Solicitor* [2005] EWHC 67 (Ch), [2005] 1 All ER 1059, [2006] 1 WLR 33, noted [2005] 67 T & ELTJ 17 (Jennifer Haywood and Ruth Jordan).

[18] *Re Harpur's Will Trusts* [1962] Ch 78, [1961] 3 All ER 588, CA.

(iii) Primary trust for non-charitable purposes, residue to charity

Where there is a trust under which a fund or the income thereof is to be applied primarily to purposes that are not charitable and accordingly void, and as to the balance or residue to purposes that are charitable, if, on the one hand, as a matter of construction, the gift to charity is a gift of the entire fund or income subject to the payments thereout required to give effect to the non-charitable purpose, the amount set free by the failure of the non-charitable gift will be caught by and pass under the charitable gift.[19] On the other hand, if the gift of the residue is to be read as a gift of the mere balance of the fund after deducting the amount of the sum previously given out of it, the gift will wholly fail, on the ground that no ascertainable part of the fund or the income is devoted to charity, unless the amount applicable to the non-charitable purpose can be quantified. If this can be done the gift will fail, in respect of that amount only, and will take effect in favour of the charitable purpose as regards the remainder.[20] Exceptionally and anomalously, if the primary non-charitable trust is the maintenance in perpetuity of a tomb not in a church, it is simply ignored, even though it may be capable of being quantified, and the whole fund or income is treated as being devoted to charitable purposes.[21]

(iv) Non-charitable trusts ancillary to charitable trusts

Purposes merely ancillary to a main charitable purpose that, if taken by themselves, would not be charitable will not vitiate the claim of an institution to be established for purposes that are exclusively charitable.[22] Thus, in *Re Coxen*,[23] a fund of some £200,000 was given to the Court of Aldermen for the City of London upon trust:

(a) to apply annually a sum not exceeding £100 to a dinner for the Court of Aldermen upon their meeting upon the business of the trust;

(b) to pay one guinea to each alderman who attended during the whole of a committee meeting in connection with the trust; and

(c) to apply the balance for a specified charitable purpose.

It was held that all of the trusts were charitable as the provisions in favour of the aldermen were given for the better administration of the principal charitable trust and not for the personal benefit of the recipients. A trust for the erection of a synagogue for religious educational and social purposes was likewise held to be exclusively charitable on the ground that the social activities were merely ancillary to the strictly religious activities.[24]

As explained by Slade J in *McGovern v A-G*,[25] a distinction of critical importance has to be drawn between:

(a) the designated purposes of the trust;

---

[19] *Re Parnell* [1944] Ch 107; *Re Coxen* [1948] Ch 747, [1948] 2 All ER 492.

[20] *Re Vaughan* (1886) 33 Ch D 187; *Re Taylor* (1888) 58 LT 538; *Re Porter* [1925] Ch 746.

[21] *Re Birkett* (1878) 9 Ch D 576; *Re Vaughan, supra; Re Rogerson* [1901] 1 Ch 715.

[22] *Incorporated Council of Law Reporting for England and Wales v A-G* [1972] Ch 73, 84, [1971] 3 All ER 1029, 1033, CA, per Russell LJ; *Stratton v Simpson* (1970) 125 CLR 138.

[23] *Supra, Royal College of Surgeons of England v National Provincial Bank Ltd* [1952] AC 631, [1952] 1 All ER 984, HL. Cf *Re Barnett* (1908) 24 TLR 788.

[24] *Neville Estates Ltd v Madden* [1962] Ch 832, [1961] 3 All ER 769.

[25] [1982] Ch 321, [1981] 3 All ER 493. See *Public Trustee v A-G of New South Wales* (1997) 42 NSWLR 600.

(b) the designated means of carrying out those purposes; and

(c) the consequences of carrying them out.

Trust purposes of an otherwise charitable nature do not lose their charitable status merely because, as an incidental consequence of the trustees' activities, there may enure to private individuals benefits of a non-charitable nature. Thus the Incorporated Council of Law Reporting was held to be charitable, notwithstanding that publication of the law reports supplies members of the legal profession with the tools of their trade.[26] On the same principle, a student's union, if it exists to further and does further the educational purposes of a college or university, may be charitable notwithstanding the personal benefits conferred on union members.[27] But the charitable purposes must be predominant, and any benefits to individual members of a non-charitable character that result from its activities must be of a subsidiary or incidental character.[28] Again, many charities are membership organizations, the members of which may be entitled to special benefits such as reduction or waiver of admission charges: for example, the National Trust. If the benefits are only given to encourage members and to carry out the main charitable purpose, they will not deprive the organization of charitable status.

Similarly, trust purposes of an otherwise charitable nature do not lose it merely because the trustees, by way of furtherance of such purposes, have incidental powers to carry on activities that are not themselves charitable. The distinction is between (i) those non-charitable activities authorized by the trust instrument that are merely subsidiary or incidental to a charitable purpose, and (ii) those non-charitable activities so authorized that in themselves form part of the trust purpose. In the latter, but not the former, case, the reference to non-charitable activities will deprive the trust of its charitable status. In drawing this distinction, Slade J recognized[29] that it might be easier to state than to apply in practice. And Scott J, in *A-G v Ross*,[30] said that the activities of an organization after its formation may serve to indicate that the power to carry on non-charitable activities was, in truth, not incidental or supplementary at all, but was the main purpose for which the organization was formed. Such activities will, however, only be relevant if they are *intra vires*, and of a nature and took place at a time that gives them probative value on the question whether the main purpose for which the organization was formed was charitable or non-charitable.

It will be convenient, at this point, to digress slightly and refer to the position in relation to trading by or on behalf of charities. The Charity Commission Guidance 'Trustees, trading and tax'[31] explains that charity law allows charities to trade,[32] provided that the trading falls within one of the following categories.

---

[26] *Incorporated Council of Law Reporting for England and Wales v A-G, supra*, CA.

[27] *London Hospital Medical College v IRC* [1976] 2 All ER 113; *A-G v Ross* [1985] 3 All ER 334; Contrast *IRC v City of Glasgow Police Athletic Association* [1953] AC 380, [1953] 1 All ER 747; and see [1978] Conv 92 (N P Gravells); [1986] T L & P 47 (J Warburton). The Attorney-General's Guidance on Expenditure by Student Unions is set out in Appendix A to the Report for 1983.

[28] See *A-G v Ross* [1985] 3 All ER 334, and RR 8.   [29] In *McGovern v A-G, supra*.

[30] [1985] 3 All ER 334.

[31] CC35 (Version April 2007) available online at <http://www.charity-commission.gov.uk/publications/cc35.asp>.

[32] Observing that there is no short answer to the question, 'what is trading?', the Guidance sets out the main factors to consider. The sale or letting of goods donated to the charity for the purposes of sale or letting is not regarded as trading.

(a) *Primary purpose trading*—that is, trading that contributes directly to one or more of the objects of the charity as set out in its governing document. Typical examples are—

   (i)   provision of educational services by a charitable school or college in return for course fees;

   (ii)   sale of goods manufactured by disabled people who are beneficiaries of a charity for the disabled;

   (iii)   holding of an art exhibition by a charitable art gallery or museum in return for admission fees;

   (iv)   provision of residential accommodation by a residential care charity in return for payment;

   (v)   sale of tickets for a theatrical production staged by a theatre charity; and

   (vi)   sale of certain educational goods by a charitable art gallery or museum.

(b) *Ancillary trading*—that is, that which contributes indirectly to the successful furtherance of the purposes of the charity. An example is the sale of food and drink in a restaurant or bar by a theatre charity to members of the audience. Trading is not, however, regarded as ancillary to the carrying out of a primary purpose of the charity simply because its purpose is to raise funds for the charity.

(c) *Non-primary purpose trading*—that is, trading in order to raise funds, that does not involve any significant risk to the resources of the charity.

If charities wish to carry out non-primary purpose trading involving significant risk, they must do so through a trading subsidiary—that is, a company owned and controlled by one or more charities, set up in order to trade.

(v) Apportionment[33]

It must be remembered that where there is a power of selection or appointment between two or more persons or objects, the whole may be appointed to one to the total exclusion of the other or others, unless there is some express provision that each object is to have a minimum amount.[34] In the first place, if each object taken by itself is a valid object, whether charitable or non-charitable, the trust will be good even though the share that each object is to take is not declared by the trust instrument, and even though the trustees, having been given a power of selection, apportionment, division, or appointment, fail to exercise it. In such case, the court will divide the property between the objects equally, unless there is some contrary intention in the trust instrument.[35]

Secondly, this principle was applied in *Re Clarke*[36] to a case in which residue was given to:

(a) indefinite charitable objects;

---

[33] It does not seem that it should make any difference whether trustees are directed to apportion a fund between different objects as opposed to being given a power of selection, division, or appointment.

[34] Section 158 of the Law of Property Act 1925, replacing earlier legislation.

[35] *Salusbury v Denton* (1857) 3 K & J 529; *Re Douglas* (1887) 35 Ch D 472, CA; *Hunter v A-G* [1899] AC 309, 324; HL, *per* Lord Davey. It seems doubtful whether the principle was properly applied in *Hoare v Osborne* (1866) LR 1 Eq 585.

[36] [1923] 2 Ch 407; *Re King* [1931] WN 232. The gift failed in *Re Wright's Will Trusts* (1981) (1999) 13 Tru LI 48, CA, in which apportionment was not possible. The whole of the gift, if valid, could have been devoted to non-charitable purposes.

(b) a definite charitable object;

(c) another definite charitable object;

(d) such indefinite charitable and non-charitable objects as the executors should think fit.

The residue was directed to be divided among the four objects, or sets of objects, in such shares and proportions as the executors should determine. It was held that the power of distribution or appointment given to the executors was void, as they could appoint the whole fund to object (d), which was void for uncertainty, and this was clearly correct. It was further held, however, that the principle of *Lambert v Thwaites*[37] applied. In this case it was held that, on its true construction, the will set up a trust for all of the children, giving them vested interests, liable to be divested if the power of appointment was exercised. Similarly, here, the residue was held to have vested in the four objects equally: prima facie, their interests were liable to be divested by exercise by the executors of their power of distribution or appointment, but this power being void, their interests were indefeasible. The gifts to objects (a), (b), and (c) were accordingly good, but the gift of the remaining one-fourth share to object (iv) failed on the ground of uncertainty, and went to the persons entitled on intestacy.

The principle of the trust power cases such as *Walsh v Wallinger*[38] does not, however, enable one, in, for instance, a gift to 'such charitable or benevolent objects as my trustees shall select', to imply a gift over in default of appointment to charitable and benevolent objects in equal shares so as to save the gift as to one half for charity. The courts are unwilling to make any apportionment in this sort of case,[39] and, as we have seen,[40] numerous decisions, including many in the House of Lords, have held such gifts altogether void. In this sort of case, there is no gift to objects, but only a power given to the trustees to distribute among an uncertain group of objects, and the court will not imply any gift in default of appointment when, as has been said[41] 'charitable purposes are mixed up with other purposes of such a shadowy and indefinite nature that the court cannot execute them'.

(vi) *Liverpool City Council v A-G*[42]

In this case, there was a gift of land to a local authority, which covenanted to use and maintain it '*as a public park or recreation ground and for no other purpose*'.[43] It was held, in the absence of any of the formalities applicable to a transfer of land to be held on charitable trusts, that no charitable trust requiring the authority to maintain the land for recreational purposes in perpetuity had been created. It was not established that there was an intention that the corporation's legal ownership was to be held beneficially for charitable purposes.

---

[37] (1866) LR 2 Eq 151, discussed in Chapter 2, section 4(b), p 37, *supra*.

[38] (1830) 2 Russ & M 78; see Chapter 2, section 4(b), p 36, *supra*.

[39] See *per* Lord Wright in *Chichester Diocesan Fund v Simpson and Board of Finance Inc* [1944] AC 341, 356, [1944] 2 All ER 60, 66, HL.

[40] See p 245, *supra*.   [41] *Hunter v A-G* [1899] AC 309, 323, HL, *per* Lord Davey.

[42] (1992) Times, 1 May, noted (1992/93) 1 CLPR 153 (D Morris).

[43] It was conceded that the provision of a recreation ground is a charitable purpose: see p 275, *infra*.

(B) PERPETUITIES

In general, the rule against perpetuities, which is shortly stated in section 1 of Chapter 11, applies to gifts to charity. As Lord Selborne LC said:[44]

> if the gift in trust for charity is itself conditional upon a future and uncertain event, it is subject...to the same rules and principles as any other estate depending for its coming into existence upon a condition precedent. If the condition is never fulfilled, the estate never arises; if it is so remote and indefinite as to transgress the limits of time prescribed by the rules of law against perpetuities, the gift fails ab initio.[45]

Thus gifts to charity to take effect on the appointment of the next lieutenant-colonel of a volunteer corps,[46] or when a candidate for the priesthood comes forward from a particular church,[47] have been held void on the ground that the event might not occur until after the expiration of the perpetuity period.[48] The general rule applies equally when the limitation to charity is by way of a gift over following a gift in favour of private individuals.[49]

Exceptionally, however, the rule against perpetuities has no application to a gift to one charity with a gift over to another charity upon some contingency, notwithstanding that the contingency may occur outside the perpetuity period.[50] The exception, however, does not cover the case of a gift over from a charity to an individual. The gift over in such case is subject to the rule.[51]

(C) THE RULE AGAINST PERPETUAL TRUSTS

As has been seen,[52] gifts for non-charitable purposes are generally void and, in the exceptional cases in which they are valid, must, if they are to be effective at all, be limited so as not to continue beyond the perpetuity period. Trusts for charitable purposes are, however, completely unaffected by the rule against perpetual trusts, and it is no objection to a charitable trust that it may continue for ever and that it may never be possible to expend the capital as opposed to the income of the property subject to the trust.

It is convenient to mention at this point some of the cases that have arisen in connection with the upkeep of tombs. Although the upkeep of a tomb, other than a tomb in a church, is not a charitable purpose, it may nevertheless be possible, to some extent, to effect the desired purpose. If the provision is limited to the perpetuity period, it is apparently valid, although unenforceable, and various devices may be adopted that may, in practice, provide for its upkeep for an even longer period. Firstly, if the gift is for the upkeep of the whole of

---

[44] *Chamberlayne v Brockett* (1872) 8 Ch App 206, 211; *Re Lord Stratheden and Campbell* [1894] 3 Ch 265; *Re Mander* [1950] Ch 547, [1950] 2 All ER 191.

[45] But see now the Perpetuities and Accumulations Act 1964, s 3.

[46] *Re Lord Stratheden and Campbell, supra.*   [47] *Re Mander, supra.*

[48] But see the Perpetuities and Accumulations Act 1964, s 3.

[49] *Re Bowen* [1893] 2 Ch 491, [1891–94] All ER Rep 238; *Re Wightwick's Will Trusts* [1950] Ch 260, [1950] 1 All ER 689.

[50] *Christ's Hospital v Grainger* (1849) 1 Mac & G 460; *Re Tyler* [1891] 3 Ch 252, CA; *Royal College of Surgeons of England v National Provincial Bank Ltd* [1952] AC 631, [1952] 1 All ER 984, HL. Cf *Re Martin* [1952] WN 339.

[51] *Re Bowen, supra*; *Gibson v South-American Stores (Gath & Chaves) Ltd* [1950] Ch 177, [1949] 2 All ER 985, CA; *Re Cooper's Conveyance Trusts* [1956] 3 All ER 28.

[52] Chapter 3, section 2(c)(v), p 57 et seq, infra.

a churchyard, including the particular tomb in question, the gift is charitable, even though the motive for it may be the non-charitable one of maintaining one particular tomb.

Secondly, advantage may be taken of the principle of *Christ's Hospital v Grainger*[53] by granting property to one charity with a gift over to another charity if the tomb is not kept in repair. Care must be taken, however, not to impose any trust for the non-charitable purpose of maintaining the tomb on the subject matter of the gift: failure to observe this point led to a failure of the scheme in *Re Dalziel*.[54] From a practical point of view, the validity of this device depends on the trust income exceeding the sums needed for the upkeep of the tomb and on the availability of other income to carry out the necessary maintenance. This device would appear to be equally available in relation to any non-charitable purpose trust that is not void for some reason, such as uncertainty or administrative unworkability.

Thirdly, it may be noted that a burial authority may undertake the maintenance of a private grave for a period not exceeding a hundred years from the date of the agreement.[55]

(D) EXEMPTIONS FROM RATES AND TAXES[56]

The income of bodies of persons or trusts established in the United Kingdom[57] for charitable purposes only, so far as it is applied accordingly,[58] is generally wholly exempt from income tax,[59] corporation tax,[60] and there is a similar exemption in relation to capital gains tax.[61]

---

[53] (1849) 1 Mac & G 460. See section 1(B), *supra*.   [54] [1943] Ch 277, [1943] 2 All ER 656.

[55] Local Authorities' Cemeteries Order 1977, SI 1977/204, art 10(7), and a monument or memorial for a period not exceeding ninety-nine years: Parish Councils and Burial Authorities (Miscellaneous Provisions) Act 1970, s 1(1).

[56] See [1972] BTR 345; (1999) 62 MLR 333 (M Chesterman). The cost in terms of lost revenues to central and local government is estimated to be £2.2–2.5bn.

[57] *Camille and Henry Dreyfus Foundation Inc v IRC* [1956] AC 39, [1955] 3 All ER 97, HL (foundation established in State of New York that carried out all of its activities in the USA not entitled to exemption in respect of royalties received from a company resident in the UK).

[58] HM Revenue and Customs may disallow a claim if it is not satisfied that the income has been used for charitable purposes. See *IRC v Educational Grants Association Ltd* [1967] Ch 993, [1967] 2 All ER 893, CA; *IRC v Helen Slater Charitable Trust Ltd* [1982] Ch 49, [1981] 3 All ER 98, CA (held to have been so applied where a charitable corporation, acting *intra vires*, made an outright transfer of money applicable to charitable purposes to another charity so as to pass to that other charity full title to the money. The opinion was expressed by the court that it would also cover the case in which income was retained by the charity or otherwise capitalized—but see (1982) 98 LQR 1); *Sheppard v IRC (No 2)* [1993] STC 240. See also [2000] BTR 144 (Jean Warburton).

[59] Income and Corporation Taxes Act 1988, ss 505–506, as amended. If a charity carries on a trade, its profits will only be exempt if they are applied solely to the purposes of the charity, and either (i) the trade is exercised in the course of the actual carrying out of a primary purpose of the charity, or (ii) the work in connection with the trade is mainly carried out by beneficiaries of the charity: s 505(1)(e). A trading subsidiary is liable to corporation tax on its profits in the same way as any other company. However, it can make payments to its parent charity (or charities) as gift aid payments, which may reduce or eliminate the trading subsidiary's potential corporation tax liability. Nor will the gift aid payments to the parent charity (or charities) be liable to corporation tax (or income tax in the case of charitable trusts) if they are applicable to charitable purposes only. Note that, under Extra Statutory Concession C4, if certain conditions are fulfilled, the profits from bazaars, jumble sales, and the like may not be charged to tax.

[60] Ibid, s 9(4).

[61] Taxation of Chargeable Gains Act 1992, s 256(1). The donor may obtain relief from capital gains tax on gifts to charities: ibid, s 257, as amended.

In relation to non-domestic rates, relief is available where, at the relevant time, the rate-payer is a charity or trustees for a charity, and the hereditament is wholly or mainly used for charitable purposes.[62] A charity is entitled to 80 per cent relief in respect of a hereditament of which it is in occupation in whole or in part,[63] and the charging authority may increase the relief to 100 per cent.[64]

Charities are generally liable to value added tax.[65] However, in relation to charities, various items are zero-rated, including the sale by a charity of goods that have been donated to it, whether new or used, and the sale of donated goods by a taxable person who has covenanted to give all of the profits of the sale to a charity.[66] There is also an exemption in respect of fund-raising events by charities.[67]

Transfers, conveyances and leases to charities are exempt from stamp duty.[68]

There is no charge to inheritance tax in respect of gifts to charities.[69]

Under gift aid arrangements, a charity can reclaim income tax at the basic rate and capital gains tax where the gift was made by a UK taxpayer, and payments made are deductible by the donor in computing his income for higher rates of tax. The donor must make an appropriate declaration stating, inter alia, that the gift is to be treated as a qualifying donation for the purposes of s 25 of the Finance Act 1990.[70] Relief is also given for donations under a payroll deduction scheme.[71] Further donations to charity by companies are, subject to certain conditions, deductible in computing their profits.[72]

---

[62] By the Local Government Finance Act 1988, s 64(10), it is provided that for this purpose a hereditament is to be treated as *'wholly or mainly used for charitable purposes, if (a) it is used wholly or mainly for the sale of goods donated to a charity; and (b) the proceeds for sale (after deduction of expenses) are applied for the purposes of a charity'*. It does not appear to provide relief to trading shops run by charities—that is, shops wholly or mainly used to sell goods bought under normal trading conditions—or to 'fifty–fifty' shops in which goods are deposited for sale, and the net proceeds of sale are divided between the donor and the charity: see *Royal Society for the Protection of Birds v Brighton Borough Council* [1982] RA 33. As to a charity setting up a trading company, see (1988) 3 TL & P 98 (J Hill and J de Souza).

[63] Local Government Finance Act 1988, s 43(5), (6). Likewise, in the case of unoccupied hereditaments, where it appears that when next in use the hereditament will be wholly or mainly used for charitable purposes: ibid, s 45(5), (6). Note *Kent County Council v Ashford Borough Council* [1998] RA 217.

[64] Ibid, ss 47, 48. Certain hereditaments, including places of religious worship and property used for the disabled, are wholly exempt from non-domestic rating: ibid, s 51, Sch 5 paras 11 (as amended by the Local Government Finance Act 1992, s 104 and Sch 10, para 3), 16.

[65] See (1995/96) 3 CLPR 37, 133 (1996/97) 4 CLPR 105; and (1997/98) 5 CLPR 77 (J Warburton).

[66] Value Added Tax Act 1994, s 30 and Sch 8, Group 15, as amended by the Finance Act 1997, ss 33, 34.

[67] Ibid, Sch 9, Group 12.   [68] Finance Act 1982, s 129, as amended.

[69] Inheritance Tax Act 1984, s 23. See *Re Benham's Will Trusts* [1995] STC 210, discussed (1995/96) 3 CLPR 11 (R Grierson) and (1998) 142 Sol Jo 1060 (J Sunnocks), not followed *Re Ratcliffe (decd)* [1999] STC 262. See [2007] PCB 458 (Alison Talbot).

[70] Finance Act 1990, s 25 as amended by the Finance Act 2000, s 39, and see SI 2000/2074. As to gift aid schemes and companies, see Finance Act 2000, s 40. As to income tax and corporation tax relief for gifts of qualifying investments to a charity by an individual or a company, see Income and Corporation Taxes Act 1988, s 587B, as amended, and (2000) 7 CLPR 23 (R Venables and J Kessler).

[71] Income and Corporation Taxes Act 1988, s 202 and Finance Act 2000, s 38.

[72] Income and Corporation Taxes Act 1988, s 338, as substituted by the Finance Act 2000, s 338A, inserted by the Finance Act 2000, s 339, as amended.

2 THE LEGAL MEANING OF 'CHARITY'

(A) THE POSITION BEFORE THE CHARITIES ACT 2006

Until the Charities Act 2006, there was no statutory definition of 'charitable purposes'. Before that Act, in order for a trust to be legally charitable, its purposes had to fall, as it was said, within the 'spirit and intendment' of the Preamble to the Statute 43 Eliz 1 c 4, sometimes referred to as the Statute of Charitable Uses 1601. In practice, for over a hundred years, the courts have followed the classification proposed by Lord Macnaghten in *Income Tax Special Purposes Commrs v Pemsel*,[73] who stated:

> Charity in its legal sense comprises four principal divisions: trusts for the relief of poverty; trusts for the advancement of education; trusts for the advancement of religion; and trusts for other purposes beneficial to the community, not falling under any of the preceding heads.

The process by which the law was enabled to develop was explained by Lord Reid as follows:[74]

> The courts appear to have proceeded first by seeking some analogy between an object mentioned in the preamble and the object with regard to which they had to reach a decision. Then they appear to have gone further, and to have been satisfied if they could find an analogy between an object already held to be charitable and the new object claimed to be charitable.

The 2006 Act builds on the pre-existing law. Most of the purposes falling within the 'new' heads of charity set out in the Act and discussed below would have fallen within Lord Macnaghten's fourth head—that is, 'other purposes beneficial to the community'. Moreover, some previously settled preliminary points remain good law. These are, firstly, that whether or not a purpose fell within the spirit and intention of the Preamble to the Statute of Elizabeth 1 c 4, or, as we shall see, since the 2006 Act, whether or not it falls within s 2(2) of that Act, was, or is, a question of law[75] to be decided by the judge in the light of the circumstances in which the institution or trust came into existence and the sphere in which it operates.[76] In reaching his decision, the judge[77] is completely unaffected by the settlor's or testator's opinion as to whether the purpose he has indicated is charitable or not.[78] Otherwise, as Russell J observed,[79] 'trusts might be established in perpetuity for the promotion of all kinds of fantastic (though not unlawful) objects, of which the training of

[73] [1891] AC 531, 583, based on the classification put forward by Sir Samuel Romilly as counsel in *Morice v Bishop of Durham* (1805) 10 Ves 522.

[74] In *Scottish Burial Reform and Cremation Society Ltd v Glasgow City Corpn* [1968] AC 138, 147, [1967] 3 All ER 215, 218.

[75] *Royal Choral Society v IRC* [1943] 2 All ER 101, CA.

[76] *Incorporated Council of Law Reporting for England and Wales v A-G* [1972] Ch 73, 91, [1971] 3 All ER 1029, 1038; CA, *per* Sachs LJ.

[77] Commonly, in practice, the Charity Commission on an application for registration: see p 321 *et seq, infra*.

[78] *Re Hummeltenberg* [1923] 1 Ch 237; *National Anti-Vivisection Society v IRC* [1948] AC 31, [1947] 2 All ER 217, HL; Cf *Re Cox* [1955] AC 627, [1955] 2 All ER 550, PC. Similarly, where the trust instrument purports to leave the matter to the opinion of the trustees: *Re Wootton's Will Trust* [1968] 2 All ER 618.

[79] In *Re Hummeltenberg, supra*, at 242, approved by the House of Lords in *National Anti-Vivisection Society v IRC, supra*.

poodles to dance might be a mild example'. Equally, the motive of the settlor or testator will not prevent a gift from being charitable if the purpose is one that is charitable in the eye of the law. Thus, a bequest to provide for the erection of a stained-glass window in a church was held to be charitable, notwithstanding that the motive of the testatrix was to perpetuate her memory and not to beautify the church or to benefit the parishioners.[80] The courts, it may be observed, are ready to give a benignant construction to ambiguous provisions if this is possible, so as to save a gift for charity.[81]

Secondly, the trust instrument generally comes into existence before, or at the same time as, the trust fund. Sometimes, however, the order may be reversed, as may be the case, for instance, where a fund is set up as a result of a public appeal that does not clearly define the trusts. The first question is to establish whether it is a private or a charitable trust.[82] If it is charitable, the position was thus explained by Cozens-Hardy LJ in *A-G v Mathieson*:[83]

> When money is given by charitable persons for somewhat indefinite purposes, a time comes when it is desirable, and indeed necessary, to prescribe accurately the terms of the charitable trust, and to prepare a scheme for that purpose. In the absence of evidence to the contrary, the individual or the committee entrusted with the money must be deemed to have implied authority for and on behalf of the donors to declare the trusts to which the sums contributed are to be subject. If the individual or the committee depart from the general objects of the original donors, any deed of trust thus transgressing reasonable limits might be set aside by proper proceedings instituted by the Attorney-General, or possibly by one of the donors. But unless and until set aside or rectified, such a deed must be treated as in all respects decisive of the trusts which, by the authority of the donor, are to regulate the charity.

Thirdly, it is clear that the mere making of a charge for the services rendered does not necessarily prevent an organization, otherwise charitable, from being charitable.[84] There are numerous cases in which beneficiaries only receive benefits from a charity by way of bargain: for example, a private hospital,[85] fee-paying schools,[86] and special housing for the elderly.[87] However, an organization that wholly excludes poor people from any benefits, direct or indirect, would not be set up, and operate, for the benefit of the public and therefore would not be a charity.[88] Nor is it necessarily fatal that incidentally it could happen that the bargain might produce a profit for the beneficiary.[89]

---

[80] *Re King* [1923] 1 Ch 243; *Re Delius* [1957] Ch 299, [1957] 1 All ER 854. See the *dicta* of Farwell J in *Re Delaney*. [1902] 2 Ch 642, 647, 648; *Northern Ireland Valuation Comr v Redemptorist Order Trustees* [1971] NI 114, CA.

[81] *Guild v IRC* [1992] 2 AC 310, [1992] 2 All ER 10, HL; *IRC v McMullen* [1981] AC 1 at 11, [1980] 1 All ER 884 at 890, HL. See also *Re Le Cren Clarke (decd)* [1996] 1 All ER 715, sub nom *Funnell v Stewart* [1996] 1 WLR 288.

[82] See Report for 1981, paras 408, Appendix A, and (1982) 132 NLJ 223 (H Picarda) discussing the Penlee Lifeboat Disaster Fund. Held not to be charitable; the £3m raised was divided among eight families.

[83] [1907] 2 Ch 383, 394, CA, applied *Re Trust Deed relating to the Darwin Cyclone Tracy Relief Fund Trust* (1979) 39 Fed LR 260.

[84] It is irrelevant that a commercial undertaking comes into the field and supplies similar services on a commercial basis. See *Scottish Burial Reform and Cremation Society Ltd v Glasgow City Corpn* [1968] AC 138, [1967] 3 All ER 215, HL.

[85] *Re Resch's Will Trusts, Le Cras v Perpetual Trustee Co Ltd* [1969] 1 AC 514, [1967] 3 All ER 915, PC. See (1993) 1 Dec Ch Com 18.

[86] *The Abbey, Malvern Wells Ltd v Ministry of Town and Country Planning* [1951] Ch 728, [1951] 2 All ER 154. Note the effect of the Charities Act 2006 on the public benefit requirement: see p 279 *et seq*.

[87] *Joseph Rowntree Memorial Trust Housing Association Ltd v A-G* [1983] Ch 159, [1983] 1 All ER 288.

[88] *Re Macduff* [1896] 2 Ch 451, 464.

[89] *Joseph Rowntree Memorial Trust Housing Association Ltd v A-G, supra.*

(B) THE STATUTORY DEFINITION IN THE CHARITIES ACT 2006

The Act[90] defines 'charity' for the purposes of the law of England and Wales as meaning an institution[91] that:

(i)   is established[92] for charitable purposes only, and

(ii)   falls to be subject to the control[93] of the High Court in the exercise of its jurisdiction with respect to charities.

It does not, however, apply to an institution established for charitable purposes outside England and Wales—that is, an institution constituted in accordance with the law of a foreign country, although if constituted here, its objects may be located abroad.[94]

A 'charitable purpose' is one that:

(i)   falls within any of the descriptions of purposes contained in s 2(2), and

(ii)   is for the public benefit.[95]

Those purposes as set out in s 2(2) are:

(a)   the prevention or relief of poverty;

(b)   the advancement of education;

(c)   the advancement of religion;

(d)   the advancement of health or the saving of lives;

(e)   the advancement of citizenship or community development;

(f)   the advancement of the arts, culture, heritage or science;

(g)   the advancement of amateur sport;

(h)   the advancement of human rights, conflict resolution or reconciliation or the promotion of religious or racial harmony or equality and diversity;

(i)   the advancement of environmental protection or improvement;

(j)   the relief of those in need by reason of youth, age, ill-health, disability, financial hardship or other disadvantage;

(k)   the advancement of animal welfare;

(l)   the promotion of the efficiency of the armed forces of the Crown, or of the efficiency of the police, fire and rescue services or ambulance services;

(m)   any other purpose within subsection (4).

---

[90] Charities Act 2006, s 1(1), substantially reproducing the definition in the Charities Act 1993, s 96(1).

[91] 'Institution' is defined as an institution whether incorporated or not, and including a trust or undertaking: Charities Act 2006, s 78(5). As to Oxbridge colleges and chartered universities, see (1999) 6 CLPR 151 (D Palfreyman); [2001] 2 ELJ 134 (GR Evans).

[92] The relevant date is the foundation date: *Incorporated Council for Law Reporting for England and Wales v A-G* [1972] Ch 73, 91, [1971] 3 All ER 1029, 1039, CA, *per* Sachs LJ.

[93] It seems from *Construction Industry Training Board v A-G* [1973] Ch 173, [1972] 2 All ER 1339, CA, that it is sufficient that the institution should be subject to the control of the court in some significant respect, even though, in other respects, the jurisdiction of the court is ousted. See (1993–94) 2 CLPR 149 (O Hyams). It is very doubtful whether there needs to be a trustee within the jurisdiction: *Re Carapiet's Trusts* [2002] EWHC 1304, [2002] WTLR 989.

[94] *Gaudiya Mission v Brahmachary* [1998] Ch 341, [1997] 4 All ER 957, CA.

[95] Charities Act 2006, s 2(1).

Subsection (4)(a) covers those purposes that do not fall within s 2(2)(a)–(l), but which were previously recognized as charitable under existing charity law or by virtue of s 1 of the Recreational Charities Act 1958. Subsection (4)(b) and (c) cover purposes analogous to, or within the spirit of, any other charitable purposes—that is, purposes falling within any of subs (2)(a)–(l), previously existing charitable purposes, or purposes that themselves have been recognised as charitable under sub-(4)(b) or (c). This use of the familiar technique of analogy allows the possibility of new charitable purposes being recognized in the future.

Having regard to subs (4)(a), and subs (5), which preserves the existing meaning of the terms used in the specific descriptions in subss (2) and (3), we will turn to consider the heads of charity set out in subs (2), taking account of the case law before the 2006 Act. Before doing so, two points may be made. Firstly, the facts of a case may easily bring it within more than one of the heads, and the courts sometimes declare a trust to be charitable without specifying under which head they are treating it as falling.

Secondly, as the Commission has explained,[96] both the courts and the Commission, in considering whether a purpose is charitable, respond to changing social and economic circumstances. They first seek an analogy, having regard to the contemporary needs of society and any relevant legislation, and then ask the question whether the proposed trust will be a real and substantial benefit to the public.

3 DESIGNATED DESCRIPTIONS OF CHARITABLE PURPOSES

(A) THE PREVENTION OR RELIEF OF POVERTY

The relief of poverty was the first head of charity set out by Lord Macnaghten; the Act expands this by adding the prevention of poverty.

> Poverty, of course, does not mean destitution. It is a word of wide and somewhat indefinite import, and, perhaps, it is not unfairly paraphrased for present purposes as meaning persons who have to 'go short' in the ordinary acceptation of that term, due regard being had to their status in life and so forth.[97]

'There may be a good charity for the relief of persons who are not in grinding need or utter destitution … [but] relief connotes need of some sort, either need for a home, or for the means to provide for some necessity or quasi-necessity, and not merely an amusement, however healthy.'[98] The Charity Commission takes the view that, generally speaking, anyone who cannot afford the normal things in life that most people take for granted would probably qualify for help, and he does not necessarily have to be 'poor' over a long period of time in order to qualify.[99] It has suggested ways in which poor people may be assisted.[100] The fact that no one in receipt of an income less than a certain amount is eligible to benefit does not necessarily prevent a trust from being charitable.[101]

---

[96] See RR 1a.   [97] *Re Coulthurst* [1951] Ch 661, 666, [1951] 1 All ER 774, 776, CA, *per* Evershed MR.
[98] *IRC v Baddeley* [1955] AC 572, 585, [1955] 1 All ER 525, 529, HL, *per* Lord Simonds.
[99] CC4, para 4.   [100] Ibid, paras 13 *et seq*, and see [1995] 4 Dec Ch Com 1.
[101] *Re De Carteret* [1933] Ch 103; *Re Lacy* [1899] 2 Ch 149.

In accordance with these dicta, gifts for ladies in reduced circumstances,[102] for the aid of distressed gentlefolk,[103] to provide a nursing home for persons of moderate means,[104] and the relief of poverty among persons who have suffered financial loss in investing in split-level investment companies[105] have all been held charitable. Neighbourhood law centres formed for the purpose of giving legal aid and advice to poor persons have also been registered as charities,[106] as have the grant of low-interest or interest-free loans to enable poor people to purchase freehold or leasehold housing accommodation.[107]

The intention that the gift shall be for the relief of poverty may be inferred from the nature of the gift, as in *Re Lucas*,[108] in which the income of a fund was given 'to the oldest respectable inhabitants in Gunville to the amount of 5s per week each'. It was held that the smallness of the amounts payable showed that the purpose of the gift was to assist the aged poor. It is, of course, sufficient if the gift is to an institution the object of which is the relief of poverty.[109]

By way of contrast, a gift to provide a contribution towards the holiday expenses of workpeople was held not to be charitable on the ground that, although employed at a very small wage, the workpeople could not be described as poor people within the meaning of the Statute of Elizabeth.[110] And it has been held that the working classes do not constitute a section of the poor for the purpose of the law of charity,[111] although a gift for the purpose of the construction of a working men's hostel has been held to fall on the other side of the line.[112] Charity funds should not be used to replace state benefits; they should be used in a way that will actually benefit the recipient in addition to any assistance that he can receive from the state.[113]

(B) THE ADVANCEMENT OF EDUCATION

Trusts for the advancement of education were Lord Macnaghten's second category, and the purposes of schools and universities prima facie fall within it. Schools are not, however, necessarily charities. While many independent non-profit-making schools, including well-known public schools, have been held to be charities, privately owned schools run for profit are not, nor are county schools funded by the state, which do not usually have assets

---

[102] *Shaw v Halifax Corpn* [1915] 2 KB 170, CA.   [103] *Re Young* [1951] Ch 344, [1950] 2 All ER 1245.

[104] *Re Clarke* [1923] 2 Ch 407.   [105] *Re The AITC Foundation* [2005] WTLR 65 (CC).

[106] See 1974 Report, paras 67–72. It does not matter that a solicitor in private practice could equally well do the work, or that there may be a contractual relationship between the centre and a beneficiary. There might, however, be a difficulty if the centre undertook a large amount of work under the Legal Aid Scheme, giving rise to payments that might be used to increase the salaries of the centre's employees.

[107] See Report for 1990, Appendix A(e); (1995) 3 Dec Ch Com 7 (Garfield Poverty Trust); (1995) 4 Dec Ch Com 13 (Habitat for Humanity Great Britain).

[108] [1922] 2 Ch 52; *Re Dudgeon* (1896) 74 LT 613; *Re Wall* (1889) 42 Ch D 510.

[109] *Biscoe v Jackson* (1887) 35 Ch D 460, CA (soup kitchens).

[110] *Re Drummond* [1914] 2 Ch 90, [1914–15] All ER Rep 223.

[111] *Re Sanders' Will Trusts* [1954] Ch 265, [1954] 1 All ER 667, compromised on appeal (1954) Times, 22 July, CA, in which it was said at first instance that the term 'working class' is now an anachronism. Cf *Westminster City Council v Duke of Westminster* [1991] 4 All ER 136; *Dano Ltd v Earl Cadogan* (2003) Times, 14 March.

[112] *Re Niyazi's Will Trusts* [1978] 3 All ER 785.   [113] See CC4, paras 21–25.

held on charitable trusts or dedicated to charitable purposes.[114] Independent schools may have difficulty in retaining their charitable status. Like any other organization claiming to be a charity, they must now satisfy the public benefit test: it is no longer to be presumed that an organization established for the advancement of education is for the public benefit unless there is evidence to the contrary.[115]

Education is not restricted to the narrow sense of a master teaching a class,[116] and includes the education of artistic taste,[117] 'the promotion or encouragement of those arts and graces of life which are, perhaps, the finest and best part of the human character',[118] and the improvement of a useful branch of human knowledge and its public dissemination.[119] So far as research is concerned, Slade J has summarized the law as follows:[120]

(1) A trust for research will ordinarily qualify as a charitable trust if, but only if (a) the subject-matter of the proposed research is a useful subject of study; and (b) it is contemplated that knowledge acquired as a result of the research will be disseminated to others; and (c) the trust is for the benefit of the public, or a sufficiently important section of the public. (2) In the absence of a contrary context, however, the court will be readily inclined to construe a trust for research as importing subsequent dissemination of the results thereof. (3) Furthermore, if a trust for research is to constitute a valid trust for the advancement of education, it is not necessary either (a) that a teacher/pupil relationship should be in contemplation or (b) that the persons to benefit from the knowledge to be acquired should be persons who are already in the course of receiving 'education' in the conventional sense. (4) In any case where the court has to determine whether a bequest for the purposes of research is or is not of a charitable nature, it must pay due regard to any admissible extrinsic evidence which is available to explain the wording of the will in question or the circumstances in which it was made.

It may be added that it is not enough that the object should be educational in the sort of loose sense in which all experience may be said to be educative.[121]

In accordance with these principles, gifts to endow and build a Cambridge college,[122] to found lectureships and professorships,[123] and to augment fellows' stipends[124] have all been held to be charitable. Of special interest is *Incorporated Council of Law Reporting for*

---

[114] See 1995 NLJ Annual Charities Review 18 (D Morris), in which the differences between types of school are explained.

[115] It was reported in October 2008 that five named independent schools were to be investigated by the Commission to see if they satisfied the public benefit requirement. See the Charities Act 2006, s 3(2), and (2007) 19 E & L 167 (D Palfreyman). The requirement of public benefit is discussed at p 279 *et seq*.

[116] *Re Koeppler Will Trusts* [1984] Ch 243, [1984] 2 All ER 111 (intensive discussion process); revsd [1986] Ch 423, [1985] 2 All ER 869, CA, but approved on this point.

[117] *Royal Choral Society v IRC* [1943] 2 All ER 101, CA.

[118] Per Vaisey J in *Re Shaw's Will Trusts* [1952] Ch 163, 172, [1952] 1 All ER 49, 55 (the wife of G Bernard Shaw). Cf Farwell J in *Re Lopes* [1931] 2 Ch 130, 136: 'a ride on an elephant may be educational. At any rate it brings the reality of the elephant and its uses to the child's mind, in lieu of leaving him to mere book learning. It widens his mind, and in that broad sense is educational.'

[119] *Incorporated Council of Law Reporting for England and Wales v A-G* [1972] Ch 73, 102, [1971] 3 All ER 1029, 1046, CA, *per* Buckley LJ.

[120] In *McGovern v A-G* [1982] Ch 321, [1981] 3 All ER 493; *Re Hopkins' Will Trusts* [1965] Ch 669, 680, [1964] 3 All ER 46, 52, *per* Wilberforce J. See (1965) 29 Conv 368 (M Newark and A Samuels); (1975) 39 Conv 183 (G S Plowright).

[121] *IRC v Baddeley* [1955] AC 572, 585, [1955] 1 All ER 525, 529, HL, *per* Lord Simonds.

[122] *A-G v Lady Downing* (1766) Amb 550; (1769) Amb 571.

[123] *A-G v Margaret and Regius Professors in Cambridge* (1682) 1 Vern 55.

[124] *The Case of Christ's College, Cambridge* (1757) 1 Wm Bl 90.

England and Wales v A-G.[125] The main object of the Council is the preparation and publication of law reports, not for profit, for the purposes of providing essential material for the study of law—in the sense of acquiring knowledge of what the law is, how it is developing, and how it applies to the enormous range of human activities that it affects. This was held to be for the advancement of education, as would be the institution and maintenance of a library for the study of any other learned subject or science.

As regards the subjects of education, a wide variety have been held to be educational. Most of those referred to later in this paragraph would now also, and more appropriately, be treated as falling within head (f), considered later. They include the promotion and advancement of the art and science of surgery,[126] of choral singing in London,[127] of organists and organ music,[128] of the music of a particular composer,[129] of Egyptology,[130] of a search for the Bacon–Shakespeare manuscripts,[131] of economic and sanitary science,[132] of industry and commerce,[133] of zoology,[134] of English classical drama and the art of acting,[135] and of ethical principles,[136] in New Zealand, the education of the public in the facts of human reproduction,[137] and, in Australia, the endowment of an annual prize for portrait painting.[138] Even a trust[139] for 'the teaching, promotion and encouragement in Ireland of self-control, elocution, oratory, deportment, the arts of personal contact, of social intercourse, and the other arts of public, private, professional and business life', described by the judge[140]

---

[125] [1972] Ch 73, [1971] 3 All ER 1029, CA. Russell LJ reached the same result, but on the ground that the case fell under Lord Macnaghten's fourth head. The fact that the reports are used by members of the legal profession for earning fees is incidental and does not detract from the exclusively charitable character of the Council's objects. See (1972) 88 LQR 171. See *Smith v Kerr* [1902] 1 Ch 774, CA (a gift to Clifford's Inn—one of the Inns of Chancery established to provide legal education).

[126] *Royal College of Surgeons of England v National Provincial Bank Ltd* [1952] AC 631, [1952] 1 All ER 984, HL.

[127] *Royal Choral Society v IRC* [1943] 2 All ER 101, CA (it is irrelevant and, according to Lord Greene, curious that incidentally people may find pleasure either in providing education or in being educated), applied *Re Perpetual Trustees Queensland Ltd* [2000] QdR 647. See also *Canterbury Orchestra Trust v Smitham* [1978] 1 NZLR 787, distinguishing between a trust for the advancement of musical education—charitable—and a society formed to promote music merely for the amusement of its members—not charitable.

[128] *Re Levien* [1955] 3 All ER 35.

[129] *Re Delius' Will Trusts* [1957] Ch 299, [1957] 1 All ER 854: a gift by the widow of the composer Delius for the advancement of his musical works. All of the counsel in the case agreed that the works were of a high standard. In *Re Pinion* [1965] Ch 85, [1964] 1 All ER 890, CA, the testator sought to found a small museum with his own paintings, and his collection of paintings and antiques. On expert evidence that, as a means of education, the collection was worthless, it was held that the gift was not charitable.

[130] *Re British School of Egyptian Archaeology* [1954] 1 All ER 887.

[131] *Re Hopkins' Will Trusts* [1965] Ch 669, [1964] 3 All ER 46.

[132] *Re Berridge* (1890) 63 LT 470, CA.

[133] *Re Town and Country Planning Act 1947 Crystal Palace Trustees v Minister of Town & Country Planning* [1951] Ch 132, [1950] 2 All ER 857n. See Report for 1987 (business in the community charitable); *Re Tennant* [1996] 2 NZLR 633.

[134] *Re Lopes* [1931] 2 Ch 130; *North of England Zoological Society v Chester RDC* [1959] 3 All ER 116, CA. Cf the narrower meaning of 'education' in the Value Added Tax Act 1994: *North of England Zoological Society v Customs and Excise Comrs* [1999] STC 1027.

[135] *Re Shakespeare Memorial Trust* [1923] 2 Ch 398.

[136] *Barralet v A-G* [1980] 3 All ER 918, sub nom *Re South Place Ethical Society* [1980] 1 WLR 1565 (both 'the study and dissemination of ethical principles' and 'the cultivation of a rational religious sentiment' held to be for the advancement of education, alternatively charitable within the fourth class).

[137] *Auckland Medical Aid Trust v IRC* [1979] 1 NZLR 382.

[138] *Perpetual Trustee Co Ltd v Groth* (1985) 2 NSWLR 278.

[139] *Re Shaw's Will Trusts* [1952] Ch 163, [1952] 1 All ER 49.   [140] Vaisey, J, *supra*, at 167, 52.

as 'a sort of finishing school for the Irish people' has been held to be charitable, as have trusts for an annual chess tournament for boys and young men in the city of Portsmouth,[141] and to provide an annual treat or field day for schoolchildren, on the ground that this would encourage nature study,[142] although not trusts for artistic purposes,[143] or to present artistic dramatic works.[144] As we have seen,[145] the advancement of the arts is now a charitable purpose under s 2(2)(f) without any need to refer to education.

Although a trust for mere sport could not be charitable before the 2006 Act,[146] it has long been settled that a gift for sport in a school is charitable as being for the advancement of education, which involves development of the body as well as the mind.[147] Without casting any doubt on *Re Nottage*,[148] the House of Lords extended *Re Mariette*[149] by holding, in *IRC v McMullen*,[150] that a trust to promote the physical education and development of pupils at schools and universities as an addition to such part of their education as relates to their mental education, by providing facilities and assistance to Association football and other games and sports, is charitable. And an Australian court has held that a trust for the establishment of a rose garden in the grounds of a university is a charitable gift for the advancement of education, since such a garden 'must of its very nature be conducive to the inspiration in all but the most blasé of students of a state of mind better attuned to the academic tasks ahead'.[151]

Alhough charitable education purposes include the discussion of political issues, political propaganda masquerading as education is not charitable.[152] Education for some purposes may lack the necessary element of public benefit and therefore not be charitable, as in the illustrations of schools or colleges for prostitutes, or pickpockets, given by Harman LJ,[153] and the college for training spiritualistic mediums in *Re Hummeltenberg*.[154] Thus, it was held, in *Southwood v A-G*,[155] that a trust for the advancement of the education of the public in the subject of militarism and disarmament, and related fields, was not charitable

---

[141] *Re Dupree's Deed Trusts* [1945] Ch 16, [1944] 2 All ER 443. See (1977) 41 Conv 8.

[142] *Re Mellody* [1918] 1 Ch 228. Cf *Re Pleasants* (1923) 39 TLR 675.

[143] *Re Ogden* (1909) 25 TLR 382, CA (too wide—might include 'merely providing for one or two individuals paints and paint-brushes', *per* Lord Greene MR in *Royal Choral Society v IRC, supra,* CA, at 107, who had no doubt that the education of artistic taste was charitable).

[144] *Associated Artists Ltd v IRC* [1956] 2 All ER 583 ('too wide and too vague').

[145] See p 269, *supra.*

[146] *Re Nottage* [1895] 2 Ch 649, CA (yacht racing); *IRC v City of Glasgow Police Athletic Association* [1953] AC 380, [1953] 1 All ER 747, HL.

[147] *Re Mariette* [1915] 2 Ch 284, [1914–15] All ER Rep 794; *London Hospital Medical College v IRC* [1976] 2 All ER 113.

[148] *Supra,* CA.   [149] *Supra.*

[150] [1981] AC 1, [1980] 1 All ER 884, HL, who left open the question whether the trust might also fall within Lord Macnaghten's fourth head.

[151] *McGrath v Cohen* [1978] 1 NSWLR 621. Cf *Re the Worth Library* [1995] 2 IR 301, and see (1994) 45 NILQ 364 (H Delany).

[152] *Bonar Law Memorial Trust v IRC* (1933) 17 TC 508; *Re Hopkinson* [1949] 1 All ER 346; *Re Bushnell* [1975] 1 All ER 721, nor is campaigning in the sense of seeking to influence public opinion on political matters: *Webb v O'Doherty* (1991) Times, 11 February. See p 278, *infra.* See also Report for 1991, Appendix D (a) in connection with a proposed Margaret Thatcher Foundation.

[153] In *Re Pinion* [1965] Ch 85, 105, [1964] 1 All ER 890, 893, CA; *Re Shaw* [1957] 1 All ER 745, 752, compromised CA, [1958] 1 All ER 245n.

[154] [1923] 1 Ch 237. See also *Re Living in Radiance* [2007] WTLR 685 (CC) (science of meditation and peace education).

[155] [2000] NLJR 1017, CA, noted (2000) 14 Tru LI 233 (J Garton); *Re Crawley Model Railway Society* [2006] WTLR 1381 (CC) (not charitable).

because the court could not determine whether or not the trust's object of securing peace by demilitarization promoted the public benefit.

It may be added that the mere fact that membership of an institution may confer some benefit on the members does not necessarily prevent the institution from being a charitable body. The test is whether the main object of the institution is the promotion and advancement of a science (using this word in a wide sense), or the protection and advantage of those practising a particular profession.[156]

(C) THE ADVANCEMENT OF RELIGION

An initial difficulty is to know what is the meaning of 'religion' in charity law. Section 2(3)(a) of the 2006 Act provides that it includes:

(i)   a religion that involves belief in more than one god; and

(ii)   a religion that does not involve belief in a god.

The Commission[157] has stated its view as follows:

The criteria that we use to decide whether an organisation is advancing religion, as that is understood by charity law, are set out in full in the Charity Commissioners' published decision (of 17 November 1999) on the application for the registration by the Church of Scientology (England and Wales). Briefly, the criteria are:[158]

- do adherents have a belief in a Supreme Being?
- do adherents worship the Supreme Being?
- does the organisation advance the religion? And
- is the organisation established for the benefit of the public?

Belief in a Supreme Being is a necessary characteristic of religion in charity law which is why the criteria that we use include reference to a Supreme Being rather than a god. The existing law allows theistic, non-theistic and polytheistic faiths to be regarded as religions in charity law and the precise nature of a Supreme Being is not defined. A Supreme Being does not necessarily have to be in the form of a personal creator god; it may be in the form of one god or many gods or no god at all in the accepted understanding of the term.

It is arguable that the effect of s 2(3)(a)(ii) is that belief in a 'Supreme Being' is no longer vital. Be that as it may, one cannot but support the view of the Commission that these criteria would benefit from further clarification and welcome its intention to consider what further guidance can be given on the definition of a religious charity.

---

[156] *Royal College of Surgeons of England v National Provincial Bank Ltd* [1952] AC 631, [1952] 1 All ER 984, HL; *Royal College of Nursing v St Marylebone Corpn* [1959] 3 All ER 663, CA: *London Hospital Medical College v IRC, supra; A-G v Ross* [1985] 3 All ER 334. See also Report for 1976, paras 30–36 and 50–53.

[157] In its 2007 'Commentary on the descriptions of charitable purposes in the Charities Act 2006'.

[158] See *Barralet v A-G* [1980] 3 All ER 918, sub nom *Re South Place Ethical Society* [1980] 1 WLR 1565, in which two of the essential attributes of religion were said to be faith and worship—faith in a god and worship of that god. This was said to be too narrow a test by the High Court of Australia in *Church of the New Faith v Comrs for Pay Roll Tax* (1983) 57 ALJR 785, noted (1984) 100 LQR 340; (1984) 14 MULR 539 (M Darian Smith); [1984] Conv 449 (St John Robilliard), in which Scientology was held to be a religion in Victoria. It has not been granted charitable status in England. It is accepted that Buddhism is a religion, although it does not have the attributes stated in *Barralet v A-G, supra.* The wider Australian view has been applied in New Zealand: *Centrepoint Community Growth Trust v IRC* [1985] 1 NZLR 673. See (1981) 131 NLJ 436 (H Picarda); (1989) 63 ALJ 834 (W Sadurski); (1999) 5 CLPR 153 (Francesca Quint and T Spring).

It is seldom, in fact, necessary to go back to first principles, because of the large body of case law relating to the question of whether or not a gift is for the advancement of religion. A preliminary point concerns the approach of the courts. As long ago as 1862, it was said[159] that:

> the Court of Chancery makes no distinction between one religion and another... [or] one sect and another... [unless] the tenets of a particular sect inculcate doctrines adverse to the very foundations of all religion and... subversive of all morality... If the tendency were not immoral and although this Court might consider the opinions sought to be propagated foolish or even devoid of foundation [the trust would nevertheless be charitable].

'As between different religions the law stands neutral, but it assumes that any religion is at least likely to be better than none.'[160] The courts are understandably reluctant to judge the relative worth of different religions or the truth of competing religious doctrines, all of which may have a place in a tolerant and culturally diverse society.

While the statement of Romilly MR remains valid as asserting judicial neutrality, his further observation cannot be supported, in so far as it conflicts with the rule that a trust for the advancement of religion must, if it is to have charitable status, satisfy the public benefit test, which, since the 2006 Act, it must do without the benefit of the presumption that applied in 1862 that a trust for the advancement of religion was for the public benefit unless the contrary was established by evidence.[161] Accordingly, it seems clear that some trusts that have been held charitable in the past would not be held charitable today.[162]

For historical reasons, most of the cases have been concerned with the Christian religion, but, even before the 2006 Act, there had been registered trusts not only for the advancement of the Jewish religion, but for wholly distinct religions including Hinduism, Sikhism, Islam, and Buddhism. The principles adopted in respect of Christianity are equally applicable to other religions.

So far as the various Christian denominations are concerned, there is no doubt as to the charitable character of religious trusts not only for the established church, but also for nonconformist bodies,[163] Unitarians,[164] Roman Catholics,[165] and the Exclusive Brethren.[166]

---

[159] Per Romilly MR in Thornton v Howe (1862) 31 Beav 14, 19; Gilmour v Coats [1949] AC 426, [1949] 1 All ER 848, HL; Re Watson, Hobbs v Smith [1973] 3 All ER 678.

[160] Per Cross J in Neville Estates Ltd v Madden [1962] Ch 832, 853, [1961] 3 All ER 769, 781. See (1992–93) 1 CLPR 87 (A Longley); (1996) 8 Auck ULR 25 (S T Woodfield). P Edge argues, in (1995–96) 3 CLPR 29, that this head of charity should be abolished, to which M King responded in (1995–96) 3 CLPR 179.

[161] Charities Act 2006, ss 2(1)(b), 3. The requirement of public benefit is discussed at p 279 et seq, infra.

[162] See, eg, Thornton v Howe, supra, which involved a trust for the publication of the works of Joanna Southcote who claimed that she was with child by the Holy Ghost and would give birth to a second Messiah. As the law then was, the effect of holding the gift charitable was that, being given out of land, it failed by reason of the Mortmain Act 1736 and went to the heir-at-law; Re Watson, Hobbs v Smith [1973] 3 All ER 678 (trust for the publication of the writings of H G Hobbs, where there was expert evidence that the intrinsic worth of the writings was nil). See also [2008] MLR 159 (M Harding).

[163] Since the Toleration Act 1688. See, eg, Re Strickland's Will Trusts [1936] 3 All ER 1027, appeal dismissed by consent, [1937] 3 All ER 676, CA (Baptist); Re Manser [1905] 1 Ch 68 (Quakers).

[164] Since the Doctrine of Trinity Act 1813. Eg Re Nesbitt's Will Trusts [1953] 1 All ER 936.

[165] Since the Roman Catholic Charities Act 1832. Eg Dunne v Byrne [1912] AC 407, [1911–13] All ER Rep 1105, PC; Re Flinn [1948] Ch 241, [1948] 1 All ER 541. As to whether there has been, or now is, an anti-Roman Catholic bias, see (1981) 2 JLH 207 (M Blakeney); [1990] Conv 34 (C E F Rickett).

[166] Holmes v A-G (1981) Times, 12 February; Broxtowe Borough Council v Birch [1981] RA 215. See also Radmanovich v Nedeljkovic (2001) 52 HSWCR 641.

More controversially, two trusts associated with the Unification Church[167] have been registered as charitable. Similarly, with regard to organizations that exist for the advancement of religion, such as the Church Army,[168] the Salvation Army,[169] the Church Missionary Society,[170] the Society for the Propagation of the Gospel in Foreign Parts,[171] the Sunday School Association,[172] the Protestant Alliance and kindred institutions,[173] and even, it has been held, a society of clergymen, in connection with a trust to provide dinners, on the ground that the free meals would increase the usefulness of the society by attracting a greater number of clergymen to the meetings.[174] Also, a faith healing movement of a religious nature[175] and a spiritualist church.[176]

Neither the objects of the Theosophical Society,[177] nor those of the South Place Ethical Society[178] or the Church of Scientology,[179] are for the advancement of religion, and it has not been thought arguable that gifts for the maintenance of a Masonic temple[180] are charitable on this ground.

The advancement of religion means the promotion of spiritual teaching in a wide sense, and the maintenance of the doctrine on which it rests, and the observances that serve to promote and manifest it,[181] such as saying masses in public.[182] Gifts for religious purposes or to religious societies have been held to be prima facie good as being restricted to such purposes as are charitable,[183] although, as we shall see,[184] religious purposes are not necessarily

---

[167] Popularly known as 'the Moonies'. The Attorney-General appealed against the refusal of the Charity Commissioners to accede to his request to remove the trusts from the register, but the appeal was eventually discontinued: see the statement of the Attorney-General in Hansard, 3 February 1988, p 977 *et seq*, and the debate in the Lords, 10 February, p 247 *et seq*.

[168] *Re Smith* (1938) 54 TLR 851.   [169] *Re Fowler* (1914) 31 TLR 102, CA; *Re Smith, supra*.

[170] *Re Clergy Society* (1856) 2 K & J 615.   [171] *Re Maguire* (1870) LR 9 Eq 632.

[172] *R v Income Tax Special Comrs, ex p Essex Hall* [1911] 2 KB 434, CA.

[173] *Re Delmar Charitable Trust* [1897] 2 Ch 163 (societies having as their object '*to maintain and defend the doctrines of the Reformation, and the principles of civil and religious liberty against the advance of Popery*').

[174] *Re Charlesworth* (1910) 26 TLR 214.

[175] *Re Le Cren Clarke (decd)* [1996] 1 All ER 715, sub nom *Funnell v Stewart* [1996] 1 WLR 288, noted [1996] Lpool LR 63 (D Morris); (1996) 112 LQR 557 (R Fletcher).

[176] *Re Sacred Hands Spiritual Centre* [2006] WTLR 873 (CC). But not a college for training spiritualistic mediums: *Re Hummeltenberg* [1923] 1 Ch 237, in which, however, it was not contended that the gift was for the advancement of religion, but as being for the advancement of education or as being otherwise beneficial to the public.

[177] *Re Macaulay's Estate* [1943] Ch 435n, HL ('to form a nucleus of Universal Brotherhood of Humanity without distinction of race, creed, caste or colour'). Cf *Re Price* [1943] Ch 422 [1943] 2 All ER 505 (Anthropological Society).

[178] *Barralet v A-G, supra* ('the study and dissemination of ethical principles' and 'the cultivation of a rational religious sentiment'—society concerned with man's relations with man, not man's relations with God: nor did it have attributes referred to in fn 158, *supra*). See (1981) 131 NLJ 761 (A Hoffer).

[179] *R v Registrar General, ex p Segerdal* [1970] 2 QB 697, [1970] 3 All ER 886, CA. The decision of the Charity Commission is reproduced [2005] WTLR 1151.

[180] *Re Porter* [1925] Ch 746.

[181] *Keren Kayemeth Le Jisroel Ltd v IRC* [1931] 2 KB 465, 477, CA, *per* Hanworth MR, affd [1932] AC 650, [1932] All ER Rep 971, HL; *Oxford Group v IRC* [1949] 2 All ER 537, CA; *Berry v St Marylebone Corpn* [1958] Ch 406, [1957] 3 All ER 677, CA.

[182] *Re Hetherington* [1990] Ch 1, [1989] 2 All ER 129, noted [1989] CLJ 373 (J Hopkins); [1989] Conv 453 (N D M Parry). See p 60, *supra*.

[183] *Re White* [1893] 2 Ch 41, CA. *Sed quaere*. See the doubts suggested in *Dunne v Bryne* [1912] AC 407, 411, [1911–13] All ER Rep 1105, 1108, PC; *Re Smith's Will Trusts* [1962] 2 All ER 563, CA. However, this principle was confirmed and applied by Browne-Wilkinson-VC in *Re Hetherington, supra*, at 135.

[184] See p 280, *infra*.

charitable, because they may, for instance, lack the vital element of public benefit, and, similarly, a religious body may engage in a number of subsidiary activities that are not purely religious. A trust in favour of such a body *simpliciter* may nevertheless be a good charitable trust, but the income can only be applied to the activities of the body that are purely religious.[185] A trust, however, which is so worded as to permit the income to be used by a religious body in activities that are not purely religious is not a good charitable trust.[186]

A gift for missionary purposes is ambiguous and may comprise objects that are not charitable,[187] but the court will readily find, in the context of surrounding circumstances, evidence to show that the gift is restricted to the popular sense of Christian missionary work, which is charitable.[188] Gifts in popular language, such as to 'the service of God'[189] or 'for God's work',[190] have also been held to be applicable only to charitable purposes for the advancement of religion, but not a gift for 'good works'.[191]

The erection, maintenance, or repair of any church, chapel, or meeting house, or any part of the fabric thereof, is charitable, and there have been held charitable gifts in connection with, inter alia, stained-glass windows,[192] the spire,[193] chancel,[194] gallery,[195] seating,[196] organ,[197] and a monument in a church.[198] By a slight extension, gifts for the upkeep of a churchyard or burial ground[199] are charitable, even though restricted to some particular denomination,[200] but not a gift for the erection or repair of a particular tomb in a churchyard,[201] although it was held otherwise in the case of a gift to erect and maintain headstones to the graves of the pensioners of certain almshouses.[202]

Trusts for the support of the clergy are clearly charitable, even though subject to a condition such as promoting some specific doctrine,[203] wearing a black gown in the pulpit,[204] or even preaching an annual sermon in commemoration of the testator.[205] Also charitable was a gift to a society for the relief of infirm, sick, and aged Roman Catholic secular priests in the Clifton diocese, on the ground that this would tend to make the ministry more efficient, by making it easy for the sick and old to retire, and give place to the young and healthy,[206] and somewhat similarly in the case of a gift for retired missionaries.[207]

---

[185] *Oxford Group v IRC* [1949] 2 All ER 537, 539, CA, *per* Tucker LJ; *Re Banfield* [1968] 2 All ER 276.

[186] *Oxford Group v IRC, supra.*

[187] *Scott v Brownrigg* (1881) 9 LR Ir 246; *McCracken v A-G for Victoria* [1995] 1 VR 67 (for Christian purposes).

[188] *Re Kenny* (1907) 97 LT 130; *Re Moon's Will Trusts* [1948] 1 All ER 300.

[189] *Re Darling* [1896] 1 Ch 50.   [190] *Re Barker's Will Trusts* (1948) 64 TLR 273.

[191] *Re How* [1930] 1 Ch 66, [1929] All ER Rep 354.

[192] *Re King* [1923] 1 Ch 243; *Re Raine* [1956] Ch 417, [1956] 1 All ER 355.

[193] *Re Palatine Estate Charity* (1888) 39 Ch D 54.   [194] *Hoare v Osborne* (1866) LR 1 Eq 585.

[195] *A-G v Day* [1900] 1 Ch 31.   [196] *Re Raine, supra.*

[197] *A-G v Oakaver* (1736) cited in 1 Ves Sen 536.   [198] *Hoare v Osborne, supra.*

[199] *Re Douglas* [1905] 1 Ch 279; *Re Vaughan* (1886) 33 Ch D 187 (*per* North J, at 192: 'I do not see any difference between a gift to keep in repair what is called "God's House" and a gift to keep in repair the churchyard round it, which is often called "God's Acre".').

[200] *Re Manser* [1905] 1 Ch 68 (Quakers). Cf *Re Eighmie* [1935] Ch 524 and see *Scottish Burial Reform and Cremation Society Ltd v Glasgow City Corpn* [1968] AC 138, [1967] 3 All ER 215, HL.

[201] *Hoare v Osborne* (1866) LR 1 Eq 585; *Re Vaughan, supra; Re Hooper* [1932] 1 Ch 38.

[202] *Re Pardoe* [1906] 2 Ch 184.   [203] *A-G v Molland* (1832) 1 You 562.

[204] *Re Robinson* [1897] 1 Ch 85, CA. Condition was subsequently removed: *Re Robinson* [1923] 2 Ch 332.

[205] *Re Parker's Charity* (1863) 32 Beav 654; cf *Re Hussey's Charities* (1861) 7 Jur NS 325.

[206] *Re Forster* [1939] Ch 22, [1938] 3 All ER 767.

[207] *Re Mylne* [1941] Ch 204, [1941] 1 All ER 405. Cf *Hester v CIR* [2005] 2 NZLR 172.

Somewhat less obviously charitable, perhaps, is a gift for the benefit of a church choir,[208] and a case that seems to be at least on the extreme limits is *Re Pardoe*,[209] in which a trust to endow the ringing of a peal of bells on 29 May in each year to commemorate the restoration of the monarchy to England was held to be for the advancement of religion as calculated to bring back 'happy thoughts', which would necessarily connote 'a feeling of gratitude to the Giver of all good gifts'.[210] This principle was not applied, however, where the bells were directed to be rung half-muffled on the anniversary of the testator's death.[211]

It is convenient to consider, at this point, the effect of a gift to a person not as an individual, but as the holder of a particular office. The relevant principles are not, in fact, restricted to gifts for the advancement of religion, and would apply equally, for instance, to a gift to the head of a school or college,[212] but they have been worked out mainly in connection with gifts to bishops and vicars.[213] The principles are, in fact, relatively easy to state, but their application has led to very fine distinctions. The basic principle is that, in determining whether or not trusts are charitable, the character of the trustee is prima facie irrelevant: what matters is the purpose of the trust, not the character of the trustee. Where, however, there is a gift to a person who holds an office, the duties of which are, in their nature, wholly charitable, and the gift is made to him in his official name and by virtue of his office, then, if the purposes are not expressed in the gift itself, the gift is assumed to be for the charitable purposes inherent in the office. But where the purposes of the gift are expressed in terms not confining them to purposes that are, in the legal sense, charitable, they cannot be confined to charitable purposes merely by reference to the character of the trustee.

Thus a gift to the bishop of a diocese, or the vicar, or vicar and church wardens, of a particular parish, *simpliciter*, is a valid charitable gift, because the bishop or vicar must use the gift exclusively for the charitable purposes inherent in his office. The gift is equally charitable where the gift is followed by words that merely indicate that the bishop or vicar is to have a full discretion in settling the particular mode of application within the charitable purposes of the gift. Thus gifts were held charitable in *Re Garrard*,[214] in which there was a legacy 'to the vicar and churchwardens—to be applied by them in such a manner as they shall in their sole discretion think fit', in *Re Flinn*,[215] in which residue was given to 'His Eminence the Archbishop of Westminster Cathedral London for the time being…to be used by him for such purposes as he shall in his absolute discretion think fit', and in *Re Rumball*,[216] in which residue was given to '*the Bishop for the time being of the Diocese of the Windward Islands to be used by him as he thinks fit in his diocese*'.

Where, however, the added words set out the purposes for which the gift is to be held, it must be seen whether or not those declared purposes are charitable. Thus, in *Dunne v Bryne*,[217] residue was left to 'the Roman Catholic Archbishop of Brisbane and his successors to be used and expended wholly or in part as such archbishop may judge most conducive to the good of religion in his diocese'. It was held this was not charitable, since a thing could be most conducive to the good of religion without being charitable in the legal sense, or

208 *Re Royce* [1940] Ch 514, [1940] 2 All ER 291.   209 [1906] 2 Ch 184.
210 *Per* Kekewich J at 186.   211 *Re Arber* (1919) Times, 13 December.
212 Compare *Re Spensley's Will Trusts* [1954] Ch 233, [1954] 1 All ER 178, CA.
213 See (1960) 24 Conv 306 (V T H Delaney).
214 [1907] 1 Ch 382; *Re Norman* [1947] Ch 349, [1947] 1 All ER 400.
215 [1948] Ch 241, [1948] 1 All ER 541.   216 [1956] Ch 105, [1955] 3 All ER 71, CA.
217 [1912] AC 407, PC.

even in itself religious. This principle was applied in *Re Stratton*,[218] in which there was a gift to the vicar of a parish 'to be by him distributed at his absolute discretion among such parochial institutions or for such parochial purposes as he shall select' and in *Farley v Westminster Bank Ltd*,[219] in which the gift was to the vicars and churchwardens of two named churches 'for parochial work'. A gift for parochial purposes or for parish work means that the gift is not a gift for ecclesiastical or religious purposes in the strict sense, but that it is a gift for the assistance and furtherance of those various activities connected with the parish church that are to be found in every parish, but which include many objects that are not charitable in the legal sense of the word. On the other hand, a gift to the vicar of a church 'to be used for his work in the parish' has been held to be charitable,[220] because the added words merely had the effect of imposing a limitation on the scope of the trust, which would have been created simply by a gift to the vicar. Again, gifts to the vicar of St Alban's Church 'for such objects connected with the Church as he shall think fit',[221] and to the vicar and churchwardens of St George's Church 'for any purpose in connection with the said church which they may select',[222] have been held to be charitable. In both cases, the objects or purposes were construed as relating to the church—its fabric and services—in contrast to the parish. The court in both cases refused to import into the objects or purposes parochial activities, holding that the funds were to be held in each case on the more limited and, accordingly, charitable trusts.

(D) THE ADVANCEMENT OF HEALTH OR THE SAVING OF LIVES

This, and the following sections (E)–(L), were not separate heads under Lord Macnaghten's classification, but largely rationalize existing case law, which we will put under what seems to be the most appropriate head. By 2(3)(b), 'the advancement of health' includes the prevention or relief of sickness, disease, or human suffering. The relief of sickness extends beyond the treatment or provision of care, such as a hospital, to the provision of items, services, and facilities to ease the suffering or to assist the recovery of people who are sick, convalescent, disabled, or infirm, or to provide comforts for patients.[223] A gift to a private non-profit-making hospital may be charitable even though charges are made, provided that the poor are not totally excluded and the public benefit requirement is satisfied;[224] but not a private hospital or nursing home run for profit.[225]

There have also been held charitable gifts to a hospital to provide accommodation for the use of relatives of patients who were critically ill,[226] and to provide a home of rest for nurses, because this would be calculated to increase the efficiency of the hospital by providing the means of restoring the efficiency of the nurses.[227] The hospital cases have been extended so as to render charitable 'Homes of Rest', as they were called, for lady teachers,[228]

---

[218] [1931] 1 Ch 197, CA.
[219] [1939] AC 430, [1939] 3 All ER 491, HL; *Ellis v IRC* (1949) 31 TC 178.
[220] *Re Simson* [1946] Ch 299, [1946] 2 All ER 220.
[221] *Re Bain* [1930] 1 Ch 224, CA.
[222] *Re Eastes* [1948] Ch 257, [1948] 1 All ER 536. [223] See CC 6, *The Relief of Sickness*.
[224] *Re Resch's Will Trusts* [1969] 1 AC 514, [1967] 3 All ER 915, PC.
[225] See *Re Smith's Will Trusts* [1962] 2 All ER 563, CA.
[226] *Re Dean's Will Trusts* [1950] 1 All ER 882. [227] *Re White's Will Trusts* [1951] 1 All ER 528.
[228] *Re Estlin* (1903) 72 LJ Ch 687.

for the sisters of a charitable community and such persons as the Mother Superior should appoint,[229] and generally so as to 'afford the means of physical and/or mental recuperation to persons in need of rest by reason of the stress and strain caused or partly caused by the conditions in which they ordinarily live and/or work'.[230]

The Commission[231] has stated that charitable purposes in relation to health are not limited to conventional medicine, but extend to complementary, alternative, or holistic methods that are concerned with healing mind, body, and spirit, in the alleviation and cure of illness. Thus treatment in the form of spiritual healing has been held to be charitable,[232] as has a trust to provide sound education in the science and art of acupuncture and traditional Chinese medicine.[233] In order to be charitable, there must be sufficient evidence of the efficacy of the method to be used. Assessing the efficacy of different therapies will depend on what benefits are claimed for it—that is, whether it is diagnostic, curative, therapeutic, and/or palliative—and whether it is offered as a complement to conventional medicine or as an alternative.

Charities for the saving of life include the Royal National Lifeboat Institution[234] and a trust for the provision of a fire brigade.[235]

(E) THE ADVANCEMENT OF CITIZENSHIP OR COMMUNITY DEVELOPMENT

This head covers a broad group of charitable purposes directed towards support for social and community infrastructure that is focused on the community rather than the individual. By s 2(3)(c), it includes:

(i)   rural or urban regeneration;[236] and

(ii) the promotion of civic responsibility, volunteering, the voluntary sector,[237] or the effectiveness or efficiency of charities.[238]

The Commission has stated[239] that the promotion of community capacity building in relation to communities that are socially and economically disadvantaged (or, in some cases, which are simply socially disadvantaged) could be accepted as a charitable purpose. The

---

[229] *Re James* [1932] 2 Ch 25.   [230] *Re Chaplin* [1933] Ch 115; *Re Banfield* [1968] 2 All ER 276.

[231] In its 2007 'Commentary on the descriptions of charitable purposes in the Charities Act 2006'.

[232] *Re Le Cren Clarke (decd)* [1996] 1 All ER 715, sub nom *Funnell v Stewart* [1996] 1 WLR 288, noted [1996] NLJ Annual Charities Review 14 (P Luxton); *Re The NFSH Charitable Trust Ltd* [2006] WTLR 629 (CC).

[233] See the entry for 'The TCM Development Trust' in the Register (also for the advancement of education).

[234] *Thomas v Howell* (1874) LR 18 Eq 198.

[235] *Re Wokingham Fire Brigade Trusts* [1951] Ch 373, [1951] 1 All ER 454.

[236] The guidance offered in RR 2, *Promotion of Urban and Rural Regeneration*, is to the effect that it must be carried out for public benefit in areas of social and economic deprivation.

[237] See RR 13, *Promotion of the Voluntary Sector for the Benefit of the Public.*

[238] See RR 14, *Promoting the Efficiency and Effectiveness of Charities and the Effective Use of Charitable Resources for the Benefit of the Public.*

[239] In RR 5, *The Promotion of Community Capacity Building*, in which this ugly phrase is said to be understood as meaning 'developing the capacity and skills of the members of a community in such a way that they are better able to identify, and help meet, their needs and to participate more fully in society'.

hundreds of local scout and guide groups previously regarded as educational[240] would now more appropriately fall within this head.

(F) THE ADVANCEMENT OF THE ARTS, CULTURE, HERITAGE OR SCIENCE

As we have seen, trusts for these purposes were at one time often held to be charitable as falling within the education head,[241] but are now clearly charitable in their own right. There may be overlap, in particular with heads (B) and (I).

The advancement of the arts covers a wide range of charitable activity, including promoting various forms of art of a national/professional and local/amateur level, the provision of arts facilities, and encouraging high standards of art.[242]

'Heritage' may be regarded as part of a country's local or national history, and traditions that are passed down through successive generations.[243] The creation and maintenance of a statue may be charitable if it enhances and improves the locality, and if it is for the benefit of its inhabitants, and advances art and education for the benefit of the public by promoting appreciation of the arts.[244]

The advancement of science includes scientific research and charities connected with various learned societies and institutions.

(G) THE ADVANCEMENT OF AMATEUR SPORT

As we have seen,[245] before the 2006 Act, a trust for mere sport was not charitable, but could be charitable as being for the advancement of education if for sport in a school or university. In 2003, the Commission recognized[246] as charitable the promotion of community participation in healthy recreation by the provision of facilities for particular sports and this is, in substance, incorporated, and possibly extended, under this new head. By s 2(3) (d), 'sport' means sports or games that promote health by involving physical or mental skill or exertion. This is consistent with the view of the Commission in RR 11 that the promotion of pastimes such as angling, billiards, pool, and snooker would not be charitable. The requirement of public benefit would seem to rule out expensive sports, such as polo, motor racing, and ocean yachting, unless there were adequate provision for the participation of the left well-off. Accordingly, although the principle of *Re Nottage*[247] has been reversed, on the facts, the actual decision might still be the same today.

The status of sport also arises under the Recreational Charities Act 1958.[248]

---

[240] *Re Webber* [1954] 3 All ER 712, 713.   [241] See p 000, *supra*.

[242] See RR 10, *Museums and Art Galleries*.

[243] See RR 9, *Preservation and Conservation*. The National Trust is a charitable body: see *Re Verrall* [1916] 1 Ch 100; likewise, a trust to preserve two ancient cottages: *Re Cranstoun* [1932] 1 Ch 537; *Re Corelli* [1943] Ch 332, [1943] 2 All ER 519. See Report for 1990, Appendix A(b); (1995) 3 Dec Ch Com 1 (Settle and Carlisle Railway Trust).

[244] *The Fine Lady upon a White Horse Appeal* [2006] WTLR 59 (CC). Note that a trust to erect and maintain the statue of a person internationally respects and of historical importance (Earl Mountbatten of Burma) was held to be charitable by the Commissioners: Report for 1981, paras 68–70. See (1983) 133 NLJ 1107 (H Picarda).

[245] See p 261, *supra*.   [246] See RR 11. *Charitable Status and Sport*.

[247] [1965] 2 Ch 649, CA (annual cup in perpetuity for the most successful yacht of the season).

[248] Discussed p 275 *et seq, infra*.

(H) THE ADVANCEMENT OF HUMAN RIGHTS, CONFLICT RESOLUTION OR RECONCILIATION, OR THE PROMOTION OF RELIGIOUS OR RACIAL HARMONY, OR EQUALITY AND DIVERSITY

All of these purposes had been recognized as charitable before the 2006 Act, but the statutory basis may make it easier to bring a case within the bounds of charity. In 2005, the Commission revised its guidance on human rights and set out a number of the ways in which human rights could be promoted.[249] It has also published its conclusions that the promotion of religious harmony, and the promotion of equality and diversity could be charitable purposes.

The advancement of conflict resolution or reconciliation includes the resolution of international conflicts and relieving the suffering, poverty, and distress arising through conflict on a national or international scale by identifying the causes of conflict and seeking to resolve such conflict. It includes the promotion of restorative justice, in which all of the parties with a stake in a particular conflict or offence come together to resolve, collectively, how to deal with the aftermath and its implications for the future. It also includes purposes directed towards mediation, conciliation, or reconciliation, as between persons, organizations, authorities, or groups involved or likely to become involved in dispute or interpersonal conflict.

(I) THE ADVANCEMENT OF ENVIRONMENTAL PROTECTION OR IMPROVEMENT

This head includes preservation and conservation of the natural environment and the promotion of sustainable development. It includes the conservation of: a particular animal, bird, or other species, or 'wildlife' in general; a specific plant species, habitat, or area of land, including areas of natural beauty and scientific interest; flora, fauna, and the environment generally.[250] Charities concerned with environmental protection or improvement may need to produce independent expert evidence that is authoritative and objective to show that the particular species, land, or habitat to be conserved is worthy of conservation.

In the light of this new head of charity, it is thought that the decision in *Re Grove-Grady*[251] can no longer by relied on with confidence. In that case, the purpose was to provide 'a refuge or refuges for the preservation of all animals, birds or other creatures not human ... so that [they] shall be there safe from molestation or destruction by man'. It was held not to be charitable, but was distinguished by an Australian court in *A-G for New South Wales v Sawtell*,[252] which accepted that, since 1929, when *Re Grove-Grady* was decided, there has

---

[249] See RR 12, *The Promotion of Human Rights*. The Concordis International Trust is an example of an organization with the purpose of conflict resolution that has been registered as a charity. Cases such as *Re Strakosch* [1949] Ch 524, [1949] 2 All ER 6, CA, and *Buxton v Public Trustee* [1986] Ch 423, [1985] 2 All ER 869, CA, would be decided differently today.

[250] See RR 9, *Preservation and Conservation*. See also *Re Cylch* [2000] WTLR 1387 (CC) (the conservation and protection of the environment by the promotion of sustainable waste management practices).

[251] [1929] 1 Ch 557, CA. See *Re The Wolf Trust* [2006] WTLR 1467 (trust purpose to reintroduce wolves into Britain not charitable).

[252] [1978] 2 NSWLR 200.

been a radical change in the recognition throughout the world of the value to mankind in the preservation of wildlife in general. The court, accordingly, on the basis of arguments and evidence not considered in *Re Grove-Grady*, held that a trust for the preservation of native wildlife (both flora and fauna) was a valid charitable gift.

(J) THE RELIEF OF THOSE IN NEED BY REASON OF YOUTH, AGE, ILL HEALTH, DISABILITY, FINANCIAL HARDSHIP OR OTHER DISADVANTAGE

By s 2(3)(e), this includes relief given by the provision of accommodation or care to the persons mentioned.

This head includes charities concerned with the care, upbringing, or establishment in life of children or young people. Thus, in *Re Sahal's Will Trusts*,[253] there was held charitable a trust for the founding of a children's home, but the Court of Appeal has decided by a majority that a gift for the general benefit and general welfare of the children for the time being in a home provided and maintained by a local authority was not charitable, as it might be possible to use the fund for non-charitable purposes, such as, it was suggested, the provision of television sets for juvenile delinquents and refractory children, or even the inmates of a Borstal institution.[254] It also includes charities concerned with the relief of the effects of old age, illness, or disability, for instance, by providing specialist advice, equipment, or accommodation.

(K) THE ADVANCEMENT OF ANIMAL WELFARE

As might be expected in English courts, gifts in favour of animals generally, or a class of animals, as opposed to gifts for specific animals,[255] have long been held to be charitable—not, however, on the ground that they benefit the animals, but on the ground that they produce a benefit to mankind. Thus, in *Re Wedgwood*,[256] a trust for the protection and benefit of animals was held to be charitable on this ground, Swinfen Eady LJ observing:[257]

> a gift for the benefit and protection of animals tends to promote and encourage kindness towards them, to discourage cruelty, and to ameliorate the condition of the brute creation, and thus to stimulate humane and generous sentiments in man towards the lower animals; and by these means promote feelings of humanity and morality generally, repress brutality, and thus elevate the human race.

Accordingly, a bequest 'for the establishment of a hospital in which animals, which are useful to mankind, should be properly treated and cured and the nature of their diseases

---

[253] [1958] 3 All ER 428.

[254] *Re Cole* [1958] Ch 877, [1958] 3 All ER 102, CA. There seems much to be said for the dissenting judgment of Lord Evershed MR.

[255] *Re Dean* (1889) 41 Ch D 552. Perhaps this was the point in the judge's mind in *Re Green's Will Trust* [1985] 3 All ER 455, when he dismissed an objection that 'cruelly treated animals are too small a section of the animal community'.

[256] [1915] 1 Ch 113, [1914–15] All ER Rep 322, CA; *Re Grove-Grady* [1929] 1 Ch 557, CA, compromised on appeal sub nom *A-G v Plowden* [1931] WN 89, HL; *National Anti-Vivisection Society v IRC* [1948] AC 31, [1947] 2 All ER 217, HL. See, generally, on animal welfare trusts (1987) 13 Mon LR 1 (P Jamieson).

[257] At 122 and 327.

investigated, with a view to public advantage' was held to be charitable in *University of London v Yarrow*,[258] and in *Re Douglas*,[259] the Home for Lost Dogs was said to be a charitable institution. Again, in *Re Moss*,[260] a gift to a lady 'for her to use at her discretion for her work for the welfare of cats and kittens needing care and protection' was held to be charitable on evidence that, for many years, she had carried on the work of receiving, sheltering, and caring for unwanted or stray cats, the judge observing[261] that:

> the care of and consideration for animals which through old age or sickness or otherwise are unable to care for themselves are manifestations of the finer side of human nature, and gifts in furtherance of these objects are calculated to develop that side and are therefore, calculated to benefit mankind.

(L) THE PROMOTION OF THE EFFICIENCY OF THE ARMED FORCES OF THE CROWN, OR OF THE EFFICIENCY OF THE POLICE, FIRE AND RESCUE SERVICES, OR AMBULANCE SERVICES

By s 2(3)(f), the term 'fire and rescue services' means 'services provided by the fire and rescue authorities under Part 2 of the Fire and Rescue Services Act 2004'.

It has long been established that to increase the efficiency of the armed forces or the police forces is a charitable purpose and gifts calculated to have this effect are accordingly charitable: for instance, gifts for the benefit of a volunteer corps,[262] and to promote the defence of the United Kingdom from the attack of hostile aircraft.[263] This principle was said to be unassailable in *IRC v City of Glasgow Police Athletic Association*,[264] but doubt was cast on whether it had been correctly applied in earlier cases in which there had been held charitable gifts to maintain a library and purchase plate for an officers' mess,[265] and for the promotion of sport in a regiment as calculated to improve the physical efficiency of the army.[266] By way of contrast, a gift for the welfare benefit or assistance of members of the Royal Navy, whether past, present, or future, was held not to be charitable as it could be used purely for the benefit of ex-members of the Navy not being necessarily poor or aged or in any other way objects of charity.[267]

(M) ANY OTHER PURPOSE WITHIN SUBS (4)

This brings in purposes recognized as charitable before the 2006 Act, but not within s 2(2), heads (A)–(L).

The House of Lords held, in *Scottish Burial Reform and Cremation Society Ltd v Glasgow City Corporation*,[268] that the purposes of the appellant company—namely, primarily, to promote and afford facilities for cremation—were charitable. Very different, but also charitable,

---

[258] (1857) 1 De G & J 72, 79.
[259] (1887) 35 Ch D 472, CA. Also the RSPCA: see *Re Wedgwood, supra*.   [260] [1949] 1 All ER 495.
[261] At 497, 498.   [262] *Re Lord Stratheden and Campbell* [1894] 3 Ch 265.
[263] *Re Driffill* [1950] Ch 92, [1949] 2 All ER 933.
[264] [1953] AC 380, [1953] 1 All ER 747, HL. See also *Downing v Taxation Comr of Commonwealth of Australia* (1971) 125 CLR 185.
[265] *Re Good* [1905] 2 Ch 60.
[266] *Re Gray* [1925] Ch 362. There would seem to be less doubt about this case than about *Re Good, supra*.
[267] *Re Meyers* [1951] Ch 534, [1951] 1 All ER 538.
[268] [1968] AC 138, [1967] 3 All ER 215, HL.

are the purposes of the Incorporated Council of Law Reporting for England and Wales, which publishes law reports, not for profit, in order to further the sound development and administration of the law in this country.[269] By analogy, the Charity Commission has taken the view that family conciliation services can be charitable as advancing the administration of the law, divorce being a judicial process.[270]

In *Re Smith*,[271] a gift of residue 'unto my country England to and for...own use and benefit absolutely' was held to be charitable, and this may be justified on the ground that, where no purpose is defined, a charitable purpose may be implicit in the context.[272] There is considerable difficulty as regards gifts limited to a particular locality. One line of cases[273] establishes the principle that if the purposes are not charitable per se, the localization of them will not make them charitable. The difficulty is really caused by *Goodman v Saltash Corpn*[274]—unfortunately, a decision of the House of Lords. Always cited in this context are words of Lord Selborne LC:[275] 'A gift subject to a condition or trust for the benefit of the inhabitants of a parish or town or of any particular class of such inhabitants is (as I understand the law) a charitable trust.' Accordingly, it would seem that, under such a charitable trust, the trust funds may properly be used for public or benevolent purposes in a parish, although a gift for public or benevolent purposes in a parish would not be charitable.

This anomalous[276] situation will not be extended. Being a House of Lords decision, it must be followed by lower courts in an appropriate case, as was done in *Re Norton's Will Trusts*,[277] in which the gift was 'for the benefit of the church and parish', but the Court of Appeal felt able to distinguish it in *Re Endacott*,[278] in which the testator gave his residuary estate 'to North Tawton Devon Parish Council for the purpose of providing some useful memorial to myself', and Jenkins LJ has even observed[279] that the line of cases based on *Goodman v Saltash Corpn*[280] 'should not now be regarded as authoritative save in so far as they can be explained on the ground that the particular purpose was regarded as falling within the spirit and intendment of the preamble to the Statute of Elizabeth I'. More recently, in *A-G of the Cayman Islands v Wahr-Hansen*,[281] Lord Browne-Wilkinson said that: 'For reasons that are obscure, [the locality] cases have been benevolently construed. They are now so long established that...they remain good law.' They are exceptions to the

---

[269] *Incorporated Council of Law Reporting for England and Wales v A-G* [1972] Ch 73, [1971] 3 All ER 1029, CA. (Also for the advancement of education in the opinion of the majority of the court: see pp 259, 260, *supra*.)

[270] Report for 1983, paras 28–34. See also *Re Restorative Justice Consortium Ltd* [2006] WTLR 1053 (CC).

[271] [1932] 1 Ch 153, CA, applied *Re Harding (decd)* [2007] EWHC 3 (Ch), [2007] 1 All ER 747. See (1940) 56 LQR 49 (M Albery).

[272] *Williams' Trustees v IRC* [1947] AC 447, 459, [1947] 1 All ER 513, 521, HL; *Re Strakosch* [1949] Ch 529, [1949] 2 All ER 6, CA.

[273] *Houston v Burns* [1918] AC 337, [1918–19] All ER Rep 817, HL; *Re Gwyon* [1930] 1 Ch 255; *Williams' Trusts v IRC*, *supra*; *Re Sanders' Will Trusts* [1954] Ch 265, [1954] 1 All ER 667, compromised on appeal (1954) Times, 22 July, CA.

[274] (1882) 7 App Cas 633, HL, applied *Peggs v Lamb* [1994] Ch 172, [1994] 2 All ER 15.   [275] At 642.

[276] See the discussion by Lord Simonds in *Williams' Trusts v IRC*, *supra*, at 459, 521; *IRC v Baddeley* [1955] AC 572, [1955] 1 All ER 525, HL; *Re Harding (decd)* [2007] EWHC 3 (Ch), [2007] 1 All ER 747.

[277] [1948] 2 All ER 842. Cf *Verge v Somerville* [1924] AC 496, [1924] All ER Rep 121, PC.

[278] [1960] Ch 232, [1959] 3 All ER 562, CA. Cf *Murray v Thomas* [1937] 4 All ER 545.

[279] In the Court of Appeal in *Baddeley v IRC* [1953] Ch 504, 527, [1953] 2 All ER 233, 246.

[280] (1882) 7 App Cas 633, HL.   [281] [2001] 1 AC 75, [2000] 3 All ER 642, PC.

well-established principle that general words are not to be artificially construed so as to be impliedly limited to charitable purposes only. *Re Endacott*[282] was itself distinguished by a Canadian court in *Re Levy Estate*,[283] in which a gift of residue was held not to lose its charitable status by reason of a direction that it was 'to be in the form of a dedication honouring and recognizing the deceased'. This was said to be a corollary to, and not to defeat, the main charitable intention.

Difficulties may arise where there is a trust, commonly as the result of a public appeal, in relation to a specified disaster that has already happened. Such a trust was held to be charitable in the case of disastrous floods in the Lyn Valley, in relation to a trust to relieve hardship and suffering by the local people, and others, who were in the area at the time of the disaster and suffered by it.[284] But if the victims are a specific and identifiable group, the trust may be non-charitable on the ground that it lacks the necessary element of public benefit.[285] Thus it was conceded in *Re Gillingham Bus Disaster Fund*,[286] in which a bus ran into a column of cadets, killing twenty-four and injuring others, that the funeral expenses and care of the boys were not, for this reason, charitable objects. To get over this difficulty, the Charity Commission advises that the trust deed in this sort of case should utilize the poverty exception[287] and restrict the benefits to those in need.[288]

The Commission[289] has listed a number of other examples, including:

(i)   the provision of public works and services, and the provision of public amenities (such as the repair of bridges, ports, havens, causeways, and highways, the provision of water and lighting, a cemetery or crematorium, as well as the provision of public libraries, reading rooms, and public conveniences);

(ii)   the relief of unemployment;[290]

(iii)   the defence of the country (such as trusts for national or local defences);

(iv)   the promotion of certain patriotic purposes (such as war memorials);

(v)   the promotion of industry and commerce;[291]

(vi)   the promotion of agriculture and horticulture;

(vii)   the promotion of mental or moral improvement;

(viii)   the promotion of the moral or spiritual welfare or improvement of the community;

(ix)   the preservation of public order;

---

[282] *Supra*, CA.   [283] [1987] 62 OR (2d) 212.

[284] *Re North Devon and West Somerset Relief Fund Trusts* [1953] 2 All ER 1032.

[285] See p 279 *et seq*. The size of the group may be relevant. This may explain the different results in the last cited and next cited cases.

[286] [1958] Ch 300, [1958] 1 All ER 37; affd [1959] Ch 62, [1958] 2 All ER 749, and see *Re Hobourn Aero Components Ltd's Air Raid Distress Fund* [1946] Ch 194, [1946] 1 All ER 501, CA.

[287] Discussed p 285 *et seq, infra*.

[288] See Report for 1965, paras 54–58, and Report for 1966, paras 9–12. Guidelines proposed by the Attorney-General are set out in CC40 (Version Jan 2002).

[289] In its 2007 'Commentary on the descriptions of charitable purposes in the Charities Act 2006'.

[290] See RR 3, *The Relief of Unemployment*.

[291] But note *IRC v Oldham Training Enterprise Council* [1996] STC 1218, noted [1997] BTR 59 (A Roycroft), in which the second main object—namely, promoting trade, commerce, or enterprise, and the ancillary object of providing support services and advice to and for new businesses, disqualified the institution from having charitable status, because they conferred freedom to provide private benefits to individuals engaged in trade, commerce, or enterprise.

(x) the promotion of ethical standards of conduct and compliance with the law in the public and private sectors;

(xi) the rehabilitation of ex-offenders and the prevention of crime.

4 RECREATIONAL CHARITIES

Until the Recreational Charities Act 1958, a trust purely for the purpose of recreation was not charitable,[292] although sport in a school might be charitable as being for the advancement of education,[293] and sport in the army might be charitable as improving its efficiency.[294] It was also accepted that the provision of land for use as a recreation ground by the community at large or by the inhabitants of a particular area is charitable.[295]

The 1958 Act, as amended by the Charities Act 2006, s 5, established the charitable status of many recreational trusts. It provides that:

> ...it shall be and be deemed always to have been charitable to provide, or assist in the provision of, facilities for recreation or other leisure-time occupation,[296] if the facilities are provided in the interests of social welfare.[297]

In construing this provision, the Charity Commission has taken the view that there is no requirement for an educative element in the provision of recreational facilities.[298]

The social welfare requirement cannot be satisfied if the basic conditions are not met. These are set out in s 2A, as follows:

(a) that the facilities are provided with the object of improving the conditions of life for the persons for whom the facilities are primarily intended,[337] and

(b) that either—
   (i) those persons have need of the facilities by reason of their youth, age, infirmity or disability, poverty, or social and economic circumstances, or
   (ii) the facilities are to be available to members of the public at large or to male,[299] or to female, members of the public at large.

In *Guild v IRC*,[300] the House of Lords unanimously approved the dissenting judgment of Bridge LJ in *IRC v McMullen*,[301] and rejected the argument that facilities are not provided

---

[292] *Re Nottage* [1895] 2 Ch 649.   [293] *Re Mariette* [1915] 2 Ch 284.

[294] *Re Gray* [1925] Ch 362.

[295] *Re Hadden* [1932] 1 Ch 133, [1931] All ER Rep 539; *IRC v Baddeley, supra*, HL; *Re Morgan* [1955] 2 All ER 632; *Bath and North East Somerset Council v A-G* [2002] EWHC 1623 (Ch), [2002] WTLR 1257; *Strathalbyn Show Jumping Club v Mayes* (2001) 79 SASR 54. Cf (1976) 54 CBR 784 (D Waters).

[296] See *Re Samford Hall Trust* [1995] 1 Qd R 60.

[297] The view of the Charity Commission in RR 4 is that the phrase 'the interests of social welfare' implies elements of both altruism and social obligation.

[298] *Re Fairfield (Croydon) Ltd* (1997) 5 Dec Ch Com 14. The provision of a cyber cafe in an area of social and economic deprivation may constitute a charitable recreational facility within the Act.

[299] 'Male' added to the original 'female' only provision thought to be incompatible with the European Convention on Human Rights. As to a registered sports club under the Finance Act 2002, see the Charities Act 2006, s 5 (4), (5).

[300] [1992] 2 AC 310, [1992] 2 All ER 10, HL, noted [1992] Conv 361 (H Norman); (1992) 51 CLJ 429 (J Hopkins); (1992/93) 1 CLPR 45 (D Morris); *Russell's Executor v IRC* 1992 SC (HL) 71, HL.

[301] [1979] 1 All ER 588, [1979] 1 WLR 130, CA; revsd [1981] AC 1, [1980] 1 All ER 884, HL on another ground: see p 261.

in the interests of social welfare unless they are provided with the object of improving the
conditions of life for persons who suffer from some form of social disadvantage. It suffices
if they are provided with the object of improving the conditions of life for members of the
community generally.

Subject to the requirement of social welfare, subs (3) provides that the Act:

> ...applies in particular to the provision of facilities at village halls, community centres
> and women's institutes, and to the provision and maintenance of grounds and buildings
> to be used for purposes of recreation or leisure-time occupation, and extends to the provi-
> sion of facilities for those purposes by the organising of any activity.

All that this means, it has been said,[302] is 'that the facilities with which the section as a
whole is dealing may be provided at these places: that is to say, on the particular premises
belonging to or associated with the examples given'.

It is specifically provided that nothing in s 1 is to derogate from the principle that a trust
or institution, to be charitable, must be for the public benefit.[303] The Charity Commission
is of the opinion that community associations and other recreational organizations that
otherwise meet the requirements of the Recreational Charities Act 1958, and which are
established for identifiable racial minority groups (including those defined by religion),
can properly be regarded as being charitable where the group in question is in special need
of the recreational facilities provided by the organization because of the group's social
and economic circumstances.[304] It has been held that s 1(2)(b)(ii) does not require that the
facilities should be available to members of the public at large primarily or without being
subject to the primary intention of benefit to others.[305]

5 TRUSTS THAT HAVE BEEN HELD
NOT TO BE CHARITABLE

Trusts that have been held not to be charitable include a trust to provide 'knickers' (short
trousers) for boys living in a certain area,[306] a trust to encourage emigration,[307] and the
trust under George Bernard Shaw's will to provide for research into, and propaganda on,
the advantages of a reform of the alphabet.[308] The Charity Commission has taken the view

---

[302] *IRC v McMullen, supra, per* Walton J at first instance, at 242.
[303] See *Wynn v Skegness UDC* [1966] 3 All ER 336, [1967] 1 WLR 52.   [304] (1995) 4 Dec Ch Com 18.
[305] *Wynn v Skegness UDC, supra.* As to the meaning of need in s 1(2)(b)(i), see *Belfast City YMCA
Trustees v Valuation Comr for Northern Ireland* [1969] NI 3, CA, esp Curran LJ at 23.
[306] *Re Gwyon* [1930] 1 Ch 255 (not for the relief of poverty and not saved by restriction to a particular
area).
[307] *Re Sidney* [1908] 1 Ch 488, CA. Cf *Re Tree* [1945] Ch 325 (a trust to help poor emigrants, charitable as
being for the relief of poverty).
[308] *Re Shaw* [1957] 1 All ER 745; compromised on appeal, [1958] 1 All ER 245n, CA. The money given up
by the residuary legatees under the compromise was spent on the creation of a forty-eight-letter alphabet and
the publication of a bi-alphabetical edition of *Androcles and the Lion*, more than 50,000 copies of which were
distributed before the compromise money was exhausted.

that the provision of a service for charities is not necessarily a charitable purpose of itself and, accordingly, refused to register as a charity a company formed to provide catering staff at cost exclusively for charities, such as voluntary hospitals and old people's homes,[309] although a different view was taken in regard to the provision to charitable organizations of advice and assistance in the field of information technology so as to improve their efficiency.[310] Again, it has been held that it is not open to one charity to subscribe to the funds of another charity unless the recipient charity is expressly, or by implication, a purpose or object of the donor charity.[311]

'Equity has always refused to recognize [political] objects as charitable.'[312] Political objects include:

(i)   furthering the interests of a political party;

(ii) procuring, or opposing[313] changes in the law of this, or a foreign, country;

(iii) procuring a reversal of government policy or a particular decision of government authority in this, or a foreign, country.[314]

One ground upon which the *National Anti-Vivisection Society's Case*[315] was decided was that a, if not *the*, main object of the Society was to obtain an alteration of the law, and that this was a political object. The law, it is said,[316] cannot stultify itself by holding that it is for the public benefit that the law itself should be changed; the court must decide on the principle that the law is right as it stands. To do otherwise, even if the court could, on the evidence, form a prima facie opinion that the proposed change in the law would be for

---

[309] Report of the Charity Commissioners for 1969, para 20.

[310] See Report for 1990, Appendix A (f).

[311] *Baldry v Feintuck* [1972] 2 All ER 81. Nor can a charity give a gratuitous guarantee in respect of the liability of a third party with whom it has no legal tie: *Rosemary Simmons Memorial Housing Association Ltd v United Dominions Trust Ltd* [1987] 1 All ER 281. See [1988] Conv 275 (Jean Warburton).

[312] *Per* Lord Parker in *Bowman v Secular Society Ltd* [1917] AC 406, 442, [1916–17] All ER Rep 1, 18, HL. See [1995] NLJ Annual Charities Review 24 (P Luxton); (1996) NLJ Christmas App Supp 30 (G Griffiths); (1999) 50 NILQ 298 (A Dunn); [1999] CLP 254 (G F K Santow); (2002) 8 Cant LR 345 (Nicola Silke). The possible effect of the Human Rights Act 1998 is discussed in (2002) KCLJ (G Moffat). See also *Public Trustee v A-G of New South Wales* (1997) 42 NSWLR 600.

[313] *Re Koeppler Will Trusts* [1984] Ch 243, [1984] 2 All ER 111; revsd [1986] Ch 423, [1985] 2 All ER 869, CA, without affecting relevant dictum; *Molloy v CIR* [1981] 1 NZLR 689. In *Hanchett-Stamford* [2008] EWHC 330 (Ch), [2008] 4 All ER 323, it was held that the Performing and Captive Animals Defence League was not a charity because one of its objects was to change the law.

[314] *McGovern v A-G* [1982] Ch 321, [1981] 3 All ER 493 (Amnesty International Trust not charitable), noted (1982) 45 MLR 704 (R Nobles) and see (1982) 10 NZULR 169 (C E F Rickett); (1983) 46 MLR 385 (F Weiss); [1984] Conv 263 (Caroline J Farder). Cf *R v Radio Authority, ex p Bull* [1997] 2 All ER 561, CA.

[315] [1948] AC 31, [1947] 2 All ER 217, HL. The other was that it lacked the required element of public benefit. In this case, Lord Simonds expressly refused to express an opinion as to whether cases such as *Re Cranston* [1898] 1 IR 431, CA, and *Re Slatter* [1905] 21 TLR 295, which decided that vegetarian societies, the object of which was to stop the killing of animals for food, were charitable, were rightly decided.

[316] See *National Anti-Vivisection Society v IRC, supra*, especially *per* Lord Wright at 50, 224–225, and *per* Lord Simonds at 62, 232. Lord Parker, dissenting, thought that political objects here should be restricted to those the only means of attainment of which is a change of law. Elsewhere in their speeches both Lord Wright and Lord Simonds frankly recognized that, in changing conditions, the same purpose may at one time be beneficial, and at another injurious, to the public. See p 285, *infra*.

the public benefit, would be to usurp the functions of the legislature, and might prejudice the reputation of the judiciary for political impartiality. As is commonly the case in
charity matters, the cases run to find distinctions; thus a gift to a temperance society, the
object of which was the promotion of temperance mainly by political means, was held
not to be charitable,[317] while, in a subsequent case, the Court of Appeal held that a gift
for the promotion of temperance generally was.[318] It should be added that some purposes
that would previously have been considered not to be charitable because of being political
would now be accepted as charitable, as a consequence of the extended meaning given to
'charitable purposes' by s 2 of the Charities Act 2006—in particular, s 2(2)(h)—and the
Human Rights Act 1998.

The law makes a distinction between 'charitable purposes' and 'charitable activities'. In
order to be a charity, an organization must be established exclusively for charitable purposes, which cannot include a political purpose. An organization that has surmounted this
hurdle and exists as a charity may, however, provided that it is permitted by its governing
document, undertake campaigning and political activity as a positive way of furthering or
supporting its purposes, but it can do so only in the context of supporting the delivery of
its charitable purposes. A charity may even choose to focus most, or all, of its resources on
political activity for a period, but the charity trustees must ensure that this activity is not,
and does not become, the reason for the charity's existence.

The Charity Commission has recently revised its *Guidance on Campaigning and Political
Activity by Charities*.[319] It focuses first on the freedoms and possibilities for charities to
campaign, and only then on the restrictions and risks that trustees must bear in mind. It
uses the term 'campaigning' to refer to the raising of awareness and to efforts to educate
or involve the public by mobilizing their support on a particular issue, or to influence or
change public attitudes. It also uses it to refer to campaigning activity that aims to ensure
that existing laws are observed. It distinguishes this from 'political activity', by which it
means activity that involves trying to secure support for, or opposition to, a change in the
law, or in the policy or decisions of central government, local authorities, or other public
bodies, whether in this country or abroad.

Before embarking on campaigning or political activity, the trustees must weigh up the
pros and cons. To take a decision to proceed, they must be satisfied, on reasonable grounds,
that the activities are likely to be an effective means of furthering or supporting the purposes of the charity, and that they are able to justify the resources applied. Some types of
campaigning and political activity—particularly those that have a high public profile—
have the potential not only to enhance, but also to damage the charity's reputation and to
compromise its independence. The trustees must take account of these risks.

Charities can campaign for a change in the law, policy, or decisions of central or local
government or other public authorities where such change would support the charity's
purposes. They can also campaign to ensure that existing laws are observed. However,
as we have seen, it is not a charitable purpose to campaign for changes in the law, in the

---

[317] *IRC v Temperance Council of Christian Churches of England and Wales* (1926) 136 LT 27.
[318] *Re Hood* [1931] 1 Ch 240, CA.
[319] See CC9. See also the Report of an Inquiry into the campaigning activities of Oxfam, and (1999) 5
CLPR 219 (Debra Morris).

United Kingdom, or elsewhere. In pursuance of its purposes, it can support, oppose, or comment on Bills before Parliament, or even promote new legislation: the Carers (Equal Opportunities) Act 2004 was the direct result of lobbying by a number of charities.

Finally, it should be noted that there is nothing to prevent an organization that has some purposes that, taken by themselves, are exclusively charitable and other related purposes that are political and non-charitable, from, in effect, dividing itself into two by founding an entirely separate organization restricted to carrying out such of the purposes as are charitable, while the original organization concentrates on the political purposes.[320] And a charity will not lose its charitable status merely because its trustees or officers are also the trustees or officers of a political and non-charitable body operating in the same field, or if, as individuals, they engage in politics.[321] Further, if a charitable organization improperly uses some of its funds for purposes that are not charitable, it does not thereby lose its charitable status. Such an act would constitute a breach of trust, making the trustees personally liable for the improper expenditure in question.

6 THE REQUIREMENT OF PUBLIC BENEFIT[322]

The Charities Act 2006, s 2(1)(b), continues the rule that, in order to be charitable, a purpose must be for the public benefit, and it is expressly provided that 'public benefit' refers to the concept as previously understood in charity law[323] under which it had to be shown that the purpose was for the benefit of the community (or public), or an appreciably important section of the community (or public). Before the Act, it was presumed that purposes for the relief of poverty, the advancement of education, or the advancement of religion were for the public benefit, subject to evidence to the contrary.[324] Other organizations had to provide evidence that their purpose was for the public benefit. Section 3(2) has abolished the presumption, putting all organizations seeking to establish charitable status on the same footing. The abolition did not, of itself, deprive existing charities for the relief of poverty, or the advancement of education, or religion of their charitable status, but they became at risk of losing it if their public benefit could not be established. The Charity Commission was required to issue guidance to promote awareness and understanding of the public benefit requirement, and to revise its guidance from time to time.[325] After due consultation, guidance was issued under the title *Charities and Public Benefit* in January 2008.[326]

---

[320] For example, the National Council of Civil Liberties—non-charitable—and the Cobden Trust, an educational charity formed to undertake 'the promotion of research into civil liberties and an understanding of the civil rights, liberties and duties of citizens and public servants in Britain'.

[321] Report for 1976, para 101.

[322] See, generally, (1956) 72 LQR 187 (G Cross); (1958) 21 MLR 138 (P S Aityah); (1993/94) 2 CLPR 203 (J Callman). For a discussion of the difficulties of making a donation to a charity coupled with an undertaking by the charity to benefit a specified individual, see (1999) 6 CLPR 31 (R Venables and Judith Morris).

[323] Charities Act 2006, s 3(3).   [324] But see (2008) 124 LQR 347 (J Hackney).

[325] Charities Act 2006, s 4.

[326] Available online at <http://www.charitycommission.gov.com>. Designed to be read with it has also published a document entitled Analysis of the Law Underpinning Charities and Public Benefit, similarly available.

Whether or not there is an identifiable benefit, which may be tangible or intangible, direct or indirect,[327] is a question of fact that must be answered by the court by means of evidence cognisable by it. Benefits must be balanced against any detriment or harm, even though the types of benefit and detriment may be of very different nature and quality. Thus, in *National Anti-Vivisection Society v IRC*,[328] the court concluded that the value of the material benefits of vivisection outweighed the moral benefits of anti-vivisection. If the evidence establishes that there is no benefit,[329] or if the benefit is not capable of proof, the claim to charitable status will fail. In *Gilmour v Coats*,[330] there was a trust for an association of strictly cloistered and purely contemplative nuns. Its purpose was clearly for the advancement of religion and, as the law then stood, was presumed to be for the public benefit. It was nevertheless held not to be charitable as lacking the element of public benefit. So far as the intercessory prayers of the nuns were alleged to be productive of public benefit, the court could not consider it; the court could only act on evidence before it and no temporal court could determine the truth of any religious belief. And the benefit alleged to be derived by others from the example of pious lives was held to be too vague and intangible to satisfy the test of public benefit.[331] Elsewhere, Farwell J has observed[332] that 'there is, in truth, no charity in attempting to improve one's own mind or save one's own soul. Charity is necessarily altruistic and involves the idea of aid or benefit to others'. Again, the courts have held that they cannot assess the benefit of a change to the law or government policy.[333]

As Lord Simonds has pointed out,[334] however:

> when a purpose appears broadly to fall within one of the familiar categories of charity, the court will assume it to be for the benefit of the community, and, therefore, charitable unless the contrary is shown, and further the court will not be astute in such a case to defeat upon doubtful evidence the avowed benevolent intention of the donor.

The most baffling problem[335] in this context is to determine whether or not the common characteristic that is shared by a number of persons is, or is not, such as to make them a

---

[327] *Income Tax Special Purposes Comrs v Pemsel* [1891] AC 531, 583.

[328] [1948] AC 33, [1947] 2 All ER 317.

[329] As in *Re Pinion* [1965] Ch 85, [1964] 1 All ER 890, CA, in which expert evidence was given that a collection of proposed exhibits 'was worthless as a means of education, and no useful purpose could be served by foisting on the public a mass of junk'.

[330] [1949] AC 426, [1949] 1 All ER 848, HL; *Cocks v Manners* (1871) LR 12 Eq 574, 585, *per* Wickens VC: '*A voluntary association of women for the purpose of working out their own salvation by religious exercises and self-denial seems to me to have none of the requisites of a charitable institution.*' These cases were rightly distinguished in *Re Banfield* [1968] 2 All ER 276. Cf the decision of the Charity Commissioners in Report for 1989, paras 56–62, (1995) 3 Dec Ch Com 11 (the Society of the Precious Blood), and see (2001) 21 LS 26 (P W Edge and J M Loughren); (2001) 7 CLPR 151 (T Haddock).

[331] As Greene MR said in the Court of Appeal, sub nom *Re Coats' Trusts* [1948] Ch 340, 353, [1949] 1 All ER 521, 528, 'they are to be paid, not to do good, but to be good'.

[332] In *Re Delany* [1902] 2 Ch 642, 648, 649.

[333] *McGovern v A-G* [1982] Ch 321, [1981] 3 All ER 493.

[334] In *National Anti-Vivisection Society v IRC* [1948] AC 31, 65, [1947] 2 All ER 217, 233, HL: *Re Watson* [1973] 3 All ER 678. See Report for 1991, Appendix D(b), in which the public benefit element is regarded as self-evident in relation to charities for the promotion of education, or of the arts generally. Evidence would be needed, however, if the education provided, or the arts promoted, were of a particular nature or type.

[335] See, eg, *Re Mead's Will Trust Deed* [1961] 2 All ER 836, 840 (members of a trade union not a section of the public for a trust under Lord Macnaghten's fourth head), in which Cross J, as he then was, said despairingly not only that this is a very difficult question, but that 'there appears to be no principle by reference to which it can be answered'.

section of the public. The test that has been most consistently applied during the last sixty or so years, often referred to as the 'Compton test',[336] was approved by the majority of the House of Lords in *Oppenheim v Tobacco Securities Trust Co Ltd.*[337] According to this test, in order to constitute a section of the public, the possible beneficiaries must not be numerically negligible, and the quality that distinguishes them from other members of the public, so that they form by themselves a section of it, must be a quality that does not depend on their relationship to a particular individual. It must be essentially impersonal and not personal. A section of the public, in this sense, has been contrasted with a fluctuating body of private individuals. Applying this test, the inhabitants of a named place normally constitute a section of the public. The principle, as expressed a little differently by Peter Gibson J in *Re Koeppler Will Trusts*,[338] is that '*the beneficiaries must not be a private class qualifying by reason of some relationship unconnected with the charitable purpose*'.

In *Re Compton* itself, a trust for the education of the lawful descendants of three named persons was held not to be for a section of the public and thus not charitable, and the same result was reached in the *Oppenheim* case, in which the trust was again for the advancement of education, and the potential beneficiaries were the children of employees and former employees of one or other of a group of companies. They were held not to constitute a section of the public, notwithstanding that the number of employees was over 110,000. In the *Oppenheim* case, counsel had pointed out some of the anomalies that may flow from an application of the *Compton* test. In his speech in the House of Lords, Lord Simonds first set out counsel's argument:

> Admittedly, those who follow a profession or calling—clergymen, lawyers, colliers, tobacco-workers and so on—are a section of the public, and how strange then it would be if, as in the case of railwaymen, those who follow a particular calling are all employed by one employer. Would a trust for the education of men employed on the railways by the Transport Board not be charitable? And what of service of the Crown, whether in the civil service or the armed forces? Is there a difference between soldiers and soldiers of the King?

His comment was short but clear: 'My Lords, I am not impressed by this sort of argument...'[339] The Charity Commission takes the view that a class whose distinguishing feature is an impersonal quality may be a sufficient section of the community even though its constituent members also happen to share some personal characteristic (for example, being tenants or related to tenants of a single landlord).[340]

The *Compton* test was, however, regarded as inadequate by Lord MacDermott, giving the only dissenting speech in the *Oppenheim*[341] case, and his views have since received

---

[336] *Re Compton* [1945] Ch 123, [1945] 1 All ER 198, CA; *Re Hobourn Aero Components Ltd's Air Raid Distress Fund* [1946] Ch 194, [1946] 1 All ER 501, CA. The Commission's approach is that it should be both cautious and flexible in the application of the *Compton* test: *Analysis of the Law Underpinning the Charities and Public Benefit*, para 3.45.

[337] [1951] AC 297, [1951] 1 All ER 31, HL.

[338] [1984] 2 All ER 111, 125; revsd [1986] Ch 423, [1986] Ch 423, [1985] 2 All ER 869, CA, without affecting this dictum.

[339] *Per* Lord Simonds in *Oppenheim v Tobacco Securities Trust Co Ltd, supra,* at 34, 35, 307.

[340] *Analysis of the Law Underpinning Charities and Public Benefit*, para 3.46.

[341] *Supra*, HL. The same judge, in *Baptist Union of Ireland (Northern) Corpn Ltd v IRC* [1945] NI 99 (NI CA), said that the test is whether the purpose is substantially altruistic in character, and this test was adopted in *Educational Fees Protection Society Inc v IRC* [1992] 2 NZLR 115. Cf *IRC v Baddeley* [1955] AC 572, 606, [1955] 1 All ER 525, 543, HL, *per* Lord Reid.

strong support from *obiter dicta* of Lord Cross in *Dingle v Turner*,[342] dicta in which all of the other Law Lords concurred. In the opinion of Lord Cross, the distinction between personal and impersonal relationships is unsatisfactory: as Lord MacDermott had pointed out in the *Oppenheim*[343] case, it is accepted that the poor and the blind are sections of the public, but what is more personal than poverty or blindness? Further, the attempt to elucidate the phrase 'a section of the public' by contrasting it with 'a fluctuating body of private individuals' is unhelpful, since a particular group of persons might equally well answer both descriptions. At the end of the day, Lord Cross said, one is left where one started with the bare contrast between 'public' and 'private', and, in his view, the question of whether or not the potential beneficiaries of a trust can fairly be said to constitute a section of the public is (as it was generally thought to be before *Re Compton*)[344] a question of degree. In the light of these dicta, the precise standing of the *Compton* test is uncertain. It may still be considered binding at first instance, but the House of Lords might well take a different view, particularly if the trust in question should be other than for the advancement of education.

In *Dingle v Turner*,[345] Lord Cross went on to say that, in his view, much must depend on the purpose of the trust:

> It may well be that, on the one hand, a trust to promote some purpose, prima facie charitable, will constitute a charity even though the class of potential beneficiaries might fairly be called a private class and that, on the other hand, a trust to promote another purpose, also prima facie charitable, will not constitute a charity even though the class of potential beneficiaries might seem to some people fairly describable as a section of the public.

This, it is submitted, is eminently reasonable and entirely consistent with the view that whether or not a class constitutes a section of the public is a question of degree, taking into account all of the facts of the case. It is difficult, however, to see that an application of the *Compton* test can permit any variation in the meaning of the phrase 'a section of the public' according to the kind of charitable purpose involved.

Yet there are clear statements and decisions recognizing that such variation exists, although, unfortunately, they do not advert to the difficulties of reconciling this with the *Compton* test. For instance, Lord Somervell, in *IRC v Baddeley*,[346] declared himself unable to accept the principle:

> that a section of the public sufficient to support a valid trust in one category must, as a matter of law, be sufficient to support a trust in any other category... There might well be a valid trust for the promotion of religion benefiting a very small class. It would not follow at all that a recreation ground for the exclusive use of the same class would be a valid charity, though it is clear... that a recreation ground for the public is a charitable purpose.

In that case, the majority of the Law Lords took the view that the social purposes were too wide to fall within Lord Macnaghten's fourth class and the trusts were, for that reason,

---

[342] [1972] AC 601, [1972] 1 All ER 878, HL noted (1972) 36 Conv 209; (1974) 33 CLJ 63 (G Jones). See also [1987] Conv 14 (Norma Dawson).

[343] [1951] AC 297, [1951] 1 All ER 31, HL.   [344] *Supra*, CA.

[345] *Supra*, HL at 624, 889. See (1976) 27 NILQ 198 (J C Brady).

[346] *Supra*, HL, at 615, 549. See also *per* Lord Simonds in *National Anti-Vivisection Society v IRC* [1948] AC 31, 65, [1947] 2 All ER 217, 233, HL.

not charitable. Lord Simonds,[347] however, went on to express the view that, had the purpose fallen within the fourth head, the trusts would still not have been charitable, as the prospective beneficiaries—members and potential members of the Methodist church in West Ham and Leyton—were 'a class within a class' and did not constitute a section of the public.[348] The Commission[349] regards the proposition that a class within a class is not a section of the public as unhelpful: what is required is a rational link, correlation, or nexus between the purpose and the restriction on the beneficial class.

By contrast, in the case of religious trusts, a similar group has been held to constitute a section of the public, as in *Neville Estates Ltd v Madden*,[350] in which the group—members, for the time being, of the Catford Synagogue—was even narrower than persons of the Jewish faith living in Catford. In this case, the judge accepted that the members of the Catford Synagogue were no more a section of the public than the members of the Carmelite priory in *Gilmour v Coats*,[351] and justified the contrasting result on the ground that the nuns of the priory lived secluded from the world, while the members of the Synagogue spent their lives in the world. The court, he said,[352] is 'entitled to assume that some benefit accrues to the public from the attendance at places of worship of persons who live in this world and mix with their fellow citizens'. Likewise, in Re Hetherington,[353] it was held that the celebration of a religious rite in public—in that case, saying masses—confers a sufficient public benefit because of the edifying and improving effect of such celebration on the members of the public who attend. The same assumption can be made in relation to attendance at an educational course.[354] In considering whether the public benefit requirement is satisfied where there is a limited beneficial class, regard must be had to the extent to which there is an indirect benefit to the wider community. It should be added that it would appear that, in order for a class to form a section of the public, the qualifications for membership must be relevant to the purposes of the trust.[355]

Several further separate points should be noted. Firstly, the charitable nature of a trust is not affected by the fact that, by its very nature, only a limited number of persons are likely

---

[347] Lord Reid took a contrary view, and Lords Porter and Tucker expressly refused to express an opinion on the point.

[348] See also *Williams' Trustees v IRC* [1947] AC 447, 457, [1947] 1 All ER 513, 520, HL, *per* Lord Simonds, who, in relation to similar trusts, expressed the opinion that Welsh people, defined as persons of Welsh nationality by birth or descent or born or educated or at any time domiciled in the Principality of Wales or the county of Monmouth, did not constitute an identifiable community for this purpose. The trust has since been registered as a charity on the grounds that the imprecision of the beneficiary class does not prevent it from being a section of the public, and that, in so far as the purposes were too wide, it was saved by the Charitable Trusts (Validation) Act 1954. See Report for 1977, paras, 71–80. See also (1977) 41 Conv 8.

[349] *Analysis of the Law Underpinning Charities and Public Benefit*, paras 3.10–3.16.

[350] [1962] Ch 832, [1961] 3 All ER 769. See *Re Dunlop* [1984] NI 408, in which it was said that the advancement of religion stands upon a different footing from the relief of poverty or the advancement of education. It is not designed to confer benefits upon those who receive it as an end in itself, but to advance the ultimate purpose of spreading the word of God and accomplishing the divine purpose.

[351] [1949] AC 426, [1949] 1 All ER 848, HL. See p 280, *supra*.

[352] *Neville Estates Ltd v Madden*, supra, at 853, 751. It is difficult to reconcile this with *Re Warre's Will Trusts* [1953] 2 All ER 99; criticized in Tudor, *Charities*, 9th edn, [2.068].

[353] [1990] Ch 1, [1989] 2 All ER 129. It was said in that case that it would be otherwise where the celebration was in private. See (1989) 139 NLJ 1767 (J M Q Hepworth); (1990) 32 Mal LR 114 (C H Sherrin).

[354] *Re Koeppler Will Trusts* [1984] 2 All ER 111, 126; revsd [1986] Ch 423, [1985] 2 All ER 869, CA, without affecting this dictum.

[355] *Davies v Perpetual Trustee Co Ltd* [1959] AC 439, PC.

to avail themselves or are, perhaps, even capable of availing themselves, of its benefits: for example, a trust for the relief of anyone in the community suffering from a particular and very rare disease. If potential beneficiaries are further limited to only some of those who are suffering (for example, those living in a specified area), the trust will only be charitable where the potential beneficiaries constitute a sufficiently important section of the community.[356] In our multicultural society, there are some groups that, although numerically small, nevertheless suffer some common disadvantage and, accordingly, many organizations have been registered as charities that are designed to cater for the education, social, and personal safety needs of Asian women and girls in a particular area. If the benefits of such an organization are available to anyone who, being suitably qualified, chooses to take advantage of them, it has a public character.

Secondly, anything in the nature of a mutual benefit society[357] does not have the necessary quality of public benefit, as in *Re Hobourn Aero Components Ltd's Air Raid Distress Fund*,[358] in which voluntary collections from employees of the munition factories belonging to a certain company were to be used to relieve, without a means test, the distress suffered by the employees from air raids. This was held not to be charitable, Greene MR observing:[359]

the point to my mind, which really puts this case beyond reasonable doubt is the fact that a number of employees of this company, actuated by motives of self-help, agreed to a deduction from their wages to constitute a fund to be applied for their own benefit without any question of poverty coming into it. Such an arrangement seems to me to stamp the whole transaction as one having a personal character, money put up by a number of people, not for the general benefit, but for their own individual benefit.

This principle does not, however, apply with full force in the case of trusts for religious purposes, which may be valid even though in favour of the members of a religious organization.[360]

Thirdly, in deciding the question of law whether or not an element of public benefit is present, it is unsettled whether regard should be had to the fiscal privileges accorded to charities. In *Dingle v Turner*,[361] Lord Cross, with whose speech Lord Simon concurred, thought that it should, but the other three Law Lords expressed their doubts, and there is no case in which fiscal privileges have been expressly taken into account. Lord Cross, however, said that, in his opinion, the *Compton*[362] and *Oppenheim*[363] cases had been influenced by fiscal considerations: a trust for the education of children of employees of a company represents a fringe benefit for the employees and does not deserve fiscal privileges. There is not the same risk of abuse in the case of trusts for the relief of poverty, the privileged position of which Lord Cross thought might be thus justified on practical grounds. Lord Cross even suggested that, for the same sort of reason, a trust to promote religion among the employees of a company might be charitable, provided that the benefits were purely

356 See *per* Lord Simonds in *IRC v Baddeley* [1955] AC 572, 592, [1955] 1 All ER 525, 533, HL.

357 Unless it comes within the 'poverty' exception discussed in the following subsection by reason of a means test for benefits.

358 [1946] Ch 194, [1946] 1 All ER 501, CA; *IRC v City of Glasgow Police Athletic Association* [1953] AC 380, [1953] 1 All ER 747, HL. Cf *London Hospital Medical College v IRC* [1976] 2 All ER 113.

359 *Supra*, at 200, 506.   360 *Neville Estates Ltd v Madden* [1962] Ch 832, [1961] 3 All ER 769.

361 [1972] AC 601, [1972] 1 All ER 878, HL. See (1977) 40 MLR 397 (N P Gravells); [1978] Conv 277 (T G Watkin).

362 [1945] Ch 123, [1945] 1 All ER 198, CA.   363 [1951] AC 297, [1951] 1 All ER 31, HL.

spiritual, although purposes under Lord Macnaghten's fourth head would normally be on a par with educational trusts.

Fourthly, it must be borne in mind that the courts' understanding of public benefit and, indeed, of what purposes are charitable may vary with the passing of time. Thus, in *National Anti-Vivisection Society v IRC*,[364] Lord Wright observed:[365]

> where a society has a religious object it may fail to satisfy the test (of public benefit) if it is unlawful, and the test may vary from generation to generation as the law successively grows more tolerant…It cannot be for the public benefit to favour trusts for objects contrary to the law. Again eleemosynary trusts may, as economic ideas and conditions and ideas of social service change, cease to be regarded as being for the benefit of the community, and trusts for the advancement of learning or education may fail to secure a place as charities, if it is seen that the learning or education is not of public value.

Lastly, it may be added that it appears that a trust may be charitable, and the test of public benefit passed, where the persons to benefit are all outside the jurisdiction.[366] The criterion to be applied is the same for all charities—namely, the one adopted by the English courts. Accordingly, the Commission doubts whether the courts would regard it as charitable to support in a foreign country a religion permitted in that country, but deemed, if carried on in the United Kingdom, contrary to the public benefit. In determining the charitable status of institutions operating abroad, one should first consider whether the organization would be regarded as a charity if its operation were confined to the United Kingdom. If it would, then the organization will be presumed also to be charitable, even though operating abroad, unless it would be contrary to the public policy of this country to recognize it.[367] It is, however, necessary to distinguish between the objects of a charity and the means by which that object is to be carried out. If the object itself is contrary to the law of the foreign state in which it is to operate, then the trust will not be charitable. On the other hand, if only the means of carrying out the object is contrary to such laws, then there will be a failure in the trusts and a case for cy-près application.

7 EXCEPTIONS TO THE REQUIREMENT OF PUBLIC BENEFIT

The major anomalous head of charity for which the requirement of public benefit is not essential or is at least greatly modified is trusts for the relief of poverty. The law of charity in relation to poverty has followed its own line, and a series of cases, beginning with

---

[364] [1948] AC 31, [1947] 2 All ER 217, HL.   [365] *Supra*, at 42, 220. Also *per* Lord Simonds, at 69, 236.

[366] *Income Tax Special Purposes Comrs v Pemsel* [1891] AC 531, HL ('for the general purposes of maintaining, supporting and advancing the missionary establishments among heathen nations of the Protestant Episcopal Church'); Re Robinson [1931] 2 Ch 122 ('to the German Government for the time being for the benefit of its soldiers disabled in the late war'); *Re Niyazi's Will Trusts* [1978] 3 All ER 785, [1978] 1 WLR 910 (working men's hostel in Cyprus); and cases on foreign missions such as *Re Kenny* (1907) 97 LT 130; *Re Redish* (1909) 26 TLR 42. *Sed quaere.* See (1965) 29 Conv 123 (D M Emrys Evans).

[367] This view was said to be clearly right in *Re Carapiet's Trusts* [2002] EWHC 1304, [2002] WTLR 989. In *Re Levy's Estate* (1989) 58 DLR (4th) 375 (followed in *Re Gray* (1990) 73 DLR (4th) 161), a Canadian court held that a gift for charitable purposes in Canada is equally valid for the same charitable purposes abroad. See also (1990) 4 TL & P 74 (G Kodilinye).

Isaac v Defriez,[368] has established the validity of trusts for 'poor relations' and other groups of persons who are not normally regarded as forming, for this purpose, a section of the community. Thus, a trust for the relief of poverty was held to be charitable in *Gibson v South American Stores (Gath and Chaves Ltd)*,[369] in which the beneficiaries were selected by the tie of common employment, and in *Re Young's Will Trusts*,[370] in which there was a gift to the trustees of the Savage Club 'upon trust to be used by them as they shall in their absolute discretion think fit for the assistance of my fellow members by way of pensions or grants who may fall on evil days'. The existing cases on this matter were considered by the Court of Appeal in *Re Scarisbrick*,[371] in which, following life interests to her children, a testatrix gave half her residue to such relations—that is, relations in any degree—of her children as should be in needy circumstances. It was held that the exceptional rule in relation to trusts for the relief of poverty applied just as much to a trust for immediate distribution as to a perpetual trust. The distinction is between (a) a gift for the relief of poverty among poor people of a particular description, which is charitable even though the class of potential beneficiaries would not normally be regarded as forming a section of the public, and even though it includes specified individuals,[372] and (b) a gift to particular poor persons, which is not charitable even though the relief of poverty may be the motive of the gift. Most of the earlier cases were reviewed by the House of Lords in *Dingle v Turner*,[373] in which the validity of the poverty exception was confirmed. Their Lordships agreed that it was a natural development of the 'poor relations' decisions to hold as charitable trusts for 'poor employees' of an individual or company (the case before the House), or poor members of a club or society, and they held that it would be illogical to draw a distinction between different kinds of poverty trust.

There seems to be a second minor, and equally anomalous, exception to the requirement of public benefit in what the Privy Council has called[374] 'the ancient English institution of educational provision for "Founder's Kin" in certain schools and colleges'. Such foundations giving preference to descendants of the donor are valid, 'though there seems to be virtually no direct authority as to the principle on which they rested and they should probably be regarded as belonging more to history than to doctrine'.[375] Most founder's fellowships at Oxford and Cambridge were abolished by the Oxford University Act 1854 and the Cambridge University Act 1856, respectively, but some still exist, and there were at least two new foundations during the twentieth century.

Although hardly an exception to the rules as to public benefit, it is convenient to refer at this point to a way in which it may be possible, from a practical point of view, to evade

---

368 (1754) Amb 595; *A-G v Price* (1810) 17 Ves 371.

369 [1950] Ch 177, [1949] 2 All ER 985, CA; *Re Coulthurst* [1951] Ch 661, [1951] 1 All ER 774, CA.

370 [1955] 3 All ER 689; *Re Hilditch* (1985) 39 SASR 469 ('*poor and distressed Freemasons who shall be members or past members*' of the specified lodge).

371 [1951] Ch 622, [1951] 1 All ER 822, CA; *Re Cohen* [1973] 1 All ER 889.

372 *Re Segelman (decd)* [1996] Ch 171, [1995] 3 All ER 676, noted [1996] NLJ Annual Charities Review 12 (P Luxton); [1996] Conv 379 (Elise Histed).

373 [1972] AC 601, [1972] 1 All ER 878, HL. See [1978] Conv 277 (T G Watkin). The Goodman Committee Report recommended that the poverty exception should be abolished.

374 In *Caffoor v Income Tax Comr, Columbia* [1961] AC 584, 602, [1961] 2 All ER 436, 444, PC. See, generally, Squibb, *Founder's Kin*.

375 *Caffoor v Income Tax Comrs, Columbia, supra*; *Spencer v All Souls College* (1762) Wilm 163; *Re Compton* [1945] Ch 123, [1945] 1 All ER 198, CA.

it. It was held, in *Re Koettgen*,[376] that the charitable character of the primary trust for the advancement of education being of a sufficiently public nature, its validity was unaffected by the expression of the testator's imperative wish that, in selecting beneficiaries, the trustees should give preference to the employees of a particular company and members of their families. It was held that it was at the stage when the primary class of eligible persons was ascertained that the question of the public nature of the trust arose to be decided. Doubts have been raised,[377] however, as to whether this decision is consistent with the principle of *Oppenheim v Tobacco Securities Trust Ltd*.[378]

Finally, it should be added that it does not follow from the general rule that, in order to be charitable, a trust must be for the public benefit that a trust for the public benefit is necessarily charitable. Referring to Lord Macnaghten's speech in *Income Tax Special Purposes Comrs v Pemsel*[379] Viscount Cave LC in *A-G v National Provincial and Union Bank of England*[380] said:

> Lord Macnaghten did not mean that all trusts for purposes beneficial to the community are charitable, but that there were certain charitable trusts which fell within that category: and accordingly to argue that because a trust is for a purpose beneficial to the community it is therefore a charitable trust is to turn round his sentence and to give it a different meaning. So here it is not enough to say that the trust in question is for public purposes beneficial to the community or for the public welfare: you must also show it to be a charitable trust.

---

[376] [1954] 1 All ER 581. Cf *Vernon v IRC* [1956] 3 All ER 14; *Trustees of George Drexler Ofrex Foundation v IRC* [1966] Ch 675, [1965] 3 All ER 529; *Re Martin* (1977) 121 Sol Jo 828. See the Report for 1976, paras 45–49, and Report for 1978, paras 86–89. See also *Public Trustee v Young* (1980) 24 SASR 407, in which the preference clause was held to be simply an administrative direction to the trustee not affecting the charitable nature of the trust. Zelling J doubted the need today for a requirement of public benefit.

[377] *Caffoor v Income Tax Comrs, Columbia, supra*; *IRC v Educational Grants Association Ltd* [1967] Ch 993, [1967] 2 All ER 893, CA.

[378] *Supra.*   [379] [1891] AC 531.

[380] [1924] AC 262 at 265, H; *Williams' Trustees v IRC* [1947] AC 447, [1947] 1 All ER 513, HL; *Scottish. Burial Reform and Cremation Society Ltd v Glasgow City Corpn* [1968] AC 138, [1967] 3 All ER 215, HL. See also *Incorporated Council of Law Reporting for England and Wales v A-G* [1972] Ch 73, [1971] 3 All ER 1029, CA; *IRC v McMullen* [1979] 1 All ER 588, revsd [1981] AC 1, [1981] 1 All ER 884, HL, without affecting this point; *Brisbane City Council v A-G for Queensland* [1979] AC 411, [1978] 3 All ER 30, PC *per* Lord Wilberforce at 422, 33.

14

THE ADMINISTRATION
OF CHARITIES

The statistics indicate the importance of charities in national life. Figures produced by the Charity Commission for England and Wales ('the commission') show that, at the end of March 2008, there were 190,387 charities on the Register,[1] and, as we shall see, not all charities are required to be registered. The total income of 'main' registered charities for the year ending 31 March 2008 was £45,910bn, a not insignificant sum. A breakdown of the figures shows that most registered charities are very small organizations. Over half have an annual income of £10,000 or less, and their combined income is less than 1 per cent of the total. Including charities with an income of £100,000 or less raises the number to 85 per cent of charities, yet their combined income is less than 4.5 per cent of the total. At the other end of the scale, around 8 per cent of charities receive more than 90 per cent of the total income recorded, and the 706 largest charities, constituting merely 0.42 per cent of those on the Register, have individual incomes of £10m or more, totalling half of the recorded income for registered charities.

Clearly, such an important sector requires regulation, and the main governing legislation is now the Charities Acts 1993 and 2006. The 2006 Act made substantial amendments to the 1993 Act, while retaining the basic framework, and also introduced some totally new provisions. In this chapter, after noting the scope of the 1993 and 2006 Acts, we shall look at the different ways in which a charity may be set up. This leads on to a consideration of, firstly, the persons and bodies who have the responsibility for running charities, and, secondly, the persons and bodies who have the responsibility for their regulation and control—in particular, the Commission. We will then turn to a device available to the courts and the Commission—namely, the establishment of what is called a 'scheme'—to remedy some difficulty that has arisen in relation to a charitable trust: one particular variant of this is the cy-près scheme, which may save for charity a trust that would otherwise fail. Next, we will discuss the Register of Charities, followed by the requirements for accounts, annual reports, and annual returns, and the powers given to certain unincorporated charities to transfer property, to spend capital, and to modify their powers. The subsequent two sections deal with the new Register of Mergers set up by the 2006 Act, and the continuing restrictions on dispositions of charity land. The final two sections do not deal with exclusively charity law: the penultimate section considers

---

[1] Of these, 21,054 were subsidiaries or constituents of other charities. This means that there were 169,333 'main' charities on the Register required to prepare accounts.

the effect of discrimination laws on charities, and the concluding section, the statutory controls on funding for charitable, benevolent, or philanthropic institutions.

From a date to be appointed, the Minister for the Cabinet Office, within five years of the passing of the Act, will be required to appoint a person to review generally the operation of the Act and compile a report to be laid before Parliament.[2]

Charities are independent of the state and, even if set up by a governmental body, cannot be directed by that body how to act.[3]

1 SCOPE OF THE REGULATORY PROVISIONS OF THE CHARITY ACTS 1993 AND 2006

At the time of writing, much of the 2006 Act has been brought into force and it is expected that most will be in force by 1 October 2009. The text is written on the assumption that this expectation will be fulfilled. It will be noted where a provision is not expected to be brought into force before 2010.

Both Acts apply to charities as defined in s 1(1) of the 2006 Act,[4] because the definition section in the 1993 Act, as amended,[5] assimilates the meaning of 'charity' in that Act to that in the 2006 Act. There are, however, charities to which the Acts, or particular provisions of the Acts, do not apply. These are considered in the following subsections.

(A) EXCLUSIONS FROM STATUTORY DEFINITION

The Acts specifically exclude from the definition[6] of 'charity' any ecclesiastical corporation—that is, any corporation in the Church of England, whether sole or aggregate, which is established for spiritual purposes—in respect of the corporate property of the corporation, except a corporation aggregate having some purposes that are not ecclesiastical in respect of its corporate property held for those purposes,[7] or any trust of property for purposes for which the property has been consecrated.[8]

(B) EXEMPT CHARITIES

Certain bodies[9] listed in Sch 2 to the 1993 Act[10] and known as 'exempt charities' are not subject to the mandatory provisions of the Act. These exempt charities, which are subject

---

[2] Charities Act 2006, s 73, which sets out particular matters that the review must address.
[3] See RR 7.   [4] See p 256 *et seq, supra*.   [5] Section 96(1), as amended by the 2006 Act.
[6] Charities Act 1993, s 96(2), as amended; Charities Act 2006, s 78(2).
[7] Also, any Diocesan Board of Finance within the meaning of the Endowments and Glebe Measure 1976 for any diocese, in respect of the diocesan glebe land of that diocese, within the meaning of that Measure: Charities Act 1993, s 96(2)(b).
[8] Ibid, s 96(2)(c).
[9] Although Sch 2 is headed 'Exempt Charities', the institutions specified in it are not thereby deemed or confirmed to be charities, but, so far as they are, they are exempt charities.
[10] See (1992–93) 1 CLPR 209 (J Hill and E Hakett). Also, certain institutions added by Order in Council under para (c) of the Schedule, eg the Royal College of Art by SI 2000/1826. See CC 23.

to their own special provisions as to supervision, include certain universities and colleges, specified national institutions (such as the British Museum and the National Gallery), and other institutions administered by them or on behalf of any of them. Although free from the supervisory provisions of the Act, exempt charities may take advantage of its enabling provisions.

Significant changes were made to Sch 2 to the 1993 Act by the 2006 Act.[11] Some specified institutions were removed and others added. The effect of the removal of a specified institution is that it will no longer be an exempt charity. The Minister for the Cabinet Office has been given power to make orders removing, or adding, particular institutions, or institutions of a particular description, from, or to, Sch 2 to the 1993 Act. Section 12 and Sch 5 to the 2006 Act make amendments to the 1993 Act that have the effect of increasing the regulation of exempt charities.

Section 13 gives the Minister for the Cabinet Office power to make regulations prescribing a body or a minister of the Crown as the principal regulator of an exempt charity. The body or minister so prescribed will have, in relation to that charity, the duty to do all that it or he reasonably can to promote compliance by the charity trustees with their legal obligations in exercising control and management of the administration of the charity.

Section 14 inserts a new s 86A into the 1993 Act, which requires the Commission to consult the principal regulator before exercising any of its specific powers in relation to that charity.

(C) EXCEPTED CHARITIES

Quite distinct from exempt charities are excepted charities, which may be excepted from some of the obligations of the Act, although, in general, subject to it.[12]

(D) TRUSTEE HOLDING SEPARATE FUNDS ON SPECIAL TRUSTS

If a trustee[13]—which may be a corporate charity with its own corporate property—holds separate funds on special trusts, each fund will, prima facie, constitute a separate institution and, accordingly, a separate charity for the purposes of the Act. However, the Commission may direct that, for all or any of the purposes of the Act, an institution established for any special purposes of or in connection with a charity (being charitable purposes) shall be treated as forming part of that charity or as forming a distinct charity,[14] and may also direct that two or more charities having the same charity trustees shall be treated as a single charity.[15] Thus, for instance, if a donor gives a fund to a school (being a charity) for the purpose of endowing a scholarship, the Commission may direct that the fund should not be treated as a distinct charity and need not be separately registered

---

[11] Sections 11–14 and 29(2).

[12] The obligations from which they may be excepted include the duty to register under the charities Act 1993, s 3, as substituted by s 9 of the 2006 Act, and in connection with annual accounts, Charities Act 1993, s 46, as amended.

[13] For example, *Re Royal Society's Charitable Trusts* [1956] Ch 87, [1955] 3 All ER 14.

[14] Charities Act 1993, s 95(5), as amended.

[15] Ibid, s 96(6), as amended, added by the Charities (Amendment) Act 1995.

under s 3.[16] A special trust does not, by itself, constitute a charity for the purposes of the statutory provisions relating to charity accounts.[17]

2 LEGAL FRAMEWORK OF CHARITY[18]

(A) CHARITABLE TRUST

A charity is, perhaps, most commonly constituted by means of a charitable trust. This is basically the same institution as a private trust: it is created, either *inter vivos* or by will, in the same way as a private trust, but is set up exclusively to carry out charitable purposes, as described in the preceding chapter.

(B) CORPORATE CHARITIES

There is no reason why a company formed in the ordinary way under the Companies Acts should not have objects that are exclusively charitable.

A charity may also be incorporated by royal charter,[19] by statute,[20] or under the provisions of the Industrial and Provident Societies Act 1965.[21]

A company formed exclusively for charitable purposes does not, by reason only of that attribute, hold its property on trust: prima facie, it owns its property beneficially as absolute owner, although it can, of course, only properly apply it to its charitable purposes. The Trustee Act 2000 does not apply to such corporate property. However, where a charitable company is a trustee of a separate charity, the Act applies to its actions as such trustee.

Like any other corporate body, a corporate charity is liable to be sued. Its charitable status gives it no immunity.[22] The directors (assuming that they have acted properly) will, even if the funds of the charity are insufficient to satisfy the liability, not be personally liable. The third party's claim will remain unsatisfied. Contrast the case of a charitable trust, in which any claim will have to be made against the trustees and although they will (assuming that they have acted properly) be entitled to reimbursement out of the trust funds, they will be personally liable in so far as this is insufficient.[23]

---

[16] Discussed p 321 *et seq, infra*.   [17] That is, ss 41–49, Charities Act 1993, as amended: ibid, s 97(1).

[18] Model forms are provided by the Charity Commission: GD 1 for corporate charities, GD 2 for charities set up under a trust, and GD3 for charities set up as unincorporated associations.

[19] See, eg, *Re Royal Society's Charitable Trusts* [1956] Ch 87, [1955] 3 All ER 14.

[20] See, eg, *Re Shipwrecked Fishermen and Mariners' Royal Benevolent Society Charity* [1959] Ch 220, [1958] 3 All ER 465.

[21] Charities incorporated under this Act are exempt charities, but only if also registered in the register of social landlords under Pt I of the Housing Act 1996: Charities Act 1993, Sch 2, para (y), as amended by s 11(8) of the 2006 Act.

[22] *Mersey Docks Trustees v Gibbs* (1866) LR 1 HL 93. It has been held in Canada that all property of a charity 'whether owned beneficially or on trust for one or more charitable purposes' is available to pay the claims of trust victims against the charity: *Re Christian Brothers of Ireland in Canada* (2000) 184 DLR (4th) 445, noted (2003) 119 LQR 44, and discussed in detail (2004) 83 CBR 805 (D R Wingfield); (2007) 92 T & ELTJ 16 (Suzanna Popovic-Montag).

[23] See p 413, *infra*, and as to reimbursement, p 475 *et seq*. As to charity trustees and exemption clauses, see Law Com No 301.

(c) UNINCORPORATED ASSOCIATIONS

It is possible for a group of persons to join together for some exclusively charitable purpose without setting up a trust and without being incorporated. The rules of the association will normally provide for it to be run by an elected committee,[24] and for any property held for this purpose to be vested in a small number of the members of the committee as trustees. However, such trustees will not be the charity trustees for the purposes of the Charities Acts 1993 and 2006: the committee, as the persons having the general control and management of the administration of the charity, will be the charity trustees for those purposes.[25] Moreover, by reason of the fact that an unincorporated association is not a separate entity in law,[26] all of the members of the association may be personally liable in respect of the acts of committee members, who, in purporting to act on behalf of the association, may be regarded as acting as agents of the members thereof, unless those acts fall outside their actual or ostensible authority having regard to the rules of the association. In an employment law case on unlawful discrimination, an industrial tribunal held that the employer was the membership of the charity as a whole, but on appeal, the Employment Appeal Tribunal held that, since employees of unincorporated associations, including charities, must have continuity of employment despite changes in the composition of the management committee, their contracts of employment were made with the management committee and its members for the time being.[27]

(d) CHARITABLE INCORPORATED ORGANIZATIONS

This new legal form is discussed in the following section.

3 CHARITY TRUSTEES AND OTHER PERSONS AND BODIES RESPONSIBLE FOR THE RUNNING OF CHARITIES

(A) TRUSTEES OF A CHARITABLE TRUST; CHARITY TRUSTEES; TRUSTEES FOR A CHARITY

(i) Kinds of trustee

Trustees in relation to charities are of three kinds, which, to some extent, overlap.

(a) *Trustees of a charitable trust*   Where a charity exists as a charitable trust, its trustees are fundamentally in the same position as trustees of a private trust, and, in general, have the same powers, duties, and liabilities.[28] Unlike the trustees of a

---

[24] In a very small association, the committee might comprise all of the members.

[25] See Charities Act 1993, s 97(1), as amended by the 2006 Act, and p 293, *infra*. As to the duties and responsibilities of members of unincorporated associations, see [2006] Conv 330 (Jean Warburton).

[26] See p 62 *et seq, supra*.   [27] *Affleck v Newcastle Mind* [1999] ICR 852, EAT.

[28] As to investment, see (1995–96) 3 CLPR 65 (H P Dale and M Gwinnell).

private trust, however, they need not act unanimously, but the decision and act of a majority will be treated as the decision and act of the whole body of trustees, and thus bind a dissenting minority.[29] Moreover, s 34 of the Trustee Act 1925, which restricts the number of trustees of land to four, does not apply to land vested in trustees for charitable purposes.[30] There is no requirement of a minimum number of trustees, but, in some circumstances, the Charity Commission may appoint add-itional trustees.[31] Trustees of a charitable trust are clearly trustees for the purposes of the Charities Acts 1993 and 2006.

(b) *Charity trustees*   Except in so far as the context otherwise requires, 'charity trust-ees', for the purposes of the Charities Acts 1993 and 2006,[32] 'means the persons having the general control and management of the administration of a charity',[33] and therefore includes not only trustees in the sense with which we are familiar, but also, for instance, the directors in the case of a charity incorporated under the Companies Acts or, in the case of an unincorporated association, the executive or management committee.

(c) *Trustees for a charity*   The funds of a charity may be vested in trustees other than the charity trustees who have the general control and management of the administration. Such trustees may be custodian trustees,[34] but this is not necessar-ily the case.[35] They are not charity trustees for the purposes of the Charities Acts 1993 and 2006.

(ii) Qualifications for trusteeship

Until 1 August 1993, anyone who could be a trustee could be a charity trustee, unless the governing document contained a relevant disqualification provision. Now, by virtue of s 72 of the Charities Act 1993,[36] a person is disqualified for being a charity trustee or trustee for a charity if:

(a) he has been convicted of any offence involving dishonesty or deception;[37]

(b) he has been adjudged bankrupt or sequestration of his estate has been awarded, and (in either case) he has not been discharged;[38] or he is the subject of a bank-ruptcy restrictions order or an interim order;

(c) he has made a composition or arrangement with, or granted a trust deed for, his creditors and has not been discharged in respect of it;

---

[29] *Wilkinson v Malin* (1832) 2 Cr & J 636; *Perry v Shipway* (1859) 1 Giff 1; *Re Whiteley* [1910] 1 Ch 600.

[30] Trustee Act 1925, s 34(3)(a). A power to execute instruments may be delegated to two or more trustees: Charities Act 1993, s 82. As to the appointment of new trustees, see Charities Act 1993, s 83.

[31] See Charities Act 1993, ss 16 and 18, as amended by the 2006 Act, discussed pp 303–306, *infra*.

[32] But not for trust law generally: see (1995–96) 3 CLPR 65 (H P Dale and M Gwinnell).

[33] Charities Act 1993, s 97(1). There are an estimated 1.1 million charity trustees.

[34] See p 392 *et seq, infra*.   [35] See p 292, *supra*.

[36] As amended by the Insolvency Act 2000, the Charities Act 2006, SIs 2004/1941, 2006/242, and 2006/1722, and the Tribunals Courts and Enforcement Act 2007, from a date to be appointed.

[37] Unless it is a spent conviction under the Rehabilitation of Offenders Act 1974: Charities Act 1993, s 72(2)(a).

[38] A person is not disqualified for being a charity trustee or trustee for a charity that is a company if he has leave under specified statutory provisions to act as director of the charity: s 72(3), as amended.

   (d) he has been removed from the office of charity trustee or trustee for a charity by an order made by the Commission, or Commissioners,[39] or by the High Court on the grounds of any misconduct or mismanagement in the administration of the charity for which he was responsible or to which he was privy, or which he by his conduct contributed to or facilitated;[40]

   (e) he has been removed by the Court of Session under similar Scottish legislation from being concerned in the management or control of any body;

   (f) he is subject to a disqualification order or disqualification undertaking under companies legislation.[41]

With some exceptions, the Commission may waive a disqualification either generally or in relation to a particular charity or class of charities, and, on an application made five years or more after a disqualification took effect, must, in some cases, do so unless it is satisfied that there is a good reason for not doing so.[42]

There is no automatic vacation of office of a disqualified trustee,[43] and acts done by him are not invalid by reason only of that disqualification.[44] However, a person who acts as a charity trustee or trustee for a charity while disqualified is guilty of an offence.[45] Moreover, the Commission may call upon him to repay to the charity the whole or part of any sums[46] that he received from the charity while so acting.[47]

(iii) Application of statutory powers relating to trustees generally

The unrepealed provisions of the Trustee Act 1925[48] apply to charity trustees. In general, the Trustee Act 2000 applies to charitable trustees, but there are modifications and limitations in relation to the appointment of agents, nominees, and custodians, and in relation to remuneration.[49]

The Trusts of Land and Appointment of Trustees Act 1996, which provides, in s 6(1), that, for the purpose of exercising their functions as trustees, the trustees of land have in relation to the land all of the powers of an absolute owner, applies to trustees of a charity, although it is expressly provided that the powers are not to be exercised in contravention of an order of any court or of the Commission.[50]

---

   [39] Under s 18(2)(i) of the Charities Act 1993 or its predecessors.

   [40] The Commission is required to keep a register available for public inspection of all persons who have been removed from office under this head: s 72(6), (7), as amended by the 2006 Act.

   [41] In relation to a charity that is a company, the disqualification order may grant him leave to act, and, in the case of an order under the Insolvency Act 1986, s 429(2)(b) (prospectively amended by the Tribunals, Courts, and Enforcement Act 2007), the court that made the order may grant leave.

   [42] Charities Act 1993, s 72(4) and (4A), as respectively amended and inserted by s 35 and Sch 8 of the 2006 Act. See (1993) 1 Dec Ch Com 26 and (1994) 2 Dec Ch Com 12 for factors taken into account.

   [43] See (1994) 2 Dec Ch Com 11.   [44] Charities Act 1993, s 73(3).

   [45] Punishable on summary conviction to imprisonment for up to six months or a fine up to the statutory maximum, or both, and on conviction on indictment to imprisonment up to two years or a fine, or both: Charities Act 1993, s 73(1). See p 321, *infra*.

   [46] Or the monetary value of any benefit in kind.

   [47] Charities Act 1993, s 73(4), as amended by the 2006 Act, Sch 8, para 157.

   [48] With the exception of s 16 (power to raise money by sale or mortgage, etc).

   [49] See pp 442 *et seq* and 452 *et seq*, *infra*. As to insurance, see CC 49.

   [50] Trusts of Land and Appointment of Trustees Act 1996, s 6(6)(7), as amended by the 2006 Act. See also s 6(8).

(iv) Payment of charity trustees

Like other trustees, charity trustees are not permitted to receive any benefit (whether money, services, facilities, or other benefits, including a token honorarium) from their trust unless they have express legal authority to do so from a clause in the charity's governing document, by the authority of the Commission[51] or the court, or under a statutory provision.[52] Where the charity has such a power, the trustees must always consider when exercising it whether to do so is in the best interests of the charity at that time.[53]

Section 73A of the Charities Act 1993, inserted by the Charities Act 2006,[54] now gives statutory power for a trustee body, subject to the conditions set out in the section being met, to pay remuneration to a person for services provided by him to the charity where either: (a) he is a charity trustee or trustee for the charity; or (b) he is connected with a charity trustee or trustee for the charity and the remuneration might result in that trustee obtaining a benefit.

Two safeguards to prevent misuse of this new provision are set out in s 73B(1) and (2), likewise inserted—namely:

(a) a duty to have regard to any guidance given by the Commission; and

(b) the requirement to act in accordance with the duty of care imposed by the Trustee Act 2000, s 1(1).[55]

(v) Insurance against personal liability of trustees

Section 73F of the Charities Act 1993, inserted by s 39 of the 2006 Act, provides trustees with a statutory power to purchase, out of the funds of the charity, indemnity insurance against any personal liability in respect of any breach of trust or breach of duty committed in their capacity as charity trustees or trustees for the charity.[56] The indemnity must exclude, inter alia, liability arising out of conduct that he knew (or must reasonably be assumed to have known) not to be in the interests of the charity.[57] The trustees must satisfy themselves that it is in the best interests of the charity for the purchase to be made and, in taking their decision, the duty of care under s 1(1) of the Trustee Act 2000 applies.[58]

The section does not allow purchase of indemnity insurance where it is expressly prohibited by the charity's trusts, but has effect notwithstanding a provision in the charity's trusts prohibiting them receiving personal benefit from the charity's funds.[59]

(vi) Relief from liability for breach of trust

Like any other trustee, a charity trustee or trustee for a charity can apply to the court for relief from personal liability for breach of trust.[60] There are similar provisions in relation to directors and auditors of a charitable company in s 727 of the Companies Act 1985. Section

---

[51] Under the Charities Act 1993, s 26, as amended, discussed p 000, *infra*.

[52] For example, Sch 1 to the Housing Act 1996.

[53] See CC 11, listing factors to be taken into account. See also Trustee Act 2000, ss 28 and 30, discussed pp 443 *et seq*, *infra*.

[54] Section 36.   [55] See also s 73C, inserted by the Charities Act 2006, s 37.

[56] Extended to any negligence, etc, in their capacity as directors or officers of a corporate charity, or of any corporate body carrying on an activity on behalf of a charity: s 73F(1)(b), as inserted.

[57] Section 73F(2), (3), as inserted.   [58] Section 73F(4), (5), as inserted.

[59] Section 73F(8), as inserted.   [60] Under s 61 of the Trustee Act 1925, discussed p 535, *infra*.

73E of the Charities Act 1993[61] extends the power of the court to auditors, independent examiners, and reporting accountants of charities that are not companies, and also to charity trustees of charitable incorporated organizations.[62]

The above provisions all require an application to the court. They are unaffected by the similar power conferred on the Commission by s 73D of the Charities Act 1993,[63] which avoids an application to the court.

(vii) Advice of the Charity Commission

Section 29 of the Charities Act 1993, as substituted by s 24 of the 2006 Act, provides that any charity trustee or trustee for a charity may make a written application to the Commission for its opinion or advice[64] in relation to any matter affecting the performance of his duties as such, or otherwise relating to the proper administration of the trust. A charity trustee or trustee for a charity who acts in accordance with such opinion or advice is deemed to have acted in accordance with his trust, unless he knows or has reasonable cause to suspect that the opinion or advice was given in ignorance of material facts, or that the decision of the court has been obtained on the matter or proceedings are pending to obtain one.[65] This provision may be useful to the trustees as a body, and may also be of particular value to an individual trustee who is concerned that the majority of his co-trustees insist on pursuing a course of action that he believes to be a breach of trust. The accuracy of the Commission's opinion or advice may be challenged under the procedure set up by s 33, discussed below,[66] but a common law action in negligence cannot be brought on the ground that the opinion or advice is not only wrong, but was given negligently.[67] The main reason for holding that there is no liability in negligence is the existence of the statutory scheme, which provides an effective right of appeal against the substance of the matter. There is no question either of the Commission being, in any sense, above the law or of aggrieved persons with sufficient *locus standi* not having a remedy. Further reasons are that to allow the concurrent exercise of rights in negligence actions at common law and rights of appeal in charity proceedings could only multiply costs, and that it would be contrary to the general good of charities for the Commission's decision to be subject to attack by so wide a class of persons as potential objects of charity.

Section 29(4) and (5) are new provisions introduced by the 2006 Act to give the Commission a more general power to give advice and guidance as part of its new function[68] of encouraging and facilitating the better administration of charities. Under this new power, the Commission may give advice or guidance to charities generally, to any class of charities, or to any particular charity, in whatever form and manner it considers appropriate.

(viii) Power to determine membership of charity

Some charities have a body of members with voting or other rights, such as a right to elect trustees of the charity. If, for instance, charity records were incomplete, it could result

---

[61] Inserted by s 38 of the 2006 Act.   [62] As to the latter see p 299, *infra.*

[63] Discussed p 309, *infra.*   [64] Which, *semble,* need not be in writing.

[65] Charities Act 1993, s 29. as substituted. A trustee of an exempt charity may take advantage of this section. See, generally, Report for 1982, paras 24–27.   [66] See pp 313–314.

[67] *Mills v Winchester Diocesan Board of Finance* [1989] Ch 428, [1989] 2 All ER 317.

[68] See s 1C(2)(2) of the 1993 Act, inserted by s 7 of the 2006 Act.

in doubt arising as to whether particular persons have been validly elected as trustees. Section 29A of the Charities Act 1993, inserted by s 25 of the Charities Act 2006, gives the Commission (or a person appointed by the Commission) power to determine who are the members[69] of the charity. The power is exercisable on the application of the charity, or at any time after the institution of a statutory inquiry under s 8 of the 1993 Act.[70]

(ix) Incorporation of charity trustees

By s 50 of the 1993 Act, as amended by the 2006 Act, the Commission is empowered, where it considers that the incorporation of the trustees would be in the interests of the charity, to grant to the charity trustees of a charity[71] a certificate of incorporation of the trustees as a body corporate. Except as regards property vested in the Official Custodian for Charities,[72] the certificate of incorporation vests in the body corporate all of the property belonging to or held in trust for the charity, but the liability of the trustees is unaffected[73] After incorporation, the trustees may sue and be sued in their corporate name,[74] and the requirements for the execution of documents are simplified.[75] However, the charity itself is not incorporated, but continues to be an unincorporated trust.

(B) CHARITABLE COMPANIES

A charitable company is normally limited by guarantee, and a model memorandum and articles of association are provided by the Commission.[76]

(i) Alteration of objects clause

There is no provision in the Charities Acts to prevent a corporate charity from altering its objects so that it ceases to be exclusively charitable. However, a company that is a charity cannot make any 'regulated alteration' without the prior written consent of the Commission.[77] A 'regulated alteration' is defined[78] as any alteration of the objects clause in the company's memorandum of association, or any alteration of any provision of its memorandum or articles of association that either directs the application of property of the company on its dissolution, or where the alteration would provide authorization for any benefit

[69] 'Members', in relation to a charity with a body of members distinct from the charity trustees, means any of those members: s 97(1), as inserted by the 2006 Act.

[70] See p 304, *supra*. The person appointed under s 8 may also be appointed to determine membership: Charities Act 1993, s 29A(3), as inserted.

[71] Other than one that should be, but is not, registered in accordance with s 3A of the Charities Act 1993, inserted by s 9 of the 2006 Act: s 50(2), as amended.

[72] See section 4(D), p 310, *infra*.

[73] Sections 51 and 54. Thirteen certificates of incorporation were granted in the year 2007–2008. It thus becomes unnecessary to change the names on documents such as share certificates and land certificates on a change of trustees. This difficulty can, however, be avoided without incorporation by the use of a custodian trustee.

[74] Charities Act 1993, s 50(4)(a).

[75] Charities Act 1993, s 60. Note, however, s 82, which achieves a somewhat similar result without incorporation: see p 293, fn 301, *supra*.

[76] The June 2003 revision is available on the Internet. See also (2004) 54 T & ELJ 11 (S Chiappini). Exceptionally, the Charity Bank, limited by shares, was recently registered as a charity.

[77] Section 64(2) of the Charities Act 1993, as substituted by the Charities Act 2006, s 31(2). A copy of the consent must be delivered to the Registrar of Companies: s 64(3), as amended by the 2006 Act.

[78] Ibid, s 64(2A), inserted by the Charities Act 2006, s 31(2).

to be obtained by directors or members of the company, or persons connected with them.[79] Where an alteration is made that has the effect that the body ceases to be a charity, it does not affect the application of property held by the company at the time of the alteration.[80]

(ii) *Ultra vires* transactions

The Companies Act 2006[81] provides:

(a) that the validity of an act done by a company cannot be called into question on the ground of lack of capacity by reason of anything in the company's constitution; and

(b) that, in favour of a person dealing with a company in good faith, the power of the directors to bind the company, or authorize others to do so, is deemed to be free of any limitation under the company's constitution.

These provisions do not apply to the acts of a company that is a charity except in favour of a person who:

(a) does not know at the time the act is done that the company is a charity, or

(b) gives full consideration in money or money's worth in relation to the act in question, and does not know (as the case may be)—
(i) that the act is not permitted by the company's constitution, or
(ii) that the act in question is beyond the powers of the directors.[82]

(iii) Certain acts by a charitable company

Where a company is a charity, the approval by members of the company required by the Companies Act 2006 to specified transactions with directors, and the affirmation by them of unapproved property transactions and loans, is ineffective without the prior written consent of the Commission.[83]

(iv) Name and status of a charitable company

Where a company is a charity and its name does not include the word 'charity' or 'charitable',[84] the fact that the company is a charity must be stated in English[85] in legible characters:

(a) in every location, and in every description of document or communication, in which it is required by regulations under s 82 of the Companies Act 2006 to state its registered name; and

---

[79] Ibid, s 64(2B), likewise inserted, which defines 'benefit' and sets out the rules for determining whether a person is connected to a director or member of the company.   [80] Ibid, s 64(1).

[81] Sections 39, 40, and 42, replacing provisions contained in the Companies Act 1985, from a date to be appointed, expected to be 1 October 2009. The text is written on the basis that the new provisions are in force.

[82] Ibid, s 42(1). Subsection (2) gives protection to a subsequent purchaser for full consideration without actual notice of the relevant circumstances.

[83] Charities Act 1993, s 66, as substituted by the Companies Act 2006, s 226. Section 66A, likewise substituted, extends the requirement to certain cases exempted from the statutory provision.

[84] Or, in the case of a document that is wholly in Welsh, the word *elusen* or *elusennol*: Charities Act 1993, s 68(2), as substituted, together with ss 68ZA and 68ZB, by SI 2008/948, arts 4(1) and 6, Sch 3, para 7.

[85] Except that, in the case of a document that is otherwise wholly in Welsh, the statement may be in Welsh if it consists of, or includes, the word *elusen* or *elusennol*: ibid, s 68(3), as substituted.

(b) in all conveyances[86] purporting to be executed by the company.[87]

(v) Winding up

A petition for the winding up of a charitable company under the Insolvency Act 1986 may be presented by the Attorney-General, as well as by any person authorized by that Act.[88] It may also be presented by the Commission with the agreement of the Attorney-General if, at any time after it has instituted an inquiry under s 8,[89] it is satisfied as mentioned in s 18(1)(a) or (b).[90]

The Commission—again, only with the agreement of the Attorney-General—may apply for a declaration that the dissolution of a company is void, or that a company name that has been struck off the Register of Companies should be restored.[91]

(vi) Offences committed by a body corporate

Where any offence under the Charities Act 1993, or the Charities Act 1992, or any regulations made under it, is committed by a body corporate and is proved to have been committed with the consent or connivance of, or to be attributable to any neglect on the part of, any director,[92] manager, secretary, or other similar officer of the body corporate, or any person who was purporting to act in any such capacity, he, as well as the body corporate, is guilty of that offence.[93]

(C) CHARITABLE INCORPORATED ORGANIZATIONS

The Charities Act 2006[94] instituted this new legal form, the first to be created specifically to meet the needs of charities. It is referred to in the Act, and generally, as a 'CIO'. Its purpose is to avoid the need for charities that wish to benefit from incorporation to register as companies and be liable to dual regulation by Companies House, as well as the Charity Commission.

(i) Nature and constitution

A CIO is a body corporate with a constitution in a specified form, stating its name, its purposes, the address of its principal office (which must be in England or Wales),[95] and whether or not its members (which may be one or more) are liable to contribute to its assets if it is wound up, and (if they are) up to what amount. The constitution must make

---

[86] 'Conveyance' means any instrument creating, transferring, varying, or extinguishing an interest in land: ibid, s 68(4), as substituted.

[87] Ibid, s 68(1), as substituted. The civil and criminal consequences of failure to make the required disclosure are set out in ss 68ZA and 68ZB, respectively.

[88] Ibid, s 63(1).   [89] See p 304, *infra*.

[90] Charities Act 1993, s 63(2), as amended by the 2006 Act.

[91] Ibid, s 63(3)–(5), as likewise amended.

[92] In relation to a body corporate, the affairs of which are managed by its members, 'director' means a member of the body corporate: Charities Act 1992, s 75, as amended; Charities Act 1993, s 95.

[93] Charities Act 1992, s 75, as amended; Charities Act 1993, s 95.

[94] Section 34 and Sch 7, which insert ss 69A–69Q and Sch 5B into the Charities Act 1993.

[95] The constitution must be in English if the principal office is in England; in English or Welsh, if in Wales: s 69B(4) of the Charities Act 1993, likewise inserted.

provision about eligibility for membership, about the appointment of one or more persons who are to be the charity trustees of the CIO, and must contain directions about the application of property of the CIO on its dissolution. There may, but need not be, overlap between the persons who are charity trustees and members of the CIO.[96]

(ii) Name and status

The name of a CIO must be stated in legible characters in, inter alia, all business letters, notices, and other official publications, bills of exchange, cheques, conveyances, invoices, and receipts.[97] Failure to comply with these requirements by a charity trustee of a CIO, or by a person acting on behalf of a CIO, is an offence, and such a person is personally liable to the holder of a bill of exchange, etc, for the amount of it unless it is duly paid by the CIO.[98] A person who holds any body out as being a CIO when it is not is guilty of an offence, unless he can prove that he believed on reasonable grounds that the body was a CIO.[99]

(iii) Registration

Any one or more persons may apply to the Commission for a CIO to be constituted and for its registration as a charity. The applicants must supply the Commission with a copy of the proposed constitution, and such other documents and information as may be specified or required. The Act sets out the circumstances in which the Commission may, or must, refuse an application.[100]

If the Commission grants an application, it must register the CIO as a charity in the Register of Charities, by virtue of which it becomes a body corporate.[101]

(iv) Conversion, amalgamation, and transfer

A charitable company, and a charity that is a registered society within the meaning of the Industrial and Provident Societies Act 1965, may apply for conversion into a CIO. An application cannot, however, be made by a company or registered society having a share capital if any of the shares are not fully paid up, or by an exempt charity.[102] The Act sets out the grounds on which the Commission may, or must, refuse an application.[103]

Any two or more CIOs may apply to the Commission to be amalgamated, and for the incorporation and registration as a new charity of a new CIO.[104] Any person who considers that he would be affected may make written representations relating to the proposal to the Commission. The Act sets out the grounds on which the Commission may, or must, refuse an application for amalgamation. If the Commission grants an application for amalgamation, it must register the new CIO in the Register of Charities, by virtue of which it becomes a body corporate.[105]

---

[96] Sections 69A and 69B, likewise inserted.

[97] Section 69C, likewise inserted. If the name of the CIO does not include 'charitable incorporated organization' or 'CIO' (or the Welsh equivalents), the fact that it is a CIO must be stated in legible characters in all of the documents referred to.

[98] Section 69D(1), (2), likewise inserted.   [99] Section 69D(3), (4), likewise inserted.

[100] Section 69E, likewise inserted.   [101] Section 69F, likewise inserted.

[102] Section 69G, likewise inserted. The section contains detailed provisions in relation to an application.

[103] Section 69H, likewise inserted. See also s 69I, likewise inserted.

[104] Detailed provisions are contained in s 69K, likewise inserted.

[105] Section 69L, likewise inserted.

A CIO may resolve that all of its property, rights, and liabilities shall be transferred to another CIO specified in the resolution. A copy, together with a copy of a resolution of the transferee CIO agreeing to the transfer, must be sent to the Commission, which may direct the transferor CIO to give public notice of its resolution. If it does so, the Commission must take account of representations received from any person interested. The Commission may, or must, refuse to confirm the resolution on specified grounds, but if it confirms the resolution, the transfer will take effect and the transferor CIO will be dissolved.[106]

4 PERSONS AND BODIES RESPONSIBLE FOR THE REGULATION AND CONTROL OF CHARITIES

(A) THE CHARITY COMMISSION—CREATION AND PURPOSES

(i) Creation of the Charity Commission

Section 1A of the Charities Act 1993, inserted by s 6(1) of the Charities Act 2006, created a body corporate called the 'Charity Commission for England and Wales' (in Welsh, *Comisiwn Elusennau Cymru a Lloegr*) to which were transferred the functions of the Charity Commissioners for England and Wales,[107] and their property, rights, and liabilities.[108] The independence of the Commission is established by s 1A(6), which provides that, in the exercise of its functions, it is not to be subject to the direction or control of any minister of the Crown or other government department.

The Commission consists of a chairman and between four and eight other members, appointed by the Minister for the Cabinet Office.[109] It is required to publish an annual report on the discharge of its functions, the extent to which its objectives have been met, the performance of its general duties, and the management of its affairs. A copy of the report must be laid before Parliament.[110] It must also hold an annual public meeting to consider the report.[111]

(ii) Objectives

Section 7 of the 2006 Act inserts new ss 1B–1E in the 1993 Act. Section 1B(3) sets out the Commission's objectives as follows:

1. The public confidence objective is to increase public trust and confidence in charities.
2. The public benefit objective is to promote awareness and understanding of the operation of the public benefit requirement.
3. The compliance objective is to promote compliance by charity trustees with their legal obligations in exercising control and management of the administration of their charities.

---

[106] Section 69M, likewise inserted.   [107] Office abolished by the Charities Act 2006, s 6(3).
[108] Ibid, s 6(4).
[109] Charities Act 1993, Sch 1A, paras 1 and 2, inserted by the Charities Act 2006, Sch 1.
[110] Ibid, para 11.   [111] Ibid, para 12.

4. The charitable resources objective is to promote the effective use of charitable resources.

5. The accountability objective is to enhance the accountability of charities to donors, beneficiaries and the general public.

(iii) General functions

Section 1C(2) sets out the Commission's general functions:

1. Determining whether institutions are or are not charities.

2. Encouraging and facilitating the better administration of charities.

3. Identifying and investigating apparent misconduct or mismanagement in the administration of charities and taking remedial or protective action in connection with misconduct or mismanagement therein.

4. Determining whether public collection certificates should be issued and remain in force, in respect of public charitable collections.[112]

5. Obtaining, evaluating and disseminating information in connection with the performance of any of the Commission's functions or meeting any of its objectives.[113]

6. Giving information or advice or making proposals, to any Minister of the Crown in matters relating to any of the Commission's functions or meeting any of its objectives.

(iv) General duties

These are set out in s 1D(2) as follows:

1. So far as is reasonably practicable, the Commission must, in performing its functions, act in a way—
   (a) which is compatible with its objectives, and
   (b) which it considers most appropriate for the purpose of meeting those objectives.

2. So far as is reasonably practicable the Commission must, in performing its functions, act in a way which is compatible with the encouragement of—
   (a) all forms of charitable giving, and
   (b) voluntary participation in charity work.

3. In performing its functions the Commission must have regard to the need to use its resources in the most efficient, effective and economic way.

4. In performing its functions the Commission must, so far as relevant, have regard to the principles of best regulatory practice....

5. In performing its functions the Commission must, in appropriate cases, have regard to the desirability of facilitating innovation by or on behalf of charities.

6. In managing its affairs the Commission must have regard to such generally accepted principles of good corporate governance as it is reasonable to regard as applicable to it.

(v) Incidental powers

Section 1E(1) grants wide incidental powers to the Commission. It is given power 'to do anything which is calculated to facilitate, or is conducive or incidental to, the performance of

---

[112] See Pt 3 of the Act referred to at p 355 *et seq, infra*.
[113] This includes the maintenance of a register of charities. See p 321 *et seq*.

any of its functions or general duties'. However, the independence of charity trustees in the administration of their charity is ensured by the express provision in s 1E(2)[114] that nothing in the Act authorizes the Commission:

(a) to exercise functions corresponding to those of a charity trustee in relation to a charity, or

(b) otherwise to be directly involved in the administration of a charity.

The Commission has issued numerous publications to assist and give guidance to actual and potential charity trustees, and, from time to time, issues consultation documents in relation to possible changes in the law. They are all available online via its website.[115]

To assist it in carrying out its duties, the Commission may, by order, require any person to furnish it with information in his possession that relates to any charity, and to furnish it with a copy or extract of any relevant documents in his custody or under his control, or to transmit the document itself for inspection.[116] It is further provided that any relevant public authority may disclose information to the Commission if the disclosure is made for the purpose of enabling or assisting the Commission to discharge any of its functions, and, conversely, that the Commission may disclose to any relevant public authority any information received by it for the purpose of enabling or assisting it to discharge any of its functions.[117]

The Commission has jurisdiction over funds raised via a charitable appeal, even if the appeal was made by an organization that is not charitable.[118]

(B) THE CHARITY COMMISSION—JURISDICTION AND POWERS

(i) Concurrent jurisdiction with the High Court

The Commission has the same powers as are exercisable by the High Court in charity proceedings for:

(a) establishing schemes;[119]

(b) appointing, discharging, or removing a charity trustee or trustee for a charity, or removing an officer or employee; and

(c) for vesting or transferring property.

The power can, however, be exercised only on the application of the charity, or on an order of the court for a scheme to be settled by the Commission,[120] or on the application of the Attorney-General.[121] The Commission may also discharge a charity trustee or trustee for a

---

[114] This does not affect the operation of ss 19A or 19B, inserted by ss 20 and 21 of the 2006 Act, discussed pp 306, 307, infra.

[115] See <http://www.charity-commission.gov.uk/publications>.

[116] Charities Act 1993, s 9(1), as amended by the 2006 Act. The right is extended to require that the information be in a legible form where it is otherwise recorded: s 9(5).

[117] Sections 10, 10A–10C, substituted for s 10 of the 1993 Act by Sch 8, para 104, of the 2006 Act. There are qualifications, in particular in connection with HM Revenue and Customs information.

[118] See Report for 1998, pp 23, 24.   [119] Discussed in section 7, p 328 et seq, infra.

[120] Under the Charities Act 1993, s 16(2), as amended by the 2006 Act.

[121] Charities Act 1993, s 16(1), (4), (5), as amended by the 2006 Act In the case of charities with a gross income that does not exceed £500 a year, on the application of a charity trustee or any other person interested

charity on his application.[122] The Commission has no jurisdiction under these provisions to try, or determine, the title to any property as between a charity or trustee for a charity and any person claiming adversely thereto, or any question as to the existence or extent of any charge or trust.[123] Moreover, the Commission is not to exercise its jurisdiction in any case that, by reason of its contentious character, or of any special question of law or of fact that it may involve, or for other reasons, it may consider more fit to be adjudicated on by the court.[124] There are provisions for appeal to the Charity Tribunal.

(ii) General power to institute inquiries

The Commission may, from time to time, institute inquiries with regard to charities or a particular charity or class of charities, either generally or for particular purposes.[125] The Commission itself may conduct the inquiry, or it may appoint someone else to conduct it and report to it; in either case, there is power to compel the attendance of witnesses and take evidence on oath.[126] It may direct any person to furnish accounts and statements in writing with respect to any matter in question at the inquiry on which he has obtained, or can reasonably obtain, information to furnish copies of relevant documents in his custody or under his control, and to attend and give evidence or produce any such documents.[127] The report of the inquiry, or some other statement of the results of the inquiry, may be printed and published, or published in some other way, so as to bring it to the attention of persons who may wish to make representations about the action to be taken.[128]

(iii) Power to act for protection of charities

Section 18 of the 1993 Act, as amended by the 2006 Act, gives the Commission wide powers to act for the protection of charities.[129] If, at any time after it has instituted an inquiry, the Commission is satisfied that:

(a) there is or has been any misconduct or mismanagement[130] in the administration of the charity; or

(b) that it is necessary or desirable to act for the purpose of protecting the property of the charity or securing a proper application for the purposes of the charity of that property or of property coming to the charity,

---

in the charity, or, in the case of any local charity, any two or more inhabitants of the area. The figure of £500 may be altered by statutory instrument: Charities Act 1993, s 16(15).

[122] Section 16(8), as amended. In many cases, a trustee will be able to retire under s 39 of the Trustee Act 1925, or, as a last resort, pay into court under s 63 of the Trustee Act 1925: see Chapter 15, section 3(C), (viii), p 386, *infra*.

[123] Section 16(3), as amended.   [124] Ibid, s 16(10), as amended.

[125] Charities Act 1993, s 8(1),as amended by the 2006 Act.

[126] Section 8, as amended. The section does not apply to exempt charities except where this has been requested by the principal regulator. See the *Report of an Inquiry into War on Want* submitted to the Commission on 15 February 1991.

[127] Section 8(3), as amended. It is an offence knowingly or recklessly to provide false or misleading information, or wilfully to alter, suppress, conceal, or destroy any relevant document: s 11, as amended. See section 4(I), p 321, *infra*.

[128] Charities Act 1993, s 8(6), as amended.

[129] Unless they are acting under subs (1), they must give notice of their intention to each of the charity trustees, except any who cannot be found or who have no known address in the UK: s 18(12), as amended.

[130] This includes the payment of excessive sums by way of remuneration or reward to persons acting in the affairs of the charity: ibid, s 18(3).

it may take various steps.

Those steps are:

(a) the suspension for a period not exceeding twelve months of any trustee, charity trustee, or other person connected with the charity from the exercise of his office or employment pending consideration being given to his removal;

(b) the appointment of additional charity trustees;

(c) the vesting in, or transfer to, the official custodian for charities of any property held by or in trust for the charity;

(d) orders not, without the approval of the Commission, to part with charity property, to make payments to the charity in discharge of a debtor's liability, or to enter into transactions or make payments in the administration of the charity;[131]

(e) to appoint an interim manager, who shall act as receiver and manager in respect of the property and affairs of the charity.[132]

If the Commission is satisfied as to *both* (a) and (b), it may:

(a) by order remove any trustee, charity trustee or other person connected with the charity who has been responsible for or privy to the misconduct or mismanagement or has by his conduct contributed to it or facilitated it; [and/or]

(b) by order establish a scheme for the administration of the charity.[133]

As an indication of the scale of the Commission' interventions, in the year to 31 March 2008, the Commission made 55 uses of its regulatory powers under s 18.

The Commission may remove a charity trustee by order made of its own motion:[134]

(a) where, within the last five years, the trustee—
    (i) having previously been adjudged bankrupt or had his estate sequestrated, has been discharged, or
    (ii) having previously made a composition or arrangement with, or granted a trust deed for, his creditors, has been discharged in respect of it;

(b) where the trustee is a corporation in liquidation;

(c) where the trustee is incapable of acting by reason of mental disorder within the meaning of the Mental Health Act 1983;

(d) where the trustee has not acted, and will not declare his willingness or unwillingness to act;

(e) where the trustee is outside England and Wales or cannot be found or does not act, and his absence or failure to act impedes the proper administration of the charity.

Similarly, it may appoint a person to be a charity trustee, and make orders with regard to the vesting and transfer of property:[135]

(a) in place of a charity trustee removed by it under this section or otherwise;

---

[131] Contravention of an order referred to in (iv) is an offence: s 18(14), as amended, and see section 4(I), p 321, *infra*.

[132] Section 18(1), (11), as amended. Detailed provisions relating to the appointment of a receiver and manager are contained in s 19, as amended, and SI 1992/2355. See Report for 1995, paras 28, 29.

[133] Section 18(2), as amended.

[134] Section 18(4), as amended. Section 18(4)(c) is unaffected by the Mental Capacity Act 2005.

[135] Section 18(5), as amended.

(b) where there are no charity trustees, or where by reason of vacancies in their number or the absence of incapacity of any of their number the charity cannot apply for the appointment;

(c) where there is a single charity trustee, not being a corporation aggregate, and the Commission is of the opinion that it is necessary to increase the number for the proper administration of the charity;

(d) where the Commission is of opinion that it is necessary for the proper administration of the charity to have an additional charity trustee, because one of the existing charity trustees who ought nevertheless to remain a charity trustee either cannot be found or does not act or is outside England and Wales.

Where the Commission makes an order under s 18, it must send a copy of the order and a statement of the reasons for making it to the charity concerned if it is a body corporate, or, if not, to each of the charity trustees.[136]

Subsection (16), as substituted by the 2006 Act, provides:

(a) sub-ss (1) to (3) apply in relation to an exempt charity, and

(b) sub-ss (4) to (6) apply in relation to such a charity at any time after the Commission have instituted an inquiry under s 8 with respect to it,

and the other provisions of the section apply accordingly.

There are provisions for appeal to the Charity Tribunal.

(iv) Power to suspend or remove trustees etc from membership of charity

Section18A of the Charities Act 1993, inserted by s 19 of the 2006 Act, applies where the Commission has made an order under s 18 suspending or removing from his office or employment any trustee, charity trustee, officer, agent, or employee of a charity who is also a member of the charity. Previously, in some cases, the person suspended or removed from office could use his membership of the charity to help vote himself back into, or reacquire in other ways, the office from which he had been suspended or removed. The Commission may now prevent this:

(a) if it makes an order suspending a person from his office or employment, it may also make an order suspending him for the like period from his membership of the charity; and

(b) if it made an order removing him from his office or employment, it may also make an order terminating his membership of the charity and prohibiting him from resuming membership of the charity without the Commission's consent.

There is a presumption, however, that, after five years, a person prohibited from resuming membership is entitled to do so unless, on an application for its consent, the Commission is satisfied that there is a good reason why the application should be refused.[137]

(v) Power to give specific directions for protection of charity

Section 19A (1)–(5) of the Charities Act 1993, inserted by s 20 of the 2006 Act, applies where the Commission has instituted an inquiry under s 8 and is satisfied as mentioned

---

[136] Charities Act 1993, s 19C, inserted by the 2006 Act, Sch 8, para 113.

[137] Section 19C applies: see fn 136, *supra*, and text thereto.

in s 18(1)(a) or (b). It empowers the Commission to make an order directing the charity trustees, any trustee for the charity, any officer or employee of the charity, or (if a body corporate) the charity itself to take any action that the Commission considers to be expedient in the interests of the charity.[138] The action directed may be something that the person does not have power to do under the charity's constitution or otherwise, provided that it is not prohibited by statute or expressly prohibited by the trusts of the charity, nor is it inconsistent with its purposes.

Anything done in accordance with the direction is deemed to have been properly done, but this does not affect any contractual or other right arising in connection with anything done under the authority of an order under the section.

(vi) Power to direct application of charity property

Section 19B of the Charities Act 1993, inserted by s 21 of the 2006 Act, applies where the Commission is satisfied that a person, or persons, in possession or control of charity property is, or are, unwilling to apply it properly for the purposes of the charity. If the Commission thinks it necessary or desirable, it may direct the person or persons concerned to apply the property in a specified manner. Subsections (3)–(5) contain similar provisions to those in section 19A(3)–(5) noted above.[139]

(vii) Publicity relating to schemes

Section 20 of the Charities Act 1993, as substituted by s 22 of the 2006 Act, now provides that, before establishing a scheme for the administration of a charity,[140] the Commission—unless it is satisfied that, in relation to a particular scheme, it is unnecessary—must give public notice of its proposals, inviting representations to be made within a specified time.[141] Any representations received must be taken into account before proceeding with the proposals either with or without modifications. A copy of any order made must be made available for public inspection for at least a month.

(viii) Publicity for orders relating to trustees or other individuals

Section 20A of the Charities Act 1993, also inserted by s 22 of the 2006 Act, provides that, unless the Commission determines that it is unnecessary in a particular case, no order to appoint, discharge, or remove a charity trustee or trustee for a charity[142] is to be made before the specified publicity requirement has been carried out. The requirement is that the Commission gives public notice of its proposals, inviting representations to be made within a specified time. In the case of an order to remove without his consent a charity trustee or trustee for a charity, or an officer, agent, or employee of a charity, there is a further requirement that the Commission give him not less than one month's notice of its proposals, inviting representations within a specified period.[143]

---

[138] Section 19C applies: see fn 136, *supra*, and text thereto.

[139] Section 19C applies: see fn 136, *supra*, and text thereto.

[140] Or submitting a scheme to the court or the Minister for an order giving it effect.

[141] There are additional requirements in relation to a local charity: s 20(2)(b).

[142] Other than an order relating to the official custodian, or an order to appoint an additional charity trustee.

[143] Section 20A(5). This does not apply if the person cannot be found or has no known address in the United Kingdom.

After taking into account any representations made within the specified time, the Commission may proceed with the proposals without modification, or with such modifications as it thinks fit.

(ix) Power to enter premises and seize documents, etc

Section 31A of the Charities Act 1993, inserted by s 26 of the 2006 Act, gives the Commission power, if certain conditions are fulfilled, to seek a warrant from a justice of the peace (JP) authorizing a member of the Commission's staff to enter and search specified premises, and to take possession, or take copies of, or extracts from, any relevant document or computer disk. The JP must be satisfied:

(a) that an inquiry has been instituted under s 8;[144]

(b) that there is, on the premises, any document or information relevant to that inquiry that the Commission could require to be produced or furnished under s 9;[145] and

(c) that, if the Commission were to make an order requiring the document or information to be so produced or furnished, the order would not be complied with, or the document or information would be removed, tampered with, concealed, or destroyed.

The section contains detailed provisions relating to the exercise of the power.

(x) Power to authorize dealings with charity property

Section 26(1)[146] of the Charities Act 1993 gives the Commission wide powers[147] to authorize dealings with charity property if it considers that any action proposed or contemplated in the administration of a charity is expedient in the interests of the charity, whether or not it would otherwise be within the powers exercisable by the charity trustees. The order may be made so as to authorize a particular transaction, compromise, or similar, or a particular application of property, or so as to give a more general authority. In practice, the procedure of establishing a scheme[148] is preferred for this last purpose. In particular, the order may authorize a charity to use common premises, or to employ a common staff, or otherwise to combine, for any purpose of administration, with any other charity,[149] and it may give directions as to the manner in which any expenditure is to be borne and as to other connected matters.[150] It may be added that the Commission may provide books in which any deed, will, or other document relating to a charity may be enrolled, and may accept for safe keeping any document of, or relating to, a charity.[151]

---

[144] See p 304, *supra*.   [145] See p 303, *supra*.

[146] As amended by the 2006 Act. This section was used in August 1962 to authorize the sale of the Leonardo cartoon by the Royal Academy of Arts at a price lower than that obtainable on the open market, on condition that, upon sale, it should be held on trust for exhibition to the public, and in 1979 to authorize investment in the Pooh Properties: Report for 1979, para 116.

[147] The wording of s 26(1) has been said to be very broad and not to be cut down by reference to more particular powers referred to in later subsections: *Seray-White v Charity Commissioners for England and Wales* [2006] EWHC 3181 (Ch), [2007] 3 All ER 60, [2007] 1 WLR 3242.

[148] See section 7, p 328 *et seq, infra*.   [149] Ibid, s 26(2).   [150] Ibid, s 26(3), (4). See CC 38.

[151] Section 30, as amended by the 2006 Act. Exempt charities may take advantage of this provision.

(xi) Power to give directions about dormant bank accounts

Where the Commission is informed by a relevant institution[152] that it holds an account in the name of or on behalf of a particular charity that is dormant,[153] and that it is unable, after making reasonable inquiries, to locate that charity or any of its trustees, it may direct that it be transferred to such other charity as it considers appropriate, subject to the willingness of that other charity to accept the transfer.[154] It will then be held for the purposes of the transferee charity, but subject to any restrictions on expenditure to which it was previously subject.[155]

(xii) Power to grant relief from liability for breach of trust or duty

The Charities Act 1993, s 73D, inserted by s 38 of the 2006 Act, empowers the Commission to grant relief (in whole or in part) to a charity trustee or trustee for a charity who appears to be personally liable for breach of trust or duty in relation to the trust where it considers that he has acted honestly and reasonably, and ought to be excused for the breach of trust or duty. The power extends to a person appointed to audit a charity's accounts and also to an independent examiner, reporting accountant, or other person appointed to examine or report on a charity's accounts.

These provisions do not affect the operation of the wide powers of the court to grant relief on a similar basis.[156] The advantage is that they avoid the need for an application to the court.

(C) THE CHARITY TRIBUNAL

Before the Charities Act 2006, there was a right of appeal to the High Court in relation to some decisions of the Charity Commissioners. Section 8 of the 2006 Act inserts a new Pt 1A in the 1993 Act (ss 2A–2D), which creates the Charity Tribunal (in Welsh, *Tribiwnlys Elusennau*)[157] to act as a 'court of first instance' for appeals and applications in respect of certain decisions, orders, or directions of the new Commission. It also enables the Tribunal to consider matters referred to it by the Attorney-General or, with the Attorney-General's consent, by the Commission, the reference being made before the Commission has made any decision on the matter.

There are detailed provisions relating to practice and procedure: Schedule 1C to the 1993 Act, inserted by s 8 and Sch 4 to the 2006 Act, lists in a table the decisions, orders, and directions of the Commission in respect of which an appeal may be brought. It prescribes, in the case of each specified matter, which persons, in addition to the Attorney-General, have a right of appeal and what powers the Tribunal has in relation to the appeal. These provisions do not apply to the 'reviewable matters' specified in para 3 of the Schedule, in

---

[152] Primarily banks and building societies: see Charities Act 1993, s 28(8)(b).

[153] Defined in s 28(8)(a), as amended by the 2006 Act, as one in which no transaction other than a payment in (or internal transaction by the institution) has been effected for the last five years.

[154] Section 28(1), (2), (3), as amended.   [155] Section 28(4).

[156] Under s 61 of the Trustee Act 1925, s 727 of the Companies Act 1985, and s 73E of the Charities Act 1993, inserted by s 38 of the 2006 Act.

[157] Details of membership, practice, and procedure, etc, are set out in Sch 1B to the 1993 Act, inserted by s 8 and Sch 3 to the 2006 Act.

respect of which the Tribunal can consider applications for review in the same way as the High Court would consider an application for judicial review.

Schedule 1D, likewise inserted, provides for references to the Tribunal. Both the Commission and the Attorney-General can refer to the Tribunal a question that involves either the operation of charity law in any respect, or its application to a of particular state of affairs. The Commission, however, can only do so with the consent of the Attorney-General, and only in relation to a question that has arisen in connection with the exercise of any of its functions.

There may be an appeal to the High Court on a point of law against a decision of the Tribunal, with the permission of the Tribunal, or, if that is refused, the High Court.[158]

The Attorney General, if not a party, may intervene in any proceedings before the Tribunal or on an appeal from the Tribunal. The Tribunal—or, on appeal, the Court—may, at any stage, direct that papers in the proceedings be sent to the Attorney-General.[159]

(D) THE OFFICIAL CUSTODIAN FOR CHARITIES

The Official Custodian for Charities, a corporation sole having perpetual succession and using an official seal, was created by s 3 of the Charities Act 1960 and continues in existence under s 2 of the 1993 Act.[160] His major function is to hold title to land on behalf of charities. The main advantage of this is that it avoids the necessity of changing the details of ownership of charity land whenever there is a change in trusteeship, and the problems that may arise if one or more of the trustees in whom the trust land is vested cannot be traced. This incidentally reduces costs and is particularly useful to unincorporated charities. It is less important to charities that are companies, or otherwise have a form of corporate status, where title to property can be held in the charity's own name.

Charity land may become vested in the Official Custodian by an order of the court,[161] either directly vesting the land in the Official Custodian, or authorizing or requiring the persons in whom the land is vested to transfer it to him, or appointing any person to transfer it to him.[162] Property other than land can only be vested in the Official Custodian by an order of the Commission or the court under s 18 for the protection of the charity.

Where property is vested in the Official Custodian in trust for a charity, he must not exercise any powers of management, but has the same powers, duties, and liabilities, and is entitled to the same rights and immunities, and is subject in the same way to the control and orders of the court, as a corporation appointed custodian trustee under s 4 of the Public Trustee Act 1906,[163] except that he has no power to charge fees.[164] Accordingly, charity trustees may bring proceedings in their own name without the need to obtain the permission of, or to join in the proceedings, the Official Custodian for Charities.[165]

(E) THE ATTORNEY-GENERAL

The Attorney-General acts in charity cases on behalf of the Crown as *parens patriae*. As a general rule, he is a necessary party to charity proceedings, in which he represents all of

---

[158] Charities Act 1993, s 2C, inserted by the 2006 Act.   [159] Ibid, s 2D, likewise inserted.
[160] As amended by the 2006 Act. See CC 13.
[161] Or, under s 16, as amended by the 2006 Act, of the Commission.   [162] Charities Act 1993, s 21.
[163] See Chapter 15, section 4(C), p 389, *infra*.   [164] Charities Act 1993, s 22(1).
[165] *Muman v Nagasena* [1999] 4 All ER 178, [2000] 1 WLR 299, CA.

the objects of the charity.[166] It has always been recognized that it is his duty to intervene for the purpose of protecting charities, and affording advice and assistance to the court in the administration of charitable trusts.[167] Until the Charities Act 1992, no one other than the Attorney-General was entitled to maintain an action against supposed trustees to establish the existence of a charitable trust, and only the Attorney-General or the trustees of a charity could bring proceedings to recover charity property from a third person.[168] 'So far as the enforcement of the trust is a matter of public interest,' it was said,[169] 'the guardian of that interest was the Attorney-General.' The Charities Act 1993 now provides that, with his agreement, the Commission may, of its own motion, exercise the same powers as the Attorney-General with respect to the taking of legal proceedings with reference to charities or the property or affairs of charities, or the compromise of claims with a view to avoiding or ending such proceedings.[170] The Commission is under a duty to inform the Attorney-General if it appears to it that it is desirable that he should bring proceedings with reference to a charity.[171]

One particular power possessed by the Attorney-General and the court is to authorize charity trustees to make *ex gratia* payments out of funds held on charitable trusts. This power is not to be exercised lightly on slender grounds, but only in cases in which it can fairly be said that, if the charity were an individual, it would be morally wrong of him to refuse to make the payment.[172] This does not, however, enable the Attorney-General to authorize an act in contravention of the express provisions of a statute.[173] By the 1993 Act,[174] the same power to make an *ex gratia* payment is conferred on the Commission, under the supervision, however, and subject to the directions of the Attorney-General. A refusal to exercise the power by the Commission does not prevent an application to the Attorney-General.[175]

The Law Officers Act 1997 allows the Solicitor-General to exercise both the statutory and non-statutory functions of the Attorney-General, and for his acts to have effect as if done by the Attorney-General.

[166] See *Brooks v Richardson* [1986] 1 All ER 952, [1986] 1 WLR 385.

[167] *Wallis v Solicitor-General for New Zealand* [1903] AC 173, PC; *Re Royal Society's Charitable Trusts* [1956] Ch 87, [1955] 3 All ER 14; *Re Belling* [1967] Ch 425, [1967] 1 All ER 105. Cf Charities Act 1993, s 33(7), as amended by the 2006 Act.

[168] *Hauxwell v Barton-upon-Humber UDC* [1974] Ch 432, [1973] 2 All ER 1022. Contrast the position with regard to 'charity proceedings', discussed p 313, *infra*.

[169] *Bradshaw v University College of Wales* [1987] 3 All ER 200, 203, *per* Hoffman J.

[170] Charities Act 1993, ss 37, 63, as amended by the 2006 Act.   [171] Ibid, s 33(7), as amended.

[172] *Re Snowden* [1970] Ch 700, [1969] 3 All ER 208; *Hobday v A-G of New South Wales* [1982] 1 NSWLR 160; and see [1968] 32 Conv 384 (P H Pettit); Report for 1969, paras 26–31, and Report for 1976, paras 113–116; [1994] PCB 416 (J Burchfield).

[173] *A-G v Trustees of the British Museum (Commission for Looted Art in Europe intervening)* [2005] EWHC 1089 (Ch), [2005] 3 WLR 396. Accordingly, the Attorney-General could not authorize the return by the British Museum of Nazi-looted Old Master drawings to the heirs of the previous owner, notwithstanding that the trustees felt under a moral obligation to do so. Under current legislation, national museums and galleries are prohibited from disposing of any of their works. In October 2008, the Department for Culture Media and Sport stated that the government was committed to introducing legislation to allow them to return works of art spoliated during the Nazi era.

[174] Section 27, as amended by the 2006 Act. See CC 7 and (2001) 32 T & ELJ 17 (P Hamlin).

[175] Section 27(4), as amended.

(F) LOCAL AUTHORITIES

Provisions designed to encourage cooperation and partnership between charity trustees and local authorities are contained in ss 76–79 of the 1993 Act.

Section 76, as amended, authorizes the council of a county or county borough, or of a district or London borough, and the Common Council of the City of London to maintain an index[176] of local charities,[177] or of any class of local charities in the council's area, and to publish information therein contained. The index is to be open to public inspection at all reasonable times.

Charity trustees, in applying their funds, should seek to avoid overlapping with the statutory welfare services or otherwise directly relieving public funds.[178] Guidance Notes issued by the Charity Commission[179] state that trustees are in breach of trust if, by making a grant, they bring about a reduction in a statutory benefit to which a person otherwise has a right; they are acting within their trusts in relieving need, hardship, and distress so long as they do not replace funds from the state.

Section 78(1) empowers any local council[180] to make, with any charity established for purposes similar or complementary to services provided by the council, arrangements for coordinating the activities of the council and those of the charity in the interests of persons who may benefit from those services or from the charity. This is carried a stage further by s 142 of the Local Government Act 1972,[181] which empowers a local authority to make, or assist in the making of, arrangements under which the public may obtain information concerning the services provided by the authority, government departments, charities, and voluntary bodies within the area of the local authority concerned.

It is convenient to mention here that s 79 of the Charities Act 1993, as amended by the 2006 Act, contains special provisions relating to parochial charities.[182] These provisions relate, in the main, to the transfer of property by the trustees to the parish council or their appointees, and to the appointment of charity trustees by the parish council or parish meeting.

[176] The Commission must provide, on request; copies of relevant entries in the Register of Charities, discussed p 321 *et seq, infra*). The index may also contain informal references to local branches of national charities that are ineligible to be placed on the Register. These have no legal consequences, but may be of considerable practical value.

[177] Defined by s 96(1) in relation to any area as 'a charity established for purposes which are by their nature or by the trusts of the charity directed wholly or mainly to the benefit of that area or of part of it'. As to reviews of local charities by local authority, see Charities Act 1993, s 77, as amended by the 2006 Act.

[178] See Report for 1978, paras 61 and 62.

[179] See CC 3, para 63, CC 4, paras 21–22, and CC 37, paras 21–32. On applications for registration as charities by the Trafford Community Leisure Trust and the Wigan Leisure and Culture Trust, the Commission considered whether they were sufficiently independent from the respective local authorities, and the extent to which they could be charities if they were established to carry out statutory duties imposed on governmental authorities: see [2006] WTLR 543.

[180] This includes councils not included in ss 76 and 77, as amended, and is defined for this purpose in s 78(1).

[181] As amended by the Local Government Act 1986, s 3.

[182] Defined by s 96(1). Voluntary and grant-maintained schools within the meaning of the Education Act 1996 are excluded: s 79(9), as amended by the Education Act 1996, Sch 37, para 119. See CC 29.

(G) THE COURT

The court has an inherent general jurisdiction[183] over charitable trusts and may accordingly enforce them, take steps to redress a breach of trust, direct a scheme[184] in order to enforce the more complete attainment of the charitable objects, and alter and amend the trusts under the cy-près doctrine. In addition to proceedings by the Attorney-General and the Commission, the Charities Act 1993 provides that charity proceedings—that is, proceedings brought under the court's jurisdiction with respect to charities, or brought under the court's jurisdiction with respect to trusts in relation to the administration of a trust for charitable purposes[185]—may be taken either by the charity, or by any of the charity trustees, or by 'any person interested in the charity', or by any two or more inhabitants of the area of the charity, if it is a local charity.[186] In *Re Hampton Fuel Allotment Charity*,[187] the Court of Appeal said that there were insuperable difficulties in attempting comprehensive definition of the phrase 'any person interested in the charity'. The interest that ordinary members of the public, whether or not subscribing to a charity, and whether or not potential beneficiaries, have in seeing that a charity is properly administered is the responsibility of the Attorney-General. To qualify as a plaintiff in his own right, a person needs to have an interest that is materially greater than, or different from, that possessed by ordinary members of the public. The Court of Appeal referred with apparent approval to Megarry V-C's reference, in *Haslemere Estates Ltd v Baker*,[188] to those 'who have some good reason for seeking to enforce the trusts of a charity or secure its due administration', which Megarry V-C contrasted with 'those who merely have some claim adverse to the charity, and seek to improve their position at the expense of the charity'. A person who founds

[183] *A-G v Sherborne Grammar School Governors* (1854) 18 Beav 256. Including, as incidental to the administration of a charity estate, jurisdiction to alien charity property where the alienation is clearly for the charity's benefit and advantage: *Oldham Borough Council v A-G* [1993] Ch 210, [1993] 2 All ER 432, CA.

[184] Either by directing a reference to chambers to settle the scheme, or by reference to the Commission under s 16(2), as amended, discussed p 303, *infra*. In a simple case, or in a case in which the fund is very small, the court may act directly without any reference.

[185] Section 33(8). See *Brookes v Richardson* [1986] 1 All ER 952, discussed [1986] All ER Rev 203 (P J Clarke). 'Charity proceedings' probably includes an application for judicial review of the decision of a charitable public body exercising its discretionary power in the management of trust property: *Scott v National Trust for Places of Historic Interest or Natural Beauty* [1998] 2 All ER 705, sub nom *Ex p Scott* [1998] 1 WLR 226 (National Trust decision to end deer hunting with hounds on Trust land; judicial review refused, as alternative remedy available under the Charities Act 1993). It does not cover proceedings by way of construction of a testamentary document to determine whether a provision was effective to create a charitable trust, where only the Attorney-General, or the trustees, can start an action: *Re Belling* [1967] Ch 425, [1967] 1 All ER 105; *Mills v Winchester Diocesan Board of Finance* [1989] Ch 428, [1989] 2 All ER 317. In appropriate circumstances, a case may be heard and judgment given in private, notwithstanding the Human Rights Act 1998: *In re Trusts of X Charity* [2003] EWHC 257 (Ch), [2003] 1 WLR 2751. See also (2006) 9 CLPR 23 (J Kilby).

[186] Section 33(1). See (1988) 2 TL & P 128 (J Thurston).

[187] [1989] Ch 484, sub nom *Richmond upon Thames London Borough Council v Rogers* [1988] 2 All ER 761, CA.

[188] [1982] 3 All ER 525. *Gunning v Buckfast Abbey Trustees* (1994) Times, 9 June (fee-paying parents of children at a preparatory school run by a charitable trust entitled to bring proceedings although neither subscribers to, nor beneficiaries of, the charity), noted (1993–94) 2 CLPR 250 (Debra Morris); (1995) 9 Tru LI 130 (R Nolan); *Royal Society for the Protection of Cruelty to Animals v A-G* [2001] 3 All ER 530 (disappointed applicant for membership has not a sufficient interest).

and finances a charity may well qualify as a person interested in that charity, although his executors would not.[189]

Apart from proceedings brought by the Attorney-General or by the Commission under s 32,[190] no charity proceedings relating to a charity[191] can be proceeded with in any court unless the taking of the proceedings is authorized by the Commission, which must not, however, without special reasons, give such authorization where, in its opinion, the case can be dealt with by it under the other powers in the Act.[192] The object of this 'protective filter', as it has been called,[193] is to prevent money of the charity being spent unnecessarily on legal proceedings. If the Commission refuses its authorization, an application for leave may nevertheless be sought from a Chancery judge.[194]

The jurisdiction is based primarily on the existence of a trust. The point has been raised several times where a testator has given property to a non-existent institution and where there is clearly a general charitable intention. In such case, if the gift is by way of trust, the court has jurisdiction and will direct a scheme; if it is by way of direct gift, the court has no jurisdiction, and the matter falls within the royal prerogative and will be disposed of by the Crown by sign manual, acting as it is said as *parens patriae*.[195]

The inherent jurisdiction was limited in relation to charities established by royal charter or by statute,[196] although it always had jurisdiction to see that the provisions of the charter or the statute were observed. There is, moreover, a difficulty as to jurisdiction over corporate charities. Where a corporate body holds property on charitable trusts, there is clearly jurisdiction, but, in many cases, a corporation with exclusively charitable purposes simply holds property as part of its corporate funds. If jurisdiction depends on the existence of a trust, a problem arises. It may be possible, in the case of a charity incorporated by charter, to evade the difficulty by holding that the corporate charity holds its property on trust for its charitable purposes,[197] but this argument is not available in the case of a company incorporated under the Companies Acts with exclusively charitable objects, because a company does not hold its property on trust either for its members or the objects set out in its memorandum of association. However, it has been held[198] that the court has jurisdiction not only where there is a trust in the strict sense, but also, in the case of a corporate

---

[189] *Re Hampton Fuel Allotment Charity, supra*, CA; *Bradshaw v University College of Wales, Aberystwyth* [1987] 3 All ER 200.

[190] Charities Act 1993, s 33(6), as amended by the 2006 Act.

[191] This does not include a charitable institution established in a foreign jurisdiction, but operating here: *Gaudiya Mission v Kamalaksha DAS Brahmachary* [1998] Ch 341, [1997] 4 All ER 957. See p 285, *supra*.

[192] That is, the powers other than those conferred by s 32 of the Charities Act 1993: ibid, s 33(2), (3), as amended by the 2006 Act. Authorization properly refused in *Seray-White v Charity Commissioners for England and Wales* [2006] EWHC 3181 (Ch), [2007] 3 All ER 60. Section 33(4) excludes an order for the taking of proceedings in a pending cause or matter or for the bringing of an appeal.

[193] By Nicholls J in *Re Hampton Fuel Allotment Charity, supra*, at 410. See also *Muman v Nagasena* [1999] 4 All ER 178, [2000] 1 WLR 299, CA.

[194] Ibid, s 33(5), as amended.

[195] See *Re Bennett* [1960] Ch 18, [1959] 3 All ER 295, (1974) 52 CBR 372 (L L Stevens). See also Report for 1964, paras 64–66. The power was delegated to the Attorney-General in 1986: the average number of directions made by the Attorney-General over the five years to 1996 is fifty, but only thirty-seven in 1996.

[196] See now p 328, *infra*.

[197] Even, it seems, although the charity came into existence before the creation of trusts: *A-G v St Cross Hospital* (1853) 17 Beav 435 (hospital founded in twelfth century).

[198] *Liverpool and District Hospital for Diseases of the Heart v A-G* [1981] Ch 193, [1981] 1 All ER 994. The particular terms of the trust or constitution in question may, however, operate substantially or partially

body, where, under the terms of its constitution, it is legally obliged to apply the assets in question for exclusively charitable purposes. In any event, such a company incorporated under the Companies Act is clearly a charity for the purposes of the Charities Acts 1993 and 2006, provision being made for its being wound up on a petition presented by the Attorney-General or by a person authorized by the Insolvency Act 1986.[199]

(H) VISITORS

(i) Position apart from statute[200]

Ecclesiastical and eleemosynary corporations[201] are subject to the jurisdiction of visitors in relation to their internal management.[202] Ecclesiastical corporations are those that exist for the furtherance of religion and perpetuating the rights of the Church. For present purposes, eleemosynary corporations[203] are such as are constituted for the perpetual distribution of the free alms or bounty of the founder of them to such persons as he has directed—originally, mainly hospitals[204] and colleges. The universities of Oxford and Cambridge are civil, and not eleemosynary, corporations and so have no visitors. However, the colleges of those universities are eleemosynary corporations, although it must be remembered that, in most cases, only the master, fellows, and scholars, and not exhibitioners or commoners, are members of the foundation.[205] Most of the more modern universities, other than those that have become universities under the Further and Higher Education Act 1992,[206] have been founded by royal charter and are eleemosynary

---

to oust the jurisdiction of the court. See (2006) 9 CLPR 19 (M C Cullity); (2007) 21 TruLI 3 (I Dawson and J Alder).

[199] Charities Act 1993, s 63(1).

[200] See, generally, (1992–93) 1 CLPR 63 (H Picarda); (1994) 18 UQLJ 106 (S Robinson); (2002) 1 ELJ 135 (T Birtwistle).

[201] *Blackstone's Commentaries*, p 470. As to civil corporations, see pp 481, 482, where he pointed out that the Court of King's Bench (now, presumably, the Queen's Bench Division) has a supervisory jurisdiction, but it is doubtful whether the court acts in the capacity of visitor. In relation to universities in Nigeria, see (1991) ICLQ 699 (M A Ikhariale), and in Western Australia, (1995) 25 UWALR 146 (P Whalley and D Price).

[202] The judges have a visitatorial jurisdiction over the Inns of Court, notwithstanding that an Inn of Court is not a corporation, does not have statutes, nor does it have a founder who nominated a visitor to hear and determine internal disputes: *R v Visitors to the Inns of Court, ex p Calder* [1994] QB 1, [1993] 2 All ER 876, CA; *Joseph v Council of Legal Education* [1994] ELR 407, CA; *R v Council of Legal Education, ex p Halstead* (1994) Times, 11 August and 7 October, DC.

[203] This phrase is not a term of art with a judicially established definition. The narrowest possible meaning has been said to be charities for the relief of poverty. In *Re Armitage's Will Trusts* [1972] Ch 438, [1972] 1 All ER 708, it was said to cover all charities directed to the relief of individual distress whether due to poverty, age, sickness, or other similar individual afflictions.

[204] In the old sense of institutions for the maintenance of the needy, infirm, or aged.

[205] The position of Oxford colleges is discussed by D Palfreyman in (1997–98) 5 CLPR 85. Cf *Herring v Templeman* [1973] 3 All ER 569, CA, in which it was held that a student at a teacher-training college was outside the visitatorial jurisdiction, because although he was a student there, he was in no position of membership. As to the visitor in New Zealand universities, see (1985) 11 NZULR 382 (F M Brookfield).

[206] Section 77. The only other non-charter university is the University of Newcastle upon Tyne, created by the Universities of Durham and Newcastle upon Tyne Act 1963, which expressly provided that the Lord Chancellor should be its visitor. Polytechnics that became universities following the 1992 Act are corporate bodies, having no visitor. As public institutions discharging public functions, their decisions are subject to judicial review on conventional grounds: *R v Manchester Metropolitan University, ex parte Nolan* [1994] ELR 380, QBD. See also *Clark v University of Lincolnshire and Humberside* [2000] 3 All ER 752, [2000] 1 WLR 1988, CA.

corporations; moreover, such charters normally—perhaps always—provide that all of the undergraduates are members of the university.[207]

Ecclesiastical corporations are generally visitable by the Ordinary.[208] So far as eleemosynary corporations are concerned, the founder is said to be a legislator,[209] and may accordingly appoint visitors, and if he appoints no visitor, he and his heirs[210] are visitors by operation of law.[211] This principle applies where the founder is the Crown. Thus, if a university is founded by royal charter and the charter reserves to the Crown the right to appoint a visitor, but no appointment has been made, the Crown is the visitor.[212] Visitatorial jurisdiction never fails through lack of a visitor.[213] If the founder's heirs die out, or cannot be found,[214] or cannot act by reason of insanity,[215] the visitatorial power becomes vested in the Crown. In any case in which visitatorial powers are exercisable by the Crown, they are, in practice, exercised by the Lord Chancellor on behalf of the Crown, acting in a capacity distinct from his judicial capacity,[216] or such other person as the Crown may nominate.[217] And, as it would be contrary to natural justice that a man should be judge in his own cause, the Court of Queen's Bench[218] has assumed jurisdiction where otherwise the same person would be both visitor and visited.[219] No technical words are required for the appointment of a visitor by the founder,[220] who may either appoint a general visitor, or divide up the visitatorial power among two or more persons,[221] or appoint special visitors for a particular purpose. If a visitatorial power is prima facie general, it requires particular words to abridge it in any respect. The mere fact that, in certain respects, the visitor's powers are limited as to the way in which they can be exercised does not cut him down from being a general visitor to a special visitor.[222]

The nature of the visitatorial power has been said to be *forum domesticum*, the private jurisdiction of the founder,[223] and in any dispute arising under the domestic law of

---

[207] *Patel v University of Bradford Senate* [1978] 3 All ER 841; affd [1979] 2 All ER 582, CA; (1970) 86 LQR 531 (J W Bridge); (1978) 4 Dal LJ 647 (W Ricquier); (1979) 12 MULR 291 (P Willis); (1981) 97 LQR 610 (P M Smith); (1985) Dal LJ 313 (C B Lewis).

[208] That is, one who has, of his own right, immediate jurisdiction in ecclesiastical cases, such as the bishop in a diocese. See 14 *Halsburys Laws of England* (4th edn) para 458. As to cathedral churches, see Cathedrals Measure 1963, s 6; Church of England (Miscellaneous Provisions) Measure 1976, s 4.

[209] *Spencer v All Souls' College* (1762) Wilm 163; *Phillips v Bury, supra; Thomas v University of Bradford* [1987] AC 795, [1987] 1 All ER 834, HL.

[210] The effect of the abolition of inheritance by the Administration of Estates Act 1925, s 45, is not clear.

[211] *Phillips v Bury, supra; Eden v Foster* (1726) 2 P Wms 325.

[212] *Thomas v University of Bradford, supra*, HL.

[213] *Re Wislang's Application* [1984] NI 63, 93, *per* Kelly LJ.

[214] *Ex p Wrangham* (1795) 2 Ves 609; *A-G v Earl of Clarendon* (1810) 17 Ves 491.

[215] *A-G v Dixie* (1805) 13 Ves 519.

[216] *Casson v University of Aston in Birmingham* [1983] 1 All ER 88.

[217] In *R v HM the Queen in Council, ex p Vijayatunga* [1990] 2 QB 444, sub nom *R v University of London Visitor, ex p Vijayatunga* [1989] 2 All ER 843, CA, the Crown nominated a Committee of the Lords of the Privy Council, in *R v Lord President of the Privy Council, ex p Page* [1993] AC 682, sub nom *Page v Hull University Visitor* [1993] 1 All ER 97, the Lord President of the Privy Council, and in *Thomas v University of Bradford (No 2)* [1992] 1 All ER 964, a Lord of Appeal in Ordinary.

[218] And presumably the High Court would now act in the same way.

[219] *R v Bishop of Chester* (1728) 2 Stra 797; *R v Bishop of Ely* (1788) 2 Term Rep 290.

[220] *A-G v Middleton* (1751) 2 Ves Sen 327; *St John's College, Cambridge v Todington* (1757) 1 Burr 158.

[221] *A-G v Middleton, supra.*   [222] *Oakes v Sidney Sussex College, Cambridge* [1988] 1 All ER 1004.

[223] *Per* Hardwicke LC in *Green v Rutherford* (1750) 1 Ves Sen 462, 472. See (1980) 7 Mon LR 59 (R T Sadler); (1981) U Tas LR 2 (R T Sadler).

the institution, the power of the visitor is absolute[224] and exclusive.[225] This is because the founder of such a body is entitled to reserve to himself or to a visitor whom he appoints the exclusive right to adjudicate upon the domestic laws that the founder has established for the regulation of his bounty.

What is meant by the 'domesticity' of the visitatorial jurisdiction was explained by Lord Griffiths giving the leading speech in *Thomas v University of Bradford*,[226] who adopted a passage from an article by Dr P M Smith.[227] Dr Smith had pointed out that the basis of the visitatorial jurisdiction is the supervision of the statutes, ordinances, regulations, etc, of the foundation, which leads to a distinction between any matter concerning the application or the interpretation of those internal laws, which is within his jurisdiction, and questions concerning rights and duties derived otherwise than from such internal laws, which are outside it:

> Thus a matter or dispute is 'domestic' so as to be within the visitatorial jurisdiction if it involves questions relating to the internal laws of the foundation of which he is visitor or rights and duties derived from such internal laws. Conversely, an issue which turns on the enforcement of or adjudication on terms entered into between an individual and his employer, notwithstanding that they may also be in the relationship of member and corporation, and which involves no enforcement of or adjudication concerning the domestic laws of the foundation, is *ultra vires* the visitor's authority and is cognizable in a court of law or equity.

Subject to any special provisions in the statutes of the foundation, the ordinary duties and powers of the visitor concern the election and removal of members[228] of the corporation and its officers, the internal management of the corporation, construction of the statutes of the foundation, and judging claims and complaints by members. He is 'a judge, not for the single purpose of interpreting laws, but also for the application of laws, that are perfectly clear: requiring no interpretation; and, farther, for the interpretations of questions of fact; involving no interpretation of laws'.[229] It is his function to ensure due compliance with the

[224] *R v Bishop of Chester* (1748) 1 Wm Bl 22, in which Wright J said 'Visitors have an absolute power; the only absolute one I know of in England', and in *Page v Hull University Visitor, supra*, HL, Lord Browne-Wilkinson said 'the position of the visitor is anomalous, indeed unique'. Where any question as to the validity of an act by the trustees of a charity was under the scheme governing it to be determined by the Charity Commissioners, the Commissioners were in the position of a visitor: *R v Charity Comrs, ex p Baldwin* [2001] WTLR 137.

[225] *Thorne v University of London* [1966] 2 QB 237, [1966] 2 All ER 338, CA (the court has no jurisdiction to hear a complaint that failure in degree examinations in, inter alia, the law of trusts was a result of negligence of the examiners); *Herring v Templeman* [1973] 2 All ER 581; affd on different grounds [1973] 3 All ER 569, CA; *Patel v University of Bradford Senate, supra*, CA; *Re University of Melborne, ex p De Dimone* [1981] VR 378; *R v University of Nottingham, ex p K* [1998] ELR 184, CA. See (1974) 37 MLR 324 (D Christie); (1974) 33 CLJ 23 (S A de Smith). It may be noted that, even if there is no visitor, the court will not hear a complaint as to the application of university regulations relating to degrees and satisfaction of examiners where the university regulations provide a proper complaints procedure: *M v London Guildhall University* [1998] ELR 149, CA.

[226] [1987] AC 795, [1987] 1 All ER 834, HL. See (1986) 136 NLJ 484, 519, 567, 571, and 665 (P M Smith); [1987] Pub L (Bridgid Hadfield); [1987] 46 CLJ 384 (C Lewis); (1987) 16 AALR 376 (G L Peiris); (1989) 8 CJQ 152 (G G Howells); (1998) Denning LJ 1 (M J Beloff).　　　　　　　　　　　　[227] Op cit, at p 568.

[228] This includes not only corporations, but all persons who can be described as members of the institution or as being on the foundation: *Hines v Birkbeck College* [1986] Ch 524, [1985] 3 All ER 156; *Thomas v University of Bradford, supra*, HL.

[229] *Per* Sir Samuel Romilly in his argument in *Ex p Kirkby Ravensworth Hospital* (1808) 15 Ves 305, 311, cited by Lord Griffiths in *Thomas v University of Bradford, supra*, HL, at 815, 842, and said to have long been accepted as authoritative.

terms of the charter and statutes. If there is a threat to do an act in breach of the charter or statutes, it is the visitor's function to prohibit such breach.[230] His jurisdiction extends beyond members to other persons who claim rights under the domestic law.[231]

The jurisdiction covers all questions of disputed membership, including claims by persons to become members of the foundation, such as rejected candidates for fellowships,[232] and disputes in which the issue is whether or not the person concerned is entitled to be reinstated or admitted to a university,[233] but does not otherwise extend to questions between the foundation and people outside it not arising under the domestic law.[234] It also covers academic matters such as the award of degrees and admission to courses, although, when dealing in educational matters with actions properly taken within the structures and discretions approved under statutory process, visitors should respect the exercise of such discretions, rather than replacing them with their own views on matters of academic judgment.[235] Contrary to the view expressed by Lord Hailsham LC,[236] the House of Lords has now[237] said that there is no reason why the visitor should not award damages in an appropriate case.

If the matter falls within his jurisdiction, a visitor can be compelled to exercise it.[238] The exercise of the visitatorial power is a judicial act so that the dictates of natural justice, which require, for example, that both sides should be heard, must be observed.[239] Provided, however, that he acts judicially, the mode of the exercise of his power is left to the discretion of the visitor, who enjoys untrammelled jurisdiction to investigate and correct wrongs done in the administration of the internal law of the foundation to which he is appointed. He has a general power to right wrongs and to redress grievances. According to the circumstances, he may act as a review court or an appellate tribunal, and he may—indeed, should—investigate the basic facts to whatever depth is appropriate.[240]

Judicial review is not available to quash the decision of the visitor on the ground of an alleged error of law. The visitor is not applying the general law of the land, but a peculiar, domestic law of which he is the sole arbiter and of which the courts have no cognisance. If

---

[230] *Pearce v University of Aston in Birmingham (No 2)* [1991] 2 All ER 469 (Visitor).

[231] *Oakes v Sidney Sussex College, Cambridge, supra.*

[232] *R v Hertford College* (1878) 3 QBD 693, CA.

[233] *Patel v University of Bradford Senate* [1978] 3 All ER 841; affd [1979] 2 All ER 582, CA: doubted as to first admission [1979] Pub L 209 (W T M Ricquier). See also *Casson v University of Aston in Birmingham* [1983] 1 All ER 88; *Thomas v University of Bradford, supra,* HL.

[234] *Oakes v Sidney Sussex College, Cambridge, supra; Thomas v University of Bradford, supra,* HL.

[235] *R v Council of Legal Education, ex p Eddis* (1995) 7 Admin LR 357; *O' v Inns of Court Law School* [1999] ELR 364 (Visitor); *Jhamat v Inns of Court School of Law* [1999] ELR 450 (Visitor); *R v University of Cambridge, ex p Persaud* [2001] ELR 64.

[236] In *Casson v University of Aston in Birmingham, supra,* at 91.

[237] *Thomas v University of Bradford, supra,* HL. In line g6 on p 848 of the All ER report, insert 'visitor' after 'university'. See *Re Macquarie University, ex p Ong* (1989) 17 NSWLR 113; *Bayley-Jones v University of Newcastle* (1990) 22 NSWLR 425.

[238] *Whiston v Dean and Chapter of Rochester* (1849) 7 Hare 532.

[239] *R v Bishop of Ely* (1788) 2 Term Rep 290.

[240] *R v University of London Visitor, ex p Vijayatunga, supra,* CA; *R v Cranfield University Senate, ex p Bashir* [1999] ELR 317, CA. See also *Thomas v University of Bradford (No 2)* [1992] 1 All ER 964, Visitor, noted (1992–93) 1 CLPR 73 (Suzy Hughes). But note *R v Visitors to the Inns of Court, ex p Calder* [1994] QB 1, [1993] 2 All ER 876, CA, in which the decision was quashed on the ground that the visitors had misapprehended their role and had acted as a reviewing, rather than an appellate, tribunal, and see [1992] Pub L 41 (J H Baker).

the visitor has power under the regulating documents to enter into the adjudication of the dispute—that is, is acting within his jurisdiction in the narrow sense—he cannot err in law in reaching his decision, since the general law is not the applicable law. Therefore he cannot be acting *ultra vires* and unlawfully by applying his view of the domestic law in reaching his decision. The court has no jurisdiction either to say that he erred in his application of the general law, since the general law is not applicable to the decision, or to reach a contrary view as to the effect of the domestic law, since the visitor is the sole judge of such domestic law.[241] Judicial review lies only where the visitor has acted outside his jurisdiction, in the narrow sense, or abused his powers, or acted in breach of the rules of natural justice.[242] The delegation of the powers of a university visitor to another could amount to a failure on the visitor's part to exercise his jurisdiction fully and such a failure would be amenable to judicial review.[243]

Thus, if, by the statutes of the foundation, he is to conduct a general visitation not more than once in five years, he has no power to visit more often. General visitation has been said to be at least obsolescent,[244] but a general visitor has a standing constant authority at all times to hear complaints and redress grievances of particular members of the foundation.[245] Apart from judicial review, the courts have no power to interfere with the visitor acting within his jurisdiction, but statute may impinge on the situation. Thus, if, in proceedings under the Employment Rights Act 1996, a question arises concerning the interpretation or application of the internal laws of the university, the proceedings will not be adjourned and the question will have to be resolved for the purpose of the case by the tribunal hearing the application.[246]

It should be added that if a corporation holds property as a trustee on a special trust, the court has jurisdiction in the ordinary way and the matter is outside the jurisdiction of the visitor.[247]

(ii) The Higher Education Act 2004

T.he jurisdiction of the visitor in relation to disputes arising in a 'qualifying institution'[248] is considerably reduced by the provisions of the above Act.

---

[241] *R v Lord President of the Privy Council, ex p Page* [1993] AC 682, sub nom *Page v Hull University Visitor* [1993] 1 All ER 97, noted (1993) 109 LQR 155 (H W R Wade); *R v Visitor of the University of Leicester* [2003] EWCA Civ 1082, [2003] ELR 562; *Denman v Lord Chancellor's Department* [2004] EWHC 930 (Admin), [2004] ELR 484. See also (1995) 7 E & L 63 (J W Parlour and L R V Burwood).

[242] *Page v Hull University Visitor, supra*, HL, and see *R v Visitors to the Inns of Court, ex p Calder, supra,* CA; *Joseph v Council of Legal Education* [1994] ELR 407, CA (jurisdiction of visitor exclusive); *Ex p Toms, Latimer and Nightingale* (1994) Times, 5 May; (1993–94) 2 CLPR 103 (P M Smith).

[243] *R (Varma) v Visitor to Cranfield University* (2004) Times, 23 July.

[244] *Patel v University of Bradford Senate, supra, per* Megarry V-C at first instance, at 846.

[245] *Philips v Bury* (1694) Carth 180, Holt KB 715.

[246] *Thomas v University of Bradford* [1987] AC 795, [1987] 1 All ER 834, HL.

[247] *Green v Rutherford* (1750) 1 Ves Sen 462, 472; *Whiston v Dean and Chapter of Rochester, supra; Thomas v University of Bradford, supra,* HL.

[248] Defined in the Higher Education Act 2004, s 11, as including a university, the entitlement of which to grant awards is conferred or confirmed by an Act of Parliament, a royal charter, or an order made by the Privy Council under the Further and Higher Education Act 1992, s 76.

(i) *Student complaints*   Part 2 of the Act provides for the setting up of a student complaints scheme for the review of a 'qualifying complaint'. This is widely defined in s 12 as:

> a complaint about an act or omission of a qualifying institution which is made by a person—
>
> (a) as a student or former student at that institution, or
>
> (b) as a student or former student at another institution . . . undertaking a course of study, or programme of research, leading to the grant of one of the qualifying institution's awards.

This is subject to the important restriction that a complaint is not 'a qualifying complaint to the extent that it relates to matters of academic judgment'.[249]

Complementarily to the scheme, s 20 provides that the visitor of a qualifying institution has no jurisdiction in respect of an application for admission to the qualifying institution as a student, or in respect of a complaint by a person referred to in (a) or (b) set out above.

(ii) *Staff disputes*   Section 46 provides that the visitor of a qualifying institution has no jurisdiction in respect of:

> (a) any dispute relating to a member of staff which concerns his appointment or employment or the termination of his appointment or employment,
>
> (b) any other dispute between a member of staff and the qualifying institution in respect of which proceedings could be brought before any court or tribunal,[250] or
>
> (c) any dispute as to the application of the statutes or other internal laws of the institution in relation to a matter falling within paragraph (a) or (b).[251]

(iii) The Human Rights Act 1998

There is, as yet, no authority as to the effect on the visitational jurisdiction of the incorporation of Art 6(1) of the European Convention for the Protection of Human Rights and Fundamental Freedoms (ECHR) into English law, but it has been contended[252] that it is likely to have a highly significant impact on the role of the visitor in universities. The contentions are, firstly, that, although a student will continue to be contractually obliged to take any complaint through the relevant university complaints procedures, any delay at a chartered university in organizing a hearing before the visitor will amount to a breach of Art 6(1) such as to enable an aggrieved student to take his case directly to court.

Secondly, it is said that, even if taken reasonably promptly, the visitor's decision will no longer be final. Recourse to the courts will lie not only for breaches of natural justice or acts in excess of jurisdiction, but also for any breach of ordinary public law principles.

---

[249] Compare the cases cited at p 318, fn 235, and text thereto.

[250] In determining whether a dispute falls within (b), it is to be assumed that the visitor does not have jurisdiction to determine the dispute.

[251] See *Labinjo v The University of Salford* [2005] ELR 1 (Visitor), noted (2005) 6 ELJ 135 (Z Leventhal).

[252] See (1999) 11 E & L 165 (T Kaye); (2001) 13 E & L 279 (M Arthur).

Thirdly, whether the student wishes to challenge the visitor's decision or goes directly to court, the judge hearing the case will normally be obliged to hear evidence as to the substantive merits and factual basis of the case.

It may be added that a private law action may, perhaps, replace an application for judicial review, because s 8(2) of the Human Rights Act 1998 gives the court power to award damages against a university that issues an improper grade or delays for an unreasonable length of time in dealing with a student's complaint, if it can be shown that the student has suffered some loss as a result, provided that the claim is made in private law and not by way of an application for judicial review.[253] Further, by s 8(1), the court may grant such relief or remedy, or make such order, within its powers as it considers just and appropriate.

(I) THE DIRECTOR OF PUBLIC PROSECUTIONS

Proceedings for certain specified offences may only be instigated by, or with the consent of, the Director of Public Prosecutions (DPP).[254] The offences specified relate to the omission of a registered charity's status on official publications,[255] supplying false or misleading information,[256] failure to comply with orders made by the Charity Commission,[257] failure to comply with requirements as to annual reports and annual returns,[258] and acting as a trustee while disqualified.[259]

5 REGISTRATION OF CHARITIES

(A) THE REGISTER OF CHARITIES

Section 3 of the Charities Act 1993, as substituted by the Charities Act 2006, s 9, provides that the Commission shall continue to keep a Register of Charities containing the name and such other particulars of, and such other information relating to, every such charity as the Commission thinks fit. It must remove from the Register:

(i) any institution that it no longer considers is a charity; and

(ii) any charity that has ceased to exist or does not operate.[260]

The Register is to be open to public inspection at all reasonable times. It is now computerized and available on the Internet.[261]

Where a charity required to be registered is not registered, it is the duty of the charity trustees to apply for registration, and to supply all of the documents and information required for this purpose; likewise, if such a charity is registered, it is the duty of the

---

[253] See *Moran v University College, Salford (No 2)* [1994] ELR 187.
[254] Charities Act 1993, s 94.   [255] See ibid, s 5, and p 324, *infra*.
[256] See ibid, s 11, as amended by the 2006 Act, and p 304, *supra*.
[257] See ibid, s 18(14), and p 305, *supra*.
[258] See ibid, s 49, as substituted by the 2006 Act, and p 328, *infra*.
[259] See ibid, s 73(1), and p 294, *supra*.
[260] Ibid s 3(4)(5), as substituted. Where a charity that does not require to be registered chooses to be registered, it must be removed at the request of the charity: s 3(6), as substituted.
[261] Ibid, s 3(7)–(9), as substituted.

charity trustees (or the last charity trustees) to notify the Commission if the institution ceases to exist, or if there is any change in its trusts or in the particulars of it entered in the Register.[262] Although no time limit is specified before which these duties must be carried out, any person who makes default may, by order of the Commission, be required to make it good. Disobedience to such an order may, on an application to the High Court, be dealt with as for disobedience to an order of the High Court.[263]

Registration is no evidence that the institution is efficiently and properly managed, or that the trustees and servants of the charity are of good character.[264]

(B) CHARITIES NOT REQUIRED TO BE REGISTERED

The general rule in s 3A(1) of the Charities Act 1993, as inserted by s 9 of the 2006 Act, is that every charity must be registered. Section 3A(2) provides that four classes of charity are not required to be registered:

  (a) any exempt charity[265] ...

  (b) any charity which for the time being—
    (i) is permanently or temporarily excepted by order of the Commission, and
    (ii) complies with any conditions of the exception,
    and whose gross income[266] does not exceed £100,000;

  (c) any charity which for the time being—
    (i) is, or is of a description, permanently or temporarily excepted by regulations made by the Secretary of State, and
    (ii) complies with any conditions of the exception,
    and whose gross income does not exceed £100,000; and

  (d) any charity whose gross income does not exceed £5,000.[267]

These provisions are significantly different from the corresponding provisions in the original s 3.

  (i)   Previously, no excepted charity—under (b) or (c), above—was required to register; now, it is required to register if its income exceeds £100,000.

  (ii) The effect of existing excepting orders and regulations is preserved, but no new exceptions can be created.[268]

  (iii) Under (d), many of the smallest charities have been released from the requirement of registration by the raising of the threshold from £1,000 to £5,000, and the removal of the rule that any charity must register, regardless of its income, if it possessed a permanent endowment or the use and occupation of any land.

---

[262] Section 3B, as inserted by the 2006 Act.   [263] Sections 87 and 88, as amended by the 2006 Act.

[264] See the Press Notice relating to the Unification Church, reprinted in the Report for 1982, Appendix C.

[265] See Sch 2, as amended by s 11 of the 2006 Act, and p 289, *supra*.

[266] 'Gross income' is defined in s 3A(10), as inserted.

[267] The Minister for the Cabinet Office is given a limited power to substitute different sums for the sums specified in s 3A(2)(b), (c), and (d): s 3A(7), (8).

[268] Section 3A(3)(4), as inserted. Section 3A(11), as inserted, contemplates the possibility of an order that s 3A(2)(b) and (c) shall cease to have effect.

An excepted charity, other than an exempt charity, may be entered on the Register at the request of the charity, for instance, to publicize its work or to establish its charitable status, if the Commission is satisfied that there is a public interest in their registration, but may at any time, and must at the request of the charity, be removed from the Register. When s 3A(6) is brought into force, which is expected to be in 2010, a charity within s 3A(2)(b), (c),or (d) must be entered in the Register if it so requests. The delay in the commencement of this provision is to allow the Commission to prepare for the large number of voluntary registrations expected when it is brought into force, particularly from charities with an income not exceeding £5,000.

(C) EFFECT OF REGISTRATION

Registration of an institution has the effect that, for all purposes other than rectification of the Register, it is conclusively presumed to be or have been a charity at any time when it is or was on the Register of Charities.[269] To some extent, the presumption operates retrospectively. Thus, in *Re Murawski's Will Trusts*,[270] the question was whether, at the date of the testatrix's death in 1964, the Bleakholt Animal Sanctuary was a charity. The Sanctuary was not registered as a charity until 1968. On evidence that, at all material times before and after registration, its objects were identical, the court felt bound to hold that the Sanctuary was a charity at the date of death. Any person who is or may be affected by the registration of an institution as a charity may, on the ground that it is not a charity, object to its being entered in the Register, or apply to the Commission for its removal, from which decision there may be an appeal to the Tribunal.[271] Even after an appeal, any question affecting the registration or removal from the Register of an institution may be reconsidered by the Commission if it considers that there has been a change of circumstances, or that the decision is inconsistent with a later judicial decision.[272]

Conversely, it should be observed that refusal of registration by the Commission on the ground that the purposes of an organization are not charitable does not conclusively establish that the organization is not charitable. Thus, the refusal by the Commission to register the Over Seventies Housing Association did not prevent that body from arguing that it was a charity and therefore entitled to rating relief, although the argument, in fact, failed.[273]

(D) CHANGE OF NAME

The Commission has power to direct a registered charity, within twelve months of registration, to change its name on the grounds that it is the same as, or too like, that of another charity,[274] that it may mislead the public as to the true nature of the purposes of the charity or of the activities it carries on, that it includes any specified word or expression the

---

[269] Charities Act 1993, s 4(1).   [270] [1971] 2 All ER 328.
[271] See s 4(2), (4), as amended by the 2006 Act; (1993) 1 Dec Ch Com 1.
[272] Ibid s 4(5), as likewise amended. See (1985) Sol Jo 886 (J M Fryer).
[273] *Over Seventies Housing Association v Westminster City Council* (1974) 230 EG 1593.
[274] For specified words and expressions, see SI 1992/1901.

inclusion of which is likely to mislead the public as to the status of the charity,[275] that it is likely to give the impression that the charity is connected in some way with the government, a local authority, or with any other body of persons or any individual, when that is not the case, or that the name is, in the opinion of the Commission, offensive.[276]

(E) STATUS TO APPEAR ON OFFICIAL PUBLICATION, ETC

Where the gross income of a registered charity in its last financial year exceeded £10,000, the fact that it is a registered charity must be stated on all official publications, including appeal documents, cheques, orders for goods, bills, receipts, and invoices.[277] There seems to be no reason why these requirements should not apply to charitable companies, which, however, are covered by more stringent requirements.[278]

(F) REVIEW OF THE REGISTER[279]

The Charity Commission is carrying out a rolling review of the Register. It has the same power as the court when determining whether an organization has charitable status, and the same powers to take into account changing social and economic circumstances— whether to recognize a purpose as charitable for the first time, or to recognize that a purpose has ceased to be charitable. The Commission interprets and applies the law in accordance with the principles laid down by the courts, to which an appeal may be made against the Commission's decision.[280]

Thus, in *Re Stephens*,[281] it had been held that teaching shooting was a charitable purpose as promoting the security of the nation and the defence of the realm. On this basis, a number of civilian rifle and pistol clubs were registered as charities. Following the Falklands and Gulf conflicts, it was seen that the skills required of modern uniformed personnel were quite different from those required when *Re Stephens* was decided in 1892 in the immediate aftermath of the First Boer War, and clubs (the principal concern of which was the benefit of members through recreational and sporting shooting) were, in no sense, a reserve for the armed forces. Most were accordingly removed from the Register.

---

[275] See (1995) 4 Dec Ch Com 23; (1996–97) 4 CLPR 1 (Debra Morris).

[276] Charities Act 1993, s 6, as amended by the 2006 Act. Consequential provisions in the case in which the charity is a company are contained in s 7. Where a charity operates under more than one name, all will be registered: see (1995) 4 Dec Ch Com 22.

[277] Ibid, s 5(1)–(3); as amended by SI 1995/2696. The statement must be in English, except that, by amendments made to subss (4), (5) and 2A inserted, by the Welsh Language Act 1993, in the case of a document that is wholly in Welsh, the statement may be in Welsh if it consists of, or includes, the words *elusen cofrestreding*. Breach of these provisions is an offence: s 5(4), (5).

[278] See ibid, s 68, as amended, discussed in section 3(b)(iv), p 298, *supra*. Unlike s 68, s 5 does not cover business letters (other than those that solicit money or other property), or conveyances.

[279] See RR 1 and RR 6. See also (2001) 32 T & ELJ 6 (S Chiappini); ibid, 10 (Catriona Syed).

[280] See RR 1a, *Recognising New Charitable Purposes*; See (2001) 21 LS 36 (P W Edge and Joan M Loughrey).

[281] (1892) 8 TLR 792.

6 CHARITY ACCOUNTS, AUDIT, ANNUAL REPORTS, AND ANNUAL RETURNS

(A) A CHARITY THAT IS NOT A COMPANY[282]

(i) General duties in relation to accounts

Charity trustees must ensure that accounting records are kept in respect of the charity that are sufficient to show and explain all of the charity's transactions and to disclose at any time, with reasonable accuracy, the financial position of the charity at that time.[283] They must prepare, in respect of each financial year, a statement of account complying with pre-scribed requirements,[284] although there are less stringent requirements where the charity's gross income in any financial year does not exceed £100,000.[285] Accounting records and statement of accounts must be preserved for at least six years from the end of the financial year of the charity.[286]

(ii) Annual audit or examination of accounts[287]

A distinction is made according to the size of the charity. A professional audit[288] is required if:

    (a) the charity's gross income in its financial year exceeds £500,000; or

    (b) the charity's gross income in that year exceeds the accounts threshold and, at the end of the year, the aggregate value of its assets (before the deduction of liabilities) exceeds £2.8m.[289]

Where the above provisions do not apply, but, in the financial year of a charity, its gross income exceeds £10,000, the accounts of the charity for that year must, at the election of the charity, either be professionally audited as above, or examined by an independ-ent person who is reasonably believed by the trustees to have the requisite ability and

---

[282] See CC 8 and 61, and the Statement of Recommended Practice (SORP 2005) issued by the Charity Commission.

[283] Charities Act 1993, s 41(1), (2).

[284] Ibid, s 42(1), as amended by SI 2006/2951, and (2). Restrictions are imposed on what the regulations can require to be disclosed during the lifetime of the creator of a charitable trust or his spouse or civil partner: s 42(2A), inserted by the 2006 Act.

[285] Ibid, s 42(3), as amended by SI 1995/2696. As to the meaning of 'income', see (1993–94) 2 CLPR 111 (C McCall). The prescribed requirements are set out in SI 2005/572, which also defines 'financial year'. As to group accounts, see the Charities Act 1993, ss 42(8), 49A, Sch 5A, inserted by the 2006 Act and amended by SI 2008/527.

[286] Ibid, s 41(3), 42(4). By s 41(4), as amended by the 2006 Act, the obligation continues on the last charity trustees of a charity that has ceased to exist unless the Commission consents in writing to the records being destroyed or otherwise disposed of.

[287] The duties of an auditor or independent examiner are set out in SI 1995/2724, as amended.

[288] The qualifications required to be an auditor for this purpose are set out in the Charities Act 1993, s 43(2), as amended by the 2006 Act and SIs 2008/527 and 2008/948.

[289] Section 43(1) of the Charities Act 1993, as substituted by s 28(1), (2), of the 2006 Act, and s 43(2), as amended. The accounts threshold is £100,000 or such other sum that may be specified under s 42(3). As to NHS charities, see ss 43A and 43B, inserted by SI 2005/1074.

practical experience to carry out a competent examination of the accounts.[290] However, where the gross income of a charity exceeds £250,000, a person qualifies as an independent examiner only if he is a member of one of the bodies specified in subs (3B), or a Fellow of the Association of Charity Independent Examiners.[291]

If the requirement of an audit (or examination) has not been complied with within ten months from the end of the relevant financial year,[292] the Commission may require the accounts to be professionally audited[293] at the expense of the charity trustees personally.[294]

None of the above provisions apply to a charity that is a company: such a charity is governed, in this respect, by the requirements of company law.[295]

The Minister for the Cabinet Office has power to amend the sums referred to in s 43 and the requirements for independent examination.[296]

(iii) Annual reports

The Charities Act 1993, s 45,[297] requires charity trustees to prepare, in respect of each financial year of the charity, an annual report on the activities of the charity and such other information as may be prescribed by regulations.[298]

Where, in any financial year of a charity, its gross income exceeds £10,000,[299] the charity trustees must, within ten months[300] from the end of the charity's financial year, transmit to the Commission the annual report, with a statement of accounts and the report of the auditor or independent examiner, as the case may be, attached. Smaller charities may be required to transmit a report on the request of the Commission.[301]

The annual reports and documents attached thereto are kept by the Commission for such period as it thinks fit, during which time, they are open to public inspection at all reasonable times.[302]

(iv) 'Whistle-blowing'

Section 44A, inserted by s 29 of the 2005 Act, provides that if, in the course of acting under s 43[303] as an auditor or independent examiner of a charity, a person becomes aware of a matter relating to the activities or affairs of the charity that he has reasonable cause

---

[290] Ibid, s 43(3), as amended by s 28 of the 2006 Act.

[291] Ibid, s 43(3A) of the Charities Act 1993, inserted by s 28(5) of the 2006 Act and amended by SI 2008/527.

[292] Or, although s 43(2) does not apply, it would be nevertheless desirable for the accounts to be professionally audited.

[293] Ibid, s 43(4).   [294] Ibid, s 43(6).

[295] Ibid, s 43(9) as substituted by SIs 2008/527 and 2008/948. Nor to NHS charities: ibid, s 43(10), inserted by SI 2005/1074.

[296] Ibid, s 43(8), as substituted by the 2006 Act and amended by SI 2008/527.

[297] As amended by SIs 2005/1074, 2006/2951, 2007/309, 2008/527, and 2008/948, the Deregulation and Contracting Out Act 1994, and the Charities Act 2006, Sch 8, para 138. Failure to comply with any of the requirements of s 45 is an offence: ibid, s 49, as substituted by the 2006 Act, Sch 8, para142.

[298] See the Charities (Accounts and Reports) Regulations 2008, SI 2008/629.

[299] But in the case of a CIO, whatever its gross income may be: s 45(3B), as inserted.

[300] Unless the Commissioners allow a longer period.

[301] Section 45(3A), inserted by the Deregulation and Contracting Out Act 1994, as amended by the 2006 Act.

[302] Ibid, ss 45(6) and 47(1), both as amended by the 2006 Act.   [303] See p 325, *supra*.

to believe is likely to be of material significance for the purposes of the exercise by the Commission of its functions under ss 8 or 18,[304] he must immediately make a written report on the matter to the Commission. Further, he has a discretionary power to report any other matter that he has reasonable cause to believe is likely to be relevant for the purpose of the exercise by the Commission of any of its functions. The section provides that no duty, such as a duty of confidentiality towards the trustees of the charity, to which he is subject is to be regarded as contravened merely because of any information or opinion contained in the report.[305]

(B) SPECIAL PROVISIONS RELATING TO PARTICULAR KINDS OF CHARITY

(i) Exempt charities

Charity trustees of these charities are required to keep proper books of account and to prepare consecutive statements of account, consisting, on each occasion, of an income and expenditure account relating to a period of not more than fifteen months, and a balance sheet relating to the end of that period. The documents must be preserved for at least six years, unless the charity ceases to exist and the Commission consents in writing to their being destroyed or otherwise disposed of.[306]

The duties discussed in section (A) above do not, in general, apply to exempt charities, which are subject to adequate alternative supervision.[307] But the 'whistle-blower' provisions apply to the auditor of an exempt charity that is not a company, with modifications[308]

(ii) Charities falling within s 3A(2)(b), (c), or (d) that are not registered

These are subject to the duty to keep accounting records and to prepare annual statements of account. However, to some extent, the provisions relating to audits, annual reports and whistle-blowing do not apply.

In the case of small charities falling within s 3A(2)(d), the requirements in respect of audits, annual reports, and whistle-blowing do not, in general, apply, but if such a charity is an exempt charity, the whistle-blowing provision applies. If such a charity is a National Health Service (NHS) charity, the provisions both in regard to annual reports and whistle-blowing apply.[309]

In the case of charities falling within s 3A(2)(b) or (c), but not s 3A(2)(d), the requirement to submit an annual report does not apply, but the charity trustees may be required by the Commission to provide an annual report.[310]

(iii) A charity that is a company

Here, the company law provisions relating to accounts apply, and not the provisions in relation to accounts and audit discussed in (A) above.[311] Further, the Commission may

---

[304] See pp 304–306, *supra*.   [305] Charities Act 1993 s 44A(5), as inserted.
[306] Charities Act 1993, s 46(1), (2), as amended by the 2006 Act.   [307] Ibid, s 46(1), as amended.
[308] Ibid, s 46(2A), (2B), as inserted.   [309] Ibid, s 46(3), (3A), (3B), as inserted.
[310] Ibid, s 46(4)–(7), as amended.
[311] Ibid, ss 41(5), 42(7), and 43(9). See the Companies Act 2006, Pt 6. As to group accounts, see Charities Act 1993, Sch 5A, inserted by the 2006 Act and amended by SI 2008/527.

require that the condition and relevant accounts of the charity be investigated by a qualified auditor, who is entitled to access to all relevant documents, and to require statements from the charity trustees, and its officers and employees. The auditor reports to the
Commission, with a copy to the charity trustees.[312] The 2006 Act modifies the circumstances in which a charitable company may be subject to a reporting accountant's report
rather than an audit.[313]

The duty to transmit annual reports applies to a charity that is a company.[314]

The Act also imposes the same whistle-blowing duty on the auditor or reporting
accountant of a charitable company as that imposed on auditors and independent examiners under s 44A.[315]

(C) PUBLIC RIGHT TO A COPY OF CHARITY'S ACCOUNTS

The charity trustees of every charity must, on written request, provide a copy of the charity's most recent accounts or its most recent annual report to any person requesting them,
subject to payment of a reasonable fee.[316]

(D) ANNUAL RETURNS

Section 48 of the Charities Act 1993[317] provides that, unless the Commission dispenses
with the requirement, every registered charity must, within ten months from the end of
the charity's financial year, submit an annual return in the form, and containing the information, prescribed by regulations made by the Commission.[318] This requirement does not
apply in relation to any financial year of a charity in which the gross income does not
exceed £10,000.[319]

7 SCHEMES

(A) GENERAL

As we have seen,[320] a charitable trust does not fail for uncertainty, and an order for the
direction of a scheme is the device available to the court under its inherent jurisdiction to

---

[312] Charities Act 1993, s 69, as amended by the 2006 Act and SI 2008/527. The expenses of the audit are
paid by the Commission.

[313] Charities Act 2006, s 32(1).

[314] Modified in that, instead of the report of the auditor or independent examiner, there must be attached
a copy of the charity's annual accounts prepared under Pt 13 of the Companies Act 2006, and the auditor's
report thereon: Charities Act 1993, s 45(5), as amended by the 2006 Act.

[315] Charities Act 1993, s 68A, inserted by s 33 of the 2006 Act and amended by SI 2008/527.

[316] The detailed provisions are contained in the Charities Act 1993, s47(2)–(5), as amended by the
Deregulation and Contracting Out Act 1994, SIs 1994/1935, 2008/527, and 2008/948, and the 2006 Act, Sch 8,
para 140. Failure to comply with s 47(2) is an offence: s 49, as substituted by the 2006 Act, Sch 8, para 142.

[317] As amended by the Deregulation and Contracting Out Act 1994, SI 2006/2951, and the 2006 Act,
Sch 7, Pt 2, and Sch 8, para 141. Failure to comply with s 48(2) is an offence: s 49, as substituted.

[318] The Commission may allow a longer period.

[319] Deregulation and Contracting Out Act 1994, s 30.

[320] Chapter 13, subsection 1(A), p 245, *supra*.

remedy uncertainty either in the substance of the trust[321] or the mode of administration, to get over some administrative difficulty or to amend the rules of the charity.[322] A scheme is not necessarily, or even generally, a scheme for the application of property cy-près,[323] under which, as will be seen later,[324] the purpose of a trust may be varied. It may be directed where the exact ambit of the charitable purpose is not clear,[325] where the trustees are dead,[326] or disclaim, or refuse to act,[327] or have misapplied the trust property,[328] where the income of the charity has substantially increased,[329] and in other cases in which it is an appropriate remedy.[330] But, sometimes, even a charitable trust cannot be saved by a scheme. Thus, 'if it is of the essence of a trust that the trustees selected by the settlor and no-one else shall act as the trustees of it and those trustees cannot or will not undertake the office, the trust must fail'.[331]

The terms of particular schemes vary considerably. Some are very simple and do no more, for example, than change the name of a charity or set up a new body of trustees to administer it, while others are long and complicated, and contain detailed provisions for the future regulation of the charity. The court has, of course, a discretion whether to order a scheme or not, even where the effect would be to defeat a gift over; however, it refused to do so in Re Hanbey's Will Trusts,[332] in which the proposed scheme, in defeating the gift over, would defeat the intention of the testator rather than give effect to it.

As we have seen, the Commission has the same power as the court for establishing a scheme, although generally only on the application of the charity.[333] Where a court directs a scheme for the administration of a charity to be established, the court may refer the matter to the Commission for it to prepare or settle a scheme and the court order may direct such scheme to come into effect without further reference to the court.[334] Further, where, in the case of a charity other than an exempt charity, the Commission is satisfied that the charity trustees ought to apply for a scheme, but have unreasonably refused or neglected to do so, and the Commission has given the charity trustees an opportunity to make representations to it, the Commission may proceed as if an application for a scheme had been

---

[321] There must be a trust: Re Bennett [1960] Ch 18, [1959] 3 All ER 295, and p 314, supra.

[322] Re Gott [1944] Ch 193, [1944] 1 All ER 293. The details of the scheme will be settled by the Master in Chambers.

[323] Re Robinson [1931] 2 Ch 122.

[324] See p 332 et seq, infra.   [325] Re White [1893] 2 Ch 41, CA; Re Gott, supra.

[326] Moggridge v Thackwell (1803) 7 Ves 36, affd (1807) 13 Ves 416, HL; Re Willis [1921] 1 Ch 44, CA. Cf Marsh v A-G (1860) 2 John & H 61.

[327] Reeve v A-G (1843) 3 Hare 191; Re Lawton [1936] 3 All ER 378; Re Lysaught [1966] Ch 191, [1965] 2 All ER 888.

[328] A-G v Coopers' Co (1812) 19 Ves 187.   [329] Re Campden Charities (1881) 18 Ch D 310, CA.

[330] For example, Re Robinson [1923] 2 Ch 332 (removing 'abiding' condition that a black gown should be worn in the pulpit); Re Dominion Students' Hall Trust [1947] Ch 183 (removing colour bar from trust for Dominion students); Re Lysaght, supra (removing provision for religious discrimination); Re J W Laing Trust [1984] 1 All ER 50 (obligation to distribute whole of capital and income within ten years of settlor's death removed where trust fund set up in 1922 with £15,000 and now worth £24m). See also [1987] NLJ Christmas Appeals Supp viii (P Luxton), who argues that the courts have sometimes, and in particular in relation to public schools, in effect varied the purpose of a trust by treating it as a matter of an administrative nature.

[331] Per Buckley J in Re Lysaght [1966] Ch 191, 207, [1965] 2 All ER 888, 896.

[332] [1956] Ch 264, [1955] 3 All ER 874.

[333] See p 303, supra. A total of 518 schemes were made in the year to March 2008. A scheme may, within limits, confer a power on trustees enabling amendments to the governing document of a charity to be made by the trustees themselves: (1995) 3 Dec Ch Com 29.

[334] Charities Act 1993, s16(2), as amended by the 2006 Act.

made by the charity.[335] Its power under this last provision does not, however, enable the Commission to alter the purposes of a charity, unless forty years have elapsed from the date of its foundation.

(B) STATUTORY EXTENSIONS OF THE JURISDICTION

(i) Charities founded by royal charter

Here, the inherent jurisdiction of the court was limited, although the limits were not altogether clear.[336] Now, it is provided[337] that a scheme relating to such a charity or the administration of its property may be made by the court,[338] notwithstanding that it cannot take effect without the alteration of the charter. In such case, the scheme must be so framed as not to come into effect unless or until Her Majesty thinks fit to make an appropriate amendment to the charter.[339]

(ii) Certain charities regulated by statute

Here, the inherent jurisdiction of the court is also limited in a somewhat similar way to that in relation to charities founded by royal charter.[340] The court[341] has now been given statutory jurisdiction with respect to certain charities relating to allotments, seamen's and regimental funds, and some educational and local charities.[342]

(iii) Other charities regulated by statute

In these cases, the Commission, but not the court, is now empowered,[343] if it considers that a scheme should be established, to settle a scheme to which effect may be given by order of the Minister made by statutory instrument.[344] The Commission can only proceed under these provisions on the like application as would be required if it was proceeding (without an order of the court) under s 16.[345]

(iv) Temporary cy-près scheme

Under s 17(8), as amended, where the Commission is satisfied—

(a) that the whole of the income of a charity cannot, in existing circumstances, be effectively applied for the purpose of the charity; and

---

[335] Section 16(6), as likewise amended.

[336] *Re Whitworth Art Gallery Trusts* [1958] Ch 461, [1958] 1 All ER 176; cf *Re Royal Society's Charitable Trusts* [1956] Ch 87, [1955] 3 All ER 14.   [337] Section 15(1).

[338] Or, in a proper case, by the Commission acting under s 16(1), as amended by the 2006 Act.

[339] By Order in Council: s 15(2). See, eg, SI 1999/656 and 1999/667.

[340] *London Parochial Charities' Trustees v A-G* [1955] 1 All ER 1; *Re Shipwrecked Fishermen and Mariners' Royal Benevolent Society Charity* [1959] Ch 220, [1958] 3 All ER 465.

[341] And, in a proper case, the Commission: s 16(1), as amended by the 2006 Act.

[342] Section 15(3) and Sch 4, as amended by the Education Act 1996, Sch 37, para 121, and the Statute Law (Repeals) Act 1993.

[343] By s 17, as amended by the 2006 Act and SI 2006/2951. The procedure set out in this section also applies where the Commission wishes to insert some provision in a scheme that otherwise would be beyond its powers, or where, in any case, it is proper for the scheme to be subject to parliamentary review. The provisions for publicity in s 20, as substituted by the 2006 Act, apply to proceedings under s 17, as amended: see p 000, *supra*.

[344] See, eg, SIs 1995/1047 and 1997/2240.   [345] See pp 303 and 329, *supra*.

(b) that, if those circumstances continue, a scheme might be made for applying the surplus cy-près; and

(c) that it is, for any reason, not yet desirable to make such a scheme—

then it may authorize the charity trustees to apply a limited[346] amount of income for any purposes for which it might be made applicable by a cy-près scheme.

(v) Reverter of Sites Act 1987, as amended

This Act confers a special scheme-making power on the Commission in relation to sites conveyed to trustees for specific purposes under Acts such as the School Sites Act 1841, where the site has ceased to be used for the particular purpose and the person to whom the site should revert cannot be ascertained.[347]

(C) COMMON INVESTMENT SCHEMES AND COMMON DEPOSIT SCHEMES

It is a frequent occurrence for a single body of trustees, particularly of a large charity, to hold and administer a number of separate funds associated with the main charity, each fund being held on separate (although possibly similar or even identical) trusts, and legally constituting a separate charity. Before the Charities Act 1960, the funds of such separate trusts had, in general, to be kept separate, even though held by the same trustees and held on similar trusts. Exceptionally, particular statutes[348] authorized particular bodies to amalgamate various trust funds held by them and to administer the amalgam as a single fund, and the court and the Commission sometimes made schemes—known as 'pooling schemes'—to the like effect, but this was only possible where the separate trusts were administered by a single body of trustees.[349] Common investment schemes were introduced by the 1960 Act and the relevant provisions are now contained in s 24 of the 1993 Act, as amended by the 2006 Act, which authorizes the court or the Commission, where two or more bodies of trustees wish to unite in pooling the endowments of the charities that they administer, to make and bring into effect schemes for the establishment of common investment funds under trusts that provide:

(a) for property transferred to the fund by or on behalf of a charity participating in the scheme to be invested under the control of trustees appointed to manage the fund; and

(b) for the participating charities to be entitled...to the capital and income of the fund in shares determined by reference to the amount or value of the property transferred to it by or on behalf of each of them and to the value of the fund at the time of the transfer.[350]

---

[346] Up to £300 income accrued before the date of the order and up to £100 out of income accruing in each of the next three years: s 17(9).

[347] See Report for 1987, Appendix C; Report for 1988, paras 78–82. See also *Re Picklenash School, Newport* (1993, unreported), but noted [1994] NLJ Charities App Supp 23 (H Picarda).

[348] For example, Liverpool University Act 1931; Birmingham University Act 1948. Cf Administration of Justice Acts 1965 and 1982, and SI 1965/1467, as amended by SI 1972/528.

[349] *Re Royal Society's Charitable Trusts* [1956] Ch 87, [1955] 3 All ER 14.

[350] See (1996–97) 4 CLPR 21 (R Marlow).

Such a scheme may involve the appointment of an entirely distinct body of trustees to manage the pooled endowments. A common investment scheme may be made on the application of any two or more charities[351]—it will be remembered that, for the purposes of the Act, each separate trust fund is prima facie a separate charity,[352] even where the trustees are the same persons[353]—and the scheme may make provision for, and for all matters connected with, the establishment, investment, management, and winding up of the common investment fund.[354] It may provide for a charity to deposit sums on such terms as to repayment and interest as may be set out in the scheme.[355] The common investment fund is itself deemed, for all purposes, to be a charity. The Commission has indicated that it will not be willing to make such schemes involving two or more bodies of trustees, unless there is some nexus, either geographical or functional, between the participating charities.[356]

Common deposit schemes were introduced by the 1992 Act and the provisions are now contained in s 25 of the 1993 Act, as amended by the 2006 Act. It provides:

(a) for sums to be deposited by or on behalf of a charity participating in the scheme and invested under the control of trustees appointed to manage the fund, and

(b) for any such charity to be entitled...to repayment of any sums so deposited and to interest thereon at a rate determined under the scheme.[357]

With minor modifications,[358] the provisions of s 24 are incorporated in s 25.

Section 23 of the Charities Act 2006, for the first time, permits the participation of Scottish and Northern Ireland charities in common investment schemes and common deposit schemes.

The provisions of the Trustee Act 2000 relating to investments, the acquisition of land, and agents, nominees, and custodians, do not apply to trustees managing a fund under a common investment scheme or a common deposit scheme.[359]

8 THE CY-PRÈS DOCTRINE

(A) GENERAL POSITION[360]

In the case of a private trust, if the trust fails, the beneficial interest results to the settlor or testator. This may be the position also in the case of a charitable trust, although

---

[351] All charities have power to participate in common investment schemes, unless expressly excluded by the trust instrument: s 24(7).   [352] See p 290, supra.

[353] Re University of London Charitable Trusts [1964] Ch 282, [1963] 3 All ER 859.

[354] Section 24(4).   [355] Section 24(5).

[356] Reports for 1962 and 1963, paras 48 and 46, respectively.   [357] Section 25(1), as amended.

[358] Different paragraphs are substituted for sub-s 4(b), (c), and sub-s (5) does not apply: s 25(2), (3).

[359] Trustee Act 2000, s 38: there is an exception in s 38(a) in relation to a common investment fund.

[360] For a review of cases in other common law jurisdictions, see (1972) 1 AALR 101 (L A Sheridan), and for comparison with the law in the USA, see [1987] NLJ Annual Charities Review 34 (P Luxton). Text below cited Re Fitzpatrick (1984) 6 DLR (4th) 644. See also (1993–94) 2 CLPR 182 (L A Sheridan); (1995–96) 3 CLPR 9 (Jean Warburton). J Garton, in (2007) 21 TruLI, argues that the traditional justifications for the doctrine are inadequate and incoherent, and contends that the most convincing justification would be simply the desirability of increasing the resources available to the charitable sector.

in practice the trust property is commonly saved for charity by the cy-près doctrine. Where this doctrine applies, even though the particular charitable trust fails, the trust property is applied for other charitable purposes cy-près. Traditionally, this meant purposes as near as possible[361] to the original purposes that cannot be carried out.[362] This has now been modified by s 14B of the 1993 Act, inserted by s 18 of the 2006 Act.

Section 14B(2) lays down how the power of the court or the Commission is to be exercised:

> Where any property given for charitable purposes is applicable cy-près, the court or the Commission may make a scheme providing for the property given[363] to be applied—
>
> (a) for such charitable purposes, and
>
> (b) (if the scheme provides for the property to be transferred to another charity) by or on trust for such other charity
>
> as it considers appropriate, having regard to the matters set out in subsection (3).

By subs (3):

> The matters are—
>
> (a) the spirit of the original gift,
>
> (b) the desirability of securing that the property be applied for charitable purposes which are close to the original purposes, and
>
> (c) the need for the relevant charity[364] to have purposes which are suitable and effective in the light of current social and economic circumstances.

It is thought that equal weight must be given to each of these matters.

By subs (4):

> If a scheme provides for the property to be transferred to another charity, the scheme may impose on the charity trustees of that charity a duty to secure that the property is applied for purposes which are, so far as is reasonably practicable, similar in character to the original purposes.

This is intended to cover cases in which the original purposes are still useful, but it is thought that the property can be more effectively used in conjunction with other property.

There are one, and often two, conditions that have to be satisfied in order for the doctrine to apply, and these, as affected by the relevant provisions of the Charities Act 1993, are considered below. The Act now imposes a statutory duty on the trustees of a charitable trust to take steps, in an appropriate case, for trust property to be applied cy-près.[365]

---

[361] *Re Prison Charities* (1873) LR 16 Eq 129; but the cy-près application may still be made even though there is no possible object closely resembling the one that has failed: *A-G v Ironmongers Co* (1841) Cr & Ph 208; affd (1844) 10 Cl & Fin 908, HL. Chesterman, *Charities, Trusts and Social Welfare*, pp 225–227, argues that s 13 has, by implication, altered the meaning of cy-près to purposes that are suitable and effective having regard, inter alia, to the spirit of the gift.

[362] The doctrine applies equally to an incorporated charity: *Liverpool and District Hospital for Diseases of the Heart v A-G* [1981] Ch 193, [1981] 1 All ER 194.

[363] This includes property for the time being representing the property originally given or property derived from it: s 14B(5).

[364] That is, the charity by or on behalf of which the property is to be applied under the scheme: s 14B(5).

[365] Section 13(5).

Before considering the cy-près doctrine in detail, one particular situation should be mentioned. Where, before the Perpetuities and Accumulations Act 1964, there was a gift to charity for a limited period only, at the end of the period, the undisposed interest resulted to the grantor, notwithstanding that the grantor had, in fact, purported to make some disposition over, if this was void for perpetuity. There was no case for cy-près application.[366] There is still no case for cy-près application, and there will still be a resulting trust, unless the case falls within s 12 of the Perpetuities and Accumulations Act 1964, which provides that, if and when it appears that the event that might cause the interest to determine must occur, if at all, outside the perpetuity period ascertained in accordance with the Act, the resulting trust becomes void and the determinable interest becomes absolute,[367] whether or not it is followed by a gift over.

(B) IMPOSSIBILITY OR IMPRACTICABILITY

Before the Charities Act 1960, the rule was that cy-près application was only possible where it was impossible or impracticable to carry out the declared trust. The rule covered both the case in which the declared trust was initially impossible[368] and the case of supervening impossibility,[369] and also cases in which there was a surplus of funds after the particular charitable purpose had been fulfilled.[370] Although impossibility and impracticability were generously construed,[371] the court had no jurisdiction to apply cy-près so long as any lawful object of the testator's bounty was available, however inexpedient such object might appear to the court as compared with other objects, and Romilly MR pointed out[372] that, in several cases, the court had considered itself bound to carry into effect 'charities of the most useless description'.

The old rule was considerably modified by s 13(1) of the Charities Act 1960, now replaced by s 13(1) of the 1993 Act, which, as amended by s 15 of the 2006 Act, provides that, subject

---

[366] *Re Rendell* (1888) 38 Ch D 213; *Re Blunt's Trusts* [1904] 2 Ch 767; *Re Cooper's Conveyance Trusts* [1956] 3 All ER 28. Cf *Re Bowen* [1893] 2 Ch 491; *Re Peel's Release* [1921] 2 Ch 218, and see (1961) 25 Conv 56 (J D Davies).

[367] See (1964) 80 LQR 486 at 527 (Morris and Wade). The resulting trust or possibility of reverter will still be valid if the determining event in fact happens within the perpetuity period and the same would be true of an express gift over.

[368] For example, *Biscoe v Jackson* (1887) 35 Ch D 460, CA: trust to establish a soup kitchen and cottage hospital in Shoreditch, but no land available for the purpose. An unusual case of initial impracticability was *Re Lysaght* [1966] Ch 191, [1965] 2 All ER 888, in which insistence on the provision for religious discrimination would have resulted in the trustee disclaiming the trusteeship. This would have occasioned complete failure of the trust, as it was the exceptional case in which the trust was conditional on acceptance of the office by the named trustee. See also *Harris v Skevington* [1978] 1 NSWLR 176, in which the legacy was held to be impractical and void because the donee by its constitution had no power to effectuate the particular charitable intention.

[369] For example, *A-G v Ironmongers Co* (1841) Cr & Ph 208; affd, sub nom *Ironmongers Co v A-G* (1844) 10 Cl & Fin 908, HL: trust for redemption of Barbary slaves.

[370] *Re Monk* [1927] 2 Ch 197, CA; *Re North Devon and West Somerset Relief Fund Trusts* [1953] 2 All ER 1032; *Re Raine* [1956] Ch 417, [1956] 1 All ER 355.

[371] For example, *Re Dominion Students' Hall Trust* [1947] Ch 183 (removing colour bar from trust for Dominion students); *Re Canada Trust Co and Ontario Human Rights Commission* (1990) 69 DLR (4th) 321 (Ont CA); *Toronto Aged Men's and Women's Homes v The Loyal True Blue and Orange Home* (2004) 68 OR (3d) 777: an unusual application of the doctrine.

[372] In *Philpott v St George's Hospital* (1859) 27 Beav 107, 111; *Re Weir Hospital* [1910] 2 Ch 124, CA.

to any other necessary conditions being fulfilled, cy-près application may be directed in any of five sets of circumstances:

(a) where the original purposes,[373] in whole or in part—
   (i) have been as far as may be fulfilled; or
   (ii) cannot be carried out, or not according to the directions given[374] and to the spirit of the gift; or

(b) where the original purposes provide a use for part only of the property available by virtue or the gift; or

(c) where the property available by virtue of the gift and other property applicable for similar purposes can be more effectively used in conjunction, and to that end can suitably, regard being had to the appropriate circumstances, be made applicable to common purposes; or

(d) where the original purposes were laid down by reference to an area which then was but has since ceased to be a unit for some other purpose, or by reference to a class of persons or to an area which has for any reason since ceased to be suitable, regard being had to the appropriate circumstances, or to be practical in administering the gift;[375] or

(e) where the original purposes, in whole or in part, have, since they were laid down—
   (i) been adequately provided for by other means;[376] or
   (ii) ceased, as being useless or harmful to the community or for other reasons, to be in law charitable; or
   (iii) ceased in any other way to provide a suitable and effective method of using the property[377] available by virtue of the gift, regard being had to the appropriate circumstances.[378]

The words 'the appropriate considerations' in s (1)(c), (d), and (e)(iii) were substituted for the previous words 'the spirit of the gift' by the 2006 Act,[379] and are defined in the inserted sub-s (1A) as meaning, on the one hand, the spirit of the gift concerned, and, on the other, the social and economic circumstances prevailing at the time of the proposed alteration of the original purposes.[380] This adds to the matters that the Commission must take into account when making a scheme to alter the purposes to which charity property is to be applied.

The court is also given a limited power to enlarge the area of a charity's operations, without any need to show that any of the above conditions are fulfilled.[381] There has been little authority on this section, but it was held, in *Re Lepton's Charity*,[382] that, in relation to a trust for payment of a fixed annual sum out of the income of a fund to charity A and payment

---

[373] Where the application of the trust property has been altered or regulated by a scheme or otherwise, 'original purposes' means the purposes for which the property is for the time being applicable: s 13(3).

[374] See *Re J W Laing Trust* [1984] Ch 143, [1984] 1 All ER 50, discussed [1985] Conv 313 (P Luxton).

[375] This paragraph applied *Peggs v Lamb* [1994] Ch 172, [1994] 2 All ER 15.

[376] For example, where the object of the charity has become the statutory responsibility of the central or local government authorities.

[377] A requirement that capital and income should be wholly distributed within ten years of the settlor's death is not a 'purpose' within s 13, nor a method of 'using the property'. Cy-près application under s 13 was therefore not appropriate: *Re J W Laing Trust, supra*—but see p 329, *supra*.

[378] *Varsani v Jesani* [1998] 3 All ER 273, CA (case held to fall within this head where the original purpose was to promote the faith of Swaminarayan and the adherents were now divided into two groups, each believing that they alone were continuing to profess the true faith; cy-près scheme directed).

[379] Section 15(1), (2).   [380] Section 15(1), (3).   [381] Section 13(4) and Sch 3.

[382] [1972] Ch 276, [1971] 1 All ER 799.

of the residue of that income to charity B, the 'original purposes' referred to in the section should be construed as referring to the trust as a whole. It has been held that mere sale of charitable property and reinvestment of the proceeds in the acquisition of other property to be held on precisely the same charitable trusts, or for precisely the same charitable purposes, does not require a scheme, but the court may act under its general jurisdiction.[383] In Victoria, Australia, there is a statutory provision in similar terms to s 13. A Victorian court has held[384] that the words 'spirit of the gift' in the section corresponding to s 13(1)(a)(ii) and (e)(iii) effect a shift in emphasis in the application of the cy-près doctrine—that is, away from the previous position of requiring the impossibility or impracticability of the testator's original objective being achieved, to those circumstances that frustrate the purposes as revealed by the terms of the will, or by evidence, being attained. On the facts, the fundamental purpose and objective of the testator to benefit all Victorian charities for ever was being frustrated by a term in the will restricting eligibility to charities in existence at the testator's death, and the restriction was accordingly removed.

As we shall see, it might have been important under the old law to know whether the case was one of initial or supervening impossibility. Suppose a testator gave a fund to trustees on trust for an individual for life and then to found a defined institution of a charitable nature, and that, at the date of the testator's death, the fund would have been adequate to carry out the charitable purpose, but was inadequate when the life tenant died, say, thirty years later: would this be a case of initial impossibility? The question of 'initial impossibility' or 'impracticability' must be determined as at the time when the gift was made, not when it falls into possession so far as charity is concerned—that is, in the case of a gift by will, on the death of the testator. The proper inquiry is therefore, in the case of a gift by will, whether, at the date of the death of the testator, it was practicable to carry the intentions of the testator into effect or whether, at that date, there was any reasonable prospect that it would be practicable to do so at some future time. If there is a negative answer to both parts of this inquiry, it is a case of initial impossibility or impracticability.[385]

If there is a vested gift to charity that is not only to take effect at some future time, but is also liable to be defeated on the happening of some event such as the birth of issue to the person holding a life interest, an inquiry as to its practicability should be approached on the footing that the gift will not be defeated, but will take effect at some future time in possession.[386]

(C) GENERAL CHARITABLE INTENTION

We must now turn to the distinction that has been drawn between 'initial' and 'supervening' impossibility, and consider whether a general charitable intention is required for the other cy-près occasions introduced by s 13(1), as amended by the 2006 Act.

---

[383] *Oldham Borough Council v A-G* [1993] Ch 210, [1993] 2 All ER 432, CA, noted (1992–93) 1 CLPR 157 (Debra Morris).

[384] *Forrest v A-G* [1986] VR 187.

[385] *Re Moon's Will Trusts* [1948] 1 All ER 300; *Re Wright* [1954] Ch 347, [1954] 2 All ER 98, CA; *Re Woodhams* [1981] 1 All ER 202. The principle has been applied where the donee had no power under its constitution to effectuate the particular charitable intention, but might be given such power by an amendment to its constitution: *Harris v Skevington* [1978] 1 NSWLR 176. Cf *Harris v Sharp* (1989) [2003] WTLR 1541, CA.

[386] *Re Tacon* [1958] Ch 447, 454, [1958] 1 All ER 163, 166, CA—but different considerations may be applicable to the case of a strictly contingent gift, *per* Evershed MR.

(i) Initial impossibility or impracticability

Here, the general rule was, and is, that cy-près application is only permitted if a paramount intention of charity on the part of the donor is established. The classic statement of the law is contained in the judgment of Parker J in *Re Wilson*,[387] in which he said the authorities were to be divided into two classes:

> First of all, we have a class of cases where, in form, the gift is given for a particular charitable purpose, but it is possible, taking the will as a whole, to say that, notwithstanding the form of the gift, the paramount intention, according to the true construction of the will, is to give the property in the first instance for a general charitable purpose rather than a particular charitable purpose, and to graft on to the general gift a direction as to the desires or intentions of the testator as to the manner in which the general gift is to be carried into effect.

If this is the proper construction and the particular purpose is initially impossible, the gift will be applied cy-près.[388] He continued:

> Then there is the second class of cases, where, on the true construction of the will, no such paramount general intention can be inferred, and where the gift, being in form a particular gift—a gift for a particular purpose—and it being impossible to carry out that particular purpose, the whole gift is held to fail.[389]

Another way of putting it is to say that the distinction is between, on the one hand, the case in which the scheme prescribed by a testator can be regarded as the mode by which a general charitable purpose is to be carried into effect and in which the mode is not of the substance of the gift, and, on the other hand, the case in which no part of the scheme prescribed by the testator can be disregarded as inessential without frustrating the testator's evident intention. One way of approaching the question of whether a prescribed scheme or project that has proved impracticable is the only way of furthering a desirable purpose that the testator or settlor contemplated or intended is to ask whether a modification of that scheme or project, which would enable it to be carried into effect at the relevant time, is one that would frustrate the intention of the testator or settlor, as disclosed by the will or trust instrument, interpreted in the light of any admissible evidence of surrounding circumstances.[390] It is a question of construction and the court will not necessarily infer a general charitable intention merely because the gift is of residue, and failure to draw the inference will result in intestacy.[391]

---

[387] [1913] 1 Ch 314, 320, 321; *Re Pettit* [1988] 2 NZLR 513. See [1957] CLJ 87 (J C Hall), who observes that the meaning of the phrase 'general charitable intention' is obscure and its application extremely difficult.

[388] *Biscoe v Jackson* (1887) 35 Ch D 460, CA; *Re Hillier* [1954] 2 All ER 59, CA; *Re Lysaght* [1966] Ch 191, [1965] 2 All ER 888.

[389] *Re Good's Will Trusts* [1950] 2 All ER 653; *Re Ulverston and District New Hospital Building Fund* [1956] Ch 622, [1956] 3 All ER 164, CA.

[390] *Re Woodhams* [1981] 1 All ER 202; *Re Currie* [1985] NI 299; *National Trust Co v Canadian Diabetes Association* (1993) 109 DLR (4th) 232. See (1984) 128 Sol Jo 760 (Jean Warburton).

[391] See *Re Crowe*, unreported, but noted in Report for 1979, paras 40–45. It does not appear whether the judge was referred to cases that suggest that, in such a case, the court will be very ready to draw the inference: *Re Raine* [1956] Ch 417, [1956] 1 All ER 355; *Re Griffiths* (23 July 1958, unreported), but cited in *Re Roberts* [1963] 1 All ER 674, 680n. See (1956) 72 LQR 170 (R E Megarry).

(ii) Anonymous donors, eg contributors to a collecting box on a flag day

This is now dealt with by s 14(1) of the 1993 Act, as amended by the 2006 Act, which provides, with retrospective effect, that:

Property given for specific charitable purposes which fail[392] shall be applicable cy-près as if given for charitable purposes generally, where it belongs—

(a) to a donor who, after
  (i) the prescribed[393] advertisements and inquiries have been published and made, and
  (ii) the prescribed period beginning with the publication of those advertisements has expired,
cannot be identified or cannot be found; or

(b) to a donor who has executed a disclaimer in the prescribed form of his right to have the property returned.

Further, sub-s (3) provides that:

For the purposes of this section property shall be conclusively presumed (without any advertisement or inquiry) to belong to donors who cannot be identified, in so far as it consists—

(a) of the proceeds of cash collections made by means of collecting boxes or by other means not adapted for distinguishing one gift from another; or

(b) of the proceeds of any lottery, competition, entertainment, sale or similar money-raising activity, after allowing for property given to provide prizes or articles for sale or otherwise to enable the activity to be undertaken.

Trustees who follow this procedure will not be liable to any person who fails to make a claim within the prescribed[394] period.[395]

And under sub-s (4), as amended by s 16 of the 2006 Act:

The court or the Commission may by order direct that property not falling within sub-s (3) above shall for the purposes of this section be treated (without any advertisement or inquiry) as belonging to donors who cannot be identified, where it appears to the court either—

(a) that it would be unreasonable, having regard to the amounts likely to be returned to the donors, to incur expense with a view to returning the property; or

(b) that it would be unreasonable, having regard to the nature, circumstances and amounts of the gifts, and to the lapse of time since the gifts were made, for the donors to expect the property to be returned.

Provision is made for a donor who cannot be identified or found to recover his contribution to property applied cy-près under these provisions, less any expenses properly incurred by the charity trustees, except in respect of property to which sub-ss (3) or (4) apply. The

---

[392] They are deemed to 'fail' by subs (7) 'where any difficulty in applying property to those purposes makes that property or the part not applicable cy-près available to be returned to the donors'. See also subs (10) as to definition of 'donor' and 'property'.

[393] That is, prescribed by regulations made by the Commission: ibid, s 14(8), as amended by the 2006 Act. The Charities (Cy-près Advertisements, Inquiries and Disclaimers) Regulations 1993 set out the forms and prescribe a period of three months.

[394] See fn 393, *supra*.   [395] Section 14(2).

scheme may direct that a sum be set aside for an appropriate period to meet any such claims. Any claim must be made within six months of the scheme being made.[396]

Section 17 of the 2006 Act has inserted a new s 14A into the 1993 Act. It applies to property given in response to a solicitation made for specific charitable purposes that was accompanied by a statement to the effect that property given in response to it will, in the event of those purposes failing, be applicable cy-près as if given for charitable purposes generally, unless the donor makes a 'relevant declaration' at the time of making the gift. A relevant declaration is a declaration in writing to the effect that, if the specific charitable purposes fail, the donor wants to have the opportunity to request the return of the property. The trustees must inform the donor if the specific purposes fail and must return the property (or a sum equal to its value) to him if he requests it. If the trustees, having taken all of appropriate prescribed steps, fail to find the donor, or if the donor does not, within the period prescribed by regulations made by the Commission, request the return of the property (or a sum equal to its value), or if no relevant declaration was made, the property can be applied cy-près as if the donor had disclaimed his right to have it returned to him. It is irrelevant whether any consideration was given, or was to be given, in return for the property in question.[397]

The first case in which the Commission used its powers under s 14 concerned the Mile End Memorial Hall Fund.[398] It is a useful illustration of how these provisions work in practice. The facts were that a fund had been opened in 1945 to provide a memorial hall at Mile End, but it was clear, in 1964, that the trusts had failed, because the fund then amounted to only £372. Of this, £346 had been raised by whist drives, dances, and concerts, and the balance of £26 represented the subscription of sixty-three subscribers. A public meeting was held to discuss the fund, at which it was agreed to apply it to the extension of a war memorial and a church hall, objects that the Commission considered satisfactory under the cy-près doctrine. By virtue of s 14(3)(b), there was no difficulty with regard to the £346, but sixty-two of the sixty-three subscribers could be traced and so could not come under s 14(1)(a). These persons were invited to execute a written disclaimer[399] so as to bring their subscriptions within s 14(1)(b). Only one of these persons desired the return of his subscription (which was, of course, returned) and the remainder could also be applied cy-près. The final result was a cy-près scheme allowing the trustees to use the money as proposed, subject to a provision for the retention of a small sum for twelve months to cover a possible claim by the one subscriber who could not be identified or found.

(iii) Supervening impossibility

Here, it is not necessary to show a paramount intention of charity. Once money is effectually dedicated to charity in perpetuity, whether in pursuance of a general or a particular

---

[396] Ibid, s 14(5). Under s 14(6), as amemded by the 2006 Act, there will normally be pro rata distribution if the amount set aside proves to be inadequate.

[397] Section 14A(8)(b) provides that where an appeal consists of solicitations within the section and those not accompanied by the statement referred to a donor is presumed to have responded to the solicitations within the section, unless he proves otherwise.

[398] Reported in the Report for 1965, paras 19–21.

[399] Under the 1960 Act, a written disclaimer was called for under s 14(1)(b), not a disclaimer in a prescribed form.

charitable intention, the testator's next of kin or residuary legatees are forever excluded and no question of subsequent failure can affect the matter so far as they are concerned. It is a case for cy-près application.[400]

The distinction between initial and supervening impossibility has commonly not been taken account of in cases in which there is a surplus over what is needed to carry out a designated purpose. It is submitted that these should properly be regarded as cases of supervening impossibility not requiring a general charitable intention for cy-près application, but the weight of authority seems to assume that a general charitable intention is required.[401]

(iv) Cy-près application on occasions introduced by s 13(1)

Although there are dicta suggesting the contrary in *Re J W Laing Trust*,[402] it is generally thought that there is no need to show a general charitable intention on occasions introduced by s 13(1).[403]

(D) GIFT TO A SPECIFIED CHARITABLE INSTITUTION THAT ONCE EXISTED, BUT CEASED TO EXIST BEFORE THE DEATH OF THE TESTATOR[404]

In this case, prima facie, the gift lapses in the same way as if it had been a gift to an individual. Thus, in *Re Rymer*,[405] there was a legacy 'to the rector for the time being of St Thomas's Seminary for the education of priests in the diocese of Westminster for the purposes of such seminary'. Shortly before the testator's death, the Seminary had been closed, the building sold, and the students transferred to another seminary near Birmingham. It was held that the legacy lapsed and fell into residue. However, as Wilberforce J observed in *Re Roberts*,[406] 'the position is that the courts have gone very far in the decided cases to resist the conclusion that a legacy to a charitable institution lapses, and a number of very refined arguments have been found acceptable with a view to avoiding that conclusion'. In practice, much depends on difficult and debatable questions of construction, and the courts may not infrequently be thought to have adopted a somewhat strained construction of the testator's words in order to reach the desired result.

There are the following possibilities.

---

[400] *Re Slevin* [1891] 2 Ch 236, CA; *Re Wright* [1954] Ch 347, [1954] 2 All ER 98, CA; *Re Tacon* [1958] Ch 447, [1958] 1 All ER 163, CA; *Re Fitzpatrick* (1984) 6 DLR (4th) 644. But see [1983] Conv 107 (P Luxton).

[401] *Re Stanford* [1924] 1 Ch 73; *Re Monk* [1927] 2 Ch 197, CA; *Re North Devon and West Somerset Relief Fund Trusts* [1953] 2 All ER 1032. Cf *Re King* [1923] 1 Ch 243; see *Re Raine* [1956] Ch 417.

[402] [1984] Ch 143, 149, [1984] 1 All ER 50, 53, *per* Peter Gibson J. See [1984] Conv 319 (Jean Warburton).

[403] See Picarda, *The Law and Practice of Charities*, 3rd edn, p 297; Luxton, *The Law of Charities*, [15.51].

[404] See, generally, (1969) 32 MLR 283 (J B E Hutton); (1972) 36 Conv 198 (R B M Cotterrell); (1974) 38 Conv 187 (Jill Martin); (1980) 39 CLJ 88 (C E F Rickett).

[405] [1895] 1 Ch 19, CA (a decision that has not received much favour in the courts *per* Wilberforce J in *Re Roberts* [1963] 1 All ER 674, 681); *Re Tacon, supra,* CA; *Re Slatter's Will Trusts* [1964] 2 All ER 469. The gift was held to lapse in *Re Prescott* [1990] 2 IR 342 (donee body had ceased to exist before the date of the will).

[406] *Supra,* at 678; *Re Broadbent's Will* [2001] WTLR 967, noted [2002] PCB 243 (G Duncan).

(i) No lapse on the ground that although the specified institution may apparently have disappeared the charity has not ceased to exist

Re Faraker[407] is the leading case in a series of decisions[408] that have established that, so long as there are funds held in trust for the purposes of a charity, the charity continues in existence and is not destroyed by any alteration in its constitution, name, or objects made in accordance with law, or even amalgamation with another charity. The vital point seems to be that there is a fund in existence forever dedicated to charity. The *Re Faraker*[409] principle is readily applied where the gift is construed as a gift to augment the funds of the named charity and there is no difficulty where, as is common, the charity was founded as a perpetual charity that no one has power to terminate. Where, however, a charitable organization was founded, not as a perpetual charity, but as one liable to termination, and its constitution provided for the disposal of its funds in that event, then, if the organization has determined and its funds have been disposed of, the charity has ceased to exist and there is nothing to prevent the operation of the doctrine of lapse.[410] There is, however, some doubt as to whether the principle was properly applied in *Re Vernon's Will Trusts*,[411] a case of an incorporated charity that had been dissolved, where its work was being carried on by another body in unbroken continuance of the work originally conducted by the dissolved charity. The funds of the incorporated charity had, however, vested in the Ministry of Health under the National Health Service Act 1946 free from any trusts and, accordingly, the funds had ceased to be dedicated to charity.

(ii) Gift construed as a gift for the purposes of the specified institution

It is well established that a gift for a particular purpose will lapse if the particular purpose has ceased to exist before the death of the testator,[412] on a similar principle to that applied in *Re Rymer*.[413] Thus, in *Re Spence*,[414] there was a gift for the benefit of the patients at 'the Old Folks Home at Hillworth Lodge, Keighley'. At the date of the will, there were patients at that home. When the testatrix died, there was no longer any home there, but offices instead, and so there were no longer any patients there, nor was there any possibility of such. The gift was a gift for a charitable purpose that at the date of the will was capable of accomplishment and at the date of death was not. Accordingly, it was held to fail.

In practice, charitable purposes are not easily destroyed and may continue, thus giving no occasion for lapse, notwithstanding the fact that the original organization or machinery for carrying out those purposes no longer exists.[415] This approach was used

---

[407] [1912] 2 Ch 488, CA.

[408] Including *Re Lucas* [1948] Ch 424, [1948] 2 All ER 22, CA (more fully reported in All ER: see *Re Spence* [1979] Ch 483, [1978] 3 All ER 92); *Re Bagshaw* [1954] 1 All ER 227; *Re Roberts, supra*; *Re Slatter's Will Trusts, supra*; *Re Broadbent's Will, supra*, CA.

[409] *Supra*, CA.

[410] *Re Stemson's Will Trusts* [1970] Ch 16, [1969] 2 All ER 517; *Re Finger's Will Trusts* [1972] Ch 286, [1971] 3 All ER 1050.

[411] Decided in 1962, but not reported until [1972] Ch 300n, [1971] 3 All ER 1061n; see *Re Finger's Will Trusts, supra*, at 295, 1057.

[412] *Re Wilson* [1913] 1 Ch 314; *Re Tacon, supra*; *Re Slatter's Will Trusts* [1964] Ch 512, [1964] 2 All ER 469, noted (1964) 28 Conv 313 (J T Farrand).

[413] *Supra*, CA.

[414] [1979] Ch 483, [1978] 3 All ER 92. See also *Re Lucas, supra*, CA; *Re Currie* [1985] NI 299.

[415] *Re Watt* [1932] 2 Ch 243n; *Re Morrison* (1967) 111 Sol Jo 758.

in several cases[416] in relation to gifts to hospitals taken over by the Minister of Health under the National Health Service Act 1946 between the date of the will and the date of death. The courts commonly held that the gift was to be construed as being for the work previously carried on by the hospital and, where the work was now being carried on by the appropriate hospital management committee, directed payment to the committee on trust to apply the money for the purposes of the particular hospital that was the object of the testator's bounty.

(iii) The approaches in (i) and (ii) above in the light of Re Vernon's Trusts[417]

In this case, Buckley J stated the principles to be applied to gifts to unincorporated charities, on the one hand, and corporate charities, on the other. He expressed the logical view that every gift to an unincorporated charity must take effect as a gift for the purpose that the charity exists to serve. Such a gift will not fail for want of a trustee and effect will be given to it by way of the scheme, notwithstanding the disappearance of the charity in the lifetime of the testator,[418] unless there is something positive to show that the continued existence of the donee was essential to the gift. In the case of a gift to a corporate charity, however, Buckley J said that there is simply a gift to the corporate body beneficially, which will lapse if that body ceases to exist before the death of the testator, unless there is positive evidence that that body took on trust for charitable purposes.[419] It has not ceased to exist if it is in insolvent liquidation, but not yet formally dissolved, and, accordingly, a gift to it will take effect and be available to the creditors of the company, and not for the charitable objects of the corporation.[420]

Re Vernon's Will Trusts[421] was adopted by Goff J in Re Finger's Will Trusts.[422] In that case, questions arose over two shares of residue: one given to the National Radium Commission, an unincorporated charity, and the other to the National Council for Maternity and Child Welfare, a corporate charity. Both charities had been dissolved between the date of the will and the date of death. Applying the above principles, it was held that the gift to the unincorporated charity, the National Radium Commission, did not fail. It was a purpose trust for the work of the Commission, which was not dependent on the continued existence of the named charitable organization. The charitable purposes of the Commission could still be carried out and the appropriate share of residue was accordingly applicable

---

[416] For example, Re Morgan's Will Trusts [1950] Ch 637, [1950] 1 All ER 1097; Re Meyers [1951] Ch 534, [1951] 1 All ER 538. The courts seem to have construed the purposes of the hospitals to these cases as that of carrying on their work on the particular premises, and this construction accordingly could not have saved a gift where the premises had ceased to be used for hospital work: Re Hutchinson's Will Trusts [1953] Ch 387, [1953] 1 All ER 996.

[417] [1972] Ch 300n, [1971] 3 All ER 1061n; Re Edis's Trusts [1972] 2 All ER 769. In Australia, it has been held that the presumption is that there is a trust for the purposes of the charity whether it is corporate or unincorporated: Sir Moses Montefiore Jewish Home v Howell & Co (No 7) Pty Ltd [1984] 2 NSWLR 406.

[418] In restating this proposition in Re Finger's Will Trusts [1972] Ch 286, [1971] 3 All ER 1050. Goff J added the proviso that the work was still being carried on. In principle, it would seem sufficient for the purpose to be capable of being carried out.

[419] Which situation applied was the main dispute in Rabin v Gerson Berger Association Ltd [1986] 1 All ER 374, CA. As to legacies to charitable corporations, see, generally, (1997) NLJ Easter App Supp 17 (P Luxton).

[420] Re AR.MS (Multiple Sclerosis Research) Ltd [1997] 1 WLR 877, noted [1997] Co Law 213 (Alison Dunn).

[421] [1972] Ch 300n, [1971] 3 All ER 1061n.

[422] Supra. The facts as stated below have been slightly simplified.

under a scheme. The gift of the share to the corporate charity failed, however, because the will did not show an intention that the gift should be held on trust for the purposes of the charity. It was an absolute gift to a corporate body that had ceased to exist before the death of the testatrix. This gift could not be claimed by the National *Association* for Maternity and Child Welfare, to which the Council had transferred its funds on its dissolution and which, to all intents and purposes, carried on the work of the Council. As will be seen later, the failure of the gift to the Council gave rise to the further question of whether the share should pass on intestacy or was applicable cy-près.

The law, as stated in *Re Vernon's Will Trusts*[423] and *Re Finger's Will Trusts*,[424] is not without its difficulties: Goff J, in the latter case, himself pointed out that the distinction between corporate and unincorporated charities produced anomalies. One such anomaly had appeared in *Re Meyers*[425] and an absurd result had only been avoided by reliance on the special context in the will. In that case, there were legacies to both unincorporated and corporate hospitals, all of which had been taken over by the Ministry of Health under the 1946 Act. There was no difficulty in construing the legacies to the unincorporated hospitals as gifts for the purposes of the work that they carried on, and on that construction, as we have seen under (ii) above, they were valid. Prima facie, however, the gifts to the corporate hospitals were gifts to them beneficially (and not for the purposes of the work they carried on) and should, accordingly, lapse. Such a result, the judge observed, would be contrary to common sense, and would produce an unacceptable difference between the gifts to corporate and unincorporated hospitals. On the true construction of that particular will, he felt able to decide that the legacies were given to the corporate hospitals for the purposes of the work they carried on, and should go to the appropriate hospital management committees on trust to apply them for those purposes.

The main difficulty, however, it is submitted, lies in the proposition, as stated by Buckley J,[426] that 'if the gift [to an unincorporated charity] is to be permitted to take effect at all, it must be a bequest for a purpose, ie that charitable purpose which the named charity exists to serve'. A gift to an unincorporated charity, it would seem to follow, must always be a gift for its purposes as under (ii) above. Both the *Re Rymer*[427] and *Re Faraker*[428] lines of cases, however, appear to assume the possibility of a gift to a charity (including an unincorporated charity) as distinct from a gift to a charitable purpose. A case that appears to raise the difficulty squarely, but which was not apparently referred to in either *Re Vernon's Will Trusts*[429] or *Re Finger's Will Trusts*,[430] is *Re Bagshaw*.[431] In this case, there was a legacy to the 'Bakewell and District War Memorial Cottage Hospital', the correct name of an unincorporated charity. Between the date of the will and the date of death, the hospital run by the charity had been taken over under the National Health Service Act 1946 and was now carried on by the defendant hospital management committee. The charity had changed its name to the Bakewell and District 1914–18 War Memorial Charity, and also changed its purposes. On the basis of the principles laid down in *Re Vernon's Will Trusts* and *Re Finger's Will Trusts*, one should, it seems, construe the legacy as a gift for the purposes of the work being carried on in

[423] *Supra.*   [424] *Supra.*   [425] [1951] Ch 534, [1951] 1 All ER 538.
[426] In *Re Vernon's Will Trusts, supra,* at 303, 1064.   [427] [1895] 1 Ch 19, CA.
[428] [1912] 2 Ch 488, CA.   [429] [1972] Ch 300n, [1971] 3 All ER 1061n.
[430] [1972] Ch 286, [1971] 3 All ER 1050.   [431] [1954] 1 All ER 227.

the hospital buildings at the date of the will; the work was, in fact, being continued on the same premises by the appropriate hospital management committee. On the posited basis, one would expect the legacy to be payable to the hospital management committee as explained in (ii) above. Such an argument was put forward, but failed. It was held that this was a gift to the charity correctly described by the testatrix as the Bakewell and District War Memorial Cottage Hospital. It was further held that the principle of *Re Faraker*[432] applied and that the legacy was accordingly payable to the Bakewell and District 1914–18 War Memorial Charity for its general purposes.

(iv) Cy-près application

If the gift would otherwise fail, it may be possible to apply the cy-près doctrine. The non-existence of the specified charity at the date of death is treated as a case of initial impossibility, and the gift will be applied cy-près, provided that a general charitable intention can be established. In *Re Harwood*,[433] it was said to be very difficult to find such an intention where a testator had selected a particular charity and taken some care to identify it. Although difficult, it depends on the circumstances and is not impossible, as is shown by *Re Finger's Will Trusts*.[434] In that case, as we have seen, the bequest of a share of residue to the National Council for Maternity and Child Welfare failed. Taking account of the facts that virtually the whole estate was dedicated to charitable purposes, that the Council had been mainly, if not exclusively, a coordinating body, and that the testatrix regarded herself as having no relatives, the judge found a general charitable intention and directed cy-près application.

The principle of *Re Harwood*[435] applies as much to a gift for a particular purpose as to a gift to a particular institution.[436]

(E)　SPECIFIED INSTITUTION CEASING TO EXIST BEFORE THE GIFT BECOMES PAYABLE OR IS IN FACT PAID OVER

In the case in which the specified institution was in existence at the death of the testator, there is no lapse and the testator's next of kin or residuary legatees are forever excluded.[437] The property will be applied to charity, though it is not clear whether the correct view is that it falls to be administered by the Crown, which, in practice, applies it to analogous charitable purposes,[438] or that it is a case of cy-près application by the court.[439]

---

[432] *Supra*, CA.

[433] [1936] Ch 285, [1935] All ER Rep 918 (gift to the Wisbech Peace Society, Cambridge). The assumption that the purposes of a peace society are charitable is probably wrong: they would seem to be political—see *Re Koeppler Will Trusts* [1984] Ch 243, [1984] 2 All ER 111; (1999) 6 CLPR 1 (H Picarda). See also *Re Collier (decd)* [1998] 1 NZLR 81, criticized, it is submitted rightly, in [1998] NZLJ 55 (C Rickett).

[434] *Supra*. The Australian courts have, indeed, held that there is no rule or principle that it is more difficult to conclude that a testator had a general charitable intention where there is a gift to a named charity that existed at the date of the will, but ceased to exist before death, than in the case in which the named charity never existed at all: *A-G for New South Wales v Public Trustee* (1987) 8 NSWLR 550.

[435] *Supra*.　　　[436] *Re Spence* [1978] 3 All ER 92.

[437] *Re Slevin* [1891] 2 Ch 236, CA; *Re Soley* (1900) 17 TLR 118; *Re Tacon, supra*; i (1984) 6 DLR (4th) 644.

[438] *Re Slevin, supra*.　　　[439] *Re Soley, supra*; *Re Tacon, supra*.

(F) GIFT TO WHAT APPEARS TO BE A SPECIFIED CHARITABLE INSTITUTION, BUT WHICH IT TURNS OUT HAS NEVER EXISTED

This is, in effect, a case of initial impossibility and a class of case, moreover, in which the court will lean in favour of a general charitable purpose, and will accept even a small indication of the testator's intention as sufficient to show that a gift for a general charitable purpose and not a particular charitable body was intended.[440] Harman LJ once declared[441] that the court has leaned so far over in this sort of case that it has become almost prone, and, expressing his preference for an upright posture, he held that there was no general charitable intention in a case of this kind, where residue was also given to charity, because this would be to favour one charity against another. There may be other circumstances in the will that may negative the existence of a general charitable intention and thus prevent a cy-près application.[442]

It is respectfully submitted that Harman LJ's preference for an upright posture showed some weakening in *Re Satterthwaite's Will Trusts*,[443] in which, simplifying the facts slightly, residue was to be divided equally between an anti-vivisection society (not, in law, charitable), seven animal charities, and the 'London Animal Hospital'. None of the claimants was able to establish a claim to this last share, which it was held must be applied cy-près, the Court finding a general charitable intention in the dispositions of residue, notwithstanding that 'one-ninth of residue was given to an anti-vivisection society which in law— unknown to the average testator—is not charitable'.[444]

In *Re Jenkins' Will Trusts*,[445] heard after *Re Satterthwaite's Will Trusts*[446] had been decided, but before it had been reported, a one-seventh share of residue was given to an anti-vivisection society expressly to be used for non-charitable purposes, and the other six one-seventh shares to animal charities. The gift of the one-seventh share to the anti-vivisection society was held to fail as being impressed with a non-charitable purpose, and Buckley J held that he could not find a general charitable intention in the residuary gift so as to enable him to apply this one-seventh share cy-près. It is not easy to distinguish this decision convincingly from *Re Satterthwaite's Will Trusts*[447] on this point. However, even if *Re Satterthwaite's Will Trusts* had been followed and a general charitable intention had been established, it is submitted that the cy-près doctrine would not have been applicable. The doctrine operates where there is failure of a gift for a particular charitable purpose, and not where there is failure of a gift for a non-charitable purpose.

It may be added that where the trust is in favour of a non-existent institution in a particular locality in a foreign country, cy-près application may, it appears, nevertheless be made and the trustees directed to make payment to an appropriate organization in that foreign country.[448]

---

[440] *Re Davis* [1902] 1 Ch 876; i [1936] Ch 285, [1935] All ER Rep 918; *Re Pettit* [1988] 2 NZLR 513. Similarly, if there are two or more possible claimants, but the one intended by the testator cannot be identified: *Re Songest* [1956] 2 All ER 765, CA; *Re Conroy* (1973) 35 DLR (3d) 752.

[441] *Re Goldschmidt* [1957] 1 All ER 513, 514; (1957) 73 LQR 166.   [442] *Re Tharp* [1942] 2 All ER 358.

[443] [1966] 1 All ER 919, CA.   [444] *Re Satterthwaite's Will Trusts, supra*, at 925, *per* Russell LJ.

[445] [1966] Ch 249, [1966] 1 All ER 926.

[446] *Supra*. It is strange that this case was apparently not referred to in *Re Jenkins' Will Trusts*, as the same person was counsel for the Attorney-General in both cases.

[447] *Supra*.   [448] See the Canadian decision of *Re Barnes* (1976) 72 DLR (3d) 651.

9 STATUTORY POWERS OF UNINCORPORATED CHARITIES

(A) POWER OF SMALL UNINCORPORATED CHARITIES TO TRANSFER PROPERTY

The charity trustees of an unincorporated charity, the gross income of which in its last financial year did not exceed £10,000 and which does not hold any land on trusts that stipulate that it is to be used for the purposes of the charity, may resolve that all of the property of the charity should be transferred to one or more other charities, whether registered or not required to be registered, specified in the resolution. The charity trustees have no power to pass such a resolution unless they are satisfied that the transfer is expedient in the interests of furthering its purposes and that the purposes (or any of the purposes) of the transferee charity are substantially similar to the purposes (or any of the purposes) of the transferor charity. The resolution must be passed by a majority of not less than two-thirds of the charity trustees voting.[449]

The charity trustees must send a copy of the resolution, together with their reasons for passing it, to the Commission, which may call for additional information or explanations. The Commission may direct the charity trustees to give public notice of the resolution and, if it does so, must take into account any representations made within twenty-eight days of the notice by persons appearing to be interested in the charity.[450]

Subject to the provisions of s 74A of the Charities Act 1993, inserted by s 40 of the 2006 Act, discussed below, a resolution takes effect sixty days after the copy was received by the Commission. The charity trustees must then arrange for all of the property of the transferor charity to be transferred to the transferee charity on the terms that, so far as is reasonably practicable, it will be applied for purposes similar in character to those of the transferor charity, but subject to any restrictions on expenditure to which it was subject as property of the transferor charity.[451]

A resolution does not, however, take effect if, before the end of the sixty-day period (or that period as modified), the Commission notifies the charity trustees in writing that it objects to the resolution, either on procedural grounds or on the merits of the proposals contained in the resolution. The sixty-day period stops running as from the date on which a direction is given to the charity trustees:

(a) to give public notice of a resolution; or

(b) to provide further information or explanations.

It will start running again in case (a) at the end of the period of forty-two days beginning with the date of the public notice, and in case (b), on the date on which the required information is, or explanations are, provided. Once the total period of time during which the

---

[449] Section 74(1)–(5) of the Charities Act 1993, as substituted by the Charities Act 2006, s 40. The Minister may substitute a different sum in subs (1): ibid, s 74(13).

[450] Ibid, s 74(6)–(8), as substituted.

[451] Ibid, s 74(9)–(11) as substituted. At the request of the charity, the Commission may make appropriate vesting orders: s 74(12).

sixty-day period has been suspended exceeds 120 days, the resolution (if not previously objected to by the Commission) is treated as if it had never been passed.[452]

Section 74B of the 1993 Act, likewise inserted by s 40 of the 2006 Act, contains specific provision for a transfer where the charity has a permanent endowment.[453]

(B) POWER TO MODIFY OR REPLACE PURPOSES

Section 74C of the Charities Act 1993, inserted by s 41 of the 2006 Act, which applies to the same unincorporated charities as discussed in (A) above, sets out corresponding provisions under which the charity trustees may alternatively resolve that the trusts of the charity should be modified by replacing all or any of the purposes of the charity with other purposes specified in the resolution that consist of, or include purposes that are similar in character to, those that are to be replaced.

(C) POWER OF UNINCORPORATED CHARITIES TO SPEND CAPITAL

Section 75 of the Charities Act 1993[454] provides that where the property of an unincorporated charity includes any available endowment fund that is subject to restrictions with respect to its expenditure, the charity trustees may resolve that the fund, or a portion of it, ought to be freed from those restrictions as from a specified date. From that date, the fund will be freed from the restrictions, without any need to seek the concurrence of the Charity Commission. The power of the charity trustees to make such a resolution is subject to the condition that they are satisfied that the purposes set out in the trusts to which the fund is subject could be carried out more effectively if the capital of the fund (or the relevant portion) could be expended as well as income accruing to it, rather than only income. These provisions do not apply to a fund if s 75A, discussed below, dealing with larger charities, applies to it.

The new s 75A, inserted by s 43 of the 2006 Act, provides the same power in relation to any available endowment fund of larger unincorporated charities—that is, where the relevant charity's gross income in its last financial year exceeded £1000, and the market value of the endowment fund exceeds £10,000. The section applies if the capital of the fund consists entirely of property given:

(i)   by a particular individual, whether in his lifetime or by his will;

(ii) by a particular institution (by way of grant or otherwise); or

(iii) by two or more individuals or institutions in pursuit of a common purpose, such as a disaster appeal.

Because of the larger funds involved, there are some safeguards. The charity must send a copy of the resolution, together with the reasons for passing it, to the Commission, which may call for additional information or explanations, and may not implement it without

---

[452] Ibid, s 74A, as inserted.   [453] Defined in the Charities Act 1993, s 96(3).
[454] As substituted by the Charities Act 2006, s 43. 'Available endowment fund' is defined in s 75(7), as substituted. 'Permanent endowment' is defined in s 96(3).

its concurrence. The Commission may direct the charity trustees to give public notice of the resolution, and must take into account any representations made within twenty-eight days by persons appearing to be interested in the charity. It must also take into account the wishes of the donor and any changes in the charity's circumstances since the gift was made to ensure that the intentions of the donor in making the gift are treated with due consideration. The fund can be expended without regard for the restrictions from the time at which the Commission notifies the charity trustees that it concurs with the resolution, or when three months have elapsed since the relevant date (defined in the section) without the Commission notifying the charity trustees that it does not concur with the resolution.[455]

(D) POWER OF UNINCORPORATED CHARITY TO MODIFY ITS POWERS OR PROCEDURES

Section 74D of the Charities Act 1993, inserted by s 42 of the 2006 Act, provides that the charity trustees of any charity that is not a company or other body corporate may resolve that any provision of the trusts of the charity relating to any of the powers exercisable, or procedures to be followed, by the charity trustees in connection with the administration of the charity shall be modified as specified in the resolution. If there is a body of members distinct from the charity trustees, a further resolution at a general meeting of the members is required approving the first resolution. The trusts are to be taken as modified as from the date specified in the first resolution, or, if a second resolution is required, from the date on which it was passed.

10 MERGER OF CHARITIES

Merger of charities takes two forms: one is where one or more charities transfer all of their property to another charity, after which the transferor charity, or charities, cease(s) to exist; the other is where two or more charities create a new charity and transfer all of their property to it. The Commission keeps a register, open to public inspection, of charity mergers that are notified to it.[456] There are special provisions in respect of mergers of charities that have both permanent endowment and unrestricted property.[457] After a registered merger, a gift to a transferor charity takes effect as a gift to the transferee charity.[458]

---

[455] Section 75B contains similar provisions to those in s 75A, which apply to any available endowment fund of a special trust, which, as the result of a direction under s 96(5), is to be treated as a separate charity for the purposes of s 75.

[456] Charities Act 1993, s 75C, inserted by the Charities Act 2006, s 44. Registration is a requirement for any charities making use of the vesting declaration provided for by the new s 75E, likewise inserted. Section 75D, likewise inserted, provides a mechanism for ensuring the automatic transfer of property that is being transferred in the course of a merger.

[457] Ibid, s 75C(5).

[458] Ibid, s 75F, likewise inserted. Subsection (5) excludes, where the transferor is a charity within s 75C(5), a gift that is intended to be held to be held as a permanent endowment.

11 DISCRIMINATION

(A) RACE RELATIONS ACT 1976

Apart from statute, it does not seem that a provision in a trust instrument discriminating against potential beneficiaries on the ground, for instance, of colour or religion is regarded as being against public policy or otherwise unlawful, even in the case of a charitable trust. This was impliedly assumed in *Re Dominion Students' Hall Trusts*,[459] a case concerning a colour bar, and expressly stated in *Re Lysaght*,[460] a case concerning a provision excluding students of the Jewish or Roman Catholic faith from benefit, although the judge stigmatized this provision as 'unamiable' and 'undesirable'.

The Race Relations Act 1976, now declares that discrimination, as defined in the Act, on racial grounds—that is, on the grounds of colour, race, nationality, or ethnic[461] or national[462] origins—is unlawful. For the purposes of the Act, a person discriminates against another if, on any of these grounds, he treats that other in certain specified situations less favourably than he treats or would treat other persons. The specified situations would prima facie seem to include the administration of a charitable, although not a private, trust.

Section 34, however, contains two special provisions relating to charities. By subs (1), a provision in a charitable instrument (whenever it took or takes effect) that provides for conferring benefits on persons of a class defined by reference to colour is to have effect for all purposes as if it provided for conferring the like benefits on persons of the class that results if the restriction by reference to colour is disregarded.[463] Thus an otherwise charitable trust for 'the Black community of Hackney, Haringey, Islington and Tower Hamlets' was held to be a valid charitable trust by removal of the reference to colour, the precise nature of the trusts to be dealt with by a scheme.[464] Otherwise, by sub-ss (2) and (3), the Act does not affect a provision in a charitable instrument that provides for conferring benefits on persons of a class defined otherwise than by reference to colour, nor does it render unlawful any act[465] that is done in order to give effect to such a provision.

---

[459] [1947] Ch 183, and see p 334, *supra*.   [460] [1966] Ch 191, [1965] 2 All ER 888.

[461] For a group to constitute itself an ethnic group, it must regard itself, and be regarded by others, as a distinct community by virtue of certain characteristics. Of these, two are essential: (i) a long shared history; and (ii) a cultural tradition of its own. Other common, but not essential characteristics, include: (iii) a common geographical origin; (iv) a common language; (v) a common literature; (vi) a common religion; and (vii) being a minority: *Mandla v Dowell Lee* [1983] 2 AC 548, [1983] 1 All ER 1062, HL, discussed [1983] Pub L 348 (St J A Robilliard); (1984) 128 Sol Jo 274 (A N Khan); (1984) 43 CLJ 218 (G T Pagone). The decision is analysed in detail in (1984) 100 LQR 120 (Helen Beynon and N Love). Gypsies have been held to be a racial group: *Commission for Racial Equality v Dutton* [1989] QB 783, [1989] 1 All ER 306, CA; Rastafarians have been held not to be a separate ethnic group: *Crown Supplies (Property Services Agency) v Dawkins* [1993] ICR 517, CA, discussed (1993) 143 NLJ 610 (N Parpworth).

[462] The Scots and the English are separate racial groups defined by reference to 'national origins', in the sense that England and Scotland are nations, but not by reference to ethnic origins: *Northern Joint Police Board v Power* [1997] IRLR 610, EAT.

[463] Or, where the original class is defined by reference to colour only, on persons generally.

[464] *Re Harding (decd)* [2007] EWHC 3 (Ch), [2007] 1 All ER 747. Section 34(1) is severely criticized in [1981] Conv 131 (T G Watkin); (1983) 47 MLR 759 (I B McKenna).

[465] Unless it is an act that is unlawful, on grounds of race or ethnic or national origins, by virtue of ss 4 or 7, which relate to employment: ibid, s 34(3A), inserted by SI 2003/1626.

It should be observed, however, that, in the administration of a charitable trust, a cy-près scheme may be made for the removal[466] of a discriminatory provision saved by s 34(2) and (3), or one altogether outside the scope of the Act, such as a provision for religious discrimination.

(B) SEX DISCRIMINATION ACT 1975

Although, in general, the Sex Discrimination Act 1975 applies to charities—for example, in advertising for, and selecting, paid staff—there is an important exception in s 43.[467] This provides that where a charitable instrument contains a provision for conferring benefits on persons of one sex only (disregarding any benefits to persons of the opposite sex that are exceptional or are relatively insignificant), nothing done by the charity trustees to comply with that provision is made unlawful by the Act. This exception applies equally to traditionally single-sex organizations, such as the Scouts and Guides, and to small parochial charities for elderly spinsters, retired schoolmasters, and so on. It was held, in *Hugh-Jones v St John's College, Cambridge*,[468] to cover the award of a research fellowship available only to men. The exception has now been qualified by the insertion of s 43(2A),[469] which provides that it is not to apply to discrimination in its application to ss 29 to 31[470] unless the conferral of benefits is:

(a) a proportionate means of achieving a legitimate aim; or

(b) for the purpose of preventing or compensating for a disadvantage linked to gender.

There are special provisions for educational charities in s 78. In the case of these charities, the trustees may apply to the Secretary of State for an order removing or modifying the restrictions so that the benefits can be made available to both sexes, and the Secretary of State may make the order if satisfied that to do so would conduce to the advancement of education without sex discrimination. However, if the trust was created by gift or bequest, no order can be made until twenty-five years after the date on which it took effect, unless the donor or his personal representatives, or the personal representatives of the testator, have consented in writing.

12 DISPOSITIONS OF CHARITY LAND

Since the Trusts of Land and Appointment of Trustees Act 1996 came into effect on 1 January 1997, all land held on charitable trusts is held on a trust of land within the meaning of that Act and, for the purposes of exercising their functions as trustees, charity

---

[466] As was done both in *Re Dominion Students' Hall Trust, supra*, and *Re Lysaght, supra*.

[467] As amended by the Sex Discrimination Act 1975 (Amendment of Section 43) Order 1977, SI 1977/528.

[468] [1979] ICR 848, EAT: college also excluded from liability under s 51, relating to things done under pre-Act statute. Sections not overriden by Directive of the Council of the European Communities.

[469] Inserted by SI 2006/1926.

[470] These sections deal with discrimination in provision of goods, facilities, or services, discrimination in disposal or management of premises, and discrimination in consent for assignment or subletting.

trustees have all of the powers of an absolute owner in relation to charity land.[471] There are, however, restrictions on disposal of charity land in the Charities Act 1993, as amended by the Charities Act 2006.[472]

The primary rule is that no land (except an advowson) held by or in trust for a charity (with the exception of an exempt charity)[473] can be conveyed, transferred, leased, or otherwise disposed of without an order of the court or of the Commission.[474] This rule will, however, in many cases, be inoperative, because it is qualified by a provision that it is not to apply to certain dispositions of such land made to a person who is not a 'connected person',[475] or a trustee for, or nominee of, a connected person.[476] There are two categories of disposition, as follow.

(A) A LEASE FOR SEVEN YEARS OR LESS (OTHER THAN ONE GRANTED WHOLLY OR PARTLY IN CONSIDERATION OF A FINE)

The primary rule does not apply provided that, before entering into an agreement for the lease, the charity trustees:

(i) obtain and consider the advice on the proposed lease by a person whom they reasonably believe to have the requisite ability and practical experience to provide them with competent advice thereon; and

(ii) decide that they are satisfied, having considered that advice, that the terms on which the lease is proposed to be made are the best that can reasonably be obtained for the charity.[477]

(B) ANY OTHER DISPOSITION OF LAND

The primary rule does not apply provided that, before entering into an agreement for the sale, lease (other than one under (A) above), or other disposition of the land, the charity

---

[471] Trusts of Land and Appointment of Trustees Act 1996, s 6(1).

[472] See [2006] Conv 219 (D Dennis).   [473] Charities Act 1993, s 36(10)(a).

[474] Ibid, s 36(1), as amended by the 2006 Act. See CC 28 and (2006) 9 CLPR 1 (S Roberts and E Millington). See also *Bayoumi v Women's Total Abstinence Educational Union Ltd* [2003] EWCA Civ 1548, [2004] 3 All ER 110 (the subsection has no application to an agreement for the sale, etc, of charity land) and [2004] PCB 118 (T Dumont and Fiona Wilson). In the view of the Commission, the section does not apply in relation to sales of land left in wills to charities, either as specific devisees or residuary legatees: (1995) 4 Dec Ch Com 26. By sub-s (9), the restrictions do not apply to a disposition expressly authorized by statute or a legally established scheme, to certain dispositions to another charity, and to certain leases to carry out the charity's purposes on the demised premises, eg in the case of a charity, the purposes of which include the provision of subsidized accommodation for the poor, a letting of premises at less than a market rent. Nor, by s 40, do they apply in many cases of the release of a rentcharge.

[475] This term is defined in the Charities Act 1993, Sch 5, as amended by the Civil Partnership Act 2004, the Charities Act 2006 and SI 2007/2194. In summary, it means: (a) charity trustee or trustee for the charity; (b) a donor of any land to the charity; (c) specified relatives of anyone in (a) or (b); (d) an officer, agent or employee of the charity; (e) the spouse or civil partner of anyone in (a)–(d); (ea) a person carrying on business in partnership with any person falling within any of the preceding sub-paragraphs; (f) an institution controlled by any person or persons in (a)–(e); (g) a body corporate in which any person or persons in (a)–(f) have a substantial interest. 'Spouse' and 'civil partner' include cohabitants.

[476] Ibid, s 36(2).   [477] Ibid, s 36(2), (5), as amended by the 2006 Act.

trustees:

(i)   obtain and consider a written report on the proposed disposition from a qualified surveyor[478] instructed by the trustees and acting exclusively for the charity;

(ii)   advertise the proposed disposition as advised by the surveyor (unless he advises against advertisement); and

(iii) decide that they are satisfied, having considered the surveyor's report, that the terms on which the disposition is proposed to be made are the best that can reasonably be obtained for the charity.[479]

There are further restrictions where any land is held by or in trust for a charity and the trusts on which it is so held stipulate that it is to be used for the purposes or any particular purposes of the charity—that is, what is sometimes called 'functional land'. In that case, the charity trustees must give public notice of the proposed disposition, inviting representations that they are under a duty to take into consideration.[480] This restriction does not, however, apply where other property is to be acquired by way of replacement of the property disposed of, or where the disposition comprises a lease for two years or less (other than one granted wholly or partly in consideration of a fine).[481]

None of the provisions in s 36 apply to a mortgage of land.[482] However, a separate section[483] provides that no mortgage of land held by or in trust for a charity (except an exempt charity)[484] can be granted without an order of the court or the Commission—but it is likewise subject to an important qualification: it does not apply to a mortgage where the charity trustees have, before executing the mortgage, obtained and considered proper advice,[485] in writing, on the relevant matters. These are, in the case of a mortgage to secure the repayment of a proposed loan or grant:

(a) whether the proposed loan or grant is necessary in order for the charity trustees to be able to pursue the particular course of action in connection with which they are seeking the loan or grant.

(b) whether the terms of the loan or grant are reasonable having regard to the status of the charity as the prospective recipient of the loan or grant, and

---

[478] Defined in s 36(4) as someone holding a specified professional qualification who is reasonably believed by the charity trustees to have ability in, and experience of, the valuation of land of the particular kind, and in the particular area, in question. As to the contents of report, see SI 1992/2980.

[479] Ibid, s 36(3), as amended. See *Bayoumi v Women's Total Abstinence Educational Union Ltd* [2003] EWCA Civ 1548, [2004] 3 All ER 110; *Re Shree Vishwaakarma Association of the UK* [2007] WTLR 829 (CC).

[480] Ibid, s 36(6), (6A), as amended and inserted by the 2006 Act. The requirements of this subsection may be waived by the Commission: s 36(8), as amended.

[481] Ibid, s 36(7).

[482] Charities Act 1993, s 36(10)(b). Nor do they apply to any disposition of an advowson: s 36(10)(c).

[483] Ibid, s 38(1), as amended by the 2006 Act. See also s 39 as amended by the Land Registration Act 2002 and the 2006 Act.

[484] Ibid, s 38(7).

[485] That is, the advice of a person: (a) who is reasonably believed by the charity trustees to be qualified by his ability in and practical experience of financial matters; and (b) who has no financial interest in relation to the loan, grant, or other transaction in connection with which his advice is given. Such advice may be given in the course of his employment by the charity or the charity trustees: ibid, s 38(4), as amended by the 2006 Act, s 27. See sub-ss (3B)–(3D) for further relaxation of the requirement of consent.

(c) the ability of the charity to repay on those terms the sum proposed to be paid by way of loan or grant.[486]

In the case of a mortgage to secure the discharge of any other proposed obligation the relevant matter is 'whether it is reasonable for the charity trustees to undertake to discharge the obligation, having regard to the charity's purposes'.[487]

13 CONTROL OF FUND-RAISING FOR CHARITABLE INSTITUTIONS

(A) CONTROL OF FUND-RAISING

Part II of the Charities Act 1992 contains provisions for the control of fund-raising[488] that extend beyond charities by reason of the fact that, in the relevant Part of that Act, 'charitable institution' is defined so as to include an institution (other than a charity) that is established for charitable, benevolent, or philanthropic purposes.

The Act[489] makes it unlawful for a professional fund-raiser[490] to solicit money or other property in any manner whatever, including by means of a statement published in any newspaper, film, or radio or television programme, for the benefit of a charitable institution unless he does so in accordance with an agreement with the institution satisfying the prescribed requirements.[491] Compliance with this requirement may be enforced by means of an injunction, but in no other way.[492]

In his solicitation, a professional fund-raiser[493] must indicate the institution or institutions[494] that are to benefit, and the method by which the fund-raiser's remuneration in connection with the appeal is to be determined and the notifiable

---

[486] Ibid, s 38(2), (3), as substituted by the 2006 Act.   [487] Ibid, s 38(3A), as likewise inserted.

[488] See, generally, CC 20. Note that when a member of the public puts money in a collecting tin, the property in the money passes at once to the charity: R v Dyke and Munro [2002] 1 Cr App R 30, CA.

[489] Ibid, s 59(1).

[490] As defined, ibid, s 58(1), (2), (3); Deregulation and Contracting Out Act 1994, s 25(3).

[491] That is, prescribed by regulations made under s 64(2)(a): see SI 1994/3024. An agreement that does not satisfy the prescribed requirements is not enforceable against the institution, nor does it give any entitlement to remuneration or expenses, save by order of the court: s 59(4), (5). It is likewise made unlawful for a commercial participator (defined in s 58(1), as amended) to represent that charitable contributions are to be given to or applied for the benefit of a charitable institution without such an agreement: s 59(2). As to a commercial participator, see (1995/96) 3 CLPR 17 (Judith Hill).

[492] Ibid, s 59(3).

[493] There are corresponding provisions relating to a commercial participator: s 60(3), as amended by the Charities Act 2006, s 67(1)(4). Section 68 of the 2006 Act inserts ss 60A and 60B (not yet fully in force), which provide that, where paid employees, officers, or trustees of a charity or connected company are acting as collectors (excluding lower paid collectors), they must make a statement including specified information when making appeals.

[494] Or, where the solicitation is for purposes rather than institutions, how the proceeds are to be distributed between different charitable institutions: s 60(2), as amended by the 2006 Act, s 67(1)(3).

amount[495] of that remuneratiom.[496] If the solicitation is made in the course of a radio or television programme inviting payment by credit card or debit card, a professional fund-raiser must also give full details of the donor's right to have any payment of £50 or more refunded by serving written notice on the fund-raiser within seven days of the solicitation.[497] Where a payment of £50 or more is made in response to a telephone solicitation, the fund-raiser must, within seven days, give the donor a written statement indicating the institutions benefiting and the arrangements for remuneration as mentioned above, and giving full details of the right to have the payment refunded and any agreement to make a payment of £50 or more cancelled.[498]

Charitable institutions are given the right to prevent unauthorized fund-raising by seeking an injunction. They may do so where the person in question is using methods of fund-raising to which the institution objects, where the court is satisfied that that person is not a fit and proper person to raise funds for the institution, or where he has represented that charitable contributions are to be given to or applied for the benefit of the institution, which, however, does not wish to be associated with the particular promotional or other fund-raising venture in which that person is engaged.[499]

It is an offence for a person to solicit money or other property for the benefit of an institution representing it to be a registered charity[500] when that is not the case, but it is a defence for the accused to prove that he believed, on reasonable grounds, that the institution was a registered charity.[501]

The Charities Act 2006[502] confers a new power on the Minister for the Cabinet Office to make regulations to control charity fund-raising if he considers it necessary or desirable. In particular, the regulations may impose a good practice requirement on charity trustees.

(B) FINANCIAL ASSISTANCE

Section 70 of the Charities Act 2006 confers on a 'relevant Minister'[503] power to give financial assistance to any charitable, benevolent, or philanthropic institution in respect of any of its activities that directly or indirectly benefit the whole, or any part, of England.[504] The assistance may be given in any form, and may be subject to terms and conditions.[505] The relevant minister must lay a report before each House of Parliament on any exercise of this power in each year.[506]

---

[495] 'Notifiable amount' means the actual amount, if known, and if not as accurate an estimate as is reasonably practicable: s 60(3A) of the 1992 Act, inserted by the 2006 Act, s 67(1)(5).
[496] Section 60(1), as amended by the 2006 Act, s 67(1)(2).
[497] Sections 60(4), and 61(1), (4).   [498] Sections 60(5), (6), and 61(2)–(4).   [499] Section 62.
[500] That is, registered under the Charities Act 1993, s 3.
[501] Charities Act 1992, s 63, as amended by the Deregulation and Contracting Out Act 1994, s 26, and the 2006 Act. A person guilty of an offence is liable on summary conviction to a fine not exceeding level 5 on the standard scale.
[502] Section 69, inserting s 64A in the Charities Act 1992.
[503] Defined in s 70(11) as the Secretary of State or the Minister for the Cabinet Office. His functions may be delegated: s 70(6), (7).
[504] Section 70(1). Similar powers in relation to institutions in Wales are devolved to the National Assembly for Wales by s 71.
[505] Section 70(2)–(4).   [506] Section 70(8), (9).

(C) PUBLIC CHARITABLE COLLECTIONS

Chapter 1 of Pt 3 of the Charities Act 2006 builds on, and will replace, the provisions in Pt 3 of the Charities Act 1992, which was never brought into force.[507]

When fully brought into force, the 2006 Act will impose controls on public charitable collections—that is, charitable appeals made in any public place or by means of visits to houses or business premises (or both). Again, the provision extends beyond charity in the legal sense, because 'charitable appeal' is defined as an appeal to members of the public to give money or other property (whether for consideration or otherwise) that is made in association with a representation that the whole or any part of its proceeds is to be applied for charitable, benevolent, or philanthropic purposes.[508]

Certain charitable appeals are not public charitable collections, and therefore do not come within the statutory licensing scheme.[509]

Section 48(1) provides:

A collection in a public place must not be conducted unless—

(i) the promoters of the collection hold a public collections certificate in force under section 52 issued by the Charity in respect of the collection,[510] and

(ii) the collection is conducted in accordance with a permit issued under section 59 by the local authority in whose area it is conducted.[511]

Section 49 provides that a door-to-door collection must not be conducted unless the promoters:

(i) likewise hold a public collections certificate; and

(ii) have duly notified the local authority in whose area the collection is to be conducted of the matters specified in subs (3).[512]

Section 50 exempts certain collections from the requirement to obtain a public collections certificate and, in the case of a collection in a public place, a permit. An exempt collection is one:

(i) that is a local, short-term collection;[513] and

---

[507] The regulations presently in force are (in the case of street collections) the Police, Factories etc (Miscellaneous Provisions) Act 1916, and (in the case of house-to-house collections) the House to House Collections Act 1939.

[508] Charities Act 1992, s 65.

[509] Ibid, s 46. These include an appeal in the course of a public meeting, an appeal made on land of a specified description, and an appeal to place money, etc, in an unattended receptacle.

[510] See ibid, ss 51–57, for detailed provisions relating to the application for and issue of certificates, the grounds on which the Commission may refuse to issue a certificate, the withdrawal or variation of certificates, appeals against the Commission's decisions, and the transfer of a certificate between trustees of an unincorporated charity.

[511] See ibid, ss 58–62, for detailed provisions relating to the application for and issue of permits, the only ground on which a local authority may refuse an application—namely, that the collection would cause undue inconvenience to the public—the withdrawal or variation of permits and appeals against the decisions of local authorities.

[512] These are: (i) the purpose for which the proceeds of the appeal are to be applied; (ii) the prescribed particulars of when the collection is to be conducted; (iii) the locality within which the collection is to be conducted; and (iv) such other matters as may be prescribed.

[513] Defined in s 50(2).

(ii) where the promoters, in due time, notify the local authority in whose area the collection is to take place of the time and place of the collection, and the purpose for which the proceeds of the appeal are to be applied.[514]

The exemption will not take effect if the local authority serves a notice that the proposed collection is not a local, short-term collection, or that the promoter has breached regulations or been convicted of a relevant offence.[515] An appeal may be made against the local authority's decision.[516]

[514] See s 50(1), (3),   [515] Section 50(1), (4),   [516] Sections 50(5) and 62.

15

TRUSTEES

A trust obviously requires trustees, but, as will be seen, little needs to be said about the appointment of the first trustees. This is normally made by the creator of the trust. Most of the first section of this chapter considers: who has the power to appoint a new trustee to fill a vacancy, to replace an existing trustee, or to appoint an additional trustee; the circumstances in which the power may be exercised; and the method by which it is to be done. It also considers who may be appointed as a trustee and the restrictions on the maximum and minimum number of trustees.

Trustees having been validly appointed, the next two sections explain how the trust property is vested in them and the ways in which trusteeship may come to an end. Certain special kinds of trustee are discussed in the final section of the chapter.

1 APPOINTMENT OF TRUSTEES

(A) APPOINTMENT BY THE SETTLOR

The first trustees are normally appointed by the settlor or testator who creates the trust.

In the case of a trust created by will, the fact that the trustees appointed all predecease the testator,[1] or otherwise cease to exist,[2] or even that no trustees were originally appointed by the testator at all,[3] or that they all disclaim the trust,[4] or that the trustee appointed is legally incapable of taking,[5] will not cause the trust to fail, even though the will may contain no provisions for the appointment of trustees. In such a case, the court will be able to appoint trustees under the powers hereafter discussed. In the meantime, the personal representatives will be deemed to be constructive trustees and, accordingly, it could not be successfully contended that the trust was not completely constituted.

In the case of a voluntary trust purported to be created *inter vivos*, it seems clear that there can be no valid trust if the document relied upon as constituting the trust is a purported conveyance or transfer to trustees who are not named or otherwise identified, or who are already dead, or have otherwise ceased to exist, or are not capable grantees. Such a document would be a nullity and completely ineffective to constitute a trust. If, however,

---

[1] *Re Smirthwaite's Trusts* (1871) LR 11 Eq 251.   [2] *A-G v Stephens* (1834) 3 My & K 347, *semble*.

[3] *Dodkin v Brunt* (1868) LR 6 Eq 580; *Pollock v Ennis* [1921] 1 IR 181.

[4] *Kynnersley v Wolverhampton City Council* [2008] WTLR 65.

[5] *Sonley v Clock Makers' Co* (1780) 1 Bro CC 81.

a trust is once completely constituted, it is another matter. Accordingly, where there is a conveyance or transfer to named persons as trustees, a trust is validly created, notwithstanding an effective disclaimer[6] by the trustees, and even though the settlor has died without having communicated the trust to the trustees. The reasoning in such case is that the conveyance or transfer is valid until disclaimer,[7] and, accordingly, the property passes to the trustees and the trust is completely constituted. On disclaimer, the trust property is, by operation of law, revested in the settlor, or his personal representatives, if he is dead, subject to the trusts, notwithstanding the fact that a disclaimer is often said to make the conveyance void *ab initio*.[8] Again, in such a case, the court has power to appoint new trustees.[9] To the above propositions, which are sometimes compendiously comprehended in the maxim that 'a trust will not fail for want of a trustee', there is one qualification that we have already met in connection with charities:[10] 'If it is of the essence of a trust that the trustees selected by the settlor and no-one else shall act as the trustees of it and those trustees cannot or will not undertake the office, the trust must fail.'[11]

Apart from his power to appoint the first trustees when creating the trust, the settlor has, as such, no power to appoint new or additional trustees, unless such a power is expressly reserved to him by the trust instrument. It should be mentioned that, in the case of an *inter vivos* trust, there is no reason why the settlor should not himself be one of the original trustees, and he will inevitably be the sole original trustee if the trust is created by the settlor simply declaring himself a trustee of property already vested in him alone.

(B) APPOINTMENT UNDER AN EXPRESS POWER

It is not usual to insert an express power of appointing new trustees, as the statutory power hereafter discussed is usually regarded as adequate. The operation and effect of an express power is, of course, a question of construction of the particular words used, and it seems that such a power will be strictly construed.[12] It is doubtful whether, under an express

---

6 As to disclaimer, generally, see section 3(A), p 380, *infra*.

7 Disclaimer does not need to be in any particular form: *Re Moss* (1977) 77 DLR (3d) 314. A transfer of property to a person without his knowledge, if made in proper form, vests the property in him at once, subject to his right to repudiate it when he learns of it—in other words, assent is presumed until dissent is signified: *Siggers v Evans* (1855) 5 E & B 367; *Standing v Bowring* (1885) 31 Ch D 282, CA. In *Dewar v Dewar* [1975] 2 All ER 728, it was held that a statement by the donee that he would only accept it as a loan did not prevent it from being an effective gift unless the donor agreed that it should be a loan, not citing the conflicting decision of *Hill v Wilson* (1873) 8 Ch App 888, as pointed out in (1976) 35 CLJ 47 (J W A Thornely) and (1975) 38 MLR 700 (S Roberts). See also (2001) 117 LQR 127 (J Hill); (1999) 28 UWALR 65 (N Crago). Cf *Re Smith (decd)* [2001] 3 All ER 552.

8 Such a statement signifies that, as regards the person to whom the grant is made, he is, in respect of his liabilities, his burdens, and his rights, in exactly the same position as though no conveyance has been made to him: *Mallott v Wilson* [1903] 2 Ch 494; but see *Re Stratton's Deed of Disclaimer* [1958] Ch 42, [1975] 2 All ER 594, CA; *J W Broomhead (Vic) Pty Ltd v J W Broomhead Pty Ltd* [1985] VR 891. It is contended in [1981] Conv 141 (P Matthews) that disclaimer should, in fact, make the conveyance void *ab initio* with consequent failure of the trust, unless established on some other ground.

9 *Jones v Jones* (1874) 31 LT 535; *Mallott v Wilson* [1903] 2 Ch 494.

10 See p 329, *supra*.

11 *Per* Buckley J in *Re Lysaght* [1966] Ch 191, 207, [1965] 2 All ER 888, 896.

12 See, eg, *Stones v Rowton* (1853) 17 Beav 308; *Re Norris* (1884) 27 Ch D 333. See also *Re Papadimitriou* [2004] WTLR 1141 (Isle of Man HC) (power given to protector).

power, the donee of the power can appoint himself to be a new trustee, either alone or jointly with other persons, even assuming that such an appointment is, prima facie, as a matter of construction, within the power.[13] Kay J has stated the equitable objection:

> A man should not be judge in his own case;…he should not decide that he is the best possible person, and say that he ought to be the trustee. Naturally no human being can be imagined who would not have some bias one way or the other as to his own personal fitness, and to appoint himself among other people, or excluding them to appoint himself, would certainly be an improper exercise of any power of selection of a fiduciary character such as this is.[14]

In order to avoid duplication, cases on the construction in express powers of common-form phrases that appear in the statutory power in identical or similar terms are discussed in relation to the latter, with an identifying note. They are not, of course, direct decisions on the statute, but are likely to be applied by analogy, and, conversely, decisions on statutory phrases would almost certainly be followed in a case on an express power in similar terms.

(C) APPOINTMENT UNDER THE PROVISIONS OF S 36 OF THE TRUSTEE ACT 1925

The statutory power contained in this section applies to all trusts, unless a contrary intention appears.[15] Such a contrary intention is not, it seems, to be inferred from the mere fact that there is an express power in certain circumstances, and, accordingly, this would not prevent the appointment of new trustees under the statutory power in other circumstances to which the express power did not apply.[16]

Subsection (1) of s 36 provides as follows:

> Where a trustee, either original or substituted, and whether appointed by a court or otherwise, is dead, or remains out of the United Kingdom for more than twelve months, or desires to be discharged from all or any of the trusts or powers reposed in or conferred on him, or refuses or is unfit to act therein, or is incapable of acting therein, or is an infant, then, subject to the restrictions imposed by this Act on the number of trustees—
>
> (a) the person or persons nominated for the purpose of appointing new trustees by the instrument, if any, creating the trust; or
>
> (b) if there is no such person, or no such person able and willing to act, then the surviving or continuing trustees or trustee for the time being, or the personal representatives of the last surviving or continuing trustee;
>
> may, by writing, appoint one or more other persons (whether or not being the persons exercising the power) to be a trustee or trustees in the place of the trustee so deceased, remaining out of the United Kingdom, desiring to be discharged, refusing, or being unfit or being incapable, or being an infant, as aforesaid.

---

[13] *Re Skeats' Settlement* (1889) 42 Ch D 522; *Re Newen* [1894] 2 Ch 297; see, however, the explanation of these cases in *Montefiore v Guedalla* [1903] 2 Ch 723; doubted in *Re Sampson* [1906] 1 Ch 435.

[14] *Re Skeats' Settlement, supra,* per Kay J at 527.

[15] Trustee Act, 1925, s 69(2). Eg, when there is a foreign trustee, the power may be varied to prevent his removal by reason of remaining outside the UK for more than twelve months.

[16] *Re Wheeler and De Rochow* [1896] 1 Ch 315; *Re Sichel's Settlements* [1916] 1 Ch 358.

It has been held[17] that, as an appointment has to be 'in place of' a retiring trustee, the section cannot be construed so that the appointment of one new trustee would be effective to discharge two retiring trustees.

The unanimous view of textbook writers, the assumption of practitioners, and the only inference to be drawn from the cases is that a trustee in this section does not include a personal representative, notwithstanding that the definition section[18] specifically provides that 'trustee, where the context admits, includes a personal representative'. In the face of such unanimity of opinion, it is not surprising that no litigant has yet been brave, or perhaps one should say rash, enough even to argue the contrary. It is, however, not easy to find in s 36 a context that clearly supplies the necessary contrary intention and it is noteworthy that, in s 41 of the Trustee Act 1925,[19] which gives power to the court to appoint new trustees in certain circumstances, it was thought necessary to provide expressly that nothing therein contained gives power to appoint a personal representative. Of course, if a personal representative has become a trustee, the statutory, or any other, power to appoint a new trustee will apply.[20]

We must now consider the provisions of the subsection set out above in more detail.

(i) The circumstances in which the statutory power may be exercised

These can be put under eight heads.

    (a) '*...where a trustee...is dead*' It is specifically provided by sub-s(8) that this includes the case of a person nominated trustee in a will, but dying before the testator, thus resolving the doubts previously caused by the differing views of the judges.[21] The statutory provision does not cover the case, which is seldom likely to occur in practice, in which, under an *inter vivos* trust, a trustee appointed is already dead. In the absence of direct authority, the cases cited in the previous note provide a close analogy, but, as stated, leave the point doubtful. Perhaps the better view is that of Parker VC in *Re Hadley*,[22] from which it would follow that, in the case of such prior death, the power of appointment would be exercisable. It will be remembered, however, that if all the trustees appointed under an *inter vivos* trust are already dead at the date of the deed, there will be no valid trust at all.[23]

    (b) '*...where a trustee...remains out of the United Kingdom*[24] *for more than twelve months*'[25] This means an uninterrupted period of twelve months, and it was

---

[17] *Adam & Co International Trustees Ltd v Theodore Goddard (a firm)* (2000) 144 Sol Jo LB 150. The principle would apply to an appointment in place of any other specified category of trustee.

[18] Trustee Act 1925, s 68(1)(17).   [19] Discussed at p 368, *infra*.

[20] The circumstances in which this transformation takes place were discussed in Chapter 2, section 5, p 39 et seq, *supra*.

[21] *Walsh v Gladstone* (1844) 14 Sim 2; *Winter v Rudge* (1847) 15 Sim 596; *Re Hadley* (1851) 5 De G & Sm 67 (all cases on express powers, where doubts still remain).

[22] *Supra.*   [23] See p 357, *supra*.

[24] This means Great Britain and Northern Ireland: Trustee Act 1925, s 68(1), (20).

[25] For the protection of purchasers, s 38 of the Trustee Act 1925 provides '(1) A statement contained in any instrument coming into operation after the commencement of this Act by which a new trustee is appointed for any purpose connected with land, to the effect that a trustee has remained out of the United Kingdom for more than twelve months or refuses or is unfit to act, or is incapable of acting... shall, in favour of a purchaser of a legal estate, be conclusive evidence of the matter stated. (2) In favour of such purchaser any appointment of a

accordingly held in *Re Walker*[26] that the event upon which the power arose had not happened when the period had been broken by a week's visit to London. If, however, the event has happened and the power has become exercisable, the trustee who has remained out of the United Kingdom can be removed against his will.[27] This head should be excluded where the trust includes a power to appoint non-resident trustees.

(c) '…*where a trustee…desires to be discharged from all or any of the trusts or powers reposed in or conferred on him*' It will be observed that this provision specifically authorizes a trustee to retire from a part only of the trusts or powers reposed in or conferred on him, thus getting over the difficulty caused by cases that held that this could only be done with the aid of the court.[28]

(d) '…*where a trustee…refuses…to act therein*'[29] This seems to cover the case of a trustee who disclaims the trust.[30]

(e) '…*where a trustee…is unfit to act therein*'[31] It seems that a trustee who is bankrupt is, prima facie, unfit to act,[32] although in *Re Wheeler and De Rochow*,[33] the court did not rely on this, saying that, whether or not a trustee who became bankrupt was for that reason alone unfit to act, one who became bankrupt and absconded certainly was.

(f) '…*where a trustee…is incapable of acting therein*'[34] The better view[35] seems to be that the incapacity to act must be personal incapacity, such as old age, with consequent bodily and mental infirmity,[36] or mental disorder,[37] but not bankruptcy.[38] Where a trustee who lacks capacity to exercise his functions as trustee is entitled in possession to some beneficial interest in the trust property, it is specially provided[39]

new trustee depending on that statement, and any vesting declaration, express or implied, consequent on the appointment, shall be valid.'

[26] [1901] 1 Ch 259. Cf *Re Moravian Society* (1858) 26 Beav 101; *Re Arbib and Class's Contract* [1891] 1 Ch 601, CA (both decisions on express provisions).

[27] *Re Stoneham's Settlement Trusts* [1953] Ch 59, [1952] 2 All ER 694.

[28] *Savile v Couper* (1887) 36 Ch D 520; *Re Moss' Trusts* (1888) 37 Ch D 513. Cf s 39 Trustee Act 1925, discussed at p 384, *infra* (retirement without appointment of new trustees).

[29] Trustee Act 1925, s 38, applies: see fn 25, *supra*.

[30] *Viscountess D'Adhemar v Bertrand* (1865) 35 Beav 19.

[31] Trustee Act 1925, s 38, applies: see fn 25, *supra*.

[32] See *Re Roche* (1842) 2 Dr & War 287; *Re Hopkins* (1881) 19 Ch D 61, 63 CA, *per* Jessel MR; *Re Matheson* (1994) 121 ALR 605; (1979) 53 ALJ 648 (R P Meagher).

[33] [1896] 1 Ch 315. Cf *Re Barker's Trusts* (1875) 1 Ch D 43 and *Re Adams' Trust* (1879) 12 Ch D 634, in which the question concerned the power of the court to appoint in place of a bankrupt trustee.

[34] Trustee Act 1925, s 38, applies: see fn 25, *supra*.

[35] See, eg, *Re Bignold's Settlement Trusts* (1872) 7 Ch App 223; *Turner v Maule* (1850) 15 Jur 761; *Re Watts' Settlement* (1851) 9 Hare 106 (all decisions on express powers).

[36] *Re Lemann's Trusts* (1883) 22 Ch D 633; *Re Weston's Trusts* [1898] WN 151 (cases on appointment by the court).

[37] *Re East* (1873) 8 Ch App 735 (express power); *Re Blake* [1887] WN 173, CA. Cf *Kirby v Leather* [1965] 2 QB 367, 387, [1965] 2 All ER 441, 446, CA, *per* Winn LJ; compromised sub nom *Leather v Kirby* [1965] 3 All ER 927n, HL.

[38] *Turner v Maule*, *supra*; *Re Watts' Settlement*, *supra* (both cases on express powers).

[39] Trustee Act 1925, s 36(9), as substituted by the Mental Health Act 1959, s 149(1) and Sch 7, and the Mental Health Act 1983, s 148 and Sch 4, amended by the Mental Capacity Act 2005, Sch 6.

that no appointment of a new trustee in his place shall be made,[40] unless leave to make the appointment has been given by the Court of Protection.

The Law of Property Act 1925[41] requires that if land subject to a trust of land is vested, either solely or jointly with any other person or persons, in a person who lacks capacity (within the meaning of the Mental Capacity Act 2005) to exercise his functions as a trustee, a new trustee must be appointed in his place, or he must be discharged from the trust, before the legal estate is dealt with by the trustees. This does not, however, prevent a legal estate being dealt with without the appointment of a new trustee, or the discharge of the incapable trustee, at a time when the donee of an enduring power of attorney or lasting power of attorney (within the meaning of the 2005 Act) is entitled to act for the trustee who lacks capacity in relation to the dealing.[42]

It was held, during the First World War, that an alien enemy was incapable of acting, on the ground that he could not bring an action to protect the trust property.[43] This decision does not appear to have been cited to the court during the Second World War in a case in which the court refused to lay down a rule, but said that, on the facts before it, there was no evidence that the trustee, resident in enemy-occupied territory, was really incapable of acting.[44] The court in fact rather avoided the issue by itself appointing a new trustee under s 41 of the Trustee Act 1925.[45]

The question of whether a trustee becomes incapable of acting by going abroad is now less likely to arise in the case of the statutory power by reason of the provision already discussed that a new trustee may be appointed in place of a trustee who remains out of the United Kingdom for more than twelve months. In cases on express powers, it was held in two early cases that a trustee did not become incapable of acting by living abroad, even in places such as Australia[46] and China[47]—at that time, very remote. In *Mesnard v Welford*,[48] however, it was held that a trustee who had been absent for twenty years and established a business in New York, was incapable of acting as a trustee of leasehold property in London, and in *Re Lemann's Trusts*,[49] residence abroad was given as an obvious illustration of incapacity.

One case is specially provided for by the section itself:[50] where a trustee is a corporation, and the corporation is or has been dissolved, it is deemed to be, and to have been from the date of the dissolution, incapable of acting in the trusts or powers reposed in or conferred on the corporation.

---

[40] Except by the person or persons nominated to appoint new trustees by the trust instrument.

[41] Section 22(2), as amended by the Trusts of Land and Appointment of Trustees Act 1996, s 25(1), Sch 3, para 4(6) and the Mental Capacity Act 2005, s 67(1), Sch 6, para 4(1), (2)(b).

[42] Ibid, s 22(3), inserted by the Trustee Delegation Act 1999, s 9, and amended by the Mental Capacity Act 2005, s 67(1), Sch 6, para 4(1), 2(c).

[43] *Re Sichel's Settlement* [1916] 1 Ch 358.   [44] *Re May's Will Trusts* [1941] Ch 109.

[45] Discussed in section 1(F), p 368 *et seq.*   [46] *Re Harrison's Trusts* (1852) 22 LJ Ch 69.

[47] *Withington v Withington* (1848) 16 Sim 104.

[48] (1853) 1 Sm & G 426 (express power). See *Re Bignold's Settlement Trusts* (1872) 7 Ch App 223 (appointment by court).

[49] (1883) 22 Ch D 633 (appointment by court).   [50] Trustee Act 1925, s 36(3).

(g) '...*where a trustee...is an infant*'   Although the appointment of an infant to be a trustee in relation to any settlement or trust is void,[51] an infant may be a trustee under a resulting, implied or constructive trust.[52]

(h) '...*where a trustee has been removed under a power contained in the instrument creating the trust*'[53]   In such a case, the statutory power arises and operates in the case of a trustee who is removed, as if he were dead, and in the case of a corporation, as if the corporation desired to be discharged from the trust. It should be observed that this provision applies only in the case in which a trustee has been removed under a power contained in the trust instrument. It does not confer any power to remove a trustee.

(ii) The persons who can exercise the statutory power

The section, it will be observed, has a primary and a secondary category, as follows.

(a) '*The person or persons nominated for the purpose of appointing new trustees*'   There is no need for the nomination to refer to the statutory power[54] and it is usual for the trust deed simply to provide that X shall have power to appoint new trustees. If someone is nominated to appoint new trustees in certain cases only, it should be noted that he is not regarded as nominated to exercise the statutory power in other cases not specifically mentioned.[55] As there is no need for the person nominated to appoint new trustees to have any beneficial interest under the trust, it is not surprising that it has been held that if a beneficiary is nominated to appoint new trustees, he may continue to exercise the power of appointment after alienating his interest, and without obtaining the consent of the alienees.[56] A curious point arises where two or more persons are jointly nominated to appoint new trustees. Here, unless a contrary intention can be found as a matter of construction, the old rule still applies that a bare power, given to two or more persons by name and not annexed to an estate or office, does not survive, but determines on the death of the first of the named persons to die.[57]

(b) '*The surviving or continuing trustees or trustee for the time being, or the personal representatives of the last surviving or continuing trustee*'   Power to appoint new trustees is given to persons in this second category where there is no one nominated to appoint, or where there is 'no such person able and willing to act'. It was held that there was no person able and willing to act where the persons jointly nominated were a husband and wife, who were at the relevant time living apart and unable to

---

[51] Law of Property Act 1925, s 20. Note Law of Property Act, s 15, which provides that the parties to a conveyance are presumed to be of full age until the contrary is proved.

[52] See, eg, *Re Vinogradoff* [1935] WN 68.   [53] Trustee Act 1925, s 36(2).

[54] See *Re Walker and Hughes' Contract* (1883) 24 Ch D 698.

[55] *Re Wheeler and De Rochow* [1896] 1 Ch 315; *Re Sichel's Settlements* [1916] 1 Ch 358.

[56] *Hardaker v Moorhouse* (1884) 26 Ch D 417 (express power). But see *Re Bedingfield and Herring's Contract* [1893] 2 Ch 332, 337.

[57] *Re Harding* [1923] 1 Ch 182. The rule was held not to be abrogated by the Trustee Act 1893, s 22, now replaced by the Trustee Act 1925, s 18. Cf *Bersel Manufacturing Co Ltd v Berry* [1968] 2 All ER 552, HL.

agree on the selection of new trustees,[58] and likewise where the donee of the power of appointment could not be found.[59]

A 'continuing trustee' normally means a trustee who is to continue to act after the appointment of the new trustee has taken effect.[60] It is, however, specifically provided that the provisions of s 36 'relative to a continuing trustee include a refusing or retiring trustee, if willing to act in the execution of the provisions' of that section.[61] It is accordingly possible for all the surviving trustees together, or a sole trustee, to retire and at the same time to appoint new trustees or a new trustee to act in their or his place, which could not be done if this power were to be given to the continuing trustees or trustee in the prima facie sense. In thus obviating one difficulty, another has arisen—namely, whether the continuing trustees or trustee *stricto sensu* can validly make an appointment without the concurrence of a refusing or retiring trustee. The answer seems to be that such an appointment is valid, unless it is shown that the refusing or retiring trustee was competent and willing to act, the onus being upon those who allege that this is so to establish it.[62] In practice, it is desirable that a refusing or retiring trustee should join in the deed of appointment of new trustees, if this is possible.

The phrase 'the last surviving or continuing trustee' has been held to include a sole trustee,[63] but where all of the trustees of a will predecease the testator, the last of them to die does not come within the meaning of the phrase and consequently his personal representatives are not entitled to appoint.[64] Where the section does apply, it seems that the personal representatives of a last surviving or continuing trustee are not bound to exercise the statutory power of appointment.[65]

Subsection (4) provides that:

the power of appointment given . . . to the personal representatives of a last surviving or continuing trustee shall be . . . exercisable by the executors for the time being (whether original or by representation) of such surviving or continuing trustee who have proved the will of their testator or by the administrators for the time being of such trustee without the concurrence of any executor who has renounced or has not proved.

But, by subs (5):

a sole or last surviving executor intending to renounce, or all the executors where they all intend to renounce, shall have . . . power, at any time before renouncing probate, to exercise the power of appointment given by this section, . . . if willing to act for that purpose and without thereby accepting the office of executor.

---

[58] *Re Sheppard's Settlement Trusts* [1888] WN 234.   [59] *Cradock v Witham* [1895] WN 75.

[60] *Travis v Illingworth* (1865) 2 Drew & Sm 344; *Re Norris* (1884) 27 Ch D 333 (both cases on express powers); *Re Coates to Parsons* (1886) 34 Ch D 370. The last two cases disapprove contrary dicta in *Re Glenny and Hartley* (1884) 25 Ch D 611. These cases would still apply to the construction of the word 'continuing' in the case of an express power.

[61] Trustee Act 1925, s 36(8). A trustee who is compulsorily removed because he has remained out of the United Kingdom for more than twelve months is not a refusing or retiring trustee within the subsection, and, accordingly, his concurrence is not required to an appointment of new trustees: *Re Stoneham's Settlement Trusts* [1953] Ch 59, [1952] 2 All ER 694.

[62] *Re Coates to Parsons* (1886) 34 Ch D 370.   [63] *Re Shafto's Trusts* (1885) 29 Ch D 247.

[64] *Nicholson v Field* [1893] 2 Ch 511.

[65] *Re Knight's Will* (1884) 26 Ch D 82, 89, *per* Pearson J (not discussed on appeal).

Although a non-proving executor can exercise the power of appointment, his title to do so can only be proved by a proper grant of representation.[66]

(iii) Mode of appointment

An appointment under s 36 is merely required to be in writing, although it is normally made by deed in order to get the benefit of the vesting provisions contained in s 40.[67] It need not be contained in an instrument expressly executed for that purpose, if it can properly be construed as having that effect.[68] If the trust deed in terms requires an appointment to be made with some unusual form of execution, or attestation, or solemnity, such provisions are ineffective by reason of s 159 of the Law of Property Act 1925, although the section expressly provides that it does not operate to defeat any direction making the consent of some person necessary to a valid appointment.[69] The appointment cannot, however, be made by will—that is, a last surviving trustee cannot appoint a new trustee to take office at his own death in place of himself.[70]

(iv) Appointment of additional trustees

Even under subs (1), the number of trustees may be increased, because this section authorizes the appointment of 'one or more other persons…to be a trustee or trustees in the place of the trustee' who has already ceased or upon the appointment ceases to hold office. Subsection (6), however, authorizes the appointment of an additional trustee or trustees in some circumstances, even where there is no vacancy in the trusteeship. As amended by the Trusts of Land and Appointment of Trustees Act 1996, it provides as follows:

Where, in the case of any trust, there are not more than three trustees—

(a) the person or persons nominated for the purpose of appointing new trustees by the instrument, if any, creating the trust; or

(b) if there is no such person, or no such person able and willing to act, then the trustee or trustees for the time being;

may, by writing, appoint another person or other persons[71] to be an additional trustee or additional trustees, but it shall not be obligatory to appoint any additional trustee, unless the instrument, if any, creating the trust, or any statutory enactment provides to the contrary, nor shall the number of trustees be increased beyond four by virtue of any such appointment.

(v) Effect of appointment

The Trustee Act 1925, s 36(7), which applies equally to a trustee appointed under ss 19 or 20 of the Trusts of Land and Appointment of Trustees Act 1996,[72] provides:

Every new trustee appointed under this section as well before as after all the trust property becomes by law, or by assurance, or otherwise, vested in him, shall have the same powers,

---

[66] *Re Crowhurst Park, Sims-Hilditch v Simmons* [1974] 1 All ER 991, [1974] 1 WLR 583.
[67] Discussed in section 2 of this chapter, p 378, *infra*.
[68] *Re Farnell's Settled Estates* (1886) 33 Ch D 399 (express power).
[69] Cf *Lancashire v Lancashire* (1848) 2 Ph 657 (express power).
[70] *Re Parker's Trusts* [1894] 1 Ch 707.
[71] Under this provision, he cannot appoint himself: *Re Power's Settlement Trusts* [1951] Ch 1074, [1951] 2 All ER 513, CA. Contrast s 36(1), p 349, *supra*. The Law Reform Committee in its 23rd Report, Cmnd 8733, para 2(6), recommended the amendment of subs (6) to bring into line with subs (1).
[72] See s 21(3). Section 20 of the 1996 Act, as amended by the Mental Capacity Act 2005: see p 366, *infra*.

authorities, and discretions, and may in all respects act as if he had been originally appointed a trustee by the instrument, if any, creating the trust.

(D) APPOINTMENT BY BENEFICIARIES UNDER THE TRUSTS OF LAND AND APPOINTMENT OF TRUSTEES ACT 1996

Where—

(i)   there is no person nominated[73] for the purpose of appointing new trustees by the instrument, if any, creating the trust; and

(ii) the beneficiaries under the trust are of full age and capacity, and (taken together[74]) are absolutely entitled to the property subject to the trust—

they may give a written direction to the trustees or trustee for the time being[75] to appoint by writing[76] to be a trustee or trustees the person or persons specified in the direction.[77] The direction may be by way of substitution for a trustee or trustees directed to retire,[78] or as an additional trustee or trustees up to the statutory maximum.[79] The section does not expressly require or empower the trustees to comply with the direction, but this is thought to be implicit.

It is further provided[80] that where—

(i)   a trustee lacks capacity (within the meaning of the Mental Capacity Act 2005) to exercise his functions as trustee;

(ii) there is no person who is both entitled and willing and able to appoint a trustee in place of him under s 36(1) of the Trustee Act 1925; and

(iii) the beneficiaries under the trust are of full age and capacity and (taken together) are absolutely entitled to the property subject to the trust—

the beneficiaries may give[81] to—

(iv) a deputy appointed for the trustee by the Court of Protection;

(v)   an attorney acting for him under the authority of an enduring power of attorney or lasting power of attorney registered under the Mental Capacity Act 2005; or

(vi) a person authorized for the purpose by the Court of Protection

---

[73] Presumably, this means no such person at the relevant time, so that if X alone is nominated and he is dead, the section will apply.

[74] This is thought to encompass the situation in which beneficiaries are entitled in succession, or are objects of a discretionary trust, as well as being co-owners. Cf the wording in s 6(2), which appears to be restricted to joint tenants and tenants in common.

[75] Or, if there are none, the personal representatives of the last person who was a trustee. 'Trustee for the time being' includes any trustee being directed to retire: see section 3(C)(vi), p 386, *infra*.

[76] In practice, it should be by deed to take advantage of s 40 of the Trustee Act 1925: see section 2, p 370, *infra*.

[77] Trusts of Land and Appointment of Trustees Act 1996, s 19(1), (2)(b). As to restrictions on who may be specified, see ibid, s 21(4).

[78] See section 3(C)(vi), p 386, *infra*.   [79] See section 1(H), p 374, *infra*.

[80] Ibid, s 20(1), as amended by the Mental Capacity Act 2005, Sch 6, para 41.

[81] Ibid, s 20(2), as likewise amended.

a written direction to appoint by writing the person or persons specified in the direction to be a trustee or trustees in place of the incapable trustee.

For the purposes of the above provisions, the direction may be a single direction given by all, or individual directions given by each; of course, in the latter case, they must specify the same persons.[82] These provisions can be excluded (in whole or in part) in any disposition on or after 1 January 1997 creating the trust.[83] They may also be excluded in a pre-1997 trust by an irrevocable deed to that effect executed by the settlor (or, if more than one settlor, such as are alive and of full capacity).[84]

(E) APPOINTMENT BY DONEE OF AN ENDURING POWER OF ATTORNEY OR A LASTING POWER OF ATTRONEY

The donee of an enduring power of attorney[85] created after the commencement of the Trustee Delegation Act 1999[86] was given a new, but limited, power to appoint new trustees. These provisions were designed to prevent the 'two trustee' rules[87] from frustrating the new power for an attorney under an enduring power of attorney to exercise the trustee functions of the donor, as provided by s 1 of the 1999 Act. For example, A holds land for himself and B. A appoints X as his attorney under an enduring power. A loses mental capacity and the power is registered. X wants to sell the land, but cannot satisfy the 'two trustee' rules unless a new trustee is appointed.

An attorney who intends to exercise a trustee function in relation to land, the capital proceeds of a conveyance of land, or income from land under s 1 of the 1999 Act, s 25 of the Trustee Act 1925, or the instrument creating the trust, may appoint a new, additional trustee if the attorney is either both a trustee and an attorney under a registered power of attorney for the other trustee or trustees (to a maximum of two), or an attorney under a registered power for all of the trustees (to a maximum of three).[88] A 'registered power' means an enduring power of attorney or a lasting power of attorney registered under the Mental Capacity Act 2005.[89] The power may be excluded or limited by the instrument creating the power of attorney or in the instrument creating the trust.[90]

The Mental Capacity Act 2005 repealed the Enduring Powers of Attorney Act 1985.[91] It introduced a lasting power of attorney,[92] in effect replacing an enduring power of attorney. Existing enduring powers of attorney, however, continue to exist, but become governed by the provisions in Sch 4 to the 2005 Act, and are capable of registration under that Act. The definition of a 'registered power' is amended so as to include both an enduring power of attorney and a lasting power of attorney registered under the 2005 Act,[93] and the above provisions[94] accordingly apply to both.

---

[82] Ibid, s 21(1), (2). [83] Ibid, s 21(5). [84] Ibid, s 21(6)–(8).
[85] See the Enduring Powers of Attorney Act 1985 (repealed).
[86] That is, 1 March 2000; Trustee Delegation Act 1999, s 8(2). [87] See p 367, infra.
[88] Trustee Act 1925, s 36(6A), (6B), inserted by the Trustee Delegation Act 1999, s 8(1).
[89] Trustee Act 1925, s 36(6C), inserted by the Trustee Delegation Act 1999, s 8(1) and amended by the Mental Capacity Act 2005.
[90] Trustee Act 1925, s 36(6D), likewise inserted.
[91] Mental Capacity Act 2005 s 67(2), Sch 7. There are transitional provisions and savings in Sch 5, Pt 2.
[92] Ibid, ss 9–14 and Sch 1. See p 458, infra. [93] The amendments are made by s 67(1), Sch 6, para 3.
[94] That is, those contained in the Trustee Act 1925, s 36(6A), (6B).

(F) APPOINTMENT BY THE COURT

(i) Under the statutory power contained in the Trustee Act 1925

Section 41(1)[95] of the Act provides as follows:

> The court[96] may,[97] whenever it is expedient to appoint a new trustee or new trustees, and it is found inexpedient difficult or impracticable so to do without the assistance of the court, make an order appointing a new trustee or new trustee either in substitution for or in addition to any existing trustee or trustees, or although there is no existing trustee.
>
> In particular and without prejudice to the generality of the foregoing provision, the court may make an order appointing a new trustee in substitution for a trustee who lacks capacity to exercise his functions as trustee, or is a bankrupt, or is a corporation that is in liquidation or has been dissolved.[98]

Cases in which the court has made an appointment under the statutory power, apart from those specifically referred to in the section, include: where all of the named trustees predeceased the testator;[99] where no trustees were named;[100] where a trustee had gone abroad with the intention of residing there permanently;[101] where a trustee was incapable of acting by reason of old age, and consequent bodily and mental infirmity;[102] where a trustee was, so far as was known, in enemy-occupied territory;[103] where there was a doubt as to whether the statutory, or an express, power of appointment was exercisable;[104] where the persons who should have exercised a power of appointment,[105] or one of them in the case of a joint power,[106] were resident abroad; where an infant had been nominated to appoint new trustees, because although an appointment by an infant may not be void, it is at least liable to be set aside and, accordingly, it would not be safe to act upon it;[107] and where there was friction between trustees, there being no dispute as to the facts, even though this involved removing a trustee against her will.[108]

There are authorities suggesting that the court will not, under s 41, interfere with an appointment of new trustees by a person having the statutory or an express power to do so,[109] even on an application by all of the beneficiaries,[110] and even though the person with

---

[95] As amended by the Mental Health Act 1959, s 149(1) and Sch 7, Pt I, and the Criminal Law Act 1967, s 10 and Sch 3, Pt III, and the Mental Capacity Act 2005, s 67(1) and Sch 6, para 3.

[96] Defined in s 67(1). It normally means the High Court, or, where the estate or fund subject to the trust does not exceed £30,000, the county court: see p 5, fn 14, *supra.*

[97] The court delayed making an appointment in *Re Pauling's Settlement (No 2)* [1963] Ch 576, [1963] 1 All ER 857 in order to protect the old trustees against possible liability for costs and estate duty.

[98] It has been held on similar provisions in Australia that although a trustee who becomes bankrupt will be removed almost as of course, in its discretion the court will not replace a corporate trustee in liquidation as a matter of course, but will approach the question with an open mind and assess where the balance of interest lies: *Wells v Wily* [2004] NSWSC 607, (2004) 83 FLR 284.

[99] *Re Smirthwaite's Trusts* (1871) LR 11 Eq 251.   [100] *Re Gillett's Trusts* (1876) 25 WR 23.

[101] *Re Bignold's Settlement Trusts* (1872) 7 Ch App 223.

[102] *Re Lemann's Trusts* (1883) 22 Ch D 633; *Re Phelps' Settlement Trusts* (1885) 31 Ch D 351, CA; *Re Weston's Trusts* [1898] WN 151.   [103] *Re May's Will Trusts* [1941] Ch 109.

[104] *Re Woodgate's Settlement* (1956) 5 WR 448; *Re Bignold's Settlement Trusts, supra.*

[105] *Re Humphry's Estate* (1855) 1 Jur NS 921.   [106] *Re Somerset* [1887] WN 122.

[107] *Re Parsons* [1940] Ch 973, [1940] 4 All ER 65; and see (1941) 57 LQR 25 (R E Megarry).

[108] *Re Henderson* [1940] Ch 764, [1940] 3 All ER 295. Cf *Letterstedt v Broers* (1884) 9 App Cas 371, PC.

[109] *Re Higginbottom* [1892] 3 Ch 132; *Re Brockbank* [1948] Ch 206, [1948] 1 All ER 287; *Re Merry* [2003] WTLR 424 (Canada). *Aliter,* where the donee of the power is an infant: *Re Parsons, supra.*

[110] But see, now, s 19 of the Trusts of Land and Appointment of Trustees Act, discussed p 366, *supra.*

the power of appointment may have intended to exercise it corruptly.[111] An Australian court has held,[112] however, it is thought rightly, that a court is not deprived of its statutory power to appoint a new trustee where there are circumstances that render it expedient to do so simply because there is an appointor who is capable of appointing and is willing to act. The exercise of the power will depend on a number of other circumstances as to whether it is expedient to make an appointment.

Even a decree for administration of the trusts by the court does not take away a power of appointing new trustees, although, after decree, the exercise of the power is subject to the supervision of the court.[113] In such case, if the person with the power of appointment nominates a fit and proper person, he must be appointed and the court will not appoint another person whom it might think more suitable. If, however, the court does not approve of the person nominated, it will call for a fresh nomination. Persistent nomination of unsuitable persons would, however, amount to a refusal to appoint and the court would then make its own choice.[114]

The exercise by the court of its power to appoint trustees under s 41 frequently involves the removal of an existing trustee, possibly against his will. This section, however, as a matter of construction, does not empower the court simply to discharge a trustee, unless at the same time it reappoints the continuing trustees in place of themselves and the retiring trustee. This, however, the court will not do in practice, either from want of jurisdiction or from a refusal to exercise it.[115]

It should be observed that s 41(4) provides in express terms that 'nothing in this section gives power to appoint an executor or administrator',[116] although the section will, of course, apply if the personal representative has become a trustee.[117] The court has now, however, been given a wide jurisdiction to appoint substituted personal representatives under s 50 of the Administration of Justice Act 1985.[118]

(ii) Under its inherent jurisdiction

Prior to the Trustee Act 1850, the court had no statutory power to appoint new trustees, but appointments were commonly made by the Court of Chancery under its inherent jurisdiction to supervise trusts and trustees.[119] There was nothing in the Act of 1850 or in the subsequent legislation replacing it to take away this jurisdiction. The statutory power should, however, be invoked if it is available and, in view of the wide wording of s 41, it is

---

[111] *Re Hodson's Settlement* (1851) 9 Hare 118. The abuse could, however, be dealt with by the court under its inherent jurisdiction in an action to restrain the corrupt exercise of the power and for the execution of the trusts by the court.

[112] *Pope v DRP Nominees Pty Ltd* (1999) 74 SASR 78.

[113] The last proposition only applies when there has been a general administration order; it does not apply to an order for partial administration, unless an enquiry is ordered as to the appointment of new trustees, or proceedings are taken for this purpose: *Re Cotter* [1915] 1 Ch 307.

[114] *Re Gadd* (1883) 23 Ch D 134, CA; *Tempest v Lord Camoys* (1882) 21 Ch D 571, CA; *Re Norris* (1884) 27 Ch D 333. See *Yusuof bin Ahmad bin Talib v Hong Kong Bank Trustees (Singapore) Ltd* (1989) 3 MLJ 84.

[115] *Re Chetwynd's Settlement* [1902] 1 Ch 692. See also *Re Dewhirst's Trusts* (1886) 33 Ch D 416, CA; *Re Gardiner's Trusts* (1886) 33 Ch D 590.

[116] The court has such power in some circumstances under the Supreme Court Act 1981, now renamed the Senior Courts Act 1981, s 114(4), and the Administration of Estates Act 1925, s 23(2).

[117] See p 40, *supra*.   [118] See p 40, *supra*.

[119] See, eg, *Buchanan v Hamilton* (1801) 5 Ves 722; *Ockleston v Heap* (1847) 1 De G & Sm 640.

seldom necessary to rely on the inherent jurisdiction,[120] unless it is desired to remove a trustee against his will and there is a dispute as to the facts.[121]

(iii) Under the Trustee Act 1925, s 54

This section[122] provides that where a person lacks capacity to exercise his functions as a trustee and a deputy is appointed for him by the Court of Protection, or an application for the appointment of a deputy has been made, but not determined, then, except as regards a trust that is being administered by the High Court, the Court of Protection will have concurrent jurisdiction with the High Court in relation to, inter alia, matters consequent on the making of provision by the Court of Protection for the exercise of a power of appointing trustees or retiring from a trust. Subject to this, the Court of Protection will not be permitted to make an order, or give a direction or authority, in relation to a person who lacks capacity to exercise his functions as trustee, if the High Court may make an order to that effect under the 2005 Act.

(iv) Under the Judicial Trustees Act 1896 and the Public Trustee Act 1906

These statutes are considered in section 4.

(v) Effect of appointment by the court

The Trustee Act 1925, s 43, provides:

> Every trustee appointed by a court of competent jurisdiction shall, as well before as after the trust property becomes by law, or by assurance, or otherwise, vested in him, have the same powers, authorities, and discretions, and may in all respects act as if he had been originally appointed a trustee by the instrument, if any, creating the trust.

(G) THE PERSONS WHO MAY BE APPOINTED TRUSTEE

(i) General

So far as legal capacity is concerned, in general,[123] any person who has capacity to hold property has capacity to be a trustee. There are however, statutory disqualifications in relation to charity trustees,[124] and trustees of an occupational pension scheme established under a trust.[125] The Crown, it seems, can be a trustee[126]—at any rate, if it deliberately

---

[120] *Dodkin v Brunt* (1868) LR 6 Eq 580, in which the court relied on the inherent jurisdiction.

[121] See p 384, *infra.*

[122] As substituted by the Mental Health Act 1959, s 149(1), and Sch 7, Pt I, and amended by the Mental Capacity Act 2005, s 67(1)(2), Schs 6, 7, and the Constitutional Reform Act 2006, s 12(2), Sch 1.

[123] As to aliens, see the Status of Aliens Act 1914, s 17, as amended by the British Nationality Act 1948. There are limitations on capacity as to ships and aircraft. As to ships, see the Merchant Shipping Act 1995 and SI 1993/3138, as amended by SI 1994/541, and as to aircraft, SI 2000/1562, art 4(3).

[124] See p 293, *supra.*

[125] Pensions Act 1995, ss 29, 30, as amended. See also ss 3–6, as amended, as to prohibition from being, or suspending, such a trustee by the Occupational Pensions Regulatory Authority.

[126] *Penn v Lord Baltimore* (1750) 1 Ves Sen 444, 453, *per* Hardwicke LC; *Lonrho Exports Ltd v Export Credits Guarantee Department* [1996] 2 Lloyd's Rep 645, 659. As to an officer of state, see *Town Investments Ltd v Department of the Environment* [1978] AC 359, [1977] 1 All ER 813, HL.

chooses to act as such[127]—but, in practice, should never be appointed a trustee if only by reason of the doubts and difficulties in enforcing the trust.[128] A local authority cannot be a trustee of an ecclesiastical charity or a charity for the relief of poverty.[129] A minor cannot be validly appointed a trustee either of real or personal property,[130] although it seems that he can hold property, other than a legal estate in land,[131] upon a resulting, implied, or constructive trust.[132]

Where an appointment of a new trustee is made by the court, it will be guided by certain rules in deciding who should be appointed. The Court of Appeal, in *Re Tempest*,[133] set out three principles:

(a) that, in selecting a person for the office of trustee, the court will have regard to the wishes of the author of the trust, expressed in, or plainly deduced from, the instrument containing it;

(b) that the court will not appoint a person with a view to the interest of some of the beneficiaries, in opposition to the interest of others;

(c) that the court will have regard to the question of whether the appointment will promote or impede the execution of the trust.

It appears from the same case, however, that the mere fact that a continuing trustee refuses to act with a proposed new trustee would not be sufficient to induce the court to refrain from appointing him. A more recent case[134] suggests a fourth principle—namely, that the court should not appoint a person who would be in a position where there would be a conflict between his duty and his interest.

In applying these principles, the courts have held that certain categories of persons will not normally be appointed trustees, although in every case 'the rule is not imperative, and when there are special circumstances, the court will exercise its discretion in judging whether the case is one in which the rule may be departed from'.[135] Thus neither the tenant for life, nor any other beneficiary, will normally be appointed.[136] If, perhaps because it is impossible to obtain the services of an independent trustee,[137] beneficiaries are appointed, an undertaking may be required in some such form as in *Re Lightbody's Trusts*,[138] in which two beneficiaries were appointed trustees, and they were required to undertake that if either of them were to become a sole trustee, he would use every endeavour to obtain the

---

[127] *Civilian War Claimants Association Ltd v R* [1932] AC 14, 27, HL, *per* Lord Atkin. Note, however, that circumstances that may at first sight appear to constitute the Crown as a trustee may well be explicable by reference to the governmental powers and obligations of the Crown, and may not set up a true trust at all: *Tito v Waddell (No 2)* [1977] Ch 106, [1977] 3 All ER 129, and see p 74, *supra*.

[128] See *Dyson v A-G* [1911] 1 KB 410, CA; *Esquimalt and Nanaimo Rly Co v Wilson* [1920] AC 358, PC; Hanbury, *Essays in Equity*, pp 87–89; Holdsworth, *History of English Law*, vol IX, pp 30–32.

[129] Local Government Act 1972, s 139(3).   [130] Law of Property Act 1925, s 20.

[131] Compare Law of Property Act 1925, s 1(6).   [132] *Re Vinogradoff* [1935] WN 68.

[133] (1866) 1 Ch App 485.   [134] *Re Parsons* [1940] Ch 973, [1940] 4 All ER 65.

[135] *Ex p Conybeare's Settlement* (1853) 1 WR 458, *per* Turner LJ.

[136] *Ex p Conybeare's Settlement*, *supra*; *Re Clissold's Settlement* (1864) 10 LT 642; *Forster v Abraham* (1874) LR 17 Eq 351.

[137] Since the Public Trustee Act 1906, it may be possible to appoint the Public Trustee (but see pp 389, 446, *infra*), or a trust corporation or other professional trustee may be appointed: see p 393, and 442–444, *infra*, as to their remuneration.

[138] (1884) 52 LT 40. Similarly, in *Re Parrott* (1881) 30 WR 97 (husband of tenant for life).

appointment of a co-trustee. Further, the court will not normally appoint the husband of a tenant for life;[139] indeed, it has been said that no near relative of parties interested should be appointed except in cases of absolute necessity.[140] This dictum was applied by an Australian court in *Re John Albert Roberts*,[141] in which the Public Trustee was trustee of the deceased's estate for the widow and their children. The court refused, on the widow's application, to appoint her as trustee in substitution for the Public Trustee. The same rule applies to the solicitor of the tenant for life, or, presumably for any other of the beneficiaries,[142] to a solicitor of an existing trustee,[143] and to the partner of an existing solicitor-trustee. It may be noticed that there is no principle that would prevent a bank from being appointed a trustee merely because one or all of the beneficiaries happen to be customers of the bank, but the special facts may justify the court in refusing to appoint a particular bank, where, for example, the trustee has a discretionary power to advance to the life tenant out of capital, and the life tenant has a large overdraft with the bank proposed as trustee.[144]

It is generally said that the donee of a power of appointment should, in making his appointment, be guided by the same principles as would guide the court. In practice, however, persons whom the court would not normally appoint are frequently appointed and the court will not normally upset such appointment.[145] Again, it has been said that it is the duty of a trustee to consult beneficiaries before appointing a new trustee,[146] but although it is a desirable and usual practice to do so, the duty seems to be unenforceable, because, as has been seen,[147] the court will not normally interfere with an appointment made by a person having power to do so, even at the instance of all of the beneficiaries.

In conclusion, it may be observed that the settlor himself is, of course, legally quite uninhibited in the choice of the original trustees, and the same appears to be the case where beneficiaries direct the appointment of trustees under the Trusts of Land and Appointment of Trustees Act 1996.[148] In practice, however, this is a vital matter, and the choice of the trustees will affect the smooth running of the trusts and the safety of the interests of the beneficiaries. Qualities to be looked for include integrity, a willingness to spend time and trouble on the trust affairs, the ability to get on with co-trustees and beneficiaries, knowledge of financial matters, business acumen, and common sense, and Megarry VC has observed that there are some who are temperamentally unsuited to being trustees.[149]

---

[139] *Re Parrott* (1881) 30 WR 97; *Re Coode* (1913) 108 LT 94.

[140] *Wilding v Bolder* (1855) 21 Beav 222; see *Re Parsons, supra.*   [141] (1983) 70 Fed LR 158.

[142] *Re Spencer's Settled Estates* [1903] 1 Ch 75; *Re Cotter* [1915] 1 Ch 307.

[143] *Re Norris* (1884) 27 Ch D 333, in which a solicitor trustee appointed his son and partner as co-trustee. The trusts were being administered by the court and the court refused to sanction the appointment.

[144] *Re Northcliffe's Settlements* [1937] 3 All ER 804, CA. Cf *Re Pauling's Settlement Trusts* [1964] Ch 303, [1963] 3 All ER 1, CA.

[145] *Re Earl of Stamford* [1896] 1 Ch 288 (solicitor of tenant for life); *Re Coode* (1913) 108 LT 94 (husband of tenant for life); *Re Norris, supra* (as to the appointment of a father and son, solicitors in partnership). As to the case in which the donee of the power of appointment is an infant, see *Re Parsons* [1940] Ch 973, [1940] 4 All ER 65; (1941) 57 LQR 25 (R E Megarry).

[146] *O'Reilly v Alderson* (1849) 8 Hare 101.   [147] See p 368, *supra.*

[148] Section 19. See section 1(D), *supra.*

[149] *Cowan v Scargill* [1985] Ch 270, [1984] 2 All ER 750. See (1988) 2 TL & P 86 (C Bell).

(ii) Exporting a trust

The power of the court to supervise a trust and give a remedy for breach of trust depends upon the trustees being within the jurisdiction of the court: the court acts *in personam*. If, therefore, trustees within the jurisdiction are replaced as trustees by persons who are outside the jurisdiction, the court ceases to be able to deal with the trust. This is referred to as 'exporting', or sometimes 'emigrating', a trust. Because of the effect that it has, persons outside the jurisdiction should not, therefore, normally be appointed. However, it is well established that there is no absolute bar to the appointment of persons resident abroad as trustees of an English trust. In *Re Whitehead's Will Trusts*,[150] Pennycuick J held that the court would only make such an appointment in exceptional circumstances, and said that it would not be right for donees of a power to do so out of court save in like exceptional circumstances. If they were to do so, presumably the court would be likely to interfere at the instance of beneficiaries. The most obvious exceptional circumstances are where the beneficiaries have settled permanently in some country outside the United Kingdom and what is proposed is to appoint new trustees in that country.[151] The court, however, refused to appoint trustees resident in Jersey in *Re Weston's Settlements*,[152] in which the appointment was sought as part of a tax avoidance scheme that would have involved removing the trusts from England to Jersey.

In *Richard v Mackay*,[153] Millett J considered that the language of Pennycuick J in *Re Whitehead's Will Trust*[154] was too restrictive for the circumstances of the present day. Although, when the court is invited to exercise an original discretion of its own, the applicants must make out a positive case for the court to exercise discretion as they request, it is a different matter where the transaction is proposed to be carried out by the trustees in the exercise of their discretion, entirely out of court, and the trustees merely seek the authorization of the court for their own protection. In that case, the court is concerned to ensure that the proposed exercise of the trustees' power is lawful and within the power, and that it does not infringe the trustees' duty to act as ordinary, reasonable, and prudent trustees might act, but it requires only to be satisfied that the trustees can properly form the view that the proposed transaction is for the benefit of beneficiaries or the trust estate. On the facts, the proposed export of about a quarter of the trust funds to a proposed similar trust in Bermuda was lawful. This approach was approved by Vinelott J in *Re Beatty's Will Trusts (No 2)*,[155] and the proposed export of the trust regarded as acceptable, although one of the three principal beneficiaries was to continue to be domiciled and resident in the United Kingdom.

(iii) Trustees of a trust for religious purposes

In the case of a charitable trust for religious purposes, in general, only members of the church, denomination, or sect in question will be appointed. It has been held in New Zealand,[156] and the law is probably the same in England, that there is no absolute rule and the court has an unfettered discretion when it is called upon to act.[157]

---

[150] [1971] 2 All ER 1334, [1971] 1 WLR 833. See Matthews, *Trusts: Migration and Change of Proper Law*.
[151] *Re Whitehead's Will Trust, supra.*   [152] [1969] 1 Ch 223, [1968] 3 All ER 338, CA.
[153] (1987), unreported until (1997) 11 Tru LI 23.
[154] *Supra.* See *Royal Society for the Protection of Animals v A-G* [2001] 3 All ER 530.
[155] (1987), unreported until (1997) 11 Tru LI 77.
[156] *Mendelssohn v Centrepoint Community Growth Trust* [1999] 2 NZLR 88. The relevant statutory provisions are similar.   [157] That is, under the Trustee Act 1925, s 41, discussed p 368, *supra*.

(H) THE NUMBER OF TRUSTEES

Apart from statute, on the one hand, a sole trustee can act effectively, while, on the other hand, there is no limit to the number of trustees who may be appointed. Statutory provisions, however, impose limitations in many cases on both the maximum and minimum number of trustees.

(i) Maximum number of trustees

Section 34(2) of the Trustee Act 1925, as amended by the Trusts of Land and Appointment of Trustees Act 1996, provides as follows:

In the case of settlements[158] and dispositions creating trusts of land[159] ... —

(a) the number of trustees thereof shall not in any case exceed four, and where more than four persons are named as such trustees, the four first named (who are able and willing to act) shall alone be the trustees, and the other persons named shall not be trustees unless appointed on the occurrence of a vacancy;

(b) the number of the trustees shall not be increased beyond four.

It should be noted that this subsection is in terms restricted to settlements and dispositions creating trusts of land,[160] and accordingly does not apply to trusts of pure personalty; further, subs (3) provides that the restrictions on the number of trustees do not apply:

(a) in the case of land vested in trustees for charitable, ecclesiastical, or public[161] purposes;[162] or

(b) where the net proceeds of the sale of the land are held for like purposes; or

(c) to the trustees of a term of years absolute limited by a settlement on trusts for raising money, or of a like term created under the statutory remedies[163] relating to annual sums charged on land.

On the appointment of a trustee, the number of trustees may, subject to the above restrictions, be increased.[164] However, where an additional trustee or additional trustees is or are appointed under the provisions of s 36(6) of the Trustee Act 1925,[165] the number of trustees cannot be increased beyond four, whether or not the trust involves land.

---

[158] Defined in Trustee Act 1925, s 68(1)(15), and Settled Land Act 1925, s 1(1), as amended.

[159] Defined in ibid, s 68(1)(6), as amended by the Trusts of Land and Appointment of Trustees Act 1996.

[160] See also s 34(3), where, however, the words 'creating trusts' would appear to have been omitted after the word 'disposition'. The section applies to appointments under s 19 of the Trusts of Land and Appointment of Trustees Act 1996: ibid, s 19(3).

[161] Trusts of land belonging to an unincorporated society coming within the provisions of the Literary and Scientific Institutions Act 1854 are public trusts: *Re Cleveland Literary and Philosophical Society's Land* [1931] 2 Ch 247.

[162] No land held on such trusts is or is deemed to be settled land: Trusts of Land and Appointment of Trustees Act 1996, s 2(5). This Act repealed (with savings) and reversed the previous position in the Settled Land Act 1925, s 29(1).

[163] See Law of Property Act 1925, s 121, as amended, and further prospectively amended by the Tribunals, Courts and Enforcement Act 2007.

[164] Trustee Act 1925, s 37(1)(a), which appears to apply to appointments under both an express and the statutory power. As to the latter, s 36(1) by itself would seem to have the same result.

[165] See p 365, *supra*.

(ii) Minimum number of trustees

Obviously, as a result of deaths of trustees, the number may be reduced to one, or, indeed, to none at all,[166] and legislation cannot prevent this happening. There are, however, two sets of relevant provisions.

Firstly, in some cases, it is provided that, for some purposes, a sole trustee (not being a trust corporation)[167] cannot act effectively. The 'two trustee' rules, as they are sometimes called, require that, save where a sole trustee is a trust corporation:

(a) capital moneys arising from land must be paid to, or at the direction of, at least two trustees;[168]

(b) a valid recept for such capital moneys must be given otherwise than by a sole trustee;[169] and

(c) a conveyance or deed must be made by at least two trustees to overreach any powers or interests affecting a legal estate in land.[170]

These provisions apply notwithstanding anything to the contrary contained in the relevant instruments.

Secondly, the better view, it is submitted, is that, provided that no contrary intention was expressed in the power of appointment, equity did not insist upon the original number of trustees being maintained. Accordingly, on the appointment of new trustees, the number of trustees might be increased[171] or reduced.[172] It followed that there was, in general, no obligation to keep up the number of trustees and where, as was commonly the case, the power of appointment was vested in the continuing trustees, failure to replace the trustees who ceased for any reason to hold office was not normally a breach of trust. This was carried to the limit by the Court of Appeal, which held, in *Peacock v Colling*,[173] that—at any rate, where the will contemplated a sole trustee acting—a sole continuing trustee was justified in refusing to appoint a second trustee, and consequently his failure to do so was not a breach of trust.

There are now statutory provisions[174] to the effect that, on the appointment of a trustee,[175] it shall not be obligatory:

(a) subject to the provisions discussed above,[176] to appoint more than one trustee where only one trustee was originally appointed; or

---

[166] But note Trustee Act 1925, s 18(2), discussed at p 383, *infra*.

[167] See section 4(E), p 393, *infra*.

[168] Settled Land Act 1925, ss 18(1)(c), 94(1); Law of Property Act 1925, s 27(2), as substituted by the Law of Property (Amendment) Act 1926, and amended by the Trusts of Land and Appointment of Trustees Act 1996.

[169] Trustee Act 1925, s 14(2), as amended by the Trusts of Land and Appointment of Trustees Act 1996.

[170] Law of Property Act 1925, s 2(1), (2), as amended by the Trusts of Land and Appointment of Trustees Act 1996.

[171] *Meinertzhagen v Davis* (1844) 1 Coll 335. See now Trustee Act 1925, s 37(1)(a).

[172] *Emmet v Clark* (1861) 3 Giff 32; *Re Cunningham and Bradley's Contract for Sale to Wilson* [1877] WN 258 (the statement in this case that there is a different rule in relation to charity trustees seems to be ill-founded: see *Re Worcester Charities* (1847) 2 Ph 284; *Re Shrewsbury Charities* (1849) 1 Mac & G 84).

[173] (1885) 53 LT 620, CA. Cf *Re Rendell's Trusts* (1915) 139 LT Jo 249.

[174] Trustee Act 1925, s 37(1)(c), as amended by the Trusts of Land and Appointment of Trustees Act 1996, Sch 3, para 12. [175] Presumably, under either an express or the statutory power.

[176] See also Trustee Act 1925, s 37(2), which provides 'Nothing in this Act shall authorise the appointment of a sole trustee, not being a trust corporation, where the trustee, when appointed, would not be able to give valid receipts for all capital money arising under the trust'.

(b) to fill up the original number of trustees where more than two trustees were
     originally appointed.

The same section[177] further provides, however, that:

> except where only one trustee was originally appointed, and a sole trustee when appointed
> will be able to give valid receipts for all capital money,[178] a trustee shall not be discharged
> from his trust unless there will be either a trust corporation or at least two persons[179] to
> act as trustees to perform the trust.

A sole surviving trustee even of pure personalty, accordingly, cannot retire from the trust
and appoint a sole trustee (not being a trust corporation) to act in his stead where more
than one trustee was originally appointed, and, in many cases a sole trustee, even though
he may be the first and only trustee originally appointed, is in the same position.[180] It has
been held,[181] however, that s 37(1)(c) can be overridden by a provision in the trust instrument since it is ancillary to s 36, which can certainly be overridden under s 69(2),[182] and as
consolidating legislation could not change the underlying law.

(iii) Appointment by the court

The court has always had power and now has statutory jurisdiction under s 41 of the Trustee
Act 1925 to increase the number of trustees on an appointment of new trustees,[183] or by
appointing an additional trustee or trustees where there is no vacancy.[184] An appointment
by the court is commonly made at the request of one or more of the beneficiaries, but
although it has been held in some cases that a beneficiary was entitled to have a second,[185]
or even a third,[186] trustee appointed, it is doubtful whether, in strictness, even all of the
beneficiaries acting together have an absolute right to require the appointment of even a
second trustee.[187] Again, the court has always had power to reduce the number of trustees
and, on the appointment of new trustees, may do so under the statutory jurisdiction,[188]
even in disregard of directions contained in the trust deed,[189] although it is not likely to
take this course without special circumstances being established.[190] As we have seen,[191]
the court either cannot, or will not, under the statutory jurisdiction, reduce the number of

---

[177] Ibid, s 37(1)(c).   [178] That is, where there is a trust of pure personalty.

[179] Prior to the 1996 Act, the subsection referred to 'individuals', which word has been held not to include
corporate trustees: *Jasmine Trustees Ltd v Wells & Hind (a firm)* [2007] EWHC 38 (Ch), [2007] 1 All ER 1142,
[2007] 3 WLR 810, noted [2007] PCB 347, 442 (Judith Harrison and Carolyn O'Sullivan).

[180] That is, where a sole trustee, when appointed, will be unable to give valid receipts for all capital
money.

[181] *London Regional Transport Pension Fund Trustee Co Ltd v Hatt* [1993] PLR 227, on this point, but relevant part of judgment cited and discussed by M Jacobs in (1993) 7 Tru LI 72.

[182] See p 359, *supra*.

[183] See, eg, *Birch v Cropper* (1848) 2 De G & Sm 255; *Plenty v West* (1853) 16 Beav 356.

[184] See, eg, *Grant v Grant* (1865) 34 LJ Ch 641; *Re Gregson's Trusts* (1886) 34 Ch D 209.

[185] *Grant v Grant, supra*.   [186] *Viscountess D'Adhemar v Bertrand* (1865) 35 Beav 19.

[187] *Re Badger's Settlement* (1915) 113 LT 150. But the position may be different since 1925 where there is
a sole trustee who cannot give a valid receipt for capital moneys, and see now s 19 of the Trusts of Land and
Appointment of Trustees Act 1996 discussed p 366, *supra*.

[188] *Re Fowler's Trusts* (1886) 55 LT 546; *Re Leslie's Hassop Estates* [1911] 1 Ch 611.

[189] *Re Leslie's Hassop Estates, supra*.   [190] *Re Fowler's Trusts* (1886) 55 LT 546.

[191] See p 369, *supra*.

trustees save on the appointment of new trustees, although it has inherent jurisdiction to do so in an action to administer the trust.

In deciding how many trustees should be appointed, the court will, of course, comply with the restriction limiting the number of trustees to four, in those cases in which s 34 of the Trustee Act 1925 applies, and, in practice, will never appoint a sole trustee where such trustee would not be able to give a valid receipt for capital moneys. Quite apart from statutory provisions, there are obvious dangers in the trust property being under the control of a sole trustee and, consequently, it has been said[192] that 'the court never commits a trust to the care of a single trustee, even in cases where no more than one was originally appointed'; one judge even affirmed[193] 'I do not think it right to leave it to two'. It seems, however, that although the court is reluctant to appoint a single trustee,[194] it will do so if special circumstances would make it more beneficial to the parties interested:[195] for instance, where the trust fund is small and shortly to be distributed, and the appointment of a second trustee would incur disproportionate expense.

(I) SEPARATE SETS OF TRUSTEES FOR DISTINCT TRUSTS

On an appointment[196] out of court of a trustee for the whole or any part of trust property, s 37(1)(b) of the Trustee Act 1925 provides:

> a separate set of trustees, not exceeding four, may be appointed for any part of the trust property held on trusts distinct from those relating to any other part or parts of the trust property, notwithstanding that no new trustees or trustee are or is to be appointed for other parts of the trust property, and any existing trustee may be appointed or remain one of such separate set of trustees, or, if only one trustee was originally appointed, then, save as hereinafter provided,[197] one separate trustee may be so appointed.

The section apparently applies in a case in which different parts of the trust property are for the time being held on distinct trusts, even though, upon a certain event, the trusts may ultimately coalesce.[198]

On an appointment of new trustees by the court,[199] it has always been possible for separate sets of trustees to be appointed for different parts of the trust property held on distinct trusts,[200] although applications to the court are now much less common by reason of the existence of the statutory power just mentioned.

---

[192] *Per* Romilly MR in *Viscountess D'Adhemar v Bertrand* (1865) 35 Beav 19, 20.

[193] *Bulkeley v Earl of Eglinton, supra,* at 994, *per* Page Wood VC. This statement goes too far.

[194] That is, an individual as opposed to a trust corporation.

[195] *Sitwell v Heron* (1850) 14 Jur 848; *Re Reynault* (1852) 16 Jur 233.

[196] Presumably, under either an express or the statutory power.

[197] By sub-s (2), set out *supra*, p 375, in fn 176.   [198] *Re Hetherington's Trusts* (1886) 34 Ch D 211.

[199] It is not clear whether the Trustee Act 1925, s 37, applies to an appointment by the court, although it seems to have been assumed that the original provision in s 5 of the Conveyancing Act 1881 did so apply in *Re Paine's Trusts* (1885) 28 Ch D 725; *Re Hetherington's Trusts, supra.* But see *Re Moss' Trusts* (1888) 37 Ch D 513.

[200] See, eg, the cases cited in fn 199, *supra.*

(J) LIABILITY[201] OF THE ORIGINAL TRUSTEES AND THE PURPORTED NEW TRUSTEES UNDER AN INVALID APPOINTMENT

If a purported appointment of new trustees in place of existing trustees is invalid, the existing trustees remain trustees and will be liable as such in case there is any loss to the trust estate, even though they act upon the assumption that the appointment was valid and take no further part in the administration of the trust. A purported new trustee under the invalid appointment may also be liable as a trustee *de son tort* if he, on the like assumption, has acted in the trust. These propositions are neatly illustrated by *Pearce v Pearce*,[202] in which A and B were trustees. A deed was prepared appointing C a new trustee in the place of B. It was executed by C, but not by the other parties, so that the appointment was invalid. At the same time, the trust fund was transferred by A and B to A and C. Afterwards, A and C authorized the husband of the tenant for life to receive the fund, and it was lost. It was held that both B and C were liable for the loss, in addition, of course, to A.

2 VESTING OF THE TRUST PROPERTY

(A) NEW TRUSTEES

When new trustees are appointed, it is clearly vital that the trust property shall be vested in them jointly with the continuing trustees, if any. Dealing firstly with an appointment out of court, the vesting of the trust property in the new trustees (including any continuing trustees) can be done by means of an ordinary conveyance or transfer by the old trustee or trustees in whom the property is vested, in the form appropriate to the particular kind of trust property. There will not always, however, be a need for this to be done, as, by statute, the trust property is, in many cases, automatically vested in the new and any continuing trustees, provided that the new trustees are appointed by deed.

The relevant provisions are contained in s 40 of the Trustee Act 1925, subs (1) of which is in the following terms:

Where by a deed[203] a new trustee is appointed to perform any trust, then:

(a) if the deed contains a declaration[204] by the appointor to the effect that any estate or interest in any land subject to the trust, or in any chattel so subject, or the right to recover or receive any debt or other thing in action so subject, shall vest in the persons who by virtue of the deed become or are the trustees for performing the trust, the deed shall operate,[205] without any conveyance or assignment, to vest in those persons

---

[201] See, generally, Chapter 23, *infra*, and in particular s 61 of the Trustee Act 1925, discussed section 3(F) of that chapter, p 535, *infra*.   [202] (1856) 22 Beav 248.

[203] An instrument in writing suffices in the case of trustees for a listed trade union: Trade Union and Labour Relations (Consolidation) Act 1992, s 13(1)–(3).

[204] See also subs (3), which deals with the possibility that there may be defects in the form of an express vesting declaration.

[205] Even where the estate, interest, or right is not vested in the person making the appointment. Cf s 9, Law of Property Act 1925. This provision conveniently covers the case in which, for instance, the person who

as joint tenants and for the purposes of the trust the estate interest or right to which the declaration relates; and

(b) if the deed ... does not contain such a declaration, the deed shall, subject to any express provision to the contrary therein contained, operate as if it had contained such a declaration by the appointor extending to all the estates interests and rights with respect to which a declaration could have been made.

There are similar provisions in s 40(2) vesting the trust property in the continuing trustees on the discharge of a trustee under s 39,[206] or under s 19 of the Trusts of Land and Appointment of Trustees Act 1996.[207]

Certain cases are, however, expressly excluded from the operation of the section by sub-s (4) and, unfortunately, they include some of the most usual kinds of trust property.[208] They comprise the following:

(a) land conveyed by way of mortgage for securing money subject to the trust except land conveyed on trust for securing debentures or debenture stock;

(b) land held under a lease[209] which contains any covenant, condition or agreement against assignment or disposing of the land without licence or consent, unless, prior to the execution of the deed containing expressly or impliedly the vesting declaration, the requisite licence or consent has been obtained, or unless, by virtue of any statute or rule of law, the vesting declaration, express or implied, would not operate as a breach of covenant or give rise to a forfeiture;

(c) any share, stock, annuity or property which is only transferable in books kept by a company or other body, or in manner directed by or under an Act of Parliament.

There are special reasons why it is necessary to exclude the implied vesting provisions in each of these cases. In the first case, concerning mortgages, the object is to keep the trusts off the face of the mortgagor's title; trustees who lend money on a mortgage of land do not disclose the fact in the mortgage deed, nor is it disclosed in the transfer of mortgage, which must be executed on the appointment of new trustees.[210] The second case, concerning leases, is to avoid the possibility of an inadvertent breach of covenant, which would render the lease liable to be forfeited. The last case is necessary because the legal title to such property as stocks and shares depends upon the appropriate entry having been made in a register consequent upon the completion of a proper instrument of transfer, and the whole system would break down if the legal title could pass in any other manner. A company deals with the registered shareholder as the legal owner of the shares, and does not recognize the existence of any trust that may affect them.

appoints the new trustees is not himself a trustee. The section presumably does not enable a legal estate outstanding in some third party holding adversely to the trust to be vested in the new trustees, or even, it seems, according to *Re King's Will Trusts* [1964] Ch 542, [1964] 1 All ER 833, where the trustee holds the legal estate in some other capacity, such as personal representative.

[206] Discussed p 384, *infra*.

[207] Discussed p 366, *supra*. Section 19, added to s 40(2), by Sch 3, para 3(14) of the 1996 Act.

[208] Paragraphs (a) and (c) do not apply in the case of trustees for a listed trade union: Trade Union and Labour Relations (Consolidation) Act 1992, s 13(4).

[209] Defined by the subsection to include an underlease and an agreement for a lease or underlease.

[210] See the Law of Property Act 1925, s 113.

(B) VESTING ORDERS

Wide powers to make vesting orders are given to the court under ss 45–56[211] of the Trustee Act 1925. In particular, it is provided that, where the court appoints or has appointed a trustee, or where a trustee has been appointed out of court under any statutory or express power, the court may make a vesting order vesting land or any interest therein in the persons who, on the appointment, are the trustees in any such manner and for any such estate or interest as the court may direct,[212] and may likewise make an order vesting in such persons the right to transfer or call for a transfer of stock, or to receive the dividends or income thereof, or to sue for or recover a thing in action.[213]

It should be mentioned that, by r 6 of the Judicial Trustee Rules 1972, on the appointment of a judicial trustee, the court is required to make such vesting or other orders as may be required for vesting the trust property in the judicial trustee either as sole trustee or jointly with other trustees as the case requires.

3 TERMINATION OF TRUSTEESHIP

(A) DISCLAIMER[214]

A person who is appointed a trustee cannot be compelled to accept the office. He may disclaim[215] the office, which will also amount to a disclaimer of the estate,[216] at any time before acceptance, but once he has accepted it, it cannot thereafter be disclaimed.[217] Acceptance may be either express, or implied from the acts or conduct of the alleged trustee. Execution by the trustee of the trust deed will normally be regarded as an express acceptance of the trust[218] and, where a person is appointed by will to be executor and trustee, it seems that if he takes out probate of the will, he will be treated as having thereby also accepted the trust.[219] It is sometimes said that in the absence of evidence to the contrary, acceptance will be presumed,[220] but the position is far from certain.

Whether, by his conduct, a person is deemed to have accepted the trust depends upon the view that the court takes of the facts of the case.[221] In general, any interference with the

---

[211] A vesting order can only be made in relation to property within the territorial jurisdiction of the court: *Webb v Webb* [1992] 1 All ER 17, [1991] 1 WLR 1410, further proceedings [1994] QB 696, [1994] 3 All ER 911, ECJ.

[212] Trustee Act 1925, s 44. Alternatively, by s 50, if it is more convenient, the court may appoint a person to convey the land or any interest therein.

[213] Trustee Act 1925, s 51, as amended.

[214] The effect of a valid disclaimer is discussed in section 1(A), p 357, *supra*.

[215] At the cost of the trust estate: *Re Tryon* (1844) 7 Beav 496.

[216] *Re Birchall* (1889) 40 Ch D 436, CA.

[217] *Re Sharman's Will Trusts* [1942] Ch 311, [1942] 2 All ER 74, and see *Re Lister* [1926] Ch 149, CA.

[218] *Jones v Higgins* (1866) LR 2 Eq 538.

[219] *Mucklow v Fuller* (1821) Jac 198; *Re Sharman's Will Trust, supra*.

[220] See, eg, Underhill and Hayton, *Law of Trusts and Trustees*, 17th edn, [39.1]—the corresponding statement in an earlier edition was cited with approval in *Re Sharman's Will Trusts* [1942] Ch 311, [1942] 2 All ER 74.

[221] See *White v Barton* (1854) 18 Beav 192.

subject matter of the trust by a person appointed trustee will be regarded as an acceptance of the trust, unless it can clearly be explained on some other ground. Thus, where a man has permitted an action to be brought in the name of himself and the other trustees,[222] or given directions as to the sale of the trust property and made enquiries as to the accounts,[223] he has been held to have accepted the trust. In another case,[224] there was a bequest of £1,100 and certain leasehold property to trustees. The only relevant act of the trustees was an assignment of the leasehold property to a beneficiary who had become absolutely entitled. It was held that the execution of the assignment amounted to an acceptance of the trusts not only of the leasehold property, but also of the sum of £1,100, because there cannot be part acceptance and part disclaimer. Acceptance of part is regarded as acceptance of the whole and, accordingly, prevents a disclaimer of any other parts.[225] Conversely, partial disclaimer is impossible: to be effective, disclaimer must be 'of the totality of the office and estate and ab initio'.[226]

On the other hand, a person appointed a trustee has been held not to have accepted the trust merely by holding the deed for about six months for safe custody;[227] similarly, in another, perhaps rather doubtful, case, in which the alleged trustee had actually signed a legacy duty receipt, which he need not have done if he were not a trustee.[228] Again, the court has sometimes allowed that the dealing with the subject matter of the trust that is alleged to constitute acceptance of the trust was merely carried out in the capacity of agent to a trustee who had accepted,[229] although the court would doubtless be suspicious of such an explanation of his conduct by an alleged trustee.[230]

If the trust has not been accepted, it may be disclaimed, the proper form being by a deed poll.[231] As has been said:[232]

It is most prudent that a deed of disclaimer[233] should be executed by a person named trustee, who refused to accept the trust, because such deed is clear evidence of the disclaimer, and admits of no ambiguity; but there may be conduct which amounts to a clear disclaimer, and such appears to be the case here.

The conduct referred to was that of the alleged trustee, who purchased real property and took a conveyance from one who could only have a title thereto on the basis of a disclaimer having been effected.[234] An effective disclaimer may be made by an alleged trustee in the pleadings in an action brought against him for enforcement of the trust,[235] or even by his counsel at the bar.[236]

---

[222] *Montfort v Cadogan* (1810) 17 Ves 485.   [223] *James v Frearson* (1842) 1 Y & C Ch Cas 370.

[224] *Urch v Walker* (1838) 3 My & Cr 702.

[225] *Re Lord and Fullerton's Contract* [1896] 1 Ch 228, CA.

[226] *Per* Sargant LJ in *Re Lister* [1926] Ch 149, 166, CA.   [227] *Evans v John* (1841) 4 Beav 35.

[228] *Jago v Jago* (1893) 68 LT 654.

[229] *Dove v Everard* (1830) 1 Russ & M 231; *Lowry v Fulton* (1838) 9 Sim 104.

[230] *Conyngham v Conyngham* (1750) 1 Ves Sen 522.

[231] *Re Schar* [1951] Ch 280, [1950] 2 All ER 1069.

[232] *Per* Leach MR in *Stacey v Elph* (1833) 1 My & K 195, 199.

[233] It has been held that what is in form a deed of release, which logically involves a prior acceptance, may operate as a disclaimer if this was the intention: *Nicolson v Wordsworth* (1818) 2 Swan 365.

[234] See also *Re Gordon* (1877) 6 Ch D 531; *Re Birchall* (1889) 40 Ch D 436, CA.

[235] *Norway v Norway* (1834) 2 My & K 278; *Bray v West* (1838) 9 Sim 429.

[236] *Foster v Dawber* (1860) 1 Drew & Sm 172.

Although it has been said[237] that 'a disclaimer, to be worth anything, must be an act whereby one entitled to an estate immediately and before dealing with it renounces it', the better view is that, although a disclaimer ought to be made without delay, there is no rule that it must be executed within any particular time,[238] and in several reported cases, a disclaimer after twenty years or so has been held to be valid.[239] It is submitted that mere inaction by the alleged trustee over a long period may by itself be sufficient evidence of disclaimer, and that the longer the period of inaction, the stronger the presumption of disclaimer.[240]

It has been said that one of several trustees cannot disclaim,[241] but it is submitted, with respect, that this *obiter dictum* cannot stand in the light of numerous cases in which such a disclaimer has been held to be effective,[242] thus making the title of those trustees who do accept valid *ab initio*.

Finally, it should perhaps be mentioned that just as acceptance of a trust makes a subsequent disclaimer impossible, so a valid disclaimer precludes the possibility of a subsequent acceptance.

(B) DEATH

Trustees are invariably joint tenants and, accordingly, on the death of one of two or more trustees, the trust estate, by reason of the *jus accrescendi*, devolves on the surviving trustees or trustee. It is now provided by statute, affirming the equitable rule[243] that the office likewise devolves on the surviving trustees or trustee. The terms of s 18(1) of the Trustee Act 1925 are as follows:

> Where a power or trust is given to or imposed on two or more trustees jointly, the same may be exercised or performed by the survivors or survivor of them for the time being.

It should be remembered that this provision does not abrogate the old rule that a bare power, given to two or more persons by name and not annexed to an estate or office, does not survive.[244] However, it has been said[245] that:

> Every power given to trustees which enables them to deal with or affect the trust property is prima facie given them ex officio as an incident of their office, and passes with the office to the holders or holder thereof for the time being: whether a power is so given ex officio or not depends in each case on the construction of the document giving it, but the mere fact that the power is one requiring the exercise of a very wide personal discretion is not enough to exclude the prima facie presumption . . . ; the testator's reliance on the individuals to the exclusion of the holders of the office for the time being must be expressed in clear and apt language.

---

[237] *Per* Kelly CB in *Bence v Gilpin* (1868) LR 3 Exch 76, 81.   [238] *Jago v Jago* (1893) 68 LT 654.

[239] *Doe d Chidgey v Harris* (1847) 16 M & W 517 (sixteen years); *Peppercorn v Wayman* (1852) 5 De G & Sm 230 (twenty or twenty-one years).

[240] *Re Clout and Frewer's Contract* [1924] 2 Ch 230; *Rajabali Jumabhoy v Ameerali R Jumabhoy* [1997] 3 SLR 802 (Singapore).

[241] *Per* Vaisey J in *Re Schar* [1951] Ch 280, 285, [1950] 2 All ER 1069, 1072.

[242] See, eg, *Peppercorn v Wayman* (1852) 5 De G & Sm 230; *Re Birchall* (1899) 40 Ch D 436, CA. McGarvie J agreed with the view in the text in *J W Broomhead (Vic) Pty Ltd v J W Broomhead Pty Ltd* [1985] VR 891, saying that Vaisey J's opinion is inconsistent with authority.

[243] See, eg, *Warburton v Sandys* (1845) 14 Sim 622.

[244] *Re Harding* [1923] 1 Ch 182, see p 363, *supra*.

[245] *Per* Farwell J in *Re Smith* [1904] 1 Ch 139, 144; *Re De Sommery* [1912] 2 Ch 622.

Upon the death of a sole or last surviving trustee, the trust estate, since 1925, devolves on his personal representatives,[246] and it is provided by s 18(2) of the Trustee Act 1925 that such personal representatives (excluding an executor who has renounced or has not proved)[247] 'shall be capable of exercising or performing any power or trust which was given to, or capable of being exercised by, the sole or last surviving or continuing trustee, or other trustees or trustee for the time being of the trust'. It will be observed that this provision does not impose any obligation on the personal representatives to act, and it would seem therefore that the old law still applies—that is, that 'such a personal representative of a deceased trustee has an absolute right to decline to accept the position and duties of trustee if he chooses so to do'.[248] Presumably, however, if such a personal representative were to choose to accept[249] the trust, he would thereafter be liable as a trustee in the ordinary way. Even if personal representatives do accept the trust, they can only act until the appointment of new trustees. In practice, they are themselves likely to be the appropriate persons to appoint new trustees, but if some other person has such a power that is validly exercised, it will operate forthwith to oust the personal representatives for all purposes from the trust.[250]

Finally, it should be mentioned that all of the above provisions are subject to the restrictions imposed in regard to receipt by a sole trustee, not being a trust corporation.[251]

(C) RETIREMENT AND REMOVAL

(i) Under an express power in the trust instrument

An express power of retirement or removal is not usually inserted under most kinds of trust. A power of removal is, however, commonly found in an equitable mortgage to a bank by a deposit of title deeds, when the mortgagor often declares himself a trustee of the legal estate for the bank, which is given an express power to remove the mortgagor as trustee and appoint itself or some other person in his place.[252]

(ii) Under the provisions of s 36 of the Trustee Act 1925

As we have seen,[253] a trustee who desires to be discharged from all or any of the trusts may retire on the appointment of a new trustee in his place, and, on the appointment of a new trustee, an existing trustee may be removed against his will if he remains out of the United Kingdom for more than twelve months, or refuses or is unfit to act therein, or is incapable of acting.

It should be noted that it has been held[254] that the appointment of a single trustee under s 36(1) would be effective to discharge only one of two or more trustees: the other trustee

---

[246] Administration of Estates Act 1925, ss 1–3, as amended. See (1977) 41 Conv 423 (P W Smith).

[247] Trustee Act 1925, s 18(4).

[248] *Per* Vaughan Williams LJ in *Re Benett* [1906] 1 Ch 216, 255, CA; *Re Ridley* [1904] 2 Ch 774.

[249] Taking out probate is not, of course, any evidence of an intention to accept a trust of which the deceased was trustee.

[250] *Re Routledge's Trusts* [1909] 1 Ch 280.   [251] Trustee Act 1925, s 18(3).

[252] *London and County Banking Co v Goddard* [1897] 1 Ch 642; and see *Key and Elphinstone's Precedents in Conveyancing*, 15th edn, vol II, p 237.

[253] See section 1(C), p 359, *supra*. Similarly, under an appropriate express power of appointment.

[254] *Adam & Co International Trustees Ltd v Theodore Goddard (a firm)* [2000] 144 SJ LB 149.

or trustees would only be effectively discharged by retirement under s 39. The decision has, however, met with convincing criticism.[255]

(iii) Under the provisions of s 39 of the Trustee Act 1925[256]

Under these provisions, a trustee may be able to retire without a new appointment. Section 39 provides as follows:

> Where a trustee is desirous of being discharged from the trust, and after his discharge there will be either a trust corporation or at least two persons to act as trustees to perform the trust, then, if such trustee as aforesaid by deed declares that he is desirous of being discharged from the trust, and if his cotrustees and such other person, if any, as is empowered to appoint trustees, by deed consent[257] to the discharge of the trustee, and to the vesting in the cotrustees alone of the trust property, the trustee desirous of being discharged shall be deemed to have retired from the trust, and shall, by the deed, be discharged therefrom under this Act, without any new trustee being appointed in his place.

It appears that under this provision, as contrasted with the provisions of s 36, a trustee cannot retire from part of the trusts, as there is no phrase equivalent to 'all or any of the trusts or powers'. However, if separate sets of trustees have been appointed under s 37, it is submitted that a trustee will be able to retire therefrom under s 39, on the ground that the distinct trust is to be regarded as a trust and not merely part of a trust.

(iv) Under the provisions of s 41 of the Trustee Act 1925

As we have seen the court may, under this section, on the appointment of a new trustee, remove an existing trustee. It will not, however, simply discharge a trustee without appointing a new trustee;[258] nor will it exercise its statutory jurisdiction to remove a trustee where there is a dispute as to the facts.[259]

It was said, in one case,[260] that 'no person can be compelled to remain a trustee and act in the execution of the trust', but retirement without good cause was discouraged by the rule that if a trustee retired from mere caprice, he would have to pay the costs,[261] although he might be justified in wishing to retire, and, accordingly, be allowed his costs when circumstances arising in the administration of the trust had altered the nature of his duties, and involved him in difficulties and responsibilities that he had never contemplated.[262] However, since the Trustee Act 1925 recognizes that a trustee has a right to retire if he desires to do so,[263] it would seem that a trustee should now normally be allowed the costs

---

[255] [2003] Conv 15 (F Barlow).

[256] As amended by the Trusts of Land and Appointment of Trustees Act 1996, Sch 3, para 3(13). Note that, in relation to trustees for a listed trade union, references to a deed are to be construed as references to an instrument in writing: Trade Union and Labour Relations (Consolidation) Act 1992, s 13(1)–(3).

[257] By the Public Trustee Act 1906, s 5(2), where the Public Trustee has been appointed a trustee, a co-trustee may retire under these provisions, notwithstanding that there are not more than two trustees, and without any consents being obtained.

[258] See pp 368–369, *supra*. Also *Re Harrison's Settlement Trusts* [1965] 3 All ER 795, [1965] 1 WLR 1492.

[259] *Re Combs* (1884) 51 LT 45, CA, applied *Popoff v Actus Management Ltd* [1985] 5 WWR 660. Cf *Re Dove's Will Trust* [1939] WN 230.

[260] *Forshaw v Higginson* (1855) 20 Beav 485, 487, *per* Romilly MR.

[261] *Forshaw v Higginson, supra; Howard v Rhodes* (1837) 1 Keen 581.

[262] *Forshaw v Higginson, supra; Gardiner v Downes* (1856) 22 Beav 395.

[263] See *Re Duke of Norfolk's Settlement Trusts* [1982] Ch 61, 81, [1981] 3 All ER 220, 231, CA, *per* Brightman LJ.

of an application to the court if, for any reason, he is unable to take advantage of the statutory provisions.

Where a sole trustee wishes to retire and it is impossible to find anyone who is willing to become the new trustee,[264] the court will not discharge him so as to leave the trust without a trustee. An order may, however, be made in such a case for the administration of the trust by the court and, although the trustee retains his office, the court will take care in working out the order that the trustee does not suffer.[265] Similar considerations will presumably apply[266] where one of two trustees wishes to retire, and the sole continuing trustee would not be able to give valid receipts for capital moneys.[267]

(v) By the court under its inherent jurisdiction

The court has an inherent jurisdiction to remove a trustee in an action[268] for the administration or execution of a trust without necessarily appointing a new trustee, and notwithstanding that the facts may be in dispute.[269] The Privy Council observed, in *Letterstedt v Broers*,[270] that there was little authority to guide it in deciding in what circumstances the jurisdiction should be exercised, and it was not prepared to lay down any general rule beyond the very broad principle that its main guide must be the welfare of the beneficiaries. It seems that although friction and hostility between a trustee and the beneficiaries is not necessarily, or even normally, a sufficient ground for the removal of a trustee,[271] the court may think it proper to take this into account and, accordingly, in some circumstances, to remove a trustee, even though he has not been guilty of any breach of trust.[272]

Clarke v Heathfield (No 2)[273] was an unusual case in which the court removed the trustees of the funds of the National Union of Mineworkers and appointed a receiver to act until new trustees were appointed, or, on a change of heart, the removed trustees were restored. Factors leading to the removal included the attempt by the trustees to place the trust property abroad and out of reach of sequestrators appointed by the court, placing the trust funds in jeopardy, and, by their actions, making the trust funds unavailable for the purposes for which they were contributed by the general membership.

Provided that the individual trustees are subject to the jurisdiction of the English courts, there is power to remove them and appoint new trustees, and to make such *in personam* orders as may be necessary to achieve vesting of the trust assets in the new trustees. This is so whether or not the trust assets are situated in England, and whether or not the proper law of the trusts in question is English law.[274]

---

[264] Since the Public Trustee Act 1906, it will usually be possible to appoint the Public Trustee (but see p 389, *infra*) or a trust corporation may be appointed.

[265] *Courtenay v Courtenay* (1846) 3 Jo & Lat 519; *Re Chetwynd's Settlement* [1902] 1 Ch 692.

[266] Compare *Re Chetwynd's Settlement, supra.*

[267] See section 1(h), p 375, *supra.*

[268] If there is a substantial dispute of fact, the claim should be made under CPR Pt 7, not CPR Pt 8.

[269] *Re Chetwynd's Settlement* [1902] 1 Ch 692; *Re Wrightson* [1908] 1 Ch 789; *Re Henderson* [1940] Ch 764, [1940] 1 All ER 295; *Scott v Scott* [1991] 5 WWR 185; *Porteous v Rinehart* (1998) 19 WAR 495.

[270] (1884) 9 App Cas 371, 385, PC, applied *Re Whitehouse* [1982] Qd R 196; *Titterton v Oates* [2001] WTLR 319 (Supreme Ct of Aust Capital Territory).

[271] *Forster v Davies* (1861) 4 De GF & J 133; *Re Wrightson, supra.*

[272] *Letterstedt v Broers, supra; Re Consiglio Trusts* (1973) 36 DLR (3d) 658.   [273] [1985] ICR 606.

[274] *Chellaram v Chellaram* [1985] Ch 409, [1985] 1 All ER 1043; (1985) 135 NLJ 18 (D Hayton).

(vi) At instance of beneficiaries under the Trusts of Land and Appointment of Trustees Act 1996

The provisions of s 19 of the 1996 Act, discussed above,[275] which, in certain circumstance,s enable beneficiaries to direct the appointment of trustees, apply equally to enable them to direct the retirement of trustees from the trust.[276] Where a trustee has been given such a direction and—

(a) reasonable arrangements have been made for the protection of any rights of his in connection with the trust;

(b) after he has retired, there will be either a trust corporation or at least two persons to act as trustees to perform the trust; and

(c) either another person is to be appointed to be a new trustee on his retirement or the continuing trustees by deed consent to his retirement—

he must make a deed declaring his retirement, and is deemed to have retired and to have been discharged from the trust.[277]

Further, as we have seen,[278] in certain circumstances, a trustee who lacks capacity (within the meaning of the Mental Capacity Act 2005) to exercise his functions as trustee can, in effect, be removed by a substitute appointment following a direction by the beneficiaries under s 20 of the Trusts of Land and Appointment of Trustees Act 1996, as amended.

The above provisions do not apply in relation to a trust created by a disposition in so far as the disposition so provides.[279]

(vii) By consent of the beneficiaries

If all of the cestuis que trust, being *sui juris*, consent to the retirement of a trustee, none of them will thereafter be able to call that trustee to account for anything that happens after the date of such retirement. In truth, this is merely a special application of the rule[280] that a beneficiary who has concurred in or consented to a breach of trust cannot have any right of action in respect thereof.

(viii) By payment into court

Under the Trustee Act 1925, s 63,[281] trustees may pay into court money or securities belonging to a trust. It has been said[282] that *'payment of a trust fund into court is a retiring from the trust'*, and it is settled that having done so the trustees cannot prevent a cestui que trust from having the fund paid out to him,[283] nor can the trustees any longer exercise any of

---

[275] Section 1(D), p 366, *supra*.   [276] Ibid, s 19(2)(a).
[277] Trusts of Land and Appointment of Trustees Act 1996, s 19(3). By sub-s (4), the retiring trustee and the continuing trustees (together with any new trustee) must do anything necessary to vest the trust property in the continuing trustees (together with any new trustee).
[278] See p 366 *et seq, supra*.
[279] Section 21(5). As to pre-1997 trusts, see sub-ss (6)–(8) and p 367, *supra*.
[280] Discussed in Chapter 23, section 3(B), p 525, *infra*.
[281] Discussed in Chapter 21, section 10(D), p 488, *infra*.
[282] *Per* Page Wood VC in *Re Williams' Settlement* (1858) 4 K & J 87, 88.
[283] *Re Wright's Trusts* (1857) 3 K & J 419.

their discretionary powers.[284] It seems, however, that he does not, in fact, altogether cease to be a trustee; neither is the court nor the Accountant-General constituted a co-trustee.[285] He remains a trustee for the purpose of receiving notices,[286] and would be a necessary party to an action in relation to the fund.[287]

4   SPECIAL KINDS OF TRUSTEE

(A)   JUDICIAL TRUSTEES

By the Judicial Trustees Act 1896,[288] the High Court[289] is empowered, on application made by or on behalf of the person creating or intending to create a trust, or of a trustee or beneficiary,[290] to appoint a person, known as a 'judicial trustee', to be a trustee of that trust. The object of the Act has been said[291] to have been:

> to provide a middle course in cases where the administration of the estate by the ordinary trustees had broken down and it was not desired to put the estate to the expense of a full administration. In those circumstances, a solution was found in the appointment of a judicial trustee, who acts in close concert with the court and under conditions enabling the court to supervise his transactions.

The provisions of the Act do not seem, however, to have found much favour with practitioners: it is often possible, and thought more convenient, to deal with cases in which a judicial trustee could be applied for by appointing a corporate trustee.

A judicial trustee may be appointed either jointly with any other person or as sole trustee, and, if sufficient cause is shown, in place of all or any existing trustees.[292] It is expressly provided that the appointment is to be made at the discretion of the court, and it follows that no one can claim to be entitled as of right to have an appointment made.[293] Thus the court, in one case,[294] refused to make an appointment on the application of the mortgagees of one fifth of the reversion where one of two trustees wished to be discharged, and the tenant for life was prepared to appoint in his place a person to whom no objection was made.

The Act does not contain any definition of 'trust' and it was held, in *Re Marshall's Will Trusts*,[295] that that word must be given its ordinary meaning, the judge for the purpose of

---

[284] *Re Tegg's Trust* (1866) 15 LT 236; *Re Nettleford's Trusts* (1888) 59 LT 315.

[285] *Thompson v Tomkins* (1862) 6 LT 305; *Barker v Peile* (1865) 2 Drew & Sm 340.

[286] *Thompson v Tomkins, supra.*   [287] *Barker v Peile, supra.*

[288] Section 1(1). See, generally, (2003) 51 T & ELJ 11 (J Ellis and P Hewitt).

[289] Proceedings under the Act are assigned to the Chancery Division.

[290] Under the doctrine of mutual wills (see p 135 *et seq, supra*), the survivor or his executor is a trustee and, accordingly, a person claiming to be entitled under the doctrine is a beneficiary within the Act: *Thomas and Agnes Carvel Foundation v Carvel* [2007] EWHC 1314 (Ch), [2007] 4 All ER 81.

[291] *Per* Jenkins J in *Re Ridsdel* [1947] Ch 597, 605, [1947] 2 All ER 312, 316–317.

[292] Judicial Trustees Act 1896, s 1(1). In *Re Martin* [1900] WN 129, Kekewich J expressed the opinion that the union of a judicial trustee and a private trustee was undesirable.

[293] Ibid, s 1(1). *Re Ratcliff* [1898] 2 Ch 352.   [294] *Re Chisholm* (1898) 43 Sol Jo 43.

[295] [1945] Ch 217, [1945] 1 All ER 550.

the case before him adopting the definition given by Underhill[296] and holding that Settled Land Act trustees were trustees within that definition. In one respect, however, the meaning of 'trust' is considerably extended for the purpose of the Judicial Trustees Act, which, by s 1(2), expressly provides that 'the administration of the property of a deceased person, whether a testator or intestate, shall be a trust, and the executor or administrator a trustee, within the meaning of this Act'. Accordingly, the court, by appointing a judicial trustee, can in effect appoint a new personal representative,[297] which, as we have seen,[298] it has no power to do either under the provisions of the Trustee Act 1925[299] or the inherent jurisdiction.[300] Unless, however, the will appointed separate executors for different parts of the estate, the court has no powers to appoint a judicial trustee of the trusts affecting a part only of the estate. Unless this were done, the executorship would be indivisible, and there would not be created separate trusts within the meaning of the Act of 1896 with regard to particular assets.[301] It may be added that the court now has a wide statutory jurisdiction to appoint substituted personal representatives under s 50 of the Administration of Justice Act 1985, and the court may treat an application to the court under that section as including an application for the appointment of a judicial trustee.

By s 1(3) of the Act:

> any fit and proper person nominated for the purpose in the application may be appointed a judicial trustee, and, in the absence of such nomination, or if the court is not satisfied of the fitness of a person so nominated, an official of the court[302] may be appointed.

An official of the court cannot, however, be appointed or act as judicial trustee for any persons in their capacity as members or debenture holders of, or being in any other relation to, any corporation or unincorporated body, or any club, or of a trust that involves the carrying on of any trade or business unless the court, with or without special conditions to ensure the proper supervision of the trade or business, specifically directs.[303] The Public Trustee Act 1906[304] provides that the Public Trustee may, if he thinks fit, be appointed to be a judicial trustee.

Except where the judicial trustee is an official of the court, the court may require a judicial trustee to give security approved by the court duly to account for what he receives as judicial trustee and to deal with it as the court directs. Security is normally by guarantee. It will not, however, normally require security to be given when the application is made by a person creating or intending to create a trust.[305]

---

[296] *Law of Trusts and Trustees*, 8th edn, p 3. The definition is modified in the current (17th) edition.

[297] *Re Ratcliff* [1898] 2 Ch 352.   [298] See p 368, *supra*.

[299] Section 41(1), discussed pp 368, 369, *supra*.

[300] Note, however, the Supreme Court Act 1981, now renamed the Senior Courts Act 1981, s 114(4), and the Administration of Estates Act 1925, s 23(2).

[301] *Re Wells* [1967] 3 All ER 908.

[302] 'Official of the court' means the holder of any paid office in or connected with the Supreme Court, and includes the Official Solicitor to the Supreme Court: Judicial Trustees Act 1896, s 5, and Judicial Trustee Rules 1983, SI 1983/370, r 2.

[303] Ibid, r 15.

[304] Section 2(1)(d). See also *Re Johnston* (1911) 105 LT 701, which seems to be authority for the proposition that, where there is an existing judicial trustee and it is desired to appoint the Public Trustee as an ordinary trustee, there must first be an order that there shall cease to be a judicial trustee of the trust.

[305] Judicial Trustee Rules 1983, r 6.

Once appointed, a judicial trustee is, in general,[306] 'in the position of any other trustee and exercises all the powers of any other trustee'. The court may give such directions as it thinks fit in relation to the custody of trust funds, property, and documents. A judicial trustee, or any person interested in the trust, may request the court to give directions as to the trust or its administration, including a direction that there shall cease to be a judicial trustee. The Judicial Trustee Rules also contain provisions relating to remuneration and accounts, and provide that, in any case of default by a judicial trustee, the court may give such directions as it thinks proper, including, if necessary, directions for the discharge of the judicial trustee and the appointment of another, and the payment of costs.[307]

(B) THE OFFICIAL SOLICITOR

The office can be traced back to medieval times, but only became statutory when the Supreme Court Act 1981, now renamed the Senior Courts Act 1981,[308] provided that the Official Solicitor should be an officer of the Supreme Court to be appointed by the Lord Chancellor. The office has been merged to a large extent with the office of Public Trustee, discussed in the following section, although they continue to have separate corporate functions. They are housed in the same building, and the same person has been appointed as Official Solicitor and Public Trustee. In general, both will continue to accept work on a 'last resort' basis—broadly, where failure to do so would result in an injustice, and where there is no other suitable person willing and able to undertake the work.

The main situations in which the Official Solicitor accepts a trust[309] are: to be an impartial trustee where disputes between the trustees and/or beneficiaries as to the administration of a trust are such that decisions cannot be made; to be trustee to facilitate the sale and purchase of real property where a trustee of the land is under a disability; and to be trustee of property held for a person under a disability pursuant to an order of the court following court proceedings. In particular, the Official Solicitor will consider accepting new matters that the Public Trustee cannot undertake because of the statutory restrictions imposed on him. Appointment of the Official Solicitor as a trustee requires the authority of the court.

(C) THE PUBLIC TRUSTEE

(i) General powers and duties

The Public Trustee, a corporation sole with perpetual succession and an official seal, is an office created by the Public Trustee Act 1906. Its main purpose was to provide a public body that could be considered by testators as a safe appointment as executor of a will, or as

---

[306] *Per* Jenkins J in *Re Ridsdel* [1947] Ch 597, 601, [1947] 2 All ER 312, 314.
[307] Judicial Trustee Rules 1983, rr 7–14; Practice Note [2003] 3 All ER 974, [2003] 1 WLR 1653.
[308] Section 90.
[309] The number of estates & trusts cases in hand 2006–07 was 419.

trustee of a trust. The need for such a body has been eroded by the availability of alternative suitably qualified professional help in the private sector.[310]

The Public Trustee may act either alone, or jointly with any person or body of persons,[311] as an ordinary trustee,[312] a judicial trustee, or as custodian trustee,[313] but he may decline to accept any trust, although he cannot do so only on the ground of the small value of the trust property.[314] He is not permitted to accept any trust exclusively for religious or charitable purposes,[315] nor any trust under a deed of arrangement for the benefit of creditors,[316] nor the trust of any instrument made solely by way of security for money.[317] He must not, as a general rule, accept any trust that involves the management or carrying on of any business.[318]

(ii) Mode of appointment

The Public Trustee may be appointed as ordinary trustee of any will or settlement or other instrument creating a trust, either as an original or a new trustee, or as an additional trustee, in the same cases and in the same manner and by the same persons or by the court, as if he were a private trustee.[319] He can always be appointed, and act,[320] as sole trustee, even though two or more trustees were originally appointed,[321] and notwithstanding a direction in the trust instrument that the number of trustees shall not be less than some specified number.[322] Indeed, the court may order that the Public Trustee be appointed as a new or additional trustee, notwithstanding an express direction to the contrary in the trust instrument.[323] Provision is, however, made for giving notice to the beneficiaries of any proposed appointment of the Public Trustee either as a new or additional trustee, and within twenty-one days of such notice, any beneficiary can apply to the court for an order prohibiting the appointment being made.[324] In deciding whether it is expedient to make

---

[310] See section 4(E), p 393, *infra*. The number of estates & trust cases in hand 2006–07 was 959.

[311] Public Trustee Act 1906, s 2(2). See, generally, (1989) 10 JLH 228 (P Polden); (2002) 33 T & ELJ 18 (C Sanders).

[312] He can accept trusteeship only of an English trust: *Re Hewitt's Settlement* [1915] 1 Ch 228.

[313] Public Trustee Act 1906, s 2(1) as amended. This section, read together with s 15 and Public Trustee Rules 1912, r 6, enables the Public Trustee to act as executor and administrator, and, in effect by s 6(2), to be appointed as a new executor or administrator, either solely or jointly with the continuing executors or administrators; he is, by s 3, also authorized to administer an estate, in lieu of administration by the court, where the gross capital is less than £1,000.

[314] Public Trustee Act 1906, s 2(3).

[315] Ibid, s 2(5). Eg a trust in which the sole object involved the selection of charitable objects for the testator's bounty: *Re Hampton* (1918) 88 LJ Ch 103.

[316] Public Trustee Act 1906, s 2(4).   [317] Public Trustee Rules 1912, r 6.

[318] For exceptions, see the Public Trustee Act 1906, s 2(4), and Public Trustee Rules 1912, r 7.

[319] Public Trustee Act 1906, s 5(1).

[320] *Re Duxbury's Settlement Trusts* [1995] 3 All ER 145, [1995] 1 WLR 425, CA, noted [1996] Conv 50 (J Snape).

[321] Ibid, s 5(1).

[322] *Re Leslie's Hassop Estates* [1911] 1 Ch 611 (appointment by the court); *Re Moxon* [1916] 2 Ch 595 (appointment by persons having statutory power of appointment).

[323] Public Trustee Act 1906, s 5(3); *Re Leslie's Hassop Estates, supra*.

[324] Public Trustee Act 1906, s 5(4). It was said, in *Re Hope Johnstone's Settlement Trusts* (1909) 25 TLR 369, that the Public Trustee should only be appointed if there was no other way out of the difficulty, but in *Re Drake's Settlement* (1926) 42 TLR 467, Romer J stated that these observations were only intended to refer

such an order, the court will not, in ordinary circumstances, take into account the fact of the expense that will be incurred by the appointment.[325]

The Public Trustee may be appointed to be custodian trustee of any trust:

(a) by order of the court made on the application of any person on whose application the court may order the appointment of a new trustee; or

(b) by the testator, settlor, or other creator of any trust; or

(c) by the person having power to appoint new trustees.[326]

There is no provision in the case of appointment as custodian trustee for giving notice to the beneficiaries.

An appointment of the Public Trustee as a judicial trustee is made by the court under the provisions of the Judicial Trustees Act 1896.

No appointment of the Public Trustee as an ordinary trustee or as custodian trustee should be made (except by a testator)[327] unless and until the Public Trustee has given his formal consent to act.[328] This is usually incorporated in the deed of appointment. It seems, however, that if formal consent is given at some time after the appointment, the appointment thereupon becomes effective and incapable of being withdrawn.[329] In any case, even under a will, the appointment will only become effective if and when the formal consent is given.[330]

(iii) Position of public trustee after appointment

The general position is set out in s 2(2) of the Act, which provides that the Public Trustee 'shall have all the same powers, duties, and liabilities, and be entitled to the same rights and immunities and be subject to the control and orders of the court, as a private trustee acting in the same capacity'.

He has no more power than a private trustee, where he is in the position of having conflicting interests, to make a bargain with himself and he must accordingly, in such circumstances, come to the court for sanction to such a bargain.[331] The more important regulations and provisions affecting the Public Trustee are referred to in their respective contexts.

(iv) Vesting of the estate of an intestate in the Public Trustee

Section 9 of the Administration of Estates Act 1925, as substituted by the Law of Property (Miscellaneous Provisions) Act 1994, s 14, provides that, where a person dies intestate, his real and personal estate vests in the Public Trustee until the grant of administration; likewise, where he dies testate, but there is no executor, or, before the grant of probate, there ceases to be any executor able to obtain probate. The vesting of the estate in the Public

---

to settlements of the kind with which the judge was dealing (spendthrift settling his own property, after payment of debts, mainly for his own benefit) and were not of general application.

[325] *Re Firth* [1912] 1 Ch 806.   [326] Public Trustee Act 1906, s 4(1).

[327] Public Trustee Rules 1912, r 8(1). Rule 8(3) provides that a person appointed by will to be co-trustee with the Public Trustee should give the Public Trustee notice of his appointment.

[328] Ibid, r 8(1) and (2).   [329] *Re Shaw* [1914] WN 141.

[330] Public Trustee Rules 1912, r 8(2); *Re Shaw, supra.*

[331] *Re New Haw Estates Trust* (1912) 107 LT 191.

Trustee is to prevent it being ownerless, but it does not, of course, confer any beneficial interest on him, nor does it impose on him any duty, obligation, or liability in respect thereof. However, if, for instance, the estate were to include a tenancy, the Public Trustee would be the proper person on whom a notice to quit should be served.[332]

(v) Public Trustee and Administration of Funds Act 1986

The effect of the 1986 Act was to merge the office of the Public Trustee with the Courts Funds Office and the property division of the Court of Protection. Section 1 of the Act provides that the office of Public Trustee and the office of Accountant-General of the Supreme Court may be held by one person, which means that funds in court and trust work may be brought together under the same person.

(D) CUSTODIAN TRUSTEES

The office of 'custodian trustee' was created by the Public Trustee Act 1906. The idea is quite simply that the trust property shall, for greater security, be vested in a custodian trustee, while the management of the trust remains in the hands of the other trustees, who are known as the 'managing trustees'. It is accordingly provided, on the one hand,[333] that the trust property shall be transferred to the custodian trustee as if he were a sole trustee, and for that purpose vesting orders may, where necessary, be made under the Trustee Act 1925, and, on the other hand,[334] that the management of the trust property and the exercise of any power or discretion exercisable by the trustees under the trust shall remain vested in the trustees other than the custodian trustee. The custodian trustee is not to be reckoned as a trustee in determining the number of trustees for the purposes of the Trustee Act 1925.[335] An incidental advantage of having a custodian trustee is that, when new managing trustees are appointed, there is no need to go to the trouble and expense of vesting the trust property in the new trustees. The trust property remains vested in the custodian trustee throughout and he, of course, is a corporate trustee who will never normally need to be replaced.

The Public Trustee Act 1906,[336] which, as we have seen, provided that the Public Trustee could act as a custodian trustee, also declared that the provisions relating to a custodian trustee should apply in like manner (including a power to charge) to any banking or insurance company, or other body corporate entitled by the rules[337] made thereunder to act as custodian trustee.

---

[332] See *Practice Direction* [1995] 3 All ER 192, [1995] 1 WLR 1120.

[333] Ibid s 4(2)(a).

[334] Ibid, s 4(2)(b). The differences between a custodian trustee and managing trustees are discussed in *Forster v Williams Deacon's Bank Ltd* [1935] Ch 359, CA.

[335] Public Trustee Act 1906, s 4(2)(g). The relevant provision is discussed at p 374, *supra*.

[336] Public Trustee Act 1906, s 4(3).

[337] The Public Trustee Rules 1912, r 30, as amended. These amended rules, inter alia, implement Council Directive 73/81/EEC, p 1, by authorizing corporations constituted in other EEC member States to act as custodian trustees if they comply with the conditions prescribed for UK corporations, including the requirement of a place of business in the UK through or at which the trust business is carried on. See *Re Bigger* [1977] Fam 203, [1977] 2 All ER 644.

The more important provisions regulating the relationship between the custodian trustee and the managing trustees are set out in s 4(2) of the Act. It provides that, as between the custodian trustee and the managing trustees, the custodian trustee is to have the custody of all securities and documents of title relating to the trust property, but the managing trustees are to have free access and are entitled to take copies. The custodian trustee must concur in and perform all acts necessary to enable the managing trustees to exercise their powers of management, without being liable for any act or default on the part of the managing trustees, unless he concurs in a breach of trust. All sums payable to or out of the income or capital of the trust property must be paid to or by the custodian trustee, who may, however, allow income to be paid to the managing trustees or as they direct. The power of appointing new trustees, when exercisable by the trustees, is exercisable by the managing trustees alone, but the custodian trustee has the same power of applying to the court for the appointment of a new trustee as any other trustee.

The Public Trustee cannot be appointed to act in the dual capacity of custodian trustee and managing trustee;[338] and accordingly, where, the Public Trustee being custodian trustee, the managing trustee died and it was desired that the Public Trustee should manage the trust, it was admitted that his custodian trusteeship had to be terminated before he could be appointed an ordinary trustee.[339]

The custodian trusteeship can be brought to an end by an order of the court, on an application for this purpose brought by the custodian trustee, or any of the managing trustees, or any beneficiary. Before making the order, the court requires to be satisfied that it is the general wish of the beneficiaries, or that, on other grounds, it is expedient, to terminate the custodian trusteeship.[340]

(E) TRUST CORPORATIONS

In various circumstances, it may be advantageous to have a corporate trustee and, when this is the case, it will commonly be desirable that the corporate trustee shall be a trust corporation. While almost any corporate trustee could provide continuity of administration, a trust corporation[341] can, in addition, be expected to provide financial stability and professional expertise in managing the trust, and can act alone in cases in which at least two individual trustees would otherwise be required by statute.[342] The most familiar trust corporations are large banks and insurance companies having trustee departments, often separately incorporated, which offer their services as professional trustees. Clearly, they will not be prepared to act unless they are remunerated, and they will now normally be entitled to remuneration whether or not there is an express charging clause.[343] These are special provisions where they are appointed by the court.[344]

---

[338] A corporation capable of being appointed custodian trustee under the Rules is in the same position: *Forster v Williams Deacon's Bank Ltd* [1935] Ch 359, CA; *Arning v James* [1936] Ch 158.

[339] *Re Squire's Settlement* (1946) 115 LJ Ch 90.   [340] Public Trustee Act 1906, s 4(2)(i).

[341] But not only a trust corporation: where, for instance, a reputable firm of accountants has formed its own trust company, with unlimited liability, such a company may be able to offer sufficient de facto protection to the beneficiaries, as well as professional skills.

[342] See p 375, *supra*.   [343] See the Trustee Act 2000, ss 28, 29, and pp 442–443, *infra*.

[344] See Chapter 19, section 1(D) and (E), pp 445, 446, *infra*.

Technically, 'trust corporation', for the purposes of the relevant 1925 Property Acts,[345] is defined therein as meaning the Public Trustee or a corporation either appointed by the court in any particular case[346] to be a trustee, or entitled by rules made under the Public Trustee Act 1906, s 4(3), to act as custodian trustee;[347] it also, as a result of the Law of Property (Amendment) Act 1926, s 3, includes the Treasury Solicitor, the Official Solicitor, and other officials prescribed by the Lord Chancellor, a trustee in bankruptcy, and a trustee under a deed of arrangement, and, in relation to charitable, ecclesiastical, and public trusts, local or public authorities and other corporations prescribed by the Lord Chancellor.[348]

[345] Law of Property Act 1925; Settled Land Act 1925; Trustee Act 1925; Administration of Estates Act 1925; Supreme Court Act 1981, now renamed the Senior Courts Act 1981, replacing the Supreme Court of Judicature (Consolidation) Act 1925.

[346] Including a corporation appointed by the Charity Commission under the Charities Act 1993: ibid, s 35.

[347] See p 392, *supra*.

[348] In addition, some other bodies are created as a trust corporation for special limited purposes: eg the Church of England Pensions Board by the Clergy Pensions Measure 1961, s 31.

16

DUTIES OF TRUSTEES

Jessell MR has pointed out[1] that 'it is a fallacy to suppose that every trustee[2] has the same duties and liabilities'. As has been mentioned,[3] for instance, the vendor under a contract for the sale of land is in a special position. And it seems that the only power of a bare trustee to deal with the trust assets is to retain them: for all other purposes, he can only deal with the assets as directed by the beneficiaries.[4] More generally, it is uncertain to what extent the following rules relating to a trustee's powers and duties apply to a constructive trustee. The question is little discussed in the cases, and it 'is a mistake to suppose that in every situation in which a constructive trust arises the legal owner is necessarily subject to all the fiduciary obligations and disabilities of an express trustee'.[5] Prima facie, however, an express trustee is under an obligation to carry out the duties and has the powers about to be considered.

Before considering these duties in detail, a general picture should perhaps be drawn. On accepting a trust, new trustees 'are bound to inquire of what the property consists that is proposed to be handed over to them and what are the trusts',[6] and they should examine all of the relevant documents in order to ascertain that everything is in order. Thereafter, 'the duty of a trustee is properly to preserve the trust fund, to pay the income and the corpus to those who are entitled to them respectively, and to give all his cestuis que trust, on demand, information with respect to the mode in which the trust fund has been dealt with, and where it is.'[7] 'A trustee cannot assert a title of his own to trust property',[8] neither can he divest himself of the trust property, nor of a power given to him as incident to the execution of his trust.[9] If he 'ventures to deviate from the letter of his trust, he does so under the obligation and at the peril of afterwards satisfying the court that the deviation was

---

[1] *Earl of Egmont v Smith* (1877) 6 Ch D 469, 475; *Knox v Gye* (1872) LR 5 HL 656, *per* Lord Westbury. Cf *Henderson v Merrett Syndicates Ltd* [1995] 2 AC 145, 206, [1994] 3 All ER 506, 543, *per* Lord Browne-Wilkinson: '*The phrase "fiduciary duties" is a dangerous one, giving rise to a mistaken assumption that all fiduciaries owe the same duties in all circumstances. That is not the case.*'

[2] As to a trustee in bankruptcy, see *Re Debtor, ex p Debtor v Dobwell (Trustee)* [1949] Ch 236, [1949] 1 All ER 510; *Ayerst v C & K (Construction) Ltd* [1976] AC 167, [1975] 2 All ER 537, HL. As to the director of a company, see *Selangor United Rubber Estates, Ltd v Cradock (No 3)* [1968] 2 All ER 1073, [1968] 1 WLR 1555.

[3] Chapter 8, section 4, p 164, *supra*.

[4] *Koorootang Nominees Pty Ltd v Australia and New Zealand Banking Group Ltd* [1998] 3 VR 16.

[5] *Lonrho plc v Fayed (No 2)* [1991] 4 All ER 961, 971, 972 [1992] 1 WLR 1, 12, *per* Millett J.

[6] *Hallows v Lloyd* (1888) 39 Ch D 686, 691, *per* Kekewich J.

[7] *Low v Bouverie* [1891] 3 Ch 82, 99, CA, *per* Lindley LJ.

[8] *Per* Page-Wood V-C in *Frith v Cartland* (1865) 2 Hem & M 417, 420. Nor can he set up, as against his cestuis que trust, the adverse title of a third party: *Newsome v Flowers* (1861) 30 Beav 461.

[9] *Re Mills* [1930] 1 Ch 654, CA; cf *Re Wills's Trust Deeds* [1964] Ch 219, [1963] 1 All ER 390; *Muir v IRC* [1966] 3 All ER 38, [1966] 1 WLR 1269, CA.

necessary or beneficial'.[10] Prima facie, a trustee must act personally, and an undertaking that fetters a trustee in the exercise of his discretionary powers is invalid.[11] 'As a general rule a trustee sufficiently discharges his duty if he takes in managing trust affairs all those precautions which an ordinary prudent man of business would take in managing similar affairs of his own.'[12] It is the paramount duty of trustees 'to exercise their powers in the best interests of the present and future beneficiaries of the trust',[13] and, accordingly, the pursuit of the interests of his beneficiaries may require him to disregard the dictates of commercial morality.[14] It has been said[15] that a 'paid trustee is expected to exercise a higher standard of diligence and knowledge than an unpaid trustee, and…a bank which advertises itself largely in the public press as taking charge of administrations is under a special duty'. Brightman J expressed a similar opinion in *Bartlett v Barclays Bank Trust Co Ltd*,[16] saying that 'a professional corporate trustee is liable for breach of trust if loss is caused to the trust fund because it neglects to exercise the special care and skill which it professes to have'. On this basis, not all paid trustees will necessarily be subject to the same higher duty of care. It may depend not merely on the fact of payment, but also on the status of the trustee and the special skills that he offers.[17] As between beneficiaries with conflicting interests, a trustee must act impartially and it is 'an inflexible rule of a Court of Equity that a person in a fiduciary position…is not, unless otherwise expressly provided, entitled to make a profit; he is not allowed to put himself in a position where his interest and duty conflict'. So far as his powers are concerned, the well-established principle is that 'a trustee shall not be permitted to use the powers which the trust may confer upon him at law, except for the legitimate purposes of his trust'.[18]

In the exercise of a discretionary power, the duty of trustees is to exercise 'the power for the purpose for which it is given, giving proper consideration to the matters which are relevant and excluding from consideration matters which are irrelevant'.[19] Relevant matters may not be limited to simple matters of fact, but will, on occasion, include taking advice from appropriate experts, whether the experts are lawyers, accountants, actuaries, scientists, or whomsoever. It is, however, for advisers to advise and for trustees to

---

[10] *Harrison v Randall* (1851) 9 Hare 397, 407, *per* Turner VC.

[11] See *Re Gibson's Settlement Trusts* [1981] Ch 179, [1981] 1 All ER 233. But see Chapter 20, *infra*.

[12] *Speight v Gaunt* (1883) 9 App Cas 1, 19, HL, *per* Lord Blackburn; *Learoyd v Whiteley* (1887) 12 App Cas 727; *Eaton v Buchanan* [1911] AC 253, HL. See (1973) 37 Conv 48 (D R Paling).

[13] *Cowan v Scargill* [1985] Ch 270, 286, 287, *per* Megarry V-C. See (2005) 114 Yale LJ 931 (J H Langbein).

[14] See *Taylors Fashions Ltd v Liverpool Victoria Trustees Co Ltd* [1982] QB 133n, [1981] 1 All ER 897, 900, 901, *per* Oliver J, and p 463, *infra*.

[15] *Per* Harman J in *Re Waterman's Will Trusts* [1952] 2 All ER 1054, 1055; *Steel v Wellcome Custodian Trustees Ltd* [1988] 1 WLR 167. Contra, *Jobson v Palmer* [1893] 1 Ch 71, *per* Romer J; *Australian Securities Commission v A S Nominees Ltd* (1995) 133 ALR 1

[16] [1980] Ch 515, [1980] 1 All ER 139, discussed [1980] Conv 155 (G A Shindler). See Law Reform Committee, 23rd Report (Cmnd 8733), paras 2.12–2.16; (1996) 146 NLJ 348 (Ann Kenny).

[17] *Bray v Ford* [1896] AC 44, 51, HL, *per* Lord Herschell. A similar distinction is made in relation to the statutory duty of care imposed by the Trustee Act 2000, s 1: see p 394, *infra*.

[18] *Per* Wigram VC in *Balls v Strutt* (1841) 1 Hare 146, 149.

[19] *Edge v Pensions Ombudsman* [2000] Ch 602, [1999] 4 All ER 546, 567, CA, *per* Chadwick LJ. In relation to pensions trusts, it has been said that, in exercising their distributive powers, trustees and managers of pensions funds should regard themselves more as giving effect to a contract than exercising discretionary trust powers: (2002) 16 Tru LI 214 (Lord Scott of Foscote). See *Wong v Burt* [2004] NZCA 174, [2005] WTLR 291, discussed (2005) 63 T & ELTJ 8 (R Myint).

decide: trustees may not (except in so far as they are authorized to do so)[20] delegate the exercise of their discretions, even to experts.[21] In reaching decisions as to the exercise of their fiduciary powers, trustees have to try to weigh up competing factors, which may be incommensurable in character. In that sense, they have to be fair. But they are not a court and are not under any general duty to give a hearing to both sides—indeed, in many situations, 'both sides' is a meaningless expression. Further, it seems that the legitimate expectation of potential beneficiaries should be taken into account.[22]

This chapter considers many of the duties of trustees, beginning with those arising on their acceptance of the office; subsequent chapters, however, discuss the duty of trustees in relation to the investment of the trust property and their obligation to keep an even hand as between the beneficiaries.

1 DUTIES ON THE ACCEPTANCE OF THE TRUST

As we have seen,[23] a trustee cannot be compelled to accept the office of trustee, 'but having once accepted it…he must discharge its duties, so long as his character of trustee subsists'.[24] The law does not recognize any distinction between active and passive trustees, and a trustee will be fully liable to the beneficiaries for any loss that occurs where he has left the management of the trust to a co-trustee, even though the co-trustee may be the solicitor to the trust.[25] A trustee who has accepted the trust has been ordered by the court to concur with the other trustees in all proper and necessary acts of administration,[26] although, in practice, it would normally, in such a case, be possible and more convenient to appoint a new trustee in his place. Before he accepts a trusteeship to which any discretionary power is annexed, a trustee must disclose any circumstances in his situation that might tend to induce him to exercise any such power unfairly. If he fails to do so and nevertheless accepts the trust, he cannot afterwards exercise the discretionary power for his own benefit.[27]

On their appointment, it is the right and duty of trustees to see that their appointment has been properly made,[28] and to ascertain of what the trust property consists and the trusts upon which they are to hold it:[29] 'They ought also to look into the trust documents and papers to ascertain what notices appear among them of incumbrances and other matters

---

[20] See Chapter 20, *infra*.

[21] *Scott v National Trust for Places of Historic Interest or Natural Beauty* [1998] 2 All ER 705, [1998] 1 WLR 226; *Dundee General Hospitals Board of Management v Walker* [1952] 1 All ER 896, HL; *Re Hastings-Bass (decd)* [1975] Ch 25, [1974] 2 All ER 193; *Mettoy Pension Trustees Ltd v Evans* [1991] 2 All ER 513, [1990] 1 WLR 1587.

[22] *Scott v National Trust for Places of Historic Interest or Natural Beauty, supra.*

[23] See Chapter 15, section 3(A), p 380, *supra*.

[24] *Moyle v Moyle* (1831) 2 Russ & M 710, 715, *per* Brougham LC. He will not be liable for failing to act in a trust of which he has no notice: *Youde v Cloud* (1874) LR 18 Eq 634.

[25] *Bahin v Hughes* (1886) 31 Ch D 390, CA; *Robinson v Harkin* [1896] 2 Ch 415; *Re Turner* [1897] 1 Ch 536.

[26] *Ouchterlony v Lord Lynedoch* (1830) 7 Bli NS 448, HL.

[27] *Peyton v Robinson* (1823) 1 LJOS Ch 191.   [28] *Harvey v Olliver* (1887) 57 LT 239.

[29] *Harvey v Olliver, supra*; *Hallows v Lloyd* (1888) 39 Ch D 686; *Nestle v National Westminster Bank plc* [1994] 1 All ER 118, [1993] 1 WLR 1260.

affecting the trust.'[30] To enable this to be done effectively, a trustee, being an individual, can be required to produce to his successors in office entries relating to the administration of the trust recorded by him in a diary or other document, and, where there are two or more trustees, they can be required to produce the minutes of their meetings. A retiring trustee is expected to answer his successor's requests for information about the trust and its affairs, and is expected to exercise due care in doing so. If, through negligence, he were to mislead his successor and loss result to the trust estate, he would have no defence to a common law action in negligence.[31] Similarly, in the case of a corporate trustee, new trustees may even be able to demand production of the internal correspondence and memoranda of such a trustee: each individual document has to be considered on its merits.[32] But a trustee is not affected by knowledge merely because a former trustee or a co-trustee has knowledge.[33]

The trustees should ensure that the legal title to the trust property is duly transferred to them and, if this is not possible, that their equitable rights are appropriately protected by notice to the legal owners, or otherwise.[34] If any part of the trust property is outstanding, it is their duty to press for the payment or transfer of such trust property to them.[35] They must not be deterred by considerations of delicacy, or regard for the feelings of relatives or friends.[36] If the payment or transfer is not completed within a reasonable time, the best course generally is to ask for the directions of the court as to whether they should bring appropriate legal proceedings for the purpose,[37] because while it has always been true that, if they do not ask for the directions of the court, they will not be liable where their failure to sue was based on a well-founded belief that an action would be fruitless, the burden of proving that such belief was well-founded will rest on the trustees who asserted it.[38] However, it now seems that, under s 15 of the Trustee Act 1925,[39] trustees who have discharged the duty of care set out in s 1(1) of the Trustee Act 2000[40] will not be liable in any case in which failure to sue is the result of the positive exercise of their discretion and not the result of a mere passive attitude of leaving matters alone.[41] Again, where a settlement contains a covenant to settle after-acquired property, a new trustee is entitled, unless there are circumstances that should put him on enquiry, to assume that everything has been duly attended to up to the time of his becoming trustee.[42]

New trustees are bound to see that the trust funds are properly invested[43] and the investment should be in the names of all the trustees.[44] Title deeds and non-negotiable securities may, however, be kept in the custody of one of the trustees, and, in such case, a co-trustee cannot, in the absence of special circumstances, require that they be removed

---

[30] *Hallows v Lloyd, supra, per* Kekewich, at 691.

[31] See *Mond v Hyde* [1999] QB 1097, [1998] 3 All ER 833, CA.

[32] *Tiger v Barclays Bank Ltd* [1952] 1 All ER 85, CA.

[33] *Re Miller's Deed Trusts* [1978] LS Gaz R 454.

[34] But see Trustee Act 1925, s 22(1) and (2), as amended by the Trustee Act 2000, Sch 2, para 22.

[35] See, eg, *M'Gachen v Dew* (1851) 15 Beav 84; *Westmoreland v Holland* (1871) 23 LT 797.

[36] *Re Brogden* (1888) 38 Ch D 546, CA.

[37] *Re Beddoe* [1893] 1 Ch 547, 557, CA; *Bennett v Burgis* (1846) 5 Hare 295. See *Young v Murphy* (1994) 13 ACSR 722.   [38] *Re Brogden, supra,* CA; *Re Hurst* (1890) 63 LT 665; affd (1892) 67 LT 96, CA.

[39] As amended by the Trustee Act 2000, Sch 2, para 20. Discussed generally in Chapter 21, section 4, p 466, *infra.*

[40] See section 2, *infra.*   [41] *Re Greenwood* (1911) 105 LT 509.

[42] *Re Strahan* (1856) 8 De GM & G 291, CA.

[43] *Re Strahan, supra,* and see Chapter 17, p 415, *infra.*

[44] *Lewis v Nobbs* (1878) 8 Ch D 591.

from such custody and placed at a bank in a box accessible only to the trustees jointly.[45] Trustees have statutory power, and, in respect of some securities, a duty to appoint custodians of trust assets and documents. This is discussed later.[46]

In the case of a trust of chattels, the trustees should ensure that there is a proper inventory,[47] which should be signed by a tenant for life who is let into possession.[48] If the trust property includes a lease containing a covenant that the tenant will, at all times, personally inhabit the demised premises, it seems that the covenant will bind the trustees.[49] In conclusion, it should be observed that no trustee can be bound by a release of a power made by a previous holder of the office, even where the power is capable of release, which is commonly not the case.[50]

2 STATUTORY 'DUTY OF CARE'

The Trustee Act 2000[51] establishes a new precisely defined duty of care applicable to trustees when carrying out their functions under the Act. As in the law generally, the phrase 'duty of care' signifies a duty to take care to avoid causing injury or loss. The new duty is intended to bring certainty and consistency to the standard of competence and behaviour expected of trustees. It is additional to existing fundamental duties, such as the duty to act in the best interests of the beneficiaries and to comply with the terms of the trust.

The new duty does not, however, alter the principles relating to the exercise of discretionary powers by trustees. The decision whether to exercise a discretion remains a matter for the trustees to determine. That decision is not subject to the new duty of care, although it is subject to the control of the court as discussed later.[52] However, once trustees have decided to exercise a discretionary function that is subject to the new duty, the manner in which they exercise it will be measured against the appropriate standard of care.

Whenever the duty applies, a trustee must exercise such care and skill as is reasonable in the circumstances, having regard in particular to:

(i) to any special knowledge or experience that he has or holds himself out as having; and

(ii) if he acts as trustee in the course of a business or profession, to any special knowledge or experience that it is reasonable to expect of a person acting in the course of that kind of business or profession.

Thus, in relation to the purchase of stocks and shares, a higher standard may be expected of a trustee who is an investment banker, specializing in equities, than of a motor mechanic, particularly if the investment banker is acting as a trustee in the course of his investment banking business.

---

[45] *Re Sisson's Settlement* [1903] 1 Ch 262; *Cottam v Eastern Counties Rly Co* (1860) 1 John & H 243.
[46] See p 455 *et seq, infra.*   [47] *England v Downs* (1842) 6 Beav 269.
[48] *Temple v Thring* (1887) 56 LT 283.   [49] *Lloyds Bank Ltd v Jones* [1955] 2 QB 298, CA.
[50] *Re Will's Trust Deeds* [1964] Ch 219, [1963] 1 All ER 390; *Muir v IRC* [1966] 3 All ER 38, [1966] 1 WLR 1269, CA and see (1968) 84 LQR 64 (A J Hawkins).
[51] Section 1. As to its application to pension schemes, see s 36(2).   [52] See pp 490–494, *infra.*

400 EQUITY AND THE LAW OF TRUSTS

The statutory functions under the Act are set out in Sch 1. The duty of care accordingly applies to a trustee:

(i) when exercising the general power of investment, or when exercising statutory duties relating to the exercise of a power of investment or to the review of investments;[53]

(ii) when exercising the statutory power to acquire land or any power in relation to land so acquired;[54]

(iii) when entering into arrangements under which a person is, under the Act, authorized to exercise functions as an agent, or is appointed to act as a nominee or custodian, or when carrying out his duties in relation to the review of an agent, nominee, or custodian;[55]

(iv) when exercising the power under s 15 of the Trustee Act 1925 to do any of the things referred to in that section;[56]

(v) when exercising the statutory power to insure property;[57]

(vi) when exercising the power under s 22(1) or (3) of the Trustee Act 1925 to do any of the things referred to there.[58]

The same duty of care applies to trustees when carrying out equivalent functions to those referred to above conferred by the trust instrument.[59] However, the duty of care does not apply if, or in so far as, it appears from the trust instrument that the duty is not meant to apply.[60]

3 DUTY OF TRUSTEES TO ACT UNANIMOUSLY

'There is no law that I am acquainted with which enables the majority of trustees to bind the minority. The only power to bind is the act of [them all].'[61] Subject to any contrary provision in the trust instrument, only the joint exercise by trustees of their powers and

---

[53] See ss 3–7, Sch 1, para 1, and p 420, *infra*.   [54] See ss 8–10, Sch 1, para 2, and p 423, *infra*.

[55] See ss 11–27, Sch 1, para 3(1), and p 452 *et seq*, *infra*. Entering into arrangements includes: (a) selecting the person who is to act; (b) determining any terms on which he is to act; and (c) if the person is being authorized to exercise asset management functions, the preparation of a policy statement under s 15 (Sch 1, para 3(2)).

[56] Schedule 1, para 4. Section 15 of the 1925 Act gives trustees wide powers to compound liabilities. See p 466 *et seq*, *infra*.

[57] See s 19 of the Trustee Act 1925, as substituted by s 34 of the Trustee Act 2000, Sch 1, para 5 of the 2000 Act, and p 464, *infra*.

[58] Schedule 1, para 6. Section 22 of the 1925 Act confers wide powers on trustees in relation to reversionary interests, valuations, and audit: see p 467, *infra*. Section 22(1) has been amended by the Trustee Act 2000, Sch 2, para 22, by substituting for the phrase 'in good faith' a reference to the duty of care in s 1(1) of the 2000 Act.

[59] Schedule 1, paras 1–6.   [60] Schedule 1, para 7.

[61] *Luke v South Kensington Hotel Co* (1879) 11 Ch D 121, 125, CA, *per* Jessel MR; *Re Mayo* [1943] Ch 302, [1943] 2 All ER 440; *Phipps v Boardman* [1965] Ch 992, [1965] 1 All ER 849, CA; affd sub nom *Boardman v Phipps* [1967] 2 AC 46, [1966] 3 All ER 721, HL. The reason behind the rule is, perhaps, to make trustees

discretions will be valid,[62] and only a receipt by all of the trustees will give a good discharge to a purchaser.[63] Accordingly, if one of two or more trustees enters into a contract to sell trust property, whether purporting to act as absolute owner, or on behalf of himself and his co-trustees (who have not authorized the sale beforehand and have refused to ratify it afterwards), the sale cannot be enforced against the trust estate.[64] The trust fund should be under the joint control of all of the trustees,[65] and if one trustee obtains control of some or all of the fund and misapplies it, his co-trustees will be fully liable,[66] although they may escape liability if they can show that the trustee properly obtained control of the fund and that the co-trustees acted promptly to get the money invested in their joint names.[67] Nor, it seems, will trustees be liable for moneys belonging to the trust that their co-trustee gets into his possession without their knowledge or consent and by a fraud upon them.[68]

Exceptionally, one of several trustees may be authorized, on the grounds of practical convenience, to receive income,[69] although no trustee should be authorized to do this whose co-trustees have any reason to believe that he is liable to misapply the income;[70] on general principles, his co-trustees must see to the money being brought under their joint control with all due despatch. Where the trust property includes an investment in a limited company, the Companies Act 2006[71] provides that no notice of any trust is to be entered on the register of members or to be receivable by the registrar, and the articles of association in practice invariably provide that trusts shall not be recognized, and that, in the case of joint holders, dividends will be payable to the first named, who can give an effectual receipt therefor.[72]

The different rules in relation to charity trustees[73] and personal representatives[74] have already been discussed, and decisions of trustees of an occupational pension scheme established under a trust may, unless the scheme provides otherwise, be taken by agreement of a majority of the trustees.[75]

more cautious: see (1986) 36 UTLJ 186 (A I Ogus). The desirability of the rule is challenged in [1991] Conv 30 (J Jaconelli).

[62] But a trustee will not be liable and the joint act of the trustees will be valid if a dissenting trustee, acting bona fide, modifies his original view in deference to the views of his cotrustees and agrees to the proposed act: *Re Schneider* (1906) 22 TLR 223.

[63] *Lee v Sankey* (1872) LR 15 Eq 204; *Re Flower and Metropolitan Board of Works* (1884) 27 Ch D 592. And see Trustee Act 1925, s 14(2), (3), discussed Chapter 21, section 2, *infra*.

[64] *Naylor v Goodall* (1877) 47 LJ Ch 53.   [65] *Consterdine v Consterdine* (1862) 31 Beav 330.

[66] *Rodbard v Cooke* (1877) 36 LT 504; *Lewis v Nobbs* (1878) 8 Ch D 591.

[67] *Thompson v Finch* (1856) 8 De GM & G 560.

[68] *Bernard v Bagshaw* (1862) 3 De GJ & Sm 355 (crossed cheque entrusted to co-trustee for delivery to beneficiary). Cf *Re Bennison* (1889) 60 LT 859, in which trustee was held liable on similar facts with the essential difference that the beneficiary should not have been paid by cheque, the strict duty of the trustees being to purchase stock to satisfy a specific legacy.

[69] *Townley v Sherborne* (1633) J Bridg 35.   [70] *Gough v Smith* [1872] WN 18.

[71] Section 126; Gower and Davies, *Principles of Modern Company Law*, 7th edn, p 342.

[72] See Table A, arts 5, 106, in SI 1985/805.   [73] In Chapter 14, section 3(A), p 292, *supra*.

[74] In Chapter 2, p 39, *supra*.   [75] Pensions Act 1995, s 32.

4 DUTIES IN RELATION TO INFORMATION, ACCOUNTS, AND AUDIT

(A) DUTY TO ACCOUNT AND GIVE INFORMATION[76]

(i) Rights of beneficiaries vis-à-vis the trustees

The extent to which a beneficiary can claim disclosure of trust documents was recently reviewed by the Privy Council in *Schmidt v Rosewood Trust Ltd*.[77] The judgment of the Board is, of course, technically not binding in England, but it is thought that it is likely to be followed. The claim has sometimes been based on proprietary right. The clearest statement to this effect is that of Lord Wrenbury in *O'Rourke v Darbishire*,[78] who said: 'The beneficiary is entitled to see all trust documents because they are trust documents and because he is a beneficiary. They are in this sense his own.' However, Lord Walker, delivering the judgment of the Board, said that this could not be regarded as a reasoned or binding decision that a beneficiary's right or claim to disclosure of trust documents or information must always have the proprietary basis of a transmissible interest in trust property. That was not an issue in *O'Rourke v Darbishire*.

The alleged proprietary right came into conflict, in *Re Londonderry's Settlement*,[79] with the principle that trustees exercising a discretionary power are not bound to disclose to their beneficiaries the reasons actuating them in coming to a decision. Although, as pointed out in *Schmidt v Rosewood Trust*,[80] the judgments in that case are not easy to reconcile, the conclusion was that the need to protect the confidentiality in communications between trustees as to the exercise of their dispositive discretions, and in communications made to the trustees by other beneficiaries, could override the prima facie proprietary right of the beneficiaries to disclosure of information.

Their Lordships, in *Schmidt v Rosewood Trust Ltd*,[81] considered that, although the right to seek disclosure of trust documents might sometimes not inappropriately be described

---

[76] As to charities, see p 325 *et seq, supra*.

[77] [2003] UKPC 26, [2003] 2 AC 709, [2003] 3 All ER 76 (technically not binding in England, but likely to be followed). It has been adopted in New Zealand: *Foreman v Kingstone* [2004] 1 NZLR 841, and noted in (2003) 17 Tru LI 90 (D Pollard); (2003) 46 T & ELJ 5 (R Colquitt); (2003) 147 Sol Jo 737 (Dawn Goodman and Henrietta Lobes); [2003] PCB 358 (C McCall); (2003) 153 NLJ 1300 (K Noel-Smith); (2003) 23 ET & PJ 1 (L Smith); (2003) 52 T & ELJ 21 (G Brown); [2004] 120 LQR 1 (J D Davies); [2006] PCB 236 (Mary Ambrose). See [2004] PCB 23 (Lightman J). See also *Broere v Mourant & Co* [2004] JCA 009, [2004] WTLR 1417; *Re the Internine and the Intertraders Trusts* [2004] JLR 325. Some Australian cases are discussed in (2006) 78 T & ELTJ 26 (Jo Summers).

[78] [1920] AC 581, 626–627, HL.   [79] [1963] Ch 918, [1964] 3 All ER 855, CA.   [80] *Supra*, PC.

[81] *Supra*, PC; *Re International Trust* [2004] JCA 158, [2006] WTLR 1551 (Jersey CA). As to pension schemes, see *Wilson v Law Debenture Trust Corpn* [1995] 2 All ER 337, discussed 145 NLJ 1414 (P O'Hagan), and see (1997) 11 Tru LI 11, 43 (D Pollard); (2003) 17 Tru LI 170 (D Pollard and Judith Clixby). Meryl Thomas, in (1997) JBL 514, argues for increasing the obligation of disclosure in occupational pension schemes. For statutory duties, see Pensions Act 1995, s 41, as amended. As to the position in which trustees are directors of a company, see *Butt v Kelson* [1952] Ch 197, sub nom *Re Butt* [1952] 1 All ER 167, and (1980) 30 UTLJ 151 (D Hughes). Cf *Hughes v Transport and General Workers' Union* [1985] IRLR 382, noted (1986) 15 Ind LJ 46 (R W Rideout). See also *Crowe v Stevedoring Employees Retirement Fund Pty Ltd* [2003] VSC 316, [2005] WTLR 1271 (Aust), and [1996] PCB 302 (P Willoughby); (2000) 13 T & ELJ 9 (C Sly).

as a proprietary right, the more principled and correct approach is to regard this right as one aspect of the court's inherent jurisdiction to supervise—and, if necessary, to intervene in—the administration of trusts. The right to seek the court's intervention does not depend on entitlement to a fixed and transmissible beneficial interest. The object of a discretionary trust, and also the object of a mere power of a fiduciary character, may also be entitled to protection from a court of equity, although the circumstances in which he may seek protection, and the nature of the protection that he may expect to obtain, will depend on the court's discretion. Sometimes, a settlor provides the trustees of a discretionary trust with what is commonly referred to as a 'wish letter', explaining, on a confidential basis and without imposing any binding obligation, the matters that he wishes the trustees to take into account in the exercise of their discretion. Applying the principle set out in *Re Londonderry's Settlement*, Briggs J held, in *Brakespear v Ackland*,[82] that, in general, trustees and the court are justified in keeping a wish letter confidential, unless, as in that case, disclosure is in the interests of the sound administration of the trust, and the discharge of their powers and discretions.

It remains to be seen whether the principles laid down by the Board in *Schmidt v Rosewood Trust*[83] will be held to be applicable to modify the law as previously understood in relation to trust accounts as distinct from other information relating to the trust. As long ago as *Pearse v Green*,[84] it was said to be 'the first duty of an accounting party [including a trustee]...to be constantly ready with his accounts', and this was recently reaffirmed by Millett LJ in *Armitage v Nurse*,[85] who stated, 'Every beneficiary is entitled to see the trust accounts, whether his interest is in possession or not'; if a trustee fails to produce accounts, he may become liable to pay the costs of proceedings by a beneficiary to obtain them.[86] There is no suggestion in *Schmidt v Rosewood Trust* that trust accounts should be treated differently from other trust documents.

It was held in *Low v Bouverie*,[87] inter alia, that it is 'no part of the duty of a trustee to tell his cestui que trust what incumbrances the latter has created, nor which of his incumbrancers have given notice of their respective charges' on the ground that 'it is no part of the duty of a trustee to assist his cestui que trust in selling or mortgaging his beneficial interest and in squandering or anticipating his fortune'. Now, however, it is provided by s 137(8) of the Law of Property Act 1925 that any person interested in the equitable interest may require, subject to the payment of costs, production of all notices in writing of dealings with the equitable interest that have been served on the trustees. But trustees are not under any duty to proffer information to their beneficiary, or to see that he has proper advice, merely

---

[82] [2008] EWHC 220 (Ch), [2008] 2 All ER (Comm) 62, [2008] 3 WLR 698, noted [2008] CLJ 252 (D M Fox); (2008) 95 T & ELTJ 12 (M Pawlowski); [2008] Conv 322 (G Griffiths); *Re The Avalon Trust* [2006] JRC 105A, [2007] WTLR 1693; *Hartigan Nominees Pty Ltd v Rydge* (1992) 29 NSWLR 403, noted (1993) 67 ALJ 703 (D Maclean). See (1995) 7 Bond LR 5 (D Davies); (2001) 26 T & ELJ 21, and 27 T & ELJ 6 (D Benest); [2001] PCB 145 (P Stibbard); [2004] PCB 23 (Lightman J).

[83] *Supra*, PC.

[84] *Pearse v Green* (1819) 1 Jac & W 135, 140, *per* Plumer MR; *Kemp v Burn* (1863) 4 Giff 348; *Foreman v Kingstone* [2004] 1 NZLR 841, noted [2005] Conv 93 (G Griffiths). See, generally, (1974) 124 NLJ 452 (D Paling). As to judicial trustees, see the Judicial Trustees Act 1896, as amended by the Administration of Justice Act 1982, s 57, and the Judicial Trustee Rules 1983, SI 1983/370, rr 9–13.

[85] [1998] Ch 241, 261, [1997] 2 All ER 705, 720. See [2004] PCB 23 (Lightman J).

[86] *James v Newington* [2004] JRC 059, [2004] WTLR 863.

[87] [1891] 3 Ch 82, 99, CA, *per* Lindley LJ.

because they are trustees for him and know that he is entering into a transaction with his beneficial interest with some person or body connected in some way with the trustees, such as a company in which the trustees own some shares beneficially.[88]

Trustees under an express trust of which there is a minor beneficiary are under a positive duty to inform him of his interest on his coming of age.[89] It seems, however, that executors are under no such duty,[90] the distinction being said to be due to the fact that a will is open to public inspection.

It may be mentioned that trustees may well be held personally liable for the costs of any proceedings made necessary by their failure to carry out the above duties.[91]

(ii) Right of beneficiaries to seek information from a third party

It is convenient to mention here that, exceptionally, the court, under its equitable jurisdiction,[92] can order a defendant, who is not otherwise an appropriate party to proceedings, to identify the name and address of a third party. Thus, in *Re Murphy's Settlements*,[93] the court, in proceedings brought by a discretionary beneficiary, ordered the settlor (who had reserved the power of appointment of trustees) to give the plaintiff information as to the names and addresses of the trustees of the settlement.[94]

(B) AUDIT[95]

There are three statutory provisions. Firstly, s 22(4) of the Trustee Act 1925 provides:

> Trustees may, in their absolute discretion, from time to time, but not more than once in every three years unless the nature of the trust or any special dealings with the trust property make a more frequent exercise of the right reasonable, cause the accounts of the trust property to be examined or audited by an independent accountant, and shall, for that purpose, produce such vouchers and give such information to him as he may require.[96]

---

[88] *Tito v Waddell (No 2)* [1977] Ch 106, 243, [1977] 3 All ER 129, 242, 243. It has, however been suggested that, in some cases, there might be a duty to see that the beneficiaries were at least warned to take proper professional advice: (1977) 41 Conv 438 (F R Cane).

[89] *Hawksley v May* [1956] 1 QB 304, [1955] 3 All ER 353. As to whether this involves an obligation to inform the beneficiary of the rule in *Saunders v Vautier* (1841) Cr & Ph 240, discussed *infra* in section 65, see (1970) 34 Conv 29 (A Samuels). See [2004] PCB 23 (Lightman J).

[90] *Re Lewis* [1904] 2 Ch 656, CA; *Re Mackay* [1906] 1 Ch 25; *Hawksley v May, supra*. See (1995) 145 NLJ 1408 (J Sunnocks).

[91] See, eg, *Re Skinner* [1904] 1 Ch 289; *Re Holton's Settlement Trusts* (1918) 119 LT 304. Illiteracy and consequent inability to keep accounts is no defence—an agent could be employed: *Wroe v Seed* (1863) 4 Giff 425.

[92] Compare what Neuberger J referred to in *Re Murphy's Settlements* [1998] 3 All ER 1, sub nom *Murphy v Murphy* [1999] 1 WLR 282, noted (1999) 115 LQR 206 (C Mitchell), as 'the discovery jurisdiction': see *Norwich Pharmacal Co v Customs and Excise Comrs* [1974] AC 133, [1973] 2 All ER 942, HL; *Ashworth Security Hospital v MGN Ltd* [2002] UKHL 29, [2002] 4 All ER 193.   [93] *Supra.*

[94] Subject to an opportunity being given to him to put in evidence as to the inconvenience or cost or other problem the order would cause. The order was extended to similar information in relation to a settlement made by the settlor's wife (now deceased) where the settlor did not have a power of appointment of trustees.   [95] As to charities, see p 325 *et seq, supra.*

[96] The subsection provides for the costs to be apportioned between capital and income by the trustees: in default, capital and income bear the costs respectively attributable to them.

Secondly, s 13 of the Public Trustee Act 1906, 'an exceedingly drastic enactment',[97] enables any trustee or beneficiary to apply to the Public Trustee for an audit of the whole accounts of a trust at any time whatever, subject to the proviso that the application cannot be made within one year after there has been a prior audit. There is no limit backwards beyond which the audit is not to be extended, and the audit can only be prevented by an application to the court to stay the exercise of the prima facie right conferred by the Act. The sanction against insisting improperly on an investigation of the trust accounts is the liability of the applicant to be ordered to pay the costs of the audit.[98] The section has been invoked only occasionally and its operation has not been found to be particularly effective, because there are no powers to enforce the Public Trustee's findings. The Law Reform Committee accordingly recommended[99] its repeal.

Lastly, there is provision for annual audit by the court in the case of a judicial trustee.[100]

5 DUTY OF TRUSTEES TO HAND OVER THE TRUST FUNDS TO THE RIGHT PERSONS

(A) THE EXTENT OF THE DUTY

Trustees are under a duty to distribute income and capital to beneficiaries without demand,[101] but must take care to distribute the trust property only to the beneficiaries who are properly entitled thereto. Accordingly, trustees have been held liable to the person rightly entitled where they have paid the wrong persons through acting on the faith of a marriage certificate that turned out to be a forgery,[102] or through acting on the wrong construction of the trust instrument.[103] Strictly, it remains a breach of trust notwithstanding the fact that the payment is made upon legal advice,[104] although, as is explained elsewhere,[105] this may be a factor that would induce the court to relieve the trustees under s 61 of the Trustee Act 1925. Since the Family Law Reform Act 1987, there is no special protection given in relation to any illegitimate relationship, and the practical course is for trustees to take advantage of s 27 of the Trustee Act 1925, discussed below. Exceptionally, under s 45 of the Adoption Act 1976, a trustee or personal representative is not under a duty to enquire before conveying or distributing any property whether any adoption has been effected or revoked if that could affect entitlement to the property, and will not be liable for any conveyance or distribution made without notice of a claim. This does not, however, prejudice the right of a person to follow the property into the hands of any person, other than a purchaser, who has received it.

---

[97] Per Parker J in Re Oddey [1911] 1 Ch 532, 537.

[98] Re Oddy, supra; Re Utley (1912) 106 LT 858.　　[99] 23rd Report, Cmnd 8733, para 4.48.

[100] Judicial Trustee Rules, SI 1972/1096, rr 13–15.

[101] Hawkesley v May [1956] 1 QB 304, [1995] 3 All ER 353.

[102] Eaves v Hickson (1861) 30 Beav 136; Sporle v Barnaby (1864) 11 LT 412.

[103] Re Hulkes (1886) 33 Ch D 552; Ministry of Health v Simpson [1951] AC 251, [1950] 2 All ER 1137, HL.

[104] National Trustees Co of Australasia Ltd v General Finance Co of Australasia Ltd [1905] AC 373, PC.

[105] See Chapter 23, section 3(F), p 535, infra.

If a trustee has received notice of a claim against the trust funds that is, prima facie, a reasonably arguable claim, he will be liable to the claimant if he deals with the trust funds in disregard of that notice should the claim subsequently prove to be well founded.[106] It should be noted, however, that, under the rule in *Cherry v Boultbee*,[107] in which a person entitled to participate in a fund is also bound to make a contribution in aid of that fund, he cannot be allowed to participate unless and until he has fulfilled his duty to contribute.[108] Trustees will not be liable if they have accounted to an apparent beneficiary on the face of the trust documents, without notice of any facts or documents that might indicate that some other person is in fact entitled. Thus, if a power of appointment has been exercised, apparently properly, in favour of X and the trustees, having made all reasonable inquiries, pay the trust funds to him, they will not be liable to pay again if it turns out that there was a prior appointment to Y of which the trustees had no notice.[109] Again, a payment to the apparent beneficiary will be a good discharge to the trustees if they have no notice of the fact that the beneficiary has assigned or charged his interest,[110] and it seems that they can safely pay to a person entitled in default of appointment on apparently satisfactory evidence that no appointment has ever been made.[111]

Conversely, trustees will be liable to pay again if they ignore a derivative title of which they have notice, whether actual or constructive.[112] Trustees have a right to call upon anyone who claims to be a beneficiary to prove his title,[113] but they cannot raise questions where the validity or invalidity of the doubt is not essential to their safety,[114] nor, on distribution of the fund, can they require delivery of the assignment or other documents whereby the beneficiary established his derivative title.[115]

Where the trustees have a reasonable doubt as to title of a claimant, as, for instance, where he claims under an appointment that may be a fraud on a power,[116] they should apply to the court and act under its directions.[117] Again, in appropriate circumstances, the court may make a *Re Benjamin*[118] order, enabling trustees to distribute on the footing that

---

[106] *Guardian Trust and Executors Company of New Zealand v Public Trustee of New Zealand* [1942] AC 115, [1942] 1 All ER 598, PC; *Sinel Trust Ltd v Rothfield Investments Ltd* [2003] WTLR 593 (Jersey CA).

[107] (1829) 2 Keen 319; *Squires v AIG Europe (UK) Ltd* [2006] EWCA Civ 7, [2006] WTLR 705; and see *Re SSSI Realisations Ltd* [2006] EWCA Civ 7, [2006] BPIR 457.

[108] *The Russell-Cooke Trust Company v Richard Prentis & Co Ltd (in liq)* [2003] EWHC 1206 (Ch), [2003] WTLR 1529.   [109] *Cothay v Sydenham* (1788) 2 Bro CC 391.

[110] *Leslie v Baillie* (1843) 2 Y & C Ch Cas 91; *Re Lord Southampton's Estate* (1880) 16 Ch D 178.

[111] *Re Cull's Trusts* (1875) LR 20 Eq 561; *Williams v Williams* (1881) 17 Ch D 437.

[112] *Hallows v Lloyd* (1888) 39 Ch D 686; *Re Neil* (1890) 62 LT 649; *Davis v Hutchings* [1907] 1 Ch 356. As to priorities relating to equitable interests in both pure personalty and land, consider the rule in *Dearle v Hall* (1828) 3 Russ 1, as affected by ss 136–138 of the Law of Property Act 1925, as amended, discussed [1999] Conv 311 and (1999) 28 AALR 87, 197 (J De Lacy). Registered land is governed by the same rules as unregistered land since the Land Registration Act 1986.   [113] *Hurst v Hurst* (1874) 9 Ch App 762.

[114] *Devey v Thornton* (1851) 9 Hare 222 (where beneficiary is dead, cannot raise doubts as to the title of apparently properly constituted executors or administrators).   [115] *Re Palmer* [1907] 1 Ch 486.

[116] It is submitted that cases such as *Campbell v Home* (1842) 1 Y & C Ch Cas 664; *Firmin v Pulham* (1848) 2 De G & Sm 99 (charging trustees with costs where the appointment was held to be valid) would not be followed. The courts are now more ready to allow costs, partly by reason of the simpler and less expensive procedure available.

[117] *Talbot v Earl of Radnor* (1834) 3 My & K 252; *Merlin v Blagrave* (1858) 25 Beav 125.

[118] [1902] 1 Ch 723; *Re Green's Will Trusts* [1985] 3 All ER 455. If the beneficiary turns out to be alive, the court order will not prevent him from pursuing the remedies dealt with in Chapter 24, but the trustees will be protected by the court order.

a theoretical beneficiary had predeceased a testator, or as the case may be. An alternative practical solution to the problem of a missing beneficiary, particularly in the case of a small trust, may be to take out missing beneficiary insurance.[119]

It may be added that, as between the trustees and a person who is wrongly paid, the trustees, under the law of restitution based on the principle of unjust enrichment, have a right to recover the payment if it was paid under a mistake, whether of fact or law, subject to the defences available in the law of restitution, such as the defence of change of position,[120] or estoppel by representation. Estoppel is a rule of evidence that prima facie defeats a claim completely, but it does not operate in full where it would be clearly inequitable or unconscionable for the defendant to retain the whole mistaken payment.[121]

(B) SECTION 27 OF THE TRUSTEE ACT 1925

This section,[122] which applies notwithstanding a provision to the contrary in the trust instrument,[123] gives considerable protection to trustees on the distribution of the trust property. Subsection 1 provides that trustees of a settlement, trustees of land, trustees for sale of personal property, or personal representatives may give notice[124] of their intention to distribute by advertisement in the *London Gazette* and, where land is involved, in a newspaper circulating in the district in which the land is situated,[125] and 'such other like notices, including notices elsewhere than in England and Wales, as would, in any special case, have been directed by a court of competent jurisdiction in an action for administration'.[126] The notice must require any person interested to send particulars of his claim to the trustees within the time, not being less than two months, fixed in the notice.[127] The notices should follow the wording of s 27 so as to indicate that it is not merely the claims of creditors that are required to be sent in, but also those of beneficiaries.[128]

---

[119] See *Re Evans (decd)* [1999] 2 All ER 777.

[120] *Kleinwort Benson Ltd v Lincoln City Council* [1999] 2 AC 349, [1998] 4 All ER 513, HL, critically noted [1999] CLJ 21 (S Hedley); [1999] Conv 40 (M P Thompson). See also [1998] SJLS 468 (A Abdullah); [2000] CLP 205 (P Birks); [2002] RLR 9 (R Sutton); [2003] RLR 26 (D Sheehan). As to overpayments to pension scheme beneficiaries, see (2000) 14 Tru LI 201 (A Simmonds). As to a restitutionary claim for tax paid under a mistake of law, see *Deutsche Morgan Grenfell Group plc v IRC* [2006] UKHL 49, [2007] 1 All ER 449, noted (2007) 123 LQR 177 (Birke Hacker); [2007] CLJ 24 (Amy Goymour); [2007] CLJ 510 (G Virgo).

[121] *Scottish Equitable plc v Derby* [2001] EWCA Civ 369, [2001] 3 All ER 818, CA; *National Westminster Bank plc v Somer International (UK) Ltd* [2001] EWCA Civ 970, [2002] 1 All ER 198, CA, both noted (2001) 60 CLJ 465 (P Key).

[122] As amended by the Law of Property Amendment Act 1926, s 7, and Schedule, and the Trusts of Land and Appointment of Trustees Act 1996. It has been pointed out that, on a strict construction, the section does not apply to trustees of personalty where there is no trust for sale, including pension scheme trustees: (1995) 9 Tru LI 127 (P Docking).

[123] Trustee Act 1925, s 27(3).

[124] At any rate, in the case of a trust arising under a will, as soon as possible: *Re Kay* [1897] 2 Ch 518.

[125] On similar language in other statutes, it has been held that *The Sporting Life* circulates in Westminster: *R v Westminster Betting Licensing Committee, ex p Peabody Donation Fund* [1963] 2 QB 750, [1963] 2 All ER 544, DC; and that *The Times* is a local paper circulating in Rickmansworth: *Re Southern Builders and Contractors (London) Ltd* (1961) Times, 10 October.

[126] See *Re Bracken* (1889) 43 Ch D 1, CA; *Re Holden* [1935] WN 52.

[127] Or the last of the notices, if more than one is given.

[128] *Re Aldhous* [1955] 2 All ER 80, [1955] 1 WLR 459.

At the expiration of the time fixed by the notice, the trustees, provided that they make all appropriate searches, can safely distribute having regard only to those claims, whether formal or not, of which they have notice, whether as a result of the advertisement or otherwise.[129] The trustees will be as fully protected as if they had administered under an order of the court.[130] So far as claimants are concerned, however, it is expressly provided that nothing in the section prejudices the right of any person to follow the property, or any property representing the same, into the hands of any person, other than a purchaser, who may have received it.[131]

(C) PROTECTION AGAINST LIABILITY IN RESPECT OF RENTS AND COVENANTS

At one time, where a trust estate included a lease, the trustees were at risk if they distributed the rest of the estate without retaining sufficient funds to meet any liability that might arise under the lease in the future. This might delay for a long time the distribution of a large part of the estate. It is now provided[132] that, where a trustee, liable as such—

(i)   satisfies all liabilities under the lease that have accrued and been claimed; and

(ii)   sets apart a sufficient sum to answer any future claim in respect of any fixed and ascertained sum that the lessee agreed to lay out on the property; and

(iii)   conveys the property to a purchaser, legatee, devisee, or other person entitled to call for a conveyance thereof—

he may distribute the remainder of the trust estate to those entitled thereto without any personal liability in respect of any subsequent claim under the lease. The section operates without prejudice to the right of the lessor to follow the trust assets into the hands of those who have received them, and applies notwithstanding anything to the contrary in the trust instrument.[133]

(D) RIGHT TO A DISCHARGE ON TERMINATION OF TRUSTS

In general, a trustee cannot demand a release by deed from the beneficiaries on handing over the trust property in accordance with the terms of the trust.[134] As Kindersley VC explained in *King v Mullins*,[135] 'in the case of a declared trust; where the trust is apparent on the face of a deed; the fund clear; the trust clearly defined; and the trustee is paying either the income or the capital of the fund; if he is paying it in strict accordance with the trusts, he has

---

[129] Trustee Act 1925, s 27(2). The Law Reform Committee, 23rd Report, Cmnd 8733, para 5.1, recommends similar protection where trustees have received the advice of counsel to distribute notwithstanding a possible adverse claim, provided that they first write to the potential creditor and no claim is made within three months.

[130] *Re Frewen* (1889) 60 LT 953.   [131] Trustee Act 1925, s 27(2)(a).

[132] Trustee Act 1925, s 26(1) as amended by the Law of Property (Amendment) Act 1926. It has been extended to cover an authorized guarantee agreement under the Landlord and Tenant (Covenants) Act 1995, s 16, which Act, by Sch 1, para 1, has added s 26(1A) to the 1925 Act.

[133] Ibid, s 26(2).

[134] *Chadwick v Heatley* (1845) 2 Coll 137; *Re Roberts' Trusts* (1869) 38 LJ Ch 708.

[135] (1852) 1 Drew 308, 311, in whichthe different position of an executor is contrasted.

no right to require a release under seal'. He has, however, a right to a receipt for the funds paid over, and an acknowledgement that the accounts are settled.[136] But if he is a trustee of two separate trusts, he cannot refuse to pay over funds to which a beneficiary is clearly entitled under one trust by reason of some dispute in connection with the other.[137]

In some cases, however, a release may be demanded. In *King v Mullins*,[138] Kindersley VC continued, on the facts of the case before him, that where 'there was no writing to indicate either what the trusts were or the amount of the trust fund; and... what the trustee has been asked to do is not in accordance with the tenor of the trusts... [it is] not illegal in the trustee to demand a release by deed'. Again, where the beneficial interest has been resettled, although the trustees of the original settlement are not entitled to a release from the trustees of the resettlement, but only an acknowledgement of the receipt of the money paid,[139] it has been said[140] that, in such case, they are entitled to a release from the cestui que trust to whom the money was due.

6 DUTIES WHERE BENEFICIARY IS SOLELY AND BENEFICIALLY ENTITLED

(A) ENTIRE EQUITABLE INTEREST PRESENTLY VESTED IN A BENEFICIARY OF FULL AGE AND CAPACITY

Such a beneficiary can require the trustee to convey the trust property to him and thus bring the trusts to an end, notwithstanding that the trust instrument may contain contrary provisions. It would, of course, be quite a different matter if the beneficiary merely had a contingent interest, contingent, for instance, upon his attaining a specified age.[141] Trustees may be validly empowered by the trust instrument to pay a beneficiary at an earlier age than eighteen, but, even so, a minor beneficiary cannot compel payment before coming of age.[142] A leading case is *Saunders v Vautier*,[143] which is commonly cited to support the general

---

[136] *Chadwick v Heatley, supra; Re Heming's Trust* (1856) 3 K & J 40. See (1981) 78 LSG 477 (A Mithani and M P Green).

[137] *Price v Loaden* (1856) 21 Beav 508.

[138] *Supra; Plimsoll v Drake* (1995) 4 Tas R 334 (release under seal can be required where at request of the beneficiaries, being *sui juris* and together absolutely entitled, the trustee acts otherwise than in accordance with terms of trust).

[139] *Re Cater's Trusts (No 2)* (1858) 25 Beav 366; *Tiger v Barclays Bank Ltd* [1951] 2 KB 556, [1951] 2 All ER 262; affd, but not on this point, [1952] 1 All ER 85, CA. Cf *Re Hoskins' Trusts* (1877) 5 Ch D 229; on appeal 6 Ch D 281, CA.

[140] *Re Cater's Trusts (No 2), supra.*

[141] See *per* Page Wood VC in (1859) John 265, 272; *Re Johnston* [1894] 3 Ch 204. The rule has been abolished in some jurisdictions and the premature termination of the trust made subject to the approval of the court. See (1984) 62 CBR 618 (J M Glenn).

[142] *Re Somech* [1957] Ch 165, [1956] 3 All ER 523, and see s 21 of the Law of Property Act 1925, whereby a married minor can give a valid receipt for income.

[143] (1841) Cr & Ph 240; *IRC v Executors of Hamilton-Russell* [1943] 1 All ER 474, CA; *Stephenson v Barclays Bank Trust Co Ltd* [1975] 1 All ER 625, [1975] 1 WLR 882. The principle has been applied to a gift to X for life, with power to appoint by deed or will, or by will alone, and a gift in default to X's personal representatives: *Re Canada Permanent Trust Co and Bell* (1982) 131 DLR (3d) 501; but not to a gift of life interests to

principle, although the ratio has been more narrowly stated by Lord Davey[144] to be:

> that where there is an absolute vested gift made payable at a future event, with direction to accumulate the income in the meantime, and pay it with the principal, the court will not enforce the trust for accumulation in which no person has any interest but the legatee or (in other words) the court holds that a legatee[145] may put an end to an accumulation which is exclusively for his benefit.

A Canadian court applied the principle more widely in *Re Lysiak*,[146] in which a testator left all of his estate to his wife and son, who resided in the Soviet Union, and gave his executors the 'sole discretion to dispose of... all my estate in such manner and at such time as they see fit, and until they are absolutely satisfied that the beneficiaries are free and unhindered to receive the said benefits without interference from the regime under which they are presently residing'. It was held that, on the construction of the will, the interests of the beneficiaries were absolutely vested and the attempt to give the executors a right to postpone the distribution of the estate was ineffective. Conversely, if the beneficiary absolutely entitled refused to accept a transfer of the trust funds, in such a case, the trustees would be entitled, if they wished, to pay them into court.[147] Again, where there is a gift of an annuity, the annuitant is entitled to demand in lieu thereof payment of the cash that would be needed to purchase it.[148] The general principle applies in the same way where the beneficiary is a charity, whether corporate or incorporated,[149] but not where the alleged beneficiary is 'charity' in the abstract, there being provisions for the future ascertainment of particular charitable institutions.[150] It may also be observed that, although an indefinite gift of income to an individual carries the right to corpus,[151] this is not so in the case of a similar gift to charity, because such a gift could be enjoyed by the charity to its fullest extent in perpetuity.[152]

(B) ENTIRE EQUITABLE INTEREST VESTED IN TWO OR MORE BENEFICIARIES, EACH OF FULL AGE AND CAPACITY

Provided they are both or all agreed, they can bring the trust to an end by requiring the trust funds to be paid over to them or as they may direct. This principle has been held applicable not only to joint tenants and tenants in common, but also to the

---

children with power to appoint by will and gift over in default to children's or testator's issue where children had agreed to appoint to each other by irrevocable wills: *Re Saracini and National Trust Co* (1987) 39 DLR (4th) 436, appeal dismissed (1989) 69 OR (2d) 640; nor in *Re Lee's Estate* (1986) 84 Fed LR 268. See also *Don King Productions Inc v Warren* [1998] 2 All ER 608; affd [2000] Ch 291, [1999] 2 All ER 218, CA, noted [1999] LMCLQ 353 (A Tettenborn) and (2006) 122 LQR 266 (P Matthews).

144 In *Wharton v Masterman* [1895] AC 186, 198, HL.

145 Assuming, of course, that he is of full age and capacity: *Re Jump* [1903] 1 Ch 129.

146 (1975) 55 DLR (3d) 161.   147 *IRC v Executors of Hamilton-Russell, supra.*

148 *Re Robbins* [1907] 2 Ch 8, CA, and cf *Parkes v Royal Botanic Society of London* (1908) 24 TLR 508. As to the valuation of the annuity, see *Re Castle* [1916] WN 195; *Westminster Bank v IRC* [1954] 1 All ER 240, [1954] 1 WLR 242.

149 *Wharton v Masterman* [1895] AC 186, HL.   150 *Re Jefferies* [1936] 2 All ER 626.

151 *Re Levy* [1960] Ch 346, [1960] 1 All ER 42, CA.

152 *Re Levy, supra; Re Beesty's Will Trusts* [1966] Ch 223, [1964] 3 All ER 82.

certificate holders under a unit trust[153] and cases in which the beneficiaries are entitled in succession.[154] It also applies to the objects of a discretionary trust where there are individuals who are, in effect, combining on a compromise basis.[155] However, it has been held in Australia that, in such a case, it is not open to the trustees of two separate charitable trusts to take action that would have the effect of varying the trusts upon which they hold or are entitled to receive property.[156] It is important to remember, moreover, as Lord Maugham has pointed out,[157] that 'the rule has no operation unless all the persons who have any present or contingent interest in the property, are sui iuris and consent'. Accordingly, it seems that the principle will not apply where the only beneficiaries who do not consent are the unborn issue of a woman, in fact, past the age of childbearing, because there remains the theoretical possibility of further beneficiaries coming into existence.[158] It is irrelevant for this purpose that the trustees, in an appropriate case, may properly distribute the trust funds on the basis that a particular woman is past the age of childbearing.[159]

In the case of any land subject to a trust of land, where each of the beneficiaries interested in the land is a person of full age and capacity who is absolutely entitled to the land, the trustees have power to convey the land to the beneficiaries even though they have not required the trustees to do so, and the beneficiaries must do whatever is necessary to secure that it vests in them.[160] Further, the trustees may, where beneficiaries are absolutely entitled in undivided shares to land subject to the trust, partition the land and provide for the payment of equality money.[161] Subject to obtaining the consent of the beneficiaries, the trustees must give effect to any such partition by conveying the partitioned land in severalty in accordance with their rights.[162]

Both of the above powers may be restricted or excluded by a provision in the disposition creating a trust of land,[163] and if a consent is required to be obtained, a power cannot be exercised without it.[164]

---

[153] *Re AEG Unit Trust (Managers) Ltd's Deed* [1957] Ch 415, [1957] 2 All ER 506.

[154] *Anson v Potter* (1879) 13 Ch D 141; *Re White* [1901] 1 Ch 570.

[155] *Re Nelson* [1928] Ch 920n, CA; *Re Smith* [1928] Ch 915; *Re Beckett's Settlement* [1940] Ch 279.

[156] *Sir Moses Montefiore Jewish Home v Howell & Co (No 7) Pty Ltd* [1984] 2 NSWLR 406.

[157] *Berry v Geen* [1938] AC 575, 582, sub nom *Re Blake, Berry v Geen* [1938] 2 All ER 362, 366, HL; *Biggs v Peacock* (1882) 22 Ch D 284, CA.

[158] *Re Whichelow* [1953] 2 All ER 1558, [1954] 1 WLR 5.

[159] See, eg, *Re Westminster Bank Ltd's Declaration of Trust* [1963] 2 All ER 400n, [1963] 1 WLR 820; *Re Pettifor's Will Trusts* [1966] Ch 257, [1966] 1 All ER 913; *Re Levy Estate Trusts* [2000] CLY 5263 and cf *Re Cazenove* (1919) 122 LT 181. See also p 510, *infra*.

[160] Trusts of Land and Appointment of Trustees Act 1996, s 6(2). If the beneficiaries fail to do what is necessary, the court may order them to do so. In relation to the conveyance by trustees of unregistered land to a beneficiary, see ibid, s 16(4), (15). For some of the difficulties in construing this subsection, see the *Encyclopaedia of Forms and Precedents*, vol 40(2), 5th edn, 2006 reissue), Part 6 paras 126, 127.

[161] Ibid, s 7(1), qualified by s 7(6), inserted by the Commonhold and Leasehold Reform Act 2002. By sub-s 5, the trustees may act on behalf of a minor and retain his share on trust for him.

[162] Ibid, s 7(2)(3).

[163] Ibid, s 8(1), except in the case of charitable, ecclesiastic, or public trusts: s 8(3).

[164] Ibid, s 8(2), and see s 10, and Chapter 21, section 11(C), p 494, *infra*.

(C) WHERE ONE OF SEVERAL BENEFICIARIES, BEING *SUI JURIS*, IS ABSOLUTELY ENTITLED IN POSSESSION TO A SHARE IN THE TRUST PROPERTY

In general, according to Cozens-Hardy MR in *Re Marshall*,[165] 'the right of a person, who is entitled indefeasibly in possession to an aliquot share of property, to have that share transferred to him is one which is plainly established by law'. So far as personalty is concerned, the rule will normally be applied, even though this may result in the undistributed shares losing value. However, in very special circumstances, where it would unduly prejudice the other beneficiaries, such a beneficiary may be unable to insist on a transfer.[166] Thus the principle discussed later,[167] that trustees are bound to hold an even hand among their beneficiaries, was successfully relied on in *Lloyds Bank plc v Duker*[168] to prevent a beneficiary from calling for his share in specie. In this case, the deceased's estate included 999 shares in a private company. The beneficiary, Duker, was entitled to 46/80ths of the estate and asked for a transfer to him of 574 shares (the nearest whole number to 46/80 of 999). The other beneficiaries argued successfully against this on the ground that, since the majority holding was worth more per share than the other shares, Duker would get more than his 46/80ths of the total value received by the beneficiaries as a body if the shares were transferred to him. The shares were directed to be sold on the general market and Duker, of course, would be entitled to 46/80ths of the proceeds of sale. In Australia, the rule has been extended to enable beneficiaries entitled in succession to combine to require payment or transfer of part of their interests in the fund, subject to the court retaining a discretion to refuse to order an inappropriate payment or transfer.[169] The question does not appear to have arisen in England.

In relation to land, the courts have taken a different view, because, as Cozens-Hardy MR went on to explain:[170]

> it is a matter of notoriety, of which the court will take judicial notice, that an undivided share of real estate never fetches quite its proper proportion of the proceeds of sale of the entire estate; therefore, to allow an undivided share to be elected to be taken as real estate by one of the beneficiaries would be detrimental to the other beneficiaries.[171]

However, an application may be made to the court under s 14 of the Trusts of Land and Appointment of Trustees Act 1996,[172] and, once all of the shares are vested in possession in persons of full age and capacity, then, as we have seen, either the beneficiaries or the trustees may take steps to bring the trust to an end.

---

[165] [1914] 1 Ch 192, 199, CA; *Stephenson v Barclays Bank Trust Co Ltd* [1975] 1 All ER 625, [1975] 1 WLR 882; *Crowe v Appleby* [1975] 3 All ER 529, [1975] 1 WLR 1539; affd without reference to this point [1976] 2 All ER 914, [1976] 1 WLR 885, CA.

[166] *Re Sandeman's Will Trusts* [1937] 1 All ER 368; *Re Weiner's Will Trusts* [1956] 2 All ER 482, [1956] 1 WLR 579. See Law Reform Committee, 23rd Report, Cmnd 8733, para 3.64–3.65.

[167] See Chapter 18, *infra*.   [168] [1987] 3 All ER 193, [1987] 1 WLR 1324.

[169] *Quinton v Proctor* [1998] 4 VR 469.   [170] In *Re Marshall*, *supra*, CA, at 199.

[171] *Re Horsnaill* [1909] 1 Ch 631; *Re Kipping* [1914] 1 Ch 62, CA. As to whether in a suitable case an appropriation could be required, *quaere: per* Harman J in *Re Weiner's Will Trusts*, *supra*.

[172] Discussed 199, *supra*.

7 RIGHTS AND LIABILITIES IN RELATION TO STRANGERS TO THE TRUST

A trustee is personally liable on the contracts into which he enters on behalf of the trust. Thus, in *Marston Thompson Evershed plc v Bend*,[173] the plaintiff lent money to finance a new clubhouse at a rugby club. The loan was secured by a mortgage of the club's property, which was held in the name of the four defendant trustees. The defendants had signed the loan agreement, which expressly described them as trustees, and had covenanted to repay the capital and interest on demand. The club failed to repay the debt and the defendants were held personally liable to the full extent of the debt. An express statement that liability is limited is needed to avoid exposure to personal risk. But a proviso that is so wide as to exclude all liability may not be upheld.[174]

Trustees may likewise be personally liable in tort in respect of their acts or omissions in connection with the administration of the trust, and this includes vicarious liability for their employees or their agents. Thus, in *Benett v Wyndham*,[175] woodcutters properly employed by a trustee to fell a tree on a settled estate negligently allowed a bough to fall on, and injure, a passer-by, who was held entitled to recover damages from the trustee.

A trustee may generally sue and be sued on behalf of, or as representing, the property of which he is trustee, and a beneficiary has no direct cause of action against a third party save in special circumstances, such as a failure, excusable or inexcusable, by the trustees in the performance of the duty owed by the trustees to the beneficiary to protect the trust estate or to protect the interests of the beneficiary in the trust estate.[176] Where he can do so, he sues in right of the trustees and in the room of the trustees, who should be joined as defendants. He is not enforcing a right reciprocal to some duty owed directly to him by the third party.[177] Thus, in *Field v Finnenich & Co*,[178] a plaintiff was allowed to sue on a cause of action vested in personal representatives where the personal representatives refused to sue, and there was no one interested in the estate except the plaintiff and the widow of the deceased, and the widow had a personal interest in the defeat of the action. Conversely, creditors do not have a direct action against either the trust estate or the beneficiaries.

---

[173] Unreported, but noted (1997) 39 LSG 38; *Perring v Draper* [1997] EGCS 109. See (1996) 10 Tru LI 45 (R Ham); (1999) 4 T & ELJ 4 (Jennifer Chambers); (1999) 6 T & ELJ 4 (D Hayton).

[174] See *Watling v Lewis* [1911] 1 Ch 414.

[175] (1862) 4 De G F & J 259; *Re Raybould* [1900] 1 Ch 199 (nuisance). As to a trustee's right to an indemnity from the trust estate, see p 478 *et seq, infra*.

[176] *Hayim v Citibank NA* [1987] AC 730, PC; *Morla Professional Services Pty Ltd v Richard Walter Pty Ltd (in liq)* (1999) 169 ALR 419. *Bradstock Trustee Services Ltd v Nabarro Nathanson (a firm)* [1995] 4 All ER 888, [1995] 1 WLR 1405; *Fried v National Australia Bank Ltd* [2001] FCR 322 (Aust). See (1997) 11 Tru LI 60 (G McCormack), in which it is suggested that in general beneficiaries cannot sue external fund managers.

[177] *Parker-Tweedale v Dunbar Bank plc* [1991] Ch 12, [1990] 2 All ER 577, CA.

[178] [1971] 1 All ER 1104.

17

THE INVESTMENT OF
TRUST FUNDS

The law of trusts developed largely in the context of the family settlement, where there was a life tenant entitled to income and, on his death, the capital of the settlement would pass to the remaindermen. Of course, the limitations of the settlement might be very complex and there might be a number of persons concurrently and/or successively entitled to income before the capital finally became vested in possession in one or more remaindermen. It is a basic duty of trustees to act fairly between the different classes of beneficiary, and, accordingly, in choosing investments, they are under a duty to hold a balance between them and must take care not to favour unduly the tenant for life against the remaindermen, or vice versa.[1] It is submitted that it is the portfolio of investments that should be balanced, not each individual investment within it.[2] The idea is that they should invest the trust funds in such a way as to provide a reasonable income for the life tenant and, at the same time, maintain the value of the capital for the remaindermen. In the view of Hoffman J (as he then was) at first instance in *Nestle v National Westminster Bank plc*,[3] this means the value in monetary terms rather than the real value. 'Preservation of real values,' he said, 'can be no more than an aspiration which some trustees may have the good fortune to achieve.' Another matter that is little discussed in the cases is whether the personal circumstances of individual beneficiaries and the relationship between them should be taken into account. In *Nestle v National Westminster Bank plc*,[4] Staughton LJ thought that they should, observing: 'If the life tenant is living in penury and the remainderman already has ample wealth, common sense suggests that a trustee should be able to take that into account.' A trustee who has a lien on the trust funds[5] is entitled to

---

[1] *Raby v Ridehalgh* (1855) 7 De G M & G 104; *Re Dick* [1891] 1 Ch 423, 431, CA; affd sub nom *Hume v Lopes* [1892] AC 112, HL. The meaning is thought to be the same whether one speaks of the obligation of a trustee to administer the trust fund impartially or fairly, having regard to the different interests of beneficiaries, or to preserving an equitable balance between them: see *Nestle v National Westminster Bank plc* [1994] 1 All ER 118, [1993] 1 WLR 1260, CA. See *Re Smith* (1971) 16 DLR (3d) 130; affd (1971) 18 DLR (3d) 405, in which the trustee was removed from office for breach of this duty; *Re Mulligan (decd)* [1998] 1 NZLR 481; *Edge v Pensions Ombudsman* [2000] Ch 602, [1999] 4 All ER 546 CA.

[2] See, generally, [1987] PCB 22, 87 (A Duckworth); (1998) 12 Tru LI 158 (G McCormack). As to modern portfolio theory, see Longstretch, *Modern Investment Management and the Prudent Man Rule*; (2000) 14 Tru LI 75 (I N Legair).

[3] See (1984) 62 CBR 577 (R E Scane); (1995) 16 NZULR 349 (A S Butler); (1997) 10 Tru LI 102 (Emma Ford).

[4] (29 June 1988, unreported), affd [1994] 1 All ER 118, [1993] 1 WLR 1260, CA.

[5] See p 479, *infra*.

take into account his own interest, but must act impartially as between himself and the beneficiaries.[6]

In this chapter, after discussing the extent to which trustees may take non-financial considerations into account in making their investment decisions, we consider, first, the effect of an express provision in the trust instrument as to the investment of the trust property, and then turn to the important provisions contained in the Trustee Act 2000, which adopted a new approach to the matter and greatly extended the investment powers of trustees. The concluding sections deal briefly with some specific situations.

1 NON-FINANCIAL CONSIDERATIONS

Until recently, there was little direct authority on the question of whether trustees could properly take non-financial considerations into account in making decisions. In *Cowan v Scargill*,[7] however, Megarry VC stated the law in clear and unambiguous terms, holding that the defendants were in breach of their fiduciary duties in refusing approval of an investment plan for the pension scheme unless it was amended so as to prohibit any increase in overseas investment, to provide for the withdrawal of existing overseas investments at the most opportune time, and to prohibit investment in energies that are in direct competition with coal.

The duty of trustees to exercise their powers in the best interests of the present and future beneficiaries, known in the USA as 'the duty of undivided loyalty to the beneficiaries',[8] is paramount. When the purpose of the trust is to provide financial benefits for the beneficiaries, as is usually the case, the best interests of the beneficiaries are normally their financial interests. It follows that a power of investment must be exercised so as to yield the best return for the beneficiaries, judged in relation to the risks of the investments in question, and that the prospects of the yield of income and capital appreciation both have to be considered in judging the return from the investment:

> In considering what investments to make trustees must put on one side their own personal interests and views. Trustees may have strongly held social or political views. They may be firmly opposed to any investment in South Africa or other countries, or they may object to any form of investment in companies concerned with alcohol, tobacco, armaments or many other things. In the conduct of their own affairs, of course, they are free to abstain from making any such investments. Yet if under a trust investments of this type would be more

---

[6] *X v A* [2000] 1 All ER 490, discussed (1999) 12 T & ELJ 4 (E Rajah); [2000] Conv 560 (Ann Kenny).

[7] [1985] Ch 270, [1984] 2 All ER 750, criticized (1984) 13 Ind LJ 167 (R Nobles) and (1986) 102 LQR 32 (J H Farrar and J K Maxton). See [1985] Conv 52 (Penelope Pearce and A Samuels); [1990] LSG 87/23/17 (Nancy Convey); (1990) 4 TL & P 25 (P Dodding and I Pittaway); (1991) 5 TruLI 157 (R Ellison); [1992] 55 MLR 587 (P Luxton); (1995) 9 Tru LI 71 (Lord Nicholls); (1998) 19 Co Law 39 (G McCormack); (2005) 19 Tru LI 127 (P Watchman, Jane Anstee-Wedderburn, and L Shipway); (2008) 22 TruLI 11 (Sir Gavin Lightman). For a general discussion of some of the special considerations in the case of a pension fund, see (1985) 14 Ind LJ 1 and (1987) 16 Ind LJ 164 (R Nobles). See also (1980) 68 Calif LR 518 (R B Ravikoff and M P Curzon); (1980) 79 Mich LR 72 (J H Langheim and R A Posner); (1987) 2 TL & P 9 (Tony Thurnham) and (1987) 61 ALJ 329 (F J Finn and P A Zeigler).

[8] See *Blankenship v Boyle* 329 F Supp 1089, 1095 (1971).

beneficial to the beneficiaries than other investments, the trustees must not refrain from making the investments by reason of the views that they hold.[9]

This was applied by Lord Murray in the Scottish case of *Martin v City of Edinburgh District Council*,[10] in which he held that a breach of trust by the council had been proved where it had acted 'in pursuing a policy of disinvesting in South Africa without considering expressly whether it was in the best interests of the beneficiaries and without obtaining professional advice on this matter'.

One interpretation might be that trustees should not take their personal views into account even if there is a choice between two equally beneficial investments, although, if they do so in such a case, it would, in practice, be difficult to sustain an attack upon their action. This interpretation is, perhaps, too extreme. In *Martin v City of Edinburgh District Council*,[11] Lord Murray considered the general proposition that trustees have a duty not to fetter their investment discretion for reasons extraneous to the trust purposes, including reasons of a political or moral nature, and presumably matters of conscience. He thought this acceptable if it means that a trustee has a duty to apply his mind genuinely and independently to a trust issue that is before him, and not simply to adhere to a decision that he has made previously in a different context, or to a policy or other principle to which he is committed. Lord Murray, however, did not consider the proposition either reasonable or practicable if it means that each individual trustee, in genuinely applying his mind and judgment to a trust decision, must divest himself of all personal preferences, of all political beliefs, and of all moral, religious, and other conscientiously held beliefs. What he must do is to recognize that he has those preferences, commitments, or principles, but nonetheless do his best to exercise fair and impartial judgment on the merits of the issue before him. If he realizes that he cannot do that, then he should abstain from participating in deciding the issue, or, in the extreme case, resign as a trustee. Further, as discussed later,[12] trustees may even have to act dishonourably (although not illegally) if the interests of their beneficiaries require it.

Megarry VC's statement of the law, that the best interests of the beneficiaries are normally their financial interests, leaves scope for the exceptional case. As he went on to observe:

> ...if the only actual or potential beneficiaries of a trust are all adults with very strict views on moral and social matters, condemning all forms of alcohol, tobacco and popular entertainments, as well as armaments, I can well understand that it might not be for the 'benefit'[13] of such beneficiaries to know that they are obtaining rather larger financial returns under the trust by reason of investments in those activities than they would have received if the trustees had invested the trust funds in other investments. The beneficiaries might well consider that it was far better to receive less than to receive more from what they consider to be evil and tainted sources...But I would emphasize that such cases are likely to be very rare, and in any case I think that under a trust for the provision of financial benefits the burden would rest, and rest heavy, on him who asserts that it is for the benefit of the beneficiaries as a whole to receive less by reason of the exclusion of some of the possibly more profitable forms of investment.

---

[9] *Cowan v Scargill, supra*, at 761, *per* Megarry VC, discussed (1984) 81 LSG 229 (S C Butler); [1985] JBL 45 (Constance Whippman).

[10] 1988 SLT 329.   [11] *Supra.*

[12] See *Buttle v Saunders* [1950] 2 All ER 193, discussed p 463, *infra.*

[13] See p 507 *et seq*, discussing the meaning of 'benefit' under the Variation of Trusts Act 1958.

The same general approach applies to charities.[14] Charity trustees may hold property for functional purposes: for example, the National Trust owns historic houses, and many charities need office accommodation in which to carry out essential administrative work. Charity trustees may also hold property for the purpose of generating money, whether from income or capital growth, with which to further the work of the charity. Where property is so held by trustees as an investment, the trustees should normally seek to obtain therefrom the maximum return, whether by way of income or capital growth, which is consistent with commercial prudence. In most cases, the best interests of the charity require that the trustees' choice of investments should be made solely on the basis of well-established investment criteria, including the need for diversification. Exceptionally if trustees are satisfied that investing in a company engaged in a particular type of business would conflict with the very objects that their charity is seeking to achieve, they should not so invest.[15] Another exceptional case might be where trustees' holdings of particular investments might hamper a charity's work either by making potential recipients of aid unwilling to be helped because of the source of the charity's money, or by alienating some of those who support the charity financially. In this case, the trustees would need to balance the difficulties that they would encounter, or likely financial loss they would sustain, if they were to hold the investments, against the risk of financial detriment if those investments were excluded from their portfolio.[16]

For the avoidance of doubt, it may be added that if an investment clause prohibits or restricts certain kinds of investment, it is the duty of the trustees to comply with the prohibition or restriction. And the clause might empower or require trustees to take non-financial considerations into account.[17]

2 EXPRESS POWER OF INVESTMENT

The effect of any particular express provision is, of course, a question of construction of the particular words used.[18] Some general observations may, however, be made. Firstly, express investment clauses are now construed more generously than was once the case. The older view[19] was that they 'should be construed strictly for the protection of trustees and remaindermen'; the modern view is that the words of such a clause will be given a natural and not a restrictive interpretation. Accordingly, it was held, in *Re Harari's Settlement*

---

[14] See CC 14 and (2006) 9 CLPR 39 (C Scanlan).

[15] For example, cancer research charities and tobacco shares. It is very unlikely that this would disable the trustees from choosing a properly diversified portfolio.

[16] *Harries v Church Comrs for England* [1993] 2 All ER 300, [1992] 1 WLR 1241 (trustees could properly adopt an ethical investment policy that left open an adequate width of alternative investments), noted [1992] Conv 115 (R Nobles). See (1982) 45 MLR 268 (Helen Beynon); Report of the Charity Commissioners for 1987, paras 41–45; [1988] NLJ Christmas Appeals Supp ii (A Phillips); (2001) 7 CPLR 137 (R Meakin); (2002) 36 T & ELJ 18 (C Cutbill); [2008] CLJ 396 (Rosy Thornton).

[17] *Harries v Church Comrs for England, supra.*

[18] It is a part of the duty of trustees to acquaint themselves with the scope of their powers and in any case of doubt to obtain legal advice and if necessary, the opinion of the court: *Nestle v National Westminster Bank plc* [1994] 1 All ER 118, [1993] 1 WLR 1260, CA,

[19] See, eg, *Re Maryon-Wilson's Estate* [1912] 1 Ch 55, 66–67, CA, *per* Farwell LJ; *Bethell v Abraham* (1873) LR 17 Eq 24; *Re Braithwaite* (1882) 21 Ch D 121.

Trusts,[20] in which the earlier authorities are discussed, that there was no justification for implying any restriction on the meaning of an investment clause authorizing trustees to invest 'in or upon such investments as to them may seem fit'.

Secondly, questions have arisen as to the meaning of the word 'invest' as used in an investment clause. The judicial definition most commonly referred to is that of P O Lawrence J in *Re Wragg*,[21] that 'to invest' includes 'as one of its meanings "to apply money in the purchase of some property from which interest or profit is expected and which property is purchased in order to be held for the sake of the income which it will yield"'. In that case, the investment clause was held to authorize the purchase of real property for the sake of the income that it would produce, but this case was distinguished in *Re Power*,[22] in which it was held that a power to invest in the purchase of freehold property did not authorize the purchase of a freehold house with vacant possession for the occupation of the beneficiaries.

Thirdly, mention may be made of the construction placed on particular provisions contained in express investment clauses in various cases. A power to invest in 'stocks' has been held to authorize an investment in fully paid shares,[23] and, conversely, a power to invest in shares an investment in stock,[24] while a power to invest in 'securities' has been held to include any stocks or shares or bonds by way of investment.[25] Only a very clear provision will be treated as authorizing an investment on personal security, in the sense that there is no security beyond the liability of the borrower to repay, as opposed to a loan on the security of personal property. In *Khoo Tek Keong v Ching Joo Tuan Neoh*,[26] there was a very wide investment clause empowering the trustees 'to invest all moneys liable to be invested in such investments as they in their absolute discretion think fit', but it was held that this did not authorize them to invest in personal security in the above sense, although it did authorize a loan on the security of personal property. One may contrast with this case *Re Laing's Settlement*,[27] in which the trustees were expressly authorized to invest 'upon such personal credit without security as the trustees or trustee shall in their or his absolute and uncontrolled discretion think fit'. On these clear words, the trustees were held to be authorized to advance by way of loan, even to the tenant for life, on his personal security, which, it was pointed out, was not really an advance on security at all.

Fourthly, it should be observed that if the trust instrument directs and requires trustees to make some specified investment, they are under a duty to do so, even if it is one of which they disapprove, and, accordingly, they will not be under any liability in doing so even though this may result in a loss to the trust estate.[28]

---

[20] [1949] 1 All ER 430; *Re Peczenik's Settlement* [1964] 2 All ER 339, [1964] 1 WLR 720.

[21] [1919] 2 Ch 58, 64, 65; *Re Peczenik's Settlement, supra.*

[22] [1947] Ch 572, [1947] 2 All ER 282. But see now section 4, p 423, *infra.*

[23] *Re McEacharn's Settlement Trusts* [1939] Ch 858. Cf *Re Willis* [1911] 2 Ch 563.

[24] *Re Boys' Will Trusts* [1950] 1 All ER 624.

[25] *Re Douglas' Will Trusts* [1959] 2 All ER 620; affd [1959] 3 All ER 785, CA, but no appeal on this point. As to the meaning of 'ordinary preferred stock or shares', see *Re Powell-Cotton's Re-Settlement* [1957] Ch 159, [1957] 1 All ER 404.

[26] [1934] AC 529, PC. See also *Pickard v Anderson* (1872) LR 13 Eq 608.

[27] [1899] 1 Ch 593; *Re Godwin's Settlement* (1918) 119 LT 643.

[28] *Beauclerk v Ashburnham* (1845) 8 Beav 322; *Cadogan v Earl of Essex* (1854) 2 Drew 227; *Re Hurst* (1890) 63 LT 665; affd (1892) 67 LT 96, CA. See (1972) 36 Conv 260 (Penelope Pearce).

Fifthly, an investment clause usually confers an express power to vary investments. In the absence of such a provision, it has been held in a series of cases[29] that a power to vary is implied in a power of investment, the court observing in one case[30] that it would be most unfortunate if it were not so.

Sixthly, there is a conflict of authority as to whether a power of investment 'with the consent of X' gives X a beneficial power that he can use for his own benefit, or effectively release, or whether it gives X a fiduciary power that he should use in the interests of all of the beneficiaries, and which he is unable to release. In the absence of a controlling context, the former view is perhaps to be preferred.[31]

Lastly, a settlor or testator can, it seems, validly confer on a trustee or someone else a power to enlarge the original investment clause.[32]

3 THE STATUTORY POWER UNDER THE TRUSTEE ACT 2000

(A) BACKGROUND

Under the Trustee Act 1925, investment by trustees was restricted in the main to fixed-interest investments that would ultimately be repayable at par—in particular, excluding investment in 'equities'. This was designed to maintain the capital value of the trust fund in money terms, and thus protect the beneficiaries from loss and the trustees from the risk of a claim for breach of trust by imprudent investment. The legislators did not, however, foresee the subsequent far-reaching changes in the economy and the investment situation—in particular, inflation. There is no real safety in the capital of a trust retaining a paper value of £10,000 if, in the meantime, the real value of the pound has, as a result of inflation, been reduced to 50p. And to a somewhat lesser extent, the same is true in relation to income beneficiaries.

The individual investor was often able to provide a hedge against inflation by investing in investments that themselves appreciated in value in money terms, so as to keep pace with the progress of inflation. In particular, he could invest in equity stock and shares that represent the right not to a fixed money income and a fixed capital sum, but to a share in the companies' profits and assets, and are thus ultimately associated with real values and not with money values. The real value may thus be maintained, or may even increase, but there is the risk of a reduction in value if the share price falls. The Trustee Investments Act 1961 was passed, somewhat belatedly, to enable trustees to invest more widely. Subject to certain safeguards, it empowered trustees to invest up to half the trust funds, later increased

---

[29] Including *Hume v Lopes* [1892] AC 112, HL; *Re Pope's Contract* [1911] 2 Ch 442; *Re Pratt's Will Trusts* [1943] Ch 326, [1943] 2 All ER 375.

[30] *Re Pope's Contract, supra, per* Neville J.

[31] *Re Wise*, unreported, discussed in (1954) 218 LT 116, following *Dicconson v Talbot* (1870) 6 Ch App 32 rather than *Re Massingberd's Settlement* (1890) 63 LT 296, CA.

[32] *Re Jewish Orphanage Endowments Trusts* [1960] 1 All ER 764, [1960] 1 WLR 344. Cf *Soldiers', Sailors' and Airmen's Families Association v A-G* [1968] 1 All ER 448n, [1968] 1 WLR 313.

to three-quarters, in the equity stock and shares of financial, industrial, and commercial companies quoted on a recognized investment exchange.

Long before the turn of the century, the 1961 Act was, in turn, generally agreed to be outdated. The Trustee Act 2000 was passed to remedy the situation. This Act embraces modern portfolio theory in which the main concern of the investor is to balance overall growth and overall risk. It repealed Pt I of the Trustee Act 1925, which contained the provisions relating to investments and, subject to savings, the Trustee Investments Act 1961, and went on to give to trustees the wide powers of investment commonly included in any contemporary professionally drawn trust.

(B) THE GENERAL POWER OF INVESTMENT

Part II of the Trustee Act 2000 is revolutionary in that it replaces the previous system, under which a trustee was only permitted to make specified 'authorized' investments, with one under which a trustee may make any kind of investment that he could make if he were absolutely entitled to the assets of the trust. This is called 'the general power of investment'.[33] The general power of investment does not, however, permit a trustee to make investments in land other than in loans secured on land, but there are special provisions in relation to the acquisition of land in s 8, discussed below.[34]

The general power of investment, which applies to trusts whenever created,[35] is additional to any powers of investment conferred on trustees otherwise than by the Act, but is subject to any restriction or exclusion imposed by the trust instrument (provided that it was made after 2 August 1961),[36] or by any enactment or any provision of subordinate legislation.[37]

Part II does not apply to trustees of pension schemes, authorized unit trusts, or funds established under schemes made under ss 24 or 25 of the Charities Act 1993.[38]

(C) GENERAL PRINCIPLES TO BE APPLIED

(i) The rules developed by equity

The mere fact that a certain type of investment is authorized by the trust instrument or by statute does not mean that it is necessarily proper to invest in it in any particular case: if it is too risky, it will constitute a breach of trust. However wide the provisions of an express investment clause may be, it is submitted that they do not absolve trustees from their duty to

---

[33] Trustee Act 2000, s 3(1), (2).

[34] Ibid, s 3(3), and see p 423, *infra*. A person invests in a loan secured on land if he has rights under any contract under which (a) one person provides another with credit, and (b) the obligation of the borrower to repay is secured on land. 'Credit' includes any cash loan or other financial accommodation and 'cash' includes money in any form: ibid, s 3(4)–(6).

[35] Ibid, s 7(1). A provision in a trust instrument made before the commencement of Pt II, which operates under the 1961 Act as a power to invest under that Act, or confers power to invest under that Act, is to be treated as conferring the general power of investment: s 7(3).

[36] Ibid, s 7(2). This is to ensure that old restrictions overcome by the 1961 Act do not revive to restrict the benefits of the new general power of investment.

[37] Ibid, s 6(1)–(3).

[38] Ibid, ss 36–38. As to ss 24 and 25 of the Charities Act 1993, see pp 331, 332, *supra*.

consider whether a proposed investment is such as, in its nature, it is prudent and right for
them as trustees to make. Even if they are given power to invest at their absolute discretion
and as if they were absolute owners, they cannot invest in an investment that is one that a
prudent man of business would have eschewed.[39] The general principles were restated in the
leading case of *Learoyd v Whiteley*.[40] In the Court of Appeal, Lindley LJ said:[41]

> care must be taken not to lose sight of the fact that the business of the trustee, and the
> business which the ordinary prudent man is supposed to be conducting for himself, is the
> business of investing money for the benefit of persons who are to enjoy it at some future
> time, and not for the sole benefit of the person entitled to the present income. The duty of
> a trustee is not to take such care only as a prudent man would take if he had only himself
> to consider; the duty rather is to take such care as an ordinary prudent man would take
> if he were minded to make an investment for the benefit of other people for whom he felt
> morally bound to provide.

In *Learoyd v Whiteley*[42] itself, although the power of investment was wide enough to cover
a mortgage on a freehold brickfield, it was held to be a breach of trust, since the property
was of a hazardous and wasting character:

> This does not mean that a trustee is bound to avoid all risk and in effect act as an insurer
> of the trust fund... The distinction is between a prudent degree of risk on the one hand,
> and hazard on the other. [The court will not] be astute to fix liability on a trustee who has
> committed no more than an error of judgment, from which no business man, however
> prudent, can expect to be immune.[43]

Particular decisions need to be looked at with care, because what a prudent man should
do depends on the economic and financial conditions of the time, not on what judges may
have said should be done in different conditions in the past.[44] Referring to the 'classic statement' of Lindley LJ cited above, Hoffman J[45] said that it set an extremely flexible standard
capable of adaptation to current economic conditions, and contemporary understanding
of markets and investments:

> For example, investments which were imprudent in the days of the gold standard may be
> sound and sensible in times of high inflation. Modern trustees acting within their invest-
> ment powers are entitled to be judged by the standards of current portfolio theory, which
> emphasizes the risk level of the entire portfolio rather than the risk attaching to each
> investment taken in isolation.

Another aspect was demonstrated in *Re David Feldman Charitable Foundation*.[46]
Mr Feldman set up an incorporated charity with a gift of US$180,000, of which he, his solic-
itor and his accountant were directors. Shortly afterwards, the charity lent US$175,000 to
Mr Feldman's company, on the security of a promissory note. This was within the charity's

---

[39] *Khoo Tek Keong v Ching Joo Tuan Neogh* [1934] AC 529, PC; *Chapman v Browne* [1902] 1 Ch 785, CA;
Bartlett v Barclays Bank Trust Co Ltd [1980] Ch 515, [1980] 1 All ER 139.

[40] (1887) 12 App Cas 727, HL. See *Jones v AMP Perpetual Trustee Co of NZ Ltd* [1994] 1 NZLR 690.

[41] *Re Whiteley* (1886) 33 Ch D 347, 355, CA; *Nestle v National Westminster Bank plc* [1994] 1 All ER 118,
[1993] 1 WLR 1260, CA.

[42] *Supra*, HL.   [43] *Bartlett v Barclays Bank Trust Co Ltd* [1980] Ch 515, [1980] 1 All ER 139.

[44] *Nestle v National Westminster Bank plc*, *supra*, CA.

[45] In *Nestle v National Westminster Bank plc* at first instance, unreported, affd on appeal, *supra*, CA. See
(1987) 62 NYULR 52 (J N Gordon); (2003) 12 Tru LI 74 (P U Ali).

[46] (1987) 58 OR (2d) 626.

powers of investment. Although there was no loss to the trust estate, it was held that, by reasons of the conflict of interest, the loan to Mr Feldman's company was an improper investment and a breach of trust.

These equitable rules have been, in effect, superseded firstly by the Trustee Investments Act 1961, and subsequently by the Trustee Act 2000, which embodies and enlarges the equitable principles.

(ii) The statutory provisions

The Trustee Act 2000 provides that, in exercising any power of investment, whether arising under the Act or otherwise, and whenever created, a trustee must have regard to the standard investment criteria. The standard investment criteria, in relation to a trust, are:

(a) the suitability to the trust of investment of the same kind as any particular investment proposed to be made or retained and of that particular investment as an investment of that kind, and

(b) the need for diversification of investments of the trust, in so far as is appropriate to the circumstances of the trust.[47]

'Suitability' includes considerations as to the size and risk of the investment, and the need to produce an appropriate balance between income and capital growth to meet the needs of the trust. It will also include any relevant ethical considerations as to the kind of investments that it is appropriate for the trust to make.

The Act also requires trustees to review the investments of the trust from time to time and to consider whether, having regard to the standard investment criteria, they should be varied.[48]

(D) OBTAINING ADVICE

Section 5(1) of the Trustee Act 2000 provides that, before exercising any power of investment,[49] a trustee must obtain and consider proper advice about the way in which, having regard to the standard investment criteria, the power should be exercised. Likewise, by s 5(2), when reviewing the investments of the trust, he must obtain and consider proper advice about whether, having regard to the standard investment criteria, the investments should be varied. 'Proper advice' is the advice of a person who is reasonably believed by the trustee to be qualified to give it by his ability in, and practical experience of, financial and other matters relating to the proposed investment.[50] The trustee is not, on the one hand, required to act on such advice, but he is not entitled to reject it merely because he sincerely disagrees with it, unless, in addition to being sincere, he is acting as an ordinary prudent man would act;[51] nor, on the other hand, is he necessarily protected if he follows it. Clearly, however, it would be difficult to establish a breach of trust if a trustee had bona fide relied on such advice, and such reliance would also normally enable him to obtain relief under s 61 of the Trustee Act 1925.[52]

---

47 Trustee Act 2000, ss 4(1), (3), and 7(1).   48 Ibid, s 4(2).
49 Whether arising under the statutory power or otherwise, and whenever created: ibid, s 7(1).
50 Trustee Act 2000, s 5(4).
51 *Cowan v Scargill* [1985] Ch 270, [1984] 2 All ER 750, *per* Megarry V-C.
52 Discussed in Chapter 23, section 3(F), p 535, *supra*.

By way of exception to the above requirements, s 5(3) provides that a trustee need not obtain such advice if he reasonably concludes that, in all of the circumstances, it is unnecessary or inappropriate to do so. This would be the case, for example, if the proposed investment were small, so that the cost of obtaining advice would be disproportionate to the benefit to be gained from doing so, or if the trustees themselves were to possess skills and knowledge making separate advice unnecessary.

In the present investment situation, the position of trustees is not easy.[53] The sort of investment that will produce a high rate of interest that will suit the life tenant is likely to be fixed-interest investment, the real value of which may well be eroded by inflation by the time that the remaindermen come into possession, while equities that it is hoped will show a capital appreciation and thus safeguard the position of remaindermen may not produce a high enough rate of interest to satisfy the tenant for life.

4 ACQUISITION OF LAND

Part III of the Trustee Act 2000 provides that a trustee may acquire freehold or leasehold land in the United Kingdom:

(i)   as an investment;

(ii)   for occupation by a beneficiary; or

(iii) for any other reason.[54]

As with Pt II, the powers conferred by Pt III are additional to any powers conferred on trustees otherwise than by the Act, but are subject to any restriction or exclusion imposed by the trust instrument or by any enactment or any provision of subordinate legislation.[55]

For the purposes of exercising his functions as a trustee, a trustee who acquires land under these provisions has all of the powers of an absolute owner in relation to the land.[56] Thus, for example, a trustee has power to hold land jointly with other persons, powers of sale and leasing, and power to grant mortgages in respect of land.

The above provisions, which apply to trusts whenever created,[57] are broadly modelled on s 6(3), (4), of the Trusts of Land and Appointment of Trustees Act 1996, but are in wider terms than that section as originally enacted. Section 6, which is still in force in relation to trustees of land, has, however, been amended by the 2000 Act so as to give trustees of land the powers conferred by s 8 of the latter Act, as set out above. Unlike the 1996 Act, the 2000 Act is not restricted to trustees of land, but applies to trustees generally. An express duty was imposed on trustees of land by s 6(5) of the 1996 Act to have regard to the interests of the beneficiaries in exercising their powers under that section. This provision is

---

[53] See (1975) 39 Conv 318 (D Paling). For a discussion of the problem in the USA, see (1978) 126 U Penn LR 1171.

[54] Ibid, s 8(1). 'Freehold or leasehold land' is defined in s 8(2). In relation to England and Wales, it means a legal estate in land: s 8(2)(a).

[55] Ibid, s 9.   [56] Ibid, s 8(3).

[57] Ibid, s 10(2). But not to settled land under the Settled Land Act 1925, or to a trust to which the Universities and College Estates Act 1925 applies: ibid, s 10(1).

not replicated in the 2000 Act, but since it is thought merely to have made statutory the pre-existing equitable duty of trustees, the omission of an equivalent provision does not diminish the obligations of trustees.

Part III does not apply to trustees of pension schemes, trustees of authorized unit trusts, or trustees managing funds established under schemes made under ss 24 or 25 of the Charities Act 1993.[58]

5 TRUSTEES HOLDING A CONTROLLING INTEREST IN A COMPANY

As already mentioned,[59] the duty of a trustee is to conduct the business of the trust in such a way as an ordinary prudent man would conduct a business of his own. In *Re Lucking's Will Trusts*,[60] Cross J had to consider how this general principle should be applied to trustees holding a controlling interest in a private company. Firstly, he asked himself: 'What steps, if any, does a reasonably prudent man who finds himself a majority shareholder in a private company take with regard to the management of the company's affairs?'

To this question, he gave answer:

> He does not, I think, content himself with such information as to the management of the company's affairs as he is entitled to as a shareholder, but ensures that he is represented on the board. He may be prepared to run the business himself as managing director or, at least, to become a non-executive director while having the business managed by someone else. Alternatively, he may find someone who will act as his nominee on the board and report to him from time to time as to the company's affairs.

Trustees holding a controlling interest, he concluded, ought in the same way to ensure, so far as they can, that they have such information as to the progress of the company's affairs as directors would have and act on that information appropriately. It has since been explained[61] that this is not to be read as imposing on such trustees a necessary requirement that one of them or a nominee must be on the board of directors. These are merely examples of what may, in some circumstances, be convenient methods for trustees to adopt, but other methods may be equally satisfactory and convenient in other circumstances. Every case will depend on its own facts.

In *Re Lucking's Will Trusts*[62] itself, trustees held a majority shareholding. One of the trustees was, indeed, on the board of the company, but he had failed to supervise adequately the drawings of the managing director in effect appointed by him, as a consequence of which the company lost some £15,000 on the managing director's bankruptcy. The failure of supervision was clearly a failure of the trustee-director's duty to the company *qua* director; the judge held that, being partly a representative of the trust, it was also a failure of his duty *qua* trustee, for which he was liable to the beneficiaries.

---

[58] Ibid, ss 36–38. As to ss 24 and 25 of the Charities Act 1993, see pp 331, 332, *supra*.

[59] See pp 396, 421, *supra*.

[60] [1967] 3 All ER 726, [1968] 1 WLR 866. See (1980) 30 UTLJ 151 (D Hughes).

[61] For instance, by Brightman J in *Bartlett v Barclays Bank Trust Co Ltd* [1980] Ch 515, [1980] 1 All ER 139; *Re Poyiadjis* [2004] WTLR 1169 (Isle of Man HC).   [62] *Supra*.

6 SETTLED LAND AND LAND HELD UPON A TRUST OF LAND

Capital money arising under a settlement within the Settled Land Act 1925 may be invested or otherwise applied in investment in securities either under the general power of investment in s 3 of the Trustee Act 2000, or under a power to invest conferred on the trustees of the settlement by the settlement, or in various other modes set out in s 73(1)[63] of the Settled Land Act 1925. Most of the modes are closely connected with the management of the settled land, but there is included[64] the purchase of land in fee simple, or of leasehold land held for sixty years or more unexpired at the time of purchase. The investment or other application of capital money by the trustees must normally be made according to the discretion of the trustees, but subject to any consent required or direction given by the settlement with respect to the investment or other application by the trustees of trust money of the settlement.[65] Any investment must be in the names or under the control of the trustees.[66] The trustees, in exercising their power to invest or apply capital money, must, so far as practicable, consult the tenant for life and, so far as consistent with the general interest of the settlement, give effect to his wishes.[67]

The general power of investment[68] applies to trustees of land as to other trustees, as does the power to acquire freehold and leasehold land.[69] As we have seen,[70] the power under the Trusts of Land and Appointment of Trustees Act 1996 for trustees of land to acquire land has been brought into line with the provisions of the Trustee Act 2000.

7 PERSONAL REPRESENTATIVES

The provisions of the Trustee Act 2000 apply in relation to a personal representative administering an estate according to the law as it applies to a trustee carrying out a trust for beneficiaries, with appropriate modifications.[71]

It may be noted that s 41[72] of the Administration of Estates Act 1925 gives a power of appropriation to personal representatives, although it is important to remember that it does not apply to trustees. Subsection 2 provides that any property duly appropriated under the statutory power shall thereafter be treated as an authorized investment, and may be retained or dealt with accordingly. The Law Reform Committee recommended[73] that trustees should be given a similar power of appropriation in all cases in which the property to be appropriated would, once appropriated, be held on trusts separate from those applying to any other trust property.

---

[63] As amended.   [64] Settled Land Act 1925, s 73(1)(xi).
[65] Settled Land Act 1925, s 75(2)(a), as substituted by the Trustee Act 2000, Sch 2, para 10(1).
[66] Settled Land Act 1925, s 75(2)(b), as likewise substituted.
[67] Ibid, s 75(4)–(4C), as likewise substituted for original s 75(4). See also ss 75(4A)–(4C) and 75A.
[68] See Trustee Act 2000, s 3, and p 420, *supra*.   [69] See ibid, s 8, and p 423, *supra*.
[70] See p 418, *supra*.   [71] Trustee Act 2000, s 35.
[72] As amended by the Mental Health Act 1959, the Mental Capacity Act 2005, the County Courts Act 1984, and the Trusts of Land and Appointment of Trustees Act 1996.
[73] 23rd Report, Cmnd 8733, para 4.42.

8 ALTERATION OF POWER OF INVESTMENT

Since the Trustee Act 2000, trustees will generally have wide powers of investment either under that Act or under an express investment clause. There are, accordingly, far fewer cases in which trustees will have any need to apply to the court for an enlargement of their investment powers. A case could arise, however, in which there is an express investment clause giving only limited powers of investment, or in which the trust instrument imposes some restriction on the statutory power.

In respect of charities, a power of investment may be altered by way of scheme,[74] or under the provisions of s 57 of the Trustee Act 1925.[75]

In the case of a private trust s 57 of the 1925 Act is equally available,[76] and there is also jurisdiction under the Variation of Trusts Act 1958.[77] It has been said,[78] where the beneficial interests under a will or settlement were unaffected, that an application for extension of investment powers should be brought under s 57 of the Trustee Act 1925 rather than under the Variation of Trusts Act 1958. The reasons for this were said to be that the trustees were the natural persons to make the application, the consent of every adult beneficiary was not essential, and the court was not required to give its consent on behalf of every category of beneficiary separately, but—more realistically—would consider their interests collectively in income and capital.

9 CLAIMS BY BENEFICIARIES IN RELATION TO THE INVESTMENT OF TRUST FUNDS

It may be difficult for beneficiaries to succeed in a claim based on mismanagement by the trustees of the trust investments. In *Nestle v National Westminster Bank plc*,[79] it was held or assumed by all of the members of the court that the trustees had, at all relevant times, been under a misunderstanding as to the scope of the investment clause in the will, in relation to which it was said to be inexcusable not to have taken legal advice. Further, they had failed

---

[74] *Re Royal Society's Charitable Trusts* [1956] Ch 87, [1955] 3 All ER 14; *Re University of London Charitable Trusts* [1964] Ch 282, [1963] 3 All ER 859; *Steel v Wellcome Custodian Trustees Ltd* [1988] 1 WLR 167 (in exceptional case, power given to invest as if trustees were absolutely and beneficially entitled), discussed (1988) 85 LSG 45/26 (N J Reville); [1988] Conv 380 (Brenda Dale), and see Chapter 14, section 7, *supra*.

[75] *Re Shipwrecked Fishermen & Mariners' Royal Benevolent Society Charity* [1959] Ch 220, [1958] 3 All ER 465; *Re Kolb's Will Trusts* [1962] Ch 531, [1961] 3 All ER 811, not following the view expressed by Vaisey J in *Re Royal Society's Charitable Trusts, supra.* See Chapter 22, section 2(B), p 499, *infra*.

[76] *Mason v Farbrother* [1983] 2 All ER 1078, and see the cases cited in fn 75, *supra*.

[77] Considered, generally, p 503 *et seq, infra*.

[78] In *Anker-Petersen v Anker-Petersen* [1991] 16 LS Gaz R 32.

[79] [1994] 1 All ER 118, [1993] 1 WLR 1260, CA, noted [1993] Conv 63 (Ann Kenny); [1997] PCB 232 (S Lofthouse). Cf *Re Mulligan (decd)* [1998] 1 NZLR 481, in which the trustees were held liable, having taken no steps over a period of forty years to protect the capital from inflation. See [1998] Conv 352 (G Watt and M Stauch), in which it is argued that courts should be prepared to acknowledge as a breach of trust any inprudent investment conduct, and to judge, in retrospect and with common sense, the probable extent of the loss caused to the fund by the breach. See also *Wight v Olswang* [2001] WTLR 291, CA.

to carry out regular reviews of the trust investments. These were symptoms of incompetence or idleness (although on the part of the predecessors of the National Westminster Bank), but not without more breaches of trust. In order to succeed, the beneficiary had to show that, through one or other or both of these causes, the trustees made decisions that they should not have made or failed to make decisions that they should have made, and further that loss to the trust estate had resulted therefrom. Staughton LJ admitted that this put on the beneficiary a burden that it might be difficult to discharge, and she failed to do so in *Nestle v National Westminster Bank plc*[80] itself. It has subsequently been held that, irrespective of breaches of trust during the decision-making process, the beneficiaries of a trust do not have a claim against trustees in respect of an investment decision that they have made unless they could establish that the decision was one that no reasonable trustee could have made.

It may be added that if a decision by trustees is objectively right, they will not be liable even if it was, in fact, made on wholly wrong grounds.[81]

10 OCCUPATIONAL PENSION SCHEMES ESTABLISHED UNDER A TRUST

Parts II (investment) and III (acquisition of land) do not apply to the trustees of any pension scheme.[82] However, the Pensions Act 1995 provides that the trustees of such a scheme have, subject to any restriction imposed by the scheme, the same power to make an investment of any kind as if they were absolutely entitled to the assets of the scheme.[83] Their duties in relation to investment cannot be excluded by an exemption clause.[84]

Similar provisions as to choosing investments to those laid down in s 4(3) of the Trustee Act 2000 are enacted by s 36 of the Pensions Act 1995, and the trustees are required to provide and maintain a written statement of the principles governing their decisions about investments.[85]

---

[80] *Supra*, CA.
[81] *Cowan v Scargill* [1985] Ch 270, [1984] 2 All ER 750; *Nestle v National Westminster Bank plc, supra*, CA.
[82] Trustee Act 2000, s 36(3).   [83] Pensions Act 1995, s 34.   [84] Ibid, s 33.
[85] Ibid, ss 35, 36. See s 40 as to restrictions on employer-related investments.

18

EVENHANDEDNESS
AS BETWEEN THE
BENEFICIARIES

One aspect of this duty that we have already come across[1] is the obligation to maintain an even hand as between the life tenant and remaindermen in considering the choice of investments. The most elaborate development, however, in connection with the conflicting interests of tenant for life and remainderman,[2] concerns the duties to convert, and to apportion income, discussed in sections 1 and 2.

Special cases considered in sections 3 and 4 are those in which stock or shares are sold or purchased cum dividend, and in which some extraordinary payment is made by a company to trustee shareholders. Section 6 looks at the way in which the principle of evenhandedness should be applied in relation to the allocation of expenditure.

The final section summarizes the Law Commission's proposals.

1 THE DUTY TO CONVERT

Where the will or settlement contains a direction, express or implied,[3] to convert, then the precise duty of the trustees will depend upon the terms of the direction, as affected by statutory provisions.[4] In the absence of any such direction, there is no duty to convert in the case of an *inter vivos* settlement, which must necessarily deal with specific

---

[1] See p 414, *supra*. For another aspect of the duty, see *Re Leigh's Settlement Trusts* (1980) [2006] WTLR 477.

[2] The different position of personal representatives in the course of administration of the deceased's estate is discussed in *Re Hayes's Will Trusts* [1971] 2 All ER 341, [1971] 1 WLR 758. For the special case in which trustees are authorized to continue a farming business, and the stock of sheep and cattle increases, see *Re Richards* [1974] 2 NZLR 60. See also *Re McClintock* (1976) 70 DLR (3d) 175; *Josephs v Canada Trust Co* (1992) 90 DLR (4th) 242; revsd (1994) 106 DLR (4th) 384. As to pension schemes, see (2000) 14 Tru LI 130 (S E K Hulme).

[3] See, eg, *Flux v Best* (1874) 31 LT 645, and cf *Re Holloway* (1888) 60 LT 46.

[4] Section 4 of the Trusts of Land and Appointment of Trustees Act 1996 provides, with retrospective effect: 'In the case of every trust for sale of land created by a disposition there is to be implied, despite any provision to the contrary made by the disposition, a power for the trustees to postpone sale of the land; and the trustees are not liable in any way for postponing sale of the land, in the exercise of their discretion, for an indefinite period.'

property;[5] nor does any such duty arise in the case of a devise of real estate, whether specific or residuary,[6] or in the case of a specific legacy of personal estate.[7] A duty to convert may, however, be implied in the case of a residuary bequest contained in a will under what is known as the 'rule in *Howe v Earl Dartmouth'*.[8] Under this rule, wasting property—such as royalties in respect of copyright[9]—and hazardous investments[10] should be converted in order to do justice to the remainderman, who might otherwise get nothing at all, or only property much depreciated in value; reversionary interests and other property not producing income should be converted in order to do justice to the tenant for life, who might otherwise obtain nothing from these parts of the trust property. The traditional reasoning behind the rule is no longer appropriate to contemporary conditions in which the remainderman may well prefer the hazard of an investment that stands a chance of maintaining its real value as against one that, while maintaining its value on paper, is certain to depreciate in real terms in an inflationary situation. Conversely, the tenant for life may well prefer a 'safe' investment such as consols bringing in, at the date of writing, nearly 5 per cent interest. The Law Reform Committee recommends[11] that the duty to convert under *Howe v Earl Dartmouth*, together with the rules as to apportionment under both that case and *Re Earl of Chesterfield's Trust*,[12] should be subsumed in a new statutory duty to hold a fair balance between the beneficiaries—in particular, those entitled to capital and those entitled to income. Coupled with such a general duty should be an express power for such purposes to convert income into capital and vice versa.

The rule in *Howe v Earl Dartmouth*, it has been observed,[13] 'has been since affirmed, as often as it has been referred to, and is unquestionably the law. But the testator may take the case of any particular bequest out of this rule...' There are a large number of reported cases in which the question has been whether, on the true construction of the will, an intention is to be found that the rule in *Howe v Earl Dartmouth* shall not apply.

Dicta are to be found in *Hinves v Hinves*[14] and other cases[15] to the effect that small indications of intention will prevent the application of the rule, but the true view, it is submitted, is that expressed by Cozens-Hardy MR in *Re Wareham*:[16] 'that the rule in Howe v Earl Dartmouth must be applied, unless it appears on the construction of the particular will that the testator has shown an intention that the rule shall not apply. The burden of providing this rests on the tenant for life who claims to enjoy the property in specie.' The willingness of

---

[5] *Re Van Straubenzee* [1901] 2 Ch 779. But see (1972) 50 CBR 116 (M C Cullity).

[6] *Re Woodhouse* [1941] Ch 332, [1941] 2 All ER 265. See (1981) 59 CBR 687 (J Smith).

[7] See, eg, *Bethune v Kennedy* (1835) 1 My & Cr 114; *Re Van Straubenzee*, *supra*, and the cases cited *infra* in connection with enjoyment in specie.

[8] (1802) 7 Ves 137 (a decision of Lord Eldon); *Hinwes v Hinves* (1844) 3 Hare 609. See, generally, (1943) 7 Conv 128 (S J Bailey); (1952) 16 Conv 349 (L A Sheridan). The suggestion in (1996) 146 NLJ 960 (R Wallington) that the incidental effect of the Trusts of Land and Appointment of Trustees Act 1996 is to exclude the rule (and the rule in *Re Earl of Chesterfield's Trusts* (1883) 24 Ch D 643) is not, it is submitted, valid.

[9] *Re Sullivan* [1930] 1 Ch 84.

[10] Unauthorized investments, ie those not authorized by the trust instrument or the Trustee Act 2000, are always deemed to be more or less hazardous: *Macdonald v Irvine* (1878) 8 Ch D 101, CA.

[11] 23rd Report (1982), Cmnd 8733, paras 3.27–3.28. See (1984) 62 CBR 577 (R E Scane).

[12] See p 434 *et seq, infra*.   [13] Per Romilly MR in *Morgan v Morgan* (1851) 14 Beav 72, 82.

[14] (1844) 3 Hare 609, 611.   [15] For example, *Morgan v Morgan, supra; Simpson v Lester, supra*.

[16] [1912] 2 Ch 312, 315, CA; *Macdonald v Irvine* (1878) 8 Ch D 101, CA; see also *Re Eaton* (1894) 70 LT 761.

the courts to hold that the duty to convert has been excluded has been criticized[17] as being inappropriate in a modern context. A testator nowadays, it is suggested,[18] 'is planning for the transmission of wealth, not for the custody of sacred icons'.

Whether the rule in *Howe v Earl Dartmouth* is held to be excluded is thus, in each case, a question of the true construction of the particular will. The intention that the rule shall not apply may be express, or may be implied from directions in the will that are inconsistent with the application of the rule. Typically, the rule will be excluded if the court finds an intention that the tenant for life should enjoy the property in specie,[19] or that the remainderman should take the identical property comprised in the residuary gift,[20] or, which indeed follows from either of the preceding intentions, that all of the beneficiaries in turn shall enjoy the estate as existing at the time of the death.[21] The intention to exclude the rule may alternatively be found not in directions as to the beneficial enjoyment, but in directions in relation to conversion. Thus the rule will be excluded by implication if the court finds an intention that the property should be converted at some time fixed by the will by reference to a given number of years after the testator's death, or to the falling in of a life,[22] or that the residuary estate should be divided on the death of the tenant for life.[23] The same result follows from finding an intention that whether the property should be sold, and, if so, when it should be sold, should be left to the discretion of the trustees or of some other person: for instance, by giving trustees power to retain existing investments, or to sell and convert the same as they should in their absolute discretion think fit,[24] or by giving them a mere power to sell if and when they should consider it expedient.[25] But a power to vary securities supports the application of the rule by showing the testator intended a conversion.[26] Contrary to what was at one time thought to be the law, in considering whether the rule in *Howe v Earl Dartmouth* is excluded, there is no distinction between hazardous and wasting investments,[27] and reversionary interests are in the same position.[28]

2   THE DUTY TO APPORTION

If there is no duty to convert, express[29] or implied, whether as a matter of construction or as a rule of law under the rule in *Howe v Earl Dartmouth*, the tenant for life is, of course, entitled to the income in specie, if any,[30] and the remainderman will in turn become

---

[17] (1984) 62 CBR 577 (R E Scane).   [18] Op cit, at p 601.
[19] See, eg, *Marshall v Bremner* (1854) 2 Sm & G 237; *Boys v Boys* (1860) 28 Beav 436.
[20] *Harris v Poyner* (1852) 1 Drew 174; *Holgate v Jennings* (1857) 24 Beav 623.
[21] *Re Gough* [1957] Ch 323, [1957] 2 All ER 193.
[22] *Alcock v Sloper* (1833) 2 My & K 699; *Rowe v Rowe* (1861) 29 Beav 276.
[23] *Re Barratt* [1925] Ch 550. Cf *Re Evans' Will Trusts* [1921] 2 Ch 309.
[24] *Re Bates* [1907] 1 Ch 22; *Re Wilson* [1907] 1 Ch 394. In *Re Bates, supra*, Kekewich J put it another way—namely, that the power to retain the shares added them to the list of authorized investments. See (1978) 56 CBR 128 (D Waters).
[25] *Re Pitcairn* [1896] 2 Ch 199; see *Re Rogers* [1915] 2 Ch 437.
[26] *Morgan v Morgan* (1851) 14 Beav 72; *Re Llewellyn's Trust* (1861) 29 Beav 171.
[27] *Re Nicholson* [1909] 2 Ch 111.   [28] *Re Pitcairn* [1896] 2 Ch 199.
[29] There is no duty to convert where trustees are merely given a discretionary power to convert if and when they think fit: *Re Leonard* (1880) 43 LT 664.
[30] *Re Pitcairn* [1896] 2 Ch 199; *Rowlls v Bebb* [1900] 2 Ch 107, CA.

entitled to the capital in specie. Suppose, however, that there is a duty to convert, no matter how it arises, and suppose, moreover, there is some lapse of time before the conversion actually takes place. In such circumstances, if the tenant for life during such period were to take the income in specie, this would be liable to result in unfairness: in the case of a wasting asset, for instance, it might be unfair to the remainderman, because the tenant for life might get a large income for a number of years and the remainderman get nothing at all; in the case of a reversionary interest producing no income, it might, conversely, be unfair to the tenant for life. Equity will not allow failure to carry out a duty to affect the rights of the beneficiaries and, basing itself on the maxim that 'equity looks upon that as done which ought to be done', has laid down somewhat elaborate rules as to the apportionment that is to take place in such circumstances. There is, of course, no reason why the testator should not make what provision he likes with regard to the intermediate income, and if, expressly or by implication, he gives the income in specie pending sale to the tenant for life, his wish will prevail.[31] Similarly, he may make what provisions he chooses where the property in question is a reversionary interest producing no income.[32] In practice, it is very common for a professionally drawn will to contain appropriate express provisions.

It may be noted that the rule in *Howe v Lord Dartmouth* is often taken to refer not only to the duty to convert, for which the case is an authority, but also to the duty to apportion when conversion is delayed, which, at most, is a corollary of the main rule.[33] Indeed, it is commonly taken[34] to refer to the corresponding duty to apportion in the case of an express trust for conversion, which would be more properly called the 'rule in *Gibson v Bott*'.[35] Subject to any such expression of a contrary intention, the rules as to apportionment are the same however the duty to convert arises.

Assuming that there is a duty to convert, the income to which the tenant for life is entitled depends to a large extent upon the type of property, in accordance with the following rules.

(A) AUTHORIZED INVESTMENTS

The tenant for life is, of course, entitled to the whole income of authorized investments as from the date of death.[36] Where there is a trust for sale of land, there is a trust of land under the Trusts of Land and Appointment of Trustees Act 1996, under which the land is an authorized investment,[37] and the tenant for life is accordingly entitled to the actual income.

It will be convenient to mention at this point the position in which there is an authorized investment upon some security such as a mortgage, the interest upon which falls into arrears, if, when the security is realized, it is not sufficient to pay the capital debt and

---

[31] *Re Crowther* [1895] 2 Ch 56; *Re Elford* [1910] 1 Ch 814.

[32] *Re Pitcairn, supra; Rowlls v Bebb, supra.*

[33] See (1952) 16 Conv 349 (L A Sheridan); (1943) 7 Conv 128 and 191 (S J Bailey).

[34] *Re Brooker* [1926] WN 93; *Re Trollope's Will Trusts* [1927] 1 Ch 596; *Re Berton* [1939] Ch 200, [1938] 4 All ER 286.

[35] (1802) 7 Ves 89. The distinction was taken by Romer J in *Re Parry* [1947] Ch 23, [1946] 2 All ER 412.

[36] *Meyer v Simonsen* (1852) 5 De G & Sm 723; *Brown v Gellatly* (1867) 2 Ch App 751.

[37] See ss 1, 6(3), as amended by the Trustee Act 2000, Sch 2, para 45, and *Re Gough* [1957] Ch 323, [1957] 2 All ER 193.

arrears of interest in full. The loss in such case has to be shared between the tenant for life and the remainderman, the sum actually realized being apportioned upon the principles laid down in *Re Atkinson*[38]—namely, in the proportion that the amount due for arrears of interest bears to the amount due in respect of the capital debt. The tenant for life, in making this calculation, is only allowed simple interest.[39]

(B) UNAUTHORIZED PURE PERSONALTY

The following rules as to how this apportionment is to be carried out where there is no express power to postpone conversion are mainly taken from the decision of Farwell J in *Re Fawcett*.[40] The tenant for life is not, in this case, entitled to the actual income, but there has to be an apportionment. In most cases, the tenant for life is likely, as a result of such apportionment, to receive less than the actual income, although, in some cases, it may operate in his favour. There is no longer any distinction made between unauthorized investments that could only be realized at a serious loss to the estate and those that could easily be realized without such loss.

(i)   Where unauthorized investments are retained unsold at the end of one year from the death of the testator, the tenant for life is entitled to receive not the actual income, but interest at the rate of 4 per cent per annum from the date of death until realization, on the value taken one year after the date of death—that is, at the end of the executors' year—by which time the conversion ought to have taken place.

(ii)   Where unauthorized investments are sold during the year following the death of the testator, the tenant for life is entitled to receive from the date of death until realization the like interest on the net proceeds of sale.[41]

(iii)   Subject to head (vi) below, upon realization, whether during or after the end of the executors' year, the net proceeds of sale must be reinvested in authorized investments and, thereafter, rule (i) above will apply.

(iv)   The unauthorized investments for the time being unsold must be treated en bloc as one aggregate.[42]

(v)   Any excess of income from unauthorized investments beyond the interest payable to the life tenant under heads (i) and (ii) above must be invested in authorized investments, to the income of which thereafter, rule (i) above will apply.

(vi)   Interest in respect of unauthorized investments is payable out of the interest arising from them or, in so far as that is insufficient, out of the proceeds of their realization; any interest for the time being in arrears is payable (but calculated as simple interest only) out of subsequent income from unauthorized investments, which are, for the time being, retained, and out of the proceeds of their sale when realized.

---

[38] [1904] 2 Ch 160, CA; *Re Walker's Settlement Trusts* [1936] Ch 280. Principles applied *Trust Company of Australia Ltd v Braid* [1998] 4 VR 97.

[39] *Re Moore* (1885) 54 LJ Ch 432.

[40] [1940] Ch 402. See also *Dimes v Scott* (1828) 4 Russ 195; *Meyer v Simonsen* (1852) 5 De G & Sm 723; *Brown v Gellatly* (1867) 2 Ch App 751.

[41] *Re Berry* [1962] Ch 97, [1961] 1 All ER 529.   [42] *Re Owen* [1912] 1 Ch 519.

(vii) Neither excess income from unauthorized investments that, at the end of any accounting period, is available under head (v) above for investment in authorized investments, nor proceeds of realization of unauthorized investments not required at the date of realization to pay interest under head (vi) above, which are accordingly available to be invested in authorized investments, are applicable towards payment of subsequently accruing interest in respect of unauthorized investments still retained.

(C) UNAUTHORIZED PURE PERSONALTY—THE EFFECT OF A POWER TO POSTPONE CONVERSION

The preliminary point is whether the inclusion of such a power shows an intention that the tenant for life should enjoy the income in specie until a conversion takes place. This depends upon whether the power is inserted for the benefit of the tenant for life, or merely for the more convenient realization of the estate.[43] In order to entitle the tenant for life in specie, there must be something more than a bare power to postpone. Where the necessary indications of the testator's intention are found, and even though there is an express provision excluding the rules as to apportionment, the tenant for life will prima facie only be entitled to the income in specie so long as the trustees postpone the sale in proper exercise of their discretion.[44]

In the absence of any indication that the tenant for life is to take the income in specie, there must be an apportionment, notwithstanding the power to postpone conversion.[45] The difference made by the insertion of a power to postpone was fully discussed by Romer J in *Re Parry*.[46] It means, he pointed out, that there is no duty upon the executor to sell at once, or within a year, or at any other time, and, accordingly, there is no reason for assuming a notional conversion at once, or within a year, or at any other time:

> The essential equity, however—the balance between the successive interests—remains equally compelling even where there is no immediate obligation to convert and property is retained for the benefit of the estate as a whole. It is accordingly rational, and indeed obvious, to substitute a valuation of the testator's assets in the place of a hypothetical sale; and, if so, it is difficult to think of a better date for the valuation than the day when the testator died and the assets passed to his executors.[47]

Accordingly, the tenant for life is entitled to receive interest at the rate of 4 per cent per annum from the date of the death until realization, on the value taken at the date of death. Subject to the consequential variations due to the different date of valuation, the directions set out in rule (B), heads (iii)–(vii), above, will, however, presumably apply.

---

[43] *Re Inman* [1915] 1 Ch 187.

[44] This seems right on principle, and may be inferred from *Rowlls v Bebb* [1900] 2 Ch 107, CA (dealing, however, with a reversionary interest); *Re Godfree* [1914] 2 Ch 110. See also *Re Slater* (1915) 113 LT 691, 693; *Re Chance* [1962] Ch 593, [1962] 1 All ER 942.

[45] *Re Chaytor* [1905] 1 Ch 233; *Re Parry* [1947] Ch 23, [1946] 2 All ER 412; *Re Berry* [1962] Ch 97, [1961] 1 All ER 529. In *Re Parry*, counsel reserved the right to contend before a higher tribunal that the power to postpone excluded the duty to apportion.

[46] *Supra*, where the relevant cases are carefully considered.

[47] *Per* Romer J in *Re Parry* [1947] Ch 23, 45, [1946] 2 All ER 412, 422.

(D) REVERSIONARY INTERESTS—THE RULE IN *RE EARL OF CHESTERFIELD'S TRUSTS*[48]

Here, the property is producing no income and, accordingly, until it falls in, there is nothing to apportion. When it eventually does fall in, or is realized, an apportionment has to be made in order to be fair to the tenant for life. The apportionment is made by ascertaining the sum that, put out at interest at 4 per cent per annum on the day of the testator's death, and accumulating at compound interest calculated at that rate with yearly rests and deducting income tax, would, with the accumulations of interest, have produced, at the day of receipt, the amount actually received. The sum so ascertained must be treated as capital and the residue as income payable to the tenant for life. The rule applies not only to a reversionary interest in its strict sense,[49] but also to other sums that have to be treated as postponed capital payments even though they may have some appearance of income. Thus, the rule has been applied to a policy of assurance on the life of another that fell in some years after the death of the testator,[50] to sums payable to the estate after the testator's death in consideration of past service,[51] to the instalments of the purchase price of a business sold by the testator and payable after his death,[52] to a determinable annuity and payments analogous thereto,[53] and to payment of a sum due from an insolvent estate that was grossly insufficient to satisfy a bond debt.[54] It was also applied to sums paid in respect of claims under Pt I of the Town and Country Planning Act 1954[55] in *Re Chance*,[56] which also decides that it makes no difference that, when the asset ultimately comes in, it brings with it or contains within it interest. It is the fact that the asset is not producing anything in the meantime that gives rise to the claim by the tenant for life for recoupment. But the court has refused to apply the rule where the interest of the testator at the date of death was not a reversionary interest, but an absolute interest, the income of which was temporarily charged in favour of a third person.[57]

(E) REVERSIONARY INTERESTS—THE EFFECT OF A POWER TO POSTPONE CONVERSION

On similar principles to those discussed under rule (C) above, a mere power to postpone does not affect the duty to apportion when the reversion eventually falls in or a sale

---

[48] (1883) 24 Ch D 643, following, with some variation, *Wilkinson v Duncan* (1857) 23 Beav 469; *Beavan v Beavan* (1869) 24 Ch D 649n. See p 429, fn 8.

[49] *Re Hobson* (1885) 53 LT 627; *Re Flower* (1890) 62 LT 216 revsd on other grounds (1890) 63 LT 201, CA; *Rowlls v Bebb* [1900] 2 Ch 107, CA. Cf *Re Holliday* [1947] Ch 402, [1947] 1 All ER 695.

[50] *Re Morley* [1895] 2 Ch 738.

[51] *Re Payne* [1943] 2 All ER 675. Cf *Re Fisher* [1943] Ch 377, [1943] 2 All ER 615.

[52] *Re Hollebone* [1919] 2 Ch 93.

[53] *Re Hey's Settlement Trusts* [1945] Ch 294, [1945] 1 All ER 618; *Re Guinness's Settlement* [1966] 2 All ER 497, [1968] 1 WLR 1355. Cf, however, *Crawley v Crawley* (1835) 7 Sim 427, followed in *Re Whitehead* [1894] 1 Ch 678, in which the court simply ordered each payment to be treated as capital and invested accordingly, the tenant for life thereafter to receive the income on the investments. It is to be noted that *Crawley v Crawley, supra*, was decided before the rule in *Re Earl of Chesterfield's Trusts* was settled, and it is submitted that on such facts an apportionment under the rule should be made.

[54] *Cox v Cox* (1869) LR 8 Eq 343; see *Re Duke of Cleveland's Estate* [1895] 2 Ch 542. For unusual applications of the rule, see *Re Godden* [1893] 1 Ch 292; *Re Hengler* [1893] 1 Ch 586 (this doubtful case is difficult to reconcile with *Re Owen* [1912] 1 Ch 519 and seems to depend on a wrong admission by counsel that the rule in *Re Earl of Chesterfield's Trusts* applied). [55] *Re Chance* [1962] Ch 593, [1962] 1 All ER 942.

[56] *Supra.* [57] *Re Holliday* [1947] Ch 402, [1947] 1 All ER 695.

eventually takes place. The apportionment must be carried out according to the principles set out in rule (D) above. If, however, there is a power to postpone that is properly[58] exercised, then there may be other indications in the will that it is the testator's intention that no apportionment is to take place, and, if so, this will be effective. In practice, it is usual to exclude the operation of the rule in *Re Earl of Chesterfield's Trusts*.

(F) RATE OF INTEREST

It will have been observed that, in making an apportionment, both in the case of wasting or hazardous investments, and in the case of reversionary interests, the rate of interest is stated to be 4 per cent. There was, however, a period in the early part of this century when the rate was reduced to 3 per cent. The rate was restored to 4 per cent in *Re Baker*[59] and *Re Beech*,[60] and has ever since continued to be applied.[61] Perhaps the time has come for a reappraisal, as has happened in other contexts. For example, the rate of interest on judgment debts, which was originally fixed at 4 per cent by the Judgments Act 1838, is now 8 per cent.[62] In Canada, it has been held[63] that the life tenant is entitled to an annual income that would be a fair equivalent for what he would have received had the assets been converted and the proceeds of such conversion invested in accordance with the provisions of the will.

(G) UNAUTHORIZED INVESTMENT BY TRUSTEES

For the avoidance of doubt, it may be observed that the above rules as to apportionment apply only to property found in a particular state of investment at the date of the death. They have no application where trustees commit a breach of trust by making an unauthorized investment. Trustees in such a case 'have discharged their liability in favour of the cestuis que trust who are entitled to the capital in remainder, when they have made good the capital and any increase which that capital has received'.[64] Increase here 'does not mean increase by way of interest, but increase by way of profit—some accumulations, something by way of accretion to the capital'.[65] Accordingly, if the tenant for life has received more than 4 per cent, he cannot be called upon to account for the balance over that amount to the remainderman, even though it be the trustee himself who is the tenant for life.[66] If the unauthorized investment proves to be insufficient, the loss[67] has to be thrown rateably on the tenant for life and remainderman. The sum available has to be divided in the

---

[58] *Rowlls v Bebb* [1900] 2 Ch 107, CA; *Re Hey's Settlement Trusts, supra*; *Re Guinness's Settlement, supra*. See (1984) 62 CBR 577 (R E Scane).

[59] [1924] 2 Ch 271.

[60] [1920] 1 Ch 40, followed in *Re Fawcett* [1940] Ch 402; *Re Parry* [1947] Ch 23, [1946] 2 All ER 412; *Re Berry* [1962] Ch 97, [1961] 1 All ER 529.

[61] In *Re Ellis* [1935] Ch 193. Farwell J refused to take judicial notice of the fact that a trustee could not then get 4 per cent on trustee securities, saying that this was a matter for evidence.

[62] SI 1993/564. See CPR 40.8 and *Cremer v General Carriers SA* [1974] 1 All ER 1, [1974] 1 WLR 341.

[63] *Re Lauer and Stekl* (1974) 47 DLR (3d) 286; affd (1975) 54 DLR (3d) 159n.

[64] *Stroud v Gwyer* (1860) 28 Beav 130, 141, *per* Romilly MR; *Slade v Chaine* [1908] 1 Ch 522, CA.

[65] *Slade v Chaine, supra*, at 526, *per* Kekewich J.   [66] *Re Hoyles* [1912] 1 Ch 67.

[67] For present purposes, it is assumed that any personal remedy against the trustee who has committed the breach of trust is worthless.

proportion that the dividends which the tenant for life would have received had the wrongful investment not been made bear to the value of the sum wrongly invested. The tenant
for life must, of course, give credit for moneys actually received, although he is not liable
to refund any over payment.[68]

3 WHERE STOCK OR SHARES ARE SOLD OR PURCHASED BY TRUSTEES CUM DIVIDEND

In such cases, the general rule is that there is no apportionment between capital and
income.[69] This is purely a rule of convenience, as a result of which the beneficiaries have to
take the rough with the smooth in order to ease the burden falling on trustees. The court,
however, may depart from the general rule where its application would cause a glaring
injustice, although it seems that this jurisdiction will only be exercised in extreme circumstances.[70] If, at the date of the purchase of stock or shares, however, dividends have been
earned and declared, although not paid, they must go to capital when they are ultimately
paid, and not to the tenant for life.[71]

4 THE 'WINDFALL' PRINCIPLE

Questions sometimes arise as to whether the tenant for life or remainderman is entitled
to extraordinary payments made by a company, which may be given some name such as
'cash bonus' or 'capital profits dividend'. It is a basic principle that a limited company not
in liquidation can make no payment by way of return of capital to its shareholders except
as a step in an authorized reduction of capital. Any other payment made by it by means
of which it parts with moneys or other property to its shareholders must, and can only,
be made by way of dividing profits. Accordingly, whatever the payment may be called,
if it is paid to a trustee shareholder, it will prima facie belong to the person beneficially
entitled to the income of the trust estate—that is, the tenant for life, as opposed to the
remainderman.[72] As Vaisey J put it:[73] 'These accretions to the normal income of the trust
fund are sometimes metaphorically described as "windfalls", and when they have left the

---

[68] *Re Bird* [1901] 1 Ch 916.

[69] *Bulkeley v Stephens* [1896] 2 Ch 241. Cf *Re Henderson* [1940] Ch 368, [1940] 1 All ER 623.

[70] *Bulkeley v Stephens, supra*; *Re Firth* [1938] Ch 517, [1938] 2 All ER 217; *Re Maclaren's Settlement Trusts*
[1951] 2 All ER 414. *Re Winterstoke's Will Trusts* [1938] Ch 158, [1937] 4 All ER 63, seems out of line with
the other cases, and in *Re Ellerman's Settlement Trusts* [1984] LSG R 430 (more fully reported and noted in
[1986] TL & P 62, sub nom *Hitch v Ruegg*), Nourse J said that it was wrong and ought not to be followed.

[71] *Re Sir Robert Peel's Settled Estates* [1910] 1 Ch 389.

[72] *Hill v Permanent Trustee Co of New South Wales Ltd* [1930] AC 720, PC; *Re Doughty* [1947] Ch 263,
[1947] 1 All ER 207, CA; *Re Harrison's Will Trusts* [1949] Ch 678; see, generally, (1951) 67 LQR 195 (S J Bailey);
Manukan City Council v Lawson [2001] 1 NZLR 599.

[73] *Re Kleinwort's Settlement Trusts* [1951] Ch 860, 863, [1951] 2 All ER 328, 330.

parent tree, I can see no principle for notionally replacing them on the boughs from which they have fallen.'

Thus, in *Re Bates*,[74] a company sold some of its assets at a price well above the value as appearing in the company's balance sheet. The profit on the sale was distributed as a cash bonus, and it was held that the tenant for life was entitled to the whole payment. Similarly, in *Re Tedlie*,[75] a company sold a considerable part of its assets to another company, receiving in payment shares and a sum of cash. Following this transaction, the company had a large surplus of assets over debts, capital, and what was required for carrying on the business retained. Shares[76] and cash were paid to the shareholders, and it was held that a trustee shareholder must pay the whole to the tenant for life. Again, in *Re Whitehead's Will Trusts*,[77] the question arose where trustees, as holders under a unit trust, received what were called 'capital distributions'. The court held that, in case of doubt, the trustees must enquire into the course of any such distribution and treat it as income or capital just as if they were the direct shareholders of the shares included in the portfolio.

These rules, however, cease to be applicable where a company has taken the necessary steps to capitalize its profits. All limited companies having a share capital now have power,[78] if authorized by their articles,[79] to increase their capital. If, instead of paying out its profits as dividend, a company uses the profits to pay for a new issue of shares that are issued as bonus shares to the shareholders, trustee-shareholders must hold the bonus shares as part of the capital of the trust and must not hand them over to the tenant for life as income. The point is that if the company does this, it is not, in fact, parting with its money at all, and the money ceases for all time to be divisible as profits and can only be paid to the shareholders on a reduction of capital or on winding up. The same principle has been applied even though no new paid-up capital in the strict sense of the word has been created, as where the profits are used to pay for an issue of unsecured loan stock:[80] 'The real application of the principle is to assets, from which any further character of divisible profits has been taken away, whatever may be the substituted character thereafter impressed upon them.'[81]

Thus, in the leading case of *Bouch v Sproule*,[82] the directors of a company proposed to distribute certain accumulated profits as a bonus dividend, to allot new shares to each shareholder, and to apply the bonus dividend in payment of the new shares. This proposal was carried out, and it was held that the real nature of the transaction was that the undivided profits should be appropriated as an increase of the capital stock, and the tenant for life accordingly had no claim either to the bonus dividend or to the new shares. Lord Herschell, in this case, approved the statement of Fry LJ in the court below[83] that the company alone decides whether to capitalize its profits or not, and provided that its decision

[74] [1928] Ch 682.
[75] (1922) 126 LT 644. See also the *Thomas Tilling* cases: *Re Sechiari* [1950] 1 All ER 417; *Re Kleinwort's Settlement Trusts* [1951] Ch 860, [1951] 2 All ER 328; *Re Rudd's Will Trusts* [1952] 1 All ER 254, discussed (1953) 17 Conv 22 (A J Bland).
[76] That is, the shares in the other company.
[77] [1959] Ch 579, [1959] 2 All ER 497; *Thomson's Trustees v Thomson* [1955] SC 476.
[78] Companies Act 2006, s 617(1).
[79] If not so authorized, the articles can be altered for the purpose.
[80] *Re Outen's Will Trusts* [1963] Ch 291, [1962] 3 All ER 478.
[81] Per Lord Summer in *IRC v Fisher's Executors* [1926] AC 395, 410, HL. Cf *IRC v Parker* [1966] AC 141, [1966] 1 All ER 399, HL.
[82] (1887) 12 App Cas 385, HL.   [83] (1885) 29 Ch D 635, 653, CA.

is properly carried out, its decision will bind beneficiaries claiming under a shareholder. Whether there has been capitalization of profits or not is, therefore, a question of fact in each case. In considering this question from one point of view, Atkin LJ observed:[84] 'the intention of the company is dominant for all purposes. Did the company intend to distribute as profits or as capital?' From another point of view, however, Lord Sumner has said:[85] 'the only intention, that the company has, is such as is expressed in or necessarily follows from its proceedings. It is hardly a paradox to say that the form of a company's resolutions and instruments is their substance.'[86] Accordingly, although the question is as to the intention of the company, the court will not be bound by a company's statement as to what it intended to do or as to the effect of what it has done, if it has failed to take the necessary steps for effective capitalization.[87] If the intention of the company to capitalize is clear, however, the fact that an option is given to the shareholders to take cash instead of new shares makes no difference and since, in practice, the cash offer is always less favourable than the offer of bonus shares, the trustees will be under a duty to accept the offer in its most favourable— that is, its capitalized—form.[88] If, however, there is such an option given, but no intention to capitalize, then, if the cash option is properly exercised, the cash will go to the tenant for life,[89] but if the trustees, as they normally should, accept the offer of new shares as being more advantageous, the tenant for life will only be entitled to so much of the value of the new shares as represented the dividend applied by the trustees in taking them up, the balance of such value forming part of the capital of the trust.[90] The point is that the issue of new shares in such circumstances necessarily depreciates the value of the old ones.

Even though the above rules may appear to operate harshly in a particular case, there is authority to support the view that the courts have power to make an apportionment only where the trustees have been guilty of some breach of trust.[91]

The question arose in an acute form in *Sinclair v Lee*.[92] In this case, ICI was about to reorganize its structure by demerging its original undertaking into two parts, each of which would be carried on as a separate undertaking by a separate company—namely, ICI and a new company (ZG). The shareholders of ICI would be issued with paid-up shares in ZG in addition to their existing holdings in ICI. These ZG shares would compensate ICI shareholders for the depreciation in the value of ICI shares caused by the transfer of assets from ICI to ZG. Nicholls V-C recognized that, as between tenant for life and remainderman, an application of established principles in their full width would produce the absurd result that the ZG shares should go to the tenant for life. In seeking to avoid this result, he observed that the principle of company law prohibiting payments by way

---

[84] *IRC v Burrell* [1924] 2 KB 52, 68, CA.   [85] *IRC v Fisher's Executors* [1926] AC 395, 411, HL.

[86] See also *IRC v Blott* [1921] 2 AC 171, HL; *Re Taylor* [1926] Ch 923; *IRC v Wright* [1927] 1 KB 333, CA.

[87] *Re Piercy* [1907] 1 Ch 289; *Re Bates* [1928] Ch 682; *Re Thomas* [1916] 2 Ch 331, 343, CA, *per* Cozens Hardy MR.

[88] *Re Evans* [1913] 1 Ch 23; *Re Malam* [1894] 3 Ch 578.

[89] *Re Despard* (1901) 17 TLR 478. The question of whether it was proper for the trustees to exercise the cash option does not seem to have been raised, although it would seem that the effect of the whole transaction must have been to reduce the value of the trust shares.

[90] *Re Northage* (1891) 64 LT 625; *Re Malam* [1894] 3 Ch 578. See (1975) 39 Conv 355 (W H Goodhart).

[91] *Re Kleinwort's Settlement Trusts, supra*; *Re Maclaren's Settlement Trusts* [1951] 2 All ER 414; *Re Rudd's Will Trusts, supra*; *Re Morris's Will Trusts* [1960] 3 All ER 548, [1960] 1 WLR 1210.

[92] [1993] Ch 497, sub nom *Re Lee (decd)* [1993] 3 All ER 926, noted [1993] PCB 294 (D Brownbill); [1993] PCB 301 (S Taube).

of return of capital to its shareholders is concerned with the protection of the company's creditors and others dealing with the company. This is far removed from the trustee's duty to hold a fair balance between income and capital beneficiaries. The rules laid down in the cases should be treated as guidelines not to be applied slavishly where to do so would produce a result manifestly inconsistent with the presumed intention of the testator or settlor. Approaching the matter in this way, Nicholls V-C decided that the ZG shares were to be held by the trustees as capital of the fund.

Finally, it should be noted that where the company is being wound up, the situation is entirely different and distributions made to shareholders are capital.[93] And as a result of statute,[94] the same rule applies to a distribution out of moneys in a company's share premium account.[95]

5 ALLOCATION OF EXPENDITURE

Trustees must equally be evenhanded in their allocation of expenditure. Lindsay J has recently, in *Revenue and Customs Commissioners v Trustees of the Peter Clay Discretionary Trust*,[96] considered in detail what principles should be applied in deciding whether the expenditure of trustees is to be regarded as a capital or income expense. The House of Lords decision in *Carver v Duncan*,[97] he said, establishes the principle or rule, within the general law of trusts, that trustees' expenditure incurred for the benefit of the whole estate is to be regarded as a capital expense. In so far as there is a rule that income has to bear all ordinary outgoings[98] of a recurrent nature, such as rates and taxes, and interest on charges and incumbrances, that rule is subservient to the principle that capital has to bear all costs, charges, and expenses incurred for the benefit of the whole estate. Of course, to the extent that expenditure is charged on capital, income beneficiaries will lose the income of the sums expended.

Thus, in *Re Bennett*,[99] capital was ordered to pay the expenses of the yearly audit and inventory of a business where money employed in the business was a capital asset of the trust. Likewise, it was held, in *Carver v Duncan*,[100] that premiums paid by trustees in respect of inheritance tax protection and on endowment policies, and fees paid to investment advisers, were capital expenses and not income expenses. In the *Peter Clay Discretionary Trust* case itself, it was held that trustees' remuneration, and investment management fees relating to how income was to be invested in order to accumulate it, or pending an expected decision to accumulate it, were chargeable only to capital.

---

[93] *Re Armitage* [1893] 3 Ch 337, CA; *Re Palmer* (1912) 28 TLR 301; *IRC v Burrell* [1924] 2 KB 52, CA.

[94] Companies Act 2006, ss 610–616.

[95] *Re Duff's Settlement* [1951] Ch 923, [1951] 2 All ER 435, CA.

[96] [2007] EWHC 2661 (Ch), [2008] 2 All ER 283, affd (2009) *Times*, 2 January. CA.

[97] [1985] AC 1082, [1985] 2 All ER 645, HL. As to insurance premiums, see Trustee Act 1925, s 19, discussed p 464, *infra*.

[98] 'Outgoing' has been said to mean 'some payment which must be made in order to secure the income of the property': *per* Lindley LJ in *Re Bennett* [1896] 1 Ch 778, 784, CA.

[99] *Supra*, CA.   [100] *Supra*, HL.

There is, of course, nothing to prevent a settlor from authorizing or directing his trustees to pay income expenses out of capital or to pay capital expenses out of income. Although such a provision is perfectly valid and effective, it does not alter the intrinsic nature of the expenditure vis-à-vis third parties.[101]

6 LAW COMMISSION CONSULTATION PAPER 175[102]

In 2004, the Law Commission proposed a new scheme for the classification and apportionment of trust receipts and expenses. Subject to any provisions to the contrary in the trust instrument, it proposes, inter alia:

(i)   instead of the 'windfall' principle, cash distributions to trustee-shareholders by corporate entities (or distributions that could have been taken in cash) should be classified as income—all other distributions by corporate entities should be classified as capital;

(ii)   trustees should have power to allocate investment returns and trust expenses as income or capital in so far as necessary to maintain a balance between income and capital;

(iii)   all existing equitable rules of apportionment should be abolished;

(iv)   the duty under the rule in *Howe v Earl Dartmouth* to convert unauthorized, hazardous, or wasting assets should be abolished. Express and statutory trusts for sale would be unaffected.

Pending work on trustee exemption clauses and cohabitation work on the project was suspended, but it is now understood that a draft Bill is to be expected in April 2009.

---

[101] *Revenue and Customs Commissioners v Trustees of the Peter Clay Discretionary Trust, supra; Carver v Duncan, supra*, HL.

[102] Discussed (2004) 62 T & ELTJ 12 (Carolyn O'Sullivan) and, in relation to charities, (2005) 63 T & ELTJ 12 (R Venables). See also (2005) 61 T & ELTJ 21 (G Shindler).

19

THE FIDUCIARY NATURE
OF TRUSTEESHIP

In *Bray v Ford*,[1] Lord Herschell said:[2] 'It is an inflexible rule of a Court of Equity that a person in a fiduciary position ... is not, unless otherwise expressly provided, entitled to make a profit; he is not allowed to put himself in a position where his interest and duty conflict.' The rule does not apply, however, where the trustee or other fiduciary has been put in that position by the testator or settlor under whose dispositions his trust or other fiduciary obligation arose.[3] Thus, for example, a trustee can be given an express power to distribute a fund among a class including himself and can exercise the power in his own favour.[4] Moreover, in exceptional circumstances, the court has jurisdiction to relax the rule.[5]

Where the rule does apply, it suffices for liability that the:

> reasonable man looking at the relevant facts and circumstances of the particular case would think that there was a real sensible possibility of conflict; not that you could imagine some situation arising which might, in some conceivable possibility in events not contemplated as real sensible possibilities by any reasonable person, result in a conflict.[6]

The liability arises from the mere fact of a profit having been made by the fiduciary. 'The profiteer, however honest and well intentioned, cannot escape that risk of being called upon to account.'[7] We have already seen that he becomes a constructive trustee of profits received

---

[1] [1896] AC 44, HL; *Regal (Hastings) Ltd v Gulliver* [1967] 2 AC 134n, [1942] 1 All ER 378, HL; *Guinness plc v Saunders* [1990] 2 AC 663, [1990] 1 All ER 652, HL, but, according to Oliver LJ in *Swain v Law Society* [1981] 3 All ER 797, 813, [1982] 1 WLR 17, 36, CA, '*the rule is not so much that it is improper for him to put himself in that position but that, if he does so, he is obliged by his trust to prefer the interest of his beneficiary*'.

[2] At 51; *Brown v IRC* [1965] AC 244, [1964] 3 All ER 119, 127, HL, *per* Lord Upjohn; *Marley v Mutual Security Merchant Bank and Trust Co Ltd* [2001] WTLR 483, PC. See (1996) 10 Tru LI 49 (J Mowbray); (2005) 121 LQR 452 (M Conaglen).

[3] *Sargeant v National Westminster Bank plc* (1990) 61 P & CR 518, CA, applied to a pensions scheme in *Edge v Pensions Ombudsman* [1998] Ch 512, [1998] 2 All ER 547; affd [2000] Ch 602, [1999] 4 All ER 546, CA.

[4] See [1998] PCB 239 (J Mowbray).

[5] *Re Drexel Burnham Lambert UK Pension Plan* [1995] 1 WLR 32, discussed (1994) 8 Tru LI 112 (D Griffiths), in which the matter arose in connection with a pension scheme under which a trustee was himself an employee and a member of the scheme. There is now a statutory exception to the rule: Pensions Act 1995, s 39.

[6] *Boardman v Phipps* [1967] 2 AC 46, 124, [1966] 3 All ER 721, 756, HL, *per* Lord Upjohn; *Queensland Mines Ltd v Hudson* (1978) 52 ALJR 399, PC. See p 146, *supra*.

[7] *Per* Lord Russell of Killowen in *Regal (Hastings) Ltd v Gulliver*, *supra*, at 386. See (1983) 46 MLR 289 (W Bishop and D D Prentice) bringing in economic considerations.

by virtue of his position as trustee.[8] Other aspects of this general principle are considered in this chapter: firstly, the duty of a trustee to act gratuitously; and secondly, the restrictions on his ability to purchase the trust property or the interest of a beneficiary.

1 DUTY TO ACT WITHOUT REMUNERATION[9]

As early as 1734,[10] it was said to be 'an established rule that a trustee . . . shall have no allowance for his care and trouble: the reason of which seems to be, for that on these pretences, if allowed, the trust estate might be loaded, and rendered of little value'. In general, the rule applies to a trustee who spends much time and trouble in managing a business to the great advantage of the beneficiaries. Prima facie, a solicitor-trustee is in no different position,[11] but he will now usually be entitled to remuneration under the provisions of the Trustee Act 2000, discussed below; nor is he now likely to need to rely on the rule in *Clack v Carlon*,[12] under which, where a solicitor-trustee could properly employ an outside solicitor, he 'may employ his partner to act as solicitor for himself and his co-trustees with reference to the trust affairs, and may pay him the usual charges, provided that it has been expressly agreed between himself and his partner that he himself shall not participate in the profits or derive any benefit from the charges'.[13] Nor will he need to rely on the rule in *Cradock v Piper*,[14] which permits a solicitor-trustee or his firm to receive the usual profit costs for work done in legal proceedings, not on behalf of the solicitor-trustee alone, but on behalf of himself and a co-trustee, provided that the costs of appearing for and acting for the two have not added to the expense that would have been incurred if he or his firm had appeared only for his co-trustee.

The rule does not mean, and has never meant, that there is necessarily anything illegal or improper in a trustee receiving remuneration, but the onus is on the trustee to point to some provision in the trust instrument or some rule of law that establishes his right thereto.[15] A trustee may establish his right to remuneration upon any of the following grounds.

(A) CHARGING CLAUSE IN THE TRUST INSTRUMENT

There has never been any doubt but that the trust instrument may authorize the payment of remuneration to a trustee,[16] although a provision to this effect always receives a strict

---

[8] See p 140 *et seq, supra.*

[9] See, generally, [1984] Conv 275 (N D M Parry); (1995) 9 Tru LI 50 (P Matthews). He can, of course, claim out-of-pocket expenses.

[10] *Robinson v Pett* (1734) 3 P Wms 249, 251.

[11] *Moore v Frowd* (1837) 3 My & Cr 45; *Todd v Wilson* (1846) 9 Beav 486.

[12] (1861) 30 LJ Ch 639.   [13] *Re Doody* [1893] 1 Ch 129, 134, *per* Stirling J.

[14] (1850) 1 Mac & G 664; *Re Corsellis* (1887) 34 Ch D 675, CA. See (1983) 46 MLR 289 (W Bishop and D D Prentice); (1998) 19 JLH 189 (Chantal Stebbings).

[15] See *Dale v IRC* [1954] AC 11, 27, [1953] 2 All ER 671, 674, HL, *per* Lord Normand.

[16] *Webb v Earl of Shaftesbury* (1802) 7 Ves 480; *Willis v Kibble* (1839) 1 Beav 559. Cf *Space Investments Ltd v Canadian Imperial Bank of Commerce Trust Co (Bahamas) Ltd* [1986] 3 All ER 75, [1986] 1 WLR 1072, PC

interpretation from the courts.[17] Thus, if a solicitor-trustee is given the right to charge for his professional services, he can only charge for services that are strictly professional, and not for business 'not strictly professional which might have been performed, or would necessarily have been performed in person by a trustee not being a solicitor'.[18] Further, where a will appoints a trustee and there is a charging clause, the right of the trustee is, for some purposes, treated as a legacy.[19] Accordingly, if the assets are insufficient, it will abate proportionately with the other legacies and will be avoided by s 15 of the Wills Act 1837 if the trustee was an attesting witness.

Section 28 of the Trustee Act 2000 introduces new rules for the construction of express charging clauses, but only where the trustee is a trust corporation or is acting in a professional capacity.[20] These new rules apply where there is a provision in the trust instrument entitling a trustee to payment out of trust funds[21] in respect of services[22] provided by him to or on behalf of the trust, whenever created.[23] The section does not apply, however, to the extent that the trust instrument makes inconsistent provision.[24]

Reversing the old rules, such a trustee is now to be treated as entitled under the trust instrument to receive payment out of the trust funds in respect of services even if they are services that are capable of being provided by a lay trustee.[25] Further, in relation to deaths occurring on or after 1 February 2001,[26] any payments to which a trustee is entitled in respect of services are to be treated as remuneration for services and not as a gift:

(i)   for the purposes of s 15 of the Wills Act 1837, which change enables trustees to be paid for work done in connection with testamentary trusts even where they witness the will under which the trust arises; and

(ii)   for the purposes of determining their priority as against other payments due from the deceased's estate.[27]

Thus, in relation to the administration of the estate, the trustee's charges are an expense of administration.

(bank trustee authorized to deposit trust money with itself as banker: on insolvency of bank no priority for trust beneficiaries).

[17] *Re Gee* [1948] Ch 284, [1948] 1 All ER 498.

[18] Per Warrington J in *Re Chalinder and Herington* [1907] 1 Ch 58, 61; see *Re Chapple* (1884) 27 Ch D 584; *Clarkson v Robinson* [1900] 2 Ch 722.

[19] *Re Pooley* (1888) 40 Ch D 1, CA; *Re White* [1898] 2 Ch 217, CA; *Re Brown* [1918] WN 118. However, it is earned income for the purposes of tax: *Dale v IRC* [1954] AC 11, [1953] 2 All ER 671, HL.

[20] That is, in the course of a profession or business that consists of or includes the provision of services in connection with the management or administration of trusts generally or a particular kind of trust, or any particular aspect thereof: Trustee Act 2000, s 28(5).

[21] 'Trust funds' means income or capital funds of the trust: ibid, s 39(1).

[22] Ibid, s 33(1). On the wording of this subsection, it seems that, in contrast to expenses, the services may have been provided before the commencement of the Act.

[23] Ibid, s 33(1).   [24] Ibid, s 28(1).

[25] Ibid, s 28(2). This subsection applies to a trustee of a charitable trust who is not a trust corporation only if he is not a sole trustee and a majority of the other trustees agree: ibid, s 28(3). A person acts as a lay trustee if he is not a trust corporation and does not act in a professional capacity: ibid, s 28(6).

[26] See ibid, s 33(2).   [27] Administration of Estates Act 1925, s 34(3).

(B) NO EXPRESS PROVISION IN TRUST INSTRUMENT RELATING TO REMUNERATION

There are new statutory provisions in the Trustee Act 2000 that apply where there is no provision (either for or against) about the entitlement of a trustee to remuneration in the trust instrument, or in any enactment or any provision of subordinate legislation.[28] It is now provided that a trustee who is a trust corporation, but who is not a trustee of a charitable trust, is entitled to receive reasonable remuneration out of the trust funds[29] for any services[30] that it provides to or on behalf of the trust.[31] A trustee who acts in a professional capacity,[32] but who is not a trust corporation, a trustee of a charitable trust, or a sole trustee, is likewise entitled, but in his case only if each other trustee has agreed in writing that he may be remunerated for the services.[33] 'Reasonable remuneration' means, in relation to the provision of services by a trustee, such remuneration as is reasonable in the circumstances for the provision of those services to or on behalf of that trust by that trustee.[34] In determining the level of remuneration that is reasonable in the circumstances, regard must be had not only to the nature of the services provided, but also to the nature of the trust and the attributes of the trustee. The above provisions apply to trusts whenever created.[35]

The above provisions apply even if the services in question could be provided by a lay trustee; they apply equally to a trustee who has been duly authorized to exercise functions as an agent of the trustees, or to act as a nominee or custodian.[36]

The above provisions do not apply to trustees of charitable trusts. However, the Secretary of State has power to make regulations for the provision of remuneration of trustees of charitable trusts.[37]

(C) CONTRACT WITH THE CESTUIS QUE TRUST

Such a contract by a trustee for remuneration may be valid, although it would be viewed with great jealousy by the courts.[38] If, however, the trustee, having accepted the trust were merely to contract to carry out his existing duties as trustee, it could be argued that the obligation to pay the remuneration would be invalid, on the ground of insufficiency of consideration, unless the contract were by deed.[39]

---

[28] Trustee Act 2000, s 29(5).

[29] 'Trust funds' means income or capital funds of the trust: ibid, s 39(1).

[30] Ibid, s 33(1) and see p 443, fn 22, *supra*.

[31] Ibid, s 29(1). 'Trust funds' means income or capital funds of the trust: ibid, s 39(1).

[32] See ibid, s 28(5), and p 443, fn 20, *supra*.   [33] Ibid, s 29(2).

[34] Ibid, s 29(3), which also provides that a trust corporation that is a recognized provider of banking services may make any reasonable charges for the provision of such services in the course of, or incidental to, the performance of its function as a trustee.

[35] Ibid, s 33(1).   [36] Ibid, s 29(4), (6).

[37] Ibid, s 30. No regulations had been made at the date of writing.

[38] *Ayliffe v Murray* (1740) 2 Atk 58.

[39] Compare Cheshire, Fifoot, and Furmston, *The Law of Contract*, 15th edn, p 114 *et seq*; (1956) 71 LQR 490 (A L Goodhart). But see *Williams v Roffey Bros & Nicholls (Contractors) Ltd* [1991] 1 QB 1, [1990] 1 All ER 512, CA, noted (1990) 53 MLR 536 (J Adams and R Brownsword), in which it was said that, today, the rigid approach to the concept of consideration to be found in *Stilk v Myrick* (1809) 2 Camp 317 was neither necessary nor desirable. The courts should now be more ready to find the presence of consideration so as to

(D) ORDER OF THE COURT

The court, under the inherent jurisdiction, can authorize the payment of remuneration to a trustee, whether appointed by the court or not.[40] The payment of remuneration may be authorized either prospectively or retrospectively, and the jurisdiction extends to increasing the remuneration authorized by the trust instrument.[41] Although the existence of the jurisdiction is undoubted, it has been said[42] that it should be exercised only sparingly and in 'exceptional cases'.

Many of the earlier cases were discussed by the Court of Appeal in *Re Duke of Norfolk's Settlement Trusts*,[43] in which it was pointed out that, in exercising this jurisdiction, the court has to balance two influences that are, to some extent, in conflict. The first is that the office of trustee is, as such, gratuitous; the court will accordingly be careful to protect the interests of the beneficiaries against claims by the trustees. The second is that it is of great importance to the beneficiaries that the trust should be well administered. If the court concludes, having regard to the nature of the trust, to the experience and skill of a particular trustee, and to the amounts that he seeks to charge when compared with what other trustees might require to be paid for their services, and to all of the other circumstances of the case, that it would be in the interests of the beneficiaries to authorize the remuneration, or increased remuneration, then the court may properly do so.

An application asking the court to exercise its jurisdiction to authorize the payment of remuneration should be made very promptly on assumption of office or after there has been a radical change in circumstances,[44] although this principle need not be rigorously applied where the individual concerned has been ignorant of his liability to account.[45]

---

reflect the intention of the parties to the contract where the bargaining powers are not unequal and where the finding of consideration reflects the true intention of the parties. See also [1991] JBL 19 (R Hooley).

[40] *Re Masters* [1953] 1 All ER 19, [1953] 1 WLR 81; *Re Jarvis* [1958] 2 All ER 336, [1958] 1 WLR 815 (constructive trustee). The jurisdiction extends to other fiduciaries: see *Boardman v Phipps* [1967] 2 AC 46, [1966] 3 All ER 721, HL; *O'Sullivan v Management Agency and Music Ltd* [1985] QB 428, [1985] 3 All ER 351, CA (remuneration allowed even though guilty of undue influence): *Badfinger Music v Evans* [2001] WTLR 1. The courts are, perhaps, even more reluctant to sanction the remuneration of trustees in the case of a charity: see Report of the Charity Commissioners for 1990, Appendix D(c). See also their Reports for 1981, para 64, and for 1988, para 38.

[41] *Boardman v Phipps, supra,* HL; *Re Keeler's Settlement Trusts* [1981] Ch 156, [1981] 1 All ER 888; *Re Duke of Norfolk's Settlement Trusts* [1982] Ch 61, [1981] 3 All ER 220, CA, and see (1981) 40 CLJ 243 (C M G Ockleton); [1982] Conv 231 (K Hodkinson); (1982) 98 LQR 181; (1982) 45 MLR 211 (B Green); (1982) 126 Sol Jo 195 (D W Fox).

[42] *Per* Upjohn J in *Re Worthington* [1954] 1 All ER 677, 678, [1954] 1 WLR 526, 528. In *Re Barbour's Settlement* [1974] 1 All ER 1188, 1192, [1974] 1 WLR 1198, 1203, Megarry J doubted whether the phrase was intended to exclude the disastrous consequences following from inflation merely because inflation is not an exception but the rule.

[43] *Supra,* CA, criticized (1982) 79 LSG 217 (A M Kenny), doubting whether the court should authorize an increase of remuneration to professional trustees who have made a bad bargain. See also *Re Berkeley Applegate (Investment Consultants) Ltd* [1989] Ch 32, [1988] 3 All ER 71; *Foster v Spencer* [1996] 2 All ER 672.

[44] See *Re Duke of Norfolk's Settlement Trusts,* at first instance, [1979] Ch 37, 58, [1978] 3 All ER 907.

[45] *Re Keeler's Settlement Trusts* [1981] Ch 156, [1981] 1 All ER 888, 893.

(E) STATUTORY PROVISIONS

By s 42 of the Trustee Act 1925, it is provided that:

> where the court appoints a corporation, other than the Public Trustee, to be a trustee[46] either solely or jointly with another person, the court may authorise the corporation to charge such remuneration for its services as trustee as the court may think fit.

The Judicial Trustees Act 1896 provides[47] that the court may assign remuneration to a person whom it appoints as a judicial trustee.

The Public Trustee is authorized[48] to charge fees fixed by the Lord Chancellor, irrespective of any provision in the trust instrument, and any body properly appointed to be a custodian trustee may likewise charge fees not exceeding those chargeable by the Public Trustee.[49] It is not, however, possible to take advantage of this latter provision by, for instance, appointing a bank separately as custodian trustee and managing trustee.[50]

(F) CUSTOM

The existence of any valid custom is very doubtful. In *Brown v IRC*,[51] a Scottish solicitor had received money from a number of his clients, too small in individual amounts or held for too short a time to make individual investment worthwhile in the interest of the client, but which, in the aggregate, amounted to a large floating sum. This money was put on deposit so as to earn interest for the solicitor, which he claimed to be entitled to retain. There was no question of professional malpractice, because the practice had been recognized as proper by the Council of the Law Society of Scotland, the opinion of which, however, was held to be ill founded. The solicitor had based his claim on the grounds of implied agreement and custom; both grounds proved to be inadequately supported by evidence, and dicta of their Lordships[52] leave it very doubtful whether the law of either Scotland or England would recognize such a custom.

(G) FOREIGN REMUNERATION

It appears from *Re Northcote's Will Trusts*[53] that if, in the course of administering assets abroad, trustees receive remuneration without their volition, they will not be called to account. In that case, executors took out an English grant and, on doing so, were required by the Inland Revenue to undertake to obtain a grant in New York state in respect of US assets. They duly obtained such a grant, and got in the US assets, for doing which the law of that state allowed them agency commission. It was held that, in those circumstances, there was no equity against the trustees requiring them to disgorge money that had come to them without their volition.

---

[46] By s 68(17), 'trustee' is defined so as to include a personal representative: *Re Youngs Estate* (1934) 151 LT 221; *Re Masters* [1953] 1 All ER 19.

[47] Section 1(5).   [48] Public Trustee Act 1906, s 9, as amended.   [49] Ibid, s 4(3).

[50] *Forster v Williams Deacon's Bank Ltd* [1935] Ch 359, CA; *Arning v James* [1936] Ch 158.

[51] [1965] AC 244, [1964] 3 All ER 119, HL.

[52] *Brown v IRC, supra, per* Lord Evershed, at 125, Lord Guest, at 126, and Lord Upjohn, at 128. As to solicitors, the law in England is now governed by the Solicitors Act 1974, s 73.

[53] [1949] 1 All ER 442.

2 DISABILITIES OF TRUSTEE RELATING TO PURCHASE OF TRUST PROPERTY OR EQUITABLE INTEREST

In *Tito v Waddell (No 2)*,[54] Megarry V-C preferred the view that the so-called 'self deal-ing' and 'fair dealing' rules are two separate rules, and not one rule with two limbs, while accepting that both rules, or both limbs, have a common origin, in that equity is astute to prevent a trustee from abusing his position or profiting from his trust. The consequences, he said, are different, and the property and the transactions that invoke the rules are differ-ent.[55] He further said that, in cases falling within these rules, what equity, in fact, does is to subject trustees to particular disabilities. Whether a rule is classified as a duty or a disabil-ity may be important in connection with the applicability of the Limitation Act 1980.[56]

(A) PURCHASE BY A TRUSTEE OF THE TRUST PROPERTY[57]—THE 'SELF DEALING' RULE[58]

The self-dealing rule is to the effect that a fiduciary—including, of course, a trustee—must not place himself in a position in which his personal interests, or his duty to other persons, are liable to conflict with his fiduciary duties to the beneficiaries. Accordingly, as Arden MR said in *Campbell v Walker*[59] as long ago as 1800: 'Any trustee purchasing[60] the trust property is liable to have the purchase set aside, if in any reasonable time the cestui que trust chooses to say, he is not satisfied with it.' The transaction is voidable at the instance of the beneficiaries,[61] even though the particular dealing may, in fact, be perfectly fair,[62] and even

---

[54] [1977] Ch 106, 247, 248, [1977] 3 All ER 129, 246, 247.

[55] But see [2006] CLJ 366 (M Conaglen), in which it is contended that both rules are most appropriately understood as applications of the fiduciary conflict principle. [56] See p 529 *et seq, infra.*

[57] See (1936) 49 HLR 521 (A W Scott); (1955) 8 CLP (O R Marshall). The rule does not apply to the pur-chase of the equity of redemption by a mortgagee: *Alec Lobb (Garages) Ltd v Total Oil GB Ltd* [1983] 1 All ER 944, 965. This point not discussed on appeal [1985] 1 All ER 303, CA, in which decision was affirmed in part. As to solicitors, see *Longstaff v Birtles* (2001) Times, 18 September, CA.

[58] *Per* Megarry V-C in *Tito v Waddell (No 2), supra,* at 241, 228; 240, 241, 255. See (1990) 10 Co Law 191 (D Hayton) as to the position of an investment manager appointed under an express provision in the trust instrument, and (1993) 137 Sol Jo 500 (L Price) as to the use of brokers/market makers. Cf *Kane v Radley-Kane* [1999] Ch 274, [1998] 3 All ER 753, noted [1998] 1 T & ELJ 7 (O Clutton), in which it was held to be a breach of the self-dealing rule for a sole personal representative of an intestate estate to appropriate to herself unquoted shares in satisfaction of her statutory legacy, unless she had been authorized to do so by the other beneficiaries, or the court had sanctioned the appropriation.

[59] In (1800) 5 Ves 678, 680; *Aberdeen Railway Co v Blaikie Bros* (1854) 1 Macq 461; *Newgate Stud Co v Penfold* [2004] EWHC 2993 (Ch), [2008] 1 BCLC 46.

[60] The rule applies equally to the grant of a lease: *Re Dumbell, ex p Hughes* (1802) 6 Ves 617; *A-G v Earl of Clarendon* (1810) 17 Ves 491. Also to a trustee who concurs in a transaction in which he has an interest and which cannot be carried into effect without his concurrence: *Re Thompson's Settlement* [1986] Ch 99, [1985] 2 All ER 720, discussed (1985) 135 NLJ 1201 (L Cane); [1986] TL & P 66 (C H Sherrin).

[61] Note that one of several beneficiaries cannot insist on the property being reconveyed to the trust with-out the consent of the other beneficiaries. His remedy is to demand a resale as discussed p 448, *infra: Holder v Holder* [1966] 2 All ER 116, 128 (this point did not arise on appeal [1968] Ch 353, [1968] 1 All ER 665, CA).

[62] See, eg, *Campbell v Walker, supra* (sale by public auction, trustee taking no unfair advantage); *Dyson v Lum* (1866) 14 LT 588.

beneficial to the trust estate.[63] The rule cannot be evaded by carrying out the transaction by means of a nominee,[64] and it applies to a sale to someone such as a partner, where the trustee may directly or indirectly benefit from the transaction;[65] it seems strictly not to apply to a sale by a trustee to his wife, but such a transaction would be viewed by the courts with great suspicion.[66] It does not apply to a sale to a company of which the trustee is a member, although the circumstances may throw upon the company the onus of showing that the sale was fair and honest,[67] and the rule will apply if the company is a mere nominee for the trustee.[68] There is no objection to a trustee completing a purchase where the contract came into existence before the fiduciary relationship.[69]

If a trustee sells to a stranger to the trust and subsequently repurchases the trust property for himself, the sale cannot always be set aside. If the sale to the stranger has not been completed, the vendor-trustee is never allowed to purchase the benefit of the contract for himself.[70] After the sale to a stranger has been completed, however, a subsequent repurchase by the trustee may be good, provided that the court is satisfied that there was no agreement or understanding for repurchase at the time of the sale to the stranger, and that the original sale price was adequate and the sale bona fide; in order to set aside a repurchase by a trustee, it is not enough merely to show that the trustee had a hope that he would be able to purchase at some time in the future, or that, having, in fact, repurchased, he ultimately made a profit on a resale many years later.[71]

The right to avoid the purchase is valid not only as against the trustee, but also against any subsequent purchaser with notice.[72] Alternatively, if the trustee has resold at a profit, the beneficiaries can adopt the sale and require the trustee to account for the profit.[73] If the trustee has not resold, the court may require him to offer the property for resale: if a greater price is offered than that paid by the trustee, the sale to the trustee will be set aside; otherwise, he will be held to his bargain.[74] On general principles, the beneficiaries, having

---

[63] It was early settled that the right of the beneficiary does not depend on the trustee making a profit: *Ex p Lacey* (1802) 6 Ves 625; *Ex p Bennett* (1805) 10 Ves 381.

[64] *Silkstone and Haigh Moore Coal Co v Edey* [1900] 1 Ch 167; *Re Walters* [1954] Ch 653, sub nom *Re Sherman* [1954] 1 All ER 893.

[65] *Ex p Moore* (1881) 45 LT 558; *Re Sparks, ex p Forder* [1881] WN 117, CA. And see *Hickley v Hickley* (1876) 2 Ch D 190 (perhaps a doubtful decision).

[66] *Burrell v Burrell's Trustees* 1915 SC 333; *Ferraby v Hobson* (1847) 2 Ph 255; (1949) 13 Conv 248 (J G Fleming). It will depend on the circumstances. '*Manifestly there are wives and wives*', per Megarry V-C in *Tito v Waddell (No 2), supra*.

[67] *Farrar v Farrar's Ltd* (1888) 40 Ch D 395, CA. *Aliter* where the trustee is a substantial shareholder and director: *Re Thompson's Settlement, supra*, said to be the high-water mark of the application of the rule in *Hillsdown Holdings plc v Pensions Ombudsman* [1997] 1 All ER 862.

[68] *Silkstone and Haigh Moore Coal Co v Edey, supra*.

[69] *Vyse v Foster* (1874) LR 7 HL 318; *Re Mulholland's Will Trusts* [1949] 1 All ER 460.

[70] *Parker v McKenna* (1874) 10 Ch App 96, 125, per Mellish LJ; *Williams v Scott* [1900] AC 499, PC; *Delves v Gray* [1902] 2 Ch 606.

[71] *Baker v Peck* (1861) 4 LT 3; *Re Postlethwaite* (1888) 60 LT 514, CA.

[72] *Cookson v Lee* (1853) 23 LJ Ch 473; *Aberdeen Town Council v Aberdeen University* (1877) 2 App Cas 544, HL. It follows that, at any rate in the case of land, the trustee will find it almost impossible to find a purchaser. On setting aside a sale to a trustee, he is liable to account for the rents and profits, but without interest: *Silkstone and Haigh Moore Coal Co v Edey* [1900] 1 Ch 167.

[73] *Baker v Carter* (1835) 1 Y & C Ex 250.

[74] *Re Dumbell, ex p Hughes* (1802) 6 Ves 617; *Ex p Lacey* (1802) 6 Ves 625; *Dyson v Lum* (1866) 14 LT 588; *Holder v Holder* [1966] 2 All ER 116, at first instance.

full knowledge of the facts,[75] may waive their rights and affirm the purchase by the trustee, and, after a long period of acquiescence, will be deemed to have done so under the equitable doctrine of laches:[76] mere lapse of time will not be enough, although it may be some evidence of laches.

The rule applies in all of its stringency to a trustee who has recently retired, whether or not with a view to the sale,[77] but ceases to apply after a long period of retirement, such as twelve years,[78] unless there are circumstances of doubt or suspicion. It does not apply to a trustee who disclaims the trust,[79] nor, it seems, to trustees who have no active duties to perform.[80] Normally, of course, the rule applies equally to an executor, but it was held, on appeal, not to do so on the special facts of *Holder v Holder*.[81] The defendant in that case was, as it was assumed, technically an executor by reason of the fact that he had intermeddled with the estate. His interference had, however, been of a minimal character, and ceased before he executed a deed of renunciation, which, at all relevant times, had been wrongly assumed to have been effective. He had taken no part in the arrangements for the sale, which had been by public auction, and the beneficiaries had not looked to him to protect their interests.

There are some exceptions to the general rule. In the first place, the court can give the trustee leave to purchase the trust property, but it will not do so, if the beneficiaries object, until all other ways of selling the property at an adequate price have failed.[82] Dicta in *Holder v Holder*,[83] however, suggest that the court might now be prepared to exercise its discretion more readily than indicated by some of the earlier cases.

Secondly, a provision in the trust instrument authorizing a purchase by a trustee will be effective according to its terms.[84]

Thirdly, under s 68 of the Settled Land Act 1925, the tenant for life, who holds the legal estate on trust for all of the beneficiaries, is permitted to purchase the settled land.

Finally, it may be noted that the rule sometimes causes difficulty in the case of family trusts, as it may make transfers between trusts with common trustees impossible without the sanction of the court. As long ago as 1982, the Law Reform Committee[85] recommended that, so long as the common trustees are not beneficiaries under either of the trusts concerned, the trustees should be able to do business with one another, with the common trustees playing such part as is thought fit, provided that the market value of any property dealt with has been certified by a truly independent valuer as being the proper market price for that property. The recommendation has not, however, been implemented.

[75] *Randall v Errington* (1805) 10 Ves 423; *Holder v Holder, supra*, CA and see p 536, *infra*.

[76] Right not lost in *Aberdeen Town Council v Aberdeen University, supra*, HL (eighty years); *Re Walters* [1954] Ch 653, sub nom *Re Sherman* [1954] 1 All ER 893 (nineteen years).

[77] *Wright v Morgan* [1926] AC 788, PC.

[78] *Re Boles and British Land Co's Contract* [1902] 1 Ch 244.

[79] *Stacey v Elph* (1833) 1 My & K 195; *Clark v Clark* (1884) 9 App Cas 733, PC.

[80] *Parkes v White* (1805) 11 Ves 209 (trustees to preserve contingent remainders).

[81] [1968] Ch 353, [1968] 1 All ER 665, CA.

[82] *Farmer v Dean* (1863) 32 Beav 327; *Tennant v Trenchard* (1869) 4 Ch App 537.

[83] *Supra*, CA, 402, 403; 398; 680, 677.

[84] Where the two trustees were also agricultural tenants of the trust property, it was held that they were entitled to sell the freehold subject to the agricultural tenancies and were under no duty to cooperate in its sale in any other way: *Sargeant v National Westminster Bank plc* (1990) 61 P & CR 518, CA. See *Edge v Pensions Ombudsman* [1998] Ch 512, [1998] 2 All ER 547; affd [2000] Ch 602, [1999] 4 All ER 546, CA.

[85] 23rd Report, Cmnd 8733, paras 3.56–3.59.

(B) PURCHASE BY THE TRUSTEE FROM THE BENEFICIARY OF HIS EQUITABLE INTEREST—THE 'FAIR DEALING' RULE[86]

There is no rigid rule that a trustee cannot purchase the equitable interest of a beneficiary, but, if challenged in proper time, the trustee, if he is to uphold the bargain, must establish that he dealt with the beneficiary at arm's length, that the bargain was beneficial to the beneficiary, that he made full disclosure to the beneficiary, and that the transaction was fair and honest.[87]

A trustee would be assisted in upholding a purchase by showing that the purchase was arranged by the beneficiary,[88] or that he pressed the trustee to purchase,[89] or that no other purchaser could be found.[90] These principles, and not those discussed in (A) above, also apply where a trustee purchases the trust property with the consent of the beneficiaries, because this is, in effect, a purchase from the beneficiaries.[91] For a purchase to be set aside, it must be possible to restore the parties to their original positions, but the court will be slow to hold that *restitutio in integrum* is impossible.[92]

The same principles apply to other persons in a fiduciary position.[93] Indeed, as Vinelott pointed out in *Movitex Ltd v Bulfield*,[94] a trustee who is in breach of the fair-dealing rule is not strictly guilty of a breach of trust, but of the duty that he owes to the beneficiary to make full disclosure and to deal fairly with him arising from his fiduciary position. Thus, for instance, on a purchase by a solicitor from his client, 'the solicitor must establish that the sale was as advantageous to the client as it could have been if the solicitor had used his utmost endeavours to sell the property to a stranger, and that the burthen of proving this lies on the solicitor, or any persons claiming through him'.[95] In practice, a solicitor who wishes to buy from his client should see to it that the client is independently advised.[96]

---

[86] *Per* Megarry V-C in *Tito v Waddell (No 2)* [1977] Ch 106, 225, 240, 241, [1977] 3 All ER 129, 228, 241.

[87] *Ex parte Lacey* (1802) 6 Ves 625, 626. *Coles v Trecothick* (1804) 9 Ves 234, 247; *Tito v Waddell, supra.* See also *Thomson v Eastwood* (1877) 2 App Cas 215, 236, HL, *per* Lord Cairns, approved in *Dougan v Macpherson* [1902] AC 197, HL, in which the trustee failed to disclose a valuation to the beneficiary.

[88] *Coles v Trecothick, supra.*

[89] *Morse v Royal* (1806) 12 Ves 355; *Luff v Lord* (1864) 34 Beav 220.

[90] *Clark v Swaile* (1762) 2 Eden 134 (actually a case of solicitor and client).

[91] See *Williams v Scott* [1900] AC 499, PC; *Coles v Trecothick, supra.*

[92] *Tate v Williamson* (1866) 2 Ch App 55. [93] *Hill v Langley* (1988) Times, 28 January.

[94] [1988] BCLC 104.

[95] *Spencer v Topham* (1856) 22 Beav 573, 577, *per* Romilly MR, in which, the sale was upheld, although the solicitor resold two years later at a considerable profit; *Luddy's Trustee v Peard* (1886) 33 Ch D 500 and cf *Johnson v Fesemeyer* (1858) 3 De G & J 13.

[96] *Cockburn v Edwards* (1881) 18 Ch D 449, CA; *Barron v Willis* [1900] 2 Ch 121, CA; affd sub nom *Willis v Barron* [1902] AC 271, HL.

20

APPOINTMENT OF AGENTS, NOMINEES, AND CUSTODIANS—DELEGATION OF TRUSTS

The original principle was that 'trustees who take on themselves the management of property for the benefit of others have no right to shift their duty on other persons'.[1] It was early recognized, however, that administration of a trust would often be impracticable unless exceptions were permitted, and thus it can now be said that 'the law is not that trustees cannot delegate: it is that trustees cannot delegate unless they have authority to do so'.[2] The equitable rules are considered in section 1. Much wider powers have been conferred by statute. The Trustee Act 2000 confers a wide power of collective delegation, discussed in section 2. Section 3 explains the power of delegation conferred on trustees individually by the Trustee Act 1925, acting by a power of attorney, including a lasting power of attorney under the Mental Capacity Act 2005. Sections 4 and 5 deal with further powers of delegation under the Trusts of Land and Appointment of Trustees Act 1996 and the Trustee Delegation Act 1999. This last Act contains provisions, noted in section 6, that are designed to strengthen and clarify the two-trustee rules.

1 THE EQUITABLE RULES AS TO DELEGATION

Lord Hardwicke[3] said that trustees could 'act by other hands' on the ground of legal necessity,[4] or what he called 'moral necessity', from the usage of mankind. The ground of moral necessity, which was much the more important of these exceptions, was fully discussed, particularly by the Court of Appeal, in *Speight v Gaunt*,[5] which, as Kay J pointed out in *Fry v Tapson*,[6] 'did not lay down any new rule, but only illustrated a very old one, viz,

---

[1] *Per* Landgale MR in *Turner v Corney* (1841) 5 Beav 515, 517.
[2] *Pilkington v IRC* [1964] AC 612, 639, [1962] 3 All ER 622, 630, HL, *per* Lord Radcliffe.
[3] In *Ex p Belchier* (1754) Amb 218.
[4] An illustration would be where a broker is employed to purchase investments, it being impossible to purchase them in any other way.
[5] (1883) 22 Ch D 727, CA; affd (1883) 9 App Cas 1, HL; *Learoyd v Whiteley* (1887) 12 App Cas 727, HL.
[6] (1884) 28 Ch D 268, 280.

that trustees acting according to the ordinary course of business, and employing agents as a prudent man of business would do on his own behalf, are not liable for the default of an agent so employed'. In deciding whether the employment of an agent by a trustee was proper, the standard adopted was the conduct of the ordinary prudent man of business in managing his own affairs.

In appointing an agent, the trustees must exercise their personal discretion in making their choice of agent;[7] an important, if obvious, limitation is that they must only employ an agent to do work within the scope of the usual business of the agent.[8]

2 PART IV OF THE TRUSTEE ACT 2000

Part IV of the Trustee Act 2000 contains new provisions for the appointment of agents, nominees, and custodians, which apply whenever the trust was created.[9] The powers conferred by Pt IV are additional to any other powers the trustees may have, but are subject to any restriction or exclusion imposed by the trust instrument, or by any enactment or any provision of subordinate legislation.[10] The previous more limited provisions in the Trustee Act 1925 have been repealed.

(A) THE APPOINTMENT OF AGENTS

Sections 11–15 confer powers of collective delegation on trustees. Section 11(1) provides that trustees may authorize any person to exercise any or all of their delegable functions as their agent. A distinction is made between charitable and non-charitable trusts. In the case of the latter, the trustees' delegable functions consist of any function other than:

   (i)   any function relating to whether or in what way any assets of the trust should be distributed;

   (ii)   any power to decide whether any fees or other payment due to be made out of the trust funds should be made out of income or capital;

   (iii)   any power to appoint a person to be a trustee of the trust; or

   (iv)   any power conferred by any other enactment or the trust instrument that permits the trustees to delegate any of their functions or to appoint a person to act as a nominee or custodian.[11]

In the case of a charitable trust, the trustees' delegable functions are:

   (i) any function consisting of carrying out a decision that the trustees have taken;

---

[7] *Re Weall* (1889) 42 Ch D 674; *Robinson v Harkin* [1896] 2 Ch 415. A direction in a will that a particular person is to be solicitor to the trust imposes no trust or duty on the trustees to employ him: *Foster v Elsley* (1881) 19 Ch D 518.

[8] *Fry v Tapson* (1884) 28 Ch D 268; *Wilkinson v Wilkinson* (1825) 2 Sim & St 237; *Rowland v Witherden* (1851) 3 Mac & G 568; *see per* Kay J in *Re Dewar, Dewar v Brooke* (1885) 52 LT 489, 492, 493.

[9] Trustee Act 2000, s 27. Part IV applies in relation to a trust having a sole trustee: ibid, s 25(1).

[10] Ibid, s 26.   [11] Ibid, s 11(2).

(ii)   any function relating to the investment of assets subject to the trust;[12]

(iii) any function relating to the raising of funds for the trust otherwise than by means of profits of a trade that is an integral part of carrying out the trust's charitable purpose;[13]

(iv)   any other function prescribed by an order[14] made by the Secretary of State.[15]

The only restrictions on whom the trustees can appoint as their agents are that they cannot authorize a beneficiary to exercise any function as their agent,[16] and they cannot authorize two or more persons to exercise the same function, unless they are to exercise it jointly.[17] The persons whom the trustees authorize to exercise functions as their agent may, however, include one or more of their number,[18] and a person so authorized may also be appointed to act as their nominee or custodian.[19]

The statutory duty of care[20] is limited to trustees. It does not apply to an agent in the performance of his agency, although such a person will owe a separate duty of care to the trust under the general law of agency. In particular, an agent is subject to any specific duties or restrictions attached to the functions. This is provided for in s 13(1), which gives as an example the case in which trustees exercise their new power to delegate their investment function. This was not possible prior to the Trustee Act 2000, except under a specific provision in the trust instrument. In such a case, the agent must have regard to the standard investment criteria in accordance with s 4, although the requirement to obtain advice[21] does not apply if the agent is the kind of person from whom it would have been proper for the trustees, in compliance with the requirement, to obtain advice.[22] Another case would be that in which charity trustees delegate functions in relation to land, when the agent would be required to comply with the restrictions on dispositions and mortagages of charity land under ss 36–39 of the Charities Act 1993.[23]

Trustees of land are, under s 11(1) of the Trusts of Land and Appointment of Trustees Act 1996, under duties to consult beneficiaries and give effect to their wishes.[24] Section 13(3)–(5) of the Trustee Act 2000 provides that trustees must ensure that, in delegating any of their functions under the 2000 Act, they do so on terms that that do not prevent them from complying with their duties under the 1996 Act.

The statutory power of trustees to employ agents does not apply to trustees of authorized unit trusts, or to trustees managing a fund under a common investment scheme or

---

[12] Including, in the case of land acquired as an investment, managing the land and creating or disposing of an interest in land: ibid, s 11(3)(b).

[13] Ibid, s 3(c), must be read together with in the definition of a trade in subs (4). A distinction is made between general fund-raising activities, and fund-raising activities that are an integral part of carrying out the trust's charitable purpose: eg the charging of fees by a school operating as a charitable trust.

[14] Made by statutory instrument as prescribed by subs (5).   [15] Ibid, 11(3).

[16] Ibid, 12(3); by s 25(1), this does not apply to a trust having a sole trustee. This is curious, as the apparent effect is that a prohibition on trustees in the plural does not apply to a sole trustee. Perhaps the reference in s 25(1) should be to s 12(4), not 12(3). This prevents the use of s 11 of the 2000 Act to avoid the restrictions on delegation by trustees of land to a beneficiary under s 9 of the Trusts of Land and Appointment of Trustees Act 1996, as amended by the Mental Capacity Act 2005, Sch 6, para 41. See p 459, infra.

[17] Trustee Act 2000, s 12(2).

[18] Ibid, s 12(1) By s 25(1), this does not apply to a trust having a sole trustee.

[19] Ibid, s 12(4).   [20] Ibid, s 1; see p 399, supra.   [21] Under ibid, s 5.   [22] Ibid, s 13(2).

[23] As amended. See p 352, supra.

[24] See p 490, infra.

common deposit scheme under ss 24 or 25 of the Charities Act 1993.[25] It does apply to trustees of a pension scheme, but subject to restrictions.[26]

(B) TERMS OF AGENCY

In general, trustees are free to determine the terms as to remuneration and other matters of the appointment of an agent. The exercise of the power to delegate is subject to the statutory duty of care.[27]

Certain terms, however, may only be authorized by the trustees where it is reasonably necessary for them to do so:

(i)   a term permitting the agent to appoint a substitute;

(ii)   a term restricting the liability of the agent or his substitute to the trustees or any beneficiary;

(iii) a term permitting the agent to act in circumstances capable of giving rise to a conflict of interest.[28]

These provisions are a response to the realities of modern fund management and are designed to ensure that adequate protection is given to beneficiaries by imposing a test of reasonable necessity on the trustees. The appointment of a fund manager will often be necessary to the efficient and effective management of assets of the trust, and would, in practice, be impossible if the trustees could not accept the terms in (ii) and (iii) above.

Special restrictions apply where trustees delegate any of their asset management functions. In this case, the delegation must be contained in an agreement made in writing or evidenced in writing. Further, the trustees must prepare a 'policy statement', giving guidance as to how the functions should be exercised, with a view to ensuring that the functions are exercised in the best interests of the trust. The agreement with the agent must include a term to the effect that the agent will secure compliance with the policy statement and any revision or replacement thereof. For example, if trustees delegate their powers of investment to an agent, they must enter into an agreement with the agent at the outset setting out the investment objectives of the trust. Such an agreement may include considerations as to the liquidity of assets to meet the needs of the trust, the desired balance between capital growth and income yield, and any 'ethical' considerations relevant to the investment policy of the trust. The policy statement may expand upon the manner in which the duties imposed by s 4 should be discharged in respect of the trust. In relation to the delegation of functions relating to the acquisition and management of land on behalf of the trust, the policy statement may include considerations as to the value and type of property that may be acquired, and the quality of title required. Where relevant, it may also consider the terms upon which land may be let, sold, or charged. The requirement for a policy statement only applies where the trustees delegate their discretion in relation to the matters concerned. It does not apply in cases in which the trustees obtain investment advice, but take decisions on investment matters themselves.[29]

---

[25] Trustee Act 2000, ss 37, 38.   [26] Ibid, s 36(4)–(7).

[27] That is, under the Trustee Act 2000, s 1, Sch 1, para 3(1)(a) and (d).   [28] Ibid, s 14(1)–(3).

[29] Ibid, s 15(1)–(4). The asset management functions of trustees are their functions relating to (a) the investment of assets subject to the trust, (b) the acquisition of property that is to be subject to the trust, and

(C) APPOINTMENT OF NOMINEES AND CUSTODIANS

A nominee is a person appointed by trustees to hold trust property in his name. Thus, a person may be registered as the owner of certain shares in a company, but may, in fact, hold them as nominee for a trust. The fact of the trust will not appear in the share register. A person is defined as a custodian in relation to assets if he undertakes the safe custody of the assets or of any documents or records concerning the assets.[30]

The trustees of a trust may appoint a person to act as a nominee or as a custodian in relation to such of the assets of the trust as they may determine.[31] Further, if they retain or invest in securities payable to bearer, they have a duty to appoint a person to act as a custodian of the securities.[32] The appointment, in each case, must be in or evidenced in writing.[33]

To be eligible for appointment as a nominee or custodian, a person must either:

(i)   carry on a business that consists of or includes acting as a nominee or custodian; or

(ii)   be a body corporate controlled by the trustees;[34] or

(iii) be a solicitor's nominee company, recognized under s 9 of the Administration of Justice Act 1985.[35]

It is intended that the use of such bodies corporate will enable trustees to use special-purpose vehicles for nominee or custodianship purposes.

The trustees may appoint one of themselves, if that one is a trust corporation, or two (or more) of their number, if they are to act as joint nominees or joint custodians.[36] The person appointed as nominee or custodian may also be appointed as custodian or nominee, as the case may be, or as agent.[37]

The terms of appointment of nominees and custodians are similar to those applicable to agents.[38]

The above provisions do not apply to any trust that has a custodian trustee or in relation to any assets vested in the official custodian for charities.[39]

(D) REVIEW OF AND LIABILITY FOR AGENTS, NOMINEES, AND CUSTODIANS

Statutory provisions for the review of, and liability for, agents, nominees, and custodians apply whether they were authorized or appointed under the provisions discussed above, or

(c) managing property that is subject to the trust and disposing of, or creating or disposing of an interest in, such property: s 15(5).

[30] Trustee Act 2000, s 17(2).

[31] Ibid, ss 16(1), 17(1). A nominee cannot, however, be appointed in relation to settled land.

[32] Ibid, s 18(1), unless exempted by a provision in the trust instrument or any enactment or provision of subsequent legislation: ibid, s 18(2). The section does not impose a duty on a sole trustee if that trustee is a trust corporation: s 25(2).

[33] Ibid, ss 16(2), 17(3), and 18(3). For the restrictions applicable to most charity trustees, see s 19(4), as amended by the Charities Act 2006, s 75(1), Sch 8, para 197.

[34] This is determined in accordance with s 840 of the Income and Corporation Taxes Act 1988: Trustee Act 2000, s 19(3).

[35] Ibid, s 19(1), (2). As to when a body is controlled by trustees, see s 19(3).   [36] Ibid, s 19(5).

[37] Ibid, s 19(6), (7).   [38] Ibid, s 20(1)–(3). See s 14 and p 454, *supra*.

[39] Ibid, ss 16(3), 17(4), and 18(4).

under express powers in the trust instrument, unless they would be inconsistent with the terms of the trust instrument.[40]

Once an agent, nominee, or custodian has been authorized or appointed, the trustees have a duty to keep under review the arrangements under which that person acts for the trust and how those arrangements are being implemented. This obligation means that the trustees must keep under review the question of whether the agent, nominee, or custodian is a suitable person to act for the trust and whether the terms of his appointment are appropriate. In addition, the trustees must keep under review the manner in which the agent, nominee, or custodian is performing his functions. The duty to keep under review does not oblige trustees to review the arrangements at specific intervals or in a particular way.[41]

Trustees have a further duty that comes into effect if circumstances make it appropriate, when they must consider whether there is a need to exercise any power of intervention[42] that they have.[43] It might become appropriate where the agent, nominee, or custodian is not carrying out his functions effectively, or where the trustees have cause to doubt the suitability of the person in question to continue to act for the trust.

Trustees are under a positive duty, if they consider that there is a need to do so, to exercise their power of intervention.[44]

If the agent has been authorized to exercise asset management functions, the above duties extend to keeping under review and, where necessary, revising or replacing, any policy statement prepared in connection with the delegation of asset management functions.[45]

(E) REMUNERATION OF AN AGENT, NOMINEE, OR CUSTODIAN

Trustees may provide for the remuneration of a person, other than a trustee, who has been authorized to exercise functions as an agent of the trustees, or who has been appointed to act as a nominee or custodian.[46] He may be remunerated out of the trust funds[47] for services if:

(i) he was engaged on terms entitling him to be remunerated for those services; and

(ii) the amount does not exceed such remuneration as is reasonable in the circumstances for the provision of those services by him to or on behalf of the trust.[48]

---

[40] Trustee Act 2000, s 21(1)–(3).   [41] Ibid, s 22(1)(a).

[42] This includes a power to give directions and a power to revoke the authorization or appointment of the agent, nominee or custodian: ibid, s 22(4).

[43] Ibid, s 22(1)(b).   [44] Ibid, s 22(1)(c).   [45] Ibid, s 22(2), (3).

[46] That is, an agent, nominee, or custodian authorized or appointed under Pt IV of the Trustee Act 2000 or any other enactment or any provision of subordinate legislation, or by the trust instrument: ibid, s 32(1). Note that Pt IV does not apply to trustees of authorized unit trusts, or to trustees managing a common investment scheme or a common deposit scheme under ss 24 or 25 of the Charities Act 1993 (as to which, see p 331, *supra*): Trustee Act 2000, ss 37, 28. Part IV applies to trustees of a pension scheme subject to restrictions: see ibid, s 36(4)–(8).

[47] 'Trust funds' means income or capital funds of the trust: ibid, s 39(1).   [48] Ibid, s 32(2).

The trustees may likewise reimburse the agent, nominee, or custodian out of the trust funds for any expenses properly incurred by him in exercising functions as an agent, nominee, or custodian.[49]

(F) LIABILITY OF TRUSTEE FOR AGENTS, NOMINEES, AND CUSTODIANS

A trustee is not liable for any act or default of an agent, nominee, or custodian unless he has failed to comply with the statutory duty of care applicable to him when entering onto the arrangements under which the person acts as agent, nominee, or custodian, or when carrying out his duties under s 22 (duty to keep under review).[50]

If a trustee has agreed a term under which the agent, nominee, or custodian is permitted to appoint a substitute, the trustee is not liable for any act or default of the substitute unless he has failed to comply with the duty of care applicable to him when agreeing the term, or when carrying out his duties under s 22, in so far as they relate to the use of the substitute.[51]

(G) PROTECTION OF THIRD PARTIES

A failure by the trustees to act within the limits of their statutory powers in authorizing a person to exercise a function of theirs as an agent, or in appointing a person to act as a nominee or custodian, does not invalidate the authorization or appointment.[52] Third parties, therefore, do not need to satisfy themselves that the trustees have complied with the requirements of the Act: for example, that a person authorized to act as an agent is not a beneficiary. The trustee will, of course, be liable for any loss to the trust estate flowing from a failure to comply with the requirements of the Act.

3 DELEGATION BY POWER OF ATTORNEY UNDER S 25 OF THE TRUSTEE ACT 1925, AS SUBSTITUTED BY S 5(1) OF THE TRUSTEE DELEGATION ACT 1999

Under this section, a power of delegation is conferred on trustees individually, not collectively,[53] and delegation under it leaves the trustee liable for the acts or defaults of the donee of the power of attorney in the same manner as if they were the acts or defaults of

---

[49] Ibid, s 32(3). In contrast to services, it seems the expenses must be incurred on or after the coming into force of the section: ibid, s 33(1).

[50] Ibid, s 23(1). As to the duty of care, see s 1, Sch 1, para 3, and p 399, *supra*.

[51] Ibid, s 23(2). See s 1, and Sch 1, para 3.   [52] Ibid, s 24.

[53] Contrast the power to appoint agents under s 11 of the Trustee Act 2000, discussed p 452, *supra*. However, it seems that each of two or more trustees may effect separate powers of attorney in favour of the same third party: see [1978] Conv 854 (J T Farrand).

the donor.[54] Section 25(1), as substituted, provides as follows:

> Notwithstanding any rule of law or equity to the contrary, a trustee may, by power of attorney, delegate[55] the execution or exercise of all or any of the trusts, powers and discretions vested in him as trustee, either alone or jointly with any other person or persons.

It will be observed that this provision authorizes the delegation of powers[56] and discretions, including investment decisions,[57] as well as merely ministerial acts. The persons who may be donees of a power of attorney under this section include a trust corporation.[58] A delegation under this section runs from the date of execution (or other date if specified) and continues for a period of twelve months or any shorter period provided by the instrument creating the power.[59] Written notice containing details of the power must be given by the trustee within seven days to each of the other trustees and any person who has power to appoint a new trustee, whether alone or jointly. The notice must contain the reason why the power is given, although this need not appear in the power itself. Failure to give notice does not, however, prejudice a person dealing with the donee of the power.[60] The Powers of Attorney Act 1971 gives protection to the donee of a power of attorney and third persons where the power of attorney has been revoked without their knowledge. The donee will not incur any liability and, in favour of the third party, the transaction will be valid.[61]

The section[62] provides a form of power of attorney, to be executed as a deed,[63] which may be used by a single trustee wishing to delegate all of his trustee functions in relation to a single trust to a single attorney. A power of attorney differing in immaterial respects only will have the same effect as a power in the prescribed form.

A power of attorney under s 25 may be a lasting power of attorney under the Mental Capacity Act 2005 Act.[64] Lasting powers of attorney replaced enduring powers of attorney under the Enduring Powers of Attorney Act 1985, which had been introduced to alter the general rule so as to enable powers of attorney to be created that would survive any subsequent mental incapacity of the donor. The 1985 Act was repealed by the 2005 Act[65] and it has not been possible to create a new enduring power of attorney since 30 September 2007, but protection is given to then existing enduring powers of attorney.[66]

Schedule 1[67] to the 2005 Act provides in Pt 1 that the instrument conferring a lasting power of attorney must be in the prescribed form and contain prescribed explanatory

---

[54] Trustee Act 1925, s 25(7), as substituted.

[55] A further power may be being granted when the first expires, but doubts have been expressed as to whether it is an appropriate exercise of the power to renew the delegation annually: (1993) 137 SJ 535 (L Price).

[56] But not including the power under s 25 itself: s 25(8), as substituted.

[57] See Law Reform Committee, 23rd Report, Cmnd 8733, paras 4.16–4.18, 4.20; (1990) 106 LQR 87 (D Hayton).

[58] Trustee Act 1925, s 25(3), as substituted.

[59] Trustee Act 1925, s 25(2), as substituted. It applies only to powers of attorney granted on or after 1 March 2000.

[60] Ibid, s 25(4), as substituted.   [61] Powers of Attorney Act 1971, s 5.

[62] Section 25(5), (6), of the Trustee Act 1925, as substituted by the Trustee Delegation Act 1999, s 5(1). These subsections are new.

[63] See the Law of Property (Miscellaneous Provisions) Act 1989, s 1(3), as amended.

[64] Sections 9–14 and Schs 1 and 2.   [65] Mental Capacity Act 2005, s 67(2), Sch 7.

[66] Ibid, s 66(3), (4), Schs 4 and 5, Pt 2.

[67] Part 1, paras 1–3. The prescribed forms and other requirements for the making and registration of lasting powers of attorney are set out in SI 2007/1253.

information. It will not, however, be effective unless and until the Public Guardian[68] has registered the instrument as a lasting power of attorney, which he must do at the end of the prescribed period, following an application made to him in the prescribed form.[69] This is, however, subject to provisions relating to objections to registration made by the donor, a donee, or a person named in the instrument.[70] Further, the Public Guardian must not register the instrument unless the court orders him to do so where the powers con-ferred on the attorney would conflict with the powers conferred on a deputy appointed by the court.[71]

4 DELEGATION UNDER THE TRUSTS OF LAND AND APPOINTMENT OF TRUSTEES ACT 1996

Trustees of land may, by power of attorney, delegate to any beneficiary or beneficiaries of full age and beneficially entitled to an interest in possession in land[72] subject to the trust any of their functions as trustees that relate to the land.[73] The delegation may be for any period or indefinite.[74] It must be given by all of the trustees jointly and may be revoked by any one or more of them.[75] Where a beneficiary to whom functions have alone been del-egated ceases to be a person beneficially entitled to an interest in possession in land subject to the trust, the power is revoked.[76]

Beneficiaries to whom functions have been delegated are, in relation to their exercise, in the same position as trustees, but they are not trustees for any other purpose.[77] Protection is given to a person who, in good faith, deals with a person to whom the trustees have pur-ported to delegate functions.[78]

In deciding whether, under the above provisions, to delegate any of their functions and, where the delegation is not irrevocable, in carrying out their obligations in relation to keeping the delegation under review, the duty of care under s 1 of the Trustee Act 2000 applies.[79] Unless the trustee fails to comply with this duty, he is not liable for any act or default of the beneficiary or beneficiaries.[80]

---

[68] As to the Public Guardian, see ibid. ss 57, 58.

[69] Ibid, s 9(2)(b), Sch 1, Pt 2, paras 4, 5, and see SI 2007/1253. Paras 6–10 impose requirements as to who must be notified of the application.

[70] See ibid, Sch 1, Pt 2, paras 12, 13.

[71] Ibid, Sch 1, Pt 2, para 11. As to deputies, see ibid, ss 16, 19, and 20. As to notification of the registration to the donor and donee (or donees), see Sch 1, Pt 2, para 14; as to evidence of registration, see para 15; as to cancellation of registration, see Sch 1, Pt 3; as to records of alterations to registered powers, see Pt 4.

[72] As to the meaning of this phrase, see p 198, *supra*.

[73] Trusts of Land and Appointment of Trustees Act 1996, s 9(1).   [74] Ibid, s 9(5).

[75] Ibid, s 9(3), unless expressed to be irrevocable and to be given by way of security.

[76] Ibid, s 9(4), which also provides for cases of delegation to two or more beneficiaries.

[77] Ibid, s 9(7). In particular, not for the purpose of any enactment permitting the delegation of functions by trustees or imposing requirements relating to payment of capital money.

[78] Ibid, s 9(2).   [79] Ibid, s 9A(1)–(5), inserted by the Trustees Act 2000, Sch 2, para 47.

[80] Ibid, s 9A(6), likewise inserted.

A power of attorney under these provisions cannot be an enduring power of attorney or a lasting power of attorney within the meaning of the Mental Capacity Act 2005.[81]

5 DELEGATION UNDER S 1 OF THE
TRUSTEE DELEGATION ACT 1999

This section created a new statutory exception to the general rule that a trustee must exercise in person the functions vested in him as a trustee. It provides that where the donee of a power of attorney created on or after 1 March 2000,[82] who is not otherwise authorized[83] to exercise trustee functions[84] would only be prevented from doing an act because doing it would involve the exercise of a function of the donor as a trustee, the donee may nevertheless do that act if:

(i) it related to land,[85] the capital proceeds of a conveyance[86] of land, or income from land; and

(ii) at the time when the act is done, the donor has a beneficial interest in the land, proceeds, or income.[87]

The person creating the trust or the donor may, however, exclude or restrict this provision in the document creating the trust, or the power of attorney, as the case may be.[88]

Subject to the provisions in the trust instrument, although a trustee is not liable for permitting the donee to exercise a function by virtue of subs (1), he remains liable for the acts and defaults of the donee in exercising such function in the same manner as if they were the acts or defaults of the donor.[89]

The above provisions are of particular benefit to co-owners of land who are essentially trustees for themselves. Firstly, it enables them to delegate without having to comply with the restrictions that apply where trustees hold land only for third parties.[90] Secondly, it enables a co-owner of land to make effective provision for the disposal of the co-owned

---

[81] Ibid, s 9(6), as amended by the Mental Capacity Act 2005, Sch 6, para 41.

[82] The date when the section came into force. For the exceptional case in which it applies to a pre-Act power, see s 4(6).

[83] Trustee Delegation Act 1999, s 1(8), ie under a statutory provision or a provision in a trust instrument, under which the donor of the power is expressly authorized to delegate the exercise of all or any of his trustee functions by power of attorney.

[84] That is, those that he has as trustee either alone or jointly with another person or persons: s 1(2)(b).

[85] Defined in s 11(1), by reference to the Trustee Act 1925. Further, by s 10(1)–(3), a reference to land in a power of attorney created after the commencement of the Act includes, subject to any contrary intention expressed in the instrument creating the power, a reference to any estate or interest of the donor of the power of attorney in the land at the time that the donee acts. In the few remaining cases in which the doctrine of conversion continues to operate, a person who has a beneficial interest in the proceeds of sale of land is treated for the purposes of ss 1 and 2 as having a beneficial interest in the land: s 1(7).

[86] Defined in s 1(2)(a) by reference to the Law of Property Act 1925.

[87] Section 1(1), (2)(b), and (9).

[88] Section 1(3), (5).   [89] Section 1(4), (5).

[90] See s 25 of the Trustee Act 1925, as substituted by s 5(1) of the Trustee Delegation Act 1999, and see p 457, *supra*.

land if he becomes mentally incapable.[91] Finally, it ensures that the donee is able to deal with the proceeds of sale and income from the land as well as the land itself.

It follows from the terms of s 1(1) that a person dealing with a donee under that section needs to know whether the donor has a beneficial interest in the relevant property. To avoid the difficulties that might otherwise arise in investigating the title of the beneficial interest, it is provided that, in favour of a purchaser,[92] a signed statement by the donee made when doing the act in question or within three months thereafter that the donor has such a beneficial interest is conclusive evidence thereof.[93]

6 ATTORNEY ACTING FOR A TRUSTEE AND THE 'TWO-TRUSTEE' RULE

The Trustee Delegation Act 1999 contains provisions intended to strengthen and clarify the operation of the 'two trustee' rules[94] by making it clear that, so long as there are at least two trustees, the rules could be satisfied either by two people acting in different capacities or by two people acting jointly in the same capacity, but not by one person acting in two capacities. It achieves this by providing that the rules are not satisfied by money being paid to or dealt with as directed, or a receipt for money being given, by a 'relevant attorney', or by a conveyance or deed being executed by such an attorney.[95] 'Relevant attorney' is defined as meaning a person (other than a trust corporation within the meaning of the Trustee Act 1925)[96] who is acting either—

(i)   both as a trustee and as attorney for one or more other trustees; or

(ii) as attorney for two or more trustees—

and who is not acting together with any other person or persons.[97] These provisions apply whenever the power under which a relevant attorney is acting was created.[98]

Applying the above provisions, where A and B are the only trustees, if A and B were each to appoint X as attorney, X (acting alone) would not satisfy the two-trustee rules. However, if A were to appoint X as his attorney and B to appoint Y as his, X and Y could act together and satisfy the requirement. Similarly, if A were to appoint X and Y as his joint attorneys, and B to appoint X and Y as his joint attorneys, X and Y can satisfy the requirement.

---

[91] So assumed in the Explanatory Notes to the Bill, but a doubt has been raised, as s 1 does not actually refer in terms to an enduring power of attorney.

[92] 'Purchaser' has the same meaning as in Pt I of the Law of Property Act 1925: s 2(1) of the 1999 Act.

[93] Section 2(1)–(3). As to liability for a false statement, see s 2(4).

[94] See p 375, *supra*.   [95] Trustee Delegation Act 1999, s 7(1).   [96] See p 393, *supra*.

[97] Trustee Delegation Act 1999, s 7(2).

[98] Ibid, s 7(3), as amended by the Mental Capacity Act 2005, s 67(2), Sch 7.

21

POWERS OF TRUSTEES

Trustees commonly have many and varied powers that may be conferred on them by the trust instrument or by statute. Many of them will be administrative, but they may be dispositive, giving them power to decide which of potential beneficiaries shall take an interest and what the extent of that interest shall be. Trustees may even be given power to amend the terms of the trust, but any such power must be exercised for the purpose for which it was granted.[1] Such a power must not be exercised beyond the reasonable contemplation of the parties.[2]

Some trustees' powers have already been discussed;[3] other important powers are discussed below. The concluding sections of this chapter discuss applications to the court, and the controls that exist over the exercise by trustees of their powers.

1 POWER OF SALE[4]

(A) EXISTENCE OF A POWER OF SALE

(i) Land

Trustees of land, for the purpose of exercising their functions as trustees, have, in relation to the land, all of the powers of an absolute owner, which must include a power of sale.[5]

Apart from statute, trustees who purchase land in breach of trust can sell it and make a good title even to a purchaser with notice, provided only that all of the beneficiaries are not at once competent and desirous to take the land in specie.[6]

(ii) Property other than land

Here, there may be an express trust for or power of sale, or one may be implied: for instance, under the rule in *Howe v Lord Dartmouth*.[7] In other cases, a power may exist

---

[1] *Hole v Garnsey* [1930] AC 472.   [2] *Society of Lloyd's v Robinson* [1999] 1 WLR 756, HL.

[3] For example, the power of investment (Chapter 17, *supra*), and the power to appoint agents (Chapter 20, *supra*).   [4] See [1999] Conv 84 (R Mitchell).

[5] Trusts of Land and Appointment of Trustees Act 1996, s 6(1), and see the Trustee Act 2000, s 8(4). If the land is settled land as defined by the Settled Land Act 1925, the power of sale given by that Act is conferred on the tenant for life, not the trustees of the settlement: Settled Land Act 1925, s 38.

[6] *Re Patten and Edmonton Union Poor Guardians* (1883) 48 LT 870; *Re Jenkins and HE Randall & Co's Contract* [1903] 2 Ch 362.

[7] Discussed in Chapter 18, p 428 *et seq, supra*.

under statutory provisions, such as s 4(2) of the Trustee Act 2000,[8] or s 16 of the Trustee Act 1925.[9]

Where the trustees were assumed to have no power of sale, it was held, in *Re Hope's Will Trust*,[10] that the court could order a sale under s 57 of the Trustee Act 1925.[11]

(B) STATUTORY PROVISIONS RELATING TO SALES

The Trustee Act 1925 contains various provisions, which are chiefly of interest to the conveyancer and, for present purposes, need not be considered in detail. By s 12(1), as amended by the Trusts of Land and Appointment of Trustees Act 1996, where a trustee has a duty or power to sell property, he:

> may sell or concur with any other person in selling[12] all or any part of the property, either subject to prior charges or not, and either together or in lots,[13] by public auction or by private contract, subject to any such conditions respecting title or evidence of title or other matter as the trustee thinks fit, with power to vary any contract for sale, and to buy in at any auction, or to rescind any contract for sale and to re-sell, without being answerable for any loss.

A duty or power to sell or dispose of land, moreover, 'includes a duty or power to sell or dispose of part thereof, whether the division is horizontal, vertical, or made in any other way'.[14] Further, no beneficiary can impeach a sale made by a trustee on 'the ground that any of the conditions subject to which the sale was made may have been unnecessarily depreciatory, unless it also appears that the consideration for the sale was thereby rendered inadequate',[15] and it cannot, after the execution of the conveyance, be impeached as against the purchaser on such ground 'unless it appears that the purchaser was acting in collusion with the trustee at the time when the contract for sale was made'.[16]

In general, it must be remembered that the trustees 'have an overriding duty to obtain the best price which they can for their beneficiaries',[17] even though accepting a higher offer

---

[8] See p 422, *supra*. The duty to review investments and vary them where appropriate implies a power to sell existing investments.

[9] This section, which applies equally to land, provides that, in any case in which trustees are authorized to pay or apply capital money subject to the trust for any purpose or on any manner, they have power to raise the money required by sale of all or any part of the trust property for the time being in possession. This section applies notwithstanding any contrary provision in the trust instrument, but does not apply to charity trustees, nor to the trustees of a settlement, not being also the statutory owners. It empowers trustees to raise money by mortgage as well as by sale. It does not, however, enable them to raise money on the security of the trust property for the purpose of acquiring further land by way of investment: *Re Suenson-Taylor's Settlement Trusts* [1974] 3 All ER 397.

[10] [1929] 2 Ch 136, [1929] All ER Rep 561.   [11] Discussed in Chapter 22, section 2(B), *infra*.

[12] Apart from statute, trustees could, and indeed should, concur with other persons, if they can thereby get a higher price: *Re Cooper and Allen's Contract for Sale to Harlech* (1876) 4 Ch D 802. There must be a proper apportionment and the apportioned part due to the trustees paid to them, unless there is some special provision in the trust instrument: *Re Parker and Beech's Contract* (1887) 56 LT 96, CA.

[13] See *Re Judd and Poland and Skelcher's Contract* [1906] 1 Ch 684, CA.

[14] Trustee Act 1925, s 12(2), as amended.

[15] Ibid, s 13(1). Cf *Dance v Goldingham* (1873) 8 Ch App 902; *Dunn v Flood* (1885) 28 Ch D 586, CA (both decided prior to any statutory conditions).

[16] Trustee Act 1925, s 13(2). This does not prevent an action against the trustees for breach of trust. See also ibid, s 17.

[17] *Buttle v Saunders* [1950] 2 All ER 193, 195, *per* Wynn Parry J; *Re Cooper and Allen's Contract for Sale to Harlech*, *supra*; (1950) 14 Conv 228 (E H Bodkin); (1975) 39 Conv 177 (A Samuels).

may mean resiling from an existing offer at a late stage in the negotiations, contrary to the dictates of commercial morality. Trustees must, however, act with proper prudence, and may accept an existing lower offer if to probe a higher one would involve a serious risk that both offers would fall through.

2 POWER TO GIVE RECEIPTS

Notwithstanding anything to the contrary in the instrument, if any, creating the trust,[18] s 14(1) of the Trustee Act 1925, as amended by the Trustee Act 2000, provides:

> The receipt in writing of a trustee for any money, securities, investments, or other personal property or effects payable, transferable, or deliverable to him under any trust or power shall be a sufficient discharge to the person paying, transferring, or delivering the same and shall effectually exonerate him from seeing to the application or being answerable for any loss or misapplication thereof.

By subs (2),[19] however, this section does not affect the statutory provisions[20] that require the proceeds of sale or other capital money arising under a trust of land not to be paid to fewer than two persons as trustees, except where the trustee is a trust corporation. Nor, it seems clear, does the section alter the rule[21] that where there are two or more trustees, a valid receipt can only be given by all of them acting jointly.

3 POWER TO INSURE

The traditional view was that unless there was some express provision in the trust instrument, trustees were under no duty to insure the trust property and, accordingly, would not be liable for failure to insure if the trust property should be destroyed or damaged.[22] Nor, originally, did they have any power to insure, unless conferred by a trust instrument expressly or by implication.[23] There are now statutory provisions.

Section 19 of the Trustee Act 1925, as substituted by the Trustee Act 2000,[24] confers power on all trustees, whenever the trust was created,[25] to insure any trust property against

---

[18] Trustee Act 1925, s 14(3).

[19] As amended by the Trusts of Land and Appointment of Trustees Act 1996.

[20] Law of Property Act 1925, s 27(2), as substituted by the Law of Property (Amendment) Act 1926, and amended by the Trusts of Land and Appointment of Trustees Act 1996. There are corresponding provisions in respect of strict settlements: Settled Land Act 1925, s 94(1).

[21] Discussed in Chapter 16, section 3, p 400, *supra*.   [22] *Re McEacharn* (1911) 103 LT 900.

[23] *Re Bennett* [1896] 1 Ch 778, CA. Where there is a power to insure, there has never been any doubt that a trustee may insure the whole beneficial interest in property in which he holds only the legal estate, and that he may recover from the insurers the entire diminution of its value, notwithstanding that the beneficial owners were not co-assured. He is, of course, accountable to the beneficiaries for such insurance proceeds as he may receive: see *Lonsdale & Thompson Ltd v Black Arrow Group plc* [1993] Ch 361, [1993] 3 All ER 648.

[24] Section 34. In relation to land, see also s 6(1) of the Trusts of Land and Appointment of Trustees Act 1996.

[25] Ibid, s 34(3).

such risks as they think fit, and to pay the premiums out of the income or capital funds of the trust.[26] Where property is held on a bare trust, however, this is subject to any direction given by the beneficiary (or each of them) that any specified property is not to be insured, or only insured on specified conditions.[27] The rationale behind this qualification is said to be that where the beneficiaries are together absolutely entitled to the trust property, they have power under the general law of trusts to bring the trust to an end.[28] Property is held on a bare trust if the beneficiary (each beneficiary if more than one) is of full age and (taken together if more than one) is absolutely entitled to the trust property.[29] To the extent that such directions are given, the trustees may not delegate their power to insure.[30]

These provisions do not impose a duty to insure. The imposition of such a duty might cause difficulties if the trustees had no funds out of which to pay premiums, and a trust fund comprising trustee investments, such as government bonds, would be secure without insurance. In *Re McEacharn*,[31] Eve J held that insurance was not to be maintained at the expense of the tenant for life, but expressly decided nothing as to whether the trustees ought to insure the premises at the expense of the estate generally, because he had not been asked that question. The Australian courts[32] have adopted the US approach[33] that a trustee would normally be under a duty to insure. It is submitted that a failure by trustees to exercise a power to insure (whether statutory or express) in circumstances under which a reasonable person would have done so would constitute a breach of the trustees' paramount duty to act in the best interests of the beneficiaries.[34] Moreover, the statutory duty of care applies to a trustee when exercising the statutory power to insure property, or any corresponding power, however conferred.[35] It will cover, for example, the selection of an insurer and the terms on which the insurance cover is taken out.

The following section[36] deals with the application of insurance moneys, the general effect of which is that money receivable by trustees or any beneficiary[37] under a policy of insurance against the loss or damage of any property subject to a trust or to a settlement within the meaning of the Settled Land Act 1925, is capital money for the purposes of the trust or settlement, as the case may be. Detailed provisions for the carrying through of the application in different circumstances are set out in subs (3). In particular, subs (3)(c), as amended by the Trusts of Land and Appointment of Trustees Act 1996, provides that money receivable in respect of land subject to a trust of land or personal property held on trust for sale is to be held upon the trusts, and subject to the powers and provisions applicable to money arising by a sale under such trust. By subs (4), subject to obtaining the

---

[26] Section 19(1), (5), of the Trustee Act 1925, as substituted. [27] Ibid, s 19(2), as substituted.

[28] See *Saunders v Vautier* (1841) 4 Beav 115, and p 409, *supra*. [29] Ibid, s 19(3), as substituted.

[30] Ibid, s 19(4), as substituted. This is so that the beneficiaries can ensure compliance with their directions.

[31] *Supra*. [32] *Pateman v Heyen* (1993) 33 NSWLR 188.

[33] See *Scott on Trusts*, 4th edn, vol IIA, p 484.

[34] The old case of *Bailey v Gould* (1840) 4 Y & C Ex 221, which suggests that trustees are not under a duty to insure trust property unless there is an obligation to insure imposed by the trust instrument, is of doubtful authority in contemporary conditions.

[35] Trustee Act 2000, s 1 and Sch 1, para 5.

[36] Ibid, s 20, as amended by the Trusts of Land and Appointment of Trustees Act 1996, and the Trustee Act 2000, s 34(3).

[37] By s 20(2) of the Trustee Act 1925, if receivable by a beneficiary, it must be paid by him to the trustees, or into court.

specified consents, the trustees are empowered to apply the money in rebuilding, reinstating, repairing, or replacing the property lost or damaged. Subsection (5), moreover, expressly saves the other rights, whether statutory or otherwise, of any person to require the insurance money to be applied in rebuilding, reinstating, or repairing the property lost or damaged—for instance, under the Fires Prevention (Metropolis) Act 1774, s 83, which, despite its title, is of general application.[38]

4 POWER TO COMPOUND LIABILITIES

Section 15 of the Trustee Act 1925[39] provides as follows:

A personal representative, or two or more trustees[40] acting together,[41] or, subject to the restrictions imposed in regard to receipts by a sole trustee not being a trust corporation, a sole acting trustee where by the instrument, if any, creating the trust, or by statute, a sole trustee is authorised to execute the trusts and powers reposed in him, may, if and as he or they think fit—

(a) accept any property, real or personal, before the time at which it is made transferable or payable; or

(b) sever and apportion any blended trust funds or property; or

(c) pay or allow any debt or claim on any evidence that he or they think sufficient; or

(d) accept any composition or any security, real or personal, for any debt[42] or for any property, real or personal, claimed; or

(e) allow any time of payment of any debt; or

(f) compromise,[43] compound, abandon, submit to arbitration, or otherwise settle any debt, account, claim, or thing whatever relating to the testator's or intestate's estate or to the trust;

and for any of those purposes may enter into, give, execute, and do such agreements, instruments of composition or arrangement, releases, and other things as to him or them seem expedient, without being responsible for any loss occasioned by any act or thing so done by

---

[38] *Sinnott v Bowden* [1912] 2 Ch 414. This Act provides that, on the request of any person interested, the insurers must cause the insurance money to be laid out and expended towards rebuilding, reinstating, or repairing the house or building burnt down, demolished, or damaged by fire, unless all of the persons interested agree as to its disposition, to the satisfaction of the insurers.

[39] As amended by the Trustee Act 2000, Sch 2, para 20. Apart from statute, see *Blue v Marshall* (1735) 3 P Wms 381.

[40] Including a judicial trustee: *Re Ridsdel* [1947] Ch 597, [1947] 2 All ER 312; see also *Re Shenton* [1935] Ch 651, [1935] All ER 920, DC.

[41] It is submitted that, under this section, trustees have no power to compromise a claim by one of themselves, unless, perhaps, there is a provision in the trust deed allowing trustees to act although personally interested. According to *Re Houghton* [1904] 1 Ch 622, however, one executor can, on other grounds, compromise a claim by a co-executor.

[42] Including a statutory debt: *Bradstock Group Pensions Scheme Trustees Ltd v Bradstock Group plc* [2002] WTLR 1281, discussed (2002) 152 NLJ 1284 (Sarah Boon).

[43] 'Compromise' in other contexts has been held to require either some dispute as to the claimant's rights, or some difficulty in enforcing them: *Mercantile Investment and General Trust Co v River Plate Trust, Loans and Agency Co* [1894] 1 Ch 578; *Chapman v Chapman* [1954] AC 429, [1954] 1 All ER 798, HL.

him or them if he has or they have discharged the duty of care set out in s 1(1) of the Trustee Act 2000.

The section, particularly (f), is drafted in very wide terms, and will not be restrictively construed. It is thought advantageous that trustees should enjoy wide and flexible powers of compromising and settling disputes, bearing in mind that such powers, however wide, must be exercised with due regard for the interests of those whose interests it is the duty of the trustees to protect. If the person who has a claim adverse to the trust happens also to be a beneficiary under it, in an appropriate case, the consideration may include the surrender of his interest. The trustees must listen to the beneficiaries and pay attention to their wishes, but have power to agree a proposed compromise even though all of the beneficiaries oppose it. The section has been held to be concerned with external disputes—that is, cases in which there is some issue between the trustees on behalf of the trust as a whole and the outside world—as opposed to internal disputes, in which one beneficiary under the trust is at issue with another beneficiary under the trust.[44] It has, however, been held to extend to the claim of one who alleges that he is a beneficiary.[45]

Re Ridsdel[46] decides the fairly obvious point that although a payment under s 15(f) must be made in compromise of a claim, it does not follow that, to justify a compromise payment, it must be established that the claim, if there had not been a compromise, would have succeeded. As the judge observed, if this were so, the power of compromise would be reduced in effect to a nullity. Further, it seems that the section only protects a trustee where he has done some act, or at least exercised some active discretion, and will not avail him where he has adopted a mere passive attitude of leaving matters alone.[47] In exercising the power, the only criterion is whether the compromise is desirable and fair as regards all of the beneficiaries.[48]

5 POWERS IN RELATION TO REVERSIONARY INTERESTS

Provisions in s 22 of the Trustee Act 1925, as amended by the Trustee Act 2000, give considerable protection to trustees where trust property includes any share or interest in property not vested in the trustees, or the proceeds of the sale of any such property, or any other thing in action. Subsection (1) provides that, on the same falling into possession, or becoming payable or transferable, the trustees may:

(a) agree or ascertain the amount or value thereof or any part thereof in such manner as they may think fit;

(b) accept in or towards satisfaction thereof, at the market or current value, or upon any valuation or estimate of value which they may think fit, any authorised investments;

---

[44] *Re Earl of Strafford* [1978] 3 All ER 18; affd [1980] Ch 28, [1979] 1 All ER 513, CA; not followed in Australia: *Re Irismay Holdings Pty Ltd* [1996] 1 Qd R 172.

[45] *Re Warren* (1884) 51 LT 561; *Eaton v Buchanan* [1911] AC 253, HL.   [46] *Supra.*

[47] *Re Greenwood* (1911) 105 LT 509.   [48] *Re Earl of Strafford, supra,* CA.

(c) allow any deductions for duties, costs, charges and expenses which they may think proper or reasonable;

(d) execute any release in respect of the premises so as effectually to discharge all accountable parties from all liability in respect of any matters coming within the scope of such release;

without being responsible in any such case for any loss occasioned by any act or thing so done by them if they have discharged the duty of care set out in s 1(1) of the Trustee Act 2000.

Subsection (2) restricts the obligations of trustees during the period before such property falls into possession, but it is expressly provided that nothing therein contained 'shall relieve the trustees of the obligation to get in and obtain payment or transfer of such share or interest or other thing in action on the same falling into possession'.

6 POWER OF MAINTENANCE OF MINORS

(A) EXPRESS POWERS

In view of the wide statutory power hereafter discussed, it is no longer so usual or vital to insert express powers of maintenance, and it is not proposed to deal with them in great detail, particularly as much turns in each case on the construction of the particular words used. A primary question may be whether the alleged power is not, in fact, an imperative trust to apply the income, or so much of it as may be required, for or towards the maintenance of the minor. Thu,s there was held to be an imperative trust in *Re Peel*,[49] and a line of cases[50] that the Court of Appeal has accepted as binding, although agreeing that criticism is well founded, has decided that 'a trust to apply the whole or part as the trustees may think fit of the income for the maintenance of the children is an obligatory trust and compels the trustees to maintain the children where that trust occurs in the marriage settlement to which the father is a party'.[51] Accordingly, the father in such case, notwithstanding his own ability to maintain his children, can compel the trustees to apply an adequate portion of the income for this purpose. It was made clear, however, that this line of cases is not to be extended.

Where the trustees have, on the construction of the instrument, a true discretionary power of maintenance, they must, in exercising it, have regard exclusively to the best interests of the minors and ignore those of the settlor or any other person. They are not, however, necessarily precluded from exercising the power by, for instance, paying children's school fees, where to do so would confer an incidental (and unintended) benefit on their father, who is bound by a consent order in divorce proceedings to pay such fees, but they can only properly do so if they honestly consider that, despite these consequences, it would be in the best interests of the minors.[52] Nor, it is thought, should they be forgetful of the principles

---

[49] [1936] Ch 161, [1935] All ER Rep 179.

[50] Including *Meacher v Young* (1834) 2 My & K 490; *Thompson v Griffin* (1841) Cr & Ph 317.

[51] *Per* Jessel MR in *Wilson v Turner* (1883) 22 Ch D 521, 515, CA.

[52] *Fuller v Evans* [2000] 1 All ER 636; *Re Lofthouse* (1885) 29 Ch D 921, CA. Applied to a statutory trust: *Re Sayers and Philip* (1974) 38 DLR (3d) 602.

that the court would apply in granting maintenance.[53] In general, the court will not interfere with or overrule the bona fide exercise by trustees of their discretion.[54] Where, however, trustees fail to exercise their discretion in one way or the other, the court may make
an appropriate order. Thus, on the one hand, past maintenance has been allowed where the
trustees were apparently unaware of their discretionary power,[55] and, on the other hand,
a father has been compelled to repay the whole of the income paid to him by the trustees
without their exercising any discretion at all;[56] where trustees had failed to exercise any
discretion as to out of which of two funds the allowance for maintenance should be paid,
the court exercised it by directing that it should be paid primarily out of that fund from
which it was most for the minor's benefit that it should be taken.[57]

It may be added that it has been held that a provision in an express maintenance clause that
no income is to be applied while the minor is in the custody or control of the father, or while
the father has anything to do with the education or bringing up of the child, is valid.[58]

(B) STATUTORY POWER

(i) The present law

The current provision is contained in s 31 of the Trustee Act 1925, as amended in relation to
instruments made on or after 1 January 1970, by the Family Law Reform Act 1969, which
reduced the age of majority to eighteen.[59] Terms in the section such as 'infant', 'infancy',
and 'minority' are to be construed accordingly. As thus amended, s 31(1), the language of
which, it has been said, '*is by no means easy to follow*',[60] provides as follows:

Where any property is held by trustees in trust[61] for any person for any interest whatso-
ever, whether vested or contingent, then, subject to any prior interests or charges affecting
that property—

(i) during the infancy of any such person,[62] if his interest so long continues, the trustees may, at their sole discretion, pay to his parent or guardian, if any, otherwise
apply for or towards his maintenance, education, or benefit,[63] the whole or such
part, if any, of the income of that property as may, in all the circumstances, be
reasonable, whether or not there is—
(a) any other fund applicable to the same purpose; or
(b) any person bound by law to provide for his maintenance or education, and

[53] See p 473, infra.   [54] See p 490, infra.   [55] *Stopford v Lord Canterbury* (1840) 11 Sim 82.
[56] *Wilson v Turner, supra.*   [57] *Re Wells* (1889) 43 Ch D 281.
[58] *Re Borwick's Settlement* [1916] 2 Ch 304.
[59] The 1969 Act does not apply to interests under a pre-1970 settlement, but does apply to an appointment thereunder incorporating s 31 made after 1969: *Begg-MacBrearty v Stilwell* [1996] 4 All ER 205, [1996] 1 WLR 951.
[60] Per Evershed MR in *Re Vestey's Settlement* [1951] Ch 209, 216, [1950] 2 All ER 891, 897, CA. See, generally, (1953) 17 Conv 273 (B S Ker).
[61] This does not include a sum of income allocated to a minor as being the object of a discretionary trust:
Re Vestey's Settlement, supra.
[62] In a class gift to persons contingently on attaining the age of twenty-one, it does not matter that one or
more members of the class have attained that age: *Re Holford* [1894] 3 Ch 30, CA.
[63] The same words, in s 53 of the Trustee Act 1925, were said to be of the widest import in *Re Heyworth's
Contingent Reversionary Interest* [1956] Ch 364, 370, [1956] 2 All ER 21, 23.

(ii) if such person on attaining the age of eighteen years has not a vested[64] interest in
such income, the trustees shall thenceforth pay the income of that property and
of any accretion thereto under subsection (2) of this section to him, until he either
attains a vested interest therein or dies, or until failure of his interest...

The principal function of s 31, it has been said:[65]

appears to be to supply a code of rules governing the disposal of income, especially during
a minority, in cases where a settlor or testator has made dispositions of capital and either
(a) being an unskilled draftsman, has not thought about income, or, (b) being a skilled
draftsman, has been content to let the statutory code apply.

A settlor may adopt the section with variations,[66] or exclude it by a contrary intention,[67]
express or implied, which may be shown even by a direction for accumulation,[68] notwithstanding that the direction itself is void.[69] The provisions of s 31 are inapplicable if, on a
fair reading of the relevant instrument, one can say that their application would be inconsistent with the purport of the instrument.[70] Obviously, as the subsection makes clear, the
power of maintenance cannot affect prior interests and charges, and by subs (3) it only
applies in the case of a contingent interest if the limitation or trust carries the intermediate income of the property, expressly including a future or contingent legacy by the parent
of, or a person standing *in loco parentis* to, the legatee, if and for such period as, under the
general law, the legacy carries interest[71] for the maintenance of the legatee.[72]

In many cases, quite irrespective of the relationship between the testator and the devisee
or legatee, a testamentary disposition will carry the intermediate income (unless otherwise
disposed of)[73] under s 175 of the Law of Property Act 1925, which provides that this shall
be so[74] in the case of a contingent or future specific devise or bequest of property, whether
real or personal, a contingent residuary devise of freehold land, and a specific or residuary
devise of freehold land to trustees upon trust for persons whose interests are contingent or
executory. Further, apart from the section, a contingent gift of residuary personalty carries
the intermediate income,[75] but probably not a residuary bequest, whether vested or contingent, expressly deferred to a future date that must come sooner or later.[76]

---

[64] This provision does not apply if such person has a vested interest, even if it is liable to be divested: *Re
McGeorge* [1963] Ch 544, [1963] 1 All ER 519.

[65] *Re Delamere's Settlement Trusts* [1984] 1 All ER 584, 587, [1984] 1 WLR 813, CA, *per* Slade LJ.

[66] For example, by substituting 'they may in their absolute discretion think fit' for '*may, in all the circumstances, be reasonable*' and deleting the proviso at the end of subs (1).

[67] Trustee Act 1925, s 69(2), as explained in *IRC v Bernstein* [1961] Ch 399, [1961] 1 All ER 320, CA; *Re Evans'
Settlement* [1967] 3 All ER 343 (both actually decisions on s 32, Trustee Act 1925); *Re McGeorge, supra.*

[68] *Re Ransome's Will Trusts* [1957] Ch 348, [1957] 1 All ER 690; *IRC v Bernstein, supra.*

[69] *Re Ransome's Will Trusts, supra.* See [1979] 43 Conv 423 (J G Riddall).

[70] *IRC v Bernstein, supra,* at 412, 325, CA, *per* Lord Evershed MR; *Re Delamere's Settlement Trusts,
supra,* CA.

[71] At 5 per cent, provided that the income available is sufficient: Trustee Act 1925, s 31(3).

[72] It is thought that s 31(3) embraces also cases (b) and (c) on p 471, *infra*, and that the specific mention of
case (i) is only for the purpose of establishing a suitable rate of interest: see Ker in (1953) 17 Conv 273, 279.

[73] See *Re Reade-Revell* [1930] 1 Ch 52; *Re Stapleton* [1946] 1 All ER 323.

[74] Subject to the provisions relating to accumulations in ss 164–166 of the Law of Property Act 1925, and
s 13 of the Perpetuities and Accumulations Act 1964.

[75] *Countess of Bective v Hodgson* (1864) 10 HL Cas 656; *Re Taylor* [1901] 2 Ch 134.

[76] *Re Geering* [1964] Ch 136, [1962] 3 All ER 1043; *Re McGeorge* [1963] Ch 544, [1963] 1 All ER 519; *Re
Nash* [1965] 1 All ER 51, [1965] 1 WLR 221; and see (1963) 79 LQR 184 (PVB).

A future or contingent pecuniary legacy is not within s 175, and prima facie does not carry the intermediate income. Exceptionally, however, the court presumes an intention that it does carry the intermediate income in three cases[77]—namely:

(a) where the legacy is given by a testator to his minor child, or to a minor to whom he stands *in loco parentis*,[78] no other fund being provided for his maintenance.[79] This exception applies to a contingent legacy,[80] but only where the contingency is the attainment of full age by the minor legatee or previous marriage;[81]

(b) where the will indicates, expressly or by implication, an intention that the income should be used for the maintenance of a minor legatee, not necessarily standing in any special relationship to the testator. It does not matter in this case that the legacy is contingent on some event other than the attainment of majority, or previous marriage.[82] The exception has been held to apply where trustees have been given a discretionary power to apply the whole or any part of the share to which the legatee might be entitled in or towards his advancement in life or otherwise for his benefit,[83] or, in another case, for the purpose of his education;[84]

(c) where a legacy is, expressly or by implication, directed to be set aside so as to be available for the legatee so soon as the contingency happens.[85]

The trustees, in deciding whether to exercise their statutory power, and, if so, to what extent, are directed[86] to have regard to the age of the minor and his requirements, and generally to the circumstances of the case, and, in particular, to what other income, if any, is applicable for the same purposes; where they have notice that the income of more than one fund is applicable, then, so far as practicable, unless the entire income of the funds is used or the court otherwise directs, a proportionate part only of the income of each fund should be applied. The principle stated in *Fuller v Evans*,[87] discussed in relation to express powers, applies equally to the statutory powers.

It has been held[88] that s 31 does not exclude the operation of the Apportionment Act 1870. This may produce a somewhat anomalous result where income is received after a beneficiary has attained the age of eighteen. In so far as such income is apportioned in respect of the period before he was eighteen, the income cannot be applied for maintenance, because the trustees cannot exercise their discretion in advance so as to affect the income when it is received, and they cannot apply it in arrear, because the infancy will have ceased.

---

[77] *Re Raine* [1929] 1 Ch 716.

[78] Only the father comes within the exception *qua* parent; if the mother is to come within it, it must be shown she was *in loco parentis*: *Re Eyre* [1917] 1 Ch 351.

[79] *Re Moody* [1895] 1 Ch 101; *Re George* (1877) 5 Ch D 837, CA.

[80] *Re Bowlby* [1904] 2 Ch 685, CA.

[81] *Re Abrahams* [1911] 1 Ch 108.   [82] *Re Jones* [1932] 1 Ch 642.

[83] *Re Churchill* [1909] 2 Ch 431. Cf *Re Stokes* [1928] Ch 716.

[84] *Re Selby-Walker* [1949] 2 All ER 178.

[85] *Re Medlock* (1886) 54 LT 828; *Re Clements* [1894] 1 Ch 665; *Re Woodin* [1895] 2 Ch 309, CA.

[86] Trustee Act 1925, s 31(1) proviso.   [87] [2000] 1 All ER 636. See p 472, *supra*.

[88] *Re Joel's Will Trusts* [1967] Ch 14, [1966] 2 All ER 482. The Law Reform Committee, 23rd Report, Cmnd 8733, para 3.41 recommends a change in the law.

(ii) Destination of any balance of the income not applied under subs (1)

Subsection (2)[89] provides that any such balance shall be accumulated during the minority (or until his interest previously determines), although, during this period, the accumulations, or any part thereof, may be applied as if they were income arising in the current year. Subsection (2) further provides for the destination of the accumulations as follows:

(i)   If any such person—
  (a) attains the age of eighteen years, or marries under that age or forms a civil partnership under that age, and his interest in such income during his infancy or until his marriage or his formation of a civil partnership is a vested interest; or
  (b) on attaining the age of eighteen years or on marriage, or formation of a civil partnership, under that age becomes entitled to the property from which such income arose in fee simple, absolute or determinable, or absolutely, or for an entailed interest;

the trustees shall hold the accumulations in trust for such person absolutely, but without prejudice to any provision with respect thereto contained in any settlement by him made under any statutory powers during his infancy, and so that the receipt of such person after marriage or formation of a civil partnership, and though still an infant, shall be a good discharge; and

(ii) In any other case the trustees shall, notwithstanding that such person had a vested interest in such income, hold the accumulations as an accretion to the capital of the property from which such accumulations arose, and as one fund with such capital for all purposes, and so that, if such property is settled land, such accumulations shall be held upon the same trusts as if the same were capital money arising therefrom.

In *Re Sharp's Settlement Trusts*,[90] it was accepted that, in para (i)(b), the words 'in fee simple, absolute or determinable' apply exclusively to realty, that the word 'absolutely' applies exclusively to personalty, and that the words 'for an entailed interest' apply alike to realty and personalty. It was further held that a person cannot be said to be entitled 'absolutely' if his interest is liable to be divested, for instance, by the exercise of a power of appointment. As Pennycuick VC pointed out in that case, the words of the subsection produce the anomalous result that a person having a determinable interest in realty qualifies to take accumulations at the age of eighteen, while a person having the like interest in personalty would not, because his interest is not absolute.

The effect of para (ii), where it applies, is to engraft upon the vested interest originally conferred on the minor a qualifying trust of a special nature that confers on the minor a title to the accumulations if, and only if, he attains the age of majority, or marries or forms a civil partnership. If he dies before attaining the age of eighteen, or marrying or entering into a civil partnership, his interest, even though vested, is defeated and the accumulations rejoin the general capital of the trust property from which they arose. The 'capital of the property from which such accumulations arose' is the share that the infant ultimately obtains. Accordingly, in a gift to a class of or including minors, the accumulations of income allocated to a minor, but not used for his maintenance under subs (1), continue to be held on trust for him, even though his share in the capital may subsequently be reduced by an increase in the size of the class. If the minor dies before attaining a vested interest, his

---

[89] As amended by the Family Law Reform Act 1969, the Trustee Act 2000 and the Civil Partnership Act 2004.
[90] [1973] Ch 331, [1972] 3 All ER 151.

share accrues to the other shares and carries the accumulations with it, becoming a part of the common fund of capital.[91]

It should be added that although the section applies to a vested annuity as if the annuity were the income of property held by trustees in trust to pay the income thereof to the annuitant for the same period for which the annuity is payable, subs (4), in contrast to subs (2)(ii), provides that accumulations made during the minority of the annuitant must be held in trust for the annuitant or his personal representative absolutely.

(iii) Interests arising under instruments made before 1 January 1970

Such interests are unaffected by the Family Law Reform Act 1969, which has to be read in its original form—that is, the age of twenty-one instead of eighteen in subss (1)(ii), and (2)(i)(a) and (b), and references to 'infant', 'infancy', and 'minority' being construed in relation to an age of majority of twenty-one.[92]

(C) POWER OF THE COURT

Although it will now seldom be necessary to invoke it, the court has an inherent jurisdiction to allow maintenance out of a minor's property. As Lord Redesdale explained in *Wellesley v Wellesley*,[93] the court has an unquestionable jurisdiction 'with respect to the income of the property, to take care of it for the benefit of the children, to apply it for the benefit of the children, as far as it may be beneficial for them that it should be so applied, and to accumulate any surplus, if any surplus there should be'. Although income will primarily be used, in exceptional circumstances, the court will even resort to capital for maintenance.[94]

The court has normally applied the rule 'that however large a child's fortune may be, whilst the father is of ability to maintain the child, he must perform his duty, and no part of the child's fortune is to be applied for that purpose'.[95] The rule, however, is not strictly applied, and the surrounding circumstances, such as the means of the father, the size of the minor's fortune, and even the effect on other members of the family, have been taken into account.[96]

As has been mentioned, where trustees have been given a power of maintenance, the court will not normally interfere with its exercise, and even where they have not been given any such power, if they in fact use income[97]—or even capital[98]—for maintenance, the court will, in a proper case, allow the payment in the accounts.

---

[91] *Re Joel's Will Trusts, supra; Re Sharp's Settlement Trusts, supra.* The Law Reform Committee, 23rd Report, Cmnd 8733, para 3.41, recommends a change in the law.

[92] Note the qualification in s 1(4) and Sch 3, para 5. Note also s 1(4), (7), and Sch 3, para 1.

[93] (1828) 2 Bli NS 124, 133, 134, HL.

[94] *Ex p Green* (1820) 1 Jac & W 253; *Ex p Chambers* (1829) 1 Russ & M 577; *Robison v Killey* (1862) 30 Beav 520, 521.

[95] *Per* Langdale MR in *Douglas v Andrews* (1849) 12 Beav 310 at 311.

[96] See *Hoste v Pratt* (1798) 3 Ves 730; *Jervoise v Silk* (1813) Coop G 52. As to means of the mother, see *Haley v Bannister* (1820) 4 Madd 275; *Douglas v Andrews, supra,* and pp 181, 182, *supra.*

[97] *Brown v Smith* (1878) 10 Ch D 377, CA. As to charging past maintenance on corpu, see *Re Hambrough's Estate* [1909] 2 Ch 620; *Re Badger* [1913] 1 Ch 385, CA.

[98] *Prince v Hine* (1859) 25 Beav 634; *Worthington v M'Craer* (1856) 23 Beav 81.

7 POWER OF ADVANCEMENT[99]

(A) EXPRESS POWERS

Before 1926, an express power of advancement was frequently conferred on trustees under settlements of personalty, although, since 1925, reliance is commonly placed on the statutory power hereafter discussed. In *Pilkington v IRC*,[100] Viscount Radcliffe explained that the general purpose and effect of such a power was to enable trustees:

> in a proper case to anticipate the vesting in possession of an intended beneficiary's contingent or reversionary interest by raising money on account of his interest and paying or applying it immediately for his benefit. By so doing they released it from the trusts of the settlement and accelerated the enjoyment of his interest (though normally only with the consent of a prior tenant for life); and where the contingency upon which the vesting of the beneficiary's title depended failed to mature or there was a later defeasance or, in some cases, a great shrinkage in the value of the remaining trust funds, the trusts as declared by the settlement were materially varied through the operation of the power of advancement.

The exact scope of a power of advancement, of course, depends upon the words of the particular clause under consideration. 'Advancement' is itself a word appropriate to an early period of life,[101] and means the establishment in life of the beneficiary who was the object of the power, or at any rate some step that would contribute to the furtherance of his establishment. To avoid uncertainties, other words were commonly inserted, such as a phrase as 'or otherwise for his benefit' being of the widest import.[102] Viscount Radcliffe has explained,[103] the combined phrases 'advancement and benefit', as meaning 'any use of the money that will improve the material situation of the beneficiary', have been held to authorize, for instance, a payment for the purpose of discharging the beneficiary's debts,[104] a payment made to the beneficiary's husband, on his personal security, for the purpose of setting him up in trade,[105] payments for the maintenance and education of a beneficiary,[106] and, of particular importance in modern conditions, an advancement made in order to avoid tax, although the beneficiary may not require it at the time it is made for any special purpose.[107]

However wide the power, the trustees must, of course, be satisfied that the proposed exercise will benefit the beneficiary.[108] There must be some sense in which the beneficiary's material situation can be said to be improved by the transaction.[109] The courts, however, do not take too narrow a view of what represents a benefit. At any rate, in the case of a

---

[99] See, generally, (1958) 22 Conv 413 (D W M Waters); [2007] PCB 282 (Natasha Hassall).

[100] [1964] AC 612, 633, [1962] 3 All ER 622, 627, HL.   [101] *Re Kershaw's Trusts* (1868) LR 6 Eq 322.

[102] *Re Halstead's Will Trusts* [1937] 2 All ER 570; *Pilkington v IRC, supra*, HL, at 633, 627, but see *Re Pinto's Settlement* [2004] WTLR 879 (Jersey Royal Court).

[103] In *Pilkington v IRC, supra*, HL, at 628, 635.   [104] *Lowther v Bentinck* (1874) LR 19 Eq 166.

[105] *Re Kershaw's Trusts* (1868) LR 6 Eq 322.

[106] *Re Breed's Will* (1875) 1 Ch D 226; *Re Garrett* [1934] Ch 477.

[107] *Pilkington v IRC, supra*, HL (on the statutory power).

[108] *Re Moxon's Will Trusts* [1958] 1 All ER 386, [1985] 1 WLR 165 (on the statutory power); *Re Pauling's Settlement Trusts* [1964] Ch 303, [1963] 3 All ER 1, CA. Cf *Molyneux v Fletcher* [1898] 1 QB 648.

[109] *X v A* [2005] EWHC 2706 (Ch), [2006] 1 All ER 952, [2006] 1 WLR 741, noted (2006) 74 T & ELTJ 9 (M Feeny).

wealthy beneficiary who regards himself as being under a moral obligation to make charitable donations, it may be for his benefit for the trustees to raise capital and pay it over to a charity in order to relieve him of his moral obligation. The trustees cannot, however, do this against the beneficiary's will, because it is of the essence of the matter that the beneficiary himself should recognize the moral obligation.[110] And it has subsequently been observed[111] that the references in *Re Clore's Settlement Trusts*[112] to the sense of obligation felt by the beneficiary were made with the view of imposing a requirement additional to the initial requirement that there should be a moral obligation capable of being recognized by the court. It has also been held to be proper, under a power to apply the capital of a fund for the benefit of a beneficiary, to resettle it on the beneficiary's children, including unborn children, with a view to avoiding tax, in a case in which the beneficiary himself was already well provided for.[113]

Four final points may be added. Firstly, if the power is given only during minority and the beneficiary has attained the age of eighteen,[114] or for a limited purpose which can no longer be effected,[115] the power ceases to be exercisable, and the trustees will, of course, be personally liable to refund if they exercise the power improperly.[116]

Secondly, where a beneficiary has an interest that will determine if he does any act whereby, if the income were payable to him, he would be deprived of the right to receive the same, it will not normally be forfeited if that beneficiary consents to the exercise of a power of advancement—whether express or statutory.[117] This is expressly provided for in the statutory protective trusts under s 33 of the Trustee Act 1925.

Thirdly, on basic equitable principles, the exercise of the power must be bona fide and, accordingly, it was held to be a breach of trust in *Molyneux v Fletcher*,[118] in which trustees advanced money to a beneficiary on the understanding that the money advanced would be used to repay a debt owed to one of the trustees by the beneficiary's husband.

Fourthly, where a power of advancement is exercised for a particular purpose specified by the trustees, the advancee is under a duty to carry out that purpose and the trustees are under a duty to see that he does so, and are under a duty not to leave the advancee free to spend the advance in any way he chooses.[119]

(B) THE STATUTORY POWER CONTAINED IN S 32 OF THE TRUSTEE ACT 1925

Subsection (1) provides as follows:

> Trustees may at any time or times pay or apply any capital money subject to a trust, for the advancement or benefit, in such manner as they may, in their absolute discretion, think fit, of any person entitled to the capital of the trust property or of any share thereof, whether absolutely or contingently on his attaining any specified age or on the occurrence of any other event, or subject to a gift over on his death under any specified age or on the occurrence

---

[110] *Re Clore's Settlement Trusts* [1966] 2 All ER 272, [1966] 1 WLR 955.

[111] *X v A, supra* (not open to trustees to make the proposed advancement).   [112] *Supra.*

[113] *Re Earl of Buckinghamshire's Settlement Trusts* (1977) Times, 29 March.

[114] *Clarke v Hogg* (1871) 19 WR 617; Family Law Reform Act 1969, s 1.

[115] *Re Ward's Trusts* (1872) 7 Ch App 727.   [116] *Simpson v Brown* (1864) 11 LT 593.

[117] *Re Rees' Will Trusts* [1954] Ch 202, [1954] 1 All ER 7.   [118] [1898] 1 QB 648.

[119] *Re Pauling's Settlement Trusts, supra,* CA, at 334.

of any other event, and whether in possession or in remainder or reversion, and such payment or application may be made notwithstanding that the interest of such person is liable to be defeated by the exercise of a power of appointment or revocation, or to be diminished by the increase of the class to which he belongs.

It adopts without qualification the accustomed wording '*for the advancement or benefit, in such manner as they may, in their absolute discretion, think fit*', which, as we have seen in connection with express powers, is of the widest import. It applies to contingent interests even where there is a double contingency, such as surviving the life interest and attaining a specified age.[120] Like s 31, a settlor may incorporate this section with variations,[121] or exclude it altogether by a contrary intention, express or implied.[122] In exceptional circumstances, the Jersey Court of Appeal has held that a trustee may exercise a power of advancement in favour of a beneficiary against his express wishes. The principle underlying the rule that no one can be forced to accept a gift was said not to preclude an indirect benefit being conferred against the objection of a donee of the power of advancement.[123]

One question is whether trustees can exercise the statutory power by transferring the sum advanced to new trustees to be held upon new trusts containing powers and discretions not contemplated in the original trust instrument. Trustees have often wished to do this in cases in which the beneficiary being advanced had no immediate need of the money, and the creation of the new trusts was designed primarily to avoid tax.[124] In *Pilkington v IRC*,[125] the House of Lords, reversing the decision of the Court of Appeal, held that it is within the scope of s 32 to exercise the power of advancement by way of resettlement, and, further, that it can make no difference whether the trustees require resettlement as a condition of advancement, or themselves appoint new trusts. It is irrelevant whether they actually raise money or merely appropriate certain investments to the new trusts, and it is also irrelevant whether or not the trustees of the new trusts are the same persons as the trustees of the original trust. It is not clear whether, in any absence of specific powers in the original settlement, the resettlement can validly include discretionary trusts, because this would involve the delegation of dispositive, not merely administrative or ministerial, discretions, in contravention of the principle *delegatus non potest delegare*.[126]

When a resettlement is made under a power that came into existence before the coming into force of the Perpetuities and Accumulations Act 1964 on 16 July 1964, one must bear in mind the operation of the rule against perpetuities, particularly where the trustees have to appoint new trusts themselves because the beneficiary being advanced is a minor and

---

[120] *Re Garrett* [1934] Ch 477, [1934] All ER Rep 129.

[121] For example, by altering or omitting proviso (a), *infra*. See *Henley v Wardell* (1988) Times, 29 January, in which the extension of the power was held, as a question of construction, not to exclude s 32(1)(c), discussed p 478, *infra*.

[122] Trustee Act 1925, s 69(2); *Re Rees' Will Trusts* [1954] Ch 202, [1954] 1 All ER 7; *IRC v Bernstein* [1961] Ch 399, [1961] 1 All ER 320, CA; *Re Evans' Settlement* [1967] 3 All ER 343, [1967] 1 WLR 1294.

[123] *Re Esteem Settlement* [2002] WTLR 337 (on the facts, a distribution to a beneficiary's creditor in reduction of his debt would not be a payment for the benefit of the beneficiary), discussed (2002) 34 T & ELJ 34 (Gilian Robinson).

[124] See *Swires v Renton* [1991] STC 490.

[125] [1964] AC 612, [1962] 3 All ER 622, HL. See (1981) 9 NZULR 247 (J Prebble).

[126] *Re Morris' Settlement Trusts* [1951] 2 All ER 528; *Re Hunter's Will Trusts* [1963] Ch 372, [1962] 3 All ER 1050; *Re Hay's Settlement Trusts* [1981] 3 All ER 786, [1982] 1 WLR 202, and see (1963) 27 Conv 65 (F R Crane); [1994] PCB 317, 402 (R Oerton).

therefore incapable of making a settlement. In such case, as regards the rule against perpetuities, there is an effective analogy between powers of advancement and special powers of appointment, and failure to realize this meant, in *Re Abraham's Will Trusts*,[127] that many of the declared trusts were void for perpetuity, so that the character of the settlement was wholly altered. It followed that the trustees had never addressed their minds to the question of whether the settlement, as modified by the rule against perpetuities, was 'for the advancement or benefit' of the beneficiary, as required by s 32. There had accordingly never been a valid exercise by the trustees of the power of advancement and the purported settlement by the trustees was ineffective.

Even in *Re Abrahams' Will Trusts*,[128] it was recognized that this drastic result would not necessarily follow where the rule against perpetuities operated to invalidate only a comparatively small part of the settlement, and the Court of Appeal in *Re Hastings-Bass*[129] declared the principle of *Re Abrahams' Will Trusts*[130] to be limited to cases in which the effect of the perpetuity rule had been to alter the intended consequences of an advancement so drastically that the trustees could not reasonably be supposed to have addressed their minds to the question relevant to the true effect of the transaction. On this basis, the advancement in *Re Hastings-Bass* was good, notwithstanding the failure for perpetuity of the ulterior trusts in the sub-settlement. The primary duty-saving aspect of the scheme, giving a clear benefit to the beneficiary being advanced, was not prejudiced thereby, and the indirect or contingent benefits that the beneficiary might have obtained under the ulterior trusts were mere makeweights.

Where the power of advancement came into existence after 15 July 1964, the effect of the Perpetuities and Accumulations Act 1964 is that it is most unlikely that the exercise of the power of advancement will be invalid, because the interests under the resettlement will be valid unless and until it becomes established that the interests thereunder must vest, if at all, after the end of the perpetuity period.

By the proviso to subs (1), the statutory power is subject to certain important restrictions—namely:

(a) the money so paid or applied for the advancement or benefit of any person shall not exceed altogether in amount one-half of the presumptive or vested share or interest of that person in the trust property;[131] and

(b) if that person is or becomes absolutely and indefeasibly entitled to a share in the trust property the money so paid or applied shall be brought into account as part of such share;[132] and

(c) no such payment or application shall be made so as to prejudice any person entitled to any prior life or other interest, whether vested or contingent, in the money paid or applied unless such person is in existence and of full age and consents in writing to such payment or application.

---

[127] [1969] 1 Ch 463, [1967] 2 All ER 1175. See also *Pilkington v IRC* [1961] Ch 488, 489, [1961] 2 All ER 340, 341, CA, *per* Upjohn LJ; [1964] AC 641, 642, [1962] 3 All ER 631, 632, HL, *per* Lord Radcliffe.

[128] *Supra.*   [129] [1975] Ch 25, [1974] 2 All ER 193, and see p 490 et seq, *infra.*   [130] *Supra.*

[131] The court may remove the limit on an application under the Variation of Trusts Act 1958: *D (a child) v O* [2004] EWHC 1036 (Ch), [2004] 3 All ER 280.

[132] The rule that advancements are brought into account on a cash basis may result in injustice in times of inflation: *Re Marquis of Abergavenny's Estate Act Trusts* [1981] 2 All ER 643, [1981] 1 WLR 843. The Law Reform Committee, 23rd Report, Cmnd 8733, paras 4.43–4.47, recomends that they should be brought into account on an index-linked or fractional basis.

Under proviso (c), it has been held that the objects of a discretionary trust are not persons whose consent to the exercise of the power is required, even where these discretionary trusts have come into operation.[133] But if there is a person whose consent is required, the court has no power to dispense with it.[134]

Section 32 does not apply to capital money arising under the Settled Land Act 1925.[135]

(C) POWER OF THE COURT

The court may, in exceptional circumstances, apply capital for the maintenance or advancement of an infant,[136] or allow such payment made by the trustee without any express power to do so,[137] and may also exercise its statutory jurisdiction for this purpose under s 53 of the Trustee Act 1925,[138] or under the Variation of Trusts Act 1958.[139]

8 RIGHT TO REIMBURSEMENT FOR COSTS AND EXPENSES

(A) REIMBURSEMENT OUT OF THE TRUST ESTATE[140]

Trustees are personally liable on any contracts they enter into in relation to the trust; creditors have no direct action against either the trust estate or the beneficiaries. However, s 31(1) of the Trustee Act 2000[141] provides:

A trustee—

(a) is entitled to be reimbursed from the trust funds,[142] or

(b) may pay out of the trust funds,

expenses properly incurred by him when acting on behalf of the trust.

The section applies equally to a trustee who has been duly authorized to exercise functions as an agent of the trustees, or to act as a nominee or custodian.[143]

---

133 *Re Harris' Settlement* (1940) 162 LT 358; *Re Beckett's Settlement* [1940] Ch 279.

134 *Re Forster's Settlement* [1942] Ch 199, [1942] 1 All ER 180. *Quaere*, if an application were made under Trustee Act 1925, s 57.

135 Section 32(2), as substituted by the Trusts of Land and Appointment of Trustees Act 1996, Sch 3, para 8.

136 For example, to pay the expenses of emigration: *Re Mary England's Estate* (1830) 1 Russ & M 499; *Clay v Pennington* (1837) 8 Sim 359.

137 *Worthington v M'Craer* (1856) 23 Beav 81.

138 Discussed in Chapter 22, section 2(a), p 498, *infra*.

139 Discussed in Chapter 22, section 3, *infra*.

140 In relation to charity trustees, see (1979) 95 LQR 99 (A J Hawkins).

141 Replacing legislation going back to the Law of Property Amendment Act 1859, s 31 (Lord St Leonard's Act). See (1996) 10 Tru LI 45 (R Ham).

142 'Trust funds' means income or capital funds of the trust: Trustee Act 2000, s 39(1).

143 Ibid, s 31(2).

The right of reimbursement has been held to include, inter alia, calls on shares that the trustee has been obliged to pay,[144] and damages and costs awarded to a third party in an action against the trustee as legal owner of the trust property.[145]

Where trustees duly authorized by will carry on a business,[146] they are personally liable on the contracts into which they enter.[147] They are, however, entitled to an indemnity,[148] which, although good as against the beneficiaries, will not prevail against the testator's creditors at the date of death, unless they have assented to the business being carried on, and such assent will not be inferred from their merely standing by with knowledge that the business was being carried on and abstaining from interfering.[149] Agents, such as solicitors, employed by the trustees, even though described as solicitors to the trust, are, in law, retained by the trustees and therefore have no direct claim against the trust estate. The trustees will, of course, be entitled to an indemnity in respect of the agent's proper fees.

Trustees may, if they wish, pay claims that are statute-barred and will be entitled to the usual indemnity in respect thereof, notwithstanding that the beneficiaries do not wish the claim to be paid.[150]

As between the beneficiaries, the trustees' costs and expenses are normally payable out of capital,[151] but so far as the trustees are concerned, their right to 'indemnity against all costs and expenses properly incurred by them in the execution of the trust is a first charge on all the trust property, both income and corpus'.[152] This indemnity, which thus gives the trustees a lien on the trust property, takes priority to the claims both of beneficiaries and third parties,[153] and is unaffected by the fact that a beneficiary has assigned his equitable interest to a stranger.[154] The lien extends to all liabilities of the trustee as such, and, in X v A,[155] was held to include liabilities under Pt IIA of the Environmental Protection Act 1990 even though they were contingent upon a number of matters, including the commencement of Pt IIA. Trustees who have such a lien may, at any time, apply to the court to enforce

---

[144] *Re National Financial Co* (1868) 3 Ch App 791; *James v May* (1873) LR 6 HL 328.

[145] *Benett v Wyndham* (1862) 4 De GF & J 259; *Re Raybould* [1900] 1 Ch 199.

[146] Under a will, the personal representatives are impliedly authorized to carry on the business for the purpose of winding it up so soon as reasonably possible. In general, the rules apply equally whether the trust is created *inter vivos* or by will, although most of the cases are on wills: *Re Johnson* (1880) 15 Ch D 548.

[147] *Farhall v Farhall* (1871) 7 Ch App 123; *Re Morgan* (1881) 18 Ch D 93, CA, esp *per* Fry J at first instance, at 99. As to the possibility of contracting in terms that avoid personal liability, see *Re Robinson's Settlement* [1912] 1 Ch 717, CA; *Hunt Bros v Colwell* [1939] 4 All ER 406, CA. See (1987) 2 TL & P 51 (D Goddard). In Australia, it has been held that a trustee's right to indemnity out of the trust assets for personal liabilities incurred in the performance of the trust constitutes a beneficial interest in the trust assets: *Chief Comr of Stamp Duties v Buckle* (1995) 38 NSWLR 574.

[148] *Re Evans* (1887) 34 Ch D 597, CA; *Dowse v Gorton* [1891] Ac 190, HL; *Re Oxley* [1914] 1 Ch 604, CA. If they are only authorized to use certain assets in the business, their indemnity will be against these assets only: *Re Johnson, supra.* Cf *Strickland v Symons* (1884) 26 Ch D 245, CA.

[149] *Dowse v Gorton, supra; Re Oxley, supra.*

[150] *Budgett v Budgett* [1895] 1 Ch 202; cf the position of executors: *Re Wenham* [1892] 3 Ch 59.

[151] *Carter v Sebright* (1859) 26 Beav 374 (costs of appointment of new trustees).

[152] Per Selborne LC in *Stott v Milne* (1884) 25 Ch D 710, 715, CA; *Re Exhall Coal Co* (1866) 35 Beav 449. Except where trustees pay off an interest-bearing debt of the estate, the court has no jurisdiction to award interest on expenses: *Foster v Spencer* [1996] 2 All ER 672.

[153] *Re Knapman* (1881) 18 Ch D 300, CA; *Dodds v Tuke* (1884) 25 Ch D 617; *Re Turner* [1907] 2 Ch 126, CA.

[154] *Re Knapman, supra.*   [155] [2000] 1 All ER 490.

it; they are not bound to wait until the trust property happens to be turned into money.[156] Exceptionally, however, the court may refuse to enforce the lien, where to do so would destroy the trusts altogether, although, in such a case, the court has held the trustees entitled to the possession of the title deeds and prohibited any disposition of the trust property without discharging the trustees' lien.[157] In any case, where the trustees have committed a breach of trust, they can only claim their indemnity after they have first made good to the trust estate the loss caused by the breach of trust.[158] As we shall see,[159] where the trustee mixes his own moneys and trust moneys, the trust has a first and paramount charge over the mixed fund, and, similarly, where a trustee expends his own money in the purchase or improvement of trust property, the claim of the trustee for indemnity is subject to the prior claim of the beneficiaries under the trust.[160]

In some cases, the above principles have been extended so as to give the trustee an indemnity and a lien on the trust property where the trustee has expended his own money in the preservation of the trust property, as by paying the premiums on an insurance policy.[161] The court, in one case, even allowed a partial indemnity where the trustee, under the impression that he would be repaid out of the estate, had bona fide used his own moneys together with trust moneys in rebuilding the mansion house, although this was a breach of trust that the court considered it would have had no jurisdiction to authorize had it been asked to do so.[162] The indemnity was, however, limited to the amount that happened to be in court,[163] this being about half the sum advanced and clearly less than the amount by which the estate had benefited. Again, in *Rowley v Ginnever*,[164] a constructive trustee of property, who expended money in improving what he bona fide believed to be his own property, was held to be entitled to recoup his expenditure to the extent of the improved value.

Creditors, or victims of tort, have no direct action against either the trust estate or the beneficiaries. However, they may be entitled to be subrogated to the rights of the trustees against the estate,[165] although they cannot be in a better position than the trustees, and if, for instance, the trustees have committed a breach of trust, this must first be made good. Each trustee has a separate right of indemnity, which will not necessarily be affected by the fact that another trustee has committed a breach of trust. Since a creditor may sue the trustee with a subsisting indemnity, it follows that he does not lose his right of subrogation by reason of the fact that one of two or more trustees is a defaulter.[166] Nevertheless, the position is that the right of a third party against the trust fund is indirect and uncertain, and this may make him reluctant to enter into contractual relations with trustees. This may cause difficulty, particularly to large commercial trusts, such as pension funds. It may well be that an appropriate and effective power could be expressly given. However,

---

[156] *Re Pumfrey* (1882) 22 Ch D 255.   [157] *Darke v Williamson* (1858) 25 Beav 622.

[158] *McEwan v Crombie* (1883) 25 Ch D 175; cf *Re Knott* (1887) 56 LJ Ch 318.

[159] See Chapter 24, section 2(B), p 546, *infra*.   [160] *Re Pumfrey* (1882) 22 Ch D 255.

[161] *Re Leslie* (1883) 23 Ch D 552; *Re Smith's Estate* [1937] Ch 636. See *Foskett v McKeown* [1998] Ch 265, [1997] 3 All ER 392, CA, revsd [2001] 1 AC 102, [2000] 3 All ER 97, HL.

[162] *Jesse v Lloyd* (1883) 48 LT 656.   [163] A somewhat haphazard solution on no clear principle.

[164] [1897] 2 Ch 503.

[165] *Benett v Wyndham* (1862) 4 De GF & J 259; *Re Blundell* (1888) 40 Ch D 370; *Re Raybould* [1900] 1 Ch 199. See (1997) NLJ Easter App Supp 28 (Emma Ford); *Belar Pty Ltd (in liq) v Mahaffey* [2000] 1 Qd R 477. See (2005) 19 TLI 75 (H Tjio).

[166] *Re Frith* [1902] 1 Ch 342.

because of doubts as to whether this is permissible, the Law Reform Committee[167] proposed legislation to make it clear that a power to create a charge upon the trust fund as a continuing entity can be conferred upon trustees by the trust deed, enabling them to give the maximum possible security to third parties.

(B) PERSONAL LIABILITY OF CESTUI QUE TRUST TO INDEMNIFY TRUSTEES

The general principle, it has been said,[168] is that a trustee is entitled to an indemnity for liabilities properly incurred in carrying out the trust, and that that right extends beyond the trust property and is enforceable in equity against a beneficiary who is *sui juris*. The basis of the principle is that the beneficiary who gets the benefit of the trust should bear its burdens unless he can show some good reason why his trustee should bear the burdens himself.

Hardoon v Belilios[169] has been thought to restrict the principle to the case in which there is a sole beneficiary, but it has been applied by Australian courts[170] to cases in which there were several beneficiaries. *Hardoon v Belilios*[171] was explained as being a case in which there was only one beneficiary and the Privy Council chose not to state the principle more widely than necessary for the case before it.

Where the settlor is also a beneficiary, Jessel MR stated, in *Jervis v Wolferstan*:[172] 'I take it to be a general rule that where persons accept a trust at the request of another, and that other is a cestui que trust, he is personally liable to indemnify the trustees for any loss accruing in the due execution of the trust.' In any case, where a cestui que trust is personally liable to indemnify his trustee, his liability is not terminated by an assignment of his beneficial interest.[173]

It may be added that, unless the rules provide to the contrary, members of a club are assumed not to be under any liability beyond their subscriptions, and are under no obligation to indemnify trustees of club property.[174]

(C) COSTS OF LEGAL PROCEEDINGS

The Civil Procedure Rules[175] provide that, where a trustee is a party to any proceedings in that capacity, the general rule is that he is entitled to the costs of those proceedings, in so far as they are not recovered from or paid by any other person, out of the trust funds, and the costs are assessed on the indemnity basis. It does not matter that, in the proceedings,

---

[167] 23rd Report, 1982, Cmnd 8733, paras 2.17–2.24. As to whether a trustee's indemnity can be excluded to the prejudice of third parties, see *RWG Management Ltd v Corporate Affairs Comr* [1985] VR 385.

[168] *J W Broomhead (Vic) Pty Ltd v J W Broomhead Pty Ltd* [1985] VR 891, 936, 937, per McGarvie J; *Hurst v Bryk* [1999] Ch 1, [1997] 2 All ER 283, CA.

[169] [1901] AC 118, PC.

[170] McGarvie J in *J W Broomhead (Vic) Pty Ltd v J W Broomhead Pty Ltd, supra; Balkin v Peck* (1998) 43 NSWLR 706; *Ron Kingham Real Estate Pty Ltd v Edgar* [1999] 2 Qd R 439. See (1990) 64 ALJ 567 (R A Hughes).

[171] *Supra*, PC.   [172] (1874) LR 18 Eq 18, 24; *Hobbs v Wayet* (1887) 36 Ch D 256.

[173] *Matthews v Ruggles-Brice* [1911] 1 Ch 194.

[174] *Wise v Perpetual Trustee Co Ltd* [1903] AC 139, PC.

[175] CPR 48.4. See *Practice Note* [2001] 3 All ER 574 as to a prospective costs order.

he is incidentally defending himself against charges made against him personally in relation to his administration of the trust provided that it is for the benefit of the trust.[176] As Ungoed-Thomas J explained in *Re Spurling's Will Trusts*:[177]

> if costs of successfully defending claims to make good to a trust fund for alleged breach of trust were excluded, it would drive a coach and four through the very raison d'etre which Sir George Jessel MR invoked[178] for the principle which he lays down; namely, the safety of trustees, and the need to encourage persons to act as such by protecting them "if they have done their duty or even if they have committed an innocent breach of trust".

To this last proposition, *Re Dargie*,[179] which, unfortunately, does not appear to have been cited to the court in *Re Spurling's Will Trusts*,[180] suggests one qualification—namely, that trustees are not necessarily entitled to costs on an indemnity basis in hostile litigation designed to define and secure the personal rights of the trustees as individuals.

In practice, the prudent course is for the trustees to apply to the court for directions before taking part in any legal proceedings:[181] if they are given leave to sue or defend, the order will normally entitle them to an indemnity for all of their costs out of the trust property, although it is essentially for the discretion of the court.[182] On such an application, the court is acting in an essentially administrative capacity: the proposed defendants are not entitled to be heard on the application, or to be furnished with the evidence on which the court is asked to act.[183]

If trustees go ahead without the leave of the court, they do so at their own risk as to costs: if they fail, they will not receive their costs unless they establish that they were properly incurred.[184] Even if they have been advised by counsel that they have a good case, they will not receive their costs unless the court is satisfied that it would have authorized the claim or defence, as the case may be, had an appropriate application been made to it.[185] Of course, even if it is proper to bring or defend the proceedings, excessive or unnecessary

---

[176] *Walters v Woodbridge* (1878) 7 Ch D 504, CA; *Re Dunn* [1904] 1 Ch 648. See (1987) 2 TL & P 55 (J Thurston).

[177] [1966] 1 All ER 745, 758. See *National Trustees Executors and Agency Co of Australasia Ltd v Barnes* (1941) 64 CLR 268.

[178] *In Turner v Hancock* (1882) 20 Ch D 303, 305.   [179] [1954] Ch 16, [1953] 2 All ER 577.

[180] *Supra.*

[181] *Re Beddoe* [1893] 1 Ch 547, CA; *Re Biddencare* [1994] 2 BCLC 160; *McDonald v Horn* [1995] 1 All ER 961, CA. The application should be made in separate proceedings: *Alsop Wilkinson (a firm) v Neary* [1995] 1 All ER 431, [1996] 1 WLR 1220.

[182] *Evans v Evans* [1985] 3 All ER 289, sub nom *Re Evans* [1986] 1 WLR 101, CA (merits of the claimant's case an important consideration); *National Anti-Vivisection Society Ltd v Duddington* (1989) Times, 23 November (other factors where a pre-emptive order for costs is sought include the likelihood that, at the trial, the court would order costs to be paid out of the fund, and the justice of the case). See *Holding and Management Ltd v Property Holdings and Investment Trust plc* [1990] 1 All ER 938, [1989] 1 WLR 1313, CA (trustee not entitled to indemnity where not a party to proceedings truly in capacity of trustee); *Professional Trustees v Infant Prospective Beneficiary* [2007] EWHC 1922 (Ch), [2007] WTLR 1631.

[183] *Re Moritz* [1960] Ch 251, [1959] 3 All ER 767; *Craig v Humberclyde Industrial Finance Group Ltd* [1999] 1 WLR 129, [1998] 2 BCLC 526, CA.

[184] *Re Beddoe, supra; Re Yorke* [1911] 1 Ch 370; *Dagnall v J L Freedman & Co (a firm)* [1993] 2 All ER 161, [1993] 1 WLR 388, HL.

[185] *Singh v Bhasin* [2000] 2 WTLR 275; *Re Beddoe, supra; Breadner v Granville-Grossman* [2001] WTLR 377. See (1999) 5 T & ELJ 10 (A Penny).

costs therein will be disallowed.[186] And where the costs are due to breach of trust or misconduct by the trustees, the court has a discretion that it will usually exercise against the trustees.[187] It was said, in *Carroll v Graham*,[188] that trustees holding a merely neutral position, and not intending to argue, ought not to appear by separate counsel on appeal, but the contrary view seems to have prevailed—that is, that trustees ought to appear in the Court of Appeal—because it is necessary for them to see that the order that relates to the administration of the estate is properly carried out.[189]

In a case in which the dispute is between rival claimants to a beneficial interest in the subject matter of the trust, the duty of the trustees is to remain neutral and offer to submit to the court's directions, leaving it to the rivals to fight their battles.[190] If, however, they actively defend the trust and succeed, for example, in challenging a claim by the settlor to set aside for undue influence, they may be entitled to costs out of the trust, because they have preserved the interests of the beneficiaries under the trust.[191] But if they fail, then, in particular in the case of hostile litigation, although in an exceptional case, the court may consider that the trustee should have his costs,[192] ordinarily, the trustees will not be entitled to any indemnity, because they have incurred expenditure and liabilities in an unsuccessful attempt to prefer one class of beneficiaries (for example, the express beneficiaries specified in the trust instrument) over another (for example, the trustee in bankruptcy or creditors), and so have acted unreasonably and otherwise than for the benefit of the trust estate.[193]

Where it appears that the cost of an application is out of proportion to the amount at stake, the Law Reform Committee recommends[194] that trustees should be empowered to take the advice of counsel (in the case of trusts having adult beneficiaries only) or Queen's Counsel practising in the Chancery Division or conveyancing counsel of the court (where there are minor beneficiaries), and to distribute on the basis of that advice if no adult beneficiary starts proceedings within three months of being sent a copy of the relevant opinion.

(D) COSTS OF BENEFICIARIES

CPR 48.4 does not apply to the costs of beneficiaries, but the courts have sometimes been willing to extend to other parties to trust litigation an entitlement to costs in any event by analogy with that accorded to trustees. In *Re Buckton*,[195] Kekewich J said trust litigation can be divided into three categories.

---

[186] *Re England's Settlement Trusts* [1918] 1 Ch 24; *Re Robertson* [1949] 1 All ER 1042; *Re Whitley* [1962] 3 All ER 45, [1962] 1 WLR 922.

[187] *Easton v Landor* (1892) 62 LJ Ch 164, CA; *Re Knox's Trusts* [1895] 2 Ch 483, CA; *Re Chapman* (1895) 72 LT 66, CA.

[188] [1905] 1 Ch 478, CA.

[189] *Re Stuart* [1940] 4 All ER 80, CA; *Chettiar v Chettiar, supra*, PC.

[190] *Alsop Wilkinson (a firm) v Neary* [1995] 1 All ER 431, adopted in New Zealand, *Re Schroder's Will* [2004] 1 NZLR 695. See the criticism of this decision in [2005] 68 T & ELTJ 25 (P Sinel).

[191] See *Re Holden* (1887) 20 QBD 43, DC.

[192] See *Bullock v Lloyds Bank Ltd* [1955] Ch 317, [1954] 3 All ER 726.

[193] *Alsop Wilkinson (a firm) v Neary, supra*.   [194] 23rd Report, Cmnd 8733, paras 5.2–5.3.

[195] [1907] 2 Ch 406. See *The Trustee Corporation Ltd v Nadir* [2000] BPIR 541. See also (2006) 20 TruLI 151 (Lightman J).

(i)   There are proceedings brought by trustees to have the guidance of the court as to the construction of the trust instrument or some question arising in the course of administration. In such cases, the costs of all parties are usually treated as necessarily incurred for the benefit of the estate and ordered to be paid out of the fund.

(ii)   There are cases in which the application is made by someone other than the trustees, but raises the same kind of point as in the first category and would have justified an application by the trustees. This second category is treated in the same way as the first.

(iii) There are cases in which a beneficiary is making a hostile claim against the trustees. This is treated in the same way as ordinary common law litigation and costs usually follow the event.

It is not always easy to determine into which category a particular case falls.[196]

In a case that clearly falls within the first or second category, parties other than the trustees can, in general, assume that an order will be made at the trial for their costs to be paid out of the fund. However, the claimant was held not to be entitled to costs out of the trust fund in *D'Abo v Paget (No 2)*,[197] in which she had successfully brought an action against the trustees and her sister (the first defendant). The trustees had been willing and able to bring the proceedings. The sole reason that the claimant brought the proceedings was to make a claim for costs in the event that the first defendant lost. In exceptional cases, trustees can ask for a prospective order that they are to have their costs in any event. The court will be reluctant to make such an order unless it is clear that the judge would be bound to do so at the trial.[198]

The principles behind CPR 48.4 were applied in *Wallersteiner v Moir (No 2)*[199] to enable a minority shareholder bringing a derivative action on behalf of a company to obtain the authority of the court to sue as if he were a trustee suing on behalf of a fund, with the same entitlement to be indemnified out of the assets against his costs and any costs that he may be ordered to pay to the other party. This was extended in *McDonald v Horn*[200] to an action primarily for breach of trust by the beneficiaries of a pension fund. Pension funds are a special form of trust,[201] and there is a compelling analogy between a minority shareholder's action for damages on behalf of a company and an action by a member of a pension fund to compel trustees or others to account to the fund.

---

[196] *McDonald v Horn* [1995] 1 All ER 961, CA; *Breadner v Granville-Grossman* [2001] WTLR 377. Cf *R v Lord Chancellor, ex p Child Poverty Action Group* [1998] 2 All ER 755.

[197] (2000) Times, 10 August, noted (2000) 22 T & ELJ 13 (J Godwin-Austen), in which it was said that a more robust attitude to costs was appropriate under the new Civil Procedure Rules, but, subject to that qualification, the guidelines in *Re Buckton, supra*, had not been superseded.

[198] Such pre-emptive costs orders have been made at the request of, or with the support of, the trustee bringing the proceedings. See *Re Exchange Securities and Commodities Ltd (No 2)* [1985] BCLC 392; *Re Charge Card Services Ltd* [1986] BCLC 316; *Re Westdock Realisations Ltd* [1988] BCLC 354; *Alsop Wilkinson (a firm) v Neary* [1995] 1 All ER 431; *Chessels v British Telecommunications plc* [2002] WTLR 719.

[199] [1975] QB 373, [1975] 1 All ER 849, CA.

[200] *Supra*, CA; *Mackin v National Power plc* [2001] WTLR 741, and see [2001] CJQ 208.

[201] See p 18, *supra*.

9 TRUSTEES OF LAND

Trustees of land[202] have, by virtue of the Trusts of Land and Appointment of Trustees Act 1996,[203] in relation to the land subject to the trust, all of the powers of an absolute owner. They have this power, however, only for the purpose of exercising their functions as trustees. Thus, they have management powers, such as letting and mortgaging, but if the land is sold, the question becomes one of investing the sale proceeds, which, in general, falls outside the scope of the Act, although, as we have seen,[204] the Act gives trustees of land power to acquire land not only as an investment, but also for occupation by a beneficiary or for any other reason.

The powers under the 1996 Act are subject to general equitable principles. Thus, it is expressly provided that, in exercising their powers, trustees of land shall have regard to the rights of the beneficiaries[205] and that the powers shall not be exercised in contravention of, or of any order made in pursuance of, any other enactment or any rule of law or equity.[206] The duty of care under s 1 of the Trustee Act 2000[207] applies to trustees of land when exercising their powers under this section.[208] Furthermore,[209] in the exercise of their functions relating to land, trustees of land have a duty to consult with beneficiaries, and, in favour of a purchaser, there are limits on the number of consents that can be required.

The powers under s 6 can be restricted or excluded by a provision in the disposition creating the trust, except in the case of charitable, ecclesiastical, or public trusts,[210] and if a consent is required to be obtained, a power cannot be exercised without it.[211]

10 APPLICATIONS TO THE COURT

(A) PROCEEDINGS FOR ADMINISTRATION, OR DETERMINATION OF QUESTION

In addition to its statutory jurisdiction,[212] the court has an inherent jurisdiction to administer trusts. Trustees, and any person claiming to be interested in the relief sought as beneficiary, may apply to the court by means of the alternative Pt 8 procedure for directions and for the determination, without an administration of the trust, of any question arising

---

[202] Including trustees holding under a bare trust: see p 74, *supra*.

[203] Section 6(1), and see Trustee Act 2000 s 8(4).

[204] See s 6(3), as amended by the Trustee Act 2000, Sch 2, para 45(1), and p 423, *supra*.

[205] Section 6(5). 'Beneficiary' is defined in s 22.

[206] Section 6(6). This includes an order of the court or of the Charity Commissioners: s 6(7), as amended by the Charities Act 2006. See also s 6(8).

[207] See p 399 *et seq, supra*.

[208] Section 6(9), inserted by the Trustee Act 2000, Sch 2, Pt II, para 45(3).   [209] See p 490, *infra*.

[210] Ibid, s 8(1), (3), and see (4). See [1997] Conv 263 (G Watt) for possible ways of escaping s 8(1) provisions.

[211] Ibid, s 8(2), and see (4). Purchases are protected under ibid, s 16(3).

[212] Trustee Act 1925, ss 41 and 44. *See Chellaram v Chellaram* [1985] 1 All ER 1043.

in the administration of the trust.[213] When a trustee surrenders his discretion to the court, the court should be put in possession of all of the material necessary to enable that discretion to be exercised. If that exercise calls for the obtaining of expert advice or valuation, it is the trustee's duty to obtain that advice, and to place it fully and fairly before the court. It should always be borne in mind that, in exercising its jurisdiction to give directions on a trustee's application, the court is essentially engaged solely in determining what ought to be done in the best interests of the trust estate and not in determining the rights of adversarial parties.[214]

It is also possible to apply by a Pt 8 claim for the administration of the trust.[215] The court, however, is not bound to make an administration order if the questions between the parties can be properly determined without it,[216] and, in fact, will only undertake the administration of a trust as a last resort. It has been said[217] that:

a general administration order will be made only in three categories of cases:

(1) where the trustees cannot pull together, or,

(2) the circumstances of the estate give rise to ever-recurring difficulties requiring the frequent direction of the court, or,

(3) where a prima facie doubt is thrown on the bona fides or the discretion of one or more of the trustees.

The beneficiary's real right is to approach the court for the appropriate order for performance of the trust, a specific order if that will meet the case, or a general decree, if that is called for, subject to the beneficiary paying the costs of any unnecessary application and subject also to the restrictions which the court has over the years put on that right to approach it.

A trustee may have to pay the costs of an application personally if he does not make out his case for administration by the court, and the court holds the view that some other process would have dealt with the difficulty more satisfactorily.[218]

The Administration of Justice Act 1985[219] may enable costs to be saved where the proceedings raise a question of construction of the terms of a will or a trust. Where an opinion

---

[213] CPR Sch 1, RSC Ord 85, r 2. See generally, (1994) 138 Sol Jo 789, 850, 878 (Dawn Goodman); (2000) 15 T & ELJ 20 (C Cutbill); correspondence at (2000) 19 T & ELJ 5. A Pt 8 claim may be brought, eg for the construction of the trust instrument, or as to whether the trustees should bring or defend an action: *Re Moritz* [1960] Ch 251, [1959] 3 All ER 767; *Re Eaton* [1964] 3 All ER 229n, [1964] 1 WLR 1269; as to whether a fund may be distributed on the basis that a person is dead: *Re Newson-Smith's Settlement* [1962] 3 All ER 963n; or a woman past childbearing: *Re Westminster Bank Ltd's Declaration of Trust* [1963] 2 All ER 400n, [1963] 1 WLR 820. New Zealand authority suggests that such an application is inappropriate where there are substantial factual disputes and/or the possibility of a breach of trust: *Neagle v Rimmington* [2002] 3 NZLR 826. As to the participation of beneficiaries in the hearing, see *Smith v Croft* [1986] 2 All ER 551, [1986] 1 WLR 580, and *Re Permanent Trustee Australia Ltd* (1994) 33 NSWLR 547. See (1978) 56 CBR 128 (D Waters).

[214] *Marley v Mutual Security Merchant Bank and Trust Co Ltd* [1991] 3 All ER 198, PC; *Patchett v Williams* [2006] WTLR 639 (NZ). Cf the case in which trustees merely seek the approval by the court of a proposed exercise by them of their discretion: see p 373, *infra*. As to costs, see *Practice Note* [2001] 3 All ER 574, and p 481, *supra*.

[215] As to the effect of an order on a trustee's powers, see (1968) 84 LQR 64 (A J Hawkins).

[216] CPR Sch 1, RSC Ord 85, r 5.

[217] *Per* Young J in *McLean v Burns Philp Trustee Co Pty Ltd* (1985) 2 NSWLR 623.

[218] See *Re Wilson* (1885) 28 Ch D 457; *Re Blake* (1885) 29 Ch D 913, CA.

[219] Section 48, as amended by the Courts and Legal Services Act 1990, s 71(2), Sch 10, para 63.

in writing of a person who has a ten-year High Court qualification[220] has been obtained on the question by the personal representatives or trustees, the High Court may, on the application of the personal representatives or trustees and without hearing argument, make an order authorizing them to take such steps in reliance on the opinion as are specified in the order. The court must not make such an order, however, if a dispute exists that would make such action inappropriate.

It should be observed that a settlor[221] or testator cannot deprive a beneficiary of his right to go to the court, at any rate, on questions of law. The reasons for this rule were explained by Danckwerts J in *Re Wynn's Will Trusts,*[222] in which he said:[223]

> a provision which refers the determination of all questions and matters of doubt arising in the execution of the trusts of a will to the trustees, and which attempts to make such determination conclusive and binding upon all persons interested under the will, is void and of no effect; because it is both repugnant to the benefits which are conferred by the will upon the beneficiaries; and also because it is contrary to public policy as being an attempt to oust the jurisdiction of the court to construe the will and control the construction and administration of a testator's will and estate.

It is submitted that the rule applies to invalidate not only wide general clauses, such as that mentioned by the judge, but any clause that purports to give trustees power to decide on a question of law, as opposed to one that gives trustees power to decide on a question of fact, provided, in this last case, that the state of affairs on which the trustees have to form their opinion is sufficiently defined. Thus, on the one hand, in *Re Raven,*[224] a provision that, in case of doubt, the trustees should decide the identity of the institution intended to benefit was held to be void, while, on the other hand, in *Re Coxen,*[225] a gift over 'if, in the opinion of my trustees, she shall have ceased permanently to reside therein' was held to be validly made dependent on the decision of the trustees, who were described as 'judges of fact for this purpose'. A similar distinction is drawn where contracting parties seek to oust the jurisdiction of the court.[226] The converse of this is that a private person cannot impose on a judge a jurisdiction or duty to adjudicate by providing, for instance, for a power of revocation 'with the consent of a judge of the Chancery Division'.[227]

(B) SURRENDER OF DISCRETION

When trustees have a discretionary power and are in genuine doubt how they ought to exercise it, they can go to the court and obtain directions as to what is the proper thing for them

---

[220] That is, has a right of audience in relation to all proceedings in the High Court: Courts and Legal Services Act 1990, s 7(3)(b).

[221] The cases concern wills, but the same principles would seem applicable in *inter vivos* trusts: *AN v Barclays Private Bank & Trust (Cayman) Ltd* [2007] WTLR 565 (Grand Court of the Cayman Islands), noted (2008) 95 T & ELTJ 15 (Sara Collins); [2008] PCB 23 (S Warnock-Smith and Morven McMillan). See (1983) 133 NLJ 915 (P Matthews).

[222] [1952] Ch 271, [1952] 1 All ER 341.   [223] At pp 278–279, 346.

[224] [1915] 1 Ch 673; *Re Wynn's Will Trusts, supra.*

[225] [1948] Ch 747, [1948] 2 All ER 492; *Re Tuck's Settlement Trusts* [1978] Ch 49, [1978] 1 All ER 1047, CA.

[226] See *Re Davstone Estates Ltd's Leases* [1969] 2 All ER 849, and cases therein cited.

[227] *Re Hooker's Settlement* [1955] Ch 55, [1954] 3 All ER 321. Cf *Allen v Distillers Co (Biochemicals) Ltd* [1974] QB 384, [1974] 2 All ER 365; *Anthony v Donges* [1998] 2 FLR 775.

to do.[228] The court will not, however, accept from trustees the surrender for the future of a discretion that involves considering, from time to time, changing circumstances. The trustees must apply their minds to future problems as and when they arise, although if they cannot arrive at a satisfactory answer, they may seek the court's directions from time to time.[229]

(C) APPEAL BY THE TRUSTEES

Contrasting views were expressed in *Re Londonderry's Settlement*[230] as to whether trustees should initiate an appeal from a decision of the court. Harman LJ said,[231] 'Trustees seeking the protection of the court are protected by the court's order and it is not for them to appeal', but Salmon LJ stated:232 'In my view the trustees were fully justified in bringing this appeal. Indeed it was their duty to bring it since they believed rightly that an appeal was essential for the protection of the general body of beneficiaries.' It is submitted that trustees should not normally appeal, but that they have a discretionary power to do so, which they may exercise in exceptional circumstances. It will only be very rarely, however, that they will be justified in bringing an appeal.

(D) PAYMENT INTO COURT

The statutory power[233] for trustees, or the majority of them, to pay trust funds into court is one that it is now seldom advisable for them to adopt, as they are likely to be made liable for at least the costs of payment out if they neglect some less expensive or more convenient procedure, such as advertising for claimants under s 27,[234] or raising a question for the decision of the court under the CPR Pt 8.[235] Moreover, 'a trustee cannot pay into court merely to get rid of a trust he has undertaken to perform', and the fact that he has been so advised by counsel will not assist him.[236] Payment into court does not affect the trusts on which the trust funds are held.[237]

Subject to what had been said, trustees may be justified in paying into court where there is a bona fide doubt as to whom they should pay,[238] or where they cannot get a valid discharge from the cestuis que trust, by reason of their incapacity, or otherwise.[239] But trustees have been held liable to pay costs where payment in was made when the trustees knew that the person claiming the fund was on his way from Australia to establish his claim,[240] and would be held liable if they paid in instead of paying a beneficiary entitled in

---

[228] *Talbot v Talbot* [1968] Ch 1, [1967] 2 All ER 920, CA. See *Thrells Ltd v Lomas* [1993] 2 All ER 546, [1993] 1 WLR 456 (conflict of interest).

[229] *Re Allen-Meyrick's Will Trusts* [1966] 1 All ER 740, [1966] 1 WLR 499; *Gailey v Gordon* [2003] 2 NZLR 192.

[230] [1965] Ch 918, [1964] 3 All ER 855, CA.   [231] At 930, 858.   [232] At 936, 862.

[233] Trustee Act 1925, s 63 (as amended by the Administration of Justice Act 1965, s 36 and Sch 3). See, generally, (1968) 84 LQR 64 (A J Hawkins).

[234] Discussed in Chapter 16, section 5(B), p 407, *supra*.   [235] *Re Giles* (1886) 55 LJ Ch 695.

[236] *Per* Romilly MR in *Re Knight's Trusts* (1859) 27 Beav 45, 49.

[237] See *Harman v Federal Comr of Taxation* (1991) 104 ALR 117.

[238] *Re Maclean's Trusts* (1874) LR 19 Eq 274; *Hockey v Western* [1898] 1 Ch 350, CA; *Re Davies' Trusts* (1914) 59 Sol Jo 234.

[239] *Re Parker's Will* (1888) 39 Ch D 303 (more fully reported in 58 LJ Ch 23), CA; *Re Salomons* [1920] 1 Ch 290. Cf Administration of Estates Act 1925, s 42.   [240] *Re Elliot's Trusts* (1873) LR 15 Eq 194.

default of appointment, satisfactory evidence having been produced that no appointment had been made.[241]

11 CONTROL OF TRUSTEE'S POWERS

So far as a trustee's duties are concerned, he is under an obligation to carry them out and, if he fails to do so, will be liable for breach of trust. In relation to the exercise of a discretionary power, however, his obligation is limited to a duty to consider from time to time whether he should exercise it and, in particular, he must consider a request by a person within the ambit of a power for it to be exercised in his favour.[242] A trustee who considers whether or not to exercise a power and acts bona fide is not likely to have his decision upset.

(A) CONTROL BY BENEFICIARIES

As we have seen,[243] all of the beneficiaries, being *sui juris*, can together terminate the trusts. They cannot, however, bind the trustees by their actions, unless power has been delegated to them by the trust document or under some statutory provision, such as s 9 of the Trusts of Land and Appointment of Trustees Act 1996.[244] Thus, in *Napier v Light*,[245] there was a trust for sale of land under which the plaintiff was the remainderman, and his mother, the life beneficiary. The plaintiff originally purported to grant a tenancy to the defendant, but, from 1952 onwards, the tenancy was treated as being between the defendant and the plaintiff's mother. It was held that the trustees were not bound in the absence of any evidence of delegation by them, or of acquiescence with knowledge of the tenancy, which might have given rise to an estoppel. Moreover, the plaintiff, who had become solely entitled in equity and acquired the legal title from the trustees, was not estopped from denying the tenancy by reason of the fact that he had been the original purported landlord.

The same case also makes it clear that the beneficiaries, even though they represent the entire beneficial interest and are all *sui juris*, cannot, so long as the trust continues, direct or control the trustees in the bona fide exercise of their powers and discretions under the trust. The point has arisen in connection with the appointment of new trustees and, in one such case, *Re Brockbank*,[246] Vaisey J observed: '*If the court, as a matter of practice and principle, refuses to interfere with the legal power to appoint new trustees,*[247] it is, in my judgment,* a fortiori *true that the beneficiaries cannot do so.*'

---

[241] *Re Cull's Trusts* (1875) LR 20 Eq 561 (although trustees were here allowed costs, as it was the first case of its kind and the trustees had been advised by counsel); see also *Re Foligno's Mortage* (1863) 32 Beav 131; *Re Leake's Trusts* (1863) 32 Beav 135.

[242] *Re Manisty's Settlement* [1974] Ch 17, 26, [1973] 2 All ER 1203, 1210.

[243] Chapter 16, section 6, p 409, *supra*.

[244] Section 9, as amended by the Mental Capacity Act 2005, s 67(1) Sch 6, para 41.

[245] (1974) 236 EG 273, CA.

[246] [1948] Ch 206, 210, [1948] 1 All ER 287, 289; *Stephenson v Barclays Bank Trust Co Ltd* [1975] 1 All ER 625; *Burns v Steel* [2006] 1 NZLR 559.

[247] As is clearly the case: *Tempest v Lord Camoys, supra*, CA; *Re Higginbottom* [1892] 3 Ch 132.

The principle remains generally valid, although substantially reversed in relation to the appointment of new trustees.[248] However, in relation to trusts of land, s 11 of the Trusts of Land and Appointment of Trustees Act 1996[249] requires that, subject to any contrary provision in the disposition,[250] trustees of land shall, in the exercise of any function relating to land subject to the trust,[251] 'so far as practicable, consult the beneficiaries of full age and beneficially entitled to an interest in possession in the land',[252] and 'so far as consistent with the general interest of the trust, give effect to the wishes of those beneficiaries, or (in case of dispute) of the majority (according to the value of their combined interests)'. A purchaser of unregistered land is not concerned to see that this requirement has been complied with.[253] The requirement is often excluded, because many draftsmen consider it to be unduly burdensome and its meaning to be, in some respects, uncertain. However, in many circumstances under which consultation is not mandatory, it is nevertheless good practice to consult.

Apart from this section, Romer LJ, in a case[254] in which the trust fund comprised shares in a private company, stated:

> the beneficiaries are entitled to be treated as though they were the registered shareholders in respect of trust shares with the advantages and disadvantages (eg restrictions imposed by the articles) which would be involved in that position and that they could compel the trustee directors, if necessary, to use their votes as the beneficiaries—or as the court, if the beneficiaries themselves are not in agreement—should think proper, even to the extent of altering the articles of association if the trust shares carry votes sufficient for that purpose.

As Upjohn J has pointed out in *Re Whichelow*,[255] however, it is difficult to reconcile this statement with the principle upon which *Re Brockbank*,[256] *Tempest v Lord Camoys*,[257] and *Re Higginbottom*[258] were decided. None of these cases was cited in *Hayim v Citibank NA*,[259] in which, on unusual facts, it seems to have been assumed that the beneficiary (itself an executor) could give binding directions to the trustee.

(B) CONTROL BY THE COURT

In *Sieff v Fox*,[260] Lloyd LJ observed that there are various grounds on which the purported exercise of a discretionary power by trustees may be held to be invalid, as follows.

---

[248] Trusts of Land and Appointment of Trustees Act 1996, ss 19–21, as amended; see p 366 *et seq, supra*.

[249] The section does not apply to a trust arising under a will made before 1997, nor to one created by a pre-1997 disposition unless the person who created it, being of full capacity, executes an appropriate deed: ibid, s 11(2)–(4).

[250] Ibid, s 11(2)(a). The corresponding provision in s 26(3) of the Law of Property Act 1925 (repealed) applied only to statutory trusts for sale unless a contrary intention appeared.

[251] See *Crawley Borough Council v Ure* [1996] QB 13, [1996] 1 All ER 724, CA; *Notting Hill Housing Trust v Brackley* [2001] WTLR 1327.

[252] As to the meaning of this phrase, see p 198, *supra*.   [253] Ibid, s 16(1), (7).

[254] *Butt v Kelson* [1952] Ch 197, 207, sub nom *Re Butt* [1952] 1 All ER 167, 172, CA (the other members of the Court of Appeal concurred in the judgment); *Kirby v Wilkins* [1929] 2 Ch 444, 454. See (1980) 30 UTLJ 151 (D Hughes).

[255] [1953] 2 All ER 1558, [1954] 1 WLR 5.   [256] *Supra*.   [257] *Supra*, CA.

[258] See p 489, fn 247, *supra*.   [259] [1987] AC 730, PC, noted [1988] Conv 60 (P McLoughlin).

[260] [2005] EWHC 1312 (Ch), [2005] 3 All ER 693, noted [2005] 19 T&E 2 at 6; [2006] CLJ 15 (R Nolan and M Conaglen); (2006) 122 LQR 35 (C Mitchell); [2006] Conv 91 (Meryl Thomas and B Dowrick); [2006] PCB 155 (S Taube); (2006) 76 T & ELTJ 13 (Susi Dunn). See also (2006) 82 T & ELTJ 13 (J Wood).

(i) There may be a formal or procedural defect, such as the failure to use the stipulated form of document—for example, a document under hand instead of a deed, or to obtain a necessary prior consent.[261]

(ii) The power may have been exercised in a way that it does not authorize—for example, with an unauthorized delegation, or by the inclusion of beneficiaries who are not objects of the power.

(iii) The exercise may infringe some rule of the general law, such as the rule against perpetuities.

(iv) The trustees may have exercised the power for an improper purpose, in cases known as a 'fraud on the power'.[262] It would likewise be an improper exercise of a power for trustees to act capriciously, which has been explained[263] as meaning where they act 'for reasons which ... could be said to be irrational, perverse or irrelevant to any sensible expectation of the settlor; for example if they chose a beneficiary by height or complexion ...'.

(v) The trustees may have been unaware that they had any discretion to exercise, as in *Turner v Turner*,[264] an extreme and highly unusual case on the facts, which has been described as equitable *non est factum*.

If the exercise of a discretionary power is not invalidated on any of the above grounds, the jurisdiction of the court to interfere is limited.[265] It has been held that where the trustees are expressly given an uncontrollable discretion by the trust instrument, the court will not interfere in the absence of mala fides, even though the court may be clearly of opinion that the trustees are not acting judiciously.[266] Where there is a simple or unenlarged discretion, some judges have asserted the jurisdiction of the court to control the exercise by trustees of discretionary powers given to them, and have interfered where the trustees have 'not exercised a sound discretion', as it was put by Fry J in *Re Roper's Trusts*.[267] However, the

---

[261] In some cases, the effect of such failure may be nullified by statute: Law of Property Act 1925, s 159; Trusts of Land and Appointment of Trustees Act 1996.

[262] For example, in *Cloutte v Storey* [1911] 1 Ch 18, the power was exercised in favour of one of the objects, but under a private arrangement whereby he passed the benefit back to his parents, who had made the appointment. Another example in a different context was *Hillsdown Holdings plc v Pensions Ombudsman* [1997] 1 All ER 862.

[263] In *Re Manisty's Settlement* [1974] Ch 17, [1973] 3 All ER 1203. See *Klug v Klug* [1918] 2 Ch 67, discussed p 494, *infra*.

[264] [1984] Ch 100, [1983] 2 All ER 745 (the trustees had executed deeds of appointment on their face effective, but executed in breach of their duties in that they signed, in all good faith, without having given any attention to the contents of the deeds), distinguished *Smithson v Hamilton* [2007] EWHC 2900 (Ch), [2008] 1 All ER 1216, at [127], [128].

[265] See, generally, (1957) 21 Conv 55 (L A Sheridan); (1967) 31 Conv 117 (A J Hawkins); (1975) 25 UTLJ 99 (M Cullity); [1992] JBL 261 (R L Nobles). N D M Parry in [1989] Conv 244 agrees that, whether or not the discretion is qualified, the court should have jurisdiction to intervene on the ground of mala fides in the sense of dishonesty, or impropriety in the sense of failing to take into account of all legally relevant factors. Cf *Asea Brown Boveri Superannuation Fund No 1 Pty Ltd v Asea Brown Boveri Pty Ltd* [1999] 1 VR 144. For a discussion of the position in New Zealand, see [1999] NZLJ 209 (R Peterson).

[266] *Gisborne v Gisborne* (1877) 2 App Cas 300, HL; *Tabor v Brooks* (1878) 10 Ch D 273.

[267] (1879) 11 Ch D 272; *Re Hodges* (1878) 7 Ch D 754 (decided immediately after, and without reference to, *Gisborne v Gisborne, supra*, HL).

better view, which seems to be supported by dicta in the more recent cases,[268] is that the court will not normally interfere if the power is exercised bona fide, and the terms of the power are duly observed: 'It is not an easy task to challenge the exercise by a trustee of a discretion.'[269] The court, however, may intervene in some circumstances by an application of what is known as the 'rule in *Re Hastings-Bass*'.[270] Lloyd LJ, sitting as a judge of the Chancery Division, carried out a careful review of the relevant cases in *Sieff v Fox*.[271] In *Re Hastings-Bass* itself, the rule was stated in a negative form:[272]

> Where by the terms of a trust...a trustee is given a discretion as to some matter under which he acts in good faith, the court should not interfere with his action notwithstanding that it does not have the full effect which he intended unless (1) what he achieved is unauthorised by the power conferred upon him, or (2) it is clear that he would not have acted as he did (a) had he not taken into account considerations which he should not have taken into account, or (b) had he not failed to take into account considerations which he ought to have taken into account.

A positive formulation was first put forward by Warner J in *Mettoy Pension Trustees Ltd v Evans*,[273] and this was elaborated in the light of the intermediate cases by Lloyd LJ in *Sieff v Fox*.

Taking account of subsequent developments, one can now summarize the principles to be applied as follows.

(i)   Where trustees act under a discretion given to them by the terms of the trust, in circumstances in which they are free to decide whether or not to exercise that discretion, but the effect of the exercise is different from that which they intended,[274] the court will interfere with their action if it is clear that they *would* not have acted as they did had they not failed to take into account considerations that they ought to have taken into account, or taken into account considerations that they ought not to have taken into account. There are, Lloyd LJ observed in *Sieff v Fox*, limits to what trustees have to consider.

(ii) Where the trustees are under an obligation to act, as in *Kerr v British Leyland (Staff) Trustees Ltd*[275] and *Stannard v Fisons Pension Trust Ltd*,[276] the position is somewhat different in that for the italicized word '*would*' in (i) above, one should read '*might*'.

---

[268] *Re Whichelow* [1953] 2 All ER 1558; *Re Gulbenkian's Settlement Trusts* [1970] AC 508, 518, [1968] 3 All ER 785, 787, HL, per Lord Reid; *Re 90 Thornhill Road, Tolworth, Surrey* [1970] Ch 261, sub nom *Barker v Addiscott* [1969] 3 All ER 685; *Edge v Pensions Ombudsman* [1998] Ch 512, [1998] 2 All ER 547, affd [2000] Ch 602, [1999] 4 All ER 546, CA.

[269] *Per* Michael Furness QC sitting as a deputy judge in *Chirkinia v Larcom Trustees Ltd* [2006] EWHC 1917 (Ch), [2006] WTLR 1523.

[270] *Re Hastings-Bass (decd)* [1975] Ch 25, [1974] 2 All ER 193, CA. See [2006] CLJ 499 (R Nolan and M Conaglen) noting *Donaldson v Smith* [2006] EWHC 1290 (Ch), [2006] All ER(D) 293 (May); (2007) 21 Tru LI 62 (Tang Hang Wu).

[271] [2005] EWHC 1312 (Ch), [2005] 3 All ER 693, noted (2005) 155 NLJ 1592 (Elaine Palser); (2005) 149 Sol Jo 1248 (Fiona Smith and A H Smart), and see (2008) 22 TruLI 81 (D Hayton).

[272] At 41, 203.   [273] [1991] 2 All ER 513, [1990] 1 WLR 1587.

[274] In *Smithson v Hamilton* [2007] EWHC 2900 (Ch), [2008] 1 All ER 1216, Sir Andrew Park suggested that a better formulation of the phrase beginning 'but' would be 'whether or not the effect of the exercise is different from that which he intended'.

[275] (1986) [2001] WTLR 1071, CA.   [276] [1992] IRLR 27, CA.

He also noted that, in two cases,[277] it had been said (not as a matter of decision) that the 'might' test applies to the voluntary exercise of a power—that is, in cases falling within (i) above—but disagreed, 'having had the benefit of what may have been fuller, and were no doubt different, submissions on the point'.

(iii) Different views have been expressed as to the necessity for the trustees to have acted in breach of duty. In *Abacus Trust Company (Isle of Man) Ltd v Barr*,[278] Lightman J said that what has to be established is that the trustee, in making his decision, has failed to consider what he was under a duty to consider. Thus, if the trustee has, in accordance with his duty, identified the relevant considerations, and used all proper care and diligence in obtaining the relevant information and advice relating to those considerations, he can be in no breach of duty and his decision cannot be impugned merely because, in fact, that information turns out to be partial or incorrect. In *Sieff v Fox*, however, Lloyd LJ did not think that the rule applies only in cases in which there has been a breach of duty by the trustees, or by their advisers or agents. And it has been held by the Grand Court of the Cayman Islands that the court may interfere even where the transaction was the result of deliberate decisions taken by a competent trustee acting on professional advice.[279]

(iv) The rule applies to things done by trustees, not to things done by settlors in the context of private trusts or by employers in the context of pension trusts. Thus, in *Smithson v Hamilton*,[280] the rule did not apply because the adoption of the defective 'definitive deed' was essentially the act of the employers and not of the trustees, although they had signed it. The fiduciary duty or responsibility that the trustees owed to the beneficiaries did not extend to identifying the deficiency in the scheme rules: this was a matter for the employers.

(v) In *Abacus Trust Company (Isle of Man) Ltd v Barr*,[281] Lightman J held that the rule 'should in principle result in the decision being held voidable and not void'. Lloyd LJ, in *Sieff v Fox*, did not need to decide between 'void' and 'voidable', but, while thinking Lightman J's conclusion attractive, was of the opinion that the question required further consideration in the light of earlier authority.

(vi) In *Sieff v Fox*, Lloyd LJ had no doubt that, as a general proposition, fiscal considerations are among the matters that may be relevant for the purposes of the rule.[282]

(vii) In an appropriate case, it is thought to be possible to set aside one provision in a larger document, leaving the rest of it to stand.[283]

(viii) One might add that there is an awareness of the danger that the principle could be developed so as to make it too easy for trustees and their professional advisers to avoid responsibility for the effect of their negligent actions.[284]

---

[277] *AMP (UK) Ltd v Barker* [2001] WTLR 1237; *Hearn v Younger* [2002] WTLR 1317.
[278] [2003] EWHC 114 (Ch), [2003] Ch 409, sub nom *Re Barr's Settlement Trusts* [2003] 1 All ER 763.
[279] *A v Rothschild Trust Cayman Ltd* [2006] WTLR 1129.   [280] *Supra.*   [281] *Supra.*
[282] Citing, inter alia, *Green v Cobham* [2000] STC 820; *Abacus Trust Company (Isle of Man) Ltd v NSPCC* [2001] STC 1344, 1353, 1354, *per* Patten J. See *Barclays Private Bank and Trust (Cayman) Ltd v Chamberlain* [2007] WTLR 1697 (Grand Court of Cayman Islands); [2002] PCB 102 (Dawn Goodman and C Graves); [2002] PCB 226 (Sir Robert Walker).   [283] *Smithson v Hamilton, supra,* at [69]–[72].
[284] See, eg, *Breadner v Granville-Grossman* [2000] 4 All ER 705, *per* Park J, at [61], [95]; [2002] 13 KCLJ 173, 185, *per* Sir Robert Walker.

(ix) In particular, where, on the face of it, rectification is the appropriate remedy, but, for some reason, is not available, the rule cannot be used, as Sir Andrew Park put it,[285] to achieve the same result 'by the back door'.

As we have seen,[286] trustees exercising a discretionary power are not bound to disclose to their beneficiaries the reasons actuating them in coming to a decision, which may make it difficult for their decision to be challenged. Thus, in *Tempest v Lord Camoys*,[287] in which no reason was given for the refusal of one of two trustees to agree with a course of action proposed by the other involving the purchase of particular land and the raising of some of the purchase money on mortgage, there was no ground on which the court could intervene. Conversely, in *Klug v Klug*,[288] in which one trustee wished to exercise a discretionary power of advancement, but the other trustee, the mother of the beneficiary, refused to do so, the court directed the advancement to be made when it appeared that the refusing trustee acted as she did for the extraneous reason that the beneficiary, her daughter, had married without her consent.

Where the court intervenes, it is usually to declare the exercise of a discretionary power void, but *Klug v Klug* was an exceptional case in which it intervened positively to exercise a power. Other exceptional cases include the pensions trust cases of *Mettoy Pension Trustees Ltd v Evans*[289] and *Thrells Ltd v Lomas*,[290] in which the person with the power could not exercise it because of a conflict of interest. A positive order was also made in the Canadian case of *Re Billes*,[291] in which a testator had given his trustees an absolute power to convert existing assets, as well as an equal and absolute power to retain. The trustees were deadlocked, and the court held that it had jurisdiction to intervene and 'cast a deciding vote'. The court's jurisdiction arose because the trustees were under a duty to exercise one power or the other and, until they did so, they were failing to discharge their duty, with the result that the testator's intention was frustrated and the beneficiaries might suffer. This may be contrasted with *Tempest v Lord Camoys*, in which there was a power, but no duty, to purchase land.

It may be added that if trustees do give reasons for the way in which they have exercised their discretion, the court can consider their soundness.[292] However, if a decision taken by trustees is directly attacked in legal proceedings, the trustees may be compelled either legally (through discovery or subpoena) or practically (in order to avoid adverse inferences being drawn) to disclose the substance of the reasons for their decision.[293]

(C) PROVISIONS OF THE TRUST INSTRUMENT—PROTECTORS

The settlor may reserve some control over the trustees—for instance, by requiring them to obtain his consent to the exercise of specified powers—or he may require them to obtain

---

[285] In *Smithson v Hamilton, supra*, at [61]–[80].   [286] See p 402, supra.
[287] (1882) 21 Ch D 571.   [288] [1918] 2 Ch 67.   [289] [1991] 2 All ER 513, [1990] 1 WLR 1587.
[290] [1993] 2 All ER 546, [1993] 1 WLR 456.
[291] (1993) 148 DLR (3d) 512, and see *Kordyban v K* (2003) 13 BCLR (4th) 50.
[292] *Re Beloved Wilkes' Charity* (1851) 3 Mac & G 440; *Re Londonderry's Settlement* [1965] Ch 918, [1964] 3 All ER 855, CA; *Wilson v Law Debenture Trust Corp* [1995] 2 All ER 337. See (1965) 81 LQR 192 (R E Megarry).
[293] *Scott v National Trust for Places of Historic Interest or Natural Beauty* [1998] 2 All ER 705, [1998] 1 WLR 226; *Maciejewski v Telstra Super Pty Ltd* (1998) 44 NSWLR 601, discussed (1999) 11 Bond LR 14 (Lisa Butler), who argues that a trustee's discretion should be somewhat circumscribed: in particular, in the limited field of superannuation, trustees should be required to disclose to beneficiaries reasons for their decisions.

the consent of a named person or persons.[294] In the case of overseas settlements with foreign trustees, it is a common practice to appoint 'protectors' for this purpose. Tax considerations may explain why the settlor appoints a protector rather than reserves powers to himself. The exact status and powers of the protector depend on the terms of his appointment; prima facie, his powers are fiduciary.[295] A settlement may confer a power to nominate a protector on the beneficiaries; if it does, they must exercise it in good faith, and for the benefit of the trust and all of the beneficiaries.[296]

Although it does not affect the liability of trustees towards their beneficiaries, if a disposition creating a trust of land (not being a charitable, ecclesiastical, or public trust) requires the consent of more than two persons to the exercise of any function relating to the land, in favour of a purchaser, the consent of any two of them will suffice.[297] Further, in favour of a purchaser, if a person whose consent is required is not of full age, his consent is not required, but the trustees must obtain the consent of his parent or guardian.[298]

A drawback to the appointment of a protector is that it complicates the administration of the trust and makes it more expensive.

A protector, who may be called by some other name, such as 'adviser', 'appointor', or 'management committee', may be given a wide variety of powers: for instance, to remove and appoint trustees, and to settle their remuneration, to add to a class of discretionary beneficiaries, to make or approve distribution decisions, to change the governing law of the trust, or to terminate the trust by triggering a final vesting provision. There are limits, however, to the powers that he may be given. He cannot be given power to determine questions of law arising in the construction or administration of the trust,[299] and it is doubtful whether he could be empowered to deprive the beneficiaries of their right to inspect the trust documents,[300] or to release the trustees from liability for breach of trust.

In exceptional circumstances, it is thought that the court has power to remove a protector if this is necessary to protect the assets of a trust or to prevent the trusts failing, or if the continuance of a protector would prevent the trusts being properly executed.[301]

---

[294] See Trusts of Land and Appointment of Trustees Act, s 8(2).

[295] See [1996] PCB 169, 245, 328 (A Duckworth); [1995] PCB 36 (H Rosen); [1995] PCB 109 (Deborah Hartnett and W Norris); [1995] PCB 288 (J Conder); [1996] PCB 24, 122 (Colloquium Report); (2004) 62 T & ELTJ 24 (R Ticehurst); (2006) 20 TruLI 180, 233 (A Duckworth); (2008) 22 TruLI 81 (D Hayton); *IRC v Schroder* [1983] STC 480. It seems that the court has the same inherent jurisdiction as in respect of trustees to appoint a person to exercise the protector's powers, or, as a last resort, to exercise those powers itself: see *Steele v Paz Ltd (in liq)* (10 October 1995, unreported), extracts from which appear in Butterworths' *Offshore Cases and Materials*, 1996, vol I, p 338. It has an inherent power to remove a protector only in exceptional circumstances, eg to protect the assets of the trust: *Re Papadimitriou* [2004] WTLR 1141 (Isle of Man HC).

[296] *Re the Circle Trust* [2007] WTLR 631 (Grand Court of the Cayman Islands).

[297] Trusts of Land and Appointment of Trustees Act 1996, s 10(1), (2).   [298] Ibid, s 10(3).

[299] See *Re Wynn's Will Trusts* [1952] Ch 271, [1952] 1 All ER 341, and p 487, *supra*.

[300] See *Re Londonderry's Settlement* [1965] Ch 918, [1964] 3 All ER 855, CA, and pp 402–404, *supra*.

[301] *Re Papadimitriou* [2004] WTLR 1141 (Isle of Man HC); *Re the Circle Trust* [2007] WTLR 631 (Grand Court of the Cayman Islands).

22

VARIATION OF TRUSTS

The fundamental principle is that a trustee must faithfully observe the directions contained in the trust instrument and, 'as a rule, the court has no jurisdiction to give, and will not give, its sanction to the performance by trustees of acts with reference to the trust estate which are not, on the face of the instrument creating the trust, authorized by its terms'.[1] There are, however, important exceptions to this principle. In this chapter, we shall consider, in section 1, the very limited extent to which the courts may permit a deviation from the terms of the trust under its inherent jurisdiction, in section 2, a number of limited statutory exceptions to the principle, and in section 3, the more general exception under the Variation of Trusts Act 1958. Two other exceptions are more conveniently considered elsewhere—namely, the rule that if all of the beneficiaries, being of full age and capacity, act together they can consent to what would otherwise be a breach of trust so as to free the trustees from any liability,[2] and, indeed, even bring the trust to an end,[3] and the cy-près doctrine in relation to charities.[4]

1 EXCEPTIONS UNDER THE INHERENT JURISDICTION

Adopting the classification used by Lord Morton in *Chapman v Chapman*,[5] the cases under the inherent jurisdiction can be grouped under four heads.

(i) *'Cases in which the court has effected changes in the nature of an infant's property, eg by directing investment of his personalty in the purchase of freeholds'* As a consequence of the substantial assimilation of the law relating to realty and the law relating to personalty, this head is no longer of practical importance.

(ii) *'Cases in which the court has allowed the trustees of settled property to enter into some business transaction which was not authorized by the settlement'* These are emergency situations not foreseen or anticipated by the settlor and in which the

---

[1] *Re New* [1901] 2 Ch 534, 544, CA, *per* Romer LJ.

[2] See Chapter 23, section 3(B), p 525 *et seq, infra*. If the proposed act can affect only some of the beneficiaries, only those who may be affected need consent in order to protect the trustees—but those beneficiaries must all be of full age and capacity.

[3] See Chapter 16, section 6, p 409, *supra*.   [4] See Chapter 14, section 8, p 332, *supra*.

[5] [1954] AC 429, 451, [1954] 1 All ER 798, 807, 808, HL.

consent of the beneficiaries cannot be obtained because some of them are under disability or not yet in existence.[6]

This exception includes, and can perhaps be regarded as,[7] an extension of the principle of the salvage cases, in which, in the case of absolute necessity, such as repairs vital to prevent further damage to settled land, the court has sanctioned a transaction such as the mortgage or sale of part of a minor's beneficial interest.[8] The Court of Appeal in *Re Montagu*,[9] following earlier cases,[10] made it quite clear that the fact that the proposed scheme would benefit the minor, or indeed all of the beneficiaries, was not enough. The application failed in *Re Montagu*[11] itself, Lopes LJ observing:[12] 'If the buildings were falling down it would be a case of actual salvage and would stand differently.'

The proposal put forward in *Re New*[13] was that the trustees, as holders of certain shares, should be empowered to concur in a proposed reconstruction of a mercantile company, as a result of which they would receive shares and debentures in the proposed new or reconstructed company. In sanctioning the scheme, the court put the trustees on an undertaking to apply for leave to retain such shares and debentures if they desired to retain them for more than a year. This decision, it was said two years later in *Re Tollemache*,[14] 'constitutes the high-water mark of the exercise by the court of its extraordinary jurisdiction in relation to trusts'. In the later case, what was sought, and refused, was authority for the trustees to acquire a mortgage of the tenant for life's interest, a transaction that it was claimed could not prejudice the remaindermen and would enable the tenant for life to enjoy a large addition to her income by reason of that fact that a higher rate of interest was payable under the mortgage than was being received on the authorized trust investments.

(iii) *'Cases in which the court has allowed maintenance out of income which the settlor or testator directed to be accumulated'* Unlike the previous two exceptions, this exception involves modification or remoulding of the beneficial trusts. The classic explanation of this exception was given by Pearson J in *Re Collins*:[15]

> that where a testator has made a provision for a family, using that word in the ordinary sense in which we take the word, that is the children of a particular stirps in succession or otherwise, but has postponed the enjoyment, either for a particular purpose or generally for the increase of the estate, it is assumed that he did not intend that these children should be left unprovided for or in a state of such moderate means that they should not be educated properly for the position and fortune which he designs them to have, and the court has accordingly found from the earliest time that where an heir-at-law is unprovided for, maintenance ought to be provided for him. Lord Hardwicke has extended that to the case of a tenant for life... [16]

---

[6] See *Re New* [1901] 2 Ch 534, 544, CA, *per* Romer LJ. Cf *Re Lotzkar* (1984) 57 BCLR 364.

[7] See (1954) 17 MLR 420 (O R Marshall).

[8] *Re Jackson* (1882) 21 Ch D 786; *Conway v Fenton* (1888) 40 Ch D 512; *Re De Teissier's Settled Estates* [1893] 1 Ch 153.

[9] [1897] 2 Ch 8, CA.   [10] For example, *Calvert v Godfrey* (1843) 6 Beav 97; *Re Jackson, supra.*

[11] *Supra.*   [12] At 11.   [13] *Supra.*   [14] [1903] 1 Ch 955, 956, CA, *per* Cozens-Hardy LJ.

[15] (1886) 32 Ch D 229, 232; *Havelock v Havelock* (1881) 17 Ch D 807.

[16] Instead of presumed intent, Farwell J, in *Re Walker* [1901] 1 Ch 879, based the jurisdiction on the construction of the will, and Denning LJ, dissenting in *Re Downshire Settled Estates* [1953] Ch 218, 273, [1953] 1 All ER 103, 134, CA, simply on the benefit to the children.

The jurisdiction here does not depend on the minority of the life tenant,[17] nor is it confined to cases of emergency or necessity.[18]

(iv) *'Cases in which the court has approved a compromise on behalf of infants and possible after-born beneficiaries'* There is no doubt that the court has jurisdiction where rights are in dispute—but if the court approves a compromise in such case, it is not really altering the trusts, which are, *ex hypothesi*, still in doubt and unascertained. The House of Lords, however, in *Chapman v Chapman*,[19] decided that there was no jurisdiction to sanction an alteration or rearrangement of beneficial interests where there was no compromise of disputed rights; the Court of Appeal has since decided that there cannot be said to be any disputed rights where there is merely an ambiguity in, for instance, an investment clause and it would be to the common advantage of all the beneficiaries to have a new clause substituted therefor.[20]

2 STATUTORY EXCEPTIONS TO DUTY NOT TO DEVIATE FROM THE TERMS OF THE TRUST

(A) SECTION 53 OF THE TRUSTEE ACT 1925[21]

The section provides as follows:

Where an infant is beneficially entitled to any property the court may, with a view to the application of the capital or income thereof for the maintenance, education, or benefit[22] of the infant, make an order—

(a) appointing a person to convey such property; or

(b) in the case of stock, or a thing in action, vesting in any person the right to transfer or call for a transfer of such stock, or to receive the dividends or income thereof, or to sue for and recover such thing in action, upon such terms as the court may think fit.

Under this section, it was held in *Re Gower's Settlement*[23] that where there was an infant tenant in tail in remainder of Blackacre with divers remainders over, the court could effectually authorize a mortgage of Blackacre (subject to the interests having priority over the infant's tenancy in tail), framed so as to vest in the mortgagee a security that would be as effective a bar against the infant's issue taking under the entail and the subsequent

---

[17] *Revel v Watkinson* (1748) 1 Ves Sen 93.

[18] *Haley v Bannister* (1820) 4 Madd 275, in which maintenance was allowed to a father, although the mother had ample means of her own to bring up the children.

[19] [1954] AC 429, [1954] 1 All ER 798, HL. See (1954) 17 MLR 427–431 (O R Marshall); *Re Barbour's Settlement, National Westminster Bank Ltd v Barbour* [1974] 1 All ER 1188, [1974] 1 WLR 1198.

[20] *Re Powell-Cotton's Re-Settlement* [1956] 1 All ER 60, CA. Cf *Mason v Farbrother* [1983] 2 All ER 1078.

[21] See (1957) 21 Conv 448 (O R Marshall).

[22] These are words of the widest import: *Re Heyworth's Settlement* [1956] Ch 364, 370, [1956] 2 All ER 21, 23.

[23] [1934] Ch 365; *Re Lansdowne's Will Trusts* [1967] Ch 603, [1967] 1 All ER 888.

remaindermen as if the infant were of full age, and had executed the conveyance in accordance with the Fines and Recoveries Act 1833.

It was expressly assumed, in *Re Gower's Settlement*,[24] that the requirement of the section that the mortgage should be made 'with a view to the application of the capital or income thereof for the maintenance, education or benefit of the infant' was satisfied. It was held that there was no such 'application' in Re Heyworth's Settlements,[25] in which it was proposed to put an end to the trusts created by the settlement by selling the infant's contingent reversionary interest to the life tenant for an outright cash payment. This decision was distinguished in *Re Meux's Will Trusts*,[26] in which the proceeds of sale were to be settled. It was held that the sale and settlement of the proceeds of the sale were to be regarded as a single transaction, which did constitute an 'application' for the purpose of the section.[27] And in *Re Bristol's Settled Estates*,[28] a person was appointed to execute a disentailing assurance to bar the infant's entail with a view to a settlement being made with the assistance of the court under the Variation of Trusts Act 1958.

(B) SECTION 57(1) OF THE TRUSTEE ACT 1925

This section, which does not apply to trustees of a settlement for the purposes of the Settled Land Act 1925,[29] provides as follows:

> Where in the management or administration of any property vested in trustees any sale, lease, mortgage, surrender, release, or other disposition, or any purchase, investment, acquisition, expenditure, or other transaction, is in the opinion of the court expedient, but the same cannot be effected by reason of the absence of any power for that purpose vested in the trustees by the trust instrument, if any, or by law, the court may by order confer upon the trustees, either generally or in any particular instance, the necessary power for the purpose, on such terms, and subject to such provisions and conditions, if any, as the court may think fit and may direct in what manner any money authorised to be expended, and the costs of any transaction, are to be paid or borne as between capital and income.[30]

Although it was conceded by counsel before the House of Lords in *Chapman v Chapman*[31] that this section could not apply, Lord Morton stated his agreement with the comments on the section contained in the majority judgment in the Court of Appeal,[32] which is authority for the following propositions. It was presumably the intention of Parliament, in enacting this section, to confer new powers on the court rather than to codify or define the existing powers under the inherent jurisdiction, although it may well be that the new extended jurisdiction does, in some degree, overlap the old. The section envisages:

(i)   an act unauthorized by a trust instrument,[33]

(ii) to be effected by the trustees thereof,

---

[24] *Supra.*   [25] [1956] Ch 364, [1956] 2 All ER 21.

[26] [1958] Ch 154, [1957] 2 All ER 630; *Re Lansdowne's Will Trusts, supra.*

[27] Compare *Re Ropner's Settlement Trust* [1956] 3 All ER 332n, [1956] 1 WLR 902 (a decision on similar words in s 32 of the Trustee Act 1925).

[28] [1964] 3 All ER 939, [1965] 1 WLR 469.   [29] Trustee Act 1925, s 57(4).

[30] An application may be made by the trustees, or any of them, or any beneficiary: see *Rennie v Proma Ltd* [1990] 1 EGLR 119, CA.

[31] [1954] AC 429, [1954] 1 All ER 798, HL.   [32] [1953] Ch 218, [1953] 1 All ER 103, CA.

[33] *Re Pratt* [1943] Ch 326, [1943] 2 All ER 375.

(iii) in the management or administration of the trust property,

(iv) which the court will empower them to perform,

(v)   if, in its opinion, the act is expedient—that is, expedient for the trust as a whole.[34]

Of primary importance is the interpretation of the words 'management' and 'administration', which are largely, although very possibly not entirely, synonymous. The subject matter of both words in s 57 is trust property that is vested in trustees, and 'trust property' cannot, by any legitimate stretch of the language, include the equitable interests that a settlor has created in that property. The application of both words is confined to the managerial supervision and control of trust property on behalf of beneficiaries, and the section accordingly does not permit the remoulding of the beneficial interests. The object of s 57, it was said,[35] is:

> to secure that trust property should be managed as advantageously as possible in the interests of the beneficiaries, and, with that object in view, to authorize specific dealings with the property which the court might have felt itself unable to sanction under the inherent jurisdiction, either because no actual 'emergency' had arisen or because of inability to show that the position which called for intervention was one which the creator of the trust could not reasonably have foreseen, but it was no part of the legislative aim to disturb the rule that the court will not re-write a trust or to add to such exceptions to that rule as had already found their way into the inherent jurisdiction.

Later in the judgment, the majority adopted the statement of Farwell J in *Re Mair*,[36] that 'if and when the court sanctions an arrangement or transaction under s 57, it must be taken to have done it as though the power which is being put into operation had been inserted in the trust instrument as an overriding power'. Perhaps Farwell J put it even more clearly later in his judgment, where he said:[37]

> the effect of the court permitting the exercise by trustees of some power which is not in the trust document itself, and, therefore, something which the trustees could not do except by the direction of the court, is the same as though that power had been inserted as an overriding power in the trust document.

Applications under s 57 are almost invariably heard and disposed of in private, and, accordingly, not reported. There are, however, a few reported cases that show that, in the exercise of its jurisdiction under this section, the court has authorized the sale of settled chattels,[38] a partition of land,[39] and a sale of land where the necessary consent could not be obtained.[40] It has authorized two residuary estates left on identical charitable trusts to be blended into one fund.[41] It has, apparently commonly, authorized capital money to be expended on paying off the tenant for life's debts, on having its replacement secured

---

[34] *Re Craven's Estate* [1937] Ch 423, [1937] 3 All ER 33.

[35] *Per* Evershed MR and Romer LJ in *Re Downshire Settled Estates* [1953] Ch 218, 248, 264, 265; [1953] 1 All ER 103, 119, 129, 132. And see *Municipal and General Securities Co Ltd v Lloyds Bank Ltd* [1950] Ch 212, [1949] 2 All ER 937.

[36] [1935] Ch 562, 565.   [37] *Supra*, at 738, 566.   [38] *Re Hope's Will Trust* [1929] 2 Ch 136.

[39] *Re Thomas* [1930] 1 Ch 194.   [40] *Re Beale's Settlement Trusts* [1932] 2 Ch 15.

[41] *Re Harvey* [1941] 3 All ER 284. The contrary decision in *Re Royal Society's Charitable Trusts* [1956] Ch 87, [1955] 3 All ER 14, in which *Re Harvey* does not appear to have been cited, would seem to be wrong in the light of *Re Shipwrecked Fishermen and Mariners' Royal Benevolent Society Charity* [1959] Ch 220, [1958] 3 All ER 465.

by a policy of insurance so that the beneficial interests remain unaltered,[42] but although it has, in exceptional circumstances, sanctioned a similar expenditure of capital to purchase the life tenant's interest, it is doubtful whether it would do so in an ordinary case, as it would come 'at least very near to altering the beneficial interests of the tenant for life'.[43] The court has also authorized the sale of a reversionary interest, which, under the trust instrument, was not to be sold until it should fall into possession.[44] All of the above cases were involved with family trusts, but it is not restricted to such trusts. It was used in *NBPF Pension Trustees Ltd v Warnock-Smith*[45] in relation to the distribution of the remaining surplus funds of a pension scheme to vary the mechanism for getting money to intended recipients. Finally, as has already been seen,[46] the section may be used to extend trustees' powers of investment.

(C) SECTION 64 OF THE SETTLED LAND ACT 1925

This section gives the court jurisdiction to authorize the tenant for life of settled land within the Act to effect any transaction. The section has five requirements:

(i) a transaction, as defined in subs (2),[47]

(ii) affecting or concerning the settled land or any part thereof,

(iii) not being a transaction otherwise authorized by the 1925 Act or the settlement,

(iv) which, in the opinion of the court, would be for the benefit of (a) the settled land or any part of it or (b) the persons interested under the settlement, and

(v) being one that could have been effected by an absolute owner.

According to the majority judgment of the Court of Appeal in *Re Downshire Settled Estates*,[48] the jurisdiction under this section is more ample in regard to the subject matter to which it relates than is s 57 of the Trustee Act 1925. The jurisdiction here is not limited to managerial and administrative acts, but also enables the court to authorize alterations in the beneficial interests, including the variation of the beneficial interests of beneficiaries who are of full age and capacity, and who do not consent.[49] It extends to the conveyance by the tenant for life of the settled land to trustees of a new settlement

---

[42] *Re Salting* [1932] 2 Ch 57; *Re Mair, supra*. These cases must be read in the light of the observations of the majority of the Court of Appeal in *Re Downshire Settled Estates* [1953] Ch 218, 249–251, [1953] 1 All ER 103, 119–121; and see *Re Forster's Settlement* [1954] 3 All ER 714, [1954] 1 WLR 1450.

[43] *Re Forster's Settlement, supra*, at 720, *per* Harman J.

[44] *Re Cockerell's Settlement Trusts* [1956] Ch 372, [1956] 2 All ER 172.

[45] [2008] EWHC 455 (Ch), [2008] 2 All ER (Comm) 740.

[46] See p 426, *supra*. Cf *James N Kirby Foundation Ltd v A-G (New South Wales)* [2004] NSWSC 1153, (2004) 62 NSWLR 276, in which, on similar words in an Australian statute, the court held that it had jurisdiction to approve the amendment of a trust deed to satisfy the requirements of a charitable trust in respect of its taxation status.

[47] As amended by the Settled Land and Trustee Acts (Court's General Powers) Act 1943 and the Statute Law (Repeals) Act 1969, to include 'any sale, exchange, assurance, grant, lease, surrender, reconveyance, release, reservation, or other disposition, and any purchase or other acquisition, and any covenant, contract, or option, and any application of capital money, and any compromise or other dealing, or arrangement'.

[48] [1953] Ch 218, [1953] 1 All ER 103, CA.

[49] *Hambro v Duke of Marlborough* [1994] Ch 158, [1994] 3 All ER 332, noted [1994] Conv 492 (Elizabeth Cooke).

to be held by them on trust for sale.[50] It is, however, essential that the court should be satisfied that the transaction proposed is for the benefit of either the settled land or some part thereof, or of the persons interested under the settlement—but not necessarily of both; and also that the transaction affects or concerns the settled land or any other land.[51] The last qualification is satisfied by transactions indirectly, as well as directly, operating upon the settled land (or other land), provided that, in the former case, the effect is real and substantial by ordinary common-sense standards, as distinct from that which is oblique or remote and merely incidental. If, however, there is no relevant property[52] that is, or is deemed to be, subject to the settlement, the settlement permanently ceases to be a settlement for the purposes of that Act.[53]

The section was used in *Re Scarisbrick Resettlement Estates*[54] to raise money by the sale of investments representing capital, to enable the tenant for life to continue to live in Scarisbrick Hall, his continued residence being essential for its preservation. In other cases,[55] the court has authorized alterations in beneficial interests with the object of avoiding estate duty. Lastly, in *Raikes v Lygon*,[56] it was held that s 64 is wide enough to allow trustees of settled property to transfer part of the property to another settlement in order to maintain other settled property of which the trustees remained the owners, even though under the second settlement bodies not beneficiaries under the first settlement would become potential beneficiaries. The transaction was said simply to involve an application of part of the capital of the settled property in a fiscally efficient way to maintain other parts of the settled property, the price of the fiscal saving being the introduction, as long stops, of certain bodies that were non-beneficiaries under the first settlement.

(D) SETTLED LAND AND TRUSTEE ACTS (COURT'S GENERAL POWERS) ACT 1943

This Act[57] permanently extends[58] the jurisdiction of the court under s 57 of the Trustee Act 1925 and s 64 of the Settled Land Act 1925, giving it power, in certain circumstances, taking all relevant matters into account,[59] to authorize any expense of action taken or proposed in or for the management of settled land, or of land subject to a trust of land, to be treated as a capital outgoing, notwithstanding that, in other circumstances, that expense could not properly have been so treated.

The circumstances referred to are that the court is satisfied that the action taken or proposed was or would be for the benefit of the persons entitled under the settlement, or

---

[50] *Hambro v Duke of Marlborough, supra.*

[51] Whether settled or not and whether within or without England.

[52] Defined in s 2(4) of the Trusts of Land and Appointment of Trustees Act 1996.   [53] Ibid, s 2(4).

[54] [1944] Ch 229, [1944] 1 All ER 404. See also *Re Mount Edgcumbe Settled Estates* [1950] Ch 615, [1950] 2 All ER 242.

[55] *Re Downshire Settled Estates, supra*, CA, in which the real object of the scheme was to preserve the land for future holders of the plaintiff's title; *Re Simmons' Trusts* [1956] Ch 125, [1955] 3 All ER 818.

[56] [1988] 1 All ER 884, [1988] 1 WLR 281.

[57] Section 9, as amended by the Emergency Laws (Miscellaneous Provisions) Act 1953, and the Trusts of Land and Appointment of Trustees Act 1996.

[58] *Re Scarisbrick Resettlement Estates* [1944] Ch 229, [1944] 1 All ER 404.

[59] Section 1(3) of the Settled Land and Trustee Acts (Court's General Powers) Act 1943.

under the trust of land; and either:

(i) that the available income from all sources of a person who, as being beneficially entitled to possession or receipt of rents and profits of the land or to reside in a house comprised therein, might otherwise have been expected to bear the expense has been so reduced as to render him unable to bear that expense, or unable to bear it without undue hardship; or

(ii) where there is no such person, that the income available for meeting that expense has become insufficient.

(E) MATRIMONIAL CAUSES ACT 1973

Part 2 of the Act confers wide powers on the court in matrimonial proceedings to make, inter alia, an order varying for the benefit of the parties to the marriage and of the children of the family, or either or any of them, any ante-nuptial or post-nuptial settlement made on the parties to the marriage. There are corresponding provisions in the Civil Partnership Act 2004 in relation to civil partnerships.

(F) MENTAL CAPACITY ACT 2005

Where a settlement has been made by virtue of s 18 of the 2005 Act[60] for a person who lacks capacity,[61] the court may vary or revoke the settlement if:

(i) the settlement makes provision for the variation or revocation;

(ii) the court is satisfied that a material fact was not disclosed when the settlement was made; or

(iii) the court is satisfied that there has been a substantial change of circumstances.[62]

(G) OCCUPATIONAL PENSION SCHEMES

Special provisions for the modification of occupational pension schemes are contained in the Pensions Act 1995, ss 67–72.

3 THE VARIATION OF TRUSTS ACT 1958[63]

This Act gives the court a discretionary power to approve on behalf of any of four classes of person any arrangement varying or revoking all[64] or any of the trusts upon which property is held, or enlarging the powers of the trustees of managing or administering

---

[60] See p 46, *supra*.   [61] As to the meaning of 'lack of capacity', see the Mental Capacity Act 2005, s 2.

[62] Ibid, s 67(1), Sch 2, para 6.

[63] Discussed (1963) 27 Conv 6 (D M Evans); (1969) 33 Conv 113 and 183 (J W Harris). See also *S v T1* [2006] WTLR 1461, noted (2007) 87 T & ELTJ 15 (Jo Summers and Rachel Brice): the effect of s 39(2) of the Adoption Act 1976 may deprive an adopted child of benefit under the estate of deceased biological father; however, the statutory trust arising on intestacy is not excluded from the 1958 Act by s 1(5) because it was not 'settled by Act of Parliament', but as a result of a combination of a disposition effected by the death of the adopted child's father and s 47 of the Administration of Estates Act 1925.

[64] *Re Seale's Marriage Settlement* [1961] Ch 574, [1961] 3 All ER 136.

any of the property subject to the trusts. The jurisdiction given to the court by the Act is not confined to settlements governed by English law.[65]

The word 'arrangement' used in the Act has been said[66] to be 'deliberately used in the widest possible sense so as to cover any proposal which any person may put forward for varying or revoking the trusts', and there is some authority as to the extent of the jurisdiction of the court in these matters. In looking at the cases, it seems that the maxim 'equity looks to the intent rather than the form' has, in effect, been applied. On the one hand, Wilberforce J has pointed out[67] that if the arrangement, although presented as a 'variation', is, in truth, a complete new resettlement, the court has no jurisdiction to approve it. If an arrangement changes the whole substratum of the trust, then it may well be that it cannot be regarded as a variation. On the other hand, Megarry J has said[68] that 'if an arrangement, while leaving the substratum, effectuates the purpose of the original trust by other means, it may still be possible to regard that arrangement as merely varying the original trusts, even though the means employed are wholly different, and even though the form is completely changed'.

The nature of the court's jurisdiction under the Act was explained in *Re Holmden's Settlement Trusts*,[69] in which Lord Reid said:

> Under the Variation of Trusts Act 1958, the court does not itself amend or vary the trusts of the original settlement. The beneficiaries are not bound by variations because the court has made the variation. Each beneficiary is bound because he has consented to the variation. If he was not of full age[70] when the arrangement was made, he is bound because the court was authorized by the Act of 1958 to approve of it on his behalf and did so by making an order. If he was of full age and did not in fact consent he is not affected by the order of the court and he is not bound. So the arrangement must be regarded as an arrangement made by the beneficiaries themselves. The court merely acted on behalf of or as representing those beneficiaries who were not in a position to give their consent and approval.

As Mummery LJ observed in *Goulding v James*,[71] the 1958 Act is viewed as a statutory extension of the consent principle embodied in the rule in *Sanders v Vautier*,[72] which recognizes the rights of beneficiaries, being *sui juris* and together absolutely entitled to the trust property, to exercise their proprietary rights to overbear and defeat the intention of a testator or settlor to subject property to the continuing trusts, powers, and limitations of a will or trust instrument.

Unfortunately, in *Re Holmden's Settlement Trusts*,[73] no mention seems to have been made of the difficulty raised by s 53(1)(c) of the Law of Property Act 1925,[74] which would seem to require that the beneficiaries, other than those on whose behalf the court was giving its approval, should sign some document in writing. The difficulty was, however,

---

[65] *Re Ker's Settlement Trusts* [1963] Ch 553, [1963] 1 All ER 801; *Re Paget's Settlement* [1965] 1 All ER 58, [1965] 1 WLR 1046.

[66] *Re Steed's Will Trusts* [1960] Ch 407, 419, [1960] 1 All ER 487, 492, CA, *per* Evershed MR.

[67] In *Re T's Settlement Trusts* [1964] Ch 158, 162, sub nom *Re Towler's Settlement Trusts* [1963] 3 All ER 759, 762.

[68] In *Re Ball's Settlement* [1968] 2 All ER 438, 442, [1968] 1 WLR 899, 905.

[69] [1968] AC 685, [1968] 1 All ER 148, HL.

[70] The principle here stated to apply to a minor must apply equally to any other class of person under s 1(1).

[71] [1997] 2 All ER 239, CA.   [72] [1841] 4 Beav 115. See p 409, *supra*.

[73] [1968] AC 685, [1968] 1 All ER 148, HL.   [74] Discussed p 91 *et seq*, *supra*.

carefully considered by Megarry J in *Re Holt's Settlement*,[75] who accepted, with some hesitation, two grounds that were put forward by counsel to defeat the argument based on s 53(1)(c): firstly, that by conferring an express power on the court to do something by order, Parliament, in the 1958 Act, had provided by necessary implication an exception to s 53(1)(c); and secondly, that where, as on the facts before him, the arrangement consisted of a specifically enforceable agreement made for valuable consideration, the beneficial interest would have passed to the respective purchasers on the making of the agreement. This would be a case of constructive trust excluded from the operation of s 53(1)(c) by sub-s (2).[76] The result appears to have been accepted as correct, and no point on s 53(1)(c) has been raised in subsequent reported cases.

(A) PERSONS ON WHOSE BEHALF THE COURT MAY ACT

The four classes of persons referred to in the Act are therein defined[77] as follows:

(a) any person having, directly or indirectly, an interest, whether vested or contingent, under the trusts who by reason of infancy or other incapacity is incapable of assenting, or

(b) any person (whether ascertained or not) who may become entitled, directly or indirectly, to an interest under the trusts as being at a future date or on the happening of a future event a person of any specified description or a member of any specified class of persons, so however that this paragraph shall not include any person[78] who would be of that description, or a member of that class, as the case may be, if the said date had fallen or the said event had happened at the date of the application to the court,[79] or

(c) any person unborn, or

(d) any person[80] in respect of any discretionary interest of his under protective trusts where the interest of the principal beneficiary[81] has not failed or determined.

The first part of para (b) gives jurisdiction in relation to any person, whether ascertained or not, who may become entitled to an interest under the trusts as being, at some future date, a person answering a specified description. This looks to someone who may become entitled in the future and excludes one who already has an interest, albeit remote. Thus the court in *Knocker v Youle*[82] had no power to give its consent on behalf of persons who

---

[75] [1969] 1 Ch 100, [1968] 1 All ER 470.

[76] See pp 91, 164, *supra*. This last ground carries more weight since *Neville v Wilson* [1997] Ch 144, [1996] 3 All ER 171, CA.

[77] Variation of Trusts Act 1958, s 1(1).

[78] It seems to be assumed that this is to be construed as 'any ascertained person': see Underhill and Hayton, *Law of Trusts and Trustees*, 17th edn, [47.46].

[79] That is, *per* Buckley J, obiter, in *Re Suffert's Settlement* [1961] Ch 1, [1960] 3 All ER 561, and *per* Warner J in *Knocker v Youle* [1986] 2 All ER 914, [1986] 1 LWR 934, the date on which the originating summons (now claim form) was issued. Underhill and Hayton, op cit, [47.44], suggest it may be the date on which the application is heard by the court.

[80] Including an unascertained or unborn person: *Re Turner's Will Trusts* [1960] Ch 122, [1959] 2 All ER 689. It appears that, under this paragraph, approval may be given on behalf of, and even against the wishes of, an adult ascertained beneficiary.

[81] Defined by s 1(2), by reference to s 33 of the Trustee Act 1925, as amended. See *Re Wallace's Settlement* [1968] 2 All ER 209, [1968] 1 WLR 711.

[82] *Supra*, discussed [1986] 136 NLJ 1057 (P Luxton).

had a merely contingent interest (in some cases, a double contingency), which, moreover, was liable to be defeated by the exercise of general testamentary power of appointment. It has been argued,[83] however, that 'interest' in s 1(1)(b) means 'vested interest' and that the court's jurisdiction is not excluded in the case of persons having a contingent interest.

Prospective next of kin, of course, do not have even a contingent interest. They have only a *spes successionis*—that is, a hope of succeeding—and are the typical category of persons who fall within the first part of para (b). They may, however, be excluded from the jurisdiction of the court if they fall within the second part of that paragraph. There has been discussion of the construction of the second half of para (b), which excludes the jurisdiction of the court in relation to persons falling within it. It apparently excludes only ascertained persons who would fit the description in the first half of the paragraph upon the occurrence of a single contingency. Thus, in *Re Suffert's Settlement*,[84] the court had no jurisdiction to give its consent on behalf of cousins who would have been entitled as next of kin if the life tenant applicant had died on the date of the application to the court, and in *Re Moncrieff's Settlement Trusts*,[85] the court had no jurisdiction in relation to an adopted son who would have been entitled had the life tenant applicant died on the date of the application to the court. In the latter case, the court did, however, have jurisdiction in relation to persons who would have been entitled as next of kin in that event had the adopted son predeceased the life tenant.

By the proviso, except as regards the last class under para (d), the court must not approve an arrangement on behalf of any person unless the carrying out thereof would be for the benefit of 'that person'.[86] In *Re Cohen's Settlement Trusts*,[87] there was a class of persons unborn. It was held that the court was not concerned with the interests of the class as a whole, but with the individual members of it. Accordingly, the court could not approve a variation where, among persons yet unborn who might become entitled to beneficial interests under the settlement in its original form, there might be a person or persons who, by the effect of the proposed variation, would be deprived of the beneficial interest that he or they might otherwise have taken without obtaining any counterbalancing advantage.

Finally, it should be noted that the court may make an order even though there may be persons with potential interests in the estate who are not parties and who will not be bound by the order. In such a case, the trustees will not be free, except at their own risk, to treat the trusts as effectively varied until they have obtained the consent of such persons.[88]

---

[83] See *Buschau v Rogers Communications Inc* (2004) 236 DLR (4th) 18, further proceedings (2004) 239 DLR (4th) 610, in which it was observed that J G Riddall appears to have resiled from his criticism of the case in [1987] Conv 144.

[84] *Supra*. See Harris, *Variation of Trusts*, pp 33–41, and fn 79, *supra*.

[85] [1962] 3 All ER 838n, [1962] 1 WLR 1344.

[86] Proviso to s 1(1) of the Variation of Trusts Act 1958; *Re Clitheroe's Settlement Trusts* [1959] 3 All ER 789, [1959] 1 WLR 1159; *Re Hessian* (1996) 153 NSR (2d) 122, 450 APR 122. It was held that the peculiar discretionary trust in *Re Bristol's Settled Estates* [1964] 3 All ER 939, [1965] 1 WLR 469, did not fall within para (d). In *Re T Settlement* [2002] JLR 204, the Royal Court of Jersey held that it was to the benefit of minor and unborn beneficiaries to vary the trust to enable tax due from the settlor, a non-beneficiary, to be paid by the settlement, in discharge of a moral obligation. By s 1(3), as amended by the Mental Capacity Act 2005, Sch 6, para 9, in the case of a person who lacks capacity (within the meaning of that Act) to give his assent, the question is to be determined by the Court of Protection.

[87] [1965] 3 All ER 139, [1965] 1 WLR 1229.

[88] *Re Suffert's Settlement, supra*; *Re Hall's Will Trusts* [1985] NI 118.

(B) MEANING OF 'BENEFIT' IN THE PROVISO

It is clear that a proposed arrangement may well involve some sort of risk to the beneficiary upon whose behalf the court is asked to give its approval, but this will not prevent the court giving its sanction if it is a risk that an adult would be prepared to take.[89] Thus, for example, it is no bar to the court giving approval on behalf of an unborn person that, in some circumstances, such a person would obtain no benefit, where probably, in fact, the arrangement would be to his advantage. This is simply the risk that the court is entitled to take, if it thinks fit, on behalf of the unborn person.[90] The court, however, starts from the principle that the beneficiary should not be materially worse off as a result of the variation, whatever happens.[91] It may be added that the fact that, as between the adult beneficiaries, the arrangement does not represent a fair bargain does not prevent the court from approving the arrangement in a proper case.[92]

According to *obiter dicta* of Megarry J in *Re Holt's Settlement*,[93] the benefit referred to is 'plainly not confined to financial benefit, but may extend to moral or social benefit'. It was, he said, 'speaking in general terms,... most important that young children "should be reasonably advanced in a career and settled in life before they are in receipt of an income sufficient to make them independent of the need to work"'. Thus it might, under the Act, be a 'benefit' to an infant to suffer the financial detriment of a postponement in the date of the absolute vesting of his interest, although, on the facts of that case, the financial advantages of the proposed arrangement were overwhelming, and there was no need for any 'balance sheet' of advantages and disadvantages. The principle that an element of financial benefit is unnecessary actually formed part of the *ratio decidendi* in *Re CL*,[94] in which the court approved an arrangement on behalf of an elderly, wealthy widow who was a patient under the Mental Health Act 1959. Under the arrangement, she gave up life interests in trust funds for no consideration at all, for the benefit of adopted daughters. The object was to save estate duty and the actual cost to the patient would be trifling, taking account of income tax and surtax, the patient's spending income being substantially in excess of her requirements. It may be added that it has been held, on similar legislation in Canada, that non-financial considerations carry greater weight where the contingent beneficiaries on whose behalf the court is asked to give consent stand no real chance of becoming entitled, and where the persons who are likely to be affected have given their consent to the proposed variation.[95]

---

[89] *Re Cohen's Will Trusts* [1959] 3 All ER 523, [1959] 1 WLR 865. The court may require the risk to be covered by insurance. See *Re Brook's Settlement* [1968] 3 All Er 416, [1968] 1 WLR 1661 for a discussion of the risk that may be involved in the possibility of the judge taking what turns out later to have been a wrong view of the law.

[90] *Re Holt's Settlement* [1969] 1 Ch 100, [1968] 1 All ER 470.

[91] *Re Robinson's Settlement Trusts* [1976] 3 All ER 61, [1976] 1 WLR 806, in which the court considered some of the implications of the change from estate duty to inheritance tax.

[92] *Re Berry's Settlement* [1966] 3 All ER 431n, [1966] 1 WLR 1515.

[93] [1969] 1 Ch 100, [1968] 1 All ER 470. See *Re an Estate Trust* [2001] WTLR 571 (Jersey Royal Court).

[94] [1969] 1 Ch 587, [1968] 1 All ER 1104 (Court of Protection).

[95] *Re Tweedie* (1975) 64 DLR (3d) 569.

Neither of these cases appears to have been cited in *Re Weston's Settlements*,[96] in which Lord Denning MR expressed a similar view:[97] 'The court should not consider merely the financial benefit to the infants or unborn children, but also their educational and social benefit. There are many things in life more worthwhile than money.' In this case, the proposed scheme involved the appointment by the court[98] of new trustees resident outside the jurisdiction, and variation of the trusts to enable the trust property to be discharged from the trusts of the existing English settlement and made subject to similar trusts under a Jersey settlement. The object was admittedly tax avoidance. Applying the principle mentioned above, Lord Denning said:

> One of these things [more worthwhile than money] is to be brought up in this our England, which is still 'the envy of less happier lands'. I do not believe it is for the benefit of children to be uprooted from England and transported to another country simply to avoid tax... The Court of Chancery should not encourage or support [the avoidance of tax]—it should not give its approval to it—if by so doing it would imperil the true welfare of the children, already born or yet to be born.

Accordingly, he dismissed the appeal from the judge's refusal to approve the scheme. The decision was criticized in *The Times*[99] on the grounds that these were matters of judgment for parents, and that the court was trespassing on the preserves of family life. Professor Crane,[100] however, is not wholly convinced by this criticism and thinks that the mathematics should carry less weight when the application involves removing the trust from the jurisdiction of the court.

(c) PRINCIPLES TO BE APPLIED

The law was reviewed by the Court of Appeal in *Goulding v James*.[101] In this case, F left her residuary estate to her daughter (D) for life, with remainder to her grandson (G) contingently on his attaining the age of forty. If G died before F or before attaining the age of forty, the residuary estate was left to F's great-grandchildren living at the death of G. The arrangement proposed by D and G was that 10 per cent of the residuary estate should be put into a trust fund for the great-grandchildren (this being considerably more than the current value of their interest in residue), and the balance of the fund divided between D and G. The first-instance judge refused to approve the arrangement, on the ground that it was the complete opposite of what was provided for under the will and the settled intention of F. In reversing this decision, Mummery LJ, who gave the leading judgment in the Court of Appeal, said that the discretion of the court whether or not to approve a proposed arrangement is fettered only by the proviso to s 1(1), which prohibits the court from approving an arrangement that is not for the benefit of the classes referred to in s 1(1)

---

[96] [1969] 1 Ch 223, [1968] 3 All ER 338, CA. See also *Re Remnant's Settlement Trusts* [1970] Ch 560, [1970] 2 All ER 554 (forfeiture clause on practising Roman Catholicism a deterrent in the selection of a husband and a source of possible family dissension; deletion accordingly a benefit), criticized by McPherson J in *Re Christmas' Settlement Trusts* [1986] 1 Qd R 372, who thought that this extended the notion of benefit much further than could fairly be justified. The criticism seems valid. Cf *Re Tinker's Settlement* [1960] 3 All ER 85n, [1960] 1 WLR 1011, not cited in *Re Remnant's Settlement Trusts*.

[97] At 245, 342.   [98] Under s 41 of the Trustee Act 1925, discussed p 368 *et seq, supra*.

[99] 1 August 1968.   [100] (1968) 32 Conv 431. See also (1969) 85 LQR 15 (P V Baker).

[101] [1997] 2 All ER 239, CA, noted (1997) 60 MLR 719 (P Luxton).

(a), (b), or (c). Actuarial benefit of the person or persons on whose behalf approval is sought does not, however, oblige the court to give its approval. The court is concerned whether the arrangement as a whole, in all of the circumstances, is such that it is proper to approve it. The court's concern involves, inter alia, a practical and business-like consideration of the arrangement, including the total amounts of the advantages that the various parties obtain, and their bargaining strength. In many cases, the intentions and wishes of the testator or settlor carry little, if any, weight on the issue of approval on behalf of those who have not the capacity to give consent themselves, and, on the facts of the case, approval should be given. *Re Steed's Will Trusts*,[102] in which the Court of Appeal had refused to approve an arrangement that 'cut at the root of the testator's wishes and intentions', was held not to have laid down any rule, principle, or guideline of general application on the importance of the intentions and wishes of a settlor or testator. It was clearly distinguishable: there, the testator had manifested a particular purpose in creating a protective trust— namely, to protect the life tenant from improvident dealings with property in favour of certain members of her family. The result of the proposed arrangement, coupled with an appointment that the life tenant had made by irrevocable deed to herself of the reversion, would have been that the applicant life tenant would have become absolutely entitled to the property. The Court of Appeal was satisfied that the testator's purpose was still justified. In the opinion of Mummery LJ, in those circumstances, there was overwhelming reason for refusal of the order.

It does not matter that the object of the proposed variation is to improve the position of the beneficiaries from the point of view of taxation or death duties, and this is, in fact, the most frequent motive behind applications under the Act.[103] The court will not, however, sanction an arrangement involving approval of an appointment that was a fraud on a power.[104] Where evidence of fraud is not clear, Megarry J has explained[105] what the attitude of the court should be: 'If to a fair, cautious and enquiring mind the circumstances of the appointment, so far as known, raise a real and not a merely tenuous suspicion of a fraud on the power, the approval of the court ought to be withheld until that suspicion is dispelled.' He added that, although the court should act as an alert and persistent watchdog, it ought not to be required to discharge the functions of a bloodhound or a ferret.

On an application under the Act, the court may remove the limit on the statutory power of advancement.[106] The Act, however, almost certainly does not empower the court to direct a settlement of an infant's property, although, in special circumstances, it may defer an infant's right to capital;[107] nor does it enable the court to get round the absence of any

---

[102] [1960] Ch 407, [1960] 1 All ER 487, CA. The approval of the court was sought on behalf of a para (d) person, the 'spectral husband' of the applicant, who was unmarried and past the age of childbearing.

[103] See *Re Holmden's Settlement Trusts* [1966] Ch 511, 517, [1966] 2 All ER 661, 665, CA per Denning MR; affd [1968] AC 685, [1968] 1 All ER 148, HL; *Re Sainsbury's Settlement* [1967] 1 All ER 878, [1967] 1 WLR 476; (1968) 32 Conv 194 (G R Bretten). Note, however, that, in *Re Weston's Settlements* [1968] 1 All ER 720, affd on different grounds [1969] 1 Ch 223, [1968] 3 All ER 338, CA, Stamp J refused to sanction what he called '*a cheap exercise in tax avoidance*' as distinct from '*a legitimate avoidance of liability to taxation*': a distinction without a difference?

[104] *Re Robertson's Will Trusts* [1960] 3 All ER 146n, [1960] 1 WLR 1050.

[105] *Re Wallace's Settlement* [1968] 2 All ER 209, [1968] 1 WLR 711. See also *Re Brook's Settlement* [1968] 3 All ER 416, [1968] 1 WLR 1661; (1969) 32 MLR 317 (S Cretney).

[106] See *D (a child) v O* [2004] EWHC 1036 (Ch), [2004] 3 All ER 780, and p 482, *supra*.

[107] *Re T's Settlement Trusts* [1964] Ch 158, sub nom *Re Towler's Settlement Trusts* [1963] 3 All ER 759.

inherent jurisdiction to order the payment out to trustees of moneys in court, being a sum recovered by way of damages by an infant, on terms that would defer the infant's entitlement beyond the age of majority. The payment out to trustees of sums in court does not give rise to the kind of trust contemplated by the Act, and, in any event, since the money recovered as damages is the infant's money absolutely, to impose such terms would not constitute a variation at all, but would be a new trust made on behalf of an absolute owner.[108] An application under the Act has been held[109] not to be appropriate to cover the contingency of the birth of a child to a woman believed, in fact, to be past the age of childbearing. In administration, the court may direct that funds be dealt with on the footing that, at a certain age—normally, in the middle or late fifties—a woman has become incapable of childbearing. In a clear case, no application to the court is necessary, but if an application is made to the court, it will be to the ordinary administrative jurisdiction.[110] As a result of medical advances (including fertility treatment), the assumptions made by the court in 1966 as to the age at which a woman becomes incapable of childbearing are now of doubtful validity. An application to the administrative jurisdiction may be combined with an application for an order under the Act in relation to other persons.[111]

As has been seen, in *Re Weston's Settlement*,[112] Lord Denning decided the case on the ground that the required benefit to the persons on whose behalf the court was asked to give consent had not been established. Harman LJ preferred to dismiss the appeal on the ground that the linchpin[113] of the scheme was the exercise by the court of its power to appoint new trustees, and that the judge was entitled in the exercise of his discretion to refuse to exercise it so as to remove the trusts to Jersey. The settlements, he said, were English settlements and should remain so unless some good reason connected with the trusts themselves could be put forward.[114]

Re Weston's Settlement[115] must not, however, be taken to decide that it is never possible to export a trust. The court did not overrule, although it did distinguish, *Re Seale's Marriage Settlement*.[116] In that case, the whole family had emigrated to Canada and become Canadian citizens. The children were being educated there. Irrespective of tax advantages, there were manifest administrative advantages in having the trust administered locally. This decision has been followed since *Re Weston's Settlement*[117] in *Re Windeatt's Will Trusts*,[118] and was extended in *Re Chamberlain*,[119] in which, to obtain freedom from capital gains tax, the

---

[108] *Allen v Distillers Co (Biochemicals) Ltd* [1974] QB 384, [1974] 2 All ER 365. See (1984) 81 LSG 977 (G W Thomas).

[109] *Re Pettifor's Will Trusts* [1966] Ch 257, [1966] 1 All ER 913. See (2001) 27 T & ELJ 10 (H Legge). In *Figg v Clarke* [1997] 1 WLR 603, it was said one should apply to the court for a declaration of the trustees' right of distribution rather than for the exercise by the court of its administrative jurisdiction.

[110] As to the test to be applied, see *Re Levy Estate Trust* [2000] 5 CL 635, discussed (2000) 21 T & ELJ 6 (R Oughton).

[111] *Re Westminister Bank Ltd's Declaration of Trust* [1963] 2 All ER 400n, [1963] 1 WLR 820.

[112] [1969] 1 Ch 223, [1968] 3 All ER 338, CA, discussed p 508, *supra*.

[113] Although commonly new trustees outside the jurisdiction could be appointed otherwise than by the court under an express, or the statutory, power.

[114] Danckwerts LJ agreed with both Lord Denning MR and Harman LJ.

[115] *Supra*, CA. The trust instrument may give power to export a trust by appointing non-resident trustees and to transfer the trust property out of the jurisdiction.

[116] [1961] Ch 574, [1961] 3 All ER 136.   [117] [1969] 1 Ch 223, [1968] 3 All ER 338, CA.

[118] [1969] 2 All ER 324, [1969] 1 WLR 692. See (1976) 40 Conv 295 (T G Watkin).

[119] (9 May 1976, unreported). See (1976) 126 NLJ 1034 (J B Morcom).

court gave its approval to an English settlement being transferred to Guernsey, a country with which the beneficiaries under the settlement—who had long since ceased to be domiciled and resident in the United Kingdom—had no connection.

(D) RELATIONSHIP TO OTHER STATUTORY PROVISIONS

It is expressly provided[120] that the jurisdiction given by the Act is additional to that given by s 57 of the Trustee Act 1925 and s 64 of the Settled Land Act 1925. Although, in most ways, the jurisdiction under the 1958 Act is wider, there are differences between these provisions that mean that it may sometimes be necessary to bring proceedings under one of the other Acts. Thus, under s 57 of the Trustee Act 1925, the court must be satisfied that the proposed transaction is expedient, but there is no requirement that all or any of the beneficiaries must give their consent for an order to be effective. Under the 1958 Act, as we have seen, approval of an arrangement will only be fully effective if all of the beneficiaries who are *sui juris* give their consent; moreover, in giving its approval on behalf of beneficiaries who are unable to give their consent, the court can, in general, only do so if the proposed arrangement is for their benefit.

Where jurisdictions overlap, practitioners seem to prefer to proceed under the 1958 Act.

---

[120] Variation of Trusts Act 1958, s 1(6), as amended by the Mental Capacity Act 2005, Sch 6, para 9. Section 1(6) provides only that nothing in the section is to be taken to limit the powers of the Court of Protection. It is thought unlikely that the omission of references to s 57 of the Trustee Act 1925 and s 64 of the Settled Land Act 1925 affects the result.

23

BREACH OF TRUST

It is clearly right that beneficiaries who suffer as a consequence of a breach of trust committed by the trustees, whether deliberately or inadvertently, and whether by a positive act—such as paying themselves remuneration to which they are not entitled—or by a failure to act—such as leaving the trust funds uninvested—should have a remedy for their loss. Section 1 of this chapter discusses the personal liability of the trustees to the beneficiaries in such circumstances, and the measure of damages where their claim succeeds. After a short section considering the liability of the trustees *inter se*, section 3 looks at the defences that a trustee may have to a claim against him. The chapter concludes with a note on the criminal liability of trustees.

1 PERSONAL LIABILITY OF TRUSTEES TO BENEFICIARIES

(A) GENERAL POSITION

At common law, there are two principles that are fundamental to the award of damages: firstly, that the defendant's wrongful act must cause the damage complained of; secondly, that the plaintiff is to be put in the same position as he would have been in had he not sustained the wrong for which he is now getting his compensation or reparation. Although equity approaches liability for making good a breach of trust from a different starting point, and although the detailed rules of equity as to causation and the quantification of loss differ from those applicable at common law, the principles underlying both systems are the same. Under both systems, liability is fault-based.[1]

The basic right of a beneficiary is to have the trust duly administered in accordance with the provisions of the trust instrument, if any, and the general law. Failure in such due administration, whether by a positive act—for instance, investing the trust funds in unauthorized investments—or by a failure to act[2]—for instance, neglecting to get the trust

---

[1] The law in this area was reviewed by Lord Browne-Wilkinson in *Target Holdings Ltd v Redferns (a firm)* [1996] AC 421, [1995] 3 All ER 785, HL. See *Friends' Provident Life Office v Hillier Parker May and Rowden (a firm)* [1997] QB 85 [1995] 4 All ER 260, CA; [1997] Conv 14 (D Capper); (2001) 60 CLJ 337 (D Capper); [2003] NZLJ 225 (C Rickett).

[2] *Grayburn v Clarkson* (1868) 3 Ch App 605. See [1983] Conv 127 (P Pearce and A Samuels). See also *Nichols v Wevill Estate* [1996] 2 WWR 408 (failure to act with care in exercising discretion).

funds transferred into his name—constitutes a breach of trust[3] for which the trustee will be liable. The liability extends to all loss thereby caused directly or indirectly[4] to the trust estate and, even where no loss can be shown, to any profit that has accrued to the trustee.[5] It is equally a breach of trust whether committed fraudulently by a trustee for his own purposes, or innocently, for the benefit of the trust estate and ignorant of the fact that it was a breach of trust.

There can, however, be cases in which, although there is an undoubted breach of trust, the trustee is under no liability at all to a beneficiary. Thus, if trustees have committed a judicious breach of trust[6] by investing in an unauthorized investment that proves to be very profitable to the trust, although a beneficiary could nevertheless insist that the unauthorized investment be sold and the proceeds invested in authorized investments, the trustees would be under no liability to pay compensation either to the trust fund or the beneficiary, because the breach has caused no loss to the trust fund.[7] In considering the liability of trustees, it is immaterial how the trust was created, and whether it was for valuable consideration, or by the voluntary gift of the very trustees who are now being sued.[8]

It is settled law that a shareholder cannot recover damages that are merely reflective of the company's loss, in respect of which the company has a cause of action (the 'reflective loss' principle).[9] Where a claimant brings an action not as a shareholder, but as a beneficiary under a trust against a trustee shareholder for a profit, the reflective loss principle would preclude the claim only if it could be shown by the defendant that the whole of the claimed profit reflected what the company had lost and which it had a cause of action to recover.[10]

Finally, it should be observed that not every legal claim arising out of a relationship of trustee and beneficiary will give rise to a claim for a breach of trust. In *Bristol and West Building Society v Mothew*,[11] the defendant solicitor held money in trust for the plaintiff society, but with the society's instructions to apply it in the completion of a transaction of purchase and mortgage. The solicitor, by an oversight, gave incorrect information to the plaintiff society, which might have revoked its instructions had the correct information been given. The defendant, acting on the unrevoked instructions, paid the money over to

---

[3] See *Tito v Waddell (No 2)* [1977] Ch 106, 247, 248, [1977] 3 All ER 129, 246, 247, in which Megarry V-C referred to two American definitions: 'every omission or violation by a trustee of a duty which equity lays on him...is a breach of trust' (*Corpus Juris Secundum*, vol 90, pp 225, 228, para 247); 'a trustee commits a breach of trust if he violates any duty which he owes as a trustee to the beneficiaries' (*Scott on Trusts*, 3rd edn, vol III, p 1605, para 201).

[4] *Bateman v Davis* (1818) 3 Madd 98; *Lander v Weston* (1855) 3 Drew 389.

[5] Where the breach of trust results in a profit for which the trustees have to account this is the limit of their liability: *Vyse v Foster* (1872) 8 Ch App 309; affd (1874) LR 7 HL 318.

[6] It has been judicially observed that the great use of a trustee is to commit judicious breaches of trust: *National Trustees Co of Australasia v General Co of Australasia* [1905] AC 373, 375, 376, PC, *per* Lindley LJ. It has been suggested that there is no such thing as a judicious breach of trust where the breach of trust involves a deliberate breach of the terms of the trust deed, whether or not the breach is in the best economic interests of the beneficiaries: (1998) 12 Tru LI 44 (V Vann).

[7] *Target Holdings Ltd v Redferns (a firm)* [1996] AC 421, [1995] 3 All ER 785, HL.

[8] *Smith v French* (1741) 2 Atk 243; *Drosier v Brereton* (1851) 15 Beav 221.

[9] *Prudential Assurance Co Ltd v Newman Industries Ltd (No 2)* [1982] Ch 204, [1982] 1 All ER 354, CA.

[10] *Shaker v Al-Bedrawi* [2002] EWCA Civ 1452, [2002] 4 All ER 835

[11] [1998] Ch 1, [1996] 4 All ER 698, CA, discussed (1999) 13 Tru LI 74 (S Elliott). See *Ratiu v Conway* [2005] EWCA Civ 1302, [2006] WTLR 101, noted (2006) 81 T & ELTJ 15 (M O'Sullivan).

the vendor. He was held liable in negligence at common law, but was held not to be guilty of a breach of trust. Although he knew that he was a trustee for the society, he did not realize that he had misled the society and could not know that his authority had determined (if, indeed, it had). He could not be bound to repay the money to the society so long as he was ignorant of the facts that had brought his authority to an end, because it would be those facts that would affect his conscience and subject him to an obligation to return the money to the society.

(B) MEASURE OF DAMAGE

(i) Equitable compensation for breach of trust[12]

This is designed to make good a loss in fact suffered by the beneficiaries and which, using hindsight and common sense, can be seen to have been caused by the breach:[13] compensation is to be assessed as at the date of judgment and not at an earlier date.

The equitable rules have largely been developed in traditional family trusts, in which the fund is held on trust for a number of beneficiaries having different, usually successive, interests. Here, if trust assets are wrongfully paid away, the only way in which all of the beneficiaries' rights can be protected is by restoring to the trust fund what ought to be there. In such a case, the basic rule is that a trustee in breach of trust must restore or pay to the trust estate either the assets that have been lost to the estate by reason of the breach or compensation for such loss. Courts of equity did not award damages, but, acting *in personam*, ordered the defaulting trustee to restore the trust estate. If specific restitution of the trust property is not possible, then the liability of the trustee is to pay sufficient compensation to the trust estate to put it back to what it would have been had the breach not been committed. Even if the immediate cause of the loss is the dishonesty or failure of a third party, the trustee is liable to make good that loss to the trust estate if, but for the breach, such loss would not have occurred. Thus the common law rules of remoteness of damage and causation do not apply. However, there does have to be some causal connection between the breach of trust and the loss to the trust estate for which compensation is recoverable, viz the fact that the loss would not have occurred but for the breach.[14] And a beneficiary who, subsequent to the breach, receives a benefit from the trustees' actions must give credit for it, and cannot recover compensation if, on balance, he has suffered no loss.[15]

If trustees have committed more than one breach of trust, a gain in one cannot be set off against a loss in another: the gain on the one transaction becomes subject to the trusts,

---

[12] See (2004) 18 Tru LI 116 (J Edelman and S Elliott).

[13] *Target Holdings Ltd v Redferns (a firm), supra,* HL. The principles laid down in this case were held to be applicable to claims for fraudulent breach of trust in *Collins v Brebner* [2000] Lloyd's Rep PN 587, CA. See also *Greater Pacific Investments Ltd (in liq) v Australian National Industries Ltd* (1996) 39 NSWLR 143 and (2003) 26 UNSWLJ 349 (R P Meagher and A Maroya).

[14] *Target Holdings Ltd v Redferns (a firm)* [1996] AC 421, [1995] 3 All ER 785, HL, discussed (1995) 9 Tru LI 86 (J Ulph); (1996) 112 LQR 27 (C E F Rickett); [1996] LMCLQ 161 (R Nolan); 8 KCLJ 86 (R Davern); (2006) 73 T & ELTJ 57 (R Dew). See *Bristol and West Building Society v May May & Merrimans (a firm)* [1996] 2 All ER 801; *Bristol and West Building Society v Mothew, supra,* CA, both noted [1997] CLJ 39 (R Nolan); [1997] LMCLQ 26 (A Alcock). See also *Bank of New Zealand v New Zealand Guardian Trust Co Ltd* [1999] 1 NZLR 213.

[15] *Hulbert v Avens* [2003] EWHC 76 (Ch), [2003] WTLR 387.

and the trustees are liable to replace the loss on the other.[16] The rule was slightly relaxed in *Bartlett v Barclays Bank Trust Co Ltd*,[17] in which the trustee was controlling shareholder in a company that made speculative investments in property development. The trustee was held liable for the loss that occurred on one of these investments, but was allowed to set off a profit arising from another investment that had stemmed from exactly the same investment policy.

(ii) Bare trusts

The position is modified where the trusts have come to an end and the trustees hold the trust fund on a bare trust for a beneficiary absolutely entitled. In relation to a breach of trust in such a case, there is no reason for compensating the breach of trust by way of an order for restitution and compensation *to the trust fund,* as opposed to the beneficiary himself. In *Target Holdings Ltd v Redferns (a firm)*,[18] Lord Browne-Wilkinson did not wholly rule out the possibility that, even in those circumstances, an order to reconstitute the fund may be appropriate.[19] However, in the ordinary case in which a beneficiary becomes absolutely entitled to the trust fund, the court orders not restitution to the trust estate, but payment of compensation directly to the beneficiary.

Lord Browne-Wilkinson further stated that although the same fundamental principles apply, it is wrong to lift wholesale the detailed rules developed in the context of traditional trusts and then seek to apply them to trusts of quite a different kind. *Target* itself was a commercial case in which the defendant solicitors held moneys as bare trustee for the plaintiff lender as part of a series of conveyancing transactions, under which they had implied authority to pay the money to or to the order of a third party, C, when the property had been transferred and C had executed charges in the plaintiff's favour. In breach of trust, the defendants paid moneys to X, but, within a short time, the legal estate became vested in C and a legal charge executed in favour of the plaintiff. This position was the one that the plaintiff had all along intended. What the plaintiff did not intend was that its security should be grossly inadequate. It had lent £1.7m on the basis of a valuation of the property at £2m made by the second defendant, against whom judgment in default had been obtained, but which was in insolvent liquidation. The property was eventually sold by the plaintiff as mortgagee for £500,000. The plaintiff alleged that it was the victim of a fraud by third parties who had induced it to advance the £1.7m, and that it had, in consequence, suffered a loss of £1.2m (the loan less the proceeds of the realization).

The way in which the case came before their Lordships was that Warner J, at first instance, had refused to give the plaintiff summary judgment and had given the defendants leave to defend the breach of trust claim, conditional on the payment into court of £1m. The Court of Appeal allowed the plaintiff's appeal against refusal to give summary judgment and gave judgment for £1,490,000 less the net sum to be realized on the subsequent sale of the property. The House of Lords had to act on the assumption (which it thought would very likely not be established at the trial) that if the defendants had not, in breach of trust,

---

[16] *Dimes v Scott* (1828) 4 Russ 195; *Wiles v Gresham* (1854) 2 Drew 258; affd 5 De GM & G 770; *Re Barker* (1898) 77 LT 712. The general rule is even clearer where there are, in fact, two separate funds, even though the trustees and the trusts may be the same: *Wiles v Gresham, supra.*

[17] [1980] Ch 515, [1980] 1 All ER 139. Cf *Fletcher v Green* (1864) 33 Beav 426.

[18] *Supra*, HL. See (1998) 114 LQR 214 (P J Millett); (2003) 25 Sydney LR 31 (C E F Rickett).

[19] Perhaps he had in mind a case in which the beneficiary is a minor or under disability.

provided moneys to X, the moneys would have been available from some other source and the series of transactions would have gone through. On this assumption, the plaintiff obtained exactly what it would have obtained had no breach occurred and, accordingly, would have suffered no compensatable loss. The defendants were therefore entitled to leave to defend to give them an opportunity to justify the assumption. However, if, at the trial, it was shown that the defendants' breach of trust in making the trust moneys available was essential to the success of the scheme, which would not have proceeded without it, the plaintiff would indeed be entitled to recover the total sum advanced to C less the proceeds of the security.

(iii) Improper retention on sale

Where the trustees were under a duty to sell unauthorized investments, and neglected or delayed doing so, they will be liable for the difference between the price for which they could have been sold at the proper time and the price eventually obtained on the actual sale.[20] Conversely, where trustees improperly realized a proper investment, they will be liable either to replace the investment sold, or to pay the difference in the price between the amount actually obtained and the value of such an investment at the date of the commencement of the proceedings or the date of judgment.[21]

(iv) Unauthorized investments

Where trustees have made an unauthorized investment, they are liable for all loss that is incurred when it is realized.[22] If an unauthorized investment has brought in a greater income than an authorized investment would have done, which income has been paid to the tenant for life, the trustees cannot call upon him to pay the excess income to capital, nor can it be set off against future income[23] even if the tenant for life and the trustee are the same person.[24] This rule may be contrasted with the position in which trustees fail to convert under the rule in *Howe v Earl of Dartmouth*,[25] or an express trust for sale.[26] Of course, as we have seen, if the unauthorized investment causes a loss to capital, the trustees must make it good.

In the case of an unauthorized investment, the beneficiaries, if they are *sui juris* and together comprehend the entire equitable interest, can, if they so agree, adopt the unauthorized investment as part of the trust property.[27] It may well be that, if they do this, they can nevertheless call on the trustee to make good any loss to the trust estate; the law

---

[20] *Grayburn v Clarkson* (1868) 3 Ch App 605; *Dunning v Earl of Gainsborough* (1885) 54 LJ Ch 991. See (1977) 55 CBR 342 (D Waters). As to the position in whichthere is a power to postpone sale and the trustees postpone for too long causing loss, and where there have been fluctuations in value, see *Fales v Canada Permanent Trust Co* (1976) 70 DLR (3d) 257.

[21] *Re Massingberd's Settlement* (1890) 63 LT 296, CA, referred to the earlier date, but Vinelott J in *Re Bell's Indenture* [1980] 3 All ER 425, [1980] 1 WLR 1217, said, without citing any authority, that this was wrong in principle and that the later date should be used. *Scott on Trusts*, 4th edn, vol III, [208.3], p 1687, could be used to support this view. See (1978) 77 Mich LR 95 (R V Wellman).

[22] *Knott v Cottee* (1852) 16 Beav 77.

[23] *Slade v Chaine* [1908] 1 Ch 522, CA; *Learoyd v Whiteley* (1887) 12 App Cas 727, HL.

[24] *Re Hoyles (No 2)* [1912] 1 Ch 67.   [25] (1802) 7 Ves 137.

[26] *Dimes v Scott* (1828) 4 Russ 195, and see Chapter 18, p 428, *supra*.

[27] *Re Patten and Edmonton Union Poor Guardians* (1883) 52 LJ Ch 787; *Re Jenkins and HE Randall & Co's Contract* [1903] 2 Ch 362; *Wright v Morgan* [1926] AC 788, PC.

is not clear:[28] 'But if there is not unanimity, then it is not trust property, but the trustee who has made it must keep the investment himself. He is debtor to the trust for the money which has been applied in its purchase.'[29] More accurately, perhaps, the duty of the trustee to sell the unauthorized investment if the cestuis que trust do not choose to adopt it is subject to the right of the trustee to take it over on replacing the trust funds.[30] Until this is done, the cestuis que trust retain a lien on the unauthorized investment.

(v) Failure to invest

Where, however, trustees were not directed to invest in one specified investment, but were given a choice and yet made no investment at all, it has been held that they are only liable to replace the trust fund, on the ground that it would be impossible to say which investment they would have chosen and for what other sum they could be held liable.[31] It is doubtful whether such a case would be decided in this way today. It is thought that the courts might well prefer to apply *obiter dicta* of Dillon and Staughton LJJ in *Nestle v National Westminster Bank plc*[32] to the effect that trustees who fail to follow a proper investment policy may be required to make good to the trust fair compensation. If trustees were directed to make a specific investment, and either made no investment at all or invested in something else, they will be required to provide the amount of that specified investment that could have been purchased with the trust funds at the time when the investment should have been made.[33]

(vi) Exemplary or punitive damages

There do not appear to be any cases in which exemplary or punitive damages have been awarded for breach of trust.[34] The Law Commission recommended[35] that punitive damages should be available for equitable wrongdoing, but the government has stated that it does not intend to take forward the draft legislation proposed, having regard to the balance of opinion disclosed at consultation.

(vii) Equitable compensation for breach of the duty of skill and care

This resembles common law damages in that it is awarded by way of compensation to the plaintiff for his loss. There is no reason in principle why the common law rules of

---

[28] *Re Lake* [1903] 1 KB 439; contra, *semble, Thornton v Stokill* (1855) 1 Jur NS 751.

[29] *Wright v Morgan, supra*, at 206, 799, PC; *Sharp v Jackson* [1899] AC 419, HL.

[30] *Re Salmon* (1889) 42 Ch D 351, CA; *Re Lake, supra; Head v Gould* [1898] 2 Ch 250.

[31] *Shepherd v Mouls* (1845) 4 Hare 500; *Robinson v Robinson* (1851) 1 De GM & G 247.

[32] [1994] 1 All ER 118, [1993] 1 WLR 1260, CA. See (1992) 142 NLJ 1279 (J Martin).

[33] *Byrchall v Bradford* (1822) 6 Madd 235; *Pride v Fooks* (1840) 2 Beav 430. See *Elder's Trustee and Executor Co Ltd v Higgins* (1963) 113 CLR 426 (failure to exercise option to purchase). Account will be taken of any payments, such as calls on shares, that they would necessarily have made if they had properly carried out the directions as to investment: *Briggs v Massey* (1882) 51 LJ Ch 447, CA.

[34] See *Vyse v Foster* (1872) 8 Ch App 309, 333, *per* James LJ. Contra *Aquaculture Corpn v New Zealand Green Mussel Ltd* [1990] 3 NZLR 299, noted (1991) 107 LQR 209 (J Beatson); (1991) 21 VUWLR 391 (P Michalik); *Harris v Digital Pulse Property Ltd* (2003) 197 ALR 626. See also (1995) 69 ALJ 773 (P M McDermott); (1996) 19 UQLJ 125 (D Jensen); (2004) 18 Tru LI 116 (J Edelman and S Elliott); (2004) 67 MLR 16 (S Elliott and C Mitchell); (2006) 29 UNSWLJ 38 (A Hughes); (2008) 11 Otago LR 603 (C Rickett).

[35] Law Com No 247 (1997). It seems to assume the equitable wrongdoing includes breach of trust.

causation, remoteness of damage, and measure of damages should not be applied by analogy in such a case.[36]

(viii) Breach of fiduciary duty

It has been said[37] that the considerations that apply to a breach of trust 'apply to a claim for breach of a fiduciary duty: fiduciary duties are equitable extensions of trustee duties'. The claimant for breach of a fiduciary duty must show that the loss that he has suffered has been caused by the defendant's breach of duty. Furthermore, it seems that unless the breach could properly be regarded as the equivalent of fraud, the claimant is not entitled to be placed financially in the same position as he was in before the breach occurred, but only in the same position as he would have been in had the breach of duty not occurred. As Evans LJ explained in *Swindle v Harrison*,[38] the positions are not necessarily the same: the claimant's position might have deteriorated, or, for that matter, improved, during the intervening period by reason of independent, extraneous events. In *Nationwide Building Society v Various Solicitors (No 3)*,[39] it was said that the correct approach to equitable compensation for breach of fiduciary duty, except where the fiduciary had acted dishonestly or in bad faith, is to assess what actual loss had resulted from the breach, having regard to the scope of the duty broken.

(ix) Profits

As we have seen,[40] different considerations apply where what is sought is not equitable compensation for breach of trust, but an account of profits improperly received by the trustee, when all of the profits must be disgorged. Profits may be assessed on the basis of the highest intermediate value of the property between the date of breach and the date of judgment, provided that there was an opportunity to realize the property during the period of the continuing breach. No distinction is made between shares and other types of property where investment is only a secondary consideration.[41]

(c) TAX

In assessing compensation for breach of trust, tax payable by the beneficiaries is not taken into account. The obligation of a trustee who is held liable for breach of trust is fundamentally different from the obligation of a contractual or tortious wrongdoer. The trustee's

---

[36] *Bristol and West Building Society v Mothew* [1998] Ch 1, [1996] 4 All ER 698, CA; *Swindle v Harrison* [1997] 4 All ER 705, CA; *ICS Ltd v West Bromwich B S* [1999] Lloyd's PN 496. See also [2002] MLR 588 (S B Elliott) and note the comments of the High Court of Australia in *Youyang Property Ltd v Minter Ellison* (2003) 196 ALR 482, 491, noted (2003) 119 LQR 545 (S Elliott and J Edelman), and see p 522, *supra*.

[37] *Per* Mummery LJ in *Swindle v Harrison* [1997] 4 All ER 705, CA, noted (1997) 11 Tru LI 72 (L Ho); (1998) 114 LQR 181 (H Tjio and T M Yeo). See (2003) 119 LQR 246 (M Conaglen). See also *Maguire v Makaronis* (1997) 188 CLR 449, noted (1998) 114 LQR 9 (S Moriarty).

[38] *Supra*, CA, at 714.

[39] [1999] PNLR 608. See *JJ Harrison (Properties) Ltd v Harrison* [2001] EWCA Civ 1467, [2002] 1 BCLC 162.

[40] See p 141 *et seq, supra*.

[41] *Jaffray v Marshall* [1994] 1 All ER 143, [1993] 1 WLR 1285 (no doubt was cast on this proposition in *Target Holdings Ltd v Redferns (a firm)*, *supra*, HL, although it was said to have been wrongly applied to a claim for compensation for breach of trust); *Nant-y-glo and Blaina Ironworks Co v Grave* (1879) 12 Ch D 738.

obligation is to restore to the trust estate the assets of which he has deprived it. The tax liability of individual beneficiaries, who have claims *qua* beneficiaries to the capital and income of the trust estate, does not enter into the picture, because it arises not at the point of restitution to the trust estate, but at the point of distribution of capital or income out of the trust estate. Accordingly, a trustee is not entitled to have an order for compensation qualified so as to restrict the compensation payable to the net loss respectively suffered by the beneficiaries by reason of non-payments of distributions that ought properly to have been made, even though the breach of trust has not enriched the defaulting trustee. The principle of *British Transport Commission v Gourley*,[42] that damages for loss of earnings should take into account the tax that would have been payable, does not apply.[43]

(D) INTEREST

Where a trustee is required to replace a loss caused to the trust estate, he is normally liable, in addition, to pay interest. Traditionally, the rate was 4 per cent, but this has been said to be unrealistic in modern conditions. Some relatively recent cases[44] have held that the proper rate of interest is 1 per cent above bank rate, while, in others, it has been said to be that allowed from time to time on the courts' special account.[45]

It is still the law that, in special circumstances, a trustee may be liable for a higher rate.[46] The earlier cases established that if he had actually received more, he was liable for what he had actually received. If he ought to have received more, he was liable for what he ought to have received, as, for instance, where he called in a mortgage carrying a high rate of interest.[47] If he was fairly presumed to have received more, as where he had used the trust money for his own purposes, he used normally to be charged an extra 1 per cent over the normal rate—in particular, where he had employed the trust money in trade, the beneficiaries had the option of claiming that higher rate, or alternatively the actual profits,[48] or, if the trustee had mixed his own moneys and the trust moneys, a proportionate share of the

---

[42] [1956] AC 185, [1955] 3 All ER 796, HL. See (1987) 103 LQR 211 (W Bishop and J Kay).

[43] *Bartlett v Barclays Bank Trust Co Ltd (No 2)* [1980] Ch 515, [1980] 2 All ER 92, noted [1980] Conv 449 (G A Shindler); *a fortiori, Re Bell's Indenture* [1980] 3 All ER 425, [1980] 1 WLR 1217, in which trust funds had been dissipated in breach of trust, and the estate duty office had waived the duty that would have been payable on the deaths of the life tenants if the funds had not been dissipated. It was held that a trustee who had taken trust moneys for his own benefit or for the benefit of others, and who was therefore liable to restore them, could not benefit from his breach of trust by retaining sums that would have been paid in tax had the breach of trust not been committed.

[44] *Belmont Finance Corpn Ltd v Williams Furniture Ltd (No 2)* [1980] 1 All ER 393, CA; *O'Sullivan v Management Agency Music Ltd* [1985] QB 428 [1985] 3 All ER 351, CA. In *Guardian Ocean Cargoes Ltd v Banco do Brasil SA (No 3)* [1992] 2 Lloyd's Rep 193, Hirst J awarded compound interest at 1 per cent over the New York prime rate applicable from time to time.

[45] See CPR 7.0.17 and *Bartlett v Barclays Bank Trust Co Ltd (No 2)* [1980] Ch 515, [1980] 2 All ER 92, in which the judge pointed out that since, to some extent, high interest rates reflect and compensate for the continual erosion in the value of money, it was arguable that a proportion of the interest should go to capital. Most recently, in *Re Evans (decd)* [1999] 2 All ER 777, a case 'involving the non-professional administrator of a small estate in times of more gentle inflation', 8 per cent was awarded. See also *Wallersteiner v Moir (No 2)* [1975].

[46] See CPR 7.0.9; *Jones v Foxall* (1852) 15 Beav 388; *A-G v Alford* (1855) 4 De GM & G 843, explained in *Berwick-on-Tweed Corpn v Murray* (1857) 7 De GM & G 497.

[47] See *Jones v Foxall* (1852) 15 Beav 388.

[48] *Vyse v Foster* (1872) 8 Ch App 309; affd (1874) LR 7 HL 318; *Gordon v Gonda* [1955] 2 All ER 762, CA. An inquiry may be ordered as to what use the defendant made of the trust money and what return on it he received: *Mathew v T M Sutton Ltd* [1994] 4 All ER 793, (1994) 1 WLR 1455.

profits.[49] They could not however, claim profits for part of the time and interest for the remainder.[50]

Prima facie the liability is for simple interest only, but compound interest may be awarded in cases in which it has been withheld or misapplied by a trustee or anyone else in a fiduciary position, by way of recouping from such a defendant an improper profit made by him. The cases commonly refer to situations in which the defendant has used trust moneys in his own trade, but it is thought that the better view is that it extends to all cases in which a fiduciary has improperly profited from his trust.[51] It may well be that there is jurisdiction in equity to award compound interest in cases in which the defendant owes no fiduciary duty, but where money has been obtained and retained by fraud: the law, however, is not settled.[52]

(E) JOINT AND SEVERAL LIABILITY TO BENEFICIARIES

It is settled that, where two or more trustees are liable for a breach of trust, their liability is joint and several: this means that the beneficiaries can claim the whole loss from any one trustee,[53] or two or more jointly, or all of them, and even where a judgment is obtained against all of them, may execute the whole judgment against any one.[54] The beneficiaries are not concerned with the liability of the trustees *inter se*. So far as the beneficiaries are concerned, 'all parties to a breach of trust are equally liable; there is between them no primary liability'.[55] The above rules apply equally where the trustees comprise or include constructive trustees.[56] The liability continues against the estate of a deceased or bankrupt trustee,[57] but the estate of a deceased trustee is not liable for what he left in a proper state of investment at his death.[58] Since the liability is joint and several, beneficiaries who have recovered in part from one trustee may prove in the bankruptcy of another trustee for the whole amount of the loss, and not merely for the balance, although they cannot, of course, in the aggregate, recover more than their loss.[59]

Retired trustees remain liable for their own breaches of trust, but are not normally liable for breaches of trust committed by their successors. If, however, a trustee is asked to commit a breach of trust and refuses, he should take care before appointing, or resigning in

---

[49] *Docker v Somes* (1834) 2 My & K 655; *Edinburgh Corpn v Lord Advocate* (1879) 4 App Cas 823, HL.

[50] *Heathcote v Hulme* (1819) 1 Jac & W 122; *Vyse v Foster* (1872) 8 Ch App 309, 334.

[51] *Westdeutsche Landesbank Girozentrale v Islington London Borough Council* [1996] AC 669, [1996] 2 All ER 961, HL, noted (1996) 112 LQR 521 (M Cope); *Equiticorp Industries Group Ltd v The Crown (No 3) (Judgment No 51)* [1996] 3 NZLR 690.

[52] *Clef Aquitaine SARL v Laporte Materials (Barrow) Ltd (sued as Sovereign Chemicals Industries Ltd)* [2001] QB 488, [2000] 3 All ER 493, CA, citing *President of India v La Pintada Cia Navegacion SA* [1985] AC 104, [1984] 2 All ER 773, HL; *Westdeutsche Landesbank Girozentrale v Islington London Borough Council, supra*, HL.

[53] *Walker v Symonds* (1818) 3 Swan 1, 75; *Re Harrison* [1891] 2 Ch 349; *McCheane v Gyles (No 2)* [1902] 1 Ch 911. But if all the trustees are dead, an action cannot normally be brought against the personal representatives of one trustee, not being the survivor of the trustees, without joining the personal representatives of the survivor, or having new trustees appointed and joining them as defendants—*Re Jordan* [1904] 1 Ch 260.

[54] *A-G v Wilson* (1840) Cr & Ph 1, 28; *Fletcher v Green* (1864) 33 Beav 426.

[55] Per Leach MR in *Wilson v Moore* (1833) 1 My & K 126, 146, affd (1834) 1 My & K 337; *Edwards v Hood-Barnes* [1905] 1 Ch 20.

[56] See Chapter 8, p 139, *supra*. *Blyth v Fladgate* [1891] 1 Ch 337; *Cowper v Stoneham* (1893) 68 LT 18.

[57] See, eg, *Dixon v Dixon* (1878) 9 Ch D 587; *Edwards v Hood-Barnes* [1905] 1 Ch 20.

[58] *Re Palk* (1892) 41 WR 28.   [59] *Edwards v Hood-Barnes, supra*.

order to enable the appointment of, a new trustee who he has reason to believe may be more accommodating. The position, according to Kekewich J in *Head v Gould*,[60] is:

> that in order to make a retiring trustee liable for a breach of trust committed by his successor you must shew, and shew clearly, that the very breach of trust which was in fact committed was not merely the outcome of the retirement and new appointment, but was contemplated by the former trustee when such retirement and appointment took place.... It will not suffice to prove that the former trustees rendered easy or even intended, a breach of trust, if it was not in fact committed. They must be proved to have been guilty as accessories before the fact of the impropriety actually perpetrated.

Again, a new trustee is not liable for breaches of trust committed by his predecessors, and 'is entitled to assume that everything has been duly attended to up to the time of his becoming trustee'.[61] However, if he discovers a breach of trust, he should take appropriate steps to remedy it, if necessary by proceedings against the old trustees, as part of his duty to get in the trust property and to see that it is in a proper state of investment.[62]

(F) LIABILITY FOR CO-TRUSTEE

It has been recognized since *Townley v Sherborne*[63] in 1634 that a trustee is not liable for the acts and defaults of his co-trustee. An innocent trustee is, however, liable for his own acts or defaults. Accordingly, he has been said to be liable for his own breach of trust in relation to a co-trustee in three cases:

(i)   where he hands over money to a co-trustee without securing its due application;

(ii) where he permits a co-trustee to receive money without making due inquiry as to his dealing with it;[64] and

(iii) where he becomes aware of a breach of trust by a co-trustee, either committed or meditated, and fails to take the needful steps to obtain restitution or redress.[65]

As Jonathan Parker J observed:[66] 'A trustee is himself in default if, by his own neglect, he allows his fellow trustees to enter into a transaction in breach of trust.'

(G) TRUSTEE-BENEFICIARY

It is settled that if a trustee who is also a beneficiary is in default and liable to the trust estate, he will not be allowed to claim, as against his beneficiaries, any beneficial interest in the trust estate until he has made good his default.[67] It makes no difference that he acquired his beneficial interest derivatively, for instance, under the will or on the intestacy

---

[60] [1898] 2 Ch 250, 273–274.   [61] *Re Strahan* (1856) 8 De GM & G 291, 309, *per* Turner LJ.

[62] See Chapter 16, section 1, *supra*.

[63] (1633) J Bridge 35. For a recent illustration, see *Re Lucking's Will Trusts* [1967] 3 All ER 726, [1968] 1 WLR 866.

[64] See, eg, *Wyman v Paterson* [1900] AC 271, HL.

[65] *Styles v Guy* (1849) 1 Mac & G 422, which referred to a duty to keep watch on co-trustees.

[66] *Segbedzi (Minors) v Segbedzi* (1999) [2001] WTLR 83, CA.

[67] *Re Rhodesia Goldfields Ltd* [1910] 1 Ch 239. See *Selangor United Rubber Estates Ltd v Cradock (No 4)* [1969] 3 All ER 965, [1969] 1 WLR 1773.

of an original beneficiary.[68] And if the trustee has assigned his beneficial interest, his assignee is in no better position, even though the default takes place after the assignment.[69] But if the same persons happen to be the trustees of two separate trusts, even though created by the same will, then their beneficial interest under one cannot be impounded to make good their default in connection with the other.[70]

(H) INJUNCTION

An injunction may be obtained in appropriate circumstances to restrain an apprehended breach of trust.[71]

2 LIABILITY OF TRUSTEES *INTER SE*

The equitable rule was that, as between themselves, trustees were equally liable, and one who was compelled to pay more than his fair share could enforce contribution from the others.[72] The right extended to the personal representatives of a deceased trustee, where the breach of trust took place before, even though the loss only occurred after, his death.[73] The rule applied as between so-called 'active' and 'passive' trustees, because, as pointed out in *Bahin v Hughes*,[74] by doing nothing, a passive trustee may neglect his duty more than a trustee who acts honestly, although erroneously.

The equitable rule has now been superseded by the Civil Liability (Contribution) Act 1978, which provides that any person liable in respect of any damage suffered by another person—defined to include damage based on breach of trust—may recover contribution from any other person liable in respect of the same damage. The amount of the contribution recoverable is such as may be found by the court to be just and equitable, having regard to the extent of that person's responsibility for the damage in question, and may be nil or 100 per cent. This gives the court a discretion to depart from the equitable rule of equal contribution, but would not otherwise appear to alter the position.

The Act does not, however, apply to an indemnity, and there are three cases in which a trustee is liable to indemnify his co-trustees:

(i)   where a trustee has got the money into his hands and made use of it;[75]

(ii) where the active trustee was a solicitor, who was relied on by the other trustees.[76] A solicitor-trustee is not, however, necessarily bound to indemnify a co-trustee

---

[68] *Jacubs v Rylance* (1874) LR 17 Eq 341; *Re Dacre* [1916] 1 Ch 344, CA.

[69] *Doering v Doering, supra; Re Towndrow* [1911] 1 Ch 662.

[70] *Re Towndrow* [1911] 1 Ch 662.   [71] This is discussed in Chapter 27, section 8, *infra*.

[72] *Chillingworth v Chambers* [1896] 1 Ch 685, CA; *Robinson v Harkin* [1896] 2 Ch 415.

[73] *Jackson v Dickinson* [1903] 1 Ch 947.

[74] (1886) 31 Ch D 390, CA; *Bacon v Camphausen* (1888) 58 LT 851; *Goodwin v Duggan* (1996–97) 41 NSWLR 158. See (1977) 55 CBR 342 (D Waters).

[75] *Bahin v Hughes, supra*, CA, at 395; *Goodwin v Duggan, supra*.

[76] *Chillingworth v Chambers, supra*, CA; *Re Linsley* [1904] 2 Ch 785. The principle is not confined to solicitors: *Bahin v Hughes* (1886) 31 Ch D 390, 395–397, *per* Cotton LJ; *Re Partington* (1887) 57 LT 654, 662; and see *Blair v Canada Trust Co* (1986) 32 DLR (4th) 515.

merely because he is a solicitor—he will be under no such obligation if it appears that the co-trustee was an active participator in the breach of trust, and is not proved to have participated merely in consequence of the advice and control of the solicitor;[77]

(iii) where a trustee is also, or subsequently becomes, a beneficiary, he is bound, at any rate, where he has received some benefit by the breach of trust,[78] to indemnify his co-trustee to the extent of his interest in the trust fund and not merely to the extent of any benefit that he may have received by the breach of trust.[79] A new trustee who is also a beneficiary, however, although he may be liable to the other beneficiaries for failure to have an existing breach of trust put right on his appointment, is not liable to indemnify the original trustees under this head, but is himself entitled to be indemnified by the original trustees who were responsible for the breach the primary cause of the loss.[80]

Finally, it may be noted that where one only of two or more trustees is excused under s 61,[81] it is strongly arguable that the effect must be to leave the other trustee or trustees fully liable without the possibility of obtaining contribution from the excused trustee.[82]

3 DEFENCES OF A TRUSTEE TO PROCEEDINGS FOR BREACH OF TRUST

(A) EXEMPTION CLAUSES

(i) The present law

The efficacy of a trustee exemption clause was affirmed by the Court of Appeal in *Armitage v Nurse*,[83] in which a clause in the settlement provided that no trustee should be liable for any loss or damage to the fund or its income 'unless such loss or damage shall be caused by his own actual fraud'. It was held that the clause was effective no matter how indolent, imprudent, lacking in diligence, negligent, or wilful the trustee might have been, so long as he had not acted dishonestly. The test of dishonesty was considered by Sir Christopher

---

[77] *Head v Gould* [1898] 2 Ch 250.

[78] *Chillingworth v Chambers, supra,* at 707, *per* Kay LJ: cf Lindley LJ, at 700.

[79] *Chillingworth v Chambers, supra,* CA.

[80] *Re Fountaine,* not reported on this point in [1909] 2 Ch 382, CA, but referred to in Underhill and Hayton, *Law of Trusts and Trustees,* 17th edn, [99.14].

[81] Discussed p 535 *et seq, infra.*

[82] See *Fales v Canada Permanent Trustee Co* (1976) 70 DLR (3d) 257 and (1977) 55 CBR 342 (D Waters). The argument is even stronger under the 1978 Act, because the excused trustee is not liable for the damage.

[83] [1998] Ch 241, [1997] 2 All ER 705, CA, noted [1998] CLJ 33 (N McBride). The Law Commission in Law Com CP 171, para 2.54, have expressed the opinion that the authority of *Armitage v Nurse* is not entirely free from doubt. In [1998] Conv 100, G McCormack argues that trustee exemption clauses should be subject to a strict construction. As to an occupational pension scheme, see Pensions Act 1995, s 33; (1999) 13 Tru LI 2 (N Moore). See also (1999) 8 T & ELJ 6 (Lord Millett); (2000) 20 T & ELJ 22 (R Vas); [1999] PCB 227 (S M Smith); [2000] All ER Rev 251 (P J Clarke); (2005) 149 Sol Jo 976 (A Hammerton).

Slade, with whose judgment the other members were content to agree, in *Walker v Stones*.[84] At first instance, Rattee J, purporting to apply dicta in *Armitage v Nurse*,[85] derived two propositions: firstly, that the deliberate commission of a breach of trust is not necessarily dishonest;[86] secondly, that it is only dishonest if the trustee committing it does so 'either knowing that it is contrary to the interests of the beneficiaries or being recklessly indifferent whether it is contrary to their interests or not'. These two propositions appeared to be accepted by the Court of Appeal, but there was a third proposition—namely: 'It seems to me impossible to call a trustee's conduct "dishonest" in any ordinary sense of that word, even if he knew he was acting in breach of the terms of the trust, if he so acted in a genuine (even if misguided) belief that what he was doing was for the benefit of the beneficiaries.' This last proposition required qualification. At least in the case of a solicitor-trustee, a qualification is necessary to take account of the case in which the trustee's so-called 'honest belief', although actually held, is so unreasonable that, by any objective standard, no reasonable solicitor-trustee could have thought that what he did or agreed to do was for the benefit of the beneficiaries. A person may act dishonestly, even though he genuinely believes that his action is morally justified. It was added that the test of honesty may vary from case to case, depending on, among other things, the role and calling of the trustee.

It is not contrary to public policy to exclude liability for gross negligence by an appropriate clause clearly worded to that effect. Further, a trustee does not lose the protection of an exemption clause by ceasing to be a trustee.[87] However, where there is a doubt on the construction of a trust whether a trustee would be exempted from liability for breach of trust by a trustee exemption clause, such doubt should be resolved against the trustee and the clause construed so as not to protect him.[88] But where a trustee falls within the clause, the fact that the judge would unhesitatingly have refused relief under s 61 of the Trustee Act 1925 is irrelevant.[89] It may be added that it has been suggested[90] that, in the case of a professional trustee, an exemption clause might be invalidated by the Unfair Contract Terms Act 1977, but this seems unlikely in the light of *Bogg v Raper*,[91] in which it was held that the solicitor draftsman of a will was entitled to rely on the provisions of an exemption clause contained therein. Indeed, the author of the suggestion now doubts whether it is right.[92]

---

[84] [2000] 4 All ER 412, [2000] 2 WLR 623, CA, noted (2000) 15 Tru LI 18 (M Doherty and R Fletcher); [2001] PCB 215 (P Stibbard). The test of dishonesty is the same as that in *Royal Brunei Airlines Sdn Bhd v Newman Industries Ltd* [1995] 2 AC 378, [1995] 3 All ER 97, PC.

[85] *Supra*, CA.

[86] Compare *per* Lindley MR in *Perrins v Bellamy* [1899] 1 Ch 797, 798: 'My old master, the late Lord Justice Selwyn, used to say, "The main duty of a trustee is to commit *judicious* breaches of trust"...' (Lindley MR's emphasis).

[87] *Seifert v Pensions Ombudsman* [1997] 1 All ER 214.

[88] *Wright v Olswang* (1998) Times, 17 September, revsd (1999) Times, 18 May, CA, on a question of construction without affecting this point. It was further held, and affirmed on the appeal, that where a settlement had two trustee exemption clauses, one protecting all trustees from liability for breach of trust and one that expressly did not apply to paid trustees, then paid trustees could not rely on the general exemption.

[89] *Re Clapham* [2006] WTLR 203, noted (2006) 78 T & ELTJ 5 (J Washington and A Smart).

[90] [1980] Conv 333 and (1986) 1 TL & P 43 (W Goodhart). See also (1995) 9 Tru LI 21 (R Ham); (1996) 146 NLJ 348 (A Kenny).

[91] (1998) Times, 22 April, CA, in which, however, the point does not appear to have been argued.

[92] (1996) 10 Tru LI 42.

There are special provisions in relation to trustees of debentures,[93] pension trust schemes,[94] and authorized unit trust schemes.[95]

(ii) The Law Commission recommendations

In its final report,[96] the Law Commission departed from the reforms provisionally favoured in the Consultation Paper.[97] It now recommends that a rule of practice should be recognized in the interests of ensuring settlor awareness of trustee exemption clauses. It recommends that the main elements of the rule should be in the following terms:

> Any paid trustee who causes a settlor to include a clause in a trust instrument which has the effect of excluding or limiting liability for negligence must before the creation of the trust take such steps as are reasonable to ensure that the settlor is aware of the meaning and effect of the clause.

The Commission further recommends that regulatory and professional bodies should make regulations to such effect in order to meet the particular circumstances of their membership, and should enforce such regulation in accordance with their codes of conduct. Bodies, the membership of which includes the drafters of trusts, should extend regulation to those who draft trust documentation containing trustee exemption provisions. It also recommends that government should promote the application of this rule of practice as widely as possible across the trust industry.

The Law Commission is awaiting a decision by the government as to whether it accepts these recommendations.

(B) CONSENT OR CONCURRENCE OF THE CESTUI QUE TRUST

A beneficiary who consents to or concurs in a breach of trust,[98] or subsequently confirms it or grants a release to the trustees,[99] or even merely acquiesces in it,[100] will not, in general, be able to succeed in a claim against the trustees[101] whether or not he has derived any benefit thereby.[102] In order to have this result, as will be elaborated later, the beneficiary must, at the relevant time, have been fully cognisant of the circumstances affecting his rights. Although a beneficiary whose interest is reversionary is not bound to assert his title until his interest falls into possession, he may, in the meantime, assent to a breach of trust so as to bar his claims in respect thereof, although the mere fact that he knows of the breach of trust and does nothing about it will not by itself be enough.[103] Further, the concurrence,

---

93 Companies Act 2006, s 750.

94 Pensions Act 1995, ss 33, 34(6). See (2004) 18 Tru LI 132 (I Greenstreet).

95 Financial Services and Markets Act 2000, s 253.

96 Law Com No 301, published June 2006. See also (2006) 81 T & ELTJ 4 (C Gothard); [2007] Conv 103 (Ann Kenny); [2007] PCB 196 (E Reed); (2007) 83 T & ELTJ 23 (R Dew).

97 Law Com CP 171. See [2003] PCB 404 (C Groves and Judith Ingham); [2003] Conv 185 (Ann Kenny).

98 *Brice v Stokes* (1805) 11 Ves 319; *Nail v Punter* (1832) 5 Sim 555; *Evans v Benyon* (1887) 37 Ch D 329, CA. See *Spellson v George* (1992) 26 NSWLR 666.

99 *Farrant v Blanchford* (1863) 1 De GJ & Sm 107.

100 *Walker v Symonds* (1818) 3 Swan 1; *Stafford v Stafford* (1857) 1 De G & J 193.

101 *A fortiori*, a beneficiary who is also a trustee cannot claim from a co-trustee in respect of a breach of trust in which they have both joined: *Butler v Carter* (1868) LR 5 Eq 276.

102 *Fletcher v Collis* [1905] 2 Ch 24, CA.

103 *Life Association of Scotland v Siddal* (1861) 3 De GF & J 58.

release, or acquiescence of a person not *sui juris* is generally ineffective;[104] although, accordingly, as Wigram VC said,[105] 'the release of infants is worth nothing in law', the court will not permit an infant who, by fraudulently misrepresenting his age, persuades trustees to pay him money in breach of trust to claim the money over again on attaining his majority.[106] Again, on general principles, a consent or release obtained by undue influence will not avail a trustee:[107] 'A consent which is not a free one is no consent at all.'[108]

Whether a beneficiary has consented to or concurred in a breach of trust is a question of fact. No particular formalities are required.[109] Similarly, a release does not need to be a formal release under seal in order to be effective; any expression of an intention to waive the breach of trust, if supported by some consideration, however slight, will be regarded as equivalent to a release.[110] A release may even be inferred from conduct,[111] but a beneficiary does not waive his rights in respect of a breach of trust merely by accepting a part of what is due to him with the knowledge that the trustee has committed a breach of trust.[112] Where a trustee relies on acquiescence by the beneficiary, he must, it seems, show more than the mere passing of time and failure to act. If a long time has passed, however, very slight acts may suffice to establish acquiescence, and Campbell LC has even said[113] that 'although the rule be that the onus lies on the party relying on acquiescence to prove the facts from which the consent of the cestui que trust is to be inferred, it is easy to conceive cases in which, from great lapse of time, such facts might and ought to be presumed'.[114]

There are many cases that stress that, whether relying on concurrence,[115] release, or acquiescence, a trustee must establish full knowledge on the part of the beneficiary.

Accordingly, releases[116] have been set aside where executed under a mistake of fact,[117] where a solicitor-trustee was allowed costs to which he was not entitled, the beneficiary not being professionally advised,[118] and where the release was executed shortly after the beneficiary

---

[104] *Lord Montfort v Lord Cadogen* (1810) 19 Ves 635.

[105] *Overton v Banister* (1844) 3 Hare 503, 506.

[106] *Overton v Banister, supra; Wright v Snowe* (1848) 2 De G & Sm 321. Cf s 3 of the Minors' Contracts Act 1987, which provides that, where a contract is unenforceable against a defendant (or he repudiates it) because he was a minor when the contract was made, the court may, if it is just and equitable to do so, require the defendant to transfer to the plaintiff any property acquired by the defendant under the contract, or any property representing it.

[107] *Farrant v Blanchford* (1863) 1 De GJ & Sm 107; *Lloyd v Attwood* (1859) 3 De G & J 614.

[108] *Per* Stuart VC in *Stevens v Robertson* (1868) 18 LT 427, 428.

[109] See *Rehden v Wesley* (1861) 29 Beav 213, 215, *per* Romilly MR.

[110] *Stackhouse v Barnston* (1805) 10 Ves 453.

[111] *Egg v Devey* (1847) 10 Beav 444. Note the observations of Nicholls J in *John v James* [1991] FSR 397, 439.

[112] *Re Cross* (1882) 20 Ch D 109, CA.

[113] *Life Association of Scotland v Siddal, supra*, at 77. Cf *Knight v Bowyer* (1858) 2 De G & J 421, 443, *per* Turner LJ.

[114] In the following cases, acquiescence was established: *Jones v Higgins* (1866) LR 2 Eq 538; *Sleeman v Wilson* (1871) LR 13 Eq 36. In the following cases it was not: *Griffiths v Porter* (1858) 25 Beav 236; *Re Jackson* (1881) 44 LT 467.

[115] *Buckeridge v Glasse* (1841) Cr & Ph 126.

[116] See *Farrant v Blanchford* (1863) 1 De GJ & Sm 107, 119; *Thomson v Eastwood* (1877) 2 App Cas 215, HL.

[117] *Hore v Becher* (1842) 12 Sim 465.

[118] *Todd v Wilson* (1846) 9 Beav 486, distinguishing *Stanes v Parker* (1846) 9 Beav 385, in which the beneficiary was professionally advised. See also *Aspland v Watte* (1855) 20 Beav 474.

attained his majority and purported to involve the examination of complicated accounts.[119] In a different context, the House of Lords has recently observed[120] that, like any other contractual provision, a release will be construed so as to give effect to what the contracting parties intended, having regard to the parties' relationship and all of the relevant facts surrounding the transaction so far as known to the parties. Although a party could, at any rate in a compromise agreement supported by valuable consideration, agree to release claims or rights of which he was not, and could not, be aware, the court would be slow to infer that he had done so in the absence of clear language to that effect.

Where a trustee relies on acquiescence, he must establish knowledge of the relevant facts by the person alleged to have acquiesced, but 'one cannot lay down a hard and fast rule to this effect that knowledge of the legal consequences of known facts is or is not essential to the success of the plea'.[121] Further, a nice distinction has to be drawn between knowledge by the beneficiary of what he is doing and its legal effect, and knowledge of the fact that what he is concurring in is a breach of trust. At any rate, where a trustee relies on the concurrence of a beneficiary—and, on principle, there seems no reason why the rule in relation to release or acquiescence should be any different—Wilberforce J, in *Re Pauling's Settlement*,[122] accepted the view of the Court of Appeal in *Evans v Benyon*[123] as correctly representing the law. In the latter case, it was said that a person who, knowing that a trustee was distributing a settled fund, consented to and was active in the distribution, could not afterwards claim against the trustee even though he did not know at the time that he was beneficially interested and although he did not know that the division was a breach of trust.[124] All of the members of the Court of Appeal in *Holder v Holder*[125] expressly approved the general statement of the law made by Wilberforce J in *Re Pauling's Settlement*,[126] in which he said,[127] after reviewing the authorities:

> The result of these authorities appears to me to be that the court has to consider all the circumstances in which the concurrence of the cestui que trust was given with a view to seeing whether it is fair and equitable that, having given his concurrence, he should afterwards turn round and sue the trustees: that, subject to this, it is not necessary that he should know that what he is concurring in is a breach of trust, provided that he fully understands what he is concurring in, and that it is not necessary that he should himself have directly benefited by the breach of trust.

[119] *Wedderburn v Wedderburn* (1838) 4 My & Cr 41; *Parker v Bloxam* (1855) 20 Beav 295.

[120] See *Bank of Credit and Commerce International SA (in liq) v Ali* [2001] UKHL 8 [2001] 1 All ER 961, HL, noted [2001] JBL 107 (D Sheehan); [2002] MLR 425 (Kay Wheat); *Ramsden v Hylton* (1751) 2 Ves Sen 304; *Lindo v Lindo* (1839) 1 Beav 496.

[121] *Per* Cross J at first instance in *Holder v Holder* [1966] 2 All ER 116, 128. Note the observations of Nicholls J in *John v James* [1991] FSR 397, 459.

[122] [1961] 3 All ER 713. The Court of Appeal expressed no opinion on this point in the same case on appeal in [1964] Ch 303, [1963] 3 All ER 1.   [123] (1887) 37 Ch D 329, CA; *Re Hulkes* (1886) 33 Ch D 552.

[124] Note, however, that the court was, in fact, of opinion that he knew both of his beneficial interest and of the breach of trust.

[125] [1968] Ch 353, [1968] 1 All ER 665, CA; *Re Freeston's Charity* [1979] 1 All ER 51, [1978] 1 WLR 741, CA; *Spellson v George* (1992) 26 NSWLR 666.

[126] *Supra*. See *Gold v Rosenberg* (1995) 129 DLR (4th) 152, appeal dismissed (1998) 35 OR (3d) 736.

[127] At 730. The proposition that it is not necessary that a consenting beneficiary should know that what he is concurring in is a breach of trust may be of a quite narrow as opposed to a general application: note the facts of *Evans v Benyon, supra*, CA. In other circumstances, such lack of knowledge may be a fact relevant to the issue of fairness and equity: see *Spellson v George* (1992) 26 NSWLR 666 , 676, *per* Hope A-JA.

(C) IMPOUNDING THE BENEFICIAL INTEREST OF THE BENEFICIARY

Quite apart from statute, a beneficiary who instigated or requested a trustee to commit a breach of trust could be called upon to indemnify the trustee, in respect of his liability to make good the loss to the trust estate, out of his beneficial interest;[128] where the beneficiary had merely consented to the breach of trust, the trustee had no right to impound his beneficial interest by way of indemnity,[129] unless the beneficiary had obtained a personal benefit from the breach of trust, when the trustee was apparently entitled to an indemnity out of the beneficial interest, although only to the extent of the benefit.[130] The right does not depend on possession of the trust fund, and so will continue in favour of a former trustee where a new trustee is appointed.[131]

The equitable right has been extended by statute, now represented by s 62 of the Trustee Act 1925. Section 62(1)[132] provides as follows:

> Where a trustee commits a breach of trust at the instigation or request or with the consent in writing[133] of a beneficiary, the court may, if it thinks fit, make such order as to the court seems just, for impounding all or any part of the interest of the beneficiary in the trust estate by way of indemnity to the trustee or persons claiming through him.

The statement with regard to the corresponding provision of the 1888 Act applies here[134]— namely, that it 'was intended to enlarge the power of the court as to indemnifying trustees, and to give greater relief to trustees, and was not intended and did not operate to curtail the previously existing rights and remedies of trustees, or to alter the law except by giving greater power to the court'.[135] Although the section gives the court a discretion, it is a judicial discretion, and in any case in which it would have impounded the interest of a beneficiary before the statutory provisions, it will be bound to make a similar order under the Act.[136] Accordingly, the power to impound is not lost, on the one hand, by an assignment, even for value, of the beneficial interest,[137] nor, on the other hand, by the appointment of new trustees.[138]

In order to rely successfully on s 62, the trustee must establish that the beneficiary at least knew the facts that rendered what he was instigating, or requesting, or consenting to, a breach of trust. It is not enough, therefore, to show that the beneficiary pressed for a particular investment if it also appears that he left it to the trustees to determine whether it was a proper one for the moneys proposed to be advanced.[139]

---

[128] *Sawyer v Sawyer* (1885) 28 Ch D 595, CA; *Chillingworth v Chambers* [1896] 1 Ch 685, CA.

[129] *Sawyer v Sawyer, supra; Fletcher v Collis* [1905] 2 Ch 24, CA.

[130] *Booth v Booth* (1838) 1 Beav 125; *Chillingworth v Chambers, supra.*

[131] *Re Pauling's Settlement (No 2)* [1963] Ch 576, [1963] 1 All ER 857.

[132] As amended by the Married Women (Restraint upon Anticipation) Act 1949, s 1(4) and Sch 2.

[133] The words 'in writing' apply only to consent and not to instigation or request: *Griffith v Hughes* [1892] 3 Ch 105; *Re Somerset* [1894] 1 Ch 231, CA.

[134] *Re Pauling's Settlement (No 2), supra.*

[135] *Bolton v Curre* [1895] 1 Ch 544, 549, *per* Romer J; *Fletcher v Collis* [1905] 2 Ch 24, CA.

[136] *Re Somerset* [1894] 1 Ch 231, CA; *Bolton v Curre, supra.*   [137] *Bolton v Curre, supra.*

[138] *Re Pauling's Settlement (No 2), supra.*

[139] *Re Somerset* [1894] 1 Ch 231, CA; *Mara v Browne* [1895] 2 Ch 69, revsd, but not on this point [1896] 1 Ch 199, CA.

It should also be observed that, again apart from statute, it has always been the practice of the court when administering the estate of a deceased person or a trust, 'in cases where trustees have under an honest mistake overpaid one beneficiary, in the adjustment of the accounts between the trustees and the cestui que trust, to make allowance for the mistake in order that the trustee may so far as possible be recouped the money which he has inadvisedly paid'.[140] The overpaid beneficiary will not, however, be compelled to refund the overpayment, but further payments will be withheld until the accounts have been put straight.[141] Exceptionally, it has been held that a trustee-beneficiary who has overpaid the other beneficiaries and underpaid himself is not allowed to correct his mistake,[142] although it is obviously different where he has overpaid himself.[143] Further, this principle only applies to trusts and estates, and not, for instance, to overpayments made under a covenant.[144]

(D) LIMITATION

The rules as to the limitation of actions against trustees are set out in s 21 of the Limitation Act 1980. There may be applied to the relevant provisions of the Act the remarks of Kekewich J in *Re Timmis*[145] on the corresponding provisions in the earlier legislation:

> The intention of the statute was to give a trustee the benefit of the lapse of time when, although he had done something legally or technically wrong, he had done nothing morally wrong or dishonest, but it was not intended to protect him where, if he pleaded the statute, he would come off with something he ought not to have, that is, money of the trust received by him and converted to his own use.

(i) Situations where there is no period of limitation

Somewhat curiously, s 21 begins by laying down the circumstances in which a trustee cannot rely upon the Act—that is, where he remains liable indefinitely. Subsection (1) provides as follows:

> No period of limitation prescribed by this Act shall apply to an action by a beneficiary under a trust, being an action—
>
> (a) in respect of any fraud or fraudulent breach of trust to which the trustee was a party or privy; or
>
> (b) to recover from the trustee trust property or the proceeds of trust property in the possession of the trustee, or previously received by the trustee and converted to his use.

(ii) Construction of sub-s (1)(a)

Subsection (1)(a) has been held to be limited to cases of fraud or fraudulent breach of trust properly so called—that is, to cases involving dishonesty.[146] Further, Lord Davey

---

[140] *Per* Neville J in *Re Musgrave* [1916] 2 Ch 417, 423; *Re Robinson* [1911] 1 Ch 502; *Re Ainsworth* [1915] 2 Ch 96.

[141] *Downes v Bullock* (1858) 25 Beav 54; affd sub nom *Bullock v Downes* (1860) 9 HL Cas 1; *Bate v Hooper* (1855) 5 De GM & G 338; *Burns & Geroff v Leda Holdings Pty Ltd* [1988] 1 Qd R 214, but cf *Hood v Clapham* (1854) 19 Beav 90.

[142] *Re Horne* [1905] 1 Ch 76, but see *Re Reading* [1916] WN 262.   [143] *Re Reading, supra.*

[144] *Re Hatch* [1919] 1 Ch 351.   [145] [1902] 1 Ch 176, 186.

[146] *Armitage v Nurse* [1998] Ch 241, [1997] 2 All ER 705, CA: *Gwembe Valley Development Co Ltd (in receivership) v Koshy (No 3)* [2003] EWCA Civ 1048, [2004] 1 BCLC 131, in which it was held that the subsection

observed,[147] on similar words in the 1888 Act, that 'if fraud, or a non-discovery of fraud, is to be relied on to take a case out of the Statute of Limitations, it must be the fraud of or in some way imputable to the person who invokes the aid of the Statute of Limitations'.

(iii) Construction of subs (1)(b)

As regards possession, or receipt and conversion to the trustee's use, under subs 1(b), the slight change in the wording from the 1888 Act probably does not alter the substance.[148] Accordingly, on the one hand, the subsection applied, and the trustees were unable to rely on the defence of limitation where they paid themselves annuities, by mistake without deduction of tax;[149] likewise where a trustee remained in occupation of trust property for his own purposes,[150] and where a company director, through an abuse of the trust and confidence reposed in him as a director, had taken a transfer of the company's property to himself.[151] In *James v Williams*,[152] an executor *de son tort* who, knowing that he was not solely entitled, took possession of property and acted as if it belonged to him was held to be a constructive trustee, and thus within s 21(1) and unprotected. This decision has been much criticized[153] as taking no account of *Paragon Finance plc v D B Thakerar & Co (a firm)*.[154] On the other hand, the subsection was held not to apply, and the trustees thus able to rely on the Act, where, for instance, the trustee had used the trust funds in the maintenance of an infant beneficiary,[155] where the trust funds had been lost,[156] and where the trust funds had been lent on mortgage and the mortgagor used the moneys to pay off a debt to a bank in which one of the trustees was a partner.[157]

(iv) Limited protection to trustees

It is clear that subs 1(b) prevents a trustee, however honest, from putting forward a defence on the ground of limitation in respect of a claim to recover trust property (or its proceeds) in his hands, although he may sometimes, as we shall see, be able to rely on the equitable

---

applies to a company director who dishonestly makes an unauthorized profit in breach of his fiduciary duty. Cf *Woodland-Ferrari v UCL Group Retirement Benefits Scheme* [2002] 3 All ER 670, [2002] 3 WLR 1154.

[147] *Thorne v Heard* [1895] AC 495, HL, and see *G L Baker Ltd v Medway Building and Supplies Ltd* [1958] 2 All ER 532, order discharged on another ground [1958] 3 All ER 540, CA.

[148] *Re Howlett* [1949] Ch 767, [1949] 2 All ER 490. On a corresponding provision in Tasmania, it was held, in *Stilbo Property Ltd v MCC Property Ltd (in liq)* (2002) 11 Tas R 63, that it covers claims for income or profit derived from trust property whenever received.

[149] *Re Sharp* [1906] 1 Ch 793. See *Nelson v Rye* [1996] 2 All ER 186, [1996] 1 WLR 1378, noted [1997] Conv 225 (J Stevens). Millett LJ pointed out in *Paragon Finance plc v D B Thakerer & Co (a firm)* [1999] 1 All ER 400, CA, that although the manager was a fiduciary, there was no trust as there was no obligation on him to keep the alleged trust property separate from his own.

[150] *Re Howlett, supra* (held chargeable with an occupation rent).

[151] *J J Harrison (Properties) Ltd v Harrison* [2001] EWCA Civ 1467, [2002] 1 BCLC 162 (liable for profits on a resale). See also *Re Pantone 485 Ltd* [2002] 1 BCLC 266.

[152] [2001] Ch 1, [1999] 3 All ER 309, CA. Cf *Gwembe Valley Development Co Ltd (in receivership) v Kosby (No 3)* [2003] EWCA Civ 1048, [2004] 1 BCLC 131.

[153] Underhill and Hayton, *Law of Trusts and Trustees*, 17th edn, [33.16], [96.9], and [100.4]; Lewin, *Law of Trusts*, 17th edn, pp 44–38; *Nolan v Nolan* [2004] VSCA 109, [2004] WTLR 1261 (Australia).

[154] *Supra*, CA.

[155] *Re Page* [1893] 1 Ch 304; *Re Timmis* [1902] 1 Ch 176.

[156] *Re Tufnell* (1902) 18 TLR 705; *Re Fountaine* [1909] 2 Ch 382, CA.

[157] *Re Gurney* [1893] 1 Ch 590.

doctrines of laches and acquiescence.[158] Exceptionally, some protection is now[159] given to a trustee who acts honestly and reasonably[160] in distributing the trust property among all those whom he believes to constitute the class of beneficiaries entitled to it, including himself. A latecomer who has a claim to a share in the distributed estate, but whose claim is barred by the Limitation Act as regards the other beneficiaries, used to be able to claim the whole of his share from a trustee-beneficiary up to the amount that the trustee had paid himself. Now, such a trustee will be liable only in respect of the share that he would have had to pay to the latecomer had all of the beneficiaries, including himself, been sued in time. Thus, if the trustee had distributed one third of the trust property to himself and one third to each of two other beneficiaries in ignorance of the existence of a fourth, he is liable to pay the newcomer only the difference between the one-third share that he has taken and the one-quarter share that is truly his.

(v) The basic limitation provision

Subject to s 21(1) discussed above, s 21(3) provides that no action by a beneficiary to recover trust property or in respect of any breach of trust[161] shall be brought after the expiration of six years from the date on which the right of action accrued. It has no application, however, to claims by the Attorney-General to enforce public charitable trusts.[162]

An action by a beneficiary includes, at least by analogy, an action brought exclusively on his behalf by trustees who have no personal interest in the outcome.[163]

(vi) Extension of limitation period

The general provisions as to the extension of the period of limitation by reason of disability,[164] fraud, deliberate concealment, and mistake[165] apply to actions against trustees. 'Fraud' is here used in the equitable sense to denote conduct by the defendant or his agent such that it would be against conscience for him to avail himself of the lapse of time.[166] Further, the periods of limitation may be extended, in appropriate cases, under the provisions of the Limitation (Enemies and War Prisoners) Act 1945.

(vii) Running of time

Where s 21(3) applies, time runs from the date of the breach of trust, not from the time at which the loss accrued,[167] for instance, where trustees pay annuities to other persons, by mistake not deducting tax,[168] where they fail to convert in accordance with the directions

---

158 See p 534, *infra*.   159 Limitation Act 1980, s 21(2).
160 Cf Trustee Act 1925, s 61, discussed p 535, *infra*.
161 See *Tito v Waddell (No 2)* [1977] Ch 106, [1977] 3 All ER 129, and pp 448, 520, *supra*.
162 *A-G v Cocke* [1988] Ch 414, [1988] 2 All ER 391, noted [1988] Conv 292 (Jean Warburton).
163 *Cattley v Pollard* [2006] EWHC 3130 (Ch), [2007] 2 All ER 1086, noted [2007] PCB 213 (Kerry Bornman).
164 Section 28.
165 Section 32, as amended; *Cattley v Pollard* [2006] EWHC 3130 (Ch), [2007] 2 All ER 1086. As to deliberate concealment, see *Cave v Robinson Jarvis & Rolf (a firm)* [2002] UKHL 18, [2003] 1 AC 384, [2002] 2 All ER 641; *Williams v Fanshaw Porter & Hazelhurst (a firm)* [2004] EWCA Civ 157, [2004] 2 All ER 616. See also *Davies v Sharples* [2006] EWHC 362 (Ch), [2006] WTLR 839.
166 *Bartlett v Barclays Bank Trust Co Ltd* [1980] Ch 515, [1980] 1 All ER 139.
167 *Re Somerset* [1894] 1 Ch 231, CA; *Want v Campain* (1893) 9 TLR 254.
168 *Re Sharp* [1906] 1 Ch 793.

of the trust instrument,[169] or where they invest on insufficient security.[170] By a proviso to this subsection, however, the right of action is not to be deemed to have accrued to any beneficiary entitled to future interest in the trust property until the interest falls into possession. It has accordingly been held that, where a person has two separate interests in property, one in possession and one reversionary, he will not be barred as to the latter merely because he is barred as to the former.[171]

(viii) Parasitic claim

Section 21(4) provides that no beneficiary whose own claim has been barred can derive any benefit from a judgment or order obtained by any other beneficiary. Thus, if a trust fund is lost and the claim of the tenant for life is barred, the trustees, if compelled to replace the trust fund by the remainderman, will be personally entitled to the income so long as the life interest subsists.[172]

(ix) To whom the Act applies

The Act applies to trustees as defined in the Trustee Act 1925, and, accordingly, includes trustees holding on implied and constructive trusts, and personal representatives.[173]

The position in relation to constructive trusts, however, is not straightforward. The matter was most recently considered by Richard Sheldon QC[174] in *Cattley v Pollard*,[175] citing, inter alia, *Paragon Finance plc v D B Thakerar & Co (a firm)*,[176] from which it is clear that, for limitation purposes, a distinction has to be drawn between the two distinct categories of constructive trust discussed earlier.[177]

The first category, it will be remembered, is where the constructive trustee, although not expressly appointed as a trustee, has assumed the duties of a trustee before the events that are alleged to constitute the breach of trust. A case in this category is, or is treated by analogy as, an action by a beneficiary for breach of trust falling within s 21(1)(a), under which subsection there is no limitation period.

The second category of constructive trust is where the trust obligation arises as a direct consequence of the unlawful transaction impeached by the claimant. As explained by Millett LJ in the *Paragon* case, in such case, the defendant is not, in fact, a trustee, although he is liable to account as if he were. Section 21(1)(a) does not apply to a case in this category that is accordingly subject to the six-year limitation period under s 21(3). Section 21(1)(a)

---

[169] *Re Swain* [1891] 3 Ch 233.

[170] *Re Bowden* (1890) 45 Ch D 444; *Re Somerset, supra*, and see *How v Earl of Winterton* [1896] 2 Ch 626, CA (failure to accumulate); *Re Tufnell* (1902) 18 TLR 705 and *Re Fountaine* [1909] 2 Ch 382, CA (allowing co-trustee, a solicitor, to receive trust moneys).

[171] *Mara v Browne* [1895] 2 Ch 69, revsd, but not on this point [1896] 1 Ch 199, CA. As to a discretionary beneficiary, see *Armitage v Nurse* [1998] Ch 24, CA; *Johns v Johns &Anor* [2004] NZCA 42, [2005] WTLR 529.

[172] *Re Somerset, supra*.   [173] Limitation Act 1980, s 38(1); Trustee Act 1925, s 68(17).

[174] Sitting as a deputy judge of the High Court.

[175] [2006] EWHC 3130 (Ch), [2007] 2 All ER 1086.

[176] [1999] 1 All ER 400, CA. See also *Coulthard v Disco Mix Club Ltd* [1999] 2 All ER 457; *Gwembe Valley Development Co Ltd (in receivership) v Koshy (No 3)* [2003] EWCA Civ 1048, [2004] 1 BCLC 131 (dishonest fiduciary liable to account for all profits whether received directly or indirectly), noted (2004) 60 T & ELJ 7 (A Thompson).

[177] See p 66 *et seq, supra*, (2005) 71 T & ELTJ 26 (N Caddick) and [2008] Conv 226 (C Mitchell). See also *Halton International Inc v Guernroy Ltd* [2006] EWCA Civ 801, [2006] WTLR 1241, noted (2007) 83 T & ELTJ 8 (T Oakley).

applies only to claims against express trustees or persons treated as express trustees, even though not appointed as such. In particular, it does not apply to persons who have dishonestly and knowingly assisted in a fraudulent breach of trust.[178]

(x) Action for breach of fiduciary duty

An action for breach of fiduciary duty *simpliciter* has been said to be outside the provisions of the Act and therefore not subject to a period of limitation.[179] However, the same distinction has to be drawn as that in relation to trustees between those whose fiduciary obligations preceded the acts complained of and those whose liability in equity was occasioned by the acts of which complaint was made.[180] It is clear that it is not possible, either in a case in which a breach of fiduciary duty gives rise to a constructive trust, or in an action for breach of an express trust, to avoid any limitation period imposed by the Act by treating the case as one of breach of fiduciary duty.[181] Further, the court will apply the statute by analogy where there is a 'correspondence' between the remedies available at law and in equity. Thus, no distinction in point of limitation is to be made between an action for damages for fraud at common law and its counterpart in equity based on the same facts.[182]

(xi) Action for an account

A claim to an account in equity, absent any trust, has no equitable element; it is based on legal, not equitable, rights and the Act will apply.[183] Accordingly, an action for an account brought by a principal against his agent is barred by the statutes of limitation unless the agent is more than a mere agent and is a trustee of the money that he received.[184] It may be added that, where an account is sought as ancillary to another claim, the period of limitation, if any, appropriate to the main claim would also be applied to the ancillary one.[185]

(xii) Actions claiming personal estate of a deceased person

Section 22(a), which applies to an action in respect of any claim to the personal estate of a deceased person or to any share or interest in any such estate (whether under a will or on intestacy), lays down a twelve-year limitation period from the date on which the right to receive the share or interest accrued. In *Re Loftus (decd)*,[186] it was explained that the section does not apply to claims against a personal representative in respect of real estate that remains unsold, or to claims in respect of personal estate at a time when the estate remains unadministered in the sense that the costs, funeral, testamentary, and administration

---

[178] *Cattley v Pollard, supra.*

[179] *A-G v Cocke, supra; Nelson v Rye* [1996] 2 All ER 186, [1996] 1 WLR 1378.

[180] *Paragon Finance plc v D B Thakerar & Co (a firm), supra,* CA.   [181] *Nelson v Rye, supra.*

[182] *Knox v Gye* (1872) LR 5 HL 656, HL; *Paragon Finance plc v D B Thakerar & Co (a firm), supra,* CA; *Coulthard v Disco Mix Club Ltd* [1999] 2 All ER 457, [2000] 1 WLR 707; *Johns v Johns & Anor, supra.* See also *Companhia de Seguros Imperio v Heath (REBX) Ltd* [2001] 1 WLR 112; (2001) 20 CJQ 171 (A McGee and G Scanlon).

[183] *How v Earl Winterton* [1896] 2 Ch 626, 639 per Lindley LJ; *Paragon Finance plc v D B Thakerar & Co (a firm)* [1999] 1 All ER 400, CA.

[184] *Burdick v Garrick* (1870) LR 5 Ch App 233; *Paragon Finance plc v D B Thakerar & Co (a firm), supra,* CA, disapproving *Nelson v Rye, supra.*

[185] *Tito v Waddell (No 2)* [1977] Ch 106, 250–252, [1977] 3 All ER 129, 248–250.

[186] [2006] EWCA Civ 1124, [2006] 4 All ER 1110, [2007] 1 WLR 591. See the discussion of the first instance decision in [2006] Conv 245 (T Prime).

expenses, debts, and other liabilities properly payable thereout have not been paid and any pecuniary legacies provided for. Where the section does apply, the better view has been said to be that time will not begin to run until administration, in that sense, has been completed.[187]

The section is expressly subject to s 21(1) and (2) discussed above. Further, it has no application to cases of trusts created by a will once the administration of the estate is complete and the personal representatives continue in office as trustees.[188] Nor does the section apply to proceedings to remove a personal representative and appoint a substitute.[189]

(xiii) Law Commission Report No 270[190]

The draft Bill appended to this report provides for a core regime, which would extend to claims for breach of trust and related claims, including claims in respect of the personal estate of a deceased person. It lays down a primary limitation period of three years from the time when the claimant knew, or ought reasonably to have known, that he had a cause of action, a period that the court would have no discretion to disapply. There would be a long-stop limitation period of ten years, starting from the date of the accrual of the cause of action. The present law in relation to future interests and to parasitic claims would be substantially continued,[191] and a cause of action to recover property held on a bare trust would not accrue unless and until the trustee acted in breach of trust.

The primary limitation would not run during the claimant's minority; the long-stop period, however, would, but not so as to bar an action before the claimant reached the age of twenty-one. Adult disability (including supervening disability) would suspend the primary limitation period, but not the long-stop period. However, the long-stop period would not run where the defendant had dishonestly concealed relevant facts.

Neither limitation period would apply to a claim for breach of trust or to recover trust property brought by the Attorney-General or the Charity Commission in relation to a charity.

(E) LACHES

Where, under s 21(1)(a) or (b), there is no statutory period of limitation, the question arises whether it can be barred by the plaintiff's delay in bringing the action—that is, by laches, in the narrow sense.[192] It has been held that these provisions do not exclude a defence of laches or acquiescence.[193] In practice, lapse of time is commonly pleaded together with acquiescence, which indeed, on one view,[194] is included in the scope of the word 'laches'

---

[187] *Re Loftus (decd), supra*, CA, at [30].

[188] *Davies v Sharples* [2006] EWHC 362 (Ch), [2006] WTLR 839.

[189] *Re Loftus (decd), supra*, CA.

[190] The report was accepted in principle by the government in July 2002, but in October 2007, the Ministry of Justice announced that it intended to consult further on the text of the Bill. It is discussed in [2003] CJQ 41 (R James).

[191] See sections 3(D)(vii) and (viii), pp 531, 532 *supra*.

[192] See Brunyate, *Limitation of Actions*, pp 188–189; *Orr v Ford* (1989) 167 CLR 316, 335–346, *per* Deane J. See also (1992) 22 VUWLR 51 (L Trevelyan).

[193] *Re Loftus (decd)* [2006] EWCA Civ 1124, [2006] 4 All ER 1110 (defence rejected on the facts).

[194] Another view is that it is simply evidence of acquiescence: *Morse v Royal* (1806) 12 Ves 355; *Life Association of Scotland v Siddal* (1861) 3 De GF & J 58.

in the wide sense. Mere delay by itself will never,[195] or almost never,[196] bar the plaintiff, but the court has to look at all of the circumstances—in particular, the period of delay, the extent to which the defendant's position has been prejudiced by the delay, and the extent to which that prejudice was caused by the actions of the plaintiff—and then decide whether the balance of justice or injustice is in favour of granting the remedy or withholding it. It is not necessary to show a causal link between the delay and the prejudice, but the plaintiff's knowledge that the delay will cause prejudice is a factor to be taken into account.[197]

It has recently been made clear that the modern approach to laches or acquiescence does not require an exhaustive inquiry into whether the circumstances could fit within the principles established in previous cases. A broader approach should be adopted—namely whether it is unconscionable for the party concerned to be permitted to assert his beneficial rights.[198]

The Law Commission recommends that nothing in the proposed new Limitation Act should be taken to prejudice any equitable jurisdiction of the court to refuse an application for equitable relief (whether final or interlocutory) on the grounds of delay (or because of any other equitable defence, such as acquiescence) even though the limitation period applicable to the claim in question has not expired.

(F) SECTION 61 OF THE TRUSTEE ACT 1925[199]

This section provides:

> If it appears to the court that a trustee...is or may be personally liable for any breach of trust...but has acted honestly and reasonably, and ought fairly to be excused for the breach of trust and for omitting to obtain the directions of the court in the matter in which he committed such breach, then the court may relieve him either wholly or partly from personal liability for the same.

'The provisions of the section,' it has been said,[200] 'were intended to enable the court to excuse breaches of trust where the circumstances of the particular case showed reasonable conduct, but it was never meant to be used as a sort of general indemnity clause for honest men who neglect their duty.' The onus of showing that he acted not only honestly, but also reasonably, rests on the trustee[201] and, unless both of these matters are established, 'the

---

[195] *Rochefoucauld v Boustead* [1897] 1 Ch 196, CA; *Re Lacey* [1907] 1 Ch 330, CA. Cf *Re Sharpe* [1892] 1 Ch 154, 168, CA, *per* Lindley LJ.

[196] *Nelson v Rye* [1996] 2 All ER 186, 201 [1996] 1 WLR 1378, 1392, *per* Laddie J.

[197] *Nelson v Rye, supra; Lindsay Petroleum Co v Hurd* (1874) LR 5 PC 221 (in which there is an important statement of the doctrine); *Erlanger v New Sombrero Phosphate Co* (1878) 3 App Cas 1218, HL; *John v James* [1991] FSR 397. See also *Baburin v Baburin (No 2)* [1991] 2 Qd R 240.

[198] *Frawley v Neill* (1999) 143 Sol Jo LB 98, CA, noted (2000) 13 T & ELJ 19 (C Taylor); As to the application of the doctrine of laches in a commercial setting, see *Patel v Shah* [2005] EWCA Civ 157, [2005] WTLR 359, noted [2005] Conv 174 (G Watt) and (2005) 63 T & ELTJ 18 (J Davey).

[199] Re-enacting, with slight alterations, Judicial Trustees Act 1896, s 3, decisions on which are usually applicable to s 61. The section need not be specially pleaded: *Singlehurst v Tapscott Steamship Co* [1899] WN 133, CA; although it is better that it should be. In relation to a charitable corporation, see *Re Freeston's Charity* [1978] 1 All ER 481; affd [1979] 1 All ER 51, [1978] 1 WLR 741, CA. Cf Companies Act 2006, s 1157 and *Coleman Taymar Ltd v Oakes* [2001] 2 BCLC 749. See generally (1955) 19 Conv 420 (L A Sheridan).

[200] *Williams v Byron* (1901) 18 TLR 172, 176, *per* Byrne J.

[201] *Re Stuart* [1897] 2 Ch 583.

court cannot help the trustees; but if both are made out, there is then a case for the court to consider whether the trustee ought fairly to be excused for the breach, looking at all the circumstances'.[202] By 'fairly' is meant in fairness to the trustee and to other people who may be affected.[203] Although the court has refused to fetter its discretion and insists that each case must be dealt with according to its own circumstances,[204] it is helpful to look at some of the decisions—particularly on the question of reasonableness. Before doing so, it may be observed that the courts have said that the section should not be narrowly construed.[205] It can even be applied to cases in which a trustee has paid the wrong person,[206] and the maxim *ignorantia juris non excusat* does not in the least prevent the court from granting relief.[207] There must, however, have been a breach of trust—the section cannot be used to excuse trustees from a breach of trust that they wish to commit in the future.[208] On another point, it seems clear that the court will be much less ready to grant relief to a professional trustee who is being paid for his services in performing his duties.[209]

Turning to the cases, in *Re Stuart*,[210] the court said that it was fair to consider whether the trustee would have acted in the same way if he had been dealing with his own property. If he would, it is a point in his favour, although not enough by itself to show that he acted reasonably.[211] The taking and acceptance of advice by someone reasonably believed to be qualified to give it has a similar effect.[212] In *Chapman v Browne*,[213] the trustees were held not to have acted reasonably where they never really considered whether the security was one that it was right and proper for a trustee to take, and in *Wynne v Tempest*,[214] the court refused relief where a trustee had left the trust money in the hands of his co-trustee, a solicitor, without sufficient reason. Indeed, Kekewich J regarded it not merely as a failure to act reasonably, but as dishonest in this context, where a trustee 'does nothing, swallows wholesale what is said by his co-trustee, never asks for explanation, and accepts flimsy explanations'.[215]

A further illustration of refusal of relief by the court is *Ward-Smith v Jebb*,[216] in which the court would assist neither a solicitor trustee nor his lay co-trustee, who had made payments out of a trust fund on the erroneous assumption that a certain person was entitled by reason of the Adoption of Children Act 1949, having failed to observe the

---

[202] *Per* Sir Ford North, giving the advice of PC in *National Trustees Co of Australasia v General Finance Co of Australasia* [1905] AC 373, 381, on the corresponding provision of the Victorian Trusts Act 1901; *Re Turner* [1897] 1 Ch 536.

[203] *Marsden v Regan* [1954] 1 All ER 475, [1954] 1 WLR 423, CA. The above passage was cited and applied by Coleman J in *Canadian Imperial Bank of Commerce v Valley Credit Union Ltd* (1989) 56 Man R (2d) 50, 65.

[204] *Re Turner, supra; Re Kay* [1897] 2 Ch 518.   [205] *Re Allsop* [1914] 1 Ch 1, CA.

[206] *Re Allsop, supra; Re Wightwick's Will Trusts* [1950] Ch 260, [1950] 1 All ER 689. But see *Ward-Smith v Jebb* (1964) 108 Sol Jo 919, discussed *infra*.

[207] *Holland v Administrator of German Property* [1937] 2 All ER 807, CA.

[208] *Re Rosenthal* [1972] 3 All ER 552, [1972] 1 WLR 1273.

[209] *National Trustees Co of Australasia v General Finance Co of Australasia* [1905] AC 373, PC; *Re Windsor Steam Coal Co (1901) Ltd* [1929] 1 Ch 151, CA; *Re Pauling's Settlement Trusts* [1964] Ch 303, [1963] 3 All ER 1, CA.

[210] [1897] 2 Ch 583; *Re Barker* (1898) 77 LT 712.

[211] *Per* Farwell J in *Re Lord De Clifford's Estate* [1900] 2 Ch 707, 716: '*The fact that he has acted with equal foolishness in both cases will not justify relief under this statute.*'

[212] *Marsden v Regan* [1954] 1 All ER 475, CA.   [213] [1902] 1 Ch 785, CA.

[214] (1897) 13 TLR 360; *Re Second East Dulwich etc Building Society* (1899) 68 LJ Ch 196.

[215] *Re Second East Dulwich etc Building Society, supra*, at 198.   [216] (1964) 108 Sol Jo 919.

provisions of the Act, which made it quite clear that it did not apply on the facts of the case. Accepting the general rule that a trustee must exercise that degree of care that a prudent man would exercise in respect of his own affairs, Buckley J applied it to the facts before him by saying:[217] 'A prudent man, whose affairs were affected by a statute would either satisfy himself that he fully understood its effect or would seek legal advice. A solicitor trustee could not be heard to say that it was reasonable to apply a lower standard to him.' The lay trustee was in no better position, in the absence of any evidence that he had relied on the advice of the solicitor or any other legal adviser. The question of any indemnity between the two trustees was not before the court. Finally, as is expressly provided by the section, the court may relieve the trustee either wholly, or to a limited extent, as it did in *Re Evans (decd)*.[218]

On the other hand, in *Re Lord De Clifford's Estate*,[219] executors were relieved where, during five years' administration of the estate and knowing that large sums were required for administration purposes, they paid various sums to their solicitors in reliance on their statements that they were required for those purposes. Over 90 per cent of the sums were, in fact, so applied, but the balance was lost on the solicitors' bankruptcy; similarly, where executors failed to call in a small debt, where the terms of the will might fairly bring a businessman to the conclusion there was no duty to do so.[220] According to the circumstances, it may[221] or may not be reasonable to act without seeking the directions of the court.

(G) DISCHARGE IN BANKRUPTCY

A claim in respect of a breach of trust is provable in bankruptcy[222] and in general, an order of discharge releases a bankrupt from all of the bankruptcy debts.[223] This provision applies to all claims in respect of a breach of trust, except where the debt was incurred in respect of any fraud or fraudulent breach of trust to which the bankrupt trustee was a party.[224] Although, as stated, in the case of a non-fraudulent breach of trust, the discharge bars the right to the original debt due from the trustee, his duties, character, and functions as debtor are perfectly distinct from those that belong to him as trustee, and those of the trustee are not affected by the bankruptcy. Accordingly, it is the duty of defaulting trustee to prove in his own bankruptcy just as much as if he were a perfect stranger to it, and it is a clear breach of trust for him to fail to do so. This further breach of trust subsequently attaching to the trustee in that character is unaffected by the discharge and the trustee accordingly remains liable for it, to the amount of the dividends that he would have received under the bankruptcy.[225]

---

[217] Ibid.

[218] [1999] 2 All ER 777 (claimant and defendant entitled equally to intestate's estate; defendant, sole administratrix, wrongfully distributed estate in belief that the claimant had long predeceased the intestate; defendant relieved against the claim of the underpaid claimant to the extent that it could not be satisfied out of a property derived from the intestate's estate, which was still at her disposal).

[219] [1900] 2 Ch 707; *Perrins v Bellamy* [1899] 1 Ch 797, CA.

[220] *Re Grindey* [1898] 2 Ch 593, CA; *Re Mackay* [1911] 1 Ch 300.

[221] *Re Gee* [1948] Ch 284, [1948] 1 All ER 498.

[222] Insolvency Act 1986, s 382(1), (3), and (4), amended from a date to be appointed by the Criminal Justice Act 1988, s 170, Sch 16, by the repeal of subs 1(c).

[223] Ibid, s 281(1).   [224] Ibid, s 281(3). See *Mander v Evans* [2001] 3 All ER 811.

[225] *Orrett v Corser* (1855) 21 Beav 52.

4 CRIMINAL LIABILITY OF TRUSTEES[226]

Under the Theft Act 1968, a trustee is liable for theft '*if he dishonestly appropriates prop-erty belonging to another with the intention of permanently depriving the other of it*'.[227] For the purposes of the Act, in the case of trust property, the persons to whom it belongs are to be regarded as including '*any person having a right to enforce the trust*'[228]—that is, the beneficiaries (including, it is thought, potential beneficiaries under a discretionary trust) or, in the case of a charitable trust, the Attorney-General. In the case of unenforceable trusts, it would presumably include the person entitled to the residue, from which it would follow that it would not be theft if the trustee were himself solely entitled to the residue.[229] Although, in general, a person cannot steal land, a trustee can and will do so if '*he appro-priates the land or anything forming part of it by dealing with it in breach of the confidence reposed in him*'.[230]

Mention may be made of the difficult decision in *A-G's Reference (No 1 of 1985)*,[231] in which the court seemed anxious lest the imposition of a constructive trust might bring within the Theft Act 1968 '*a host of activities which no layman would think were stealing*'. The facts were that the salaried manager of a tied public house was under contract to sell on his employer's premises only goods supplied by his employer and to pay all of the takings into his employer's account. He bought beer elsewhere and sold it to customers in the public house, making a secret profit, of which he was held not to be a constructive trustee.[232] It was held that there was no difference in principle between the facts of this case and a bribe, and, at that time, it was generally assumed that a fiduciary was not a constructive trustee of a bribe he received. In the light of *A-G for Hong Kong v Reid*,[233] it seems unlikely that this assumption is valid, and this casts doubt on this ground of the decision in *A-G's Reference (No 1 of 1985)*.[234] A further ground for the decision seems very doubtful. It was said that there could be no trust until the profit is identifiable as a separate piece of property. Equity, however, has never found any difficulty in relation to mixed funds.[235] The actual decision may perhaps be supported on the basis of absence of *mens rea*: the manager clearly knew that he was breaking the terms of his contract, but the idea that he might be stealing from his employers the profit element in the transactions may well never have occurred to him.

Finally, it may be mentioned that, under the Debtors Act 1869, s 4, a trustee who has been ordered by the court to pay any sum in his possession or under his control is, on default, liable to imprisonment for a period of up to a year.

---

[226] See (1975) 39 Conv 29 (R Brazier).
[227] Theft Act 1968, s 1(1). As to 'borrowing' trust funds, see (1985) 5 LS 183 (G Williams). See also *Re Wain* (1993) unreported, but noted (1994) 2 Dec Ch Com 34.
[228] Theft Act 1968, s 5(2).
[229] Nor, of course, would the trustee in such case be liable for breach of trust.
[230] Theft Act 1968, s 4(2)(a).   [231] [1986] QB 491, [1986] 2 All ER 219, CA.
[232] Disregarding the use by the manager of his employer's property.
[233] [1994] 1 AC 324, [1994] 1 All ER 1, PC. See pp 149–150, *supra*.
[234] *Supra*, CA.   [235] See pp 546 *et seq*, *infra*.

24

FOLLOWING AND TRACING

It may be helpful to begin by giving an illustration of the sorts of circumstances that may call for following or tracing. Suppose a trustee (T), now bankrupt so that any remedy against him would be inadequate, in breach of trust had transferred an asset of the trust to X, who has transferred it to Y. The beneficiaries (B) can *follow* the asset through X into the hands of Y, assert their equitable title, and call on Y to restore the asset to the trust. B will normally succeed in their claim unless Y can show that either he or X was a bona fide purchaser for value of the asset without notice of the trust.

Suppose, further, that X and Y are volunteers, and that Y has sold the asset to Z, a bona fide purchaser for value without notice, and used the proceeds of sale to purchase another asset. B can no longer *follow* the original asset, but they can *trace* it into the substituted asset held by Y.

Alternatively, suppose that X was a purchaser for value without notice of the trust and had given T a cheque for its full value, which he paid into a new account in his own name. Suppose, further, that the account has been exhausted in the purchase by T of shares in his own name, which he continues to hold. B can *trace* the original asset into the account and out of the account into the shares.

This illustration adopts the new approach that appears to have been established by Lord Millett in *Foskett v McKeown*.[1] He said, in relation to beneficiaries under a trust, that following and tracing:

> ...are both exercises in locating assets which are or may be taken to represent an asset belonging to the [claimants] and to which they assert ownership. The processes of following and tracing are, however distinct. Following is the process of following the same asset as it moves from hand to hand. Tracing is the process of identifying a new asset as the substitute for the old.

It enables the claimant to substitute the traceable proceeds for the original asset as the subject matter of his claim. Although there are undoubtedly two different processes, the distinction has by no means always been made in this way, and the past language of judges and academics must be looked at with care. Unfortunately, Lord Millett did not explain

---

[1] [2001] 1 AC 102, [2000] 3 All ER 97, HL noted [2001] Conv 94 (J Stevens); [2000] 63 MLR 905 (R Grantham and C Rickett); (2000) 14 Tru LI 194 (P Jaffey); [2001] LMCLQ 1 (D Fox); [2001] NZLJ 276 (C Cato and M Connell); [2003] RLR 56 (C Rotherham); (2001) 117 LQR 366 (A Berg). Lord Millet's opinion set out above was not expressly referred to by any of the other Law Lords. Lord Browne-Wilkinson and Lord Hoffman can, perhaps, be taken to have implicitly agreed, and neither Lord Steyn nor Lord Hope expressed dissent. See also (2001) 117 LQR 412 (A Burrows); [2001] CLP 231 (P Birks); [2002] CLP 262 (P Jaffey); *Ultraframe (UK) Ltd v Fielding* [2005] EWHC 1638 (Ch), [2006] WTLR 835.

the change of approach from that he had previously expressed, extrajudicially,[2] that it is
'...necessary to distinguish between two kinds of tracing: (i) following the same asset from
one person to another; and (ii) following an asset into a changed form in the same hands'.
The change is one of classification and terminology, rather than of substance. The matter is
complicated by the fact that one set of facts may well involve both following and tracing.

Lord Millett explained the law of tracing as follows:

> The transmission of a claimant's property rights from one asset to its traceable proceeds is
> part of our law of property, not of the law of unjust enrichment. There is no 'unjust factor'
> to justify restitution (unless 'want of title' be one, which makes the point). The claimant
> succeeds if at all by virtue of his own title, not to reverse unjust enrichment. Property
> rights are determined by fixed rules and settled principles. They are not discretionary.
> They do not depend upon ideas of what is 'fair, just and reasonable'. Such concepts, which
> in reality mask decisions of legal policy, have no place in the law of property.[3]
>
> A beneficiary of a trust is entitled to a continuing beneficial interest not merely in the trust
> property but in its traceable proceeds also, and his interest binds everyone who takes the
> property or its traceable proceeds except a bona fide purchaser for value without notice.

Lord Millett further stated that tracing is neither a claim nor a remedy.[4] After the process is
complete, the beneficiaries may be able to make a claim.[5] Where a beneficiary can follow a
trust asset into the hands of a third party, without the intervention of a bona fide purchaser
for value without notice, he can assert his equitable proprietary interest and require the
asset to be restored to the trust. Where one asset is exchanged for another, a claimant can
elect whether to follow the original asset into the hands of the new owner or to trace its
value into the new asset in the hands of the original owner, although he cannot, of course,
recover twice. In practice, his choice is often dictated by circumstances. If, for instance, the
asset had been transferred to a bona fide purchaser for value without notice of the trust, it
would be pointless to try to follow it even if it could physically be located. In this case, or if
the trust property had ceased to exist in traceable form, the beneficiary will seek to claim
against the trustee. He has a choice of remedy where the trustee has wrongfully misappropriated trust property and used it exclusively to acquire other property for his own
benefit. He may either assert his beneficial ownership of the proceeds, or bring a personal
claim against the trustee for breach of trust and enforce an equitable lien or charge on the
proceeds to secure restoration of the trust fund. If the traceable proceeds are worth more
than the original asset, it will be to his advantage to assert his beneficial ownership and
obtain the profit for himself. If they are worth less, he will take the whole of the proceeds

---

[2] (1991) 107 LQR 71.

[3] Dicta of Millett LJ, as he then was, in *Boscawen v Bajwa* [1995] 4 All ER 769, 776, [1996] 1 WLR 328, 334,
CA, which, surprisingly, was not cited by any of their Lordships in *Foskett v McKeown, supra*, HL, are difficult to reconcile with this statement. There, he seemed to say that the claim following successful completion
of a tracing exercise is based on unjust enrichment, to which there could, applying *Lipkin Gorman (a firm) v
Karpnale* [1991] 2 AC 548, [1992] 4 All ER 512, HL, be raised the defence of innocent change of position.

[4] *Foskett v McKeown, supra*, HL at 128, 120. Unfortunately, he did not refer to *Agip (Africa) Ltd v Jackson*
[1990] 1 Ch 265, [1992] 4 All ER 385; affd [1991] Ch 547, [1992] 4 All ER 451, CA, in which he said, at 285, 398:
'*Tracing at common law, unlike its counterpart in equity, is neither a cause of action nor a remedy but serves
as evidential purpose.*'

[5] The successful completion of a tracing exercise may be preliminary to a personal claim (as in *El Ajou
v Dollar Land Holdings plc* [1993] 3 All ER 717; revsd [1994] 2 All ER 685, CA, on a company law point) or
a proprietary one, to the enforcement of a legal right (as in *F C Jones & Sons (a firm) v Jones* [1997] Ch 159,
[1996] 4 All ER 721, CA) or an equitable one.

either by asserting his beneficial ownership or by enforcing his lien, and have a personal claim for the deficiency.

In so far as he does not rely on his personal claim, his remedies are proprietary and can be maintained not only against the wrongdoing trustee, but also against anyone who derives title from him other than a bona fide purchaser without notice of the breach of trust. It does not matters how many successive transactions there may have been, so long as tracing is possible and no bona fide purchaser for value without notice has intervened.

The proprietary remedy may have various advantages. Suppose, for instance, a trustee, who has since become bankrupt, used the trust funds in clear breach of trust to buy a diamond brooch, which he gave to Marilyn. The beneficiary can, of course, bring a personal action against the trustee for breach of trust, but the effect of the bankruptcy will be to make the remedy worthless, or, at best, lead to a claim to a dividend in the bankruptcy. If, however, Marilyn still has the brooch, the beneficiary can trace the trust funds into her hands in their altered form, assert his proprietary right, and require that the brooch be transferred to the trust. One advantage of a proprietary remedy is that if a trustee becomes bankrupt, the trust property does not pass to the trustee in bankruptcy and does not become available to the trustee's creditors.[6] Further, as we shall see, a proprietary remedy may enable the beneficiary to take advantage of any increase that there may be in the value of the property, and entitle him to any income that the property has produced in the defendant's hands.

So far, we have been considering the position in equity. Following and tracing, however, are available at law as well as in equity, but the rules are generally thought to be more restricted. Lord Millett[7] has said that there is nothing inherently legal or equitable about the tracing exercise, and that there is no sense in maintaining different rules for tracing at law and in equity. These observations were obiter, however, and elsewhere[8] he has accepted that presently differences exist. It has been pointed out[9] that a more restricted right to trace at law may be justified because a legal right, unlike an equitable one, is not defeated by a bona fide purchase without notice. Since we are concerned with the position of beneficiaries under a trust, we will concentrate on the rules in equity, but it will be helpful first to refer briefly to the rules at law.

1 FOLLOWING AND TRACING AT COMMON LAW

These are preliminary steps towards obtaining an appropriate remedy necessary in some circumstances. Completion of the process enables the defendant to be identified as the recipient of the plaintiff's money or chattels.[10] In the case of chattels, he may then be

---

[6] See Insolvency Act 1986, s 283(3)(a).

[7] In *F C Jones & Sons (a firm) v Jones, supra*, CA, at 169, 729; and *Foskett v McKeown, supra*, HL, at 128, 121.

[8] *Agip (Africa) Ltd v Jackson, supra*, at first instance; *El Ajou v Dollar Land Holdings plc, supra*, at first instance.   [9] [2001] Conv 94 (J Stevens).

[10] See *Agip (Africa) Ltd v Jackson, supra*, CA; *Bank Tejarat v Hong Kong & Shanghai Banking Corp (CI) Ltd* [1995] 1 Lloyd's Rep 239, discussed (1995) 9 Tru LI 91 (P Birks).

liable in conversion. Conversion does not, however, lie for money taken and received as currency, but there may be a remedy by the old action for 'money had and received'— nowadays, called a 'personal claim in restitution at common law'.[11]

At common law, the legal owner of an asset who is deprived of its possession has a right to follow or trace it no matter into whose hands it might come, notwithstanding that it may change its form, so long as the means of identifying the asset in its original or converted form continue to exist. The right is not restricted to tangible assets, such as the sovereigns in a bag or a strong box referred to in the older cases, but applies equally to a chose in action, such as a banker's debt to his customer.[12] In *Lipkin Gorman (a firm) v Karpnale Ltd*,[13] Cass, one of the partners in a firm of solicitors, had withdrawn some £223,000 from the firm's client account and lost it in gambling at the Playboy Club, owned and operated by the defendant. Cass himself had been convicted of theft, and was presumably not worth suing. It was held that the claimant solicitors could trace their original property, a chose in action that is a debt owed to them by the bank, into its product, cash drawn from their client account at the bank, and thence follow it into the hands of the defendant. The defendant, the recipient of the stolen money traced into his hands, albeit innocent, was further held, under the law of restitution, obliged to pay an equivalent sum to the true owner where he had not given full consideration for it and had thus been unjustly enriched at the expense of the true owner.

One difficulty that may arise is as to the continued identification of the asset, particularly if, at some stage of the chain of events, it has been converted into money. Lord Goff, in *Lipkin Gorman (a firm) v Karpnale Ltd*,[14] has recently restated the rule that 'at common law, property in money, like other fungibles, is lost as such when it is mixed with other money', and it was mixing that caused the common law claims to fail in *Agip (Africa) Ltd v Jackson*[15] and *El Ajou v Dollar Land Holdings*.[16] Professor Goode, however, has argued forcefully[17] that the inability of the common law to allow money to be followed into a mixed fund is a myth. In any case, it is clear that mixing can only refer to mixing by a prior recipient. Mixing by the defendant himself is irrelevant, because the cause of action for money had and received is complete when the plaintiff's money is received by the defendant. But mixing by a prior recipient will defeat a claim because it will prevent proof that the money received by the defendant was the money paid by the plaintiff.[18]

---

[11] See *Lipkin Gorman (a firm) v Karpnale Ltd, supra*, HL, and *Westdeutsche Landesbank Girozentrale v Islington London Borough Council* [1996] AC 669, [1996] 2 All ER 961, 967, HL, *per* Lord Goff.

[12] *Agip (Africa) Ltd v Jackson, supra*, CA; (1991) 107 LQR 71 (P Millett) (1992) 55 MLR 377 (E McKendrick); [1992] Conv 124 (Margaret Halliwell); [1995] CLJ 377 (A J Oakley); [1995] LMCLQ 240 (L D Smith); (1995) 9 Tru LI 113 (Sarah Worthington). But see (1979) 95 LQR 78 (S Khurshid and P Matthews).

[13] *Supra*, HL, noted (1991) 107 LQR 521 (P Watts); [1991] CLJ 407 (W R Cornish); (1992) 55 MLR 377 (E McKendrick); [1992] Conv 124 (Margaret Halliwell). See also (2002) 31 CLWR 165 (S Baughen); *F C Jones & Sons v Jones, supra*, CA, noted [1997] 113 LQR 21 (N H Andrews and J Beatson); (1997) 8 KCLJ 123 (C Mitchell); (1997) 6 Nott LJ 90 (G McMeel); (1997) 11 Tru LI 12 (P Birks).

[14] *Supra*, HL, at 527. See (1992) 45(2) CLP 69 (P Birks); (1992) All ER Rev 263, 264 (W J Swadling).

[15] *Supra*, CA. See *Solomon v Williams* [2001] BPIR 1123.   [16] *Supra*, CA.

[17] (1976) 92 LQR 360.

[18] *Agip (Africa) Ltd v Jackson* [1992] 4 All ER 385, 399, *per* Millett J, affd [1991] Ch 547, [1992] 4 All ER 451, CA.

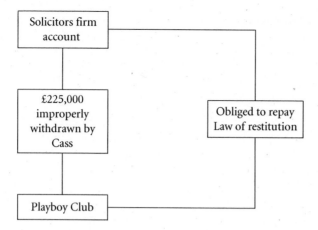

Figure 24.1 Following at common law—*Lipkin Gorman (a firm) v Karpnale Ltd* [1991] 2 AC 548, [1992] 4 All ER 512, HL

With regard to physical mixtures, in *Indian Oil Corpn Ltd v Greenstone Shipping SA*,[19] it was held that justice required that, in a case of wrongful mixing of similar goods, the mixture should be held in common and that each party should be entitled to receive out of the bulk a quantity equal to that of his goods that went into the mixture, any doubt as to that quantity being resolved in favour of the innocent party. This was carried one stage further in *Glencore International AG v Metro Trading Inc*,[20] another case concerning oil, in which it was held that when one person wrongfully blends his own oil with oil of a different grade belonging to another person, with the result that a new product is produced, that new product is owned by them in common, the proportions in which the contributors own the new blend reflecting both the quantity and the value of the oil that each has contributed. Any doubts about the quantity or value of the oil contributed by the innocent party are to be resolved against the wrongdoer. But if the 'mixing' destroys the claimant's contribution, there is nothing that he can trace.[21] The essence of tracing through a mixed fund is the ability to redivide the mixed fund into its constituent parts pro rata according to the value of the contributions made to it. There was, however, an inevitable limitation at common law, as the common law did not recognize equitable interests in property. A beneficiary under a trust could not, at law, follow the property in the hands of the trustee, although he could take steps in equity to compel the trustee to follow the trust property into the hands of a stranger to the trust.

It should be added that the right at law is not restricted to cases in which there is fiduciary relationship.[22]

---

[19] [1988] QB 345, [1988] 3 All ER 893, noted (1987) 46 CLJ 369 (P Stein).

[20] [2001] 1 All ER (Comm) 103. See (2003) 66 MLR 368 (R W J Hickey).

[21] See, eg, *Borden (UK) Ltd v Scottish Timber Products Ltd* [1981] Ch 25, [1979] 3 All ER 961, CA.

[22] *Sinclair v Brougham* [1914] AC 398, 420, HL, *per* Haldane LC.

2 TRACING IN EQUITY

(A) GENERAL POSITION

In *Re Diplock's Estate*,[23] Caleb Diplock, who died in 1936, by his will directed his executors to apply his residuary estate of over a quarter of a million pounds 'for such charitable institution or institutions or other charitable or benevolent object or objects in England as my acting executors or executor may in their or his absolute discretion select'. The executors had distributed over £200,000 among 139 charitable institutions before the validity of this disposition was successfully challenged by the next of kin.[24] Having exhausted their primary remedy against the personal representatives for their misapplication of the residuary estate,[25] the next of kin sought to recover the balance from the wrongly paid charities, claiming alternatively *in personam* and *in rem*. The claim *in personam* was allowed by the House of Lords, affirming the Court of Appeal. The claim *in rem*—that is, the right of the next of kin to trace their claims into the hands of the charities—did not come before the House of Lords, but was considered at length by the Court of Appeal. It is, of course, the claim *in rem* with which we are now concerned.[26]

The general principle laid down in *Re Diplock's Estate* is that whenever there is an initial fiduciary relationship,[27] the beneficial owner of an equitable proprietary[28] interest in property can follow or trace it into the hands of anyone holding the property, except a bona fide purchaser for value without notice, whose title is, as usual, inviolable.[29] The requirement

---

[23] [1948] Ch 465, [1948] 2 All ER 318, CA, affd sub-nom *Ministry of Health v Simpson* [1951] AC 251, [1950] 2 All ER 1137, HL. See *Equity and Contemporary Legal Developments* (ed S Goldstein), p 407 (P J Millett); *Re Goldcorp Exchange Ltd (in receivership)* [1994] 2 All ER 806, PC, noted [1994] CLJ 443 (L S Sealy); (1994) 110 LQR 509 (E McKendrick); [1995] CLJ 377 (A J Oakley); (1995) 9 Tru LI 43 (P Birks); (1995) 9 Tru LI 78 (P Oliver); (1996) 70 ALJ 54 (April Mountfort); (1996) 17 Co Law 3; [1996] JBL 225 (G McCormack). Also, (1995) 6 Cant LR 123; (1996) 8 Otago LR 467 (S R Scott); (1996) 34 Osg Hall LJ 321 (C Rotherham); [1997] LMCLQ 65 (Christa Bond); (1999) 115 LQR 438 (S Evans); (2003) 26 UNSWLJ 377 (Margaret Stone and A McKeogh).

[24] *Chichester Diocesan Fund v Simpson* [1944] AC 341, [1944] 2 All ER 60, HL, and see Chapter 3, section 2(c), *supra*.

[25] Not surprisingly, the executors could not satisfy the claims of the next of kin and terms of compromise were approved by the court. It is believed that at least one of the executors committed suicide as a consequence of taking on the executorship.

[26] *Supra*, CA.

[27] *Re Diplock's Estate*, *supra*, CA; *Agip (Africa) Ltd v Jackson*, *supra*, CA; *Boscawen v Bajwa* [1995] 4 All ER 769, [1996] 1 WLR 328, CA; *Westdeutsche Landesbank Girozentrale v Islington London Borough Council* [1996] AC 669, [1996] 2 All ER 961, HL. But see (1976) 40 Conv 277 (R A Pearce). Heydon, Gummow, and Austin, *Cases & Materials on Equity & Trusts* 4th edn, para 3702, ask, in the light of *Stamp Duties Comr (Queensland) v Livingston* [1965] AC 694, [1964] 3 All ER 692, PC, discussed p 41, *supra*, why the next of kin were allowed to trace in *Re Diplock's Estate* itself.

[28] See (1959) 75 LQR 234, 243 *et seq* (R H Maudsley); [1975] CLP 64 (A J Oakley). In the administration of a deceased's estate, a mere unsatisfied creditor has a similar equitable right to follow assets of the estate into the hands of devisees and legatees and those claiming through them for the purpose of obtaining payment: see *Salih v Atchi* [1961] AC 778, PC. See *Moriarty v Atkinson* (2009) *Times*. 14 January (no proprietary right—no tracing).

[29] *Sinclair v Brougham* [1914] AC 398, [1914–15] All ER Rep 622, HL; *Re Diplock's Estate* [1948] Ch 465, 539, [1948] 2 All ER 318, 356, CA; *McTaggart v Boffo* (1975) 64 DLR (3d) 441, in which Lieff J cited and applied the statement in the text; *Millican v Robinson* [1993] 6 WWR 539. *Polly Peck International plc v Nadir (No 2)* [1992] 4 All ER 769, 781, 782, *per* Scott LJ, CA. *Clarke v Cutland* [2003] EWCA Civ 810, [2003] 4 All ER 733.

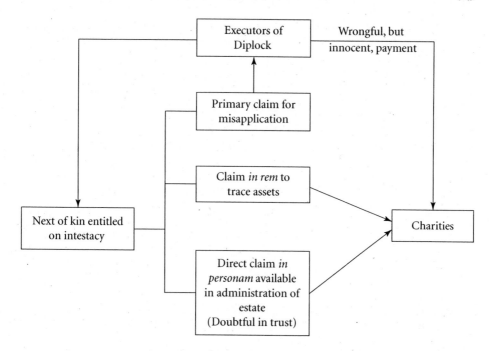

Figure 24.2 *Re Diplock's Estate* [1048] Ch 465, [1948] 2 All ER 318, CA, affd sub nom *Ministry of Health v Simpson* [1951] AC 251, [1950] 2 All ER 1137, HL

of a fiduciary relationship has been much criticized,[30] and Peter Leaver QC[31] appears to have treated *Foskett v McKeown*[32] as deciding that there is no longer any necessity for there to be a pre-existing fiduciary relationship in order for tracing to be permitted. However, the dictum of Lord Millett[33] that he cites does not form part of the *ratio decidendi* and it is thought that Rimer J, in *Shalson v Russo*,[34] was right to take the view that the requirement remains. It may well be, however, that the requirement would not survive an appeal to the House of Lords in some future case. Trustees, of course, occupy a fiduciary position, and there is probably a rebuttable presumption that bailees and agents do so. It may also be established by evidence in other situations.[35]

The wide meaning given to 'fiduciary relationship' may have important repercussions in commercial transactions, because if an appropriate reservation of title clause is incorporated into a contract of sale, not only may the property sold remain the property of the vendor until he has been fully paid, but, on a sub-sale, the head vendor may be able to

---

[30] (1959) 75 LQR 234 (R H Maudsley); Goff and Jones, *The Law of Restitution*, 6th edn, [2.031]–[2.033].

[31] Sitting as a deputy judge of the High Court in *Bracken Partners Ltd v Gutteridge* [2003] EWHC 1064 (Ch), [2003] 2 BCLC 84, appeal dismissed [2003] EWCA Civ 1875, [2004] 1 BCLC 377.

[32] [2000] 3 All ER 97, HL.

[33] In *Foskett v McKeown, supra*, HL, at 121. See *Governor and Company of the Bank of Scotland v A Ltd* [2001] EWCA Civ 52, [2001] 3 All ER 58, *per* Lord Woolf, at [30].

[34] [2003] EWHC 1637 (Ch), [2003] WTLR 1165, 1199.

[35] *Hendy Lennox (Industrial Engines) Ltd v Grahame Puttick Ltd* [1984] 2 All ER 152, [1984] 1 WLR 485. See [1975] CLP 39 (J D Stephens).

trace the proceeds of sale and recover them in priority to other creditors.[36] Stolen moneys
have been said to be traceable in equity on the ground that, when property is obtained by
fraud, equity imposes a constructive trust on the fraudulent recipient,[37] but this has been
doubted by Rimer J in *Shalson v Russo*,[38] pointing out that a thief has no title to property
that he steals and it is accordingly difficult to see how he can become a trustee of it: the true
owner retains the legal and beneficial title. Further, a recipient of money under a contract
subsequently found to be void for mistake or as being *ultra vires* does not hold the money
on a resulting trust. In these cases, the transferor intended that the whole legal and beneficial ownership should pass to the transferee.[39] It is a different matter where a transfer of
property to an agent of the transferor was obtained by fraudulent misrepresentation, and
the transferor never intended that the whole legal and beneficial interest should pass to the
transferee.[40]

(B) MIXING OF TRUST PROPERTY WITH THE TRUSTEE'S[41] OWN PROPERTY

In *Foskett v McKeown*,[42] Lord Millett cited, with approval Page Wood V-C in *Frith v
Cartland*[43]—'...if a man mixes trust funds with his own, the whole will be treated as trust

---

[36] See, eg, *Aluminium Industrie Vaasen BV v Romalpa Aluminium Ltd* [1976] 2 All ER 552, CA; *Armour v
Thyssen Edelstahlwerke AG* [1991] 2 AC 339, [1990] 3 All ER 481, HL, noted (1991) 54 MLR 726 (R Bradgate).
Re Highway Foods International Ltd [1995] 1 BCLC 209; *Chaigley Farms Ltd v Crawford, Kaye & Grayshire
Ltd* [1996] BCC 957, noted [1997] CLJ 28 (L S Sealy); [1998] Conv 52 (J de Lacy). See, generally, [1996] Denning
LJ 23 (M D J Conaglen); (1997) 9 SAcLJ Pt II 250 (V Yeo).

[37] *Westdeutsche Landesbank Girozentrale v Islington London Borough Council* [1996] AC 669, 716, [1996] 2
All ER 961, 998, HL, *per* Lord Browne-Wilkinson, noted [1996] CLJ 432 (G Jones) ; *Lipkin Gorman v Karpnale
Ltd* [1991] 2 AC 548, 565–566, [1992] 4 All ER 512, 522, HL, *per* Lord Templeman. See also *El Ajou v Dollar
Land Holdings plc* [1993] 3 All ER 717, noted (1994) 15 Co Law 148 (R Nolan), revsd [1994] 2 All ER 685, CA,
on a company law point. In *Robb Evans of Robb Evans & Associates v European Bank Ltd* (2004) NSWCA 82,
(2004) 61 NSWLR 75, Spigelman CJ thought it better described as a presumed or resulting trust.

[38] [2003] EWHC 1637 (Ch), [2003] WTLR 1165, noted (2003) 49 T & ELJ 7. The principle in relation to
property obtained by fraud was reaffirmed in *Commerzbank Aktiengesellschaft v IMB Morgan plc* [2004]
EWHC 2771 (Ch), [2005] 1 Lloyd's Rep 298 (not involving stolen property).

[39] *Westdeutsche Landesbank Girozentrale v Islington London Borough Council, supra,* HL. In this case,
Lords Browne-Wilkinson and Lloyd thought that the 'bewildering authority' of *Sinclair v Brougham* [1914]
AC 398, HL, should be overruled, and Lord Slynn agreed that it should be departed from. Lord Woolf,
however, was unwilling to go so far, and Lord Goff was not prepared to depart from it. Further, in the light
of the *Westdeutsche* case, the reasoning in *Chase Manhattan Bank NA v Israel-British Bank (London) Ltd*
[1981] Ch 105, [1979] 3 All ER 1025, that a person who pays money to another under a mistake of fact retains
an equitable property in it and that the conscience of that other is subjected to a fiduciary duty to respect
his proprietary right, '*is at best doubtful*': *Hillsdown Holdings plc v Pensions Ombudsman* [1997] 1 All ER
862, *per* Knox J; although the actual result may be supported on the ground that the retention of the moneys
after the recipient bank learned of the mistake may well have given rise to a constructive trust: see *per* Lord
Browne-Wilkinson, at 997. Notwithstanding criticism of this dictum in Goff and Jones, *Restitution*, 6th edn,
paras 4.35 and 4.36, the judge in *Papamichael v National Westminster Bank plc* [2003] EWHC 164 (Comm),
[2003] 1 Lloyd's Rep 341, agreed with it. It has not, however, been followed in Singapore: *Re Pinkroccade
Educational Services Pte Ltd* [2002] 4 SLR 867. See [1997] JBL 48 (G C G McCormack); (1997) 10 Tru LI 84
(C Mitchell); (2000) 12 Bond LR 30 (D S K Ong); (2005) 71 T & ELTJ 12 (Julia Clark).

[40] *Collings v Lee* [2001] 2 All ER 332, CA, noted (2001) 60 CLJ 477 (R Nolan).

[41] Trustee in this section is used, where the context admits, to include other fiduciary agents.

[42] [2001] 1 AC 102, 133, [2000] 3 All ER 97, 125, HL; *Re Global Finance Group Pty Ltd (in liq), ex p Read
& Herbert* (2002) 26 WAR 385.   [43] (1865) 2 Hem & M 417, 420.

property, except so far as he may be able to distinguish what is his own'—and went on to say that this does not exclude a pro rata division where this is appropriate, as in the case of money and other fungibles, such as grain, oil, and wine.

Equity, by contrast with the position at common law, recognized and protected equitable interests, and the metaphysical approach of equity, coupled with and encouraged by the far-reaching remedy of a declaration of charge, enabled equity to identify money in a mixed fund: 'Equity, so to speak, is able to draw up a balance sheet, on the right hand side of which appears the composite fund, and on its left hand side the two or more funds of which it is deemed to be made up.'[44]

In relation to physical mixtures, the rule is the same in equity as at law. Pro rata division is the best that the wrongdoer and his donees can hope for. If this is not possible, the beneficiary takes the whole; there is no question of confining him to a lien. *Jones v De Marchant*[45] illustrates the rules—namely, that an innocent recipient who receives misappropriated property by way of gift obtains no better title than his donor, and that if a proportionate sharing is inappropriate, the wrongdoer and those who derive title under him take nothing. In that case, the claimant's husband used eighteen beaver skins belonging to his wife, together with four of his own, and had them made up into a coat, which he gave to his mistress, the defendant, who knew nothing of the true ownership of the skins. The coat was clearly not divisible and the claimant, on the above principles, was held entitled to recover the coat. The determinative factor was that the mixing was the act of the wrongdoer through whom the mistress acquired the coat otherwise than for value.

Most cases, in practice, will be those in which a trustee in breach of trust has mixed money in his own bank account with trust moneys. In this case, the moneys in the account belong to the trustee personally and to the beneficiaries under the trust rateably according to the amounts respectively provided. On a proper analysis, there are 'no moneys in the account' in the sense of physical cash. Immediately before the improper mixture, the trustee had a chose in action, being his right against the bank to demand payment of the credit balance in the account. Immediately after the mixture, the trustee had the same chose in action, but its value reflected, in part, the amount of the beneficiaries' money wrongly paid in. The credit balance on the account belongs to the trustee and the beneficiaries rateably according to their respective contributions.[46]

Commonly, the mixing takes place in an active banking account when, under the rule in *Re Hallett's Estate*,[47] the trustee is presumed to draw out his own moneys first, and is deemed not to draw on the trust moneys until his own moneys have been exhausted, no matter in what order the moneys were paid in. This is said to be based on a presumption against a breach of trust—or rather, a further breach of trust, because any mixing of trust moneys and other moneys is, of course, improper. Thus, if a trustee has £1,000 of his own money in his account, pays in first £2,000 of trust moneys and then a further £1,000 of his own money, and subsequently withdraws £2,000 for his own purposes, the beneficiaries are entitled to say that the £2,000 remaining in the account is trust property. The presumption is not, however, extended to enable a beneficiary to claim, once the trust funds have been drawn upon, that any subsequent payment in of private moneys is to be

[44] *Re Diplock's Estate* [1948] Ch 465, 520, [1948] 2 All ER 318, 346, CA.   [45] (1916) 28 DLR 561.
[46] See *Foskett v McKeown, supra,* HL, *per* Lord Browne-Wilkinson, at 110, 103.
[47] (1880) 13 Ch D 696, CA.

treated as being made in replacement of such withdrawals in breach of trust. Thus, if in the illustration given above, the £2,000 were to have been withdrawn before the £1,000 private moneys had been paid in, the beneficiary would only have been able to claim £1,000 of the balance in the account as trust property. Tracing is only possible to such an amount of the balance ultimately standing to the credit of the trustee as does not exceed the lowest intermediate balance standing to the credit of the account after the date of the mixing and before the date when the claim is made.[48] It is, of course, impossible to trace through an overdrawn bank account because, in that case, there is no fund into which the trust moneys can be traced. This is so whether the account was already overdrawn at the time that the relevant money was paid in, or was then in credit, but subsequently became overdrawn.[49]

The rule in Re Hallett's Estate[50] does not, however, operate so as to derogate from the basic principle that the beneficiary is entitled to a first charge on the mixed fund or any property that is purchased thereout. In Re Oatway,[51] the trustee had mixed his own and trust moneys in a banking account. He drew on this account to purchase shares, leaving a balance exceeding the amount of the trust moneys paid in. He subsequently made further drawings that exhausted the account, so that it was useless to proceed against the account: these later drawings were dissipated and did not result in traceable assets. On these facts, it was held that the beneficiary had a charge on the shares for the trust money paid into the account. The original charge on the mixed fund would, it was said, continue on each and every part thereof, notwithstanding changes of form, unless and until the trust money paid into the mixed account was restored and the trust money reinstated by the due investment of the money in the joint names of the proper trustees. Equity's power to charge a mixed fund with the repayment of trust moneys enables the claimant to follow the money, not because it is his, but because it is derived from a fund that is treated as if it were subject to a charge in his favour.[52]

Since equity treats money in a mixed account as charged with the repayment of the claimant's money, if it is paid out into a number of different accounts, the claimant can claim a similar charge over each of the recipient accounts. He is not bound to choose between them.[53]

Re Oatway[54] did not raise the question of whether a beneficiary is entitled to any profit made out of the purchase of property by a trustee out of a fund consisting of his personal moneys that he mixed with the trust moneys. In such a case of a mixed substitution—that is, where a trustee buys property partly with his own money and partly

---

[48] James Roscoe (Bolton) Ltd v Winder [1915] 1 Ch 62; Dewar v Nustock Pastoral Co Pty Ltd (1994) 10 State Rep (W A) 1.

[49] Bishopsgate Investment Management Ltd v Homan [1995] Ch 211, [1995] 1 All ER 347, CA, noted [1996] Conv 129 (Alison Jones); Shalson v Russo [2003] EWHC 1637 (Ch), [2003] WTLR 1165. If the payment in were to put the account into credit and it continued in credit, to that extent, tracing would be possible subject to the lowest intermediate balance rule. The possibility of 'backward tracing' apparently accepted by Dillon LJ was approved by Millett LJ, writing extrajudicially, in KCLJ 6 (1995–96) 1, 12. However, the contrary view expressed by Leggatt LJ is preferred by Oakley in [1995] CLJ 377. See also (1994) 8 Tru LI 102 (L Smith); [1995] LMCLQ 446 (Louise Gallifer).

[50] Supra.   [51] [1903] 2 Ch 356.

[52] Boscawen v Bajwa [1995] 4 All ER 769, 778, [1996] 1 WLR 328, 336, CA.

[53] El Ajou v Dollar Land Holdings plc [1993] 3 All ER 717, 735, revsd [1994] 2 All ER 685, CA, on a company law point.

[54] Supra.

with trust money—*Foskett v McKeown*[55] now lays down that where a trustee wrongfully uses trust money to provide part of the cost of acquiring an asset, the beneficiary is entitled at his option either to claim a proportionate share of the asset, or to enforce a lien upon it to secure his personal claim against the trustee for the amount of the misapplied money. It does not matter whether the trustee mixed the trust money with his own in a single fund before using it to acquire the asset, or made separate payments (whether simultaneously or sequentially) out of differently owned funds to acquire a single asset.

In *Re Tilley's Will Trusts*,[56] a sole trustee, who was also the life tenant of the trust, had mixed the trust moneys with her own moneys in her bank account, which became overdrawn on the purchase of an asset, although subsequent payments in of her own moneys left the account in credit to an amount exceeding the amount of the trust fund. The trustee carried out many property dealings, had ample overdraft facilities, and had no need, nor, as the judge found, any intention, of relying on the trust moneys for the purchase. Ungoed-Thomas J's view[57] was:

> that if, having regard to all the circumstances of the case objectively considered, it appears that the trustee has in fact, whatever his intention, laid out trust moneys in or towards a purchase, then the beneficiaries are entitled to the property purchased and any profits which it produces to the extent to which it has been paid for out of the trust moneys.

Applying this test, he nevertheless held that the trust moneys were not so laid out: they were not invested in properties at all, but merely went in reduction of the trustee's overdraft, which was, in reality, the source of the purchase moneys. The application of the test was perhaps unduly favourable to the trustee.

(C) MIXING OF TWO TRUST FUNDS, OR OF TRUST MONEYS WITH MONEYS OF AN INNOCENT VOLUNTEER

Where the contest is between two claimants to a mixed fund made up of moneys held on behalf of the two of them respectively and mixed together by the trustee, they share *pari passu*, and if property is acquired by means of the mixed fund, each is entitled to a charge *pari passu* and neither is entitled to priority over the other.[58] Further, as against the trustee, they can agree to take the property itself, so as to become tenants in common in shares proportional to the amounts for which either could claim a charge.[59] The same rules apply where moneys of a beneficiary and an innocent volunteer are mixed, whether the mixing is done by the innocent volunteer or the trustee,[60] although it has been argued[61] that this puts the innocent volunteer in too favourable a position. The suggestion is that it is

---

[55] [2001] 1 AC 102, [2000] 3 All ER 97, HL, overruling a dictum of Jessel MR to the contrary in *Re Hallett's Estate, supra*, CA. In (2001) 117 LQR 366, Berg argues that the beneficiaries should have been held entitled to the whole of the profit. See also (2001) 117 LQR 412 (A Burrows).

[56] [1967] Ch 1179, [1967] 2 All ER 303.   [57] *Supra*, at 1193, 313.

[58] *Foskett v McKeown* [2001] 1 AC 102, [2000] 3 All ER 97, HL; *Re Diplock's Estate* [1948] Ch 465, 533, 534, 539, [1948] 2 All ER 318, 353, 354, 356, CA; *Sinclair v Brougham* [1914] AC 398, HL. See Maudsley (1959) 75 LQR 234, 246 *et seq*.

[59] *Sinclair v Brougham, supra*, at 643, 442, *per* Lord Parker; *Re Tilley's Will Trusts, supra*.

[60] *Re Diplock's Estate, supra*, at 524, 536, 539, and at 349, 354, 357, CA; *Sinclair v Brougham, supra*.

[61] Maudsley, op cit. But see [1983] Conv 135 (K Hodkinson), pointing out that if an innocent volunteer dissipates an unmixed fund, there is no action *in rem* against him.

unreasonable that, as is the law, an innocent volunteer who purchases, say, £2,000 stock, half with his own and half with trust moneys, and then withdraws half and spends it on living expenses is regarded as withdrawing it rateably from the trust funds and his own funds, and is accordingly entitled to share the remaining half equally with the beneficiary. The position, as will be seen, might be even more extreme if the funds were in an active banking account to which the rule in Clayton's *Case*[62] applied, when the innocent volunteer might be entitled to the whole remaining funds.

The above rules as to mixing are modified where the mixing takes place in an active banking account. Where a trustee mixes the funds of two separate trusts,[63] or a volunteer mixes trust moneys with his own moneys,[64] the rule in *Clayton's Case*[65] applies. This rule of convenience, based on so-called 'presumed intention', is to the effect that withdrawals out of the account are presumed to be made in the same order as payments in—that is, first in, first out. It was reaffirmed, in *Barlow Clowes International Ltd (in liq) v Vaughan*,[66] as the prima facie rule, although it was also said that, being a rule of convenience, it will not be applied if to do so would be impracticable or result in injustice. More recently, in *Russell-Cooke Trust Co v Prentis*,[67] Lindsay J said that it was plain from *Barlow Clowes* that the rule could be 'displaced by even a slight counterweight. Indeed in terms of its actual application between beneficiaries who have in any sense met a shared misfortune, it might be more accurate to refer to the exception that is, rather than the rule in, *Clayton's* case'. In *Barlow Clowes* itself, the rule in *Clayton's Case* was not applied and the available assets were ordered to be distributed *pari passu* among all unpaid investors rateably in proportion to the amounts due to them, and a similar result was reached in *Commerzbank Aktiengesellschaft v IMB Morgan plc*.[68]

The North American solution has not found favour in England. It was held to be impractical on the facts in *Barlow Clowes*, and Lindsay J said[69] it was complicated and could be difficult to apply. This solution involves treating credits to a bank account made at different times and from different sources as a blend with the result that, when a withdrawal is made from the account, it is treated as a withdrawal in the same proportions as the different interests in the account bear to each other at the moment before the withdrawal is made.[70]

---

[62] *Devaynes v Noble, Clayton's Case* (1816) 1 Mer 529, 572.

[63] *Re Hallett's Estate* (1880) 13 Ch D 696; *Re Stenning* [1895] 2 Ch 433.

[64] *Re Diplock's Estate, supra*, at 364, 554, CA.

[65] *Supra*. For application in another context, see *Re Yeovil Glove Co Ltd* [1965] Ch 148, [1964] 2 All ER 849, CA; held inapplicable in *Re Eastern Capital Futures Ltd (in liq)* [1989] BCLC 371. See *Re Global Finance Group Pty Ltd (in liq), ex p Read and Herbert* (2002) 26 WAR 385, discussed (2003) 52 T & ELJ 11, (2004) 53 T & ELJ 18 (J Hockley). For an unorthodox view, see (1963) 79 LQR 388 (D A McConville).

[66] [1992] 4 All ER 22, CA, noted (1993) 137 Sol Jo 770 (R S J Marshall); [1993] Conv 370 (Jill Martin). See *Re Registered Securities Ltd* [1991] 1 NZLR 545, in which it was said that the presumed intent must give way to an express contrary intention or to circumstances that point to a contrary conclusion. See also [1995] CLJ 377 (A J Oakley).

[67] [2002] EWHC 2227 (Ch), [2003] 2 All ER 478, noted [2003] Conv 339 (M Pawlowski); [2005] CLJ 45 (M Conaglen). After a full consideration of the cases both in England and Australia, it was held, in *Re French Caledonia Travel Service Pty Ltd (in liq)* (2004) 204 ALR 353, that *Clayton's Case* does not apply in Australia to allocate losses suffered by beneficiaries where funds are mixed, regardless of whether or not there is sufficient information to enable an allocation of withdrawals to deposits to be made in any particular case.

[68] [2004] EWHC 2771 (Ch), [2005] 1 Lloyd's Rep 298.

[69] In *Russell-Cooke Trust Co v Prentis, supra*.

[70] *Re Ontario Securities Commission and Greymac Credit Corpn* (1986) 30 DLR (4th) 1, appeal dismissed (1988) 52 DLR (4th) 767n; *Re Elliott* (2002) 333 AR 39. See [1997] Denning LJ 431 (Sarah Lowrie and P Todd); *Re Graphicshoppe Ltd* (2006) 260 DLR 713.

The rule, where it applies, will not be extended beyond banking accounts and only applies where there is one unbroken account. Moreover, the rule will not apply if the fund is 'unmixed' and a specific withdrawal is earmarked as trust money. Accordingly, in *Re Diplock's Estate*,[71] a charity that paid £1,500 trust moneys into its current account and later drew out the same sum, which it placed in a Post Office Savings Bank account and treated as 'Diplock' money, was held bound by its own appropriation. The whole sum could accordingly be traced by the next of kin, the rule in *Clayton's Case*[72] not being applicable.

(D) IDENTIFICATION

Tracing is only possible so long as the fund can be followed in a true sense—that is, so long as, whether mixed or unmixed, it can be located and identified. It presupposes the continued existence of the money either as a separate fund, or as part of a mixed fund, or as latent in property acquired by means of such a fund. If, on the facts of any individual case, such continued existence is not established, equity is as helpless as the common law itself.[73] Thus tracing is impossible where an innocent volunteer spends the trust money on a dinner,[74] or on education or general living expenses. Where trust money is used in the alteration and improvement of property that the defendant already owns, it was said, in *Re Diplock's Estate*,[75] that this would not necessarily increase its value, in which case, the money would have disappeared leaving no monetary trace behind. However, it has been said more recently[76] that where the value of the defendant's land has been enhanced by the use of the plaintiff's money, the court may treat the land as charged with the payment to the plaintiff of a sum representing that increase in value: the most that a claimant can hope for is a proprietary lien to recover the money expended.[77]

In *Foskett v McKeown*,[78] M effected a life assurance policy on his own life, which he later declared to be held on trust for his children. He paid the first two premiums out of his own funds, but at least the fourth and fifth premiums were paid out of funds in a bank account under M's name to which the claimants were entitled under an express trust. The claimants' money had been moved in and out of various bank accounts where, in breach of trust, it had been inextricably mixed by M with his own money. M committed suicide and the death benefit of £1m was paid out to the trustees. Under the terms of the policy, the

---

[71] [1948] Ch 465, 551, 552, [1948] 2 All ER 318, 363, 364, CA (revsd on the facts at 559, 429–432); *Boscawen v Bajwa* [1995] 4 All ER 769, 778, CA.

[72] (1816) 1 Mer 529.

[73] It has been pointed out, eg by Goulding in [1992] Conv 367, that this seems to have been overlooked or disregarded in *Agip (Africa) Ltd v Jackson* [1991] Ch 547, [1992] 4 All ER 451, CA, in which there was said to be no difficulty about the mechanics of tracing in equity, although, at one stage, Lloyds Bank had taken a delivery risk and paid out of its own money. *See McTaggart v Boffo* (1975) 64 DLR (3d) 441.

[74] *Re Diplock's Estate*, *supra*, at 521, 347, CA.

[75] *Supra*, at 547, 361, CA. Another difficulty in such case might be as to whether the charge should be on the whole of the land or only on that part which was altered or reconstructed.

[76] *Boscawen v Bajwa*, *supra*, CA, *per* Millett LJ, at 777.

[77] *Foskett v McKeown* [2001] 1 AC 102, 133, [2000] 3 All ER 97, 102, HL, *per* Lord Browne-Wilkinson. In *Re Esteem Settlement* [2002] JLR 53, the Royal Court of Jersey held that the claimant could trace his money spent on improvements into the increased value of the property. On the one hand, there can be no tracing if there is no increase in value attributable to the claimant's money. On the other hand, if tracing is possible, the claimant will be entitled not merely to a lien to recover the money expended, but to a proportionate share of any subsequent increase in total value.

[78] *Supra*, HL.

same benefit would have been paid even if only the first two premiums had been paid. The claimants claimed to be entitled to a share proportionate to the premiums paid.

The essence of the competing arguments was whether the correct analogy was with an improvement of property, as discussed above, or with a mixed bank account, as discussed earlier.[79] It was held by the majority that the correct analogy was with a bank account. The claimants could trace the premiums paid out of their funds into the policy—that is, the bundle of rights to which the policyholder was entitled in return for the premiums and which collectively constituted a chose in action. That chose in action represented the traceable proceeds of the premium, and it followed that the claimants were entitled to a proportionate share of the policy, in so far as they could show that the premiums were paid with their money. Such an interest arose immediately upon the payment of the premiums, and thus the claimants were entitled to the insurance money paid on M's death in the same shares and proportions as they were entitled in the policy immediately before his death.

Re Diplock's Estate[80] also appears to hold that the right to trace comes to an end if an innocent volunteer uses the trust money to pay off a debt, even though secured, and even though the money was given to him for this purpose. The effect of such payment was said to be that the debt is extinguished and any security ceases to exist, and the cestui que trust cannot claim to be subrogated to the rights of the creditor.[81] In *Boscawen v Bajwa*,[82] however, Millett LJ could see no reason why, in the case of a secured debt, subrogation should not be available and explained *Re Diplock's Estate*[83] as a case in which, in the particular circumstances, it was considered unjust to grant the remedy of subrogation. Those circumstances would today, he said, be regarded as relevant to a change of position defence rather than as going to liability.

It may be added that a volunteer who has received trust property cannot be made subject to a personal liability to account for it as a constructive trustee if he has parted with it without having previously acquired some knowledge of the existence of the trust.[84]

(E) CLAIM INEQUITABLE

The general principle that a remedy will not be granted in a case in which it would lead to an inequitable result was said, in *Re Diplock's Estate*,[85] to be an additional reason why trust moneys used by an innocent volunteer in alterations to his house could not be traced. The equitable remedy is a declaration of charge, enforceable by sale. This would be equitable where the land was purchased with moneys of the innocent volunteer mixed with trust moneys, but it would be different where the innocent volunteer has contributed not money, but the land itself. It is not clear how this relates to the defence of change of position recognized in *Lipkin Gorman (a firm) v Karpnale Ltd*.[86]

---

[79] See p 547, *supra*.   [80] *Supra*, at 549, 362, CA. See [1995] CLJ 290 (L D Smith).

[81] *Re Diplock's Estate, supra*, at 521, 347, CA.

[82] *Supra*, CA. And see *Banque Financière de la Cité v Parc (Battersea) Ltd* [1991] 1 AC 221, [1998] 1 All ER 737, HL, discussed [1998] JBL 323 (M Bridge); (1998) 114 LQR 341 (P Watts).

[83] *Supra*, CA.

[84] *Re Montagu's Settlement Trusts* [1987] Ch 264, [1992] 4 All ER 308; *Agip (Africa) Ltd v Jackson* [1992] 4 All ER 385, 403, *per* Millett J, affd [1991] Ch 457, [1992] 4 All ER 451, CA; *Westdeutsche Landesbank Girozentrale v Islington London Borough Council* [1996] AC 669, [1996] 2 All ER 961, HL.

[85] *Supra*, at 547–548, 361, CA.   [86] [1991] 2 AC 548, [1992] 4 All ER 512, HL.

(F) INTEREST

Where a tracing claim succeeds, it appears that the claimant is entitled to interest—that is, the interest, in fact, earned by the trust moneys or the property into which they have been traced.[87]

3 THE CLAIMS *IN PERSONAM*

It is convenient to mention here the alternative claim by the next of kin in *Re Diplock's Estate*[88] against the innocent recipients by means of a direct action *in personam* in equity. The House of Lords expressly affirmed the Court of Appeal judgment on this point, which had asserted the right of an unpaid or underpaid creditor, legatee, or next of kin to bring a direct action in equity against the persons to whom the estate had been wrongfully distributed. Contrary to what had previously been commonly thought, it makes no difference whether the wrongful distribution was due to a mistake of law or fact; it does not matter that the wrongful recipient has no title at all and was a stranger to the estate, and there is no requirement that the estate must be administered by the court. The Court of Appeal observed:[89] 'as regards the conscience of the defendant on which in this, as in other jurisdictions, equity is said to act, it is prima facie, at least, a sufficient circumstance that the defendant, as events have proved, has received some share of the estate to which he was not entitled.' Nevertheless, it seems somewhat inequitable that an innocent volunteer can be called upon to refund—admittedly without interest—until the claim is barred by the Limitation Act, because he may well alter his position on the assumption that the payment was valid.[90] However, in the light of *Lipkin Gorman v Karpnale Ltd*,[91] it may be that a defence of change of position would now have a chance of success.

The claim, in any case, is subject to the qualification that the primary remedy is against the wrongdoing executor or administrator, and the direct claim in equity against those overpaid or wrongly paid is limited to the amount that the beneficiary cannot recover in the primary action.[92] And it seems that no claim will lie if, when the payment was made to the defendant, the assets were sufficient to pay all claims in full, but a deficiency has subsequently arisen.[93]

It must be made clear that it is uncertain whether a direct action in equity lies in similar circumstances in the execution of a trust as opposed to the administration of the estate of

---

[87] *Re Diplock's Estate* [1948] Ch 465, 517, 557, [1948] 2 All ER 318, 345, 346, CA.

[88] *Supra.*   [89] In *Re Diplock's Estate, supra*, at 503, 337, CA.

[90] (1957) 73 LQR 48 (G H Jones), cf (1961) 24 MLR 85 (R Goff).

[91] [1991] 2 AC 548, [1992] 4 All ER 512, HL. In this case, it was held that change of position is a good defence to a claim for restitution based on unjust enrichment. But an illegal change of position cannot be relied on: *Barros Mattos Jnr v MacDaniels Ltd* [2004] EWHC 1188 (Ch), [2004] 3 All ER 299, criticized [2005] LMCLQ 6 (A Tettenborn); [2005] Conv 357 (Margaret Halliwell).

[92] *Re J Leslie Engineers Co Ltd* [1976] 2 All ER 85, [1976] 1 WLR 292. The same qualification appears to apply to the claim *in rem*: *Re Diplock's Estate, supra*, at 556, 365. The qualification has been statutorily modified in some jurisdictions: eg the Western Australian Trustees Act, s 65(7), provides that the volunteer must be sued first. See also Queensland Trusts Act 1973, s 109; New Zealand Administration Act 1969, s 50.

[93] *Fenwick v Clarke* (1862) 4 De GF & J 240; *Peterson v Peterson* (1866) LR 3 Eq 111.

a deceased person. In the House of Lords, Lord Simonds, whose speech was concurred in by all the other Law Lords, said:[94]

> it is important in the discussion of this question to remember that the particular branch of the jurisdiction of the Court of Chancery with which we are concerned relates to the administration of assets of a deceased person. While in the development of this jurisdiction certain principles were established which were common to it and to the comparable jurisdiction in the execution of trusts, I do not find in history or in logic any justification for an argument which denies the possibility of an equitable right in the administration of assets because, as it is alleged, no comparable right existed in the execution of trusts.

However, although the claims failed on other grounds, Templeman J, in *Butler v Broadhead*,[95] was inclined to think that there was a sufficient analogy between the position of an executor and the liquidator of a company in a winding up to enable equity to intervene in favour of unpaid creditors against overpaid contributories; Oliver J took a similar view in *Re J Leslie Engineers Co Ltd*,[96] in which a liquidator sought to recover the company's money wrongfully procured by its controlling director and paid to the respondent after the commencement of the winding up.

It would now appear that a claim could be made by an application of the law of restitution based on the principle of unjust enrichment, under which, it is submitted, as between trustees and a person who is wrongly paid, the trustees have a right to recover the payment if it was paid under a mistake, whether of fact or law, subject to the defences available in the law of restitution such as the defence of change of position.[97] This defence requires some causal link between the innocent receipt of the mistaken payment and the defendant's change of position, which makes it inequitable for the recipient to be required to make restitution.[98] The change of position must have occurred after the receipt of the mistaken payment.[99] Since the emphasis is upon whether it would be unjust or inequitable to allow restitution, the defence may be defeated if it can be shown that the recipient acted in bad faith, even though he was not (subjectively) dishonest.[100]

---

[94] *Ministry of Health v Simpson* [1951] AC 251, 265–266, [1950] 2 All ER 1137, 1140, HL. But see *G L Baker Ltd v Medway Building and Supplies Ltd* [1958] 3 All ER 540, [1958] 1 WLR 1216, CA; *Eddis v Chichester Constable* [1969] 1 All ER 546, affd without reference to this point [1969] 2 Ch 345, [1969] 2 All ER 912, CA. Professor Goode (1976) 92 LQR 528, 541, considers the restriction to be justified, but Professor Martin [1998] Conv 13, argues for coherence in equity's treatment of the rights of beneficiaries of trusts and beneficiaries of estates.

[95] [1975] Ch 97, [1974] 2 All ER 401.   [96] *Supra*.

[97] *Lipkin Gorman (a firm) v Karpnale Ltd* [1991] 2 AC 548, [1992] 4 All ER 512, HL; *Kleinwort Benson Ltd v Lincoln City Council* [1999] 2 AC 349, [1998] 4 All ER 513, HL; See [2002] RLR 69 (D Sheehan).

[98] *Scottish Equitable plc v Derby* [2001] EWCA Civ 369, [2001] 3 All ER 818; *Maersk Air Ltd v Expeditors International (UK) Ltd* [2003] 1 Lloyd's Rep 491. See also [2000] CLP 205 (P Birks); (2004) 15 KCLJ 301 (H Liu).

[99] *South Tyneside Metropolitan BC v Svenska International plc* [1994] 4 All ER 972, doubted Goff and Jones, *The Law of Restitution*, 6th edn, at [4.004].

[100] *Niru Battery Manufacturing Co v Milestone Trading Ltd* [2003] EWCA Civ 1446, [2004] 1 All ER (Comm) 193, noted [2005] CLJ 35 (G Virgo) and *Commerzbank AG v Gareth Price-Jones* [2003] EWCA Civ 1663, both noted [2004] CLJ 276 (A Burrows); (2004) 120 LQR 373 (P Birks); *Fea v Roberts* [2005] EWHC 2186 (Ch), [2006] WTLR 255, noted (2007) 85 T & ELTJ 12 (Harriet Atkinson).

25

INJUNCTIONS I—NATURE; DAMAGES IN LIEU; ENFORCEMENT

The injunction is the most potent of equity's remedies and has played an important part in its development. This chapter begins with an explanation of what exactly an injunction is, and continues in section 2 with an account of the ways in which they may be classified. Sometimes, an injunction is not an appropriate remedy and section 3 considers the possibility of damages being awarded in lieu. The final section discusses the ways in which an injunction may be enforced.

1 MEANING AND NATURE OF AN INJUNCTION

(A) MEANING

An injunction is an order[1] of the court directing a person or persons to refrain from doing some particular act or thing or, less often, directing a person or persons to do some particular act or thing. It is an equitable remedy that originally could only be obtained in the Court of Chancery or the Court of Exchequer in equity.[2] A limited power to grant injunctions was first given to the common law courts by the Patent Law Amendment Act 1852 and then, by the Common Law Procedure Act 1854,[3] the common law courts were given so wide a jurisdiction to grant injunctions in all cases of breach of contract or other

---

[1] The Supreme Court Act 1981, now renamed the Senior Courts Act 1981, s 31(2), provides that an injunction may be granted on an application for judicial review. In *Re M* [1994] 1 AC 377, sub nom *M v Home Office* [1993] 3 All ER 537, HL, noted [1994] CLJ 1 (T R S Allan), it was held that the language of the section being unqualified in its terms, there was no warrant for restricting its application so that, in respect of ministers and other officers of the Crown alone, the remedy of an injunction, including an interim injunction, was not available, but the jurisdiction should be exercised only in the most limited circumstances. So far as final relief was concerned, a declaration would continue to be an appropriate remedy. See (1996) 146 NLJ (J Algazy).

[2] The equity jurisdiction of the Court of Exchequer was abolished by the Court of Chancery Act 1841.

[3] Common Law Procedure Act 1854, ss 79 and 82.

injury that, as Baggalay LJ observed,[4] they had a more extensive jurisdiction as regards the granting of injunctions than the Court of Chancery itself.

These statutes have been repealed and the Judicature Acts[5] have transferred to the High Court all of the jurisdiction, including the jurisdiction to grant injunctions, previously exercised both by the Court of Chancery and the common law courts. The jurisdiction may, of course, be exercised by every division of the High Court, although in practice most applications for an injunction are made to the Chancery Division.[6]

The Supreme Court Act 1981, now renamed the Senior Courts Act 1981, replacing earlier provisions, now provides, in s 37(1) and (2):

> (1) The High Court may by order (whether interlocutory or final) grant an injunction or appoint a receiver in all cases in which it appears to the court to be just and convenient to do so.
>
> (2) Any such order may be made either unconditionally or on such terms and conditions as the court thinks just.

In ordinary litigation affecting the private rights of litigants, s 37 does not entitle the court to exercise its discretion to grant an injunction unless there is some substantive right, the infringement of which is threatened.[7] Thus in *Day v Brownrigg*,[8] in which the plaintiff lived in a house that, for some sixty years, had been called 'Ashford Lodge'. The defendant's adjoining house had been known for some forty years as 'Ashford Villa'. The plaintiff was held to have no claim to an injunction when the defendant altered the name of his house to 'Ashford Lodge', notwithstanding the resulting inconvenience. The plaintiff had suffered no legal injury because there is no right of property in the name of a house, or, it may be added, of a political party.[9] Again, a husband has no legal right enforceable at law or in equity to stop his wife having, or a registered medical practitioner performing, a legal abortion and, accordingly, he cannot obtain an injunction for this purpose.[10] And in *Medina Housing Association Ltd v Case*,[11] the claimant had obtained a possession order on the grounds of the tenant's antisocial behaviour in breach of the terms of the tenancy agreement from the county court judge. At the same time, he granted an injunction in effect prohibiting the defendant from continuing her antisocial behaviour for some five

[4] In *Quartz Hill Consolidated Gold Mining Co v Beall* (1882) 20 Ch D 501, 509, CA.

[5] Judicature Act 1873, s 16, now the Supreme Court Act 1981, s 19(2).

[6] Under s 38 of the County Courts Act 1984 (as substituted by s 3 of the Courts and Legal Services Act 1990), in proceedings in which a county court had jurisdiction, the county court has the same remedies available to it as the High Court, save that it cannot grant a search order or a freezing injunction, except in family cases. The jurisdiction extends to a district judge sitting as a small claims arbitrator: *Joyce v Liverpool City Council* [1996] QB 252, [1995] 3 All ER 110, CA. As to sequestration of a company's assets, see *Rose v Laskington* [1990] 1 QB 562, [1989] 3 All ER 306, DC.

[7] *Siskina (Cargo Owners) v Distos Cia Naviera SA* [1979] AC 210, [1977] 3 All ER 803, HL; *Mercedes-Benz AG v Leiduck* [1996] 1 AC 284, [1995] 3 All ER 929, PC; *Morris v Murjani* [1996] 2 All ER 384, [1996] 1 WLR 848, CA. See [1996] LMCLQ 268 (P Devonshire).

[8] (1878) 10 Ch D 294, CA; *Sports and General Press Agency Ltd v Our Dogs Publishing Co Ltd* [1917] 2 KB 125, CA; *The Siskina* [1979] AC 210, [1977] 3 All ER 803, HL; *Richards v Richards* [1984] AC 174, [1983] 2 All ER 807, HL.

[9] *Kean v McGivan* [1982] FSR 119, CA (Social Democratic Party).

[10] *Paton v Trustees of British Pregnancy Advisory Service* [1979] QB 276, [1978] 2 All ER 987, noted (1979) 42 MLR 325 (I M Kennedy). The position is different in Canada: *Tremblay v Daigle* (1989) 59 DLR (4th) 609. See also *Patel v Patel* [1988] 2 FLR 179, CA; *Burris v Azadani* [1995] 4 All ER 802, [1995] 1 WLR 1372, CA.

[11] [2002] EWCA Civ 2001, [2003] 1 All ER 1084.

years after the tenancy came to an end. The Court of Appeal held that the judge had no jurisdiction to grant an injunction extending beyond the time at which the possession order would become effective, thereby bringing to an end the claimant's contractual rights.

In some other situations, it is not necessary to establish the infringement or threatened infringement of a substantive right. Thus a chief constable was granted an injunction in *Chief Constable of Kent v V*[12] to prevent the dissipation of identifiable money in a bank account alleged to have been obtained by fraud, explained in *Chief Constable of Hampshire v A Ltd*[13] on the basis that the chief constable has a general duty to recover stolen property and restore it to the true owner. In *Re Oriental Credit Ltd*,[14] an injunction was granted in aid of, and ancillary to, an order made by the registrar under s 561 of the Companies Act 1985 on the ground that the defendant had a public duty to obey that order, although the section created no cause of action and no legal or equitable right in the liquidation. And in *Morris v Murjani*,[15] an injunction was granted to secure the appellant's compliance with his duty under s 333 of the Insolvency Act 1986. Further, in some family proceedings, the infringement of a legal or equitable right is not necessarily a precondition for the grant of an injunction. Non-molestation orders are commonly made between both spouses[16] and former spouses,[17] apparently without the infringement of a legal or equitable right being considered essential, and likewise a wide-ranging variety of orders have been made in wardship proceedings.[18]

The words 'just and convenient' do not confer an arbitrary or unregulated discretion on the court:[19] 'what is right or just must be decided, not by the caprice of the judge, but according to sufficient legal reasons or on settled legal principle.'[20] When it is said that equitable remedies are 'discretionary', what is meant is that the court is entitled to take into account certain collateral matters, such as the conduct of the parties, in addition to considering their bare legal rights, in deciding whether to grant an equitable remedy. It may be added that it follows that an appeal court will be slow to interfere with an order made by the trial judge in his discretion, unless it appears that he has acted on wrong principles.

Further, it should be noted that where statute provides that a statutory duty is enforceable by injunction, the court has little, if any, discretion to exercise.[21]

(B) REMEDY IN PERSONAM

In granting an injunction, 'the court acts in personam, and will not suffer anyone within its reach to do what is contrary to its notions of equity, merely because the act to be done

---

[12] [1983] QB 34, [1982] 3 All ER 36, CA.   [13] [1985] QB 132, [1984] 2 All ER 385, CA.

[14] [1988] Ch 204, [1988] 1 All ER 892.   [15] *Supra*, CA.

[16] For example, *Horner v Horner* [1982] Fam 90, [1982] 2 All ER 495, CA, in which the meaning of 'molestation' is discussed.

[17] For example, *Vaughan v Vaughan* [1973] 3 All ER 449, [1973] 1 WLR 1159, CA.

[18] See, eg, *Re C (a minor) (No 2)* [1990] Fam 39, [1989] 2 All ER 791, CA.

[19] *Per* Davey LJ in *Harris v Beauchamp Bros* [1894] 1 QB 801, 809, CA.

[20] *Per* Jessel MR in *Beddow v Beddow, supra*, at 93. See (1959) 17 MULR 133 (Patricia Loughlon).

[21] *Taylor v Newham London Borough Council* [1993] 2 All ER 649, [1993] 1 WLR 444, CA. In this case, Bingham MR found it almost impossible to imagine circumstances in which a discretion would arise or be properly exercisable.

may be, in point of locality, beyond its jurisdiction'.[22] A person who is residing abroad, and physically outside the jurisdiction, is nevertheless within the reach of the court if service out of the jurisdiction can properly be made upon him under rules of court,[23] and the same is true of a company incorporated abroad.[24] The court, however, will consider carefully before it grants an injunction in these cases, and, as a general rule, will not adjudicate on questions relating to the title or the right to the possession of immovable property out of the jurisdiction,[25] nor will it give effect to a contractual or equitable right u which the *lex situs* would treat as incapable of creation.[26]

Until recently, it has been generally thought that the court has no jurisdiction to grant an injunction against the world at large, relying on the dictum of Lord Eldon in *Iveson v Harris*[27] that '*you cannot have an injunction except against a party to the suit*'. It was said, in *Venables v News Group Newspapers Ltd*,[28] however, that we are now entering into a new era following the implementation of the Human Rights Act 1998, and the requirements that the courts act in a way that is compatible with the Convention[29] and have regard to European jurisprudence; this adds a new dimension, enabling the court to grant an injunction openly *contra mundum*, or 'against the world'.

An injunction may be granted against a representative defendant under CPR 19.6, and it may also be granted against a defendant by description, provided that the description is sufficiently certain so as to identify both those who are included and those who are not.[30] Thus, in *Bloomsbury Publishing Group Ltd v News Group Newspapers Ltd*,[31] injunctive relief was granted against a defendant referred to as '*the person or persons who have offered the publishers of* The Sun, *the* Daily Mail *and the* Daily Mirror *newspapers a copy of the book* Harry Potter and the Order of the Phoenix *by J K Rowling*', referred to at an earlier hearing[32] as effectively a 'John Doe' order. In a subsequent unreported case,[33] the claimant had been the victim of a hoaxer who had written forged letters in her name, published in the national press, expressing views that she did not hold and which led to her receiving vicious hate mail. Evans J granted an injunction restraining 'John Doe' from continuing to send such letters. Although the hoaxer might not learn of the existence of

---

[22] *Per* Cranworth LC in *Carron Iron Co v Maclaran* (1855) 5 HL Cas 416, 436, 437; *Hope v Carnegie* (1868) LR 7 Eq 254. See, however, '*Morocco Bound' Syndicate Ltd v Harris* [1895] 1 Ch 534. Cf *Chellaram v Chellaram* [1985] Ch 409, [1985] 1 All ER 1043.

[23] Now CPR 6.17–6.31. See *Re Liddell's Settlement Trusts* [1936] Ch 365, [1936] 1 All ER 239, CA, applied *Re D (a minor)* [1992] 1 All ER 892 [1992] 1 WLR 315, CA.

[24] *Hospital for Sick Children v Walt Disney Productions Inc* [1968] Ch 52, [1967] 1 All ER 1005, CA.

[25] *Deschamps v Miller* [1908] 1 Ch 856.   [26] *Bank of Africa Ltd v Cohen* [1909] 2 Ch 129, CA.

[27] (1802) 7 Ves 251, 257.

[28] [2001] Fam 430, [2001] 1 All ER 908; *X (a woman formerly known as Mary Bell) v O'Brien* [2003] EWHC 1101 (QB), [2003] FCR 686, both discussed at p 615, *infra*. See *Re Z (a minor)* [1997] Fam 1, [1995] 4 All ER 961, in which the Court of Appeal affirmed the grant of an injunction *in rem*.

[29] That is, the European Convention for the Protection of Human Rights and Fundamental Freedoms 1950.

[30] J Seymour argues, in [2007] CLJ 605, that there is no material difference between a claim under CPR 19.6 and a claim against a party by description.

[31] [2003] EWHC 1205 (Civ), [2003] 3 All ER 736, [2003] 1 WLR 1633. Any other person who knowing of the order assisted in its breach would be liable for contempt of court: see p 576, *infra*.

[32] [2003] EWHC 1087 (Ch).

[33] Referred to by S Smith and A Sithamparanathan in a feature in *The Times* on 23 December 2003. See also an article by Dan Tench in *The Times* on 23 May 2006.

the injunction, if served on the media, it would effectively prevent publication.[34] Finally, in *South Cambridgeshire DC v Persons Unknown*,[35] an interim injunction was granted, under the statutory power contained in the Town and Country Planning Act 1990, s 187B,[36] against persons unknown, restraining them from perpetrating identified breaches of planning control.

(C) WHERE A PARTICULAR REMEDY IS PROVIDED BY STATUTE

If a right of property that is created or confirmed by statute is infringed, it is settled that the fact that a particular remedy is provided for an infringement of that right by statute does not oust the jurisdiction of the court to grant an injunction. Even though the statutory remedy may be the only remedy available for the past infringement, the court may grant an injunction to prevent further infringements in the future,[37] unless the statute expressly or by implication provides to the contrary.[38] If no right of property is created, the question of whether legislation that makes the doing or omitting to do a particular act a criminal offence renders the person guilty of such offence liable also in a civil action for damages or an injunction at the suit of any person who thereby suffers loss or damage is a question of construction of the legislation.[39] The presumption is that there is no civil action at the suit of a private individual. The exceptions are discussed later.[40]

(D) INJUNCTIONS AGAINST PERSONS UNDER DISABILITY

The fact of disability is not in itself a bar to the granting of an injunction against the person under disability or to the enforcement of an order that has been made. In the case of mental incapacity, the question is whether the person under that disability understands the proceedings, and the nature and requirements of the order sought. In the case of a person incapable of understanding what he is doing or that it is wrong, an injunction should not be granted against him, since he would not be capable of complying with it. An injunction could not have the desired deterrent effect, nor could any breach be the subject of effective enforcement proceedings, since he would have a clear defence to an application for committal to prison for contempt.[41]

In the case of a person under the age of seventeen, he may well understand the order and its consequences. However, the court has no power to commit him to prison for breach of an injunction. The court should investigate other alternatives—in particular, the possibility of a fine. If this would be an appropriate means of enforcement, the penal notice attached to the injunction should substitute the threat of a fine for the threat of imprisonment. But

---

[34] See fn 31, *supra*, and p 576, *infra*.

[35] [2004] EWCA Civ 1280, (2004) Times, 11 November, discussed [2005] JPEL 595 (R Langham). The court also ordered that service of the claim form and the injunction be effected by placing copies in clear plastic envelopes and nailing them to gateposts, etc, on the site.

[36] As inserted by the Planning and Compensation Act 1991.

[37] *Stevens v Chown* [1901] 1 Ch 894; *Devonport Corpn v Tozer* [1903] 1 Ch 759, CA; *Carlton Illustrators v Coleman & Co* [1911] 1 KB 771.

[38] *Evans v Manchester, Sheffield and Lincolnshire Rly Co* (1887) 36 Ch D 626; *Stevens v Chown, supra*.

[39] *Cutler v Wandsworth Stadium Ltd* [1949] AC 398, [1949] 1 All ER 544, HL.

[40] See Chapter 27, section 7, *infra*.

[41] *Wookey v Wookey, Re S (a minor)* [1991] Fam 121, [1991] 3 All ER 365, CA.

in the vast majority of cases in which the minor is still of school age, or unemployed, it would be inappropriate to grant an injunction.[42]

2 CLASSIFICATION OF INJUNCTIONS

(A) PROHIBITORY AND MANDATORY

The prohibitory or restrictive injunction, by which a person is directed to refrain from doing some particular act or thing, is the original basic form, the mandatory injunction, by which a person is directed to perform some positive act, being a later development. This is demonstrated by the fact that, until the turn of the nineteenth century, an order, even though mandatory in substance, had to be drafted in a prohibitory form. Thus the court would not, for instance, make an order directing a building to be pulled down, but would order the defendant not to allow it to remain on the land. Since the decision in *Jackson v Normandy Brick Co*,[43] however, it has been the rule that if an injunction is mandatory in substance, it should be made in direct mandatory form.

At one time, it was thought that particular caution had to be exercised by the court in granting a mandatory injunction,[44] but it is now settled that there is no distinction in principle between granting a prohibitory and a mandatory injunction: every injunction requires to be granted with care and caution, but it is not more needed in one case than the other.[45] The court will not hesitate to grant a mandatory injunction in an appropriate case,[46] but whenever it does so, it must be careful to see that the defendant knows exactly what he has to do, and this means not as a matter of law, but as a matter of fact.[47]

There is obviously an analogy between a mandatory injunction and a decree of specific performance. As we shall see, there are certain contracts of which specific performance cannot be obtained,[48] and one cannot get round this by making a claim for a mandatory injunction. Thus, for example, the court will not grant an injunction ordering the defendant to do something that is impossible,[49] or which cannot be enforced, or which is unlawful.[50] Again, the court will not normally make an order requiring a defendant to perform

[42] Ibid.

[43] [1899] 1 Ch 438, CA. Occasionally, orders were made in the positive form even before this date: *Bidwell v Holden* (1890) 63 LT 104. See [1981] Conv 55 (C D Bell); [1983] Conv 29 (R Griffith).

[44] *Great North of England, Clarence and Hartlepool Junction Rly Co v Clarence Rly Co* (1845) 1 Coll 507; *Isenberg v East India House Estate Co Ltd* (1863) 3 De GJ & Sm 263.

[45] *Smith v Smith* (1875) LR 20 Eq 500; *Lawrence v Hornton* (1890) 59 LJ Ch 440.

[46] *Hermann Loog v Bean* (1884) 26 Ch D 306, CA; *Kelsen v Imperial Tobacco Co (of Great Britain and Ireland) Ltd* [1957] 2 QB 335; *Evans v BBC and IBA* (1974) Times, 27 February (mandatory injunction to ensure political programme during election campaign transmitted as originally arranged). See *Charrington v Simons & Co Ltd* [1971] 2 All ER 588, [1971] 1 WLR 598, CA; *John Trenberth Ltd v National Westminster Bank Ltd* (1979) 39 P & CR 104, and see p 605, *infra*.

[47] *Redland Bricks Ltd v Morris* [1970] AC 652, [1969] 2 All ER 576, HL; *Stephen & Co Ltd v Post Office* [1978] 1 All ER 939, [1977] 1 WLR 1172, CA.

[48] See Chapter 28, section 2, *infra*. See also *Sanderson Motors (Sales) Pty Ltd v Yorkstar Motors Pty Ltd* [1983] 1 NSWLR 513.   [49] *A-G v Colney Hatch Lunatic Asylum* (1868) 4 Ch App 146.

[50] *Pride of Derby and Derbyshire Angling Association Ltd v British Celanese Ltd* [1953] Ch 149, 198, [1953] 1 All ER 179, 181, CA, *per* Evershed MR.

personal services,[51] nor one to enforce an obligation entered into by a person that he will not apply to Parliament, or that he will not oppose an application to Parliament by another person,[52] or to compel the sale and delivery of chattels not specific or ascertained.[53]

(B) PERPETUAL AND INTERIM

A perpetual injunction is one that has been granted after the right thereto has been established in an action in which both sides have been fully heard; it is intended to settle finally the relationship between the parties in connection with the matter in dispute, so as to relieve the plaintiff from the need to bring a series of actions as his rights are from time to time infringed by the defendant. The word 'perpetual' does not necessarily signify that the order is to remain permanently effective: for instance, where a man has entered into a valid contract not to enter into competition with his former employer in a defined area for, say, three years after leaving the employment, any injunction granted will be limited to that specific period.

An interim injunction (previously[54] called an 'interlocutory injunction'), on the other hand, is only a temporary measure framed normally so as to continue in force until the trial of the action, or until further order.[55] In an appropriate case, however, one may be granted even though, from a practical point of view, it disposes of the matter. This has been done, for instance, where it has been applied for in order to remove a trespasser, who had plainly no defence to the action and merely sought to delay his eviction as long as possible,[56] and, again, to prevent a member of a private association from being deprived of his right to vote at the annual general meeting.[57] Generally, where an injunction, although in form interim, will be irreversible in effect, the court will not grant it unless it feels a high degree of assurance that the claimant would be successful at the trial in obtaining the remedy that he seeks at the interlocutory stage.[58]

Exceptionally, an interim injunction may be granted after judgment. In a case involving a freezing injunction,[59] Bingham J observed[60] that *an injunction is to be regarded as interlocutory, whether given before judgment or after, if it is not finally determinative of the rights of the parties but is merely in aid of the court's procedure and safeguarding the rights of the parties in the proceedings*.

---

[51] *Lumley v Wagner* (1852) 1 De GM & G 604. Cf *Hill v CA Parsons & Co Ltd* [1972] Ch 305, [1971] 3 All ER 1345, CA; and see pp 657–660, *infra*.

[52] *Bilston Corpn v Wolverhampton Corpn* [1942] Ch 391, [1942] 2 All ER 447.

[53] *Sky Petroleum Ltd v VIP Petroleum Ltd* [1974] 1 All ER 954, [1974] 1 WLR 576, an exceptional case in which order made; decision said to be 'almost certainly wrong' by Professor Goode (1976) 92 LQR 383, n 98 and 540. See p 668, *infra*.

[54] That is, before the Civil Procedure Rules 1998.

[55] If an application for an interim injunction is dismissed, the judge has jurisdiction to grant the unsuccessful applicant a limited interim injunction in the same terms pending appeal against the dismissal: *Erinford Properties Ltd v Cheshire County Council* [1974] Ch 261, [1974] 2 All ER 448. See *Ketchum International plc v Group Public Relations Holdings Ltd* [1996] 4 All ER 374, [1997] 1 WLR 4, CA.

[56] *Manchester Corpn v Connolly* [1970] Ch 420, [1970] 1 All ER 961, CA.

[57] *Woodford v Smith* [1970] 1 All ER 1091n, [1970] 1 WLR 806. Cf *Cayne v Global Natural Resources plc* [1984] 1 All ER 225, CA, with this case and that cited in the previous footnote.

[58] *Ford Sellar Morris Developments Ltd v Grant Seward Ltd* [1989] 2 EGLR 40.

[59] See pp 624–638, *infra*.   [60] In *Hill Samuel & Co Ltd v Littaur* [1985] NLJ Rep 57, 58.

Generally, an interim injunction will only be granted on notice so as to give the defendant a full opportunity to resist the claim. In a case of urgency, however, it may be granted without notice to the other party.[61] Although the claimant is under a duty to make the fullest possible disclosure of all material facts within his knowledge,[62] it is an anomaly that the court should have power to act against a defendant without having heard his side of the story. Although it is essential that the court should have such a power, it must be used only in circumstances in which it is really necessary to act immediately.[63]

The temporary character of an interim injunction means that it is generally of a prohibitory nature, although, in exceptional circumstances, it may be mandatory.[64] This is not because different principles apply to the grant of mandatory and prohibitory interim injunctions—in every case, the fundamental principle is that the court should take whichever course appears to carry the lower risk of injustice if it should turn out that the successful party at this stage should ultimately fail. In practice, this means that the features that justify describing an injunction as 'mandatory' will usually also have the consequence of creating a greater risk of injustice if it is granted rather than withheld at the interim stage. The merits threshold is a flexible one and, in some circumstances, the court requires a high degree of assurance that the claimant will be able to establish his right at a trial.[65] Cases in which mandatory interim injunctions were granted include *Von Joel v Hornsey*,[66] in which the defendant, knowing that the plaintiff wished to serve a writ upon him deliberately evaded service of the writ for some days and, in the meantime, hurried on with the building of which the plaintiff, as he well knew, was complaining. Another case is *Esso Petroleum Co Ltd v Kingswood Motors (Addlestone) Ltd*,[67] in which there was a five-year solus tie agreement between Esso and Kingswood. As part of a scheme to defeat the tie, Kingswood's garage was conveyed to a third party, Impact. The facts were somewhat complex, but the judge had no doubt that Impact had unlawfully procured a direct breach of Kingswood's contract with Esso. Accordingly, a mandatory injunction was granted, ordering a reconveyance of the garage to Kingswood. Finally, a mandatory order was made in *Parker v Camden London Borough Council*,[68] in which the defendant landlord

---

[61] For guidance on the information to be provided and the procedure to be followed in seeking without notice relief, see the cases referred to *B Borough Council v S (by the Official Solicitor)* [2006] EWHC 2584 (Fam), [2007] 1 FLR 1600, at [40]. Likewise, an injunction will normally only be varied or discharged on notice: *London City Agency (J C D) Ltd v Lee* [1970] Ch 597, [1969] 3 All ER 1376. As to the procedures, see *Pickwick International Inc (GB) Ltd v Multiple Sound Distributors Ltd* [1972] 3 All ER 384.

[62] *Bank Mellat v Nikpour* [1985] FSR 87, CA; *Memory Corpn plc v Sidhu (No 2)* [2000] 1 WLR 1443, CA.

[63] *Ansah v Ansah* [1977] Fam 138, [1977] 2 All ER 638, CA; *G v G* [1990] 1 FLR 395, CA; *Re First Express Ltd* [1992] BCLC 824.

[64] *Daniel v Ferguson* [1891] 2 Ch 27, CA; *Astro Exito Navegacion SA v Southland Enterprise Co Ltd (No 2)* [1983] 2 AC 787, [1982] 3 All ER 335, CA (an interlocutory mandatory order compelling the execution of a contractual obligation), noted (1983) 99 LQR 5; *Locabail International Finance Ltd v Agroexport and Atlanta (UK) Ltd* [1986] 1 All ER 901, [1986] 1 WLR 657, CA.

[65] *Films Rover International Ltd v Cannon Film Sales Ltd* [1986] 3 All ER 772, [1987] 1 WLR 670, discussed (1988) 47 CLJ 34 (N H Andrews); *Leisure Data v Bell* [1988] FSR 367, CA; *Channel Tunnel Group Ltd v Balfour Beatty Construction Ltd* [1992] 2 All ER 609, 626, CA, per Staughton LJ, affd [1993] AC 334, [1993] 1 All ER 664, HL, without discussing this point; *Edwin Shirley Productions Ltd v Workspace Management Ltd* [2001] 2 EGLR 10.

[66] [1895] 2 Ch 774, CA. But refused in *Shepherd Homes Ltd v Sandham* [1971] Ch 340, [1970] 3 All ER 402 (breach of negative covenant). [67] [1974] QB 142, [1973] 3 All ER 1057.

[68] [1986] Ch 162, [1985] 2 All ER 141, CA. The actual order was for an inspection of the boiler installations with a view to an appropriately drafted injunction being granted if necessary. Also in *London and Manchester Assurance Co Ltd v O and H Construction Ltd* [1989] 2 EGLR 185.

was admittedly in breach of its obligation to keep in repair the services for space heating and heating water. The breach, during a spell of cold weather, was causing severe hardship to the plaintiff tenants, particularly the elderly and the young, giving rise to an immediate fear as to the health of the tenants, going even to the risk of death.

In an appropriate case, at the trial of the action where the defendant intends to appeal, the judge may refuse to grant a successful claimant a perpetual injunction forthwith, but, pending appeal by the defendant, may instead continue an interim injunction. This may be done where, if the defendant were to succeed on appeal, he would otherwise have no claim for compensation for the loss that he might suffer by being subject to the injunction between the trial and appeal. If only an interim injunction is granted, it may be made subject to the usual undertaking in damages.[69] The claimant would be given the right to come back to court to ask for a perpetual injunction if the defendant failed to enter an appeal in due time or if an appeal were not prosecuted with due diligence.[70]

(c) *QUIA TIMET* INJUNCTION

Although an injunction is directed to the future, it is, in general, based on some infringement or, in the case of an interim injunction, alleged infringement of the claimant's rights. It is, however, possible to obtain injunctions, both interim and perpetual, based on an injury by the defendant[71] that is merely threatened or apprehended, although no infringement of the claimant's rights has yet occurred.[72] The House of Lords, in *Redland Bricks Ltd v Morris*,[73] said that there are two types of case: firstly, that in which the defendant has as yet done no hurt to the plaintiff, but is threatening and intending (so the plaintiff alleges) to do works that will render irreparable harm to him or his property if carried to completion, which cases are normally concerned with negative injunctions; secondly, the type of case in which the plaintiff has been fully recompensed both at law and in equity for the damage that he has suffered, but in which he alleges that the earlier actions of the defendant may lead to future causes of action. The typical case is that in which the defendant has withdrawn support from the plaintiff's land. Such withdrawal of support only constitutes a cause of action when damage is suffered, and any further damage arising from the original withdrawal will constitute a fresh cause of action. In such cases, a mandatory injunction may well be the appropriate remedy. Professor Jolowicz contends, however, that the term 'quia timet injunction' should be restricted to the first type of case.[74]

The jurisdiction to grant a *quia timet* injunction has been said to be 'as old as the hills',[75] but 'no one can obtain a quia timet order by merely saying "Timeo"'.[76] Chitty J said[77] 'that

---

[69] See p 581 *et seq, infra*.   [70] *American Cyanamid Co v Ethicon Ltd* [1979] RPC 215, 275 *et seq*.

[71] *Trawnik v Gordon Lennox* [1985] 2 All ER 368, [1985] 1 WLR 532, CA.

[72] As to the power of a county court see p 556, fn 6, *supra*. As to *quia timet* injunctions in libel and slander actions, see *British Data Management plc v Boxer Commercial Removals plc* [1996] 3 All ER 707, CA; as to an injunction restraining someone from using the plaintiff's name or trademark as a domain name on the Internet, see *British Telecommunications plc v One in a Million* [1998] FSR 265.

[73] [1970] AC 652, [1969] 2 All ER 576, HL.   [74] (1975) 34 CLJ 224.

[75] *A-G v Long Eaton UDC* [1915] 1 Ch 124, 127, CA, *per* Cozens-Hardy.

[76] *Per* Lord Dunedin in *A-G for Dominion of Canada v Ritchie Contracting and Supply Co Ltd* [1919] AC 999, 1005, PC.

[77] *A-G v Manchester Corpn* [1893] 2 Ch 87, 92; *Redland Bricks Ltd v Morris* [1970] AC 652, [1969] 2 All ER 576, HL.

the plaintiff must show a strong case of probability that the apprehended mischief will, in fact, arise'—in other words, the plaintiff must prove that the threatened or intended act would be an inevitable violation of his right. 'Inevitable' has been explained as meaning, in this context, a 'very great probability',[78] or that 'the result is one which all reasonable men skilled in the matter would expect would happen'.[79] More recently, Russell LJ has suggested[80] that the degree of probability of future injury is not an absolute standard. 'What is to be aimed at,' he said, 'is justice between the parties having regard to all the relevant circumstances.'

Not surprisingly, in the light of what has been said above, the dividing line between the cases is not altogether clear. It may be helpful to look at a few cases on either side. On the one hand, the court thought that there was a sufficient degree of probability in *Dicker v Popham, Radford & Co*,[81] in which the defendant was erecting a building that, if completed, would infringe the plaintiff's alleged right to light; in *Goodhart v Hyett*,[82] in which the plaintiff had a right to have pipes to convey water through the defendant's land, and the defendant was building a house over part of the line of pipes, which would render their repair more difficult and expensive; and in *Torquay Hotel Co Ltd & Cousins*,[83] in which defendant members of a trade union had begun to picket the plaintiff's hotel in order to prevent the delivery of fuel oil. The evidence was that the defendants threatened or intended to interfere with the delivery of fuel oil, if necessary for months, by placing pickets. This showed a manifest intention to interfere directly and deliberately with the execution of contracts for the supply of fuel oil to the plaintiff's hotel, which warranted the granting of a *quia timet* injunction. On the other hand, the court will not grant an injunction where there is nothing more than a mere possibility of future injury, or mere speculation of possible mischief, which may never happen at all.[84] Thus the plaintiff failed to make out a case of sufficient probability, and an injunction was refused, in *Fletcher v Bealey*,[85] to restrain a defendant from polluting a river by depositing chemicals, from which, in time, a noxious liquid would flow, on certain land close to the river, on the ground that the liquid could be prevented from reaching the river and that, by the time the flow began, some method of rendering it innocuous might have been discovered; nor in *A-G v Manchester Corpn*,[86] to restrain the erection of a smallpox hospital, on the ground that the danger to the health of the neighbourhood was not sufficiently established; nor in *Draper v British Optical Association*,[87] to restrain the holding of a meeting to consider the removal of the plaintiff from the defendant association, because it was to be assumed that they would not remove him unless entitled to do so.

In particular, a *quia timet* injunction will readily be granted where the plaintiff establishes his right, and the defendant has claimed and insisted on his right to do an act that

---

[78] *Per* Jessel MR in *Pattisson v Gilford* (1874) LR 18 Eq 259, 264.

[79] *Per* Chitty J in *Phillips v Thomas* (1890) 62 LT 793, 795.

[80] In *Hooper v Rogers* [1975] Ch 43, [1974] 3 All ER 417, CA. This approach was followed in Australia in *Kestrel Coal Property Ltd v Construction, Forestry, Mining & Energy Union* [2001] 2 Qd R 634.

[81] (1890) 63 LT 379; *Hepburn v Lordan* (1865) 2 Hem & M 345.

[82] (1883) 25 Ch D 182.   [83] [1969] 2 Ch 106, [1969] 1 All ER 522, CA.

[84] *Worsley v Swann* (1882) 51 LJ Ch 576, CA.

[85] (1885) 28 Ch D 688 (the plaintiff's right to bring another action later in case of actual injury or imminent danger, was expressly reserved).

[86] [1893] 2 Ch 87; *A-G v Nottingham Corpn* [1904] 1 Ch 673.   [87] [1938] 1 All ER 115.

would be an infringement of the plaintiff's right,[88] or has threatened or given notice of his intention to do such act.[89] In any case, it is not as a rule a sufficient defence to a claim for an injunction for the defendant to say that he has no present intention of doing the act in question.[90] Conversely, in *Lord Cowley v Byas*,[91] an injunction was refused where the defendant not only stated that he had no present intention of using the land as a cemetery, but said also that if he should, at any time thereafter, wish to do so, he would give the plaintiff two months' prior notice of his intention in order to give him an opportunity to bring proceedings to try and prevent his doing so. The general principle seems to be that 'it would be wrong for [the] court in quia timet proceedings to grant relief by way of injunction to compel the defendants to do something which they appear to be willing to do without the imposition of an order of the court'.[92]

Where a mandatory injunction is sought in *quia timet* proceedings, the question of the cost to the defendant of doing works to prevent or lessen the likelihood of a future apprehended wrong must be an element to be taken into account. On the one hand, where the defendant has acted wantonly and quite unreasonably in relation to his neighbour, he may be ordered to repair his wanton and unreasonable acts by doing positive work to restore the status quo even if the expense to him is out of all proportion to the advantage thereby accruing to the claimant. On the other hand, where the defendant has acted reasonably, although in the event wrongly, the cost of remedying by positive action his earlier activities is more important for two reasons: firstly, because *ex hypothesi* no legal wrong has occurred (for which the claimant has not been recompensed) and may never occur or only on a small scale; secondly, because if ultimately heavy damage does occur, the claimant is in no way prejudiced, because he has his action at law and all of his consequential remedies in equity. The cost to the defendant of carrying out a mandatory order must be balanced against the anticipated possible damage to the plaintiff, and if, on such balance, it seems unreasonable to inflict such expenditure on one who, for this purpose, is no more than a potential wrongdoer, then the court must exercise its jurisdiction accordingly.[93]

3 DAMAGES IN LIEU OF AN INJUNCTION

(A) JURISDICTION

Whether, before Lord Cairns' Act,[94] the Court of Chancery had power to award damages is not altogether clear.[95] If it had such power, it would only exercise it in exceptional

---

[88] *Shafto v Bolckow, Vaughan & Co* (1887) 34 Ch D 725; *Philips v Thomas* (1890) 62 LT 793.

[89] *McEacharn v Colton* [1902] AC 104, PC; *Thornhill v Weeks* [1913] 1 Ch 438.

[90] *Hext v Gill* (1872) 7 Ch App 699; *Leckhampton Quarries Co Ltd v Ballinger* (1904) 20 TLR 559.

[91] (1877) 5 Ch D 944, CA; *Jenkins v Hope* [1896] 1 Ch 278.

[92] *Bridlington Relay Ltd v Yorkshire Electricity Board* [1965] Ch 436, 445, [1965] 1 All ER 264, 269, *per* Buckley J. [93] *Redland Bricks Ltd v Morris* [1970] AC 652, [1969] 2 All ER 576, HL.

[94] Chancery Amendment Act 1858. For a valuable discussion of this Act, see (1975) 34 CLJ 224 (J A Jolowicz); [1981] Conv 286 (T Ingman and J Wakefield). As to its application to the county court, see p 556, fn 6, *supra*. See also (1985) 34 ICLQ 317 (A Burgess); (1989) 12 Dal LJ 131 (P M McDermott).

[95] See *Grant v Dawkins* [1973] 3 All ER 897, 899, 900, [1973] 1 WLR 1406, 1408; Spry, *Equitable Remedies*, 5th edn, pp 623–625, and p 7, *supra*. It is clear that an account might be ordered in certain cases in which the defendant had made a profit. As to equitable damages in Singapore, see (1988) 30 Mal LR 79 (Soh Kee Bun).

circumstances, and there seems to be no reported case of its exercise since Lord Cairns' Act, which, by s 2, empowered the court to award damages in addition to or in substitution for an injunction 'in all cases in which the Court of Chancery has jurisdiction to entertain an application for an injunction'.[96] This statutory power enabled the court to give damages in some cases in which damages could not have been obtained in a court of common law: where, for instance, the injury was merely threatened or apprehended;[97] where the writ was issued prematurely for a common law action;[98] or where the right was purely equitable.[99] It applied even though the damage was only nominal.[100] Again, at common law, damages are recoverable only in respect of causes of action that are complete at the date of the writ; damages for future or repeated wrongs—for instance, a continuing trespass—must be made the subject of fresh proceedings. Damages in substitution for an injunction, however, relate to the future, not the past, and inevitably extend beyond the damages to which the claimant may be entitled at law. They compensate the claimant for those future wrongs that an injunction would have prevented, and make it impossible for him to bring an action in respect thereof in the future.[101] Although Lord Cairns' Act has been repealed,[102] the jurisdiction has been preserved, as explained by the House of Lords in *Leeds Industrial Co-operative Society Ltd v Slack*.[103] The relevant provision of Lord Cairns' Act is now substantially re-enacted in s 50 of the Supreme Court Act 1981, now renamed the Senior Courts Act 1981, and the present position is that all divisions of the High Court now have both this jurisdiction and also, under the Judicature Acts,[104] the jurisdiction that the common law courts had to award damages before 1875. It may be added that, in a proper case, the court may grant damages as to the past and an injunction as to the future.[105] It may also, in an appropriate case, award a restricted injunction and damages as compensation for the restriction.[106]

The object of Lord Cairns' Act was said, in *Ferguson v Wilson*,[107] to be to prevent a litigant being bandied about from one court to another, and to enable the Court of Chancery to do complete justice by awarding damages where, before the Act, it would have refused

---

[96] Or specific performance. Since the same principles apply, the cases referred to below include cases on specific performance.

[97] *Leeds Industrial Co-operative Society Ltd v Slack* [1924] AC 851, HL.

[98] *Oakacre Ltd v Claire Cleaners (Holdings) Ltd* [1982] Ch 197, [1981] 3 All ER 667, discussed p 649, *infra*.

[99] For example, a restrictive covenant, in respect of a subsequent purchaser to whom the burden did not pass at common law: *Eastwood v Lever* (1863) 4 De GJ & Sm 114; *Baxter v Four Oaks Properties Ltd* [1965] Ch 816, [1965] 1 All ER 906.

[100] *Sayers v Collyer* (1884) 28 Ch D 103, CA.

[101] *Jaggard v Sawyer* [1995] 2 All ER 189, [1995] 1 WLR 269, CA.

[102] By the Statute Law Revision Act 1883, s 3.   [103] *Supra*.

[104] See now Supreme Court Act 1981, s 49.

[105] *Martin v Price* [1894] 1 Ch 276, CA; *Gilling v Gray* (1910) 27 TLR 39. At least in the case of breach of a restrictive covenant, notwithstanding that the covenantee cannot establish actual financial loss: *WWF–World Wide Fund for Nature v World Wrestling Federation Entertainment Inc* [2007] EWCA Civ 286, [2008] 1 All ER 74, at [53].

[106] *Chiron Corpn v Organon Teknika Ltd (No 10)* [1995] FSR 325.

[107] (1866) 2 Ch App 77, *per* Turner LJ (a case on specific performance). But Jessel MR thought, in *Aynsley v Glover* (1874) LR 18 Eq 544, 555, that the Act was designed to prevent a man obtaining an extortionate sum as the price of giving up his legal right to an injunction, for instance, against some comparatively trifling infringement of a right to light by a property developer. Cf Buckley J in *Cowper v Laidler* [1903] 2 Ch 337, who did not think it extortionate to ask a price that a property for exceptional reasons, in fact, commands.

an injunction and left the plaintiff to bring his action for damages at law. Since Lord Cairns was himself a member of the court in which this explanation was given, it is presumably accurate, but it seems at first sight to be contradicted by cases[108] that appear to hold that the court could only exercise the jurisdiction to award damages where it would have granted an injunction before the Act, or in cases in which the injunction was refused by reason of a change in circumstances between the filing of the bill and the trial, but would have been granted on the facts at the time of the filing of the bill. As Professor Jolowicz observes,[109] this 'comes close to the reductio ad absurdum that the jurisdiction to award damages under the Act exists only when, by definition, it should not be exercised'.

The difficulty, as pointed out by Professor Jolowicz,[110] lies in defining the scope of the jurisdiction conferred by the Act, which grants a discretionary power to substitute damages in lieu of a remedy that is itself discretionary. The correct view appears to be that damages may be granted in substitution for an injunction in any case in which, as at the date of the writ, the court *could* (not *would*) have granted an injunction apart from Lord Cairns' Act.[111] If the plaintiff does not make out even a prima facie claim to equitable relief, there can, of course, be no question of damages under Lord Cairns' Act. Thus, in *Ferguson v Wilson*[112] itself, specific performance of the alleged contract for the allotment of shares to the plaintiff was impossible because the shares had already been allotted to third parties. Accordingly, it was held that damages could not be awarded under Lord Cairns' Act. But if he makes out a case that requires the court to exercise its general equitable discretion as to whether, in all of the circumstances, an injunction should be awarded, it is a different matter. If, in the exercise of that discretion, the judge decides against an injunction, he should then consider whether to award damages under Lord Cairns' Act, by reference to the circumstances as they exist at the date of the hearing.

In this context, *Price v Strange*[113] suggests that the courts will be slow to hold that a matter alleged as a defence to a claim for equitable relief goes to jurisdiction rather than discretion. That case concerned want of mutuality[114] in a claim for specific performance, which was unhesitatingly held to go to discretion. Likewise the fact that it concerned a contract to do repairs was held not to go to jurisdiction, because although the court does not often order specific performance of a contract to build or do repairs, it can do so in exceptional circumstances.[115] It has further been held that the jurisdiction to grant damages in lieu of specific performance exists in any case in which, when the proceedings were begun, the court had jurisdiction to grant specific performance, and continues notwithstanding that thereafter, but before judgment, specific performance has become impossible,[116] and also,

---

[108] For example, *Aynsley v Glover, supra*; *Holland v Worley* (1884) 26 Ch D 578 (in which Pearson J observed that the authorities added to rather than removed the difficulties); *Proctor v Bayley* (1889) 42 Ch D 390, CA.

[109] (1975) 34 CLJ 224, 240.   [110] Op cit, pp 240–242.

[111] *Jaggard v Sawyer* [1995] 2 All ER 189, [1995] 1 WLR 269, CA; *Hooper v Rodgers* [1975] Ch 43, [1974] 3 All ER 417; *Harris v Williams-Wynne* [2006] EWCA Civ 104, [2006] 2 P & CR 595.

[112] *Supra*. See *Surrey County Council v Bredero Homes Ltd* [1993] 3 All ER 705, [1993] 1 WLR 1361, CA, as explained in *Jaggard v Sawyer, supra*, CA.

[113] [1978] Ch 337, [1977] 3 All ER 371, CA.   [114] See p 660, *infra*.

[115] See p 671, *infra*. Goff LJ in *Price v Strange, supra*, at 385, 386, CA, thought the same was true of a contract for personal services, but Buckley LJ, at 394, seems to have thought that this went to the jurisdiction.

[116] *Johnson v Agnew* [1978] Ch 176, [1978] 3 All ER 314, CA; appeal dismissed on other grounds [1980] AC 367, [1979] 1 All ER 883, HL.

it is thought, where a right to decree equitable relief has accrued after the commencement of the action.[117]

It is not necessary for the plaintiff to include a claim for damages in his claim. Nor, conversely, need he ask for an injunction if he recognizes that he is unlikely to obtain one, although he should make it clear whether he is claiming damages for past injury at common law, or damages under the Act in substitution for an injunction.[118]

(B) PRINCIPLES TO BE APPLIED

The result of the Act was, where it applied, to give the court a discretion whether to grant an injunction or to award damages in substitution therefor. The court has assumed a similar discretion where, as a result of the Judicature Acts, it has both the equitable jurisdiction to grant an injunction and the common law jurisdiction to award damages. The courts do not seem to distinguish between these two discretions in considering whether to award an injunction or damages.

In exercising their discretion, the courts have made it clear that if, according to ordinary principles, a plaintiff has made out his case for an injunction, the court will not award damages in substitution therefor, except under very exceptional circumstances.[119] The mere fact that an injunction would almost certainly do no good to the plaintiff does not seem to be sufficient.[120] In particular, as Lindley LJ said in *Shelfer v City of London Electric Lighting Co*:[121]

> ever since Lord Cairns' Act was passed the Court of Chancery has repudiated the notion that the legislature intended to turn that court into a tribunal for legalizing wrongful acts; or in other words, the court has always protested against the notion that it ought to allow a wrong to continue simply because the wrongdoer is able and willing to pay for the injury he may inflict.

This is so even if the wrongdoer is, in some sense, a public benefactor.[122] Lord Sumner expressed the same idea in colourful language in *Leeds Industrial Co-operative Society Ltd v Slack*,[123] which involved the infringement of a right to light:

> For my part, I doubt, as Sir George Jessel doubted,[124] whether it is complete justice to allow the big man, with his big building and his enhanced rateable value and his improvement of the neighbourhood, to have his way, and to solace the little man for his darkened and stuffy little house by giving him a cheque that he does not ask for.

---

[117] See McDermott, *Equitable Damages*, p 82 *et seq.*

[118] *Jaggard v Sawyer, supra,* CA. Cf *Surrey County Council v Bredero Homes Ltd, supra,* CA.

[119] *Shelfer v City of London Electric Lighting Co* [1895] 1 Ch 287, CA, referred to as a binding authority in *Regan v Paul Properties Ltd* [2006] EWCA Civ 1391, [2007] 4 All ER 48, [2006] 3 WLR 1131. The latter case reviews the authorities and sets out the general principles applicable.

[120] *Per* Stamp J at first instance in *Sefton v Tophams Ltd* [1964] 3 All ER 876, 894. Lord Cairns' Act was not discussed at either stage of the appeal.

[121] [1895] 1 Ch 287, 315, 316, CA, referred to with approval in *Elliott v London Borough of Islington* [1991] 1 EGLR 167, CA.

[122] *Supra; Biogen Inc v Medeva plc* [1993] RPC 475 discussing the point in relation to life-saving drugs. See also *Sampson v Hodson-Pressinger* [1981] 3 All ER 710, CA.

[123] [1924] AC 851, 872, HL.

[124] In *Krehl v Burrell* (1878) 7 Ch D 551, 554; affd (1879) 11 Ch D 146, CA.

In *Shelfer v City of London Electric Lighting Co*,[125] A L Smith LJ gave it as his opinion that 'as a good working rule' damages in substitution for an injunction may[126] be given if:

(i)   the injury to the plaintiff's legal right is small; and

(ii) is one that is capable of being estimated in money; and

(iii) is one that can be adequately compensated by a small money payment; and

(iv) the case is one in which it would be oppressive to the defendant to grant an injunction.

It was pointed out in *Slack v Leeds Industrial Co-operative Society Ltd*,[127] in which the rule was accepted as valid, that it must be read in its context, including, in particular, the judge's preceding observation that if the plaintiff's legal right has been invaded, he is prima facie entitled to an injunction. It came in for more severe criticism in *Fishenden v Higgs and Hill Ltd*,[128] in which it was said[129] 'to be the high water mark of what might be called definite rules'. It was further said[130] that the rule was not intended to be exhaustive or to be rigidly applied, and that the tests were, as A L Smith LJ himself recognized, of imperfect application—what, for instance, is meant by a 'small' injury, or 'adequate' compensation? Another member of the court,[131] after noting that the rule was contained in an *obiter dictum*, observed that, although it might have been valid in the sort of case then before the court—that is, nuisance by noise and vibration—it was 'not a universal or even sound rule in all cases of injury to light'. However, in the more recent cases, the Court of Appeal has accepted the rule as valid, pointing out that it has been applied time and again over the years, but reiterating that it is only a working rule: it does not purport to be an exhaustive statement of the circumstances in which damages may be awarded instead of an injunction. Moreover, it is clearly wrong to place the onus on the claimant to show why damages should not be awarded.[132] Thus, in *Jaggard v Sawyer*,[133] the award of damages at first instance was confirmed by the Court of Appeal, Millett LJ observing that the outcome of any particular case usually depends on the application of the fourth of A L Smith's rules.

By way of contrast, in *Kennaway v Thompson*,[134] the judge at first instance had awarded £15,000 damages, but the Court of Appeal granted an injunction restricting the activities

---

[125] [1895] 1 Ch 287, 322, 323, CA. Cf *Aynsley v Glover* (1874) LR 18 Eq 544.

[126] The word 'may' was emphasized by Lord Donaldson, with whom the other LJJ agreed, in *Elliott v London Borough of Islington* [1991] 1 EGLR 167, CA.

[127] [1924] 2 Ch 475, CA. Dicta in *Woollerton and Wilson Ltd v Richard Costain Ltd* [1970] 1 All ER 483, [1970] 1 WLR 411, doubting whether the rule applied to trespass where only nominal damages are recoverable were disapproved in *Jaggard v Sawyer* [1995] 2 All ER 189, [1995] 1 WLR 269, CA.

[128] (1935) 153 LT 128, CA.   [129] *Per* Hanworth MR, at 138.

[130] Some assistance is obtained from *Slack v Leeds Industrial Co-operative Society Ltd, supra*, which says that this is meant comparatively and not absolutely, and *Fishenden v Higgs and Hill Ltd, supra*, which decided that it does not matter if 'comparatively small damages' constitute absolutely a 'not inconsiderable sum'.

[131] Maugham LJ, at 144.

[132] *Regan v Paul Properties Ltd* [2006] EWCA Civ 1391, [2007] 4 All ER 48, [2006] 3 WLR 1131 (injunction awarded on appeal).

[133] *Supra*, CA.

[134] [1981] QB 88, [1980] 3 All ER 329, CA, discussed (1981) 131 NLJ 108 (B S Markesinis and A M Tettenborn); (1982) 41 CLJ 87 (S Tromans), who argues that the time is ripe for a review of the rule in *Shelfer's Case* and that the courts should exercise their discretion more readily in favour of damages; *Wakeham v Wood* (1981) 43 P & CR 40, CA (conditions not satisfied—mandatory injunction awarded); *Daniells v Mendonca* (1999) 78 P & CR 401, CA (rule applied: mandatory injunction granted); *Midtown Ltd v City*

of a club that organized motor boat races causing a nuisance by noise to the plaintiff. None of the first three conditions in A L Smith LJ's 'good working rule' was satisfied. Rather surprisingly *Kennaway v Thompson* was not referred to in *Watson v Croft Promosport Ltd*,[135] which involved nuisance by noise caused by motor racing. In that case, Simon J adopted the same approach as the court in *Regan v Paul Properties Ltd*, observing that 'the guidance in the *Shelfer* case is not a forensic straight-jacket for what is ultimately a matter of judgment and discretion'. On the facts, however, he came to a different conclusion and gave two reasons for awarding damages in lieu of an injunction: firstly, although falling short of giving rise to a defence of acquiescence, there had been considerable delay in commencing proceedings; secondly the claimant's willingness to accept compensation for noise on more than twenty days up to forty days was a matter that counted against granting an injunction. He added that he thought that the effect that an injunction would have on local employment and the enjoyment of followers of motor racing, for which limited sites were available, were legitimate matters to take into account, although he had reached his conclusion without doing so.

The exercise of the court's discretion has been discussed in several cases. On the one hand, Lord Macnaghten has stated[136] that while the amount of damages that it is supposed could be recovered does not furnish a satisfactory test, an injunction and not damages should be awarded if the injury cannot fairly be compensated by money, or if the defendant has acted in a high-handed manner, or if he has endeavoured to 'steal a march' upon the plaintiff or to evade the jurisdiction of the court. Jessel MR has suggested[137] that, as a general rule, an injunction should be awarded if the defendant knew that he was doing wrong and took his chance about being disturbed in doing it. And it has been held[138] that, in general, damages will not be granted in lieu of an injunction against the pollution of a stream, or nuisance by noise or smell,[139] as it is impossible to measure what the future damage would be; nor in the case of a continuing trespass, where refusal of an injunction would, in effect, compel the landowner to grant a right to the trespasser.[140] On the other

of London Real Property Co Ltd [2005] EWHC 33 (Ch), [2005] 1 EGLR 65; *Tamares (Vincent Square) Ltd v Fourpoint (Vincent Square) Ltd* [2006] EWHC 3589, [2007] 1 WLR 2148; *Morris v Redland Bricks Ltd* [1967] 3 All ER 1, CA, in which, however, the LJJ disagreed as to the application of the rule of the facts. Note, however, that this decision was reversed on appeal in the House of Lords, sub nom *Redland Bricks Ltd v Morris* [1970] AC 652, [1969] 2 All ER 576, in which this point was not discussed. All of their Lordships agreed with Lord Upjohn that the Court of Appeal should not have considered Lord Cairns' Act at all. The question at issue was said to be simply whether or not a mandatory *quia timet* injunction should be granted. Lord Cairns' Act was said not to be applicable because neither party had sought to rely on it, but the better view is that the Act applies whether or not the parties themselves invoke it: see (1975) 34 CLJ 224 (J A Jolowicz). See *Hooper v Rogers* [1975] Ch 43, [1974] 3 All ER 417, in which, on similar facts, Lord Cairns' Act was applied. See also (1977) 36 CLJ 369, (1978) 37 CLJ 51 (P H Pettit).

[135] [2008] EWHC 759 (QB), [2008] 3 All ER 1171.

[136] In *Colls v Home and Colonial Stores Ltd* [1904] AC 179, 193, HL; *Shelfer's Case*, CA, *supra*; *Wakeham v Wood*, CA, *supra*.

[137] *Smith v Smith* (1875) LR 20 Eq 500; *Pugh v Howells* (1984) 48 P & CR 298, CA discussed (1985) 135 NLJ 1005 (H W Wilkinson). But see *Ketley v Gooden* (1996) 73 P & CR 305, in which delay in seeking relief was an important factor against the award of an injunction.

[138] *Pennington v Brinsop Hall Coal Co* (1877) 5 Ch D 769.

[139] *Wood v Conway Corpn* [1914] 2 Ch 47, CA.

[140] Damages in lieu were, however, awarded in *Tollemache and Cobbold Breweries Ltd v Reynolds* (1983) 268 Estates Gazette 52, CA, having regard to the minor nature of the trespass and the appellant's behaviour.

hand, Lord Macnaghten, in the same case,[141] observed that where there is a real question as to whether the plaintiff's rights have been infringed, and the defendant has acted fairly and not in an unneighbourly spirit, the court should incline to damages rather than an injunction, and Lindley LJ has suggested,[142] as examples of circumstances in which the court would exercise its discretion by awarding damages, trivial and occasional nuisances, cases in which a plaintiff has shown that he only wants money, vexatious and oppressive cases, cases in which the plaintiff has so conducted himself as to render it unjust to give him more than pecuniary relief, and cases in which damages is really an adequate remedy. And in several cases,[143] it has been held that a fairly weak case of acquiescence by the plaintiff may be a ground for awarding damages in lieu of an injunction.

Most of the cases in which an injunction has been refused and damages awarded are cases in which the plaintiff has sought a mandatory injunction to pull down a building that infringes his right to light or which has been built in breach of a restrictive covenant. In such cases, the court is faced with a fait accompli and to grant an injunction would subject the defendant to a loss out of all proportion to that which would be suffered by the plaintiff if it were refused. A similar situation arises where a prohibitory injunction is sought to restrain access to the defendant's house, which, if granted, would render the house landlocked and incapable of beneficial enjoyment.[144] One may note also *Sharp v Harrison*,[145] in which Astbury J stated the general proposition that damages, and not an injunction, should be granted where the plaintiff had not really suffered any damage and an injunction would inflict damage upon the defendant out of all proportion to the relief that the plaintiff ought to obtain.

Finally, Lord Denning MR has indicated, obiter, that damages should be awarded where the effect of an injunction would be '*to stop a great enterprise and render it useless*'.[146]

(C) MEASURE OF DAMAGE

Where damages are recoverable in respect of the same cause of action either at common law or under Lord Cairns' Act, the same compensatory principle applies to both situations.[147] As previously mentioned, Lord Cairns' Act applies equally to claims for specific performance and claims for an injunction, and, in *Wroth v Tyler*,[148] the point arose in a specific

---

[141] *Colls v Home and Colonial Stores Ltd, supra*, HL. It is pointed out in *Regan v Paul Properties Ltd, supra*, CA, that Lord Macnaghten prefaced what he described as 'practical suggestions' with the comment that he did not put them forward as carrying any authority. See also *Kine v Jolly* [1905] 1 Ch 480, CA.

[142] In *Shelfer v City of London Electric Lighting Co* [1895] 1 Ch 287, 317, CA.

[143] *Sayers v Collyer* (1884) 28 Ch D 103, CA, esp per Fry LJ, at 110; *H P Bulmer Ltd and Showerings Ltd v J Bollinger SA* [1977] 2 CMLR 625, 681, per Goff LJ. In *Ludlow Music Inc v Robbie Williams* [2001] FSR 271, an injunction was refused, although the appropriate compensation might be substantial, where there was clearly an element of acquiescence, and the evidence suggested strongly that the claimants were only interested in money.

[144] *Jaggard v Sawyer* [1995] 2 All ER 189, [1995] 1 WLR 269, CA. Cf cases such as *Goodson v Richardson* (1874) 9 Ch App 221.   [145] [1922] 1 Ch 502.

[146] *Allen v Gulf Oil Refining Ltd* [1980] QB 156, [1979] 3 All ER 1008, 1016, CA.

[147] *Johnson v Agnew* [1980] AC 367, [1979] 1 All ER 883, HL; *Jaggard v Sawyer, supra*, CA. See (1980) CLJ 58 (A J Oakley); (1981) 97 LQR 445 (S M Waddams); (1999–2000) 4 Deak LR 61 (T H Ong); Jones and Goodhart, *Specific Performance*, 2nd edn, pp 280 *et seq*.

[148] [1974] Ch 30, [1973] 1 All ER 897; *Tito v Waddell (No 2)* [1977] Ch 106, 334, 335, [1977] 3 All ER 129, 318, 319; *Suleman v Shahsavari* [1989] 2 All ER 460, [1988] 1 WLR 1181; *Souster v Epsom Plumbing*

performance action. Specific performance of a contract for the sale of land was refused and the question was whether the damages should be £1,500, the difference between the contract price and the market price of the property as at the date of the breach—that is, the date fixed for completion—or £5,500, being the same difference as at the date of the trial. Although damages are normally assessed as at the date of the breach, Megarry J took the view that damages under Lord Cairns' Act are not necessarily the same as at common law, and awarded damages of £5,500. In *Johnson v Agnew*,[149] the House of Lords disagreed with this case, in so far as it might be taken to hold that the measure of damage differs in common law from equity. Although damages are normally assessed as at the date of the breach, this is not an absolute rule either at common law or under Lord Cairns' Act. As Lord Wilberforce observed:[150]

> In cases where a breach of a contract of sale has occurred, and the innocent party reasonably continues to try to have the contract completed, it would to me appear more logical and just rather than tie him to the date of the original breach, to assess damages as at the date when (otherwise than by his default) the contract is lost.

In a few cases, damages may be awarded in substitution for an injunction under Lord Cairns' Act where damages could not be recovered at common law: for example, in lieu of a *quia timet* injunction, or for breach of a restrictive covenant to which the defendant was not a party.[151] An instance of this is *Wrotham Park Estate Co v Parkside Homes Ltd*,[152] in which the houses were built in breach of a restrictive covenant, and a mandatory injunction to demolish them was refused. The value of the covenantee's retained land was not diminished by the breach, but he was nevertheless awarded substantial damages in lieu of the injunction, assessed by reference to the sum he might reasonably have demanded as a quid pro quo for relaxing the covenant. This method of assessment was approved and applied by the Court of Appeal in *Jaggard v Sawyer*,[153] and approved by the House of Lords in *A-G v Blake*.[154]

Contractors Ltd [1974] 2 NZLR 515; *Semelhago v Paramadevan* [1996] 2 SCR 415. See [1974] 48 ALJ 273 (R P Austin); (1975) 91 LQR 337 (M Albery); (1997) 76 CBR 551 (N Siebrasse), in which *Wroth v Tyler* is said to be wrong in principle.

[149] *Supra*, HL.

[150] *Supra*, HL, at 896. All of the other Law Lords agreed with the speech of Lord Wilberforce.

[151] See p 566, *supra*.

[152] [1974] 2 All ER 321, [1974] 1 WLR 799; *Bracewell v Appleby* [1975] Ch 408, [1975] 1 All ER 993; *Carr-Saunders v Dick McNeil Associates Ltd* [1986] 2 All ER 888, [1986] 1 WLR 922. See (1979) 95 LQR 581 (Harris, Ogus, and Phillips); (1953) 99 LQR 443 (G Jones).

[153] *Supra*, CA, noted [1995] 14 CJQ 16 (F M); *Harris v Williams-Wynne* [2006] EWCA Civ 104, [2006] 2 P & CR 595. Since *A.G. v Blake, Supra*, HL, in so far as *Surrey County Council v Bredero Homes Ltd* [1993] 3 All ER 705, [1993] 1 WLR 1361, CA, decided that damages on the *Wrotham Park* basis were not available at common law, the decision can no longer be regarded as authoritative: *WWF—World Wide Fund for Nature v World Wresteins Federation Entertainment Inc, supra*, CA at [41]. Exceptionally, an account of profits may be the most appropriate remedy for breach of contract: *A-G v Blake* [2001] 1 AC 268, [2000] 4 All ER 385, HL; *Experience Hendrix LCC v PPX Enterprises Inc* [2003] EWCA Civ 323, [2003] 1 All ER (Comm) 830, noted (2003) RLR 101 (J Edelman); [2003] LMCLQ 301 (Pey-Woan Lee); (2004) 120 LQR 26 (M Graham); *Tamares (Vincent Square) Ltd v Fourpoint (Vincent Square) Ltd (No 2)* [2007] EWHC 212 (Ch), [2007] 1 WLR 2167 (damages in lieu for infringement of right to light). See (2002) 118 LQR 377 (J Beatson); [2003] CLJ 605 (D Campbell and P Wylie). See *Stoke-on-Trent City Council v W & J Wass Ltd* [1988] 3 All ER 394, [1988] 1 WLR 1405, CA; *Gafford v Graham* (1999) 77 P & CR 73, CA, noted (1998) 114 LQR 555 (P Milne). See also [1995] Conv 141 (T Ingman).

[154] *Supra*, HL. Subsequently applied *Amec Development Ltd v Jury's Hotel Management (UK) Ltd* (2001) 82 P & CR 286, noted (2001) 66 PLJ 16 (B Leighton). See [2001] Conv 453 (D Halpern); [2001] LMCLQ 9 (J Edelman); (2002) 22 LS 208 (D Campbell and D Harris).

Chadwick LJ, with whose judgment the other members of the court agreed, said, in *WWF–World Wide Fund for Nature v World Wrestling Federation Entertainment Inc*,[155] that when the court makes an award of damages on the *Wrotham Park* basis, it does so because it is satisfied that it is a just response to circumstances in which the compensation that is the claimant's due cannot be measured (or cannot be measured solely) by reference to identifiable financial loss. He also said,[156] obiter, that, in a case in which a covenantor has acted in breach of a restrictive covenant, the court may award damages on the *Wrotham Park* basis, notwithstanding that there is no claim for an injunction, and notwithstanding that there could be no claim for an injunction.

4 ENFORCEMENT OF AN INJUNCTION[157]

(A) POWERS OF THE COURT

(i) Enforcement against defendant

A person who is restrained by injunction from doing a particular act is liable for contempt of court[158] if he, in fact, does the act, and it is no answer to say that the act was not contumacious, in the sense that, in doing it, there was no direct intention to disobey the order; an act, however, which is merely casual, or accidental and unintentional, would not give rise to liability.[159] It is not sufficient, by way of answer to an allegation that a court order has

---

[155] [2007] EWCA Civ 286, [2008] 1 All ER 74, at [59], and see *Lunn Poly Ltd v Liverpool and Lancashire Properties Ltd* [2000] EWCA Civ 430, [2006] 2 EGLR 29.

[156] Ibid, at [54].

[157] An undertaking given to the court has all of the force of an injunction: *Roberts v Roberts* [1990] 2 FLR 111, CA; *Kensington Housing Trust v Oliver* (1997) 30 HLR 608, CA; but the procedural requirements for enforcement are not so strict as in the case of an order: *Hussain v Hussain* [1986] Fam 134, [1986] 1 All ER 961, CA. But it is not a contempt of court to refuse to comply with a declaratory order: *Webster v Southwark London Borough Council* [1983] QB 698; *D v D* (1990) Times, 16 November, CA. Where a breach by the defendant of an undertaking to the court necessarily involves a breach of a contract between the plaintiff and the defendant, the court may, on the hearing of an application to commit the defendant for breach of the undertaking, award damages without need for the plaintiff to bring a separate action: *Midland Marts Ltd v Hobday* [1989] 3 All ER 246. In this case, Vinelott J said, at 250, that the court cannot impose a fine and direct that the fine be paid to someone other than the Crown, but a different view has been taken in New Zealand: *Taylor Bros Ltd v Taylors Group Ltd* [1991] 1 NZLR 91 (NZ CA). Contempt proceedings in industrial disputes are discussed by J Bowers in (1985) 135 NLJ 1143, and in relation to the disobeying spouse by M Chesterman and P Waters (1985) 8 UNSWLJ 106.

[158] This is technically 'civil contempt', ie contempt by a party to proceedings in matters of procedure. A finding of contempt may be made against a government department or a minister of the Crown in his official capacity: *Re M* [1994] 1 AC 377, sub nom *M v Home Office* [1993] 3 All ER 537, HL, noted [1994] Pub L 568 (M Gould), in which Lord Templeman said that to hold otherwise would be to '*establish the proposition that the executive obeyed the law as a matter of grace, not of necessity, a proposition that would reverse the result of the Civil War*'. A finding of contempt can, of course, be made against a minister personally, provided that the contempt related to his own default. See also *R v IRC, ex p Kingston Smith (a firm)* [1996] STC 1210.

[159] *Fairclough v Manchester Ship Canal* (1897) 41 Sol Jo 225, CA; *Heatons Transport (St Helens) Ltd v Transport and General Workers Union* [1973] AC 15, [1972] 3 All ER 101, HL; *Director General of Fair Trading v Pioneer Concrete UK Ltd* [1995] 1 AC 456, HL; *Bird v Hadkinson* [1999] BPIR 653. In *Pereira v Beanlands*

not been complied with, for the person concerned to say that he 'did his best'; nor is bona fide reliance on legal advice that turns out to be wrong, although this may be relevant as mitigation.[160] The party enjoined is, of course, liable for its agents, and has some responsibility for the acts of its licensees. There is implied in the standard form of an injunction a requirement on the party enjoined to take such steps as are within its power to prevent its independent contractors from performing acts that, if performed by the party enjoined, would be in breach; failure unreasonably to exercise such power would be a contempt of court.[161] In the case of a company, disobedience to an injunction by its employees, acting in the course of their employment, amounts to contempt of court by the employing company, notwithstanding that the act of disobedience contravenes a specific instruction given by senior management, unless the conduct of the employees could be described as merely casual, or accidental and unintentional.[162]

The quality of non-compliance, which varies over an enormous range, from a flat defiance of the court's authority to a genuine wholehearted use of the best endeavours to comply with the order that, nevertheless, has been unsuccessful, is of the utmost importance to the court in deciding what penalty should be imposed. The penalty, in fact, reflects faithfully the court's view of the conduct of the person to whom the order was addressed.[163] However, the history that led to the imposition of an injunction is not relevant when sentencing for breach of the injunction, which has to be examined for what it is and sentenced accordingly.[164] An injunction, or an undertaking given, operates until it is revoked on appeal or by the court itself, and must be obeyed whether or not it should have been granted or accepted in the first place.[165]

The traditional sanction for contempt of court is imprisonment in the case of an individual, or sequestration in the case of a corporation, although in the case both of an individual and a corporation, it seems that the court could always impose the lesser penalty of a fine,[166] or merely order the offending party to pay costs and, if it thought fit, damages.[167]

[1996] 3 All ER 528, it was said that the word 'defiant' was possibly one that combined some of the flavour of both 'contumelious' and 'contumacious' in more everyday language.

[160] *Z Bank v DI* [1994] 1 Lloyd's Rep 656. *Parker (t/a NBC Services) v Rasalingham (t/a Micro Tec)* (2000) Times, 25 July.

[161] *World Wide Fund for Nature v THQ/Jakks Pacific LLC* [2004] FSR 161 CA.

[162] *Director General of Fair Trading v Pioneer Concrete (UK) Ltd, supra,* HL.

[163] *Howitt Transport Ltd v Transport and General Workers Union* [1973] ICR 1, *per* Donaldson J, esp at 10 and 11. See *A-G v Newspapers Publishing plc* (1990) Times, 28 February, CA, discussed (1991) 141 NLJ 173 (A Halpin).

[164] *Cambridgeshire County Council v D* [1999] 2 FLR 42, CA (sentence of twelve months' imprisonment reduced to three months for writing love letters to his pregnant girlfriend in breach of an injunction taken out by the local authority to prevent violence on the girlfriend in its care).

[165] *Johnson v Walton* [1990] 1 FLR 350, CA.

[166] *Ronson Products Ltd v Ronson Furniture Ltd* [1966] Ch 603, [1966] 2 All ER 381; *The Jarlinn* [1965] 3 All ER 36, [1965] 2 Lloyd's Rep 191; *The Calyx* [1966] 1 Lloyd's Rep 701 (Mayor's and City of London Court). The fine may be large, eg £525,000: see *Messenger Newspapers Group Ltd v National Graphical Association* [1984] IRLR 397. But is limited to £2,500 in the case of an inferior court: Contempt of Court Act 1981, s 14(2); Criminal Justice Act 1991 s 17(3)(a), Sch 4, Pt I. As to the level of sentencing for contempt proceedings associated with domestic and other violence, see *H v O (Contempt of Court: Sentencing)* [2004] EWCA Civ 1691, [2005] 2 FLR 329.

[167] *Fairclough v Manchester Ship Canal, supra; Re Agreement of Mileage Conference Group of the Tyre Manufacturers' Conference Ltd* [1966] 2 All ER 849 (RPC).

These powers remain and rules of court[168] now provide that one or more of the following means are available for enforcing an injunction against both an individual and a body corporate, viz:

(i) with the permission of the court, a writ of sequestration against the property of that person;

(ii) where that person is a body corporate, with the permission of the court, a writ of sequestration against the property of any director or other officer of the body;[169]

(iii) subject to the provisions of the Debtors Act 1869 and 1878, an order of committal against that person or, where that person is a body corporate, against any such officer.

The High Court has jurisdiction to commit for contempt whenever contempt involves a degree of fault or misconduct, including negligence.[170] However, the power is discretionary and is not automatically available at the demand of the plaintiff whose rights are being infringed. Indeed, where an application for committal is a wholly disproportionate response to a trivial or blameless breach of a court order, the court will dismiss the application with costs in favour of the respondent.[171]

The fundamental purpose of proceedings for contempt of court consisting of disobedience of an injunction is to uphold the supremacy of the rule of law and the court's authority to administer it. It is punitive in character. That it provides the beneficiary of such an order with an enforcement remedy is incidental.[172] Nevertheless, the court seldom takes the initiative in punishing a person who disobeys an injunction; the initiative is normally taken by the beneficiary of the order, who is entitled to consult his own interests in deciding whether or not to enforce it, and, if he chooses not to, the court will not, generally speaking, intervene. Where a public element is involved, the Attorney-General may intervene if he thinks fit. If neither the litigant nor the Attorney-General seeks to enforce the order, the court may act to punish the contempt of its own volition, but will only do so in exceptional cases of clear contempts that cannot wait to be dealt with.[173] However, once proceedings for contempt have been launched, they cannot be abandoned without the leave of the court, because the court itself has a major interest in the proceedings.[174]

Six final points may be added.

---

[168] CPR Sch 1, RSC Ord 45, r 5. See *AMIEU v Mudginberri Station Pty Ltd* (1986) 66 ALR 577; *A-G for Tuvalu v Philatelic Distribution Corpn Ltd* [1990] 2 All ER 216, [1990] 1 WLR 926, CA.

[169] An officer of a company is not liable in contempt merely by virtue of his office and his knowledge that the order sought to be enforced was made. He will only be liable if he can otherwise be shown to be in contempt under the general law of contempt: *Director General of Fair Trading v Buckland* [1990] 1 All ER 545, [1990] 1 WLR 920.

[170] *Guildford Borough Council v Valler* (1993) Times, 15 October, CA; *Heaton's Transport (St Helens) Ltd v Transport and General Workers Union* [1973] AC 15, 109, [1972] 3 All ER 101, 117, HL, *per* Lord Wilberforce.

[171] *Adam Phones Ltd v Goldschmidt* [1999] 4 All ER 486.

[172] *Re Supply of Ready Mixed Concrete* [1992] QB 213, sub nom *Director-General of Fair Trading v Smiths Concrete Ltd* [1991] 4 All ER 150, CA, overruled *Re supply of Ready Mixed Concrete (No 2)*; *Director-General of Fair Trading v Pioneer Concrete (UK) Ltd* [1995] 1 AC 456, [1995] 1 All ER 135, HL, without affecting this point.

[173] *Clarke v Chadburn* [1985] 1 All ER 211, [1985] 1 WLR 78, in which Megarry V-C debated whether the law was satisfactory.

[174] *Re Supply of Ready Mixed Concrete, supra,* CA.

(a) Under CPR Sch 1, RSC Ord 45, r 8, the court, without prejudice to its powers in relation to contempt, may direct that an act to be done be carried out by some person appointed by the court at the cost of the disobedient party.

(b) The court has jurisdiction to commit for contempt for breach of an injunction even though the injunction has ceased to have effect,[175] or has been discharged as having been irregularly obtained.[176]

(c) An act done in disobedience to an order of the court is an illegal and invalid act that cannot effect any change in the rights and liabilities of others.[177]

(d) The contempt jurisdiction of the court is quite separate from the criminal jurisdiction of any other court, notwithstanding that it may arise out of the same set of factual circumstances. The judge at first instance was accordingly held to have acted rightly in *Szczepanski v Szczepanski*[178] in refusing to adjourn contempt proceedings pending completion of criminal proceedings.

(e) When imposing a sentence of imprisonment for contempt of court, the court has no jurisdiction to direct that the contemnor should not be released from prison until a certain date. This would override the early release provisions in the Criminal Justice Act 1991.[179]

(f) There is no general rule that a court will not hear an application for his own benefit by a person in contempt unless and until he has purged his contempt. Whether the interests of justice are best served by hearing the application or by refusing to do so depends on the circumstances of a particular case.[180]

(ii) Enforcement against third parties

A third party who assists—that is, by aiding and abetting—a breach of an injunction is an accessory to breach of the injunction and equally liable with the defendant for what is a civil contempt.[181]

Further, in the case of an interim, but not a final, injunction,[182] a third party may be liable for criminal contempt even though he is acting independently of the party against whom the order was made. This is where his act constitutes a wilful interference with the administration of justice in the proceedings in which the order was made. One species of such interference is the deliberate publication information that the court has ordered someone else to keep confidential. Such publication interferes with the administration of justice because it destroys the subject matter of proceedings. Once the information has been published, the court can no longer do justice between the parties by enforcing the obligation of confidentiality.[183]

---

[175] *Jennison v Baker* [1972] 2 QB 52, [1972] 1 All ER 997, CA, in which it was held on this point that the county court has the same power as the High Court.

[176] *Wardle Fabrics Ltd v G Myristis Ltd* [1984] FSR 263.   [177] *Clarke v Chadburn, supra.*

[178] [1985] FLR 468, CA, in which the appellant had been committed to prison for twelve months; *Keeber v Keeber* [1995] 2 FLR 748, CA.   [179] *Thompson v Mitchell* (2004) Times, 13 September.

[180] *Raja v van Hoogstraten* [2004] EWCA Civ 968, [2004] 4 All ER 793.

[181] *Acrow (Automation) Ltd v Rex Chainbelt Inc* [1971] 3 All ER 1175, CA; *A-G v Punch Ltd* [2002] UKHL 50, [2003] 1 All ER 289.

[182] *Jockey Club v Buffham* [2002] EWHC 1866 (QB), [2003] QB 462, noted [2003] CLJ 241 (A T H Smith). See also (2002) 33 VUWLR 51 and (2003) 81 CBR 207 (J Berryman).

[183] *A-G v Times Newspapers Ltd* [1992] UKHL 50, [2003] 1 All ER 289, noted (2003) 119 LQR 384 (P Devonshire); (2003) 24 Co Law 310 (R Sarker). As to freezing injunctions, see p 624 *et seq, infra.*

(B) SERVICE OF THE INJUNCTION

Unless the court dispenses with the requirement, a mandatory injunction cannot be enforced unless a copy of the order has been served personally on the person required to do the act in question.[184] In the case of a prohibitory injunction, however, it suffices if the defendant was present when the order was made, or has been notified informally by telephone, or telegram, or in some other way.[185] A defendant who has merely had informal notice will not, however, be committed for contempt if he can establish a bona fide and reasonable belief that no injunction has, in fact, been granted.[186] In the case of an undertaking, the defendant is presumed to have known that he has given it, although, if he can satisfy the court that he was unaware of the terms of an undertaking given on his behalf, but not by him personally, this may be a mitigating circumstance.[187]

The court has a general power to dispense with service of a copy of an order if it thinks it just to do so.[188] In the case of a mandatory order, the power is exercisable not only prospectively—that is, before the expiration of the time limited for compliance with it—but also retrospectively—that is, after the occurrence of the events alleged to constitute its breach.[189]

(C) COMMITTAL TO PRISON

Guidance as to the proper approach was given by Lord Woolf MR in *Nicholls v Nicholls*.[190] Since committal orders involve the liberty of the subject, it is particularly important that the relevant rules are duly complied with. However, where defects have occurred in a committal order, or in an application to commit, but the contemnor has had a fair trial and the order for committal has been made on valid grounds, the court will not, in the absence of prejudice to the contemnor, set aside the order, since it has power to rectify the order and it would be contrary to the interests of justice to set aside the order purely on the grounds of a technicality.

By s 14(1) of the Contempt of Court Act 1981, imprisonment must be for a fixed term not exceeding two years in the case of committal by a superior court,[191] including, for this purpose, a county court,[192] or one month in the case of committal by an inferior court. Both the High Court and the county court have power on making an order of committal to prison to suspend the order conditional on compliance with stated conditions, and have power to impose consecutive sentences of imprisonment in appropriate cases.[193]

---

[184] CPR Sch 1, RSC Ord 45, r 7(2) and (7). In the case of a body corporate, if enforcement is sought against an officer, personal service on that officer is normally required: Ord 45, r 7(3).

[185] CPR Sch 1, RSC Ord 45, r 7(6). See *Blome v Blome* (1976) 120 Sol Jo 315 and (1977) 40 MLR 220 (P H Pettit).

[186] *Re Bishop, ex p Langley* (1879) 13 Ch D 110, CA.

[187] *Hussain v Hussain* [1986] Fam 134, [1986] 1 All ER 961, CA. See *Watkinson v AJ Wright (Electrical) Ltd* [1996] 3 All ER 31.

[188] CPR Sch 1, RSC Ord 45, r 7(7).

[189] *Davy International Ltd v Tazzyman* [1997] 3 All ER 183, CA.

[190] [1997] 2 All ER 97, CA, applying *M v P* [1992] 4 All ER 833, CA.

[191] As defined in s 19. See *Villiers v Villiers* [1994] 2 All ER 149, [1994] 1 WLR 493, CA.

[192] County Courts (Penalties for Contempt) Act 1983.

[193] *Lee v Walker* [1985] QB 1191, [1985] 1 All ER 781, CA. See *Re R (a minor)* [1994] 2 FCR 629, CA.

The reasons for a committal to custody for contempt are twofold: firstly, to punish the contemnor for disobedience of an order of the court; and secondly, to attempt to coerce him to comply with the order. Once the contemnor has been sufficiently punished for disobeying a court order, he should not be punished further for continuing to do the same thing. If it becomes clear that continuance of imprisonment will have no coercive effect and he has been punished enough, there is no justification for continuing to keep him in prison.[194] And a person cannot be committed more than once for a single breach.[195] Although, as a general rule, the court should not commit where there is a reasonable alternative available,[196] a prison sentence may be appropriate where there has been flagrant defiance of an order.[197]

It may be added that, on an application to the court to purge contempt, the judge can only say 'yes', 'no', or 'not yet'. He cannot release him on terms that the remaining part of sentence be suspended.[198]

(D) FAMILY LAW ACT 1996

Section 47 provides that if the court makes an occupation order (as defined by s 39), or a non-molestation order (as defined by s 42(1)), and it appears to the court that the respondent has used or threatened violence against the applicant or a relevant child (as defined in s 62(2), as amended) it must attach a power of arrest to one or more provisions of the order unless satisfied that, in all of the circumstances of the case, the applicant or child will be adequately protected without such power of arrest.[199]

The effect of this is to empower a constable to arrest without warrant a person whom he has reasonable cause to suspect of being in breach of any such provision. The person arrested must be brought before a judge within twenty-four hours.[200]

---

[194] *Enfield London Borough Council v Mahoney* [1983] 2 All ER 901, [1983] 1 WLR 749, CA (refusal to deliver up the Glastonbury Cross).

[195] *Kumari v Jalal* [1996] 4 All ER 65, [1997] 1 WLR 97, CA (failure to comply with delivery order by a fixed date; committal and continued non-compliance after release).

[196] *Danchevsky v Danchevsky* [1975] Fam 17, [1974] 3 All ER 934, CA.

[197] *Burton v Winters* [1993] 3 All ER 847, [1993] 1 WLR 1077, CA, in which the maximum sentence of two years was held to be justified; *Aubrey v Damollie* [1994] 1 FCR 131, CA.

[198] *Harris v Harris* [2002] 1 All ER 185, CA.

[199] There are restrictions to attaching a power of arrest in the case of without notice orders: s 47(3)–(5).

[200] Excluding Christmas Day, Good Friday, or any Sunday: Family Law Act 1996, s 47(7).

26

INJUNCTIONS II—PRINCIPLES GOVERNING GRANT OF INJUNCTIONS

Different principles apply to interim, as opposed to perpetual, injunctions. In the case of an interim injunction, the court is making an order against a defendant when the claimant has not yet established that some right of his has been infringed by the defendant, and, indeed, may never do so. If an injunction is granted and the claimant ultimately fails in his claim, the defendant will have suffered unjustly. Conversely, if an injunction is refused and the claimant ultimately succeeds in his claim, he may have suffered in the meantime from a continued violation of his rights in respect of which he may be unable to obtain adequate compensation. There is a good deal of authority as to how the court should balance these competing considerations, which will be considered in section 1 of this chapter.

A perpetual injunction can only be granted where the claimant has established the infringement of some right of his by the defendant. Since the grant of an injunction is always discretionary, the question is usually whether the circumstances are such that, in the discretion of the court, an injunction should be granted or refused, although where the injunction is sought in aid of a legal right, it will be refused if damages would be an adequate remedy.

1 INTERIM INJUNCTIONS

(A) INTRODUCTORY CONSIDERATIONS

In *American Cyanamid Co v Ethicon Ltd*,[1] Lord Diplock explained the rationale of interim injunctions as follows:

> When an application for an interlocutory injunction to restrain a defendant from doing acts alleged to be in violation of the plaintiff's legal right[2] is made on contested facts, the

---

[1] [1975] AC 396, [1975] 1 All ER 505, HL, most recently reaffirmed in *Bath and North East Somerset DC v Mowlem plc* [2004] EWCA Civ 722, [2004] BLR 153. See (1981) 40 CLJ 307 (Christine Gray), and for a general discussion of the position in Canada, (1982) 60 CBR 1 (B M Rogers and G W Hately). As to US law, see (1978) 91 HLR 525 (J Leubsdorf). See also *Smith v Peters* (1875) LR 20 Eq 511, 513, cited with approval in *Astro Exito Navegacion SA v Southland Enterprise Co Ltd (No 2)* [1982] QB 1248, [1982] 3 All ER 335, CA; *Bayer AG v Winter* [1986] 1 All ER 733, [1986] 1 WLR 497, CA.

[2] An injunction to restrain a defendant from presenting a winding-up petition is in a different category to which special rules apply: *Bryanston Finance Ltd v de Vries (No 2)* [1976] Ch 63, [1976] 1 All ER 25, CA.

decision whether or not to grant an interlocutory injunction has to be taken at a time when ex hypothesi the existence of the right or the violation of it, or both, is uncertain and will remain uncertain until final judgment is given in the action. It was to mitigate the risk of injustice to the plaintiff during the period before that uncertainty could be resolved that the practice arose of granting him relief by way of interlocutory injunction...The object of the interlocutory injunction is to protect the plaintiff against injury by violation of his right for which he could not be adequately compensated in damages recoverable in the action if the uncertainty were resolved in his favour at the trial.

An interim injunction is never granted as a matter of course;[3] it is always a matter of discretion. However, it is a judicial discretion and, in appropriate circumstances, it is a 'matter of right that upon proper terms the property shall be maintained *in statu quo* pending the trial'. As one would expect, the plaintiff has a harder task on a without-notice application.[4] Claimants who seek relief without notice are under a duty to make full and frank disclosure of all of the material facts. Those who fail in that duty, and those who misrepresent matters to the court, expose themselves to the very real risk of being denied interim relief whether or not they have a good arguable case or even a strong prima facie case.[5] On the other hand, the rule must not be allowed itself to become an instrument of injustice, nor must it be carried to extreme lengths.[6] In every case, the court retains a discretion to continue or to grant interim relief even if there has been non-disclosure, or worse. In deciding how that discretion should be exercised, the court will have regard to all of the circumstances of the case, including the degree and extent of the culpability with regard to the non-disclosure or misrepresentation.[7]

The discretion is vested in the judge of first instance and, accordingly, on an appeal from the judge's grant or refusal of an interim injunction, the function of an appellate court is not to exercise an independent discretion of its own. It must not interfere merely on the ground that the members of the appellate court would have exercised the discretion differently. It may, however, interfere on the ground that the judge's exercise of his discretion was based on a misunderstanding of the law or of the evidence before him, or on an inference that particular facts existed or did not exist that new evidence shows to be wrong, or that there has been a change of circumstances that would have justified the trial judge in acceding to an application to vary his order.[8]

At the hearing of an interim injunction, the court does not decide finally on the rights of the parties, but confines itself to the immediate object of the proceedings and, so far as possible, will not prejudge the case.[9] It will impose only such a restraint as may be required

---

[3] *Potter v Chapman* (1750) Amb 98. *Saunders v Smith* (1838) 3 My & Cr 711, 728, *per* Cottenham LC (in which an injunction was refused to restrain the sale of the first edition of Smith's *Leading Cases*, as being an infringement of copyright in various law reports).

[4] *Eothen Films Ltd v Industrial and Commercial Education—Macmillan Ltd* [1966] FSR 356, CA.

[5] *Behbehani v Salem* [1989] 2 All ER 143, [1989] 1 WLR 723n, CA; *W v H (Family Division: without notice orders)* [2001] 1 All ER 300.

[6] *Brink's-MAT Ltd v Elcombe* [1988] 3 All ER 188, [1988] 1 WLR 1350, CA.

[7] See the cases referred to in the previous two notes.

[8] *Hadmor Productions Ltd v Hamilton* [1983] 1 AC 191, [1982] 1 All ER 1042, HL, discussed (1984) 128 Sol Jo 325 (A N Khan); *The Abidin Daver* [1984] AC 398, [1984] 1 All ER 470, HL; *Bouygues Offshore SA v Caspian Shipping Co* [1998] 2 Lloyd's Rep 461, CA.

[9] *Skinners' Co v Irish Society* (1835) 1 My & Cr 162; *Preston v Luck* (1884) 27 Ch D 497, CA.

to stop the mischief complained of and to keep things as they are until the hearing.[10] The court has jurisdiction to make, at this stage, an order that would not be appropriate at the final trial.[11]

(B) UNDERTAKINGS

The court has no power to award damages to a defendant who suffers injury as a consequence of the grant of an interim injunction to which it is subsequently held that the clamant was not entitled.[12] To deal with the unfairness that might otherwise result, the Civil Procedure Rules[13] provide that, on the grant of an interim injunction, the claimant must enter into the 'usual undertaking' unless the court otherwise orders.[14] He cannot be compelled to enter into the undertaking, but if he does not, the injunction will normally be refused. This applies in the Chancery and Queen's Bench Divisions, but not in the Family Division, where it will be assumed that there is no undertaking as to damages unless it has been expressly given.[15] The usual undertaking requires that the claimant will abide by any order as to damages that the court may make if it should eventually turn out that he was not entitled to the interlocutory injunction and the defendant has suffered damage thereby.[16] Although the undertaking is extracted for the defendant's benefit, it is, in fact, given to the court,[17] and non-performance is accordingly a contempt of court. The court therefore retains a discretion not to enforce the undertaking if the conduct of the

[10] *Blakemore v Glamorganshire Canal Navigation, supra.*

[11] *Fresh Fruit Wales Ltd v Halbert* (1991) Times, 29 January, CA.

[12] See *F Hoffman-la Roche & Co AG v Secretary of State for Trade and Industry* [1975] AC 295, 360, [1974] 2 All ER 1128, 1150, HL, *per* Lord Diplock.

[13] CPR PD 25.5(1). See, generally, [1994] CLJ 546 (A A S Zuckerman).

[14] If omitted in the court order by mistake, it may be inserted under the 'slip rule': CPR 40.12. However, it is the practice not to require the usual undertaking if (a) the applicant is legally aided, or, (b) the applicant is a public authority enforcing the general law. As to lack of means of the applicant, see *Bunn v British Broadcasting Corpn* [1998] 3 All ER 552.

[15] *W v H (Family Division: without notice orders)* [2001] 1 All ER 300, in which Munby J summarizes the history of the rule.

[16] Possibly exemplary damages if the injunction was obtained fraudulently or maliciously: *Smith v Day* (1882) 21 Ch D 421, 428, *per* Brett LJ; *Digital Equipment Corpn v Darkcrest Ltd* [1984] Ch 512, [1984] 3 All ER 381. The possibility of exemplary damages is not consistent with the statement of Lewison J in *Smithkline Beecham plc v Apotex Europe Ltd* [2005] EWHC 1655 (Ch), [2006] 2 All ER 53, [2006] 1 WLR 872, at [43], affd in part [2006] EWCA Civ 658, [2006] 4 All ER 1078, that the nature of the claim on an undertaking is not a claim for *damages* at all, but for compensation for loss. Note that the court will not make an order as to damages until either the plaintiff has failed on the merits of the trial, or it is established before the trial that the injunction ought not to have been granted in the first instance: *Ushers Brewery Ltd v P S King & Co (Finance) Ltd* [1972] Ch 148, [1971] 2 All ER 468; *Colledge v Crossley, supra,* CA. The possibility of a claim where a freezing order is made for an excessive sum is discussed in [2004] 36 Sol Jo 1081 (Z Mavrogardato).

[17] *Digital Equipment Corpn v Darkcrest Ltd, supra; Cheltenham and Gloucester Building Society v Ricketts* [1993] 4 All ER 276, [1993] 1 WLR 1545, CA; *Balkanbank v Taher* [1994] 4 All ER 239, 256 (in which, in dismissing an appeal [1995] 2 All ER 904, [1995] 1 WLR 1056, CA, it was held that, on the proper construction of a consent order providing for an inquiry as to damages, the court still retained a discretion whether to award damages at all).

defendant makes it inequitable to do so;[18] but if the undertaking is enforced, the measure of damages payable under it is not discretionary.

The 'cross-undertaking', as it is commonly called, probably extends to all defendants who become parties while the interim injunction is in force, although with only prospective, rather than retrospective, effect.[19] Since the cross-undertaking is given to the court, it may be enforced by one who is not a party to the action, if the cross-undertaking is given for his benefit.[20] It became, and remains, the standard practice for the court to require cross-undertakings for the benefit of third parties to be given by applicants for a freezing order,[21] but it is not the standard practice in other cases, although the court has jurisdiction to do so.[22] It was contended at first instance in *Smithkline Beecham plc v Apotex Europe Ltd*[23] that the position was radically changed by the introduction of the Practice Direction supplementing CPR Pt 25.[24] The judge considered that the position was unclear, and was content to assume (without deciding) that the Practice Direction requires that a non-party to the litigation is entitled to the benefit of the cross-undertaking unless the judge otherwise orders. This point was not discussed by the Court of Appeal.

Damages, it has been said,[25] are to be assessed on the same basis as damages for breach of contract would be assessed if the undertaking had been a contract between the claimant and the defendant, that the claimant would *not* prevent the defendant from doing that which he was restrained from doing by the terms of the injunction. It has been suggested[26] that this basis may be too narrow in some cases, and that, in an appropriate case, the courts will have to examine the principles more closely.

Contrary to the view expressed by Jessel MR,[27] an undertaking is perfectly valid and enforceable even though the injunction was obtained by the claimant bona fide, without any misrepresentation, suppression of the facts, or other default on his part.[28] It makes no difference whether, in granting the injunction, the judge made an error of law or of fact.[29] The court has technically no power to compel the claimant to enter into an undertaking, but it has power in practice, since it can indicate that an injunction will be refused unless the undertaking is given.[30]

---

[18] As to the possible courses of action where an interlocutory injunction is discharged before trial, see *Cheltenham and Gloucester Building Society v Ricketts, supra,* CA.

[19] *Smithkline Beecham plc v Apotex Europe Ltd, supra.*

[20] But a party identified in a cross-undertaking as one whom the injunctor would compensate cannot claim compensation for others who were adversely affected by the injunction: *Smithkline Beecham plc v Apotex Europe Ltd, supra,* CA.

[21] As to freezing injunctions see p 625 *et seq, infra.*

[22] See *Allied Irish Bank v Ashford Hotels Ltd* [1997] 3 All ER 309, CA; *Smithkline Beecham plc v Apotex Europe Ltd, supra,* CA, at [31]. See also [2007] CJQ 10 (A J Phipps).

[23] *Supra.*   [24] See CPR Pt 25; PD 25A, para 5.1, as revised in March 2005.

[25] *F Hoffman-La Roche & Co AG v Secretary of State for Trade and Industry* [1975] AC 295, 361, [1974] 2 All ER 1128, 1150, HL, *per* Lord Diplock. The undertaking remains effective even though the action is dismissed: *Ross v Buxton* [1888] WN 55, or the plaintiff discontinues his action; *Newcomen v Coulson* (1878) 7 Ch D 764. See *Tharros Shipping Co Ltd v Bias Shipping Ltd* [1994] 1 Lloyd's Rep 577.

[26] *R v Medicines Control Agency, ex p Smith & Nephew Pharmaceuticals Ltd* [1999] RPC 705, 714, 715, *per* Jacob J.

[27] In *Smith v Day* (1882) 21 Ch D 421, CA, in which the history of undertakings is discussed.

[28] *Griffith v Blake* (1884) 27 Ch D 474, CA.   [29] *Hunt v Hunt* (1884) 54 LJ Ch 289.

[30] See, eg, *F Hoffman-La Roche & Co A-G v Secretary of State for Trade and Industry* [1975] AC 295, 361, [1974] 2 All ER 1128, 1150, HL, *per* Lord Diplock. The undertaking is nonetheless regarded as voluntary, and a party is not normally entitled to appeal against it: *Secretary of State for Trade and Industry v Bell*

It is not unusual, on an application for an injunction, for no injunction to be granted, but for the defendant to offer and the claimant to accept an undertaking by the defendant in terms similar to those claimed in the injunction.[31] In such cases, a cross-undertaking in damages, similar to the usual undertaking mentioned above, will automatically be inserted in the order, unless the contrary is expressly agreed at the time.[32]

Where an injunction is granted on the usual undertaking, the court may, if it doubts the claimant's ability to pay any damages that may be ordered under the undertaking, make the injunction conditional on the claimant's depositing a specified sum of money with the parties' solicitors,[33] or giving security to the satisfaction of the court.[34]

Likewise, the court may require the defendant to enter into an undertaking as a condition of refusing an injunction: thus the defendant, in appropriate circumstances, may be required to undertake to keep an account to assist the court, should the claimant succeed at the trial, in ascertaining what damage he has suffered in the meantime.[35]

There is no reason why a settlement agreement should not provide that the defendant is to be contractually bound to the claimant not to do the acts that would breach the undertakings that they have agreed in the settlement agreement to give to the court. In this case, if the undertaking is breached, the defendant will be at risk of proceedings for breach of contract as well as for contempt.[36]

Finally, special mention should be made of the position in which an injunction is sought by the Attorney-General on behalf of the Crown. In general, when the Crown applies for an interim injunction in an action brought against a subject to enforce or protect its proprietary or contractual rights, it should be put on the same terms as a subject as respects the usual undertakings as to damages.[37] There is, however, a kind of action by the Crown that has no counterpart in ordinary litigation between subject and subject. This has been called a 'law enforcement action', in which civil proceedings are brought by the Crown to restrain a subject from breaking a law where the breach is harmful to the public or some section of it, but does not necessarily effect any proprietary or contractual rights of the Crown. The action is brought by the Attorney-General, as guardian of the public interest, who may sue *ex officio* or under the relator procedure. Under this latter procedure, a member of the public, known as the 'relator', may seek the Attorney-General's consent to the institution of proceedings in which the Attorney-General is the nominal claimant. If the Attorney-General gives his consent, the relator becomes responsible for the conduct

---

Davis Trading Ltd [2004] EWCA Civ 1066, [2005] 1 BCLC 516 (an exceptional case in which an appeal was allowed).

[31] But if the defendant wishes to appeal, an injunction, not an undertaking, is appropriate: *McConnell v McConnell* (1981) 131 NLJ 116. It was pointed out, in *London and Manchester Assurance Co Ltd v O and H Construction Ltd* [1989] 2 EGLR 185, that an undertaking is just as binding and even more effective than an order, because it does not need service and a penal notice endorsed on it in order to bite. See *Gantenbrink v BBC* [1995] FSR 162.

[32] *Practice Note* [1904] WN 203; *Oberrheinische Metallwerke GmbH v Cocks* [1906] WN 127; *W v H (Family Division: without notice orders)* [2001] 1 All ER 300.

[33] *Baxter v Claydon* [1952] WN 376.

[34] *Harman Pictures N V v Osborne* [1967] 2 All ER 324, [1967] 1 WLR 723.

[35] *Mitchell v Henry* (1880) 15 Ch D 181, CA; *Holophane Ltd v Berend & Co Ltd* (1897) 15 RPC 18. See also *Wall v London and Northern Assets Corpn* [1898] 2 Ch 469, CA; *Wright v Hennessey* (1894) 11 TLR 14, DC.

[36] *Independiente Ltd v Music Trading On-Line (HK) Ltd* [2007] EWCA Civ 111, [2007] 4 All ER 736.

[37] See *F Hoffman-La Roche and Co A-G v Secretary of State for Trade and Industry* [1975] AC 295, [1974] 2 All ER 1128, HL.

of the proceedings and is liable for the costs, and, if an interim injunction is sought, the relator will be called upon to give the usual undertaking.

Where, however, the Attorney-General sues *ex officio*, the court will consider the propriety of requiring such an undertaking in the light of the particular circumstances of the case. It seems that an undertaking is unlikely to be thought proper where the Attorney-General is proceeding directly under a statute that provides expressly that compliance with some provision of the Act shall be enforceable by civil proceedings by the Crown for an injunction. This was the position in *F Hoffman-La Roche & Co A-G v Secretary of State for Trade and Industry*,[38] in which the interim injunction was granted without any undertaking being given. A similar view has been taken in relation to a law enforcement action by a local authority under s 222 of the Local Government Act 1972,[39] an application by the Director-General of Fair Trading for an interim injunction to restrain the publication of misleading advertisements,[40] and an application by the Securities and Investments Board for interim injunctions under the Financial Services Act 1986, including a worldwide freezing injunction.[41]

Analogous to a law-enforcement action is an action by the Attorney-General in the exercise of the Crown's power to act as protector of charity. In such an action, the Crown is not asserting any proprietary or contractual claim of its own, and it is not therefore a case in which the cross-undertaking will be demanded as of course. However, in *A-G v Wright*,[42] the Crown was asserting proprietary rights on behalf of the charity and was seeking to recover property alleged to belong to or to be owed to the charity. It was thought right to protect the interests of the defendant by a cross-undertaking limited to the funds of the charity.

(C) THE APPROACH OF THE COURTS

Until *American Cyanamid Co v Ethicon Ltd*,[43] it was the accepted rule that, in order to get an interim injunction, the claimant must first make out a prima facie case. In that case, Lord Diplock, in a speech with which all of the other Law Lords agreed, appeared to have laid down that there is no such rule. The court must be satisfied that the claim is not 'frivolous or vexatious'—in other words, that there is 'a serious question to be tried', or 'a real prospect of succeeding in his claim to a permanent injunction at the trial'.[44] But unless the

---

[38] *Supra*, HL. Cf *Customs and Excise Comrs v Anchor Foods Ltd* [1999] 3 All ER 268, [1999] 1 WLR 1139, in which, on the unusual facts of the case, a cross-undertaking was required.

[39] *Kirklees Metropolitan Borough Council v Wickes Building Supplies Ltd* [1993] AC 227, [1992] 3 All ER 717, HL, discussed (1992) 136 Sol Jo 1084 (R Galinsky); *Chisholm v Kirklees Metropolitan Borough Council* [1993] ICR 826.

[40] *Director General of Fair Trading v Tobyward Ltd* [1989] 2 All ER 266, [1989] 1 WLR 517; *Re Agreement between Members of the Institute of Insurance Brokers* [1991] ICR 822.

[41] *Securities and Investment Board v Lloyd-Wright* [1993] 4 All ER 210. As to a worldwide freezing injunction, see p 634 *et seq, infra*.

[42] [1987] 3 All ER 579, [1988] 1 WLR 164.

[43] [1975] AC 396, [1975] 1 All ER 504, HL. See (1975) 91 LQR 168 (P Prescott); (1975) 38 MLR 672 (A Gore); (1976) 35 CLJ 82 (P Wallington); (1980) 30 UTLJ 240 (R Grant Hammond).

[44] In *Mothercare Ltd v Robson Books Ltd* [1979] FSR 466 Megarry V-C pointed out that this phrase could give rise to misunderstanding. All that has to be seen is whether the claimant has prospects of success that, in substance and reality, exist.

material available to the court at the hearing of the application fails to disclose that the claimant has any real prospect of succeeding in his claim for a permanent injunction at the trial, the court should at once proceed to consider whether the balance of convenience lies in favour of granting or refusing the interim relief that is sought.[45]

Shortly afterwards, in two cases in the Court of Appeal, *Fellowes & Son v Fisher*[46] and *Hubbard v Pit*,[47] it was noted that the previous House of Lords decision of *J T Stratford & Son v Lindley*[48] had not been cited to the House in the *American Cyanamid* case. There, all of the members of the House of Lords had expressed the view that a claimant was not entitled to an interim injunction unless he established a prima facie case. Notwithstanding this, the Court of Appeal in the two cases cited agreed that the *American Cyanamid* case had laid down an entirely different approach to be followed in connection with interim relief from that which had hitherto been habitually applied, and accepted that the principles stated by Lord Diplock in the *American Cyanamid* case must be followed even on the assumption that the two House of Lords decisions were in conflict. It was the more recent decision, and the point was not argued in the earlier case.

In *Series 5 Software v Clarke*,[49] Laddie J has sought to reinterpret the decision. He stresses the discretionary nature of the jurisdiction to grant an interim injunction and the absence of fixed rules. The view of the court as to the relative strength of the parties' cases is, in his opinion, a major factor to take into account. Laddie J found it difficult to accept that Lord Diplock had performed a volte-face within four months, because, in *F Hoffman-La Roche & Co A-G v Secretary of State for Trade and Industry*,[50] he had said that the claimant must first satisfy the court that there was a strong prima facie case. On the other hand, although he referred to *NWL Ltd v Woods*,[51] decided after the change of approach had been highlighted by the two Court of Appeal cases cited above, he did not quote Lord Diplock's statement in that case that the *American Cyanamid* case 'enjoins the judge on an application for an interim injunction to direct his attention to the balance of convenience as soon as he has satisfied himself that there is a serious question to be tried', which seems consistent with the interpretation of the *American Cyanamid* case in the Court of Appeal decisions mentioned, to which Laddie J did not refer. Laddie J has adhered to his view in subsequent cases,[52] and his approach has received the support of Robert Walker LJ.[53] In *Rilett v Greet and Greet*,[54] Park J referred to the judgment of Laddie J as 'thought-provoking', but applied the *American Cyanamid* principles; on appeal,[55] it was argued that the judge below should have complied with *Series 5* guidelines, to which Chadwick LJ responded that the judge was not at liberty to disregard the well-settled approach founded on *American Cyanamid*. It is far from clear that the reinterpretation will prevail and it seems appropriate, therefore, to consider the traditional approach.

---

[45] The court was not satisfied in *John Hayter Motor Underwriting Agencies Ltd v R B H S Agencies Ltd* [1977] 2 Lloyd's Rep 105, CA; but was in *Losinka v Civil and Public Services Association* [1976] ICR 473, CA.

[46] [1976] QB 122, [1975] 2 All ER 829, CA.   [47] [1976] QB 142, [1975] 3 All ER 1, CA.

[48] [1965] AC 269, [1964] 3 All ER 102, HL.   [49] [1996] 1 All ER 853.

[50] [1975] AC 295, [1974] 2 All ER 1128, HL.   [51] [1979] 3 All ER 614, [1979] 1 WLR 1294, HL.

[52] See, eg, *Barclays Bank plc v RBS Advanta* [1996] RPC 307, and *Antec International Ltd v South Western Chicks (Warren) Ltd* [1997] FSR 278.

[53] See, eg, *Barnsley Brewery Co Ltd v RBNB* [1997] FSR 462; *SIG Architectural Products Ltd v Castle House Windows Ltd* (1996, unreported), but referred to in [1997] JBL 486.

[54] [1999] BPIR 145.   [55] (11 March 1999, unreported), but available on Lexis.

It has been observed[56] that the principles laid down in the *American Cyanamid* case[57] apply even though the life of the injunction may be brief and the decision on the application for an interim injunction may influence future proceedings. The principles are not, however, applicable where it is clear that if an injunction were granted to the claimants, they would not pursue their claim to trial. They apply in cases, such as the *American Cyanamid* case itself, in which the application for the interim injunction is merely a holding operation pending a contemplated trial. If the grant of an injunction would have the effect of putting an end to the action, the court should approach the case on the broad principle: 'what can the court do in its best endeavour to avoid injustice?'[58] On this basis, an interim injunction was granted in *Dyno-Rod v Reeve*,[59] in respect of a restrictive covenant in a franchising agreement, although the action could not be tried before all or a substantial proportion of the period of restraint had expired.

(D) THE PRINCIPLES LAID DOWN IN THE *AMERICAN CYANAMID* CASE

Lord Goff has pointed out[60] that, in many cases, the court will be able to decide the application on the basis of the first two principles (the first stage). It is only where there is doubt as to the adequacy of either or both of the respective remedies in damages that the court proceeds to the second stage—that is, the balance of convenience. In any event, it has been made clear that the House in the *American Cyanamid* case[61] did not intend to lay down rigid rules, and, indeed, the principles themselves contain flexible words such as 'normally'. As was reaffirmed by Lord Goff in *Factortame Ltd v Secretary of State for Transport (No 2)*,[62] they are guidelines rather than rules.

The principles are as follows.

(i)

> The governing principle is that the court should first consider whether if the plaintiff were to succeed at the trial in establishing his right to a permanent injunction he would be adequately compensated by an award of damages for the loss he would have sustained as a result of the defendant's continuing to do what was sought to be enjoined between the time of the application and the time of the trial.[63] If damages in the measure recoverable at common law would be an adequate remedy and the defendant would be in a financial position to pay them,[64] no interlocutory injunction should normally be granted, however strong the plaintiff's claim appeared to be at that stage.[65]

---

[56] *Budget Rent A Car International Inc v Mamos Slough Ltd* (1977) 121 Sol Jo 374, CA, *per* Geoffrey Lane LJ.

[57] *Supra*, HL. See (2004) 23 CJQ 132 (A Keay).

[58] *Cayne v Global Natural Resources plc* [1984] 1 All ER 225, CA.   [59] [1999] FSR 148.

[60] In *Factortame Ltd v Secretary of State for Transport (No 2)* [1991] 1 All ER 70, 118, HL.

[61] *Supra*, HL. See [2004] 23 CJQ 132 (A Keay).

[62] *Supra*, HL, at 118,; *Fellowes & Son v Fisher* [1976] QB 122, 139, [1975] 2 All ER 829, 841, *per* Browne LJ; *Cayne v Global Natural Resources plc* [1984] 1 All ER 225, CA; *Cambridge Nutrition Ltd v BBC* [1990] 3 All ER 523, CA.

[63] Damages will seldom be adequate compensation in a passing-off action: *GMG Radio Holdings Ltd v Tokyo Project Ltd* [2005] EWHC 2188 (Ch), [2006] FSR 239.

[64] Damages can only be an adequate remedy if the defendants will be good for the money: *Dyrlund-Smith A/S v Turberville Smith Ltd* [1998] FSR 774, CA.

[65] Applied in *Polaroid Corpn v Eastman Kodak Co* [1977] RPC 379, CA.

This is, in effect, a restatement of the established rule that a claimant should not be granted an interim injunction unless he is able to show that, if it was not granted, he would suffer irreparable damage[66]—that is, *'the damage must be substantial and one which could not be adequately remedied by a pecuniary payment'.*[67] Illustrations of irreparable damage in the cases include *Express Newspapers Ltd v Keys,*[68] in which the defendant trade union proposed unlawfully to induce the claimant's employees to break their contracts by participating in a political strike. The claimant did not want money, but wanted its newspaper published, and would find it difficult to prove its loss; in *Hubbard v Pitt,*[69] the defendants were picketing the claimant's premises and there was a real prospect that, if it continued, it would seriously interfere with the claimant's business and that damages would be an inadequate remedy, even if the defendants could pay damages.

(ii) On the other hand, Lord Diplock continued, if damages:

> would not provide an adequate remedy for the plaintiff in the event of his succeeding at the trial, the court should then consider whether, on the contrary hypothesis that the defendant were to succeed at the trial in establishing his right to do that which was sought to be enjoined, he would be adequately compensated under the plaintiff's undertaking as to damages for the loss he would have sustained by being prevented from doing so between the time of the application and the time of the trial. If damages in the measure recoverable under such an undertaking would be an adequate remedy and the plaintiff would be in a financial position to pay them, there would be no reason on this ground to refuse an interlocutory injunction.

Accordingly, an injunction was granted in *Chancellor, Masters and Scholars of Oxford University v Pergamon Press Ltd*[70] to restrain the defendants from passing off Pergamon's *Dictionary of Perfect Spelling* as and for one of the claimant's dictionaries by the use in the title of the word 'Oxford' in conjunction with the word 'dictionary'. The claimant would otherwise suffer very great, but unascertainable, damage and the defendants would be amply covered by the claimant's undertaking.

(iii) 'It is where there is doubt as to the adequacy of the respective remedies in damages available to either party or both, that the question of balance of convenience arises.' The matters that will have to be considered, and their relative weight, will vary from case to case, and have been said to include the nature of the injunction that is being sought.[71] Although the phrase 'balance of convenience' is one commonly used, Donaldson MR has referred[72] to it as 'an unfortunate expression', saying that the business of the court is justice not convenience. Making a similar point, May

---

[66] *Johnson v Shrewsbury and Birmingham Rly Co* (1853) 3 De GM & G 914. See (1989) 68 CBR 538 (P M Perell).

[67] *Litchfield-Speer v Queen Anne's Gate Syndicate (No 2) Ltd* [1919] 1 Ch 407, 411, *per* P O Lawrence J; *Pinchin v London and Blackwall Rly Co* (1854) 5 De GM & G 851.

[68] [1980] IRLR 247.

[69] [1976] QB 142, [1975] 3 All ER 1, CA. See also *A-G v Guardian Newspapers Ltd* [1987] 3 All ER 316, [1987] 1 WLR 1248, HL (the 'Spycatcher' case).

[70] (1977) 121 Sol Jo 758, CA.

[71] *Potters-Ballotini Ltd v Weston-Baker* [1977] RPC 202, 209, CA, *per* Scarman LJ.

[72] *Francome v Mirror Group Newspapers Ltd* [1984] 2 All ER 408, [1984] 1 WLR 892, CA.

LJ observed[73] that the '*balance of the risk of doing an injustice*' better describes the process involved.

(iv) 'Where other factors appear to be evenly balanced it is a counsel of prudence to take such measures as are calculated to preserve the status quo'—that is, the state of affairs existing during the period immediately preceding the issue of the writ claiming the permanent injunction.[74] It will clearly cause less inconvenience to stop the defendant temporarily from doing something he has not done before, than to interrupt him in the conduct of an established enterprise.

(v) In many cases, the unsuccessful party on the application for an interim injunction, if ultimately successful at the trial, will have suffered some disadvantage for which he will not be fully compensated by damages. 'The extent to which the disadvantages to each party would be incapable of being compensated in damages in the event of his succeeding at the trial is always a significant factor in assessing where the balance of convenience lies.'

(vi)

> If the extent of the uncompensatable disadvantages to each party would not differ widely, it may not be improper to take into account in tipping the balance the relative strength of each party's case as revealed by the affidavit evidence adduced on the hearing of the application. This, however, should be done only where it is apparent on the facts disclosed by evidence as to which there is no credible dispute that the strength of one party's case is disproportionate to that of the other party.

This seems to mean that the relative strength of each party's case is the last factor to be taken into consideration, instead of being, as was thought in the past, the first.

In *Fellowes & Son v Fisher*,[75] this proposition was thought to cause some difficulty by both Browne LJ and Sir John Pennycuick. Thus Browne LJ observed:[76] 'I cannot see how the "balance of convenience" can be fairly or reasonably considered without taking some account as a factor of the relative strength of the parties' cases, but the House of Lords seems to have held that this is only the last resort.' And Sir John Pennycuick felt[77] that there would be difficulty in disregarding the prospect of success where this is a matter within the competence of a judge—in particular, in cases depending in whole or in great part on the construction of a written instrument. He was also concerned about cases in which immediate judicial interference is essential—for example, trespass—or the internal affairs of a company, where the court cannot do justice without, to some extent, considering the probable upshot of the action if it ever came to be fought out. And it has also been said that in matters involving trade restrictions, where the decision on the application, whichever way it goes, profoundly affects the rights of the parties in a way that cannot easily

[73] In *Cayne v Global Natural Resources plc, supra*, CA, echoed by Lord Jauncey in *Factortame Ltd v Secretary of State for Transport (No 2)* [1991] 1 All ER 70, 128, HL and reaffirmed *Fleming Fabrications v Albion Cylinders Ltd* [1989] RPC 47, CA.

[74] *Garden Cottage Foods Ltd v Milk Marketing Board* [1984] AC 130, 140, [1983] 2 All ER 770, 774, 775, HL.

[75] [1976] QB 122, [1975] 2 All ER 829, CA.   [76] *Fellowes v Fisher, supra*, at 138, 841, CA.

[77] Ibid, at 141, 843, 834, CA.

be undone if, at the trial, a different result is reached, it is necessary to consider rather more than in the usual case the strength of the plaintiff's case in law.[78]

Lord Diplock himself added a gloss to his *American Cyanamid* speech in *N W L Ltd v Woods*[79] when he observed that there was nothing in the earlier decision to suggest that, in considering whether or not to grant an interim injunction, the judge ought not to give full weight to all of the practical realities of the situation to which the injunction will apply. He pointed out that, in the *American Cyanamid* case, the court was not dealing with a case in which the grant or refusal of an injunction at that stage would, in effect, dispose of the action finally in favour of whichever party was successful in the application. In such a case, where the harm that will have already been caused to the losing party by the grant or refusal of the injunction is complete and a kind for which money cannot constitute any worthwhile recompense, the degree of likelihood that the claimant would have succeeded in establishing his right to an injunction if the action had gone to trial is a factor to be brought into the balance by the judge in weighing the risks that injustice may result from his deciding the application one way rather than the other.

(vii) 'In addition...there may be many other special factors to be taken into consideration in the particular circumstances of individual cases.' There was a special factor in the *American Cyanamid* case,[80] in which an interim injunction was sought for the infringement of a patent relating to a pharmaceutical product. This was that, once doctors and patients had got used to the defendant's product in the period prior to the trial, it might well be commercially impractical for the claimant to deprive the public of it by insisting on a permanent injunction at the trial, owing to the damaging effect that this would have on its goodwill in a specialized market and thus on the sale of its other pharmaceutical products.

(E) DECISIONS ON SPECIAL FACTORS

It is not yet clear how the 'special factors' principle will develop, although it is submitted that it is doubtful whether it will be used so as to emasculate the first six principles, as, in effect, suggested by Lord Denning MR in *Fellowe & Son v Fisher*.[81] In particular, Lord

---

[78] *Athletes Foot Marketing Associates Inc v Cobra Sports Ltd* [1980] RPC 343, 348, 349, *per* Walton J.

[79] [1979] 3 All ER 614, 625, 626, [1979] 1 WLR 1294, 1306; *Cambridge Nutrition Ltd v BBC* [1990] 3 All ER 523, CA (injunction refused: chances of success to be taken into account in cases concerning the right to publish an article, or to transmit a broadcast, the importance of which may be transitory, but the impact of which depends on timing, news value, and topicality); *Lansing Linde Ltd v Kerr* [1991] 1 All ER 418, [1991] 1 WLR 251, CA (covenant in restraint of trade where neither party would be adequately compensated by damages: judge rightly took into account strength of claimant's claim where trial could not take place until period of restraint had almost expired); *Entec (Pollution Control) Ltd v Abacus Mouldings* [1992] FSR 332, CA (injunction refused: granting it likely to put defendants out of business; witholding it unlikely to cause claimants very substantial damage); *Douglas v Hello! Ltd* [2001] 2 All ER 289, CA, noted (2001) 60 CLJ 231 (M Elliott). See (1991) 107 LQR 196 (A A S Zuckerman).

[80] *Supra*, HL. Cf *Walker v Standard Chartered Bank plc* [1992] BCLC 535, CA.

[81] [1976] QB 122, 133, 134, [1975] 2 All ER 829, 836, 837, CA, but see *Hubbard v Pitt* [1976] QB 142 at 185, [1975] 3 All ER 1, 16, CA, *per* Stamp LJ.

Denning's view in that case that covenants in restraint of trade are in a special category has been held to be mistaken.[82]

(i)   In *Bryanston Finance Ltd v de Vries (No 2)*,[83] the claimant sought an interim injunction to restrain the bringing of a winding-up petition. Buckley LJ said it was 'a special factor' that the injunction sought was designed to prevent the commencement of proceedings *in limine*. The other two judges in the Court of Appeal reached the same result on the ground that the principles of the *American Cyanamid* case were not concerned with such a case, but only with applications seeking interim relief pending determination of the rights of the parties at the hearing of the action.

(ii) The impact of the public interest is a special factor in cases in which a public authority is seeking to enforce the law against some person and either the authority seeks an interim injunction to restrain that person from acting contrary to the law, and that person claims that no injunction should be granted on the ground that the relevant law is, for some reason, invalid, or that other person seeks an interim injunction to restrain the action of the authority on the same ground. As a general rule, the problem cannot be solved at the first stage,[84] and it will be necessary to proceed to the second stage, concerned with the balance of convenience. In cases in which a party is a public authority performing duties to the public, Lord Goff, in *Factortame Ltd v Secretary of State for Transport (No 2)*,[85] agreed with Brown LJ in *Smith v Inner London Education Authority*[86] that the interests of the public in general to whom those duties are owed constitute a special factor. The court should not restrain a public authority by interim injunction from enforcing an apparently authentic law unless it is satisfied, having regard to all of the circumstances, that the challenge to the validity of the law is, prima facie, so firmly based as to justify so exceptional a course being taken.[87]

---

[82] *Lawrence David Ltd v Ashton* [1991] 1 All ER 385, CA. But see (1989) 133 Sol Jo 232 (M Jefferson), in which unreported cases to the contrary are referred to.

[83] [1976] Ch 63, [1976] 1 All ER 25, CA. See also *Dunford and Elliot Ltd v Johnson and Firth Brown Ltd* [1977] 1 Lloyd's Rep 505, CA (injunction to stop takeover bid refused, Lord Denning MR found 'special factors'; Roskill and Lawton LJJ reached the same result on other grounds).

[84] See *Factortame Ltd v Secretary of State for Transport (No 2)* [1991] 1 All ER 70, 118, 119, HL, *per* Lord Goff, and p 600, *supra*. The difficulties at the first stage are that: the usual undertaking in damages is not normally imposed on the Crown (see pp 583, 584, *supra*); there is no general right to indemnity by reason of damage suffered through invalid administrative action (see *Bourgoin SA v Ministry of Agriculture, Fisheries and Food* [1986] QB 716, [1985] 3 All ER 585, CA); an authority acting in the public interest cannot normally be protected by a remedy in damages because it will itself have suffered none.

[85] *Supra*, HL, applied *Belize Alliance of Conservation Non-Governmental Organisations v Department of the Environment of Belize* (2003) UKPC 63, [2004] P & CR 13.

[86] [1978] 1 All ER 411, 422, CA. See *Express Newspapers Ltd v Keys* [1980] IRLR 247. See also *Lewis v Heffer* [1978] 3 All ER 354, [1978] 1 WLR 1061, CA (rules not applicable in a political context where no question of quantifying anyone's loss in terms of cash).

[87] An interim injunction was granted in *Factortame Ltd v Secretary of State for Transport (No 2)*, *supra*, HL, in which English legislation was held to contravene Community law. See (1991) 107 LQR 1, 4 (H W R Wade). See also *R v Secretary of State for Health, ex p Imperial Tobacco Ltd* [2000] 1 All ER 572, CA, in which it was held that where a party sought an injunction restraining the government from implementing a Community measure pending a challenge to its validity, the court is required to apply the principles governing interim relief to be found in the Community jurisprudence; no order made on appeal, [2001] 1 All ER 850, HL.

(iii) Prior to the *American Cyanamid* case, the court would not normally restrain a defendant in a libel action who said he was going to justify,[88] nor a defendant in a copyright action who had a reasonable defence of fair dealing, nor a defendant in an action for breach of confidence who had a reasonable defence of public interest. The reason in all of those cases was that the defendant, if he was right, was entitled to publish, and the law is reluctant to intervene to suppress freedom of speech.[89]

In cases in which the grant of relief might affect the exercise of the right to freedom of expression under Art 10 of the European Convention for the Protection of Human Rights and Fundamental Freedoms,[90] the Human Rights Act 1998, s 12(3), provides that an interim injunction should not be granted 'so as to restrain publication before trial unless the court is satisfied that the applicant is likely to establish that publication should not be allowed'.

In *Cream Holdings Ltd v Banerjee*,[91] it was said that the intention of Parliament must be taken to be that 'likely' should have an extended meaning setting as the normal prerequisite to the grant of an injunction before trial a likelihood of success at the trial higher than the *American Cyanamid*[92] standard of 'real prospect', but permitting the court to dispense with this higher standard where particular circumstances make this necessary. The effect of the section is that the court should not make an interim restraint order unless satisfied the applicant's prospects of success at the trial are sufficiently favourable to justify such an order being made in the particular circumstances of the case. As to what degree of likelihood makes the prospects of success 'sufficiently favourable', the general approach should be that courts should be exceedingly slow to make interim restraint orders where the applicant has not satisfied the court that he will probably ('more likely than not') succeed at the trial. But, in some circumstances, a lesser degree of likelihood will suffice as a prerequisite: for instance, where the potential adverse consequences of disclosure are particularly grave, or where a short-lived injunction is needed to enable the court to hear and give proper consideration to an application for interim relief pending the trial or any relevant appeal.

---

[88] *Bonnard v Perryman* [1891] 2 Ch 269, CA. Although there are exceptions—eg where the statement is obviously untrue and defamatory: *Al-Fayed v Observer* Ltd (1986) Times, 14 July—neither the defendant's motive nor the manner in which he threatens publication nor the potential damage to the claimant is normally a basis for making an exception: *Holley v Smyth* [1998] QB 726, [1998] 1 All ER 853, CA. An injunction will not be granted even in relation to allegations that cannot be proven if they are inseparable from other allegations the common sting of which the defendant intends to justify: *Khashoggi v IPC Magazines Ltd* [1986] 3 All ER 577, [1986] 1 WLR 1412, CA.

[89] *Hubbard v Vosper* [1972] 2 QB 84, [1972] 1 All ER 1023, CA. In particular, an injunction will not be granted to restrain political controversy: *Kennard v Lewis* [1983] FSR 346. See *per* Laws J in *R v Advertising Standards Authority, ex p Vernons Organisation Ltd* [1993] 2 All ER 202, 205, [1992] 1 WLR 1289, 1293.

[90] Incorporated into English law by the Human Rights Act 1998. The Convention is to be found in Sch 1. See Chapter 27, section 6, *infra*. See also *London Regional Transport v Mayor of London* [2001] EWCA Civ 1491, [2003] EMLR 66, *per* Sedley LJ.

[91] [2004] UKHL 44, [2004] 4 All ER 617, noted [2005] CLJ 4 (A T H Smith); [2005] CJQ 194 (P Devonshire); *E v Channel Four Television Corp* [2005] EWHC 1144 (Fam), [2005] EMLR 709; *John v Associated Newspapers Ltd* [2006] EWHC 1611 (QB), [2006] EMLR 772; *Lord Browne of Madingley v Associated Newspapers Ltd* [2007] EWCA Civ 295, [2007] 3 WLR 289.

[92] [1975] AC 396, [1975] 1 All ER 504, HL. See p 584 *et seq, supra*.

Cream Holdings Ltd v Banerjee,[93] which involved a claim for breach of confidence, was distinguished in *Greene v Associated Newspapers Ltd,*[94] in which it was held that the 1998 Act had not affected the rule in *Bonnard v Perryman*[95] that, in a claim for defamation where the defendant maintains that he intends to justify the alleged libel, a claimant will not obtain an interim injunction to restrain publication unless it is clear that the plea of justification is bound to fail.

(iv) In *Hubbard v Pitt,*[96] Stamp LJ said[97] that it was not necessary to consider to what extent the *American Cyanamid* case is applicable where there is no relevant conflict of evidence and no difficult question of law. Previously, the claimant was regarded almost as having a right to an injunction where there was a plain and uncontested breach of a clear covenant not to do a particular thing,[98] or where there was an admitted trespass, even though it might do no harm to the claimant.[99] This seems to have been the view of the Court of Appeal in *Office Overload Ltd v Gunn,*[100] *Patel v W H Smith (Eziot) Ltd,*[101] and *Lawrence David Ltd v Ashon,*[102] since the *American Cyanamid* case. In such cases, there is no serious question to be tried. Further, in the most recent cases, it has been held that if it is clear that the defendant is acting unlawfully, an injunction should normally be granted.[103]

(v) The approach called for by the *American Cyanamid* case has, as such, no application to the grant or refusal of freezing injunctions,[104] which proceed on principles that are quite different from those applicable to other interim injunctions.[105]

---

[93] *Supra,* HL.

[94] [2004] EWCA Civ 1462, [2005] QB 972 [2005] 1 All ER 30, noted [2006] CJQ 27 (N Hatzis), and in *Coys v Autocherish Ltd* [2004] EWHC 1334 (QB), [2004] EMLR 482.

[95] *Supra,* CA.   [96] [1976] QB 142, [1975] 3 All ER 1, CA.

[97] At 185, 16, CA. See also *Newsweek Inc v BBC* [1979] RPC 441, CA.

[98] *Hampstead and Suburban Properties Ltd v Diomedous* [1969] 1 Ch 248, [1968] 3 All ER 545, applying the rule in *Doherty v Allman* (1878) 3 App Cas 709, which undoubtedly applies to perpetual injunctions: see p 619, *infra.* The rule was applied post-*Cyanid* by Nourse LJ in *A-G v Barker* [1990] 3 All ER 257, CA, although it was not referred to by the other members of the court. See *McDonald's Restaurants of Canada Ltd v West Edmonton Mall Ltd* (1994) 11 Alta LR (3rd) 402.

[99] *Patel v W H Smith (Eziot) Ltd* [1987] 2 All ER 569, CA; *Woollerton and Wilson Ltd v Richard Costain Ltd* [1970] 1 All ER 483. The suspension of the operation of the injunction in this last case, so as virtually to nullify its effect, was criticized in (1970) 33 MLR 552 (G Dworkin), and opinion on the correctness of the decision reserved by CA in *Charrington v Simons & Co Ltd* [1971] 2 All ER 588, 592. It was not followed on this point in *John Trenberth Ltd v National Westminster Bank Ltd* (1979) 39 P & CR 104, noted [1980] Conv 308 (H Street), or in *Anchor Brewhouse Developments Ltd v Berkeley House (Docklands Developments) Ltd* [1987] 2 EGLR 173. See (1988) 138 NLJ 23 (E McKendrick); (1988) 138 NLJ 385 (H W Wilkinson).

[100] [1977] FSR 39, CA.   [101] [1987] 2 All ER 569, CA.

[102] [1991] 1 All ER 385, CA. Some other cases suggest that the court retains a larger discretion: *Texaco Ltd v Mulberry Filling Station Ltd* [1972] 1 All ER 513, [1972] 1 WLR 814; *Harlow Development Corpn v Cox Bros (Butchers) Ltd* (1975) 233 Estates Gazette 765.

[103] *Express Newspapers Ltd v Keys* [1980] IRLR 247; *Ekland v Scripglow Ltd* [1982] FSR 431 (clear non-compliance with Performers' Protection Act 1963, repealed). See also *Redler Grain Silos Ltd v BICC Ltd* [1982] 1 Lloyds' Rep 435, CA.

[104] See p 625 *et seq, infra.*

[105] *Polly Peck International plc v Nadir (No 2)* [1992] 4 All ER 769, 786, CA, *per* Lord Donaldson MR. Note that where there is a proprietary claim, a freezing injunction is not appropriate, but an interim injunction may be granted restraining the disposal of property over which the claimant has a proprietary claim. In this case, the approach prescribed by the *American Cyanamid* case should be followed: ibid, and see (1992) 108 LQR 559 (A A S Zuckerman).

(vi) Letter of credit cases are special cases within the *American Cyanamid* guidelines because of the special factors that apply in such cases, or, perhaps, they fall outside the guidelines altogether.[106]

(F) INTERIM MANDATORY INJUNCTIONS

The principles laid down in the *American Cyanamid* case are not really relevant to interim mandatory, as contrasted with prohibitory, injunctions. The Court of Appeal has approved the observations of Megarry J in *Shepherd Homes Ltd v Sandham*[107] that, at this stage, the case has to be unusually strong and clear before a mandatory injunction will be granted,[108] and has said that these observations are unaffected by the *American Cyanamid* case. Thus, in *De Falco v Crawley Borough Council*,[109] Bridge LJ said that the principles of the *American Cyanamid* case had no relevance to a claim for a mandatory injunction ordering a local authority to provide accommodation for the plaintiffs under the Housing (Homeless Persons) Act 1977.[110]

In relation to industrial disputes, Geoffrey Lane LJ, in *Harold Stephen & Co Ltd v Post Office*,[111] observed: 'It can only be in very rare circumstances and in the most extreme circumstances that this court should interfere by way of mandatory injunction in the delicate mechanism of industrial disputes and industrial negotiations.' However, it should be noted that interim prohibitory injunctions were granted in *Thomas v National Union of Mineworkers (South Wales Area)*[112] to working miners who were being unreasonably harassed, in exercise of their right to use the highway for the purpose of entering and leaving their place of work, by the presence and behaviour of pickets and demonstrators.

(G) DELAY AND ACQUIESCENCE

Delay or laches, and, *a fortiori*, acquiescence by the claimant in the infringement of his rights may disentitle him to an interim injunction,[113] particularly if the defendant has

---

[106] See *Deutsche Ruckversicherung AG v Walbrook Insurance Co Ltd* [1996] 1 All ER 791, CA.

[107] [1971] Ch 340, [1970] 3 All ER 402; *Leisure Data v Bell* [1988] FSR 367, CA; *Zockall Group Ltd v Mercury Communications Ltd* [1998] ESR 354, CA.

[108] A recent clear case in which a mandatory injunction was granted is *London and Manchester Assurance Co Ltd v O and H Construction Ltd* [1989] 2 EGLR 185. But even where the court is unable to feel any high degree of assurance that the claimant will establish his right, it may yet be appropriate to grant the mandatory injunction where the risk of injustice if the injunction is refused sufficiently outweighs the risk of injustice if it is granted: *Nottingham Building Society v Eurodynamics Systems plc* [1993] FSR 468; *Psychometric Services Ltd v Merant International Ltd* [2002] FSR 147. 'The merits threshold is a flexible one', per Lawrence Collins J in *Edwin Shirley Productions Ltd v Workspace Management Ltd* [2001] 2 EGLR 16.

[109] [1980] QB 460, [1980] 1 All ER 913, CA, applied *R v Kensington and Chelsea Royal London Borough Council, ex p Hammell* [1989] QB 518, [1989] 1 All ER 1202, CA.

[110] Now repealed and replaced by ss 58–78, Housing Act 1985.

[111] [1978] 1 All ER 939, 944, CA, applied *Meade v London Borough of Haringey* [1979] 2 All ER 1016, 1034, CA, per Sir Stanley Rees. See (1979) 38 CLJ 228 (J Griffiths). But the *American Cyanamid* principles should normally be applied in the ordinary way in trade union discipline and expulsion cases: *Porter v National Union of Journalists* [1980] IRLR 404, HL; see (1981) 97 LQR 214 (D Newell).

[112] [1986] Ch 20, [1985] 2 All ER 1, noted [1985] Pub L 542 (H Carty). See also *Parker v Camden London Borough Council* [1986] Ch 162, [1985] 2 All ER 141, CA, discussed p 562, *supra*, in which, in exceptional circumstances, a mandatory order was made, notwithstanding that it might give rise to an extension of an industrial dispute.

[113] *Great Western Rly Co v Oxford, Worcester and Wolverhampton Rly Co* (1853) 3 De G M & G 341; *Bovill v Crate* (1865) LR 1 Eq 388; *Isaacson v Thompson* (1871) 41 LJ Ch 101.

incurred expenditure in the meantime. The meaning of 'acquiescence' has been discussed in a number of cases.[114] It involves a knowledge by the claimant of his rights infringed by the defendant,[115] and an encouragement, or even merely passive inaction, by the claimant, on the strength of which the defendant has expended money or altered his position in violation of the claimant's rights. The fact that the claimant has indicated that he is willing to accept the payment of a sum of money as the price of giving up his rights may well persuade the court not to grant an injunction, although it does not take away its jurisdiction to do so in a proper case,[116] and a demand for payment will not constitute acquiescence if it is shown that the defendant had statutory power to do the thing complained of.[117] If it is shown that the claimant took no steps to enforce a restrictive covenant on prior breaches, this may show acquiescence and an intent to abandon any building scheme that there may be, in which case, no injunction will be granted,[118] but the mere fact that the claimant has waived his right to sue for breaches in the past does not constitute acquiescence as to the future so as to prevent him from suing for some subsequent infraction, particularly if the earlier infractions were trivial in character.[119] Even acquiescence, however, may be explained away, for instance, where the claimant has been led to believe that the violation of his right would only be temporary,[120] or where he had not, at the earlier time, the necessary documents to establish his right,[121] or where he had been assured by the defendant that steps were being taken to prevent continued violation of his rights;[122] if he has acquiesced in some infringement of his rights causing him only slight injury, this does not prevent him from obtaining an interim injunction if the injury is subsequently considerably increased.[123] Moreover, no equity arises if the defendant expended money with knowledge of the true legal position.[124]

(H) 'CLEAN HANDS'[125]

'The jurisdiction to interfere is purely equitable and it must be governed by equitable principles.'[126] One of the principles is that the court will not grant equitable relief to a litigant unless he comes, as it is said, 'with clean hands'. On this principle, as Lord Eldon

---

[114] See, eg, *Duke of Leeds v Earl Amherst* (1846) 2 Ph 117, and *Rochdale Canal Co v King* (1853) 16 Beav 630.

[115] *Ramsden v Dyson* (1866) LR 1 HL 129; *Wilmott v Barber* (1880) 15 Ch D 96; *Armstrong v Sheppard & Short Ltd* [1959] 2 QB 384, [1959] 2 All ER 651, CA; *Shaw v Applegate* [1978] 1 All ER 123, [1977] 1 WLR 970, CA.

[116] *Viscountess Gort v Clark* (1868) 18 LT 343. Cf *Ainsworth v Bentley* (1866) 14 WR 630; *McKinnon Industries Ltd v Walker* (1951) 95 Sol Jo 559, PC.

[117] *Pentney v Lynn Paving Comrs* (1865) 12 LT 818.   [118] *Roper v Williams* (1822) Turn & R 18.

[119] *Kilbey v Haviland* (1871) 24 LT 353; *German v Chapman* (1877) 7 Ch D 271, CA; *Shaw v Applegate* [1978] 1 All ER 123, [1977] 1 WLR 970, CA.

[120] *Gordon v Cheltenham and Great Western Union Rly Co* (1842) 5 Beav 229.

[121] *Coles v Sims* (1854) 5 De GM & G 1.

[122] *A-G v Birmingham Borough Council* (1858) 4 K & J 528; *Innocent v North Midland Rly Co* (1839) 1 Ry & Can Cas 242.

[123] *Bankart v Houghton* (1860) 27 Beav 425.   [124] *Rennie v Young* (1858) 2 De G & J 136.

[125] The principle is more fully discussed in connection with perpetual injunctions, p 598, *infra*.

[126] Per Turner LJ in *Great Western Rly Co v Oxford, Worcester and Wolverhampton Rly Co* (1853) 3 De GM & G 341, 359.

observed,[127] many cases have occurred in which injunctions are applied for, and are granted or refused, not upon the ground of the right possessed by the parties, but upon the ground of their conduct and dealings before they applied to the court for the injunction to preserve and protect that right.

(I) TRADE DISPUTES

The Trade Union and Labour Relations (Consolidation) Act 1992, s 221, provides that a without-notice injunction shall not be granted against a defendant who would be likely to claim that his acts were in contemplation or furtherance of a trade dispute[128] without an opportunity being given to the defendant to be heard. Subsection (2) further provides that, on the hearing of an application for an interim injunction where the defendant makes such a claim, the court, in exercising its discretion, is to have regard to the likelihood of the defendant's establishing any of the specified matters that, under the Act, confer immunity from liability in tort.[129] This likelihood is only one of the factors to be taken into consideration by the court and different views have been expressed as to whether it is one of the elements of the balance of convenience,[130] or a separate factor. An injunction will normally be refused in cases in which the defendant has shown that it is more likely than not that the defence of statutory immunity would succeed.[131]

2   PERPETUAL INJUNCTIONS

(A) GENERAL PRINCIPLES

(i) Injunctions to restrain legal wrongs

There are two important principles that have to be kept in mind. What has been called 'the very first principle of injunction law is that prima facie you do not obtain injunctions to restrain actionable wrongs, for which damages are the proper remedy'.[132] A perpetual injunction, as we have seen, is intended to relieve the claimant from the necessity of bringing a series of actions to protect his right each time it is infringed, and is, therefore, particularly appropriate where the injury is continuous, or in any case in which the repetition—or, in the case of a *quia timet* application, the commission—of an injury is

---

[127] *Blakemore v Glamorganshire Canal Navigation* (1832) 1 My & K 154, 168; *Sheard v Webb* (1854) 23 LTOS 48; *Jarvis v Islington Corpn* (1909) 73 JP Jo 323.

[128] As to the meaning of this phrase, see s 244; *Mercury Communications Ltd v Scott-Garner* [1984] Ch 37, [1984] 1 All ER 179, CA; (1983) 46 MLR 463 (B Simpson).

[129] See *Duport Steels Ltd v Sirs* [1980] 1 All ER 529, [1980] 1 WLR 142, HL; *Dimbleby & Sons Ltd v National Union of Journalists* [1984] 1 All ER 751, [1984] 1 WLR 427, HL.

[130] See *NWL Ltd v Woods* [1979] 3 All ER 614, [1979] 1 WLR 1294, HL; (1980) 96 LQR 189 (A B Clarke and J Bowers); (1980) 43 MLR 319 (Lord Wedderburn) and 327 (R C Simpson); (1987) 50 MLR 506 (B Simpson).

[131] Ibid, *Hadmor Productions Ltd v Hamilton* [1983] 1 AC 191, [1982] 1 All ER 1042, HL.

[132] *Per* Lindley LJ in *London and Blackwell Rly Co v Cross* (1886) 31 Ch D 354, 369, CA; *Dollfus v Pickford* (1854) 2 WR 220; *Straight v Burn* (1869) 5 Ch App 163.

reasonably apprehended and the remedy of damages would be inadequate,[133] as is typically the case in nuisance or infringement of rights such as patents or copyrights.[134] But even if an infringement of a patent or copyright has been established, an injunction should not be granted if there is no reason to think that there will be any further infringement after the claimant's right has been established by the court.[135] The second principle is that, being an equitable remedy, the award of an injunction is discretionary. This proposition, although generally[136] true, tends to be misleading, and, even if it is recognized that the discretion is a judicial discretion to be exercised in accordance with precedent, it is easy to overestimate the discretion that the court has. From a practical point of view, Lord Evershed MR's statement[137] is more helpful:

> It is, I think, well settled that, if A proves that his proprietary rights are being wrongfully interfered with by B, and that B intends to continue his wrong, then A is prima facie entitled to an injunction, and he will be deprived of that remedy only if special circumstances exist, including the circumstance that damages are an adequate remedy for the wrong that he has suffered.

The existence of the discretion merely means that, to a limited extent largely dictated by precedent, the court may, indeed must, 'have regard not only to the dry strict rights of the plaintiff and defendant, but also to the surrounding circumstances, to the rights or interests of other persons which may be more or less involved'.[138] The main illustrations of special circumstances that have to be taken into account are discussed in the following subsections.[139]

(ii) Injunctions in aid of an equitable right or title

The first of the two principles just discussed has no relevance where it is sought to enforce an equitable right by means of an injunction. The question of whether damages would be an adequate remedy does not arise, because the Court of Chancery originally had no power to award damages. Consequently, section (B) below does not apply, but the other subsections are relevant.

(B) SMALL DAMAGE

When it was necessary to bring separate actions in different courts for damages and an injunction, it was held that the fact that, at law, only a very small or nominal sum

---

[133] See *Hodgson v Duce* (1856) 28 LTOS 155, in which the court took into account that the defendant was a pauper, and a mere award of damages would, accordingly, be a mockery of justice. In *Pride of Derby and Derbyshire Angling Association Ltd v British Celanese Ltd* [1953] Ch 149, 181, Evershed MR pointed out that damages would be a wholly inadequate remedy for the association, which had '*not been incorporated in order to fish for monthly sums*'.

[134] See *Phonographic Performance Ltd v Maitra* [1998] 2 All ER 638, CA.

[135] *Proctor v Bayley* (1889) 42 Ch D 390, CA; *Coflexip SA v Stolt Comex Seaway MS Ltd* [1999] 2 All ER 593, revsd on another point [2000] IP & T 1332, CA.

[136] See, however, for an exception, Chapter 27, section 1(A), *infra*.

[137] In *Pride of Derby and Derbyshire Angling Association Ltd v British Celanese Ltd, supra*, at 181, 197; in effect, repeated in *Armstrong v Sheppard & Short Ltd* [1959] 2 QB 384, 394, [1959] 2 All ER 651, 655, CA.

[138] *Per* Kindersley VC in *Wood v Sutcliffe* (1851) 2 Sim NS 163, 165.

[139] See also Chapter 25, section 3, *supra*, as to the award of damages in lieu of an injunction, and *Ocular Sciences Ltd v Aspect Vision Care Ltd* [1997] RPC 289, 395 *et seq*.

was recovered by way of damages was not, per se, a sufficient ground for refusing an injunction,[140] particularly where there was the possibility of a series of actions to recover damages from time to time. In general, the fact that the claimant has not suffered substantial damage does not prevent him from obtaining an injunction if he can establish an infringement of a legal right.[141] Sometimes, however, the court may regard the matter as too trivial to entitle the claimant to 'the formidable weapon of an injunction',[142] and an injunction will not necessarily be granted to restrain a trespass or a nuisance where the infringement is only temporary or occasional. Thus the court refused an injunction in *Society of Architects v Kendrick*,[143] in which members of the claimant society were accustomed to use the letters 'MSA' after their names. The claimant society sought to restrain the defendant, a non-member, from doing likewise, but the court refused an injunction on the ground that the matter was too trivial. Again, the court refused an injunction in *Behrens v Richards*,[144] in which it was sought to restrain members of the public from using tracks on the claimant's land situated on an unfrequented part of the coast, which use caused no damage. However, in *Patel v W H Smith (Eziot) Ltd*,[145] it was made clear that it is only in very exceptional circumstances that an injunction will be refused where a continuing trespass is proved or admitted. Further, in exceptional circumstances, particularly where a mandatory injunction is sought, the court may take into account the fact that an injunction would inflict serious damage on the defendant with no compensating advantage to the claimant, as in *Doherty v Allman*,[146] in which the court refused an injunction to restrain ameliorating waste by a tenant under a lease with over 900 years left to run.

(C) DELAY AND ACQUIESCENCE[147]

Delay or laches has been said not to affect the claimant's right to a perpetual injunction, unless the claim itself is barred,[148] but recent cases suggest that the court may decline

---

[140] *Rochdale Canal Co v King* (1851) 2 Sim NS 78; *Wood v Sutcliffe* (1851) 2 Sim NS 163, in which sums of one shilling and one farthing were referred to.

[141] *Goodson v Richardson* (1874) 9 Ch App 221; *Marriott v East Grinstead Gas and Water Co* [1909] 1 Ch 70 (both cases of pipes being laid in soil under a highway, which was of no value to the owner). Cf *Armstrong v Sheppard and Short Ltd, supra.*

[142] Per Buckley J in *Behrens v Richards* [1905] 2 Ch 614, 621.

[143] (1910) 26 TLR 433. Cf *Society of Accountants and Auditors v Goodway* [1907] 1 Ch 489 (incorporated accountant) and *Society of Accountants in Edinburgh v Corpn of Accountants Ltd* (1893) 20 R 750 (Court of Session), in which injunctions were granted. It seems to depend on the status of the plaintiff body.

[144] *Supra; Ward v Kirkland* [1967] Ch 194, [1966] 1 All ER 609, (right to use drain to convey bath water: court refused injunction to restrain additional user of same drains for effluent from water closets).

[145] [1987] 2 All ER 569, CA; *Kelsen v Imperial Tobacco Co (of Great Britain and Ireland) Ltd* [1957] 2 QB 335 (mandatory injunction granted for removal of advertising sign that constituted a trespass to claimant's airspace although no damage suffered); *Jaggard v Sawyer* [1995] 2 All ER 189, CA; *Harrow London Borough Council v Donohue* [1995] 1 EGLR 257, CA (grant of mandatory injunction for demolition of encroaching building works said to be inevitable). Cf *Ketley v Gooden* (1996) 73 P & CR 305, CA (mandatory injunction discharged and damages awarded: *Harrow London Borough Council v Donohue* not cited); see (1996) 140 Sol Jo 1002 (A Westwood).

[146] (1878) 3 App Cas 709, HL; *Meux v Cobley* [1892] 2 Ch 253; *Sharp v Harrison* [1922] 1 Ch 502.

[147] As to the meaning of 'acquiescence', see p 594, *supra.*

[148] *Rochdale Canal Co v King* (1851) 2 Sim NS 78; *Savile v Kilner* (1872) 26 LT 277; *Fullwood v Fullwood* (1878) 9 Ch D 176.

to interfere by injunction where the delay has been 'inordinate'.[149] Delay is, however, commonly, although not necessarily, an important factor to be taken into account in deciding whether there has been acquiescence. However:

> to justify the court in refusing to interfere at the hearing of a cause there must be a much stronger case of acquiescence than is required upon an interlocutory application, for at the hearing of a cause it is the duty of the court to decide upon the rights of the parties, and the dismissal of the bill upon the ground of acquiescence amounts to a decision that a right which has once existed is absolutely and for ever lost.[150]

The test has been said to be whether, in the circumstances, it has become unconscionable for the claimant to rely upon his legal right,[151] or, in other words, whether the owner of the legal right has done something beyond mere delay to encourage the wrongdoer to believe that he does not intend to rely on his strict rights, in which belief, the wrongdoer has acted to his prejudice.[152] It has been said that it may be easier to establish a case of acquiescence where the right is equitable only,[153] but this is perhaps doubtful.[154]

Failure to seek an interim injunction is a factor that can be taken into account, but does not automatically equate to 'standing by' so as to bar the grant of a final injunction.[155]

(D) 'CLEAN HANDS'

Being an equitable remedy, the principle expressed in the maxim that 'he who comes into equity must come with clean hands' applies.[156] Thus an injunction has been refused to a claimant who had wrongfully taken away partnership books,[157] and, in *Telegraph Despatch and Intelligence Co v McLean*,[158] a claimant in breach of an implied undertaking in a contract was held not entitled to an injunction to enforce an express undertaking therein entered into by the defendant. Again, in *Litvinoff v Kent*,[159] a landlord had reserved a right of re-entry only for breach of the covenant in the lease to pay rent. This covenant had not been broken, but the landlord nevertheless re-entered and excluded the tenant from the demised premises. The tenant, the claimant in the proceedings, sought an injunction, but this was refused on the grounds that he had been guilty of breaches of other covenants in the lease and was using the premises for an illegal purpose.

---

[149] *H P Bulmer Ltd and Showerings Ltd v J Bollinger SA* [1977] 2 CMLR 625, 681, CA.

[150] *Johnson v Wyatt* (1863) 2 De G J & Sm 18, 25, *per* Turner LJ; *Patching v Dubbins* (1853) Kay 1.

[151] *Shaw v Applegate* [1978] 1 All ER 123, CA; *Gafford v Graham* (1998) 77 P & CR 73. CA, noted (1988) 114 LQR 555 (P Milne).

[152] *H P Bulmer Ltd v J Bollinger SA, supra*, at 682, CA, *per* Goff LJ.

[153] *Shaw v Applegate, supra*, CA, at 132, *per* Goff LJ.

[154] *Habib Bank Ltd v Habib Bank A G Zurich* [1981] 2 All ER 650, 666, CA, *per* Oliver LJ; *Gafford v Graham, supra*, CA, considered *WWF–World Wildlife Fund for Nature v World Wrestling Federation Entertainment Inc* [2006] EWHC 184 (Ch), [2006] FSR 663.

[155] *Mortimer v Bailey* [2004] EWCA Civ 1514, [2005] 1 EGLR 75, noted [2005] Conv 460 (G Griffiths).

[156] See [1990] Conv 416 (P H Pettit), suggesting it is a last resort defence where it would be unconscionable for the claimant to have an equitable remedy. See also *Equity and Contemporary Legal Developments* (ed S Goldstein), p 72 (P Jackson); *Chocosuisse Union des Fabricants Suisses de Chocolat v Cadbury Ltd* [1998] RPC 117; *Equiticorp Industries Group Ltd (in statutory management) v The Crown (Judgment No 47)* [1998] 2 NZLR 481, 519–529.

[157] *Littlewood v Caldwell* (1822) 11 Price 97; *Williams v Roberts* (1850) 8 Hare 315.

[158] (1873) 8 Ch App 658; *Stiff v Cassell* (1856) 2 Jur NS 348.   [159] (1918) 34 TLR 298.

The point has often arisen in connection with a building scheme where numerous pur-chasers have entered into restrictive covenants with their common vendor for each other's benefit. In such a case, a claimant who has not complied with the covenants himself may be unable to enforce them against another,[160] but there is no rigid rule and an injunction may yet be obtained where the claimant's breach was only trifling, or where he has broken a much less important covenant than the one that he seeks to enforce.[161] The same qualifi-cation applies to other types of case: thus, in *Besant v Wood*,[162] a husband was not debarred from enforcing provisions in a separation deed by reason of trifling breaches of covenant on his part. Further 'the cleanliness required is to be judged in relation to the relief that is sought'.[163] Thus, in *Duchess of Argyll v Duke of Argyll*,[164] the claimant was held not to be disentitled to an injunction to restrain the publication by her ex-husband of intimate confidences between husband and wife by reason of the fact that it was her subsequent immorality that was the basis for the divorce and the termination of the marriage.

The same basic idea is behind the maxim that 'he who seeks equity must do equity', although, here, one is looking to the future rather than the past. The equitable remedy of an injunction will not be granted to a claimant, even though his past conduct is impec-cable, if he is not both able and willing to carry out any obligation that he has undertaken towards the defendant.[165]

It should be added that, according to *Holmes v Eastern Counties Rly Co*,[166] in which it would be unduly hard to refuse the claimant an injunction on the ground of his conduct, because this would leave him with no adequate remedy, the court may grant the injunction and register its disapproval of his conduct by depriving him of costs. It does not seem from the reports, however, that the courts are very ready to adopt this course.

Finally, some cases that are, at first sight, apparently decided on the ground that the claimant has forfeited his right to an injunction by his conduct are, in fact, decided on the ground that the alleged contractual right has ceased to exist, either because the claimant has himself repudiated the contract, or acted in such a way as to entitle the defendant to treat it as being at an end.[167]

(E) THIRD PARTIES

Again, owing to the fact that it is an equitable remedy, the court, in deciding whether or not an injunction should be granted, may take into consideration the effect that the

---

[160] *Goddard v Midland Rly Co* (1891) 8 TLR 126.

[161] *Chitty v Bray* (1883) 48 LT 860; *Meredith v Wilson* (1893) 69 LT 336; *Hooper v Bromet* (1903) 89 LT 37; affd (1904) 90 LT 234, CA. In *Cantor Fitzgerald International v Bird* [2002] IRLR 867, the court refused to punish the claimant, by the refusal of equitable relief, because of his conduct in 1994.

[162] (1879) 12 Ch D 605.

[163] *Duchess of Argyll v Duke of Argyll* [1967] Ch 302, 332, [1965] 1 All ER 611; *Grobbelaar v News Group Newspapers Ltd*, [2002] UKHL 40, [2002] 4 All ER 732; *Lewis v Nortex Pty Ltd* [2004] NSWSC 1143, [2005] 214 ALR 634.

[164] *Supra*. This was a motion for an interlocutory injunction, but the principle seems equally applicable to a claim for a perpetual injunction.

[165] *Measures Bros Ltd v Measures* [1910] 2 Ch 248, CA; *Re Berkeley (Applegate) Investment Consultants Ltd* [1989] Ch 32, [1988] 3 All ER 71.   [166] (1857) 3 K & J 675.

[167] *Fechter v Montgomery* (1863) 33 Beav 22; cf *General Billposting Co Ltd v Atkinson* [1909] AC 118, HL; *Measures Bros Ltd v Measures*, *supra*.

grant of an injunction would have on third parties.[168] Thus, in *Maythorn v Palmer*,[169] the defendant employee had entered into a limited and valid covenant not to enter into the employment of anyone other than the claimant. He entered into the employment of a third party who knew nothing about his undertaking to the claimant. The claimant's claim to an injunction was refused, partly on the ground of the injury that this would do to the third party, who was not a party to the action.

In *Miller v Jackson*,[170] a village cricket club was sued by the owner of a newly erected house adjoining the ground where cricket had been played for some seventy years, in respect of sixes hit into his property. Lord Denning MR was in favour of allowing the appeal against the grant of an injunction on the ground that the club was liable neither in negligence nor nuisance. The other members of the court, however, thought the club guilty of both torts, but while Geoffrey Lane LJ would have dismissed the appeal (although postponing the operation of the injunction for twelve months), Cumming-Bruce LJ took the view that, in the special circumstances, the interests of the public required that the injunction should be discharged:

> A court of equity must seek to strike a fair balance between the right of the plaintiffs to have quiet enjoyment of their house and garden without exposure to cricket balls occasionally falling like thunderbolts from the heavens, and the opportunity of the inhabitants of the village in which they live to continue to enjoy the manly sport which constitutes a summer recreation for adults and young persons.[171]

A further statement by Lord Denning MR, that the public interest should prevail over the private interest, was said, by a differently constituted Court of Appeal in *Kennaway v Thompson*,[172] to run counter to the well-established principles enunciated in *Shelfer v City of London Electric Lighting Co*,[173] and in *Elliott v London Borough of Islington*,[174] Lord Donaldson referred to the improbability of a situation arising in which the interests of the public would be decisive. Such a situation arose, however, in *Dennis v Ministry of Defence*,[175] although the claim being against the Crown, it was for a declaration and/or damages, and not an injunction.[176] The use of an airfield for training Harrier jump jet pilots was held to cause a nuisance by noise, but a declaration was refused on the ground of the serious public interest. However, substantial compensation was awarded at the public expense.

---

[168] *Maythorn v Palmer* (1864) 11 LT 261; *Hartlepool Gas and Water Co v West Hartlepool Harbour and Rly Co* (1865) 12 LT 366; cf *PSM International plc v Whitehouse* [1992] FSR 489, CA; *Silktone Pty Ltd v Devreal Capital Pty Ltd* (1990) 21 NSWLR 317.

[169] *Supra*.

[170] [1977] QB 966, [1977] 3 All ER 338, CA. See (1984) 134 NLJ 183 (J Sharrock); (1985) 129 Sol Jo 139 and 163 (D Grant and S R Wilson).

[171] *Per* Cumming-Bruce LJ in *Miller v Jackson, supra*, at 350, CA.

[172] [1981] QB 88, [1980] 3 All ER 329, CA; *Tetley v Chitty* [1986] 1 All ER 663. See (1981) 131 NLJ 108 (B S Markesinis and A M Tettenborn); (1982) 41 CLJ 87 (S Tromans).

[173] [1895] 1 Ch 287, CA, and see p 568 *et seq, supra*.

[174] [1991] 1 EGLR 167, CA (mandatory injunction affirmed to remove tree invading claimant's property; the other LJJ agreed with Lord Donaldson). See *Biogen Inc v Medeva plc* [1993] RPC 475, in which Aldous J discussed the matter in relation to life-saving drugs infringing a patent, and *Chiron Corpn v Murere Diagnostics Ltd (No 9)* [1995] FSR 318.

[175] [2003] 19 EG 118 CS, discussed [2003] Conv 526 (J Hartshorne).

[176] See Crown Proceedings Act 1947, s 21.

(F) DECLARATIONS AND SUSPENSION OF INJUNCTION

(i) Claimant prima facie entitled to an immediate injunction

In some circumstances, where prima facie the claimant is entitled to an immediate injunction, the court may merely make a declaration as to the claimant's right, with liberty to apply for an injunction should this become necessary. This may be done, for instance, where there seems to be no probability that the violation of the claimant's rights will be repeated.[177] The court also took this course in *Stollmeyer v Trinidad Lake Petroleum Co Ltd*,[178] in which there was a clear infringement of the claimant's right, but the damage caused to the claimant was insignificant, although the grant of an injunction would seriously affect local industry. In this case, the right to apply for an injunction was suspended for two years.

In other cases—for example, those in which it would be impossible, difficult, or unduly hard on the defendant to comply with an injunction forthwith—the court may adopt the device of granting an immediate injunction, but suspending its operation for a specified time, and the defendant may even be given liberty to apply for an extension of the suspension.[179] This has frequently been done in cases against a local authority for the pollution of a stream by sewage and similar cases in which immediate cessation of the nuisance would, in fact, be impossible,[180] or on the ground of considerations of public welfare.[181] And it has also been done where the defendant body is in the course of promoting a Bill in Parliament authorizing it to do the thing complained of,[182] or even to enable it to promote such a Bill.[183] This course may also be followed where the grant of an immediate injunction coming into effect forthwith would cause difficulties with third parties.[184]

In any case in which either of the above devices is adopted, the court may require the defendant, if he wishes to avoid an immediately operative injunction, to undertake to pay damages from time to time as any damage is, in fact, suffered by the claimant.[185]

(ii) Proposed action by claimant may prima facie give a defendant right to an injunction

In exceptional circumstances, the court may grant a claimant a declaration that the defendant will not be entitled to claim an injunction if the claimant carries out work that prima facie would infringe the defendant's rights. The court has jurisdiction to grant such a declaration if three conditions are satisfied—namely, that the question under consideration is

---

[177] *A-G v Birmingham, Tame and Rea District Drainage Board* [1910] 1 Ch 48, CA, affd [1912] AC 788, HL; *Race Relations Board v Applin* [1973] QB 815, [1973] 2 All ER 1190, CA (no repetition of acts complained of for twenty months).

[178] [1918] AC 485, PC.

[179] *Frost v King Edward VII Welsh etc Association* [1918] 2 Ch 180; compromised on appeal (1918) 35 TLR 138; *Pride of Derby and Derbyshire Angling Association Ltd v British Celanese Ltd* [1953] Ch 149, [1953] 1 All ER 179, CA.

[180] *A-G v Lewes Corpn* [1911] 2 Ch 495; *Phillimore v Watford RDC* [1913] 2 Ch 434.

[181] *Price's Patent Candle Co Ltd v LCC* [1908] 2 Ch 526, 544, CA, *per* Cozens-Hardy MR.

[182] *A-G v South Staffordshire Waterworks Co* (1909) 25 TLR 408.

[183] *Roberts v Gwyrfai District Council* [1899] 2 Ch 608, CA.

[184] *Tubbs v Esser* (1909) 26 TLR 145.

[185] *Stollmeyer v Trinidad Lake Petroleum Co Ltd* [1918] AC 485, PC; *Stollmeyer v Petroleum Development Co Ltd* [1918] AC 498n, PC.

a real question, that the person seeking the declaration has a real interest, and that there has been proper argument.[186] These conditions were satisfied in *Greenwich Health Service Trust v London and Quadrant Housing Trust*,[187] in which the grant of a negative declaration that the claimant was not exposed to possible action seeking injunctive relief was a matter of the highest utility, since it was a precondition to the ability of the claimant to secure the building of a new modern National Health Service (NHS) hospital.

[186] See *Re F (mental patient: sterilisation)* [1990] 2 AC 1, sub nom *F v West Berkshire Health Authority (Mental Health Act Commission intervening)* [1989] 2 All ER 545, HL.

[187] [1998] 3 All ER 437.

27

INJUNCTIONS III—
INJUNCTIONS IN PARTICULAR
TYPES OF CASE

It is impossible to consider exhaustively the various circumstances that may give rise to a claim for an injunction. An injunction is commonly claimed in aid of a legal right, in which case, a mere equitable owner, although he may obtain an interlocutory injunction, can only obtain a perpetual injunction by joining the legal owner in the action,[1] but it may also be granted to give effect to a purely equitable right, for instance, to restrain a breach of trust,[2] equitable waste,[3] or the breach of a restrictive covenant enforceable only in equity under the doctrine of *Tulk v Moxhay*.[4] It is also available to restrain a breach of Art 86 of the EC Treaty, which prohibits abuse of a dominant market position.[5] Some of the types of case in which an injunction is commonly claimed will now be considered.

1 TO RESTRAIN A BREACH OF CONTRACT

There is a close relationship between an injunction to restrain a breach of contract and a decree of specific performance. The terms of a contract may be affirmative or negative, or partly one and partly the other. Subject to the restrictions dealt with in the following chapter, specific performance is the natural remedy to enforce an affirmative term, while the injunction is appropriate to enforce a negative one. So far as jurisdiction to grant an interlocutory injunction is concerned, the general principles discussed above apply, but there are special considerations in regard to a claim for a perpetual injunction.

---

[1] *Performing Right Society Ltd v London Theatre of Varieties Ltd* [1924] AC 1, HL. Cf *Weddell v J A Pearce & Major* [1988] Ch 26; *MCC Proceeds Inc v Lehman Bros International (Europe)* [1998] 4 All ER 675, CA.

[2] See section 8, p 622, *infra*.

[3] See *Standard Chartered Bank v Walker* [1992] 1 WLR 561 (injunction to restrain shareholders in the exercise of his voting rights in a very unusual situation perhaps an extension of jurisdiction in relation to waste).

[4] (1848) 2 Ph 774; *Windsor Hotel (Newquay) Ltd v Allan* [1981] JPL 274, CA. See; eg, Megarry and Wade, *The Law of Real Property*, 6th edn, p 1012 *et seq*; Cheshire and Burn, *Modern Law of Real Property*, 16th edn, p 671 *et seq*.

[5] *Garden Cottage Foods Ltd v Milk Marketing Board* [1984] AC 130, [1983] 2 All ER 770, HL, although, on the facts, the House of Lords discharged the injunction.

(A) PURELY NEGATIVE TERMS

Where it is sought to restrain by perpetual injunction the threatened breach of a purely negative contract or covenant, the court, in general, has no discretion to exercise. The classic statement on this point, although strictly only an *obiter dictum*, is that of Lord Cairns in *Doherty v Allman*:[6]

> If parties for valuable consideration, with their eyes open, contract that a particular thing shall not be done, all that a Court of Equity has to do is to say, by way of injunction, that which the parties have already said by way of covenant, that the thing shall not be done; and in such case the injunction does nothing more than give the sanction of the process of the Court to that which already is the contract between the parties. It is not then a question of the balance of convenience or inconvenience, or of the amount of damage or of injury—it is the specific performance, by the Court, of that negative bargain which the parties have made, with their eyes open, between themselves.

Thus, in *Viscount Chelsea v Muscatt*,[7] a mandatory injunction was granted requiring the tenant to reinstate the top three courses of a parapet wall taken down in clear breach of a covenant in the lease and in the face of a clear indication from the landlords that they were not prepared to consent thereto.

In these cases, there is no need for the claimant to prove damage, except, it seems, in an action by a reversioner.[8] The general rule is that 'if the construction of the instrument be clear and the breach clear, then it is not a question of damage, but the mere circumstance of the breach of covenant affords sufficient ground for the court to interfere by injunction'.[9] It is no defence, therefore, to show that the claimant had not suffered any loss by reason of the breach, or even that the breach is more beneficial to him than strict performance of the contract would have been,[10] and, accordingly, in *Marco Productions Ltd v Pagola*,[11] in which theatrical performers expressly agreed not to perform for any other person during the period of the contract, the plaintiffs were entitled to an injunction although they could not show that they would suffer greater damage by the defendants performing elsewhere than by their remaining idle. Nor can the court take into account that the matter is one of public importance, and that the granting of an injunction would cause inconvenience to the public.[12] The principles as to the granting of injunctions are the same whether the injunction is sought in aid of the legal right, where there is privity of contract or privity of estate,[13] or in aid of an equitable claim only, as in the case of restrictive covenants enforceable under the rule of *Tulk v Moxhay*.[14]

---

[6] (1878) 3 App Cas 709, 720, HL: cited *John Trenberth Ltd v National Westminster Bank Ltd* (1979) 39 P & CR 104. See *Martin v Nutkin* (1724) 2 P Wms 266, and note *Dalgety Wine Estate Pty Ltd v Rizzon* (1979) 53 ALJR 647, 655, *per* Mason J.

[7] [1990] 2 EGLR 48, CA.   [8] *Johnstone v Hall* (1856) 2 K & J 414.

[9] *Per* Page Wood VC in *Tipping v Eckersley* (1855) 2 K & J 264, 270; *Wells v Attenborough* (1871) 24 LT 312; *Cooke v Gilbert* (1892) 8 TLR 382, CA.

[10] *Earl Mexborough v Bower* (1843) 7 Beav 127; *Dickinson v Grand Junction Canal Co* (1852) 15 Beav 260.

[11] [1945] KB 111, [1945] 1 All ER 155.

[12] *Lloyd v London, Chatham and Dover Rly Co* (1865) 2 De GJ & Sm 568; *Price v Bala and Festiniog Rly Co* (1884) 50 LT 787.

[13] *Spencer's Case* (1583) 5 Co Rep 16a; Law of Property Act 1925, ss 140–142.

[14] (1848) 2 Ph 774; *Lord Manners v Johnson* (1875) 1 Ch D 673; *Richards v Revitt* (1877) 7 Ch D 224. See [1996] Conv 329 (Jill Martin).

The principle stated by Lord Cairns must, however, be applied in the light of the surrounding circumstances and the court is not prevented from considering the effect of delay, acquiescence, or other supervening circumstances.[15] This discretionary element is of greater significance when a mandatory injunction is sought. Thus, in *Sharp v Harrison*,[16] a mandatory injunction was refused, where the claimant had suffered no damage, an injunction would inflict damage upon the defendant out of all proportion to the relief that the claimant ought to obtain, and the defendant was willing to give certain undertakings. Similarly, in *Wrotham Park Estate Co v Parkside Homes Ltd*,[17] the judge unhesitatingly declined to grant a mandatory injunction, which would have involved the demolition of houses—'now the homes of people'—built in breach of a restrictive covenant. The claimant had suffered no financial damage from the breach, their use of the land for the benefit of which the covenant had been imposed would not be impeded, and the integrity of the restrictive covenant for the future would not be impaired by allowing the existing homes to remain. Substantial damages in lieu of an injunction were awarded.

The extent of this residual discretion must not be overrated, however, even in the case of a mandatory injunction, and dicta at first instance in *Charrington v Simons & Co Ltd*[18] and in *Shepherd Homes Ltd v Sandham*,[19] to the effect that the criterion is whether a mandatory order, and if so what kind of mandatory order, will produce a fair result, were treated with some reservation by the Court of Appeal in the former case,[20] although this proposition seems subsequently to have met with the approval of a differently constituted Court of Appeal in *Viscount Chelsea v Muscatt*.[21] In this case, and also in *Wakeham v Wood*,[22] mandatory injunctions were awarded for breaches of restrictive covenants.

(B) CONTRACT CONTAINING BOTH AFFIRMATIVE AND NEGATIVE STIPULATIONS

In many cases, a party's obligation under a contract will expressly involve both affirmative and negative stipulations. It seems that, as a general rule, the negative stipulations will be enforced by means of an injunction,[23] notwithstanding the fact that the affirmative stipulations may not be enforceable by means of a decree of specific performance. The negative stipulation to be enforceable must, however, be negative in substance as well as in form.

---

[15] *Shaw v Applegate* [1978] 1 All ER 123, [1977] 1 WLR 970, CA (damages awarded in lieu of injunction that would have operated in a mandatory fashion); *Baxter v Four Oaks Properties Ltd* [1965] Ch 816, [1965] 1 All ER 906 (damages in lieu of prohibitory injunction).

[16] [1922] 1 Ch 502. Cf *Sutton Housing Trust v Lawrence* (1987) 55 P & CR 320, CA (wrong to refuse prohibitory injunction on ground that defendant might disobey order, and would be unlikely to be committed for contempt, or fined for lack of means).

[17] [1974] 2 All ER 321. Cf *Pugh v Howells* (1984) 48 P & CR 298. Failure to apply for an interim injunction does not necessarily disentitle the claimant to a final mandatory injunction at the trial: see *Deakins v Hookings* [1994] 1 EGLR 190 (Mayors and City of London Cty Ct).

[18] [1970] 2 All ER 257, 261, *per* Buckley J (order varied [1971] 2 All ER 588, CA).

[19] [1971] Ch 340, 351, [1970] 3 All ER 402, 412, *per* Megarry J.

[20] *Charrington v Simons & Co Ltd* [1971] 2 All ER 588, CA.

[21] [1990] 2 EGLR 48, CA (*Charrington v Simons & Co Ltd, supra*, CA, not cited).

[22] [1981] 43 P & CR 40, CA, in which Watkins LJ criticized *Achilli v Tovell* [1927] 2 Ch 243, in so far as it decided that, in some circumstances, the court has no discretion. See [1984] Conv 429 (P Polden).

[23] *Donnell v Bennett* (1883) 22 Ch D 835. In relation to charterparties, see *Lauritzencool AB v Lady Navigation Inc* [2004] EWHC 2607 (Comm), [2005] 1 Lloyd's Rep 260.

In *Davis v Foreman*,[24] there was, in a contract of personal service, a stipulation in negative form by an employer not to give notice except for misconduct or breach of agreement. It was held that this was affirmative in substance, to retain the employee in his employment, and an injunction was consequently refused.

Problems have arisen where the grant of an injunction would amount to an indirect way of compelling specific performance of an agreement where that remedy could not be obtained directly. Although there may be a reluctance to grant an injunction in such a situation, there is no general principle totally debarring the grant of an injunction where this would be its practical effect.[25] The position may be illustrated[26] by reference to contracts of personal service, which cannot be enforced by a decree of specific performance. The foundation of this branch of the law is *Lumley v Wagner*,[27] in which the defendant had agreed to sing at the claimant's theatre during a certain period of time, and had also expressly agreed not to sing elsewhere without the claimant's written authority. The court would not grant specific performance of the affirmative stipulation, but granted an injunction to restrain the defendant from singing anywhere other than in the claimant's theatre. This decision has been consistently followed, although it has been said to be 'an anomaly which it would be very dangerous to extend'.[28] In particular, an injunction is unlikely to be granted where its effect would be to leave the defendant with the two alternatives only of remaining idle[29] or performing his contract. So, in *Rely-A-Bell Burglar and Fire Alarm Co Ltd v Eisler*,[30] the court, while granting a declaration as to the claimant's legal right and awarding damages, refused to grant an injunction to enforce a stipulation by an employee not to enter into *any* other employment during the term of the contract.

The niceness of the distinctions that have been drawn in this context appears by comparing the *Rely-A-Bell* case with *Warner Bros Pictures Inc v Nelson*,[31] in which the defendant film actress agreed not to render any services *in that capacity* for any other person during the term of the contract,[32] and the court granted an injunction. The defendant here was not confronted with the dilemma faced by the defendant in the *Rely-A-Bell* case:[33] there were other ways in which she might earn a living, and it was irrelevant that the alternative ways might well be less remunerative. She might be tempted to perform her contract, although she must not be compelled to do so. Some doubt was cast on this decision in *Warren v Mendy*,[34] in which it was said[35] to represent the high-water mark of the application of *Lumley v Wagner*.[36]

[24] [1894] 3 Ch 654; *Kirchner & Co v Gruban* [1909] 1 Ch 413; *Warner Bros Pictures Inc v Nelson* [1937] 1 KB 209, [1936] 3 All ER 160.

[25] *Lauritzencool AB v Lady Navigation Inc* [2005] EWCA Civ 579, [2005] 1 WLR 3686 (a case involving charterparties), noted (2005) 121 LQR 560 (P Devonshire).

[26] See [1991] Cambrian LR 26 (E Macdonald); (1994) 138 Sol Jo 152 (J Brown). See also, as to contracts requiring constant supervision, *Ryan v Mutual Tontine Westminster Chambers Association* [1893] 1 Ch 116, CA.

[27] (1852) 1 De GM & G 604. See (2001) 117 LQR 430 (S M Waddams).

[28] *Whitwood Chemical Co v Hardman* [1891] 2 Ch 416, 428, CA, *per* Lindley LJ.

[29] It was said, in *Evening Standard Co Ltd v Henderson* [1987] IRLR 64, CA, to be unclear what is meant by 'being idle'.   [30] [1926] Ch 609; *Whitwood Chemical Co v Hardman, supra*.

[31] [1937] 1 KB 209, [1936] 3 All ER 160. For a sideways look, see (1989) 86 LSG 36 (M L Nash).

[32] The court was prepared to sever the covenants as drafted.

[33] *Supra*. See also *Hawthorn Football Club Ltd v Harding* [1988] VR 49.   [34] *Supra*, CA.

[35] *Per* Oliver J in *Nicholas Advance Vehicle Systems Inc v De Angelis* (21 December 1979, unreported, Ch D), but cited in *Warren v Mendy, supra*, CA.

[36] *Supra*.

The above cases were considered in *Page One Records Ltd v Britton*,[37] in which a group of musicians known as 'The Troggs' had appointed the claimant company as their manager for five years, and had agreed not to engage any other person to act as manager or agent for them. An argument based on *Warner Bros Pictures Inc v Nelson*,[38] to the effect that The Troggs could, without employing any other manager or agent, continue as a group on their own or seek other employment of a different nature, failed, however. Stamp J held that, as a practical matter on the evidence before him, to grant an injunction would compel The Troggs to continue to employ the claimant company as their manager and agent:

> It would be a bad thing to put pressure on The Troggs to continue to employ as a manager and agent in a fiduciary capacity one, who, unlike the plaintiff in those cases[39] who had merely to pay the defendant money, had duties of a personal and fiduciary nature to perform and in whom The Troggs, for reasons, good, bad or indifferent, have lost confidence and who may, for all I know, fail in its duty to them.

In *Nichols Advance Vehicle Systems Inc v De Angelis*,[40] Oliver J found *Warner Bros Pictures Inc v Nelson*[41] difficult to reconcile with *Page One Records Ltd v Britton*,[42] as did the Court of Appeal in *Warren v Mendy*,[43] which preferred the approach of Stamp J in the latter case, both on grounds of realism and practicality, and because that approach is more consistent with the earlier authorities. In *Warren v Mendy*, it was said that the most significant feature of cases in which an injunction had been granted before *Warner Bros Pictures Inc v Nelson*[44] was that the term of engagement was short, in none exceeding twenty weeks. Although it was impossible to lay down a rule where the line between short and long-term engagements should be drawn, an injunction for two years (the period applicable in *Warren v Mendy*)[45] would practically compel performance of the contract. The other chief consideration was said to be the presence of obligations involving mutual trust and confidence, not merely because they are not mutually enforceable, but also because their enforcement—more especially where the servant's trust in the master may have been betrayed, or his confidence in him has genuinely gone—will serve the better interests of neither party. *Warren v Mendy*[46] itself involved a contract between a boxer and his manager, and an injunction was refused. Where, as in that case, there are negative obligations in a contract for personal services inseparable from the exercise of some special skill or talent, the court ought not to enforce the performance of the negative obligations if their enforcement will effectively compel the servant to perform his positive obligations under the contract. Compulsion is a question to be decided upon the facts of each case, with a realistic regard for the probable reaction of an injunction on the psychological and material, and, sometimes, the physical need of his servant to maintain his skill or talent. It was added that the assumption that

---

[37] [1967] 3 All ER 822. Cf *Thomas Borthwick & Sons (Australasia) Ltd v South Otago Freezing Co Ltd* [1978] 1 NZLR 538; *Dataforce Pty Ltd v Brambles Holdings Ltd* [1988] VR 771.

[38] *Supra.* Cf *Thomas Marshall (Exporters) Ltd v Guinle* [1979] Ch 227, [1978] 3 All ER 193.

[39] *Lumley v Wagner, supra*; *Warner Bros Pictures Inc v Nelson, supra.*

[40] *Supra.* See (1989) 139 NLJ 1716 (A Jennings); [1990] CLJ 28 (Hazel McLean).

[41] *Supra.* Cf *Thomas Marshall (Exporters) Ltd v Guinle, supra.*   [42] *Supra.*

[43] [1989] 3 All ER 103, [1989] 1 WLR 853, CA.   [44] *Supra.*

[45] *Supra*, CA. In relation to sports cases, see (1997) 17 LS 65 (P McCutcheon), who prefers the North American approach, which shows a greater willingness to enforce the negative stipulation by means of an injunction.

[46] *Supra*, CA.

has usually been made that damages will not be an adequate alternative remedy is not justified now that damages are invariably assessed by a judge or master.

An unusual feature of *Warren v Mendy*[47] was that the injunction was sought not against the servant, but only against a third party, who, for the purpose of the proceedings for an interim injunction, had to be taken to have induced a breach of the contract between the boxer and the manager. The court held that an injunction should usually be refused against such a third party if, on the evidence, its effect would be to compel performance of the contract.

Evening Standard Co Ltd v Henderson[48] suggests a way in which an employer may be able to get round the decision in *Rely-A-Bell Burglar and Fire Alarm Co Ltd v Eisler,*[49] although possibly at some cost. In the *Evening Standard* case, the defendant employee's contract provided that it was terminable by one year's notice on either side, and that the employee would not work for anyone else during the currency of the contract. The employee gave two months' notice only, and intended to work for a rival newspaper. An interim injunction was granted to enforce the negative restriction in the contract, on the basis of an undertaking by the employer to pay the employee his salary and other contractual benefits throughout the contractual notice period, whether he chose to continue working for it or not. However, in *Provident Financial Group plc v Hayward,*[50] the Court of Appeal refused to disturb the exercise of his discretion by the first-instance judge against the grant of an injunction restraining the employee from taking up employment with a rival employer during the period of his notice, notwithstanding that the employer was prepared to pay the employee his salary during that period. Here, unlike the *Evening Standard* case, the employer was not prepared to allow the employee to continue to work, but was being offered 'garden leave'. On the facts of the case, there was no real prospect of serious or significant damage to the claimants from the defendant working for the rival, and they should be left to their remedy in damages for the plain breach of contract.

(C) NO EXPRESS NEGATIVE STIPULATION

Where there is no express negative stipulation, the question arises whether one should be implied from an affirmative stipulation that is incapable of being directly enforced by specific performance, or, which often comes to the same thing, whether what on the face of it is an affirmative stipulation is, in substance, a negative one and should be treated as such.

The court is slow to draw this inference.[51] Mere inconsistency of the proposed course of conduct with the positive obligation under the contract is not enough. It is necessary to point to something specific that the defendant has, by implication, agreed not to do.[52] Accordingly, on the one hand, the court will not import a negative quality into an agreement if this would, in effect, result in specific performance of a contract for which that remedy is not directly available. Thus, so far as contracts for personal service are concerned,

---

[47] *Supra*, CA.
[48] [1987] IRLR 64, CA. See *GFI Group Inc v Eaglestone* [1994] IRLR 119, and [1997] Denning LJ 107 (I G C Stratton).
[49] [1926] Ch 609.   [50] [1989] 3 All ER 298, CA.
[51] See *Peto v Brighton, Uckfield and Tunbridge Wells Rly Co* (1863) 1 Hem & M 468, 486.
[52] *Bower v Bantam Investments Ltd* [1972] 3 All ER 349.

although the Court of Appeal has indicated[53] that it is not impossible for a negative stipulation to be implied, it is extremely difficult and no negative stipulation will be implied simply from an employee's covenant to devote all of his time to his employer's business[54] or to act exclusively for his employer.[55] Again, it has been held[56] that where specific performance of an agreement of a lease could not be obtained by reason of the infancy of one of the two defendants, no injunction against the granting of a lease to any other person should be decreed. Further, no injunction will be granted where it would really be ancillary to a decree of specific performance that cannot be obtained.[57]

On the other hand, in *Metropolitan Electric Supply Co Ltd v Ginder*,[58] a covenant by the defendant 'to take the whole of the electric energy required' for certain premises from the claimant was held to be, in substance, a covenant not to take it from anyone else; in *Manchester Ship Canal Co v Manchester Racecourse Co*,[59] a contract to give 'first refusal' was held to involve a negative covenant not to part with the property without giving that first refusal, which could be enforced by injunction.

(D) *DE MATTOS V GIBSON* [60]

In *De Mattos v Gibson*, Knight Bruce LJ laid down the principle that:

> reason and justice seems to prescribe that, at least as a general rule, where a man, by gift or purchase, acquires property from another, with knowledge of a previous contract, lawfully and for valuable consideration made by him with a third person, to use and employ the property for a particular purpose in a specified manner, the acquirer shall not, to the material damage of the third person, in opposition to the contract and inconsistently with it, use and employ the property in a manner not allowable to the giver or seller.

The principle, discredited in *London County Council v Allen*[61] and *Barker v Stickney*,[62] but resuscitated by the Privy Council in *Lord Strathcona Steamship Co Ltd v Dominion Coal Co*,[63] was held to be invalid by Diplock J in *Port Line Ltd v Ben Line Steamers Ltd*.[64]

The authorities were reviewed by Browne-Wilkinson J at first instance in *Swiss Bank Corpn v Lloyds Bank Ltd*,[65] who came to the conclusion that this principle is good law and represents the counterpart in equity of the tort of knowing interference with contractual

---

[53] *Mutual Reserve Fund Life Assurance v New York Life Assurance Co* (1896) 75 LT 528, 530, CA, *per* Lindley LJ.

[54] *Whitwood Chemical Co v Hardman* [1891] 2 Ch 416, CA; *Mortimer v Beckett* [1920] 1 Ch 571. Cf *Frith v Frith* [1906] AC 254, PC.

[55] *Mutual Reserve Fund Life Assurance v New York Life Insurance Co, supra.*

[56] *Lumley v Ravenscroft* [1895] 1 QB 683, CA. See *Fothergill v Rowland* (1873) LR 17 Eq 132.

[57] *Baldwin v Society for Diffusion of Useful Knowledge* (1838) 9 Sim 393; *Phipps v Jackson* (1887) 3 TLR 387.

[58] [1901] 2 Ch 799; *Esso Petroleum Co Ltd v Harper's Garage (Stourport) Ltd* [1968] AC 269, [1967] 1 All ER 699, HL. Cf *Clegg v Hands* (1890) 44 Ch D 503, CA.

[59] [1901] 2 Ch 37, CA. Cf *Gardner v Coutts & Co* [1967] 3 All ER 1064 (an action for damages only), and note *Pritchard v Briggs* [1980] Ch 338, [1980] 1 All ER 294, CA.

[60] (1858) 4 De G & J 276, 282, dist *Mac-Jordan Construction Ltd v Brookmount Erostin Ltd (in receivership)* [1992] BCLC 350, CA. See [2003] Conv 61 (G Watt).

[61] [1914] 3 KB 642, CA.   [62] [1919] 1 KB 121, CA.   [63] [1926] AC 108, PC.

[64] [1958] 2 QB 146, [1958] 1 All ER 78. See (1958) 21 MLR 433 (G H Trietel).

[65] [1979] Ch 548, [1979] 2 All ER 853. The *De Mattos v Gibson* point was not discussed on appeal: [1982] AC 584, [1980] 2 All ER 419, CA; [1982] AC 584, [1981] 2 All ER 449, HL. See (1982) 45 MLR 241

rights.[66] A person proposing to deal with property in such a way as to cause a breach of a contract affecting that property will be restrained by injunction from so doing if, when he acquired the property, he had actual knowledge of that contract. The claimant does not have to have any proprietary interest in the property: his right to have his contract performed is a sufficient interest. He must, however, establish actual, as opposed to constructive, notice of the contract by the defendant. And it seems that the principle will not be used to impose on a purchaser a positive duty to perform the covenants of his predecessor.[67]

(E) DEFENCES

Finally, it may be added that the 'clean hands' doctrine[68] applies, and a claimant may also become disentitled to an injunction by reason of his laches or acquiescence,[69] or by reason of the effect that the grant of an injunction would have on third parties.[70]

2 TO RESTRAIN LEGAL PROCEEDINGS

Before the coming into operation of the Judicature Act 1873, the Court of Chancery would restrain by injunction the prosecution of proceedings in a common law court where their continuance was inequitable, such an injunction being known as a 'common injunction', as opposed to other injunctions, which were 'special'. On the fusion of the courts by the Judicature Acts, the common injunction ceased to exist, it being expressly provided[71] that no cause or proceeding at any time pending in the High Court of Justice or before the Court of Appeal should be restrained by prohibition or injunction, although every matter of equity on which an injunction against the prosecution of any such cause or proceeding might formerly have been obtained, either unconditionally or on any terms or conditions, might be relied on by way of defence thereto.

The Judicature Acts do not, however, prohibit the High Court from granting an injunction to restrain a person from instituting proceedings,[72] or continuing pending proceedings, in other courts, such as a county court,[73] or a magistrates' court.[74]

(N Cohen-Grabelsky). See also *Binions v Evans* [1972] 2 All ER 70, 78, CA, *per* Megaw LJ; *Mac-Jordan Construction Ltd v Brookmount Erostin Ltd (in receivership), supra*, CA.

[66] See *Lumley v Gye* (1853) 2 E & B 216.

[67] *Law Debenture Trust Corpn plc v Ural Caspian Oil Corpn Ltd* [1993] 2 All ER 355, [1993] 1 WLR 138. See [1992] LMCLQ 448 (Alison Clarke).

[68] See Chapter 26, section 2(D), p 598, *supra*.

[69] Lord Cairns' dictum in *Doherty v Allman* (1878) 3 App Cas 709, considered on p 604, *supra*, does not prevent the court from considering the effect of delay, or other supervening circumstances: *Shaw v Applegate* [1978] 1 All ER 123 CA. See p 613, *supra*.

[70] See Chapter 26, section 2(E), p 599, *supra*.   [71] Judicature Act 1873, s 4(5).

[72] *Besant v Wood* (1879) 12 Ch D 605.

[73] *Murcutt v Murcutt* [1952] P 266, [1952] 2 All ER 427. In *Johns v Chatalos* [1973] 3 All ER 410, however, the court expressly left open the question of whether or not the Chancery Division has jurisdiction to grant an injunction to restrain a party from enforcing an order of a county court that is said to be a nullity.

[74] *Thames Launches Ltd v Corpn of the Trinity House of Deptford Strond* [1961] Ch 197, [1961] 1 All ER 26; *Stannard v St Giles, Camberwell Vestry* (1882) 20 Ch D 190, CA.

On traditional principles, an anti-suit injunction restraining a party from commencing or pursuing legal proceedings in a foreign jurisdiction may be granted when the ends of justice require it. The order is, of course, directed not against the foreign court, but against the parties so proceeding or threatening to proceed. It will only be issued restraining a party who is amenable to the jurisdiction of the court, against whom an injunction will be an effective remedy. Since it indirectly affects a foreign court, the jurisdiction must be exercised with caution.[75] However, in relation to the European Union, the Court of Justice of the European Communities has recently held[76] that the courts of a contracting state are precluded by the Brussels Convention[77] from prohibiting a party to proceedings pending before it from commencing or continuing legal proceedings before a court of another contracting state, even where the party was acting in bad faith with a view to frustrating the existing proceedings.

3 TO PROTECT MEMBERSHIP OF CLUBS, TRADE UNIONS, AND OTHER UNINCORPORATED BODIES

Members of unincorporated bodies can only be expelled from membership if the rules so provide and the procedure there set out is strictly complied with. The court, accordingly, can only intervene it if can be shown that the purported expulsion was not authorized by the rules,[78] or that the proceedings were irregular,[79] or not consonant with the principles of natural justice,[80] or that there was mala fides or malice in arriving at the decision.[81] If, however, a member is wrongfully expelled, he may seek a declaration that the purported expulsion is null and void, and an injunction to restrain the club, trade union, or other body from acting on the basis that he is not a member. At one time, the jurisdiction of the court to grant an injunction was thought to be based purely on the member's right of property,[82] but recent decisions indicate that the jurisdiction is founded on the contractual rights of the expelled member.[83] An injunction will, however, only be granted to prevent

---

[75] See *Airbus Industrie GIE v Patel* [1999] 1 AC 119, 132–133, [1998] 2 All ER 257, 263–264, HL, *per* Lord Goff; *Donohue v Armco Inc* [2002] 1 All ER 749, HL; *American International Specialty Lines Insurance Co v Abbott Laboratories* [2002] EWHC 2714 (Comm), [2003] 1 Lloyd's Rep 267; *Sabah Shipyard (Pakistan) Ltd v Islamic Republic of Pakistan* [2002] EWCA Civ 1643, [2003] 2 Lloyd's Rep 570; *Turner v Grovit* [2002] 1 WLR 107, HL noted [2003] ICLQ 401 (Clare Ambrose); *Cadre SA v Astra Asigurari SA* [2005] EWHC 2626 (Comm), [2006] 1 Lloyd's Rep 560. In relation to arbitration, see [2005] LMCLQ 10 (P Gross).

[76] *Turner v Grovit*, C-159/02, [2004] All ER (EC) 485. This regrettable decision is discussed in (2004) 120 LQR 529 (A Briggs); (2004) 154 NLJ 798 (L Flannery); and see [2003] ICLQ 697 (Look Chan Ho).

[77] See Civil Jurisdiction and Judgments Act 1982, Sch 1.

[78] *Lee v Showmen's Guild of Great Britain* [1952] 2 QB 329, [1952] 1 All ER 1175, CA; *Bonsor v Musicians' Union* [1956] AC 104, [1955] 3 All ER 518, HL.

[79] *Young v Ladies' Imperial Club* [1920] 2 KB 523, CA.

[80] *Lawlor v Union of Post Office Workers* [1965] Ch 712, [1965] 1 All ER 353.

[81] *Bryne v Kinematograph Renters Society Ltd* [1958] 2 All ER 579; *Annamunthodo v Oilfields Workers' Trade Union* [1961] AC 945, [1961] 3 All ER 621, PC.   [82] *Rigby v Connol* (1880) 14 Ch D 482.

[83] *Lee v Showmen's Guild of Great Britain, supra*, CA at 341, 342, 1180, *per* Denning LJ; *Bonsor v Musicians' Union, supra, per* Lord Morton, at 127, 524; *Bryne v Kinematograph Renters Society Ltd* [1958] 2 All ER 579.

a member's expulsion if it is necessary to protect a proprietary right of his, or to protect him in his right to earn his livelihood.[84] It will not be granted to give a member the right to enter a social club, unless there are proprietary rights attached to it, because, purely as a matter of contract, it is too personal to be specifically enforced.[85]

4 TO RESTRAIN THE COMMISSION OR REPETITION OF A TORT [86]

Injunctions have frequently been granted to prevent a threatened or apprehended trespass to land,[87] nuisance,[88] and waste, whether legal or equitable, but never, it seems, so as to stop a man being negligent;[89] also where a person, without just cause or excuse, deliberately interferes with the trade or business of another, and does so by unlawful means.[90] An injunction has been granted to a mother against her son to restrain the commission of assaults,[91] and the court has jurisdiction in nuisance to grant an injunction restraining persistent harassment by unwanted telephone calls.[92] Harassment has now been made a criminal offence,[93] and an actual or apprehended act of harassment within the Act may be the subject of civil proceedings in respect of which an injunction may be granted.[94] In exceptional cases, the court has power to impose an exclusion zone prohibiting the defendant from coming or remaining within a specified distance of a specified property.[95]

So far as an injunction to restrain the publication of a libel is concerned, this was wholly impossible prior to the Common Law Procedure Act 1854. Courts of equity had no jurisdiction in matters of libel,[96] and courts of law had no power to issue injunctions. Such a

---

[84] As to a right to membership when this is necessary to enable him to earn his living, see *Faramus v Film Artistes' Association* [1964] AC 925, [1964] 1 All ER 25, HL; *Nagle v Feilden* [1966] 2 QB 633, [1966] 1 All ER 689, CA, noted (1966) 82 LQR 319 (A L Goodhart); (1966) 29 MLR 424 (R W Rideout).

[85] *Baird v Wells* (1890) 44 Ch D 661, CA; *Lee v Showmen's Guild of Great Britain, supra*. It follows that no injunction will lie at the suit of a member of a proprietary club.

[86] See (1992) 22 Fam Law 158 (N Fricker); [2007] Ox JLS 509 (J Murphy).

[87] *League Against Cruel Sports Ltd v Scott* [1986] QB 240, [1985] 2 All ER 489.

[88] For example, *Halsey v Esso Petroleum Co Ltd* [1961] 2 All ER 145, and see *Rugby Joint Water Board v Walters* [1967] Ch 397, [1966] 3 All ER 497 (to restrain riparian owner from abstracting water for extraordinary purposes). See (1977) 36 CLJ 294 (A I Ogus and G M Richardson).

[89] *Miller v Jackson* [1977] QB 966 [1977] 3 All ER 338, 343, CA, *per* Lord Denning MR.

[90] *Acrow (Automation) Ltd v Rex Chainbelt Inc* [1971] 3 All ER 1175, CA; *Esso Petroleum Co Ltd v Kingswood Motors (Addlestone) Ltd* [1974] QB 142, [1973] 3 All ER 1057. See (1972) 88 LQR 177 (P Rayner).

[91] *Egan v Egan* [1975] Ch 218, [1975] 2 All ER 167. It had been held in Australia that an injunction to restrain apprehended or threatened assaults should only be granted in exceptional circumstances: *Corvisy v Corvisy* [1982] 2 NSWLR 557.

[92] *Khorasandjian v Bush* [1993] QB 727, [1993] 3 All ER 669, CA. This decision was overruled by the House of Lords in *Hunter v Canary Wharf Ltd* [1997] AC 655, [1997] 2 All ER 426, noted (1997) 113 LQR 515 (P Cane); [1998] Conv 309 (P R Ghandhi); (1998) 61 MLR 870 (J Wightman), in so far as it held that a mere licensee could sue in nuisance; only someone with a right to the land, such as the freeholder, a tenant in possession or a licensee with exclusive possession, can sue in nuisance. Cf *Manchester Airport plc v Dutton* [2000] 1 QB 133, sub nom *Dutton v Manchester Airport plc* [1999] 2 All ER 675, CA, noted p 216, *supra*.

[93] Protection from Harassment Act 1997, ss 1 and 2.   [94] Ibid, s 3.

[95] *Burris v Azadani* [1995] 4 All ER 802, [1995] 1 WLR 1372, CA.

[96] *Prudential Assurance Co v Knott* (1875) 10 Ch App 142.

power was conferred on the common law courts by the Common Law Procedure Act 1854, although there is no reported instance of its exercise prior to *Saxby v Easterbrook*.[97] By the Judicature Act 1873, the High Court acquired the powers previously possessed by both common law and equity courts, and after that Act, the Chancery Division began to grant injunctions to restrain the publication of libels.[98]

It may be added that the jurisdiction to restrain the publication of a libel does not distinguish between a libel affecting trade or property and one affecting character only, and extends to an action of slander, as well as to an action of libel.[99]

5 TO PROTECT COPYRIGHT, PATENT RIGHTS, AND TRADE MARKS

An injunction is the appropriate remedy to restrain the infringement of any of these rights, the substantive law now being largely statutory.[100]

6 TO RESTRAIN A BREACH OF CONFIDENCE

In origin, the gist of the cause of action for breach of confidence was that information of a confidential nature had been disclosed in circumstances in which there was a duty of confidence arising by reason of the relationship between the parties—for example, employer and employee—or by contract. Now, however, the limiting constraint of the need for an initial confidential relationship has been shaken off, and the law imposes a duty of confidence whenever a person receives information that he knows or ought to know is fairly and reasonably to be regarded as confidential.[101]

Lord Nicholls has pointed out[102] that, as the law has developed, breach of confidence, or misuse of confidential information, now covers two distinct causes of action, protecting two different interests—secret ('confidential') information and privacy[103]—although the two may overlap. In the second sense, when the action is used as a remedy for the

---

[97] (1878) 3 CPD 339, DC.

[98] *Bonnard v Perryman* [1891] 2 Ch 269, CA; *White v Mellin* [1895] AC 154, HL.

[99] *Hermann Loog v Bean* (1884) 26 Ch D 306, CA.

[100] Copyright Designs and Patents Act 1988; Patents Acts 1949 and 1977; Trade Marks Act 1994.

[101] See *A-G v Guardian Newspapers Ltd (No 2)* [1990] 1 AC 109, 291, [1988] 3 All ER 545, 658–659, HL *per* Lord Goff; *Campbell v MGN Ltd* [2004] UKHL 22, [2004] 2 AC 457, [2004] 2 All ER 995, *per* Lord Nicholls, at [13], [14].

[102] In *Douglas v Hello! Ltd (No 3)* [2007] UKHL 21, [2008] 1 AC 1 [2007] 4 All ER 545, at [255]. Their Lordships, by a majority, restored the decision of Lindsay J in [2003] EWHC 786 (Ch), [2003] 3 All ER 996, which had been reversed by the Court of Appeal in [2005] EWCA Civ 595, [2006] QB 125,[2005] 4 All ER 128.

[103] It has been said that no claim of confidence can be made in relation to matters properly described as shocking or immoral: *Maccaba v Lichtenstein* [2004] EWHC 1579, [2005] EMLR 109, applied in *Harrods v Times Newspapers Ltd* [2006] EWHC 83 (Ch), [2006] EMLR 320. As Page Wood VC put it in *Gartside v Outram* (1856) 26 LJ Ch 113, 114: 'there is no confidence in the disclosure of iniquity.' However, in *Mosley v News Group Newspapers Ltd* [2008] EWHC 1777 (QB), [2008] All ER (D) 322 (Jul), Eady J said 'it is highly

unjustified publication of personal information, rather than being based on the duty of good faith, it focuses on the protection of human autonomy and dignity—that is, the right to control the dissemination of information about one's private life, and the right to the esteem and respect of other people.[104]

(A) BREACH OF CONFIDENCE

Under the head of 'breach of confidence' in the first sense, injunctions have been granted to restrain an employee or ex-employee from divulging trade secrets, whether they are in the nature of secret processes,[105] or a list of customers.[106] An injunction has been granted to restrain the improper use or disclosure of trade secrets, even though the details of the secrets were not disclosed to the court at the trial,[107] but the usual procedure is for this difficulty to be dealt with by having the matter heard in private.[108] In particular, as between traders, where the question most often arises, the broad principle is 'that if information be given by one trader to another in circumstances which make that information confidential then the second trader is disentitled to make use of the confidential information for purposes of trade by way of competition with the first trader'.[109] The principle is not, however, restricted to traders, and thus, for instance, a printer is not entitled to make additional copies for his own purposes of a drawing that he has undertaken to reproduce,[110] a person who attends oral lectures can be restrained from publishing them for profit,[111] a spouse can be prevented from publishing confidences communicated during marriage,[112] and a Cabinet minister can be restrained from publishing information relating to discussions at Cabinet meetings.[113] Again, the former client of a solicitor or accountant may be able to obtain an injunction restraining him from acting for another client if he can establish:

(i) that the defendant is in possession of confidential information; and

(ii) that the information is or may be relevant to the new matter in which the interest of the other client is or may be adverse to his own.[114]

---

questionable whether in modern society that is a concept that can be applied to sexual activity, fetishist or otherwise, conducted between consenting adults in private'.

[104] See *Campbell v MGN Ltd* [2004] UKHL 22, [2004] 2 AC 457, [2004] 2 All ER 995, *per* Lord Hoffman, at [51].

[105] *Morrison v Moat* (1851) 9 Hare 241; *Cranleigh Precision Engineering Ltd v Bryant* [1964] 3 All ER 289; *Lancashire Fires Ltd v S A Lyons & Co Ltd* [1996] FSR 629, CA.

[106] *Robb v Green* [1895] 2 QB 315, CA.

[107] *Amber Size and Chemical Co Ltd v Menzel* [1913] 2 Ch 239.

[108] *Mellor v Thompson* (1885) 31 Ch D 55, CA.

[109] *Per* Evershed MR, in *Terrapin Ltd v Builders' Supply Co (Hayes) Ltd* [1960] RPC 128, 131, CA, based on *Saltman Engineering Co Ltd v Campbell Engineering Co Ltd* (1948) 65 RPC 203, CA. And see *Seager v Copydex Ltd* [1967] 2 All ER 415, CA.

[110] *Prince Albert v Strange* (1849) 1 Mac & G 25; *Tuck & Sons v Priester* (1887) 19 QBD 629, CA.

[111] *Abernethy v Hutchinson* (1825) 1 H & Tw 28.

[112] *Duchess of Argyll v Duke of Argyll* [1967] Ch 302, [1965] 1 All ER 611.

[113] *A-G v Jonathan Cape Ltd* [1976] QB 752, [1975] 3 All ER 484 (the 'Crossman diaries' case), although the injunction was refused because, the events dealt with being ten years old, the need for confidentiality had ceased.

[114] *Prince Jefri Bolkiah v KPMG (a firm)* [1999] 1 All ER 517, HL (injunction granted, but the possibility of an effective Chinese wall within a defendant organization was accepted); *Young v Robson Rhodes (a firm)* [1999] 3 All ER 524.

In *A-G v Guardian Newspapers Ltd*,[115] an interim injunction was granted restraining newspapers from publishing information already published abroad in breach of a clear duty of confidence by a former member of the British security service. Whether a final injunction would be obtained at the trial was said to be arguable, and the House of Lords affirmed that it would be a denial of justice to refuse to allow the injunction to continue until the trial. Following the trial of the action, the matter returned to the House of Lords, which discharged the injunction,[116] because there was no longer any secrecy attached to the contents of the book and no damage would be done to the public interest by further publication. However, it was affirmed that members and former members of the Security Service have a lifelong obligation of confidence owed to the Crown. In a different context, on grounds of public policy, an undoubted duty of confidence has been held not to extend so as to bar disclosure to the Financial Intermediaries, Managers and Brokers Regulatory Association (FIMBRA) or HM Revenue and Customs (HMRC) of matters that it is the province of those authorities to investigate.[117]

In *Venables v News Group Newspapers Ltd*,[118] which might well now be treated as a privacy case, two ten-year-old boys had been convicted of murdering a two-year-old toddler and had been sentenced to detention during Her Majesty's pleasure. At the conclusion of the trial, injunctions were granted restraining publication of further information about them, based on the court's jurisdiction in relation to minors. The boys had now reached the age of eighteen, and there was a likelihood that the Parole Board would release them into the community before long. Permanent injunctions were now sought to protect, inter alia, information regarding changes in their physical appearances since their detention and the new identities that would probably be given to them on their release. The evidence was that there was a real and substantial risk of death or serious physical harm if they could be identified after release. The court, taking account of the potential conflict between Art 10 (the right to freedom of expression) of the European Convention for the Protection of Human Rights and Fundamental Freedoms 1950, incorporated into English law by the Human Rights Act 1998, on the one hand, and Arts 2 (the right to life), 3 (the prohibition of torture), and 8 (the right to respect for private and family life, held that it had jurisdiction, in exceptional circumstances, to extend the protection of confidentiality of information, even to impose restrictions on the press, where not to do so would be likely to lead to serious physical injury, or death, of the person seeking that confidentiality, and there was no other way to protect the applicants other than by seeking relief from the court. Appropriate injunctions were accordingly granted. Again, in another exceptional case, *X (a woman formerly known as Mary Bell) v O'Brien*,[119] an injunction *contra mundum* was granted to protect the identity and whereabouts of X and her daughter Y. X had, some thirty-five years earlier, been convicted, at the age of eleven, of killing two children. Since her release, she had been rehabilitated into society and had not reoffended.

---

[115] [1987] 3 All ER 316, HL (the 'Spycatcher' case).

[116] *A-G v Guardian Newspapers Ltd (No 2)*, *supra*, HL. See [1989] Pub L 13 (Y Cripps); [1989] 56 MLR 389 (J Michael); (1989) 105 LQR 501 (P Birks); [1989] CLP 49 (G Jones).

[117] *Re a Company's Application* [1989] Ch 477, [1989] 2 All ER 248.

[118] [2001] 1 All ER 908. See [2002] CJQ 29 (Linda Clark).

[119] [2003] EWHC 1101(QB). [2003] 2 FCR 686.

The law was extended, in *Douglas v Hello! Ltd (No 3)*,[120] to the publication of unauthorized photographs of a private event. In that case, the magazine *OK!* contracted with a celebrity couple, Michael Douglas and Catherine Zeta-Jones ('the Douglases'), for the exclusive right to publish photographs of their wedding, at which all other photography would be forbidden. The rival magazine *Hello!* published photographs that it knew to have been surreptitiously taken by an unauthorized photographer pretending to be a waiter or guest. In joint proceedings by the Douglases and *OK!*, various claims were made, including a claim by the Douglases for invasion of privacy, which is considered later,[121] and a claim by *OK!* for breach of confidence. Lord Hoffman, who gave the leading speech for the majority, said that Lindsay J, in rightly holding *Hello!* liable for breach of confidence, had applied the well-known criteria summarized by Megarry J in *Coco v AN Clark (Engineers) Ltd*:[122]

> First, the information itself… "must have the necessary quality of confidence about it". Secondly, that information must have been imparted in circumstances importing an obligation of confidence. Thirdly, there must be an unauthorized use of that information to the detriment of the party communicating it.

To this, one might add the limitations to the principle of confidentiality stated by Lord Goff in *A-G v Guardian Newspapers Ltd (No 2)*[123]—namely, that it applies neither to useless information, nor to trivia, and that the public interest protecting confidence may be outweighed by some other countervailing public interest that favours disclosure. As to the latter, before the Human Rights Act 1998, the circumstances in which the public interest in publication overrode a duty of confidence were very limited. The test was whether exceptional circumstances justified disregarding the confidentiality that would otherwise prevail. Today, the test is different. It is whether a fetter on the right of freedom of expression set out in Art 10 of the Convention is, in the particular circumstances, necessary in a democratic society. It is a test of proportionality, in which a significant element is the importance of upholding duties of confidence that exist between individuals.[124]

In *Douglas v Hello! Ltd (No 3)*, *OK!* had paid £1m for the benefit of the obligation of confidence imposed upon those present in respect of any photographs of the wedding. Lord Hoffman held that there was no conceptual or policy reason why it should not have the benefit of the obligation. He also said that while it is certainly the case that, once information gets into the public domain, it can no longer be the subject of confidence, whether there is still a point in enforcing the obligation of confidence depends on the facts and the nature of the information. If the purpose of publishing the photographs had simply been to convey the information that the marriage had taken place, it would, like a verbal description, have put that information into the public domain. In this case, however, each photograph was to be treated as a separate piece of information that *OK!* would have the exclusive right to publish. When published by *OK!*, they were put into the public domain and *OK!* would have to rely on the law of copyright, not the law of confidence, to prevent

---

[120] [2007] UKHL 21, [2008] 1 AC 1 [2007] 4 All ER 545.   [121] See p 617 *et seq, infra*.

[122] [1969] RPC 41, 47. The relevant information in *Douglas v Hello! Ltd (No 3)*, was the photographic images of the wedding. Not information about the wedding generally.

[123] [1990] 1 AC 109, [1988] 3 All ER 545, HL.

[124] *HRH Prince of Wales v Associated Newspapers Ltd* [2006] EWCA Civ 1776, [2007] 2 All ER 139, at [67], and see Arts 8 and 10 of the Convention.

their reproduction. No other pictures were in the public domain and they did not enter the public domain merely because they resembled other pictures that had.

It is at least doubtful whether a duty of confidentiality assumed under contract carries more weight, when balanced against the right of freedom of expression, than a duty of confidentiality not buttressed by express agreement.[125] Nor is it clear what is the effect on a contractual duty of confidence when the contract in question has been wrongfully repudiated.[126]

(B) INVASION OF PRIVACY—MISUSE OF PRIVATE INFORMATION

The House of Lords has held that there is no general tort of invasion of privacy,[127] but the law of breach of confidence has been extended so as to give a remedy in some cases. This development has been significantly influenced by the European Convention for the Protection of Human Rights and Fundamental Freedoms 1950, incorporated into English law by the Human Rights Act 1998. Lord Phillips, delivering the judgment of the court in *Douglas v Hello! Ltd (No 3)*,[128] said that the court should, so far as possible, develop the action for breach of confidence in such a manner as will give effect to both Arts 8[129] and 10[130] of the Convention. He referred to *Campbell v MGN Ltd*,[131] in which, he said, the House was agreed that knowledge, actual or imputed, that information is private will normally impose on anyone publishing that information the duty to justify what, in the absence of justification, would be a wrongful invasion of privacy. Further, when Arts 8 and 10 are both engaged, neither has pre-eminence, and a difficult question of proportionality may arise.

In *Murray v Express Newspapers plc*,[132] Clarke MR, giving the judgment of the court, referred to Arts 8 and 10 of the Convention, and summarized the principles to be derived from *Campbell v MGN Ltd*. The first question is whether there is a reasonable expectation of privacy. This is an objective question: it is a question of what a reasonable person of ordinary sensibilities would feel if he were to be placed in the same position as the claimant and faced with the same publicity. Account should be taken of all of the circumstances of the case. In the case of a child, it is not limited by whether the child was physically aware of the photograph being taken or published, or was personally affected by it. The court can

---

[125] *A-G v Parry* [2002] EWHC 3201 (Ch), [2004] EMLR 13.

[126] *Campbell v Frisbee* [2002] EWCA Civ 1374, [2003] EMLR 76.

[127] *Wainwright v Home Office* [2003] UKHL 53, [2004] 2 AC 406 [2003] 4 All ER 969; *Campbell v MGN Ltd* [2004] UKHL 22, [2004] 2 AC 457, [2004] 2 All ER 995 (newspaper publication of covertly taken photograph of celebrated fashion model leaving meeting of Narcotics Anonymous), noted (2004) 120 LQR 563 (J Morgan). See [2003] CLJ 444 (J Morgan); [2003] 66 MLR 726 (G Phillipson); [2004] SJLS 311 (Megan Richardson); (2005) 121 LQR 628 (N A Moreham); (2005) 149 Sol Jo 976 (A Hammerton).

[128] *Douglas v Hello! Ltd (No 3)* [2005] EWCA Civ 595, [2006] QB 125, [2005] 4 All ER 128, at [53] (there was no appeal against this part of the decision); *Green Corns Ltd v Claverley Group Ltd* [2005] EWHC 958 (QB), [2005] EMLR 31.

[129] Right to respect for private and family life.   [130] Freedom of expression.

[131] *Supra*, HL, followed *Murray (by his litigation friends) v Express Newspapers plc* [2007] EWHC 1908 (Ch), [2007]3 FCR 331.

[132] [2008] EWCA Civ 446, [2008] 3 WLR 13 (May) (action brought in name and on behalf of infant son of Dr and Mrs Murray—better known as J K Rowling—for an injunction against further publication of a photograph taken covertly of him and his parents in a public street).

attribute to the child reasonable expectations about his private life, based on matters such as how it has, in fact, been conducted by those responsible for his welfare and upbringing.

If the answer to the first question is 'yes', the court has to carry out a balancing exercise in the context of Arts 8 and 10 of the Convention. The position has been explained by Lord Hope[133] in the following terms:

> The rights guaranteed by these articles are qualified rights. Article 8(1) protects the right to respect for private life, but recognition is given by [A]rt 8(2) to the protection of the rights and freedoms of others. Article 10(1) protects the right to freedom of expression, but [A]rt 10(2) recognizes the need to protect the rights and freedoms of others. The effect of these provisions is that the right to privacy which lies at the heart of an action for breach of confidence has to be balanced against the right of the media to impart information to the public. And the right of the media to impart information to the public has to be balanced in its turn against the respect that must be given to private life.

The balancing exercise is now routinely applied. It came down in favour of the claimants in *Douglas v Hello! Ltd (No 3)*,[134] *McKennitt v Ash*,[135] *Campbell v MGN Ltd*,[136] *Murray v Express Newspapers plc*,[137] and *Mosley v News Group Newspapers Ltd*.[138] Other recent cases include *A v B plc*,[139] in which the court, while taking account of the Human Rights Act 1998, set aside an interim injunction granted to the claimant, a married Premier League footballer, to prevent the first defendant newspaper publishing stories concerning his sexual relationships with two named women. Balancing the protection of the claimant's privacy against the defendant's right to freedom of expression, the freedom of the press should prevail. Account was taken of the fact that the two women involved chose to disclose their relationships with the claimant to the defendant newspaper: their right to freedom of expression was also engaged.

A v B plc was distinguished in *CC v AB*,[140] in which the claimant had an adulterous relationship with the defendant's wife. In this case, neither of the parties to the sexual relationship in question wished the fact of it, or any details about it, to be made public. The claimant obtained a limited injunction restraining the defendant, who was motivated by a desire for revenge and an opportunity to make money, from communicating, directly or indirectly, with the media or the Internet on the subject of the claimant's former relationship with his wife.

---

133 In *Campbell v MGN Ltd*, *supra*, HL, at 1023.

134 [2003] EWHC 786 (Ch), [2003] 3 All ER 996, affd on this point [2005] EWCA Civ 595, [2006] QB 125, [2005] 4 All ER 128. For the facts, see p 616, *supra*. The Douglases were not involved in the further appeal to the House of Lords.

135 [2006] EWCA Civ 1714, [2007] 3 WLR 194. See *BBC v Rochdale MBC* [2005] EWHC 2862 (Fam), [2007] 1 FLR 101; *T v BBC* [2007] EWHC 1683 (QB), [2008] 1 FLR 281. See also [2007] LS 404 (G Gomery).

136 [2004] UKHL 22, [2004] 2 AC 457, [2004] 2 All ER 995 (a claim for damages only, being too late for an injunction). As to damages in breach of confidence actions, with particular reference to privacy cases, see [2007] LS 43 (N Witzleb), who refers to most of the relevant periodical literature.

137 See p 617 and fn 132, *supra*.

138 [2008] EWHC 1777, (QB), [2008] EMLR 679 (again, a claim in damages only).

139 [2002] EWCA Civ 337, [2003] QB 195, sub nom *A v B (a company)* [2002] 2 All ER 545, criticized [2002] CLJ 264 (D Howarth). The case turned on whether the information in question was properly to be regarded as confidential. Cf *Archer v Williams* [2003] EWHC 1670 (QB), [2003] EMLR 869 (claimant not a public figure; her right to preserve her privacy outweighed the defendant's right to freedom of expression). See also *Mills v News Group Newspapers Ltd* [2001] EMLR 960; and pp 591–592, *supra*.

140 [2006] EWHC 3083, [2007] EMLR 312.

Again, in *X v Persons Unknown*,[141] the claimants X (a famous model) and her husband obtained a limited injunction against persons unknown, served on newspapers so that they would be aware, if they received approaches from 'persons unknown', that publication of relevant confidential information about the state of the claimants' marriage would be a breach of the order.

It has recently been held that where the public interest justifies the publication of confidential information, there is no prepublication obligation on the publisher to disclose to the owner of that information the material that he proposes to publish and to give the owner an opportunity to reply to it.[142]

As a general rule, an injunction can be obtained not only against the original guilty party, but also against any third party who knowingly obtained the confidential information in breach of confidence or in any other fraudulent manner.[143] Indeed, even if a man obtains the confidential information innocently, once he gets to know that it was originally given in confidence, he can, according to the circumstances, be restrained from breaking that confidence:[144] 'Each case will depend upon its own facts and the decision of the judge as to...whether the conscience of the third party is affected by the confidant's breach of duty.'[145]

The Law Commission[146] has recommended that the present action for breach of confidence should be abolished and replaced by a new statutory tort of breach of confidence.

7 TO PROTECT PUBLIC RIGHTS[147]

Although, as we have seen,[148] where a statute creates an offence without creating a right of property and provides a summary remedy, an individual cannot normally claim an injunction, the Attorney-General can do so if the public interest is affected,[149] unless,

---

[141] [2006] EWHC 2783(QB), [2007] EMLR 290.

[142] *Tillery Valley Foods Ltd v Channel Four Television Corporation* (2004) Times, 21 May.

[143] *Morrison v Moat* (1851) 9 Hare 241; *Lord Ashburton v Pape* [1913] 2 Ch 469, CA; *Duchess of Argyll v Duke of Argyll* [1967] Ch 302, [1965] 1 All ER 611.

[144] *Fraser v Evans* [1969] 1 QB 349, [1969] 1 All ER 8; *Butler v Board of Trade* [1971] Ch 680, [1970] 3 All ER 593. The above paragraph was cited and applied by Helsham CJ in *Wheatley v Bell* [1984] FSR 16, and by Seaton JA in *GEAC Canada Ltd v Prologic Computer Corpn* (1989) 35 BCLR (2d) 143.

[145] *Per* Lord Griffiths in *A-G v Guardian Newspapers Ltd (No 2)*, *supra*, HL, at 652; *Lord Advocate v Scotsman Publications Ltd* [1990] 1 AC 812, [1989] 2 All ER 852, HL.

[146] Law Com No 110. See, generally, (1982) 11 AALR 273 (A M Tettenborn); (1989) 7 Otago LR 3; (1990) 14 NZULR 144 (D Laster); (1992) 12 LS 302 (G Wei). The origins are discussed in (1979) 8 AALR (R G Hammond). For a US view, see (1982) 82 Col LR (A B Vickery). The defence of public interest is discussed in *Lion Laboratories Ltd v Evans* [1985] QB 526, [1984] 2 All ER 417, CA; *X v Y* [1988] 2 All ER 648; *A-G v Guardian Newspapers Ltd (No 2)*, *supra*, HL; and in Australia in *Sullivan v Sclanders* (2000) 77 SASR 419.

[147] See, generally, (1979) 42 MLR 369 (D Feldman). Note also the novel case of *West Mercia Constabulary v Wagener* [1981] 3 All ER 378, [1982] 1 WLR 127, discussed (1982) 98 LQR 190 (D Feldman); *Chief Constable of Kent v V* [1983] QB 34, [1982] 3 All ER 36, CA, noted (1983) 99 LQR 1; (1983) 42 CLJ 51 (A Tettenborn); (1983) 133 NLJ 926 (D Feldman); (1983) Crim LR 723 (C P Walker); (1984) 133 NLJ 829 (Suzanne Bailey); (1989) 17 MULR 56 (J Duns). Cf *Chief Constable of Hampshire v A Ltd* [1985] QB 132, [1984] 2 All ER 385, CA, noted (1984) 100 LQR 537 (G Samuel), and see *Chief Constable of Leicestershire v M* [1988] 3 All ER 1015; *Chief Constable of Surrey v A* (1988) Times, 27 October. The Criminal Justice Act 1988 now provides for restraint orders and confiscation orders. See also *A-G v Blake* [2000] 4 All ER 385, HL.

[148] See p 559, *supra*. But note that an individual may sue to enforce legal rights vested in the inhabitants of a parish: *Wyld v Silver* [1963] 1 QB 169, [1962] 3 All ER 309, CA.

[149] *A-G v Smith* [1958] 2 QB 173, [1958] 2 All ER 557; *A-G v Harris* [1961] 1 QB 74, [1960] 3 All ER 207, CA.

it would seem, the statute expressly provides that the statutory remedy is to be the only one.[150] The House of Lords, however, in *Gouriet v Union of Post Office Workers*,[151] has stressed the anomalous character of the civil remedy of an injunction prohibiting conduct solely because it is criminal. The effect of an injunction in such circumstances is to add a discretionary penalty for contempt of court to the criminal penalty, which, in the case of a statutory offence, will have been fixed by Parliament. Further, breach of an injunction will be dealt with in the civil court by the judge alone, whereas, in the criminal court, the accused may be entitled to be tried by a jury. Scott J has recently[152] referred to an injunction in aid of the criminal law as a remedy of last resort, which should not be granted if other less draconian means of securing obedience to the law are available. Long used for this purpose in cases of public nuisance, the grant of an injunction has only been extended to statutory offences comparatively recently. It has been said[153] that this use of the injunction should be confined to statutes the objects of which are to promote the health, safety, or welfare of the public, and to particular cases under such statutes in which either the prescribed penalty for the summary offence has proved to be insufficient to deter the offender from numerous repetitions of the offence, or the defendant's disobedience to the statutory prohibition may cause grave and irreparable harm.

Public rights are normally asserted by the Attorney-General, as representing the public. A private person is entitled to sue in respect of interference with a public right[154] if there is also interference with a private right of his, which case, however, does not depend on the existence of a public right in addition to the private one. Lord Diplock, who gave the only reasoned speech in *Lohnro Ltd v Shell Petroleum Co Ltd (No 2)*,[155] said that there were two classes of exception to the general rule. The first is where, on the true construction of the Act, it is apparent that the obligation or prohibition was imposed for the benefit or protection of a particular class of individuals, as in the case of the Factories Acts and similar legislation.[156] The second is where the statute creates a public right—that is, a right to be enjoyed by all of those of Her Majesty's subjects who wish to avail themselves of it—and a particular member of the public suffers particular, direct, and substantial damage other and different from that which was common to all of the rest of the public. A mere prohibition on members of the public generally from doing what it would otherwise be lawful for them to do is not enough.

[150] *Evans v Manchester, Sheffield and Lincolnshire Rly Co* (1887) 36 Ch D 626; *Stevens v Chown* [1901] 1 Ch 894.

[151] [1978] AC 435, [1977] 3 All ER 70, HL. For a discussion of this decision in an Australian context, see (1978) 5 Mon LR 133 (G A Flick). See also *Stoke-on-Trent City Council v B & Q (Retail) Ltd* [1984] AC 754, [1984] 2 All ER 332, HL; *Kirklees Metropolitan Borough Council v Wickes Building Supplies Ltd* [1993] AC 227, [1992] 3 All ER 717, HL.

[152] *Waverley Borough Council v Hilden* [1988] 1 All ER 807, [1988] 1 WLR 246.

[153] Per Lord Diplock in *Gouriet v Post Office Engineering Union*, supra, HL, at 500, 99.

[154] But, in some circumstances, a prerogative remedy may be available: see (1978) 94 LQR 4 (HWRW); *R v IRC, ex p National Federation of Self-Employed and Small Business Ltd* [1980] QB 407, [1980] 2 All ER 378, CA; (1982) Cambrian LR 32 (J A Jolowicz).

[155] [1982] AC 173, [1981] 2 All ER 456, HL; *Gouriet v Post Office Engineering Union*, supra, HL, at 518, 114, per Lord Fraser of Tullybelton; *RCA Corpn v Pollard* [1983] Ch 135, [1982] 3 All ER 771, CA, discussed (1983) 133 NLJ 527 (G Mitchell); (1983) 99 LQR 182 (G Samuel); [1983] Conv 451 (H Carty); *X (minors) v Bedfordshire County Council* [1995] 2 AC 633, [1995] 3 All ER 353, HL; *Mid Kent Holdings plc v General Utilities plc* [1996] 3 All ER 132. See also (1987) 38 NILQ 118 (A M Tettenborn).

[156] *Rickless v United Artists Corpn* [1988] QB 40, [1987] 1 All ER 679, CA.

The Attorney-General, however, may sue, either *ex officio*, or under the relator procedure. In the latter case, although, as we have seen,[157] the relator is liable for the costs and although the conduct of the proceedings is left in his hands, it is in his hands as agent for the Attorney-General, who retains control. The Attorney-General not only can, but does, scrutinize and criticize draft pleadings, and directs what interlocutory steps should be taken. He may continue relator proceedings even though the relator has died, and no compromise can be arrived at without his concurrence. It is entirely a matter for the Attorney-General to decide whether he should commence litigation or not, and the court has no jurisdiction to control the exercise of his discretion. The only control is parliamentary.[158]

It should be added that local authorities have been given various powers to initiate proceedings without the intervention of the Attorney-General. These include, inter alia, proceedings in respect of a statutory nuisance under the Environmental Protection Act 1990,[159] and, more generally, under the Local Government Act 1972, where the local authority considers it expedient for the promotion or protection of the interests of the inhabitants of their area.[160] But something more than infringement of the criminal law must be shown before the assistance of civil proceedings, by way of injunction, can be invoked by a local authority. The broad question to be asked is whether, in the circumstances, criminal proceedings are likely to prove ineffective to achieve the public interest purposes for which the legislation in question was enacted, or if there are good grounds for thinking that compliance would not be secured by prosecution. An injunction should only be granted in an exceptional case.[161]

Once the matter is before the court, it is for the court to decide what the result of the litigation shall be,[162] although, in a case in which the Attorney-General is acting *ex officio*, the very fact that he has initiated proceedings, thereby showing that, in his opinion, the acts of the defendant warrant an injunction, will carry weight with the court.[163] In particular, where the Attorney-General establishes deliberate and still continuing breaches of the law, the court will, in the exercise of its discretion, normally grant an injunction, unless, after hearing both sides, it comes to the conclusion that the matter is too trivial to warrant it, or that an injustice would be caused by it, or that there is some other good reason for refusing to enforce the general right of the public to have its laws obeyed. The mere fact that there is no immediate injury in a narrow sense to the public is not a ground for refusing an injunction at the instance of the Attorney-General who, representing the community, has

---

[157] See p 583, *supra*.

[158] *Gouriet v Post Office Engineering Union*, *supra*, HL. See *Imperial Tobacco Ltd v A-G* [1979] QB 555, [1979] 2 All ER 592, CA; (1978) 41 MLR 58 (T C Hartley) and [1979] Pub L 214 (P P Mercer).

[159] Section 81(5).

[160] Section 222. See *Stoke-on-Trent City Council v B & Q (Retail) Ltd* [1984] AC 754, [1984] 2 All ER 332, HL; *Runnymede Borough Council v Ball* [1986] 1 All ER 629, CA; *Waverley Borough Council v Hilden* [1988] 1 WLR 246; (1979) 95 LQR 174 (D Feldman); [1983] JPEL 511 (E F Cousins and R Anthony).

[161] *Guildford Borough Council v Hein* [2005] EWCA Civ 979, (2005) Times, 21 September, CA. The exercise by the local authority of its statutory powers may be the subject of judicial review. As to the grant of an injunction under the Town and Country Planning Act 1990, s 187B, in relation to breaches of planning control, see *South Bucks D C v Porter* [2003] UKHL 26, [2003] 3 All ER 1: *South Cambridgeshire D C v Persons Unknown* [2004] EWCA Civ 1280, (2004) Times, 11 November, CA, and p 572, *supra*. See also [2004] JPEL 8 (I Loveland).

[162] *A-G v Birmingham, Tame and Rea District Drainage Board*, *supra*; *A-G v Harris*, *supra*.

[163] A local authority application under s 222 of the Local Government Act 1972 seems not to carry any special weight: see (1986) 45 CLJ 374 (S Tromans).

a larger and wider interest in seeing that the laws are obeyed and order maintained. Thus, in a narrow sense, there was no public injury—there may possibly even have been a public benefit—in, for instance, *A-G v Sharp*,[164] in which the defendant persistently ran omnibuses without the proper licence, and *A-G v Harris*,[165] in which the defendants sold flowers from stalls erected on the pavement near a cemetery in breach of the Manchester Police Regulation Act 1844. Further, in an action by the Attorney-General, the court, although retaining its discretion, ought to be slow to say that the Attorney-General should first have exhausted other remedies.[166]

Where the Attorney-General or a local authority seeks an injunction to restrain the commission of a statutory offence, the court, in deciding how it should exercise its discretion, will consider the extent to which the statutory remedies have been exhausted. In *A-G v Harris*,[167] the two defendants had been prosecuted and convicted no fewer than 142 and 95 times, respectively, before proceedings were brought for an injunction, but there are exceptions to the prima facie rule that the High Court will intervene only in the case of persistent lawbreaking. These include, inter alia, cases in which some permanent damage to the public interest is being done,[168] in which the intervention of the court is required as a matter of urgency,[169] in which the defendant is quite deliberately organizing and maintaining a system that is designed to break the law,[170] in which resort to the statutory remedy would be futile,[171] or in which the court draws the inference that the defendant's unlawful operations will continue unless and until effectively restrained by the law, and that nothing short of an injunction will be effective to restrain him.[172] In an appropriate case, it may even be possible to obtain an injunction before there has been any resort to the statutory remedies at all.[173]

8 TO RESTRAIN A BREACH OF TRUST

In the exercise of its inherent jurisdiction over trustees, the court will inquire what personal obligations are binding on them and, in an appropriate case, will enforce those obligations by the grant of an injunction.[174] Here, an injunction is granted not in aid of a legal

---

[164] [1931] 1 Ch 121, CA.

[165] [1961] 1 QB 74, [1960] 3 All ER 207, CA; *A-G v Chaudry* [1971] 3 All ER 938, CA.

[166] *A-G v Bastow* [1957] 1 QB 514, [1957] 1 All ER 497.   [167] *Supra.*

[168] *A-G v Ashborne Recreation Ground Co* [1903] 1 Ch 101.

[169] *A-G v Chaudry, supra,* CA; *Kirklees Metropolitan Borough Council v Wickes Building Supplies Ltd* [1993] AC 227, [1992] 3 All ER 717, HL.

[170] *Stafford Borough Council v Elkenford Ltd* [1977] 2 All ER 519, CA (Sunday market: one enforcement notice under planning law and one prosecution and conviction under the Shops Act 1950); *Stoke-on-Trent City Council v B & Q (Retail) Ltd* [1984] AC 754, [1984] 2 All ER 332, HL; *Kirklees Metropolitan Borough Council v Wickes Building Supplies Ltd, supra,* HL.

[171] *Runnymede Borough Council v Ball* [1986] 1 All ER 629, CA. See (1992) 142 NLJ 428 (M Beloff).

[172] *City of London Corpn v Bovis Construction Ltd* [1992] 3 All ER 697, CA; *Kirklees Metropolitan Borough Council v Wickes Building Supplies Ltd, supra,* HL.

[173] *A-G v Chaudry, supra,* CA; *Stafford Borough Council v Elkenford Ltd, supra,* CA; *Hammersmith London Borough v Magnum Automated Forecourts Ltd* [1978] 1 All ER 401, CA.

[174] *Chellaram v Chellaram* [1985] Ch 409, [1985] 1 All ER 1043.

right, but to protect a purely equitable claim. Thus, for instance, in *Dance v Goldingham*,[175] trustees for sale of land inserted depreciatory conditions of sale without reasonable cause. An injunction to restrain completion of the sale was issued against both the trustees and the purchaser,[176] the court holding it irrelevant that the claimant had only a small interest under the trust, that she was an infant, and that the action may have been started from some other motive. More recently, in *Waller v Waller*,[177] a wife sought an injunction to restrain her husband from making or completing any sale of the matrimonial home without her consent. She and her husband were tenants in common in equity, but the legal estate was vested in the husband alone. Notwithstanding the imposition of the statutory trust for sale,[178] the husband alone entered into a contract of sale with a third party, without having appointed another trustee and without consulting his wife. The injunction was granted.[179] Other cases show that an injunction may be granted to restrain trustees from distributing the estate otherwise than in accordance with the terms of the trust instrument,[180] from introducing ministers into the pulpit who were not ministers of the Church of Scotland, in breach of the provisions of the trust,[181] or otherwise disturbing the management of a chapel by the majority of trustees,[182] from demolishing a building,[183] from mortgaging the trust property unnecessarily,[184] or from selling it to anyone at a lower price than that offered by the reversioner and without first communicating with him.[185]

9 IN MATRIMONIAL AND OTHER FAMILY MATTERS

The Family Law Act 1996, replacing and extending earlier legislation, gives the courts wide powers both in divorce and other matrimonial proceedings, and in cases in which a man and a woman have been living together without being married to each other. The Act gives the courts jurisdiction to grant orders to restrain one party from forcing his or her society on another, or otherwise molesting that other, and/or prohibiting him or her from entering on, or coming within a specified distance of, property occupied by the person seeking the order. Injunctions may also be granted under the Housing Act 1996[186] and the Protection from Harassment Act 1997.[187] The details of these provisions are primarily matters of family law, and are not dealt with in this work.[188]

---

[175] (1873) 8 Ch App 902. See, generally, *Balls v Strutt* (1841) 1 Hare 146.

[176] The question of whether the purchaser might have a personal right of action against the trustees was left open.   [177] [1967] 1 All ER 305.

[178] *Bull v Bull* [1955] 1 QB 234, [1955] 1 All ER 253, and see Megarry and Wade, *Law of Real Property*, 7th edn, [13.051] *et seq*.

[179] The third party was not a party to the proceedings, and the injunction was granted on an undertaking by the wife to join him as a defendant, and he was given liberty to apply to discharge the injunction.

[180] *Fox v Fox* (1870) LR 11 Eq 142.   [181] *Milligan v Mitchell* (1837) 3 My & Cr 72.

[182] i(1859) 4 De G & J 353.   [183] *Ludlow Corpn v Greenhouse* (1827) 1 Bli NS 17.

[184] *Rigall v Foster* (1853) 18 Jur 39.   [185] *Wheelwright v Walker* (1883) 23 Ch D 752.

[186] See *Moat Housing Group South Ltd v Harris* [2005] EWCA Civ 287, [2006] QB 606, [2005] 4 All ER 1051.   [187] See *Hipgrave v Jones* [2004] EWHC 2901 (QB), [2005] 2 FLR 174.

[188] As to the balance between the freedom of the press and the protection of children, see *Re S (a child) (identification: restriction on publication)* [2004] UKHL 47, [2005] 1 AC 593 [2004] 4 All ER 683; *Re X, Y (children)* [2004] EWHC 762 (Fam), [2004] EMLR 29.

10 IN COMPANY MATTERS

The legal capacity of a company regulated by the Companies Act 2006 is defined by the memorandum of association, and if a company attempts to do an *ultra vires* act—that is, one beyond its legal powers—even a single shareholder has a right to resist it, notwithstanding that it may have been sanctioned by all of the directors and a large majority of the shareholders, and the court will interpose on his behalf by injunction.[189] A mere creditor, as opposed to a shareholder, however, has no such right, and, as Lord Hatherley LC observed,[190] he cannot claim 'the interference of this court on the ground that he, having no interest in the company, except the mere fact of being a creditor, is about to be defrauded by reason of their making away with their assets'.

11 FREEZING INJUNCTIONS[191] AND SEARCH ORDERS[192]

In *Bank Mellat v Nikpour*,[193] Donaldson LJ referred to the 'Mareva injunction' (the freezing injunction) and the 'Anton Piller order' (the search order) as the law's two 'nuclear' weapons. The object of a freezing injunction is to freeze the defendant's assets so as to ensure that they are not spirited away before judgment, leaving nothing on which the claimant's judgment can bite.[194] It is a prohibitory injunction. By contrast, the search order is a mandatory injunction. It orders the defendant to permit the claimant to enter his, the defendant's, premises for specified purposes. It came into being to deal with situations created by infringements of patents, trade marks, and copyright, and, in particular, with acts of so-called 'video piracy'. It is designed to provide a quick and efficient means of recovering infringing articles, and of discovering the sources from which the articles have been supplied and the persons to whom they are distributed, before those concerned have had time to destroy or conceal them.

As we have seen,[195] an interim injunction—and freezing injunctions and search orders are invariably interim orders—will normally only be granted upon notice, so as to give the defendant a full opportunity to resist the claim. However, it has long been accepted that, in

---

[189] *Simpson v Westminster Palace Hotel Co* (1860) 8 HL Cas 712; *Mosely v Koffyfontein Mines Ltd* [1911] 1 Ch 73, CA; affd sub nom *Koffyfontein Mines Ltd v Mosely* [1911] AC 409, HL; *Parke v Daily News Ltd* [1962] Ch 927, [1962] 2 All ER 929 (principle unaffected, but decision would now be different by reason of Companies Act 2006, s 247).

[190] *Mills v Northern Rly of Buenos Ayres Co* (1870) 5 Ch App 621, 628.

[191] Formerly, Mareva injunctions.

[192] Formerly, Anton Pillar orders. See, generally, (1989) Supreme Court Journal 1 (P H Pettit); (1990) 20 UWALR 143 (J Martin); (1990) 20 UWALR 169 (I C F Spry); (1993) 109 LQR 432 (A A S Zuckerman); Equity & Contemporary Legal Developments (ed S Goldstein), p 793 (P H Pettit); (1999) 62 MLR 539 (P Devonshire); (1999) 49 UTLJ 1 (R J C Deane).

[193] [1985] FSR 87, 92, CA.

[194] See *Derby & Co v Weldon (Nos 3 & 4)* [1990] Ch 65, sub nom *Derby & Co v Weldon (No 2)* [1989] 1 All ER 1002, CA, and *Derby & Co Ltd v Weldon (No 6), supra*, CA; *C Inc plc v L* [2001] 2 All ER (Comm) 446.

[195] See p 562, *supra*.

a case of urgency, an interim injunction may be granted without notice, and, for obvious reasons, both freezing injunctions and search orders are invariably applied for without notice in the first instance, although the courts have laid down guidelines to be applied to try to ensure that the defendant is not treated unfairly. In a matter of extreme urgency, the injunction may be obtained before issue of the claim, and may even be granted over the telephone.[196]

It may be noted that a freezing injunction is often sought on its own, but a claim for a search order is almost invariably accompanied by a claim for a freezing injunction, and many of the same considerations apply to both forms of relief. There is, however, one important distinction. In both cases, the defendant will be given the right to apply on short notice for the injunction to be discharged. This provides a reasonable safeguard in the case of a freezing injunction, which can be lifted on very short notice. The defendant may have suffered some damage, but it is likely to be limited. In the case of a search order, his theoretical right to apply to have the order discharged is likely to be of little, if any, value to him. He does not know that the order has been made until it has been served upon him. At the same time as the order is served, he comes under an immediate obligation to consent to the entry into and search of his premises, and the removal therefrom of material specified in the order. If he does not consent, he is at risk of committal to prison for contempt of court even if the reason for his refusal to consent is his intention to apply to have the order discharged. Accordingly, it is right to regard a search order as an even more drastic remedy than the freezing injunction, and for the courts to act with even greater caution in granting it.

(A) THE FREEZING INJUNCTION

(i) Origins

In *Mareva Compania Naviera SA v International Bulkcarriers SA*,[197] the Court of Appeal was following and applying its own decision given a month earlier in *Nippon Yusen Kaisha v Karageorgis*.[198] Lord Denning MR presided over both these decisions, which he subsequently observed[199] set in motion '*The greatest piece of judicial law reform in my time*'. Until these cases, the conventional wisdom[200] was that *Lister & Co v Stubbs*[201] prevented a claimant from obtaining an injunction restraining the defendant from removing or disposing out of the jurisdiction property that would otherwise be available to satisfy a judgment that it the claimant was likely to obtain against him. In the *Nippon* case,[202] the court was well aware of the position, and Lord Denning, with whom the other members of the court agreed, quite deliberately enunciated a change in the practice. There was nothing, he said, to prohibit such an order, and it was warranted by the predecessor[203] of s 37(1) of the Supreme Court Act 1981, now renamed the Senior Courts Act 1981, which empowers

---

[196] See *P S Refson & Co Ltd v Saggers* [1984] 3 All ER 111. It is not the practice in the Chancery Division to grant a without-notice order for more than seven days. See the Chancery Guide, para 1.35.

[197] [1980] 1 All ER 213n, [1975] 2 Lloyd's Rep 509, CA.   [198] [1975] 3 All ER 282, CA.

[199] In *The Due Process of Law*, p 134. See [1999] Denning LJ 25 (J Stevens).

[200] See, eg, *The Siskina* [1977] 3 All ER 803, 828, HL, *per* Lord Hailsham LC.

[201] (1890) 45 Ch D 1, CA.   [202] *Supra*, CA.

[203] Section 45(1) of the Supreme Court of Judicature (Consolidation) Act 1925.

the High Court to grant an injunction in all cases in which it appears to the court to be just and convenient to do so. This provision, it has been held, enables the court not only to grant a freezing injunction, but also to grant any ancillary order that appears just and convenient for the purpose of ensuring that the freezing injunction is effective.[204] It may also be granted after judgment has been entered, but before execution has been successfully levied, to restrain a judgment debtor from dealing with or disposing of his assets pending execution.[205]

The juridical basis of a freezing injunction remains unclear. It is quite a different injunction from any other: it is not connected with the subject matter of the cause of action in issue in the proceedings, and it does not prevent the defendant from doing something that, if done, would be a wrong attracting a remedy. Section 37(3) of the 1981 Act, a new provision, did not, as has sometimes been said, turn the freezing injunction into a statutory remedy, but it assumed that the remedy existed, and tacitly indorsed its validity. It is, perhaps, best regarded as a special exception to the general law.[206] It has a direct effect on third parties who are notified of it and who hold assets comprised in the order.[207]

A freezing order acts *in personam* only, and does not entitle a party in whose favour it was granted to say that he has a property or security interest in the defendant's assets in question, even where the order fixes on a single asset and even where that asset is land.[208]

When freezing injunctions were first granted, no maximum amount was inserted. Quite soon,[209] however, it became the preferred and usual practice to make 'maximum sum' orders—that is, injunctions that freeze the defendant's assets only up to the level of the claimant's prima facie justifiable claim, leaving him free to deal with the balance. The freezing injunction has been held to be inappropriate where relatively small sums are involved.[210]

(ii) Extent of the jurisdiction

The extent of the jurisdiction of the court was explained by Lord Scott in *Fourie v Le Roux*,[211] in a speech with which, on this issue, all of the other Law Lords agreed. In that case, the question was raised whether the first-instance judge had jurisdiction to grant an injunction. Lord Scott observed that 'jurisdiction' is a word of some ambiguity. He cited

---

[204] *Derby & Co Ltd v Weldon (No 6)* [1990] 3 All ER 263, [1990] 1 WLR 1139, CA. See also *Camdex International Ltd v Bank of Zambia (No 2)* [1997] 1 All ER 728, CA.

[205] *Orwell Steel (Erection and Fabrication) Ltd v Asphalt & Tarmac (UK) Ltd* [1985] 3 All ER 747; *Hill Samuel & Co Ltd v Littaur* [1985] NLJ Rep 57. And, in aid of enforcement of a judgment against one defendant, against a co-defendant in respect of whom all causes of action had been abandoned: *Mercantile Group (Europe) AG v Aiyela* [1994] QB 366, [1994] 1 All ER 110, CA.

[206] *Mercedes-Benz AG v Leiduck* [1996] AC 284, [1995] 3 All ER 929, PC.

[207] See *Babanaft International Co SA v Bassatne* [1990] Ch 13, [1989] 1 All ER 433, CA. See also (1989) 8 CJQ 263 (J Dine and J MacEvoy Jnr).

[208] *Kastner v Jason* [2004] EWCA Civ 1599, [2005] 1 Lloyd's Rep 397; *Technocrats International Inv v Fredic Ltd* [2004] EWHC 2674 (QB), [2006] BPIR 317; *Customs and Excise Commissioners v Barclays Bank plc* [2006] UKHL 28, [2007] 1 AC 181, [2006] 4 All ER 256.

[209] See *A v C* [1980] 2 All ER 347, 351, per Robert Goff; *Z Ltd v A-Z and AA-LL* [1982] 1 All ER 556 CA, per Lord Denning MR, at 565, and Kerr LJ, at 575 (there is a misprint in 575, b1, where 'plaintiff' should read 'defendant'); *Charles Church Developments plc v Cronin* [1990] FSR 1.

[210] *Sions v Price* (1988) Independent, 19 December, CA.

[211] [2007] UKHL 1, [2007] 1 All ER 1087, [2007] 1 WLR 320, noted (2007) 123 LQR 361 (P Devonshire); [2007] 16(2) Nott LJ 78 (Jane Ching); [2007] CJQ 181 (D Capper).

from the judgment of Pickford LJ in *Guaranty Trust Co of New York v Hannay & Co*,[212] who said:

> The first and, in my opinion, the only really correct sense of the expression that the Court has no jurisdiction is that it has no power to deal with and decide the dispute as to the subject-matter before it, no matter in what form or by whom it is raised. But there is another sense in which it is often used, i.e., that, although the Court has power to decide the question it will not according to its settled principles do so except in a certain way and under certain circumstances.

Lord Scott went on to say:

> The power of a judge sitting in the High Court to grant an injunction against a party to proceedings properly served is confirmed by, but does not derive from, s 37 of the Supreme Court Act 1981 [now renamed the Senior Courts Act 1981] and its statutory predecessors. It derives from the pre-Judicature Act 1873 powers of the Chancery courts, and other courts, to grant injunctions.

He then considered to the line of House of Lords' authority on the power of the court to grant an injunction under s 37 of the 1981 Act, starting from *Siskina (cargo owners) v Distos Cia Naviera SA, The Siskina*,[213] and ending with *Channel Tunnel Group Ltd v Balfour Beatty Construction Ltd*,[214] and concluded that they showed that, 'provided the court has in personam215 jurisdiction over the person against whom an injunction, whether interlocutory or final is sought, the court has jurisdiction, in the strict sense, to grant it'.

Where there is jurisdiction in the strict sense, whether an injunction should be granted in any particular case depends on the practice of the court, as established by judicial precedent and rules of court. This, Lord Scott said, has not stood still even since *The Siskina* and is unrecognizable from that to which Cotton LJ referred in *North London Railway Co v Great Northern Railway Co*.[216] Prior to 1982, the effect of the decision of the House of Lords in *The Siskina*[217] was that the court could not grant a freezing injunction unless there was in existence an action, actual or potential, claiming substantive relief[218] that it was within

---

[212] [1915] 2 KB 536, 563.

[213] [1979] AC 210, [1977] 3 All ER 803, continuing with *Castanho v Brown & Root (UK)* Ltd [1981] AC 557, [1981] 1 All ER 143; *British Airways Board v Laker Airways Ltd* [1985] AC 58, [1984] 3 All ER 39; *South Carolina Insurance co v Assurantie Maatschappij 'de Zeven Provincien' NV* [1987] AC 24, [1986] 3 All ER 487.

[214] [1993] AC 334, [1993] 1 All ER 664.   [215] See p 557, *supra*.

[216] (1883) 11 QBD 30, 39–40, referred to by Lord Diplock in *The Siskina*, *supra*, HL, at 256, 824.

[217] *Supra*, HL. It is available to the Securities and Investments Board: *Securities and Investments Board v Pantell SA* [1990] Ch 426, [1989] 2 All ER 673, discussed [1994] JBL 8 (D Crighton).

[218] See *Siporex Trade SA v Comdel Commodities Ltd* [1986] 2 Lloyd's Rep 428 (injunction will be refused where declaration sought but no legal or equitable right). In *A v B* [1989] 2 Lloyd's Rep 423, a conditional freezing injunction was granted only to come into effect if, as, and when a vessel was delivered, at which point of time, the plaintiffs might acquire a cause of action. This beneficial development was halted by the Court of Appeal in *Veracruz Transportation Inc v VC Shipping Co Inc* [1992] 1 Lloyd's Rep 353, noted [1992] LMCLQ 161 (P Marshall); (1992) 108 LQR 175 (L Collins); and argued to be wrongly decided by D Wilde in [1993] LMCLQ 309; and *Zucker v Tyndall Holdings plc* [1992] 1 All ER 124, [1992] 1 WLR 1127, CA, discussed (1992) 142 NLJ 1511 (R Harrison). However, it has been held that, where the claimant seeks a freezing injunction before accrual of a cause of action, the court may indicate that it will be willing in principle to grant the injunction once the cause of action has accrued: this happened in *Re Q's Estate* [1999] 1 All ER (Comm) 499, and the injunction was subsequently granted 25 minutes after the cause of action accrued.

the jurisdiction of the court to grant.[219] Accordingly, if a claimant had a claim against the defendant in the courts of a foreign country, but where the defendant had no assets in the foreign country, he could not obtain a freezing order freezing assets in this country, with the consequence that the claimant would have no effective remedy.[220] Now, however, as a consequence of the Civil Jurisdiction and Judgments Act 1982, s 25,[221] as extended by the Civil Jurisdiction and Judgments Act 1982 (Interim Relief) Order 1997,[222] the position has been reached in which the High Court has power to grant interim relief in aid of substantive proceedings of whatever kind and wherever taking place.[223] It was observed, in *Fourie v Le Roux*,[224] that interim relief is defined in s 25(7) as being the kind of relief that the English courts have power to grant in proceedings relating to matters within its jurisdiction. This emphasizes that where there are foreign proceedings, those proceedings must have a claim, the equivalent of which in England would be sufficient for the English court to accept jurisdiction for granting a freezing order.

Originally, the remedy was regarded as exceptional, but it rapidly became extremely popular.[225] It will, however, only be granted where there is a good reason to apprehend that a debtor would remove assets out of the jurisdiction, or otherwise dispose of them to defeat a creditor's claim.[226] It cannot be used simply to improve the position of claimants in an insolvency,[227] merely to exert pressure on the defendant to settle the action, or to safeguard in advance the making of an unjustifiable payment, such as an illegal premium on the assignment of a lease.[228] And the claimant must always at least show that he has a good arguable case,[229] the ultimate test being whether, in the words of s 37(1) of the 1981 Act, 'it

---

[219] But the mere fact that the defendant, otherwise subject to the jurisdiction of the court, is entitled to a stay does not deprive the court of the power to grant an interlocutory injunction: *Channel Tunnel Group Ltd v Balfour Beatty Construction Ltd* [1993] AC 334, [1993] 1 All ER 664, HL. See (1993) 109 LQR 342 (L Collins). It was held, in *Department of Social Security v Butler* [1995] 4 All ER 193, [1995] 1 WLR 1528, CA, that there is no jurisdiction to grant a freezing injunction in relation to the duty to pay under a maintenance assessment made under the Child Support Act 1991, a duty that cannot be enforced by action in any civil court.

[220] See *Mercedes-Benz AG v Leiduck* [1996] AC 284, [1995] 3 All ER 929, PC.

[221] As amended by the Civil Jurisdiction and Judgments Act 1991, s 3, Sch 2, para 12.

[222] SI 1977/302. See (1997) 18 Co Law 188 (S Robert-Tissot).

[223] See *Crédit Suisse Fides SA v Cuoghi* [1998] QB 818, [1997] 3 All ER 724, CA; (1998) 17 CJQ 35 (D Capper). In granting interim relief, a court should generally seek to avoid making orders inconsistent with those of the courts in which the primary litigation was taking place, even where the primary court had made orders of a kind that would not have been made in domestic litigation: *State of Brunei Darussalam v Bolkiah* (2000) Times 5 September.

[224] [2005] EWCA Civ 204, [2006] 2 BCLC 537, affd [2007] UKHL 1, [2007] 1 All ER 1087, [2007] 1 WLR 320.

[225] See *The P* [1992] 1 Lloyd's Rep 470.

[226] *Montecchi v Shimco (UK) Ltd* [1979] 1 WLR 1180, CA; *Bakarim v Victoria P Shipping Co Ltd* [1980] 2 Lloyd's Rep 193; *Re Bank of Credit and Commerce International SA (No 9)* [1994] 3 All ER 764, CA. An injunction may be discharged or varied if there is no longer a risk that the assets will be dissipated, as may be the case where administrative receivers are appointed under a company debenture: *Capital Cameras Ltd v Harold Lines Ltd* [1991] 3 All ER 389, [1991] 1 WLR 54.

[227] *Iraqi Ministry of Defence v Arcepey Shipping Co SA, The Angel Bell* [1981] QB 65, [1980] 1 All ER 480; *K/S A/S Admiral Shipping v Portlink Ferries Ltd* [1984] 2 Lloyd's Rep 166, CA; *Investment and Pensions Advisory Service Ltd v Gray* [1990] BCLC 38.

[228] *Z Ltd v A-Z and AA-LL* [1982] QB 558, [1982] 1 All ER 556, CA; *P C W (Underwriting Agencies) Ltd v Dixon* [1983] 2 All ER 158.

[229] *Establishment Esefka International Anstalt v Central Bank of Nigeria* [1979] 1 Lloyd's Rep 445, CA; *Ninemia Maritime Corpn v Trave Schiffahrtsgesellschaft mbH & Co KG* [1984] 1 All ER 398, [1983] 1 WLR 1412, CA.

appears to the court to be just and convenient' to grant the injunction. In a time of rapidly growing commercial and financial sophistication, the courts have adapted the remedy to meet the current wiles of those defendants who are prepared to devote as much energy to making themselves immune to the courts' orders as to resisting the making of such orders on the merits of their case. The trial judge has to exercise a discretion with which, on general principles, the Court of Appeal will be reluctant to interfere.[230] Further, the exercise by a judge of his discretion in one case cannot provide a precedent binding upon another court concerned with another case, save in so far as that exercise is based upon basic principles applicable in both cases.[231]

Where an injunction is sought under s 25 of the Civil Jurisdiction and Judgments Act 1982, subs (2) provides that the court may refuse to grant relief if, in the opinion of the court, the fact that the court has no jurisdiction apart from the section makes it inexpedient for the court to grant it. The meaning of this 'inelegant' provision was explained in *Crédit Suisse Fides Trust SA v Cuoghi*,[232] in which it was observed that the English court should not be deterred from granting relief in support of proceedings taking place elsewhere by the fact that its role is only an ancillary one unless the circumstances of the particular case make the grant of relief inexpedient. The question is not whether the circumstances are exceptional or very exceptional, but whether it would be inexpedient to make the order. An order may be made even though to make such an order would be beyond the powers of the court seized of the substantive proceedings; in making an order in such a case, the court would be supplementing the jurisdiction of the foreign court in accordance with Art 24 of the Lugano Convention,[233] and principles that are internationally accepted.

Where an application is made for *in personam* relief in ancillary proceedings, two considerations that are highly material are the place in which the person sought to be enjoined is domiciled and the likely reaction of the court that is seized of the substantive dispute. Where a similar order has been applied for and refused by that court, it would generally be wrong for the English court to interfere. But where the other court lacks jurisdiction to make an effective order against a defendant because he is resident in England, it does not at all follow that it would find an order by an English court objectionable. It would obviously weigh heavily, probably conclusively, against the grant of interim relief if such a grant would obstruct or hamper the management of the case by the court seized of the substantive proceedings, or give rise to a risk of conflicting, inconsistent or overlapping orders in other courts.

(iii) Guidelines[234]

Lord Denning MR set out guidelines to be borne in mind in *Third Chandris Shipping Corpn v Unimarine SA*.[235] These have been added to and elaborated in later cases.

---

[230] *Avant Petroleum Inc v Gatoil Overseas Inc* [1986] 2 Lloyd's Rep 236, CA; *Derby & Co Ltd v Weldon (No 2) and (Nos 3 & 4), supra*, CA.

[231] *Derby & Co Ltd v Weldon (Nos 3 & 4), supra*, CA.

[232] [1997] 3 All ER 724, CA. See *Motorola Credit Corpn v Uzon (No 2)* [2003] EWCA Civ 752, [2004] 1 WLR 113. See also [2007] CLJ 495 (Louise Merrett)

[233] That is, the 1988 European Convention on Jurisdiction and the Enforcement of Judgments in Civil and Commercial Matters.   [234] For standard forms of order, see CPR 25, PD-014–015.

[235] [1979] QB 645, [1979] 2 All ER 972, CA. See also *Flightwise Travel Services Ltd v Gill* (2003) Times, 5 December. As to the practice, see *ALG Inc v Uganda Airlines Corpn* (1992) Times, 31 July.

(a) The claimant should make full and frank disclosure of all matters within his knowledge[236] that are material for the judge to know[237] and, so long as the proceedings are on a without-notice basis, should bring to the attention of the court any subsequent material changes in the situation.[238] If material non-disclosure is established, the court will be astute to ensure that a plaintiff who obtains a without-notice injunction without full disclosure is deprived of any advantage that he may have derived by the breach of duty. Thus, if there has been non-disclosure of a substantial kind, the freezing injunction will normally be discharged and not immediately reimposed. It has been said that:[239]

> The parties should be restored to the position they were in prior to the ex parte application, that is when no freezing injunction was in force. No doubt this means that a defendant will have the opportunity of making away with his assets but that is due to the plaintiff's failure properly to make his initial application.

But Ferris J insisted, in *Lagenes Ltd v It's At (UK) Ltd*,[240] that the court retains a discretion. The court must take into account all of the relevant circumstances, including the gravity of the breach of the duty of disclosure, the excuse or explanation offered, and the severity and duration of the prejudice occasioned to the defendant, always bearing in mind the overreaching objective and the need for proportionality.[241] It is no answer to say that the orders improperly obtained have in fact been fruitful.[242]

(b) The claimant should give particulars of his claim against the defendant, stating the ground of his claim and the amount thereof, and fairly stating the points made against it by the defendant.

(c) The claimant should normally give some grounds for believing that the defendants have assets here. There are 'no limitations put on the word "assets", from which it follows that this word includes chattels such as motor vessels,[243] jewellery, objets d'art and other valuables as well as choses in action'.[244] It may include goodwill.[245] Existence of a bank account in England is enough, whether in overdraft or not.[246] It is not restricted to movable assets.[247]

---

[236] He will be deemed to know matters that would have been revealed if proper enquiries had been made: *Behbehani v Salem* [1989] 2 All ER 143, [1989] 1 WLR 723n, and see (1989) 139 NLJ 407 (J de B Bate).

[237] This was elaborated by Ralph Gibson LJ in *Brink's-MAT v Elcombe* [1988] 3 All ER 188, CA, in which the relevant cases are referred to.

[238] *Commercial Bank of the Near East plc v A, B, C and D* [1989] 2 Lloyd's Rep 319; *W v H (Family Division: without notice orders)* [2001] 1 All ER 300. As to overlap between an advocate's individual duty to the court, and the collective duty to the court of a claimant and his team of legal advisers, see *Memory Corpn v Sidhu plc (No 2)* [2000] 1 WLR 1443, CA.

[239] *Ali & Fahd Shobokshi Group Ltd v Moneim* [1989] 2 All ER 404, 414, per Mervyn Davies J; *Dubai Bank Ltd v Galadari* [1990] 1 Lloyd's Rep 120, CA; *Gulf Interstate Oil Corpn v ANT Trade and Transport Ltd of Malta* [1999] 1 All ER (Comm) 97.

[240] [1991] FSR 492.   [241] *Memory Corpn v Sidhu (No 2)* [2000] 1 WLR 1443, CA.

[242] *Manor Electronics Ltd v Dickson* [1988] RPC 618.

[243] See *Clipper Maritime Co Ltd of Monrovia v Mineralimportexport* [1981] 3 All ER 664, [1981] 1 WLR 1262.

[244] *CBS United Kingdom Ltd v Lambert* [1982] 3 All ER 237, 241, CA, per Lawton LJ, giving the judgment of the court.   [245] *Darashah v UFAC (UK) Ltd* (1982) Times, 30 March, CA.

[246] But a bank guarantee providing for payment outside the jurisdiction is not an asset here, even though it may be a chose in action, the situs of which under English rules of conflict of laws is in London: *Intraco Ltd v Notis Shipping Corpn* [1981] 2 Lloyd's Rep 256, CA.

[247] *Derby & Co Ltd v Weldon (No 2), supra*, CA.

The words 'his assets and/or funds' in the standard form of freezing order are not apt to cover assets and funds that belong, or are assumed to belong, beneficially to someone other than the person restrained. They are confined to assets and funds belonging to the defendant, and which are, and should remain, available to satisfy the claim against him. The court could, however, make an appropriately worded order to cover assets and funds that might not belong beneficially to the defendant, although such an order would be discharged or modified if it were subsequently established that the assets belonged beneficially to a third party.[248]

Assets should be identified with as much precision as is reasonably practicable.[249]

(d) The claimant should give some grounds for believing that there is a risk of the assets being removed from the jurisdiction, or otherwise dealt with so as to defeat the ends of justice, before the judgment or award is satisfied. The test is whether the court should conclude that the refusal of a freezing injunction would involve a real risk that a judgment or award in favour of the claimant would remain unsatisfied.[250]

(e) The claimant must, as in the case of any interim injunction, give an undertaking in damages, which will normally extend to the costs of third parties.[251] The claimant must disclose any material change for the worse in his financial position.[252] However, the undertaking need not always be supported by assets: a legally aided claimant may be granted an injunction even though his undertaking may be of little value.[253]

(f) As regards any asset to which the injunction applies, but which has not been identified with precision (for example, money held in an identified bank account), the claimant may also be required to give an undertaking to pay reasonable costs incurred by any third party to whom notice of the terms of the injunction is given. This applies to the costs of ascertaining whether or not any asset to which the order applies, but which has not been identified in it, is within his possession or control.[254]

(g) The standard form of order[255] permits the defendant to spend specified sums to meet reasonable living expenses,[256] defend himself in the action,[257] and carry

---

[248] *Federal Bank of the Middle East Ltd v Hadkinson* [2000] 2 All ER 395, CA.

[249] As to assets that may belong to a third party, see *SCF Finance Co Ltd v Masri* [1985] 2 All ER 747, CA; *Allied Arab Bank Ltd v Hajjar* [1989] Fam Law 68, CA; *TSB Private Bank International SA v Chabra* [1992] 2 All ER 245, [1992] 1 WLR 231; *Yukong Line v Rendsburg* [2001] 2 Lloyd's Rep 113, CA. See (1999) 62 MLR 539 (P Devonshire).

[250] *Ninemia Maritime Corpn v Trave Schiffahrtsgesellschaft mbH & Co KG* [1984] 1 All ER 398, CA. For the somewhat different approach in matrimonial proceedings, see *Shipman v Shipman* [1991] 1 FLR 250; *Ghoth v Ghoth* [1992] 2 All ER 920, CA, and (1991) 141 NLJ 1340 (S Edwards and A Halpern); [1995] PCB 368 (P Moor and J Humphreys).

[251] See p 582, *supra*.   [252] *Staines v Walsh* (2003) Times, 1 August.

[253] *Allen v Jambo Holdings Ltd* [1980] 2 All ER 502 [1980] 1 WLR 1252, CA. See *DPR Futures Ltd* [1989] 1 WLR 778, on undertaking by liquidator; *Belize Alliance of Conservation Non-Governmental Organisations v Department of the Environment of Belize* [2003] UKPC 53, [2004] 2 P & CR 13, and [2007] CLJ 495 (Louise Merrett).

[254] *Searose Ltd v Seatrain (UK) Ltd* [1981] 1 All ER 806, [1981] 1 WLR 894.   [255] See CPR 2A-161.

[256] *TDK Tape Distributor (UK) v Videochoice Ltd* [1985] 3 All ER 345. See CPR 25 PD-014.

[257] *PCW (Underwriting Agencies) Ltd v Dixon* [1983] 2 All ER 158; *Mansour v Mansour* [1990] FCR 17, CA, in which it was said that it had never been the purpose of freezing injunctions to inhibit people from taking part in litigation.

out transactions in the ordinary course of business, such as the payment of trade creditors,[258] which may include repayment of a loan that is unenforceable by virtue of the Consumer Credit Act 1974.[259] It may, however, be granted even where a defendant proposed to effect a bona fide transfer of assets for a price in accordance with a valuation from an independent and respectable firm of accountants.[260]

As to legal costs, where the claimant has a proprietary claim, safeguards may be inserted in the order to give an ultimately successful claimant some protection from the defendant, in effect, paying his legal costs out of the claimant's property. Further, although the effect of the usual proviso is that it is not a breach of the order to use funds to pay reasonable legal expenses, it is no guarantee in advance that, if at trial the claimant is successful in establishing a proprietary claim against the defendant such that money so expended turns out to have been the claimant's, the solicitors acting for the defendant could avoid a claim of constructive trust for knowing receipt being raised against them.[261]

(h) A claimant who succeeds in obtaining a freezing injunction is under an obligation to press on with his action as rapidly as he can so that, if he should fail to establish liability in the defendant, the disadvantage that the injunction imposes on the defendant will be lessened so far as possible.[262]

Finally, it may be noted that if the court makes an order within its jurisdiction, then a party is bound to obey it at the risk of contempt proceedings if he does not, and the subsequent discharge of the order as having been irregularly obtained does not affect the disobedient party's liability to penalties for contempt.[263]

(iv) Third parties

(a) *Third party with notice of freezing injunction against defendant* Although the freezing injunction is an *in personam* order against the defendant, any third party who has notice of a freezing injunction that affects money or other assets of the defendant in his hands will be guilty of contempt of court if he knowingly assists in

---

[258] *X v Y* [1990] 1 QB 220, [1989] 3 All ER 689. In *Normid Housing Association Ltd v Ralphs and Mansell (No 2)* [1989] 1 Lloyd's Rep 274, CA, the court refused to grant a freezing injunction sought with the sole purpose of preventing the defendant entering into a bona fide settlement with his insurers.

[259] *Iraqi Ministry of Defence v Arcepey Shipping Co SA, The Angel Bell* [1981] QB 65, [1980] 1 All ER 480. As to subsequent qualifications to the injunction, see ibid, *per* Robert Goff J, at 71, 486; *A v C (No 2)* [1981] QB 961n, [1981] 2 All ER 126. See (1989) 86 Sol Jo 22 (T Taylor).

[260] *Customs and Excise Comrs v Anchor Foods Ltd* [1999] 3 All ER 268.

[261] *United Mizrahi Bank Ltd v Doherty* [1998] 2 All ER 230, [1998] 1 WLR 435. See [1998] NLJ Easter Appeals Supp 11 (A P Thomas).

[262] *Lloyds Bowmaker Ltd v Britannia Arrow Holdings plc* [1988] 3 All ER 178, CA; *Town and Country Building Society v Daisystar Ltd* [1989] NLJR 1563, CA; *A/S D/S Svendborg v Awada* [1999] 2 Lloyd's Rep 244 (notwithstanding delay application to discharge injunction refused: it was not a case in which there had been a deliberate tactical decision by the claimants to obtain a freezing injunction and then sit on it without taking any steps in the action whatever using the freezing injunction as a weapon of attack, whereby the freezing injunction is abused).

[263] *Wardle Fabrics Ltd v G Myristis Ltd* [1984] FSR 263; *Columbia Picture Industries Inc v Robinson* [1986] 3 All ER 338, 368. These are both cases on search orders, but the same principle must apply to freezing injunctions.

the disposal of assets, whether or not the defendant has notice of the injunction.[264] Thus, as soon as a bank is given notice of a freezing injunction, it should freeze the defendant's bank account, but the standard form of order does not prevent any bank from exercising any right of set-off that it may have in respect of any facility that it gave to the defendant before it was notified of the order.[265] However, unlike the strict liability of a defendant against whom the injunction is made, or a third party who aids and abets him, a third party who is notified of an injunction is guilty of contempt of court only if he knowingly takes a step that will frustrate the court's purpose in granting the order. So a bank will be in contempt only if it knowingly fails to freeze a customer's account and pays away sums in the account after being notified of an order.[266] If guilty, the penalty imposed depends on the degree of culpability. Thus, where a bank mistakenly releases assets in breach of an injunction, in some circumstances, the gravity of the offence may justify sequestration of the bank's assets equivalent to the amount covered by the injunction.[267] Such an order would not, however, be a direct source of compensation for the claimant; it could only be used as a lever to enforce the court's original freezing order. In other circumstances, there may not be such justification and the party in whose favour the injunction was made may consequently suffer loss irremediable by operation of the contempt procedure. Moreover, in such case, a third party who has notified the bank of a freezing injunction granted against one of the bank's customers cannot sue the bank in negligence, because the bank would owe no duty of care to the third party to take reasonable care to comply with the terms of the injunction.[268]

In justice to banks or other innocent third parties, the claimant comes under an obligation to indemnify them against any expenses or liabilities that they are required to incur,[269] and they should be told with as much certainty as possible what they are to do or not to do. A freezing injunction is not intended to interfere with the ordinary rights and remedies of a third party in the ordinary course of its business,[270] as is well illustrated by *Galaxia Maritime SA v Mineralimportexport, The Eleftherios*,[271] in which Kerr LJ said that it was a clear abuse of the jurisdiction to seek to prevent a ship belonging to an innocent third party, with the defendant's

---

[264] *Z Ltd v A-Z and AA-LL* [1982] QB 558. [1982] 1 All ER 556, CA; *Bank Mellat v Kazmi* [1989] QB 541, [1989] 1 All ER 925, CA.

[265] *Gangway Ltd v Caledonian Park Investments (Jersey) Ltd* [2001] 2 Lloyd's Rep 715. As to joint bank accounts, see [1994] LMCLQ 651 (P Matthews). As to the duty of claimant's counsel and solicitors to provide a full note of the hearing to parties affected, see *Interroute Telecommunications (UK) Ltd v Fashion Group Ltd* (1999) Times, 10 November.

[266] *Customs and Excise Commissioners v Barclays Bank plc* [2006] UKHL 28, [2006] 4 All ER 256, at [63], and see p 576, *supra*.

[267] *Z Bank v D1* [1994] 1 Lloyd's Rep 656.

[268] *Customs and Excise Commissioners v Barclays Bank plc* [2006] UKHL 28, [2007] 1 AC 181, [2006] 4 All ER 256.

[269] *Searose Ltd v Seatrain (UK) Ltd* [1981] 1 All ER 806; *Clipper Maritime Co Ltd of Monrovia v Mineralimportexport* [1981] 3 All ER 664. See p 582, *supra*.

[270] *Oceanica Castelana Armadora SA v Mineralimportexport* [1983] 2 All ER 65. In particular, the court is slow to interfere with routine banking transactions: *Lewis & Peat (Produce) Ltd v Almata Properties Ltd* [1993] 2 Bank LR 45, CA.

[271] [1982] 1 All ER 796, [1982] 1 WLR 539, CA. See also *Guinness Peat Aviation (Belgium) NV v Hispania Lineas Aereas SA* [1992] 1 Lloyd's Rep 190.

cargo on board, from sailing out of the jurisdiction. The rights of the innocent third party must prevail over the desire of the claimant to secure his position.

(b) *Freezing injunction against third parties*   The English courts have cited with approval[272] and, in substance, adopted the view of the High Court of Australia in *Carlile v LED Builders Pty Ltd*,[273] in which it was said that it may be appropriate, assuming the existence of other relevant criteria and discretionary factors, to grant a freezing injunction against a third party in circumstances in which:

> (i) the third party holds, is using, or has exercised or is exercising a power of disposition over, or is otherwise in possession of, assets, including "claims and expectancies", of the judgment debtor or potential judgment debtor, or
>
> (ii) some process, ultimately enforceable by the courts, is or may be available to the judgment creditor as a consequence of a judgment against that actual or potential judgment debtor, pursuant to which, whether by appointment of a liquidator, trustee in bankruptcy, receiver or otherwise, the third party may be obliged to disgorge property or otherwise contribute to the funds or property of the judgment debtor to help satisfy the judgment against the judgment debtor.

Thus, in *C Inc plc v L*,[274] the claimant had obtained a default judgment against Mrs L, who, arguably, had a right to an indemnity from Mr L, which could be enforced by Mrs L, or if she would not do so, by a receiver appointed by the court. A freezing order was made against Mr L as well as Mrs L. And in *Revenue and Customs Commissioners v Egleton*,[275] a company was liable for value-added tax (VAT) as a consequence of fraud in which the respondents were allegedly implicated. In principle, it was held that there was jurisdiction to grant the provisional liquidator of the company, who could pursue the respondents, a freezing order against them.

(v) Whereabouts of defendant

In some of the early cases,[276] it seems to have been assumed that the remedy was only available against foreign-based defendants. The Supreme Court Act 1981,[277] now renamed the Senior Courts Act 1981, now makes it clear that there is no distinction between English-based and foreign-based defendants.

(vi) Whereabouts of assets

The whereabouts of the assets to be subject to the order raises quite different issues and is a fast-developing topic.[278] As a matter of English law, the court has jurisdiction to grant

---

[272] See *TSB Private Bank International SA v Chabra* [1992] 2 All ER 245, [1992] 1 WLR 231; *C Inc plc v L* [2001] 2 All ER (Comm) 446; *Dadourian Group International Inc v Simms* [2005] EWHC 1768 (Ch), [2006] WTLR 239, affd on different grounds [2006] EWCA Civ 399, [2006] 3 All ER 48; *Revenue and Customs Commissioners v Egleton* [2006] EWHC 2313 (Ch), [2007] 1 All ER 606, noted (2006) 122 LQR 535 (S Gee). See also (2002) 118 LQR 124 (P Devonshire).

[273] (1999) 162 ALR 294.   [274] *Supra*.

[275] *Supra*. In fact, a provisional liquidator had not been appointed and the claim was made by a petitioning creditor: a freezing order was nevertheless made, but only by reason of exceptional circumstances.

[276] For example, *Rasu Maritime SA v Pertamina*, *supra*, CA; *The Agrabele* [1979] 2 Lloyd's Rep 117.

[277] Section 37(3).

[278] The possibility of an order for disclosure of assets is discussed later. See (1989) 105 LQR 262 (L Collins); (1989) 48 CLJ 199 (N H Andrews); (1990) LMCLQ 88 (A Malek and Caroline Lewis); (1991) 54 MLR 324 (D Capper).

relief against any party properly before it in relation to assets wherever situated, because the freezing jurisdiction is not a territorial jurisdiction, but depends on the unlimited jurisdiction of the court *in personam* against any person (whether an individual or a corporation) who, under English procedure, was properly made a party to proceedings pending in England.[279] However, in the ordinary case—that is, a case in which there is no question of extending the order beyond local assets—the practice is to require some grounds for believing that the defendant has assets locally situated within the jurisdiction of the court.[280] In *Derby & Co Ltd v Weldon (Nos 3 & 4), (No 2)*,[281] the Court of Appeal followed and applied three other of its recent decisions,[282] and it can now be regarded as established that the court has jurisdiction to issue a freezing injunction over the defendant's assets wherever they may be.

Such a worldwide injunction may be made before, as well as after, judgment.[283] In the Court of Appeal, Lord Donaldson MR agreed with the statement of Browne-Wilkinson VC, at first instance, that three requirements needed to be satisfied before taking what he referred to as 'the extreme step that is asked for in this case'. Firstly, he said, the special circumstances of the case must justify the exceptional order sought.

Secondly, the order must be in accordance with the rationale on which a freezing injunction is based. The basic requirement is that the court should make an effective order to preserve assets against which an effective enforcement can be obtained eventually if the claimant is successful at the trial. In the Court of Appeal,[284] Lord Donaldson MR pointed out that while the existence of *sufficient* assets within the jurisdiction is an excellent reason for confining the jurisdiction to such assets, other considerations apart, the fewer the assets within the jurisdiction, the greater the necessity for taking protective measures in relation to those outside it.

Thirdly, the order of the court should not conflict with the ordinary principles of international law. To deal with this, the standard form[285] provides:

(1) Except as provided in paragraph (2) the terms of this order do not affect or concern anyone outside the jurisdiction of this court.

(2) The terms of this order will affect the following persons in a country or state outside the jurisdiction of this court
   (a) the Respondent or his officer or agent appointed by power of attorney
   (b) any person who
      (i) is subject to the jurisdiction of this court
      (ii) has been given written notice of this order at his residence or place of business within the jurisdiction of this court; and

---

[279] See *Derby & Co Ltd v Weldon (No 6)* [1990] 3 All ER 263, [1990] 1 WLR 1139, CA.

[280] *Third Chandris Shipping Corpn v Unimarine SA, supra*, CA; *A J Bekhor & Co Ltd v Bilton, supra*, CA; *Ashtiani v Kashi* [1987] QB 888, [1986] 2 All ER 970, CA; *Derby & Co Ltd v Weldon (Nos 3 and 4)* [1990] Ch 65, sub nom *Derby & Co Ltd v Weldon (No 2)* [1989] 1 All ER 1002, CA.

[281] *Supra*, CA; *Re Bank of Credit and Commerce International SA (No 9)* [1994] 3 All ER 764, CA. See (1989) 86 LSG 17/22 (I T Taylor); [1990] CJQ 12 (P Kaye); (1996) 59 MLR 460 (J A Epp); [1996] 15 CJQ 211 (D Capper).

[282] *Babanaft International Co SA v Bassatne* [1990] Ch 13, [1989] 1 All ER 433, CA; *Republic of Haiti v Duvalier* [1990] 1 QB 202, [1989] 1 All ER 456, CA; *Derby & Co Ltd v Weldon* [1990] Ch 48, [1989] 1 All ER 469, CA.

[283] *Masu v Consolidated Contractors International UK Ltd (No 2)* [2007] EWHC 3010 (Comm), [2008] 1 All ER (Comm) 305.

[284] *Derby & Co Ltd v Weldon (Nos 3 and 4), (No 2), supra*, CA.   [285] CPR 2A-161.

(iii) is able to prevent acts or omissions outside the jurisdiction of this court which constitute or assist in a breach of the terms of this order; and

(iv) any other person, only to the extent that this order is declared enforceable by or is enforced by a court in that country or state.

The so-called *Baltic* proviso[286] should normally be added—namely, that nothing in the order should, in respect of assets located outside England and Wales, prevent a party from complying with:

(a) what it reasonably believes to be its obligations, contractual or otherwise, under the laws and obligations of the country or state in which those assets are situated, or under the proper law of any bank account in question; or

(b) any orders of the courts of that country or state, provided that reasonable notice of any application for such an order has been given to the claimant's solicitors.[287]

Two further points may be made. Firstly, a freezing injunction may relate not only to specified assets, but also to unspecified, but ascertainable, assets that may increase during the life of the injunction, such as all of the defendant's assets within the jurisdiction.[288]

Secondly, it may be noted that it was held in *Derby & Co Ltd v Weldon (No 6)*[289] that there is no reason, in principle, why, in an appropriate case, the court should not order the transfer of assets to a jurisdiction in which the order of the English court after the trial would be recognized, from a jurisdiction in which the order would not be recognized and the issues would have to be relitigated, if the only connection of the latter jurisdiction with the matters in issue is financial in nature. However, in considering whether to make such an order, the court will proceed with great caution.

(vii) Disclosure of assets[290]

A v C[291] seems to have been the first reported case in which the question arose whether the court has jurisdiction to make an order for discovery in aid of a freezing injunction. In that case, Goff J held that it had, and less than ten years later, Nicholls LJ was able to say, in *Derby & Co Ltd v Weldon*,[292] that it was now established law that the English courts have jurisdiction to make a disclosure order in respect of assets outside England and Wales,[293] both before judgment[294] and after judgment.[295] The Civil Procedure Rules[296] now provide

---

[286] From *Baltic Shipping v Translink Shipping Ltd* [1995] 1 Lloyd's Rep 673. See CPR 2A-161.

[287] *Bank of China v NBM LLC* [2002] 1 All ER 717, CA.

[288] *Cretanor Maritime Co Ltd v Irish Marine Management Ltd* [1978] 3 All ER 164.

[289] [1990] 3 All ER 263, [1990] 1 WLR 1139, CA, noted [1991] LMCLQ 26 (D Capper).

[290] See (1989) 139 NLJ 875 (P Kaye); (1998) 47 ICLQ 3 (C McLachlan).

[291] [1981] QB 956n, [1980] 2 All ER 347.

[292] [1990] Ch 48, [1989] 1 All ER 469, CA. The jurisdiction is conferred by s 37(1) of the Supreme Court Act 1981, now renamed the Senior Courts Act 1981. It also appears to arise within the court's inherent jurisdiction: *Grupo Torras SA v Sheikh Fahad Mohammed Al-Sabah* [1996] 1 Lloyd's Rep 7, CA. See (1994) 144 NLJ 932 (P D Friedman).

[293] *A fortiori* they may do so in respect of assets within the jurisdiction.

[294] See *Republic of Haiti v Duvalier* [1990] 1 QB 202, [1989] 1 All ER 456, CA.

[295] *Interpool Ltd v Galani* [1988] QB 738, [1987] 2 All ER 981, CA; *Maclaine Watson & Co Ltd v ITC (No 2)*, *supra*, CA.

[296] CPR 25.1g. Risk of personal violence is no defence to disobedience to an order: *Coca Cola and Schweppes v Gilbey* [1996] FSR 23, CA.

that the court may grant an order directing a party to provide information about the location of relevant property or assets, or to provide information about relevant property or assets that may be the subject of an application for a freezing injunction.[297]

(viii) Enforcement of worldwide freezing order

In order to cure the oppression potentially inherent in the worldwide enforcement of a worldwide freezing order (WFO), the standard form of order contains undertakings not, without the leave of the court:

(a) to seek to enforce the order, or seek a similar order, outside England and
Wales; and

(b) to use information obtained by the order for the purpose of civil or criminal
proceedings in England or Wales, or any other jurisdiction.

The court may, of course, modify the terms of the undertaking to suit the facts of any particular case.

Guidelines relating to the exercise by the court of its discretion to permit a WFO to be enforced abroad were set out in *Dadourian Group International Inc v Simms*,[298] as follows:

Guideline 1: The principle applying to the grant of permission to enforce a WFO abroad is that the grant of that permission should be just and convenient for the purpose of ensuring the effectiveness of the WFO, and in addition that it is not oppressive to the parties to the English proceedings or to third parties who may be joined to the foreign proceedings.

Guideline 2: All the relevant circumstances and options need to be considered. In particular consideration should be given to granting relief on terms, for example, terms as to the extension to third parties of the undertaking to compensate for costs incurred as a result of the WFO and as to the type of proceedings that may be commenced abroad. Consideration should also be given to the proportionality of the steps proposed to be taken abroad, and in addition to the form of any order.

Guideline 3: The interests of the applicant should be balanced against the interests of the other parties to the proceedings and any new party likely to be joined to the foreign proceedings.

Guideline 4: Permission should not normally be given in terms that would enable the applicant to obtain relief in the foreign proceedings which is superior to the relief given by the WFO.

Guideline 5: The evidence in support of the application for permission should contain all the information (so far as it can reasonably be obtained in the time available) necessary to enable the judge to reach an informed decision, including evidence as to the applicable law and practice in the foreign court, evidence as to the nature of the proposed proceedings to be commenced and evidence as to the assets believed to be located in the jurisdiction of the foreign court and the names of the parties by whom such assets are held.

Guideline 6: The standard of proof as to the existence of assets that are both within the WFO and within the jurisdiction of the foreign court is a real prospect, that is the applicant must show that there is a real prospect that such assets are located within the jurisdiction of the foreign court in question.

---

[297] Cross-examination on an affidavit of assets may be ordered as an exceptional measure, but should not become a routine feature: *Yukong Line Ltd v Rendsburg Investments Corpn of Liberia* [1996] 2 Lloyd's Rep 604. See also *Den Norske Bank ASA v Antonatos* [1999] QB 271, [1998] 3 All ER 74, CA; *Memory Corpn plc v Sidhu* [2000] Ch 645, [2000] 1 All ER 434.

[298] [2006] EWCA Civ 399, [2006] 3 All ER 48. See [2007] CJQ 171 (F Meisel).

Guideline 7: There must be evidence of a risk of dissipation of the assets in question.

Guideline 8: Normally the application should be made on notice to the respondent, but in cases of urgency, where it is just to do so, the permission may be given without notice to the party against whom relief will be sought in the foreign proceedings but that party should have the earliest practicable opportunity of having the matter reconsidered by the court at a hearing of which he is given notice.

In further proceedings,[299] the court had to consider the exercise of its discretion to release a party who had obtained a freezing order from his undertaking not to use information obtained from the party against whom the freezing order had been made in contempt proceedings against that party. More often than not, Longmore LJ said, a court exercises its powers in contempt proceedings for the purpose of punishing a party for disobedience to or non-compliance with a court order. The formal position is that permission to use information obtained pursuant to a freezing order should be granted where it is convenient for that information to be used for the purpose of establishing that contempt. However, it may well be that, as is commonly the case, the contempt proceedings had actually been initiated to 'improve' a defendant's compliance with the original order—a fact that is unlikely to be openly stated. There is no requirement that exceptional circumstances should be found. The threat of contempt proceedings is more likely to motivate a person to give information frankly if the court is willing to give permission for the use of information obtained under a freezing order in any appropriate case.

(ix) Privilege against self-incrimination

The same principles apply in relation to freezing injunctions and search orders, and they are discussed in relation to the latter, in respect of which the question more often arises.[300]

(x) Other orders in support of freezing injunction

The court has jurisdiction, under s 37, to appoint a receiver by way of, or in support of, a freezing injunction,[301] and in an appropriate case, it may be just and convenient to order a defendant to make a payment, or periodic payments, into a special account out of money already in his hands or coming into his hands from time to time. This may be a simpler and cheaper way of putting the money out of the reach of the defendant, although, in most cases, a freezing injunction can be buttressed adequately by notification of the injunction to banks and others.[302]

(B) THE SEARCH ORDER

(i) Origins

The search order slightly predates the freezing injunction. The first reported case is *EMI Ltd v Pandit*,[303] decided on 5 December 1974, and the first Court of Appeal decision—the one

---

[299] *Dadorian Group International Inc v Simms (No 2)* [2006] EWCA Civ 1745, [2007] 2 All ER 329, [2007] 1 WLR 2967.

[300] See p 642 *et seq, infra.*

[301] *Derby & Co Ltd v Weldon (Nos 3 and 4)* [1990] Ch 65, sub nom *Derby & Co Ltd v Weldon (No 2)* [1989] 1 All ER 1002, CA. See p 675 *et seq, infra.*

[302] *3 Style Ltd v Goss* (11 April 1990, unreported), CA, but available on Lexis.

[303] [1975] 1 All ER 418. See, generally, (1983) 46 MLR 274 (Anne Staines); (1983) 80 LSG 467 (A Rosen); [1986] All ER Rev 225 (A A S Zuckerman). As to the position in Canada, see (1996) 54 UT Fac LR 107 (P D Godin).

that gave its original name to the order—was *Anton Piller KG v Manufacturing Processes Ltd*,[304] decided at the end of 1975. The practice of granting search orders was approved in principle by the House of Lords in *Rank Film Distributors Ltd v Video Information Centre*.[305]

Let us consider the sort of situation that may give rise to a claim for a search order. A claimant may believe that it is essential to his case to have inspection of documents or other things in the possession of the defendant, and may have reason to fear that, if the defendant is forewarned, there is a grave danger that vital evidence will be destroyed—for example that papers will be burnt, or lost, or hidden, or taken beyond the jurisdiction— and thus the ends of justice will be defeated. It was established long ago, in the leading case of *Entick v Carrington*,[306] that no court has any power to use a search warrant to enter a man's house so as to see if there are papers or documents there that are of an incriminating nature, whether libels or infringements of copyright, or anything else of the kind. In the *Anton Piller* case[307] itself, Lord Denning MR said, 'None of us would wish to whittle down that principle in the slightest', and no doubt, in theory, that principle remained unimpaired.

The defendant served with a search order might well have regarded this as a lawyer's quibble, and Lord Denning MR himself said that it might seem to be a search warrant in disguise,[308] because what such an order did was to direct the defendant *in personam* by what is, in effect, a mandatory injunction to give permission to the person serving the order, and such other persons duly authorized by the claimant not exceeding a specified number, commonly four or five, forthwith to enter the defendant's premises, for the purpose of inspecting and photographing, and looking for and removing, the things specified in the order.[309] It is true that the defendant could refuse to allow entry and inspection, but he did so at his peril. Disobedience of the order to permit entry and inspection may be a contempt of court,[310] and, in the action, refusal is almost certain to lead to adverse inferences being drawn against him. Most applications for a search order are made at a very early stage, but it was held, in *Distributori Automatici Italia SpA v Holford General Trading Co Ltd*,[311] that the court has jurisdiction to make an order after judgment for the purpose of eliciting documents that are essential to execution and which would otherwise be unjustly denied to the judgment creditor.

---

[304] [1976] Ch 55, [1976] 1 All ER 779, CA.   [305] [1982] AC 380, [1981] 2 All ER 76, HL.

[306] (1765) 2 Wils 275.   [307] *Supra*, CA.

[308] See also *Bhimji v Chatwani* [1991] 1 All ER 705, [1991] 1 WLR 989, where Scott J said that such orders 'involve the court in the hypocrisy of pretending that the entry and search are carried on because the owners of the premises have consented to it'.

[309] The standard form of order set out in CPR 25, PD-016, extends to vehicles on or around the premises. The defendant is entitled to refuse access to anyone who could gain commercially from anything that he might read or see on the premises.

[310] It has been held that a defendant will not be in breach until after a reasonable time for legal advice to be obtained has passed: *Bhimji v Chatwani*, *supra*, in which the refusal of the defendants to permit entry until after the hearing of an application to discharge or vary the order heard in the afternoon of the day of service was held, on the facts, to be a mere technical breach of the order that did not justify committal or the imposition of any other penalty.

[311] [1985] 3 All ER 750, [1985] 1 WLR 1066.

(ii) The Civil Procedure Act 1997

Section 7 of the above Act put the search order on a statutory footing, without any intention to limit or reduce the jurisdiction that had hitherto been exercised. The main purpose of the section was to dispense with the fiction that the entry on the premises is with the consent of the owner. It makes it clear that it is the court order that is the basis of the requirement to permit entry, not the implied consent of the owner.

The Act provides that the court may make an order [312] for the purpose of securing, in the case of any existing or proposed proceedings in the court:

(a) the preservation of evidence that is or may be relevant; or

(b) the preservation of property that is or may be the subject matter of the proceedings, or as to which any question arises or may arise in the proceedings.

The order may direct any person to permit [313] any person described in the order, or secure that any person so described is permitted:

(a) to enter premises in [314] England and Wales; and

(b) while on the premises, to take, in accordance with the terms of the order, any of the steps specified in the Act.

These steps are:

(a) to carry out a search for or inspection of anything described in the order; and

(b) to make or obtain a copy, photograph, sample, or other record of anything so described.

The order may also direct the person concerned:

(a) to provide any person described in the order, or secure that any person so described is provided, with any information or article described in the order; and

(b) to allow any person described in the order, or secure that any person so described is allowed, to retain for safe keeping anything described in the order.

(iii) Preconditions to making order

According to Ormrod LJ in the *Anton Piller* case, there are three essential preconditions to the making of an order:

> First, there must be an extremely strong prima facie case. Secondly, the damage, potential or actual, must be very serious for the plaintiff. Thirdly, there must be clear evidence that the defendants have in their possession incriminating documents or things, and that there is a real possibility [315] that they may destroy such material before an application inter partes can be made.

---

[312] On the application of any person who is, or appears to the court to be likely to be, a party to proceedings in the court: Civil Procedure Act 1997, s 7(2).

[313] The meanings of the words 'any person' and 'permit' are considered in (1998) 17 CJQ 272 (M Dockray and Katherine R Thomas).   [314] 'Premises' includes any vehicle: ibid, s 7(8).

[315] *Lock International plc v Beswick* [1989] 3 All ER 373, [1989] 1 WLR 1268. Because there is no such possibility it is inappropriate to make an order against a practising barrister: *Randolph M Fields v Watts* (1984) 129 Sol Jo 67, CA.

To these, one may add Lord Denning MR's dictum[316] that the inspection must do no real harm to the defendant or his case.

Lastly, the court will normally want to be satisfied that the plaintiff is good for any damages that might ultimately be ordered against him on the undertaking in damages that he will be called upon to give as a condition of the order.[317]

(iv) Safeguards to defendant

Guidelines have been promulgated and a standard form of order provided.[318] They provide for the order to be served by a supervising solicitor, and carried out in his presence and under his supervision. The supervising solicitor should be an experienced solicitor, having some familiarity with the operation of search orders, who is not a member or employee of the firm acting for the applicant. Where the premises are likely to be occupied by an unaccompanied woman and the supervising solicitor is a man, at least one of the persons attending on the service of the order should be a woman. Where appropriate, the applicant should be required to insure items removed. Entry is limited to working days between 9.30 am and 5.30 pm. The supervising solicitor must offer to explain to the person served with the order its meaning and effect fairly and in everyday language, and inform him of his right to seek legal advice, provided that he does so at once.

The applicant must give the usual undertaking in damages, and an undertaking to issue a writ of summons as soon as possible. Any information or documents that he obtains as a result of the order can only be used for the purposes of the proceedings.

To prevent other defendants being alerted, the standard form of order provides that, except for the purpose of obtaining legal advice, the defendant must not directly or indirectly inform anyone of the proceedings or the contents of the order, or warn anyone that proceedings have been brought against him by the applicant, until a specified date.

As we have already seen, on a without-notice application, the court is concerned to see that the defendant is not treated unfairly. Just as in the case of an application for a freezing injunction, the claimant should make full and frank disclosure of all matters within his knowledge that are material for the judge to know. The principles that have already been discussed in relation to freezing injunctions apply with at least equal force in applications for a search order.[319]

Two additional points may be made. Firstly, reference may be made to *Guess? Inc v Lee Seck Mon*,[320] in which a search order in relation to a claim for infringement of copyright had been discharged for substantial and serious non-disclosure of relevant facts by the claimant. In the Hong Kong Court of Appeal, the question arose whether the judge, on a subsequent application for a fresh search order and an interim injunction, was entitled to take into account the 'yield' from the original search order. It was held that the judge

---

[316] In the *Anton Piller* case, *supra*, CA, at 783.

[317] *Vapormatic Co Ltd v Sparex* [1976] 1 WLR 939. But see *Allen v Jambo Holdings Ltd* [1980] 2 All ER 502, [1980] 1 WLR 1252, CA; *Belize Alliance of Conservation Non-Governmental Organisations v Department of the Environment of Belize* [2003] UKPC 53, [2004] 2 P & CR 13.

[318] See CPR 25, PD-016; *Gadget Shop Ltd v Bug.Com Ltd* [2001] FSR 383.

[319] See *Columbia Picture Industries Inc v Robinson* [1987] Ch 38, [1986] 3 All ER 338; *Lock International plc v Beswick* [1989] 3 All ER 373, [1989] 1 WLR 1268; *Intergraph Corp v Solid Systems CAD Services Ltd* [1993] FSR 617.

[320] [1987] FSR 125, applied *Naf Naf SA v Dickens (London) Ltd* [1993] FSR 424.

had a discretion whether to exclude evidence thus obtained. However, even where non-disclosure was innocent, in that it was not done for improper motives, the court should not lightly allow a party to keep the benefit of it. Where non-disclosure was both serious and substantial, the court should allow it only if good and compelling reasons for doing so are shown.

Secondly, in the case of an executed search order, the court will not normally entertain an interim application for its discharge. Normally, the only consequence of discharge is to enable the defendant to enforce the cross-undertaking in damages and that is a decision that can wait until the trial. Exceptionally, as in *Lock International plc v Beswick*,[321] justice may require that the order should be discharged at an earlier point of time.

(v) Privilege against self-incrimination

In *Rank Film Distribution Ltd v Video Information Centre*,[322] the House of Lords held that a defendant would not be compelled to answer questions or disclose documents where compliance might involve self-incrimination, including self-incrimination for civil contempt.[323] There is no way in which a court can compel disclosure while, at the same time, protecting the defendant from the consequences of self-incrimination. While there seems to be no privilege against self-incrimination in the case of offences under foreign criminal law, Morritt J, in *Arab Monetary Fund v Hashim*,[324] could see no reason why the possibility of self-incrimination—or, indeed, the incrimination of others—should not be a factor to be taken into account in deciding whether—and, if so, in what terms—a disclosure order should be made. The standard form of order informs the defendant of his right to refuse to disclose documents or answer questions that might incriminate him,[325] and the Civil Procedure Act 1997 expressly provides[326] that it does not affect any right of a person to refuse to do anything on the ground that to do so might expose him, or his spouse or civil partner, to proceedings for an offence or for the recovery of a penalty.

It should be noted, however, that the privilege against self-incrimination does not extend to independent matters coming to light in the course of executing a proper order of the court. Thus where, in intellectual property proceedings, a computer seized under a search order was found to contain highly objectionable images of children, it was held that the privilege claimed did not cover this material, which existed independently of the order, and, accordingly, there was no bar to its disclosure to the police if it was otherwise right do so.[327]

Further, s 72 of the Supreme Court Act 1981, now renamed the Senior Courts Act 1981, as amended, imposes an important restriction on the privilege against self-incrimination. It provides that, in proceedings to which it applies—primarily, proceedings for infringement

---

[321] *Supra*; *O'Regan v Iambic Productions Ltd* [1989] NLJR 1378.

[322] [1982] AC 380, [1981] 2 All ER 76, HL, discussed (1981) 44 MLR 580 (A Stains) and (1982) 132 NLJ 471 (P Davis and P Russell).

[323] *Cobra Golf Ltd v Rata* [1998] Ch 109, [1997] 2 All ER 150.

[324] [1989] 3 All ER 466, [1989] 1 WLR 565; *Crédit Suisse Fides Trust SA v Cuoghi* [1998] QB 818, [1997] 3 All ER 724, CA; *Memory Corp plc v Sidhu* [2000] Ch 645, [2000] 1 All ER 434.

[325] See *Cobra Golf Ltd v Rata*, *supra*; *Den Norske Bank ASA v Antonatos* [1998] 3 All ER 74, CA.

[326] In s 7(7), as amended.

[327] *C Ltd v P (Secretary of State for Home Office and anor intervening)* [2007] EWCA Civ 493, [2007] 3 All ER 1034.

of rights pertaining to any intellectual property or for passing off—but not otherwise, a person is not to be excused from answering any question or complying with any order by reason that to do so would expose that person, or his or her spouse or civil partner, to proceedings for a related offence or for the recovery of a related penalty.[328]

The withdrawal of the privilege against incrimination of self, or spouse or civil partner, in these cases is qualified by a provision that statements or admissions made in answering questions or complying with an order shall not be admissible against the maker of the statement or admission, or his spouse or civil partner, in proceedings for any related offence or for the recovery of any related penalty,[329] except in proceedings for perjury or contempt of court.[330]

Where s 72 does not apply, the principle of the *Rank Film Distribution* case remains fully effective, which may give rise to great difficulties of proof in fraud cases. If there is a real risk of a conspiracy charge, the judge will be unable to make a search order and, in consequence, vital evidence may be destroyed. This has led to judicial calls for an amendment to the legislation.[331]

Apart from the question of privilege, the court will not require a defendant to reveal breaches that he has committed either of an undertaking given by him or of an order made upon him in exercise of the ancillary jurisdiction to secure enforcement of a court's order, such as a freezing injunction or a search order, unless that disclosure is necessary for the actual working out or the proper operation of the court's order.[332]

(vi) Exceptional or routine?

Between 1974 and 1986, the search order had ceased to be the very rare and exceptional remedy that had been envisaged in the early cases, and such orders were, according to Scott J in *Columbia Pictures Industries Inc v Robinson*,[333] '*regularly applied for and granted in all divisions of the High Court*'. In no previous case had the propriety of the obtaining and execution of a search order been examined otherwise than in interim proceedings.

Scott J, of course, accepted that search orders have become established as one of the tools of the administration of justice in civil cases, with the main purpose of preserving evidence necessary for the claimant's case. He was, however, concerned with the effect that such an order, made in secrecy *ex parte*, may have on the defendant. It had to be realized, he said,[334] 'that a common, perhaps the usual, effect of the service and execution of an Anton Piller order is to close down the business which, on the applicants' evidence, is being

---

[328] As defined in s 72(5) of the Supreme Court Act 1981, now renamed the Senior Courts Act 1981, as amended. Section 72 is discussed in (1982) 132 NLJ 983 (N Garnham). See *Crest Homes plc v Marks* [1987] AC 829, [1987] 2 All ER 1074, HL; *Cobra Golf Ltd v Rata, supra*. Cf the provisions in s 31 of the Theft Act 1968 in relation to offences under that Act; *Khan v Khan* [1982] 2 All ER 60, [1982] 1 WLR 513, CA.

[329] Section 72(3), as amended. See *Charles of the Ritz Group Ltd v Jory* [1986] FSR 14.

[330] Section 72(4).

[331] *Sociedade Nacional de Combustiveis de Angola UEE v Lundquist* [1991] 2 QB 310, [1990] 3 All ER 283, CA, noted (1990) 106 LQR 389 (A Zuckerman), (1990) 134 Sol Jo 1365 (N Padfield). *Den Norske Bank ASA v Antonatos* [1999] QB 271, [1998] 3 All ER 74, CA. See (1986) 13 Co Law 66 (B Strong); (1990) 106 LQR 601 (M Dockray and H Laddie). See also *AT & T Istel Ltd v Tully* [1993] AC 45, [1992] 3 All ER 523, HL, noted (1994) 15 Co Law 26 (J Cotton); (1993) CLJ 42 (N H Andrews).

[332] *Bhimji v Chatwani (No 3)* [1992] 4 All ER 912.   [333] [1986] 3 All ER 338, 369.

[334] In *Columbia Picture Industries Inc v Robinson, supra*, at 369.

carried on in violation of their rights'. If that is the intention of the applicants, it is, he later stated,[335] an improper one and an abuse of the search order procedure.

He also pointed out[336] that the service and execution of a search order may well have a personal, as well as a commercial, effect:

> Anton Piller orders are often granted not simply in respect of business premises but in respect of the respondent's home. He is required, on pain of committal, to open the doors of his house to the plaintiff's representatives and to permit a search of the contents thereof. The plaintiffs and their representatives are at liberty to search and rummage through the personal belongings of any occupant of the house and to remove the material they consider to be covered by the terms of the order. The traumatic effect and the sense of outrage likely to be produced by an invasion of home territory in the execution of an Anton Piller order is obvious.

He asked the question:[337]

> What is to be said of the Anton Piller procedure which, on a regular and institutionalized basis, is depriving citizens of their property and closing down their businesses by orders made ex parte, on applications of which they know nothing and at which they cannot be heard, by orders which they are forced, on pain of committal, to obey, even if wrongly made?

Scott J concluded[338] that the:

> decision whether or not an Anton Piller order should be granted requires a balance to be struck between the plaintiff's need that the remedies allowed by the civil law for the breach of his rights should be attainable and the requirements of justice that a defendant should not be deprived of his property without being heard.

In his view, the practice of the court had swung much too far in favour of the claimants, and search orders had been too readily granted and with insufficient safeguards for respondents. This view was indorsed by Hoffman J in *Lock International plc v Beswick*,[339] and it has been stated[340] that the warning signals in these two cases have been heeded and that search orders are now made much more sparingly than previously.

(vii) Guidelines

Scott LJ[341] went on to lay down guidelines that should be applied, bearing in mind the draconian and essentially unfair nature of the order from the point of view of the defendant:

(i) Search orders should be drawn so as to extend no further than the minimum extent necessary to achieve the purpose for which they are granted,

(ii) a detailed record of the material taken should always be required to be made by the solicitors who execute the order before the material is removed from the defendant's premises,

(iii) no material should be taken from the defendant's premises by the executing solicitors unless it is clearly covered by the terms of the order. The practice which had grown

---

[335] Ibid, at 377.　　[336] Ibid, at 368, 369.　　[337] Ibid, at 369.　　[338] Ibid, at 371.

[339] [1989] 3 All ER 373, [1989] 1 WLR 1268. See (1990) 106 LQR 173 (L Collins).

[340] By Nicholls V-C in *Universal Thermosensors Ltd v Hibben* [1992] 3 All ER 257, [1992] 1 WLR 840.

[341] In *Columbia Picture Industries Inc v Robinson, supra*, at 371, 372; *Araghchinchi v Araghchinchi* [1997] 2 FLR 142, CA.

up whereby the defendant is procured by the executing solicitors to give consent to additional material being removed is wholly unacceptable,

(iv) seized material the ownership of which is in dispute, such as allegedly pirated tapes, should not be retained by the plaintiff's solicitors pending trial. It should be delivered to the defendant's solicitor as soon as he is on the record subject to an undertaking for its safe custody and production, if necessary, at the trial. All documents which are removed should be immediately photocopied and returned,[342]

(v) affidavits in support of an application for a search order ought to err on the side of excessive disclosure. In the case of the material falling into the grey area of possible relevance, the judge, not the plaintiff's solicitors, should be the judge of relevance.

It may be added that a solicitor in charge of the execution of a search order who does not observe the exact terms of the court's order may be held to be in contempt of court.[343]

(c) EXTENSION OF FREEZING INJUNCTIONS AND SEARCH ORDERS

The Court of Appeal has been prepared to extend the jurisdiction by making further orders, even if of a novel character, if that is thought necessary for the proper protection of the claimant. In *Bayer AG v Winter*,[344] the judge had granted relief in the freezing injunction and search order forms, including orders requiring the defendants to disclose all documents relating to the counterfeit insecticide with which the case was concerned, and to make an affidavit detailing all transactions relating thereto. The judge at first instance, however, refused to make further orders restraining the defendant from leaving the jurisdiction for a specified time and ordering him to deliver up his passport to the claimant. The Court of Appeal made the orders sought. It was said that if the defendant were to fail to provide the information ordered to be given by the first-instance judge, the defendant, if within the jurisdiction, could be compelled to attend for cross-examination. However, the order of the court would be frustrated if he were to leave the jurisdiction without having done so. The further order sought would prevent this happening and any risk of hardship to the defendant was covered by his right to apply to the court for the order to be varied or discharged. Both Ralph Gibson and Fox LJJ referred to the observations of Cumming-Bruce LJ in *House of Spring Gardens Ltd v Waite*:[345]

> The court has the power (and, I would add, the duty) to take such steps as are practicable upon an application of the plaintiff to procure that where an order has been made that the defendants identify their assets and disclose their whereabouts, such steps are taken as will enable the order to have effect as completely and successfully as the powers of the court can procure.

---

[342] *L T Piver SARL v S & J Perfume Co Ltd* [1987] FSR 159. As to the duty of a solicitor in relation to items obtained by him, see *Gordon v Summers* [2003] FSR 719.

[343] *VDU Installations Ltd v Integrated Computer Systems and Cybernetics Ltd* [1989] FSR 378.

[344] [1986] 1 All ER 733, [1986] 1 WLR 497, CA; *Re M (Freezing Injunction)* [2006] 1 FLR 1031. A disclosure order contained in an injunction carries with it an obligation to do more than simply tell the truth. Accordingly, a party who gave a truthful, but inaccurate, answer, without taking reasonable steps to investigate its truth, has been held to be in contempt of court: *Bird v Hadkinson* [1999] BPIR 653.

[345] [1985] FSR 173, 183, CA. In this case in aid of a freezing injunction, an order had been made that the defendants identify their assets and disclose their whereabouts.

This principle was held to justify the orders made, although the restraint on leaving the country was limited to two days, since it was recognized that it was an interference with the liberty of the subject. *Bayer AG v Winter*[346] was cited in *Re J (a minor),*[347] in which it was said that if the orders made in that case were available to protect a claimant's financial position, *a fortiori* they should be available to provide for the welfare and future upbringing of a ward of court.

The order in *Bayer AG v Winter* was served on the defendant on 22 December, and on Christmas Eve Scott J[348] was asked for orders that the defendant be directed to attend the court at a suitable time for cross-examination, and that his liberty to leave the country be further restricted to enable the cross-examination to take place. Scott J again[349] referred to the tendency of the courts to make *ex parte* orders of an increasingly extensive sort, and thought that the basis on which *ex parte* orders can properly be made requires to be very carefully examined. Although he accepted that the court has, through its *in personam* jurisdiction, power to subject citizens to an interrogatory process designed to enforce court orders, he found it very difficult to envisage any circumstances in which, as a matter of discretion, it would be right to make such an order as was sought in the case before him. In ringing tones reminiscent of Lord Denning, he said:[350] 'Star Chamber interrogatory procedure has formed no part of the judicial process in this country for several centuries. The proper function of a judge in civil litigation is to decide issues between parties. It is not, in my opinion, to preside over an interrogation.' Accordingly, Scott J refused to order the defendant to submit himself to cross-examination, or to restrict his liberty to leave the country for a further period.

In another case, *Coca-Cola Co v Gilbey,*[351] a search order required the defendant, inter alia, to disclose information about the activities of a criminal organization manufacturing counterfeits of the claimant's products and the names of other individuals involved. It was accepted that there was a prima facie case for the defendant's involvement. He applied for the discharge of the disclosure part of the order on the ground of the risk of violence to him and his family if he complied with it. In the exercise of its discretion, the court had no hesitation in holding that the interest of the claimant and the public in the provision of the information outweighed the interest of the defendant in avoiding any risk of violence to which the disclosure might expose him.

It may be useful to look in a little more detail at *House of Spring Gardens Ltd v Waite.*[352] A freezing injunction and a search order having been granted, there was a hearing at which there was affidavit evidence in opposition to the continuance of the freezing injunction described by Vinelott J as 'almost insultingly brief and inexplicit'. He proceeded to order disclosure of the defendant's assets, which was, he said, 'essential if the Mareva injunction is to be properly policed'. The claimants did not think that the affidavits sworn by the

---

[346] *Supra.* See *O'Neill v O'Keeffe* [2002] IR 1.

[347] [1988] 1 FLR 65; *Den Norske Bank ASA v Antonatos* [1999] QB 271, [1998] 3 All ER 74, CA.

[348] *Bayer AG v Winter (No 2)* [1986] 2 All ER 43, [1986] 1 WLR 540.

[349] *Bayer AG v Winter (No 2), supra,* was decided a few days after *Columbia Picture Industries Inc v Robinson, supra.*

[350] *Bayer AG v Winter (No 2), supra,* at 46.

[351] [1995] 4 All ER 711 (the CA refused leave to appeal).

[352] *Supra,* CA. See *Arab Monetary Fund v Hashim* [1989] 3 All ER 466, [1989] 1 WLR 565. See (1990–91) 1 KCLJ 1 (Jill Martin).

defendants in purported compliance with Vinelott J's orders were a proper compliance, and sought an order that they should be at liberty to cross-examine the defendants.

The applications came before Nourse J and the order was made by consent. The cross-examination was arranged for hearing before Scott J, who was troubled by the fact that there was no specific present issue that would call for immediate decision by him after the cross-examination. He commented, '*It is not the business of the court to "police" its orders. The business of the court is to decide issues between parties*', and discharged Nourse J's order, apparently on the ground that Nourse J had not, in fact, had power to make an order in that form. The Court of Appeal, as already indicated, reversed this ruling and affirmed the wide power of the court to implement a lawful order by ancillary orders required for their efficacy, such as an order calling for cross-examination on an affidavit. Slade LJ, giving the leading judgment, said that the court would always take care to ensure that the defendant is not unfairly treated, and will be particularly on guard against potential oppression in a case in which there is no immediate issue calling for decision. But although, in general, as Scott J said, the business of the court is to decide issues between parties, in the special context of the freezing injunction, there is the function of protecting the parties to the litigation in such manner as may be just and convenient pending the final resolution of the issues at the trial.

It is convenient to mention here *B v B*,[353] in which Wilson J fully accepted that, under s 37(1) of the Supreme Court Act 1981, now renamed the Senior Courts Act 1981, there are a number of circumstances in which it is possible to restrain a party from leaving the jurisdiction and to make a consequential order for the surrender of his or her passport. The jurisdiction exists where the other party has established a right to interlocutory relief, such as a search order, which would otherwise be rendered nugatory, and, indeed, exists in principle in aid of all of the court's procedures leading to the disposal of the proceedings. It can also be invoked after judgment. However, it was not available, in the case before the court, to enable the court to restrain a judgment debtor from leaving the jurisdiction indefinitely until the debt was paid, since it was ancillary to other powers of the court and was not a free-standing enforcement procedure in its own right.

[353]   [1997] 3 All ER 258, [1998] 1 WLR 329.

28

SPECIFIC PERFORMANCE

This equitable remedy consists of an order of the court directing a party to a contract to perform his obligations thereunder according to its terms. It has been said[1] that it 'presupposes an executory as distinct from an executed agreement, something remaining to be done, such as the execution of a deed or a conveyance, in order to put the parties in the position relative to each other in which by the preliminary agreement they were intended to be placed'. In this passage, Lord Selborne was drawing a broad distinction between the class of executory agreements, such as agreements for the sale of land and marriage articles, and the principles applicable to specific performance of them, on the one hand, and, on the other, a very different class of agreements, which he described[2] as 'ordinary agreements for work and labour to be performed, hiring, and service, and things of that sort', for which specific performance is not available. The strict or proper sense of the term 'specific performance' apparently designates the first type of case, in which an executory agreement is to be followed by the execution of a more formal instrument. However, the term is commonly used, and will henceforward be used in this work, as including the equitable right to specific relief in respect of an intermediate class of agreements that do not call for the execution of a further instrument. The principles applicable seem to be the same.[3]

Section 1 of this chapter discusses the nature of the remedy, section 2, the grounds on which it may be refused, and section 3, the defences that may be put forward to defeat a claim.

1 NATURE OF THE REMEDY OF SPECIFIC PERFORMANCE

(A) BASIS OF THE JURISDICTION

The basis of the jurisdiction to grant specific performance has always been the inadequacy of the common law remedy of damages for breach of contract: 'The court gives specific

---

[1] Per Lord Selborne LC in *Wolverhampton and Walsall Rly Co v London and North Western Rly Co* (1873) LR 16 Eq 433, 439; approved by Lord Macnaghten in *Tailby v Official Receiver* (1888) 13 App Cas 523, 547, HL. For a review of New Zealand law, see (1987) 6 Otago LR 420 (A Beck). [2] *Supra*.

[3] *Australian Hardwoods Pty Ltd v Railways Comr* [1961] 1 All ER 737, PC. But see Meagher, Gummow and Lehane, *Equity: Doctrine and Remedies*, 3rd edn, pp 495–498; Heydon, Gummow, and Austin, *Cases and Materials on Equity and Trust*, 4th edn, para 3801.

performance instead of damages, only when it can by that means do more perfect and complete justice.'[4] An alternative way of putting it is to say that the question is whether it is just, in all circumstances, for the plaintiff to be confined to his remedy in damages.[5] Thus the common law remedy may be regarded as inadequate and specific performances may be available in an appropriate case, where only nominal damages could be recovered by an action at law,[6] although it is not clear why this should be so. Nominal damages are awarded because the claimant is regarded as having suffered no loss, and they should accordingly be regarded as adequate in principle. Specific performance may also be available where there is a continuing obligation that would necessitate a series of actions at law for damages.[7] Further, there are, on the one hand, as we shall see, many cases in which specific performance is not available although damages may be obtained, and, on the other hand, although originally specific performance was not granted unless the claimant had first recovered damages at law,[8] it has long since been recognized that, in some cases, specific performance may be granted although there is no right to recover damages at law at all. Thus damages at law can only be awarded for a *breach* of contract, but a breach of contract is not absolutely essential to a claim for specific performance. Accordingly, the claimant in *Marks v Lilley*[9] was held to be justified in issuing a writ for specific performance of a contract for the sale of land after the date fixed for completion had passed, although no notice had been served making time the essence of the contract, and in *Hasham v Zenab*,[10] even before the date for completion had been reached. Further, it seems that the fact that an action of law will not lie,[11] or even that it is doubtful if it will,[12] may itself be a ground for granting specific performance. And specific performance may be granted where equity takes a less rigid view than the common law: thus, in *Mortlock v Buller*,[13] Lord

---

[4] *Per* Lord Selborne LC in *Wilson v Northampton and Banbury Junction Rly Co* (1874) 9 Ch App 279, 284; *Chinn v Collins* [1979] Ch 447, [1979] 2 All ER 529, CA; reversed without affecting this point [1981] AC 533, [1981] 1 All ER 189, HL. See, generally, Reiter and Swan, *Studies in Contract Law*, pp 123 *et seq* (R J Sharpe); (1987) 38 NILQ 244 (Elizabeth Macdonald); (1999) 10 KCLJ 1 (R Austen-Baker).

[5] *C N Marine Inc v Stena Line A/B (No 2)* [1982] 2 Lloyd's Rep 336, 348, CA, *per* May LJ; Jones and Goodhart, *Specific Performance*, 2nd edn, p 5, say: 'Specific performance should be decreed if it is the *appropriate* remedy.'

[6] *Beswick v Beswick* [1968] AC 58, [1967] 2 All ER 1197, HL.

[7] See *Beswick v Beswick, supra*, HL.   [8] *Dodsley v Kinnersley* (1761) Amb 403.

[9] [1959] 2 All ER 647. It has now been held that failure to complete a contract for the sale of land on the date specified in the contract constitutes a breach thereof both at law and in equity, even though the time for completion was not expressed to be of the essence of the contract: *Raineri v Miles* [1981] AC 1050, [1980] 2 All ER 145, HL. See [1982] Conv 191 (M P Thompson).

[10] [1960] AC 316, PC; *Manchester Diocesan Council for Education v Commercial and General Investments Ltd* [1969] 3 All ER 1593, [1970] 1 WLR 241. Of course, the decree would not order performance to take place before the date of completion. And damages 'in addition' may be awarded under Lord Cairns' Act, even though no decree of specific performance is made because the contract has been completed by the date of the hearing: *Oakacre Ltd v Claire Cleaners (Holdings) Ltd* [1982] Ch 197, [1981] 3 All ER 667, in which damages could not have been awarded at law, because the writ was premature, having been issued five days before the completion date, at which time there had been no breach of contract. See also (1960) 76 LQR 200 (R E Megarry).

[11] *Wright v Bell* (1818) 5 Price 325.

[12] *Buxton v Lister* (1746) 3 Atk 383; *Doloret v Rothschild* (1824) 1 Sim & St 590.

[13] (1804) 10 Ves 292 at 306. As to a condition substantially, but not exactly, performed, see *Davis v Hone* (1805) 2 Sch & Lef 341, esp *per* Lord Redesdale, at 347.

Eldon pointed out that specific performance with compensation might be granted where some unessential misdescription would defeat an action at law.

The question has not infrequently arisen as to the effect of a clause in the contract that, if the primary obligation is not performed, a specified sum of money is to be paid either by way of penalty or as liquidated damages. The answer depends upon whether, on the true construction of the contract, the defendant is intended to be able to choose either to do the thing specified in the contract or, alternatively, to pay the specified sum, or whether the intention is that he is bound to do the specified thing, the money clause being added by way of security. If the first construction is the correct one, specific performance cannot be obtained, because the parties have, in effect, agreed that damages will be an adequate remedy and thus taken away the basis of a claim for specific performance.[14] If, however, the second construction is the true one, the court will decide the claim for specific performance disregarding the presence of the money clause. It makes no difference for this purpose whether the sum is intended as a penalty[15] or as liquidated damages, such as the common case of forfeiture of a deposit on a sale of land.[16]

It should be noted that, although a contract for the sale of land continues to exist after an order for its specific performance has been made, the rights conferred by the contract do not remain unaffected. By applying for an order of specific performance and obtaining it, the applicant puts into the hands of the court how the contract is to be carried out. If the order for specific performance is not complied with, the claimant may either apply to the court for enforcement of the order, or may apply to the court to dissolve the order and ask the court to put an end to the contract.[17]

(B) REMEDY *IN PERSONAM*

In relation to specific performance, equity, as always, acts *in personam*. The leading case is *Penn v Lord Baltimore*,[18] in which Lord Hardwicke LC decreed specific performance of an English agreement relating to the boundaries between Pennsylvania and Maryland, despite the inability of the court to enforce its remedy *in rem*. And in *Richard West Partners (Inverness) Ltd v Dick*,[19] specific performance was decreed of a contract for the sale of land outside the jurisdiction[20] against a defendant within it.

---

[14] *Magrane v Archbold* (1813) 1 Dow 107; *Legh v Lillie* (1860) 6 H & N 165.

[15] *Howard v Hopkyns* (1742) 2 Atk 371; *Logan v Weinholt* (1833) 7 Bli NS 1.

[16] *Crutchley v Jerningham* (1817) 2 Mer 502, 506, *per* Lord Eldon. Cf cases of negative contract specifically enforced by an injunction, such as *Bird v Lake* (1863) 1 Hem & M 111. See *Ranger v Great Western Rly Co* (1854) 5 HL Cas 72.

[17] *Johnson v Agnew* [1980] AC 367, [1979] 1 All ER 883, HL, and see p 706 *et seq*, *infra*.

[18] (1750) 1 Ves Sen 444. Cf *Re Hawthorne* (1883) 23 Ch D 743, in wihch the claim was not for specific performance, but for account. There was no contract. The question was as to the title to land in a foreign country, and the court had no jurisdiction. See also *Chellaram v Chellaram* [1985] Ch 409, [1985] 1 All ER 1043.

[19] [1969] 1 All ER 289; affd [1969] 2 Ch 424, [1969] 1 All ER 943, CA. See also *Webb v Webb* [1992] 1 All ER 17, [1991] 1 WLR 1410, further proceedings [1994] QB 696, [1994] 3 All ER 911, ECJ; *Ashurst v Pollard* [2001] Ch 595, [2001] 2 All ER 75, CA.

[20] It was actually in Scotland.

(C) DISCRETIONARY CHARACTER

'From the very first, when specific performance was introduced it has been treated as a question of discretion whether it is better to interfere and give a remedy which the common law knows nothing at all about, or to leave the parties to their rights in a Court of Law.'[21] It is undoubted, however, that this discretion is not arbitrary or capricious, but is governed so far as possible by fixed rules and principles.[22] The result is that, in many cases, where the parties are under no disability and there is nothing objectionable in the nature or circumstances of the contract, a decree of specific performance is as much a matter of course in equity as damages are in common law,[23] and will be ordered even though the judge may think it to be a hard case for the defendant.[24] But, as will be seen, matters that would be irrelevant at common law, such as the conduct of the claimant, may be material in a claim for specific performance.[25] Further, the court may have to take into account other equitable doctrines. Thus, in *Langen and Wind Ltd v Bell*,[26] the purchaser brought a specific performance action for the sale of shares under a contract whereby the purchase price could not be ascertained for about two years after the agreed date for the transfer of the shares. The court had regard to the equitable principle that an unpaid vendor is entitled to a lien on the subject matter of the sale, and refused to grant an order for specific performance except in a form that would effectively safeguard the equitable lien.

(D) DAMAGES IN ADDITION TO, OR IN SUBSTITUTION FOR, SPECIFIC PERFORMANCE

The same statutory provisions apply in the case of a claim for an injunction, which were discussed, together with the relevant cases, in Chapter 25.[27]

(E) SPECIFIC PERFORMANCE WITH COMPENSATION

This is discussed later in this chapter.[28]

(F) SPECIFIC PERFORMANCE AND FREEZING INJUNCTION

In an appropriate case, a court that had made an order for specific performance could, by a separate freezing injunction, restrain the vendor from dealing with all or some part of the purchase money. In *Seven Seas Properties Ltd v Al-Essa*,[29] Hoffman J said that it would be excessively formalistic to insist upon two separate orders, and that they could be combined into one.

---

[21] *Per* Rigby LJ in *Re Scott and Alvarez's Contract* [1895] 2 Ch 603, 615, CA.

[22] *White v Damon* (1802) 7 Ves 30; *Lamare v Dixon* (1873) LR 6 HL 414. See *Haywood v Cope* (1858) 25 Beav 140, 151.

[23] *Hall v Warren* (1804) 9 Ves 605.   [24] *Haywood v Cope* (1858) 25 Beav 140.

[25] *Cox v Middleton* (1854) 2 Drew 209; *Lamare v Dixon* (1873) LR 6 HL 414.

[26] [1972] Ch 685, [1972] 1 All ER 296.   [27] See section 3, p 565, *supra*.

[28] See section 2(E)(iii), p 661, *infra*.   [29] [1989] 1 All ER 164, [1988] 1 WLR 1272.

2 GROUNDS ON WHICH SPECIFIC PERFORMANCE MAY BE REFUSED

Specific performance will not, of course, be granted unless there is, in accordance with the law of contract, a concluded contract, complete and certain;[30] even such a contract will not be enforced by specific performance if it is illegal or against the policy of the law,[31] even though valid according to the law of the country in which it was made.[32] Moreover, a claimant who seeks specific performance can obtain it only if there is, before the court, every other person entitled to join with him in enforcing the contract.[33] Assuming, however, that these matters are satisfied, there are certain classes of contract in relation to which specific performance will nevertheless not be granted, and certain defences may be available. Those more commonly arising will now be discussed.

(A) CONTRACT RELATING TO PURE PERSONALTY

In general, specific performance of a contract relating to land[34] is granted as a matter of course, but it was settled at an early date that specific performance would not, as a general rule, be granted of a contract relating to other forms of property, primarily on the ground that damages is an adequate remedy. Thus, for instance, specific performance will not be granted of a contract to transfer government, or other, stocks or shares freely available on the market,[35] or coal,[36] or other merchandise.

Where, however, for some reason, damages would not be an adequate remedy, specific performance may be granted. Thus it may properly be granted where there is a contract for the purchase of articles of unusual beauty, rarity, and distinction, or of a chattel of peculiar

[30] See *Waring and Gillow Ltd v Thompson* (1912) 29 TLR 154, CA; *Fountain Forestry Ltd v Edwards* [1975] Ch 1, [1974] 2 All ER 280 (administrator purported to enter into a contract for the sale of land on behalf of himself and his co-administrator, who never ratified the contract; purchaser refused specific performance against administrator); *Sudbrook Trading Estate Ltd v Eggleton* [1981] 3 All ER 105, [1981] 3 WLR 361, CA (option to purchase at price to be fixed by valuers nominated by parties; one party refused to appoint valuer; no concluded contract), reversed [1983] 1 AC 444, [1982] 3 All ER 1, HL, on ground that there was, on its true construction, a complete contract for a sale at a fair and reasonable price, and the court would substitute its own machinery for the agreed machinery which had broken down.

[31] *Rees v Marquis of Bute* [1916] 2 Ch 64; *Stuart v Kingman* (1979) 90 DLR (3d) 142 (contract document understated price to defraud revenue authorities). It is not clear how heavy is the burden of proof: see *De Hoghton v Money* (1866) 2 Ch App 164. Cf *Ailion v Spiekermann* [1976] Ch 158, [1976] 1 All ER 497 (specific performance decreed free of illegal premium).

[32] *Hope v Hope* (1857) 8 De GM & G 731, 743.   [33] *Tito v Waddell (No 2), supra*, at 325, 310.

[34] Including a contractual licence: see *Verrall v Great Yarmouth Borough Council* [1981] QB 202, [1980] 1 All ER 839, CA, discussed p 680, *infra*. Cf *Webster v Newham London Borough Council* (1980) Times, 22 November (damages an adequate remedy; no specific performance). See [1984] Conv 130 (J Berryman), suggesting there may be a reappraisal where, for instance, the land is being purchased as an investment and damages would be an inadequate remedy; (1985) 17 OLR 295 (J Berryman), for an historical perspective. And, in Canada, it has been held that specific performance should not be granted as a matter of course absent evidence that the property is unique to the extent that its substitute would not be readily available: *Semelhago v Paramadevan* [1996] 2 SCR 415.

[35] *Cud v Rutter* (1720) 1 P Wms 570, sub nom *Cuddee v Rutter* 5 Vin Abr 538 pl 21; *Adderley v Dixon* (1824) 1 Sim & St 607; *Pooley v Budd* (1851) 14 Beav 34. For a US suggestion for extending the remedy, see (1979) Yale LJ 271 (A Schwartz).

[36] *Dominion Coal Co Ltd v Dominion Iron and Steel Co Ltd* [1909] AC 293, PC.

value to the plaintiff.[37] Although refused on other grounds, it would have been granted in *Falcke v Gray*[38] of a contract to purchase two china jars apparently worth at least £200, and no objection seems to have been taken to the jurisdiction in *Thorn v Public Works Comrs*,[39] which involved a contract for the purchase of the arch-stone, the spandrill stone, and the Bramley Fall stone contained in the old Westminster Bridge, which had been pulled down. Again, specific performance may be granted of a contract for the transfer of shares,[40] or other property,[41] not freely available on the market. Specific performance may also be granted in relation to goods where there is an entire contract of land and goods,[42] and the goods are of such a nature that it would damage the land to remove them, or where there is a contract for the sale of a house and chattels in it, with the furnishings *in situ*, if damages would not be an adequate remedy.[43]

Finally, statute[44] has intervened to empower the court to grant the buyer, but not the seller, a decree of specific performance in any action for breach of contract to deliver specific or ascertained goods. 'Specific goods' means 'goods identified and agreed upon at the time a contract of sale is made', and includes an undivided share, specified as a fraction or percentage, of goods identified and agreed as aforesaid,[45] and 'ascertained' probably means identified in accordance with the agreement after the time at which a contract of sale is made.[46] The court will exercise its discretionary power on established equitable principles.[47] In no case does it matter whether the property has passed to the buyer or not.[48] A new Pt 5A added to the Sale of Goods Act 1979[49] gives the court power to order specific performance of goods that do not conform to the contract of sale. It remains to be seen whether this provision will be held to apply to ordinary goods readily available on the market.

(B) VOLUNTARY CONTRACTS

Lord Hardwick's dictum[50] that 'the court never decrees specifically without a consideration' has been consistently followed, and it makes no difference that the contract is by deed. The

---

[37] Ships seem to be readily so regarded: *Behnke v Bede Shipping Co Ltd* [1927] 1 KB 649, [1927] All ER Rep 689; *Société Des Industries Métallurgiques SA v Bronx Engineering Co Ltd* [1975] 1 Lloyd's Rep 465, CA; *C N Marine Inc v Stena Line A/B (No 2)* [1982] 2 Lloyds Rep 336, CA (but it must depend on the facts).

[38] (1859) 4 Drew 651. See also *Phillips v Lamdin* [1949] 2 KB 33, [1949] 1 All ER 770.

[39] (1863) 32 Beav 490.

[40] *Duncuft v Albrecht* (1841) 12 Sim 189; cf *Sri Lanka Omnibus Co Ltd v Perera* [1952] AC 76, PC. As to choses in action, see *Cogent v Gibson* (1864) 33 Beav 557.

[41] *Sky Petroleum Ltd v V I P Petroleum Ltd* [1974] 1 All ER 954 (petroleum where no alternative source of supply; the order was in form an injunction, but, in substance, specific performance). Cf *Re Wait* [1927] 1 Ch 606, CA, in which, however, the claim to specific performance was based solely on the predecessor of s 52 of the Sale of Goods Act 1979, discussed below. See (1984) 4 LS 102 (A S Burrows).

[42] *Nutbrown v Thornton* (1804) 10 Ves 159.

[43] *Record v Bell* [1991] 4 All ER 471, [1991] 1 WLR 853.

[44] Sale of Goods Act 1979, s 52, replacing earlier legislation.

[45] Ibid, s 61(1), as amended by the Sale of Goods (Amendment) Act 1995, s 2.

[46] *Per* Atkin LJ in *Re Wait* [1927] 1 Ch 606, 630, CA.

[47] *Behnke v Bede Shipping Co Ltd*, supra; *Société Des Industries Metallurgiques SA v Bronx Engineering Co Ltd*, supra, CA.

[48] *Re Wait, supra*, at 617, *per* Hanworth MR; *Cohen v Roche* [1927] 1 KB 169, 180.

[49] Added by the Sale and Supply of Goods to Consumers Regulations 2002, SI 2002/3045. See (2003) 119 LQR 541 (D R Harris).

[50] In *Penn v Lord Baltimore* (1750) 1 Ves Sen 444, 450; *Groves v Groves* (1829) 3 Y & J 163; *Dean and Westham Holdings Pty Ltd v Lloyd* [1990] 3 WAR 235.

rule, which can be regarded as an application of the maxim that 'equity will not assist a volunteer',[51] applies equally to a contract to create a trust or settlement.[52] It is thought not to have been affected by the Contracts (Rights of Third Parties) Act 1999.[53]

It should be noted that if a valid option to purchase is duly exercised, there will be constituted a perfectly ordinary contract for sale and purchase to which the remedy of specific performance may be applicable in the ordinary way. It is irrelevant that the contract may have arisen in pursuance of an option granted for valuable consideration, even though that consideration may be described as a token payment or, if by deed, may in fact have been granted without any payment.[54]

(c) CONTRACTS TO CARRY ON A BUSINESS OR ANY COMPARABLE SERIES OF ACTIVITIES

Although it is a matter for the judge's discretion, it is the settled practice of the court not to grant a decree of specific performance that would have the effect of compelling the defendant to carry on a business indefinitely, or, indeed, any comparable series of activities. The House of Lords has recently reaffirmed, in *Co-operative Insurance Society Ltd v Argyll Stores (Holdings) Ltd*,[55] that this practice should be applied in all but exceptional circumstances. The facts of the case were that the defendants had taken a thirty-five-year lease of the anchor unit at a shopping centre, and had covenanted to use the premises as a supermarket and to keep it open for retail trade during the usual hours of business. Some fourteen years into the lease, the defendants, who were making a considerable loss on the operation, gave short notice that they intended to close the supermarket, and, within little more than a month, the shop was closed and stripped out. It would cost £1m to reinstate the premises. In allowing the appeal against the order of specific performance made by the Court of Appeal, Lord Hoffman said that the most frequent reason given for declining to order someone to carry on a business was that it would require constant supervision by the court.[56] It was the possibility of the court having to give an indefinite series of rulings to ensure the execution of the order that had been regarded as undesirable. The only means available to it to enforce its order was the quasi-criminal procedure of punishment for contempt, and the use of such a heavy-handed mechanism had undesirable consequences.

There were, he continued, other objections. If the terms of the court's order, reflecting the terms of the obligation, could not be precisely drawn, the possibility of wasteful

---

[51] *Ford v Stuart* (1852) 15 Beav 493, 501. See p 105, *supra*.

[52] *Jefferys v Jefferys* (1841) Cr & Ph 138; *Lister v Hodgson* (1867) LR 4 Eq 30.

[53] See p 109, *supra*.

[54] *Mountford v Scott* [1975] Ch 258, [1975] 1 All ER 198, CA (option to purchase a house for £10,000 in consideration of payment of £1 valid; purported withdrawal ineffective; option exercised and specific performance granted of contract thereby created). See (1958) 74 LQR 242 (W J Mowbray), and, for an unorthodox view, (1977) 127 NLJ 806 and 897 (K Davies).

[55] [1998] AC 1, [1997] 3 All ER 297, HL, noted [1997] CLJ 488 (G Jones); (1998) 114 LQR 43 (G McMeel); [1998] Conv 396 (P Luxton); [1998] SJLS 150 (Yeo Hwee Ying); (1998) 61 MLR 421 (A Phang). See also (1999) 50 NILQ 102 (O Breen).

[56] See *Ryan v Mutual Tontine Westminster Chambers Association* [1893] 1 Ch 116, CA (contract to appoint a porter to carry out certain specified duties); *Barnes v City of London Real Property Co* [1918] 2 Ch 18 (contract to appoint a housekeeper to be in attendance during certain fixed hours); *Peto v Brighton, Uckfield and Tunbridge Wells Rly Co* (1863) 1 Hem & M 468 (contract to construct railway).

litigation over compliance was increased; so was the oppression caused by the defendant having to do things under threat of proceedings for contempt. Further, an order requiring the defendant to carry on a business might cause injustice by allowing the claimant to enrich himself at the defendant's expense. The loss that the defendant might suffer through having to comply with the order might be far greater than that which the claimant would suffer from the contract being broken. A remedy that enabled the claimant to secure, in money terms, more than the performance due to him was unjust.

From a wider perspective, it could not be in the public interest for the courts to require someone to carry on business at a loss if there was any plausible alternative by which the other party could be given compensation.[57] The cumulative effect of the various reasons for it showed that the settled practice was based on sound sense. The decision has, nevertheless, been criticized[58] as an unfortunate failure to liberalize the rules of specific performance and grant an effective remedy to a plaintiff who is clearly deserving, and who is likely to be severely short-changed by a mere award of damages. It also sits ill with the idea that it should be the function of the courts to make sure, as far as possible, that contracts are performed rather than broken.

Relatively recent cases in which the objection relating to supervision did not prevail include *Posner v Scott-Lewis*,[59] in which the claimants sought specific performance of a covenant to employ a resident porter for certain specified purposes. In granting the order, it was said that the relevant considerations were:

(i)   is there a sufficient definition of what has to be done in order to comply with the order of the court?

(ii) will enforcing compliance involve superintendence by the court to an unacceptable degree?

(iii) what are the respective prejudices or hardships that will be suffered by the parties if the order is made or not made?

In *Co-operative Insurance Society v Argyll Stores (Holdings) Ltd*,[60] Lord Hoffman pointed out the distinction between orders that require a defendant to carry on an activity, such as running a business over a more or less extended period of time, and orders that require him to achieve a result. In the latter type of case, there is a much-reduced risk of repeated applications for rulings, and this distinction explains why the courts have, in appropriate circumstances, ordered specific performance of building contracts and repairing covenants.

The conditions that have to be fulfilled if specific performance of a building contract is to be granted were set out by Romer LJ in *Wolverhampton Corpn v Emmons*,[61] and his

---

[57] *A-G v Colchester Corpn* [1955] 2 QB 207, [1955] 2 All ER 124; *Gravesham Borough Council v British Railways Board* [1978] Ch 379, [1978] 3 All ER 853 (mandatory injunction to maintain frequency of ferry refused).

[58] [1998] Conv 23 (A Tettenborn).

[59] [1987] Ch 25, [1986] 3 All ER 513, noted (1987) 46 CLJ 21 (G Jones); *Barrow v Chappell & Co Ltd* [1976] RPC 355.

[60] *Supra*, HL.

[61] [1901] 1 KB 515, 525, CA; *Rainbow Estates Ltd v Tokenhold Ltd* [1999] Ch 64, [1998] 2 All ER 860, noted [1999] CLJ 283 (S Bridge); [1998] Conv 495 (M Pawlowski and J Brown).

statement would appear still to hold good:

> The first is that the building work, of which he seeks to enforce the performance, is defined by the contract; that is to say, that the particulars of the work are so far definitely ascertained that the court can sufficiently see what is the exact nature of the work of which it is asked to order the performance.[62]

The second is that the claimant has a substantial interest in having the contract performed, which is of such a nature that he cannot adequately be compensated for breach of contract by damages.[63]

The third is that the defendant has, by the contract, obtained possession of land on which the work is contracted to be done. This last condition was criticized in *Carpenters Estates Ltd v Davies*,[64] and it is submitted that the formulation in that case is to be preferred—namely, that the claimant must establish that the defendant is in possession of the land on which the work is contracted to be done. The point is that the claimant cannot go on the land in order to do the work himself or through other agents.

In the two cases last mentioned, the conditions were fulfilled and specific performance was granted. Their facts, slightly simplified, were, in *Wolverhampton Corpn v Emmons*,[65] that the claimant corporation, in pursuance of a scheme of street improvement, sold and conveyed to the defendant a plot of land abutting on a street, the defendant covenanting with the corporation that he would erect buildings thereon in accordance with certain plans and specifications within a certain time. The defendant failed to erect the buildings. In the other case, *Carpenters Estates Ltd v Davies*,[66] a vendor who sold certain land to purchasers for building development, retaining other land adjoining it, failed to perform his covenant to make certain roads, and lay certain mains, sewers, and drains on the land retained.

In relation to a covenant to repair contained in a lease, Lord Eldon laid down[67] that a landlord cannot obtain an order for specific performance in the case of a tenant's covenant to repair. This no longer represents the law. It has recently been held[68] that a modern law of remedies requires specific performance to be available in appropriate circumstances, and that there are no constraints of principle or binding authority against the availability of the remedy. Subject to the overriding need to avoid injustice or oppression, the remedy should be available when damages are not an adequate remedy or, in the more modern formulation, when specific performance is the appropriate remedy. The court, however, should be astute to ensure that the landlord was not seeking the decree simply in order to harass the tenant. In so doing, it may take into account considerations similar to those it must take into account under the Leasehold Property (Repairs) Act 1938.[69] In practice, it

---

[62] *South Wales Rly Co v Wythes* (1854) 5 De GM & G 880, CA.

[63] If the building is to take place on the plaintiff's land, damages will normally be adequate because some other contractor can be paid to do the job and any increased price be recovered as damages.

[64] [1940] Ch 160, [1940] 1 All ER 13.   [65] *Supra*, CA.

[66] *Supra*. Cf *Hounslow London Borough Council v Twickenham Garden Development Ltd* [1971] Ch 233, [1970] 3 All ER 326, and comments of Jones and Goodhart, *Specific Performance*, 2nd edn, p 187.

[67] In *Hill v Barclay* (1810) 16 Ves 402.   [68] In *Rainbow Estates Ltd v Tokenhold Ltd*, *supra*.

[69] The 1938 Act imposes restrictions on the recovery of damages or forfeiture, but does not apply to decrees of specific performance.

was said that it would be a rare case in which the remedy of specific performance would be the appropriate one.[70]

In the case of a landlords' covenant to repair, it had previously been held, in *Jeune v Queen's Cross Properties Ltd*,[71] that an order could be made where there has been a plain breach of a covenant to repair and there is no doubt at all what is required to be done to remedy the breach. Further, in the case of a dwelling, it is now provided, by s 17 of the Landlord and Tenant Act 1985, that, in the case of a breach on the part of the landlord of a repairing covenant[72] relating to any part of the premises in which the dwelling is comprised, the court may order specific performance. The statutory jurisdiction is discretionary, but may be exercised whether or not the breach relates to a part of the premises let to the tenant, and notwithstanding any equitable rule restricting the scope of the remedy of specific performance.

(D) CONTRACTS FOR PERSONAL WORK OR SERVICE

'The courts, as such, have never dreamt of enforcing agreements strictly personal in their nature.'[73] Accordingly, equity would not normally order specific performance of a contract of employment, whether at the instance of employer or employee, nor could the same result be achieved indirectly by means of an injunction. In addition to the ordinary contract of service, such as the employment of a valet, coachman, or cook referred to in *Johnson v Shrewsbury and Birmingham Rly Co*,[74] specific performance has been refused on this ground of a contract between a company and its managing director,[75] of an agreement to compose and write reports of cases in the Court of Exchequer,[76] of an agreement to supply drawings or maps,[77] of a claim to fill the office of receiver to the Bishop of Ely,[78] of an agreement to sing at a theatre,[79] and of articles of apprenticeship.[80] The same principle applies to any contract of agency.[81] Relief was also refused in *R v Incorporated Froebel Institute, ex p L*,[82] in which a pupil had been suspended from a private school for alleged misconduct, including theft. In refusing to order specific performance of the contract between the school and the parents, Tucker J observed that the courts are reluctant to force one body of persons into daily contact with another against the will of one

---

[70] In the case of commercial leases, the landlord would normally have the right to forfeit or to enter and do the repairs at the expense of the tenant; in residential leases, the landlord would normally have the right to forfeit in appropriate cases.

[71] [1974] Ch 97, [1973] 3 All ER 97.

[72] *Quaere*, whether the section applies to an obligation assumed under hand only: see *Gordon v Selico Co Ltd* [1985] 2 EGLR 79. It was held in that case that, given a deed, the word 'covenant' extended to implied promises, and this seems to have been accepted on appeal [1986] 1 EGLR 71, CA.

[73] Per Jessel MR in *Rigby v Connol* (1880) 14 Ch D 482. See, generally, [1991] Cambrian LR 26 (Elizabeth Macdonald); (1994) 138 Sol Jo 152 (Jillian Brown); (1998) 27 Ind LJ 37 (D Brodie).

[74] (1853) 3 De GM & G 914, 926.   [75] *Bainbridge v Smith* (1889) 41 Ch D 462, CA.

[76] *Clarke v Price* (1819) 2 Wils Ch 157.

[77] *Baldwin v Society for the Diffusion of Useful Knowledge* (1838) 9 Sim 393.

[78] *Pickering v Bishop of Ely* (1843) 2 Y & C Ch Cas 249.

[79] *Lumley v Wagner* (1852) 1 De GM & G 604.

[80] *Webb v England* (1860) 29 Beav 44; *De Francesco v Barnum* (1890) 45 Ch D 430.

[81] *Chinnock v Sainsbury* (1860) 3 LT 258; *Brett v East India and London Shipping Co* (1864) 2 Hem & M 404; *Morris v Delobbel-Flipo* [1892] 2 Ch 352.

[82] [1999] ELR 488.

of the parties. In cases such as that before the court, there are difficulties inherent in the breakdown of trust and the undesirability of requiring parties to coexist in a pastoral or educational relationship.

So far as contracts of employment are concerned, the Trade Union and Labour Relations (Consolidation) Act 1992[83] provides that no court can decree specific performance so as to compel an employee to do any work, nor can the same result be achieved by means of an injunction to restrain a breach of contract. Moreover, although, in a case of unfair dismissal, a tribunal may make an order for reinstatement or re-engagement, there is no provision for such an order being specifically enforced. If not complied with, however, the employer will not only have to pay compensation for unfair dismissal, but an additional award of compensation may be made.[84]

The reasons commonly put forward for the above rules are, partly, the difficulty of supervision, and partly, the undesirability on grounds of public policy of compelling persons to continue personal relations with each other against their will. Fry LJ put the latter reason rather dramatically in *De Francesco v Barnum*,[85] when he said that 'the courts are bound to be jealous, lest they should turn contracts of service into contracts of slavery'. Other factors are that damages is normally an adequate remedy, and in many cases, where an employee has been replaced, the difficulty of reinstatement. Megarry J has recently suggested,[86] however, that the reasons are 'more complex and more firmly bottomed on human nature'. He speculated on the effect of a decree of specific performance of a contract to sing:

> If a singer contracts to sing, there could no doubt be proceedings for committal, if ordered to sing, the singer remained obstinately dumb. But if instead the singer sang flat, or sharp, or too fast or too slowly, or too loudly, or too quietly...the threat of committal would reveal itself as a most unsatisfactory weapon; for who could say whether the imperfections of the performance were natural or self-induced? To make an order with such possibilities of evasion would be vain; and so the order will not be made.

Nevertheless, in Megarry J's view, it depends on the circumstances of the particular case, and although there is always a reluctance on the part of the court to decree specific performance of a contract for personal services, the rule is not a rigid one. *Hill v C A Parsons & Co Ltd*[87] supports the view that the courts do not regard themselves as bound by an inflexible rule. The case was actually concerned with a motion for an interim injunction, but is directly relevant, as this could only be granted with a view to specific performance of the contract at the hearing. The majority[88] of the Court of Appeal granted the injunction on the ground of special circumstances—in particular, that damages would not be an

---

[83] Section 236.   [84] Employment Rights Act 1996, s 117, as amended.

[85] (1890) 45 Ch D 430. See (1969) 32 MLR 532 (G de N Clark).

[86] *C H Giles & Co Ltd v Morris* [1972] 1 All ER 960, 969.

[87] [1972] Ch 305, [1971] 3 All ER 1345, CA, applied *Irani v Southampton and South West Hampshire Health Authority* [1985] ICR 590, noted (1985) 14 Ind LJ 248 (G Smith); and see *Dietman v Brent London Borough Council* [1987] ICR 737. See (1983) 133 NLJ 68 (B W Napier); (1984) 4 LS 102 (A S Burrows); (1988) 85 LSG (5) 29 (J Hendy and J McMullen).

[88] The two common law members, reversing the Chancery judge at first instance. Per Lord Denning MR, at 1359: '*It is the common lawyers who now do equity!*' Cf *Associated British Ports v Transport and General Workers' Union* [1989] 3 All ER 796, [1989] 1 WLR 939, CA; revsd on other grounds [1989] 3 All ER 822, [1989] 1 WLR 939, HL.

adequate remedy, and that a combination of the injunction and the coming into operation of the Industrial Relations Act 1971 would safeguard the claimant's position.

It has, however, subsequently been stressed by the Court of Appeal[89] that the facts of *Hill v C A Parsons & Co Ltd*[90] were unusual, if not unique, and it is clear that it is extremely difficult, in practice, to find exceptional circumstances that will take a case outside the general rule. In affirming that *Hill v C A Parsons & Co Ltd* is an exception to the long-standing general rule, the Court of Appeal in *Powell v London Borough of Brent*[91] said that the court would not, by injunction—and the same must apply to specific performance:

> require an employer to let a servant continue in his employment, when the employer has sought to terminate that employment and to prevent the servant carrying out his work under the contract, unless it is clear on the evidence not only that it is otherwise just to make such a requirement but also that there exists sufficient confidence[92] on the part of the employer in the servant's ability and other necessary attributes for it to be reasonable to make the order.

However, in *Wadcock v London Borough of Brent*,[93] notwithstanding an affidavit by the Deputy Director of Social Services deposing to a breakdown of confidence such that it was quite unrealistic to expect the employer–employee relationship to be re-established, the court made an order that, on undertakings by the claimant to work in accordance with proper instructions, he should be employed by the defendants pending trial.

An important distinction was drawn in *Robb v Hammersmith and Fulham London Borough Council*,[94] in which it was accepted that if an injunction is sought to reinstate an employee dismissed in breach of contract, so that when reinstated he can actually carry out the job for which he was employed, trust and confidence are highly relevant. The all-important criterion, it was said, is whether the order is workable. A breakdown of trust and confidence does not necessarily bar injunctive relief, and is of little relevance where the employee seeks an order that would have the effect of requiring the employer to treat him as suspended with pay until contractual disciplinary procedures have been complied with. On the facts, an order should be made.

Apart from these recent cases, there are also earlier decisions in which it has been held that, in exceptional circumstances, specific performance may be decreed of some personal

---

[89] *Chappell v Times Newspapers Ltd* [1975] 2 All ER 233, [1975] ICR 145, CA. See also *Price v Strange* [1978] Ch 337, CA, in which Goff LJ expressly approved the opinion of Megarry J referred to above, although Buckley LJ said that there was no jurisdiction to grant specific performance of a contract for personal services; *Gunton v London Borough of Richmond upon Thames* [1981] Ch 448, [1980] 3 All ER 577, CA; *Regent International Hotels (UK) Ltd v Pageguide Ltd* (1985) Times, 13 May, CA.

[90] [1972] Ch 305, [1971] 3 All ER 1345, CA.

[91] [1988] ICR 176, CA, noted (1989) 48 CLJ (K D Ewing), dist *Wishart v National Association of Citizens Advice Bureaux Ltd* [1990] ICR 794, CA. See also *Hughes v London Borough of Southwark* [1988] IRLR 55; (1990) 140 NLJ 1007 (A Burrows).

[92] The confidence may be comparative. In *Alexander v Standard Telephones and Cables plc* [1990] IRLR 55, noted (1992) Ind LJ 58 (Aileen McColgan), redundancies were inevitable. So far as the dismissed plaintiffs were concerned, 'it cannot be said that the defendant has complete confidence in the plaintiffs, as it has less confidence that they can do the work than the other members of the workforce that have been retained'.

[93] [1990] IRLR 223.

[94] [1991] ICR 514, noted (1991) 42 NILQ 374 (Elizabeth MacDonald); *Gryf-Lowezowski v Hinchingbrooke Healthcare NHS Trust* [2005] EWHC 2407 (QB), [2006] IRLR 100.

obligation, where it forms only a small part of a larger contract that is otherwise suitable for such an order.[95]

It should be added that there is a vital distinction between an order to perform a contract for services and an order to procure the execution of such a contract. The mere fact that the contract to be made is one of which the court would not order specific performance—such as the service agreement as managing director of a company in *C H Giles & Co Ltd v Morris*[96]—is no ground for refusing to decree that the contract be entered into. In the last-cited case, the defendants were properly ordered to procure the execution of the service agreement.

(E) CONTRACTS WANTING IN MUTUALITY

(i) General rule

English judges and writers[97] commonly state and apply the general rule that specific performance will not be granted unless the remedy is mutual—that is, if, by reason of personal incapacity, the nature of the contract, or any other matter, A cannot obtain specific performance against B, then B will not be granted specific performance against A even though, taking A's obligation by itself, this would be an appropriate remedy. The defence of mutuality may be waived.[98]

In accordance with this general rule, a minor cannot obtain a decree of specific performance,[99] because specific performance cannot be decreed against him,[100] and a claimant against whom specific performance should not be decreed because his obligation is to do something of a personal or a continuous nature cannot obtain specific performance even though this is prima facie appropriate to the defendant's obligation.[101] It should be observed, however, that it has been long settled that, in the case of the ordinary contract for the sale and purchase of land, the vendor is as much entitled to a decree of specific performance as the purchaser, notwithstanding that the purchaser's obligation is merely to pay the purchase price. This has been explained by Lord St Leonards[102] on the ground that damages would not be an adequate remedy:

> a seller wants the exact sum agreed to be paid to him, and he wants to divest himself legally of the estate, which after the contract was no longer vested in him beneficially. This is accomplished by specific performance, whereas, at law, he would be left with the estate on his hands, and would recover damages...

---

[95] *Fortescue v Lostwithiel and Fowey Rly Co* [1894] 3 Ch 621; *Kennard v Cory Bros & Co Ltd* [1922] 2 Ch 1; *Beswick v Beswick* [1968] AC 58, 97, [1967] 2 All ER 1197, 1218, HL, *per* Lord Upjohn; *C H Giles & Co Ltd v Morris* [1972] 1 All ER 960, 969.

[96] *Supra.*

[97] See Ames in *Lectures On Legal History*, pp 370 *et seq*; (1992) 108 LQR 280 (C Harpum). See *per* Kekewich J in *Wylson v Dunn* (1887) 34 Ch D 569, 576.

[98] *Price v Strange* [1977] 3 All ER 371, 384, CA, *per* Goff LJ.

[99] *Flight v Bolland* (1828) 4 Russ 298. See Law Commission Working Paper No 81 on minors' contracts, proposing that specific performance should be available to a minor, and against him if he has first sued the adult. However, in its Report No 134, the Commission did not recommend legislation on this point.

[100] *Lumley v Ravenscroft* [1895] 1 QB 683, CA.

[101] *Johnson v Shrewsbury and Birmingham Rly Co* (1853) 3 De GM & G 914; *Page One Records Ltd v Britton* [1967] 3 All ER 822.

[102] In *Eastern Counties Rly Co v Hawkes* (1855) 5 HL Cas 331, 376, and see *per* Lord Campbell, at 360.

(ii) Time when mutuality has to be shown

This was given detailed and careful consideration by the Court of Appeal in *Price v Strange*.[103] The essential facts were that the defendant orally[104] agreed to grant the claimant a new underlease at an increased rent of the maisonette in which the claimant was living, in consideration of the claimant executing certain repairs to the interior and exterior of the building in which the maisonette was situated. The claimant completed the interior repairs, but was not allowed to carry out the external repairs because the defendant repudiated the agreement and had the exterior repairs done at her own expense, nevertheless accepting rent at the increased rate for some months. The claimant's specific performance action was dismissed at first instance on the ground that the remedies were not mutual at the date of the contract, since the claimant's obligation to execute the repairs could not be specifically enforced. The decision was unanimously reversed by the Court of Appeal, where Buckley LJ stated:[105]

> The time at which the mutual availability of specific performance and its importance must be considered is, in my opinion, the time of judgment, and the principle to be applied can I think be stated simply as follows: the court will not compel a defendant to perform his obligations specifically if it cannot at the same time ensure that any unperformed obligations of the plaintiff will be specifically performed, unless, perhaps, damages would be an adequate remedy to the defendant for any default on the plaintiff's part.

An unusual feature of the facts in *Price v Strange*[106] was that, although all of the agreed repairs had been done, they had not all been done by the claimant. It was held that the claimant should nevertheless succeed, because the failure of the claimant to do the work was not due to any default of his, but to the defendant's unjustified repudiation of the contract. Nevertheless, it was only equitable that specific performance should be ordered on the terms that the claimant should pay the defendant proper compensation for the work done by her.

(iii) Exceptions to the requirement of mutuality

Firstly, it has been said that the holder of an option to purchase may be able to obtain specific performance even though the other party may have no such right against him.[107] This may be explained, however, on the ground that specific performance could not be obtained prior to the exercise of the option, after which there would be mutuality.

Secondly, an exception arises in connection with the grant of specific performance with compensation,[108] a special variant of the remedy limited to cases of misdescription in a

---

[103] [1977] 3 All ER 371, CA, applied *Sutton v Sutton* [1984] Ch 184, [1984] 1 All ER 168; *E Johnson & Co (Barbados) Ltd v NSR Ltd* [1997] AC 400, [1996] 3 WLR 583, PC.

[104] It was conceded that there were sufficient acts of part-performance to make the contract enforceable as the law stood before the Law of Property (Miscellaneous Provisions) Act 1989.

[105] At 392. See also *per* Goff LJ at 383, who accepted as valid the established rule that, where the vendor has no title, the purchaser can on discovering the defect repudiate the contract forthwith, the vendor losing any right to specific performance albeit he is able to make title before the date fixed for completion. This is a special right arising out of the difficulty of making title to land in England. See also (1977) 41 Conv 18 (C T Emery).

[106] *Supra*, CA.

[107] *McCarthy & Stone Ltd v Julian S Hodge & Co Ltd* [1971] 2 All ER 973, 980, *per* Foster J.

[108] See (1981) 40 CLJ 47 (C Harpum), and *Rutherford v Acton-Adams* [1915] AC 866, 869, 870, PC. The contract in practice commonly contains special provisions. As to the extent of a claim for damages where

contract for the sale of land, whether the misdescription relates to the title, or the quantity or quality of the land. In other words, it is only available where the vendor is unable to convey to the purchaser property exactly corresponding to that which he has contracted to convey, and not even in the case in which there has been a misstatement not incorporated in the contract, but in the form of a misrepresentation inducing it.[109] When specific performance with compensation is granted, the court, exceptionally, does more than simply enforce the agreement between the parties: it enforces an agreement somewhat different from that agreed upon, and compels the acceptance of compensation that the parties never agreed to give or receive. 'Compensation', in every case, means compensation to the purchaser and not to the vendor. The general position is, on the one hand, that where the vendor cannot fulfil the exact terms of the contract, but can convey to the purchaser substantially what he had contracted to get,[110] either the vendor or the purchaser may obtain a decree of specific performance with compensation. If, however, it is impossible to estimate the amount of compensation, specific performance will be refused.[111] Where, on the other hand, the vendor cannot even convey to the purchaser substantially what he contracted to get, the remedies are not mutual. In such case, the vendor is not entitled to specific performance at all, but the purchaser can, as a general rule,[112] elect to take all that the vendor is able to convey to him, and to have a proportionate abatement from the purchase money, provided that this is capable of computation.[113] The purchaser may alternatively, of course, rescind the contract.[114]

Lastly, by s 17 of the Landlord and Tenant Act 1985, there is no need for mutuality where the tenant of a dwelling sues his landlord for breach of a repairing covenant.[115]

(F) CONTRACTS CAPABLE OF PARTIAL PERFORMANCE ONLY[116]

Suppose that a contract contains two terms, under one of which X is obliged to do an act for which, taken by itself, specific performance would be an appropriate remedy, and, under the other, he is obliged to do an act, say, of a personal nature, for which it is not. Here, the rule[117] is that a contract cannot be specifically performed in part; it must be wholly performed, or not at all. Thus, in *Ogden v Fossick*,[118] an agreement was entered

---

even extinguishment of the purchase price would not be adequate compensation, see *Grant v Dawkins* [1973] 3 All ER 897, noted (1974) 38 Conv 45 (F R Crane); (1974) 90 LQR 299 (P H Pettit).

[109] A purchaser may have other remedies in such cases, eg rescission, or damages for deceit if the vendor has been fraudulent, or possibly damages for breach of a collateral contract. See *Rutherford v Acton-Adams, supra*, PC.

[110] As to what is meant by 'substantial' in this context, reference should be made to Fry, *Specific Performance*, 6th edn, and works on conveying such as *Williams on Vendor and Purchaser*, 4th edn, vol I, p 723 *et seq.*

[111] *Westmacott & Robins* (1862) 4 De GF & J 390; *Cato v Thompson* (1882) 9 QBD 616, CA.

[112] Not, however, if innocent third parties would be prejudiced: *Thomas v Dering* (1837) 1 Keen 729. And some general defence, such as those discussed below, may be available.

[113] *Westmacott v Robins* (1862) 4 De GF & J 390; *Cato v Thompson* (1882) 9 QBD 616, CA.

[114] See Chapter 29, section 3, *infra*.   [115] See p 657, *supra*.

[116] See also Chapter 27, section 1, as to the enforcement by injunction of a contract of which specific performance will not be granted.

[117] See *per* Romilly MR in (1852) 15 Beav 493, 501; *Merchant's Trading Co v Banner* (1871) LR 12 Eq 18, 23.

[118] (1862) 4 De GF & J 426; *Barnes v City of London Real Property Co* [1918] 2 Ch 18.

into between Fossick and Ogden that Fossick should grant Ogden a lease of a coal wharf at a certain rent, and should be employed throughout the tenancy at a salary of £300 per annum plus a commission on the coal sold at the wharf. Although the first part of the agreement was typical of the kind of matter of which specific performance is decreed, this remedy was refused on the ground that it was inseparably connected with the second part of the agreement, which was clearly of the kind of which specific performance is not granted. It is an *a fortiori* case in which the term sought to be enforced by specific performance is merely an ancillary or subsidiary term of a contract, the principal terms of which are unenforceable by specific performance.[119] Megarry J's observations in *C H Giles & Co Ltd v Morris*[120] suggest that the rule may be less strictly applied nowadays. The presence of a provision not, by itself, specifically enforceable does not, in his view, necessarily prevent the contract as a whole from being specifically enforced.

There is an exception or apparent exception to the traditional rule where the contract is divisible—that is, where, on its true construction, there is not one contract containing two or more parts, but two or more separate agreements. In such a case, specific performance will lie in appropriate circumstances for breach of a separate agreement.[121] This is what happened in *Wilkinson v Clements*,[122] from which it seems that the burden of proof that the contract is divisible lies upon the person who alleges that this is so, Mellish LJ observing[123] that, as a general rule, all agreements must be considered as entire and indivisible. Where, however, property is sold in separate lots, specific performance can normally be obtained in relation to one lot, even though it may be unobtainable in relation to the others.[124]

What has been called 'the doctrine of partial performance' may apply in a rather different situation—namely, where a person has represented that he can grant a certain property, or is entitled to a certain interest in that property, and it later appears that there is a deficiency in his title or interest. In such a case, the other party can obtain an order compelling him to grant what he has got.[125]

(G) WHERE A DECREE OF SPECIFIC PERFORMANCE WOULD BE USELESS

In such cases, a decree will not be granted. Thus it has been refused of an agreement to enter into a partnership at will, which could be dissolved immediately afterwards,[126] of an agreement to grant a deputation of an office, which was clearly revocable,[127] and of an agreement to grant a lease for a term expired before proceedings were commenced.[128]

---

[119] *South Wales Rly Co v Wythes* (1854) 5 De GM & G 880; *Brett v East India and London Shipping Co Ltd* (1864) 2 Hem & M 404.

[120] [1972] 1 All ER 960, 969. Jones and Goodhart, *Specific Performance*, 2nd edn, p 58, suggest that the general rule no longer exists.

[121] *Wilkinson v Clements* (1872) 8 Ch App 96; *Odessa Tramways Co v Mendel* (1878) 8 Ch D 235, CA.

[122] *Supra.*

[123] *Wilkinson v Clements, supra,* at 110; *Roffey v Shallcross* (1819) 4 Madd 227.

[124] *Lewin v Guest* (1826) 1 Russ 325; *Casamajor v Strode* (1834) 2 My & K 706.

[125] *Thames Guaranty Ltd v Campbell* [1985] QB 210, [1984] 2 All ER 585, CA; *United Bank of Kuwait plc v Sahib* [1995] 2 All ER 973; affd [1996] 3 All ER 215, CA, without discussing this point.

[126] *Hercy v Birch* (1804) 9 Ves 357.   [127] *Wheeler v Trotter* (1737) 3 Swan 174n.

[128] *Gilbey v Cossey* (1912) 106 LT 607; *McMahon v Ambrose* [1987] VR 817.

Somewhat similarly, a decree will not be granted if it would be substantially impossible to carry it out. Thus, if X and Y are joint tenants of Blackacre, and X contracts to sell Blackacre to P without the knowledge or subsequent approbation of Y, it has been held that P will be unable to obtain specific performance against X. X could not convey the legal estate, as he is only one of the two trustees of land, and a transfer of X's beneficial interest would be a transfer of something substantially different from the subject matter of the contract.[129] It has been doubted[130] whether this latter ground can be sustained in the light of *William and Glyn's Bank Ltd v Boland*.[131] Another example would be where there was a contract to grant a lease at a rent greater than that which could be lawfully recovered at the time when the contract is due to be performed.[132]

It may be added that it was held, in *Verrall v Great Yarmouth Borough Council*,[133] that there was no reason why the court should not order specific performance of a contractual licence of short duration—in that case, two days—and the same principle must surely apply to an agreement for a lease for a short term. The court expressly disapproved earlier cases to the contrary, and further held that, in an appropriate case, such as the case before it, specific performance could be ordered where a licensee's licence had been wrongfully repudiated before he entered into possession.

(H) CONTRACTS TO LEND OR ADVANCE MONEY

Such contracts are not enforceable by specific performance, whether or not the loan is to be secured by mortgage. The reason is that the remedy at law is adequate—the borrower can borrow the money elsewhere, and claim at law, if he is compelled to pay a higher rate of interest, and likewise the lender has a simple money demand if his money has laid idle or been invested less advantageously.[134] Exceptionally, by statute,[135] a contract with a company to take up and pay for any debentures of a company may be enforced by an order for specific performance.

Specific performance can, however, be obtained of a contract to execute a mortgage—that is, of an agreement to give security—when the money has been actually advanced.[136]

It should be observed that it is quite possible for a decree of specific performance to be obtained in appropriate circumstances of a contract to make a money payment. For instance, a purchaser of land is commonly compelled to pay the purchase price in a specific performance action at the instance of a vendor, in relation to which, as has been seen,[137] damages is not regarded as an adequate remedy, and it has been held that it makes no difference that the price is payable by instalments, or that the price is not payable to the

---

[129] *Watts v Spence* [1976] Ch 165, [1975] 2 All ER 528. And see (1977) 41 Conv 141 (Angela Sydenham); [1980] Conv 191 (P W Smith).

[130] (1981) 40 CLJ 47 (C Harpum).   [131] [1981] AC 487, [1980] 2 All ER 408, HL.

[132] See *Newman v Dorrington Developments Ltd* [1975] 3 All ER 928, in which, however, the principle did not apply on the facts of the case and specific performance was granted.

[133] [1981] QB 202, [1980] 1 All ER 839, CA (attempt by local authority, after a change of control following local elections, to withdraw licence to National Front to hold annual conference in council premises).

[134] *Larios v Bonany y Gurety* (1873) LR 5 PC 346; *Western Wagon and Property Co v West* [1892] 1 Ch 271; *Loan Investment Corpn of Australasia v Bonner* [1970] NZLR 724, PC.

[135] Companies Act 2006, s 740.

[136] *Ashton v Corrigan* (1871) LR 13 Eq 76; *Hermann v Hodges* (1873) LR 16 Eq 18.

[137] See p 660, *supra*.

plaintiff, but to some third party.[138] Similarly, the Minister of Transport can sue for specific performance of the agreement between himself and the Motor Insurers' Bureau,[139] under which the Bureau agreed that if a judgment for an injured person against a motorist were not satisfied in full within seven days, the Bureau would pay the amount of the judgment to the injured person.[140] Hitherto, it has generally been thought that the courts would be unwilling to extend the limited type of case in which specific performance of a contract to make a money payment would be granted, but *Beswick & Beswick*[141] perhaps heralds a more liberal approach.

(I) A CONTRACT TO REFER TO ARBITRATION

Such a contract is not specifically enforceable.[142] It may, however, be indirectly enforced under the provisions of the Arbitration Act 1996,[143] which gives the court a discretionary power to stay an action in respect of any dispute that the parties have, by writing, agreed to refer to arbitration. If the court exercises this power, the plaintiff must either give up his claim or proceed by arbitration.

Specific performance may, however, be granted of the award of the arbitrator, 'because the award supposes an agreement between the parties, and contains no more than the terms of that agreement ascertained by a third person'.[144] It follows that it is enforceable on the same principles and subject to the same limitations as an ordinary contract.

(J) PARTNERSHIP AGREEMENTS

As a general rule, the court will not decree specific performance of an agreement to perform and carry on a partnership,[145] because this would involve the court in constant superintendence of the partnership affairs. *A fortiori*, the rule applies in the case of a partnership at will, in relation to which specific performance would be useless, as either party could forthwith dissolve the partnership.[146]

Exceptionally, it seems that, where there has been part-performance of the partnership agreement, the parties may be compelled specifically to perform a term to execute a partnership deed, incorporating any subsequent variations to the original agreement that may have been made between the partners.[147]

---

[138] *Beswick v Beswick* [1968] AC 58, [1967] 2 All ER 1197, HL. And see (1967) 30 MLR 690–693 (G H Treitel).

[139] The agreement is set out in a note to *Hardy v Motor Insurers' Bureau* [1964] 2 QB 745, 770–775.

[140] *Gurtner v Circuit* [1968] 2 QB 587, [1968] 1 All ER 328, CA.

[141] *Supra*, HL. See p 112, *supra*.

[142] *South Wales Rly Co v Wythes* (1854) 5 De GM & G 880, CA; *Doleman & Sons v Ossett Corpn* [1912] 3 KB 257, CA.

[143] Section 9, replacing earlier legislation.

[144] *Per* Lord Eldon in *Wood v Griffith* (1818) 1 Swan 43, 54.

[145] *Scott v Rayment* (1868) LR 7 Eq 112.   [146] *Hercy v Birch* (1804) 9 Ves 357.

[147] *England v Curling* (1844) 8 Beav 129; *Sichel v Mosenthal* (1862) 30 Beav 371. See Lindley and Banks on *Partnership*, 18th edn, pp 23–46.

(K) CONTRACTS TO LEAVE PROPERTY BY WILL

In these cases, an action for damages will clearly lie against the covenantor's estate if the contract is not carried out, and the Court of Appeal had no doubt, in *Synge v Synge*,[148] of the power of the court, where the contract related to a defined piece of real property, to decree a conveyance of that property after the death of the covenantor against all persons claiming under him as volunteers.[149] Specific performance will not, however, be decreed where the covenantor is merely donee of a testamentary power of appointment.[150]

3 DEFENCES TO AN ACTION FOR SPECIFIC PERFORMANCE

(A) MISREPRESENTATION AND MISTAKE

As we shall see,[151] both misrepresentation and mistake[152] may be grounds for rescission, and, in such cases, will *a fortiori* be a defence to an action for specific performance. Both pleas have, however, a wider scope for the latter purpose. Misrepresentation, even though not sufficient to induce a court to rescind a contract, may be sufficient to defeat a claim for specific performance,[153] the point being that rescission has the drastic effect of avoiding the contract for all purposes, while refusing specific performance leaves it open to the claimant to seek other remedies, such as damages. It is commonly the wiser course to seek rescission, if this is possible, rather than to wait to raise the defence of misrepresentation if a specific performance action is brought[154]—particularly as, in the latter case, the burden of proof rests on the defendant to show that he repudiated the contract upon, or at least within a reasonable time after, discovery of the truth.[155]

Mistake may be a defence to a specific performance action even where there has been a mistake in a popular, rather than a technical, sense. This does not mean that a man can be careless in entering into a contract, and then avoid liability simply by alleging or even proving that he did so under a mistake,[156] because to allow this would open the door to

---

[148] [1894] 1 QB 466, CA; *Schaefer v Schuhmann* [1972] AC 572, [1972] 1 All ER 621, PC.

[149] There seems no reason to doubt that other persons may be bound by the equitable interest and liable to specific performance according to the ordinary rules.

[150] *Re Parkin* [1892] 3 Ch 510; *Re Evered* [1910] 2 Ch 147, CA; *Re Coake* [1922] 1 Ch 292.

[151] Chapter 29, section 3(C), *infra*.

[152] Mistake may also give the court jurisdiction to rectify the contract. See Chapter 29, section 4, *infra*.

[153] *Re Banister* (1879) 12 Ch D 131, 142, CA; *Re Terry and White's Contract* (1886) 32 Ch D 14, 29, CA. As to the duty of a vendor to disclose defects in title of which he is aware, see *Faruqi v English Real Estates Ltd* [1979] 1 WLR 963.

[154] *Fenn v Craig* (1838) 3 Y & C Ex 216, 222; Cf *Aaron's Reefs Ltd v Twiss* [1896] AC 273, 293, HL.

[155] *United Shoe Machinery Co of Canada v Brunet* [1909] AC 330, 338, PC; *First National Reinsurance Co v Greenfield* [1921] 2 KB 260, 266, DC.

[156] *Goddard v Jeffreys* (1881) 51 LJ Ch 57; *Tamplin v James* (1880) 15 Ch D 215, CA. Cf *Williams v Bulot* [1992] 2 Qd R 566, in which it was held no defence to an action for specific performance that the defendant would only have been prepared to sell at a much higher price if he had known that the other contracting party was the undisclosed agent of the claimant.

perjury and fraud. If, however, he can establish that he made a bona fide mistake and that he had a reasonable ground for the mistake, it may well be thought inequitable to grant specific performance. This is likely to be the case where the claimant has contributed to the defendant's mistake,[157] even though unintentionally.[158] Thus, in *Denny v Hancock*,[159] on a sale by auction, the plan annexed to the particulars showed, on the western side, a shrubbery with an iron fence outside it, and, within the fence, three very large and fine elm trees. He successfully bid for the property, in the belief that he was buying everything up to the fence, but the real boundary was denoted by stumps largely concealed by shrubs, and the elm trees were outside it. It was held, on appeal, that the defendant's mistake was induced by the plan for which the vendors were responsible, and the vendor's specific performance action was accordingly dismissed. Further, Lord Macnaghten has said[160] that it cannot be disputed that a unilateral mistake by the defendant may be a good defence to a specific performance action even when the mistake has not been induced or contributed to by any act or omission on the part of the claimant, although most of such cases have been cases in which a hardship amounting to injustice would have been inflicted upon the defendant by holding him to his bargain, and it was unreasonable to hold him to it. It has, indeed, been judicially suggested[161] that some of the cases have gone too far. *Malins v Freeman*[162] may, perhaps, be one of these cases, in which specific performance was refused against a purchaser, whose agent had mistakenly bid for the wrong property, the mistake being an unreasonable one not in any way contributed to by the vendor.

The mistake has, in effect, been held to a reasonable one and specific performance refused, where it was caused by some ambiguity, even though the defendant was the author of the ambiguity.[163] One case is *Webster v Cecil*,[164] in which the defendant, due to an arithmetical error, offered his property to the plaintiff for £1,250, instead of £2,250. The claimant, although his previous offer of £2,200 had been refused and he must have known of the mistake, accepted the offer and brought his action for specific performance. The action was dismissed. A case may arise for refusing specific performance in which, through the ignorance, neglect, or error of the vendor's agent, property not intended to be sold is included in the sale.[165]

(B) HARDSHIP AND WANT OF FAIRNESS

Even though there may not be fraud or other vitiating element that would support a claim for rescission, unfairness or hardship on the defendant, or oppression or sharp practice on the part of the claimant may be a sufficient reason for the court to refuse a decree of

---

[157] *Higginson v Clowes* (1808) 15 Ves 516; *Moxey v Bigwood* (1862) 4 De GF & J 351.

[158] *Baskcomb v Beckwith* (1869) LR 8 Eq 100; *Bray v Briggs* (1872) 26 LT 817.

[159] (1870) 6 Ch App 1.

[160] In *Stewart v Kennedy* (1890) 15 App Cas 75, 105, HL; *Jones v Rimmer* (1880) 14 Ch D 588, CA.

[161] *Tamplin v James, supra, per* James LJ, at 221.

[162] (1836) 2 Keen 25, doubted by Kekewich J in *Van Praagh v Everidge* [1902] 2 Ch 266, revsd on another ground [1903] 1 Ch 434, CA.

[163] *Butterworth v Walker* (1864) 11 LT 436; *Wycombe Rly Co v Donnington Hospital* (1866) 1 Ch App 268; *Douglas v Baynes* [1908] AC 477, PC.

[164] (1861) 30 Beav 62. See the comment of James LJ in *Tamplin v James, supra*, at 221. See also *Deputy Comr of Taxation (NSW) v Chamberlain* (1990) 93 ALR 729.

[165] *Leslie v Tompson* (1851) 9 Hare 268; *Re Hare and O'More's Contract* [1901] 1 Ch 93.

specific performance, while leaving open the possibility of a claim for damages.[166] Mere inadequacy of consideration is not, however, by itself, a ground for refusing a decree, even though it may, in fact, cause considerable hardship to the defendant,[167] and this principle applies to a sale at a valuation. Thus specific performance was granted[168] where it was admitted that the valuation appeared very high and perhaps exorbitant, in the absence of any other factor such as fraud, mistake, or misconduct by the valuer, but the additional presence of any of these factors may be a defence to such a claim.[169] On the same principle, it is no defence that the purpose for which the defendant entered into the contract cannot be carried out, as where he had purchased a lease and it turned out that the activities intended to be carried on there were prohibited by the lease.[170] Inadequacy of consideration may, however, be an important factor where combined with other circumstances,[171] and may be evidence—and, in an extreme case, conclusive evidence—of fraud.[172]

Questions of fairness, hardship, and the like are normally to be judged as at the time when the contract was entered into,[173] and subsequent events are, in general, irrelevant. Exceptionally, specific performance may be refused because of a change of circumstances subsequent to the contract such that a decree of specific performance would inflict on the defendant 'a hardship amounting to injustice'.[174] This is particularly the case where the hardship is attributable to the claimant;[175] the more so if his conduct has acted as a trap for the defendant, even though unintentionally.[176] But, clearly, hardship that the defendant has brought upon himself is no defence.[177]

In deciding questions as to the fairness of a contract, the court considers the surrounding circumstances: if the consideration is inadequate and there are suspicious circumstances, the court may refuse a decree, although there may not be enough to enable it to set the contract aside. Relevant factors may include weakness of mind (not amounting to insanity), age, illiteracy, poverty, want of advice, and financial distress.[178] The fact that

---

[166] *Willan v Willan* (1810) 16 Ves 72; *Martin v Mitchell* (1820) 2 Jac & W 413. Jones and Goodhart, *Specific Performance*, 2nd edn, p 113, point out that, in most of the more recent cases in which a court has refused to order specific performance on the ground of unfair conduct, it has also set aside the contract.

[167] *Kimberley v Jennings* (1836) 6 Sim 340. It is submitted that the early cases to the contrary, followed in *Falcke v Gray* (1859) 4 Drew 651, are no longer good law.

[168] *Collier v Mason* (1858) 25 Beav 200; *Weekes v Gallard* (1869) 21 LT 655.

[169] *Chichester v M'Intire* (1830) 4 Bli NS 78; *Eads v Williams* (1854) 4 De GM & G 674.

[170] *Morley v Clavering* (1860) 29 Beav 84; *Haywood v Cope* (1858) 25 Beav 140.

[171] *Cockell v Taylor* (1851) 15 Beav 103; and see *James v Morgan* (1663) 1 Lev 111 (the geometric progression trick where a horse was sold at a barleycorn a nail, doubling it for each nail on the horse's feet). See also *K v K* [1976] NZLR 31.

[172] *Griffith v Spratley* (1787) 1 Cox Eq Cas 383; *Stilwell v Wilkins* (1821) Jac 280.

[173] *Francis v Cowcliffe Ltd* (1976) 239 EG 977 (financial inability to complete not hardship; specific performance decreed although it was said that it would inevitably result in the defendant company being wound up). See *Stewart v Ambrosina* (1975) 63 DLR (3d) 595; *Roberts v O'Neil* [1981] ILRM 403.

[174] *Patel v Ali* [1984] Ch 283, [1984] 1 All ER 978, in which long delay was also a factor. See (1984) 134 NLJ 927 & 949 (J A Priest); (1984) 100 LQR 337.

[175] *Duke of Bedford v British Museum Trustees* (1822) 2 My & K 552; *Shell UK Ltd v Lostock Garage Ltd* [1976] 1 WLR 1187, 1202, CA, esp per Ormrod LJ.

[176] *Dowson v Solomon* (1859) 1 Drew & Sm 1.

[177] *Storer v Great Western Rly Co* (1842) 2 Y & C Ch Cas 48.

[178] *Martin v Mitchell* (1820) 2 Jac & W 413; *Stanley v Robinson* (1830) 1 Russ & M 527; *Huttges v Verner* (1975) 64 DLR (3d) 374. Cf *Mountford v Scott* [1975] Ch 258, [1975] 1 All ER 198, CA (decree granted although defendant could not read; he was intelligent, had been given an oral explanation, and the price was adequate).

an agreement was obtained from the defendant while he was intoxicated may also be a defence.[179] The question is whether, in all of the circumstances, it would be unfair and inequitable to grant specific performance. It is not, on the other hand, necessary to show any intentional unfairness or misconduct on the part of the claimant.[180]

In general, the court will not grant specific performance of an agreement relating to a lease if the consequence would be a forfeiture,[181] although it is, of course, otherwise if the state of affairs is due to the defendant's own acts.[182] Cases in which specific performance was refused on the ground of hardship include: *Wedgwood v Adams*,[183] in which trustees personally undertook with the purchaser of trust property to see it freed from incumbrances, and it appeared that the purchase money would be inadequate to an uncertain extent; *Denne v Light*,[184] in which the purchaser might have found himself with no means of access to his land; and *Hope v Walter*,[185] in which the court refused to 'thrust down the throat of an innocent buyer the obligation of becoming the landlord of a brothel'.

The hardship or unfairness that may cause the court to refuse a decree may be suffered by a third party,[186] rather than the defendant.[187] In particular, the court will not normally grant specific performance if this would necessarily involve breach of a prior contract with a third party,[188] or would require a person to do an act that he is not lawfully competent to do.[189] And an order for partial performance was refused, in *Thames Guaranty Ltd v Campbell*,[190] of a husband's contract to create an equitable charge, because an order, if made, would expose the wife to proceedings under s 30 of the Law of Property Act 1925,[191] likely to result in an order for sale of the matrimonial home that she occupied. Again, there are many cases in which the court has refused a decree against trustees on the ground that performance by them would constitute a breach of trust,[192] or even that it is reasonably and seriously doubtful whether it is a breach of trust.[193] If, however, an innocent breach of trust has already been committed as a result of a contract, the court may grant specific performance and compel the other party to carry out his part of the bargain.[194]

---

[179] *Cooke v Clayworth* (1811) 18 Ves 12; *Cox v Smith* (1868) 19 LT 517. Cf *Matthews v Baxter* (1873) LR 8 Exch 132. *Lightfoot v Heron* (1839) 3 Y & C Ex 586.

[180] *Mortlock v Buller* (1804) 10 Ves 292; *Huttges v Verner, supra*.

[181] *Helling v Lumley* (1858) 3 De G & J 493; *Warmington v Miller* [1973] QB 877, [1973] 2 All ER 372, CA.

[182] *Helling v Lumley, supra*.   [183] (1843) 6 Beav 600; *Watson v Marston* (1853) 4 De GM & G 230.

[184] (1857) 8 De GM & G 774 (the judgment of Knight Bruce LJ is worth reading for its entertainment value alone).

[185] [1900] 1 Ch 257, 258, CA, *per* Lindley MR; *Talbot v Ford* (1842) 13 Sim 173.

[186] But not, *semble*, by the public: *Raphael v Thames Valley Rly Co* (1866) LR 2 Eq 37; revsd (1867) 2 Ch App 147. *Aliter* if it would be a fraud on the public: *Post v Marsh* (1880) 16 Ch D 395.

[187] *Thomas v Dering* (1837) 1 Keen 729; *McKewan v Sanderson* (1875) LR 20 Eq 65.

[188] *Willmott v Barber* (1880) 15 Ch D 96; *Manchester Ship Canal Co v Manchester Racecourse Co* [1901] 2 Ch 37, CA; (*Earl*) *Sefton v Tophams Ltd* [1965] Ch 1140, [1965] 3 All ER 1, CA. This point was not discussed on appeal sub nom *Tophams Ltd v (Earl) Sefton* [1967] 1 AC 50, [1966] 1 All ER 1039, HL.

[189] *Tolson v Sheard* (1877) 5 Ch D 19, CA; *Warmington v Miller, supra*, CA.

[190] [1985] QB 210, [1984] 2 All ER 585, CA. The husband, now bankrupt, who was co-owner with his wife, had purported to charge the whole legal and beneficial interest.

[191] This section has been repealed and replaced by s 14 of the Trusts of Land and Appointment of Trustees Act 1996.

[192] *Maw v Topham* (1854) 19 Beav 576.   [193] *Rede v Oakes* (1864) 4 De GJ & Sm 505.

[194] *Briggs v Parsloe* [1937] 3 All ER 831.

(C) RIGHTS OF THIRD PARTIES

In contracts for the sale of land, problems have sometimes arisen where a purchaser has sought specific performance against a vendor who is unable to give a good title without the consent of some third person, or where he has contracted to give vacant possession and some third person is in possession. Megarry J summarized the position in *Wroth v Tyler*[195] as follows:

> A vendor must do his best to obtain any necessary consent to the sale; if he has sold with vacant possession he must, if necessary, take proceedings to obtain possession from any person in possession who has no right to be there or whose right is determinable by the vendor, at all events if the vendor's right to possession is reasonably clear; but I do not think that the vendor will usually be required to embark on difficult or uncertain litigation in order to secure any requisite consent or obtain vacant possession. Where the outcome of any litigation depends on disputed facts, difficult questions of law or the exercise of a discretionary jurisdiction, then I think the court would be slow to make a decree of specific performance against the vendor which would require him to undertake such litigation.

In *Wroth v Tyler*[196] itself, the judge refused to decree specific performance, which would compel the defendant to take legal proceedings against his wife, who had, after the contract and without his knowledge, registered rights of occupation under the Matrimonial Homes Act 1967,[197] and with whom he was still living.

If, however, a defendant vendor has it in his power to compel a third party to convey the property in question, specific performance will be decreed against the defendant. Indeed, an order may be made against the third party if it is the creature of the defendant, such as a limited company in the defendant's ownership and control.[198]

(D) CONDUCT OF THE CLAIMANT

In general, a claimant who seeks specific performance must 'come with clean hands'—that is he must have fulfilled all conditions precedent and performed, or at least have tendered performance of all of the terms of the contract that he has been under a duty to perform—and he must, seeking equity, be prepared to do equity—that is, to perform all of his future obligations under the contract.[199] It has been held that a contractual term purporting to oust this principle cannot fetter the courts' discretion to grant or refuse specific performance after taking account of the claimant's conduct.[200]

---

[195] [1974] Ch 30, 50, [1973] 1 All ER 897, 913.

[196] *Supra; Watts v Spence* [1976] Ch 165, [1975] 2 All ER 528. On the damages award in the latter case, see *Sharneyford Supplies Ltd v Edge* [1987] Ch 305, [1987] 1 All ER 588, CA.

[197] Now replaced by the Family Law Act 1996.

[198] *Jones v Lipman* [1962] 1 All ER 442, [1962] 1 WLR 832.

[199] *Australian Hardwoods Pty Ltd v Railways Comr* [1961] 1 All ER 737, 742, PC; *Chappell v Times Newspapers Ltd* [1975] 2 All ER 233, [1975] ICR 145, CA. A defence alleging that a wife claiming specific performance did not come to equity with clean hands because of the conduct of her husband was rightly held to be unarguable in *Boulding Group plc v Newett* (1991) Independent, 24 June, CA. As to the correct approach where there are alleged improprieties on both sides, see *Sang Lee Investment Co Ltd v Wing Kwai Investment Co Ltd* (1983) Times, 14 April, PC.

[200] *Quadrant Visual Communications Ltd v Hutchinson Telephone (UK) Ltd* [1993] BCLC 442, CA. See [1992] CLJ 263 (C Harpum).

Firstly, it is clear that where a contract is subject to the performance of some condition precedent, there can be no decree of specific performance unless and until the condition has been performed.[201] Thus specific performance has been refused of a covenant to renew a lease conditional on compliance with repairing covenants,[202] and of an agreement to take a lease of a public house conditional on the grant of a licence,[203] where the respective conditions had not been fulfilled. The condition remains capable of fulfilment, in a case between vendor and purchaser, at any time until the time fixed for completion of the contract.[204] Conditions may be express or implied, as a matter of construction of the contract,[205] and the performance of a condition precedent may be waived by the person or persons who alone benefit therefrom.[206]

Turning to the terms of the contract, the claimant must be able to show that he has performed all of the essential terms of the contract, express or implied, which he was under a duty to have performed by the time at which the writ was issued.[207] The breach of a non-essential or trivial term is not, however, necessarily fatal to a specific performance action,[208] nor is it absolutely vital to show the exact performance that would be required at law.[209] Non-performance of a term by the claimant cannot be used as a defence where the defendant has waived performance,[210] or where non-performance has been caused by the defendant's acts or defaults.[211] Moreover, if the term that has not been performed is independent and collateral to the contract sought to be enforced, even though contained in the same document, the non-performance will not prevent specific performance being obtained.[212] If there is a stipulation in the contract intended to benefit the claimant, he may waive it and obtain specific performance, provided that the stipulation is in terms for the exclusive benefit of the claimant.[213]

Somewhat similar to what has just been discussed are the cases that show that a claimant who has repudiated his obligation under a contract, or who has done acts at variance with it, may be refused specific performance. Thus, an employer who has wrongfully dismissed a servant cannot specifically enforce a term in restraint of trade contained in the service contract,[214] and a vendor who, having given possession under the contract, repossesses the property cannot obtain specific performance.[215] There is also a line of cases

---

[201] *Regent's Canal Co v Ware* (1857) 23 Beav 575; *Scott v Liverpool Corpn* (1858) 3 De G & J 334.

[202] *Bastin v Bidwell* (1881) 18 Ch D 238; *Greville v Parker* [1910] AC 335, PC.

[203] *Modlen v Snowball* (1861) 4 De GF & J 143.

[204] *Smith v Butler* [1900] 1 QB 694, CA; *Re Sandwell Park Colliery Co* [1929] 1 Ch 277; *Aberfoyle Plantations Ltd v Cheng* [1960] AC 115, [1959] 3 All ER 910, PC.

[205] *Williams v Brisco* (1882) 22 Ch D 441, CA.

[206] See *Graham v Pitkin* [1992] 2 All ER 235, [1991] 1 WLR 403, PC, discussed [1992] Conv 318 (C Harpum).

[207] *Modlen v Snowball* (1861) 4 De GF & J 143; *Tildesley v Clarkson* (1862) 30 Beav 419.

[208] *Dyster v Randall & Sons* [1926] Ch 932; cf *Oxford v Provand* (1868) LR 2 PC 135.

[209] *Davis v Hone* (1805) 2 Sch & Lef 341.   [210] *Lamare v Dixon* (1873) LR 6 HL 414.

[211] *Murrell v Goodyear* (1860) 1 De GF & J 432.

[212] *Green v Low* (1856) 22 Beav 625; *Phipps v Child* (1857) 3 Drew 709.

[213] *Heron Garage Properties Ltd v Moss* [1974] 1 All ER 421, noted (1974) 33 CLJ 211 (R J Smith); *Federated Homes Ltd v Turner* (1974) 233 Estates Gazette 845, and see (1975) 39 Conv 251 (S Robinson). Cf *Scott v Bradley* [1971] Ch 850, [1971] 1 All ER 583. See also *BICC plc v Burndy Corpn* [1985] Ch 232, [1985] 1 All ER 417, CA, noted (1985) 101 LQR 146.

[214] *Measures Bros Ltd v Measures* [1910] 2 Ch 248, CA.

[215] *Knatchbull v Grueber* (1815) 1 Madd 153; affd (1817) 3 Mer 124.

that shows that a tenant under an agreement for a lease who is in breach of his obligations thereunder cannot compel a lease to be granted.[216] Again, the act must not be merely trivial and unsubstantial,[217] and the doctrine of waiver applies.[218]

Failure to perform representations that induced the defendant to enter into the contract may also be a defence to a claim for specific performance, even though the representations were not such as would ground an action at law.[219] Further, the claimant must be ready and willing to perform all of the terms of the contract that have yet to be performed by him. Thus, a purchaser who has committed an available act of bankruptcy of which the vendor has notice cannot enforce the contract, because he is incapable of so paying the purchase money to the vendor as that the latter shall be certain of being able to retain it against the trustees, should bankruptcy supervene.[220] And in one case, the fact that the vendor could not produce the title deeds, which had been destroyed by fire, prevented him from getting specific performance.[221]

(E) LACHES

In equity, in general, the rule has always been that time is not of the essence of the contract—that is, of the particular contractual term that has been breached[222]—and, accordingly, a claimant may obtain specific performance even though he has not performed the terms of the contract to be carried out by him at the time specified.[223] The parties may, however, agree that time should be of the essence of the contract, in which case, specific performance will not be granted if the time limit has not been observed by the claimant as to his part.[224] Likewise, the circumstances of the case or the subject matter of the contract may indicate that the time for completion is of the essence, and even though not originally of the essence, time may be made of the essence by serving an appropriate notice at the proper time.[225]

---

[216] *Coatsworth v Johnson* (1885) 55 LJQB 220, CA; *Swain v Ayres* (1888) 21 QBD 289, CA. See (1960) 24 Conv 125 (P H Pettit); *Equity and Contemporary Legal Developments* (ed S Goldstein), p 829 (C Harpum).

[217] *Parker v Taswell* (1858) 2 De G & J 559; *Besant v Wood* (1879) 12 Ch D 605.

[218] *Gregory v Wilson* (1852) 9 Hare 683.

[219] *Myers v Watson* (1851) 1 Sim NS 523; *Lamare v Dixon, supra.*

[220] *Dyster v Randall & Sons* [1926] Ch 932. Similarly as to the vendor's bankruptcy: *Lowes v Lush* (1808) 14 Ves 547.

[221] *Bryant v Busk* (1827) 4 Russ 1. But secondary evidence may suffice: *Moulton v Edmonds* (1859) 1 De GF & J 246.

[222] *British and Commonwealth Holdings plc v Quadrex Holding Inc* [1989] 3 All ER 492, 504, *per* Browne-Wilkinson VC.

[223] Compare s 41 of the Law of Property Act 1925, replacing s 25(7) of the Judicature Act 1873, and note *Raineri v Miles* [1981] AC 1050, [1980] 2 All ER 145, HL, in which it was held that damages may be available for failure to adhere to the original completion date.

[224] *Steedman v Drinkle* [1916] 1 AC 275, PC; *Union Eagle Ltd v Golden Achievement Ltd* [1997] 2 All ER 215, PC (order refused where purchaser 10 minutes late), noted (1997) 113 LQR 385 (J D Heydon); [1997] Conv 382 (M P Thompson); (1998) 61 MLR 255 (J Stevens).

[225] *Behzadi v Shaftesbury Hotels Ltd* [1992] Ch 1, [1991] 2 All ER 477, CA, noted (1991) 107 LQR 536 (P V Baker).

Even though time is not of the essence of the contract, delay by the claimant[226] in performing his part, or in bringing proceedings, may defeat his claim to specific performance. It has been said that the claimant must come to the court promptly, and as soon as the nature of the case will permit,[227] but Megarry VC observed,[228] in a case in which over two years' delay was held not to be a bar, that specific performance should not be regarded as a prize to be awarded by equity to the zealous and denied to the indolent. In his view, if it is just that the claimant should obtain a decree, it should not be withheld merely because he has been guilty of delay. It is not settled whether simple delay, where there is no evidence that the defendant or any third party has altered his position in the meantime, will suffice.[229] Three-and-a-half years' delay was a good defence in *Eads v Williams*,[230] and less than two years in *Lord James Stuart v London and North Western Rly Co*.[231] As little as three-and-a-half months was held to be enough in *Glasbrook v Richardson*,[232] a case concerning the sale of a colliery, said however to be 'a property of an extremely speculative character, approaching a trade' to which special considerations applied.

If the writ has been issued promptly, it seems that delay in bringing the action to trial will not normally defeat the claimant's claim to specific performance. This result will only follow if the claimant by his conduct has lulled the defendant into a belief that he is going to ask for damages only and not specific performance.[233]

Laches will not, however, defeat a claim nearly so soon, if at all, where the claimant is in possession and is the equitable owner, and the action is brought merely to clothe the claimant with the legal estate. Thus, in such circumstances, specific performance was decreed of an agreement for a lease after eighteen years' delay in *Sharp v Milligan*,[234] and of a contract for the sale of land after ten years in *Williams v Greatrex*.[235] To have this effect, the possession of the claimant must be possession under the contract.[236] It may well be different where the transaction that brought the proprietary interest into being is disputed.[237]

It need hardly be said that the defendant may waive, or by his conduct be deemed to have waived, the defence on the ground of laches.[238]

The six-year limitation period applicable to an action founded on a simple contract does not apply by analogy to a claim for specific performance.[239]

---

[226] Whether vendor or purchaser: *Rich v Gale* (1871) 24 LT 745.

[227] *Eads v Williams* (1854) 4 De GM & G 674.

[228] *Lazard Bros & Co Ltd v Fairfield Properties Co (Mayfair) Ltd* (1977) 121 Sol Jo 793.

[229] See *P & O Nedlloyd BV v Arab Metals Co (No 2)* [2006] EWCA Civ 1717, [2007] 1 WLR 2288, *per* Moore-Bick LJ, at [61].

[230] *Supra.*   [231] (1852) 1 De GM & G 721.

[232] (1874) 23 WR 51. Cf *Wroth v Tyler* [1974] Ch 30, [1973] 1 All ER 897.

[233] *Du Sautoy v Symes* [1967] Ch 1146, [1967] 1 All ER 25. As to delay in enforcing a decree once obtained, see *Easton v Brown* [1981] 3 All ER 278.

[234] (1856) 22 Beav 606; *Shepheard v Walker* (1875) LR 20 Eq 659.

[235] [1956] 3 All ER 705, CA, applying a dictum of Lord Redesdale in *Crofton v Ormsby* (1806) 2 Sch & Lef 583, who contemplated forty or fifty years' delay. See *Frawley v Neill* (1999) 143 Sol Jo LB 98, CA.

[236] *Mills v Haywood* (1877) 6 Ch D 196, CA.

[237] *Joyce v Joyce* [1979] 1 All ER 175, [1978] 1 WLR 1170.

[238] *Seton v Slade* (1802) 7 Ves 265; *King v Wilson* (1843) 6 Beav 124.

[239] Limitation Act 1980, s 36; *P & O Nedlloyd BV Arab Metals Co (No 2)* [2006] EWCA Civ 1717, [2007] 1 WLR 2288.

(F) ABSENCE OF WRITING

Section 2(1) of the Law of Property (Miscellaneous Provisions) Act 1989,[240] which provides that *'A contract for the sale or other disposition of an interest in land can only be made in writing and only by incorporating all the terms which the parties have expressly agreed in one document or, where contracts are exchanged, in each'*, applies just as much to a claim for specific performance as to a claim for damages. It is more stringent than s 40 of the Law of Property Act 1925, which it repeals and replaces, and is generally thought to leave no scope for the application of the doctrine of part-performance.[241]

Where the 1989 Act applies, specific performance of the void contract cannot be obtained, but in some circumstances, a remedy may be available on the basis of propri-etary estoppel or constructive trust.[242]

---

[240] As amended by the Trusts of Land and Appointment of Trustees Act 1996.

[241] See *Yaxley v Gotts* [2000] Ch 162, [2000] 1 All ER 711, CA, which silences the doubts expressed by Neill LJ in *Singh v Beggs* (1996) 71 P & CR 120, CA. See also *Grossman v Harper* [2001] 2 EGLR 82, CA; [2002] Conv 216 (G Griffiths).

[242] See pp 213, 214, *supra*.

29

OTHER EQUITABLE REMEDIES

The Court of Chancery invented a number of other remedies to deal with particular situations and these are considered below. The power to appoint a receiver is still regarded as an equitable remedy, although, like the grant of an injunction, it is now statutory under s 37 of the Supreme Court Act 1981, now renamed the Senior Courts Act 1981.

1 THE APPOINTMENT OF A RECEIVER, OR RECEIVER AND MANAGER

(A) RECEIVERS

The jurisdiction of the Court of Chancery to appoint a receiver has been said to be one of the oldest equitable remedies.[1] It is now statutory and, like an injunction, may be granted 'in all cases in which it appears to the court to be just and convenient to do so'.[2] A receiver may be appointed, on the one hand, in order to preserve property that is in danger, or, on the other hand, to enable a person to obtain the benefit of his rights over property, or to obtain payment of his debt, where the legal remedies are inadequate. Generally, the appointment may extend over any form of property,[3] provided that it is capable of assignment, but there are important restrictions, which are discussed later,[4] on the kinds of property over which a receiver by way of equitable execution may be appointed. A receiver has been described[5] as 'a person who receives rents or other income paying ascertained outgoings, but who does not...manage the property in the sense of buying or selling or anything of that kind'. This description is not comprehensive, because the purpose of the appointment may be simply to preserve property pending the settlement of legal proceedings, the property in the meantime bringing in no income. It is the duty of a receiver to take

---

[1] *Hopkins v Worcester and Birmingham Canal Proprietors* (1868) LR 6 Eq 437, 447, *per* Giffard VC; *A-G v Schonfeld* [1980] 3 All ER 1, 5, *per* Megarry VC.

[2] Supreme Court Act 1981, now renamed the Senior Courts Act 1981, s 37(1), (2). See also CPR Sch 1, RSC Ord 30.

[3] Including property situated out of the jurisdiction: *C Inc plc v L* [2001] 2 All ER (Comm) 446.

[4] See p 683 *et seq, infra.*

[5] *Per* Jessel MR in *Re Manchester and Milford Rly Co* (1880) 14 Ch D 645, 653, CA.

possession of the relevant property, and the order appointing him will usually direct any parties to the action in possession to deliver it up to him.

A person appointed receiver may be required to give security[6] for what he receives as such receiver; the appointment may be conditional upon security being given, or the receiver may be ordered to give security by a given date, with liberty to act at once, on an undertaking by the applicant to be answerable for what he receives or becomes liable to pay.

In so far as the appointment of a receiver is made as a protective measure, it is an *in personam* remedy, It is only when an English court orders the money received to be paid out to the judgment creditor that any *in rem* effect takes place.[7]

(B) MANAGERS

Where it is desired to continue a trade or business, it is not sufficient to appoint a receiver, because, as we have seen, he has no authority for this purpose. Although not so old a remedy as appointing a receiver,[8] the court has for many years, however, had jurisdiction for this purpose to appoint a manager, and, normally, the same person is appointed and known as the receiver and manager.[9] The effect is that the management of the business is carried on by the court, through its officer, but the court will do this only for a limited period of time, for the purpose of preserving the assets:[10] 'Nothing is better settled than that this Court does not assume the management of a business or undertaking except with a view to the winding up and sale of the business or undertaking.'[11] Accordingly, in the first instance, a manager will not normally be appointed for longer than three months, although this may be extended from time to time if a proper case is made out.

(C) WHO MAY BE APPOINTED AS RECEIVER, OR
RECEIVER AND MANAGER

Any party to the action, but not a stranger thereto,[12] may nominate a person to be appointed as receiver. In making the appointment, the general principle is that the person appointed, who must be an individual,[13] should be independent and impartial. Prima facie, therefore, the court will not appoint a party to the action,[14] or anyone who has shown a partiality for one of the parties,[15] or whose interest may conflict with his duties.[16] Again, the court will not normally appoint a person who should act as a check on the receiver. Thus a trustee will not normally be appointed receiver of the trust property, because the beneficiaries should be able to rely on him to control the receiver,[17] nor will the court appoint the next friend of

---

[6] CPR, Pt 69.5.

[7] *Masu v Consolidated Contractors International UK Ltd (No 2)* [2007] EWHC 3010 (Comm), [2008] 1 All ER (Comm) 305.

[8] *Re Newdigate Colliery Ltd* [1912] 1 Ch 468, CA.

[9] *Re Manchester and Milford Rly Co* (1880) 14 Ch D 645, 653, CA.

[10] *Waters v Taylor* (1808) 15 Ves 10; *Taylor v Neate* (1888) 39 Ch D 538.

[11] *Gardner v London Chatham and Dover Rly Co (No 2)* (1867) 2 Ch App 201, 212, *per* Cairns LJ; *Re Andrews* [1999] 2 All ER 751, CA.

[12] *A-G v Day* (1817) 2 Madd 246.   [13] CPR Part 69.2(2).   [14] *Re Lloyd* (1879) 12 Ch D 447, CA.

[15] *Blakeway v Blakeway* (1833) 2 LJ Ch 75; *Wright v Vernon* (1855) 3 Drew 112.

[16] *Fripp v Chard Rly Co* (1853) 11 Hare 241.

[17] *Sykes v Hastings* (1805) 11 Ves 363; *Sutton v Jones* (1809) 15 Ves 584.

a minor claimant.[18] Similarly, the court will not normally appoint the solicitor having the conduct of the case,[19] nor any member of the firm of solicitors acting for the claimant.[20]

The court may, however, and frequently does, depart from this general principle if the parties consent—and even without their consent, if a proper case is made out. Thus, if a receiver is appointed on the dissolution of a partnership, a solvent partner will usually be appointed as receiver, if he has not behaved improperly,[21] in order that the partnership business may be wound up to the best advantage of all concerned.[22] Again, where a company is in liquidation, and the duties to be performed by the liquidator and the receiver are identical, the court will, in general, appoint the liquidator as receiver to avoid additional expense and to prevent conflict between them.[23] However, in *Boyle v Bettws Llantwit Colliery Co*,[24] the claimants successfully applied to be appointed receivers. They were the unpaid vendors of the property of a company in voluntary liquidation. The liquidator had no funds to reopen the colliery or carry on the workings, while the claimants, who were said to be 'really the owners of the colliery',[25] were willing to provide funds for this purpose.

A minor cannot be appointed as receiver.[26] In an old case,[27] the court refused to appoint a peer on the ground that parliamentary privilege would protect him from the ordinary remedies against a receiver; however, a member of the House of Commons was appointed in *Wiggin v Anderson*.[28] And where a receiver and manager is to be appointed, which will involve trading, it seems that a beneficed clergyman of the Church of England[29] is ineligible, as is a practising barrister. Moreover, by statute,[30] a body corporate is not qualified for appointment as receiver[31] of the property of a company, and it is an offence for an undischarged bankrupt to act as receiver or manager of a company on behalf of debenture holders,[32] save in the unlikely event of his being appointed by the court. An administrative receiver, as defined in s 29(2) of the Insolvency Act 1986, must be an individual—that is, a natural person—who is qualified to act as an insolvency practitioner.

Two or more persons may be appointed as joint receivers,[33] or, exceptionally, as separate receivers of different parts of the assets.[34]

---

[18] *Stone v Wishart* (1817) 2 Madd 64, nor the son of the next friend in *Taylor v Oldham* (1822) Jac 527.

[19] *Garland v Garland* (1793) 2 Ves 137.   [20] *Re Lloyd, supra.*

[21] *Young v Buckett* (1882) 51 LJ Ch 504.

[22] *Collins v Barker* [1893] 1 Ch 578; *Harrison-Broadley v Smith* [1964] 1 All ER 867, 872, CA.

[23] *Re Joshua Stubbs Ltd* [1891] 1 Ch 475, CA; *British Linen Co v South American and Mexican Co* [1894] 1 Ch 108, CA.

[24] (1876) 2 Ch D 726.   [25] At 728.   [26] Co Litt 171b, 172a.

[27] *A-G v Gee* (1813) 2 Ves & B 208, but see *Re Gent* (1888) 40 Ch D 190; *Earl of Aylesford v Earl Poulett* [1892] 2 Ch 60.

[28] (1982, unreported), but referred to in Picarda, *The Law relating to Receivers, Managers and Administrators*, 3rd edn, p 357. See, however, *Re Armstrong* [1892] 1 QB 327.

[29] Pluralities Act 1838, s 29.

[30] Insolvency Act 1986, s 30; *Portman Building Society v Gallwey* [1955] 1 All ER 227.

[31] The disqualification apparently does not apply to appointment as manager.

[32] Insolvency Act 1986, s 31.   [33] *Duder v Amsterdamsch Trustees Kantoor* [1902] 2 Ch 132.

[34] *British Linen Co v South American and Mexican Co* [1894] 1 Ch 108, CA.

(D) REMUNERATION

It has always been a basic principle of receivership that the receiver is entitled to be indemnified in respect of his costs, expenses, and remuneration, if he is entitled to remuneration, out of the assets in his hands as receiver. He has no personal claim, however, against the parties to the action, even if they all consented to his appointment.[35] In most cases, it would be an extreme hardship to the parties if they were to be held personally liable for expenses incurred by receivers over which they have no control. The matter of remuneration is now governed by the procedural code set out in the Civil Procedure Rules, Pt 69,[36] which does not make any fundamental change in the law. The code provides that a receiver may only charge for his services if the court:

  (i) so directs; and

  (ii) specifies the basis on which the receiver is to be remunerated.[37]

Unless the court orders otherwise, in determining the remuneration of a receiver, it will award such sum as is reasonable and proportionate in all of the circumstances.[38] The court will also be likely in its order to specify who is to be responsible for paying the receiver, and the fund or property from which the receiver is to recover his remuneration.[39] A party to an action who is appointed receiver will normally be required to act without remuneration,[40] but it seems that remuneration may be allowed in partnership cases.[41] A receiver may be paid for any extraordinary trouble and expense beyond what his duties as receiver required, provided that it was for the benefit of the estate.[42] In practice, a receiver should apply to the court for directions before undertaking the exceptional work or expense, otherwise he runs the risk that additional remuneration will not be allowed. The court has no power to order that a receiver's remuneration should rank before prior securities.[43]

CPR, Pt 69, does not deal with expenses, which it is well established fall to be met out of the realisable assets in the receiver's hands.[44]

(E) POSITION OF RECEIVER

A receiver is an officer of the court. It is his duty to take possession of the property over which he is appointed, and his possession and acts are the possession and acts of the court.[45]

---

[35] *Boehm v Goodall* [1911] 1 Ch 155; *Capewell v Revenue and Customs Commissioners* [2007] UKHL 2, [2007] 2 All ER 370.

[36] In general, this code applies to the new species of statutory receiverships (as to which see p 000, *infra*), although it cannot override any detailed provisions contained in such Acts: *Capewell v Revenue and Customs Commissioners, supra,* HL.

[37] CPR Part 69.7(1).

[38] CPR Part 69.7(4), which also specifies the circumstances to be taken into account.

[39] CPR Part 69.7(2).   [40] *Sargant v Read* (1876) 1 Ch D 600; *Taylor v Neate* (1888) 39 Ch D 538.

[41] *Davy v Scarth* [1906] 1 Ch 55.

[42] *Potts v Leighton* (1808) 15 Ves 273; *Harris v Sleep* [1897] 2 Ch 80, CA.

[43] *Choudhri v Palta* [1994] 1 BCLC 184, [1992] BCC 787, CA.

[44] In reversing the decision of the Court of Appeal, the House of Lords, in *Capewell v Revenue and Customs Commissioners, supra,* HL, cast no doubt on Carnwath LJ's statement to this effect.

[45] *Aston v Heron* (1834) 2 My & K 390; *Re Flowers & Co* [1897] 1 QB 14, CA.

As Chitty J expressed it:[46] 'A receiver is not an agent for any other person, and a receiver is not a trustee. The receiver is appointed by the order of the court and is responsible to the court, and cannot obey the directions of the parties in the action.' By reason of the fact that the receiver is an officer of the court, any interference by anyone with his possession of the property that he has been directed to receive is a contempt of court, even though the order appointing him is perfectly erroneous.[47] Interference may be punished by committal,[48] and restrained by the issue of an injunction.[49] Thus, in *Dixon v Dixon*,[50] an injunction was granted to the receiver and manager of a partnership business to restrain one of the old partners from inducing employees of the receiver to leave his employment and enter the employment of a rival business set up by the old partner, even though due notice was given to the receiver and breach of contract was neither instigated nor committed. Apart from physical interference, it would be a contempt of court to institute legal proceedings to assert a right over property of which the receiver has either taken or been directed to take possession[51] without first obtaining the leave of the court, which will, however, readily be given unless it is perfectly clear that there is no foundation for the claim.[52] There will, however, be no actionable interference if the order for a receiver does not make it clear, on its face, that he is to be receiver over the property in dispute,[53] nor where the order is made conditional on the giving of security, and security has not yet been given.[54]

Not being an agent for anyone, a receiver is personally liable for his acts: for instance, contracts entered into in carrying on a business,[55] or existing contracts adopted as his own.[56] He is, however, entitled to an indemnity out of the assets for all costs and expenses not improperly incurred,[57] including the costs of an action brought against him as receiver where the defence was for the benefit of the trust estate,[58] but, as with a claim for remuneration, he is not entitled to any personal indemnity,[59] even though he has been appointed with the consent of all parties.[60] Further, by the doctrine of subrogation, the receiver's creditors will be entitled to the same rights against the property as the receiver himself.[61] Where multiple receivers have been appointed, it is an issue of construction whether they can act severally as well as jointly.[62]

---

[46] In *Bacup Corpn v Smith* (1890) 44 Ch D 395, 398. See *Re Andrews, supra*, CA.

[47] *Ames v Birkenhead Docks Trustees* (1855) 20 Beav 332.

[48] *Helmore v Smith (No 2)* (1886) 35 Ch D 449, CA.   [49] *Dixon v Dixon* [1904] 1 Ch 161.

[50] *Supra.*   [51] *Ames v Birkenhead Docks Trustees, supra; Defries v Creed* (1865) 12 LT 262.

[52] *Hawkins v Gathercole* (1852) 1 Drew 12; *Lane v Capsey* [1891] 3 Ch 411; *Brenner v Rose* [1973] 2 All ER 535. Provided that such leave is obtained, an action may be brought against a receiver even by the person at whose instance he was appointed: *L P Arthur (Insurance) Ltd v Sisson* [1966] 2 All ER 1003, [1966] 1 WLR 1384.

[53] *Crow v Wood* (1850) 13 Beav 271.   [54] *Edwards v Edwards* (1876) 2 Ch D 291, CA.

[55] *Burt, Boulton and Hayward v Bull* [1895] 1 QB 276, CA; *Moss Steamship Co Ltd v Whinney* [1912] AC 254, HL. Cf *Land Rover Group Ltd v UPF(UK) Ltd (in administrative receivership)* [2002] EWHC 3183(QB), [2003] 2 BCLC 222, in relation to the effect of breach by receiver as agent of company.

[56] *Re Botibol* [1947] 1 All ER 26.

[57] *Burt, Boulton and Hayward v Bull, supra*, CA; *Strapp v Bull Sons & Co* [1895] 2 Ch 1, CA.

[58] *Re Dunn* [1904] 1 Ch 648; cf *Walters v Woodbridge* (1878) 7 Ch D 504, CA, in which the defence was merely to vindicate the receiver's character against charges of personal fraud and misconduct in his office, and not to benefit the estate.

[59] *Re Bushell, ex p Izard* (1883) 23 Ch D 75, CA; *Batten v Wedgwood Coal and Iron Co* (1884) 28 Ch D 317.

[60] *Boehm v Goodall* [1911] 1 Ch 155; *Rosanove v O'Rourke* [1988] 1 Qd R 171.

[61] *Re London United Breweries Ltd* [1907] 2 Ch 511.

[62] *Gwembe Valley Development Co Ltd (in Receivership) v Koshy* (2000) Times, 8 February.

(F) CASES IN WHICH A RECEIVER MAY BE APPOINTED BY THE COURT

Except where the appointment is to enforce an equitable mortgage or charge, or by way of equitable execution, the general ground on which a receiver is appointed is for the protection and preservation of property for the benefit of the persons who are, or, as a result of litigation are ultimately held to be, beneficially interested.[63] It was said, in *Owen v Homan*,[64] that where 'the property is as it were in medio, in the enjoyment of no one, the court can hardly do wrong in taking possession. It is the common interest of all parties that the court should prevent a scramble'.

The main types of case in which a receiver may be appointed are as follows.

(i) Pending the grant of probate or letters of administration

Where the assets of a deceased person are in jeopardy, a receiver may be appointed to protect the assets of the estate,[65] and similarly, if a sole executor dies, a receiver may be appointed, pending a fresh grant being obtained.[66] If, however, probate proceedings have been started, the proper procedure is to apply for an administrator *pendente lite*.

(ii) As against executors and trustees

The court may dispossess an executor or trustee of the trust estate by appointing a receiver if a strong case is made out.[67] Gross misconduct or personal disability on the part of the executor or trustee, such as wasting or misapplication of the assets, may justify the appointment of a receiver,[68] or even mere mismanagement without any corrupt intention.[69] Mere poverty is not a sufficient ground,[70] but insolvency is a different matter, although, in this case, as in others in which a receiver has been appointed in the past, it will now commonly be possible and better to deal with the matter by removal of the trustee and the appointment of a new one.[71]

(iii) In partnership cases

The court will readily appoint a receiver if it can be shown, when the application is made, that the partnership is at an end.[72] The court, however, finds itself in a difficulty if the defendant claims that the partnership is continuing. On the one hand, if a receiver is appointed, the effect is to bring to an end the partnership, which one party claims to have a right to be continued; on the other hand, if a receiver is not appointed, it leaves the defendant at liberty to go on with the business, with risk of loss and prejudice to the

---

[63] *Bertrand v Davis* (1862) 31 Beav 429.   [64] (1853) 4 HL Cas 997, 1032.

[65] *Re Oakes* [1917] 1 Ch 230; *Re Sutcliffe* [1942] Ch 453, sub nom *Jackman v Sutcliffe* [1942] 2 All ER 296.

[66] *Re Parker* (1879) 12 Ch D 293; *Re Clark* [1910] WN 234.

[67] *Middleton v Dodswell* (1806) 13 Ves 266; *Bainbridge v Blair* (1835) 4 LJ Ch 207.

[68] *Evans v Coventry* (1854) 5 De GM & G 911; *Swale v Swale* (1856) 22 Beav 584; *Re Brooker's Estate, Brooker v Brooker* (1857) 3 Sm & G 475. For an exceptional case in which the order was made *ex parte*, see *Clarke v Heathfield* [1985] ICR 203, CA.

[69] *Whitehead v Bennett* (1845) 6 LTOS 185.

[70] *Anon* (1806), *supra*; *Howard v Papera* (1815) 1 Madd 142.

[71] See Chapter 15, *supra*. Older cases include *Re H's Estate* (1875) 1 Ch D 276; *Dickens v Harris* (1866) 14 LT 98 (sole executor remaining outside the jurisdiction).

[72] *Pini v Roncoroni* [1892] 1 Ch 633; *Taylor v Neate* (1888) 39 Ch D 538.

claimant.[73] The court tries to weigh the various factors, but will not, in general, appoint a receiver unless it appears reasonably clear either that the partnership is already at an end or that the court will order a dissolution at the trial.[74] For similar reasons, the court will be slow to appoint a receiver if the defendant denies the existence of the alleged partnership, although there is no rigid rule preventing it.[75]

(iv) Companies

Receivers are usually appointed under express powers in debentures or debenture trust deeds,[76] although any such appointment may be superseded by an appointment by the court.[77] An appointment may be made by the court at the instance of shareholders or the company itself where, for instance, there is no governing body, or such disputes between the directors that the management is not being carried on.[78] Debenture holders may ask the court to appoint a receiver if their security is in jeopardy,[79] even though they have reserved a power under the debenture that has not yet become exercisable.[80] The mere fact that the security is insufficient is not enough;[81] there must also be evidence that the security is in jeopardy, as, for instance, where the company is threatening to distribute all of its assets among the shareholders,[82] or where it has ceased to be a going concern.[83]

(v) Mortgages

The court may appoint a receiver at the instance of a legal mortgagee when it thinks it just and convenient to do so,[84] and it may do so, if a special case is made out, even though the mortgagee has gone into possession or himself appointed a receiver under the express power that is almost invariably included in a mortgage deed.[85]

An equitable mortgagee or chargee has, however, always had a right to have a receiver appointed by the court,[86] where there has been no prior incumbrancer in possession,[87] on the ground that he was unable to take possession for himself.[88] He has this right whenever there has been a breach of any of the mortgagor's obligations, or even without this, where the security is in jeopardy.[89] Where the application is made by a subsequent incumbrancer, and the appointment is made in the usual form, expressly without prejudice to the rights

---

[73] *Madgwick v Wimble* (1843) 6 Beav 495.

[74] *Goodman v Whitcomb* (1820) 1 Jac & W 589; *Smith v Jeyes* (1841) 4 Beav 503.

[75] *Floydd v Cheney* [1970] Ch 602, [1970] 1 All ER 446.　　[76] See p 685, *infra*.

[77] *Re Maskelyne British Typewriter Ltd* [1898] 1 Ch 133, CA; *Re Slogger Automatic Feeder Co Ltd* [1915] 1 Ch 478.

[78] *Trade Auxiliary Co v Vickers* (1873) LR 16 Eq 303, CA; *Stanfield v Gibbon* [1925] WN 11.

[79] *McMahon v North Kent Ironworks Co* [1891] 2 Ch 148; *Edwards v Standard Rolling Stock Syndicate* [1893] 1 Ch 574.

[80] *McMahon v North Kent Ironworks Co, supra.*　　[81] *Re New York Taxicab Co Ltd* [1913] 1 Ch 1.

[82] *Re Tilt Cove Copper Co Ltd* [1913] 2 Ch 588.

[83] *Hubbuck v Helms* (1887) 56 LT 232. See also *Re London Pressed Hinge Co* [1905] 1 Ch 576; *Re Braunstein and Marjorlaine* [1914] WN 335.

[84] *Tillett v Nixon* (1883) 25 Ch D 238; *Re Prytherch* (1889) 42 Ch D 590.

[85] *Gloucester County Bank v Rudry Merthyr Coal Co* [1895] 1 Ch 629, CA. See p 702, *infra*.

[86] *Sollory v Leaver* (1869) LR 9 Eq 22; *Re Crompton & Co Ltd* [1914] 1 Ch 954, 967.

[87] *Berney v Sewell* (1820) 1 Jac & W 647.

[88] The ground, however, seems doubtful as regards an equitable mortgagee. See *Barclays Bank Ltd v Bird* [1954] Ch 274, [1954] 1 All ER 449; Megarry & Wade, *Law of Real Property*, 6th edn, pp 1214, 1215.

[89] See cases cited in, fnn 79–82, *supra*.

of prior incumbrancers, a prior incumbrancer can take possession without leave of the court.[90] Where no reservation is made of the rights of prior incumbrancers, they are not, in fact, destroyed, but can only be exercised if the leave of the court is first obtained, which will not, in practice, be refused.[91]

(vi) Creditors

In *Cummins v Perkins*,[92] Lindley MR observed that the authorities clearly showed 'that, quite independently of the Judicature Act 1873, if a plaintiff had a right to be paid out of a particular fund he could in equity obtain protection to prevent that fund from being dissipated so as to defeat his rights'. It was, he said, 'settled that a person who had a right to be paid out of a particular fund could obtain an injunction (and if an injunction, it followed on principle that he could obtain a receiver) in a proper case to protect the fund from being misapplied'.[93]

(vii) Between vendor and purchaser

In appropriate cases, a receiver may be appointed both in actions for specific performance and for rescission. Thus it has been done where proceedings had been brought to set aside a sale for fraud, where the court thought it hardly possible that the transaction could stand, although it was also said that this was not the usual practice.[94] More commonly, it has been done in order to preserve the property, for instance, where the property is a mine and it is clearly desirable to keep it working,[95] or a farm, which should clearly be kept in a state of cultivation.[96] And an unpaid vendor may be granted a receiver for the protection of his lien.[97]

(viii) Other instances

These have included cases in which the owner of a chattel was suing for its return from a bailee, who claimed a lien over it,[98] pending a reference to arbitration,[99] pending litigation in a foreign court,[100] in aid of a freezing injunction,[101] where the affairs of a charity were in a state of disarray and controversy,[102] and where a landlord has failed to comply with

---

[90] *Underhay v Read* (1887) 20 QBD 209, CA.

[91] *Re Metropolitan Amalgamated Estates Ltd* [1912] 2 Ch 497.   [92] [1899] 1 Ch 16, 19, 20, CA.

[93] See also *Kearns v Leaf* (1864) 1 Hem & M 681; *Owen v Homan* (1853) 4 HL Cas 997.

[94] *Stilwell v Wilkins* (1821) Jac 280.

[95] *Boehm v Wood* (1820) 2 Jac & W 236; *Gibbs v David* (1875) LR 20 Eq 373.

[96] *Hyde v Warden* (1876) 1 Ex D 309, CA.

[97] *Munns v Isle of Wight Rly Co* (1870) 5 Ch App 414; cf *Cook v Andrews* [1897] 1 Ch 266.

[98] *Hattan v Car Maintenance Co Ltd* [1915] 1 Ch 621, [1911–13] All ER Rep 890, in which the receiver was authorized to allow the owner to use the chattel.

[99] *Law v Garrett* (1878) 8 Ch D 26, CA; *Compagnie du Senegal v Smith* (1883) 49 LT 527.

[100] *Transatlantic Co v Pietroni* (1860) John 604.

[101] *A-G v Schonfeld* [1980] 3 All ER 1, [1980] 1 WLR 1182; *International Credit and Investment Co (Overseas) Ltd v Adharn* [1998] BCC 134 (where worldwide freezing injunctions had been granted over property, it was right for the court to pierce the corporate veil and appoint a receiver over the property in circumstances in which there appeared to the court a real risk that the freezing orders might be breached).

[102] *Derby and Co Ltd v Weldon (Nos 3 and 4)* [1990] Ch 65, sub nom *Derby & Co Ltd v Weldon (No 2)* [1989] 1 All ER 1002, CA (against a foreign company with no assets in this country).

his repairing obligations.[103] However, a court will not appoint a receiver and manager to manage houses owned by a local authority.[104]

(ix) Appointment of a receiver under special statutory provisions

The appointment of a receiver has proved such a useful procedure that statute has, from time to time, extended the range of situations in which an appointment may be made. These include the Insolvency Act 1986,[105] the Landlord and Tenant Act 1987,[106] and the Proceeds of Crime Act 2002.[107] These statutory receiverships are, in general, treated like any other receivership, but any particular provisions in the relevant statute will, of course, prevail. The circumstances in which appointments can be made under these Acts, and their effects, are outside the scope of this book.

(x) Equitable execution

Lastly, there is the rather separate case of the receiver by way of equitable execution.[108] Before the Judicature Acts, the Court of Chancery would come to the aid of a judgment creditor who was unable to enforce his judgment by a common law writ of execution, by appointing a receiver over certain assets of the debtor. Despite its title, 'equitable execution' is not really execution at all, but equitable relief that the court gives because execution at law cannot be had: 'It is not execution, but a substitute for execution.'[109] Accordingly, the executors of a deceased judgment creditor, who may obtain leave to issue a writ of execution under CPR, Sch 1, RSC, Ord 46, cannot, under this order, obtain the appointment of a receiver.[110]

Before the Judicature Acts, the Court of Chancery would only appoint a receiver where the plaintiff could show that he had exhausted his legal remedies. Since the Judicature Acts, which, as we have seen, give the court jurisdiction to appoint a receiver whenever it appears just and convenient to do so,[111] it has been unnecessary to go through the 'useless and absurd form'[112] of issuing a barren writ of execution,[113] although, apart from cases within the Supreme Court Act 1981, now renamed the Senior Courts Act 1981,[114] it is still, in general, necessary to show that there is no remedy available at law. It is still not sufficient merely to show that to appoint a receiver by way of equitable execution would be a more convenient mode of obtaining satisfaction of a judgment than the usual modes of execution.[115] What has to be shown is that there is some hindrance arising from the nature

---

[103] *Hart v Emelkirk Ltd* [1983] 3 All ER 15; *Daiches v Bluelake Investment Ltd* (1985) 275 Estates Gazette 462; *Clayhope Properties Ltd v Evans* [1986] 2 All ER 795, CA; see (1985) 135 NLJ 1215 (N Madge).

[104] *Parker v Camden London Borough Council* [1986] Ch 162, [1985] 2 All ER 141, CA.

[105] Section 286. See *Dunn v Rio Properties* [2004] EWCA Civ 1043, [2004] 1 WLR 2702.

[106] Section 21.   [107] Sections 48, 50, 52, and 61.

[108] For a Canadian view, see [1988] 67 CBR 306 (E R Edinger).

[109] *Per* Bowen LJ in *Re Shephard* (1889) 43 Ch D 131, 137, CA; *Levasseur v Mason and Barry Ltd* [1891] 2 QB 73, CA; *Holmes v Millage* [1893] 1 QB 551, CA.

[110] *Norburn v Norburn* [1894] 1 QB 448.   [111] See p 675, *supra*.

[112] *Per* Jessel MR in *Anglo-Italian Bank v Davies* (1878) 9 Ch D 275, 285, CA: *Re Watkins, ex p Evans* (1879) 13 Ch D 252, 260, CA.

[113] *Re Whiteley* (1887) 56 LT 846; *Hills v Webber* (1901) 17 TLR 513, CA.

[114] Section 37(4), discussed *infra*.

[115] *Harris v Beauchamp Bros* [1894] 1 QB 801, CA; *Holmes v Millage, supra*, CA; *Morgan v Hart* [1914] 2 KB 183, CA; *Maclaine Watson & Co Ltd v International Tin Council* [1988] Ch 1, [1987] 3 All ER 787; affd [1989] Ch 253, [1988] 3 All ER 257, CA; on appeal [1990] 2 AC 418, [1989] 3 All ER 523, HL.

of the property that prevents the judgment creditor from obtaining execution at law, but which the appointment of a receiver can overcome. It has not been settled whether it must be shown that execution at law is impossible, or whether it will suffice to show that it is difficult or impractical.[116]

Obvious cases for the appointment of a receiver are over an interest in a settlement of personalty,[117] even when reversionary,[118] or a legacy or share of residue under a will.[119] Other property over which a receiver by way of equitable execution has been appointed includes debts and sums of money payable to a judgment debtor, and a claim to be indemnified by a third party,[120] to which garnishee proceedings are not applicable,[121] rents of land outside the jurisdiction,[122] and goods in the possession of a third party, subject to that third party's lien.[123] Generally, in determining whether it is just and convenient to appoint a receiver by way of equitable execution, the court must have regard to the amount of the debt claimed, the amount likely to be obtained by the receiver, and the probable cost of his appointment.[124]

If the nature of the property is such that it could not be reached by either law or equity, an appointment will be refused.[125] Thus a receiver has been refused over a patent that was not producing any profits,[126] and a sum, the payment of which to the debtor was wholly contingent and dependent on the will of another person.[127] These cases may require reconsideration in the light of *Soinco SACI v Novokuznetsk Aluminium Plant*,[128] in which, not following earlier decisions, it was held that the court had jurisdiction under s 37(1) of the Supreme Court Act 1981, now renamed the Senior Courts Act 1981, to appoint a receiver by way of equitable execution to receive future debts as well as debts due and accruing due at the date of his appointment.

It remains to say that, by s 36 of the Administration of Justice Act 1956, now repealed and replaced by s 37(4) of the 1981 Act, which has 'made a revolutionary change in the enforcement of judgments',[129] the power of the court to appoint a receiver by way of equitable execution was extended[130] so as to operate in relation to all legal estates and interests in land, whether or not a charge has been imposed on that land under s 1 of the Charging Orders Act 1979 for the purpose of enforcing the judgment; the power is in addition to,

---

[116] *Maclaine Watson & Co Ltd v International Tin Council, supra*, at first instance and in CA. See also *Bourne v Colodense Ltd* [1985] ICR 291, CA.

[117] *Oliver v Lowther* (1880) 42 LT 47; *Webb v Stenton* (1883) 11 QBD 518, CA; *Ideal Bedding Co v Holland* [1907] 2 Ch 157.

[118] *Fuggle v Bland* (1883) 11 QBD 711, DC; *Tyrrell v Painton* [1895] 1 QB 202, CA.

[119] *Re Marquis of Anglesey* [1903] 2 Ch 727.

[120] *Maclaine Watson & Co Ltd v International Tin Council, supra*, HL.

[121] *Westhead v Riley* (1883) 25 Ch D 413.

[122] *Mercantile Investment and General Trust Co v River Plate Trust Loan and Agency Co* [1892] 2 Ch 303 (although, in the circumstances, the court refused to make the appointment).

[123] *Levasseur v Mason and Barry Ltd* [1891] 2 QB 73, CA.

[124] CPR, Sch 1, RSC, Ord 51, r 1.

[125] *Maclaine Watson & Co Ltd v International Tin Council, supra*, at first instance and in CA.

[126] *Edwards & Co v Picard*, [1909] 2 KB 903, CA.

[127] *R v Lincolnshire County Court Judge* (1887) 20 QBD 167, DC.

[128] [1998] QB 406, [1997] 3 All ER 523. As to future earnings, see the Attachment of Earnings Act 1971, which is a complete code and excludes any power to appoint a receiver of future earnings.

[129] *Per* Danckwerts LJ in *Barclays Bank Ltd v Moore* [1967] 3 All ER 34, CA.

[130] But see *Re Pope* (1886) 17 QBD 743, CA.

and not in derogation of, any power of any court to appoint a receiver in proceedings for enforcing such a charge. The remedy of a judgment creditor against land is, accordingly, either the imposition of a charge,[131] or the appointment of a receiver, or, perhaps,[132] both.[133] In practice, because of the greatly increased scope of charging orders, the appointment of a receiver by way of equitable execution is rarely necessary.

(G) APPOINTMENT OUT OF COURT

It is possible for a receiver to be appointed out of court, and, indeed, this is commonly done under mortgages and debentures, and may be done in other cases: for instance, where partners by agreement appoint a receiver and manager to wind up the partnership business.[134] An express power to appoint a receiver was, at one time, commonly inserted in mortgage deeds, but reliance is now usually placed on the statutory power contained in the Law of Property Act 1925.[135] On the other hand, although, in most cases, debentures and debenture trust deeds are mortgages to which the statutory power would apply,[136] they still commonly include an express power in order to confer extended powers on the receiver. Strictly speaking, any discussion of a receiver appointed out of court is out of place in a chapter on equitable remedies, but it seems desirable to consider briefly the position of such a receiver by way of contrast and comparison.

Unlike a receiver appointed by the court, a receiver or manager appointed out of court is prima facie an agent for the person appointing him.[137] However, the statutory provisions in the case of mortgages and the usual express provisions in debentures make the receiver the agent of the mortgagor or company, as the case may be, with the object of making the mortgagor or company liable for the receiver's acts or defaults, and this is now made a statutory rule in the case of the administrative receiver of a company under the Insolvency Act 1986.[138] The better view is that the agency is nevertheless a real one,[139] and certainly the receiver is under a duty to account to the mortgagor or company.[140] The receiver is, however, primarily concerned to look after the interests of the person who appointed

---

[131] Under the Charging Orders Act 1979. See *National Westminster Bank Ltd v Stockman* [1981] 1 All ER 800, [1981] 1 WLR 67.

[132] See (1985) 82 LSG 674 (J M Dyron).

[133] As to the effect of a charging order in the event of the debtor subsequently becoming bankrupt or being wound up, see *Roberts Petroleum Ltd v Bernard Kenny Ltd* [1983] 2 AC 192, [1983] 1 All ER 564, HL.

[134] *Turner v Major* (1862) 3 Giff 442. For different examples, see *Knight v Bowyer* (1858) 2 De G & J 421; *Cradock v Scottish Provident Institutions* [1893] WN 146; affd [1894] WN 88, CA.

[135] Sections 101(1)(iii) and 109, prospectively amended by the Tribunals, Courts, and Enforcement Act 2007.

[136] Compare *Knightsbridge Estates Trust Ltd v Byrne* [1940] AC 613, [1940] 2 All ER 401, HL. Contra, *Blaker v Herts and Essex Waterworks Co* (1889) 41 Ch D 399, 405, 306.

[137] *Knight v Bowyer* (1858) 2 De G & J 421; *Ford v Rackham* (1853) 17 Beav 485.

[138] Section 44(1). See Insolvency Act 1994, s 2; *Powdrill v Watson* [1995] 2 AC 394, [1995] 2 All ER 65, HL.

[139] *Hibernian Bank v Yourell (No 2)* [1919] 1 IR 310, 312, per O'Connor MR; *Ratford v Northavon District Council* [1987] QB 357, [1986] 3 All ER 193, CA; *Kerr on Receivers*, 17th edn, p 341. Contra, (1977) 41 Conv 83 (P J Millett).

[140] *Smiths Ltd v Middleton* [1979] 3 All ER 842. As to the ownership of documents created during receivership, see *Gomba Holdings UK Ltd v Minories Finance Ltd* [1989] 1 All ER 261, CA. As to his duty towards guarantors, see *Standard Chartered Bank Ltd v Walker* [1982] 3 All ER 938, [1982] 1 WLR 1410, CA; *American Express International Banking Corpn v Hurley* [1985] 3 All ER 564, noted [1986] JBL 154 (R M Goode), which

him,[141] and he cannot, in general, short of misconduct, be controlled by the court at the suit of the mortgagor or company.[142] The relationship is, in fact, tripartite, and involves the mortgagor, the receiver, and the debenture holder.[143] He is receiver for the benefit of all those interested in the property of which he is receiver.[144] He does not, however, owe a duty to the general creditors, to contributors, to officers of the company, or to members.[145] A receiver appointed out of court ceases to be an agent for any person if he is superseded by a receiver appointed by the court,[146] and, on general principles of agency, his authority will be terminated by the death of the principal.[147] It is however, no longer possible for an administrative receiver to be removed from office by the appointor, thus strengthening the receiver's independence.[148] If, under a debenture, a receiver is appointed as agent for the company, winding up will deprive the receiver of power to bind the company personally by acting as its agent. It will not, however, affect his powers to hold and dispose of the company's property comprised in the debenture, including his power to use the company's name for that purpose, because such powers are given by the disposition of the company's property that it made (in equity) by the debenture itself.[149]

As we have seen, a receiver appointed out of court is prima facie a mere agent, and, accordingly, he incurs no personal liability for acts properly done by him as receiver,[150] although he may make himself personally liable for some transaction by giving his personal promise to carry it out,[151] and may always make himself liable for breach of warranty of authority. However, in the case of a receiver or manager of the property of a company, the Insolvency Act 1986[152] provides that he is to be personally liable on any contract entered into by him in the performance of his functions to the same extent as if he had

---

also discuss the duty of care owed by the receiver in realizing assets. See (1982) 132 NLJ 1137 (G Mitchell); (1982) 132 NLJ 883 (H W Wilkinson).

[141] *Re B Johnson & Co (Builders) Ltd* [1955] Ch 634, [1955] 2 All ER 775, CA; *Gomba Holdings UK Ltd v Minories Finance Ltd, supra,* CA. As to the effect on the powers of the directors, see *Newhart Developments Ltd v Co-operative Commercial Bank Ltd* [1978] QB 814, [1978] 2 All ER 896, CA.

[142] *Rottenberg v Monjack* [1993] BCLC 374, in which, however, it was held that where the debenture holder who had appointed the receiver had been paid in full, but there was a dispute as to the receiver's remuneration, the company was entitled to an interlocutory injunction to restrain him from selling any further property, which might be unnecessary.

[143] See *Gomba Holdings UK Ltd v Minories Finance Ltd, supra,* CA, per Fox LJ, at 263; *Re Leyland DAF Ltd* [1994] 1 BCLC 264.

[144] A receiver managing mortgaged property owes duties to the mortgagor and anyone else with an interest in the equity of redemption. The duties include, but are not necessarily confined to, a duty of good faith: *Medforth v Blake* [2000] Ch 86, [1999] 3 All ER 97, noted [1999] Conv 434 (A Kenny); (1999) 143 Sol Jo 950 (M Griffiths); (2000) 63 MLR 413 (Sandra Fisher). See *Downsview Nominees Ltd v First City Corpn Ltd* [1993] AC 295, [1993] 3 All ER 626, PC, noted [1993] Conv 401 (R Grantham); [1994] Co Law 28 (R Nolan); (1994) 45 NILQ 61 (M Fealy); *Raja (administratrix of the estate of Raja (decd)) v Austin Gray (a firm)* [2002] EWCA Civ 1965, [2003] 1 EGLR 91; *Silven Properties Ltd v Royal Bank of Scotland plc* [2003] EWCA Civ 1409, [2004] 4 All ER 484. See also *Meretz Investments NV v ACP Ltd* [2006] EWHC 74 (Ch), [2006] 3 All ER 1029.

[145] *Lathia v Dronsfield Bros Ltd* [1987] BCLC 321.

[146] *Hand v Blow* [1901] 2 Ch 721, CA; *Ratford v Northavon District Council, supra,* CA.

[147] *Semble,* this is not the case when the appointment is made under the statutory power by reason of the definition in the Law of Property Act 1925, s 205(1)(xvi).

[148] Insolvency Act 1986, s 45(2).

[149] *Sowman v David Samuel Trust Ltd* [1978] 1 All ER 616; *Barrows v Chief Land Registrar* (1977) Times, 20 October. See (1977) 41 Conv 83 (P J Millett).

[150] *Owen & Co v Cronk* [1895] 1 QB 265, CA.

[151] *Robinson Printing Co Ltd v Chic Ltd* [1905] 2 Ch 123.   [152] Section 37.

been appointed by order of the court, except in so far as the contract otherwise provides. And he may incur personal liability after a winding up when he ceases to be the agent of the company, and is not apparently the agent for the debenture holders.[153]

In general, there are no restrictions as to who may be appointed receiver out of court, but the statutory restrictions in relation to receivers, already discussed,[154] apply.

The statutory power provides for the payment of remuneration,[155] and the Insolvency Act 1986[156] contains provisions for remuneration where a receiver of a company is appointed for debenture holders. If there is no provision for remuneration, a receiver may be entitled to claim on a *quantum meruit*.[157]

2 ACCOUNT

(A) ACTIONS OF ACCOUNT[158]

At common law, an action of account could be brought in certain special cases, but it was said by Alderson B[159] to be 'so inconvenient, that it has been long discontinued, and parties have gone into a court of equity in preference',[160] 'partly on account of the difficulty attending the process under the old writ of account, but chiefly from the advantage of compelling the party to account upon oath, according to the practice of courts of equity'.[161]

It did not follow from this that a person with a legal claim had a right to an account in equity, as he would normally have in an equitable matter, such as where a beneficiary sought an account from his trustee, or a mortgagor from a mortgagee in possession. The Court of Chancery refused to lay down definite rules as to when it would allow a bill for an account, and when it would leave the plaintiff to his action at law. The principle on which the court acted was, however, reasonably clear: jurisdiction would not be exercised where the matter could be as fully and conveniently dealt with by a court of common law.[162]

In practice, equity would normally exercise its jurisdiction in the following cases:

(i) where there were mutual accounts, unless these were extremely simple;[163]

---

[153] *Bacal Contracting Ltd v Modern Engineering (Bristol) Ltd* [1980] 2 All ER 655.

[154] See p 677, *supra*.

[155] Law of Property Act 1925, s 109(6). There is no need to apply to the court unless the receiver wants more than 5 per cent: *Marshall v Cottingham* [1982] Ch 82, [1981] 3 All ER 8.

[156] Section 58. This enables the court to interfere with the receiver's remuneration, but not his right to an indemnity for costs, retrospectively: *Re Potters Oil Ltd (No 2)* [1986] 1 All ER 890.

[157] *Prior v Bagster* (1887) 57 LT 760.

[158] See, generally, (1987) 11 Adel LR 1 (Fiona Patfield). As to whether it is a personal or proprietary remedy, see *Ultraframe (UK) Ltd v Fielding* [2005] EWHC 1628 (Ch), [2006] WTLR 835.

[159] In *Sturton v Richardson*, (1844) 13 M & W 17, 20; *Blackstone's Commentaries*, vol III, p 164.

[160] It was resuscitated, however, by the plaintiff in *Godfrey v Saunders* (1770) 3 Wils 73, because his action in Chancery had been 'fruitlessly depending there for more than twelve years'.

[161] *Per* Lord Redesdale in *A-G v Dublin Corpn* (1827) 1 Bli NS 312, 337, HL.

[162] *Shepard v Brown* (1862) 4 Giff 203; *Southampton Dock Co v Southampton Harbour and Pier Board* (1870) LR 11 Eq 254; (1964) 80 LQR 203 (S J Stoljar).

[163] *Phillips v Phillips* (1852) 9 Hare 471; *Fluker v Taylor* (1855) 3 Drew 183.

(ii)   where there was some confidential relationship between the parties, as between principal and agent, or between partners.[164] A principal could normally maintain an action of account against the agent by reason of the confidence reposed and the fact that the only way of ascertaining the state of the account was by the equitable procedure of discovery,[165] but the agent had no corresponding right, because the facts were within his knowledge and he placed no special confidence in his principal;[166]

(iii) where the account was so complicated that a court of law would be incompetent to examine it, a question of degree left somewhat indefinite;[167]

(iv)   Lindley LJ has said[168] that an account would be ordered where the plaintiff would have had a legal right to have money ascertained and paid to him by the defendant, if the defendant had not wrongfully prevented it from accruing;

(v)   as regards waste, although this was normally a tort for which a remedy lay at law, an account would be ordered where an injunction was also sought, and waste had already been committed, in order to prevent the need for two actions,[169] and in any case of equitable waste, which was not recognized at common law;[170]

(vi)   an account was also ordered as incident to an injunction, but not otherwise, in cases of infringement of patent rights.[171]

The Judicature Acts[172] have now assigned actions for an account to the Chancery Division. Being an equitable remedy, it is a discretionary remedy and the court may decide that it is not appropriate to grant it, as was the case in *Laskar v Laskar*.[173]

Provisions as to taking accounts are contained in the Civil Procedure Rules.[174] Any party who wishes to contend—

(i)   that an accounting party has received more than the amount shown by the account to have been received;

(ii)   that an accounting party should be treated as having received more than he has actually received;

(iii) that any item in the account is erroneous in respect of amount; or

(iv)   that, in any other respect, the account is inaccurate—

must, unless the court otherwise orders, give written notice to the accounting party of his objections with appropriate details and a statement of the ground on which the contention is based.

---

[164] But there is no such relationship between a banker and his customers: *Foley v Hill* (1848) 2 HL Cas 28.

[165] *Beaumont v Boultbee* (1802) 7 Ves 599; *Mackenzie v Johnson* (1819) 4 Madd 373.

[166] *Padwick v Stanley* (1852) 9 Hare 627.

[167] *Taff Vale Rly Co v Nixon* (1847) 1 HL Cas 111; *Phillips v Phillips, supra*.

[168] In *London, Chatham and Dover Rly Co v South Eastern Rly Co* [1892] 1 Ch 120, 140, CA; affd [1893] AC 429, HL.   [169] *Jesus College v Bloom* (1745) 3 Atk 262; *Parrott v Palmer* (1834) 3 My & K 632.

[170] *Duke of Leeds v Earl of Amherst* (1846) 2 Ph 117.

[171] *Price's Patent Candle Co v Bauwen's Patent Candle Co* (1858) 4 K & J 727; *De Vitre v Betts* (1873) LR 6 HL 319; see now Patents Act 1977, s 61.

[172] Now the Supreme Court Act 1981, renamed as the Senior Courts Act 1981, s 61(1) and Sch 1, para 1.

[173] [2008] EWCA Civ 347, [2008] All ER(D) 104 (Feb).

[174] CPR 40 PD. See *Satnam Investments Ltd v Dunlop Heywood & Co Ltd* [1999] 3 All ER 652, CA; *Ultraframe (UK) Ltd v Fielding* [2005] EWHC 1628 (Ch), [2006] WTLR 835.

3 RESCISSION

(A) MEANING OF 'RESCISSION'[175]

Rescission is a remedy available both at common law and in equity, although more widely in the latter. In *Buckland v Farmer and Moody*,[176] Buckley LJ said that the word 'rescind' had no primary meaning. The sense in which it was used in a particular case must be discovered from the context. This has sometimes given rise to confusion.

One should distinguish between the following.

(i) Rescission in the strict sense, with which we are solely concerned, arises when the contract contains an inherent cause of invalidity—for example, mistake, fraud, or lack of consent—which makes it voidable at the suit of one of the parties. If and when that party declares his intention not to be bound by the contract, he is said to 'rescind' it.

(ii) Rescission in a looser sense, includes one of the options that the innocent party may have where a perfectly valid contract is broken by the other party. He may, of course, affirm the contract, and sue for damages for breach of contract, or, in an appropriate case, pursue the equitable remedy of specific performance. This does not absolve the innocent party from carrying out his obligations under the contract. If, however, the breach is a serious one going to the root or substance of the contract, the innocent party may treat it as a repudiation of the contract by the other party that relieves him from performing his part of it, while retaining his right to sue for damages for breach of contract.[177] This may also be called 'rescission' and, in this looser sense, is a matter of contract law. An innocent party who thus accepts the repudiation cannot thereafter seek specific performance.

(iii) Further questions have arisen where a vendor has chosen to affirm a contract for the sale of land and has obtained a decree of specific performance, with which the purchaser has failed to comply. In such case, the vendor may either apply to the court for enforcement of the decree, or apply for an order of the court rescinding the contract at this stage, the latter application being no mere formality. In this context, 'rescission' means that the vendor will be permitted to retain the land on the basis that he is no longer bound to perform his part of the contract in consequence of the purchaser's repudiation of it. At the same time, he is entitled to claim damages at common law for breach of contract.[178] It should be remembered that, since the court is, at this stage, necessarily exercising its equity jurisdiction, it will act in accordance with equitable principles and would not accede to the plaintiff's claim; it would not make an order dissolving the decree of specific performance

---

[175] See the valuable article in (1975) 91 LQR 337 (M Albery); see also (1976) 92 LQR 5 (W Gummow); (1976) 39 MLR 214 (F Dawson); (1980) 39 CLJ 58 (A J Oakley); [2000] CLJ 509 (Janet O'Sullivan); [2002] RLR 28 (Sarah Worthington). Partial rescission is not permissible, but see (2005) 121 LQR 273 (J Poole and A Keyser).

[176] [1978] 3 All ER 929; CA; *Johnson v Agnew* [1980] AC 367, [1979] 1 All ER 883, HL.

[177] *Johnson v Agnew, supra*, HL. See also *Millichamp v Jones* [1983] 1 All ER 267, [1982] 1 WLR 1422.

[178] *Johnson v Agnew* [1980] AC 367, [1979] 1 All ER 883, HL (which also decides what is the measure of damage—see p 571, *supra*). See (1980) 9 Sydney LR 71 (Marion Hetherington).

and terminating the contract (with recovery of damages) if to do so would be unjust, in the circumstances then existing, to the purchaser.[179]

(iv) A contract may confer on a party to it a power of rescission on certain terms, in certain events. There is no reason why effect should not be given to such a provision, but the meaning of the term 'rescission' in a contract is whatever the contract gives it.

(B) RESCISSION IN ITS STRICT SENSE

Where there is a right of rescission in the strict sense, the contract remains fully valid and binding unless and until the party entitled to do so repudiates it, which repudiation must normally be communicated to the other party.[180] A valid repudiation, however, terminates the contract, puts the parties in *statu quo ante* and restores things, as between them, to the position in which they stood before the contract was entered into. Strictly speaking, rescission is the act of a party and not the act of a court: if the court makes an appropriate order, this has been said to be 'merely the judicial determination of the fact that the expression by the plaintiff of his election to rescind was justified, was effective, and put an end to the contract'.[181] It may be asked, therefore, why the matter should come before the court at all. This may happen for a variety of reasons: for instance, the other party may refuse to accept the repudiation and bring an action on the contract, to which the defence may be that the contract has been rescinded, or, the party who claims the right to rescind, perhaps knowing that his claim is not accepted by the other party, may prefer to bring an action to have the contract set aside, or, commonly, there may be some consequential question on which the decision of the court is required, as to the steps that have to be taken to arrive at the *restitutio in integrum*—that is, the restoring of the parties to their original positions—which is an essential concomitant of rescission. It was because of the ancillary relief commonly sought that, originally, questions of rescission generally arose in the Court of Chancery. The accounts and inquiries that might be necessary to enable *restitutio in integrum* to be implemented could not usually be carried out in a court of common law.[182] Also, a court of equity might be prepared to set aside a contract in circumstances that would not render it voidable at common law. But if *restitutio in integrum* merely required the repayment of

---

[179] *Johnson v Agnew, supra*, HL, discussed (1980) 96 LQR 403 (Marion Hetherington), (1981) 97 LQR 26 (D Jackson); *G K N Distributors Ltd v Tyne Tees Fabrication Ltd* [1985] 2 EGLR 181.

[180] Exceptionally, communication is not required where election to rescind is shown by retaking goods transferred under the contract, or, at any rate in a case of fraud, where the other party has made communication impossible: *Car and Universal Finance Co Ltd v Caldwell* [1965] 1 QB 525, [1964] 1 All ER 290, CA; *Newtons of Wembley Ltd v Williams* [1965] 1 QB 560, [1964] 3 All ER 532, CA.

[181] Per Lord Atkinson in *Abram Steamship Co Ltd v Westville Shipping Co Ltd* [1923] AC 773, 781, cited *Baird v BCE Holdings Pty Ltd* [1996] 134 Fed LR 279. See also *Aaron's Reefs Ltd v Twiss* [1896] AC 273, HL; *United Shoe Machinery Co of Canada v Brunet* [1909] AC 330, PC; *Horsler v Zorro* [1975] Ch 302, [1975] 1 All ER 584. It was submitted, in *Halpern v Halpern (No 2)* [2006] EWHC 1728 (Comm), [2006] 3 All ER 1139, that rescission in equity on grounds that were not recognized at common law was a judicial remedy that takes effect from the date of the court's order and not from the date of the party's decision to avoid or rescind the contract. In the event, the judge did not find it necessary to rule on the submission.

[182] *Erlanger v New Sombrero Phosphate Co* (1878) 3 App Cas 1218, 1278, per Lord Blackburn. See also *Cheese v Thomas* [1994] 1 All ER 35, [1994] 1 WLR 129, CA, discussed (1994) 144 NLJ 264 (Jill Martin); [1994] LMCLQ 330 (J Mee); (1994) 110 LQR 173 (M Chen-Wishart); and *O'Sullivan v Management Agency and Music Ltd* [1985] QB 428, [1985] 3 All ER 351, CA, per Dunn LJ.

money paid or the recovery of property transferred, and the contract was voidable at common law, the matter could be completely remedied by a common law action for money had or received,[183] or trover.[184] Actions for setting aside deeds or other written instruments are now assigned to the Chancery Division.[185]

It may be, of course, that the act relied upon as a ground for rescission will also be a ground for an independent action in tort. Thus a fraudulent misrepresentation that induces a man to enter into a contract may give him a right of action for damages at common law for the tort of deceit. If this is so it may be either, alternative, or additional to rescission:[186] the party defrauded may either affirm the contract and be compensated for his loss by damages for the tort, or rescind and yet bring his action for deceit to cover any loss beyond *restitutio in integrum*, which, however, in many cases, will be merely nominal.

(C) GROUNDS UPON WHICH RESCISSION MAY BE GRANTED

The main grounds on which a contract may be rescinded are mentioned briefly below, but for a fuller discussion, the reader is referred to books on the law of contract.[187]

(i) Fraudulent misrepresentation

This rendered a contract voidable both at law and in equity.[188] For this purpose, what is relevant is fraud in the common law sense, sometimes called 'actual fraud', which will sustain an action of deceit. A fraud is proved when it is shown that a false representation has been made knowingly, or without belief in its truth, or recklessly, careless of whether it is true or false.[189] The fraudulent party need not have acted with a corrupt motive,[190] but the false statement must have been made with the intent that it should be acted on,[191] and it must actually have been acted on by the other party.[192]

(ii) Innocent misrepresentation

As such, this had no effect at common law, unless incorporated into the contract. In equity, although it might be a good defence to a specific performance action, it was for a long time, somewhat illogically, not regarded as sufficient to enable a court of equity to set the contract aside.[193] From the middle of the nineteenth century, however, the courts of equity have asserted this jurisdiction,[194] which Jessel MR explained, in *Redgrave v Hurd*,[195]

---

[183] *Stone v City and County Bank* (1877) 3 CPD 282, CA; *Kettlewell v Refuge Assurance Co* [1908] 1 KB 545, CA; affd [1909] AC 243, HL.

[184] *Jones v Keene* (1841) 2 Mood & R 348.

[185] Supreme Court Act 1981, now renamed the Senior Courts Act 1981, s 61(1) Sch 1.

[186] *Newbigging v Adam* (1886) 34 Ch D 582, 592, CA, *per* Bowen LJ; affd sub nom *Adam v Newbigging* (1888) 13 App Cas 308, HL.

[187] For example, Cheshire, Fifoot, and Furmston, *The Law of Contract*, 15th edn p 352 *et seq.*

[188] But see *Halley v The Law Society* [2003] EWCA (Civ) 97, [2003] WTLR 845, noted [2004] CLJ 30 (Tang Hang Wu).

[189] *Derry v Peek* (1889) 14 App Cas 337, HL.   [190] *Polhill v Walter* (1832) 3 B & Ad 114.

[191] *Peek v Gurney* (1873) LR 6 HL 377.   [192] *Smith v Chadwick* (1884) 9 App Cas 187, HL.

[193] *Attwood v Small* (1838) 6 Cl & Fin 232; *Bartlett v Salmon* (1855) 6 De GM & G 33.

[194] *Reese River Silver Mining Co v Smith* (1869) LR 4 HL 64; *Torrance v Bolton* (1872) 8 Ch App 118; *Walker v Boyle* [1982] 1 All ER 634, [1982] 1 WLR 495.

[195] (1881) 20 Ch D 1, 12, 13, CA.

either on the ground that equity would not permit a man to get a benefit from a statement made by him that has, in fact, been proved false, or that it would be fraudulent to allow a man to insist upon a contract obtained by the aid of his own false statement. Since the Misrepresentation Act 1967,[196] rescission has been equally available where the misrepresentation has become a term of the contract. Any misrepresentation that, in fact, induces a person to enter into a contract entitles him to rescind; the question of whether or not it would have induced a reasonable person to enter into the contract relates only to the question of onus of proof.[197]

(iii) Mere silence

This does not usually amount to a representation, but it may do so if the concealment gives to the truth that is told the character of falsehood,[198] or if there is a duty to make disclosure, as is the case where the contract is one *uberrimae fidei*.[199]

(iv) Executed contracts entered into as a result of misrepresentation

If the misrepresentation was fraudulent, the fact that the contract has been completed does not destroy the right of rescission. Before the Misrepresentation Act 1967, it was the law that there could be no rescission for innocent misrepresentation after completion of a contract for the sale of land,[200] or, probably, the execution of a formal lease.[201] This rule was less firmly established in other cases.[202] The Act now provides[203] that rescission may be allowed for innocent misrepresentation where the contract has been performed in the same way as where the representation is fraudulent.

(v) Constructive fraud

A contract may be rescinded in equity on the ground of constructive fraud. There has been held to be constructive fraud in cases involving taking advantage of weakness or necessity, including catching bargains with expectant heirs, breach of fiduciary duty, such as a purchase by a trustee of the trust property, and frauds on a power.[204] In particular, it includes undue influence.

'Undue influence' has long been a ground on which equity might relieve a party to a transaction where it was entered into by reason of the undue influence of the other party, thus enabling a gift to be recovered or a contract to be set aside. In *Allcard v Skinner*,[205] a woman was persuaded to join a religious order that involved a strict vow of poverty, as a

---

[196] Section 1. See (1967) 30 MLR 369 (P S Atiyah and G H Treitel); (1967) 31 Conv 234 (J R Murdock).

[197] *Museprime Properties Ltd v Adhill Properties Ltd* (1990) 61 P & CR 111.

[198] *Oakes v Turquand* (1867) LR 2 HL 325.

[199] Principally, contracts of insurance of all kinds. See *Wales v Wadham* [1977] 2 All ER 125.

[200] *Early v Garrett* (1829) 9 B & C 928; *Wilde v Gibson* (1848) 1 HL Cas 605.

[201] *Angel v Jay* [1911] 1 KB 666, DC; *Edler v Auerbach* [1950] 1 KB 359, [1949] 2 All ER 692.

[202] *Seddon v North Eastern Salt Co Ltd* [1905] 1 Ch 326, [1904–7] All ER Rep 817; cf *Leaf v International Galleries* [1950] 2 KB 86, [1950] 1 All ER 693, CA; *Long v Lloyd* [1958] 2 All ER 402, [1958] 1 WLR 753, CA.

[203] Section 1.

[204] For the doctrine of unconscionable bargains, see *Portman Building Society v Dusangh* [2000] 2 All ER (Comm) 221, CA, and cases there cited. See (2000) 21 T & ELJ 12 (M Hardwick); [2000] Conv 573 (L McMurtry).

[205] (1887) 36 Ch D 145, CA. This case, in the Australian context, is considered in (2003) 26 UNSWLJ 66 (P Ridge). See, generally, [2007] JBL 541 (J Devenney and A Chandler).

consequence of which she gave some £7,000 to the order. All but £1,671 had been spent by the order when the woman left it. Subsequently, she sought to recover this money. It was held that, as the gift had been made under a pressure that she could not resist, she was, in principle, entitled to recover it in so far as it had not been disbursed with her consent for the purposes of the order. On the facts, however, her claim was barred by her laches and acquiescence.[206] The leading case is now *Royal Bank v Etridge (No 2).*[207]

Whether a transaction was brought about by the exercise of undue influence is a question of fact, and, in general, the person who alleges undue influence must prove it. It must be affirmatively established that the donor's trust and confidence in the donee has been betrayed or abused. The principle is not confined to cases of abuse of trust and confidence; it includes other cases in which a vulnerable person has been exploited. Various expressions have been used: 'trust and confidence', 'reliance', 'dependence', or 'vulnerability', on the one hand, and 'ascendency', 'domination', or 'control', on the other. But 'None of these descriptions is perfect. None is all embracing. Each has its proper place'.[208] Moreover, the fact that the donee's conduct was unimpeachable and that there was nothing sinister in it is no sufficient answer to a claim.[209] The evidence required depends on the nature of the alleged undue influence, the personality of the parties, the extent to which the transaction cannot readily be accounted for by the ordinary motives of ordinary persons in that relationship, and all of the circumstances of the case.

A distinction is drawn between 'actual undue influence' and 'presumed undue influence'. Actual undue influence does not depend upon a pre-existing relationship between the two parties, although it is most commonly associated with, and derived from, such a relationship. The party who alleges actual undue influence must prove affirmatively that he entered into the impugned transaction not of his own will, but as a result of actual undue influence exerted against him.[210] He must show that the other party to the transaction, or someone who induced the transaction for his own benefit, had the capacity to influence the complainant, that the influence was exercised, that the exercise was undue, and that its exercise brought about the transaction. It is not necessary, however, to show domination. Whether actual undue influence has been exercised is a question of fact.[211]

The evidential burden may, however, shift to the defendant if the complainant can show that he placed trust and confidence in the defendant in relation to the management of his financial affairs, coupled with a transaction that calls for explanation—that is, one that is

---

[206] See p 534, *supra.*

[207] *Royal Bank of Scotland v Etridge (No 2)* [2001] UKHL 44, [2002] 2 AC 773, [2001] 4 All ER 449. The salient points in the speech of Lord Nicholls, which reflected the views of the House of Lords, were summarized in *Randall v Randall* [2004] EWHC 2258 (Ch), [2005] WTLR 119. For New Zealand, see (2006) 11 Otago LR 247 (B Allen).

[208] See *Royal Bank of Scotland v Etridge (No 2)*, *supra*, HL, at [11]; *Macklin v Dowsett* [2004] EWCA Civ 904, [2005] WTLR 1561.

[209] *Hammond v Osborn* [2002] EWCA (Civ) 885, [2002] WTLR 1125; *Niersmans v Pesticcio* [2004] EWCA (Civ) 372, [2004] WTLR 699; *Goodchild v Bradbury* [2006] EWCA Civ 1868, [2007] WTLR 463, noted [2008] Conv 1.

[210] See *Royal Bank of Scotland v Etridge (No 2)*, *supra*, HL; *Daniel v Drew* [2005] EWCA Civ 507, [2005] WTLR 807, noted [2005] Sol Jo 757 (M Pawlowski); (2006) 73 T & ELTJ 10 (M Farren and Penelope Reed).

[211] *Langton v Langton* [1995] 2 FLR 890; *UCB Corporate Services Ltd v Williams* [2002] EWCA Civ 555, [2003] 1 P & CR 168; *Wright v Cherrytree Finance Ltd* [2001] 2 All ER (Comm) 877.

not readily explicable by the relationship between the parties.[212] This is commonly referred to as a case of 'presumed undue influence'. Once the presumption is raised, it is presumed, unless and until it is rebutted, that the donee has preferred his own interests and has not behaved fairly to the donor.[213] In such a case, the court interferes not on the ground that any wrongful act has, in fact, been committed by the donee, but on the ground of public policy, and to prevent the relationship that existed between the parties and the influence arising therefrom being abused. The presumption may be rebutted by proof that the gift was 'the spontaneous act of the donor acting under circumstances which enabled him to exercise an independent will and which justifies the court in holding that the gift was a free exercise of the donor's will', or, to put it more shortly, where it is proved that the gift was made by the donor 'only after full, free and informed thought about it'—that is, fully informed not only of the nature of the gift, but also of its effect.[214]

Moreover, in the case of certain well-known relationships, such as solicitor and client, and trustee and beneficiary,[215] the law presumes, irrebuttably, that one party had influence over the other. In these cases, the complainant need not prove that he actually reposed trust and confidence in the other party; it is sufficient to prove the existence of the relationship. But, even here, he must show that the transaction was wrongful in that it constituted an advantage taken of the person subjected to the influence, which, failing proof

---

[212] *Michael v Cansick* [2004] EWHC 1684 (Ch), [2004] WTLR 961. See *Turkey v Awadh* [2003] EWCA Civ 382, [2005] 2 FCR 7, in which the transaction, curious as it might otherwise seem, was explicable by the ordinary motives of people in the position of the parties. The classification of presumed undue influence cases in *Bank of Credit and Commerce International SA v Aboody* [1990] 1 QB 923, 953, [1992] 4 All ER 955, 964, CA (overruled on other grounds by *CIBC Mortgages plc v Pitt* [1994] 1 AC 200, [1993] 4 All ER 417, HL), adopted in *Barclays Bank plc v O'Brien* [1994] 1 AC 180, [1993] 4 All ER 417, HL, into Class 2A, in which the law presumes the legal relationship between the parties to be one of trust and confidence, and Class 2B, in which the claimant must establish by affirmative evidence that he or she was accustomed to repose trust and confidence in the alleged wrongdoer, has lost most of its significance since *Royal Bank of Scotland v Etridge (No 2), supra*, HL, esp *per* Lord Clyde, at [92], Lord Hobhouse, at [107], and Lord Scott, at [158] and [161]. The presumption was not rebutted in *Goldsworthy v Brickell* [1987] Ch 378, [1987] 1 All ER 853, CA, in *Hammon v Osborn, supra*, CA, noted [2003] LMCLQ 145 (Karen Scott); (2004) 120 LQR 34 (P Birks), in which a very large gift, both in absolute and comparative terms, was not made after 'full, free and informed thought', or in *Goodchild v Bradbury* [2006] EWCA Civ 1868, [2007] WTLR 463. Cf *Re Brocklehurst* [1978] 1 Ch 14, CA; *Chater v Mortgage Agency Services Number Two Ltd* [2003] EWCA Div 490, [2003] HLR 61, and see *In the Estate of Bennett (decd)* [2004] EWHC 396 (Ch), [2004] WTLR 485, in which the relationship did not give rise to any evidential presumption of undue influence, and the unusual case of *Hughes v Hughes* [2005] EWHC 469 (Ch), [2005] 1 FCR 679.

[213] *Wright v Hodgkinson* [2004] EWHC 3091 (Ch), [2005] WTLR 435.

[214] *Randall v Randall, supra*, in which it was that the two formulations have consistently been treated as expressing an identical test.

[215] Also parent and child, guardian and ward, medical, religious, and other advisers and their patients, etc. In *Leeder v Stevens* [2005] EWCA Civ 50, [2005] All ER (D) 40 (Jan), it was assumed to be well settled that the presumption applies between fiancé and fiancée, and it was extended to a relationship between a man and a woman who were not engaged to be married (the man was already married to someone else), but where there had been some discussion of marriage. In (2005) 1221 LQR 567, N Enonchong contends that the matter is not 'well settled' and that the law ought not to persist in what he argues is an anomaly, let alone be extended. The presumption does not apply between husband and wife, but the undue influence may, of course, be established by evidence, although it was not in *Re Barker-Benfield (decd)* [2006] EWHC 1119 (Ch), [2006] WTLR 1141. Nor does the presumption arise in the case of an adult child and his or her elderly parent, although this may be a factor in establishing the necessary trust and confidence. As to undue influence and elderly persons generally, see (2003) 23 LS 251 (Fiona R Burns). In relation to banker and customer, see (1986) 65 CBR 37 (D Waters).

to the contrary, was explicable only on the basis that undue influence had been exercised to procure it.[216]

One way in which a claim of undue influence may be defeated is by showing that the claimant received independent legal advice, but the involvement of a solicitor does not necessarily prevent a finding that a transaction was tainted by undue influence.[217] It is a question of fact whether the outside advice had an appropriate emancipating effect.[218] It has been said[219] that it would be sensible for a person who may be at risk of being alleged to have exercised undue influence, whether presumed or actual, to ensure that the solicitor who gives legal advice to the potential claimant is wholly unconnected with that person.

So long as the undue influence persists, a claim can be brought regardless of how much time has passed since the transaction.[220]

Many cases have come before the courts in recent years in which a wife has charged her interest in the matrimonial home to a bank as security for her husband's indebtedness or the indebtedness of a company through which he carried on business. Subsequently, when the bank seeks to realize its security, the wife alleges that she is not bound because she has executed the charge under the undue influence of her husband. Assuming that undue influence is established, the wife would have no difficulty in claiming a remedy against the husband. The difficulty in these cases is that (commonly supported by her husband) she seeks to prevent a third party, the bank, which has not exercised any undue influence, from enforcing its security.

The traditional view of equity in this tripartite situation was that the wife could only succeed if the third party was privy to the conduct that led to the wife's entry into the transaction. There is no legal obligation on one party to a transaction to check whether the other party's concurrence was obtained by undue influence. The leading case of *Barclays Bank plc v O'Brien*[221] has now introduced into the law the concept that, in certain circumstances, a party to a contract may lose the benefit of his contract, entered into in good faith, if he ought to have known that the other's concurrence had been procured by the misconduct of a third party. The *O'Brien* principle, as it has been called, was affirmed and elaborated in *Royal Bank of Scotland v Etridge (No 2)*.[222] Although most of the cases have involved a wife

---

[216] See *National Westminster Bank plc v Morgan* [1985] AC 686, 703–707, [1985] 1 All ER 821, 826–829, HL, *per* Lord Scarman; *Allcard v Skinner, supra,* CA, *per* Lindley LJ, at 185. In citing and applying these dicta in *Royal Bank of Scotland v Etridge (No 2), supra,* HL, Lord Nicholls said that the label 'manifest disadvantage' that had been attached to this latter requirement had given rise to misunderstanding and should be discarded. See (2005) 121 LQR 29 (N Enonchong). See also *Jennings v Cairns* [2003] EWCA Civ 1935, [2004] WTLR 361.

[217] *Randall v Randall, supra; Vale v Armstrong* [2004] EWHC 1160 (Ch), [2004] WTLR 1471, noted (2004) 18(7) T & E 2.

[218] *Randall v Randall, supra.*

[219] *Per* Neuberger J in *Pesticcio v Huet* [2003] EWHC 2293 (Ch), [2003] WTLR 1327, at [106], affd sub nom *Niersmans v Pesticcio* [2004] EWCA (Civ) 37, [2004] WTLR 699 (the evidence established that the brother had the necessary degree of trust and confidence in his sister).

[220] *Humphreys v Humphreys* [2004] EWHC 2201 (Ch), [2004] WTLR 1425.

[221] *Supra,* HL. As to the possibility of severing from an instrument affected by undue influence the objectionable parts, leaving the part uncontaminated by undue influence enforceable, see *Barclays Bank plc v Caplan* [1998] 1 FLR 532.

[222] *Supra,* HL, noted (2002) 118 LQR 337 (D O'Sullivan), 351 (P Watts); [2002] MLR 435 (R Bigwood); [2002] Conv 174 (M P Thompson) and 456 (Georgina Andrews); (2002) 61 CLJ 29 (Mika Oldham); [2002] JBL 439 (S Wong); [2002] LMCLQ 231 (A Phang and H Tjio); [2002] RLR 100 (D Capper). See also *Meredith v Lackschwitz-Martin* [2002] EWHC 1462 (Ch), [2002] WTLR 1451; *A-G v R* [2003] UKPC 22, [2003] EMLR

becoming surety for her husband, the principle is not restricted to cases in which a creditor obtains a security from a guarantor whose sexual relationship with the debtor gives rise to a heightened risk of undue influence. It applies equally where a husband stands surety for his wife, and, in the case of unmarried couples, whether heterosexual or homosexual, where the bank is aware of the relationship. Cohabitation is not essential.[223] It has been applied where the relationship was employer and employee,[224] and is applicable in every case in which the relationship between the surety and the debtor is non-commercial.[225]

In the above cases, the bank (or other creditor) is, as it is said, 'put on inquiry', and, in *Royal Bank of Scotland v Etridge (No 2)*,[226] detailed guidance was given as to the steps that the bank should take to protect itself in these circumstances. One way is for the bank to insist that the wife attends a private meeting with a representative of the bank, at which she is told of the extent of her liability as surety, warned of the risk that she is running, and urged to take independent advice. In practice, banks are reluctant to follow this course and prefer to rely on the wife having obtained independent advice from a solicitor. To obtain protection in this way, the bank must communicate directly with the wife, informing her that, for her own protection, it will require written confirmation from a solicitor, acting for her, to the effect that the solicitor has fully explained to her the nature of the documents and the practical implications that they will have for her. She should be told that the purpose of this requirement is that thereafter she should not be able, once she has signed the documents, to dispute that she is legally bound by them. She should be asked to nominate a solicitor (not necessarily a different solicitor from the one advising her husband) whom she is willing to instruct to advise her, separately from her husband, and act for her in giving the necessary confirmation to the bank. The bank must supply the solicitor with all of the necessary financial information.

Where a mortgage is voidable for undue influence as against a husband and against a bank, a replacement mortgage would itself be voidable, at any rate, if the replacement mortgage were taken out as a condition of discharging the earlier voidable mortgage, even if undue influence were not operative at the time of such replacement, and even if there were a new contract rather than a mere variation.[227]

499, noted [2003] RLR 110 (A Phang and H Tjio); [2003] LMCLQ 341 (Joan Wadsley); *Nel v Kean* [2003] EWHC 190 (QB), [2003] WTLR 501.

[223] *Massey v Midland Bank plc* [1995] 1 All ER 929, 933, *per* Steyn LJ, approved by Lord Nicholls in *Royal Bank of Scotland v Etridge (No 2)*, *supra*, HL, at [47].

[224] *Credit Lyonnais Bank Nederland NV v Burch* [1997] 1 All ER 144, CA.

[225] See, eg, *Avon Finance Co Ltd v Bridger* [1985] 2 All ER 281, CA (son and elderly parents); *National Westminster Bank plc v Amin* [2002] UKHL 9, [2002] 1 FLR 735 (English-speaking son and non-English-speaking parents), noted [2002] Conv 499 (M Haley).

[226] *Supra*, HL. The guidance was said to be applicable to future transactions. In relation to past transactions, the test applicable was said to be that set out by Lord Browne-Wilkinson in *Barclays Bank plc v O'Brien*, *supra*, HL, at 196–197, 629–630. See also *McGregor v Michael Taylor & Co* [2002] Lloyd's Rep 468; *UCB Corporate Services Ltd v Williams*, *supra*, CA; *UCB Group Ltd v Hedworth* [2003] EWCA Civ 1717, [2003] 3 FCR 737; [2001] PLJ 16 (M Pawlowski); *First National Bank plc v Achampong* [2003] EWCA Civ 487, [2004] 1 FCR 18, discussed [2003] LMCLQ 307 (N Enonchong); [2003] Conv 314 (M P Thompson).

[227] *Yorkshire Bank plc v Tinsley* [2004] EWCA Civ 816, [2004] 3 All ER 463, noted [2004] Conv 399 (M P Thompson); [2005] CLJ 42 (N P Gravells).

(vi) Mistake

After a full discussion of the cases, the Court of Appeal held in *Great Peace Shipping Ltd v Tsavliris Salvage (International) Ltd*,[228] disapproving *Solle v Butcher*[229] as being unable to stand with *Bell v Lever Bros Ltd*,[230] that there is no jurisdiction to grant rescission of a contract on the ground of common mistake where that contract is valid and enforceable on ordinary principles of contract law. The court observed, however, that just as the Law Reform (Frustrated Contracts) Act 1943 was needed to temper the effect of the common law doctrine of frustration, so there is scope for legislation to give greater flexibility to the law of mistake than the common law allows.

It seems, however, that the equitable jurisdiction to set aside a transaction for unilateral mistake continues.[231]

(vii) Bribery

Bribery is committed where one person makes, or agrees to make, a payment to the agent of another person with whom he is dealing without the knowledge and consent of the agent's principal. Where a contract ensues from those dealings, the principal is entitled to rescission if he neither knew nor consented to the payment. If he knew of it, but did not give his informed consent, the court may award rescission as a discretionary remedy, if it is just and proportionate to do so.[232]

(D) LOSS OF THE RIGHT TO RESCISSION

This may occur in various ways.

(i) Affirmation of the contract

Where a man has a right of rescission, he may elect either to rescind the contract or to affirm it. If, with full knowledge not only of the relevant facts, but also of his legal right to rescind, he, either by express words or by unequivocal acts, affirms the contract, his election has been determined forever.[233] Although the question remains open until he elects one way or the other, lapse of time and acquiescence will furnish evidence of an election to affirm the contract, and when the lapse of time is great, it would probably, in practice, be treated as conclusive evidence to show that he had so determined. The court will, of course,

---

[228] [2002] EWCA Civ 1407, [2002] 4 All ER 689, discussed [2002] NLJ 132 (M Pawlowski); [2002] NLJ 1654 (D Dabbs); [2002] LMCLQ 449 (G McMeel); (2003) 119 LQR 177 (F M B Reynolds); (2003) 119 LQR 180 (S B Midwinter); [2003] CLJ 29 (C Hare); [2004] JBL 34 (A Chandler, J Devenney, and J Poole); [2003] RLR 93 (J Cartwright); (2004) KCLJ 127 (J Edelman); [2003] Conv 247 (A Phang); [2005] 16(1) KCLJ 69 (M de Gregorio).

[229] [1950] 1 KB 671, [1949] 2 All ER 1007, CA.   [230] [1932] AC 161, HL.

[231] See [2005] LQR 393 (T M Yeo), citing *Chwee Kin Keong v Digilandmall. com Pte Ltd* [2005] 1 SLR 202.

[232] *Ross River Ltd v Cambridge City Football Club Ltd* [2007] EWHC 2115 (Ch), [2008] 1 All ER 1004.

[233] *Clough v London and North Western Rly Co* (1871) LR 7 Exch 26; *Peyman v Lanjani* [1985] Ch 457, [1984] 3 All ER 703, in which the point is also made that if A has acted to his detriment in reliance on an *apparent* election by B, he will, in most cases, be able to rely on an estoppel by conduct; *Cornish v Midland Bank plc* [1985] 3 All ER 513, CA.

on equitable principles, take all of the circumstances into account,[234] including the nature of the contract[235] and the presence or absence of fraud.[236]

(ii) *Restitutio in integrum*

The basic rule is that rescission is not permitted unless it is possible for the contract to be rescinded *in toto*,[237] and the parties replaced in *statu quo ante*. On the one hand, this means that rescission necessarily involves the restoration of money paid or property transferred under the contract that has been avoided; where there is no independent right of action for damages, as may still be the case even after the Misrepresentation Act 1967 where rescission is decreed for innocent misrepresentation,[238] this includes a right to an indemnity against liabilities necessarily incurred or created under the contract that has been avoided, but this may well be something less than what would be recoverable in an action for damages. On the other hand, it follows that, if it is not possible to restore the parties to their pre-contract position, then the remedy of rescission will not lie.[239] In applying this rule, the courts are primarily concerned with the restoration of the defendant to his pre-contract position and do not lay stress on the restoration of the plaintiff.[240]

The requirement of *restitutio in integrum* seems to have been strictly enforced at common law,[241] but the equitable rules were, or became, more flexible. The result is that the doctrine is not applied too literally, the court fixing its eyes on the goal of doing what is practically just in the individual case, even though *restitutio in integrum* is impossible, and being more drastic in exercising its discretionary remedy of rescission in a case of fraud than in a case of innocent misrepresentation.[242] Fraud includes constructive fraud—in particular, a transaction that has been procured by undue influence, or where one party is

---

[234] See, generally, *Erlanger v New Sombrero Phosphate Co* (1878) 3 App Cas 1218, HL; *Senanayake v Cheng* [1966] AC 63, [1965] 3 All ER 296, PC; *Laurence v Lexcourt Holdings Ltd* [1978] 2 All ER 810. And see *William Sindall plc v Cambridgeshire County Council, supra*, CA.

[235] *Leaf v International Galleries* [1950] 2 KB 86, [1950] 1 All ER 693, CA (in which a claim to rescind an executed contract for the sale of goods for innocent misrepresentation was barred by five years' delay, although the plaintiff brought his action as soon as he knew the true facts); *Re Scottish Petroleum Co* (1883) 23 Ch D 413, 434, CA (where shares are allotted in a going concern, it is doubtful if repudiation in a fortnight would be soon enough).

[236] *Charter v Trevelyan* (1844) 11 Cl & Fin 714; *Spackman v Evans* (1868) LR 3 HL 171.

[237] *Thorpe v Fasey* [1949] Ch 649, [1949] 2 All ER 393, severely criticized on other grounds in (1975) 91 LQR 337 (M Albery).

[238] Section 2(1) of the Misrepresentation Act 1967 did not altogether abolish the common law rule laid down in *Gilchester Properties Ltd v Gomm* [1948] 1 All ER 493. A misrepresentor may defend an action for damages by proving that '*he had reasonable ground to believe and did believe up to the time the contract was made that the facts represented were true*'. Quaere, whether non-disclosure can ever constitute misrepresentation for the purposes of this section.

[239] *Clarke v Dickson* (1858) EB & E 148; *Urquhart v Macpherson* (1878) 3 App Cas 831, PC; and cases cited in the following three footnotes.

[240] *Western Bank of Scotland v Addie* (1862) LR 1 Sc & Div 145; *Spence v Crawford* [1939] 3 All ER 271, HL.

[241] See *Halpern v Halpern (No 2)* [2006] EWHC 1728 (Comm), [2007] QB 88, [2006] 3 All ER 1139 (rescission on the ground of duress), reversed in part [2007] EWCA Civ 291, [2007] 3 All ER 478, which suggests that the common law approach may now be assimilated to that of equity.

[242] *O'Sullivan v Management Agency and Music Ltd* [1985] QB 428, [1985] 3 All ER 351, CA; *De Molestian v Ponton* [2002] 1 Lloyds Rep 270. Where the victim of a fraudulent misrepresentation has lost the right of rescission because *restitutio in integrum* is no longer possible, he could still rely on the misrepresentor's reprehensible conduct in resisting on application for specific performance, provided that he has not affirmed the contract: *Geest plc v Fyffes plc* [1999] 1 All ER (Comm) 672.

in breach of a fiduciary duty to another. Thus, in *O'Sullivan v Management Agency & Music Ltd*,[243] it was held that the wrongdoer must give up his profits and advantages, while at the same time being compensated for work that he had actually performed under the contract. At least in relation to a transaction entered into in breach of a fiduciary relationship, the transaction:

> may be set aside even though it is impossible to place the parties precisely in the position in which they were before, provided that the court can achieve practical justice between the parties by obliging the wrongdoer to give up his profits and advantages, while at the same time compensating him for any work that he has actually performed pursuant to the transaction.[244]

The equitable course may not be rescission at all, but rather to enforce specific performance with compensation.

(iii) Rights of third parties

If an innocent third party has acquired for value an interest in property affected by the contract that would be prejudiced by rescission, the person who would otherwise have a right to rescind will be precluded from exercising it.[245] The right of rescission being, it is submitted, a mere equity, this is a correct application of the basic principle that such a right is ineffective against a subsequent purchaser for value without notice of either a legal estate or an equitable interest.[246]

(iv) Misrepresentation Act 1967

In any case of innocent misrepresentation giving rise to a right of rescission, the court may declare the contract subsisting and award damages in lieu of rescission, if of the opinion that it would be equitable to do so, having regard to the nature of the misrepresentation and the loss that would be caused by it if the contract were upheld, as well as to the loss that rescission would cause the other party.[247] According to *Government of Zanzibar v British Aerospace (Lancaster House) Ltd*,[248] however, the court has no power to award damages if the right of rescission has been lost.

4 RECTIFICATION OF DOCUMENTS

(A) GENERAL

Where a transaction is embodied in a written instrument that, by mistake, does not express the true agreement of the parties, the remedy of rectification may be available.

---

[243] *Supra*, CA. See also *Mahoney v Purnell* [1997] 1 FLR 612; (2002) 16 Tru LI 151 (T Akkouh); (2003) 17 Tru LI 66 (V J Vann).

[244] *O'Sullivan v Management Agency and Music Ltd, supra*, CA, *per* Dunn LJ, at 466.

[245] *Clough v London and North Western Rly Co* (1871) LR 7 Exch 26, 35; *Oakes v Turquand* (1867) LR 2 HL 325.　　　　　　　　　　　　　　　　　　　　[246] See Chapter 1, section 5, p 21 *et seq, supra*.

[247] See [1987] Conv 423 (J Cartwright).

[248] [2000] 1 WLR 2333, critically noted (2001) 117 LQR 524 (D Malet).

Where it is ordered, such alterations or amendments will be made in the written instrument as may be necessary to express the true agreement, and, after such rectification, 'the written agreement does not continue to exist with a parol variation; it is to be read as if it had been originally drawn in its rectified form'.[249] This may have the result of validating with retrospective effect some act that was invalidly done under the instrument in its original form.[250] It is vital to realize that it is only the written expression of the parties' agreement that is rectified, never the agreement itself: 'Courts of Equity do not rectify contracts; they may and do rectify instruments purporting to have been made in pursuance of the terms of contracts.'[251]

Rectification will only be granted if the court is satisfied that there is an issue, capable of being contested, between the parties (or the grantor/covenantor and the persons he intended to benefit). If there is such an issue, it is irrelevant that rectification is sought or consented to by all parties, or that rectification is desired because of the fiscal consequences. But rectification cannot be granted if the rights of the parties will be unaffected and the only effect is to receive a fiscal benefit.[252]

> In order to get rectification, it is necessary to show that the parties were in complete agreement on the terms of their contract, but by an error wrote them down wrongly...If you can predicate with certainty what their contract was, and that it is, by a common mistake, wrongly expressed in the document, then you rectify the document.[253]

It is not a bar to relief that the need for rectification arises from an error of the claimant's solicitors: and, generally speaking, negligence is an irrelevant consideration.[254] The remedy is available in respect of nearly all kinds of documents, such as a conveyance of land,[255] a lease,[256] a settlement,[257] a bill of exchange,[258] a policy of life[259] or marine[260] insurance, a building contract,[261] and a disentailing deed,[262] but not the articles of association of a company.[263]

---

[249] Per Sterndale MR in *Craddock Bros Ltd v Hunt* [1923] 2 Ch 136, 151, [1923] All ER Rep 394, 402, CA; *Johnson v Bragge* [1901] 1 Ch 28.

[250] *Malmesbury v Malmesbury* (1862) 31 Beav 407, 418.

[251] Per James VC in *Mackenzie v Coulson* (1869) LR 8 Eq 368, 375.

[252] *Whiteside v Whiteside* [1950] Ch 65, [1949] 2 All ER 913, CA; *Sherdley v Sherdley* [1986] 2 All ER 202, CA; *Racal Group Services Ltd v Ashmore* [1995] STC 1151, CA, noted [1996] Conv 228 (I Ferrier); [1996] 146 NLJ 1589 (Sarah Lacey); *Price v Williams-Wynn* [2006] EWHC 788 (Ch), [2006] WTLR 1633. See also *Martin v Nicholson* [2004] EWHC 2135 (Ch), [2005] WTLR 175.

[253] Per Denning LJ in *Frederick E Rose (London) Ltd v William H Pim Jnr & Co Ltd* [1953] 2 QB 450, 461, [1953] 2 All ER 739, 747, CA. See also *Olympia Sauna Shipping Co SA v Shinwa Kaiun Kaisha Ltd* [1985] 2 Lloyd's Rep 364.

[254] *Weeds v Blaney* (1977) 247 EG 211, CA.   [255] *White v White* (1872) LR 15 Eq 247.

[256] *Murray v Parker* (1854) 19 Beav 305. Cases on leases are reviewed in (1984) 270 EG 1012 (D W Williams) and (1984) 81 LSG 1577 (S Tromans).

[257] *Welman v Welman* (1880) 15 Ch D 570.   [258] *Druiff v Lord Parker* (1868) LR 5 Eq 131.

[259] *Collett v Morrison* (1851) 9 Hare 162.   [260] *Motteux v London Assurance Co* (1739) 1 Atk 545.

[261] *Simpson v Metcalf* (1854) 24 LTOS 139; *A Roberts & Co Ltd v Leicestershire County Council* [1961] Ch 555, [1961] 2 All ER 545.

[262] Notwithstanding s 47 of the Fines and Recoveries Act 1833: *Hall-Dare v Hall-Dare* (1885) 31 Ch D 251, CA; *Meeking v Meeking* [1917] 1 Ch 77.

[263] *Evans v Chapman* (1902) 86 LT 381; *Scott v Frank F Scott (London) Ltd* [1940] Ch 794, [1940] 3 All ER 508, CA.

Prior to the Administration of Justice Act 1982, it was not available in the case of a will, but s 20 of that Act now empowers a court to order rectification of a will, if satisfied that it is so expressed that it fails to carry out the testator's intentions in consequence of either a clerical error,[264] or of a failure to understand his instructions. However, in the case of a will, an application for rectification cannot be made, except with the permission of the court, more than six months after the date on which representation with respect to the estate of the deceased was first taken out.[265]

Rectification must be kept distinct from the power of the court to correct an obvious mistake or error on the face of the instrument as a matter of construction, where this can be done without recourse to extrinsic evidence. As Amphlett LJ said in *Burchell v Clark*,[266] 'the courts of law and equity—for the rule was the same in both—where there is a manifest error in a document will put a sensible meaning on it by correcting or reading the error as corrected'. There are innumerable instances in the reports of this being done. Thus, in *Re Doland*,[267] a testator disposed of his residuary estate in percentages and gave 2 per cent to WFL. The testator further provided that, if the gift of any share should fail, his trustees should hold 'my residuary estate' upon trust for HC and PRC absolutely. The gift to WFL having failed, it was argued that the whole of the residuary estate passed to HC and PRC. The court, however, held that the words 'such share of' must be inserted before 'my residuary estate'. The mistake may be corrected on this principle whether it involves inserting words omitted, as in the case cited, deleting words,[268] altering words (as, for instance, in *Wilson v Wilson*),[269] by reading Mary for John, where in a separation deed the trustees had apparently covenanted to indemnify the husband against liability for *his* debts, or rearranging them.[270]

It must be emphasized that this constructional escape is only available where, without the aid of extrinsic evidence, both the error on the face of the document and the intention of the parties are manifest from the document itself.

(B) COMMON MISTAKE

A party seeking rectification must show that:

(i) the parties had a common continuing intention, whether or not an actual concluded contract, in respect of a particular matter in the instrument to be rectified;

---

[264] That is, an error made in the process of recording the intended words of the testator in the drafting or transcription of his will: *Re Segelman (decd)* [1996] Ch 171, [1995] 3 All ER 676, noted [1996] Conv 379 (E Histed); *Re Bell (decd)* [2002] EWHC 1080 (Ch), [2002] WTLR 1105; *Re Martin* [2007] WTLR 329, noted [2007] Conv 558 (R Kerridge and A H R Brierley); *Pengelly v Pengelly* [2007] WTLR 1619. See [2003] CLJ 250 (R Kerridge and A H R Brierley).

[265] See (1983) 80 LSG 2589 (A Mithani); (1989) 86 LSG 26 (D A Chatterton).

[266] (1876) 2 CPD 88, 97, CA; *Key v Key* (1853) 4 De GM & G 73, 84. See [1992] 1 MLJ cxiii (J C C Tik).

[267] [1970] Ch 267, [1969] 3 All ER 713; *Coles v Hulme* (1828) 8 B & C 568 (the accidental omission of the word 'pounds' said to be a 'moral certainty'). Cf *East v Pantiles (Plant Hire) Ltd* (1982) 263 EG 61, CA, in which the rectification claim failed on appeal.

[268] For example, deleting 'not': *Wilson v Wilson* (1854) 5 HL Cas 40, 67, *per* Lord St Leonards.

[269] *Supra*; *Fitch v Jones* (1855) 5 E & B 238; *Nittan (UK) Ltd v Solent Steel Fabrication Ltd* [1981] 1 Lloyd's Rep 633, CA.

[270] *Re Bacharach's Will Trusts* [1959] Ch 245, [1958] 3 All ER 618; *Schneider v Mills* [1993] 3 All ER 377.

(ii)   there was an outward expression of accord;

(iii) the intention continued at the time of the execution of the instrument sought to be rectified;

(iv)   by mistake, the instrument did not reflect that common intention.[271] Contrary to earlier decisions,[272] the rule is now settled that, while it is necessary to show that the parties were in complete agreement on the terms of their contract, it is not necessary to find a concluded and binding contract between the parties antecedent to the instrument that it is sought to rectify.[273] There must, however, be some outward expression of their continuing common intention in relation to the provision in dispute.[274] Moreover, that common intention must be formulated with certainty. Accordingly, claimants who pleaded two claims for rectification in the alternative, based on inconsistent assertions of the parties' common continuing intentions, failed. They had demonstrated at the outset that there was no certain intention that would found a claim.[275]

Where the necessary antecedent agreement is established, rectification can be granted of a written agreement, even though that agreement is complete in itself and has been carried out by a more formal document based upon it.[276] Nor is it a valid objection to a claim for rectification that the contract in question is one that is required by law to be in writing, and that the evidence of the antecedent agreement is merely oral,[277] because the jurisdiction to order rectification is outside the scope of such provisions, and the contract, when rectified, will satisfy them. If a contract is rectified, the court may order specific performance of the contract as rectified in the same action.

It is not enough to establish the existence of an antecedent agreement the terms of which differ from those of the instrument that is sought to be rectified, unless it is also established that the instrument was intended to carry out the terms of the agreement and not to vary them. If the evidence shows that the parties have changed their intentions and the instrument represents their altered intentions, there is no case for rectification.[278] As Simonds J said in *Gilhespie v Burdis*,[279] 'in order to establish [rectification], it must be shown beyond

---

[271]   *Grand Metropolitan plc v The William Hill Group Ltd* [1997] 1 BCLC 390; *Swainland Builders Ltd v Freehold Properties Ltd* [2002] EWCA Civ 560, [2002] 2 EGLR 71. See (2005) 150 PLJ 7 (Allyson Colby).

[272]   See *Mackenzie v Coulson* (1869) LR 8 Eq 368, 375; *W Higgins Ltd v Northampton Corpn* [1927] 1 Ch 128.

[273]   *Joscelyne v Nissen* [1970] 2 QB 86, [1970] 1 All ER 1213, CA, expressly approving the judgment of Simonds J in *Crane v Hegeman-Harris Co Inc* [1939] 1 All ER 662; affd [1939] 4 All ER 68, CA (but not on this point). Omitted passage at first instance printed as note to *Prenn v Simmonds* [1971] 3 All ER 237, 245, HL. See also *Rooney and McParland Ltd v Carlin* [1981] NI 138, CA, and (2007) 123 LQR 116 (A T Williams).

[274]   Per Denning LJ in *Frederick E Rose (London) Ltd v William H Pim Jnr & Co Ltd* [1953] 2 QB 450, [1953] 2 All ER 739, CA; *Joscelyne v Nissen, supra*, CA. The necessity for an outward expression is attacked in (1971) 87 LQR 532 (L Bromley).

[275]   *C H Pearce & Sons Ltd v Stonechester Ltd* (1983) Times, 17 November, dist *Swainland Builders Ltd v Freehold Properties Ltd, supra*. It is not enough to show that there had been confusion between the parties and their solicitors as to what land should be included in the conveyance: *Cambro Contractors Ltd v John Kennelly Sales Ltd* (1994) Times, 14 April, CA.

[276]   *Craddock Bros Ltd v Hunt* [1923] 2 Ch 136, [1923] All ER Rep 394, CA.

[277]   *Craddock Bros Ltd v Hunt, supra; United States of America v Motor Trucks Ltd* [1924] AC 196, PC.

[278]   *Breadalbane v Chandos* (1837) 2 My & Cr 711.   [279]   (1943) 169 LT 91, 92.

all reasonable doubt that up till the moment of execution of the agreement, it was the common intention of the parties that something should find a place in the agreement which is not there as expressed by the agreement'. Thus, where a written agreement for a lease has been followed by a regular lease with, however, some differences in the terms, it has been held that the prima facie conclusion must be that there was a new agreement with which the lease is in conformity.[280]

Since the principle behind rectification is to make the written instrument correspond with the parties' intentions, there can be no rectification where some term is deliberately omitted or put in a particular form,[281] even though this may have been done because of a mistaken belief by the parties that the inclusion of the term would be supererogatory,[282] or (in a sublease) a breach of covenant contained in the head lease,[283] or illegal.[284] The documents in such a case express the parties' intentions, and it is irrelevant that they might have had different intentions if all of the material facts had been present to their minds.[285] Again, there was held to be no case for rectification of a contract for horse beans, although it was established that both parties were under the mistaken belief that 'horse beans' were the same things as 'feveroles'.[286] On similar grounds, rectification will not be granted where a person has deliberately executed a document, although under protest and threatening in due course to bring proceedings for rectification.[287] Rectification can, however, be granted notwithstanding that the clause in question is a perfectly proper one usually contained in documents of that kind;[288] the fact that the instrument may have been drawn up by the plaintiff or his agent is not a bar to relief—even though the common mistake was engendered by the negligence of the plaintiff or his solicitors.[289]

Another question is whether rectification is possible where there is a mistake of law, as opposed to a mistake of fact—that is, where the mistake is as to the legal effect and consequences of the words used. Although dicta can be found denying the possibility of rectification on this ground, it now appears to be settled that if the parties addressed their minds to, and were under a common mistake as to the legal effect of a provision in a deed, rectification may be an appropriate remedy. Thus, in *Re Butlin's Settlement Trust*,[290] rectification was decreed where both the settlor and his solicitor were under a misapprehension as to the effect of a clause giving power to the trustees to decide by a majority. Similarly,

---

[280] *Hills v Rowland* (1853) 4 De GM & G 430. Cf *Bold v Hutchinson* (1855) 5 De GM & G 558; *Viditz v O'Hagan* [1899] 2 Ch 569, in connection with marriage settlements.

[281] *Rake v Hooper* (1900) 83 LT 669.   [282] *Worrall v Jacob* (1817) 3 Mer 256.

[283] *City and Westminster Properties (1934) Ltd v Mudd* [1959] Ch 129, [1958] 2 All ER 733.

[284] *Lord Irnham v Child* (1781) 1 Bro CC 92.

[285] *Barrow v Barrow* (1854) 18 Beav 529; *Tucker v Bennett* (1887) 38 Ch D 1, CA; cf *Carpmael v Powis* (1846) 10 Beav 36.

[286] *Frederick E Rose (London) Ltd v William H Pim Jnr & Co Ltd* [1953] 2 QB 450, [1953] 2 All ER 739, CA.

[287] *Eaton v Bennett* (1865) 34 Beav 196.   [288] *Torre v Torre* (1853) 1 Sm & G 518.

[289] *Weeds v Blaney* (1977) 247 Estates Gazette 211, CA.

[290] [1976] Ch 251, [1976] 2 All ER 483; *Farmer v Sloan* [2004] EWHC 606 (Ch), [2005] WTLR 521 (clause added to deed by draftsman produced a document contrary to parties' true intentions; rectification granted); *Stamp Duties Comr (NSW) v Carlenka Pty Ltd* (1996–97) 41 NSWLR 329. See also *Whiteside v Whiteside* [1950] Ch 65, [1949] 2 All ER 913, CA. Cf *Frederick E Rose (London Ltd v William H Pim Jnr & Co Ltd* cited in fn 278, *supra* (no rectification when mistake as to material fact which led to the words used); see (1976) 92 LQR 325.

rectification is available where the parties believe that certain wording will give effect to their bargain, but mistakenly overlook some other aspect of their arrangements, with the result that the wording will not, in fact, do so.[291] It may be added that 'if there is a written contract which accurately gives effect to the agreement or common intention of the parties, the fact that a statute, passed later, in effect provides that that intention shall be frustrated and that the instrument shall not operate according to its tenor, seems to afford no ground for rectification'.[292]

(C) UNILATERAL MISTAKE

The general rule is that there cannot be rectification if the mistake is merely unilateral.[293] Thus there could be no rectification of a separation deed although the husband, and the husband's and wife's, respective solicitors were under a common mistake, where the wife thought that she was getting under the deed what, in fact, the deed, according to its terms, gave her.[294]

To this general rule, there are exceptions. Firstly, on general principles, the court can rectify an instrument where one party only is mistaken, but the other party is guilty of fraud, whether actual, or constructive, or equitable. Thus, in several cases,[295] a marriage settlement has been rectified where the intended husband acted as the intended wife's fiduciary agent in the preparation of the settlement, and failed to inform or explain to her the inclusion therein of unusual provisions advantageous to him. The principle is not restricted to marriage settlements.[296]

Secondly, it was held, in *A Roberts & Co Ltd v Leicestershire County Council*,[297] that 'a party is entitled to rectification of a contract on proof that he believed a particular term to be included in the contract and that the other party concluded the contract with the omission or a variation of that term in the knowledge that the first party believed the term to be included'.[298] In that case, Pennycuick J suggested[299] that possible bases for the doctrine were estoppel or fraud. More recently, Buckley LJ said in the Court of Appeal, in *Thomas Bates & Son Ltd v Wyndham's (Lingerie) Ltd*,[300] that it depends on the equity of the position.

---

[291] *Co-operative Insurance Society Ltd v Centremoor Ltd* (1983) 268 Estates Gazette 1027, CA.

[292] *Per* Asquith J in *Pyke v Peters* [1943] KB 242, 250.

[293] *Fowler v Fowler* (1859) 4 De G & J 250; *Sells v Sells* (1860) 1 Drew & Sm 42; *Earl Bradford v Earl of Romney* (1862) 30 Beav 431.

[294] *Gilhespie v Burdis* (1943) 169 LT 91; *Fowler v Scottish Equitable Insurance Co* (1858) 28 LJ Ch 225.

[295] *Clark v Girdwood* (1877) 7 Ch D 9, CA; *Lovesy v Smith* (1880) 15 Ch D 655.

[296] *Hoblyn v Hoblyn* (1889) 41 Ch D 200; *McCausland v Young* [1949] NI 49.

[297] [1961] Ch 555, [1961] 2 All ER 545; *Riverlate Properties Ltd v Paul* [1975] Ch 133, [1974] 2 All ER 656, CA; *Weeds v Blaney* (1977) 247 EG 211, CA.

[298] *Per* Pennycuick J in *A Roberts & Co Ltd v Leicestershire County Council, supra*, at 570, 551.

[299] *A Roberts & Co Ltd v Leicestershire County Council, supra*, at 570, 552. See (1961) 77 LQR 313 (R E Megarry).

[300] [1981] 1 All ER 1077, [1981] 1 WLR 505, CA (omission of provision in rent review clause for fixing rent in default of agreement; tenant claimed to hold either rent free or at original rent; lease rectified). Note (1982) 126 Sol Jo 251 (P Matthews), criticizing Buckley LJ's *obiter dictum* that if rectification were not available, the tenant 'on construction and by a process of implication' would have to pay a fair rent.

Buckley LJ went on to explain that, for the doctrine to apply, it must be shown:

(i)   that one party, A, erroneously believed[301] that the document sought to be rectified contained a particular term or provision, or possibly did not contain a particular term or provision that, mistakenly, it did contain;[302]

(ii)   that the other party, B, was aware of the omission or the inclusion, and that it was due to a mistake on the part of A;

(iii) that B has omitted to draw the mistake to the notice of A;

(iv)   that the mistake must be one calculated to benefit B.

On this last point, Eveleigh LJ thought that it would suffice that the inaccuracy of the instrument as drafted would be detrimental to A. According to some cases, it must be shown that B had actual knowledge of the existence of the relevant mistaken belief at the time when the mistaken A signed the contract.[303] Most recently, it has been said to be sufficient that B had wilfully shut his eyes to the obvious, or had wilfully and recklessly failed to make such inquiries as an honest and reasonable man would make.[304] However, where B, intending A to be mistaken as to the construction of the agreement, so conducts himself that he diverts A's attention from discovering the mistake by making false and misleading statements, and A, in fact, makes the very mistake that B intends, then, notwithstanding that B does not actually know, but merely suspects that A is mistaken, and that it cannot be shown that the mistake was induced by any misrepresentation, rectification may be granted.[305] Although the court must be satisfied that it would be unconscionable to deny the remedy of rectification, it is unnecessary to show sharp practice as such on the part of B.[306]

Thirdly, in a few cases[307] of unilateral mistake, the court has given the defendant the option of accepting rectification of the instrument against him or having the contract rescinded. These cases can no longer be relied on, particularly since *Riverlate Properties Ltd v Paul*,[308] which, in effect, decides that unilateral mistake is not a ground for

---

[301] In *Coles v William Hill Organisation Ltd* [1998] 11 LS Gaz R 37, it was held sufficient that the inclusion of a break clause in a lease had been overlooked by the plaintiff's solicitors, although they had had every opportunity to check it.

[302] No rectification in *Kemp v Neptune Concrete* (1988) 57 P & CR 369, CA, in which requirement that there was, in fact, a mistake made by the party seeking relief when executing the deed was not satisfied.

[303] See *Agip SpA v Navigazione Alta Italia SpA* [1984] 1 Lloyd's Rep 353, CA; *Irish Life Assurance Ltd v Dublin Land Securities Ltd* [1986] IR 333 (no knowledge; no sharp practice; no rectification); *KPMG LLP v Network Rail Infrastructure Ltd* [2006] EWHC 67, [2006] 2 P & CR 7.

[304] *Coles v William Hill Organisation Ltd, supra.* In *George Wimpey UK Ltd v V I Construction Ltd* [2005] EWCA Civ 77, (2006) 103 Con LR 67, the claim for rectification failed. The claimant had failed to prove that VIC shut its eyes to the obvious, or willfully and recklessly failed to do what an honest and reasonable person would have done, nor had it led any evidence as to what the board of Wimpey, the decision taker, thought. The inference was that it intended to approve the contract in the form put before it. It also failed in *Chartbrook Ltd v Persimmon Homes Ltd* [2008] 2 All ER (Comm) 387. See (2008) 124 LQR 608 (D McLauchlan).

[305] *Commission for the New Towns v Cooper (Great Britain) Ltd* [1995] Ch 259, [1995] 2 All ER 929, CA.

[306] *Coles v William Hill Organisation Ltd, supra.*

[307] *Garrard v Frankel* (1862) 30 Beav 445; *Harris v Pepperell* (1867) LR 5 Eq 1; *Bloomer v Spittle* (1872) LR 13 Eq 427; *Paget v Marshall* (1884) 28 Ch D 255.

[308] [1975] Ch 133, [1974] 2 All ER 656, CA.

rectification unless there is fraud, or the principle of *A Roberts & Co Ltd v Leicestershire County Council*[309] applies.

Fourthly, a quasi-exception appeared in *Wilson v Wilson*.[310] In that case, the defendant wished to purchase a house and, his own income being insufficient to qualify him for a loan, he requested that the plaintiff to join him in an application to a building society for this purpose. The plaintiff agreed to do so, and, in due course, the house was conveyed into their joint names and the conveyance expressly declared that they were beneficially interested as joint tenants. It was held, on the facts, that the plaintiff never made any contribution to the purchase price, and that the common intention of the plaintiff and the defendant was that the beneficial ownership should be solely vested in the defendant. It was held that the conveyance should be rectified by striking out that part of it which declared the beneficial interests, notwithstanding the fact that the vendor was not a party to the action.[311] It was pointed out by the court that the vendor would not be concerned with, or affected by, the part of the deed that was being rectified, and that the declaration of beneficial trusts could perfectly well have been contained in a separate document. Although superficially a unilateral mistake by the purchasers, in substance, there was a common mistake by the plaintiff and defendant, in that the expressed declaration of beneficial interests did not represent the terms of their agreement.

(D) VOLUNTARY SETTLEMENTS

The court has jurisdiction to rectify a voluntary settlement, not only at the instance of the settlor,[312] but even at the instance of a beneficiary who is a volunteer.[313] Rectification will not, however, be decreed against the wishes of the settlor,[314] even though it is clear that the document does not represent his intentions at the time of the execution thereof: 'No amount of evidence, however conclusive, proving that he did so intend, will at all justify the court in compelling him to introduce a clause into the deed which he does not choose to introduce now, although he might at the time have wished to have done so.'[315] However, if the settlor is dead 'and it is afterwards proved, from the instructions or otherwise, that beyond all doubt the deed was not prepared in the exact manner which he intended, then the deed may be reformed, and those particular provisions necessary to carry his intention into effect may be introduced'.[316] In the case of a voluntary settlement, the burden of proof is perhaps even heavier, and, in particular, the court is slow to act on the evidence of the settlor alone, unsupported by other evidence, such as written instructions, even though the rectification sought would make the settlement more in accord with recognized precedents and may have reasonably been intended.[317] Further, in *Weir v Van Tromp*,[318] Byrne J, while

---

[309] [1961] Ch 555, [1961] 2 All ER 545.   [310] [1969] 3 All ER 945, [1969] 1 WLR 1470.

[311] The consequence was that the property was held on trust for the defendant who had put up the purchase price.

[312] *Re Butlin's Settlement Trust* [1976] Ch 251, [1976] 2 All ER 483.

[313] *Thompson v Whitmore* (1860) 1 John & H 268.

[314] *Broun v Kennedy* (1863) 33 Beav 133, 147; affd (1864) 4 De GJ & Sm 217; *Lister v Hodgson* (1867) LR 4 Eq 30; *Weir v Van Tromp* (1900) 16 TLR 531.

[315] Per Romilly MR in *Lister v Hodgson, supra*, at 34.

[316] *Van der Linde v Van der Linde* [1947] Ch 306.

[317] *Rake v Hooper* (1900) 83 LT 669; *Constandinidi v Ralli* [1935] Ch 427; *Van der Linde v Van der Linde* [1947] Ch 306.   [318] (1900) 16 TLR 531.

accepting that there was jurisdiction, observed that he had not been referred to any case in which judgment had, in fact, been given in favour of reforming a voluntary settlement at the instance of a volunteer.

In *Re Butlin's Settlement Trust*,[319] the court had to decide whether a settlor, seeking rectification of a voluntary settlement to which trustees were parties, was required to establish that the mistake was mutual, or whether it was enough to prove that he alone made a mistake. If the settlement involved an actual bargain between the settlor and the trustees, a mutual mistake would presumably be required. In other cases, the judge stressed the discretionary nature of the remedy and put forward the following propositions:

(i) a settlor may seek rectification by proving that the settlement does not express his true intention, or the true intention of himself and any party with whom he has bargained, such as a spouse in the case of an ante-nuptial settlement;

(ii) it is not essential for him to prove that the settlement fails to express the true intention of the trustees if they have not bargained; but

(iii) the court may in its discretion decline to rectify a settlement against a protesting trustee who objects to rectification, and, perhaps, would normally refuse where the objection was reasonable and the trustee had accepted office on the faith of the settlement as executed, and in ignorance of the mistake.

On the facts of the case (which did not involve a bargain with trustees), rectification was granted, because the only trustee to oppose rectification gave no evidence to support her opposition. Rectification was also ordered in *AMP(UK) plc v Barker*[320] in relation to amendments to a pension scheme that, in terms, benefited all early leavers, but where there was overwhelming evidence that the trustees and the employer intended to improve the benefits only of those leaving on account of incapacity; similarly, with some hesitation as to whether the high standard of proof required was satisfied, in *Martin v Nicholson*,[321] in which, in a deed of variation of a will, the upper limit of the nil rate band applicable to the estate was substituted for £200,000. Rectification was also granted in *Bartlam v Coutts & Co*[322] by substituting the age of twenty-five for the age of thirty in an accumulation and maintenance (A&M) settlement, which otherwise would utterly fail to achieve the intended tax savings, notwithstanding that there was no explanation as to how the age of thirty had come to be inserted. But it was refused in *Tankel v Tankel*,[323] in which it could not be said that the settlement in question differed, by reason of some mistake, from that which the settlor intended to execute. It was not enough for the judge to consider that the proposed rectification would improve the settlement, or that, if the settlor's attention had been drawn to the point, he would have approved it. And in *Allnutt v Allnutt*,[324] in which the rectification sought was, in effect, the substitution for the settlement as executed a settlement in a materially different form, the settlor must be assumed to have understood the meaning and effect of the settlement as executed, and to have intended to execute a

---

[319] [1976] Ch 251, [1976] 2 All ER 483; *Re Frey's Settlement* [2001] WTLR 1009 (Bahamas Supreme Court).

[320] [2001] WTLR 1237.   [321] [2004] EWHC 2135 (Ch), [2005] WTLR 175.

[322] [2006] EWHC 1502 (Ch), [2006] WTLR 1165. Also in *Wills v Gibbs* [2007] EWHC 3361 (Ch), [2008] STC 808.

[323] [1999] 1 FLR 676.   [324] [2006] EWHC 1905 (Ch), [2006] WTLR 1317.

settlement in that form and having the legal effect it did. His only mistake was that a payment into it would be a potentially exempt transfer. It may be added that, in the case of a unilateral document, the need for a common mistake is necessarily modified and it may well be sufficient to prove a mistake on the part of the maker of the document.[325]

(E) EVIDENCE

The rule that applies in the construction of documents—that is, that parol evidence is not admissible to add to, vary, or subtract from a written instrument—clearly cannot apply in an action for rectification, which is, of course, based on the proposition that the written instrument fails to carry out the true agreement of the parties. Evidence must necessarily be admitted of the true agreement that is allegedly not expressed in the written instrument.[326] There are many dicta to the effect that 'the burden of proof lies upon the plaintiff,[327] and that this court, upon an application to reform an executed deed, looks at the evidence in a very jealous manner'.[328] In *Joscelyne v Nissen*,[329] Russell LJ, giving the judgement of the Court of Appeal, discussed what the plaintiff has to show and adopted the phrase 'convincing proof'. He expressly approved the judgment of Simonds J in *Crane v Hegeman-Harris Co Inc*,[330] who said that the jurisdiction is one 'which is to be exercised only upon convincing proof that the concluded instrument does not represent the common intention of the parties...and [where the court] is further satisfied as to what their common intention was'.

Another way in which it has been put is that the court must be 'sure' of the mistake and of the existence of a prior agreement or common intention, before granting the remedy.[331] Brightman LJ has, however, pointed out[332] that this does not mean that the standard of proof is other than the normal civil standard of balance of probability:

> But as the alleged common intention ex hypothesi contradicts the written instrument, convincing proof is required in order to counteract the cogent evidence of the parties' intention displayed by the instrument itself. It is not...the standard of proof which is high, so differing from the normal civil standard, but the evidential requirement needed to counteract the inherent probability that the written instrument truly represents the parties' intention because it is a document signed by the parties.

The court has jurisdiction, on the one hand, to rectify a document solely on the evidence afforded by a perusal of it,[333] and, on the other hand, may act purely on oral evidence[334]

---

[325] *Wright v Goff* (1856) 22 Beav 207; *Killick v Gray* (1882) 46 LT 583; *Re Farepak Food & Gifts Ltd* [2006] EWHC 3272 (Ch), [2007] WTLR 1407. See *Pappadakis v Pappadakis* (2000) Times, 19 January, in which the court refused to rectify a purported declaration of trust in the absence of clear and convincing evidence both (a) that although it has said one thing, the party concerned intended it to say something else, and (b) of what that 'something else' was intended to be.

[326] See, eg, *per* Cozens-Hardy MR in *Lovell and Christmas Ltd v Wall* (1911) 104 LT 85, 88, CA.

[327] That is, the person claiming rectification.

[328] *Per* Romilly MR in *Wright v Goff* (1856) 22 Beav 207, 214; *Tucker v Bennett* (1887) 38 Ch D 1, CA.

[329] [1970] 2 QB 86, [1970] 1 All ER 1213, CA.   [330] [1939] 1 All ER 662; see p 720, fn 265, *supra*.

[331] *Etablissements Georges et Paul Levy v Adderley Navigation Co Panama SA* [1980] 2 Lloyd's Rep 67.

[332] In *Thomas Bates & Son Ltd v Wyndham's (Lingerie) Ltd* [1981] 1 All ER 1077, 1090, CA, discussed (1981) 131 NLJ 967 (H W Wilkinson); *Agip SpA v Navigazione Alta Italia SpA* [1984] 1 Lloyd's Rep 353, CA.

[333] *Banks v Ripley* [1940] Ch 719, [1940] 3 All ER 49; *Fitzgerald v Fitzgerald* [1902] 1 IR 477, CA.

[334] *Lackersteen v Lackersteen* (1860) 30 LJ Ch 5; *M'Cormack v M'Cormack* (1877) 1 LR Ir 119. But see *Re Distributors and Warehousing Ltd* [1986] BCLC 129.

and on the uncontradicted evidence of the person seeking relief.[335] It is too late to seek rectification after an agreement has been construed by the court and money paid under a judgment founded on that construction,[336] or if the contract is no longer capable of performance,[337] and rectification will not be decreed to the prejudice of a bone fide purchaser for value who has acquired an interest in the property dealt with by the instrument.[338] In accordance with familiar equitable principles, a claim may be barred by laches and acquiescence.[339] It may be added that it may be more difficult to persuade the court that there has been a common mistake where the matter has been dealt with through professional advisers.[340]

5 DELIVERY UP AND CANCELLATION OF DOCUMENTS

In some circumstances, a court of equity was prepared to order a void document to be delivered up for cancellation. The idea behind this remedy is that it is inequitable that the defendant should be allowed to remain in possession of an apparently valid document, with the risk to the plaintiff that an action may possibly be brought against him on the document many years later, when evidence to support his defence may have become difficult or impossible to obtain. Thus, if a document is voidable, and avoided, for fraud, whether actual or constructive, delivery up can be ordered.[341] Where, however, the document is void at law and the invalidity appears on its face, so that there is no risk of a successful action being brought on it, delivery up will not be ordered.[342] Where the invalidity does not so appear, however, it has long been held that the court has jurisdiction to order delivery up,[343] although there was, at one time, doubt as to the position.[344]

All kinds of document may be ordered to be delivered up: for instance, negotiable instruments,[345] forged instruments,[346] policies of insurance,[347] and documents that, as it has been said, form a cloud upon title to land.[348] The document must, however, be altogether void, and not merely void as against creditors;[349] nor will a document be

---

[335] *Edwards v Bingham* (1879) 28 WR 89; *Hanley v Pearson* (1879) 13 Ch D 545.

[336] *Caird v Moss* (1886) 33 Ch D 22, CA.   [337] *Borrowman v Rossell* (1864) 16 CBNS 58.

[338] *Garrard v Frankel* (1862) 30 Beav 445; *Smith v Jones* [1954] 2 All ER 823; *Lyme Valley Squash Club Ltd v Newcastle under Lyme Borough Council* [1985] 2 All ER 405.

[339] *Fredensen v Rothschild* [1941] 1 All ER 430 (thirty years); *Burroughs v Abbott* [1922] 1 Ch 86 (twelve years; rectification granted).

[340] *Hazell, Watson and Viney Ltd v Malvermi* [1953] 2 All ER 58.

[341] *Duncan v Worrall* (1822) 10 Price 31; *Hoare v Bremridge* (1872) 8 Ch App 22; *Brooking v Maudslay, Son and Field* (1888) 38 Ch D 636.

[342] *Gray v Mathias* (1800) 5 Ves 286; *Simpson v Lord Howden* (1837) 3 My & Cr 97.

[343] *Davis v Duke of Marlborough* (1819) 2 Swan 108, 157; *Underhill v Horwood* (1804) 10 Ves 209.

[344] *Ryan v Mackmath* (1789) 3 Bro CC 15.   [345] *Wynne v Callander* (1826) 1 Russ 293.

[346] *Peake v Highfield* (1826) 1 Russ 559.

[347] *Bromley v Holland* (1802) 7 Ves 3; *Kemp v Pryor* (1802) 7 Ves 237.

[348] *Bromley v Holland, supra; Hayward v Dimsdale* (1810) 17 Ves 111.

[349] *Ideal Bedding Co Ltd v Holland* [1907] 2 Ch 157.

ordered to be delivered up where it is alleged that there would be a good defence to an action at law, but the document is neither void nor voidable.[350]

Delivery up and cancellation being an equitable remedy, it has been said that it will only be granted on terms that will do justice to both parties—an application of the maxim that 'he who seeks equity must do equity'. Thus, in *Lodge v National Union Investment Co Ltd*,[351] in which a borrower gave certain securities to the lender under a money-lending contract that was illegal and void under the Moneylenders Act 1900,[352] the court was only prepared to order delivery up of the securities on the terms that the borrower should repay such of the money borrowed as was still outstanding. The Privy Council, however, has declared[353] that this case 'cannot be treated as having established any wide general principle that governs the action of courts in granting relief in moneylending cases'. It seems that where the money-lending contract is merely unenforceable[354] as opposed to illegal and void, the lender is, paradoxically, in a worse position, because, in such a case, the borrower can recover his securities without any terms being imposed. To impose terms would be an indirect way of enforcing a contract declared unenforceable by statute.[355]

It should be added that the Court of Appeal has held,[356] on similar facts to those in *Lodge v National Union Investment Co Ltd*,[357] that a declaration that the transaction is illegal and void may be made without any terms being imposed, on the ground that a declaration is not 'equitable relief' or 'true equitable relief'. This ground is not altogether convincing, because a declaration has long been recognized in equity, although under the inherent jurisdiction there was only power to make a declaration as ancillary to some other remedy.[358]

Finally, it should be made clear that no attempt has been made above to set out the present law relating to money-lending contracts. This is largely contained in the Consumer Credit Act 1974, which repealed the Moneylenders Act 1927.

6 NE EXEAT REGNO

The issue of the writ *ne exeat regno* is a process whereby an equitable creditor can have the debtor arrested and made to give security if, but only if, the debtor is about to leave the realm. It is essential that the debt shall be an equitable and not a legal one. In connection with this writ, the provisions of s 6 of the Debtors Act 1869 are applied by analogy. This means that four conditions have to be satisfied before the writ can be issued—namely:

(i) the action is one in which the defendant would formerly have been liable to arrest at law;

---

[350] *Brooking v Maudslay, Son and Field* (1888) 38 Ch D 636.

[351] [1907] 1 Ch 300, [1904–7] All ER Rep 333.

[352] Section 2, repealed by the Moneylenders Act 1927.

[353] *Kasumu v Baba-Egbe* [1956] AC 539, 549, [1956] 3 All ER 266, 270, PC.

[354] This was the effect of the Moneylenders Act 1927, s 6, repealed by the Consumer Credit Act 1974.

[355] *Kasuma v Baba-Egbe, supra*; *Barclay v Prospect Mortgages Ltd* [1974] 2 All ER 672.

[356] *Chapman v Michaelson* [1909] 1 Ch 238, CA.   [357] [1907] 1 Ch 300, [1904–7] All ER Rep 333.

[358] *Ferrand v Wilson* (1845) 4 Hare 344, 385; *Clough v Ratcliffe* (1847) 1 De G & Sm 164, 178. The only case to the contrary seems to be *Taylor v A-G* (1837) 8 Sim 413. See, generally, Zamir, *The Declaratory Judgment*.

(ii) a good cause of action for at least £50 is established;

(iii) there is 'probable cause' for believing that the defendant is 'about to quit England' unless he is arrested; and

(iv) the absence of the defendant from England will materially prejudice the plaintiff in the prosecution of his action, as opposed to the execution of any judgment he may obtain.

Even if these four conditions are satisfied—and the standard of proof is high—the issue of an order is discretionary.

The law was fully reviewed by Megarry J in an unsuccessful application in *Felton v Callis*,[359] and, after a long period during which the writ was rarely issued, if at all, it is now clear that, in appropriate cases, its validity is unimpaired. In many cases, the freezing injunction will sufficiently protect the claimant, but, in a small number of cases, the additional power in support of the freezing order may assist the cause of justice. The writ was issued in *Al Nahkel for Contracting and Trading Ltd v Lowe*[360] to prevent the defendant fleeing the jurisdiction with assets in order to frustrate a lawful claim before the court. Tudor Price J's observation in that case that the writ can issue in support of a freezing injunction gave Leggatt J some anxiety in *Allied Arab Bank Ltd v Hajjar*.[361] He agreed if the statement was intended to refer only to cases in which both remedies might properly issue, with the result that the arrest of the debtor might incidentally prevent him from breaching the freezing injunction; he disagreed if it was intended to go further and to suggest that the writ might be ordered for the purpose of enforcing the freezing injunction—for which purpose, the appropriate remedy is an injunction to restrain him from leaving the jurisdiction. A freezing injunction is a remedy in aid of execution. It is not part of the prosecution of the action. Condition (iv) is therefore not satisfied if the purpose of the writ is to enforce a freezing injunction.

7 SETTING ASIDE A JUDGMENT OBTAINED BY FRAUD

Shortly after the Judicature Acts came into force, the Court of Appeal held, in *Flower v Lloyds*,[362] that it had no power to review its own decision on the ground of the subsequent discovery of facts indicating that its order had been obtained by fraud. It held, however, that the jurisdiction of the old Court of Chancery under which, if a decree had been obtained by fraud, it could be impeached by Bill, had been transferred to the High Court with the effect that, since the Acts, a fresh action could be brought to set aside a judgment that has been obtained by fraud.

---

[359] [1969] 1 QB 200, [1968] 3 All ER 673; *Re B* [1997] 3 All ER 258. See (1972) 88 LQR 83 (J W Bridge).

[360] [1986] QB 235, [1986] 1 All ER 729; *Ali v Naseem* (2003) Times, 3 October. See (1987) 104 LQR 246 (Lesley J Anderson); (1986) 45 CLJ 189 (G Marston); (1987) 137 NLJ 584 (Lesley J Anderson).

[361] [1988] QB 787, [1987] 3 All ER 739, noted (1988) 47 CLJ 364 (N H Andrews). Point not discussed in further proceedings reported [1989] Fam Law 68, CA.

[362] (1877) 6 Ch D 297, CA.

In the Australian case of *Wentworth v Rogers (No 5)*,[363] Kirby J summarized the principles that govern proceedings of this kind.

(i)   The essence of the action is fraud. As in all actions based on fraud, particulars of the fraud claimed must be exactly given and the allegations must be established by the strict proof that such a charge requires.[364]

(ii) It must be shown, by the party asserting that a judgment was procured by fraud, that there has been a new discovery of something material, in the sense that fresh facts have been found that, by themselves or in combination with previously known facts, would provide a reason for setting aside the judgment.[365]

(iii) Mere suspicion of fraud, raised by fresh facts later discovered, will not be sufficient to secure relief. The claimant must establish that the new facts are so evidenced and so material that it is reasonably probable that the action will succeed.[366]

(iv) Although perjury by the successful party or a witness or witnesses may, if later discovered, warrant the setting aside of a judgment on the ground that it was procured by fraud, and although there may be exceptional cases in which such proof of perjury could suffice, without more, to warrant relief of this kind, the mere allegation, or even the proof, of perjury will not normally be sufficient to attract such drastic and exceptional relief as the setting aside of a judgment. The other requirements must be fulfilled.[367]

(v)   It must be shown by admissible evidence that the successful party was responsible for the fraud that taints the judgment under challenge. The evidence in support of the charge ought to be extrinsic.[368]

(vi) The burden of establishing the components necessary to warrant the drastic step of setting aside a judgment, allegedly affected by fraud or other relevant taint, lies on the party impugning the judgment. It is for that party to establish the fraud and to do so clearly.

8 SETTING ASIDE A DEED FOR MISTAKE

Needless to say, gifts cannot be revoked, nor can deeds of gift be set aside, simply because the donors wish that they had not made them, and would like to have back the property given. However:

wherever there is a voluntary transaction[369] by which one party intends to confer a bounty on another, the deed will be set aside if the court is satisfied that the disponer did not intend the

---

[363] [1986] 6 NSWLR 534. See, generally, (1995) 14 U Tas LR 129 (G D Pont).

[364] *Jonesco v Beard* [1930] AC 298, HL.

[365] *Boswell v Coaks (No 2)* (1894) 6 R 167, 170, 174, *per* Lord Selborne; *Birch v Birch* [1902] P 130, 136–138; *Everett v Ribbands* [1946] 175 LT 143, 145, 146.

[366] *Birch v Birch, supra,* at 136, 139.   [367] *Everett v Ribbands, supra,* at 145, 146.

[368] *Perry v Meddowcroft* (1846) 10 Beav 122, 136–139.

[369] Equitable relief will not be granted in the context of non-voluntary transactions such as pension schemes: *Smithson v Hamilton* [2007] EWHC 2900 (Ch), [2008] 1 All ER 1216.

transaction to have the effect which it did. It will be set aside for mistake whether the mistake is a mistake of law or of fact, so long as the mistake is as to the effect of the transaction and not merely as to its consequences or to the advantages to be gained by entering into it.[370]

This is so provided that the mistake is of '*so serious a character as to render it unjust on the part of the donee to retain the property given to him*'.[371] Lewison J observed, in *Re Griffiths (decd)*,[372] that the distinction between the effect of the transaction and its consequences or advantages had proved a difficult one to grasp, and one that he did not need to resolve. In the case before him, he held that a mistake about a fact existing at the time of the transaction (the state of the disponer's health) was a mistake entitling him to set aside the transaction. If, which he doubted, Millett J intended to limit the scope of the equitable jurisdiction to a mistake about the effect of a transaction, he disagreed.

The effect of an operative mistake is to make the transaction voidable; the court has a discretion whether or not to set it aside.

---

[370] *Per* Millett J in *Gibbon v Mitchell* [1990] 3 All ER 338, 343, [1990] 1 WLR 1304, 1309.

[371] *Per* Lindley LJ in *Ogilvie v Littleboy* (1897) 13 TLR 399, 400, CA, affd sub nom *Ogilvie v Allen* (1899) 15 TLR 294, HL.

[372] [2008] EWHC 118 (Ch), [2008] 2 All ER 654, citing *Anker-Petersen v Christensen* [2002] WTLR 313, noted (2002) 38 T & ELTJ 10 (T Dumont); *Sieff v Fox* [2005] EWHC 1312 (Ch), [2005] 3 All ER 693, [2005] 1 WLR 3811; *Wolff v Wolff* [2004] EWHC 2110 (Ch), [2004] STC 1633, noted (2004) 61 T & ELTJ 11 (Clarissa Vallat). See [2004] PCB357, [2005] PCB 159 (J Hilliard); *Clarkson v Barclays Private Bank and Trust (Isle of Man) Ltd* [2007] WTLR 1703 (Deemster), in which the Deemster accepted that there was no rational basis for restricting recovery to cases in which there had been a mistake as to the operative effect of a transaction.

GLOSSARY

administrator A person authorized to administer the estate of a person who dies without having made a valid will, or where, having made a valid will, there is no proving **executor**

advancement, power of The power of trustees to make a payment to a **beneficiary** in anticipation of his interest becoming vested in possession

advancement, presumption of The presumption that the payment of money or transfer of property by a parent to a child, or a husband to a wife, is made by way of gift

assent An act by a **personal representative** vesting property in the person beneficially entitled

attorney, power of The authority given by one person to another to act for him in his absence

beneficial owner A person entitled for his own benefit, in contrast to a person, such as a trustee, who holds property for the benefit of others

beneficiary A person entitled to a beneficial interest under a trust or a will

bequest A gift of **personal property** contained in a will

bona vacantia Goods without an owner

cestui que trust A person for whose benefit a trust is created; a person entitled to an equitable interest in the trust property

cestui que use A person for whose benefit a **use** was created

chose in action A personal right of property that can only be claimed or enforced by action, and not by taking physical possession

codicil A supplement to a will

condition precedent A condition that must happen or be performed before an estate or interest can vest

condition subsequent A condition on the failure or non-performance of which an estate or interest already vested may be defeated

contingent Dependent on an event that may never happen

contra mundum Against the world at large

conversion A change in the nature of property. See **personal property** and **real property**, and the Online Resource Centre

covenant A promise or undertaking contained in a **deed**

cy-près As near as possible

deed A document that complies with the formalities required by the Law of Property (Miscellaneous) Provisions Act 1989

dehors Outside; not within the scope of

determine Come to an end; terminate

devise A gift of **real property** contained in a will

discretionary trust A trust in which the trustees have a discretionary power to decide which of the potential **beneficiaries** shall benefit and what their benefit will be

donatio mortis causa A gift made in contemplation of death by delivery of the subject matter of the gift, only to take effect on death and revocable in the meantime

eleemosynary corporation A corporation constituted for the perpetual distribution of the free alms or bounty of the founder to such persons as he has directed

en ventre sa mère Conceived, but not yet born

estoppel A rule that prevents a person from denying what he has led another person to assume

executed trust A trust that defines precisely the interests of the **beneficiaries**. Cf **executory trust**

executor A person appointed by a **testator** to administer his estate

executor *de son tort* A person who, without authority, meddles with the property of a deceased person as if he had been appointed executor

executory trust A trust that declares the **settlor**'s general intention directing how a formal **settlement** should be made, Cf **executed trust**

feoffment with livery of seisin The original method of conveying land—the grantor was the feoffor and the grantee, the feoffee

feoffee to uses A person to whom land was conveyed and directed to hold it for the benefit of another

fixed trust A trust in which the interests of the **beneficiaries** are precisely defined in the trust **deed**

forum domesticum The private jurisdiction of the founder of a charity

freezing injunction Formerly known as a 'Mareva' injunction, this freezes the defendant's assets so as to ensure that they are not spirited away before judgment, leaving nothing on which the claimant's judgment can bite

functus officio Where a person has discharged his duty, or where his office or authority has come to an end

infant Before the Family Law Reform Act 1969, a person under the age of twenty-one; since that Act, a person under the age of eighteen, usually now termed a 'minor'

in loco parentis In the situation of a parent, with particular reference to a parent's duty to provide for a child

in personam A proceeding in which a claim is made against a specific person, eg against a trustee to replace trust funds lost through a breach of trust

in rem A proceeding in which a claim is made in relation to specific property, eg a claim against a stranger to the trust to restore trust property that has wrongfully come into his hands

inter vivos Between living persons

intestacy The state of affairs when a person—'the intestate'—dies without having made a valid will

issue Descendants of a person, whether children or more remote

legacy A **bequest** or gift of **personal property** contained in a will

letters of administration Authorization to persons (**administrators**) to administer the estate of a deceased person

limitation of actions Barring of the right of a person to pursue a claim after a period of time

malum in se An act that is intrinsically and morally wrong, eg murder

malum prohibitum An act that offends against a rule of law, but is not intrinsically wrong, such as smuggling

marriage articles The preliminary agreement for the execution of a marriage **settlement**

minority The state of being a minor. See **infant**

mutatis mutandis With the obviously necessary changes

perpetuities, rule against The rule making void an interest that would vest at too remote a point of time

personal property (or 'personalty') All property other than **real property**

personal representative A term that includes both an **executor** and an administrator

probate The **executor**(s) prove the will and the grant of probate by the court is formal confirmation of its validity

quia timet **injunction** An injunction obtained before there has been any infringement of the claimant's rights, but where one is threatened or apprehended

real property (or 'realty') Interests in land, with the exception of leases (or 'terms of years'), which are **personal property**

restitutio in integrum Restoring parties to their original position

search order Formerly known as an 'Anton Piller' order, this authorizes entry into premises and the search for, and copying or seizure of, property that is the subject matter of the proceedings or required as evidence

sequestration A process whereby the property of the defendant can be seized

settlement A **deed** by which property is 'settled' on the intended **beneficiaries**, specifying who they are and what their interests are to be

settlor A person creating a **settlement** or trust

testator A male person who has made a valid will

testatrix A female person who has made a valid will

trustee *de son tort* A person who, not being a trustee and without authority, intermeddles with trust affairs

use The ancestor of the modern trust (see Chapter 1)

volunteer A person who takes under a disposition without having given valuable consideration

INDEX